PRAISE FOR THE ULTIMATE SCHOLARSHIP BOOK BY GEN AND KELLY TANABE

"Upbeat, well-organized and engaging, this comprehensive tool is an exceptional investment for the college-bound."

—*Publishers Weekly*

"Gen and Kelly Tanabe are by far the best experts on winning scholarships. Not only will their books help you find scholarships that you qualify for, they will show you how to win them. Soon after applying the strategies in their book, I won a $1,000 scholarship. I couldn't have done it without them. The Tanabes can help you win scholarships too!"

—*Doug Wong, University of California, San Diego*

"A present for anxious parents."

—*The Honolulu Advertiser*

"Upbeat tone and clear, practical advice."

—*Book News*

"Unlike other authors, the Tanabes use their experiences and those of other students to guide high school and college students and their parents through the scholarship and financial aid process."

—*Palo Alto Daily News*

"If the Tanabes could earn over $100,000 in scholarships and graduate from an Ivy League institution owing nothing, others can, too."

—*Star-Bulletin*

"This is a helpful, well-organized guide. A good resource for all students."

—*KLIATT*

"A common sense approach to scholarship searches. *The Ultimate Scholarship Book* gives a down to earth step by step method of finding, applying for and winning scholarships. The scholarship list has many opportunities for students to showcase their talents for financial reward."

—*Lynda McGee, College Counselor, Downtown Magnets High School, Los Angeles*

"This guide (has) ... practical tips on where to find scholarships; how to write effective applications, resumes and winning essays; and how to get glowing recommendations and ace scholarship interviews."

—*C.E. King, Iowa State University, Choice Magazine*

"Getting into college is only half of the game. How to pay for it offers the second big challenge. Whether they qualify for financial need or are just looking for ways to help their parents with this heavy burden, all students will profit from *The Ultimate Scholarship Book* which both outlines the process of finding financial help for college as well as it provides an extensive and up to date list of current scholarship sources.

"Take these important tips from two experienced writers who are nationally recognized for their expertise on all facets of the college application process. Both members of this impressive husband and wife team paid for their Harvard educations by following the precepts which they share with you now in this easy to read guidebook."

—*David Miller, Director of College Counseling, Stevenson School, Pebble Beach, California*

Dedication

To our families for shaping who we are.

To Harvard for four of the best years of our lives.

To the many students and friends who made this book possible by sharing their scholarship experiences, secrets, successes and failures.

To all the students and parents who understand that paying for college is a challenging but worthwhile endeavor.

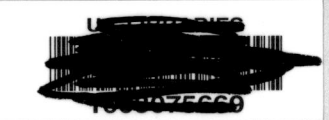

The Ultimate Scholarship Book 2012

Billions of Dollars in Scholarships, Grants and Prizes

Gen and Kelly Tanabe

Winners of over $100,000 in college scholarships and award-winning authors of *Get Free Cash for College* and *How to Write a Winning Scholarship Essay*

- Comprehensive scholarship directory to over 1.5 million awards worth more than $2 billion
- Scholarships for high school and college students of every background, talent and achievement level
- Easy to use indexes to quickly find the best matching scholarships

The Ultimate Scholarship Book 2012: Billions of Dollars in Scholarships, Grants and Prizes

By Gen and Kelly Tanabe

Published by SuperCollege, LLC
3286 Oak Court
Belmont, CA 94002
650-618-2221
www.supercollege.com

Credits: Cover: Monica Thomas, www.tlcgraphics.com. Cover photograph: ©iStockphoto.com/Kaleido. Layout: The Roberts Group, www.editorialservice.com. Back cover photograph: Alvin Gee, www.alvingee.com.

The Ultimate Scholarship Book is the #1 bestselling scholarship guide based on Nielsen/BookScan sales data of the 2011 editions of comparable titles.

Special Sales: For information on using SuperCollege books in the classroom or special prices for bulk quantities, please contact our Special Sales Department at 650-618-2221.

ISBN-13: 978-1-932662-94-8
ISBN-10: 1-932662-94-4

Manufactured in the United States of America
10 9 8 7 6 5 4 3 2 1

Library of Congress Cataloging-in-Publication Data

Tanabe, Gen S.
The ultimate scholarship book 2012 : billions of dollars in scholarships, grants, and prizes / Gen Tanabe and Kelly Tanabe.
p. cm.
Includes indexes.
ISBN-13: 978-1-932662-94-8 (alk. paper)
ISBN-10: 1-932662-94-4 (alk. paper)
1. Scholarships--United States--Directories. I. Tanabe, Kelly Y. II. Title.
LB2338.T36 2011
378.3'402573--dc22

2011014761

CONTENTS

How to Use the Ultimate Scholarship Book

chapter 1

A Scholarship Book That's Better Than a Website

Is it crazy to say that a bound stack of paper and glue is superior to the high speed bits and bytes of a scholarship website? Absolutely not! Because it is true.

Let us explain.

Unless you're starting out, you've probably used a scholarship website. Typically you fill out a profile questionnaire to provide information about yourself before hitting the "search" button. So far, this seems much easier than using a book.

Until you get your results.

No matter what website you use, there will be an unusually large number of scholarships that aren't good matches. After reading the eligibility requirements, you will discover that only a small handful are worth your time to apply.

You've just discovered the first major weakness of every scholarship website: your life (background, experiences, goals, talents, awards, interests and accomplishments) cannot be defined or summarized by a computer-generated questionnaire.

Your Life is MORE Than a 30-Question Profile

The simple truth is that no computer can match you to scholarships as well as you can. You are a complex individual with a variety of passions, interests and goals. Nothing—person or machine—knows you better than you know yourself.

And think about that profile form. That's the only information the computer has about you. But what if you don't know all the answers? Are you really set on becoming an orthopedic surgeon, or did that just sound cool? Even worse, you are limited by the choices provided on that profile questionnaire. Imagine that you wrote a poem that was published in your town's community newspaper. Should you select "poet" as a future career? Will that trigger a great poetry scholarship? Or maybe under hobbies, you should select "writing and journalism"? Of course, that might trigger a flood of journalism scholarships that wouldn't apply to you. Or maybe, even though your school doesn't have a poetry club, you should still tell the computer that you are a member of one in order to trick it into showing you a sweet poetry award?

Do you see where we're going?

The very fact that you need to give the computer information about yourself while only using the choices the computer provides, without any clue about how those answers will affect your results, almost guarantees that you are going to miss out on some good scholarships. How do you know that because you answered a single question in the way that you did, that you are not missing out on some fantastic scholarship opportunities?

The answer is, you don't.

About Your Authors

What makes us qualified to write *The Ultimate Scholarship Book*? Primarily it's because at one time we were exactly where you are now. We needed money to pay for college, and scholarships turned out to be our only answer. Not only did we do pretty well (winning more than $100,000 in free cash for college) but since then, we've continued to help thousands of students do the same.

Here's our story:

Kelly grew up in Los Angeles and when she got accepted to Harvard (which costs about $45,000 per year!), her family just didn't have the money to pay for it. Gen grew up in Hawaii and faced a similar financial crunch when he got into Harvard. In fact, his father even tried to bribe him to attend his state university by offering him a new car if he would give up his idea of attending the ivy-league college. Even considering the cost of a brand new car, it would have been cheaper for Gen's family to make car payments than pay Harvard tuition!

Since we both had our hearts set on attending a very expensive college that our families could not afford, we had little choice but to become fanatics about applying for scholarships. While we made a lot of beginner mistakes and it was by no means a quick or easy process, we were ultimately successful in winning more than $100,000 in scholarships. It was only because of this money that we were able to attend Harvard and were both able to graduate from college debt free.

As you may have guessed by now, we met while at college. We were actually next door neighbors in the dorm, and we were married a few years after we graduated from Harvard. Knowing first-hand how hard it can be for families to pay for college, we decided to share what we had learned as a result of our own pursuits to find funds for tuition. Our first books were about how to win scholarships and get financial aid. In fact, you can find *1001 Ways to Pay for College* and *How to Write a Winning Scholarship Essay* in bookstores. But despite the success of these books, we found that whenever we spoke to groups of students or parents, the number one question they asked was, "Do you know of scholarships for such-and-such a student?"

At the same time, we were also noticing a growing dissatisfaction from students who only relied on websites for scholarship information. This was somewhat of a mystery to us since we knew of thousands of great scholarships that were available. Why weren't these awards being found? Why wasn't every student applying for these scholarships?

All of this led to our decision to build our own database of scholarships and publish the results in *The Ultimate Scholarship Book*. We have a team of researchers who help us investigate scholarships, verify awards and ensure that the scholarships that make it into the book are the best and most up-to-date possible.

So that's our story and why we feel so passionate about what we write in this book. It's not just a collection of words on paper; it's really the collective experience and intelligence of our own quest for scholarships along with thousands of hours of research by our scholarship staff.

How This Book Overcomes the Disadvantages of Websites

A book has certain advantages over websites; for example, a book can work for you without the necessity of input. In many ways, a book is more flexible than a computer site because you are not penalized for not having an answer to a specific question that is worded in a narrow and inflexible way. Likewise, you are not forced to fit yourself into a predetermined, inflexible category. A book also lets you do the matching, a tool which we have found to be far better than outsourcing that work to some machine.

The Ultimate Scholarship Book is designed to be browsed. Spend an hour with this book and you will be able to evaluate hundreds of scholarships quickly and efficiently. By scanning the descriptions, you (not some computer) can decide if you have the right combination of background, interests or skills to qualify. By seeing all of the possibilities, you remain in control of how you prioritize which awards are right for you.

Now it is true that this is a slower process than using a website. But the trade-off is that it is far more accurate, and accuracy is what it's all about. You're not trying to find hundreds of awards that you may or may not win. Who has time to apply for that many scholarships anyway?! Your goal is to find the best awards that you have highest chances of winning. So while you'll invest more time in the finding of scholarships by using a book, we guarantee that the payoff (which in this case is literally thousands of extra dollars in scholarships) will be worth it.

If the time aspect of using a book versus a website still bothers you, here's one more thought. You can use books practically anywhere—especially when you have downtime. Try using a scholarship website while you're waiting for the bus, hanging out at school or even in the bathroom! In other words, you can transform the natural wasted time during your day into highly productive scholarship time.

A Dirty Secret of Websites: They're Out-of-Date

It's natural to assume that anything online is more current than something printed on paper. But is this really true? Use a few scholarship websites and you'll soon realize that many are horribly out of date. Does it make you angry? Do you want to demand a refund? Of course not! Most scholarship websites are free services! Now it is true that many so-called "free" websites do actually make money by reselling your information; and once they get this from your profile form, you are of little value to the site. This is very annoying. However, we digress. Our point is that as a free service, there is really very little incentive for the website to maintain a high level of accuracy in their data.You really do get what you pay for with most scholarship websites!

It's a lot different with a book. There are two strong incentives that ensure the data in this book is up-to-date and accurate. The first is that we know once we commit something to paper, it's permanent. That creates a very strong desire to get it right the first time. This degree of permanence—the finality of words on paper—is a huge responsibility for us. Once the book goes to press, it is very difficult and expensive to update a mistake. The second powerful incentive is that you're paying hard earned money for this book! It's not free. Because of this, you expect to receive only the best product. If we don't deliver, we'll hear from you!

Together, these two incentives guarantee that each award in this book has been checked and re-checked. We have a small army of researchers whose only job is to verify each award in the book before it goes to press. We also send out letters twice a year to every scholarship listed to ask the providers themselves to verify and update their information. The end result is that this book is extremely accurate and up-to-date.

We also never keep this book in print for longer than a year—which is what we have found to be the typical time in which scholarships change. So as long as you are buying this book new, you are guaranteed to have the latest information possible.

Given how diligent and thorough our researchers are and the rigorous process we apply to every award we publish, we would happily pit this book against any website!

Another Dirty Secret of Websites: They Don't Actually List Millions of Awards

Here's a controversial statement: Websites often claim to list millions of awards worth billions of dollars, but the truth is that these numbers are just marketing hype. To arrive at these numbers, the websites use the most liberal definitions possible. For example, the Coca-Cola Foundation awards $3.4 million per year to over 1,400 students. So the website counts their single listing of the Coca-Cola Foundation Scholarship as being 1,400 awards valued at $3.4 million. Or consider that each Target department store gives a scholarship to a student in the community. Even though you can apply only at the store in your community, the website still counts each individual award, which totals into the thousands. The results are highly inflated numbers.

Now before we claim the high road in this debate, we have to admit that we do the exact same thing! Take a look at the front cover of this book. Our numbers are just as impressive as many scholarship websites. But unlike the websites, we don't hide reality. All you need to do is pick up our book and see how thick it is to know how many awards we have inside. But you can't do this with a website. There is no way to know (and the website will never tell you) how many actual awards they have. They want you to think that they have millions when in reality they often contain no more—and often much less—than what you'll find in this book!

The Bottom Line: Books Can Beat Websites

It should be obvious by now that we are just a little bothered when we hear that websites—just because they are online—are superior to books.

It's just not true.

This is not to say that websites don't have any value. They absolutely do and inside this book, we list a number of websites that we think are worth your time. However, you need to understand that you must go beyond websites if you hope to find the best scholarships. In fact, you need to go beyond books too! The entire next chapter is dedicated to places in which to find scholarships other than books and websites. We highly recommend that you explore all these sources in order to find the best scholarships for you.

Why Choose *This* Book?

We know that there are other books that provide directories of scholarships, so why choose this one?

- Discover the best scholarships for you with awards in the humanities, academics, public service, extracurricular activities, talents, athletics, religion, ethnicity, social science and science based on career goals and more.
- Find scholarships that are not based on grades.
- Get all the information you need in one place with the application details, eligibility requirements, deadlines, contact information and website addresses.
- Find scholarships you can use at any college.
- Avoid wasting money on scholarship competitions that require a fee to enter.
- Save time and find the best scholarships that fit you with the easy-to-use indexes.
- Access the most up-to-date information that has been checked and double-checked.
- Learn not only how to find scholarships but how to win them! Get insider advice from judges and scholarship winners.

Common Scholarship Myths Busted

Now that we've cleared up some of the misconceptions about books and websites, let's debunk some of the common scholarship myths. We hate these myths because not only are they untrue, but they often prevent students from applying for scholarships.

Myth: You need to be financially destitute to be eligible to apply for scholarships.

Busted: While it is true that financial need is a consideration for some scholarships, the definition of "need" varies considerably. Given the cost of a college education, many families who consider themselves to be "middle class" actually qualify for some need-based scholarships. In addition, there are many scholarships where financial need is not even a factor. These "merit-based" scholarships are based on achievements, skills, career goals, family background and a host of other considerations that have nothing to do with a family's financial situation. You could actually be the son or daughter of Donald Trump and still win a "merit-based" scholarship.

Myth: You can only win scholarships as a high school senior.

Busted: It is never too early or too late to apply for scholarships. There are awards for students as young as seventh grade. If you win, the money is usually held in an account until it is time for you to actually go to college. But even if there are not as many awards for younger students as there are for seniors, it doesn't mean it's not important to look. Finding awards that you can apply for next year or even two years from now is a huge advantage. Keep a list of these awards since you are going to be super busy as a senior (think college apps and AP classes!) and you are going to be so thankful when you can just refer to your file of previously found awards and don't have to spend time searching. At the same time, you also don't want to stop applying for scholarships after you graduate from high school. There are many awards for college students. Once you are in college, you should continue to apply for scholarships, especially those geared toward specific majors and careers.

Myth: Only star athletes get college scholarships.

Busted: While star running backs receiving full-tuition scholarships are often what make the news, the majority of scholarships awarded by colleges are not for athletics. As you will see in this book, there are literally thousands of scholarships for those of us who don't know the difference between a touchdown and a touchback. Even if you are an athlete, you might also be surprised to know that many colleges give scholarships to student athletes who may not be destined to become the next Michael Jordan. The needs of a college's athletic program depend on the level of their competition. You may find that at one college your soccer skill wouldn't earn you a place on the team as a bench warmer; but at another school, you might not only be a starter but also earn a half-tuition scholarship.

Myth: You need straight A's to win money for college.

Busted: While straight A's certainly don't hurt, most students mistakenly assume that grades are the primary determinate for selecting scholarship winners. This is just not true. Most scholarships are based on criteria other than grades and reward specific skills or talents such as linguistic, athletic or artistic ability. Even for scholarships in which grades are considered, GPAs are often not the most important factor. What's more relevant is that you best match the qualities the scholarship committee seeks. Don't let the lack of a perfect transcript prevent you from applying for scholarships.

Myth: You should get involved in as many extracurricular activities as possible to win a scholarship.

Busted: Scholarship competitions are not pie eating contests where you win through volume. They are more like baking contests in which you create an exquisite dessert with an appearance and flavor that matches the tastes of the judges. Scholarships are won by quality, not quantity. Scholarship judges are looking for students who have made quality contributions. For example, for a public service scholarship, the judges would be more impressed if you organized a school-wide volunteer day than if you were a member of 20 volunteer organizations but did little to distinguish yourself in any one of them.

Myth: If you qualify for financial aid, you don't need to apply for scholarships.

Busted: Financial aid and scholarships are not mutually exclusive but complimentary. You need to do both—apply for financial aid and scholarships—at the same time! Relying only on financial aid is dangerous. First, financial aid is "need based" which means if you're a middle or upper middle class family, you may not receive any free money (i.e. grants) but only student loans which you need to pay back. Even if you do qualify for grants, it may not be enough. The maximum Pell Grant, for example, is $4,050 per year, which is still far short of what tuition plus room and board costs at most schools. While financial aid is important, we consider scholarships to be far superior. With few, if any, strings attached, scholarships represent free cash that does not have to be paid back and which you can use at almost any school. Best of all, you can win scholarships regardless of your family's income!

Myth: You should apply to every scholarship that you find.

Busted: When you turn 35, you technically are eligible to run for President of the United States. This hardly means you should start packing your bags for the White House. Let's apply that same logic to scholarships. Just because you are technically eligible for a scholarship does not mean you should start filling out the paperwork for it. Why? You have a limited amount of time to spend on scholarship applications. It is necessary to allocate your time to those that you have the best chance of winning. You may find that you are eligible for 500 scholarships. Unless you're willing to make applying to scholarships your full-time avocation, it's unlikely that you can apply for more than several dozen awards. Thus, you need to be selective about which scholarships fit you the best. One caveat: This does not mean that you should only apply to two or three scholarships. You should still apply to as many scholarships as you can—just make sure you have them prioritized.

How a Solid Scholarship Strategy Helps Win You Money

Back in high school, Kelly applied for a scholarship from her father's employer. She was confident she would win since academically she had both high grades and test scores—which she diligently listed on the application. After turning in her application, she eagerly waited for the check to arrive. But the check never came. In fact, when Kelly found out who did win, she was surprised to learn that he had lower grades and lower test scores. What happened? How did this guy win instead of Kelly?

The answer was that Kelly relied solely on grades and test scores to win while the other applicant clearly used the entire application to stand out. That was when Kelly learned the importance of having a strategy.

So what does it take to win a scholarship?

The answer is that scholarship winners are not superstars. Rather, they are the students who have prepared—those young men and women that have invested the time to create applications that highlight their strengths. It's really sad to see students who don't apply for scholarships because they mistakenly assume that they don't have a chance to win.

Unlike a lottery, scholarships are not based on luck. To win scholarships, you need to show the scholarship judges how you fit the award. Often this is through the scholarship application, essay and interview. In fact, almost all scholarship competitions come down to one key factor—how well you can show that you fit the purpose of the scholarship. In this respect, you have power over the outcome. Through what you choose to highlight (and ignore) in the scholarship application, you are able to construct a case for why you deserve to win.

In the following chapters we will lay out what we found to be the keys to a winning strategy. Now turn the page and let's get started!

Where to Find the Best Scholarships

chapter 2

Scholarships Beyond this Book

We know you bought this book because it's the largest and most up-to-date directory of scholarships available. However, we do want to show you how to find even more scholarships above and beyond the ones listed in this book.

We learned how to find scholarships through trial and often painful error. For example, when we first started to search for scholarships, we spent a lot of time tracking down scholarships that we later discovered were listed in our high school counseling office. But we did learn from each mistake and slowly developed an efficient strategy for finding scholarships.

Our approach to finding scholarships consists of two important steps. First, you must create a list of as many scholarships as possible that fit you. Second, once you have a big list of scholarships, prioritize the awards. Here is where you will do some detective work that will show you which scholarships are worth your time to fill out.

By following this two-step approach, you will end up with a prioritized list of scholarships that are closely matched to your background and achievements. So, even before you fill out a single scholarship application form, you will have greatly improved your chances of winning. Plus, you saved time by not wasting energy on awards that you won't win.

Start Your Scholarship Search in Your Own Backyard

When we began looking for scholarships, we made what is perhaps the biggest mistake of the novice scholarship hunter—we started by looking as far away as possible. We were mesmerized by the big prizes of the large (and often well-publicized) national awards. We thought, "If I won just one of these national scholarship competitions, I'd be set and could end my search." This turned out to be a big mistake and an even bigger time-waster. It seemed that everyone and his brother, sister and cousin were also applying to these competitions. The Coca-Cola scholarship competition, for example, receives more than 100,000 applications each year.

It turned out that the last place we looked for scholarships was our most lucrative source. Best of all, this place turned out to be in our own backyard!

What are backyard scholarships and where do you find them? Think about all the civic groups, clubs, businesses, churches and organizations in your community. Each of these is a potential source for scholarships. (If you are already in college, you have two communities: your hometown and the city in which you go to school.) Since these awards are usually only available to students in your community, the competition is a lot less fierce.

You may be thinking, "What good is a $500 Lions Club scholarship when my college costs 20 grand a year?" It's true that local scholarships don't award the huge prizes that some of the national competitions do. You already know that we won over $100,000 in scholarships. What we haven't told you is that the majority of this money came from local scholarships! We literally won $500 here and $1,500 there. By the time we graduated from Harvard and added up all the awards, it turned out to be a huge amount. Plus, some of the local scholarships that we won were "renewable," which meant that we received that money each year we were in college. So a $500 renewable scholarship was really worth $2,000 over four years.

If you still can't get excited because these local awards seem small compared to the cost of tuition, try this exercise: Take the amount of the award and divide it by the time you invested in the application. For the $500 Lions Club award, let's say that you spent one hour each night for three days to complete the application and write the essay. Take $500 and divide it by three hours. That works out to a little over $166 per hour. (Now imagine that the award was for $1,000 instead. That would make it $333 per hour!) Not bad by any measure. If you can find a job that pays you more than $166 an hour, then take it and forget applying to scholarships. If not, get back to applying for scholarships–even the little ones!

Let's get specific and look at all of the places in your backyard to find scholarships.

✓ High school counselor or college financial aid officer

If you are a high school student, start with your counselor. Ask if he or she has a list of scholarship opportunities. Most counselors have a binder filled with local scholarships. It's helpful if before your meeting, you prepare information about your family's financial background as well as special interests or talents you have that would make you eligible for scholarships. Don't forget that your own high school will have a variety of scholarships from such places as the parent-teacher organization, alumni group and athletic booster clubs.

If you are a college student, make an appointment with your school's financial aid office. Before the appointment, think about what interests and talents you have and what field you may want to enter after graduation. Take a copy of your Free Application for Federal Student Aid (FAFSA) as background (www.fafsa.ed.gov). Mention any special circumstances about your family's financial situation. Ask the financial aid officer for recommendations of scholarships offered by the college or by community organizations.

Also, if you have already declared a major, check with the department's administrative assistant or chair for any awards that you might be eligible to win.

It's important whenever you speak to a counselor (either in high school or college) that you inquire about any scholarships that require nomination. Often these scholarships are easier to win since the applicant pool is smaller. You have nothing to lose by asking, and if anything, it shows how serious you are about financing your education.

High school websites

You may not visit your school's website daily, but when you are looking for scholarships, it pays to search the site for lists of scholarships. Most high schools post scholarship opportunities for students on their websites. (You may have to dig down a few levels to find this list.)

Other high school websites

If your school does not post scholarship opportunities, surf over to the websites of other high schools in the area. You'll find that many offer a wealth of scholarship resources.

Nearby colleges

While your college has great scholarship resources, wouldn't it be great if you had double or triple these resources? You can. Simply seek the resources of other local colleges. Ask permission first, but you'll find that most neighboring schools are more than willing to help you. If you are in high school, nothing prevents you from visiting a local college and asking for scholarship information. Because you are a prospective student, the college will often be happy to provide whatever assistance it can.

Student clubs and organizations

Here's a reason to enjoy your extracurricular activities even more. One benefit of participating may be a scholarship sponsored by the organization. Inquire with the officers or advisors of the organization about scholarship funds. Bands, newspapers, academic clubs, athletic organizations and service organizations often have scholarships that are awarded to outstanding members. If the organization has a national parent organization (e.g. National Honor Society) visit the national organization website. There are often awards that are given by the parent organization for members of local chapters.

Community organizations

Maybe you've wondered why community organizations have so many breakfast fundraisers—one reason is that some provide money for scholarships.

You usually don't have to be a member of these organizations to apply. In fact, many community groups sponsor scholarships that are open to all students who live in the area. As we have mentioned, college students really have two communities: their hometown and where they go to college. Don't neglect either of these places.

How do you find these organizations? Many local government websites list them. Visit the websites for your town, city and state. Also visit or call your community association or center. You can use the phone book to look up organizations. Some phone books even have a calendar of annual events that are sponsored by various civic groups. Finally, don't forget to pay a visit to the public library and ask the reference librarian for help. Here is a brief list of some of the more common civic groups to track down:

- Altrusa
- American Legion and American Legion Auxiliary
- American Red Cross
- Association of Junior Leagues International
- Boys and Girls Clubs
- Boy Scouts and Girl Scouts
- Circle K
- Civitan
- Elks Club
- Lions Club
- 4-H Clubs
- Fraternal Order of Eagles
- Friends of the Library
- Kiwanis International
- Knights of Columbus
- National Exchange Club
- National Grange
- Optimist International
- Performing Arts Center
- Rotary Club
- Rotaract and Interact
- Ruritan
- Sertoma International

- Soroptimist International of the Americas
- U.S. Jaycees
- USA Freedom Corps
- Veterans of Foreign Wars
- YMCA and YWCA
- Zonta International

Local businesses

Businesses like to return some of their profits to employees and students in the community. Many offer scholarships as a way to reward students who both study and work. Ask your manager if your employer has a scholarship fund and how you can apply. Some companies—particularly large conglomerates that have offices, distributorships or factories in your community—offer scholarships that all students in the community are eligible to win. Check with the chamber of commerce for a list of the largest companies in the area. You can call the public relations or community outreach department in these companies to inquire about any scholarship opportunities. Visit the large department and chain stores in the area and ask the store manager or customer service manager about scholarships.

Parents' employer

Your parents may hate their jobs, but they'll love the fact that many companies award scholarships to the children of employees as a benefit. They should speak with someone in the human resources department or with their direct managers about scholarships and other educational programs offered by their company.

Parents' or grandparents' military service

If your parents or grandparents served in the U.S. Armed Forces, you may qualify for a scholarship from a military association. Each branch of the service and even specific divisions within each branch have associations. Speak with your parents and grandparents about their military service and see if they belong to or know of these military associations.

Your employer

Flipping burgers may have an up side. Even if you work only part-time, you may qualify for an educational scholarship given by your employer. For example, McDonald's offers the National Employee Scholarship to reward the accomplishments of its student-employees. There is even a McScholar of the Year prize that includes a $5,000 scholarship. If you have a full- or part-time job, ask your employer about scholarships.

Parents' union

Don't know if your parents are in a union? Ask and find out. Some unions sponsor scholarships for the children of their members. Ask your parents to speak with the union officers about scholarships and other educational programs sponsored by their union.

Interest clubs

Performing arts centers, city orchestras, equestrian associations and amateur sports leagues are just a few of the many special interest clubs that may offer scholarships. While some limit their awards to members, many simply look for students who are interested in what they support. A city performing arts center, for example, may offer an award for a talented performing artist in the community.

Professional sports teams

They may not have won a World Series since the 1950s, but don't discount them as a viable scholarship source. Many local professional athletic teams offer community awards (and not necessarily for athletes) as a way to contribute to the cities in which they are based.

Church or religious organizations

Religious organizations may provide scholarships for members. If you or your parents are members of a religious organization, check with the leaders to see if a scholarship is offered.

Local government

Some cities and counties provide scholarships specifically designated for local students. Often, local city council members and state representatives sponsor a scholarship fund. Even if you didn't vote for them, call their offices and ask if they offer a scholarship.

Local newspaper

Local newspapers often print announcements about students who win scholarships. Keep a record of the scholarships featured or go to the library or look online at back issues of the newspaper. Check last year's spring issues (between March and June) for announcements of scholarship recipients. Contact the sponsoring organizations to see if you're eligible to enter the next competition.

Is There a Magic Number of Scholarships?

We often are asked, "How many scholarships should I apply to?" The truth is that there is no magic number of scholarships for which you should apply. But you should avoid the extremes. Don't select only a couple of scholarships with the intention of spending countless hours crafting the perfect application. While it is true that to win you need to turn in quality applications, there is also a certain amount of subjective decision making. So even with the perfect application, you may not win. This means that you need to apply to more than a few scholarships. On the other hand, don't apply for 75 awards, sending in the same application to each. You'll just waste your time. You need to strike a balance between quantity and quality.

Searching Beyond Your Backyard

Once you have exhausted the opportunities in the community, it is time to broaden your search. Although the applicant pool is often larger with national awards, you shouldn't rule them out. Because many national award programs have marketing budgets, finding these awards may actually be easier than local awards. Most national awards will be advertised and the following places will help you track them down:

Internet

Forget the time-wasting social networks, and let's use the Internet for something productive. We recommend that you use as many online scholarship databases as possible as long as they are free. There are enough quality free databases that you should not have to pay for any online search. Here are a few we recommend:

- SuperCollege (www.supercollege.com)
- moolahSPOT (www.moolahspot.com)
- Sallie Mae (www.salliemae.com/scholarships)
- BrokeScholar (www.brokescholar.com)
- FastWeb (www.fastweb.com)
- Careers and Colleges (www.careersandcolleges.com)
- The College Board (www.collegeboard.com)
- Scholarships.com (www.scholarships.com)
- AdventuresinEducation (www.adventuresineducation.org)
- CollegeNet (www.collegenet.com)

Just remember that while many online databases claim to have billions of dollars in scholarships listed, they represent only a tiny fraction of what is available. We have personally used nearly every free scholarship database on the Internet and know from experience that none of them (including our own at www.supercollege.com) lists every scholarship that you might win. Think of these databases as starting points, and remember that they are not the only places to find awards.

Professional associations

There is an association for every profession you can imagine. Whether you want to be a doctor, teacher or helicopter pilot, there are professional organizations that exist not only to advance the profession, but also to encourage students to enter that field by awarding grants and scholarships.

To find these associations, contact people who are already in the profession. If you think you want to become a computer programmer, ask computer programmers about the associations to which they belong. Also look at the trade magazines that exist for the profession since they have advertisements for various professional organizations.

Another way to find associations is through books like *The Encyclopedia of Associations*. This multi-volume set found at most college libraries lists nearly every professional association in the United States. Once you find these associations, contact them or visit their websites to see if they offer scholarships.

Professional associations often provide scholarships for upper-level college students, graduate school or advanced training. But even high school students who know what they want to do after college can find money from associations.

Big business

If you've never received a personal "thank you" from large companies like Coca-Cola, Tylenol or Microsoft, here it is. A lot of these have charitable foundations that award scholarships. Companies give these awards to give something back to the community (and the positive PR sure doesn't hurt either). When you visit company websites, look for links to their foundations, which often manage the scholarship programs.

Many companies offer similar types of scholarships. What if you're a student film maker? Think about all the companies that make money or sell products to you from cameras to editing software to tripods. Are you into industrial music? What special equipment or instruments do you use? Consider the companies that will benefit from more people using their products and services. Some companies also offer awards to attract future employees. For example, Microsoft, the software company, sponsors a scholarship program for student programmers. Be sure to investigate companies that employ people in your field of study—especially if it is highly competitive—to see if they offer scholarships.

Colleges

You may think that checks only travel from your pocket to your college to pay for tuition. But colleges actually give a lot of money to students. Some of this money comes from the college itself while other money is from generous donations of alumni. Every college administers a number of scholarships, some based on financial need and some based on merit. What many students don't know is that often a student's application for admission is also used by the college to determine if he or she may win a scholarship. This is one reason it is worth the submission of any optional essay suggested on a college application. Even if the essay does not impact your admission, it could be used to award you some scholarship dollars.

Don't Look for Scholarships Alone

One of the biggest mistakes we made when looking for scholarships was that we did so alone. Maybe we didn't want to share what we found with our friends and thereby increase competition, or perhaps we just didn't see the benefits of working in groups. Whatever the reason, it probably cost us a ton of money.

Since then we've met thousands of students who have won scholarships. Of these the most successful are those who did not look for scholarships alone. In fact, they made it the biggest group project imaginable.

Take for example the three guys we met in Los Angeles. Essentially, all three young men are going to college for free because they were able to win way more money than they could ever use! How did they do it? They formed a "scholarship group". Every Saturday morning they met at Starbucks and one of their parents agreed to pick up the tab for Frappuccinos. The only rule was that each had to bring at least two new scholarships. What happened was that one guy might find an award that was not right for him but was perfect for someone else in the group. This sharing of information was a tremendous advantage over laboring individually and literally tripled their chances of finding scholarships.

Another benefit was that working in a group kept these guys motivated. There certainly must have been weeks when searches were fruitless and the scholarship pickings were slim. The guys might have been tempted to give up, but being in a group brings with it a sense of responsibility not to disappoint the other members of the unit. Searching for scholarships alone is very difficult and it's so easy to just quit. But when you work in a group, you keep one another motivated and you have a natural support base that keeps you going when you feel like quitting.

So did these guys increase the competition by sharing scholarships? In some cases they did. But this was far outweighed by the sheer number of scholarships that they found collectively that they never would have found working alone.

As a general rule, students who worked with others discovered that by sharing the awards they found and pooling their resources, they were able to find more scholarships in less time than they would have found individually. The end result was that these students had more scholarships to apply to and more time to focus on their applications. Hence, they won more money.

Let this be a lesson to all of us. Look around you and find others who are also hunting for scholarships. Convince them that the way to really win lots of free money for college is to work in groups.

Prioritize the Scholarships You Find

Until now, we have focused on where to find scholarships. If you invest time exploring these areas, you should have a fairly long list of potential scholarships. It may be tempting to start cranking out applications. We actually have a name for the methodology used by students that apply to anything and everything they find—it's called the "shotgun" approach and it never works. Just because you find an award for which you qualify does not mean that you should immediately apply. You want to focus your energies (and limited time) only on those awards that you have the best chance of winning.

It would save a lot of time if you knew beforehand which scholarships you'd win and which you wouldn't. With this information, you'd only spend time applying for the scholarships that you knew would result in cash in your pocket. While there is no way to be 100 percent certain that you'll win any scholarship, you can do some research and make an educated guess.

Here are the steps you should take with each scholarship to determine if you have a reasonable chance of winning it. By prioritizing your list based on these criteria, you'll be able to focus time on awards that you have the best odds of winning while not wasting time on the ones where being a match is a long shot.

Step 1 Learn the Purpose

Nobody, and we mean nobody, gives away money without a reason. Every sponsor of a scholarship has a concrete reason for giving away their hard-earned cash to students like you. For example, a teachers' organization might award a scholarship to encourage students to enter the teaching profession. An environmental group might sponsor a scholarship with the purpose of promoting environmental awareness, or it might reward students who have done environmental work in school. A local bank might give money to a student who has done a great deal of public service as a way to give back to the community in which it does business.

Your job is to uncover the purpose of every scholarship on your list. If you're lucky, it will be stated in the description of the award. Look at the eligibility requirements to see what kind of questions the scholarship sponsors are asking. Is there a GPA requirement? If there is and it's relatively high, academic achievement is probably important. If the GPA requirement is low, then grades are probably not important. Does the application ask for a list of extracurricular activities? If so, they are probably a significant part of the selection criteria. Do you need to submit an essay on a specific topic or a project to demonstrate proficiency in a field of study? All these requirements are clues about what the scholarship judges think will (and won't) be important.

For example, the sole purpose of a public service scholarship may be to reward a student's philanthropic acts. If that is the case, the application will most likely be focused on descriptions of a student's selfless deeds. On the other hand, a scholarship given by a major corporation may be based on a combination of grades, leadership and character.

If you cannot determine the purpose of the scholarship by reading its description and eligibility requirements, then you need to look for the purpose of the group that sponsors the award. For example, even if the scholarship description does not directly state it, you can be sure that an award given by an organization that is composed of local physicians will probably prefer that the winner have a connection with medicine or an intention to enter the medical field.

The membership of the organization can be a big clue. Just as your friends are a reflection of who you are, most clubs and organizations want to reach students who are similar to their membership. If you don't know much about the organization, contact them to learn background information regarding the history, purpose or contributions of the group. Visit the organization's website. Read their brochures or publications. The more you know about why the organization is giving the award, the better you'll understand how you may or may not fit.

Somewhere on your list of potential scholarships, note in a few words its purpose. You'll be using this information in the next step which is to determine if you can make a case that you are the type of person the scholarship committee is looking for.

Beware of Scholarship Scams

While the great majority of scholarship providers and services have philanthropic intentions, not all do. There are some scholarship services and even scholarships themselves that you need to avoid. According to the Federal Trade Commission, in one year there were more than 175,000 cases reported of scholarship scams, costing consumers $22 million. And this is a low estimate since most scholarship scams go unreported!

While we were fortunate to have not been victims of a scholarship scam, we have to admit that the offers we received were tempting. We both received letters in high school and college from companies that promised to help us find and win "unclaimed" scholarships. The pitch was tempting: There is money out there that no one is claiming. All we needed to do was purchase their service to get a list of these awards. Had we done so, we would have been $400 poorer and certainly none the richer. In this chapter, we will describe some of the common scams that you may encounter. You must avoid these offers, no matter how glamorous they seem.

The key to avoiding a scholarship scam is to understand the motivation of the people behind these scams. Those who operate financial aid rip-offs know that paying for college is something that makes you extremely nervous. They also know that most people don't have extensive experience when it comes to scholarships and may therefore believe that there are such things as "hidden" or "unclaimed" scholarships. These charlatans take advantage of your fears and discomfort by offering an easy answer with a price tag that seems small compared to the promised benefits. Be aware that you are vulnerable to these kinds of inducements. Think about it this way. If you have a weakness for buying clothes, you need to be extra vigilant when you are at the shopping mall. Similarly, because you need money for college, you are more susceptible to tempting scholarship offers. Acknowledging that these fears make you a target of scam artists is the first step to spotting their traps.

Step 2 Think Like a Judge

Once you know the purpose of the scholarship, you need to see if you are a match for the organization that sponsors it. At this point students often make one of two mistakes. Either they 1) overestimate how well they fit the purpose or, more commonly, 2) underestimate their qualifications and don't apply. After working with thousands of students, we have learned that students more often underestimate their abilities than overestimate. Try to be realistic, but also don't sell yourself short. Remember that scholarship judges are not looking for the perfect match. There are a lot of factors that will influence their decision, and many of these things—like personality, character and motivation—are difficult to measure.

Let's look at an example. If you are your school's star journalist, naturally you should apply for journalism scholarships. But if all you have done is write a single letter to the editor, then spend your time applying to scholarships that better match what you have accomplished. You can still apply for a journalism scholarship, especially if you only recently realized that you want to become a journalist, but you will be at a disadvantage compared to the other applicants and therefore should prioritize this award below other awards on your to-do list.

As you go through your list of scholarships, move to the bottom those which are the weakest matches to the goal of the scholarships. Make those awards that fit you best your highest priority. These are the ones that you want to focus on first.

Step 3 Take a Reality Check

Scholarship deadlines are not like tax deadlines, where there is a single day when all forms are due. The deadlines for scholarships vary. Be aware of these crucial dates. Unless you plan carefully, you may miss out on a scholarship simply because you don't have the time to create a decent application. Sandwiched among studying, sleeping and everything else in your busy life, there is limited time to spend on applying for scholarships. If you find a great scholarship that is due next week but requires a yet to-be-written original composition that would take a month, you should probably pass on the competition. If you know that, given the amount of time available, you won't be able to do an acceptable job, it's better to pass and move on to awards in which you have the time to put together a winning application. Remember too that you may be able to apply for the award next year.

Review Your List Daily

After you prioritize your scholarships with the ones you feel fit you best at the top of the list, push yourself to apply to as many as you can, working from top to bottom. You probably won't get to the end. This is okay since you have the least chance of winning the awards at the bottom anyway. By prioritizing and working methodically down your list, you will have hedged your bets by making sure that your first applications are for the scholarships that you have the best chance of winning while also not limiting yourself to only a handful of awards.

How to Win the Scholarships You Find

Chapter 3

Attacking the Scholarship Application

At first glance, scholarship applications look easy—most are only a single page in length. Piece of cake, right? Don't let their diminutive size fool you. The application is a vital part of winning any scholarship. Scholarship judges must sift through hundreds or even thousands of applications, and the application form is what they use to determine which applicants continue to the next stage. It's crucial that you ace your application to make this first cut.

In this chapter, we'll look at strategies you can use to transform an ordinary scholarship application form into a screaming testament of why you deserve to win free cash for college.

Five Steps to Crafting a Winning Application

Step 1 Strategically Choose What to List

Imagine that you need to give a speech to two groups of people. Without knowing who your audience is, you would have a difficult time composing a speech that would appeal to them, right? It would make a huge difference if one were a group of mathematicians and the other a group of fashion designers. To grab the attention of each of these audiences, you'd need to adjust your speech accordingly. References to mathematical theorems would hardly go over well with the designers, just as the mathematicians probably couldn't care less about how black the "new" black really is.

In much the same way, you need to decide what to highlight on your scholarship application based on the purpose of the award. When you know what the scholarship judges are looking for, it makes it easier to decide what to include or omit. As we mentioned earlier, organizations don't give away scholarships and expect nothing in return. Behind their philanthropic motives lies an ulterior motive—to promote their organization's purpose. If you prioritized your list of scholarships correctly, you've already uncovered the purpose for each award. Now look at all your activities, interests, hobbies and achievements. Ask yourself which ones fit the purpose of each award and would make a positive impression on the scholarship judges.

Let's imagine that you are applying for an award given by an organization of professional journalists. In visiting their website, you learn that print and broadcast journalists join this group because they are passionate about the profession of journalism and want to encourage public awareness about the importance of a free press. Immediately, you know that you need to highlight those experiences that demonstrate your zeal for journalism and, if applicable, your belief in the value of a free press.

Among your activities and accomplishments are the following:

- Soccer team captain
- Vice President of the Writers' Club
- Key Club treasurer
- Columnist for your high school newspaper
- English essay contest winner
- Summer job working at a pet store
- Summer internship at a radio station

As you look at this list, you can eliminate some activities outright. Your involvement on the soccer team, with the Key Club, and your job at the pet store are not relevant and don't show how you fit with the purpose of the scholarship.

However, even looking at what's left, you still have to decide which ones to list first. As you think about the purpose of the scholarship, you remember that in the Writers' Club you participated in a workshop that helped a local elementary school start its own newspaper. Since this achievement almost perfectly matches the mission of our hypothetical journalism organization, use your limited space in the application to list it first and to add an explanation.

You might write something like this:

```
Writers' Club, Vice President, organized "Writing Counts"
workshop at Whitman Elementary School, which resulted in the
launch of the school's first student-run newspaper.
```

Think of the impact this would have on the scholarship judges. "Look here, Fred!" one journalist on the judging committee would say. "This student does what we do! Definitely someone we should interview!"

When choosing accomplishments to list, don't be afraid to eliminate any that don't fit—even good ones. You have limited space in which to cram a lot of information. As you fill out the application, you may find that you are trying to squeeze in too many details or simply too many things. You need to be ruthless in trimming down what you submit to the judges. Make sure to include the accomplishments that *best fit* the purpose of the award.

At the same time you are picking which things to include in your application, be sure to also be aware of what might be offensive to the organization's members. Just imagine what would happen if you thoughtlessly mentioned that you were the author of an economics project entitled "How Labor Unions Make the U.S. Unable to Compete and Lower Our Standard of Living" to judges who are members of the International Brotherhood of Teamsters.

Clearly you can't use the same list of activities and accomplishments for every scholarship. You must take the time to craft a unique list that matches what each of the scholarships is intended to reward.

Create a Timeline

Every scholarship has a deadline. Even though you have created a prioritized list of awards, you need also be aware of the deadlines. In fact, the due date for an award may also influence how you prioritize it. It's also helpful to set yourself deadlines and create a schedule for applying. Set deadlines for when you will have the application forms completed, essays written and any required recommendations submitted. Post this schedule where you can see it every day. We also recommend that you share it with your parents. Moms and dads are great at nagging (we mean reminding) you to meet deadlines, so you might as well use their nagging (we mean motivating) skills to your advantage.

Step 2 List Important Accomplishments First

In movies, the most dare-devilish car chase, the most harrowing showdown and the most poignant romantic revelations are usually saved until the end. While this works for Hollywood, it does not for scholarship applications. Since scholarship judges review so many applications and the space on the form is limited, you must learn to highlight your most impressive points first.

If you have listed four extracurricular activities, assume that some judges won't read beyond the first two. This doesn't mean that all judges will be this rushed, but there are always some who are. It's extremely important that you prioritize the information that you present and rank your accomplishments according to the following criteria—which should not come as too much of a surprise.

Fit: The most important factor in ordering your achievements is how they fit with the purpose of the scholarship. This is, after all, why these kind people want to hand you some free dough. Emphasize accomplishments that match the purpose of the scholarship. If you are applying for an award that rewards athleticism, stress how well you've done in a particular sport before listing your volunteer activities.

Scope: Next prioritize your accomplishments by their scope, or how much of an impact they have made. How many people have been affected by your work? To what extent has your accomplishment affected your community? Did your contribution produce measurable results? In simple terms, put the big stuff before the small stuff.

Uniqueness: Since your application will be compared to those of perhaps thousands of others, include accomplishments that are uncommon. Give priority to those that are unique or difficult to win. Being on your school's honor roll is certainly an achievement, but it is an honor that many others have received. Try to select honors that fewer students have received—you want to stand out in order to be selected.

Timeliness: This is the least-important criterion, but if you get stuck and aren't sure how to arrange some of your accomplishments, put the more recent achievements first. Having won an election in the past year is more relevant than having won one three years ago. Some students ask us if they should list junior high or even elementary school achievements. Generally, stick to accomplishments from high school if you're a high school student and to college if you're a college student. An exception is if your accomplishment is extremely impressive and relevant—such as publishing your own book in the eighth grade. Of course, if you run out of recent achievements and there is still space on the form, go ahead and reach back to the past—but try to limit yourself to only one or two items.

You want your application to be as unforgettable as the best Hollywood movies. The only difference between your work and Spielberg's—besides the millions of dollars—is that you need to place the grand finale first.

You Can Recycle Your Applications

The first scholarship for which you apply will take the most time. But with each application you complete, it will get easier. This is because for each successive application, you can draw on the materials you developed for the previous one. To complete your first application, you need to think about your activities and recall achievements that you have forgotten. If there is an essay component, you will need to find a topic and craft an articulate essay. When you work on your second application, you can benefit from the work you've already done for the first. As you're building your timeline, look for scholarships in which you can recycle information from one application to another. Recycling will save you time. In addition, you can improve on your work each time that you use it. For example, the second time you answer a question about your plans after graduation, you can craft your response more effectively than the first. As you recycle Information, don't just reuse it—improve it!

Step 3 Spin Your Application to Impress the Judges

Politicians are notorious for telling voters what they want to hear. Good politicians never lie, but they do put a flattering "spin" on their words depending on whom they're addressing. While you must never lie on your application forms, you do want to present yourself in the best possible way so that you appeal to your audience. In other words, employ a little spin.

We know that some politicians have a difficult time distinguishing between lying and spinning. You shouldn't. Let's say you are applying for a scholarship that rewards students who are interested in promoting literacy. You have been a volunteer at your local library where, aside from typical page duties each week, you also read stories to a dozen children for story time. Here are three ways you could describe this activity on your application:

Non-spin description:

```
Library volunteer.
```

Lie:

```
Library reading program founder. Started a national program
that reaches thousands of children every day to promote
literacy.
```

Spin:

```
Library volunteer. Promoted literacy among children through
weekly after-school reading program at public library.
```

At one extreme, you can see that a lie exaggerates well beyond the truth. At the other extreme, the non-spin description is not very impressive because it does not explain how the activity relates to the purpose of the scholarship. The spin version is just right. It does not stretch the truth, but it does make clear how this activity fits within the context of the purpose of the scholarship. It focuses on what is important to the judges while at the same time, it ignores other aspects of your job that are not relevant—such as shelving books.

To take this example one step further, let's say that now you are applying for a scholarship that rewards student leaders. One of your other responsibilities as a library volunteer is to maintain the schedule for volunteers and help with the recruitment of new volunteers. Your description for this scholarship might read something like this:

```
Library volunteer. In charge of volunteer schedule and re-
cruitment of new members.
```

Notice how you have "spun" your activity so that it highlights a different aspect of what you did and better shows the judges how you fit their criteria. In the application, you should use the opportunity to spin your accomplishments to match the purpose of the award.

To be able to spin effectively, you need to know your audience. When you prioritized your scholarships earlier, you should have discovered the purpose of each scholarship. Remember that in most cases the scholarship judges want to give their money to students who are the best reflections of themselves. For example, the Future Teachers of America judges will want to fund students who seem the most committed to pursuing a teaching career. The American Congress of Surveying and Mapping judges, on the other hand, want to award their money to students who have the strongest interest in cartography.

Step 4 Write to Impress

The inspiring words of Martin Luther King Jr.'s "I Have a Dream" speech were punctuated with his dramatic, emotion-filled voice, hopeful expression and confident presence. His delivery would not have been as forceful had he spoken in a drab, monotone, with hands stuffed into his pockets and eyes lowered to avoid contact with the audience. Nor would his dramatic presentation have been as effective had his message been unimportant. The lesson? Both content and delivery count. While you don't have the opportunity for person-to-person delivery with your scholarship applications, you can and should present information in a compelling way. Here are some time-tested writing strategies for creating a positive impression through your applications:

Showcase Your Smarts. There's a reason why your parents wanted you to study and do well in school. In addition to the correlation between studying and success in college, almost all scholarship judges (even those of athletic awards) are impressed by academic achievement. College is, after all, about learning (at least that's what you want your parents to believe).

As you are completing your applications, keep in mind that while you may be applying for a public service scholarship, you should also include at least one academic achievement. For example, it does not hurt to list on an athletic scholarship form that you also came in second place at the science fair. This should not be the first thing you list, but it should be included somewhere to show the committee that you have brains in addition to brawn.

Extracurricular Activities and Hobbies Show Your Passion. If your only activity were studying, your life would be severely lacking in excitement. Scholarship organizers recognize this and thus the criteria for many scholarships include extracurricular activities or hobbies. Scholarship committees want evidence that you do more than read textbooks, take exams and watch television. They want to know that you have other interests. This makes you a more well-rounded person.

As always, when completing your applications, select extracurricular activities and hobbies that fit with the scholarship's mission. If you are applying for a music scholarship, describe how you've been involved in your school's orchestra or how you've taken violin lessons. By showing that you not only have taken classes in music theory but have also been involved with music outside of your studies, the scholarship committee will get a more complete picture of your love for music. Remember to use your activities and hobbies to illustrate your passion for a subject.

Leadership Is Always Better Than Membership. If you've ever tried to motivate a group of peers to do anything (without taking the easy way out—bribery) you know that it takes courage, intelligence and creativity to be a leader. Because of this, many scholarships give extra points to reward leadership. Scholarship judges want to know that the dollars will be awarded to someone who will not only make a difference in the future but who will also be a leader and motivate others to do the same. Think of it this way: If you were a successful businessperson trying to encourage entrepreneurship, wouldn't you want to give your money to a young person who is not only an entrepreneur but who also motivates others to become entrepreneurs?

Describing leadership in your activities or hobbies will also help set you apart from the other applicants. Many students are involved with environmental groups, but what if you are the only one to actually help increase recycling on your campus? Wouldn't that make your application a standout?

To show scholarship judges that you are a leader, list any activities in which you took responsibility for a specific project. Use action verbs when describing your work:

- Organized band fundraiser to purchase new instruments
- Led a weeklong nature tour in Yosemite Valley
- Founded first website to list volunteer activities
- Directed independent musical performance

Remember that you don't need to be an elected officer to be a leader. Many students have organized special projects, led teams or helped run events. Even if you didn't have an official title, you can include these experiences. Here's an example:

```
Environmental Action Committee Member. Spearheaded subcom-
mittee on reducing waste and increasing recycling on campus.
```

When describing your leadership, include both formal and informal ways you have led groups. This shows the scholarship committee that you are a worthy investment.

Honors and Awards Validate Your Strengths. There's a reason why all trophies are gold and gaudy. They shout to the world in a deafening roar, "Yes, this glittery gold miniature figure means I am the best!" For applications that ask for your honors and awards, impart some of that victorious roar and attitude. In no way are we recommending that you ship your golden statuettes off with your applications. We are saying that you should highlight honors and awards in a way that gets the scholarship committee to pay attention to your application. What makes an award impressive is scope. Not a minty mouthwash, scope in this case is the impact and influence of the award. You worked for the award and earned every golden inch of it. Show the committee that they don't just hand these statuettes out to anybody. One way to do this is to point out how many awards are given:

```
English Achievement Award. Presented to two outstanding ju-
niors each year.
```

By itself, the English Achievement Award does not tell the scholarship committee very much. Maybe half the people in your class were given the award. By revealing the scope of the award (particularly if it was given to only a few) it becomes much more impressive.

In competitions that reach beyond your school, it is important to qualify your awards. For example, while everyone at your school may know that the Left Brain Achievement Award is given to creative art students, the rest of the world does not.

Don't write:

```
Left Brain Achievement Award.
```

Do write:

```
Left Brain Achievement Award. Recognized as an outstanding
creative talent in art as conferred upon by vote of art de-
partment faculty.
```

You've worked hard to earn the honors and awards that you have received, and you should not hesitate to use them in your applications to help you win scholarships.

Know when to leave a space blank. An official mom rule from childhood is this: "If you don't have anything nice to say, don't say it." While this is a good lesson on self-restraint, it does not always hold true for scholarship applications. In general, it is not a good idea to leave any area blank. You don't need to fill the entire space, but you should make an effort to list something in every section. However, before you try to explain how the handmade certificate that your mom presented you for being Offspring of the Year qualifies as an "award," realize that there are limits. If you've never held a job, don't list anything under work experience. If, however, you painted your grandmother's house one summer and got paid for it, you might consider listing it if you don't have any other options.

Perfect every sentence. Succinct and terse, scholarship application forms bear the well-earned reputation for having less space than you need. Often offering only a page or less, scholarship and award forms leave little room for much more than just the facts. As you are completing your applications, remember to abbreviate where appropriate and keep your sentences short. Often judges are scanning the application form. If they want an essay, they will ask for one. However, you do not want to take instructions so literally that you miss their intent. For instance, if the instructions say to list your awards, don't feel like you can't add explanation if you need to. And, as always, be selective in what you list. If you have three great awards, it is better to use your space to list those three with short explanations rather than cram in all 15 awards that you've won in your life. (No argument can be made for the timeliness of your Perfect Attendance Award from kindergarten.) You are trying to present the most relevant information that shows the scholarship judges why you deserve their money. Use the space to explain how each award, job or activity relates to the scholarship.

Also, feel free to interpret some instructions. Work experience does not have to be limited to traditional jobs. Maybe you started your own freelance design business or cut lawns on the weekends—those count! The same goes for leadership positions. Who said that leadership has to be an elected position within an organization? Just be sure to explain the entry if the relationship is not totally clear. Here's an example:

```
Volunteer Wilderness Guide. Led clients through seven-day
trek in Catskills. Responsible for all aspects of the trip
including group safety.
```

Always remember that the application is you. A scholarship application is more than a piece of paper. In the eyes of the scholarship judges, it is *you*. It may not be fair, but in many cases the application is the only thing that the judges will have as a measurement standard. The last thing you want to be is a dry list of academic and extracurricular achievements. You are a living, breathing person. Throughout the application, take every opportunity—no matter how small—to show the judges who you really are. Use descriptions and vocabulary that reveal your passion and commitment. Always remember that the application is a reflection of you.

Step 5 Separate Yourself from the Competition

Think of the scholarship competition as a reverse police lineup where you want to stand out and be picked by the people behind the one-way mirror. You want the judge to say without hesitation, "That's the one!" The only way this will happen is if your application is noticed and doesn't get lost in the stack. One of the best ways to accomplish this is to know what you're up against—in other words, think about who else will be in the lineup with you.

Try to anticipate your competition—even if it's just an educated guess. Depending on to whom the scholarship is offered, you may have a limited or broad pool of competitors. If the award is confined to your school, you may know everyone who will enter on a first-name basis. If it's national, all you may know is that all the applicants have a similar interest in a broad field. For a medical scholarship, for instance, the applicants might be students interested in becoming doctors or nurses. More important than the scope of the competition is the type of students who will apply. One of the biggest challenges in any competition is to break away from the pack. If 500 pre-med students are applying for a $10,000 scholarship from a medical association, you need to make sure that your application stands out from those of the 499 other applicants. If you are lucky, you may have done something that few have done. (Inventing a new vaccine in your spare time would certainly set you apart!) Unfortunately, most of us will have to distinguish ourselves in more subtle ways, such as through the explanation of our activities and accomplishments.

Say you are applying for a scholarship given by a national medical association that seeks to promote the medical sciences. It just so happens that you are considering a pre-med major and you have interned at a local hospital. If you hadn't read this book, you might have listed under activities something like this entry:

```
Summer Internship at Beth Israel Children's Hospital.
```

But you did read this book! So you know that this is a great activity to elaborate on since it demonstrates your commitment to medicine and shows that you truly are interested in entering the medical field. You also know that you need to stand out from the competition; and as great as this activity is, you know that a lot of other applicants also will have volunteered at hospitals. So instead of simply listing the internship, you add detail to make the experience more unique. You could write it this way:

```
Summer Internship at Beth Israel Children's Hospital; as-
sisted with clinical trial of new allergy medication.
```

This description is much more unique and memorable. By providing details, you can illustrate to the judges how your volunteer work is different from that of other students. Remember that you can add short descriptions in most applications even if the instructions do not explicitly ask for them.

If you can anticipate who your competition will be and what they might write in their applications, you will be able to find a way to go one step further to distinguish yourself from the crowd. Even the simple act of adding a one-sentence description to an activity can make the difference between standing out or being overlooked.

Now that you know the five steps to insure that your application is a winner, here is our Top Ten list of application form do's and don'ts which will serve as a final reminder of how to create that stunning application!

Be a Neat Freak

You may have dirty laundry strewn across your room and a pile of papers large enough to be classified as its own life form, but you don't want the scholarship judges to know that. When it comes to applications, neatness does count. We would not ordinarily be neatness zealots—we admit to having our own mountains of life-imbibed papers—but submitting an application with globs of correction fluid, scratched out words or illegible hieroglyphics will severely diminish your message. Think how much less impressive the Mona Lisa would be if da Vinci had painted it on a dirty old bed sheet. You may have the most incredible thoughts to convey in your applications, but if your form is filled with errors, none of it will matter. In a sea of hundreds and even thousands of other applications, you don't want yours to be penalized by sloppy presentation.

Top Ten Application Do's and Don'ts

With money on the table, it's much better to learn from others' successes and mistakes before you risk your own fortunes. From interviews with students and scholarship judges and firsthand experience reviewing scholarship applications, we've developed our Top Ten list of scholarship application do's and don'ts. Let's shed the negative energy first and start with the don'ts.

Don'ts

1. DON'T prioritize quantity over quality. It's not the quantity of your accomplishments that is important. It's the quality of your contributions.
2. DON'T stretch the truth. Tall tales are prohibited.
3. DON'T squeeze to the point of illegibility. Scholarship applications afford minimal space. It's impossible to fit in everything that you want to say. Don't try by sacrificing legibility.
4. DON'T write when you have nothing to say. If you don't have something meaningful to present, leave it blank.
5. DON'T create white-out globs. If it's that sloppy, start over.
6. DON'T procrastinate. Don't think you can finish your applications the night before they're due.
7. DON'T settle for less than perfect. You can have imperfections. Just don't let the selection committee know.
8. DON'T miss deadlines. No matter the reason, if you miss the deadline, you won't win the scholarship.
9. DON'T turn in incomplete applications. Make sure your application is finished before sending it.

10. DON'T underestimate what you can convey. Scholarship applications may appear to be short and simple. Don't undervalue them. In a small space, you can create a powerful story of why you should win.

And now the good stuff.

Do's

1. DO understand the scholarship's mission. Know why they're giving out the dough.
2. DO remember who your audience is. You need to address animal rights activists and retired dentists differently.
3. DO show how you fit with the scholarship's mission. You're not going to win unless you have what the selection committee wants.
4. DO be proud of your accomplishments. Don't be afraid to brag.
5. DO focus on leadership and contributions. Make your contributions known.
6. DO make your application stand out.
7. DO practice to make sure everything fits. Make practice copies of the original form before you begin filling it out. Then use your spare copies for trial and error.
8. DO get editors. They'll help you create the best, error-free applications you can.
9. DO include a resume. Whether they ask for it or not, make sure you include a tailored scholarship resume. See the next chapter for how to create a great resume.
10. DO make copies of your finished applications for reference. Save them for next year when you do this all over again.

Double Check Your App

Once you've completed your applications, check and double-check for accuracy. Look at every line and every question to make sure you've filled out all the information that is requested on the form. Make sure you have someone else take a look at your application. A second set of eyes may catch mistakes that you invariably will miss. Remember that presentation affects how scholarship judges view applications. You want to convey that you are serious about winning the scholarship by submitting an application that is complete and error-free.

Finally, before handing your applications off to the post office, make application twins. Photocopy all your application materials. If for some reason your scholarship form is lost in the mail, you have a copy you can resend. Plus, by saving this year's applications, you have recycling possibilities (especially the essays: you'll see what we mean in Chapter 4!) and a great starting place for next year's scholarships.

How to Write a Winning Scholarship Essay

chapter 4

The Essay Can Make or Break Your Chances of Winning

Here's a situation repeated a million times each year. A student receives a scholarship application and quickly glances over the form. It looks pretty straightforward, so it's tossed into the "to do" pile. The day before it's due, the student finally gets around to filling it out. Breezing through the application form, the student is about to celebrate finishing when he or she encounters the final requirement. It reads as follows:

```
In 1894 Donald VonLudwig came to America with 10 cents in
his pocket and within a decade built an empire. Write an
800-word essay on how you would incorporate the lessons
of VonLudwig's success into your life.
```

Uh, oh. Life just got harder. Meet the dreaded scholarship essay. The hypothetical student described above—the one we are poking fun at—was one of us! After a few experiences like this one, (which were usually accompanied by all night writing sessions), we learned to work on the essay first and never underestimate how much time it requires.

For most scholarship competitions, it is the essay that will make or break your chances of winning. Why? Because the essay offers you the best chance to show the scholarship judges why you deserve to win. While your application form will get you to the semifinals, it is the essay that will carry you into the winner's circle.

Since the essay is so important, you must not assume that you can crank out a quality essay the night before it's due. A quality essay will take both time and effort. In this chapter we will take you step by step through the process of crafting a winning essay—don't worry, it's easier than you may have imagined. Plus, you will read examples of essays that won thousands of dollars in scholarships. From these, you can see firsthand how the strategies presented in this chapter are actually put to use in real life.

All Essays Ask the Same Underlying Question

Regardless of the specific wording, the underlying question for almost all essay questions is the same: "Why do you deserve to win?" (Your answer should *not* be, "Because I need the money!")

Think about these questions: The Future Teachers of America scholarship asks you to write about the "future of education". The Veterans of Foreign Wars asks you to define "patriotism". The National Sculpture Society asks you to "describe your extracurricular passions". Believe it or not, all these seemingly different questions are asking for the same answer: Why do you deserve to win our money?

Your answers to each must address this underlying question. When writing the Future Teachers of America essay, you can discuss the general state of education and quote a few facts and figures, but you'd better be sure to include how you personally fit into the future of education. If you are planning to be a teacher, you might elaborate on how you will contribute to shaping students' lives. Similarly use the topic of patriotism to impress the VFW judges with not only what you perceive patriotism to be but also how you have actually acted upon those beliefs. And if you answer the National Sculpture Society question with an essay on how much you love to play the guitar, then you really don't deserve to win!

Six Steps to Writing a Winning Scholarship Essay

By now you should be tired of hearing us repeat our mantra of knowing the purpose of the scholarship. You have used this to guide your selection of those scholarships you are most likely to win and how to complete the application form for them. It shouldn't surprise you that you must also use it to guide your essay. Remember, when you are writing about why you deserve to win, the answer and all the examples that you use should show how you fulfill that mission of the scholarship. With this in mind, let's begin our six steps to writing a winning scholarship essay.

Step 1 Find the Right Topic and Approach

You will encounter two types of essay questions. The first asks you to write about a specific topic. For example, "Why is it important to protect our natural environment?" The second type of question gives you a very broad topic such as, "Tell us about yourself." In the first case you don't need to think about a topic, but you do need to develop an approach to answering the question. In the latter you need to come up with both a topic and an approach. Let's look at how this is done, starting with the more difficult task of finding a topic.

Finding a Topic

Let's imagine that you are applying for a scholarship that presents an essay question so broad that you can essentially choose your own topic. To get the ideas flowing, you should use that idea-generating technique you learned in fifth grade—brainstorming. Take out a notebook or start a new file on your computer and just start listing possible topics and themes. Ask yourself questions like these:

- What was a significant event in my life?
- What teacher, relative or friend has influenced who I am?
- What have I learned from my experiences?
- What are my goals for the future?
- Where will I be ten years from now?
- What motivates me to achieve my goals?

When brainstorming, don't be critical of the topics you unearth—just let the creativity flow. Ask parents and friends for suggestions.

Once you have a list of topics, you can start to eliminate those that don't help you answer the question of why you deserve to win. For example, if you apply to a scholarship that rewards public service, you would not want to write about the time you got lost in the woods for three days and had to survive on a single candy bar and wild roots. While that might make an interesting and exciting essay, it does not show the scholarship judges why you are the epitome of public service. This topic, however, may come in handy when you need to write an essay for a scholarship based on character or leadership or why you love Snickers bars.

After you whittle down your list to a few topics that will help show why you deserve to win this particular scholarship, then choose the topic that is the most interesting to you or that you care about the most. It seems self-evident, but surprisingly many students do not select topics that excite them. Why is it important to pick a topic that you are passionate about? Because if you truly like your topic, you will write a better essay. In fact, your enthusiasm and excitement will naturally permeate your writing, which will make it interesting and memorable. It's so much easier to stay motivated writing about something you enjoy rather than something you find boring.

How to Develop a Unique Approach

Whether you have to think of a topic yourself or one is given to you, the next task is to figure out how you are going to approach it. For any given topic there are probably a hundred ways you could address the subject matter in an essay. Most topics are also way too large to completely cover in an 800- to 1,000-word essay, so you are going to have to narrow it down and only share a small part of the larger story. All this involves coming up with an approach to what you will present in your essay—an approach that must convince the judges that you deserve to win their money.

Let's take a look at writing about the traumatic experience of being lost in the woods for three days. You choose this topic since the scholarship wants to reward students with strong character and leadership and this is an experience that you believe shows both. But how do you write about it? If you just retell the story of the ordeal, it will not help the judges see why such an experience reveals the quality of your character or leadership. You need to dig deeper and think about how this experience revealed your strengths. To do this, ask yourself questions like these:

- What does this topic reveal about me?
- How has my life been changed by this experience?
- Why did I do what I did?
- What is the lesson that I learned from this experience?
- What aspect of this topic is most important to making my point?

In thinking about your experience alone in the woods, you may realize that on the second day you came close to breaking down and losing all hope of being rescued. This was the critical point where you had to make a decision to give up or push forward. You decide to focus your essay only on this small sliver of time, what went through your mind and how you decided that you were not going to give up. The details of how you got lost and of your eventual rescue would be unimportant and may be mentioned in only a sentence or two. Focusing your essay on just the second day—and more particularly on how you were able to conquer your fears and not lose hope—would clearly demonstrate to the judges that even under extreme pressure, your true character was revealed. Since you also need to address the leadership aspect, you decide to focus on how you took charge of your fears on the second day. To do this, your essay will describe specific actions you took to lead yourself successfully through this ordeal.

Finding the right approach is just as important as finding the right topic. This is especially true if you answer a question that provides a specific topic. With every scholarship applicant writing about the same topic, you need to be sure that your approach persuasively shows the judges why you deserve to win more than anyone else.

Step 2 Share a Slice of Life

Now that you have a topic and an idea for your approach, you need to decide how you are going to convey your message on paper. Keep in mind that scholarship judges are going to read hundreds if not thousands of essays. Often the essays will be on similar topics, particularly if the topic was given in the scholarship application. Therefore, you need to make sure that your writing is original. The best way to do this is to share a "slice of your life" in the essay.

Imagine that you are writing about your summer trip to Europe. Travel is a very common topic. If you decide to write about how your trip made you realize people from around the world are really quite similar, then you run the real risk of sounding just like every other travel essay. The same would be true for writing about sports. If you tell the story of how your team rallied and came from behind to win the game, you can be sure that it will sound like many other essays about sports. To make sure your essay is original, you need to share a "slice of life." Find one incident that happened during your travels or pick one particular moment in the game and use that to make your point. By focusing on a single day, hour or moment, you greatly reduce your chances of having an essay that sounds like everyone else's. Plus, essays that share a slice of life are usually a lot more interesting and memorable.

Let's look at an example. What if you choose to write about how your mom has been your role model? Moms are one of the most popular role models for essays (and they should be, considering the pain of childbirth). How do you make your mom distinct from all the other applicants writing about their moms? Go ahead and take a moment to think about your mom. Be very specific. Can you find one character trait or incident that really influenced you? Let's say your mom has an obsession with collecting porcelain figurines and this passion led to you becoming interested in collecting baseball cards. Because of this, you are now considering a career in sports management. Now we have something! Imagine that first day when you realized how much your mom loved collecting figurines. Maybe you even bought her one as a present and now she cherishes it above all others. Perhaps it was that moment that jump-started your love for baseball cards, which has now developed into a full blown obsession with sports to the point that you intend to make it a career. You've just succeeded in turning a very popular topic—Mom—into an entirely original essay by finding that slice of life. No two people share the exact same slice of life, so by finding one to share, you are almost always guaranteed to have an original essay.

Want another example? Let's set the stage. Imagine that you are applying to a scholarship for students who major in psychology. The question posed on the application is this: "Tell us about an influential person who inspired you to pursue psychology." As you brainstorm, you list the authors of books you've read and some professors whose classes you have enjoyed. But how many students will be writing about these same people? You could even wager money that every other essay will be about Freud!

As you brainstorm, you recall the worst fight you have ever had with your best friend Susan. As you think about this fight that nearly destroyed a 10-year friendship, you realize that it was one of the first times you applied classroom knowledge to a real life experience. In analyzing the fight, you realize that those psychology principles you studied have practical applications beyond the textbook. So for your essay you decide to write about the fight and how it made you even more committed than ever to become a psychology major.

You don't have to look far to find originality. We all have experiences that are unique to us. Even common experiences can be made original, depending on how you approach them. So don't exclude a topic just because it is common.

By spending some time thinking about how you will write about it, you may be surprised at how original it could be.

Step 3 Stop Thinking, Start Writing

The most challenging part of writing a scholarship essay is getting started. Our advice: Just start writing. The first words you put down on paper may not be brilliant, but don't worry. You can always return to edit your work. It's easier to edit words you've already written than words that don't exist.

Do you think you have a bad case of writer's block? If so, the cure may surprise you. The best cure for writer's block is to just start writing!

We all have different writing styles, but certain points should be kept in mind as you are writing something that is focused on winning over a scholarship committee. Think about these things as you craft that winning essay:

Write for the Scholarship Judges. Let's pretend you're a stand-up comedian who has two performances booked: one at the trendiest club in town where all cool college students congregate and the other at a retirement home. As a skilled comedian, you would prepare different material aimed at the different audiences. The college crowd would be able to relate to jokes about relationships and dating, while your jokes about dentures and arthritis would probably—and this is a hunch—go over better with the senior citizens. The same goes for writing your essays. Since many are given by specialized organizations or for specific purposes, you need to write an essay that is appropriate for the audience. Think about who is going to read your essay. Is your audience natural science professors, circus performers or used car salesmen? Write your essay so it appeals to that audience. This should guide not only your selection of topics but also your word choice, language and tone.

Be Yourself. While you want to present yourself in a way that attracts the attention of the scholarship judges, you don't want to portray yourself as someone you are not. It's okay to present selected highlights from your life that fit with the award, but it's not ethical to exaggerate or outright lie. If you apply for a scholarship to promote the protection of animals, don't write about your deep compassion for helping animals when you've never ventured closer than 10 feet to one because of your allergies. Feel comfortable about everything you write, and don't go overboard trying to mold yourself into being the student you think the scholarship judges want to read about. If you've done your job of picking scholarships that match you best, you already know that you are a good fit. Your task in the essay is to demonstrate this to the judges.

Personalize Your Essay. Think of the scholarship judges as an audience that has come to see your Broadway show. You are the star. To keep them satisfied, give them what they want. In other words, the scholarship judges want to know about your life and experiences. When you write your essay, write about what has happened to you personally or about how you personally have been affected by something. If you are writing about drug abuse for an essay about a problem that faces college students today, do more than recite the latest national drug use statistics and the benefits of drug rehabilitation programs. Otherwise, your essay may be informative, but it won't be interesting. Instead, write about how a friend nearly overdosed on drugs, how others tried to pressure you into trying drugs or about your volunteer work at a rehabilitation clinic. Instantly, your essay will be more interesting and memorable. Plus, the judges really do want to learn more about you, and the only way for them to do this is if you share something about yourself in your essay.

Make Sure You Have a Point. Try this exercise: See if you can encapsulate the point of your essay into a single sentence. If you can't, you don't have a main point. So, you'd better get one! You may think this is obvious, but many students' essays don't have a main point. Use that most basic lesson from Composition 101: Have a thesis statement that states the main point of your essay. Let's say you are writing about growing up in the country. You might structure your essay around the idea that growing up in the country gave you a strong work ethic. This is the essay's main point. You can describe all the flat land and brush you like, but unless these descriptions help to support your point, you don't have a quality essay.

Support Your Statement. Once you put your main point out there, you can't abandon it. Like a baby learning to walk, you have to support your thesis statement because it can't stand on its own. This means you have to provide reasons why your statement is true. You can do this by giving detailed and vivid examples from your personal experiences and accomplishments.

Use Examples and Illustrations. When a reader can visualize what you are writing, it helps to make an impression. Anecdotes and stories accomplish this very effectively. Examples and illustrations also make your ideas clearer. If you want to be a doctor, explain how you became interested in becoming one. You might describe the impact of getting a stethoscope from your father when you were a child. Or maybe you can write about your first day volunteering at the hospital. Examples help readers picture what you are saying and even relate to your experiences. The scholarship judge may have never volunteered at a hospital; but by reading your example, that judge can easily understand how such an experience could be so influential. The one danger of examples is that you need to be sure to keep them concise. It is often too easy to write a long and detailed example when only a few sentences are sufficient. Remember, in an example you are not retelling an entire story but just pulling out a few highlights to illustrate the point you are trying to make.

Show Activity. If you were forced to sit in an empty room with nothing but a bare wall to stare at, you would probably get bored pretty quickly. The same goes for an essay. Don't force the scholarship judges to read an essay that does nothing. Your essay needs activity and movement to bring it to life. This may consist of dialogue, action, stories and thoughts. The last thing you want to do is bore your readers. With action, you won't have to worry about that!

Highlight Your Growth. You may not have grown an inch since seventh grade, but scholarship judges will look for your growth in other ways. They want to see evidence of emotional and intellectual growth, what your strengths are and how you have developed them. Strengths may include—but certainly aren't limited to—mastery of an academic course, musical talent, a desire to help others, athletic ability, leadership of a group and more. Overcoming adversity or facing a challenge may also demonstrate your growth.

Be Positive. You don't need to break out the pompoms and do a cheer, but you need to convey a positive attitude in your essay. Scholarship committees want to see optimism, excitement and confidence. They prefer not to read essays that are overly pessimistic, antagonistic or critical. This doesn't mean that you have to put a happy spin on every word written or that you can't write about a serious topic or problem. For example, if you were a judge reading the following essays about the very serious topic of teen pregnancy, to which author's education fund would you rather make a contribution?

Thesis 1:
`We could reduce the number of pregnant teens if we shifted our efforts away from scare tactics to providing responsible sex education combined with frank discussions regarding the responsibilities of caring for a child.`

Thesis 2:
`Teen pregnancy is incurable. Teenagers will always act irresponsibly and it would be futile for us to believe that we can control this behavior.`

Scholarship committees favor authors who not only recognize problems but also present potential solutions. Leave being pessimistic to adults. You are young, with your entire future ahead of you. Your optimism is what makes you so exciting and why organizations want to give you money to pursue your passion for changing the world. Don't shy away from this opportunity.

Be Concise. The scholarship essay may not have the strict limits of a college admission essay, but that does not give you a license to be verbose. Keep your essay tight, focused and within the recommended length of the scholarship guidelines. If no parameters are given, one or two pages should suffice. You certainly want the readers to get through the entirety of your masterpiece. Remember that most scholarship selection committees are composed of volunteers who are under no obligation to read your entire essay. Make your main points quickly and keep your essay as brief and to the point as possible.

Step 4 Don't Neglect Your Introduction and Conclusion

Studies have found that the most important parts of a speech are the first and last minutes. In between, listeners fade in and out rather than constantly pay attention. It is the introduction and conclusion that leave a lasting impact. This holds true for scholarship essays as well. You need to have a memorable introduction and conclusion. If you don't, the readers may not make it past your introductory paragraph or they may discount your quality essay after reading a lackluster ending. Spend extra time making sure these two parts deliver the message you want. Here are some tips to create knockout introductions and conclusions:

For Introductions

Create action or movement. Think of the introduction as the high-speed car chase at the beginning of a movie that catches the audience's attention.

Pose a question. Questions draw the readers' attention for two reasons. First, they think about how they would answer the query as you have posed it. Second, they are curious to see how you will answer or present solutions to the question in your essay.

Describe. If you can create a vivid image for readers, they will be more likely to want to read on.

For Conclusions

Be thoughtful. Your conclusion should make the second most powerful statement in your essay because this is what your readers will remember. (The most powerful statement should be in your introduction.)

Leave a parting thought. The scholarship committee members have already read your essay (we hope), so you don't need to rehash what you have already said. It's okay to summarize in one sentence, but you want to do more than just "wrap it up". You have one final opportunity to make an impression, so add a parting thought. This should be one last observation or idea that ties into the main point of your essay.

Don't be too quick to end. Too many students tack on a meaningless conclusion or even worse, don't have one at all. Have a decent conclusion that goes with the rest of your essay. Never end your essay with the two words, "The End."

Step 5 Find Editors

Despite what you may think, you're not infallible. Stop gasping—it's true. This means it's important to get someone else to edit your work. Roommates, friends, family members, teachers, professors or advisors make great editors. When you get another person to read your essay, he or she will find errors that eluded you, as well as parts that are unclear to someone reading your essay for the first time. Ask your editors to make sure your ideas are clear, that you answer the question appropriately and that your essay is interesting. Take their suggestions seriously. The more input you get from others and the more times you rewrite your work, the better.

You want your essay to be like silk—smooth and elegant. When you read your work, make sure the connections between ideas are logical and the flow of your writing is understandable. (This is where editors can be extremely helpful.) Also check that you have not included any unnecessary details that might obscure the main point of your essay. Be careful to include any information that is vital to your thesis. Your goal is to produce an essay with clear points and supporting examples that logically flow together.

You also want to make sure that your spelling and grammar are perfect. Again, the best way to do this is to have someone else read your work. If you don't have time to ask someone, then do it yourself—but do it carefully. Read your essay at least once with the sole purpose of looking for spelling and grammatical mistakes. (Your computer's spell check is not 100 percent reliable and won't catch when you accidentally describe how you bake bread with one cup of "flower" instead of "flour.") Try reading your work out loud to listen for grammatical mistakes.

Step 6 Recycle Your Essays

This has no relation to aluminum cans or newspapers. In this case recycling means reusing essays you have written for college applications, classes or even other scholarships. Because colleges and scholarship committees usually ask very broad questions, this is generally doable and saves you a tremendous amount of time. Later in this chapter you will read an example essay. You may be surprised to learn that the author recycled her essay with minimal changes to answer such differing questions as these: "Tell us about one of your dreams," "What is something you believe in strongly?" and "What past experience continues to influence you today?"

However, be careful not to recycle an essay when it just doesn't fit. It's better to spend the extra time to write an appropriate essay than to submit one that doesn't match the scholarship or answer the question.

Seven Sins of the Scholarship Essay

Instead of writing an essay, one student placed the sheet of paper on the floor and tap danced on it. She then wrote that she hoped the scuff marks on the paper were evidence of her enthusiasm. In the judges' eyes, this was a silly stunt and, of course, her application was sent to the rejection pile. While you may not make such an egregious error, there are common mistakes that you need to avoid. Most of these lessons were learned the hard way—through actual experience.

1. DON'T Write a Sob Story

Everyone who applies for a scholarship needs money. Many have overcome obstacles and personal hardships. However, few scholarships are designed to reward students based on the "quantity" of hardships. Scholarship judges are not looking to give their money to those who have suffered the most. On the contrary, they want to give money to students who came up with a plan to succeed despite an obstacle. Therefore, if you are writing about the hardships you have faced, be sure that you spend as much time, if not more, describing how you have overcome or plan to rise above those challenges.

2. DON'T Use the Shotgun Approach

A common mistake is to write one essay and submit it without any changes to dozens of scholarships—hoping that maybe one will be a winner. While we do recommend that you recycle your essays, you should not just photocopy your essays and blast them out to every scholarship committee. This simply does not work. Unless the scholarships have identical questions, missions and goals, your essay cannot be reused verbatim. Spend the time to craft an essay for each scholarship, and you will win more than if you write just one and blindly send it off to many awards.

3. DON'T Be Afraid to Get Words on Paper

One common cause of writer's block is the fear of beginning. When you sit down to write, don't be afraid to write a draft, or even ideas for a draft, that are not perfect. You will have time to revise your work. What you want to do is get words on paper. They can be wonderfully intelligent words or they can be vague concepts. The point is that you should just write. Too many students wait until the last minute and get stuck at the starting line.

4. DON'T Try to Be Someone Else

Since you want to be the one the scholarship judges are seeking to reward with money, you need to highlight achievements and strengths that match the criteria of the scholarship. But you don't want to lie about yourself or try to be someone you are not. Besides being dishonest, the scholarship judges will probably pick up on your affectation and hold it against you.

5. DON'T Try to Impress with Feats of Literary Gymnastics

You won't get any bonus points for overusing clichés, quotes or words you don't understand. Too many students think that quotes and clichés will impress scholarship judges; but unless they are used sparingly and appropriately, they will win you no favors. (Remember that quotes and clichés are not your words and are therefore not original.) The same goes for overusing the thesaurus.

Do experiment with words that are less familiar to you, but do not make the thesaurus your co-author. It's better to use simple words correctly than to make blunders with complicated ones.

6. DON'T Stray Too Far from the Topic

A mistake that many students make is that they don't actually answer the question. This is especially true with recycled essays. Make sure that your essays, whether written from scratch or recycled from others, address the question asked.

7. DON'T Write Your Stats

A common mistake is to repeat your statistics from your application form. Often these essays begin with "My name is" and go on to list classes, GPAs and extracurricular activities. All this information is found in your application. On top of that, it's boring. If you are going to write about a class or activity, make it interesting by focusing on a specific class or activity.

Example Winning Scholarship Essays

It's one thing to study the theory behind the pheromones of love, but it is entirely a different thing to experience the euphoria, quickened heartbeat and walking-on-clouds feeling that goes with love. In a similar way, you have seen the theory behind writing a powerful scholarship essay. It is now time to see this theory in action.

The following two essays were written by students who won scholarships. In each essay you will see how winning principles are put to use. The results are essays that inspire, provoke and most important, win money. As with any example essay, please remember that this is not necessarily the way your essay should be written. Use these sample essays as illustrations of how a good essay might look. Your essay will naturally be different and unique to your own style and personality.

Winning Essay: My Two Dads

This essay was written by Gregory James Yee, a graduate of Whitney High School in Cerritos, California. Although Gregory is a student at Stanford University, he wrote this essay as part of his application to the University of Southern California. Besides garnering an acceptance to USC, this essay also earned him a $7,500 per year Trustee Scholarship. Remember that many colleges use your college application to automatically consider you for scholarships they offer.

The topic of the essay is Gregory's musical talent, which was discovered early in his life. At the age of two, he could hum *The Star-Spangled Banner* in perfect rhythm and pitch; and at age four, he began piano lessons. Throughout his 15 years of lessons, he won numerous awards, including the Raissa Tselentis Award given to one student nationwide for outstanding performance in the Advanced Bach category of the National Guild Audition. He is also a composer.

My Two Dads

I have two fathers. My first and biological father is the one who taught me how to drive a car, throw a baseball and find the area under a curve using integral calculus, among the innumerable other common duties of a good dad. He has been there for me through the ups of my successful piano career and the downs of my first breakup, and has always offered his insightful hand of guidance. My second father is who I connect with on a different level; he is the only person I know who thinks like I do. My second dad is my music composition teacher, Tony Fox, and he shares the one passion that has been a part of my life since the age of two: music.

Tony is a hardworking professor who can spend hours illustrating the meaning of a particular chord in a famous classical composition or ease an extraordinarily stressful situation with his colorful wit. He may appear intimidating to a new student at USC as the Assistant Band Director, but once someone mentions music, there is no one more adept, more creative or more dedicated to making music for the world to hear than Tony.

Tony has touched my life in a way few people have experienced. At my lessons with him, I bring compositions I am in the progress of perfecting, and with a few words of his guidance, I can almost see the changes needed before he mentions them. Almost instantly after I ask a question - such as which chord progression works best at a certain point in the music or why a certain counter melody sounds so beautiful—we agree on what is best for the music. It is almost as if we know what the other is thinking and merely state aloud our thoughts just in case one or the other is caught off guard. It is truly rare to find two people who agree with each other on what it is exactly that makes compositions aesthetically pleasing. Last year when I was working on a composition, I ran into a discouraging roadblock that could have delayed my progress significantly. No one in my family and none of my friends could help.

However, as soon as I shared the piece with Tony, he made some suggestions and together we made the necessary amendments to the music. The result was a finished project, a beautiful mosaic of our collective design, and it was debuted last year by my high school wind ensemble. When I first heard my music performed, I thought back to the hours I had spent tinkering at my piano and Tony's thoughtful guidance. This is how Tony and I relate. It's a common frequency upon which the most advanced radio cannot even begin to comprehend.

Tony has filled in areas of my life where few people, including my real father, could understand. He is the teacher of lessons big and small, from looking into the eyes of those whose hands I shake to recognizing that time is the most valuable gift one can give or receive. Whereas many of my peers have only one father, I have been fortunate enough to have two of them.

Why This Essay Won

An accomplished musician like Gregory could have written an essay that was simply a retelling of all the musical awards he had won. Instead, Gregory gives insight into what music means to him and takes us into his mind to see the creative and learning process at work. Writing about what he goes through to create a composition allows even those of us who are tone deaf to experience vicariously what it is like to create music.

Notice how Gregory uses powerful imagery to show us how he interacts with his music teacher and overcomes difficulties while composing. Gregory also subtly includes some of his most important musical accomplishments. Although he listed many of his awards in his application, this essay takes us beyond those achievements and really lets us see the wonderful person behind those awards.

Winning Essay: Leadership

Donald H. Matsuda, Jr. is the kind of person who doesn't just act. He inspires others to act as well. In his application for the Truman Scholarship, Donald shared how he directed community leaders and health professionals to start a series of health insurance drives. This is one of the essays that he wrote to become one of 80 Truman Scholars in the country.

From Sacramento and a graduate of Stanford University, Donald also founded the San Mateo Children's Health Insurance Program, directed the United Students for Veterans' Health and founded the Nepal Pediatric Clinical Internship.

Leadership

A few years ago, I saw a shocking headline on the front page of the New York Times that read: "Forty-Four Million Americans Without Health Insurance." Upon reading the article, I was stunned to discover that one-third of these uninsured Americans were children. Such figures made it clear to me that work needed to be done to remedy this problem, and I was ready to take action.

At this time, I was working at the Health for All Clinic as a public health and community outreach intern, and I decided to approach the director about this problem. He clearly agreed that immediate action needed to be taken to control the growing numbers of America's uninsured. However, he admitted that the clinic did not have the time, energy or the funds to invest in such an ambitious endeavor. I was not discouraged by his response. Instead, I saw this challenge as an opportunity to gain firsthand experience as a change agent in the field of public policy.

After completing extensive research, I discovered a unique program called Healthy Families. The ultimate goal of this government program is to provide low-cost insurance coverage to children who do not qualify for traditional insurance plans. I decided to develop my own project from scratch, proposing to launch a sustainable series of Healthy Families insurance drives at the Health for All Clinic. I applied for funding through the Haas Center for Public Service Fellowship program, and the clinic director signed on as my community partner for the project.

During the next six months, I worked very closely with the clinic staff to organize and plan this series of insurance drives. I recruited various ethnic community leaders and healthcare professionals to help generate support for the program and assembled several advertising campaigns in the surrounding communities. The clinic director and I also developed a workshop on immigrant health to attract more diverse populations to our insurance drives. After holding three Healthy Families drives, the clinic managed to sign up over 150 children for this program. The director was elated by this turnout and established an entire Healthy Families division to build upon the success of this project. Upon completion of this project, I started directing other insurance drives with the hope of improving the health and well-being of America's children.

Why This Essay Won

Donald's essay only scratches the surface of his accomplishments, which is exactly how it should be. Instead of listing every leadership role he has ever had, Donald explains how he created a health care program in his community. He begins with his motivation for starting the program and then recounts the initial skepticism that he faced when he first proposed the idea. Donald's essay describes the various difficulties and ultimate success of his project.

Notice that Donald does not describe a typical leadership role, one in which he was elected as a leader. This is an excellent example of how you can take a project in which you played a significant role and show how it demonstrates your leadership abilities. Remember, leadership is not just an elected position.

Where to Find More Winning Scholarship Essays

We believe that reading real essays is the best way for you to really see what works, and these essays are certainly a start. Unfortunately, we could not include more than two examples in this book. If you want more scholarship essay examples, take a look at our book, *How to Write a Winning Scholarship Essay.* In it you will find 30 additional winning essays from students who tested the waters of many topics and wrote in a variety of styles. Also, take a look at our website, SuperCollege (www.supercollege.com), where we post additional example essays. We think you'll be inspired.

The Scholarship Resume

Chapter 5

Write Your Own One-Page Autobiography

If you want to say that your life is a book, then be ready to follow with the analogy that your scholarship resume is the *CliffsNotes* summary. A scholarship resume is your opportunity to tout your greatest achievements and life's accomplishments. The only catch is that you are limited to one page. Some scholarship committees require resumes as a part of the application process so that they can use them to get a quick overview of your achievements. Others don't, but including a resume will always enhance your application.

A scholarship resume is not the same as one that you would use to get a job. It's unlikely that your work experience (if you have any) will be the focus. However, the principles and format are the same. A good resume that scores you a job shows employers that you have the right combination of work experience and skills to be their next hire. Similarly, your scholarship resume should show the committee why you are the most qualified student to win their award.

Think of the scholarship resume as a "cheat sheet" that you give to the judges. By looking at your resume, the judges get a quick overview of your achievements and interests. The resume is not an exhaustive list of everything you have done. It rather highlights and summarizes the most impressive and relevant achievements.

To make sure that it really focuses on the crème de la crème, your resume should fit on a single sheet of paper. This is sometimes harder than it sounds.

Here is the information you need for a scholarship resume:

- **Contact information:** Your vital statistics, including name, address, phone number and email.

- **Education:** Schools you've attended beginning with high school, expected or actual graduation dates.
- **Academic achievements:** Relevant coursework, awards and honors received.
- **Extracurricular experience.** Relevant extracurricular activities, locations and dates of participation, job titles, responsibilities and accomplishments.
- **Work experience:** Where and when you've worked, job titles, responsibilities and accomplishments on the job.
- **Skills and interests:** Additional relevant technical, lingual or other skills or talents that do not fit in the categories above.

Don't worry if your resume presents the same information that's in the application form. Some judges will read only the application or your resume, so it's important your key points are in both. However, in the resume, try to expand on areas that you were not able to cover fully in the application.

Example Resume that Worked

There are many good ways to format a resume. Most important, your resume should be easy to skim and be organized in a logical manner. Here is an example of a well-written scholarship resume. Remember that there are other equally good formats in which to present this information.

Melissa Lee
1000 University Drive
San Francisco, CA 94134
(415) 555-5555
melissa@email.com

Education
University of San Francisco; San Francisco, CA
B.A. candidate in sociology. Expected graduation in 2015. Honor roll.

Lowell High School; San Francisco, CA
Graduated in 2011 with highest honors. Principal's Honor Roll, 4 years.

Activities and Awards
SF Educational Project; San Francisco, CA
Program Assistant. Recruited and trained 120 students for various community service projects in semester-long program. Managed and evaluated student journals, lesson plans and program participation.
2009-present.

Lowell High School Newspaper; San Francisco, CA
Editor-In-Chief. Recruited and managed staff of 50. Oversaw all editorial and business functions.
Newspaper was a finalist for the prestigious Examiner Award for excellence in student journalism. 2007-2011.

Evangelical Church; San Francisco, CA
Teacher. Prepared and taught weekly lessons for third grade Sunday School class. Received dedication to service award from congregation. 2007-2011.

Asian Dance Troupe; San Francisco, CA
Member. Performed at community functions and special events. 2009-present.

Employment
Palo Alto Daily News; Palo Alto, CA
Editorial Assistant. Researched and wrote eight feature articles on such topics as education reform, teen suicide and summer fashion. Led series of teen-reader response panels. Summer 2011.

Russian Hill Public Library; San Francisco, CA
Library Page. Received "Page of the Month" Award for outstanding performance. Summers 2009-2010.

Interests
Fluent in Mandarin and HTML. Interests include journal writing, creative writing, photography, swimming and aerobics.

Some points to note about this resume:

- Notice how this resume is concise and very easy to read. By limiting herself to a single page, Melissa makes sure that even if you just scan her resume, you will pick up her key strengths.
- See how each description includes examples of leadership as well as awards or special recognition.
- Melissa conveys the impact of her work by pointing out concrete results (which you should also do on the application form).
- Notice how her description of summer jobs highlights some of her key accomplishments.
- The final section adds a nice balance by describing some of her other hobbies and interests.

Elements of a Powerful Resume

Your resume should be descriptive enough for the judges to understand each item but not so wordy that they can't find what they need. It should be neatly organized and easy to follow. Having reviewed hundreds of resumes, here are some simple strategies that we've developed to help you:

Include only the important information. Remember to incorporate only the most relevant items and use what you know about the scholarship organization to guide how you prioritize what you share in your resume. Only include things that support your fit with the scholarship's mission. For each piece of information, ask yourself these two questions: Will including this aid the selection committee in seeing that I am a match for the award? Is this information necessary to convince them that I should receive the award?

Focus on responsibilities and achievements. In describing your experiences in work and activities, focus on the responsibilities you held and highlight measurable or unique successes such as starting a project, reaching goals or implementing one of your ideas. For example, if you were the treasurer of the Literary Club, you would want to include that you were responsible for managing a $10,000 annual budget.

Demonstrate in your resume how you showed leadership. Leadership could include leading a project or team, instructing others or mentoring your peers. What's more important than your title or where you worked is the quality of your involvement. Explaining your successes and your role as a leader will provide concrete evidence of your contribution.

Be proud. Your resume is your time to shine. Don't be afraid to draw attention to all that you've accomplished. If you played a key role in a project, say so. If you exceeded your goals, advertise it. No one else is going to do your bragging for you.

Use action verbs. When you are describing your achievements, use action verbs such as these: founded, organized, achieved, created, developed, directed and (our personal favorite) initiated.

Don't tell tall stories. On the flip side of being proud is being untruthful. It's important that you describe yourself in the most glowing way possible, but stay connected with the truth. If you developed a new filing system at your job, don't claim that you single-handedly led a corporate revolution. With your complete scholarship application, selection committees can see through a resume that is exaggerated and doesn't match the rest of the application, essay and recommendations.

Get editors. After the hundredth time reading your resume, you'll probably not notice an error that someone reading it for the first time will catch. Get others to read and edit your resume. Editors can let you know if something doesn't make sense, offer you alternative wording and help correct your boo-boos. Some good choices for editors may be teachers or professors, work supervisors or parents. Work supervisors may be especially helpful since part of their job is to review resumes of job applicants. Your school may also offer resume help in the counseling department or career services office.

Avoid creating an eye test. In trying to squeeze all the information onto a single page, don't make your font size so small that the words are illegible. Try to leave space between paragraphs. The judges may have tired, weary eyes from reading all those applications. Don't strain them even more.

Strive for perfection. It's a given that your resume should be error-free. There's no excuse for mistakes on a one-page document that is meant to exemplify your life's work.

Include Your Resume in Every Application

Once you have a resume, include it with every scholarship application. In addition, you should also give it to your recommenders so that they have a "cheat sheet" that highlights your accomplishments when it comes time to write those letters of recommendations. They will no doubt want to mention some of your successes to make their letters on point and personal. Remember, your resume is *you*!

Getting Great Recommendations

Chapter 6

Letters of Recommendation Count

If you need a reason to kiss up to your teachers or professors, here's one: recommendations. Scholarships sometime require that you submit recommendations from teachers, professors, school administrators, employers or others who can vouch for your accomplishments. Scholarship judges use these testaments to get another perspective of your character and accomplishments. Viewed together with your application and essay, the recommendation helps the judges get a more complete picture of who you are. Plus, it's always impressive when someone else extols your virtues.

Many students believe that they have no control over the recommendation part of their application. This isn't true. You actually can have a lot of input regarding the letters that your recommenders write. In this chapter we will explore several ways—all perfectly ethical—to ensure that you get great recommendations.

A recommendation is an important opportunity for someone else to tell scholarship judges why you deserve to win. You may assume that because others do the actual writing, recommendations are completely out of your control. Banish that thought. The secret is to not only pick the right people but to also provide them with all of the information they need to turn out a great letter of recommendation. Many applicants overlook this fact. But not you, right? Armed with superb recommendations, your scholarship application is sure to rise to the top.

Find People to Say Nice Things about You

Your first task is to find recommenders. Unfortunately, Mom, Dad and anyone else related to you is excluded. So, how do you get those recommendations without familial ties to sing your praises?

First, think about all the people in your life who can speak meaningfully about you and your accomplishments. Your list may include teachers, professors, advisors, school administrators, employers, religious leaders, coaches or leaders of organizations and activities in which you are involved. While some scholarships require recommendations from specific people (like a teacher or professor), most are pretty liberal and allow you to select anyone who knows you.

Second, once you have a list of potential recommenders, analyze which of these people could present information about you that best matches the goals of the scholarships.

If you apply for an academic scholarship, you'll want at least one teacher or professor to write a recommendation. If you apply for an athletic scholarship, a coach would be a good choice. Select people who are able to write about the things that are most important to the scholarship judges. A good exercise is to imagine what your potential recommender would write and whether or not this would enhance your case for winning the scholarship.

After considering these two questions, you should be left with only a few people from which to choose. If you can't decide between two equally qualified people, choose the one who knows you the best as a person. For example, if you got A's in three classes and are trying to decide which professor to ask for a recommendation, pick the one who can write *more* than a testament to your academic ability. This is important because a recommendation that contains comments on your character is extremely memorable. Maybe one of the professors knows you well enough to include a few sentences on your drive to succeed or your family background. Ideally, your recommender is able to describe not only your performance in the classroom but also the values and character traits that make you special.

Give Your Recommender the Chance to Say "No"

Once you've selected those you'd like to write your recommendations, ask them to do so—early. A general rule is to allow at least three weeks before the recommendation is due. Explain that you are applying for scholarships and are required to submit recommendations from people who know you and who can comment on some of your achievements.

It's important to ask the person a question like this: "Do you feel comfortable writing a recommendation letter for me?" This allows the person the opportunity to decline your request if he or she doesn't feel comfortable or doesn't have the time. If you get a negative or hesitant response, don't assume that it's because he or she has a low opinion of you. It could simply be that the person doesn't know you well enough or is too busy to write a thoughtful recommendation. It's much better to have the recommender decline to write a letter than to get one that is rushed or not entirely positive. In most cases, however, potential recommenders are flattered and happy to oblige.

Don't Play the Name Game

From being recognized by strangers to getting preferential reservations at the hottest restaurants, there are a lot of perks to being famous. You might think that this special treatment carries over to recommendations, and that scholarship judges will be star-struck by a letter from someone with a fancy title. However, don't assume that just because you ask someone well known to write your recommendations that you are a shoo-in for the scholarship. In fact, you might be surprised to learn that doing so could actually hurt your chances of winning.

So the question is this: "Should I try to find someone famous to write a letter of recommendation for me?" The answer comes down to the principles outlined above. How well does the person know you, and can he or she write about you in a way that presents you as a viable candidate for the scholarship? If the answer is "yes," then by all means ask the person to help you. However, if you don't know the person very well or if what he or she will write could lack a connection to the qualities that the scholarship committee is looking for, it's better to forgo the value of high name recognition and ask someone who can address what's most important in a letter of recommendation.

For example, if you work as a summer intern for your state senator, you may think that a letter from such a political luminary would give your application the star power to set it apart from others with recommendations from mere mortals. However, if you spent more time photocopying or stuffing envelopes than you did developing keen political strategies, and you saw the senator as many times as you have fingers on your left hand, chances are that he or she would have very few meaningful things to say about your performance. "A skilled photocopier" and "brewed a mean cup of coffee" are not compliments you want sent to the scholarship judges.

If you ask someone well known to write your recommendations, make sure that he or she really knows you and can speak about your accomplishments personally and meaningfully. The quality of what is said in the recommendations is much more important than whose signature is at the bottom of the page.

Do the Grunt Work for Your Recommenders

Once you've selected your recommenders, give them everything they need to get the job done. Since they are doing you a favor, make the process as easy as possible for them. This is also where you can most influence what they write and actually direct what accomplishments they highlight. But before we delve into the specifics, here is an overview of what you need to provide each recommender:

Cover letter: This describes the scholarships you are applying for. In the letter, you should list deadlines and give the recommenders direct guidance on what to write. More on this in a bit.

Resume: A resume provides a quick overview of your most important achievements in an easy to follow one-page format. It is also what your recommenders will use as they cite your important achievements.

Recommendation form: Some scholarships provide an actual form that your recommenders need to complete. Fill in the parts that you can, such as your name and address.

Pre-addressed, stamped envelopes: Read the application materials to find out if you need to submit your recommendations separately or with the rest of your application. For letters that are to be mailed separately, provide your recommenders with envelopes that are stamped and have the scholarship's mailing address on them. If you are supposed to submit the letters with your application, provide your recommenders with envelopes on which you have written your name. Many recommenders prefer to write letters that are confidential and that you don't get to read. Once you have everything, place it in a folder or envelope and label it with your recommender's name.

Give Your Recommenders a Script

Because you know yourself better than anyone else, you would probably receive the best recommendations if you sat down and wrote them yourself. Unfortunately, this practice is frowned upon by scholarship judges. Short of writing your own recommendations, you can influence how they turn out by providing your recommenders with detailed descriptions of your accomplishments that can help them decide which aspects of you to highlight in their letters. This is best done through the cover letter that you send to the prospective recommender.

Your cover letter provides your recommenders with all the information that they need to write your recommendations, including details about the scholarships and suggestions for what you'd like the recommendations to address. Since the cover letter also includes other essentials like deadlines, mailing instructions and a thank you, you will not sound as if you are giving orders but rather that you are providing helpful assistance. In fact, your recommenders will appreciate your reminding them what's important and what they should include.

Here are the elements to include in your cover letter:

Details on the scholarships: List the scholarships for which you will use their letters. Give a brief one-paragraph description of the mission of each of the awards and what qualities the scholarship committee seeks. This information will help your recommenders understand which of your qualities are important to convey and who will read the letters.

How you fit the scholarship: This is the most important part of your cover letter because it's your chance to remind your recommenders of your accomplishments and to offer suggestions for what to write. Make sure that you highlight how you match the goals of the scholarships. For example, if you are applying for a scholarship for future teachers, include information about your student teaching experience and the coursework you've taken in education. Leave out the fact that you were on the tennis team.

Deadlines: Inform your recommenders of how long they have to compose the letters. If time permits, ask them to mail the letters a week before the actual deadlines.

What to do with the letters when they're done: Give your recommenders instructions about what to do with the completed letters. You may want to offer to pick them up, or you might explain that you have included addressed, stamped envelopes so that the letters can be mailed.

Thank you: Recommendations may take several hours to complete, and your recommenders are very busy people. Don't forget to say thank you in advance for writing you a great letter of recommendation.

To illustrate the power of a good cover letter, read the example on the following page as if you were a recommender. Remember that this is only one example and your cover letter will naturally be different. However, regardless of your individual writing style, your cover letter should include the same points as the following example.

Some notes about this cover letter:

- Beth describes each scholarship she is applying for, its goal and deadline, and why she feels she is a match for the award.
- The heart of the cover letter is here, where Beth gives a quick summary of information she suggests her professor include in the letter.
- Beth provides instructions about what to do with the letters when completed.
- This is a well-written cover letter that is brief and easy to understand.

Dear Dr. Louis,

Thank you again for writing my scholarship recommendations. I want to do my best to be competitive for these awards. They are very important for my family as they will help me to pay for my education. Here are the scholarships I am applying for:

SuperCollege.com Scholarship Deadline: July 31
This is a national scholarship based on academic and non-academic achievement, including extracurricular activities and honors. I believe I'm a match for this scholarship because of my commitment to academics (I currently have a 3.85 grade point average) and because of the volunteer work I do with the Youth Literacy Project and the PLUS program.

Quill & Scroll Scholarship Deadline: April 20
This scholarship is for students who want to pursue a career in journalism. As you know, I am an editor for our school newspaper, contributing a column each week on issues that affect our student body. Journalism is the field I want to enter after graduation.

Community Scholarship Deadline: May 5
This scholarship is for students who have given back to their communities through public service. I have always been committed to public service. Outside of class, I not only formed the Youth Literacy Project but have also volunteered with the PLUS program.

To help you with your recommendation, I've enclosed a resume. Also, here are some highlights of specific accomplishments that I was hoping you might comment on in your letter:

* The essay I wrote for your class that won the Young Hemingway competition

* How I formed the Youth Literacy Project with you as the project's advisor

* My three years of volunteer work with the PLUS program

* The weekly column I've written for the newspaper on school issues

After you've finished, please return the recommendations to me in the envelopes I've enclosed. If you have any questions, please feel free to contact me at 555-5555. Again, thank you very much for taking the time to help me.

Sincerely,

Beth

Don't Let Your Recommenders Miss Deadlines

All recommenders have one thing in common: Too much to do and not enough time. It's important that you check with your recommender a couple of weeks before the letters are due. You need to monitor the progress of your recommendations. You may find that they're complete and already in the mail. A more common discovery is that they won't have been touched. Be polite yet diligent when you ask about the progress. It's crucial that you work with your recommenders to get the letters in on time.

The "You Can't Spell Success Without U" Mug

You now have everything you need to receive stellar recommendations. It's important to remember that even if it is a part of their job description, your recommenders are spending their time to help you. Remember this as you ask others to write recommendation letters and be sure to let them know that you appreciate their efforts.

Sometimes, a thank you gift is appropriate. Every time my (Kelly) mother wants to say thank you to a friend or acquaintance, she writes a note and gives a small token gift. My favorite is the "You Can't Spell Success Without U" mug because of its campy play on words.

Whether or not you select an equally campy token of appreciation, it's important that you thank your recommenders. After all, they are dedicating their free time to help you win funds for college.

Ace the Scholarship Interview

The Face-to-Face Encounter

A judge for the Rotary International Ambassadorial Scholarship shared with us the following true story. For the last phase of the scholarship competition for his region, the finalists met with the selection committee for an interview. The interview was very important and was the final step in determining who would win the $25,000 scholarship.

One finalist was an Ivy League student who flew across the country for the interview. Within the first five minutes, it was painfully clear to all the judges that the applicant didn't have the foggiest idea what the Rotary Club stood for. It's as if the applicant thought that his resume and Ivy League pedigree would make him a winner. As you can guess, this applicant had a very disappointing flight back to his college. Lesson number one for the scholarship interview: At the very least, know what the organization stands for.

Many students dread the interview. If your heart beats faster or your palms moisten when you think about the prospect of sitting face to face with the judges, you are not alone. While the other parts of the scholarship application take time and effort, they can be done in the privacy of your home. Interviews, on the other hand, require interaction with—gasp—a real live human.

The good news is that the interview is usually the final step in the scholarship application process and if you make it that far, you're a serious contender. In this chapter, we show you what most scholarship committees are looking for and how you should prepare to deliver a winning interview. We also show you how to make the most of your nervousness and how to turn it into an asset rather than a liability.

There are two secrets for doing well in scholarship interviews. The first is this: Remind yourself over and over again that scholarship interviewers are real people. Repeat it until you believe it. As such, your goal is to have as normal a conversation as possible, despite the fact that thousands of dollars may hang in the balance. It's essential that you treat interviewers as real people, interact with them and ask them questions.

The second secret is just as important: The best way to have successful interviews is to train for them. The more you practice interviewing, the more comfortable you'll be during the real thing. Don't worry—we'll tell you what kinds of questions to expect and how to perfect your answers.

Why Human Interaction Is Necessary

The first step to delivering a knockout interview is to understand why some scholarships require interviews in the first place. With the popularity of technology like e-mail and instant messaging, there seems to be less need for human interaction. (Believe it or not, there was a time when telephones were answered by a person instead of a maze of touchtone options.)

For some scholarship committees, a few pieces of paper with scores and autobiographical writing are not enough to get a full picture of who the applicants really are. They are giving away a lot of cash and the judges are responsible for making sure they are giving it to the most deserving students possible.

Scholarship judges use interviews as a way to learn how you compare in person versus on paper. Having been on both sides of the interview table, we can attest to the fact that the person you expect based on the written application is not always the person you meet at the interview. It's important to know that the purpose of interviews is not to interrogate you, but rather for the scholarship committee to get to know you better and probe deeper into the reason that you deserve their money.

Interviewers Are Real People Too

If you've ever met someone famous, you've probably realized that while celebrities' faces may grace the covers of magazines and they have houses big enough to merit their own ZIP code, they eat, drink and sleep and have likes and dislikes just like other people. The same thing holds true for interviewers.

Interviewers can be high-profile professors or high-powered businesspeople, but they are all passionate about some topics and bored with others. They enjoy speaking about themselves and getting to know more about you. Acknowledging this will help keep your nerves under control. Throughout the interview, remind yourself that your interviewer is human, and strive to make the interview a conversation, not an interrogation.

Interview Homework

You'd never walk into a test and expect to do well without studying the material. The same is true for interviews. Don't attempt them without doing your homework. There is basic information you need to know before starting your interviews so that you appear informed and knowledgeable. It's not difficult information to obtain, and it goes a long way in demonstrating that you care enough about winning to have put in some effort. Here are some things you should know before any interview:

Purpose of the scholarship: What is the organization hoping to accomplish by awarding the scholarship? Whether it's promoting students to enter a certain career area, encouraging a hobby or interest or rewarding students for leadership, every scholarship has a mission.

Criteria for selecting the winner: From the scholarship materials, you can get information about what the judges are hoping to find in a winner. From the kinds of information they request in the application to the topic of the essay question, each piece is a clue about what is important to the judges. Scholarships can be based on academic achievement, nonacademic achievement or leadership, to name a few criteria. Understand what kind of student the organization is seeking and stress that side of yourself during the interview.

Background of the awarding organization: Do a little digging on the organization itself. Check out its website or publications. Attend a meeting or speak with someone who's a member. From this detective work, you will get a better idea of who the organization's members are and what they are trying to achieve. It can also be a great topic of conversation during the interview.

Background of your interviewer: If possible, find out as much as you can about who will be interviewing you. In many cases, you may know little more than their names and occupations, but if you can, find out more. You already have one piece of important information about your interviewers: You know that they are passionate about the organization and its mission. They wouldn't be volunteering their time to conduct interviews if they weren't.

Use Your Detective Work to Create an Advantage

Once you've done your detective work on the above topics, it's time to use the information you've uncovered. For example, if you are in front of a group of doctors and they ask you about your activities, you would be better off discussing your work at the local hospital than your success on the baseball diamond. As much as possible, focus the conversation on areas where your activities, goals, interests and achievements match the goal of the awarding organization. By discussing what matters most to the scholarship judges, you will insure that this will be a memorable conversation—one that will set you apart from the other applicants that are interviewed.

By knowing something about your interviewers beforehand, you can think of topics and questions that will be interesting to them. Most interviewers allow some time for you to ask questions. Here again your detective work will come in handy since you can ask them about their background or the history of the organization. By asking intelligent questions (i.e. not the ones that can be answered by simply reading the group's mission statement) you will demonstrate that you've done your homework.

You'll also give interviewers something interesting to talk about—either themselves or their organization. The more information you can get before the interview, the better you will perform. Having this background material will also allow you to answer unexpected questions better and come up with thoughtful questions for the judges if you are put on the spot.

You Are Not the Center of the Universe

Despite what Mom or Dad says, the Earth revolves around the sun, not you. It helps to remember this in your interviews. Your life may be the most interesting ever lived, but this is still no excuse for speaking only about yourself for the duration of the interview.

The secret to successful interviews is simply this: They should be *interactive*. The surest way to bore your interviewers is to spend the entire time speaking only about yourself. You may have had the unfortunate experience of being on the receiving end of a conversation like this if you have a friend who speaks nonstop about herself and who never seems to be interested in your life or what you have to say. Don't you just hate this kind of conversation? So will your scholarship interviewers.

To prevent a self-centered monologue, constantly look for ways to interact with your interviewers. In addition to answering questions, ask some yourself. Ask about their experiences in school or with the organization. Inquire about their thoughts on some of the questions they pose to you. Take time to learn about your interviewers' experiences and perspectives.

Also, speak about topics that interest your interviewers. You can tell which topics intrigue them by their reactions and body language. From the detective work you've done, you also have an idea of what they are passionate about.

Try to make your interviews a two-way conversation instead of a one-way monologue. Engage your interviewers and keep them interested. If you do this, they will remember your interview as a great conversation and you as a wonderful, intelligent person deserving of their award.

Look and Sound the Part

Studies on the effectiveness of speeches have shown that how you sound and how you look when you present your material is more important than what you actually say. From that, we can learn that it is positively essential that you make a good visual presentation. Here are some tips to make sure that you look and sound your best, an important complement to what you actually say to the judges:

Dress appropriately: A backward-turned baseball cap and baggy jeans slung down to your thighs may be standard fare for the mall (at least they were last season), but they are not appropriate for interviews.

You probably don't have to wear a suit unless you find out through your research that the organization is very conservative, but you should dress appropriately. No-no's include the following: hats, bare midriffs, short skirts or shorts, open-toe shoes and iron-free wrinkles. Think about covering obtrusive tattoos or removing extra ear/nose/tongue/eyebrow rings. Don't dress so formally that you feel uncomfortable, but dress nicely. It may not seem fair, but your dress will affect the impression you make and influence the decision of the judges. Save making a statement of your individuality for a time when money is not in question.

Sit up straight: During interviews, do not slouch. Sitting up straight conveys confidence, leadership and intelligence. It communicates that you are interested in the conversation. Plus, it makes you look taller.

Speak in a positive tone of voice: One thing that keeps interviewers engaged is your tone. Make sure to speak in a positive one. This will not only maintain your interviewers' interest but will also suggest that you have an optimistic outlook. Of course, don't try so hard that you sound fake.

Don't be monotonous: If you've ever had a teacher or professor who speaks at the same rate and tone without variation, you know that this is the surest reason for a nap. Don't give your interviewers heavy eyelids. Tape record yourself and pay attention to your tone of voice. There should be natural variation in your timbre.

Speak at a natural pace: If you're like most people, the more nervous you are, the faster you speak. Be aware of this so that you don't speed talk through your interview.

Make natural gestures: Let your hands and face convey action and emotions. Use them as tools to illustrate anecdotes and punctuate important points.

Make eye contact: Eye contact engages interviewers and conveys self-assurance and honesty. If it is a group interview, make eye contact with all your interviewers—don't just focus on one. Maintaining good eye contact can be difficult, but just imagine little dollar signs in your interviewers' eyes and you shouldn't have any trouble. Ka-ching!

Smile: There's nothing more depressing than having a conversation with someone who never smiles. Don't smile nonstop, but show some teeth at least once in a while. If you use these tips, you will have a flawless look and sound to match what you're saying. All these attributes together create a powerful portrait of who you are. Unfortunately, not all these things come naturally, and you'll need to practice so that they can become unconscious actions.

The Practice Interview

One of the best ways to prepare for an interview is to do a dress rehearsal. This allows you to run through answering questions you might be asked and to practice honing your interview skills, including demeanor and style. You will feel more comfortable when it comes time for the actual interview. If anything will help you deliver a winning interview, it's practice. It may be difficult, but force yourself to set aside some time to run through a practice session at least once. Here's how:

Find a mock interviewer. Bribe or coerce a friend or family member to be your mock interviewer. Parents or teachers often make the best interviewers because they are closest in age and perspective to most actual scholarship interviewers.

Prep your mock interviewer. Share with your interviewer highlights from this chapter such as the purpose of scholarship interviews, what skills you want to practice and typical interview questions, which are described in the next section. If you're having trouble with eye contact, for example, ask them to take special notice of where you are looking when you speak and to make suggestions for correcting this.

Set up a video camera. If you have access to a tape recorder or camcorder, set it up to tape yourself so that you can review your mock interview afterward. Position the camera behind your interviewer so you can observe how you appear from their perspective.

Do the dress rehearsal. Grab two chairs and go for it. Answer questions and interact with your mock interviewer as if you were at the real thing. Get feedback. After you are finished, get constructive criticism from your mock interviewer. Find out what you did well and what you need to work on. What were the best parts of the interview? Which of your answers were strong, and which were weak? When did you capture or lose your mock interviewer's attention? Was your conversation one-way or two-way?

Review the tape. Evaluate your performance. If you can, watch or listen to the tape with your mock interviewer so you can get additional feedback. Listen carefully to how you answer questions so you can improve on them. Pay attention to your tone of voice. Watch your body language to see what you are unconsciously communicating.

Do it again. If you have the time and your mock interviewer has the energy or you can find another mock interviewer, do a second interview. If you can't find anyone, do it solo. Practice your answers, and focus on making some of the weaker ones more interesting. The bottom line is the more you practice, the better you'll do.

How to Answer to the Most Common Interview Questions

The best way to ace an exam would be to know the questions beforehand. The same is true for interview questions. From interviewing dozens of judges and applicants as well as having judged dozens of scholarship competitions ourselves, we've developed a list of commonly asked questions along with suggestions for answering them. This list is by no means comprehensive. There is no way to predict every question you will be asked, and in your actual interviews, the questions may not be worded in exactly the same way. However, the answer that interviewers are seeking is often the same.

Before your interviews, take the time to review this list. Add more questions particular to the specific scholarship to which you are applying. Practice answering these questions to yourself and in your mock interviews with friends and family. You will find that the answers you prepare to these questions will be invaluable during your real interviews. Even though the questions you are asked may be different, the thought that you put in now will help you formulate better answers. To the interviewer, you will sound incredibly articulate and thoughtful. Let's take a look at those questions.

Why did you choose your major?

- For major-based scholarships and even for general scholarships, interviewers want to know what motivated you to select the major, and they want a sense of how dedicated you are to that area of study. Make sure you have reasons for your decision. Keep in mind that an anecdote will provide color to your answer.
- If you are still in high school, you will probably be asked about your intended major. Make sure you have reasons for considering this major.

Why do you want to enter this career field?

- For scholarships that promote a specific career field, interviewers want to know your inspiration for entering the field and how committed you are to it. You will need to articulate the reasons and experiences that prompted your interest in this career and also anything you have done to prepare yourself for associated studies in this area.
- Be prepared to discuss your plans for after graduation, i.e. how will you use your education in the field you have chosen. You may be asked what kind of job you plan to have and why you would like it.
- Know something about the news in the field associated with the scholarship. For example, if you are applying for an information technology award, read up on the trends in the IT industry. There may be some major changes occurring that you will be asked to comment on.

What are your plans after graduation?

- You are not expected to know precisely what you'll do after graduation, but you need to be able to respond to this common question. Speak about what you are thinking about doing once you have that diploma in hand. The more specific you can be, the better.
- Provide reasons for your plans. Explain the process in which you developed your plans and what your motivation is.
- It's okay to discuss a couple of possible paths you may take, but don't bring up six very different options. Even if you are deciding among investment banking, the Peace Corps, banana farming and seminary, don't say so. The interviewer will think that you don't have a clear direction of what you want to do. This may very well be true, but it's not something you want to share. Select the one or two possible paths that you are most likely to take.

Why do you think you should win this scholarship?

- Focus your answer on characteristics and achievements that match the mission of the scholarship. For example, if the scholarship is for biology majors, discuss your accomplishments in the field of biology. Your answer may include personal qualities as well as specific accomplishments.
- Be confident but not arrogant. For this type of question, be careful about balancing pride and modesty in your answer. You want to be confident enough to have reasons why you should win the scholarship, but you don't want to sound overly boastful. To avoid sounding pompous, don't say that you are better than all the other applicants or put down your competition. Instead, focus on your strengths independent of the other people who are applying.
- Have three reasons. Three is the magic number that is not too many or too few. To answer this question just right, offer three explanations for why you fulfill the mission of the scholarship.

Tell me about times when you've been a leader.

- Interviewers ask this type of question (although sometimes worded a little differently) to gauge your leadership ability and your accomplishments as a leader. They want to award scholarships to students who will be leaders in the future. When you answer, try to discuss leadership you've shown that matches what the scholarship is meant to achieve.
- Don't just rattle off the leadership positions you've held. Instead, give qualitative descriptions of what you accomplished as a leader. Did your group meet its goals? Did you start something new? How did you

shape the morale of the group you led? For this kind of question, anecdotes and short stories are a good way to illustrate how you've been effective.

- Remember that leadership doesn't have to be a formally elected position. You can describe how you've informally led a special project or group. You could even define how you are a leader among your siblings.
- Be prepared to discuss what kind of leader you are. Your interviewer may ask about your approach to leadership or your philosophy on being a good leader. Have examples ready that show how you like to lead. For example, do you lead by example? Do you focus on motivating others and getting their buy-in?

What are your strengths? Weaknesses?

- As you are applying for jobs, you will answer this question more times than you will shake hands. It is a common job interview question that you may also get asked in scholarship interviews. Be prepared with three strengths and three weaknesses. Be honest about your weaknesses.
- Your strengths should match the mission of the scholarship and should highlight skills and accomplishments that match the characteristics the judges are seeking.
- You should be able to put a positive spin on your weaknesses. (And you'd better say you have some!) For example, your perfectionism could make you frustrated when things don't go the way you plan but could also make you a very motivated person. Your love of sports could detract from your studies but could provide a needed break and be representative of your belief in balance for your life. Just make sure that the spin you put on your weakness is appropriate and that your weakness is really a weakness.

Where do you see yourself ten years from now?

- We know that nobody knows exactly what he or she is going to be doing in ten years. The interviewers don't need specific details. They just want a general idea of what your long-term goals are and what you aspire to become. If you have several possibilities, at least one should be in line with the goals of the scholarship.
- Try to be as specific as possible without sounding unrealistic. For example, you can say that you would like to be working at a high-tech company in marketing, but leave out that you plan to have a daughter Rita, son Tom and dog Skip. Too much detail will make your dreams sound too naive.

Tell me about yourself. Or, is there anything you want to add?

- The most difficult questions are often the most open-ended. You have the freedom to say anything. For these kinds of questions, go back to the mission of the scholarship and shape your answer to reflect the characteristics that the judges are seeking in the winner. Practice answering this question several times because it is the one that stumps applicants the most.
- Have three things to say about yourself that match the goal of the scholarship. For example, you could discuss three personal traits you have, such as motivation, leadership skills and interpersonal skills. Or, you could discuss three skills applicable to academics, such as analytical skills, problem-solving skills and your love of a good challenge.
- The alternative, "Is there anything you want to add?" is typically asked at the end of the interview. In this case, make your response brief but meaningful. Highlight the most important thing you want your interviewer to remember.

Other Questions

In addition to these, here are some more common questions:

- What do you think you personally can contribute to this field?
- How do you plan to use what you have studied after graduation?
- Do you plan to continue your studies in graduate school?
- What do you want to specifically focus on within this field of study?
- Do you plan to do a thesis or senior project?
- Who are your role models in the field?
- What do you see as the future of this field?
- How do you see yourself growing in your career?
- What can you add to this field?
- What do you think are the most challenging aspects of this field?
- What is your ideal job after graduating from college?
- Tell me about a time that you overcame adversity.
- What are your opinions about (fill in political or field-related issue)?
- Tell me about your family.
- What do you hope to gain from college?
- Who is a role model for you?

- What is your favorite book? Why?
- What is the most challenging thing you have done?

Remember that with all these questions your goal is to demonstrate that you are the best fit for the scholarship. Be sure to practice these with your mock interviewer. The more comfortable and confident you feel answering these questions, the better you'll do in your interviews.

Questions for the Questioner

There is a huge difference between an interview and an interrogation. In an interview, you also ask questions. Make certain that your interview does not become an interrogation. Ask questions yourself throughout the conversation. Remember that you want to keep the conversation two-way.

Toward the end of your interview, you will probably have the opportunity to ask additional questions. Take this opportunity. If you don't ask any questions, it will appear that you are uninterested in the conversation or haven't put much thought into your interview. Take time before the interview to develop a list of questions you may want to ask. Of course you don't have to ask all your questions, but you need to be prepared to ask a few.

To get you started, we've developed some suggestions. Adapt these questions to the specific scholarship you are applying for and personalize them.

- How did you get involved with this organization?
- How did you enter this field? What was your motivation?
- Who do you see as your mentors in this field?
- What do you think are the most exciting things about your career?
- What advice do you have for someone starting out?
- What do you see as the greatest challenges for this field?
- What do you think will be the greatest advancements in ten years?
- What effect do you think technology will have on this field?
- I read that there is a (insert trend) in this field. What do you think?

The best questions are those that come from your detective work. Let's say that in researching an organization you discover that they recently launched a new program to research a cure for diabetes. Inquiring about this new program would be a perfect question to ask. It not only shows that you have done your homework, but it is also a subject about which the organization is deeply concerned.

Use Time to Your Advantage

The best time to ask Mom or Dad for something is when they're in a good mood. It's all about timing. Timing is also important in interviews. If you have more than one scholarship interview, time them strategically. Schedule less important and less demanding interviews first. This will allow you the opportunity to practice before your more difficult interviews. You will improve your skills as you do more interviews. It makes sense to hone your skills on the less important ones first.

If you are one of a series of applicants who will be interviewed, choose the order that fits you best. If you like to get things over with, try to be interviewed in the beginning. If you need more time to prepare yourself mentally, select a time near the end. We recommend that you don't choose to go first because the judges will use your interview as a benchmark for the rest. They may not recognize you as the best applicant even though it turns out to be true.

The Long-Distance Interview

If you've ever been in a long-distance relationship, you know there's a reason why most don't last. You simply can't communicate over the telephone in the same way you can in person. Scholarship interviews are the same. You may find that an interview will not be face to face but over the telephone instead. If this happens, here are some strategies to help bridge the distance:

Find a quiet place to do the interview where you won't be interrupted. You need to be able to give your full attention to the conversation you are having.

Know who's on the other end of the line. You may interview with a panel of people. Write down each of their names and positions when they first introduce themselves to you. They will be impressed when you are able to respond to them individually and thank each of them by name.

Use notes from your practice interviews. One of the advantages of doing an interview over the telephone is that you can refer to notes without your interviewers knowing. Take advantage of this.

Look and sound like you would in person. Pretend that your interviewers are in the room with you, and use the same gestures and facial expressions that you would if you were meeting in person. It may sound strange, but your interviewers will actually be able to hear through your voice when you are smiling, when you are paying attention and when you are enthusiastic about what you're saying. Don't do your interview lying down in your bed or slouched back in a recliner.

Don't use a speaker phone, cordless phone or cell phone. Speaker phones often echo and pick up distracting surrounding noise. Cordless and cell phones can generate static, and the battery can die at the worst possible moment.

Turn off call waiting. Nothing is more annoying than hearing the call waiting beep while you are trying to focus and deliver an important thought. (And, this may sound obvious, never click over to take a second call.) Use the techniques of regular interviews. You'd be surprised how much is translated over the telephone. Don't neglect good speaking and delivery points just because the interviewers can't see you!

Secrets to the Group Interview

So it's you on one side of the table and a panel of six on the other side. It's certainly not the most natural way to have a conversation. How do you stay calm when you are interviewed by a council of judges?

Think of the group as individuals. Instead of thinking it's you versus the team, think of each of the interviewers as an individual. Try to connect with each person separately.

Try to get everyone's name if you can. Have a piece of paper handy that you can use to jot down everyone's name and role so that you can refer to them in the conversation. You want to be able to target your answers to each of the constituents. If you are interviewing with a panel of employees from a company and you know that Ms. Sweeny works in accounting while Mr. Duff works in human resources, you can speak about your analytical skills to appeal to Ms. Sweeny and your people skills to appeal to Mr. Duff.

Make eye contact. Look into the eyes of each of the panelists. Don't stare, but show them that you are confident. Be careful not to focus on only one member of the group.

Respect the hierarchy. You may find that there is a leader in the group like the scholarship chair or the CEO of the company. Pay a little more attention to stroke the ego of the person or persons in charge. They are used to it, they expect it and a little kissing up never hurt anyone.

Include everyone. In any group situation, there are usually one or two more vocal members who take the lead. Don't focus all your attention only on the loud ones. Spread your attention among the panelists as evenly as possible.

The Disaster Interview

Even if you do your interview homework and diligently practice mock interviewing, you may still find that you and your interviewer(s) just don't connect or that you just don't seem to have the right answers. For students who spend some time preparing, this is a very rare occurrence. Interviewers are not trying to trick you or make you feel bad. They are simply trying to find out more about you and your fit with the award. Still, if you think that you've bombed, here are some things to keep in mind:

Avoid should have, would have, could have. Don't replay the interview in your head again and again, thinking of all the things you should have said.

It's too easy to look back and have the best answers. Instead, use what you've learned to avoid making the same mistakes in your next interview.

There are no right answers. Remember that in reality there really are no right answers. Your answers may not have been perfect, but that doesn't mean that they were wrong. There are countless ways to answer the same question.

The toughest judge is you. Realize that you are your own greatest critic. While you may think that you completely bombed an interview, your interviewer will most likely not have as harsh an opinion.

The Post-Interview

After you complete your interviews, follow up with a thank you note. Remember that interviewers are typically volunteers and have made the time to meet with you. If you feel that there is very important information that you forgot to share in your interview, mention it briefly in your thank you note. If not, a simple note will suffice. You will leave a polite, lasting impression on your interviewer(s).

Final Thoughts

Chapter 8

How to Keep the Money You Win

When you learn to skydive, your first lesson does not start with jumping out of an airplane. First you go through training in which you learn techniques and safety measures—on the ground. Only after practicing on the ground can you take to the sky. In your scholarship education, you have just completed the ground training and are ready to take the plunge. As you move from the *strategies* for applying for scholarships to actually *applying* for them, we have a few words of advice on how to keep the dollars you earn and how to stay motivated.

Let's jump ahead to after you win a cache of scholarship dollars. It would be nice once the scholarship checks were written if you could run off for that well-deserved trip to the Bahamas. Alas, there are restrictions on how you can spend the cash and how you must maintain your scholarship. (Besides, everyone knows that Hawaii is the place to go.) Here are some tips to keep in mind:

Get to know your scholarship and financial aid administrators. These people will be able to answer questions about your award and make sure you are spending it in the way that you should.

Give the scholarship committee members proof if they want it. Some awards require that you provide proof of enrollment or transcripts. Send the committee whatever they need.

Be aware of your award's requirements and what happens if something changes. How long does the award last? What happens if you take a leave of absence, study part time, study abroad, transfer schools or quit your studies? College is full of possibilities! Do you have to maintain a minimum grade point average or take courses in a certain field?

Know if there are special requirements for athletic scholarships. If you've won an athletic scholarship, you are most likely required to play the sport. (You didn't get that full ride scholarship for nothing!) Understand the implications of what would happen if you were not able to play because of circumstances such as an injury or not meeting academic requirements.

Find out if the award is a cash cow (renewable). If an award is renewable, you are eligible to get it every year that you are in school. If so, find out what you need to do, and when you need to do it, to renew your scholarship. Some awards just require a copy of your transcript, while others require you to submit an entirely new application.

Understand restrictions for spending the dough. Some awards are limited to tuition. Others can be used for books, travel or even living expenses. Some provide the money directly to your school; others provide a check made out to you. Be aware of what you can spend the money on and what sort of records you need to keep.

Learn the tax implications of your award. Speak with the award administrator or your pals at the IRS (www.irs.gov or 800-829-1040). Be aware of requirements after you graduate. Some awards such as ROTC scholarships require employment after graduation. Because these arrangements can drastically affect your future, learn about the requirements now.

Keep the awarding organization up to date on your progress as a student. Write the organization a thank you note, and keep them updated on your progress at the end of the year. This is not only good manners, but it will also help ensure that the award is around in the future.

Parting Words

I (Gen) remember when I won the Sterling Scholarship, one of the highest honors for students in Hawaii. The awards ceremony was televised live throughout the state. For weeks before submitting my application, I prepared for the competition, compiling a 50-page application book, practicing for the eight hours of interviews and enlisting the help of no less than three teachers from my high school. Even though the scholarship was only $1,000, my parents still keep the trophy on display and share with unwitting visitors the videotape of my triumph. I realize now that I was able to put in such extensive effort because of my outlook on the award. I knew whether I won or lost, I would gain the experience of building a portfolio, becoming a skilled interviewee, working closely with my teachers and meeting some incredible students.

While scholarships are primarily a source of funding for your education, approach them in the same way you do your favorite sport or hobby. I also played for my school's tennis team—and lost just about every match. Yet, I continued because I enjoyed the sport and found the skills a challenge. If you approach your scholarships in this manner, you'll probably win more of them and have fun in the process. Treat them like a chore, and you'll hate every minute, neglecting to put in the effort required to win.

The bottom line is that if you are going to take the time to apply, you should take the time to win. The secrets, tips and strategies in this book will put you within striking distance. Follow them and you'll win more and more often. This book is unique in that it really is two books in one. Now that you know how to win, it's time to begin finding scholarships to put these strategies to use. The second half of this book is a complete listing of scholarships and awards and is indexed by various criteria so you can quickly find those that match your interests and qualifications. And, because we know you just can't get enough of us, we also encourage you to visit our website, SuperCollege.com, for the most up-to-date information on scholarships and financial aid.

We both wish you the best of luck.

A SPECIAL REQUEST

As you jump headlong into the wonderful world of scholarships, we have a special request. We would love to hear about your experiences with scholarships and how this book has helped you. Please send us a note after you've finished raking in your free cash for college.

Gen and Kelly Tanabe
c/o SuperCollege
3286 Oak Court
Belmont, CA 94002

Onward! Flip the page and start finding scholarships. It's time to put all the strategies and tips you've just learned to work for you!

approach your scholarship in this manner you'll probably [illegible] and have fun in the process. Treat them like a game, and you'll have even more [illegible] as you [illegible] the effort required to win.

The bottom line is that if you are going to take the time to apply, you should take the time to win. The secrets, tips and strategies in this book will put you within striking distance. Follow them and you'll win more and more often. This book is unique in that it really is two books in one. Now that you know how to win, it's time to begin finding scholarships to put these strategies to use. The second half of this book is a complete listing of scholarships and awards indexed by various criteria so you can quickly find those that match your interests and qualifications. And because we know you can never get enough money, we also encourage you to visit our website, SuperCollege.com, for more up-to-date information on scholarships and financial aid.

We wish you the best of luck.

A SPECIAL REQUEST

As you jump headlong into the wonderful world of scholarships, we have a special request. We would love to hear about your experiences with scholarships and how this book has helped you. Please send us your most amusing, moving or [illegible] stories or [illegible] you have used for college.

Gen and Kelly Tanabe
c/o SuperCollege
2713 Old Road [illegible]
Belmont, CA 94002

Onward! Flip the page and start finding scholarships. It's time to put all the strategies and advice in this book to work for you!

The Ultimate Scholarship Directory

Now it's time to put into action all that you learned in the first half of the book. We've done the hard work of scouring the country to find the best scholarships that you can win. We've made a special effort to select awards with broad eligibility requirements, which means you'll find plenty of scholarships that fit your background, goals and interests.

Before you jump into the directory, spend a few moments to learn how the scholarships are organized so you don't miss out on any awards for which you might be a good fit.

To help find the awards that match you best, we've conveniently organized our directory of scholarships into eight major categories.

Below is the complete list of categories and descriptions of the types of awards you'll find in each one. Remember to also use the various indexes in the back of the book to help you zero in on more scholarships.

General

This section lists scholarships that have the broadest eligibility requirements. Included are awards based on **academics**, **leadership** and **community service** to name a few. While some of the scholarships have GPA requirements, you'll be surprised at how many are not based on grades. Some are even awarded by random drawing.

Humanities / Arts

This section includes awards for students interested in **English** and **writing** as well as **foreign language** and **area studies**. It also includes all of the **visual and performing arts** such as **dancing**, **singing**, **acting**, **music**, **drawing**, **painting**, **sculpture**, **photography** and **graphic art**.

Social Sciences

This section deals with the study of the human aspects of the world. Often called the "soft sciences" it includes:

- Anthropology
- Accounting / Finance
- Archaeology
- Business Management
- Communications
- Criminology
- Economics
- Education / Teaching
- Geography
- History
- Hospitality / Travel
- International Relations
- Journalism / Broadcasting
- Law / Legal Studies
- Marketing / Sales
- Political Science
- Psychology
- Public Administration / Social Work
- Sociology
- Urban Studies

Sciences

Typically known as the "hard sciences," this category includes:

- Aerospace / Aviation
- Agriculture / Horticulture / Animals
- Anatomy
- Architecture
- Astronomy
- Biological Sciences / Life Sciences
- Biochemistry
- Chemistry
- Computer and Information Science
- Dentistry
- Earth and Planetary Sciences
- Ecology
- Engineering
- Forestry / Wildlife
- Geology
- Health Professions / Medicine
- Mathematics
- Neuroscience
- Nursing
- Oceanography
- Paleontology
- Pathology

- Pharmacology
- Physics
- Zoology

State of Residence

Here's your opportunity to get something back from your (or your parents') state tax dollars. Every state offers scholarships and grants for their residents. Some states even offer awards to out-of-state students who study in their states. Be sure to look at both your home state as well as any of the states you are planning to go to college in to find the most awards.

Membership

Many large **companies**, **unions**, **organizations** and **religious organizations** give awards to their members. If you or your parents are members of any of the groups in this category, you may qualify for a scholarship.

Ethnicity /Race/Gender/Family Situation/Sexual Orientation

There are a lot of awards for members of minority and nonminority ethnic groups, women and students with unique family situations.

Disability / Illness

This section has awards for students with physical, hearing, vision, mental and learning disabilities. It also includes awards for students who have been afflicted with certain illnesses.

"Take Off the Blinders" to Find the Most Scholarships

Now that you know the categories, the best way to find scholarships is to jump right in and head to the sections that fit you best.

Do you remember when your elementary school teacher used to say, "Take off the mental blinders"? Ours did to encourage us to think broadly. In the same way, we want to encourage you to "take off the scholarship blinders" and not think about yourself too narrowly. Consider your accomplishments, activities, goals and background as broadly as possible. Look through some of the categories even if you don't immediately see a fit. You might discover that you actually fit one of the leadership scholarships even if you haven't held a formal leadership position. Or you may find an award in the sciences category in a field that you love but never realized was a science.

Don't be afraid to be forward-thinking. Write down any scholarships that fit, even if you have to wait a year to apply. The awards we have selected are from the larger organizations and businesses, so you can be certain that they are going to be around for a long time.

We are really excited that you can now put everything that you learned to good use to help you find and win some free cash for college.

Happy scholarship hunting!

GENERAL AWARDS

(1) • $1,000 Moolahspot Scholarship

MoolahSPOT
3286 Oak Court
Belmont, CA 94002
http://www.moolahspot.com/scholarship/

Purpose: To help students pay for college or graduate school.
Eligibility: Students must be at least 16 years or older and plan to attend or currently attend college or graduate school. Applicants may study any major or plan to enter any career field at any accredited college or graduate school. A short essay is required.
Target applicants: High school students. College students. Adult students.
Amount: $1,000.
Number of awards: Varies.
Deadline: April 30.
How to apply: Applications are available only online.
Exclusive: Visit www.UltimateScholarshipBook.com and enter code MO112 for updates on this award.

(2) • $1,500 College JumpStart Scholarship

College JumpStart Scholarship Fund
4546 B10 El Camino Real
No. 325
Los Altos, CA 94022
http://www.jumpstart-scholarship.net

Purpose: To recognize students who are committed to using education to better their life and that of their family and/or community.
Eligibility: Applicants must be 10th, 11th or 12th grade high school, college or adult students. Applicants may study any major and attend any college in the U.S. Applicants must be legal residents of the U.S. and complete the online application form including the required personal statement. The award may be used for tuition, room and board, books or any related educational expense.
Target applicants: High school students. College students. Adult students.
Amount: Up to $1,500.
Number of awards: 3.
Deadline: April 15.
How to apply: Applications are available online.
Exclusive: Visit www.UltimateScholarshipBook.com and enter code CO212 for updates on this award.

(3) • $1,500 Scholarship Detective Launch Scholarship

Scholarship Detective
4546 B10 El Camino Real, No. 325
Los Altos, CA 94022
http://www.scholarshipdetective.com/scholarship/

Purpose: To help college and adult students pay for college or graduate school.
Eligibility: Applicants must be high school, college or graduate students (including adult students) who are U.S. citizens or permanent residents. Students may study any major. The funds may be used to attend an accredited U.S. institution for undergraduate or graduate education.
Target applicants: High school students. College students. Adult students.
Amount: $1,500.
Number of awards: 2.
Deadline: May 31.
How to apply: Applications are available online.
Exclusive: Visit www.UltimateScholarshipBook.com and enter code SC312 for updates on this award.

(4) • 100th Infantry Battalion Memorial Scholarship Fund

Hawaii Community Foundation - Scholarships
1164 Bishop Street, Suite 800
Honolulu, HI 96813
Phone: 888-731-3863
Fax: 808-521-6286
Email: scholarships@hcf-hawaii.org
http://www.hawaiicommunityfoundation.org

Purpose: To support students who promote the legacy of the 100th Infantry Battalion of World War II.
Eligibility: Applicants must be full-time undergraduate or graduate students at a two- or four-year college or university. They must be a direct descendant of a 100th Infantry Battalion World War II veteran and demonstrate excellence in academics and community service. A minimum 3.5 GPA is required. Students do not need to be a Hawaii resident.
Target applicants: College students. Adult students.
Minimum GPA: 3.5
Amount: $2,000.
Number of awards: Varies.
Deadline: March 15.
How to apply: Applications are available online. An application form, transcript and two letters of recommendation are required.
Exclusive: Visit www.UltimateScholarshipBook.com and enter code HA412 for updates on this award.

(5) • 1st Marine Division Association Scholarship

1st Marine Division Association Inc.
410 Pier View Way
Oceanside, CA 92054
Phone: 877-967-8561
Fax: 760-967-8567
Email: oldbreed@sbcglobal.net
http://www.1stmarinedivisionassociation.org

Purpose: To provide financial aid to undergraduate students who are the dependents of deceased or disabled veterans of the 1st Marine Division.
Eligibility: Applicants must be dependents of honorably discharged veterans of the 1st Marine Division or units attached to or supporting the Division who are now deceased or totally and permanently disabled for any reason. Applicants must attend an accredited university as full-time undergraduate students.
Target applicants: College students. Adult students.
Amount: Up to $1,750.
Number of awards: Varies.
Scholarship may be renewable.
Deadline: Varies.
How to apply: Applications are available online.
Exclusive: Visit www.UltimateScholarshipBook.com and enter code 1S512 for updates on this award.

(6) • Academic Competitiveness Grant

Federal Student Aid
U.S. Department of Education

400 Maryland Avenue, SW
Washington, DC 20202
Phone: 800-433-3243
http://studentaid.ed.gov
Purpose: To help students who have finished a rigorous secondary school program of study.
Eligibility: Applicants must be full-time students who are Federal Pell Grant recipients and have enrolled or been accepted by a two- or four-year degree-granting institution of higher education. The grants are available to students for the first and second years of college with up to $750 for the first year and up to $1,300 for the second year. Second year students must also have a minimum 3.0 GPA.
Target applicants: High school students. College students. Adult students.
Minimum GPA: 3.0
Amount: Up to $1,300.
Number of awards: Varies.
Scholarship may be renewable.
Deadline: Varies.
How to apply: Applicants must complete the Free Application for Federal Student Aid (FAFSA).
Exclusive: Visit www.UltimateScholarshipBook.com and enter code FE612 for updates on this award.

(7) · Accepting the Challenge of Excellence Award

National Exchange Club
3050 Central Avenue
Toledo, OH 43606
Phone: 800-924-2643
Fax: 419-535-1989
Email: info@nationalexchangeclub.org
http://www.nationalexchangeclub.org
Purpose: To support students who have overcome hardships in order to graduate from high school and to encourage students who are "often overlooked for their accomplishments."
Eligibility: Students must be nominated by their local National Exchange Club or guidance counselor. Applicants must be high school seniors who have overcome obstacles including physical, emotional or social obstacles to graduate from high school. These obstacles may include physical, language, child abuse, delinquency or substance abuse.
Target applicants: High school students.
Amount: $10,000.
Number of awards: 1.
Deadline: June 1.
How to apply: The application is prepared by the student's sponsoring club or counselor. The student must write two essays to be submitted with the application.
Exclusive: Visit www.UltimateScholarshipBook.com and enter code NA712 for updates on this award.

(8) · ACJA/Lambda Alpha Epsilon Scholarship

American Criminal Justice Association
P.O. Box 601047
Sacramento, CA 95860-1047
Phone: 916-484-6553
Fax: 916-488-2227
Email: acjalae@aol.com
http://www.acjalae.org
Purpose: To assist criminal justice students.
Eligibility: Applicants must be undergraduate or graduate students who are studying criminal justice. Students must be ACJA/LAE members, but they may submit a membership form at the time of application. Applicants must have completed at least two semesters or three quarters of their education while earning at least a 3.0 GPA. Applicants must submit transcripts, letters of enrollment and goals statements.
Target applicants: College students. Graduate school students. Adult students.
Minimum GPA: 3.0
Amount: $100-$400.
Number of awards: Up to 9.
Deadline: December 31.
How to apply: Applications are available online and by written request.
Exclusive: Visit www.UltimateScholarshipBook.com and enter code AM812 for updates on this award.

(9) · Admiral Mike Boorda Scholarship Program

Navy-Marine Corps Relief Society
875 North Randolph Street Suite 225
Arlington, VA 22203
Phone: 703-696-4960
Fax: 703-696-0144
Email: education@hq.nmcrs.org
http://www.nmcrs.org
Purpose: To help eligible Navy and Marine Corps members.
Eligibility: Applicants must be enrolled or planning to enroll as full-time undergraduate students at an eligible post-secondary, technical or vocational institution. Applicants must have a minimum 2.0 GPA and be active duty servicemembers accepted to the Enlisted Commissioning Program, the Marine Enlisted Commissioning Education Program or the Medical Enlisted Commissioning Program.
Target applicants: College students. Adult students.
Minimum GPA: 2.0
Amount: $3,000.
Number of awards: Varies.
Scholarship may be renewable.
Deadline: May 1.
How to apply: Applications are available online.
Exclusive: Visit www.UltimateScholarshipBook.com and enter code NA912 for updates on this award.

(10) · AFCEA General Emmett Paige Scholarships

Armed Forces Communications and Electronics Association (AFCEA)
4400 Fair Lakes Court
Fairfax, VA 22033
Phone: 703-631-6149
Fax: 703-631-4693
http://www.afcea.org
Purpose: To offer scholarships to members of the armed forces.
Eligibility: Applicants must be on active duty in the uniformed military services, honorably discharged veterans or their spouses or dependents who are full-time students in an accredited four-year U.S. college or university. Applicants must also be U.S. citizens, majoring in electrical, computer, chemical or aerospace engineering, computer science, physics or mathematics and have a minimum 3.4 GPA. Veterans may apply for the scholarship as college freshmen. All others must apply as college sophomores or juniors.
Target applicants: College students. Adult students.
Minimum GPA: 3.4
Amount: $2,000.

Number of awards: Varies.
Deadline: March 1.
How to apply: Applications are available online.
Exclusive: Visit www.UltimateScholarshipBook.com and enter code AR1012 for updates on this award.

(11) • AFCEA ROTC Scholarships

Armed Forces Communications and Electronics Association (AFCEA)
4400 Fair Lakes Court
Fairfax, VA 22033
Phone: 703-631-6149
Fax: 703-631-4693
http://www.afcea.org
Purpose: To assist ROTC sophomores or juniors who are majoring in aerospace engineering, electronics, computer science, computer engineering, physics or mathematics.
Eligibility: Applicants must major in electrical or aerospace engineering, electronics, computer science, computer engineering, physics or mathematics at an accredited U.S. four-year college or university. Applicants must also be enrolled full-time as college sophomores or juniors and be nominated by professors of military science, naval science or aerospace studies. Applicants must be U.S. citizens enrolled in ROTC, have good moral character, demonstrate academic excellence and the potential to serve as an officer in the U.S. Armed Forces and have financial need.
Target applicants: College students. Adult students.
Amount: $2,000.
Number of awards: Varies.
Deadline: March 1.
How to apply: Applications are available online.
Exclusive: Visit www.UltimateScholarshipBook.com and enter code AR1112 for updates on this award.

(12) • AFCEA Sgt Jeannette L. Winters, USMC Memorial Scholarship

Armed Forces Communications and Electronics Association (AFCEA)
4400 Fair Lakes Court
Fairfax, VA 22033
Phone: 703-631-6149
Fax: 703-631-4693
http://www.afcea.org
Purpose: To support active duty Marine Corps members or veterans.
Eligibility: Applicants must be on active duty in the U.S. Marine Corps or honorably discharged veterans of the U.S. Marine Corps. Applicants must also be current undergraduate sophomores, juniors or seniors attending an accredited U.S. college or university majoring in electrical, aerospace or computer engineering, computer science, physics or mathematics with a minimum 3.0 GPA. Distance-learning or online programs are eligible as long as all other criteria are met.
Target applicants: College students. Adult students.
Minimum GPA: 3.0
Amount: $2,000.
Number of awards: Varies.
Deadline: September 1.
How to apply: Applications are available online.
Exclusive: Visit www.UltimateScholarshipBook.com and enter code AR1212 for updates on this award.

(13) • AFSA National Essay Contest

American Foreign Service Association (AFSA)
2101 East Street NW
Washington, DC 20037
Phone: 202-944-5504
Fax: 202-338-6820
Email: dec@afsa.org
http://www.afsa.org/
Purpose: To support students interested in writing an essay on foreign service.
Eligibility: Students must attend a public, private, parochial school, home school or participate in a high school correspondence program in any of the 50 states, the District of Columbia or U.S. territories or must be U.S. citizens attending schools overseas. Students must be the dependent of a US government Foreign Service employee (active, retired with pension, deceased or separated). The current award is $2,500 to the student, $500 to his/her school and all expenses paid trip to Washington, DC, for the winner and parents.
Target applicants: High school students.
Amount: $2,500.
Number of awards: 1.
Deadline: April 15.
How to apply: The registration form is available online. Applicants must write a 750- to 1,000 word essay on the topic provided.
Exclusive: Visit www.UltimateScholarshipBook.com and enter code AM1312 for updates on this award.

(14) • Air Force ROTC ASCP

Air Force Reserve Officer Training Corps
AFROTC Admissions
551 E. Maxwell Boulevard
Maxwell AFB, AL 36112-5917
Phone: 866-423-7682
Fax: 334-953-6167
http://www.afrotc.com
Purpose: To allow active duty Air Force personnel to earn a commission while completing their bachelor's degree.
Eligibility: Applicants must be active-duty Air Force personnel who are U.S. citizens under the age of 31, with the exception of nurses, who must be under the age of 42. They must also meet all testing and waiver requirements and be recommended by their commanding officer.
Target applicants: High school students. College students. Adult students.
Minimum GPA: 2.5
Amount: Up to $24,900.
Number of awards: Varies.
Scholarship may be renewable.
Deadline: July 15 and September 1.
How to apply: Application details are available online.
Exclusive: Visit www.UltimateScholarshipBook.com and enter code AI1412 for updates on this award.

(15) • Air Force ROTC Enhanced HBCU Scholarships

Air Force Reserve Officer Training Corps
AFROTC Admissions
551 E. Maxwell Boulevard
Maxwell AFB, AL 36112-5917
Phone: 866-423-7682
Fax: 334-953-6167
http://www.afrotc.com

Purpose: To increase enrollment at Historically Black Colleges or Universities and to meet officer production requirements.
Eligibility: Applicants must be college freshmen or sophomores enrolled at Jackson State University, Tuskegee University, Alabama State University, Howard University, Grambling State University, North Carolina A&T University, Fayetteville State University or Tennessee State University.
Target applicants: College students. Adult students.
Amount: Up to $18,900.
Number of awards: Varies.
Deadline: Varies.
How to apply: Applications are available from your school's Air Force ROTC detachment.
Exclusive: Visit www.UltimateScholarshipBook.com and enter code AI1512 for updates on this award.

(16) • Air Force ROTC Enhanced Hispanic Serving Institutions (HSI) Scholarships

Air Force Reserve Officer Training Corps
AFROTC Admissions
551 E. Maxwell Boulevard
Maxwell AFB, AL 36112-5917
Phone: 866-423-7682
Fax: 334-953-6167
http://www.afrotc.com
Purpose: To enhance enrollment at Hispanic Serving Institutions and to meet officer production requirements.
Eligibility: Applicants must be college freshmen or sophomores at California State University (Fresno or San Bernardino), New Mexico State University, University of Miami, University of New Mexico, University of Puerto Rico (Rio Piedras or Mayaguez) or University of Texas-San Antonio.
Target applicants: College students. Adult students.
Amount: Up to $18,900.
Number of awards: Up to 75.
Scholarship may be renewable.
Deadline: Varies.
How to apply: Applications are available from your school's Air Force ROTC detachment.
Exclusive: Visit www.UltimateScholarshipBook.com and enter code AI1612 for updates on this award.

(17) • Air Force ROTC Express Scholarships

Air Force Reserve Officer Training Corps
AFROTC Admissions
551 E. Maxwell Boulevard
Maxwell AFB, AL 36112-5917
Phone: 866-423-7682
Fax: 334-953-6167
http://www.afrotc.com
Purpose: To meet Air Force ROTC officer production requirements.
Eligibility: Applicants must be U.S. citizens who are college students, have passed the Air Force ROTC Physical Fitness Test and have either passed the Air Force Officer Qualifying Test or had their failing scores waived. Students must have a GPA of 2.5 or higher and major in computer engineering, electrical engineering, environmental engineering, aeronautical engineering, aerospace engineering, astronautical engineering, civil engineering, mechanical engineering or meteorology/atmospheric sciences.
Target applicants: College students. Adult students.
Minimum GPA: 2.5
Amount: Up to $18,900.
Number of awards: Varies.
Scholarship may be renewable.
Deadline: Varies.
How to apply: Applications are available from your school's Air Force detachment.
Exclusive: Visit www.UltimateScholarshipBook.com and enter code AI1712 for updates on this award.

(18) • Air Force ROTC HBCU Minority School Scholarships

Air Force Reserve Officer Training Corps
AFROTC Admissions
551 E. Maxwell Boulevard
Maxwell AFB, AL 36112-5917
Phone: 866-423-7682
Fax: 334-953-6167
http://www.afrotc.com
Purpose: To assist students who are attending minority institutions that offer Air Force ROTC programs.
Eligibility: Applicants must be U.S. citizens who are college students and have passed the Air Force ROTC Physical Fitness Test and have either passed the Air Force Officer Qualifying Test or had their failing scores waived. They must also have a 2.5 or higher GPA.
Target applicants: College students. Adult students.
Minimum GPA: 2.5
Amount: Up to $18,900.
Number of awards: Varies.
Scholarship may be renewable.
Deadline: Varies.
How to apply: Applications are available from your school's Air Force ROTC detachment.
Exclusive: Visit www.UltimateScholarshipBook.com and enter code AI1812 for updates on this award.

(19) • Air Force ROTC High School Scholarship Program

Air Force Reserve Officer Training Corps
AFROTC Admissions
551 E. Maxwell Boulevard
Maxwell AFB, AL 36112-5917
Phone: 866-423-7682
Fax: 334-953-6167
http://www.afrotc.com
Purpose: To help students with financial need who are also interested in joining the Air Force pay for college.
Eligibility: Applicants must pass the physical fitness assessment and demonstrate academic achievement or outstanding leadership skills. There are three types of award: one that pays full tuition, most fees and for books, one that pays tuition up to $15,000, most fees and for books and one that pays full tuition at a college or university that costs less than $9,000 per year. In return for the scholarship, recipients must serve in the Air Force.
Target applicants: High school students.
Amount: Up to full tuition plus fees, books and stipend.
Number of awards: Varies.
Scholarship may be renewable.
Deadline: December 1.
How to apply: Applications are available online.
Exclusive: Visit www.UltimateScholarshipBook.com and enter code AI1912 for updates on this award.

(20) • Air Force ROTC Hispanic Serving Institutions (HSI) Minority School Scholarships

Air Force Reserve Officer Training Corps
AFROTC Admissions
551 E. Maxwell Boulevard
Maxwell AFB, AL 36112-5917
Phone: 866-423-7682
Fax: 334-953-6167
http://www.afrotc.com

Purpose: To increase enrollment at Hispanic Serving Institutions and to meet officer production requirements.
Eligibility: Applicants must be college freshmen or sophomores enrolled at a Hispanic Serving Institution that hosts an Air Force ROTC detachment or is a crosstown of another school with a detachment.
Target applicants: College students. Adult students.
Amount: Up to $18,900.
Number of awards: Varies.
Scholarship may be renewable.
Deadline: Varies.
How to apply: Applications are available from your school's Air Force ROTC detachment.
Exclusive: Visit www.UltimateScholarshipBook.com and enter code AI2012 for updates on this award.

(21) • Air Force ROTC In-College Program

Air Force Reserve Officer Training Corps
AFROTC Admissions
551 E. Maxwell Boulevard
Maxwell AFB, AL 36112-5917
Phone: 866-423-7682
Fax: 334-953-6167
http://www.afrotc.com

Purpose: To promote the Air Force ROTC program.
Eligibility: Applicants must be U.S. citizens who have passed the Air Force Officer Qualifying Test, the Air Force ROTC Physical Fitness Test and a Department of Defense medical examination. Students must also be college freshmen or sophomores and have a GPA of 2.5 or higher.
Target applicants: College students. Adult students.
Minimum GPA: 2.5
Amount: Up to $18,900.
Number of awards: Varies.
Scholarship may be renewable.
Deadline: Varies.
How to apply: Applications are available from your school's Air Force ROTC detachment.
Exclusive: Visit www.UltimateScholarshipBook.com and enter code AI2112 for updates on this award.

(22) • Air Force ROTC Professional Officer Course-Early Release Program

Air Force Reserve Officer Training Corps
AFROTC Admissions
551 E. Maxwell Boulevard
Maxwell AFB, AL 36112-5917
Phone: 866-423-7682
Fax: 334-953-6167
http://www.afrotc.com

Purpose: To allow active duty Air Force personnel the opportunity for early release in order to complete their bachelor's degrees.
Eligibility: Applicants must be active-duty Air Force personnel who are U.S. citizens under the age of 31, with the exception of nurses, who must be under the age of 42. They must also meet all testing and waiver requirements, be recommended by their commanding officer and not be within one year of receiving their degree.
Target applicants: College students. Adult students.
Minimum GPA: 2.5
Amount: Up to $6,900.
Number of awards: Varies.
Scholarship may be renewable.
Deadline: October 15.
How to apply: Application details are available online.
Exclusive: Visit www.UltimateScholarshipBook.com and enter code AI2212 for updates on this award.

(23) • Air Force ROTC SOAR Program

Air Force Reserve Officer Training Corps
AFROTC Admissions
551 E. Maxwell Boulevard
Maxwell AFB, AL 36112-5917
Phone: 866-423-7682
Fax: 334-953-6167
http://www.afrotc.com

Purpose: To give active duty Air Force personnel the opportunity to earn their commissions while completing their bachelor's degrees.
Eligibility: Applicants must be active-duty Air Force personnel who are U.S. citizens under the age of 31, with the exception of nurses, who must be under the age of 47. They must also meet all testing and waiver requirements and be recommended by their commanding officer. Students must also have a minimum college GPA of 2.5 or a minimum ACT score of 24 or minimum SAT reading comprehension and math score of 1100.
Target applicants: College students. Adult students.
Minimum GPA: 2.5
Amount: Up to $24,900.
Number of awards: Varies.
Scholarship may be renewable.
Deadline: Varies.
How to apply: Application details are available online.
Exclusive: Visit www.UltimateScholarshipBook.com and enter code AI2312 for updates on this award.

(24) • Air Force Spouse Scholarship

Air Force Association
1501 Lee Highway
Arlington, VA 22209
Phone: 800-727-3337
Fax: 703-247-5853
Email: lcross@afa.org
http://www.afa.org

Purpose: To aid U.S. Air Force spouses who wish to pursue undergraduate and graduate degrees.
Eligibility: Applicants must be the spouses of active duty members of the U.S. Air Force, Air National Guard or Air Force Reserve. They must be accepted or enrolled at an accredited college or university and have a GPA of 3.5 or higher. Applicants who are themselves Air Force members or in ROTC are not eligible. Selection is based on the overall strength of the application.
Target applicants: High school students. College students. Graduate school students. Adult students.
Minimum GPA: 3.5

Amount: $2,500.
Number of awards: Varies.
Deadline: April 30.
How to apply: Applications are available online. An application form, official transcript, personal essay, applicant photo, proof of college acceptance (rising freshmen only) and two letters of recommendation are required.
Exclusive: Visit www.UltimateScholarshipBook.com and enter code AI2412 for updates on this award.

(25) • Airmen Memorial Foundation Scholarship Program

Air Force Sergeants Association
5211 Auth Road
Suitland, MD 20746
Phone: 301-899-3500
Fax: 301-899-8136
Email: staff@afsahq.org
http://www.afsahq.org
Purpose: To assist dependents of Air Force enlisted personnel in obtaining higher education.
Eligibility: Applicants must be dependents of Air Force enlisted personnel who are attending high school or college. They must have a GPA of 3.5 or higher and be accepted to the college of their choice.
Target applicants: High school students. College students. Adult students.
Minimum GPA: 3.5
Amount: Up to $2,000.
Number of awards: Varies.
Deadline: March 31.
How to apply: Applications are available online.
Exclusive: Visit www.UltimateScholarshipBook.com and enter code AI2512 for updates on this award.

(26) • Alpha Kappa Alpha Financial Need Scholars

Alpha Kappa Alpha Educational Advancement Foundation Inc.
5656 S. Stony Island Avenue
Chicago, IL 60637
Phone: 800-653-6528
Fax: 773-947-0277
Email: akaeaf@akaeaf.net
http://www.akaeaf.org
Purpose: To assist undergraduate and graduate students who have overcome hardship to achieve educational goals.
Eligibility: Applicants must be studying full-time at the sophomore level or higher at an accredited institution and have a GPA of 2.5 or higher. Students must also demonstrate leadership, volunteer, civic or academic service. The program is open to students without regard to sex, race, creed, color, ethnicity, religion, sexual orientation or disability. Students do NOT need to be members of Alpha Kappa Alpha. Deadline is April 15 for undergraduate students and August 15 for graduate students.
Target applicants: College students. Graduate school students. Adult students.
Minimum GPA: 2.5
Amount: $750-$2,500.
Number of awards: Varies.
Deadline: April 15 for undergraduate students, August 15 for graduate students.
How to apply: Applications are available online. An application form, personal statement and three letters of recommendation are required.
Exclusive: Visit www.UltimateScholarshipBook.com and enter code AL2612 for updates on this award.

(27) • Alphonso Deal Scholarship Award

National Black Police Association
NBPA Scholarship Award
30 Kennedy Street NW
Suite 101
Washington, DC 20011
Phone: 202-986-2070
Fax: 202-986-0410
Email: nbpanatofc@worldnet.att.net
http://www.blackpolice.org
Purpose: To support students who plan careers in law enforcement.
Eligibility: Applicants must be collegebound high school seniors planning to study law enforcement who are U.S. citizens and are recommended by their high school principal, counselor or teacher.
Target applicants: High school students.
Amount: $500.
Number of awards: Varies.
Deadline: June 1.
How to apply: Applications are available online.
Exclusive: Visit www.UltimateScholarshipBook.com and enter code NA2712 for updates on this award.

(28) • American Darts Organization Memorial Scholarships

American Darts Organization
230 N. Crescent Way
Suite K
Anaheim, CA 92801
Phone: 714-254-0212
Fax: 714-254-0214
Email: adooffice@aol.com
http://www.adodarts.com
Purpose: To support participants in the American Darts Organization Youth Playoff Program.
Eligibility: Applicants must be ADO members, and they must have been at least quarter-finalists in the ADO Youth Playoff Program. Students must be under 21 years old on December 1 of the year in which they intend to start school. They must be enrolled or accepted in a degree-granting program on a full-time basis with at least a 2.0 GPA.
Target applicants: High school students. College students.
Minimum GPA: 2.0
Amount: $500-$1,500.
Number of awards: 8.
Deadline: Varies.
How to apply: Applications are available online.
Exclusive: Visit www.UltimateScholarshipBook.com and enter code AM2812 for updates on this award.

(29) • American Fire Sprinkler Association Scholarship Program

American Fire Sprinkler Association
12750 Merit Drive
Suite 350
Dallas, TX 75251
Phone: 214-349-5965
Fax: 214-343-8898
Email: acampbell@firesprinkler.org

http://www.afsascholarship.org
Purpose: To provide financial aid to high school seniors and introduce them to the fire sprinkler industry.
Eligibility: Applicants must be high school seniors who plan to attend a U.S. college, university or certified trade school. Students must read the "Fire Sprinkler Essay" available online and then take an online quiz. Applicants receive one entry in the scholarship drawing for each question answered correctly.
Target applicants: High school students.
Amount: $2,000.
Number of awards: 10.
Scholarship may be renewable.
Deadline: May 3.
How to apply: Applications are available online.
Exclusive: Visit www.UltimateScholarshipBook.com and enter code AM2912 for updates on this award.

(30) · American Legion Baseball Scholarship

American Legion Baseball
700 N. Pennsylvania Street
Indianapolis, IN 46204
Phone: 317-630-1249
Fax: 317-630-1369
Email: baseball@legion.org
http://www.legion.org/baseball
Purpose: To award scholarships to members of American Legion-affiliated baseball teams.
Eligibility: Applicants must be graduating high school seniors and be nominated by a head coach or team manager. One player per department (state) will be selected. Nominations should be sent to the local Department Headquarters. Scholarships may be used to further education at any accredited college, university or other institution of higher education.
Target applicants: High school students.
Amount: $1,000.
Number of awards: 51.
Deadline: July 15.
How to apply: Applications are available online.
Exclusive: Visit www.UltimateScholarshipBook.com and enter code AM3012 for updates on this award.

(31) · American Legion Junior Air Rifle National Championship Scholarships

American Legion
Attn.: Americanism and Children and Youth Division
P.O. Box 1055
Indianapolis, IN 46206
Phone: 317-630-1249
Fax: 317-630-1369
Email: acy@legion.org
http://www.legion.org
Purpose: To reward outstanding young marksmen and women.
Eligibility: Applicants must be 18 years of age or younger. They must qualify for and compete in the Junior Air Rifle National Championship. Winners receive a $2,500 scholarship.
Target applicants: Junior high students or younger. High school students.
Amount: $2,500.
Number of awards: 2.
Deadline: Varies.
How to apply: Applications are available from your local American Legion chapter.
Exclusive: Visit www.UltimateScholarshipBook.com and enter code AM3112 for updates on this award.

(32) · American Legion Legacy Scholarships

American Legion
700 North Pennsylvania Street
P.O. Box 1055
Indianapolis, IN 46206
Phone: 317-630-1202
Fax: 317-630-1223
http://www.legion.org
Purpose: To support the children of deceased U.S. military personnel.
Eligibility: Applicants must be the children or adopted children of a parent who was in the U.S. military and died in active duty on or after September 11, 2001. Students must be pursuing or planning to pursue undergraduate study in the U.S.
Target applicants: High school students. College students. Adult students.
Amount: Varies.
Number of awards: Varies.
Deadline: April 15.
How to apply: Applications are available online.
Exclusive: Visit www.UltimateScholarshipBook.com and enter code AM3212 for updates on this award.

(33) · American Police Hall of Fame Educational Scholarship Fund

American Police Hall of Fame and Museum
6350 Horizon Drive
Titusville, FL 32780
Phone: 321-264-0911
Email: info@aphf.org
http://www.aphf.org/scholarships.html
Purpose: To provide financial assistance for children of fallen law enforcement officers.
Eligibility: Applicants must be sons or daughters of law enforcement officers who were killed in the line of duty. They may attend a public, private or vocational school. A current transcript, letter of acceptance to an institution of higher learning or a student ID is required.
Target applicants: High school students. College students. Adult students.
Amount: $1,500.
Number of awards: Varies.
Scholarship may be renewable.
Deadline: Varies.
How to apply: Applications are available online.
Exclusive: Visit www.UltimateScholarshipBook.com and enter code AM3312 for updates on this award.

(34) · American Society of Crime Laboratory Directors Scholarship Program

American Society of Crime Laboratory Directors
139K Technology Drive
Garner, NC 27529
Phone: 919-773-2600
Fax: 919-773-2602
http://www.ascld.org

Purpose: To help students who are enrolled in a forensics-related degree program and who plan to pursue a career in the forensics field.
Eligibility: Applicants must be rising undergraduate juniors, rising undergraduate seniors or graduate students who are enrolled in a degree program in forensic science, forensic chemistry or a related physical or natural science. They must attend an accredited university and must be interested in pursuing a career in the field of forensics. Preference is given to students who are enrolled in degree programs accredited by the Forensic Science Education Program Accreditation Commission (FEPAC). Selection is based on overall academic achievement, achievement in forensics coursework, personal statement, level of interest in forensics careers and recommendation letter.
Target applicants: College students. Graduate school students. Adult students.
Amount: $1,000.
Number of awards: Varies.
Deadline: April 15 and May 15.
How to apply: Applications are available online. An application form, transcripts, personal statement and one recommendation letter are required.
Exclusive: Visit www.UltimateScholarshipBook.com and enter code AM3412 for updates on this award.

(35) • Americorps National Civilian Community Corps

AmeriCorps
1201 New York Avenue NW
Washington, DC 20525
Phone: 202-606-5000
Fax: 202-606-3472
Email: questions@americorps.org
http://www.americorps.gov/Default.asp
Purpose: To strengthen communities and develop leaders through community service.
Eligibility: Applicants must be U.S. citizens who are between 18 and 24 years of age. Recipients must live on one of four AmeriCorps campuses in Denver, Colorado; Sacramento, California; Perry Point, Maryland or Vicksburg, Mississippi. Applicants must commit to 10 months of service on projects in areas such as education, public safety, the environment and other unmet needs. The projects are located within the region of one of the four campuses.
Target applicants: High school students. College students. Graduate school students. Adult students.
Amount: $5,350.
Number of awards: Varies.
Deadline: Varies.
How to apply: Applications are available online.
Exclusive: Visit www.UltimateScholarshipBook.com and enter code AM3512 for updates on this award.

(36) • Americorps Vista

AmeriCorps
1201 New York Avenue NW
Washington, DC 20525
Phone: 202-606-5000
Fax: 202-606-3472
Email: questions@americorps.org
http://www.americorps.gov/Default.asp
Purpose: To provide education assistance in exchange for community service.
Eligibility: Applicants must be United States citizens who are at least 17 years of age. They must be available to serve full-time for one year at a nonprofit organization or local government agency with an objective that may include to fight illiteracy, improve health services, create businesses or strengthen community groups.
Target applicants: High school students. College students. Graduate school students. Adult students.
Amount: $5,350.
Number of awards: Varies.
Deadline: Varies.
How to apply: Applications are available online.
Exclusive: Visit www.UltimateScholarshipBook.com and enter code AM3612 for updates on this award.

(37) • AMVETS National Scholarship for Veterans

AMVETS National Headquarters
4647 Forbes Boulevard
Lanham, MD 20706-4380
Phone: 877-726-8387
Fax: 301-459-7924
Email: thilton@amvets.org
http://www.amvets.org
Purpose: To provide financial assistance for veterans.
Eligibility: Applicants must be United States citizens and veterans who demonstrate financial need. They must have been honorably discharged or be on active duty and eligible for release. They must agree to allow AMVET to publicize their award if selected.
Target applicants: High school students. College students. Adult students.
Amount: $1,000.
Number of awards: 3.
Deadline: April 15.
How to apply: Applications are available online.
Exclusive: Visit www.UltimateScholarshipBook.com and enter code AM3712 for updates on this award.

(38) • AMVETS National Scholarships for Entering College Freshman

AMVETS National Headquarters
4647 Forbes Boulevard
Lanham, MD 20706-4380
Phone: 877-726-8387
Fax: 301-459-7924
Email: thilton@amvets.org
http://www.amvets.org
Purpose: To provide education assistance for graduating JROTC cadets.
Eligibility: Applicants must be high school seniors with a minimum GPA of 3.0 or documented extenuating circumstances. They must be United States citizens and children or grandchildren of U.S. veterans. They must show academic potential and financial need.
Target applicants: High school students.
Minimum GPA: 3.0
Amount: $1,000.
Number of awards: 1.
Deadline: April 15.
How to apply: Applications are available online.
Exclusive: Visit www.UltimateScholarshipBook.com and enter code AM3812 for updates on this award.

(39) • Anchor Scholarship Foundation Scholarship

Anchor Scholarship Foundation
P.O. Box 9535
Norfolk, VA 23505

Phone: 757-374-3769
Email: admin@anchorscholarship.com
http://www.anchorscholarship.com
Purpose: To assist the dependents of current and former members of the Naval Surface Forces, Atlantic and Naval Surface Forces, Pacific.
Eligibility: Applicants must be high school seniors or college students planning to attend or currently attending an accredited, four-year college or university full-time. Applicants must also be dependents of service members who are on active duty or retired and have served a minimum of six years in a unit under the administrative control of Commander, Naval Surface Forces, U.S. Atlantic Fleet or U.S. Pacific Fleet. The award is based on academics, extracurricular activities, character, all-around ability and financial need.
Target applicants: High school students. College students. Adult students.
Amount: Varies.
Number of awards: 40+.
Deadline: March 15.
How to apply: Applications are available online.
Exclusive: Visit www.UltimateScholarshipBook.com and enter code AN3912 for updates on this award.

(40) • Armed Services YMCA Annual Essay Contest

Armed Services YMCA
6359 Walker Lane
Suite 200
Alexandria, VA 22310
Phone: 703-313-9600
Fax: 703-313-9668
Email: essaycontest@asymca.org
http://www.asymca.org
Purpose: To promote reading among children of service members and civilian Department of Defense employees.
Eligibility: Applicants must be K-12 students who are children of active duty or Reserve/Guard military personnel. Entrants up to eighth grade should write an essay of 300 words or less. High school entrants should write an essay of 500 words or less.
Target applicants: Junior high students or younger. High school students.
Amount: Up to $1,000.
Number of awards: 12.
Deadline: March 18.
How to apply: Applications are available online.
Exclusive: Visit www.UltimateScholarshipBook.com and enter code AR4012 for updates on this award.

(41) • Army College Fund

U.S. Army
Building 1307
Third Avenue
Fort Knox, KY 40121
Phone: 502-626-1587
Email: brian.shalosky@usaac.army.mil
https://www.hrc.army.mil
Purpose: To provide incentives for Army enlistees to pursue needed occupational specialties.
Eligibility: Applicants must be enlisting in the Army with no prior service and have a high school diploma at time of entry. A minimum score of 50 on the Armed Forces Qualification Test is required. Students must be enrolled in the basic Montgomery G.I. Bill and must enlist in a specified military occupational specialty. Funding amounts vary by occupational specialty.
Target applicants: High school students. College students. Adult students.
Amount: Varies.
Number of awards: Varies.
Scholarship may be renewable.
Deadline: Varies.
How to apply: Applications are available from your local Army recruiting office.
Exclusive: Visit www.UltimateScholarshipBook.com and enter code U.4112 for updates on this award.

(42) • Army Nurse Corps Association Scholarships

Army Nurse Corps Association (ANCA)
Education Committee
P.O. Box 847
Manhattan, KS 66505
Phone: 210-650-3534
Fax: 210-650-3494
Email: education@e-anca.org
http://e-anca.org
Purpose: To support nursing and nurse anesthesia students who are or plan to become affiliated with the U.S. Army.
Eligibility: Applicants must be enrolled in a bachelor's or graduate degree program in nursing or nurse anesthesia. They must be in the U.S. Army, planning to enter the U.S. Army or be the parent, spouse or child of a U.S. Army officer. They cannot already be receiving funding from any source that is associated with the U.S. Army. Selection is based on the overall strength of the application.
Target applicants: College students. Graduate school students. Adult students.
Amount: $3,000.
Number of awards: Varies.
Deadline: April 1.
How to apply: Applications are available online. An application form, personal statement, endorsement from student's academic dean, official transcript and military service documents (if applicable) are required.
Exclusive: Visit www.UltimateScholarshipBook.com and enter code AR4212 for updates on this award.

(43) • Army ROTC Advanced Course

U.S. Army
Building 1307
Third Avenue
Fort Knox, KY 40121
Phone: 502-626-1587
Email: brian.shalosky@usaac.army.mil
https://www.hrc.army.mil
Purpose: To prepare ROTC members for service as officers.
Eligibility: Applicants must be rising college juniors who have completed the ROTC Basic Course or Leader's Training Course who have made a commitment to serve as an officer in the Army after they graduate. Students must take an ROTC class or lab each semester of their final two years of school and attend a summer leadership camp.
Target applicants: College students. Adult students.
Amount: Varies.
Number of awards: Varies.
Scholarship may be renewable.
Deadline: Varies.

How to apply: Applications are available from your school's military science department.
Exclusive: Visit www.UltimateScholarshipBook.com and enter code U.4312 for updates on this award.

(44) • Army ROTC Four-Year Scholarship Program

Headquarters
U.S. Army Cadet Command
55 Patch Road
Fort Monroe, VA 23651
Email: atccps@monroe.army.mil
http://www.goarmy.com/rotc/
Purpose: To bolster the ranks of the Army, Army Reserve and Army National Guard by providing monetary assistance to eligible student candidates.
Eligibility: Applicants must be U.S. citizens and high school seniors, graduates or college freshmen with at least four years of college remaining who wish to attend one of 600 colleges and earn a commission. Recipients must serve in the Army for four to eight years after graduation.
Target applicants: High school students. College students. Adult students.
Minimum GPA: 2.5
Amount: Up to full tuition.
Number of awards: Varies.
Scholarship may be renewable.
Deadline: January 10.
How to apply: Applications are available online.
Exclusive: Visit www.UltimateScholarshipBook.com and enter code HE4412 for updates on this award.

(45) • Army ROTC Green To Gold Scholarship Program

Headquarters
U.S. Army Cadet Command
55 Patch Road
Fort Monroe, VA 23651
Email: atccps@monroe.army.mil
http://www.goarmy.com/rotc/
Purpose: To provide scholarship funds for Army enlisted soldiers.
Eligibility: Applicants must be active duty enlisted members of the Army who wish to complete their baccalaureate degree requirements and obtain a commission. Recipients are required to serve in the U.S. Army.
Target applicants: College students. Adult students.
Amount: Varies.
Number of awards: Varies.
Deadline: Varies.
How to apply: Applications are available online.
Exclusive: Visit www.UltimateScholarshipBook.com and enter code HE4512 for updates on this award.

(46) • Arnold Sobel Endowment Fund Scholarships

Coast Guard Foundation
2100 Second Street SW
Washington, DC 20593
http://www.uscg.mil
Purpose: To provide financial assistance to children of Coast Guard members.
Eligibility: Applicants must be dependent children of men or women who are enlisted in the Coast Guard or who are in the Coast Guard Reserve on extended active duty. Children of retired or deceased Coast Guard members are also eligible.
Target applicants: High school students. College students. Adult students.
Amount: $5,000.
Number of awards: 4.
Deadline: April 1.
How to apply: Applications are available online after January 2.
Exclusive: Visit www.UltimateScholarshipBook.com and enter code CO4612 for updates on this award.

(47) • AWSEF Scholarship

American Water Ski Educational Foundation (AWSEF)
1251 Holy Cow Road
Polk City, FL 33868-8200
Phone: 863-324-2472
Email: info@waterskihalloffame.com
http://www.waterskihalloffame.com
Purpose: To support those involved in USA WATER SKI.
Eligibility: Applicants must be full-time undergraduates at a two- or four-year college as incoming sophomores to incoming seniors. Applicants must also be active members of USA WATER SKI all divisions: AWSA-ABC-AKA-WSDA-NSSA-NCWSA-NCWSRA-USAWB-HYD. Students should submit an application, two reference letters, an essay and a transcript.
Target applicants: College students. Adult students.
Amount: $1,500.
Number of awards: 6.
Scholarship may be renewable.
Deadline: March 1.
How to apply: Applications are available online.
Exclusive: Visit www.UltimateScholarshipBook.com and enter code AM4712 for updates on this award.

(48) • AXA Achievement Community Scholarship

AXA Achievement Scholarship
c/o Scholarship America
One Scholarship Way
St. Peter, MN 56082
Phone: 800-537-4180
Email: axaachievement@scholarshipamerica.org
http://www.axa-equitable.com/axa-foundation/community-scholarships.html
Purpose: To aid outstanding college-bound high school seniors.
Eligibility: Applicants must be U.S. citizens or legal residents and be high school seniors in the U.S. or Puerto Rico. They must be planning to attend an accredited two- or four-year postsecondary institution no later than the fall following high school graduation. They must be ambitious, goal-oriented, respectful of others and able to succeed in college. Selection is based on the overall strength of the application.
Target applicants: High school students.
Amount: $2,000.
Number of awards: Varies.
Deadline: February 15.
How to apply: Applications are available online. An application form, transcript, personal essay and one recommendation letter are required.
Exclusive: Visit www.UltimateScholarshipBook.com and enter code AX4812 for updates on this award.

(49) · AXA Achievement Scholarships

AXA Achievement Scholarship
c/o Scholarship America
One Scholarship Way
St. Peter, MN 56082
Phone: 800-537-4180
Email: axaachievement@scholarshipamerica.org
http://www.axa-equitable.com/axa-foundation/community-scholarships.html

Purpose: To provide financial assistance to ambitious students.

Eligibility: Applicants must be U.S. citizens or legal residents who are current high school seniors and are planning to enroll full-time in an accredited college or university in the fall following their graduation. They must show ambition and drive evidenced by outstanding achievement in school, community or workplace activities. A recommendation from an unrelated adult who can vouch for the student's achievement is required.

Target applicants: High school students.

Amount: $10,000-$25,000.

Number of awards: 52.

Deadline: December 15.

How to apply: Applications are available online.

Exclusive: Visit www.UltimateScholarshipBook.com and enter code AX4912 for updates on this award.

(50) · Babe Ruth League Scholarships

Babe Ruth League Inc.
1770 Brunswick Avenue
P.O. Box 5000
Trenton, NJ 08638
http://www.baberuthleague.org/scholarship.html

Purpose: To provide educational assistance to players in the Babe Ruth Baseball and Softball divisions.

Eligibility: Applicants must be members or former members of the Babe Ruth Baseball or Softball leagues. They must be graduating seniors. A short essay, copy of high school transcript and a letter of recommendation are required.

Target applicants: High school students.

Amount: $1,000.

Number of awards: Varies.

Deadline: July 1.

How to apply: Applications are available online.

Exclusive: Visit www.UltimateScholarshipBook.com and enter code BA5012 for updates on this award.

(51) · Best Buy @15 Scholarship Program

Best Buy Children's Foundation
7601 Penn Avenue S.
Richfield, MN 55423
Phone: 612-292-6397
Email: bestbuy@scholarshipamerica.org
http://www.bestbuy-communityrelations.com/scholarship.htm

Purpose: To assist students in grades 9-12 who will be attending a college, university or vocational school immediately following high school graduation.

Eligibility: Applicants must be currently in grades 9-12 living in the United States or Puerto Rico, have a minimum cumulative GPA of 2.5 (on a 4.0 scale), and demonstrate commitment to and involvement in community volunteer service or work experience. Selection is based on academic performance and exemplary community volunteer service or work experience. Consideration may also be given to participation and leadership in school activities. Financial need is not considered. Best Buy employees and relatives of employees who meet the requirements are eligible to apply.

Target applicants: High school students.

Minimum GPA: 2.5

Amount: $1,000.

Number of awards: 1200.

Deadline: February 16.

How to apply: Applications are only available online.

Exclusive: Visit www.UltimateScholarshipBook.com and enter code BE5112 for updates on this award.

(52) · Best Buy Scholarships

Best Buy Children's Foundation
7601 Penn Avenue S.
Richfield, MN 55423
Phone: 612-292-6397
Email: bestbuy@scholarshipamerica.org
http://www.bestbuy-communityrelations.com/scholarship.htm

Purpose: To assist students in obtaining a higher education.

Eligibility: Applicants must be high school students residing in the U.S. or Puerto Rico, live within 75 miles of a Best Buy store, have a minimum GPA of 2.5 and have community service or work experience. They must plan to enter a full-time undergraduate program at an accredited two- or four-year institution of higher learning in the United States or Puerto Rico no later than the fall term following graduation.

Target applicants: High school students.

Minimum GPA: 2.5

Amount: $1,000.

Number of awards: Up to 1,200.

Deadline: February 16.

How to apply: Students may apply online only. An application form and transcript are required.

Exclusive: Visit www.UltimateScholarshipBook.com and enter code BE5212 for updates on this award.

(53) · Better Chance Scholarship

Associates of Vietnam Veterans of America
8605 Cameron Street
Suite 400
Silver Spring, MD 20910-3710
Phone: 800-822-1316
Fax: 301-585-0519
Email: pvarnell@avva.org
http://www.avva.org

Purpose: To provide financial assistance to the families of veterans.

Eligibility: Applicants must be VVA or AVVA members or their spouses, children or grandchildren, or spouses, children or grandchildren of KIA or MIA Vietnam Veterans. They must be registered at an accredited institution of higher learning, and they must demonstrate financial need according to an official FAFSA printout.

Target applicants: High school students. College students. Adult students.

Amount: Up to $1,000.

Number of awards: Varies.

Deadline: June 30.

How to apply: Applications are available online.

Exclusive: Visit www.UltimateScholarshipBook.com and enter code AS5312 for updates on this award.

(54) • Big Dig Scholarship

Antique Trader
4216 Pacific Coast Highway
#302
Torrance, CA 90505
Phone: 310-294-9981
Email: henryk@antiquetrader.tv
http://www.antiquetrader.tv

Purpose: To aid the student who has written the most interesting essay on a specific antiques-related topic.
Eligibility: Applicants must be current undergraduate freshmen or sophomores or must be graduating high school seniors who are planning to enroll in college during the year following the application due date year. They must write an essay on a sponsor-defined question that relates to antiques. Selection is based on the content, grammatical correctness and originality of the essay.
Target applicants: High school students. College students. Adult students.
Amount: $3,000.
Number of awards: 1.
Deadline: December 3.
How to apply: Application instructions are available online. An essay is required.
Exclusive: Visit www.UltimateScholarshipBook.com and enter code AN5412 for updates on this award.

(55) • Billy Welu Scholarship

United States Bowling Congress
5301 S. 76th Street
Greendale, WI 53129
Phone: 800-514-2695 x3168
Email: smart@bowl.com
http://www.bowl.com

Purpose: To recognize exemplary qualities in amateur bowlers who are in college.
Eligibility: Applicants must be amateur bowlers who are currently attending college. They must have a 2.5 or higher GPA.
Target applicants: College students. Graduate school students. Adult students.
Minimum GPA: 2.5
Amount: $1,000.
Number of awards: 1.
Deadline: May 31.
How to apply: Applications are available online.
Exclusive: Visit www.UltimateScholarshipBook.com and enter code UN5512 for updates on this award.

(56) • Blogging Scholarship

CollegeScholarships.org
150 Caldecott Lane #8
Oakland, CA 94618
Phone: 888-501-9050
Email: info@collegescholarships.org
http://www.collegescholarships.org/our-scholarships/blogging.htm

Purpose: To provide financial assistance for students who blog.
Eligibility: Applicants must maintain blogs with unique and interesting information. They must be U.S. citizens or permanent residents who are currently enrolled full-time in a U.S. institution of higher learning. Winners must agree to have their name and blog listed on the website.
Target applicants: College students. Adult students.
Amount: Up to $10,000.
Number of awards: Varies.
Deadline: October 31.
How to apply: Applications are available online. An essay is required.
Exclusive: Visit www.UltimateScholarshipBook.com and enter code CO5612 for updates on this award.

(57) • Bob Warnicke Scholarship

National Bicycle League (NBL)
3958 Brown Park Drive
Suite D
Hilliard, OH 43026
Phone: 614-777-1625
Fax: 614-777-1680
Email: administration@nbl.org
http://www.nbl.org

Purpose: To help students who have participated in BMX racing events.
Eligibility: Applicants must be members, have a current NBL competition license or official's license and have participated in BMX racing events for at least a year. Students must also be high school graduates and plan to or currently attend a postsecondary institution full- or part-time.
Target applicants: College students. Graduate school students. Adult students.
Amount: Varies.
Number of awards: Varies.
Deadline: November 1.
How to apply: Applications are available online, by mail or by phone.
Exclusive: Visit www.UltimateScholarshipBook.com and enter code NA5712 for updates on this award.

(58) • Bobby Sox High School Senior Scholarship Program

Bobby Sox Softball
P.O. Box 5880
Buena Park, CA 90622-5880
Phone: 714-522-1234
Fax: 714-522-6548
http://www.bobbysoxsoftball.org/scholar.html

Purpose: To provide educational assistance for Bobby Sox softball players.
Eligibility: Applicants must be eighth grade girls who have participated in Bobby Sox for four or more seasons, or high school seniors who have participated for five or more seasons. They must have a GPA of 2.0 or higher.
Target applicants: High school students.
Minimum GPA: 2.0
Amount: Up to $2,500.
Number of awards: 45.
Deadline: Varies.
How to apply: Applications are available online.
Exclusive: Visit www.UltimateScholarshipBook.com and enter code BO5812 for updates on this award.

(59) • Bonner Scholarship

Bonner Foundation
10 Mercer Street
Princeton, NJ 08540
Phone: 609-924-6663
Fax: 609-683-4626

Email: info@bonner.org
http://www.bonner.org
Purpose: To award four-year community service scholarships to students planning to attend one of 27 participating colleges.
Eligibility: Students must complete annual service requirements as stipulated by the organization. Awards are geared toward students demonstrating significant financial need. Scholarship recipients are named Bonner Scholars.
Target applicants: High school students.
Amount: Varies.
Number of awards: Varies.
Deadline: Varies.
How to apply: Contact the admission office at each participating school to request an application.
Exclusive: Visit www.UltimateScholarshipBook.com and enter code BO5912 for updates on this award.

(60) • Buddy Pelletier Surfing Foundation Scholarship

Buddy Pelletier Surfing Foundation Fund
5121 Chalk Street
Morehead City, NC 28557
Phone: 252-727-7917
Fax: 866-925-7125
Email: lynne.pelletier@bbandt.com
http://www.myspace.com/buddypelletier
Purpose: To support the education and humanitarian needs of the East Coast surfing community.
Eligibility: Applicants must be members of the East Coast surfing community. Rising high school seniors, current undergraduate college students and returning students may apply regardless of age. Two letters of recommendation and a 500-word essay are required. Previous applicants and winners may reapply each year.
Target applicants: High school students. College students. Adult students.
Amount: $1,000.
Number of awards: 3-4.
Deadline: June 1.
How to apply: Applications are available online.
Exclusive: Visit www.UltimateScholarshipBook.com and enter code BU6012 for updates on this award.

(61) • Burger King Scholars Program

Burger King Scholars Program
5505 Blue Lagoon Drive
Miami, FL 33126
Phone: 305-378-3000
Email: bdorado@whopper.com
http://www.haveityourwayfoundation.org/burger_king_scholars_program.html
Purpose: To provide financial assistance for high school seniors who have part-time jobs.
Eligibility: Applicants may apply from public, private, vocational, technical, parochial and alternative high schools in the United States, Canada and Puerto Rico and must be U.S. or Canadian residents. Students must also have a minimum 2.5 GPA, work part-time an average of 15 hours per week unless there are extenuating circumstances, participate in community service or other activities, demonstrate financial need and plan to enroll in an accredited two- or four-year college, university or vocational/technical school by the fall term of the graduating year. Applicants do NOT need to work at Burger King, but Burger King employees are eligible.
Target applicants: High school students.
Minimum GPA: 2.5
Amount: $1,000-$25,000.
Number of awards: Varies.
Deadline: Varies.
How to apply: Applications are available online and may only be completed online.
Exclusive: Visit www.UltimateScholarshipBook.com and enter code BU6112 for updates on this award.

(62) • C.I.P. Scholarship

College Is Power
San Francisco, CA 94102
http://www.collegeispower.com/content.cfm?area=4
Purpose: To assist adult students age 18 and over with college expenses.
Eligibility: Applicants must be adult students currently attending or planning to attend a two-year or four-year college or university within the next 12 months. Students must be 18 years or older and U.S. citizens or permanent residents. The award may be used for full- or part-time study at either on-campus or online schools.
Target applicants: High school students. College students. Adult students.
Amount: $1,500.
Number of awards: Varies.
Deadline: May 31.
How to apply: Applications are available online.
Exclusive: Visit www.UltimateScholarshipBook.com and enter code CO6212 for updates on this award.

(63) • Capt. James J. Regan Scholarship

Explorers Learning for Life
P.O. Box 152079
Irving, TX 75015
Phone: 972-580-2433
Fax: 972-580-2137
Email: pchestnu@lflmail.org
http://www.learningforlife.org/exploring
Purpose: To support students who are Law Enforcement Explorers.
Eligibility: Students must be at least in their senior year of high school. Applicants must submit three letters of recommendation and an essay.
Target applicants: High school students. College students. Adult students.
Amount: $500.
Number of awards: 2.
Deadline: March 31.
How to apply: Applications are available online.
Exclusive: Visit www.UltimateScholarshipBook.com and enter code EX6312 for updates on this award.

(64) • Captain Caliendo College Assistance Fund Scholarship

U.S. Coast Guard Chief Petty Officers Association
5520-G Hempstead Way
Springfield, VA 22151-4009
Phone: 703-941-0395
Fax: 703-941-0397
Email: cgcpoa@aol.com
http://www.uscgcpoa.org
Purpose: To provide financial assistance for children of CPOA/CGEA members.

Eligibility: Applicants must be dependents of a living or deceased USCG CPOA/CGEA member who are under the age of 24 as of March 1 of the award year. The age limit does not apply to disabled children. Proof of acceptance or enrollment in an institution of higher learning is required.
Target applicants: High school students. College students.
Amount: $5,000.
Number of awards: 1.
Deadline: March 1.
How to apply: Applications are available online.
Exclusive: Visit www.UltimateScholarshipBook.com and enter code U.6412 for updates on this award.

---

(65) · Carson Scholars

Carson Scholars Fund
305 W Chesapeake Avenue
Suite L-020
Towson, MD 21204
Phone: 877-773-7236
Email: caitlin@carsonscholars.org
http://www.carsonscholars.org
Purpose: To recognize students who demonstrate academic excellence and commitment to the community.
Eligibility: Applicants must be nominated by their school. They must be in grades 4 through 11 and have a GPA of 3.75 or higher in English, reading, language arts, math, science, social studies and foreign language. They must have participated in some form of voluntary community service beyond what is required by their school. Scholarship recipients must attend a four-year college or university upon graduation to receive funds.
Target applicants: Junior high students or younger. High school students.
Minimum GPA: 3.75
Amount: $1,000.
Number of awards: Varies.
Deadline: January 14.
How to apply: Applications are available from the schools of those nominated. Only one student per school may be nominated.
Exclusive: Visit www.UltimateScholarshipBook.com and enter code CA6512 for updates on this award.

---

(66) · Castle Ink's Green Scholarship

Castle Ink
37 Wyckoff Street
Greenlawn, NY 11740
Phone: 800-399-5193
Fax: 404-460-5001
Email: scholarships@castleink.com
http://www.castleink.com
Purpose: To aid environmentally-minded students.
Eligibility: Applicants must be U.S. citizens or permanent residents who are college-bound high school seniors or current college students at an accredited institution. They must have a GPA of 2.5 or higher and submit an essay describing their own efforts in recycling and conservation. Selection is based on the strength of the essay.
Target applicants: High school students. College students. Graduate school students. Adult students.
Minimum GPA: 2.5
Amount: $2,500.
Number of awards: 1.
Deadline: July 31.
How to apply: Application instructions are available online. A personal essay is required.
Exclusive: Visit www.UltimateScholarshipBook.com and enter code CA6612 for updates on this award.

---

(67) · Challenge Scholarship

National Strength and Conditioning Association (NSCA) Foundation
1885 Bob Johnson Drive
Colorado Springs, CO 80906
Phone: 800-815-6826
Fax: 719-632-6367
Email: nsca@nsca-lift.org
http://www.nsca-lift.org
Purpose: To support NSCA members pursuing studies related to strength and conditioning.
Eligibility: Applicants must be NSCA members for one year before applying and be pursuing careers in strength and conditioning. Students must submit an essay detailing their course of study, career goals and financial need. Applications are evaluated based on grades, courses, experience, honors, recommendations and involvement in the community and with NSCA.
Target applicants: College students. Graduate school students. Adult students.
Amount: $1,500.
Number of awards: Varies.
Deadline: March 15.
How to apply: Applications are available with membership.
Exclusive: Visit www.UltimateScholarshipBook.com and enter code NA6712 for updates on this award.

---

(68) · Charles Shafae' Scholarship

Papercheck
Phone: 866-693-3348
Email: scholarships@papercheck.com
http://www.papercheck.com
Purpose: To reward the students who have written the most compelling essays.
Eligibility: Applicants must be legal residents of the U.S. or must hold a valid student visa and be enrolled as full-time undergraduates at an accredited U.S. four-year postsecondary institution. They must have a GPA of 3.2 or higher, must be in good academic standing and must write an essay that addresses a question that has been predetermined by the scholarship sponsor. Selection is based on the strength of the essay.
Target applicants: College students. Adult students.
Minimum GPA: 3.2
Amount: $500.
Number of awards: Varies.
Deadline: September 1.
How to apply: Application instructions are available online. An entry form and essay are required.
Exclusive: Visit www.UltimateScholarshipBook.com and enter code PA6812 for updates on this award.

---

(69) · Charlie Logan Scholarship Program for Seamen

Seafarers International Union of North America
Mr. Lou Delma, Administrator
Seafarers Welfare Plan Scholarship Program
5201 Auth Way
Camp Springs, MD 20746

Phone: 301-899-0675
Fax: 301-899-7355
http://www.seafarers.org
Purpose: To offer scholarships to members of the SIU.
Eligibility: Applicants must be active seamen who are high school graduates or equivalent, are eligible to receive Seafarers Plan benefits and have credit for two years (730 days) of employment with an employer who is obligated to make contributions to the Seafarers' Plan on the employee's behalf prior to the date of application. Recipients may attend any U.S. accredited institution (college or trade school). Selection is based on high school equivalency scores or secondary school records, college transcripts, if any, SAT/ACT scores, references on character or personality and autobiography. The $6,000 scholarships are for two-year study, and the $20,000 scholarship is for four-year study.
Target applicants: College students. Adult students.
Amount: $6,000-$20,000.
Number of awards: 3.
Scholarship may be renewable.
Deadline: April 15.
How to apply: Applications are available by written request.
Exclusive: Visit www.UltimateScholarshipBook.com and enter code SE6912 for updates on this award.

(70) • Chick Evans Caddie Scholarships

Western Golf Association
1 Briar Road
Golf, IL 60029
Phone: 847-724-4600
Fax: 847-724-7133
Email: evansscholars@wgaesf.com
http://www.evansscholarsfoundation.com
Purpose: To support golf caddies.
Eligibility: Applicants must have completed their junior year of high school and be nominated by their clubs. They must have caddied regularly for at least two years. A B average or higher in college preparatory courses is required, and applicants must have taken the ACT. Financial need and outstanding character, integrity and leadership are required. Applicants must apply to eligible universities in their home state. Scholarship finalists must participate in an interview with the scholarship committee.
Target applicants: High school students.
Minimum GPA: 3.0
Amount: Tuition and housing.
Number of awards: Varies.
Scholarship may be renewable.
Deadline: September 30.
How to apply: Applications are available from your sponsoring club. An application form, high school evaluation, transcript, caddy evaluation, letters of recommendation, copy of parents' latest federal tax return and financial aid profile are required.
Exclusive: Visit www.UltimateScholarshipBook.com and enter code WE7012 for updates on this award.

(71) • Chief Master Sergeants of the Air Force Scholarships

Air Force Sergeants Association
5211 Auth Road
Suitland, MD 20746
Phone: 301-899-3500
Fax: 301-899-8136
Email: staff@afsahq.org
http://www.afsahq.org
Purpose: To provide financial assistance to the families of Air Force enlistees.
Eligibility: Applicants must be dependents of enlisted Air Force members, either on active duty or retired. They must meet the eligibility requirements and participate in the Airmen Memorial Foundation Scholarship Program. An unweighted GPA of 3.5 or higher is required. Extenuating circumstances are considered.
Target applicants: High school students. College students. Adult students.
Minimum GPA: 3.5
Amount: $500-$3,000.
Number of awards: Varies.
Deadline: March 31.
How to apply: Applications are available online.
Exclusive: Visit www.UltimateScholarshipBook.com and enter code AI7112 for updates on this award.

(72) • Chief Petty Officer Scholarship Fund

Chief Petty Officer Scholarship Fund
8401 Hampton Boulevard
Suite 3
Norfolk, VA 23505
Phone: 757-233-9136
Email: cposfboard@cposf.org
http://www.cposf.org
Purpose: To aid the families of Chief Petty Officers of the US Navy.
Eligibility: Applicants must be spouses or children of active, retired or reserve Chief, Senior Chief or Master Chief Petty Officers of the US Navy. They must be high school graduates or have earned a GED and plan to attend a college or university to earn an AA, BA or BS degree. Current college students may also apply. Selection criteria include scholastic proficiency, character and all-around ability.
Target applicants: High school students. College students. Adult students.
Amount: Varies.
Number of awards: Varies.
Deadline: April 1.
How to apply: Applications are available online. An application form, three letters of recommendation, a copy of your dependents ID card and a personal statement are required.
Exclusive: Visit www.UltimateScholarshipBook.com and enter code CH7212 for updates on this award.

(73) • Church Hill Classics "Frame My Future" Scholarship

Church Hill Classics
594 Pepper Street
Monroe, CT 06468
Phone: 800-477-9005
Fax: 203-268-2468
Email: info@diplomaframe.com
http://www.framemyfuture.com
Purpose: To help success-driven students attain their higher education goals.
Eligibility: Applicants must be high school seniors or otherwise eligible for graduation in the school year of application or current college students. They must plan to enroll in college full-time the following academic year. Applicants must be residents of the United States,

including APO/FPO addresses but excluding Puerto Rico. Employees of Church Hill Classics and affiliated companies, their family members and individuals living in the same household are not eligible. A photograph, essay, painting or other creative entry is required to demonstrate what the applicants want to achieve in their personal and professional life after college.
Target applicants: High school students. College students. Adult students.
Amount: $1,000.
Number of awards: 5.
Deadline: March 2.
How to apply: Applications are available online. An entry form and original piece of artwork are required.
Exclusive: Visit www.UltimateScholarshipBook.com and enter code CH7312 for updates on this award.

(74) • CIA Undergraduate Scholarship Program

Central Intelligence Agency
Office of Public Affairs
Washington, DC 20505
Phone: 703-482-0623
Fax: 703-482-1739
http://www.cia.gov
Purpose: To encourage students to pursue careers with the CIA.
Eligibility: Applicants must be high school seniors or college sophomores. High school students must have an SAT score of 1000 or higher or an ACT score of 21 or higher, while all applicants must have a GPA of at least 3.0. Applicants must demonstrate financial need, defined as a household income of less than $70,000 for a family of four or $80,000 for a family of five or more. They must meet all criteria for regular CIA employees, including security checks and medical examinations. Applicants must commit to a work experience each summer during college and agree to CIA employment for 1.5 times the length of their CIA-sponsored scholarship.
Target applicants: High school students. College students. Adult students.
Minimum GPA: 3.0
Amount: Annual salary including benefits and up to $18,000 for tuition.
Number of awards: Varies.
Scholarship may be renewable.
Deadline: August 1-October 15.
How to apply: Applications are available online. A resume, SAT/ACT scores, family income information, copy of FAFSA or Student Aid Report, transcript and two letters of recommendation are required.
Exclusive: Visit www.UltimateScholarshipBook.com and enter code CE7412 for updates on this award.

(75) • CKSF Scholarships

Common Knowledge Scholarship Foundation
P.O. Box 290361
Davie, FL 33329-0361
Phone: 954-262-8553
Email: info@cksf.org
http://www.cksf.org
Purpose: To support high school and college students.
Eligibility: Applicants must register online with CKSF and complete quizzes on various topics. Students may be U.S. high school students in grades 9 to 12 or college students.
Target applicants: High school students. College students. Graduate school students. Adult students.
Amount: Varies.
Number of awards: 1.
Deadline: Monthly.
How to apply: Applications are available online. Online registration is required.
Exclusive: Visit www.UltimateScholarshipBook.com and enter code CO7512 for updates on this award.

(76) • Coast Guard College Student Pre-Commissioning Initiative

U.S. Coast Guard
4200 Wilson Boulevard
Suite 730
Arlington, VA 22203-1800
Phone: 877-663-8724
Fax: 703-235-1880
http://www.gocoastguard.com
Purpose: To train future Coast Guard officers for success.
Eligibility: Applicants must be between 19 and 27 years of age and be college sophomores or juniors with at least 60 credits completed toward their degrees. They must be enrolled in a four-year degree program at a Coast Guard-approved institution with at least a 25 percent minority population. Students must be U.S. citizens, have a 2.5 or higher GPA and meet all physical requirements of the Coast Guard. Applicants must have a minimum score of 1000 on the SAT, 23 on the ACT or 109 on the ASVAB.
Target applicants: College students. Adult students.
Minimum GPA: 2.5
Amount: Tuition plus salary.
Number of awards: Varies.
Scholarship may be renewable.
Deadline: January 12 for Coast Guard members, February 9 for civilians.
How to apply: Applications are available online. An application form, physical exam results, immunization record, copy of Social Security card and driver's license, transcript, test results, proof of enrollment and tuition statement are required.
Exclusive: Visit www.UltimateScholarshipBook.com and enter code U.7612 for updates on this award.

(77) • Coast Guard Foundation Scholarship Fund

Coast Guard Foundation
2100 Second Street SW
Washington, DC 20593
http://www.uscg.mil
Purpose: To provide financial assistance to children of Coast Guard members.
Eligibility: Applicants must be unmarried dependent children of U.S. Coast Guard members, living, retired or deceased or Coast Guard reservists on extended active duty. They must be high school seniors or full-time undergraduate students in a four-year program or vocational/technical program. They must be under 23 years old.
Target applicants: High school students. College students.
Amount: Up to $5,000.
Number of awards: Varies.
Scholarship may be renewable.
Deadline: April 1.
How to apply: Applications are available online.
Exclusive: Visit www.UltimateScholarshipBook.com and enter code CO7712 for updates on this award.

(78) · Coca-Cola All-State Community College Academic Team

Coca-Cola Scholars Foundation
P.O. Box 442
Atlanta, GA 30301
Phone: 800-306-2653
Email: questions@coca-colascholars.org
http://www.coca-colascholars.org

Purpose: To assist community college students with college expenses.

Eligibility: Applicants must be enrolled in community college, have a minimum GPA of 3.5 on a four-point scale and be on track to earn an associate's or bachelor's degree. Students attending community college in the U.S. do NOT need to be members of Phi Theta Kappa. One student from each state will win a $2,000 scholarship. Fifty students will win a $1,500 scholarship, fifty students will win a $1,250 scholarship and fifty students will win a $1,000 scholarship.

Target applicants: College students. Adult students.

Minimum GPA: 3.5

Amount: $1,000-$2,000.

Number of awards: 200.

Deadline: December 1.

How to apply: Applications are available online. Nomination from the designated nominator at your school is required. A list of nominators is available at http://www.ptk.org/schol/allusacontacts/

Exclusive: Visit www.UltimateScholarshipBook.com and enter code CO7812 for updates on this award.

(79) · Coca-Cola Scholars Program

Coca-Cola Scholars Foundation
P.O. Box 442
Atlanta, GA 30301
Phone: 800-306-2653
Email: questions@coca-colascholars.org
http://www.coca-colascholars.org

Purpose: Begun in 1986 to celebrate the Coca-Cola Centennial, the program is designed to contribute to the nation's future and to assist a wide range of students.

Eligibility: Applicants must be high school seniors in the U.S. and must use the awards at an accredited U.S. college or university. Selection is based on character, personal merit and commitment. Merit is shown through leadership, academic achievement and motivation to serve and succeed.

Target applicants: High school students.

Amount: $10,000-$20,000.

Number of awards: 250.

Scholarship may be renewable.

Deadline: August 1-October 31.

How to apply: Applications are available online.

Exclusive: Visit www.UltimateScholarshipBook.com and enter code CO7912 for updates on this award.

(80) · College Answer $1,000 Scholarship

College Answer
Sallie Mae
12061 Bluemont Way
Reston, VA 20190
http://www.collegeanswer.com

Purpose: To help students pay for college.

Eligibility: Applicants may be high school, undergraduate or graduate students and must register on the CollegeAnswer website. Each month one registered user is selected in a random drawing to receive the scholarship. When you are registered for the website or the Sallie Mae Scholarship Search, you are automatically entered into the scholarship drawing.

Target applicants: High school students. College students. Graduate school students. Adult students.

Amount: $1,000.

Number of awards: 1 per month.

Deadline: Monthly.

How to apply: Enter the scholarship by registering on the website. If you have already registered on the website or have a screen name and password, you are already entered for the scholarship.

Exclusive: Visit www.UltimateScholarshipBook.com and enter code CO8012 for updates on this award.

(81) · College Prep Scholarship for High School Juniors

QuestBridge
120 Hawthorne Avenue
Suite 103
Palo Alto, CA 94301
Phone: 888-275-2054
Fax: 650-653-2516
Email: questions@questbridge.org
http://www.questbridge.org

Purpose: To equip outstanding low-income high school juniors with the knowledge necessary to compete for admission to leading colleges.

Eligibility: Applicants must be high school juniors who have a strong academic record and an annual household income of less than $60,000. Many past award recipients have also been part of the first generation in their family to attend college. Scholarships are open to all qualified students, regardless of race or ethnicity.

Target applicants: High school students.

Amount: Varies.

Number of awards: Varies.

Deadline: March 29.

How to apply: Applications are available on the QuestBridge website in February. An application form, transcript and one teacher recommendation are required.

Exclusive: Visit www.UltimateScholarshipBook.com and enter code QU8112 for updates on this award.

(82) · CollegeNET Scholarship

CollegeNET Scholarship Review Committee
805 SW Broadway
Suite 1600
Portland, OR 97205
Phone: 503-973-5200
Fax: 503-973-5252
Email: scholarship@collegenet.com
http://www.collegenet.com

Purpose: To assist college applicants.

Eligibility: Applicants must sign up at the website and visit and participate in forums. Recipients are determined by votes on the website.

Target applicants: High school students. College students. Adult students.

Amount: $1,000-$5,000.

Number of awards: 4.

Deadline: Monthly.

How to apply: Applications are available online.

Exclusive: Visit www.UltimateScholarshipBook.com and enter code CO8212 for updates on this award.

(83) • Congressional Black Caucus Spouses Education Scholarship

Congressional Black Caucus Foundation
1720 Massachusetts Avenue NW
Washington, DC 20036
Phone: 202-263-2800
Fax: 202-775-0773
Email: info@cbcfinc.org
http://www.cbcfinc.org

Purpose: To support students who are pursuing undergraduate or graduate degrees.
Eligibility: Applicants do NOT need to be African American but must reside or attend school in a congressional district represented by a CBC member. Students must be attending or planning to attend school on a full-time basis. Students must have at least a 2.5 GPA, and they must demonstrate leadership and community service participation.
Target applicants: High school students. College students. Graduate school students. Adult students.
Minimum GPA: 2.5
Amount: Varies.
Number of awards: Varies.
Deadline: June 1.
How to apply: Applications are available online.
Exclusive: Visit www.UltimateScholarshipBook.com and enter code CO8312 for updates on this award.

(84) • Congressional Medal of Honor Society Scholarships

Congressional Medal of Honor Society
40 Patriots Point Road
Mount Pleasant, SC 29464
Phone: 843-884-8862
Fax: 843-884-1471
Email: medalhq@earthlink.net
http://www.cmohs.org

Purpose: To provide education assistance to children of Congressional Medal of Honor recipients.
Eligibility: Applicants must be natural or adopted children of Congressional Medal of Honor recipients or of other combat veterans if recommended by a Medal of Honor recipient.
Target applicants: High school students. College students. Adult students.
Amount: Up to $500.
Number of awards: Varies.
Deadline: Varies.
How to apply: Applications are available from the Congressional Medal of Honor Society.
Exclusive: Visit www.UltimateScholarshipBook.com and enter code CO8412 for updates on this award.

(85) • CrossLites Scholarship Contest

CrossLites
1000 Holt Avenue
1178
Winter Park, FL 32789
Phone: 407-833-3886
Email: crosslites@gmail.com
http://www.crosslites.com

Purpose: To encourage students to learn about Dr. Charles Parker.
Eligibility: Applicants must be high school, undergraduate or graduate students. There are no minimum GPA, SAT, ACT, GMAT, GRE or any other test score requirements. Students must write a reflective essay of 400 to 600 words based on one of Dr. Charles Parker's quotes or messages, which are listed on the website. There are winners for the high school, undergraduate and graduate school levels. Selection is based on the judges' score (10 percent) and votes from website visitors (90 percent).
Target applicants: High school students. College students. Graduate school students. Adult students.
Amount: Up to $2,000.
Number of awards: 33.
Deadline: December 15.
How to apply: Applications are available online. An essay, contact information and transcript are required.
Exclusive: Visit www.UltimateScholarshipBook.com and enter code CR8512 for updates on this award.

(86) • Curt Greene Memorial Scholarship

Harness Horse Youth Foundation
16575 Carey Road
Westfield, IN 46074
Phone: 317-867-5877
Fax: 317-867-5896
Email: ellen@hhyf.org
http://www.hhyf.org

Purpose: To support students who are interested in harness racing.
Eligibility: Students must demonstrate financial need, and they must be at least in their senior year of high school. Applicants must submit an essay and two letters of reference.
Target applicants: High school students. College students. Adult students.
Amount: Varies.
Number of awards: Varies.
Deadline: April 30.
How to apply: Applications are available online.
Exclusive: Visit www.UltimateScholarshipBook.com and enter code HA8612 for updates on this award.

(87) • Daedalian Foundation Matching Scholarship Program

Daedalian Foundation
P.O. Box 249
Randolph AFB, TX 78148
Phone: 210-945-2113
Fax: 210-945-2112
Email: icarus2@daedalians.org
http://www.daedalians.org

Purpose: To aid undergraduates who are studying to become military pilots.
Eligibility: Applicants must be rising or current undergraduates attending a four-year institution and must have a demonstrated interest in pursuing a career in military aviation. Selection is based on the overall strength of the application.
Target applicants: High school students. College students. Adult students.
Amount: Varies.
Number of awards: Varies.
Deadline: Varies.

How to apply: Applications are available online. An application form and applicant photo are required.
Exclusive: Visit www.UltimateScholarshipBook.com and enter code DA8712 for updates on this award.

(88) · Daughters of the Cincinnati Scholarship

Daughters of the Cincinnati
National Headquarters
122 East 58th Street
New York, NY 10022
Phone: 212-319-6915
http://fdncenter.org/grantmaker/cincinnati/
Purpose: To support daughters of Armed Services commissioned officers.
Eligibility: Applicants must be daughters of career officers in the United States Army, Navy, Air Force, Coast Guard or Marine Corps (active, retired or deceased). Daughters of reserve officers or enlisted personnel cannot apply. Applicants must also be high school seniors.
Target applicants: High school students.
Amount: Varies.
Number of awards: Varies.
Scholarship may be renewable.
Deadline: March 15.
How to apply: Applications are available by mailing the organization your parent's rank and branch of service and enclosing a self-addressed, stamped envelope.
Exclusive: Visit www.UltimateScholarshipBook.com and enter code DA8812 for updates on this award.

(89) · Davidson Fellows Award

Davidson Institute for Talent Development
9665 Gateway Drive
Suite B
Reno, NV 89521
Phone: 775-852-3483
Email: davidsonfellows@ditd.org
http://www.davidson-institute.org
Purpose: To award young people for their works in mathematics, science, technology, music, literature, philosophy or "outside the box."
Eligibility: Applicants must be under the age of 18 and be able to attend the awards reception in Washington, DC. In addition to the monetary award, the institute will pay for travel and lodging expenses. Three nominator forms, three copies of a 15-minute DVD or VHS videotape and additional materials are required.
Target applicants: Junior high students or younger. High school students.
Amount: $10,000-$50,000.
Number of awards: Varies.
Deadline: March 2.
How to apply: Applications are available online.
Exclusive: Visit www.UltimateScholarshipBook.com and enter code DA8912 for updates on this award.

(90) · Davis-Putter Scholarship Fund

Davis-Putter Scholarship Fund
P.O. Box 7307
New York, NY 10116
Email: information@davisputter.org
http://www.davisputter.org
Purpose: To assist students who are both academically capable and who aid the progressive movement for peace and justice both on campus and in their communities.
Eligibility: Applicants must be undergraduate or graduate students who participate in the progressive movement, acting in the interests of issues such as expansion of civil rights and international solidarity, among others. Applicants must also have demonstrated financial need as well as a solid academic record.
Target applicants: College students. Graduate school students. Adult students.
Amount: Up to $10,000.
Number of awards: Varies.
Deadline: April 1.
How to apply: Applications are available online.
Exclusive: Visit www.UltimateScholarshipBook.com and enter code DA9012 for updates on this award.

(91) · Dell Scholars Program

Michael and Susan Dell Foundation
P.O. Box 163867
Austin, TX 78716
Phone: 512-329-0799
Fax: 512-347-1744
Email: apply@dellscholars.org
http://www.dellscholars.org
Purpose: To support underprivileged high school seniors.
Eligibility: Students must be participants in an approved college readiness program, and they must have at least a 2.4 GPA. Applicants must be pursuing a bachelor's degree in the fall directly after graduation. Students must also be U.S. citizens or permanent residents and demonstrate financial need. Selection is based on "individual determination to succeed," future goals, hardships that have been overcome, self motivation and financial need.
Target applicants: High school students.
Minimum GPA: 2.4
Amount: Varies.
Number of awards: Varies.
Scholarship may be renewable.
Deadline: January 15.
How to apply: Applications are available online. An online application is required.
Exclusive: Visit www.UltimateScholarshipBook.com and enter code MI9112 for updates on this award.

(92) · Dinah Shore Scholarship

Ladies Professional Golf Association
100 International Golf Drive
Daytona Beach, FL 32124-1092
Phone: 386-274-6200
Fax: 386-274-1099
http://www.lpga.com
Purpose: To honor the late Dinah Shore.
Eligibility: Applicants must be female high school seniors who have been accepted into a full-time course of study at an accredited U.S. institution of higher learning. They must have played golf regularly for the past two years but not played on a competitive collegiate golf team. A minimum GPA of 3.2 is required.
Target applicants: High school students.
Minimum GPA: 3.2
Amount: $5,000.
Number of awards: 1.
Deadline: May 15.

How to apply: Applications are available online.
Exclusive: Visit www.UltimateScholarshipBook.com and enter code LA9212 for updates on this award.

(93) · Directron.com College Scholarship

Directron
10402 Harwin Drive
Houston, TX 77036
Phone: 713-773-3636 x1500
Fax: 281-754-4959
Email: customer_service@directron.us
http://www.directron.com
Purpose: To aid U.S. college students.
Eligibility: Applicants must be high school seniors or current college students and submit an essay on the provided topic related to computers. Essays are judged on academic merit (50 percent) and originality and creativity (50 percent). Photos are not required but recommended.
Target applicants: High school students. College students. Adult students.
Amount: $1,000-$3,000.
Number of awards: 8.
Deadline: March 1.
How to apply: No application is required. Applicants should send their contact information and essays to information@directron.com.
Exclusive: Visit www.UltimateScholarshipBook.com and enter code DI9312 for updates on this award.

(94) · Discover Scholarship Program

Discover Card
c/o International Scholarship and Tuition Services Inc.
200 Crutchfield Avenue
Nashville, TN 37210
Phone: 866-756-7932
Email: info@applyists.com
http://www.discoverfinancial.com/community
Purpose: To recognize high school juniors for their accomplishments beyond academics.
Eligibility: Applicants must be high school juniors at an accredited U.S. high school and have a minimum cumulative 2.75 GPA for their 9th and 10th grades. Applicants must also demonstrate accomplishments in community service and leadership and have faced a significant roadblock or challenge.
Target applicants: High school students.
Minimum GPA: 2.75
Amount: $25,000.
Number of awards: Up to 10.
Deadline: January 31.
How to apply: Requests for applications are available online.
Exclusive: Visit www.UltimateScholarshipBook.com and enter code DI9412 for updates on this award.

(95) · DiscoverScholars.org Scholarship

DiscoverScholars.org
5062 27th Street N.
Arlington, VA 22207
Phone: 413-454-5233
Email: mail@discoverscholars.org
http://www.discoverscholars.org
Purpose: To distribute scholarship funds to the types of students that individual donors wish to support.
Eligibility: Applicants must be United States citizens or permanent residents. They must be high school seniors who have accepted an offer to attend a four-year undergraduate college or university during the coming school year or currently enrolled undergraduate students at an accredited four-year college or university.
Target applicants: High school students. College students. Adult students.
Amount: Varies.
Number of awards: Varies.
Deadline: March 15, June 15, September 15, December 15 of each year.
How to apply: Applications are available online. An application form, transcript, standardized test scores, copy of Student Aid Report and copy of financial aid package are required.
Exclusive: Visit www.UltimateScholarshipBook.com and enter code DI9512 for updates on this award.

(96) · Discus Awards College Scholarships

Discus Awards
7101 Wisconsin Avenue, Suite 750
Bethesda, MD 20814
Email: info@discusawards.com
http://www.discusawards.com
Purpose: To aid well-rounded, college-bound high school students.
Eligibility: Applicants must be U.S.-based high school students who have involvement or achievements in at least three of the following areas: academics, arts, athletics, community service, faith, government, green, technology, work or other achievements. Students may be in grades 9 to 12. Selection is based on merit.
Target applicants: High school students.
Amount: $2,000.
Number of awards: 10.
Deadline: Monthly.
How to apply: Applications are available online. An application form and supporting materials are required.
Exclusive: Visit www.UltimateScholarshipBook.com and enter code DI9612 for updates on this award.

(97) · Dixie Boys Baseball Scholarship Program

Dixie Boys Baseball
P.O. Box 8263
Dothan, AL 36304
Phone: 334-793-3331
Fax: 334-793-3331
Email: jjones29@sw.rr.com
http://www.dixie.org
Purpose: To help high school seniors who have participated in a franchised Dixie Boys Baseball Inc. program.
Eligibility: Applicants must plan to pursue undergraduate studies at a college or university. An application, financial statement, two recommendation letters, proof of baseball participation, transcript and essay are required. Selection is based on class rankings, strong school and community leadership and financial need. Programs are located in Alabama, Arkansas, Florida, Georgia, Louisiana, Mississippi, North Carolina, South Carolina, Tennessee, Texas and Virginia.
Target applicants: High school students.
Amount: $1,250.
Number of awards: 11.
Deadline: March 15.
How to apply: Applications are available online.
Exclusive: Visit www.UltimateScholarshipBook.com and enter code DI9712 for updates on this award.

(98) • Dixie Youth Scholarship Program

Dixie Youth Baseball
P.O. Box 877
Marshall, TX 75671
Phone: 903-927-2255
Email: dyb@dixie.org
http://www.dixie.org

Purpose: To help high school seniors who have participated in a franchised Dixie Youth Baseball league.

Eligibility: Applicants must have been registered on a Dixie Youth Baseball team participating in a franchised Dixie Youth Baseball Inc. league prior to reaching age thirteen. Selection is based on financial need, scholastic record and citizenship. Programs are located in Alabama, Arkansas, Florida, Georgia, Louisiana, Mississippi, North Carolina, South Carolina, Tennessee, Texas and Virginia.

Target applicants: High school students.

Amount: $2,000.

Number of awards: 70.

Deadline: March 1.

How to apply: Contact your local league officials or a district, state or national director for an application, and applications are also available online.

Exclusive: Visit www.UltimateScholarshipBook.com and enter code DI9812 for updates on this award.

(99) • Do Something Awards

Do Something
24-32 Union Square East
4th Floor
New York, NY 10003
Phone: 212-254-2390
Email: aashton@dosomething.org
http://www.dosomething.org/awards

Purpose: To award scholarships and community grants to young social entrepreneurs who make a measurable difference in their communities.

Eligibility: Young community leaders up to age 25 may apply. Emphasis is on those who take a leadership role in creating a positive, lasting impact on the community. Focus areas include health, environment and community building.

Target applicants: High school students. College students. Graduate school students.

Amount: Varies.

Number of awards: Varies.

Deadline: March 1.

How to apply: Applications are available online.

Exclusive: Visit www.UltimateScholarshipBook.com and enter code DO9912 for updates on this award.

(100) • Dollars for Scholars Scholarship

Citizens' Scholarship Foundation of America
One Scholarship Way
P.O. Box 297
St. Peter, MN 56082
Phone: 800-537-4180
http://scholarshipamerica.org/index.php

Purpose: To encourage students to aim for and achieve loftier educational goals.

Eligibility: Applicants must be members of a local Dollars for Scholars chapter. There are more than 1,200 Dollars for Scholars chapters that award more than $29 million in awards each year.

Target applicants: High school students.

Amount: Varies.

Number of awards: Varies.

Deadline: Varies.

How to apply: Contact your local Dollars for Scholars chapter for more information. A list of chapters is available online.

Exclusive: Visit www.UltimateScholarshipBook.com and enter code CI10012 for updates on this award.

(101) • Dolphin Scholarship

Dolphin Scholarship Foundation
5040 Virginia Beach Boulevard
Suite 104A
Virginia Beach, VA 23462
Phone: 757-671-3200
Fax: 757-671-3330
Email: info@dolphinscholarship.org
http://www.dolphinscholarship.org

Purpose: To assist the children of members of the Navy Submarine Force and other Navy submarine support personnel.

Eligibility: Applicants must be the unmarried children or stepchildren of navy submariners or navy members who have served in submarine support activities and must be under 24 years old at the time of the application deadline. The parents must have been part of the Submarine Force for at least eight years, have served in submarine support activities for at least 10 years or died on active duty while in the Submarine Force. The children of submariners who served less than the required number of years due to injury or illness occurring in the line of duty may also be eligible. Applicants must attend an accredited four-year college, working for a bachelor's degree.

Target applicants: High school students. College students.

Amount: Varies.

Number of awards: Varies.

Scholarship may be renewable.

Deadline: Varies.

How to apply: Applications are available online.

Exclusive: Visit www.UltimateScholarshipBook.com and enter code DO10112 for updates on this award.

(102) • Dorothy Harris Endowed Scholarship

Women's Sports Foundation
Eisenhower Park
1899 Hempstead Turnpike, Suite 400
East Meadow, NY 11554
Phone: 800-227-3988
Fax: 516-542-4716
Email: info@womenssportsfoundation.org
http://www.womenssportsfoundation.org

Purpose: To support female students who are majoring in physical education, sport management, sport psychology or sport sociology.

Eligibility: Students must be enrolled full-time in a graduate program. Applicants must submit two letters of recommendation.

Target applicants: Graduate school students. Adult students.

Amount: $1,500.

Number of awards: Up to 3.

Deadline: December 31.

How to apply: Applications are available online.

Exclusive: Visit www.UltimateScholarshipBook.com and enter code WO10212 for updates on this award.

(103) • Dr. Arnita Young Boswell Scholarship

National Hook-Up of Black Women Inc.
1809 East 71st Street
Suite 205
Chicago, IL 60649
Phone: 773-667-7061
Fax: 773-667-7064
Email: nhbwdir@aol.com
http://www.nhbwinc.com
Purpose: To reward adult students for their academic achievement.
Eligibility: Applicants must be undergraduate or graduate continuing education students. Selection is based on academic accomplishments as well as involvement in school and community activities and an essay.
Target applicants: Graduate school students. Adult students.
Minimum GPA: 2.75
Amount: $1,000.
Number of awards: Varies.
Scholarship may be renewable.
Deadline: March 15.
How to apply: Applications are available by mail and must be requested by March 1.
Exclusive: Visit www.UltimateScholarshipBook.com and enter code NA10312 for updates on this award.

(104) • Dr. Wynetta A. Frazier "Sister to Sister" Scholarship

National Hook-Up of Black Women Inc.
1809 East 71st Street
Suite 205
Chicago, IL 60649
Phone: 773-667-7061
Fax: 773-667-7064
Email: nhbwdir@aol.com
http://www.nhbwinc.com
Purpose: To assist women who are returning to school without the support of a spouse or family.
Eligibility: Applicants may have taken a break in their educations to seek employment, care for their children or because of financial burden.
Target applicants: Graduate school students. Adult students.
Amount: $500.
Number of awards: At least 2.
Deadline: April.
How to apply: Applications are available by mail.
Exclusive: Visit www.UltimateScholarshipBook.com and enter code NA10412 for updates on this award.

(105) • Dream Deferred Essay Contest on Civil Rights in the Mideast

Hands Across the Mideast Support Alliance
263 Huntington Avenue, #315
Boston, MA 02115
Phone: 617-266-0080
Fax: 617-812-4789
Email: info@hamsaweb.org
http://www.hamsaweb.org
Purpose: To award American and Middle Eastern youth who have written outstanding essays on civil rights in the Middle East.
Eligibility: Entrants must be age 25 or younger at the time of the entry deadline. They must be living in an Arab League nation, the U.S., Afghanistan or Iran. They must write an essay of 600 to 1,500 words responding to one of the civil rights topics presented in the official entry rules. Selection is based on the strength and relevance of the essay response.
Target applicants: Junior high students or younger. High school students. College students. Graduate school students.
Amount: $500-$2,000.
Number of awards: 10.
Deadline: February 20.
How to apply: Applications are available online. The completion of an online essay submission form is required.
Exclusive: Visit www.UltimateScholarshipBook.com and enter code HA10512 for updates on this award.

(106) • Earl Anthony Memorial Scholarships

United States Bowling Congress
5301 S. 76th Street
Greendale, WI 53129
Phone: 800-514-2695 x3168
Email: smart@bowl.com
http://www.bowl.com
Purpose: To recognize USBC members for community involvement and academic achievement.
Eligibility: Applicants must be USBC members in good standing who are high school seniors or current college students. They must have a GPA of 2.5 or higher. Community involvement, academic achievement and financial need are considered.
Target applicants: High school students. College students. Adult students.
Minimum GPA: 2.5
Amount: $5,000.
Number of awards: 5.
Deadline: May 1.
How to apply: Applications are available online.
Exclusive: Visit www.UltimateScholarshipBook.com and enter code UN10612 for updates on this award.

(107) • Education Exchange College Grant Program

ACCEL/Exchange Network
250 Johnson Road
Morris Plains, NJ 07950
Phone: 800-519-8883
Email: eftbasupport@fiserv.com
http://www.accelexchange.com
Purpose: To assist hardworking and talented students in the pursuit of higher education.
Eligibility: Applicants must be graduating seniors and U.S. citizens. Selection criteria include scholastic achievement, extracurricular activities, character, leadership, essay and financial need. Judging is done from March to May of each year, and recipients are announced in June.
Target applicants: High school students.
Amount: $1,000-$5,000.
Number of awards: 34.
Deadline: March.
How to apply: Applications are available from ACCEL/Exchange member institutions.
Exclusive: Visit www.UltimateScholarshipBook.com and enter code AC10712 for updates on this award.

(108) · Education Memorial Scholarship Awards / George and Rosemary Murray Scholarship Award

25th Infantry Division Association (TIDA)
P.O. Box 7
Flourtown, PA 19031
http://www.25thida.com

Purpose: To aid in the education of the members of the 25th Infantry Division Association or the children and grandchildren of active and former members of the association.
Eligibility: Applicants must be high school seniors who are the child or grandchild of an active association member, the child of a former member who died during combat with the Division or an active member who will be discharged before the end of the award year. Applicants must be entering a four-year college or university as a freshman. Selection is based on future plans, school activities, interests, financial status and academic achievement.
Target applicants: High school students.
Amount: Up to $1,500.
Number of awards: Varies.
Deadline: February 15.
How to apply: Applications are available throughout the year in Tropic Lightning Flashes, the quarterly newsletter of the 25th Infantry Division Association.
Exclusive: Visit www.UltimateScholarshipBook.com and enter code 2510812 for updates on this award.

(109) · Educational Advancement Foundation Merit Scholarship

Alpha Kappa Alpha Educational Advancement Foundation Inc.
5656 S. Stony Island Avenue
Chicago, IL 60637
Phone: 800-653-6528
Fax: 773-947-0277
Email: akaeaf@akaeaf.net
http://www.akaeaf.org

Purpose: To support academically talented students.
Eligibility: Applicants must be full-time college students at the sophomore level or higher, including graduate students, at an accredited school. They must have a GPA of at least 3.0 and demonstrate community involvement and service. The program is open to students without regard to sex, race, creed, color, ethnicity, religion, sexual orientation or disability. Students do NOT need to be members of Alpha Kappa Alpha. The application deadline is April 15 for undergraduates and August 15 for graduates.
Target applicants: College students. Graduate school students. Adult students.
Minimum GPA: 3.0
Amount: $750-$2,500.
Number of awards: Varies.
Deadline: April 15 (undergraduates) and August 15 (graduates).
How to apply: Applications are available online. An application form, personal statement and three letters of recommendation are required.
Exclusive: Visit www.UltimateScholarshipBook.com and enter code AL10912 for updates on this award.

(110) · EOD Memorial Scholarship

Explosive Ordnance Disposal (EOD) Memorial Committee
P.O. Box 594
Niceville, FL 32588
Phone: 850-729-2401
Fax: 850-729-2401
Email: admin@eodmemorial.org
http://www.eodmemorial.org

Purpose: To support those connected to Explosive Ordnance Disposal (EOD) technicians.
Eligibility: Applicants must be accepted or enrolled as full-time undergraduates in a U.S. accredited two-year, four-year or vocational school. Students must also be the family member of an active duty, guard/reserve, retired or deceased EOD technician. The award is based on academic achievement, community involvement and financial need. Applicants should submit the Free Application for Federal Student Aid form.
Target applicants: High school students. College students. Adult students.
Amount: Varies.
Number of awards: Varies.
Deadline: March 1.
How to apply: Applications are available online.
Exclusive: Visit www.UltimateScholarshipBook.com and enter code EX11012 for updates on this award.

(111) · Ethnic Minority and Women's Enhancement Scholarship

National Collegiate Athletic Association
700 W. Washington Street
P.O. Box 6222
Indianapolis, IN 46206
Phone: 317-917-6222
Fax: 317-917-6888
Email: ahightower@ncaa.org
http://www.ncaa.org/wps/portal/ncaahome?WCM_GLOBAL_CONTEXT=/ncaa/NCAA/NCAA News/NCAA Home Pages/

Purpose: To assist minority and female students in intercollegiate athletics with postgraduate scholarships at the NCAA national office.
Eligibility: Applicants must be planning to attend a sports administration program and plan to pursue a career in intercollegiate athletics such as athletic administration, coaching or athletic training.
Target applicants: College students. Graduate school students. Adult students.
Amount: $6,000.
Number of awards: 26.
Deadline: December 2.
How to apply: Application details are available online.
Exclusive: Visit www.UltimateScholarshipBook.com and enter code NA11112 for updates on this award.

(112) · Families of Freedom Scholarship Fund

Families of Freedom c/o Scholarship America
One Scholarship Way
P.O. Box 297
St. Peter, MN 56082
Phone: 877-862-0136
Email: familiesoffreedom@scholarshipamerica.org
http://www.familiesoffreedom.org

Purpose: To support dependents of victims of the 9/11 attacks.
Eligibility: Applicants must be dependent children, spouses or domestic partners of 9/11 victims. Children of victims must enroll in a postsecondary program by age 24 and must continue studies uninterrupted after their 24th birthday to continue to receive assistance. Spouses and domestic partners can apply through the year 2012. Financial need is required.

Target applicants: High school students. College students. Adult students.
Amount: Varies.
Number of awards: Varies.
Scholarship may be renewable.
Deadline: May 15.
How to apply: Applications are available online. An application form, copy of most recent tax return, transcript and copy of school billing statement are required.
Exclusive: Visit www.UltimateScholarshipBook.com and enter code FA11212 for updates on this award.

(113) • Family Travel Forum Teen Travel Writing Scholarship

Family Travel Forum
891 Amsterdam Avenue
New York, NY 10025
Phone: 212-665-6124
Fax: 212-665-6136
Email: editorial@travelbigo.com
http://www.travelbigo.com
Purpose: To aid college-bound students who have written the best travel essays.
Eligibility: Applicants must be members of the TravelBIGO.com online community and be between the ages of 13 and 18. They must be in grades 8 through 12 and must be attending a U.S. or Canadian high school, U.S. or Canadian junior high school, U.S. home school or an American school located outside of the U.S. They must submit an essay about a significant travel experience that occurred within the past three years and that happened when the applicant was between the ages of 12 and 18. Selection is based on originality, quality of storytelling and grammar.
Target applicants: Junior high students or younger. High school students.
Amount: $200-$1,000.
Number of awards: 3.
Deadline: August 1.
How to apply: Application instructions are available online. An essay submission form and essay are required.
Exclusive: Visit www.UltimateScholarshipBook.com and enter code FA11312 for updates on this award.

(114) • Federal Criminal Investigators' Service Award

Explorers Learning for Life
P.O. Box 152079
Irving, TX 75015
Phone: 972-580-2433
Fax: 972-580-2137
Email: pchestnu@lflmail.org
http://www.learningforlife.org/exploring
Purpose: To support students who are Law Enforcement Explorers.
Eligibility: Students must by nominated by the sponsoring agency of their Explorer post. Applicants must submit three letters of recommendation and an essay.
Target applicants: High school students. College students. Adult students.
Amount: $500.
Number of awards: Varies.
Deadline: March 31.
How to apply: Applications are available online.
Exclusive: Visit www.UltimateScholarshipBook.com and enter code EX11412 for updates on this award.

(115) • Financial Connects Scholarship

Net Literacy Alliance
426 Springwood Drive
Carmel, IN 46032
Email: danielkent@netliteracy.org
http://www.netliteracyalliance.org
Purpose: To encourage financial literacy amongst America's youth.
Eligibility: Applicants must be legal residents of the U.S. They must be in grades 6-12 or must be college students who are enrolled at least part-time at a U.S. two- or four-year postsecondary institution. Applicants whose video entry proposals are approved will be invited to submit a video on a topic that relates to financial literacy. Selection is based on the quality of the video.
Target applicants: Junior high students or younger. High school students. College students. Graduate school students. Adult students.
Amount: Up to $5,000.
Number of awards: Varies.
Deadline: June 30.
How to apply: Application instructions are available online. Submission of applicant contact information and a video proposal, followed by the video itself if requested, is required.
Exclusive: Visit www.UltimateScholarshipBook.com and enter code NE11512 for updates on this award.

(116) • First Cavalry Division Association Scholarship

Foundation of the First Cavalry Division Association
Alumni Of The First Team
302 North Main Street
Copperas Cove, TX 76522
Phone: 254-547-6537
Email: firstcav@1cda.org
http://www.1cda.org
Purpose: To assist the children of First Cavalry troopers who have become disabled or who died while serving in the Division.
Eligibility: Applicants must be First Cavalry Division troopers who have become totally disabled while serving in the division or active duty members, their spouses or children. Applicants may also be the spouses or children of First Cavalry Division troopers who have died while serving in the division.
Target applicants: High school students. College students. Adult students.
Amount: $1,200.
Number of awards: Varies.
Deadline: Varies.
How to apply: Applications are available by request.
Exclusive: Visit www.UltimateScholarshipBook.com and enter code FO11612 for updates on this award.

(117) • FiSCA Scholarship

Financial Service Centers of America
Attn.: FiSCA Scholarship Program
Court Plaza South, East Wing
21 Main Street, 1st Floor, P.O. Box 647
Hackensack, NJ 07602
Phone: 201-487-0412
Fax: 201-487-3954
Email: info@fisca.org
http://www.fisca.org
Purpose: To help collegebound high school seniors from areas served by FiSCA centers.

Eligibility: Applicants must be high school seniors. Selection is based on leadership, academic achievement and financial need. There are more than 7,000 locations nationwide.
Target applicants: High school students.
Amount: $2,000.
Number of awards: At least 10.
Deadline: April 26.
How to apply: Applications are available online.
Exclusive: Visit www.UltimateScholarshipBook.com and enter code FI11712 for updates on this award.

(118) • Flashcard Scholarship

SimpleLeap Software
48 Peachtree Avenue
Suite 313
Atlanta, GA 30305
http://www.flashcardscholarship.com
Purpose: To reward the student who has created the most interesting paper flashcard disposal video.
Eligibility: Applicants must be high school or college students. They must create a video depicting how to get rid of paper flashcard study aids. Selection is based on the video's popularity and creativity.
Target applicants: High school students. College students. Graduate school students. Adult students.
Amount: $500.
Number of awards: 1.
Deadline: August 1.
How to apply: Applications are available online. An application form and video are required.
Exclusive: Visit www.UltimateScholarshipBook.com and enter code SI11812 for updates on this award.

(119) • Frank Newman Leadership Award

Campus Compact
45 Temple Place
Boston, MA 02111
Phone: 617-357-1881
Email: campus@compact.org
http://www.compact.org
Purpose: To provide scholarships and opportunities for civic mentoring to students with financial need.
Eligibility: Emphasis is on students who have demonstrated leadership abilities and significant interest in civic responsibility. Students must attend one of the 1,000 Campus Compact member institutions and be nominated by the Campus Compact member president.
Target applicants: College students. Adult students.
Amount: $5,000.
Number of awards: 2.
Deadline: Varies.
How to apply: Nominations must be made by the Campus Compact member president.
Exclusive: Visit www.UltimateScholarshipBook.com and enter code CA11912 for updates on this award.

(120) • Fraternal Order of Eagles Memorial Foundation

Fraternal Order of Eagles
1623 Gateway Circle S.
Grove City, OH 43123
Phone: 614-883-2200
Fax: 614-883-2201
Email: assistance@foe.com
http://www.foe.com
Purpose: To provide financial support for post-secondary education to the children of Eagles.
Eligibility: Applicants must be the children of Eagles who lost their lives while serving in the military or in the commission of their daily employment. Applicants must have a 2.0 minimum GPA.
Target applicants: High school students. College students. Graduate school students.
Minimum GPA: 2.0
Amount: Up to $30,000.
Number of awards: Varies.
Scholarship may be renewable.
Deadline: Varies.
How to apply: Eligible juniors in high school will be sent a form requesting post high school plans, and eligible seniors will be mailed the scholarship application form.
Exclusive: Visit www.UltimateScholarshipBook.com and enter code FR12012 for updates on this award.

(121) • Fulbright Grants

U.S. Department of State
Office of Academic Exchange Programs, Bureau of Educational and Cultural Affairs
U.S. Department of State, SA-44
301 4th Street SW, Room 234
Washington, DC 20547
Phone: 202-619-4360
Fax: 202-401-5914
Email: academic@state.gov
http://fulbright.state.gov
Purpose: To increase the understanding between the people of the United States and the people of other countries.
Eligibility: Applicants must be graduate students, scholars or professionals. Funds are generally used to support students in university teaching, advanced research, graduate study or teaching in elementary and secondary schools.
Target applicants: Graduate school students. Adult students.
Amount: Varies.
Number of awards: 4,500.
Deadline: August 1.
How to apply: Applications are available online.
Exclusive: Visit www.UltimateScholarshipBook.com and enter code U.12112 for updates on this award.

(122) • Gen and Kelly Tanabe Student Scholarship

Gen and Kelly Tanabe Scholarship Program
3286 Oak Court
Belmont, CA 94002
Phone: 650-618-2221
Email: tanabe@gmail.com
http://www.genkellyscholarship.com
Purpose: To assist high school, college and graduate school students with educational expenses.
Eligibility: Applicants must be 9th-12th grade high school students, college students or graduate school students who are legal U.S. residents. Students may study any major and attend any college in the U.S.
Target applicants: High school students. College students. Adult students.

Amount: $1,000.
Deadline: July 31.
How to apply: Applications are available online.
Exclusive: Visit www.UltimateScholarshipBook.com and enter code GE12212 for updates on this award.

---

(123) • Gene Carte Student Paper Competition

American Society of Criminology Gene Carte Student Paper Competition
Nancy Rodriguez
Department of Criminology and Criminal Justice, Arizona State University West
4701 W. Thunderbird Road
Glendale, AZ 85306
Phone: 602-543-6601
Fax: 602-543-6658
Email: nancy.rodriguez@asu.edu
http://www.asc41.com
Purpose: To recognize outstanding student works in criminology.
Eligibility: Applicants must be full-time undergraduate or graduate students. The writing competition requires applicants to write on a topic directly related to criminology and must be accompanied by a letter signed by the dean or department chair. Other paper formatting requirements are listed on the website. The first place winner also receives a travel award.
Target applicants: College students. Graduate school students. Adult students.
Amount: $200-$500.
Number of awards: 3.
Deadline: April 15.
How to apply: There is no application form. Paper must be mailed in. The paper specifications are on the website.
Exclusive: Visit www.UltimateScholarshipBook.com and enter code AM12312 for updates on this award.

---

(124) • General Henry H. Arnold Education Grant Program

Air Force Aid Society Inc.
Education Assistance Department
241 18th Street S, Suite 202
Arlington, VA 22202
Phone: 800-429-9475
Fax: 703-607-3022
http://www.afas.org
Purpose: To help Air Force members and their families realize their academic goals.
Eligibility: Applicants must be the dependent sons and daughters of Air Force members, spouses of active duty members or surviving spouses of Air Force members who died while on active duty or in retired status. They must also be high school seniors or college students enrolled or accepted as full-time undergraduates for the following school year and maintain a minimum 2.0 GPA.
Target applicants: High school students. College students. Adult students.
Minimum GPA: 2.0
Amount: $2,000.
Number of awards: Varies.
Scholarship may be renewable.
Deadline: March 9.
How to apply: Applications are available online.
Exclusive: Visit www.UltimateScholarshipBook.com and enter code AI12412 for updates on this award.

---

(125) • Generation 'E' Scholarship

WHOmentors.com Inc.
110 Pacific Avenue, Suite 250
San Francisco, CA 94111
Phone: 888-946-6368
Email: rauhmel@whomentors.com
http://www.whomentors.com
Purpose: To support students with academic merit and financial need.
Eligibility: Students must have at least a 2.0 GPA. They must be graduating high school seniors or full-time college students. Preference will be given to graduates of the CEO@18 Youth and College Development Program. Selection is based on academic record, academic goals, financial need, community service, essay and letter of recommendation.
Target applicants: High school students. College students. Adult students.
Minimum GPA: 2.0
Amount: $1,500.
Number of awards: Varies.
Deadline: May 15.
How to apply: Applications are available online.
Exclusive: Visit www.UltimateScholarshipBook.com and enter code WH12512 for updates on this award.

---

(126) • Get Well Soon Grant

Do Something
24-32 Union Square East
4th Floor
New York, NY 10003
Phone: 212-254-2390
Email: aashton@dosomething.org
http://www.dosomething.org/awards
Purpose: To reward the person who has submitted the best project proposal for helping youth in hospitals.
Eligibility: Applicants must submit a proposal detailing a project that helps children in hospitals. Selection is based on the overall strength of the proposal.
Target applicants: High school students. College students. Graduate school students. Adult students.
Amount: $1,000-$5,000.
Number of awards: 20.
Deadline: Varies.
How to apply: Applications are available online. An application form and supporting materials are required.
Exclusive: Visit www.UltimateScholarshipBook.com and enter code DO12612 for updates on this award.

---

(127) • Gift for Life Scholarships

United States Bowling Congress
5301 S. 76th Street
Greendale, WI 53129
Phone: 800-514-2695 x3168
Email: smart@bowl.com
http://www.bowl.com
Purpose: To provide financial assistance to high school students with financial need.

Eligibility: Applicants must be USBC Youth members who are current high school students in grades 9-12. They must have a GPA of 2.0 or higher and demonstrate financial need. Two awards each year are reserved for children of fire department, emergency rescue or police personnel. Candidates may win once per year up until graduation.
Target applicants: High school students.
Minimum GPA: 2.0
Amount: $1,000.
Number of awards: 12.
Deadline: April 1.
How to apply: Applications are available online.
Exclusive: Visit www.UltimateScholarshipBook.com and enter code UN12712 for updates on this award.

(128) · Global Citizen Awards

EF Educational Tours
EF Center Boston
One Education Street
Cambridge, MA 02141
Phone: 617-619-1300
Fax: 800-318-3732
Email: marisa.talbot@ef.com
http://www.eftours.com
Purpose: To help students reflect on their place in the world through writing and then have a chance to experience it first-hand.
Eligibility: Applicants must be college-bound high school sophomores and juniors in the U.S. or Canada nominated by their schools and must write an essay on a topic related to global citizenship. The award involves a paid educational trip to Europe.
Target applicants: High school students.
Amount: Educational tour expenses.
Number of awards: Varies.
Deadline: Varies.
How to apply: Applications are available online.
Exclusive: Visit www.UltimateScholarshipBook.com and enter code EF12812 for updates on this award.

(129) · GNC Nutritional Research Grant

National Strength and Conditioning Association (NSCA) Foundation
1885 Bob Johnson Drive
Colorado Springs, CO 80906
Phone: 800-815-6826
Fax: 719-632-6367
Email: nsca@nsca-lift.org
http://www.nsca-lift.org
Purpose: To fund nutrition-based research.
Eligibility: Applicants must be NSCA members for one year before applying and pursuing careers in strength and conditioning. Students must also plan a research project that falls within the mission of the NSCA and submit a proposal describing the rationale, purpose and methods of the planned research. Applications are evaluated based on grades, courses, experience, honors, recommendations and involvement in the community and with NSCA.
Target applicants: College students. Graduate school students. Adult students.
Amount: $2,500.
Number of awards: 1.
Deadline: March 15.
How to apply: Applications are available with membership.
Exclusive: Visit www.UltimateScholarshipBook.com and enter code NA12912 for updates on this award.

(130) · GoCollege Lucky Draw Scholarship

GoCollege.com
Phone: 800-975-7150
Email: giovanna@gocollege.com
http://www.gocollege.com/lucky-draw-scholarship.html
Purpose: To support students looking for college and scholarship advice.
Eligibility: Applicants must use the GoCollege.com website and complete a form telling how the website can be improved. A winner is drawn each month.
Target applicants: College students. Adult students.
Amount: $250.
Number of awards: 1.
Deadline: Monthly.
How to apply: Enter by registering online and completing a questionnaire.
Exclusive: Visit www.UltimateScholarshipBook.com and enter code GO13012 for updates on this award.

(131) · Graduate Research Grant - Master and Doctoral

National Strength and Conditioning Association (NSCA) Foundation
1885 Bob Johnson Drive
Colorado Springs, CO 80906
Phone: 800-815-6826
Fax: 719-632-6367
Email: nsca@nsca-lift.org
http://www.nsca-lift.org
Purpose: To support research in strength and conditioning.
Eligibility: Applicants must be master's or doctoral students and submit a proposal for a research project in the field of strength and conditioning that fulfills the mission of the NSCA. Students must be NSCA members for one year before applying and pursuing careers in strength and conditioning. Applications are evaluated based on grades, courses, experience, honors, recommendations and involvement in the community and with NSCA.
Target applicants: Graduate school students. Adult students.
Amount: $5,000-$10,000.
Number of awards: Varies.
Deadline: March 15.
How to apply: Applications are available with membership.
Exclusive: Visit www.UltimateScholarshipBook.com and enter code NA13112 for updates on this award.

(132) · Graduate Scholarship

Jack Kent Cooke Foundation
44325 Woodridge Parkway
Lansdowne, VA 20176
Phone: 800-498-6478
Fax: 703-723-8030
Email: jkc-g@act.org
http://www.jkcf.org
Purpose: To help students with academic merit and financial need attend graduate school.
Eligibility: Applicants must be college seniors or recent graduates of an accredited U.S. college or university who plan to attend full-time graduate or professional programs for the first time. Applicants may not apply directly to the foundation but must be nominated by the Jack Kent Cooke Foundation faculty representatives at their institutions and must be recipients of Jack Kent Cooke Foundation undergraduate awards. The award is based on academic merit and unmet financial need. A GPA of 3.5 or higher is required.

Target applicants: College students. Adult students.
Minimum GPA: 3.5
Amount: Up to $50,000.
Number of awards: Varies.
Scholarship may be renewable.
Deadline: January 19.
How to apply: Applications are available online.
Exclusive: Visit www.UltimateScholarshipBook.com and enter code JA13212 for updates on this award.

(133) • Hanscom Air Force Base Spouses' Club Scholarship

Hanscom Officers' Spouses' Club
P.O. Box 557
Bedford, MA 01730
Phone: 781-538-5361
Email: scholarship@hanscomsc.org
http://www.hanscomsc.org
Purpose: To aid dependents of past and present members of the military.
Eligibility: Applicants must be children or spouses of retired, deceased or current active duty members of any branch of the military. They must hold a valid military ID card. Children of military members must be high school seniors.
Target applicants: High school students.
Amount: Varies.
Number of awards: Varies.
Deadline: Varies.
How to apply: Applications are available online. An application form and copy of military ID are required.
Exclusive: Visit www.UltimateScholarshipBook.com and enter code HA13312 for updates on this award.

(134) • Harness Racing Scholarship

Harness Horse Youth Foundation
16575 Carey Road
Westfield, IN 46074
Phone: 317-867-5877
Fax: 317-867-5896
Email: ellen@hhyf.org
http://www.hhyf.org
Purpose: To encourage the education of young people about harness racing.
Eligibility: Applicants must be pursuing a horse-related career, have financial need, demonstrate scholastic achievements and have experience with horses and harness racing. Applicants must also be at least a high school senior and under the age of 25.
Target applicants: High school students. College students. Graduate school students.
Amount: Varies.
Number of awards: Varies.
Deadline: April 30.
How to apply: Applications are available by mail.
Exclusive: Visit www.UltimateScholarshipBook.com and enter code HA13412 for updates on this award.

(135) • Hayek Fund for Scholars

Institute for Humane Studies at George Mason University
3301 N. Fairfax Drive
Suite 440
Arlington, VA 22201
Phone: 800-697-8799
Fax: 703-993-4890
Email: ihs@gmu.edu
http://www.theihs.org
Purpose: To make awards of up to $1,000 to graduate students and untenured faculty members for career-enhancing activities.
Eligibility: Applicants must be graduate students or untenured faculty members and must submit a cover letter explaining how participation will advance their careers and how their understanding of the classical liberal/libertarian tradition will be broadened. Applicants must also submit an abstract of the paper they are going to present (if applicable), an itemized expense list and resume.
Target applicants: Graduate school students. Adult students.
Amount: $1,000.
Number of awards: Varies.
Deadline: Abstracts accepted year round.
How to apply: There is no application form.
Exclusive: Visit www.UltimateScholarshipBook.com and enter code IN13512 for updates on this award.

(136) • Healthy Respect Win-Win Scholarship

Healthy Respect
3250 Westchester Avenue
Suite 202
Bronx, NY 10461
Phone: 718-409-0800
Fax: 718-409-1081
Email: info@healthrespect.org
http://www.healthrespect.org
Purpose: To aid students who would be good role models for at-risk children.
Eligibility: Applicants must be high school or college students. They must have personal qualities that would make for a good role model. Selection is based on the overall strength of the application.
Target applicants: High school students. College students. Graduate school students. Adult students.
Amount: Varies.
Number of awards: Varies.
Deadline: December 30.
How to apply: Application instructions are available online. An application form is required.
Exclusive: Visit www.UltimateScholarshipBook.com and enter code HE13612 for updates on this award.

(137) • High School Scholarship

National Strength and Conditioning Association (NSCA) Foundation
1885 Bob Johnson Drive
Colorado Springs, CO 80906
Phone: 800-815-6826
Fax: 719-632-6367
Email: nsca@nsca-lift.org
http://www.nsca-lift.org
Purpose: To support high school students entering the strength and conditioning field.
Eligibility: Applicants must be high school seniors planning to graduate with a degree related to strength and conditioning with a current 3.0 GPA. Students must be NSCA members, although applicants may enroll at the time of application, and pursuing a career in strength and conditioning. Applications are evaluated based on grades, courses, experience, honors, recommendations and involvement in the community and with NSCA.

Target applicants: High school students.
Minimum GPA: 3.0
Amount: $1,500.
Number of awards: Varies.
Deadline: March 15.
How to apply: Applications are available by contacting the organization.
Exclusive: Visit www.UltimateScholarshipBook.com and enter code NA13712 for updates on this award.

(138) • Horatio Alger Association Scholarship Program

Horatio Alger Association
Attn.: Scholarship Department
99 Canal Center Plaza
Alexandria, VA 22314
Phone: 703-684-9444
Fax: 703-684-9445
Email: association@horatioalger.com
http://www.horatioalger.com
Purpose: To assist students who are committed to pursuing a bachelor's degree and have demonstrated integrity, financial need, academic achievement and community involvement.
Eligibility: Applicants must enter college the fall following their high school graduation, be in need of financial aid ($50,000 or less adjusted gross income per family is preferred) and be involved in extracurricular and community activities.
Target applicants: High school students.
Minimum GPA: 2.0
Amount: Varies.
Number of awards: Varies.
Deadline: October 30.
How to apply: Applications are available online.
Exclusive: Visit www.UltimateScholarshipBook.com and enter code HO13812 for updates on this award.

(139) • Howard R. Swearer Student Humanitarian Award

Campus Compact
45 Temple Place
Boston, MA 02111
Phone: 617-357-1881
Email: campus@compact.org
http://www.compact.org
Purpose: Awards granted to college students for use in strengthening or maintaining a service program/project. Emphasis is on college students who work to improve their communities while encouraging others to do the same.
Eligibility: Applicants must be undergraduate students attending institutions that are Campus Compact members and must be nominated by the Campus Compact member president. Students of any class year are eligible.
Target applicants: College students. Adult students.
Amount: Varies.
Number of awards: 5.
Deadline: February.
How to apply: Nominations must be made by the Campus Compact member president.
Exclusive: Visit www.UltimateScholarshipBook.com and enter code CA13912 for updates on this award.

(140) • Humane Studies Fellowships

Institute for Humane Studies at George Mason University
3301 N. Fairfax Drive
Suite 440
Arlington, VA 22201
Phone: 800-697-8799
Fax: 703-993-4890
Email: ihs@gmu.edu
http://www.theihs.org
Purpose: To award scholarships to students who are interested in the classical liberal/libertarian tradition of individual rights and market economies and wish to apply these principles in their work.
Eligibility: Applicants must be one of the following: undergraduates who will be juniors or seniors during the academic year of funding, graduate students who are in any field and at any stage before completion of the Ph.D., law students, MBA students or other professional students. The fellowships can be used for study in the U.S. or abroad. Applicants must also be enrolled as full-time students at an accredited degree-granting institution.
Target applicants: College students. Graduate school students. Adult students.
Amount: $2,000-$12,000.
Number of awards: Varies.
Scholarship may be renewable.
Deadline: December 31.
How to apply: Applications are available online.
Exclusive: Visit www.UltimateScholarshipBook.com and enter code IN14012 for updates on this award.

(141) • IAFC Foundation Scholarship

International Association of Fire Chiefs Foundation
4025 Fair Ridge Drive
Fairfax, VA 22033-2868
Phone: 571-344-5410
Email: iafcfoun@msn.com
http://www.iafcf.org
Purpose: To assist students in fire sciences or related academic programs.
Eligibility: Applicants must be active members with a minimum of three years volunteer work, two years paid work or a combination of paid and volunteer work of three years with a state, county, provincial, municipal, community, industrial or federal fire department who will use the scholarship at an accredited institution of higher education. Students must submit application forms, statements, a list of credits and a transcript. Preference is given to those demonstrating need, desire and initiative.
Target applicants: College students. Graduate school students. Adult students.
Amount: $4,000.
Number of awards: Varies.
Deadline: June 1.
How to apply: Applications are available online.
Exclusive: Visit www.UltimateScholarshipBook.com and enter code IN14112 for updates on this award.

(142) • Imagine America Promise

Imagine America Foundation
1101 Connecticut Avenue NW
Suite 901
Washington, DC 20036
Phone: 202-336-6800
Fax: 202-408-8102

Email: scholarships@imagine-america.org
http://www.imagine-america.org
Purpose: To further assist recipients of the Imagine America high school scholarship.
Eligibility: Prospective recipients must be nominated by a participating college and meet the following scholarship criteria: student must have been an Imagine America (high school) scholarship recipient; student must be currently enrolled in his/her course of study; student's graduation date must be after December 31; student must have a cumulative 3.5 or higher GPA; student must currently have a 95 percent or higher attendance record; student must obtain a written recommendation from a faculty/administrator representative of his/her career college and student's transcripts must be sent with the nomination form.
Target applicants: College students. Adult students.
Minimum GPA: 3.5
Amount: $500-$1,000.
Number of awards: Varies.
Deadline: November.
How to apply: Nomination forms are available online.
Exclusive: Visit www.UltimateScholarshipBook.com and enter code IM14212 for updates on this award.

(143) · IMCEA Scholarships

International Military Community Executives Association (IMCEA)
1530 Dunwoody Village
Parkway Suite 203
Atlanta, GA 30338
Phone: 770-396-2101
Fax: 770-396-2198
Email: imcea@imcea.com
http://www.imcea.com
Purpose: To provide scholarships for high school students and military welfare and recreation professionals seeking to further their educations.
Eligibility: High school or college applicants must be children of IMCEA members. Candidates must provide information about their activities, honors and awards and submit an essay on the provided topic.
Target applicants: High school students. College students. Graduate school students. Adult students.
Amount: Varies.
Number of awards: 1.
Deadline: Varies.
How to apply: Applications are available online.
Exclusive: Visit www.UltimateScholarshipBook.com and enter code IN14312 for updates on this award.

(144) · Indianhead Division Scholarships

Second Indianhead Division Association
P.O. Box 460
Buda, TX 78610
Phone: 512-295-5324
Email: warriorvet@verizon.net
http://www.2ida.org
Purpose: To support the children and grandchildren of veterans from the Second Indianhead Division Association.
Eligibility: Applicants' parents or grandparents must have been members of the association for at least three years, or they must have been killed while serving with the Second Infantry Division.
Target applicants: High school students. College students. Adult students.
Amount: Varies.
Number of awards: Varies.
Scholarship may be renewable.
Deadline: June 1.
How to apply: Applications are available by phone.
Exclusive: Visit www.UltimateScholarshipBook.com and enter code SE14412 for updates on this award.

(145) · International Association of Fire Chiefs Foundation Scholarship

Explorers Learning for Life
P.O. Box 152079
Irving, TX 75015
Phone: 972-580-2433
Fax: 972-580-2137
Email: pchestnu@lflmail.org
http://www.learningforlife.org/exploring
Purpose: To support students who are pursuing careers in fire sciences.
Eligibility: Students must be graduating high school seniors, active fire service Explorers and members of a fire department. Applicants must submit three letters of recommendation and an essay.
Target applicants: High school students.
Amount: $500.
Number of awards: 2.
Deadline: July 1.
How to apply: Applications are available online.
Exclusive: Visit www.UltimateScholarshipBook.com and enter code EX14512 for updates on this award.

(146) · ISIA Education Foundation Scholarship

Ice Skating Institute of America (ISIA) Education Foundation
17120 N. Dallas Parkway, Suite 140
Dallas, TX 75248
Phone: 972-735-8800
Fax: 972-735-8815
http://www.skateisi.com
Purpose: To encourage skaters to make athletic and educational achievements.
Eligibility: Applicants must have completed at least three years of high school with a minimum 3.0 GPA during the last two years and enroll as full-time undergraduate students. Applicants must also have been members of the Ice Skating Institute (ISI) and have participated in the ISI Recreational Skater Program for at least four years, have participated in ISI competitions or classes within the last two years and have completed 240 hours of verified service, with 120 hours volunteered. Applicants must also submit two evaluation forms and an essay of 500 words or less explaining why they should receive the award.
Target applicants: High school students. College students. Adult students.
Minimum GPA: 3.0
Amount: $4,000.
Number of awards: Varies.
Deadline: March 1.
How to apply: Applications are available online.
Exclusive: Visit www.UltimateScholarshipBook.com and enter code IC14612 for updates on this award.

(147) · James M. and Virginia M. Smyth Scholarship

Community Foundation for Greater Atlanta Inc.
50 Hurt Plaza
Suite 449
Atlanta, GA 30303

Phone: 404-688-5525
Fax: 404-688-3060
Email: info@cfgreateratlanta.org
http://www.cfgreateratlanta.org
Purpose: To support students who are pursuing undergraduate degrees.
Eligibility: Students must have at least a 3.0 GPA, and they must have community service experience. Applicants must plan to obtain a degree in the arts and sciences, music, ministry or human services. Preference will be given to students from the following states: Missouri, Mississippi, Georgia, Illinois, Oklahoma, Texas and Tennessee. Applicants must demonstrate financial need. Adult students may also apply.
Target applicants: High school students. College students. Adult students.
Minimum GPA: 3.0
Amount: $2,000.
Number of awards: 12-15.
Scholarship may be renewable.
Deadline: March 15.
How to apply: Applications are available online.
Exclusive: Visit www.UltimateScholarshipBook.com and enter code CO14712 for updates on this award.

(148) • Jewell Hilton Bonner Scholarship

Navy League Foundation
2300 Wilson Boulevard
Arlington, VA 22201
Phone: 800-356-5760
Fax: 703-528-2333
Email: lhuycke@navyleague.org
http://www.navyleague.org
Purpose: To support the dependents and descendants of sea personnel.
Eligibility: Service personnel may be active, reserve, retired or honorably discharged members of the U.S. Navy, Coast Guard, U.S. Flag Merchant Marine, Marine Corps or U.S. Naval Sea Cadet Corps. Students must be high school seniors who plan to enter a college or university in the fall.
Target applicants: High school students.
Amount: Varies.
Number of awards: Varies.
Deadline: March 1.
How to apply: Applications are available online.
Exclusive: Visit www.UltimateScholarshipBook.com and enter code NA14812 for updates on this award.

(149) • John F. Duffy Scholarship/Grant Program

California Peace Officers' Memorial Foundation
P.O. Box 2437
Fair Oaks, CA 95628
Email: cpomf@camemorial.org
http://www.camemorial.org
Purpose: To provide financial assistance to survivors of California peace officers who have died in the line of duty.
Eligibility: Applicants must be spouses, children, stepchildren or adopted children of peace officers who died in the line of duty and are enrolled on the California memorial monument. They must carry no less than six units per quarter or eight units per semester at an accredited college or university, and they must maintain a 2.5 or higher GPA.
Target applicants: High school students. College students. Graduate school students. Adult students.
Minimum GPA: 2.5
Amount: Up to $4,000.
Number of awards: Varies.
Deadline: June 1.
How to apply: Applications are available online.
Exclusive: Visit www.UltimateScholarshipBook.com and enter code CA14912 for updates on this award.

(150) • John Foster Memorial College Scholarship

Kansas Peace Officers Association
1620 S.W. Tyler
Topeka, KS 66612
Phone: 785-296-8200
Email: kpoa@kpoa.org
http://www.kpoa.org/fosterscholarship.asp
Purpose: To assist children of Kansas law enforcement officers in obtaining higher education.
Eligibility: Applicants must be sons or daughters of full-time active Kansas law enforcement officers. They must attend an accredited college or university in the state of Kansas and take at least 12 hours of credit per semester.
Target applicants: High school students. College students. Adult students.
Amount: $2,100.
Number of awards: Varies.
Deadline: April 1.
How to apply: Applications are available online.
Exclusive: Visit www.UltimateScholarshipBook.com and enter code KA15012 for updates on this award.

(151) • John Jowdy Scholarship

Columbia 300
P.O. Box 746
Hopkinsville, KY 42241
Phone: 800-531-5920
Email: columbiainfo@columbia300.com
http://www.columbia300.com
Purpose: To support graduating high school seniors who are involved in bowling.
Eligibility: Students must submit an essay and two letters of recommendation. Recipients must maintain at least a 3.0 GPA for award renewal.
Target applicants: High school students.
Amount: $500.
Number of awards: 1.
Scholarship may be renewable.
Deadline: April 1.
How to apply: Applications are available online.
Exclusive: Visit www.UltimateScholarshipBook.com and enter code CO15112 for updates on this award.

(152) • Jolly Green Memorial Scholarship

Jolly Green Association
P.O. Box 965
O'Fallon, IL 62269
Email: bill6100@aol.com
http://www.jollygreen.org/jolly_green_memorial_scholarship.htm
Purpose: To provide financial assistance to dependents of present or former Air Force Combat Rescue or rescue support organization members.
Eligibility: Applicants must be eligible for admission to a college or university and must have demonstrated aptitude for college-level study.
Target applicants: High school students.

Amount: Varies.
Number of awards: Varies.
Deadline: April 15.
How to apply: Applications are available by mail or email.
Exclusive: Visit www.UltimateScholarshipBook.com and enter code JO15212 for updates on this award.

(153) • Jon C. Ladda Memorial Foundation Scholarship

Jon C. Ladda Memorial Foundation
P.O. Box 55
Unionville, CT 06085
Email: info@jonladda.org
http://www.jonladda.org
Purpose: To provide financial assistance to children of Naval Academy graduates and Navy members who have died or become disabled while on active duty.
Eligibility: Applicants must be children of United States Naval Academy graduates or Navy members who served in the submarine service. The Navy member or Academy graduate must have died on active duty or have 100 percent disability and be medically retired. Applicants must also be accepted and enroll in an accredited institution of higher learning.
Target applicants: High school students. College students. Adult students.
Amount: Varies.
Number of awards: Varies.
Scholarship may be renewable.
Deadline: March 15.
How to apply: Applications are available by mail.
Exclusive: Visit www.UltimateScholarshipBook.com and enter code JO15312 for updates on this award.

(154) • Jonathan Jasper Wright Award

National Association of Blacks in Criminal Justice
North Carolina Central University
P.O. Box 19788
Durham, NC 27707
Phone: 919-683-1801
Fax: 919-683-1903
Email: office@nabcj.org
http://www.nabcj.org
Purpose: To award regional and national leadership in the field of criminal justice.
Eligibility: Award recipients will be involved in affecting policy change. Nominator should be a member of NABCJ.
Target applicants: College students. Graduate school students. Adult students.
Amount: Varies.
Number of awards: 1.
Deadline: May 15.
How to apply: Nomination applications are available online.
Exclusive: Visit www.UltimateScholarshipBook.com and enter code NA15412 for updates on this award.

(155) • Joseph P. and Helen T. Cribbins Scholarship

Association of the United States Army
2425 Wilson Boulevard
Arlington, VA 22201
Phone: 800-336-4570
Email: ausa-info@ausa.org
http://www.ausa.org
Purpose: To aid U.S. army soldiers who are studying engineering or a related subject.
Eligibility: Applicants must be active duty or honorably discharged enlisted soldiers in the U.S. Army or one of its affiliate entities (Army Reserve, National Guard, etc.). They must be accepted or enrolled at an accredited college or university and majoring in or planning to major in engineering or a related subject. Selection is based on the overall strength of the application.
Target applicants: High school students. College students. Adult students.
Amount: $2,000.
Number of awards: Varies.
Deadline: July 1.
How to apply: Applications are available online. An application form, two recommendation letters, applicant autobiography, an official transcript, a course of study outline, certificates of completion for other training courses (if applicable) and a copy of form DD-214 (for discharged soldiers) are required.
Exclusive: Visit www.UltimateScholarshipBook.com and enter code AS15512 for updates on this award.

(156) • Josephine De Karman Fellowship

Josephine De Karman Fellowship Trust
P.O. Box 3389
San Dimas, CA 91773
Phone: 909-592-0607
Email: info@dekarman.org
http://www.dekarman.org
Purpose: To recognize students who demonstrate academic achievement.
Eligibility: Applicants must be undergraduate students entering their senior year or Ph.D. candidates nearing completion of their degree (all requirements except for the dissertation must be completed by January 31). Applicants may not be post-doctoral students. Special consideration is given to doctoral students in the humanities. The award is open to international students living in the U.S.
Target applicants: College students. Graduate students. Adult students.
Amount: $14,000-$22,000.
Number of awards: At least 10.
Deadline: January 31.
How to apply: Applications are available online.
Exclusive: Visit www.UltimateScholarshipBook.com and enter code JO15612 for updates on this award.

(157) • Judith Haupt Member's Child Scholarship

Navy Wives Clubs of America (NWCA)
P.O. Box 54022
NSA Mid-South
Millington, TN 38053-6022
Phone: 866-511-6922
Email: scholarships@navywivesclubsofamerica.org
http://www.navywivesclubsofamerica.org
Purpose: To aid college students who are the adult children of members of the Navy Wives Clubs of America (NWCA).
Eligibility: Applicants must be college students who are the adult children of NWCA members. They cannot be carrying a military ID card and must have been accepted into a college no later than the application due date. Selection is based on academic merit and financial need.
Target applicants: High school students. College students. Adult students.
Amount: Varies.

Number of awards: Varies.
Deadline: May 30.
How to apply: Applications are available online. An application form and an official transcript are required.
Exclusive: Visit www.UltimateScholarshipBook.com and enter code NA15712 for updates on this award.

(158) • Kathern F. Gruber Scholarship Program

Blinded Veterans Association (BVA)
477 H Street, NW
Washington, DC 20001-2694
Phone: 202-371-8880
Email: bva@bva.org
http://www.bva.org
Purpose: To assist the spouses and children of blinded veterans with their higher-learning goals.
Eligibility: Applicants must be the spouses or children of a blind veteran and be accepted or enrolled at an accredited higher learning institution.
Target applicants: High school students. College students. Graduate school students. Adult students.
Amount: $2,000.
Number of awards: 6.
Deadline: April 16.
How to apply: Contact the BVA for application materials.
Exclusive: Visit www.UltimateScholarshipBook.com and enter code BL15812 for updates on this award.

(159) • KFC Colonel's Scholars Program

KFC Kentucky Fried Chicken
P.O. Box 725489
Atlanta, GA 31139
Phone: 866-532-7240
Email: kfcscholars@act.org
http://www.kfcscholars.org
Purpose: To assist students with financial need in obtaining a college education.
Eligibility: Applicants must be high school seniors who are enrolling in a public college or university within their state of residence and pursuing a bachelor's degree. They must also have a GPA of 2.75 or higher and demonstrate financial need. The award is up to $5,000 per year and renewable for up to four years. To renew the scholarship, recipients must maintain a 2.75 minimum GPA, take a minimum of 12 credit hours per semester and during the second year of funding work an average of 10 hours per week.
Target applicants: High school students.
Minimum GPA: 2.75
Amount: Up to $5,000.
Number of awards: At least 50.
Scholarship may be renewable.
Deadline: February 9.
How to apply: Applications are available online. An online application is required.
Exclusive: Visit www.UltimateScholarshipBook.com and enter code KF15912 for updates on this award.

(160) • Kohl's Kids Who Care Scholarship

Kohls Corporation
N56 W17000 Ridgewood Drive
Menomonee Falls, WI 53051
Phone: 262-703-7000
Fax: 262-703-7115
Email: community.relations@kohls.com
http://www.kohlskids.com
Purpose: To recognize young people who volunteer in their communities.
Eligibility: Applicants must be nominated by parents, educators or community members. There are two categories: one for kids ages 6-12 and another for ages 13-18. Nominees must be legal U.S. residents who have not graduated from high school.
Target applicants: Junior high students or younger. High school students.
Amount: Up to $10,000.
Number of awards: 2,136.
Deadline: March 15.
How to apply: Applications are available online and at Kohl's stores.
Exclusive: Visit www.UltimateScholarshipBook.com and enter code KO16012 for updates on this award.

(161) • Kymanox's James J. Davis Memorial Scholarship for Students Studying Abroad

Kymanox
Attn.: Scholarship Administrator
2220 Sedwick Road, Suite 201
Durham, NC 27713
Phone: 847-433-2200
Fax: 610-471-5101
http://www.kymanox.com/scholarship
Purpose: To assist students who are interested in studying abroad.
Eligibility: Applicants must be U.S. citizens or permanent residents planning to attend an accredited program abroad for at least eight weeks. Strong preference is given to students with financial need, and preference is given to applicants studying in a non-English speaking country and to applicants who are majoring in engineering, math or science.
Target applicants: High school students. College students. Graduate school students. Adult students.
Amount: $1,000.
Number of awards: 1.
Deadline: April 16.
How to apply: Applications are available online. An application form, an acceptance letter to a study abroad program, a financial needs verification form and an essay are required.
Exclusive: Visit www.UltimateScholarshipBook.com and enter code KY16112 for updates on this award.

(162) • La Fra Scholarship

Ladies Auxiliary of the Fleet Reserve Association
125 N. West Street
Alexandria, VA 22314
Phone: 800-372-1924 x123
Email: mserfra@fra.org
http://www.la-fra.org
Purpose: To support the female descendants of sea personnel.
Eligibility: Students must have a father or grandfather who was in the Marine Corps, Coast Guard, Navy, Fleet Reserve, Coast Guard Reserve or Fleet Marine Corps Reserve.
Target applicants: High school students. College students. Adult students.
Amount: Varies.
Number of awards: Varies.
Deadline: April 15.
How to apply: Applications are available online.

Exclusive: Visit www.UltimateScholarshipBook.com and enter code LA16212 for updates on this award.

(163) • Leaders and Achievers Scholarship Program

Comcast
1500 Market Street
Philadelphia, PA 19102
Phone: 800-266-2278
http://www.comcast.com

Purpose: To provide one-time scholarship awards of $1,000 each to graduating high school seniors. Emphasis is on students who take leadership roles in school and community service and improvement.

Eligibility: Students must be high school seniors with a minimum 2.8 GPA, be nominated by their high school principal or guidance counselor and attend school in a Comcast community. See the website for a list of eligible communities by state. Comcast employees, their families or other Comcast affiliates are not eligible to apply.

Target applicants: High school students.
Minimum GPA: 2.8
Amount: $1,000.
Number of awards: Varies.
Deadline: Varies.
How to apply: Applications are available from the nominating principal or counselor.
Exclusive: Visit www.UltimateScholarshipBook.com and enter code CO16312 for updates on this award.

(164) • Lewis A. Kingsley Foundation Scholarship

Naval Sea Cadet Corps
2300 Wilson Boulevard
Arlington, VA 22201-3308
Phone: 800-356-5760
Email: alewis@seacadets.org
http://www.seacadets.org

Purpose: To provide financial assistance to Sea Cadets.

Eligibility: Applicants must be former Sea Cadets attending college full-time at the sophomore level or higher. They musts be employed, earning at least $5,000 per year and maintain a 2.0 or higher GPA. A one- to two- page personal statement, a letter of recommendation and a resume are required.

Target applicants: College students. Adult students.
Minimum GPA: 2.0
Amount: At least $2,000.
Number of awards: Varies.
Deadline: May 15.
How to apply: Applications are available online.
Exclusive: Visit www.UltimateScholarshipBook.com and enter code NA16412 for updates on this award.

(165) • Life Lessons Essay Contest

Life and Health Insurance Foundation for Education
1655 N. Fort Myer Drive
Suite 610
Arlington, VA 22209
Phone: 202-464-5000
Fax: 202-464-5011
Email: info@lifehappens.org
http://www.lifehappens.org

Purpose: To support students who have been affected financially and emotionally by the death of a parent.

Eligibility: Applicants must submit either a 500-word essay or a three-minute video describing the impact of losing a parent at a young age. The grand prize winner of the video contest is selected by an online public vote.

Target applicants: High school students. College students. Adult students.
Amount: Up to $10,000.
Number of awards: 59.
Deadline: April 15.
How to apply: Applications are available online.
Exclusive: Visit www.UltimateScholarshipBook.com and enter code LI16512 for updates on this award.

(166) • LTG and Mrs. Joseph M. Heiser Scholarship

U.S. Army Ordnance Corps Association
P.O. Box 377
Aberdeen Proving Ground, MD 21005
Phone: 410-272-8540
Fax: 410-272-8425
http://www.usaocaweb.org/scholarships.htm

Purpose: To honor the memory of LTG Joseph M. Heiser.

Eligibility: Applicants must be active or reserve Ordinance soldiers or OCA members or members or their immediate family. They must write a 300- to 500- word essay about the reasons they are seeking the grant and why they feel they deserve it and a 1,000- to 1,500-word essay on the missions, heritage or history of the U.S. Army Ordnance Corps.

Target applicants: High school students. College students. Adult students.
Amount: Varies.
Number of awards: Varies.
Deadline: June 30.
How to apply: Applications are available online.
Exclusive: Visit www.UltimateScholarshipBook.com and enter code U.16612 for updates on this award.

(167) • Marine Corps League Scholarships

Marine Corps League
P.O. Box 3070
Merrifield, VA 22116
Phone: 800-625-1775
Fax: 703-207-0047
http://www.mcleague.org

Purpose: To provide educational opportunities to spouses and descendants of Marine Corps League members.

Eligibility: Applicants must be Marine Corp League or Auxiliary members in good standing, their spouses or their descendants, children of Marines who died in the line of duty or honorably discharged Marines who need rehabilitation training that is not being subsidized by government programs.

Target applicants: High school students. College students. Adult students.
Amount: Varies.
Number of awards: Varies.
Scholarship may be renewable.
Deadline: July 1.
How to apply: Applications are available online.
Exclusive: Visit www.UltimateScholarshipBook.com and enter code MA16712 for updates on this award.

(168) · Marine Corps Scholarship Foundation Scholarship

Marine Corps Scholarship Foundation
P.O. Box 3008
Princeton, NJ 08543-3008
Phone: 800-292-7777
Fax: 609-452-2259
Email: mcsfnj@mcsf.org
http://www.marine-scholars.org

Purpose: To provide financial assistance to sons and daughters of U.S. Marines and children of former Marines in their pursuit of higher education.
Eligibility: Applicants must be children of one of the following: an active duty or reserve U. S. Marine, a U.S. Marine who has received an Honorable Discharge, Medical Discharge or was killed while serving in the U.S. Marine Corps, an active duty or reserve U.S. Navy Corpsman who is serving, or has served, with the U.S. Marine Corps, a U.S. Navy Corpsman who has served with the U.S. Marine Corps and has received an Honorable Discharge, Medical Discharge or was killed while serving in the U.S. Navy. Applicants can also be grandchildren of one of the following: A U.S. Marine who served with the 4th Marine Division during World War II and is/was a member of their association, a U.S. Marine who served with the 6th Marine Division during World War II and is/was a member of their association, or a U.S. Marine who served in the 531 Gray Ghost Squadron and is/was a member of their association. Applicants must be either high school graduates or undergraduate students. There is a family income limit.
Target applicants: College students. Adult students.
Minimum GPA: 2.0
Amount: Varies.
Number of awards: Varies.
Deadline: April 1.
How to apply: Applications are available online.
Exclusive: Visit www.UltimateScholarshipBook.com and enter code MA16812 for updates on this award.

(169) · Markley Scholarship

National Association for Campus Activities
13 Harbison Way
Columbia, SC 29212
Phone: 803-732-6222
Fax: 803-749-1047
Email: info@naca.org
http://www.naca.org

Purpose: To support undergraduate and graduate students who have made exceptional contributions in the field of student activities. The focus is on involvement with NACA Central, along with contributions to other activities-based organizations.
Eligibility: Applicants must attend a college/university in the former NACA South Central Region (AR, LA, NM, OK, TX); must be enrolled as juniors, seniors or graduate students at a four-year institution or as sophomores at a two-year institution and must have a minimum 2.5 GPA.
Target applicants: College students. Graduate school students. Adult students.
Minimum GPA: 2.5
Amount: Varies.
Number of awards: Up to 2.
Deadline: September 1.
How to apply: Applications are available online.
Exclusive: Visit www.UltimateScholarshipBook.com and enter code NA16912 for updates on this award.

(170) · Marsh Scholarship Fund

Eastern Surfing Association
P.O. Box 321
Ormond Beach, FL 32175
Phone: 386-672-4905
Email: scholastics@surfesa.org
http://www.surfesa.org

Purpose: To assist Eastern Surfing Association (ESA) student surfers.
Eligibility: Applicants must be current ESA members. Transcripts, a recommendation letter, purpose letters and applications are required. The award is based on academics and citizenship, not athletic ability.
Target applicants: College students. Graduate school students. Adult students.
Amount: Varies.
Number of awards: Varies.
Deadline: May 15.
How to apply: Applications are available online and by email.
Exclusive: Visit www.UltimateScholarshipBook.com and enter code EA17012 for updates on this award.

(171) · Marshall Memorial Fellowship

German Marshall Fund of the United States
1744 R Street NW
Washington, DC 20009
Phone: 202-683-2650
Fax: 202-265-1662
Email: info@gmfus.org
http://www.gmfus.org

Purpose: To provide fellowships for future community leaders to travel in Europe and to explore its societies, institutions and people.
Eligibility: Applicants must be nominated by a recognized leader in their communities or professional fields. They must be between 28 and 40 years of age and demonstrate achievement within their profession, civic involvement and leadership. They must be U.S. citizens or permanent residents. Candidates should have little or no previous experience traveling through Europe. Fellows visit five or six cities and meet with policy makers, business professionals and other community leaders.
Target applicants: College students. Graduate school students. Adult students.
Amount: Varies.
Number of awards: 100+.
Deadline: Varies.
How to apply: Applications are available online.
Exclusive: Visit www.UltimateScholarshipBook.com and enter code GE17112 for updates on this award.

(172) · Marshall Scholar

Marshall Aid Commemoration Commission
Email: info@marshallscholarship.org
http://www.marshallscholarship.org

Purpose: Established in 1953 and financed by the British government, the scholarships are designed to bring academically distinguished Americans to study in the United Kingdom to increase understanding and appreciation of the British society and academic values.
Eligibility: Applicants must be U.S. citizens who expect to earn a degree from an accredited four-year college or university in the U.S.

with a minimum 3.7 GPA. Students may apply in one of eight regions in the U.S.
Target applicants: College students. Adult students.
Minimum GPA: 3.7
Amount: Varies.
Number of awards: 40.
Deadline: October.
How to apply: Contact your regional center at the address listed on the website.
Exclusive: Visit www.UltimateScholarshipBook.com and enter code MA17212 for updates on this award.

(173) · Mary Church Terrell Award

National Association of Blacks in Criminal Justice
North Carolina Central University
P.O. Box 19788
Durham, NC 27707
Phone: 919-683-1801
Fax: 919-683-1903
Email: office@nabcj.org
http://www.nabcj.org
Purpose: To award activism for positive change in criminal justice on city and state levels.
Eligibility: The nominator should be a member of NABCJ. This award is given to an individual who has initiated relationships with churches, courts, councils and assemblies.
Target applicants: College students. Graduate school students. Adult students.
Amount: Varies.
Number of awards: Varies.
Deadline: May 1.
How to apply: Nomination applications are available online.
Exclusive: Visit www.UltimateScholarshipBook.com and enter code NA17312 for updates on this award.

(174) · Mary Paolozzi Member's Scholarship

Navy Wives Clubs of America (NWCA)
P.O. Box 54022
NSA Mid-South
Millington, TN 38053-6022
Phone: 866-511-6922
Email: scholarships@navywivesclubsofamerica.org
http://www.navywivesclubsofamerica.org
Purpose: To aid students who are members of the Navy Wives Clubs of America (NWCA).
Eligibility: Applicants must have been accepted into a college no later than the application due date. Selection is based on academic merit and financial need.
Target applicants: High school students. College students. Adult students.
Amount: Varies.
Number of awards: Varies.
Deadline: May 30.
How to apply: Applications are available online. An application form, official transcript and tax form copies are required.
Exclusive: Visit www.UltimateScholarshipBook.com and enter code NA17412 for updates on this award.

(175) · Maurice B. Cohill, Jr. Young Investigator Award

National Center for Juvenile Justice (NCJJ)
3700 South Water Street
Suite 200
Pittsburgh, PA 15203
Phone: 412-227-6950
Fax: 412-227-6955
Email: ncjj@ncjj.org
http://www.ncjj.org
Purpose: To encourage young people to be interested in law and justice research.
Eligibility: Applicants must be high school seniors. They must complete a research paper on a topic relating to juvenile crime, law, public policy, delinquency, courts, law data analysis or probation. Selection is based on the overall strength of the paper.
Target applicants: High school students.
Amount: Up to $500.
Number of awards: 4.
Deadline: April 1.
How to apply: Applications are available online. An application form, cover sheet, research paper and abstract are required.
Exclusive: Visit www.UltimateScholarshipBook.com and enter code NA17512 for updates on this award.

(176) · Medal of Honor AFCEA ROTC Scholarships

Armed Forces Communications and Electronics Association (AFCEA)
4400 Fair Lakes Court
Fairfax, VA 22033
Phone: 703-631-6149
Fax: 703-631-4693
http://www.afcea.org
Purpose: To support students who are members of the ROTC and committed to serving in the United States armed forces.
Eligibility: Applicants must be enrolled in college full-time, and they must be in their sophomore or junior year. Students must have at least a 3.0 GPA.
Target applicants: College students. Adult students.
Minimum GPA: 3.0
Amount: $4,000.
Number of awards: 4.
Deadline: March 1.
How to apply: Applications are available online.
Exclusive: Visit www.UltimateScholarshipBook.com and enter code AR17612 for updates on this award.

(177) · Medger Evers Award

National Association of Blacks in Criminal Justice
North Carolina Central University
P.O. Box 19788
Durham, NC 27707
Phone: 919-683-1801
Fax: 919-683-1903
Email: office@nabcj.org
http://www.nabcj.org
Purpose: To award efforts to ensure that all people, including those in institutions, receive equal justice under the law.

Eligibility: This award honors the slain civil rights leader. Nominator should be a member of NABCJ.
Target applicants: College students. Graduate school students. Adult students.
Amount: Varies.
Number of awards: 1.
Deadline: May 15.
How to apply: Nomination applications are available online.
Exclusive: Visit www.UltimateScholarshipBook.com and enter code NA17712 for updates on this award.

(178) · Mediacom World Class Scholarship Program

Mediacom
3737 Westown Parkway
Suite A
West Des Moines, IA 50266
Email: scholarship@mediacomcc.com
http://www.mediacomworldclass.com
Purpose: To aid students in Mediacom service areas.
Eligibility: Applicants must be graduating high school seniors. Those who have earned college credits may apply as long as they have not yet graduated high school. Applicants may not be children of Mediacom employees and must live in areas serviced by Mediacom.
Target applicants: High school students.
Amount: $1,000.
Number of awards: Varies.
Deadline: February 11.
How to apply: Applications are available online. An application form, essay, transcript and two reference forms are required.
Exclusive: Visit www.UltimateScholarshipBook.com and enter code ME17812 for updates on this award.

(179) · Memorial Scholarship Fund

Third Marine Division Association
MFySgt. James G. Kyser, USMC (Ret)
15727 Vista Drive
Dumfries, VA 22025-1810
Phone: 352-726-2767
Email: scholarship@caltrap.org
http://www.caltrap.com
Purpose: To assist veterans and their families.
Eligibility: Applicants must be the children of Marines (Corpsman or other) who served with the Third Marine Division or in support of the Division at any time and who have been members of the Third Marine Division Association for at least two years. Applicants must be 16-23 and unmarried dependents. Applicants must attend school in the U.S. or Canada.
Target applicants: High school students. College students.
Amount: Varies.
Number of awards: Varies.
Scholarship may be renewable.
Deadline: April 15.
How to apply: Applications are available by written request after September 1.
Exclusive: Visit www.UltimateScholarshipBook.com and enter code TH17912 for updates on this award.

(180) · Mensa Education and Research Foundation Scholarship Program

Mensa Education and Research Foundation
1229 Corporate Drive West
Phone: 817-607-5577
Fax: 817-649-5232
Email: info@mensafoundation.org
http://www.mensafoundation.org
Purpose: To support students seeking higher education.
Eligibility: Applicants do not need to be members of Mensa but must be residents of a participating American Mensa Local Group's area. They must be enrolled in a degree program at an accredited U.S. college or university in the academic year after application. They must write an essay explaining career, academic or vocational goals.
Target applicants: High school students. College students. Adult students.
Amount: Varies.
Number of awards: Varies.
Deadline: January 15.
How to apply: Applications are available online in September. Please do NOT write to the organization to request an application. An application form and essay are required.
Exclusive: Visit www.UltimateScholarshipBook.com and enter code ME18012 for updates on this award.

(181) · MG James Ursano Scholarship Fund

Army Emergency Relief (AER)
200 Stovall Street Rm. 5N13
Alexandria, VA 22332
Phone: 703-428-0035
Fax: 703-325-7183
Email: education@aerhq.org
http://www.aerhq.org
Purpose: To assist the children of Army families with their undergraduate education, vocational training and service academy education.
Eligibility: Applicants must be dependent children of Army soldiers who are unmarried and under the age of 22. Students must also be registered with the Defense Eligibility Enrollment Reporting System, have a minimum 2.0 GPA and be enrolled and accepted or pending acceptance as full-time students in post-secondary educational institutions. Awards are based primarily on financial need.
Target applicants: High school students. College students.
Minimum GPA: 2.0
Amount: Varies.
Number of awards: Varies.
Scholarship may be renewable.
Deadline: March 1.
How to apply: Applications are available online and by mail.
Exclusive: Visit www.UltimateScholarshipBook.com and enter code AR18112 for updates on this award.

(182) · Mike Nash Memorial Scholarship Fund

Vietnam Veterans of America
8605 Cameron Street
Silver Spring, MD 20910
Phone: 800-882-1316
Email: finance@vva.org
http://www.vva.org
Purpose: To provide financial assistance to Vietnam veterans, their widows and their children.

Eligibility: Applicants must be Vietnam Veterans of America members or their spouses, children, stepchildren or grandchildren, or spouses, children, stepchildren or grandchildren of Vietnam veterans who are deceased, MIA or KIA. They must enroll at least half time at an accredited institution of higher learning.
Target applicants: High school students. College students. Adult students.
Amount: Varies.
Number of awards: Varies.
Deadline: May 31.
How to apply: Applications are available online.
Exclusive: Visit www.UltimateScholarshipBook.com and enter code VI18212 for updates on this award.

(183) · Military Award Program (MAP)

Imagine America Foundation
1101 Connecticut Avenue NW
Suite 901
Washington, DC 20036
Phone: 202-336-6800
Fax: 202-408-8102
Email: scholarships@imagine-america.org
http://www.imagine-america.org
Purpose: To help those who have served in the military with their education and make the transition from military to civilian life.
Eligibility: Applicants must be enrolling into a participating college and be active duty, reservist, honorably discharged or retired veterans of the U.S. military. They must be likely to enroll in and successfully complete their postsecondary education and may not be a previous recipient of any other Imagine America Foundation scholarships/awards. Applicants must also have financial need.
Target applicants: College students. Graduate school students. Adult students.
Amount: $1,000.
Number of awards: Varies.
Deadline: June 30.
How to apply: Applications are available online.
Exclusive: Visit www.UltimateScholarshipBook.com and enter code IM18312 for updates on this award.

(184) · Military Officers' Benevolent Corporation Scholarships

Military Officers' Benevolent Corporation
1010 American Eagle Boulevard
Box 301
Sun City Center, FL 33573
Phone: 813-634-4675
Fax: 813-633-2412
Email: president@mobc-online.org
http://www.mobc-online.org
Purpose: To provide financial assistance to children and grandchildren of military members and others who have served their country.
Eligibility: Applicants must be children or grandchildren of current or former military members, federal employees of GS-7 or higher equivalent officer grade, foreign services officers (FSO-8 and below) and honorably discharged or retired foreign military officers of Allied Nations living in the U.S. The applicant must be a high school senior who has been recommended by his or her principal and have a minimum score of 21 on the ACT, 900 on the two-part SAT or 1350 on the three-part SAT. The minimum GPA required is 3.0.
Target applicants: High school students.
Minimum GPA: 3.0
Amount: $500-$3,000.
Number of awards: 14.
Scholarship may be renewable.
Deadline: March 1.
How to apply: Applications are available online.
Exclusive: Visit www.UltimateScholarshipBook.com and enter code MI18412 for updates on this award.

(185) · Military Order of the Purple Heart Scholarship

Military Order of the Purple Heart
MOPH National Headquarters
5413-B Backlick Road
Attn.: Scholarship
Springfield, VA 22151
Phone: 703-642-5360
Fax: 703-642-2054
Email: scholarship@purpleheart.org
http://www.purpleheart.org
Purpose: To recognize outstanding achievement.
Eligibility: Applicants must be a member of the Military Order of the Purple Heart (MOPH) or a child, step-child, grandchild or great grandchild of a member of the MOPH or a veteran killed in action or a veteran who died of injuries but did not have the chance to join the Military Order of the Purple Heart. Applicants must also be U.S. citizens, be high school graduates or high school seniors, have a 2.75 minimum GPA and be enrolled in a full-time program in a college. Applicants must write an essay and send a non-refundable $15 fee. Note: We do not recommend applying to scholarships that charge application fees. However, some scholarships of this type charge fees and are included for completeness.
Target applicants: High school students. College students. Graduate school students. Adult students.
Minimum GPA: 2.75
Amount: $3,000.
Number of awards: 83.
Deadline: February 15.
How to apply: Applications are available online.
Exclusive: Visit www.UltimateScholarshipBook.com and enter code MI18512 for updates on this award.

(186) · Montgomery GI Bill - Active Duty

Department of Veterans Affairs
Veterans Benefits Administration
810 Vermont Avenue NW
Washington, DC 20420
Phone: 888-442-4551
http://www.gibill.va.gov
Purpose: To provide educational benefits to veterans.
Eligibility: Applicants must have an Honorable Discharge and high school diploma and meet other service requirements. The bill provides up to 36 months of educational benefits to veterans for college, technical or vocational courses, correspondence courses, apprenticeship/job training or flight training, high-tech training, licensing and certification tests, entrepreneurship training and certain entrance examinations. In most cases the award must be used within 10 years of being discharged.
Target applicants: College students. Graduate school students. Adult students.
Amount: Varies.
Number of awards: Varies.
Deadline: None.

How to apply: Applications are available online.
Exclusive: Visit www.UltimateScholarshipBook.com and enter code DE18612 for updates on this award.

(187) • Montgomery GI Bill - Selected Reserve

Department of Veterans Affairs
Veterans Benefits Administration
810 Vermont Avenue NW
Washington, DC 20420
Phone: 888-442-4551
http://www.gibill.va.gov
Purpose: To support members of the United States military Selected Reserve.
Eligibility: Applicants must have a six-year commitment to the Selected Reserve signed after June 30, 1985. The Selected Reserve includes the Army Reserve, Navy Reserve, Air Force Reserve, Marine Corps Reserve and Coast Guard Reserve, and the Army National Guard and the Air National Guard. Applicants must have completed basic military training, meet the requirements to receive a high school diploma or equivalency certificate and may use the funds for degree programs, certificate or correspondence courses, cooperative training, independent study programs, apprenticeship/on-the-job training and vocational flight training programs.
Target applicants: High school students. College students. Graduate school students. Adult students.
Amount: Varies.
Number of awards: Varies.
Scholarship may be renewable.
Deadline: Varies.
How to apply: Applications are available online.
Exclusive: Visit www.UltimateScholarshipBook.com and enter code DE18712 for updates on this award.

(188) • Montgomery GI Bill Tuition Assistance Top-Up

Department of Veterans Affairs
Veterans Benefits Administration
810 Vermont Avenue NW
Washington, DC 20420
Phone: 888-442-4551
http://www.gibill.va.gov
Purpose: To support students who are receiving tuition assistance from the military that doesn't cover the full cost of courses.
Eligibility: Applicants must be eligible for MGIB-Active Duty benefits, and they must have served on active duty in the United States military for at least two years.
Target applicants: College students. Graduate school students. Adult students.
Amount: Varies.
Number of awards: Varies.
Scholarship may be renewable.
Deadline: Varies.
How to apply: Applications are available online. Contact your education services officer or education counselor for more information.
Exclusive: Visit www.UltimateScholarshipBook.com and enter code DE18812 for updates on this award.

(189) • Most Valuable Student Scholarships

Elks National Foundation Headquarters
2750 North Lakeview Avenue
Chicago, IL 60614
Phone: 773-755-4732
Fax: 773-755-4733
Email: scholarship@elks.org
http://www.elks.org
Purpose: To support high school seniors who have demonstrated scholarship, leadership and financial need.
Eligibility: Applicants must be graduating high school seniors who are U.S. citizens and who plan to pursue a four-year degree on a full-time basis at a U.S. college or university. Male and female students compete separately.
Target applicants: High school students.
Amount: $1,000-$15,000.
Number of awards: 500.
Scholarship may be renewable.
Deadline: Varies.
How to apply: Contact the scholarship chairman of your local Lodge or the Elks association of your state.
Exclusive: Visit www.UltimateScholarshipBook.com and enter code EL18912 for updates on this award.

(190) • NABF Scholarship Program

National Amateur Baseball Federation
Awards Committee Chairman
P.O. Box 705
Bowie, MD 20718
Phone: 301-464-5460
Fax: 301-352-0214
Email: nabf1914@aol.com
http://www.nabf.com
Purpose: To support students who have been involved with the federation.
Eligibility: Applicants must be enrolled in an accredited college or university, must have participated in a federation event and must be sponsored by a member association. Selection is based on grades, financial need and previous awards.
Target applicants: College students. Adult students.
Amount: $1,000.
Number of awards: Varies.
Deadline: Varies.
How to apply: Applications are available online.
Exclusive: Visit www.UltimateScholarshipBook.com and enter code NA19012 for updates on this award.

(191) • NACA Regional Council Student Leader Scholarships

National Association for Campus Activities
13 Harbison Way
Columbia, SC 29212
Phone: 803-732-6222
Fax: 803-749-1047
Email: info@naca.org
http://www.naca.org
Purpose: To provide educational assistance to students in each of NACA's regions.
Eligibility: Applicants must be undergraduate college students in good standing, hold leadership positions on campus and have made significant contributions to their respective campuses.
Target applicants: College students. Adult students.
Amount: Varies.
Number of awards: Varies.
Deadline: May 1.

How to apply: Applications are available online.
Exclusive: Visit www.UltimateScholarshipBook.com and enter code NA19112 for updates on this award.

(192) • NACOP Scholarship

National Association of Chiefs of Police
NACOP Scholarship Program
6350 Horizon Drive
Titusville, FL 32780
Phone: 321-264-0911
Email: kimc@aphf.org
http://www.aphf.org
Purpose: To recognize law enforcement individuals.
Eligibility: Applicants must be disabled officers wishing to retrain through education or the collegebound children of a disabled officer. Students must maintain a 2.0 GPA and be enrolled in a minimum of six credit hours.
Target applicants: High school students. College students. Graduate school students. Adult students.
Minimum GPA: 2.0
Amount: $500.
Number of awards: Varies.
Deadline: Varies.
How to apply: Applications are available by written request.
Exclusive: Visit www.UltimateScholarshipBook.com and enter code NA19212 for updates on this award.

(193) • Nancy Reagan Pathfinder Scholarships

National Federation of Republican Women
124 N. Alfred Street
Alexandria, VA 22314
Phone: 703-548-9688
Fax: 703-548-9836
Email: mail@nfrw.org
http://www.nfrw.org/programs/scholarships.htm
Purpose: To honor former First Lady Nancy Reagan.
Eligibility: Applicants must be college sophomores, juniors, seniors or master's degree students. Two one-page essays and three letters of recommendation are required. Previous winners may not reapply.
Target applicants: College students. Graduate school students. Adult students.
Amount: $2,500.
Number of awards: 3.
Deadline: June 1.
How to apply: Applications are available online. An application form, three letters of recommendation, transcript, two essays and State Federation President Certification are required.
Exclusive: Visit www.UltimateScholarshipBook.com and enter code NA19312 for updates on this award.

(194) • NATA Scholarship

National Athletic Trainers' Association
National Athletic Trainer's Association Research and Education Foundation Inc.
2952 Stemmons Freeway
Dallas, TX 75247
Phone: 214-637-6282
Fax: 214-637-2206
Email: barbaran@nata.org
http://www.nata.org
Purpose: To encourage study among athletic trainers.
Eligibility: Applicants must be at least a junior in college with a minimum 3.2 GPA, be sponsored by a certified athletic trainer and be a member of the NATA.
Target applicants: College students. Graduate school students. Adult students.
Minimum GPA: 3.2
Amount: $2,300.
Number of awards: Varies.
Deadline: Varies.
How to apply: Applications are available online.
Exclusive: Visit www.UltimateScholarshipBook.com and enter code NA19412 for updates on this award.

(195) • National College Match Program

QuestBridge
120 Hawthorne Avenue
Suite 103
Palo Alto, CA 94301
Phone: 888-275-2054
Fax: 650-653-2516
Email: questions@questbridge.org
http://www.questbridge.org
Purpose: To connect outstanding low-income high school seniors with admission and full four-year scholarships to some of the nation's most selective colleges.
Eligibility: Applicants must have demonstrated academic excellence in the face of economic obstacles. Students of all races and ethnicities are encouraged to apply. Many past award recipients have been among the first generation in their families to attend college.
Target applicants: High school students.
Amount: Varies.
Number of awards: Varies.
Scholarship may be renewable.
Deadline: September 30.
How to apply: Applications are available on the QuestBridge website in August of each year. An application form, two teacher recommendations, one counselor recommendation (Secondary School Report), a transcript and SAT and/or ACT score reports are required.
Exclusive: Visit www.UltimateScholarshipBook.com and enter code QU19512 for updates on this award.

(196) • National Junior Girls Scholarships

Ladies Auxiliary VFW
406 West 34th Street
10th Floor
Kansas City, MO 64111
Phone: 816-561-8655 x19
Fax: 816-931-4753
Email: jmillick@ladiesauxvfw.org
http://www.ladiesauxvfw.org
Purpose: To award Junior Girls who excel academically, are actively involved in Junior Girls and demonstrate leadership at school.
Eligibility: Applicants must be Junior Girls ages 13 to 16 and active members of a Ladies Auxiliary VFW Junior Girls Unit for at least a year who have held an office. Applicants must also submit letters of recommendation, a transcript and a list of activities.
Target applicants: Junior high students or younger. High school students.
Amount: $7,500.
Number of awards: 1.

Deadline: March 11.
How to apply: Applications are available online.
Exclusive: Visit www.UltimateScholarshipBook.com and enter code LA19612 for updates on this award.

(197) • National Merit Scholarship Program and National Achievement Scholarship Program

National Merit Scholarship Corporation
1560 Sherman Avenue, Suite 200
Evanston, IL 60201-4897
Phone: 847-866-5100
Fax: 847-866-5113
http://www.nationalmerit.org
Purpose: To provide scholarships through a merit-based academic competition.
Eligibility: Applicants must be enrolled full-time in high school, progressing normally toward completion and planning to enter college no later than the fall following completion of high school, be U.S. citizens or permanent legal residents in the process of becoming U.S. citizens and take the PSAT/NMSQT no later than the 11th grade. Participation in the program is based on performance on the exam.
Target applicants: High school students.
Amount: $2,500.
Number of awards: Varies.
Scholarship may be renewable.
Deadline: Varies.
How to apply: Application is made by taking the PSAT/NMSQT test.
Exclusive: Visit www.UltimateScholarshipBook.com and enter code NA19712 for updates on this award.

(198) • National Oratorical Contest

American Legion
Attn.: Americanism and Children and Youth Division
P.O. Box 1055
Indianapolis, IN 46206
Phone: 317-630-1249
Fax: 317-630-1369
Email: acy@legion.org
http://www.legion.org
Purpose: To reward students for their knowledge of government and oral presentation skills.
Eligibility: Applicants must be high school students under the age of 20 who are U.S. citizens or legal residents. Students first give an oration within their state and winners compete at the national level. The oration must be related to the Constitution of the United States focusing on the duties and obligations citizens have to the government. It must be in English and be between eight and ten minutes. There is also an assigned topic which is posted on the website, and it should be between three and five minutes.
Target applicants: High school students.
Amount: Up to $18,000.
Number of awards: Varies.
Deadline: Local American Legion department must select winners by March 14.
How to apply: Applications are available from your local American Legion post or state headquarters. Deadlines for local competitions are set by the local Posts.
Exclusive: Visit www.UltimateScholarshipBook.com and enter code AM19812 for updates on this award.

(199) • National President's Scholarship

American Legion Auxiliary
8945 N. Meridian Street
Indianapolis, IN 46260
Phone: 317-569-4500
Fax: 317-569-4502
Email: alahq@legion-aux.org
http://www.legion-aux.org
Purpose: To award scholarships to children of veterans who served in the Armed Forces.
Eligibility: Applicants must be the daughters or sons of veterans who served in the Armed Forces for membership in The American Legion, be high school seniors and complete 50 hours of community service. Selection is based on character, application/essay, scholastic achievement, leadership and financial need.
Target applicants: High school students.
Amount: $1,500-$2,500.
Number of awards: 15.
Deadline: March 1.
How to apply: Applications are available online. Applicants should submit applications, four recommendation letters, essays, proof of volunteering, transcripts, ACT or SAT scores and parent's military service description.
Exclusive: Visit www.UltimateScholarshipBook.com and enter code AM19912 for updates on this award.

(200) • National Scholarship Program

National Scholastic Surfing Association
P.O. Box 495
Huntington Beach, CA 92648
Phone: 714-378-0899
Fax: 714-964-5232
Email: jaragon@nssa.org
http://www.nssa.org
Purpose: To assist NSSA members in their pursuit of post-high school education.
Eligibility: Applicants must be competitive student NSSA members and have a minimum 3.0 GPA in the current school year. Scholastic achievement, leadership, service, career goals and recommendations are considered.
Target applicants: High school students. College students. Adult students.
Minimum GPA: 3.0
Amount: Varies.
Number of awards: Varies.
Deadline: Varies.
How to apply: Applications are available with organization membership.
Exclusive: Visit www.UltimateScholarshipBook.com and enter code NA20012 for updates on this award.

(201) • Naval Enlisted Reserve Association Scholarships

Naval Enlisted Reserve Association
6703 Farragut Avenue
Falls Church, VA 22042-2189
Phone: 800-776-9020
Email: secretary@nera.org
http://www.nera.org
Purpose: To recognize the service and sacrifices made by Navy, Marine and Coast Guard members, retirees and their families.

Eligibility: Applicants must be members of the Naval Enlisted Reserve Association in good standing or their spouses, children or grandchildren. Children and grandchildren of members must be single and under 23 years of age on the application deadline. Applicants must be graduating high school seniors or students who are already pursuing an undergraduate degree.
Target applicants: High school students. College students. Adult students.
Amount: $2,500-$3,000.
Number of awards: 6.
Deadline: June 15.
How to apply: Applications are available online.
Exclusive: Visit www.UltimateScholarshipBook.com and enter code NA20112 for updates on this award.

(202) · Navin Narayan Scholarship

American Red Cross Youth
2025 E Street NW
Washington, DC 20006
Phone: 202-303-4498
http://www.redcrossyouth.org
Purpose: The scholarship is named after Navin Narayan, a former youth volunteer with the Red Cross who died from cancer at the age of 23. In his honor, the Red Cross awards this scholarship to youth volunteers who have made significant humanitarian contributions to the organization and who have also achieved academic excellence in high school.
Eligibility: Applicants must plan to attend a four-year college or university and have volunteered a minimum of two years with the Red Cross.
Target applicants: High school students.
Amount: $2,500.
Number of awards: 1.
Deadline: February 11.
How to apply: Application forms are available online.
Exclusive: Visit www.UltimateScholarshipBook.com and enter code AM20212 for updates on this award.

(203) · Navy College Fund

U.S. Navy Personnel
5720 Integrity Drive
Millington, TN 38055
Phone: 866-827-5672
Email: bupers_webmaster@navy.mil
http://www.npc.navy.mil/Channels/
Purpose: To encourage entry into the Navy for recruits who have skills and specialties for which there is a critical shortage.
Eligibility: Applicants must be Navy recruits who are qualified for training in selected Navy ratings as non-prior service enlistees and agree to serve on active duty for at least three years. They must have graduated from high school, be 17 to 30 years old, agree to a $1,200 pay reduction and receive an "Honorable" Character of Service.
Target applicants: High school students. College students. Adult students.
Amount: Varies.
Number of awards: Varies.
Scholarship may be renewable.
Deadline: Varies.
How to apply: Applications are available from Navy recruiters.
Exclusive: Visit www.UltimateScholarshipBook.com and enter code U.20312 for updates on this award.

(204) · Navy League Endowed Scholarships

Navy League Foundation
2300 Wilson Boulevard
Arlington, VA 22201
Phone: 800-356-5760
Fax: 703-528-2333
Email: lhuycke@navyleague.org
http://www.navyleague.org
Purpose: To help military dependents attend college.
Eligibility: Applicants must be dependents or direct descendants of an active, reserve, retired or honorably discharged member of the U.S. Navy, Coast Guard, U.S.-Flag Merchant Marine, Marine Corps or U.S. Naval Sea Cadet Corps; be high school seniors or the equivalent and enter an accredited college or university. Students should submit a list of scholastic and extracurricular activities, transcripts, no more than two recommendations, SAT or ACT scores, FAFSA information, proof of qualifying sea service duty and personal statement. There are various scholarships available.
Target applicants: High school students. College students. Adult students.
Amount: Varies.
Number of awards: Varies.
Scholarship may be renewable.
Deadline: March 1.
How to apply: Applications are available online.
Exclusive: Visit www.UltimateScholarshipBook.com and enter code NA20412 for updates on this award.

(205) · Navy Supply Corps Foundation Scholarship

Navy Supply Corps Foundation Inc.
1425 Prince Avenue
Athens, GA 30606-2205
Phone: 706-354-4111
Fax: 706-354-0334
Email: evans@usnscf.com
https://www.usnscf.com
Purpose: To provide financial aid for undergraduate studies to family members of Supply Corp members and enlisted Navy personnel.
Eligibility: Applicants must be family members of a Navy Supply Corps officer or an enlisted member, active duty, reservist or retired. Awards are based on character, leadership, academic performance and financial need.
Target applicants: Junior high students or younger. High school students. College students. Adult students.
Amount: $2,500-$10,000.
Number of awards: Varies.
Deadline: March 26.
How to apply: Applications are available online.
Exclusive: Visit www.UltimateScholarshipBook.com and enter code NA20512 for updates on this award.

(206) · Navy-Marine Corps ROTC College Program

U.S. Navy Naval Reserve Officers Training Corps (NROTC)
Naval Service Training Command Officer Development
NAS Pensacola
250 Dallas Street, Suite A
Pensacola, FL 32508
Phone: 800-628-7682
Fax: 850-452-2486
Email: pnsc_nrotc.scholarship@navy.mil
https://www.nrotc.navy.mil

Purpose: To provide education opportunities for NROTC students.
Eligibility: Applicants must be accepted to or attending a college with an NROTC program. They must complete naval science and other specified university courses and attend a summer training session. Scholarships are available for two or four years, depending on time of application.
Target applicants: College students. Adult students.
Amount: Varies.
Number of awards: Varies.
Scholarship may be renewable.
Deadline: Varies.
How to apply: Applications are available online.
Exclusive: Visit www.UltimateScholarshipBook.com and enter code U.20612 for updates on this award.

(207) • Navy-Marine Corps ROTC Four-Year Scholarships

U.S. Navy Naval Reserve Officers Training Corps (NROTC)
Naval Service Training Command Officer Development
NAS Pensacola
250 Dallas Street, Suite A
Pensacola, FL 32508
Phone: 800-628-7682
Fax: 850-452-2486
Email: pnsc_nrotc.scholarship@navy.mil
https://www.nrotc.navy.mil
Purpose: To provide education opportunities for ROTC members.
Eligibility: Applicants must plan to attend an eligible college or university. They must commit to eight years of military service, four of which must be on active duty. The scholarship pays full tuition and fees plus a stipend for textbooks.
Target applicants: High school students.
Amount: Tuition plus stipend.
Number of awards: Varies.
Scholarship may be renewable.
Deadline: January 31.
How to apply: Applications are available online.
Exclusive: Visit www.UltimateScholarshipBook.com and enter code U.20712 for updates on this award.

(208) • Navy-Marine Corps ROTC Two-Year Scholarships

U.S. Navy Naval Reserve Officers Training Corps (NROTC)
Naval Service Training Command Officer Development
NAS Pensacola
250 Dallas Street, Suite A
Pensacola, FL 32508
Phone: 800-628-7682
Fax: 850-452-2486
Email: pnsc_nrotc.scholarship@navy.mil
https://www.nrotc.navy.mil
Purpose: To provide education opportunities for NROTC students.
Eligibility: Applicants must be attending a college with an NROTC program as a freshman or sophomore. They must complete naval science and other specified university courses and attend a summer training session. They must also attend a Naval Science Institute program during the summer between their sophomore and junior year.
Target applicants: College students. Adult students.
Amount: Varies.
Number of awards: Varies.
Scholarship may be renewable.
Deadline: Varies.
How to apply: Applications are available online.
Exclusive: Visit www.UltimateScholarshipBook.com and enter code U.20812 for updates on this award.

(209) • Navy/Marine Corps/Coast Guard (NMCCG) Enlisted Dependent Spouse Scholarship

Navy Wives Clubs of America (NWCA)
P.O. Box 54022
NSA Mid-South
Millington, TN 38053-6022
Phone: 866-511-6922
Email: scholarships@navywivesclubsofamerica.org
http://www.navywivesclubsofamerica.org
Purpose: To provide financial assistance to spouses of certain military members.
Eligibility: Applicants must be spouses of enlisted Navy, Marine Corps and Coast Guard personnel. They must be accepted to an institution of higher learning by May 30 of the year of application.
Target applicants: High school students. College students. Adult students.
Amount: Varies.
Number of awards: Varies.
Deadline: May 30.
How to apply: Applications are available online. Financial information and a transcript are required.
Exclusive: Visit www.UltimateScholarshipBook.com and enter code NA20912 for updates on this award.

(210) • NCAA Division I Degree Completion Award Program

National Collegiate Athletic Association
700 W. Washington Street
P.O. Box 6222
Indianapolis, IN 46206
Phone: 317-917-6222
Fax: 317-917-6888
Email: ahightower@ncaa.org
http://www.ncaa.org/wps/portal/ncaahome?WCM_GLOBAL_CONTEXT=/ncaa/NCAA/NCAA News/NCAA Home Pages/
Purpose: To aid athletes who have exhausted their student aid.
Eligibility: Applicants must have competed at a NCAA Division I institution and received athletics-related aid. They must be within 30 semester hours or 45 quarter hours of completing their degrees. Funds are awarded to 40 to 45 percent of applicants. Recipients are chosen by consultants from seven Division I member institutions.
Target applicants: College students. Adult students.
Amount: Full tuition and fees.
Number of awards: Varies.
Deadline: April and September.
How to apply: Applications are available online. An application form, copy of tax forms, transcript, personal statement, list of extracurricular activities and leadership roles and statement from the director of athletics is required.
Exclusive: Visit www.UltimateScholarshipBook.com and enter code NA21012 for updates on this award.

(211) • NCAA Division II Degree Completion Award Program

National Collegiate Athletic Association
700 W. Washington Street
P.O. Box 6222
Indianapolis, IN 46206
Phone: 317-917-6222
Fax: 317-917-6888
Email: ahightower@ncaa.org
http://www.ncaa.org/wps/portal/ncaahome?WCM_GLOBAL_CONTEXT=/ncaa/NCAA/NCAA News/NCAA Home Pages/
Purpose: To assist student-athletes who are no longer eligible for athletics-based aid.
Eligibility: Applicants must have exhausted athletics eligibility at an NCAA Division II school within the past calendar year. They must be within their first 10 semesters or 15 quarters of full-time attendance and must have received athletics-related aid from the institution. Applicants must be within 32 semester or 48 quarter hours of earning their first undergraduate degree and have a GPA of 2.5 or higher.
Target applicants: College students. Adult students.
Minimum GPA: 2.5
Amount: Up to $6,000.
Number of awards: Varies.
Deadline: First Tuesday in April.
How to apply: Applications are available online. An application form, personal statement, financial aid information, endorsement from director of athletics, senior woman administrator or coach and transcript are required.
Exclusive: Visit www.UltimateScholarshipBook.com and enter code NA21112 for updates on this award.

(212) • NCAA Postgraduate Scholarship

National Collegiate Athletic Association
700 W. Washington Street
P.O. Box 6222
Indianapolis, IN 46206
Phone: 317-917-6222
Fax: 317-917-6888
Email: ahightower@ncaa.org
http://www.ncaa.org/wps/portal/ncaahome?WCM_GLOBAL_CONTEXT=/ncaa/NCAA/NCAA News/NCAA Home Pages/
Purpose: To reward student athletes who perform well in both sports and academics.
Eligibility: Student athletes must show achievement in their last year of varsity-level intercollegiate athletics at an NCAA school. Applicants must be nominated by the faculty athletic representative or athletic director and be enrolling as a full- or part-time graduate student.
Target applicants: College students. Adult students.
Minimum GPA: 3.2
Amount: $7,500.
Number of awards: Up to 174.
Deadline: January 14 (fall), March 18 (winter), May 13 (spring).
How to apply: Applications are available online.
Exclusive: Visit www.UltimateScholarshipBook.com and enter code NA21212 for updates on this award.

(213) • NLUS Stockholm Scholarship Fund

Naval Sea Cadet Corps
2300 Wilson Boulevard
Arlington, VA 22201-3308
Phone: 800-356-5760
Email: alewis@seacadets.org
http://www.seacadets.org
Purpose: To provide financial assistance to a selected cadet.
Eligibility: Applicants must have been Sea Cadets for at least two years and be a member at the time of application. They must be rated NSCC E-3 or higher and receive a recommendation from their commanding officer, NSCC Committee Chairman and a high school principal or counselor. A B+ average or better is required, and SAT/ACT scores and class rank are considered. Applicants must present evidence of acceptance from an accredited institution of higher learning. Stockholm Scholars are selected every four years or when the previous scholar ceases to meet continuation criteria.
Target applicants: High school students.
Minimum GPA: 3.3
Amount: Varies.
Number of awards: 1.
Scholarship may be renewable.
Deadline: May 15.
How to apply: Applications are available online.
Exclusive: Visit www.UltimateScholarshipBook.com and enter code NA21312 for updates on this award.

(214) • No Excuses Wear Student Athlete Annual Scholarship

No Excuses Wear
c/o Student Athlete Scholarship Committee
976 Lake Isabella Way
San Jose, CA 95123
Phone: 408-927-7027
Email: noexcuseswear@yahoo.com
http://www.noexcuseswear.com
Purpose: To aid college-bound high school athletes.
Eligibility: Applicants must be high school seniors who are athletes. They must have a GPA of 3.0 or higher. Selection is based on the overall strength of the application.
Target applicants: High school students.
Minimum GPA: 3.0
Amount: Varies.
Number of awards: Varies.
Deadline: August 1.
How to apply: Application instructions are available online. A nomination letter, transcript and list of extracurricular activities are required.
Exclusive: Visit www.UltimateScholarshipBook.com and enter code NO21412 for updates on this award.

(215) • North American Rolex Scholarship

Our World-Underwater Scholarship Society
P.O. Box 4428
Chicago, IL 60680
Phone: 630-969-6690
Fax: 630-969-6690
Email: info@owuscholarship.org
http://www.owuscholarship.org
Purpose: To support students planning careers in underwater world or associated disciplines.
Eligibility: Applicants must be certified scuba divers with a minimum of 25 open-water dives, be academically excellent, not have earned graduate degrees and be at least 21 and no older than 26 at the time of the application deadline. Applicants must also pass a preliminary

medical examination for diving fitness and pass a NOAA diving physical if selected. A personal interview will be required of all scholarship finalists. There is a $25 fee. Note: We do not recommend applying to scholarships that charge application fees. However, some scholarships of this type charge fees and are included for completeness.
Target applicants: College students. Adult students.
Amount: $20,000.
Number of awards: Varies.
Deadline: December 31.
How to apply: Applications are available online.
Exclusive: Visit www.UltimateScholarshipBook.com and enter code OU21512 for updates on this award.

(216) • NRA Outstanding Achievement Youth Award

National Rifle Association
11250 Waples Mill Road
Fairfax, VA 22030
Phone: 703-267-1505
Email: youth_programs@nrahq.org
http://www.nrahq.org
Purpose: To recognize NRA Junior Members who actively participate in shooting sports.
Eligibility: Applicants must be NRA Junior Members (or Regular or Life Members under 18 years old) and have completed five core and five elective requirements. Core requirements are being current members of the NRA, attending and completing an NRA Basic Firearm Training Course, earning a rating in a shooting discipline and submitting an essay. Applicants must also complete five elective requirements from those listed on the website.
Target applicants: High school students.
Amount: $2,00-$5,000.
Number of awards: 3.
Deadline: May 1.
How to apply: Applications are available online.
Exclusive: Visit www.UltimateScholarshipBook.com and enter code NA21612 for updates on this award.

(217) • NROTC Nurse Corps Scholarship

U.S. Navy Naval Reserve Officers Training Corps (NROTC)
Naval Service Training Command Officer Development
NAS Pensacola
250 Dallas Street, Suite A
Pensacola, FL 32508
Phone: 800-628-7682
Fax: 850-452-2486
Email: pnsc_nrotc.scholarship@navy.mil
https://www.nrotc.navy.mil
Purpose: To aid students who are planning to pursue nursing degrees at an NROTC college or university.
Eligibility: Applicants must be in the second semester of their junior year of high school. They must plan to attend an NROTC college or university that offers the bachelor's degree in nursing. They must be in the top 10 percent of their class or have a combined critical reading and math SAT score of 1080 or higher or have a combined English and math ACT score of 43 or higher. Selection is based on the overall strength of the application.
Target applicants: High school students.
Amount: Varies.
Number of awards: Varies.
Scholarship may be renewable.
Deadline: Varies.
How to apply: Applications are available online. An application form, official transcript, standardized test scores and three references are required.
Exclusive: Visit www.UltimateScholarshipBook.com and enter code U.21712 for updates on this award.

(218) • NROTC Scholarship Program

Chief of Naval Education and Training/NROTC
Phone: 800-NAV-ROTC
https://www.nrotc.navy.mil
Purpose: To prepare young men and women for leadership roles in the Navy and Marine Corps.
Eligibility: Applicants must be U.S. citizens who are at least 17 years old as of September 1 of their first year of college, no older than 23 on June 30 of that first year and must be younger than 27 at the time of anticipated graduation. Students must attend an NROTC college and have no moral or personal convictions against military service. Those interested in the Navy program, including Nurse-option, must have an SAT critical reading score of 530 and a math score of 520 or an ACT score of 22 in English and 22 in math. For the Marine Corps option, students must have an SAT composite score of 1000 or an ACT composite score of 22. Applicants must also meet all Navy or Marine Corps physical standards.
Target applicants: High school students. College students.
Amount: Full tuition and fees, books, uniforms and monthly stipend.
Number of awards: Varies.
Scholarship may be renewable.
Deadline: January 31.
How to apply: Applications are available online. Contact information for regional offices is available online.
Exclusive: Visit www.UltimateScholarshipBook.com and enter code CH21812 for updates on this award.

(219) • NSCC Scholarship Funds

Naval Sea Cadet Corps
2300 Wilson Boulevard
Arlington, VA 22201-3308
Phone: 800-356-5760
Email: alewis@seacadets.org
http://www.seacadets.org
Purpose: To provide financial assistance for Sea Cadets.
Eligibility: Applicants must have been Sea Cadets for at least two years and be members at the time of application. They must have attained the rate of NSCC E-3 or higher and be recommended by their commanding officers, NSCC Committee Chairmen and principals or counselors. They must have a B+ or higher GPA and present evidence of acceptance to an accredited institution of higher learning. SAT or ACT scores and class rank are considered.
Target applicants: High school students.
Minimum GPA: 3.3
Amount: Varies.
Number of awards: Varies.
Deadline: May 15.
How to apply: Applications are available online.
Exclusive: Visit www.UltimateScholarshipBook.com and enter code NA21912 for updates on this award.

(220) • Off to College Scholarship Sweepstakes

SunTrust
P.O. Box 27172
Richmond, VA 23261-7172

Phone: 800-786-8787
http://www.suntrusteducation.com
Purpose: To assist a student for the first year of expenses at any accredited college.
Eligibility: Applicants must be high school seniors who are at least 13 years old and plan to attend a college accredited by the U.S. Department of Education the following fall. U.S. residency is required. Financial need and academic achievement are not considered. Note that this is a sweepstakes drawing every two weeks.
Target applicants: High school students.
Amount: $1,000.
Number of awards: 15.
Deadline: May 14.
How to apply: Applications are available online. Mail-in entries are also accepted. Contact information is required.
Exclusive: Visit www.UltimateScholarshipBook.com and enter code SU22012 for updates on this award.

(221) • OP Loftbed Scholarship Award

OP Loftbed
P.O. Box 573
Thomasville, NC 27361-0573
Phone: 866-567-5638
Email: info@oploftbed.com
http://www.oploftbed.com
Purpose: To reward students who excel at creative writing.
Eligibility: Applicants must be U.S. citizens who plan to attend an accredited college or university in the upcoming school year. They must have a mailing address in the United States. Essay topics and requirements vary from year to year.
Target applicants: High school students. College students. Adult students.
Amount: $500.
Number of awards: Varies.
Deadline: July 31.
How to apply: Applications are available online.
Exclusive: Visit www.UltimateScholarshipBook.com and enter code OP22112 for updates on this award.

(222) • Parent Answer Scholarship Sweepstakes

Parent Answer Scholarship Sweepstakes
P.O. Box 9500
Wilkes-Barre, PA 18773-9500
https://www1.salliemae.com/content/parent_answer/index.html
Purpose: To support the parents of college students.
Eligibility: This $10,000 sweepstakes is open to all U.S. residents who are parents of undergraduate college students. Applicants must have children who are undergraduate students at a Title IV school. They must sign up for Sallie Mae's Parent Answer e-Newsletter and not opt out prior to the sweepstakes drawing.
Target applicants: College students. Adult students.
Amount: $10,000.
Number of awards: 1.
Deadline: May 31.
How to apply: Applicants may enter the sweepstakes online or by mail. An online registration form or 4" x 6" card with contact information is required.
Exclusive: Visit www.UltimateScholarshipBook.com and enter code PA22212 for updates on this award.

(223) • Paul and Daisy Soros Fellowships for New Americans

Paul and Daisy Soros
400 W. 59th Street
New York, NY 10019
Phone: 212-547-6926
Fax: 212-548-4623
Email: pdsoros_fellows@sorosny.org
http://www.pdsoros.org
Purpose: Named after Hungarian immigrants, the Paul and Daisy Soros Fellowships are designed to assist the graduate studies of immigrant children.
Eligibility: Applicants must be immigrants who are resident aliens, have been naturalized or are the children of two parents who have been naturalized. The potential winner of a fellowship must already have a bachelor's degree or be a college senior and must not be over the age of 30 by the application deadline.
Target applicants: College students. Graduate school students. Adult students.
Amount: Up to $45,000.
Number of awards: 30.
Scholarship may be renewable.
Deadline: November 1.
How to apply: Applications are available online.
Exclusive: Visit www.UltimateScholarshipBook.com and enter code PA22312 for updates on this award.

(224) • Pauline Langkamp Memorial Scholarship

Navy Wives Clubs of America (NWCA)
P.O. Box 54022
NSA Mid-South
Millington, TN 38053-6022
Phone: 866-511-6922
Email: scholarships@navywivesclubsofamerica.org
http://www.navywivesclubsofamerica.org
Purpose: To aid college students who are the adult children of members of the Navy Wives Clubs of America (NWCA).
Eligibility: Applicants must be the child of an NWCA member. They must not be carrying a military ID card and must be enrolled or planning to enroll at an accredited postsecondary institution. High school seniors must have been accepted into a college or university no later than the application due date. Selection is based on academic merit and financial need.
Target applicants: High school students. College students. Adult students.
Amount: Varies.
Number of awards: Varies.
Deadline: May 30.
How to apply: Applications are available online. An application form and an official transcript are required.
Exclusive: Visit www.UltimateScholarshipBook.com and enter code NA22412 for updates on this award.

(225) • Pentagon Assistance Fund

Navy-Marine Corps Relief Society
875 North Randolph Street Suite 225
Arlington, VA 22203
Phone: 703-696-4960
Fax: 703-696-0144
Email: education@hq.nmcrs.org

http://www.nmcrs.org
Purpose: To provide financial assistance to spouses of military personnel who died as a result of the September 11, 2001 terrorist attack on the Pentagon.
Eligibility: Applicants must be spouses of deceased victims of the 9/11/2001 terrorist attack on the Pentagon who have not remarried. They must be pursuing an undergraduate degree and demonstrate financial need. They must have a Dependent's Uniformed Services Identification and Privilege Card and maintain a GPA of 2.0 or higher. They must also be enrolled or accepted to an eligible institution of higher learning.
Target applicants: High school students. College students. Adult students.
Amount: Varies.
Number of awards: Varies.
Deadline: March 1 (children) and two months prior to start of school (unmarried spouses).
How to apply: Applications are available online.
Exclusive: Visit www.UltimateScholarshipBook.com and enter code NA22512 for updates on this award.

(226) • Phoenix Scholarship Program

Phoenix Scholarship Program
159 Concord Avenue
Suite 1C
Cambridge, MA 02138
Email: phoenixawards@gmail.com
Purpose: To provide financial assistance to deserving high school seniors who plan to seek higher education.
Eligibility: Applicants must be U.S. high school seniors or they must have graduated within 13 months prior to the application deadline. They must have a 2.75 or higher GPA and have already taken the SAT or ACT. They must be in good standing with their high school, possess good moral character and plan to enroll in an accredited college or university upon graduation.
Target applicants: High school students.
Minimum GPA: 2.75
Amount: Varies.
Number of awards: Up to 4.
Deadline: April 30.
How to apply: Applications are available via email.
Exclusive: Visit www.UltimateScholarshipBook.com and enter code PH22612 for updates on this award.

(227) • Principal's Leadership Award

Herff Jones
c/o National Association of Secondary School Principals
1904 Association Drive
Reston, VA 20191
Phone: 800-253-7746
Email: carrollw@principals.org.
http://www.principals.org/awards/
Purpose: To recognize students for their leadership.
Eligibility: Applicants must be seniors and nominated by their high school principal. Each principal can nominate one student leader from the senior class. Application packets are mailed each fall to every secondary school.
Target applicants: High school students.
Amount: $1,000-$12,000.
Number of awards: 100.
Deadline: December 3.
How to apply: Nomination forms are available online.
Exclusive: Visit www.UltimateScholarshipBook.com and enter code HE22712 for updates on this award.

(228) • Prudential Spirit of Community Awards

Prudential Spirit of Community Awards
Prudential Financial Inc.
751 Broad Street, 16th Floor
Newark, NJ 07102
Phone: 877-525-8491
Email: spirit@prudential.com
http://spirit.prudential.com
Purpose: To recognize students for their self-initiated community service.
Eligibility: Applicants must be a student in grades 5-12 and a legal resident one of the 50 states of the U.S. or District of Columbia and engaged in a volunteer activity that occurred at least in part after the year prior to date of application.
Target applicants: Junior high students or younger. High school students.
Amount: $1,000-$5,000.
Number of awards: 102.
Deadline: November 2.
How to apply: Applications are available online.
Exclusive: Visit www.UltimateScholarshipBook.com and enter code PR22812 for updates on this award.

(229) • Return 2 College Scholarship

R2C Scholarship Program
Belmont, CA 94002
http://www.return2college.com/scholarship.cfm
Purpose: To provide financial assistance for college and adult students with college or graduate school expenses.
Eligibility: Applicants must be college or adult students currently attending or planning to attend a two-year or four-year college or graduate school within the next 12 months. Students must be 17 years or older and U.S. citizens or permanent residents. The award may be used for full- or part-time study at either on-campus or online schools.
Target applicants: High school students. College students. Adult students.
Amount: $1,500.
Number of awards: Varies.
Deadline: March 31.
How to apply: Applications are available online.
Exclusive: Visit www.UltimateScholarshipBook.com and enter code R222912 for updates on this award.

(230) • Rhodes Scholar

Rhodes Scholarship Trust
Attn.: Elliot F. Gerson
8229 Boone Boulevard, Suite 240
Vienna, VA 22182
Email: amsec@rhodesscholar.org
http://www.rhodesscholar.org
Purpose: To recognize qualities of young people that will contribute to the "world's fight."
Eligibility: Applicants must be U.S. citizens between the ages of 18 and 24 and have a bachelor's degree at the time of the award. The awards provides for two to three years of study at the University of Oxford

including educational costs and other expenses. Selection is extremely competitive and is based on literary and scholastic achievements, athletic achievement and character.
Target applicants: College students.
Amount: Full Tuition plus stipend.
Number of awards: 32.
Deadline: October 4.
How to apply: Applications are available online.
Exclusive: Visit www.UltimateScholarshipBook.com and enter code RH23012 for updates on this award.

(231) • Ronald McDonald House Charities Scholarship Program

Ronald McDonald House Charities
One Kroc Drive
Oak Brook, IL 60523
Phone: 630-623-7048
Email: scholarships@us.mcd.com
http://www.rmhc.org
Purpose: To help high school seniors attend college.
Eligibility: Applicants must be high school seniors less than 21 years of age who are eligible to attend a two- or four-year institution of higher learning full-time. They must be U.S. residents who live in a participating Ronald McDonald House Charities chapter's geographic area. A list of chapters is on the website.
Target applicants: High school students.
Amount: $1,000.
Number of awards: Varies.
Deadline: January 28.
How to apply: Applications are available online. An application form, transcript, personal statement, letter of recommendation and parents' tax forms are required.
Exclusive: Visit www.UltimateScholarshipBook.com and enter code RO23112 for updates on this award.

(232) • Ronald Reagan College Leaders Scholarship Program

Phillips Foundation
7811 Montrose Road
Suite 100
Potomac, MD 20854
Phone: 301-340-7788
Email: jhollingsworth@phillips.com
http://www.thephillipsfoundation.org
Purpose: To recognize students who demonstrate leadership on behalf of freedom, American values and constitutional principles.
Eligibility: Applicants must be enrolled full-time at any accredited, four-year degree-granting institution in the U.S. or its territories. Applicants may apply for a Ronald Reagan College Leaders Scholarship Program grant during their sophomore or junior year in high school. Selection is based on merit and financial need.
Target applicants: High school students.
Amount: $1,000-7,500.
Number of awards: Varies.
Scholarship may be renewable.
Deadline: January 15.
How to apply: Applications are available online.
Exclusive: Visit www.UltimateScholarshipBook.com and enter code PH23212 for updates on this award.

(233) • Ruth Stanton Community Grant

Action Volunteering
Ruth Stanton Community Grant
P.O. Box 1013
Calimesa, CA 92320
Email: painter5@ipsemail.com
http://www.actionvolunteering.com
Purpose: To aid those who are interested in furthering their community service activities.
Eligibility: Applicants must be active in community service work. Selection is based on the overall strength of the application.
Target applicants: High school students. College students. Graduate school students. Adult students.
Amount: $500.
Number of awards: Varies.
Deadline: November 1.
How to apply: Application instructions are available online. An essay and letter of recommendation are required.
Exclusive: Visit www.UltimateScholarshipBook.com and enter code AC23312 for updates on this award.

(234) • Salvatore J. Natoli Dissertation Award in Geographic Education

National Council for Geographic Education
Jacksonville State University
206-A Martin Hall
700 Pelham Road North
Jacksonville, AL 36265-1602
Phone: 256-782-5293
Fax: 256-782-5336
Email: ncge@jsu.edu
http://www.ncge.org
Purpose: To recognize outstanding doctoral research.
Eligibility: This award is not restricted to dissertations in geography. Applicants must have received the doctoral degree within the previous two years and are expected to present their research at the annual meeting. Applicants must submit papers drawn from the dissertation, plus abstracts; cover letters that state the title of the dissertation, date of the degree, major professor's name and institution and applicant's social security number; verification letters from the major professors and applications for program participation for the NCGE Annual Meeting. The meeting registration fee will be refunded to finalists and winners after the meeting. Note: We do not recommend applying to scholarships that charge application fees. However, some scholarships of this type charge fees and are included for completeness.
Target applicants: Graduate school students. Adult students.
Amount: $500.
Number of awards: 2.
Deadline: March 15.
How to apply: Application materials are stated online.
Exclusive: Visit www.UltimateScholarshipBook.com and enter code NA23412 for updates on this award.

(235) • Sam Walton Community Scholarship

Wal-Mart Foundation
c/o ACT Scholarship and Recognition Services
Email: https://www.act.org/walmart/contact.html
http://www.walmartfoundation.org
Purpose: To support local communities and to help students achieve their educational dreams.

Eligibility: Applicants must be high school seniors. Selection is based on academic record, test scores, community and extracurricular involvement, work experience and financial need. Each Wal-Mart Store and Sam's Club awards up to two scholarships. Wal-Mart employees and the children of employees are not eligible.
Target applicants: High school students.
Amount: $3,000.
Number of awards: Varies.
Deadline: Varies.
How to apply: Applications are only available at your local Wal-Mart Store or Sam's Club during the first week of December.
Exclusive: Visit www.UltimateScholarshipBook.com and enter code WA23512 for updates on this award.

(236) • Samuel Huntington Public Service Award

National Grid
25 Research Drive
Westborough, MA 01582
Phone: 508-389-2000
http://www.nationalgridus.com
Purpose: To assist students who wish to perform one year of humanitarian service immediately upon graduation.
Eligibility: Applicants must be graduating college seniors, and must intend to perform one year of public service in the U.S. or abroad. The service may be individual work or through charitable, religious, educational, governmental or other public service organizations.
Target applicants: College students. Adult students.
Amount: $10,000.
Number of awards: 1-2.
Deadline: January 18.
How to apply: Applications are available online.
Exclusive: Visit www.UltimateScholarshipBook.com and enter code NA23612 for updates on this award.

(237) • Scholar Athlete Milk Mustache of the Year Award (SAMMY)

National Fluid Milk Processor Promotion Board
Scholar Athlete Milk Mustache of Year
P.O. Box 9249
Medford, NY 11763
http://www.bodybymilk.com/
Purpose: To reward outstanding student athletes.
Eligibility: Applicants must be legal residents of the 48 contiguous United States or the District of Columbia, high school seniors and participate in a high school or club sport. Applicants must describe in 75 words or less how drinking milk has been a part of their life and training regimen.
Target applicants: High school students.
Amount: $7,500.
Number of awards: 25.
Deadline: March 4.
How to apply: Applications may be obtained online, and only applications submitted online will be accepted.
Exclusive: Visit www.UltimateScholarshipBook.com and enter code NA23712 for updates on this award.

(238) • Scholarship Drawing for $1,000

Edsouth
eCampusTours
P.O. Box 36014
Knoxville, TN 37930
Phone: 865-342-0670
Email: info@ecampustours.com
http://www.ecampustours.com
Purpose: To assist students in paying for college.
Eligibility: Eligible students include U.S. citizens, U.S. nationals and permanent residents or students enrolled in a U.S. institution of higher education. Winners must be enrolled in an eligible institution of higher education, as stipulated in the eligibility requirements, within one year of winning the award. Scholarship awards will be paid directly to the college.
Target applicants: High school students. College students. Graduate school students. Adult students.
Amount: $1,000.
Number of awards: 2.
Deadline: March 31.
How to apply: Applications are available online or by mail. Registration with eCampusTours is required.
Exclusive: Visit www.UltimateScholarshipBook.com and enter code ED23812 for updates on this award.

(239) • Scholarships for Military Children

Defense Commissary Agency
Attn: OC
1300 E Avenue
Fort Lee, VA 23801-1800
Phone: 804-734-8860
Email: info@militaryscholar.org
http://www.militaryscholar.org
Purpose: To provide educational opportunities for children of military personnel.
Eligibility: Applicants must be unmarried dependents under the age of 21 (23 if full-time students) of active duty, reserve, retired or deceased members of the military. They must be enrolled in the Defense Enrollment Eligibility Reporting System database. Applicants must be enrolled or plan to enroll in a full-time undergraduate degree-seeking program. Community or junior college students must be in a program that will allow transfer directly into a four-year program. Applicants also must not be accepted to a U.S. Military Academy or be the recipients of full scholarships at any accredited institution.
Target applicants: High school students. College students.
Minimum GPA: 3.0
Amount: $1,500.
Number of awards: Varies.
Deadline: February 22.
How to apply: Applications are available online or from military commissaries.
Exclusive: Visit www.UltimateScholarshipBook.com and enter code DE23912 for updates on this award.

(240) • Scholarships for Student Leaders

National Association for Campus Activities
13 Harbison Way
Columbia, SC 29212
Phone: 803-732-6222
Fax: 803-749-1047
Email: info@naca.org
http://www.naca.org
Purpose: The NACA foundation is committed to developing professionals in the field of campus activities.

Eligibility: Applicants must be current undergraduate students who hold a significant campus leadership position, have made significant contributions to their campus communities and have demonstrated leadership skills and abilities.
Target applicants: College students. Adult students.
Amount: Varies.
Number of awards: Varies.
Deadline: November 1.
How to apply: Applications are available online.
Exclusive: Visit www.UltimateScholarshipBook.com and enter code NA24012 for updates on this award.

---

(241) · Seabee Memorial Scholarship

Seabee Memorial Scholarship Association
P.O. Box 6574
Silver Spring, MD 20916
Phone: 301-570-2850
Email: smsa@erols.com
http://www.seabee.org
Purpose: To provide scholarships for the children of Seabees, both past and present, active, reserve or retired.
Eligibility: Applicants must be sons, daughters or step-children of Regular, Reserve, Retired or deceased officers or enlisted members who have served or are now serving with the Naval Construction Force or Naval Civil Engineer Corps, or who have served but have been honorably discharged. Scholarships are for bachelor's degrees.
Target applicants: High school students. College students. Adult students.
Amount: $1,500.
Number of awards: 100.
Deadline: April 15.
How to apply: Applications are available online or by written request.
Exclusive: Visit www.UltimateScholarshipBook.com and enter code SE24112 for updates on this award.

---

(242) · Second Chance Scholarship Contest

American Fire Sprinkler Association
12750 Merit Drive
Suite 350
Dallas, TX 75251
Phone: 214-349-5965
Fax: 214-343-8898
Email: acampbell@firesprinkler.org
http://www.afsascholarship.org
Purpose: To help U.S. students pay for higher education.
Eligibility: Applicants must be U.S. citizens or legal residents and be high school graduates or GED recipients. They must be enrolled at an institution of higher learning no later than the spring semester of the upcoming academic year. American Fire Sprinkler Association (AFSA) staff and board member relatives are ineligible, as are past contest winners. Selection is made by random drawing from the pool of contest entrants.
Target applicants: College students. Graduate school students. Adult students.
Amount: $1,000.
Number of awards: 5.
Deadline: August 25.
How to apply: Contest entrants must read an informational article on fire sprinklers before taking a ten-question multiple choice test on the material covered in the article. The number of correct responses on the test is equal to the number of entries that will be made in the entrant's name, giving each entrant up to 10 entries to the random drawing that will determine the winners of the contest.
Exclusive: Visit www.UltimateScholarshipBook.com and enter code AM24212 for updates on this award.

---

(243) · Sergeant Major Douglas R. Drum Memorial Scholarship Fund

American Military Retirees Association
5436 Peru Street
Suite 1
Plattsburgh, NY 12901
Phone: 800-424-2969
Fax: 518-324-5204
Email: info@amra1973.org
http://www.amra1973.org
Purpose: To provide funds for AMRA members, their spouses, dependent children and their grandchildren.
Eligibility: Applicants must be full-time students pursuing or planning to pursue an undergraduate degree at a two- or four-year accredited college or university.
Target applicants: High school students. College students. Adult students.
Amount: $1,000-$5,000.
Number of awards: 24.
Deadline: March 1.
How to apply: Applications are available online.
Exclusive: Visit www.UltimateScholarshipBook.com and enter code AM24312 for updates on this award.

---

(244) · Shepherd Scholarship

Ancient and Accepted Scottish Rite of Freemansonry Southern Jurisdiction
1733 16th Street NW
Washington, DC 20009-3103
Phone: 202-232-3579
Fax: 202-464-0487
http://www.srmason-sj.org
Purpose: To provide financial assistance to students pursuing degrees in fields associated with service to country.
Eligibility: Applicants must have accepted enrollment in a U.S. institution of higher learning. No Masonic affiliation is required. Up to four letters of recommendation will be considered. Selection is based on "dedication, ambition, academic preparation, financial need and promise of outstanding performance at the advanced level."
Target applicants: High school students. College students. Adult students.
Amount: $1,500.
Number of awards: Varies.
Scholarship may be renewable.
Deadline: April 1.
How to apply: Applications are available online. An application form, transcript and up to four letters of recommendation are required.
Exclusive: Visit www.UltimateScholarshipBook.com and enter code AN24412 for updates on this award.

---

(245) · Sheryl A. Horak Memorial Scholarship

Explorers Learning for Life
P.O. Box 152079
Irving, TX 75015
Phone: 972-580-2433

Fax: 972-580-2137
Email: pchestnu@lflmail.org
http://www.learningforlife.org/exploring
Purpose: To support students who are pursuing careers in law enforcement.
Eligibility: Students must be in their senior year of high school, and they must be members of a Law Enforcement Explorer post. Applicants must submit three letters of recommendation and an essay.
Target applicants: High school students.
Amount: $1,000.
Number of awards: Varies.
Deadline: March 31.
How to apply: Applications are available online.
Exclusive: Visit www.UltimateScholarshipBook.com and enter code EX24512 for updates on this award.

(246) · Siemens Awards for Advanced Placement

Siemens Foundation
170 Wood Avenue South
Iselin, NJ 08330
Phone: 877-822-5233
Fax: 732-603-5890
Email: foundation.us@siemens.com
http://www.siemens-foundation.org
Purpose: To aid outstanding Advanced Placement students.
Eligibility: Students do not apply for this award directly but are instead chosen by the College Board based on Advanced Placement (AP) test scores. Award winners will have the greatest number of scores of 5 on eight Advanced Placement science and math exams. Selection is based on AP exam scores.
Target applicants: High school students.
Amount: Up to $5,000.
Number of awards: Up to 102.
Deadline: Varies.
How to apply: Applications are not required for this award. Winners are chosen automatically by the College Board.
Exclusive: Visit www.UltimateScholarshipBook.com and enter code SI24612 for updates on this award.

(247) · Simon Youth Foundation Community Scholarship

Simon Youth Foundation
225 W. Washington Street
Indianapolis, IN 46204
Phone: 800-509-3676
Fax: 317-263-2371
Email: syf@simon.com
http://www.syf.org
Purpose: To assist promising students who live in communities with Simon properties.
Eligibility: Applicants must be high school seniors who plan to attend an accredited two- or four-year college, university or technical/vocational school full-time. Scholarships are awarded without regard to race, color, creed, religion, gender, disability or national origin, and recipients are selected on the basis of financial need, academic record, potential to succeed, participation in school and community activities, honors, work experience, a statement of career and educational goals and an outside appraisal. Awards are given at every Simon mall in the U.S.
Target applicants: High school students.
Amount: $1,400-$2,500.
Number of awards: Varies.
Deadline: Varies.
How to apply: Applications are available online.
Exclusive: Visit www.UltimateScholarshipBook.com and enter code SI24712 for updates on this award.

(248) · Skateboard Scholarship

Patrick Kerr Skateboard Scholarship
P.O. Box 2054
Jenkintown, PA 19046
Fax: 215-663-5897
Email: info@skateboardscholarship.org
http://www.skateboardscholarship.org
Purpose: To provide scholarships for skateboarders.
Eligibility: Applicants must be skateboarders who are high school seniors with at least a 2.5 GPA. They must be U.S. citizens and be planning to enroll full-time at a post-secondary school. Applicants must submit an essay on how skateboarding has influenced their lives, two letters of recommendation and a high school transcript. Special consideration will be given to students who are involved in skateboarding activism. Skateboarding skill will not be considered in awarding the scholarship.
Target applicants: High school students.
Minimum GPA: 2.5
Amount: $1,000-$5,000.
Number of awards: 4.
Deadline: April 20.
How to apply: Applications are available online.
Exclusive: Visit www.UltimateScholarshipBook.com and enter code PA24812 for updates on this award.

(249) · SOAR Scholarship

Students Overcoming Adversity Responsibly (SOAR)
P.O. Box 481030
Charlotte, NC 28269
Email: emergedevelopment2@yahoo.com
http://www.adriannemccauley.com/scholarship.html
Purpose: To support students who have overcome adversity.
Eligibility: Applicants must be U.S. citizens who are high school seniors who will graduate in the year of application. They must write a 750- to 2,000-word essay on a topic chosen by the organization. Selection is based solely on the applicant's essay.
Target applicants: High school students.
Amount: $1,000.
Number of awards: 1.
Deadline: April 15.
How to apply: Applications are available online. An application form and essay are required.
Exclusive: Visit www.UltimateScholarshipBook.com and enter code ST24912 for updates on this award.

(250) · Sons of Union Veterans of the Civil War Scholarships

Sons of Union Veterans of the Civil War
John R. Ertell, Chair
654 Grace Avenue
Spring City, PA 19475
Phone: 610-948-1278
Email: jertell@verizon.net
http://www.suvcw.org/
Purpose: To assist students connected with the Sons of Union Veterans of the Civil War in obtaining higher education.

Eligibility: Male applicants must be members or associates of the Sons of Union Veterans of the Civil War. Female applicants must be daughters or granddaughters of members or associates and must be current members of the Women's Relief Corps, Ladies of the Grand Army of the Republic, Daughters of Union Veterans of the Civil War 1861-1865 or Auxiliary to the Sons of Union Veterans of the Civil War. All applicants must rank in the upper quarter of their graduating class, have a record of school and community service and provide three letters of recommendation.
Target applicants: High school students. College students. Adult students.
Amount: $1,000.
Number of awards: 2.
Deadline: March 31.
How to apply: Applications are available online.
Exclusive: Visit www.UltimateScholarshipBook.com and enter code SO25012 for updates on this award.

---

(251) · Sportquest All-American Scholarships for Females

Sportquest All-American Program
P.O. Box 53433
Indianapolis, IN 46253-0433
Phone: 317-270-9495
Fax: 317-244-0495
Email: info@allamericanaward.org
http://www.allamericanaward.org
Purpose: To support Christian athletes.
Eligibility: Athletes must be one of the top three female Christian athletes in their class and be nominated by their schools. They must have a GPA of 3.0 or higher and be current high school sophomores, juniors or seniors. They must exert a positive influence upon their schools and communities.
Target applicants: High school students.
Minimum GPA: 3.0
Amount: Up to $500 plus travel expenses.
Number of awards: 6.
Deadline: February 18.
How to apply: Applications are available online.
Exclusive: Visit www.UltimateScholarshipBook.com and enter code SP25112 for updates on this award.

---

(252) · Sportquest All-American Scholarships for Males

Sportquest All-American Program
P.O. Box 53433
Indianapolis, IN 46253-0433
Phone: 317-270-9495
Fax: 317-244-0495
Email: info@allamericanaward.org
http://www.allamericanaward.org
Purpose: To support Christian athletes.
Eligibility: Applicants must be high school sophomores, juniors or seniors. They must be one of the top three male Christian athletes in their class and be nominated by their schools. A GPA of 3.0 or better is required. Applicants must exert a positive influence upon their schools and communities.
Target applicants: High school students.
Minimum GPA: 3.0
Amount: Up to $500 plus travel expenses.
Number of awards: 6.
Deadline: February 18.
How to apply: Applications are available online.
Exclusive: Visit www.UltimateScholarshipBook.com and enter code SP25212 for updates on this award.

---

(253) · Standout Student College Scholarship

College Peas LLC
1210 Forest Avenue
Highland Park, IL 60035
Phone: 847-681-0698
http://www.collegepeas.com
Purpose: To aid college-bound high school students who have interests that make them stand out from their peers.
Eligibility: Applicants must be current high school students, have a GPA of 2.0 or higher on a four-point scale and have plans to enroll full-time at a four-year postsecondary institution after graduation. They must submit an essay describing a unique interest or skill that teens typically do not have.
Target applicants: High school students.
Minimum GPA: 2.0
Amount: $500.
Number of awards: Varies.
Deadline: October 31.
How to apply: Applications are available online. An application form and essay are required.
Exclusive: Visit www.UltimateScholarshipBook.com and enter code CO25312 for updates on this award.

---

(254) · Stokes Educational Scholarship Program

National Security Agency (NSA)
9800 Savage Road, Suite 6779
Ft. George G. Meade, MD 20755-6779
Phone: 410-854-4725
https://www.cia.gov/index.html
Purpose: To recruit those with skills useful to the NSA, especially minority high school students.
Eligibility: Students must be seniors at the time of application, be U.S. citizens, have a 3.0 GPA, have a minimum ACT score of 25 or a minimum SAT score of 1600 and demonstrate leadership skills. Applicants must be planning to major in one of the following fields: computer science, electrical or computer engineering, languages, mathematics or intelligence analysis.
Target applicants: High school students.
Minimum GPA: 3.0
Amount: Tuition, fees, salary and summer employment expenses.
Number of awards: Varies.
Scholarship may be renewable.
Deadline: November 30.
How to apply: Applications are available online.
Exclusive: Visit www.UltimateScholarshipBook.com and enter code NA25412 for updates on this award.

---

(255) · Stuck at Prom Scholarship

Henkel Consumer Adhesives
32150 Just Imagine Drive
Avon, OH 44011-1355
http://www.stuckatprom.com
Purpose: To reward students for their creativity with duct tape.
Eligibility: Applicants must attend a high school prom as a couple in the spring wearing the most original attire that they make from duct

tape. Both members of the couple do not have to attend the same school. Photographs of past winners are available on the website.
Target applicants: High school students.
Amount: $500-$3,000.
Number of awards: Varies.
Deadline: June 7.
How to apply: Applications are available online. Contact information, release form and prom picture are required
Exclusive: Visit www.UltimateScholarshipBook.com and enter code HE25512 for updates on this award.

(256) · Student Activist Awards

Freedom from Religion Foundation
P.O. Box 750
Madison, WI 53701
Phone: 608-256-5800
Email: info@ffrf.org
http://www.ffrf.org
Purpose: To assist high school and college student activists.
Eligibility: Selection is based on activism for free thought or separation of church and state.
Target applicants: High school students. College students. Adult students.
Amount: $1,000.
Number of awards: Varies.
Deadline: Varies.
How to apply: Contact the organization for more information.
Exclusive: Visit www.UltimateScholarshipBook.com and enter code FR25612 for updates on this award.

(257) · Student Paper Competition

American Criminal Justice Association
P.O. Box 601047
Sacramento, CA 95860-1047
Phone: 916-484-6553
Fax: 916-488-2227
Email: acjalae@aol.com
http://www.acjalae.org
Purpose: To encourage scholarship in criminal justice students.
Eligibility: Applicants must be student members (undergraduate or graduate) of the American Criminal Justice Association-Lambda Alpha Epsilon and submit an original paper on criminology, law enforcement, juvenile justice, courts, corrections, prevention, planning and evaluation or career development and education in the field of criminal justice. Students may apply for membership along with their paper submission. Applicants should submit applications and three copies of the paper.
Target applicants: College students. Graduate school students. Adult students.
Amount: $50-$150.
Number of awards: 9.
Deadline: January 31.
How to apply: Applications are available online and by written request.
Exclusive: Visit www.UltimateScholarshipBook.com and enter code AM25712 for updates on this award.

(258) · Study Abroad Grants

Honor Society of Phi Kappa Phi
7576 Goodwood Boulevard
Baton Rouge, LA 70806
Phone: 800-804-9880
Fax: 225-388-4900
Email: awards@phikappaphi.org
http://www.phikappaphi.org
Purpose: To provide scholarships for undergraduate students who will study abroad.
Eligibility: Applicants do not have to be members of Phi Kappa Phi but must attend an institution with a Phi Kappa Phi chapter, have between 30 and 90 credit hours and have at least two semesters remaining at their home institution upon return. Students must have been accepted into a study abroad program that demonstrates their academic preparation, career choice and the welfare of others. They must have a GPA of 3.5 or higher.
Target applicants: College students. Adult students.
Minimum GPA: 3.5
Amount: $1,000.
Number of awards: 45.
Deadline: April 1.
How to apply: Applications are available online. An application form, personal statement, transcript, letter of acceptance and two letters of recommendation are required.
Exclusive: Visit www.UltimateScholarshipBook.com and enter code HO25812 for updates on this award.

(259) · Summer Graduate Research Fellowships

Institute for Humane Studies at George Mason University
3301 N. Fairfax Drive
Suite 440
Arlington, VA 22201
Phone: 800-697-8799
Fax: 703-993-4890
Email: ihs@gmu.edu
http://www.theihs.org
Purpose: To support graduate students who are interested in scholarly research in the classical liberal tradition.
Eligibility: Applicants must be graduate students in areas related to the classical liberal tradition and should be focusing on a discrete writing project. Selection is based on resume, GRE or LSAT scores and graduate transcripts, writing sample and research proposal and bibliography for thesis chapter or publishable paper.
Target applicants: Graduate school students. Adult students.
Amount: $3,000 + travel and housing allowance.
Number of awards: Varies.
Deadline: Varies.
How to apply: Applications are available online.
Exclusive: Visit www.UltimateScholarshipBook.com and enter code IN25912 for updates on this award.

(260) · SuperCollege Scholarship

SuperCollege.com
Scholarship Dept. 673
3286 Oak Court
Belmont, CA 94002
Email: supercollege@supercollege.com
http://www.supercollege.com/scholarship/
Purpose: SuperCollege donates a percentage of the proceeds from the sales of its books to award scholarships to high school, college, graduate and adult students.
Eligibility: Applicants must be high school seniors, college undergraduates, graduate students or adult students residing in the U.S. and attending or planning to attend any accredited college or university within the next 12 months. The scholarship may be used to

pay for tuition, books, room and board, computers or any education-related expenses.
Target applicants: High school students. College students. Adult students.
Amount: $1,500.
Number of awards: 1.
Deadline: March 31.
How to apply: Applications are available online.
Exclusive: Visit www.UltimateScholarshipBook.com and enter code SU26012 for updates on this award.

(261) • Tailhook Educational Foundation Scholarship

Tailhook Association
The Tailhook Educational Foundation
9696 Businesspark Avenue
San Diego, CA 92131-1643
Phone: 800-269-8267
Email: thookassn@aol.com
http://www.tailhook.org
Purpose: To assist the members of and the children of the members of the United States Navy carrier aviation.
Eligibility: Applicants must be high school graduates who are accepted at an undergraduate institution and are the natural or adopted children of current or former Naval Aviators, Naval Flight Officers or Naval Aircrewmen. Applicants may also be individuals or children of individuals who are serving or have served on board a U.S. Navy Aircraft Carrier in the ship's company or the air wing. Educational and extracurricular achievements, merit and citizenship will be considered.
Target applicants: High school students. College students. Adult students.
Amount: Varies.
Number of awards: Varies.
Deadline: March 16.
How to apply: Applications are available online.
Exclusive: Visit www.UltimateScholarshipBook.com and enter code TA26112 for updates on this award.

(262) • Talbots Scholarship Foundation

Talbots
Scholarship Management Services, Scholarship America
One Scholarship Way
P.O. Box 297
Saint Peter, MN 56082
Phone: 507-931-1682
http://www.talbots.com/scholarship
Purpose: To provide scholarships for women returning to college.
Eligibility: Applicants must be female U.S. residents who have earned their high school diploma or GED at least 10 years ago and who are now enrolled or planning to attend undergraduate study at a two- or four-year college or university or vocational-technical school. The deadline is January 2 or when the first 1,000 applications are received, whichever is earlier.
Target applicants: College students. Adult students.
Amount: $15,000-$30,000.
Number of awards: 11.
Deadline: January.
How to apply: Applications are available online.
Exclusive: Visit www.UltimateScholarshipBook.com and enter code TA26212 for updates on this award.

(263) • Telluride Association Summer Programs

Telluride Association
217 West Avenue
Ithaca, NY 14850
Phone: 607-273-5011
Fax: 607-272-2667
Email: telluride@cornell.edu
http://www.tellurideassociation.org
Purpose: Summer program to provide high school students with a college-level, intellectually enriching experience.
Eligibility: Applicants must be high school juniors. The association seeks applicants from a variety of socio-economic backgrounds and provides for their tuition and room and board during summer programs in New York, Texas and Michigan. Students are invited to apply either by receiving a score on the PSAT/NMSQT that is usually in the top 1 percent or by nomination by a teacher or counselor.
Target applicants: High school students.
Amount: Summer program tuition.
Number of awards: 64.
Deadline: January 24.
How to apply: Applications are sent to nominated students.
Exclusive: Visit www.UltimateScholarshipBook.com and enter code TE26312 for updates on this award.

(264) • The Lowe's Scholarship

Lowe's Company
1000 Lowe's Boulevard
Mooresville, NC 28117
Phone: 800-44-LOWES
http://www.lowes.com
Purpose: To help young people in the communities where Lowe's does business to get a strong educational foundation.
Eligibility: Applicants must be high school seniors who will enroll in an accredited two- or four-year college or university in the United States. Leadership ability, community involvement and academic achievement are considered when making the selection for the scholarships.
Target applicants: High school students.
Amount: $2,500.
Number of awards: 140.
Scholarship may be renewable.
Deadline: February 28.
How to apply: Applications are available online.
Exclusive: Visit www.UltimateScholarshipBook.com and enter code LO26412 for updates on this award.

(265) • Truman Scholar

Truman Scholarship Foundation
712 Jackson Place NW
Washington, DC 20006
Phone: 202-395-4831
Fax: 202-395-6995
Email: office@truman.gov
http://www.truman.gov
Purpose: To provide college junior leaders who plan to pursue careers in government, non-profits, education or other public service with financial support for graduate study and leadership training.
Eligibility: Applicants must be juniors, attending an accredited U.S. college or university and be nominated by the institution. Students may not apply directly. Applicants must be U.S. citizens or U.S. nationals, complete an application and write a policy recommendation.

Target applicants: College students. Adult students.
Amount: $30,000.
Number of awards: 60-65.
Deadline: February 1.
How to apply: See your school's Truman Faculty Representative or contact the foundation.
Exclusive: Visit www.UltimateScholarshipBook.com and enter code TR26512 for updates on this award.

(266) · Tweeddale Scholarship

U.S. Navy Naval Reserve Officers Training Corps (NROTC)
Naval Service Training Command Officer Development
NAS Pensacola
250 Dallas Street, Suite A
Pensacola, FL 32508
Phone: 800-628-7682
Fax: 850-452-2486
Email: pnsc_nrotc.scholarship@navy.mil
https://www.nrotc.navy.mil
Purpose: To aid undergraduate chemistry, computer science, engineering, mathematics and physics majors who wish to enter the Naval Reserve Officers Training Corps (NROTC).
Eligibility: Applicants must have a GPA that is above the peer mean GPA or above 3.0 (whichever is higher), have a C average or better in all courses taken and have completed at least one but no more than four academic terms. They must be interested in entering the Naval Reserve Officers Training Corps (NROTC). Selection is based on the overall strength of the application.
Target applicants: College students. Adult students.
Minimum GPA: 3.0
Amount: Varies.
Number of awards: Varies.
Scholarship may be renewable.
Deadline: Varies.
How to apply: Applications are available by request. An application form and supporting materials are required.
Exclusive: Visit www.UltimateScholarshipBook.com and enter code U.26612 for updates on this award.

(267) · U.S. Bank Internet Scholarship Program

U.S. Bank
U.S. Bancorp Center
800 Nicollet Mall
Minneapolis, MN 55402
Phone: 800-242-1200
http://www.usbank.com/cgi_w/cfm/studentloans/marketing.cfm
Purpose: To support graduating high school seniors who plan to attend college.
Eligibility: Applicants must be high school seniors who plan to attend full-time an accredited two- or four-year college and be U.S. citizens or permanent residents. Recipients are selected through a random drawing.
Target applicants: High school students.
Amount: $1,000.
Number of awards: Up to 30.
Deadline: March 31.
How to apply: Applications are only available online.
Exclusive: Visit www.UltimateScholarshipBook.com and enter code U.26712 for updates on this award.

(268) · U.S. JCI Senate Scholarship Grants

U.S. JCI Senate
106 Wedgewood Drive
Carrollton, GA 30117
Email: tom@smipc.net
http://www.usjcisenate.org
Purpose: To support high school students who wish to further their education.
Eligibility: Applicants must be high school seniors and U.S. citizens who are graduating from a U.S. accredited high school or state approved home school or GED program. Winners must attend college full-time to receive funds. Applications are judged at the state level.
Target applicants: High school students.
Amount: $1,000.
Number of awards: Varies.
Deadline: Varies.
How to apply: Applications are available from your school's guidance office.
Exclusive: Visit www.UltimateScholarshipBook.com and enter code U.26812 for updates on this award.

(269) · UDT-SEAL Scholarship

Naval Special Warfare Foundation
P.O. Box 5965
Virginia Beach, VA 23471
Phone: 757-363-7490
Email: info@nswfoundation.org
http://www.nswfoundation.org
Purpose: To assist the dependents of UDT-SEAL Association members.
Eligibility: Students must be single dependents of a UDT-SEAL Association member who has served in or is serving in the U.S. Armed Forces and the Naval Special Warfare community. Selection is based on academic achievement, a written essay and extracurricular involvement.
Target applicants: High school students. College students.
Amount: Varies.
Number of awards: Varies.
Deadline: First quarter of the year.
How to apply: Applications are available by contacting the NWSF.
Exclusive: Visit www.UltimateScholarshipBook.com and enter code NA26912 for updates on this award.

(270) · Undergraduate Transfer Scholarship

Jack Kent Cooke Foundation Undergraduate Transfer Scholarship
44325 Woodridge Parkway
Lansdowne, VA 20176
Phone: 800-498-6478
Fax: 319-337-1204
Email: jkc-u@act.org
http://www.jkcf.org
Purpose: To help community college students attend four-year universities.
Eligibility: Applicants must be students or recent alumni from accredited U.S. community colleges or two-year institutions who plan to pursue bachelor's degrees at four-year institutions. Applicants may not apply directly to the foundation but must be nominated by the Jack Kent Cooke Foundation faculty representatives at their institutions. The award is based on academic merit and unmet financial need. A GPA of 3.5 or higher is required.
Target applicants: College students. Adult students.
Minimum GPA: 3.5

Amount: Up to $30,000.
Number of awards: About 50.
Scholarship may be renewable.
Deadline: January 26.
How to apply: Applications are available online and must be mailed to Jack Kent Cooke Undergraduate Transfer Scholarship Program, 301 ACT Drive, PO Box 4030 Iowa City, IA 52243-4030.
Exclusive: Visit www.UltimateScholarshipBook.com and enter code JA27012 for updates on this award.

(271) • United Daughters of the Confederacy Scholarship

United Daughters of the Confederacy
328 North Boulevard
Richmond, VA 23220
Phone: 804-355-1636
Fax: 804-353-1396
Email: hqudc@rcn.com
http://www.hqudc.org
Purpose: To support the descendants of Confederates.
Eligibility: Applicants must be lineal descendants of Confederates or other eligible descendants.
Target applicants: College students. Graduate school students. Adult students.
Minimum GPA: 3.0
Amount: Varies.
Number of awards: Varies.
Scholarship may be renewable.
Deadline: June 15.
How to apply: Contact any Division Second Vice President as listed on the website.
Exclusive: Visit www.UltimateScholarshipBook.com and enter code UN27112 for updates on this award.

(272) • University Language Services College Scholarship

University Language Services
15 Maiden Lane
Suite 300
New York, NY 10038
Phone: 800-419-4601
Fax: 866-662-8048
Email: service@universitylanguage.com
http://www.universitylanguage.com
Purpose: To aid college-bound high school students.
Eligibility: Applicants must be current high school students at an accredited high school. They must submit a photo that they took while visiting a college campus along with a description of why the photo represents college life. Selection is based on the originality and creativity of the photo.
Target applicants: High school students.
Amount: $100-$500.
Number of awards: 3.
Deadline: Varies.
How to apply: Application instructions are available online. A photo and description are required.
Exclusive: Visit www.UltimateScholarshipBook.com and enter code UN27212 for updates on this award.

(273) • University Language Services Scholarship

University Language Services
15 Maiden Lane
Suite 300
New York, NY 10038
Phone: 800-419-4601
Fax: 866-662-8048
Email: service@universitylanguage.com
http://www.universitylanguage.com
Purpose: To support students who have studied outside the United States.
Eligibility: Applicants must be currently enrolled or planning to enroll in an accredited United States institution of higher learning and must have studied outside the United States for at least one semester and be legal U.S. residents. Students must submit a photo taken while studying abroad.
Target applicants: High school students. College students. Adult students.
Amount: $100-$500.
Number of awards: 3.
Deadline: September 24.
How to apply: Applications are available online. An online application, photo and 200-word essay are required.
Exclusive: Visit www.UltimateScholarshipBook.com and enter code UN27312 for updates on this award.

(274) • USA Funds Access to Education Scholarships

USA Funds
Scholarship Management Services, CSFA
1505 Riverview Road
St. Peter, MN 56082
Phone: 888-537-4180
Email: scholarship@usafunds.org
http://www.usafunds.org
Purpose: To assist students in achieving their higher education goals.
Eligibility: This is a need-based scholarship program with aid for full-time and half-time students. Applicants must be high school seniors or other individuals who plan to enroll or are enrolled in full- or half-time undergraduate or graduate coursework at an accredited two- or four-year college, university or vocational or technical school. Students must be U.S. citizens or eligible noncitizens and must have an adjusted gross family income of $35,000 or less. Selection is based on academic performance, leadership, activities, work experience and career and educational goals.
Target applicants: High school students. College students. Graduate school students. Adult students.
Amount: $1,500.
Number of awards: Varies.
Deadline: February 15.
How to apply: Applications are available online.
Exclusive: Visit www.UltimateScholarshipBook.com and enter code US27412 for updates on this award.

(275) • USBC Alberta E. Crowe Star of Tomorrow

United States Bowling Congress
5301 S. 76th Street
Greendale, WI 53129
Phone: 800-514-2695 x3168
Email: smart@bowl.com
http://www.bowl.com

Purpose: To recognize star qualities in female students in high school or college who are competitive bowlers.
Eligibility: Applicants must be female high school seniors or college students 22 years of age or younger and USBC members who compete in certified events. They must hold an average of 175 or higher and must not have competed in professional tournaments except for Pro-AM's. They must also have a GPA of 2.5 or higher.
Target applicants: High school students. College students.
Minimum GPA: 2.5
Amount: $6,000.
Number of awards: 1.
Deadline: October 1.
How to apply: Applications are available online.
Exclusive: Visit www.UltimateScholarshipBook.com and enter code UN27512 for updates on this award.

(276) · USBC Annual Zeb Scholarship

United States Bowling Congress
5301 S. 76th Street
Greendale, WI 53129
Phone: 800-514-2695 x3168
Email: smart@bowl.com
http://www.bowl.com
Purpose: To reward USBC Youth members with high academic achievement who have participated in community service.
Eligibility: Applicants must be high school juniors or seniors who are USBC Youth members in good standing. They must have a GPA of 2.0 or higher and must not have competed in any professional bowling tournament except for Pro-Am's.
Target applicants: High school students.
Minimum GPA: 2.0
Amount: $2,500.
Number of awards: 1.
Deadline: April 1.
How to apply: Applications are available online.
Exclusive: Visit www.UltimateScholarshipBook.com and enter code UN27612 for updates on this award.

(277) · USBC Chuck Hall Star of Tomorrow

United States Bowling Congress
5301 S. 76th Street
Greendale, WI 53129
Phone: 800-514-2695 x3168
Email: smart@bowl.com
http://www.bowl.com
Purpose: To recognize star qualities in male high school and college students who are competitive bowlers.
Eligibility: Applicants must be United States Bowling Congress members who compete in certified events, are age 22 or younger and are high school seniors or college students with a GPA of 2.5 or higher. They must also have a bowling average of 175 or greater and not have competed in a professional bowling tournament except for Pro-AM's.
Target applicants: High school students. College students.
Minimum GPA: 2.5
Amount: $6,000.
Number of awards: 1.
Scholarship may be renewable.
Deadline: October 1.
How to apply: Applications are available online.
Exclusive: Visit www.UltimateScholarshipBook.com and enter code UN27712 for updates on this award.

(278) · USBC Youth Ambassador of the Year

United States Bowling Congress
5301 S. 76th Street
Greendale, WI 53129
Phone: 800-514-2695 x3168
Email: smart@bowl.com
http://www.bowl.com
Purpose: To recognize contributions to the sport of bowling, academic achievement, and community service.
Eligibility: Students must be USBC Youth members who will be 18 years of age or older by August 1 of the year of their selection. They must also be high school seniors and be nominated by a USBC member. The award is given to one male and one female student each year.
Target applicants: High school students.
Amount: $1,500.
Number of awards: 2.
Deadline: November 1.
How to apply: Applications are available online.
Exclusive: Visit www.UltimateScholarshipBook.com and enter code UN27812 for updates on this award.

(279) · VADM E. P. Travers Scholarship and Loan Program

Navy-Marine Corps Relief Society
875 North Randolph Street Suite 225
Arlington, VA 22203
Phone: 703-696-4960
Fax: 703-696-0144
Email: education@hq.nmcrs.org
http://www.nmcrs.org
Purpose: To aid Navy and Marine Corps families.
Eligibility: Applicants must be enrolled or planning to enroll as full-time undergraduate students at an eligible post-secondary, technical or vocational institution. Applicants must also have a minimum 2.0 GPA and be unmarried dependent sons or daughters of active duty or retired Navy or Marine Corps service members or spouses of active duty Navy or Marine Corps service members.
Target applicants: College students. Adult students.
Minimum GPA: 2.0
Amount: $500-$3,000.
Number of awards: Varies.
Scholarship may be renewable.
Deadline: March 1.
How to apply: Applications are available online.
Exclusive: Visit www.UltimateScholarshipBook.com and enter code NA27912 for updates on this award.

(280) · Veterans Caucus Scholarship

Veterans Caucus of the American Academy of Physician Assistants
Email: shanley@veteranscaucus.org
http://www.veteranscaucus.org
Purpose: To aid U.S. military veterans who are enrolled in a physician assistant training program.
Eligibility: Applicants must be U.S. military veterans. They must be enrolled in an accredited physician assistant (PA) training program. Selection is based on the overall strength of the application.
Target applicants: College students. Graduate school students. Adult students.
Amount: Varies.
Number of awards: Varies.

Deadline: March 1.
How to apply: Applications are available online. An application form and personal statement are required.
Exclusive: Visit www.UltimateScholarshipBook.com and enter code VE28012 for updates on this award.

(281) · Violet Richardson Award

Soroptimist International of the Americas
1709 Spruce Street
Philadelphia, PA 19103
Phone: 215-893-9000
Fax: 215-893-5200
Email: siahq@soroptimist.org
http://www.soroptimist.org
Purpose: To recognize young women who contribute to the community through volunteer efforts.
Eligibility: Applicants must be young women between the ages of 14 and 17 who make outstanding contributions to volunteer efforts. Efforts that benefit women or girls are of particular interest. This award is administered by local, participating Soroptimist clubs and is not available in all communities.
Target applicants: High school students.
Amount: Up to $2,500.
Number of awards: Varies.
Deadline: Varies.
How to apply: Contact your local Soroptimist club.
Exclusive: Visit www.UltimateScholarshipBook.com and enter code SO28112 for updates on this award.

(282) · Voice of Democracy Audio Essay Contests

Veterans of Foreign Wars
406 W. 34th Street
Kansas City, MO 64111
Phone: 816-968-1117
Fax: 816-968-1149
Email: kharmer@vfw.org
http://www.vfw.org
Purpose: To encourage patriotism with students creating audio essays expressing their opinion on a patriotic theme.
Eligibility: Applicants must submit a three- to five-minute audio essay on tape or CD focused on a yearly theme. Students must be in the 9th to 12th grade in a public, private or parochial high school, home study program or overseas U.S. military school. Foreign exchange students are not eligible for the contest, and students who are age 20 or older also may not enter. Previous first place winners on the state level are ineligible.
Target applicants: High school students.
Amount: $1,000-$30,000.
Number of awards: Varies.
Deadline: November 1.
How to apply: Applications are available online but must be submitted to a local VFW post.
Exclusive: Visit www.UltimateScholarshipBook.com and enter code VE28212 for updates on this award.

(283) · VRG Scholarship

Vegetarian Resource Group
P.O. Box 1463
Baltimore, MD 21203
Phone: 410-366-8343
Fax: 410-366-8804
Email: vrg@vrg.org
http://www.vrg.org
Purpose: To award high school seniors who promote vegetarianism.
Eligibility: Applicants must be graduating U.S. high school students who have promoted vegetarianism in their schools or communities. Vegetarians do not eat meat, fish or fowl. The award is based on compassion, courage and commitment to promoting a "peaceful world through a vegetarian diet or lifestyle." Applicants should submit transcripts and at least three recommendations.
Target applicants: High school students.
Amount: $5,000.
Number of awards: 2.
Deadline: February 20.
How to apply: Applications are available online, by mail, by phone or by email. A typed document containing the application's information will be accepted.
Exclusive: Visit www.UltimateScholarshipBook.com and enter code VE28312 for updates on this award.

(284) · W. H. Howie McClennan Scholarship

International Association of Fire Fighters
1750 New York Avenue, NW
Washington, DC 20006
Phone: 202-737-8484
Fax: 202-737-8418
http://www.iaff.org
Purpose: To provide scholarships for the children of firefighters who died in the line of duty.
Eligibility: Applicants must be the children (natural or legally-adopted) of firefighters who died in the line of duty. Applicants' parent must have been a member in good standing of the International Association of Fire Fighters, AFL-CIO/CLC at time of death. Selection is based on financial need, academic record and promise.
Target applicants: High school students. College students. Adult students.
Amount: $2,500.
Number of awards: 1.
Scholarship may be renewable.
Deadline: February 1.
How to apply: Applications are available by written request.
Exclusive: Visit www.UltimateScholarshipBook.com and enter code IN28412 for updates on this award.

(285) · Watson Travel Fellowship

Thomas J. Watson Fellowship
11 Park Place
Suite 1503
New York, NY 10007
Phone: 212-245-8859
Fax: 212-245-8860
Email: tjw@watsonfellowship.org
http://www.watsonfellowship.org
Purpose: To award one-year grants for independent study and travel outside the U.S. to graduating college seniors.
Eligibility: Only graduating seniors from the participating colleges are eligible to apply. A list of these colleges is available online. Applicants must first be nominated by their college or university. An interview with a representative will follow. Recipients must graduate before the fellowship can begin.
Target applicants: College students. Adult students.
Amount: Up to $35,000.

Number of awards: 40.
Deadline: Second Wednesday in November.
How to apply: Interested students should contact their local Watson liaison to begin the application process. Once nominated, applicants must complete an online application form, project proposal and personal statement. A photo, transcripts and letters of recommendation are also required.
Exclusive: Visit www.UltimateScholarshipBook.com and enter code TH28512 for updates on this award.

---

(286) • Wendy's High School Heisman Award

Wendy's Restaurants
Phone: 800-205-6367
Email: wendys@act.org
http://www.wendyshighschoolheisman.com
Purpose: To recognize high school students who excel in academics, athletics and student leadership.
Eligibility: Applicants must be entering their high school senior year and participate in one of 27 officially sanctioned sports. Eligible students have a minimum 3.0 GPA. Selection is based on academic achievement, community service and athletic accomplishments.
Target applicants: High school students.
Minimum GPA: 3.0
Amount: Varies.
Number of awards: Varies.
Deadline: October 3.
How to apply: Application forms are available online.
Exclusive: Visit www.UltimateScholarshipBook.com and enter code WE28612 for updates on this award.

---

(287) • Where's FRANKIE the Diploma Frame? Scholarship Photo Contest

Church Hill Classics
594 Pepper Street
Monroe, CT 06468
Phone: 800-477-9005
Fax: 203-268-2468
Email: info@diplomaframe.com
http://www.framemyfuture.com
Purpose: To help college students pay for textbooks.
Eligibility: Applicants must be U.S. legal residents, be age 18 or older and be full-time college students or family members of full-time college students. They must submit a photo depicting the sponsor's mascot participating in a summer activity. Selection is based on the creativity and popularity of the photo.
Target applicants: College students. Graduate school students. Adult students.
Amount: $500.
Number of awards: 3.
Deadline: August 13.
How to apply: Entry forms are available online. An entry form and photo are required.
Exclusive: Visit www.UltimateScholarshipBook.com and enter code CH28712 for updates on this award.

---

(288) • WikiAnswers Scholarship Program

WikiAnswers Scholarship
c/o The Center for Scholarship Administration
P.O. Box 1465
Taylors, SC 29687
Phone: 864-268-3363
Email: allisonlee@bellsouth.net
http://wiki.answers.com/static/scholarship_program.html
Purpose: To support students who contribute to WikiAnswers.
Eligibility: Applicants must be high school seniors or undergraduate college students. They must be citizens of the U.S., Canada or the United Kingdom. Applicants must have answered at least fifty questions on the WikiAnswers website and plan to enroll in undergraduate classes the following fall.
Target applicants: High school students. College students. Adult students.
Amount: $1,000-$5,000.
Number of awards: 13.
Deadline: March 28.
How to apply: Applications are available online. An application form and list of questions answered are required.
Exclusive: Visit www.UltimateScholarshipBook.com and enter code WI28812 for updates on this award.

---

(289) • William L. Hastie Award

National Association of Blacks in Criminal Justice
North Carolina Central University
P.O. Box 19788
Durham, NC 27707
Phone: 919-683-1801
Fax: 919-683-1903
Email: office@nabcj.org
http://www.nabcj.org
Purpose: To award demonstrations of national leadership in criminal justice and the pursuit of policy change within the field.
Eligibility: The award honors the first African American appointed to the bench in 1937 by President Franklin Roosevelt. Nominator should be a member of NABCJ.
Target applicants: College students. Graduate school students. Adult students.
Amount: Varies.
Number of awards: 1.
Deadline: May 15.
How to apply: Nomination applications are available online.
Exclusive: Visit www.UltimateScholarshipBook.com and enter code NA28912 for updates on this award.

---

(290) • Win Free Tuition Giveaway

Next Step Magazine
86 W. Main Street
Victor, NY 14565
Phone: 800-771-3117
Email: webcopy@nextstepmag.com
http://www.nextstepmagazine.com/winfreetuition
Purpose: To support higher education.
Eligibility: Entrants must be legal residents of the U.S. and Canada (except for Puerto Rico or Quebec) who are age 14 or older. They must also be planning to enroll or currently enrolled in college by September 30 three years after the application date. This is an annual sweepstakes drawing for one year's tuition up to $10,000 and 11 monthly drawings for a $1,000 scholarship.
Target applicants: High school students. College students. Graduate school students. Adult students.
Amount: $1,000-$10,000.
Number of awards: 12.
Deadline: June 30.

How to apply: Applications are available online. Students may also apply by mailing a 3x5 postcard with their name, address, city, state, zip code, age, phone number and email address or using a reply card found in Next Step Magazine.
Exclusive: Visit www.UltimateScholarshipBook.com and enter code NE29012 for updates on this award.

(291) · Women Marines Association Scholarship Program

Women Marines Association
P.O. Box 8405
Falls Church, VA 22041-8405
Phone: 888-525-1943
Email: wma@womenmarines.org
http://www.womenmarines.org
Purpose: To aid Marines and their families.
Eligibility: Applicants must be sponsored by a Women Marines Association member. They must have served or be serving in the Marine Corps or Reserve, be a direct descendant, sibling or descendant of a sibling of a member of the Marines or have completed two years in a Marine ROTC program. A minimum GPA of 3.5 is required. High school students must have a minimum SAT score of 1100 or a minimum ACT score of 25.
Target applicants: High school students. College students. Adult students.
Minimum GPA: 3.5
Amount: $1,500.
Number of awards: Varies.
Deadline: March 31.
How to apply: Applications are available online. An application form, copy of sponsor's membership card, photo, three letters of recommendation, proof of Marine or ROTC status or relationship to a Marine and proof of draft registration (for males) are required.
Exclusive: Visit www.UltimateScholarshipBook.com and enter code WO29112 for updates on this award.

(292) · Women's Overseas Service League Scholarships for Women

Women's Overseas Service League
Scholarship Committee
P.O. Box 7124
Washington, DC 20044-7124
Email: kelsey@openix.com
http://www.wosl.org/scholarships.htm
Purpose: To assist women in the military and other public service careers.
Eligibility: Applicants must demonstrate a commitment to advancement in their careers and must have completed at least 12 semester or 18 quarter hours of study at an institution of higher learning and be working toward a degree. Students must agree to enroll for at least six semester or nine quarter hours each academic period. A GPA of 2.5 or higher is required.
Target applicants: College students. Adult students.
Minimum GPA: 2.5
Amount: Up to $1,000.
Number of awards: Varies.
Scholarship may be renewable.
Deadline: March 1.
How to apply: Applications are available online. An application form, statement of financial need, resume, three letters of reference, essay and transcript are required.
Exclusive: Visit www.UltimateScholarshipBook.com and enter code WO29212 for updates on this award.

(293) · Women's Western Golf Foundation Scholarship

Women's Western Golf Foundation
393 Ramsay Road
Deerfield, IL 60015
Phone: 608-274-0173
Email: cocomc2000@comcast.net
http://www.wwga.org
Purpose: To support female students who are involved in golf.
Eligibility: Applicants must be in their senior year of high school. Students must demonstrate academic excellence, good character and financial need. Recipients must maintain a 3.0 GPA for award renewal.
Target applicants: High school students.
Amount: $2,000.
Number of awards: Varies.
Scholarship may be renewable.
Deadline: March 1.
How to apply: Applications are available by mail.
Exclusive: Visit www.UltimateScholarshipBook.com and enter code WO29312 for updates on this award.

(294) · Young People for Fellowship

Young People For
2000 M Street, NW
Suite 400
Washington, DC 20036
Phone: 202-467-4999
Email: zdryden@fpaw.org
http://www.youngpeoplefor.org
Purpose: To encourage and cultivate young progressive leaders.
Eligibility: Applicants must be undergraduate students and be interested in promoting social change on their campuses and in their communities. Selection is based on the overall strength of the application.
Target applicants: College students. Adult students.
Amount: Varies.
Number of awards: Varies.
Deadline: Varies.
How to apply: Applications are available online. An application form is required.
Exclusive: Visit www.UltimateScholarshipBook.com and enter code YO29412 for updates on this award.

(295) · Young Scholars Program

Jack Kent Cooke Foundation Young Scholars Program
301 ACT Drive
P.O. Box 4030
Iowa City, IA 52243
Phone: 800-498-6478
Fax: 703-723-8030
Email: jkc@jackkentcookefoundation.org
http://www.jkcf.org
Purpose: To help high-achieving students with financial need and provide them with educational opportunities throughout high school.
Eligibility: Applicants must have financial need, be in the 7th grade and plan to attend high school in the United States. Academic achievement and intelligence are important, and students must display strong academic records, academic awards and honors and submit a strong letter of recommendation. A GPA of 3.5 is usually required, but exceptions are

made for students with unique talents or learning differences. The award is also based on students' will to succeed, leadership and public service, critical thinking ability and participation in the arts and humanities. During two summers, recipients must participate in a Young Scholars Week and Young Scholars Reunion in Washington, DC.
Target applicants: Junior high students or younger.
Amount: Varies.
Number of awards: 50.
Scholarship may be renewable.
Deadline: April 25.
How to apply: Applications are available online and at regional talent centers. An application form, parental release, financial and tax forms, school report, teacher recommendation, personal recommendation and survey form are required.
Exclusive: Visit www.UltimateScholarshipBook.com and enter code JA29512 for updates on this award.

(296) · Your Point of View Contest

Transitions to Complete Education
1125 Linda Vista Drive
Suite 101
San Marcos, CA 92078
Phone: 760-591-0719
http://www.t2ce.org
Purpose: To encourage teens to take a more active role in improving high school education.
Eligibility: Applicants must be U.S. citizens or legal residents and be between the ages of 14 and 19. They must submit an essay or video describing how they would change high school education for the better. Selection is based on the overall strength of the submission.
Target applicants: High school students.
Amount: $300-$1,000.
Number of awards: 3.
Deadline: September 30.
How to apply: Application instructions are available online. An entry form and an essay or video are required.
Exclusive: Visit www.UltimateScholarshipBook.com and enter code TR29612 for updates on this award.

HUMANITIES / ARTS

(297) • Academic Fellowships and Grants

American-Scandinavian Foundation
58 Park Avenue
New York, NY 10016
Phone: 212-879-9779
Email: grants@amscan.org
http://www.amscan.org
Purpose: To encourage research projects related to Scandinavia.
Eligibility: Applicants must have completed their undergraduate educations and have a research or study project requiring a stay in Scandinavia. Some language proficiency is required.
Target applicants: Graduate school students. Adult students.
Amount: $5,000-$23,000.
Number of awards: Varies.
Scholarship may be renewable.
Deadline: November 1.
How to apply: Applications are available online and by written request.
Exclusive: Visit www.UltimateScholarshipBook.com and enter code AM29712 for updates on this award.

(298) • ACES Copy Editing Scholarships

American Copy Editor's Society
c/o Kathy Schenck
333 W. State Street
Milwaukee, WI 53203
Email: kschenck@journalsentinel.com
http://www.copydesk.org/scholarships.htm
Purpose: To support students who are interested in copy editing.
Eligibility: Applicants must be college juniors, seniors or graduate students. Graduating students who will take full-time copy editing jobs or internships are eligible. They must demonstrate interest in and aptitude for copy editing.
Target applicants: College students. Graduate school students. Adult students.
Amount: $1,000-$2,500.
Number of awards: 5.
Deadline: November 15.
How to apply: Applications are available online. An application form, list of course work related to copy editing, list of copy editing experience, two letters of recommendation, copies of 5 to 10 headlines written by applicant and a copy of a story edited by applicant are required.
Exclusive: Visit www.UltimateScholarshipBook.com and enter code AM29812 for updates on this award.

(299) • ACL/NJCL National Greek Examination Scholarship

American Classical League
Miami University
Oxford, OH 45056
Phone: 513-529-7741
Fax: 513-529-7742
Email: info@aclclassics.org
http://www.aclclassics.org
Purpose: To support outstanding students of Greek.
Eligibility: Applicants must be high school seniors who have earned purple or blue ribbons in the upper level National Greek Exam. They must agree to earn six credits in Greek during their freshman year in college.
Target applicants: High school students.
Amount: $1,000.
Number of awards: 1.
Deadline: Varies.
How to apply: Applications are sent to teachers of eligible students by mail.
Exclusive: Visit www.UltimateScholarshipBook.com and enter code AM29912 for updates on this award.

(300) • ACL/NJCL National Latin Examination Scholarships

American Classical League
Miami University
Oxford, OH 45056
Phone: 513-529-7741
Fax: 513-529-7742
Email: info@aclclassics.org
http://www.aclclassics.org
Purpose: To support outstanding students of Latin.
Eligibility: Applicants must Latin students and gold medal winners in the National Latin Exam Awards. They must also be high school seniors and must agree to take at least one Latin or classical Greek course each semester of their first year of college.
Target applicants: High school students.
Amount: $1,000.
Number of awards: 21.
Scholarship may be renewable.
Deadline: Varies.
How to apply: Applications are mailed to NLE gold medal winners who are high school seniors.
Exclusive: Visit www.UltimateScholarshipBook.com and enter code AM30012 for updates on this award.

(301) • Actors' Work Program

Actors' Fund of America/Actors' Work Program
729 Seventh Avenue
11th Floor
New York, NY 10019
Phone: 800-221-7303
Fax: 212-921-4295
Email: info@actorsfund.org
http://www.actorsfund.org
Purpose: To assist members of the entertainment industry with finding sideline work and pursuing new careers.
Eligibility: Applicants must be members in good standing of an entertainment industry union and have a referral from the Fund's social service department or other organization able to document entertainment industry work.
Target applicants: Junior high students or younger. High school students. College students. Graduate school students. Adult students.
Amount: Varies.
Number of awards: Varies.
Deadline: Varies.
How to apply: Applicants must attend an Actors' Work Program Orientation to learn more about the program.
Exclusive: Visit www.UltimateScholarshipBook.com and enter code AC30112 for updates on this award.

(302) • AMCA Music Scholarship

Associated Male Choruses of America
Robert H. Torborg, Scholarship Chair
P.O. Box 342
Cold Spring, MN 56320
Phone: 320-685-3848
Email: scholarship@amcofa.net
http://www.amcofa.net

Purpose: To promote the study of chorus and music studies in college.
Eligibility: Applicants must be full-time students obtaining their bachelor's degree in a music-related field (with preference given to voice or choral concentrations) and be sponsored by a chorus of the Associated Male Choruses of America. Applicants must submit references and a personal letter.
Target applicants: College students. Adult students.
Amount: $1,000-$1,200.
Number of awards: Varies.
Deadline: Varies.
How to apply: Applications are available online or by contacting your local AMCA chorus.
Exclusive: Visit www.UltimateScholarshipBook.com and enter code AS30212 for updates on this award.

(303) • America's First Freedom Student Competition

First Freedom Center
1321 E. Main Street
Richmond, VA 23219-3629
Phone: 804-643-1786
Fax: 804-644-5024
Email: competition@firstfreedom.org
http://www.firstfreedom.org

Purpose: To encourage students to examine religious freedom.
Eligibility: Applicants must be 9th-12th grade students in public, private or parochial schools or home-schooled or distance-learning students living in the U.S. and U.S. territories. The competition is also open to 9th-12th grade American students living outside of the U.S., non-American students attending American and international schools outside of the U.S., foreign-exchange students studying in the U.S. and legal aliens and legal visitors studying in the U.S. Students participating in dual enrollment programs, which combine classes for a high-school diploma and college credit, whether studying on a high school or college campus are eligible; and American GED-program students, 20 years of age and younger, are eligible.
Target applicants: High school students.
Amount: Up to $3,000.
Number of awards: 3.
Deadline: November 23.
How to apply: Registration and all essay materials (guidelines, topic, etc.) are available online. Online registration, a signed registration form, six copies of essay and bibliography and an essay and bibliography saved on a CD or disk are required.
Exclusive: Visit www.UltimateScholarshipBook.com and enter code FI30312 for updates on this award.

(304) • America's Next Top Namer Scholarship

Strategic Name Development Inc.
1650 West 82nd Street
Suite 1000
Minneapolis, MN 55431
Phone: 952-830-4100
Email: stephanie@namedevelopment.com
http://www.namedevelopment.com

Purpose: To reward undergraduate students who have devised creative brand names for the internet.
Eligibility: Applicants must be undergraduate students at an accredited U.S. institution and be majoring in mass communication, marketing, English or linguistics. They must have a GPA of 3.0 or higher and devise five original brand names for the internet. Current employees of Strategic Name Development are ineligible. Selection is based on creativity and originality.
Target applicants: College students. Adult students.
Minimum GPA: 3.0
Amount: $2,500.
Number of awards: 1.
Deadline: August 15.
How to apply: Applications are available online. An application form and personal essay are required.
Exclusive: Visit www.UltimateScholarshipBook.com and enter code ST30412 for updates on this award.

(305) • American String Teachers Association National Solo Competition- Senior Division

American String Teachers Association (ASTA)
4153 Chain Bridge Road
Fairfax, VA 22030
Phone: 703-279-2113
Fax: 703-279-2114
Email: asta@astaweb.com
http://www.astaweb.com

Purpose: To support outstanding musicians.
Eligibility: Applicants must be ASTA members or students of professional ASTA members. They must be musicians age 19-25 who play violin, viola, cello, bass, classical guitar or harp. They may enter the competition in their home state or in the state in which they are studying. Previous grand prize and first prize winners may not enter the competition again.
Target applicants: High school students. College students. Graduate school students.
Amount: Varies.
Number of awards: Varies.
Deadline: Varies.
How to apply: Applications are available online. An application form and proof of birth date are required.
Exclusive: Visit www.UltimateScholarshipBook.com and enter code AM30512 for updates on this award.

(306) • American Theatre Organ Society Scholarships

American Theatre Organ Society
Carlton B. Smith, Director
2175 N. Irwin Street
Indianapolis, IN 46219
Phone: 317-356-1240
Fax: 317-322-9379
Email: smith@atos.org
http://www.atos.org

Purpose: To provide students with an opportunity to study with professional theatre organ teachers or to further their organ performance education in college.
Eligibility: Applicants must be between the ages of 13 and 27 as of July 1 and either working toward college organ performance degrees or be studying with professional organ instructors. Students' names must

be submitted by their present organ instructor or the school's music department head. An essay is also required.
Target applicants: Junior high students or younger. High school students. College students. Adult students.
Amount: Up to $1,500.
Number of awards: Varies.
Deadline: April 15.
How to apply: Applications are available online.
Exclusive: Visit www.UltimateScholarshipBook.com and enter code AM30612 for updates on this award.

(307) · Amy Lowell Poetry Travelling Scholarship

Choate, Hall and Stewart
Two International Place
Boston, MA 02110
Phone: 617-248-5253
Email: amylowell@choate.com
http://www.amylowell.org
Purpose: To support travel abroad for American-born poets.
Eligibility: Applicants should submit applications, curriculum vitae and poetry samples. Recipients should not accept another scholarship during the scholarship year, must travel outside North America and should have three poems by the end of scholarship year.
Target applicants: College students. Graduate school students. Adult students.
Amount: $52,000.
Number of awards: 1-2.
Deadline: October 15.
How to apply: Applications are available online.
Exclusive: Visit www.UltimateScholarshipBook.com and enter code CH30712 for updates on this award.

(308) · Annual Music Student Scholarships

School Band and Orchestra Magazine
21 Highland Circle
Suite One
Needham, MA 02494
Phone: 800-964-5150
Fax: 781-453-9389
Email: pgalileos@symphonypublishing.com
http://www.sbomagazine.com
Purpose: To support music students.
Eligibility: Applicants must be public, private or home school students in grades 4 through 12, be music students and write an essay on the given topic. Five scholarships are awarded to students in grades 4 through 8, and five are awarded to students in grades 9 through 12. Schools of winners will receive merchandise prizes.
Target applicants: Junior high students or younger. High school students.
Amount: $1,000.
Number of awards: 10.
Deadline: December 31.
How to apply: Applications are available online. An essay, contact information, school contact information and instrument played are required.
Exclusive: Visit www.UltimateScholarshipBook.com and enter code SC30812 for updates on this award.

(309) · Anthem Essay Contest

Ayn Rand Institute Anthem Essay Contest
Department W
P.O. Box 57044
Irvine, CA 92619-7044
Phone: 949-222-6550
Fax: 949-222-6558
Email: essay@aynrand.org
http://www.aynrand.org
Purpose: To honor high school students who distinguish themselves in their understanding of Ayn Rand's novel *Anthem*.
Eligibility: Applicants must be high school freshmen or sophomores who submit a 600-1200 word essay that will be judged on both style and content, with an emphasis on writing that is clear, articulate and logically organized. Winning essays must demonstrate an outstanding grasp of the philosophic meaning of *Anthem*.
Target applicants: Junior high students or younger. High school students.
Amount: $30-$2,000.
Number of awards: 236.
Deadline: March 20.
How to apply: Application request information is available online.
Exclusive: Visit www.UltimateScholarshipBook.com and enter code AY30912 for updates on this award.

(310) · Art Awards

Scholastic
557 Broadway
New York, NY 10012
Phone: 212-343-6100
Fax: 212-389-3939
Email: a&wgeneralinfo@scholastic.com
http://www.artandwriting.org
Purpose: To reward America's best student artists.
Eligibility: Applicants must be in grades 7 through 12 in American or Canadian schools and must submit artwork in one of the following categories: art portfolio, animation, ceramics and glass, computer art, design, digital imagery, drawing, mixed media, painting, photography, photography portfolio, printmaking, sculpture or video and film. There are regional and national levels.
Target applicants: Junior high students or younger. High school students.
Amount: Up to $10,000.
Number of awards: Varies.
Deadline: Varies.
How to apply: Applications are available online.
Exclusive: Visit www.UltimateScholarshipBook.com and enter code SC31012 for updates on this award.

(311) · Atlas Shrugged Essay Contest

Ayn Rand Institute Atlas Shrugged Essay Contest
Department W
P.O. Box 57044
Irvine, CA 92619-7044
Phone: 949-222-6550
Fax: 949-222-6558
Email: essay@aynrand.org
http://www.aynrand.org
Purpose: To honor college students who distinguish themselves in their understanding of Ayn Rand's novel *Atlas Shrugged*.

Eligibility: Applicants must be college students and high school students entering college in the fall who submit an 800-1,600 word essay which will be judged on both style and content with an emphasis on writing that is clear, articulate and logically organized. Winning essays must demonstrate an outstanding grasp of the philosophic meaning of *Atlas Shrugged*.
Target applicants: High school students. College students. Adult students.
Amount: $2,000-$10,000.
Number of awards: 49.
Deadline: September 17.
How to apply: Application request information is available online.
Exclusive: Visit www.UltimateScholarshipBook.com and enter code AY31112 for updates on this award.

(312) • Bridging Scholarships for Study Abroad in Japan

Association of Teachers of Japanese
Bridging Project Clearinghouse
Campus Box 279
240 Humanities Building, University of Colorado
Boulder, CO 80309
Phone: 303-492-5487
Fax: 303-492-5856
Email: atj@colorado.edu
http://www.colorado.edu/ealc/atj
Purpose: To assist students with travel and living expenses while studying in Japan.
Eligibility: Applicants must be undergraduates, U.S. citizens and be enrolled in a U.S. college. Study in Japan must be for at least three months and take place during the academic year (summer programs are not eligible). Students must submit a letter of recommendation and an essay on their interest in studying in Japan.
Target applicants: College students. Adult students.
Amount: $4,000.
Number of awards: 70.
Deadline: October 6 and April 6.
How to apply: Applications are available online.
Exclusive: Visit www.UltimateScholarshipBook.com and enter code AS31212 for updates on this award.

(313) • Bronislaw Kaper Award

Los Angeles Philharmonic
Education Department
151 S. Grand Avenue
Los Angeles, CA 90012
Phone: 213-972-3454
Fax: 213-972-7650
Email: education@laphil.org
http://www.laphil.org
Purpose: To encourage the development of young musicians.
Eligibility: Applicants must be current residents of the state of California and are required to prepare and perform a piano or string piece for competition. The category alternates between piano and string each year. The maximum level in school is a senior in high school.
Target applicants: Junior high students or younger. High school students.
Amount: $1,000-$2,500.
Number of awards: 4.
Deadline: December 14.
How to apply: Applications are available online.
Exclusive: Visit www.UltimateScholarshipBook.com and enter code LO31312 for updates on this award.

(314) • Carl A. Ross Student Paper Award

Appalachian Studies Association Carl A. Ross Student Paper Award
William Schumann
Emory and Henry College
P.O. Box 947
Emory, VA 24327
Phone: 304-696-2904
Fax: 276-944-6170
http://www.appalachianstudies.org
Purpose: To promote Appalachian studies.
Eligibility: Applicants must submit a 20- to 30-page research paper on an Appalachian studies topic. Selections will be made from two categories: middle/high school and undergraduate/graduate.
Target applicants: Junior high students or younger. High school students. College students. Graduate school students. Adult students.
Amount: $100.
Number of awards: Varies.
Deadline: December 8.
How to apply: Submission of research paper is the application.
Exclusive: Visit www.UltimateScholarshipBook.com and enter code AP31412 for updates on this award.

(315) • Caroline H. Newhouse Scholarship Fund

Career Transition for Dancers
Caroline and Theodore Newhouse Center for Dancers
165 West 46th Street, Suite 701
The Actors' Equity Building
New York, NY 10036
Phone: 212-764-0172
Fax: 212-764-0343
Email: info@careertransition.org
http://www.careertransition.org
Purpose: To provide educational grants for dancers seeking second careers.
Eligibility: Applicants must provide documentation of 100 weeks or more of paid employment as a dance performer in the U.S. over at least seven years. For work not performed under union jurisdiction, applicants must also provide documentation of total gross earnings of at least $56,000. Choreographers and dance teachers are not eligible for this program.
Target applicants: College students. Graduate school students. Adult students.
Amount: Up to $2,000.
Number of awards: Varies.
Deadline: Every other month.
How to apply: Applicants must call to confirm their eligibility.
Exclusive: Visit www.UltimateScholarshipBook.com and enter code CA31512 for updates on this award.

(316) • ChiGems Art and Poetry Scholarship

ChiGems
24695 Monita Circle
Laguna Niguel, CA 92677
Phone: 949-547-9427
Email: info@chigems.com
http://www.chigems.com/scholarshipapplication.htm

Purpose: To reward artistically and academically talented students who contribute to their schools and communities.
Eligibility: Applicants must be students in grades 9 through 12 who are enrolled in any U.S. public or private school or adult non-professionals who want to continue their art education. Financial need and merit are considered. An art or poetry submission is required.
Target applicants: High school students.
Amount: $250.
Number of awards: Varies.
Deadline: Varies.
How to apply: Applications are available online. There are six deadlines per year, with one award distributed every other month.
Exclusive: Visit www.UltimateScholarshipBook.com and enter code CH31612 for updates on this award.

(317) • Christianson Grant

InterExchange Inc.
161 Sixth Avenue
New York, NY 10013
Phone: 212-924-0446
Fax: 212-924-0575
Email: grants@interexchange.org
http://www.interexchange.org/content/1/en/Home.html
Purpose: To further international understanding and promote cultural awareness by supporting young Americans in working abroad.
Eligibility: Applicants must have arranged their own work abroad programs and be U.S. citizens or permanent residents aged 18 to 28.
Target applicants: High school students. College students. Graduate school students. Adult students.
Amount: $2,500-$10,000.
Number of awards: Varies.
Deadline: March 15, July 15 and October 15.
How to apply: Applications are available online.
Exclusive: Visit www.UltimateScholarshipBook.com and enter code IN31712 for updates on this award.

(318) • Clan MacBean Foundation Grant Program

Clan MacBean Foundation
441 Wadsworth Boulevard, Suite 213
Denver, CO 80226
http://www.clanmacbean.net
Purpose: To provide financial assistance to those studying Scottish culture.
Eligibility: Applicants must be pursuing a course of study related directly to Scottish culture. If pursuing a project, applicants must pick a project that reflects direct involvement in the preservation or enhancement of Scottish culture.
Target applicants: College students. Adult students.
Amount: Varies.
Number of awards: Varies.
Deadline: Varies.
How to apply: Applications are available by written request.
Exclusive: Visit www.UltimateScholarshipBook.com and enter code CL31812 for updates on this award.

(319) • Clauder Competition Prize

Portland Stage Company
P.O. Box 1458
Portland, ME 04104
Email: dburson@portlandstage.com
http://www.portlandstage.com
Purpose: To support playwrights.
Eligibility: Applicants must live or attend school in Connecticut, Maine, Massachusetts, New Hampshire, Rhode Island or Vermont. This requirement may be waived for playwrights who have previously lived in New England and produce material relevant to the area. They must submit a full-length play that is an original work and has not been produced or published.
Target applicants: High school students. College students. Graduate school students. Adult students.
Amount: Up to $2,500.
Number of awards: Varies.
Deadline: Varies.
How to apply: No application form is required.
Exclusive: Visit www.UltimateScholarshipBook.com and enter code PO31912 for updates on this award.

(320) • College Television Awards

Academy of Television Arts and Sciences Foundation
5220 Lankershim Boulevard
North Hollywood, CA 91601
Phone: 818-754-2800
Fax: 818-761-2827
Email: collegeawards@emmys.org
http://www.emmys.org
Purpose: To award college student film or video producers.
Eligibility: Applicants must produce an original film or video in one of the following categories: drama, comedy, music, documentary, news, magazine show, traditional or computer-generated animation, children's programming or commercials. Professionals may not be involved in the production of the piece, including producers, directors, camera operators, lighting or sound technicians and production managers. Applicants must also be full-time students who have produced their video for course credit at an American college or university from January 1 to December 31 of the current year.
Target applicants: College students. Graduate school students. Adult students.
Amount: $500-$10,000.
Number of awards: Varies.
Deadline: Varies.
How to apply: Applications are available online from September 1 to January 15 and are also sent to college film and television departments.
Exclusive: Visit www.UltimateScholarshipBook.com and enter code AC32012 for updates on this award.

(321) • Congressional Black Caucus Spouses Performing Arts Scholarship

Congressional Black Caucus Foundation
1720 Massachusetts Avenue NW
Washington, DC 20036
Phone: 202-263-2800
Fax: 202-775-0773
Email: info@cbcfinc.org
http://www.cbcfinc.org
Purpose: To support students who are pursuing careers in performing arts.
Eligibility: Applicants do NOT need to be African American but must reside or attend school in a congressional district represented by a CBC member. Students must have at least a 2.5 GPA, and they must be enrolled or accepted into a full-time undergraduate degree

program. Applicants must show leadership qualities and community service participation.
Target applicants: High school students. College students. Adult students.
Minimum GPA: 2.5
Amount: Varies.
Number of awards: Varies.
Deadline: April 30.
How to apply: Applications are available online.
Exclusive: Visit www.UltimateScholarshipBook.com and enter code CO32112 for updates on this award.

(322) • Congressional Black Caucus Spouses Visual Arts Scholarship

Congressional Black Caucus Foundation
1720 Massachusetts Avenue NW
Washington, DC 20036
Phone: 202-263-2800
Fax: 202-775-0773
Email: info@cbcfinc.org
http://www.cbcfinc.org
Purpose: To support students who are pursuing careers in visual arts.
Eligibility: Applicants do NOT need to be African American but must reside or attend school in a congressional district represented by a CBC member. Students must have at least a 2.5 GPA, and they must be enrolled or accepted into a full-time undergraduate degree program. Applicants must show leadership qualities and community service participation.
Target applicants: High school students. College students. Adult students.
Minimum GPA: 2.5
Amount: Varies.
Number of awards: Varies.
Deadline: April 30.
How to apply: Applications are available online.
Exclusive: Visit www.UltimateScholarshipBook.com and enter code CO32212 for updates on this award.

(323) • Constance Eberhardt Memorial Award, AIMS Graz Experience Scholarship and Banff Center School of Fine Arts Scholarship

National Opera Association
Vocal Competition
P.O. Box 60869
Canyon, TX 79016-0001
Phone: 806-651-2857
Email: rhansen@mail.wtamu.edu
http://www.noa.org
Purpose: To provide financial support for young opera singers.
Eligibility: Applicants must be enrolled in undergraduate or graduate programs or the equivalent and be between the ages of 18 and 24. The applicants' teachers must be members of the National Opera Association. Selection is based on a recording of two arias for preliminary hearings and a live audition of four arias for the final judging. There is a $20 entry fee. Note: We do not recommend applying to scholarships that charge application fees. However, some scholarships of this type charge fees and are included for completeness.
Target applicants: High school students. College students. Graduate school students.
Amount: $500-$2,000.
Number of awards: Varies.
Deadline: October 15.
How to apply: Applications are available online.
Exclusive: Visit www.UltimateScholarshipBook.com and enter code NA32312 for updates on this award.

(324) • Corporate Leadership Scholarships

Gravure Education Foundation
1200-A Scottsville Road
Rochester, NY 14624
Phone: 315-589-8879
Fax: 585-436-7689
Email: lwshatch@gaa.org
http://www.gaa.org
Purpose: To provide scholarships to undergraduate and graduate students pursuing degrees in printing or graphic arts.
Eligibility: Applicants must be enrolled full-time at a GEF Learning Resource Center at Arizona State University, California Polytechnic State University, Clemson University, Murray State, Rochester Institute of Technology, University of Wisconsin - Stout or Western Michigan University. Students must major in printing, graphic arts or graphic communications and be a sophomore, junior or senior at the time the scholarship is awarded.
Target applicants: College students. Graduate school students. Adult students.
Minimum GPA: 3.0
Amount: $1,500.
Number of awards: 5.
Deadline: May 31.
How to apply: Applications are available online.
Exclusive: Visit www.UltimateScholarshipBook.com and enter code GR32412 for updates on this award.

(325) • Council on International Educational Exchange (CIEE) Scholarships

Council on International Educational Exchange
7 Custom House Street, 3rd Floor
Portland, ME 04101
Phone: 800-40-STUDY
Fax: 207-553-7699
Email: scholarships@ciee.org
http://www.ciee.org
Purpose: To make the study abroad program available to a wider audience and to provide assistance to CIEE Study Center (CSC) members who have demonstrated academic talent and financial need in order to study abroad.
Eligibility: Applicants must plan to participate in a CIEE study abroad program. Financial need is strongly considered along with other materials from the study abroad application. Other eligibility requirements vary according to the specific scholarship. If awarded a scholarship, applicants are required to submit a one-page essay on their experiences after returning.
Target applicants: College students. Graduate school students. Adult students.
Amount: Up to $8,000.
Number of awards: Varies.
Deadline: April 1 and November 1.
How to apply: Applications are available online.
Exclusive: Visit www.UltimateScholarshipBook.com and enter code CO32512 for updates on this award.

(326) • DAAD/AICGS Research Fellowship Program

American Institute for Contemporary German Studies - (AICGS)
1755 Massachusetts Avenue NW
Suite 700
Washington, DC 20036
Phone: 202-332-9312
Fax: 202-265-9531
Email: jwindell@aicgs.org
http://www.aicgs.org

Purpose: To bring scholars and specialists working on Germany, Europe and/or transatlantic relations to AICGS for research stays.
Eligibility: Applicants must have a Ph.D. or be enrolled in a Ph.D. program and hold U.S. or German citizenship. The grant provides a research stay of two months at AICGS.
Target applicants: Graduate school students. Adult students.
Amount: Up to $4,725 monthly stipend.
Number of awards: Varies.
Deadline: February 28.
How to apply: Apply via email to jwindell@aicgs.org.
Exclusive: Visit www.UltimateScholarshipBook.com and enter code AM32612 for updates on this award.

(327) • DiversityAbroad.com Summer Abroad Scholarship

Diversity Abroad
1731 Delaware Street
Berkeley, CA 94703
Phone: 510-647-5100
Fax: 510-647-5032
Email: feedback@diversityabroad.com
http://www.diversityabroad.com

Purpose: To support minority students who plan to study abroad in a summer session.
Eligibility: Applicants must be African American, Asian American, Hispanic or Native American. Students must have at least a 2.5 GPA in a full-time undergraduate program. Applicants must submit an essay and one letter of recommendation. Recipients must enroll in a study abroad program sponsored by a Diversity Abroad member organization, and they must be willing to share their experiences through blogs and online forums at DiversityAbroad.com.
Target applicants: College students. Adult students.
Minimum GPA: 2.5
Amount: $1,000.
Number of awards: 20.
Deadline: April 1.
How to apply: Applications are available online.
Exclusive: Visit www.UltimateScholarshipBook.com and enter code DI32712 for updates on this award.

(328) • Doodle 4 Google

Google
1600 Amphitheatre Parkway
Mountain View, CA 94043
Phone: 650-253-0000
Fax: 650-253-0001
Email: doodle4google-team@google.com
http://www.google.com/doodle4google

Purpose: To encourage creativity in United States school students through a logo contest.
Eligibility: Participants must be elementary or secondary school students in the 50 U.S. states or the District of Columbia that have registered for the contest. They must be U.S. residents who have obtained parental consent to enter. Employees, interns, contractors and office-holders of Google Inc. and their immediate families are not eligible.
Target applicants: Junior high students or younger. High school students.
Amount: $10,000.
Number of awards: 1.
Deadline: March 17.
How to apply: Applications are available from participating schools.
Exclusive: Visit www.UltimateScholarshipBook.com and enter code GO32812 for updates on this award.

(329) • Dr. Randy Pausch Scholarship Fund

Academy of Interactive Arts and Sciences (AIAS)
c/o Randy Pausch Scholarship
23622 Calabasas Road
Suite 220
Calabasas, CA 91302
Phone: 818-876-0826
Fax: 818-876-0850
Email: gabriel@interactive.org
http://www.interactive.org

Purpose: To support students pursuing careers in game design, development and production.
Eligibility: Applicants must be full-time students who are currently enrolled in an accredited college or university at the undergraduate or graduate level. They must plan to enter the video game industry and have a GPA of 3.3 or higher. Selection is based on application, required documentation, service, leadership, character and financial need.
Target applicants: College students. Graduate school students. Adult students.
Minimum GPA: 3.3
Amount: $2,500.
Number of awards: 4.
Deadline: May 31.
How to apply: Applications are available online. An application form, verification of enrollment, personal statement, two letters of recommendation and transcript are required.
Exclusive: Visit www.UltimateScholarshipBook.com and enter code AC32912 for updates on this award.

(330) • Dumbarton Oaks Fellowships

Dumbarton Oaks
1703 32nd Street NW
Washington, DC 20007
Phone: 202-339-6401
Fax: 202-339-6419
Email: dumbartonoaks@doaks.org
http://www.doaks.org

Purpose: To provide fellowships to scholars engaged in Byzantine studies, Pre-Columbian studies and garden and landscape studies
Eligibility: Applicants must hold a doctorate (or appropriate final degree) or have established themselves in their field and wish to pursue their own research or expect to have the Ph.D. in hand prior to taking up residence at Dumbarton Oaks. The fellowships are in the following areas: Byzantine Studies (including related aspects of late Roman, early Christian, western medieval, Slavic and Near Eastern Studies), Pre-Columbian Studies (of Mexico, Central America and Andean South America) and garden and landscape studies. Fellowships are based on

demonstrated scholarly ability and preparation (including knowledge of the required languages), interest and value of the study or project and its relevance to Dumbarton Oaks.
Target applicants: Graduate school students. Adult students.
Amount: $42,500-$75,000 plus allowance and health benefits.
Number of awards: Varies.
Deadline: November 1.
How to apply: Applicants must submit ten complete, collated sets of the application letter, proposal and personal and professional data. Applicants must also submit three recommendation letters.
Exclusive: Visit www.UltimateScholarshipBook.com and enter code DU33012 for updates on this award.

(331) • Edna Meudt Memorial Award and the Florence Kahn Memorial Award

National Federation of State Poetry Societies
NFSPS College/University-Level Competition
N. Colwell Snell
P.O. Box 520698
Salt Lake City, UT 84152
Phone: 801-484-3113
Email: SBSenior@juno.com
http://www.nfsps.com
Purpose: To recognize the importance of poetry on the nation's culture.
Eligibility: Applicants can be college students at any level.
Target applicants: College students. Adult students.
Amount: $500.
Number of awards: 2.
Deadline: February 14.
How to apply: Applications are available online.
Exclusive: Visit www.UltimateScholarshipBook.com and enter code NA33112 for updates on this award.

(332) • Elizabeth Greenshields Foundation Grants

Elizabeth Greenshields Foundation
1814 Sherbrooke Street West Suite #1
Montreal
Quebec, Canada H3H 1E4
Phone: 514-937-9225
Fax: 514-937-0141
http://www.elizabethgreenshieldsfoundation.org/main.html
Purpose: To promote an appreciation of painting, drawing, sculpture and the graphic arts by supporting art students, artists or sculptors.
Eligibility: Applicants must have already started or completed training at an established school of art, and/or demonstrated, through past work and future plans, a commitment to make art a lifetime career. Applicants must be in the early stages of their careers working in painting, drawing, printmaking or sculpture. Abstract work will not be considered.
Target applicants: High school students. College students. Graduate school students. Adult students.
Amount: $12,500 CDN.
Number of awards: Varies.
Deadline: Rolling.
How to apply: Applications are available by phone or written request.
Exclusive: Visit www.UltimateScholarshipBook.com and enter code EL33212 for updates on this award.

(333) • FALCON - Full Year Asian Language CONcentration

FALCON Program
Department of Asian Studies, Cornell University
338 Rockefeller Hall
Ithaca, NY 14853
Phone: 607-255-6457
Fax: 607-255-1345
Email: falcon@cornell.edu
http://lrc.cornell.edu/falcon/
Purpose: To provide scholarships for undergraduate and graduate students seeking intensive, long-term instruction in Chinese and Japanese.
Eligibility: The program is conducted at Cornell University, and students receive Cornell credits.
Target applicants: College students. Graduate school students. Adult students.
Amount: Varies.
Number of awards: Varies.
Deadline: Varies.
How to apply: Applications are available online.
Exclusive: Visit www.UltimateScholarshipBook.com and enter code FA33312 for updates on this award.

(334) • Federal Junior Duck Stamp Program and Scholarship Competition

U.S. Fish and Wildlife Service
Junior Duck Stamp Program
4401 N. Fairfax Drive
MBSP-4070
Arlington, VA 22203
Phone: 703-358-2073
Email: duckstamps@fws.gov
http://www.fws.gov/juniorduck
Purpose: To encourage students to paint waterfowl and learn about the importance of habitat and wildlife conservation.
Eligibility: Applicants must be in kindergarten to 12th grade and submit their artwork to their state or local department. Students must be U.S. citizens, resident aliens or nationals. The first place national winner has their art made into the next Federal Junior Duck Stamp, wins $5,000 and travels with a parent to the next First Day of Sale event for their stamp. The second place winner receives $3,000, and the third place winner receives $2,000. A $500 prize is also awarded to the best conservation message.
Target applicants: Junior high students or younger. High school students.
Amount: $100-$5,000.
Number of awards: 100.
Deadline: March 15.
How to apply: Applications are available online.
Exclusive: Visit www.UltimateScholarshipBook.com and enter code U.33412 for updates on this award.

(335) • Fellowships for Regular Program in Greece

American School of Classical Studies at Athens
6-8 Charlton Street
Princeton, NJ 08540
Phone: 609-683-0800
Fax: 609-683-0800
Email: ascsa@ascsa.org

http://www.ascsa.edu.gr
Purpose: The institution is devoted to allowing advanced graduate students enrolled in North American colleges and institutions to study the classics and related fields of language, literature, art, history, archaeology and philosophy of Greece and the Greek world.
Eligibility: Applicants must have completed at least one to two years of graduate study and must take exams in ancient Greek language, history and either literature or art and archaeology. Students must be able to read French, German, ancient Greek and Latin with an ability to also read modern Greek and Italian considered helpful. Applicants must be graduate students who are preparing for an advanced degree in classical and ancient Mediterranean studies or a related field. The fellowships provide study in Athens or Greece for nine months and may not be used for costs at the student's home institution.
Target applicants: Graduate school students. Adult students.
Amount: $11,500 plus housing, board, fees.
Number of awards: Varies.
Deadline: February 19.
How to apply: Applications are available online.
Exclusive: Visit www.UltimateScholarshipBook.com and enter code AM33512 for updates on this award.

(336) • FFTA Scholarship Competition

Flexographic Technical Association
900 Marconi Avenue
Ronkonkoma, NY 11779
Phone: 631-737-6020
Fax: 631-737-6813
Email: education@flexography.org
http://www.flexography.org
Purpose: To advance the state of the flexographic industry.
Eligibility: Applicants must demonstrate interest in a career in flexography and must be high school seniors with plans to attend a post-secondary institution or be presently enrolled at a post-secondary institution offering a course of study in flexography. Applicants must exhibit exemplary performance in their studies, particularly in the area of graphic communications and must have a minimum 3.0 GPA.
Target applicants: High school students. College students. Adult students.
Minimum GPA: 3.0
Amount: $2,000.
Number of awards: Varies.
Scholarship may be renewable.
Deadline: March 19.
How to apply: Applications are available online.
Exclusive: Visit www.UltimateScholarshipBook.com and enter code FL33612 for updates on this award.

(337) • Finlandia Foundation National Student Scholarships Program

Finlandia Foundation
470 W. Walnut Street
Pasadena, CA 91103
Phone: 626-795-2081
Fax: 626-795-6533
Email: ffnoffice@mac.com
http://www.finlandiafoundation.org
Purpose: To support undergraduate and graduate students in Finland and the United States for conducting studies or research related to Finnish culture and society.
Eligibility: Applicants must be full-time undergraduate or graduate students enrolled in a college or university in the U.S. or Finland and must plan research on Finnish culture in the U.S. They must be studying at the sophomore level or higher and have a minimum GPA of 3.0. Financial need, course of study and citizenship are considered in evaluating applications. Students may not receive funds for two consecutive years.
Target applicants: College students. Graduate school students. Adult students.
Minimum GPA: 3.0
Amount: Varies.
Number of awards: Varies.
Deadline: February 1.
How to apply: Applications are available online. Application form and cover letter are required.
Exclusive: Visit www.UltimateScholarshipBook.com and enter code FI33712 for updates on this award.

(338) • Fountainhead Essay Contest

Ayn Rand Institute Fountainhead Essay Contest
Department W
P.O. Box 57044
Irvine, CA 92619-7044
Phone: 949-222-6550
Fax: 949-222-6558
Email: essay@aynrand.org
http://www.aynrand.org
Purpose: To honor high school students who distinguish themselves in their understanding of Ayn Rand's novel *The Fountainhead*.
Eligibility: Applicants must be high school juniors or seniors who submit a 800-1,600 word essay which will be judged on both style and content with an emphasis on writing that is clear, articulate and logically organized. Winning essays must demonstrate an outstanding grasp of the philosophic and psychological meaning of *The Fountainhead*.
Target applicants: High school students.
Amount: $50-$10,000.
Number of awards: 236.
Deadline: April 26.
How to apply: Application request information is available online.
Exclusive: Visit www.UltimateScholarshipBook.com and enter code AY33812 for updates on this award.

(339) • GEF Resource Center Scholarships

Gravure Education Foundation
1200-A Scottsville Road
Rochester, NY 14624
Phone: 315-589-8879
Fax: 585-436-7689
Email: lwshatch@gaa.org
http://www.gaa.org
Purpose: To award scholarships to undergraduate and graduate students majoring in printing, graphic arts or graphic communications.
Eligibility: Applicants must be enrolled at one of the following GEF Learning Resource Centers: Arizona State University, California Polytechnic State University, Clemson University, Murray State University, Rochester Institute of Technology, University of Wisconsin - Stout or Western Michigan University.
Target applicants: College students. Graduate school students. Adult students.
Minimum GPA: 3.0
Amount: Varies.

Number of awards: Varies.
Deadline: May 31.
How to apply: Applications are available online.
Exclusive: Visit www.UltimateScholarshipBook.com and enter code GR33912 for updates on this award.

(340) • General Heritage and Culture Grants

Sons of Norway Foundation
1455 West Lake Street
Minneapolis, MN 55408
Phone: 800-945-8851
Fax: 612-827-0658
Email: foundation@sofn.com
http://www.sofn.com
Purpose: To preserve Norwegian heritage.
Eligibility: Applicants may be individuals, groups or organizations dedicated to the preservation of Norwegian heritage. Selection is based on applicants' record or activities and adherence to the goals and objectives of the Sons of Norway Foundation.
Target applicants: High school students. College students. Adult students.
Amount: Up to $3,000.
Number of awards: Varies.
Deadline: April 1.
How to apply: Applications are available online.
Exclusive: Visit www.UltimateScholarshipBook.com and enter code SO34012 for updates on this award.

(341) • German Studies Research Grant

German Academic Exchange Service
DAAD
871 UN Plaza
New York, NY 10017
Phone: 212-758-3223
Fax: 212-755-5780
Email: thomanek@daad.org
http://www.daad.org
Purpose: To encourage the research of cultural, political, historical, economic and social aspects of modern and contemporary German affairs.
Eligibility: Applicants must be junior or senior undergraduates pursuing a German studies major or minor, or master's degree students or Ph.D. candidates in the humanities or social sciences who are working on a certificate in German studies at U.S. or Canadian institutions of higher education or a dissertation on a modern German topic, respectively. Applicants must be nominated by their department and must have completed two years of college German and a minimum of three courses in German studies (literature, history, politics or other fields). Applicants should submit applications, resumes, project descriptions, budget reports, lists of German courses taken, two recommendation letters, language evaluation forms and transcripts.
Target applicants: College students. Graduate school students. Adult students.
Amount: $1,500-$2,500.
Number of awards: Up to 5.
Deadline: May 1 and November 1.
How to apply: Applications are available online.
Exclusive: Visit www.UltimateScholarshipBook.com and enter code GE34112 for updates on this award.

(342) • Gilman International Scholarship

Institute of International Education
1400 K Street NW
Washington, DC 20005
Phone: 202-326-7672
Fax: 202-326-7835
Email: boren@iie.org
http://www.iie.org
Purpose: To support students with financial need who are planning to study abroad.
Eligibility: Students must be recipients of a Pell Grant. They must be currently attending a two-year or four-year college in the United States. Recipients must study abroad for at least four weeks in any country excluding Cuba and the countries on the Travel Warning list.
Target applicants: College students. Adult students.
Amount: Up to $5,000.
Number of awards: Varies.
Deadline: March 1 and October 8.
How to apply: Applications are available online.
Exclusive: Visit www.UltimateScholarshipBook.com and enter code IN34212 for updates on this award.

(343) • Glenn Miller Scholarship Competition

Glenn Miller Birthplace Society
107 East Main Street
P.O. Box 61
Clarinda, IA 51632
Phone: 712-542-2461
Fax: 712-542-2461
Email: gmbs@heartland.net
http://www.glennmiller.org
Purpose: To honor Glenn Miller by recognizing future musical leaders.
Eligibility: Applicants may apply as instrumentalists or vocalists. They must be high school seniors or college freshmen who plan to focus on music in their future lives. Applicants must submit an audition CD or tape in addition to an application form. High school seniors may reapply as college freshmen as long as they weren't first-place winners the previous year.
Target applicants: High school students. College students. Adult students.
Amount: $1,000-$4,000.
Number of awards: 6.
Deadline: March 15.
How to apply: Applications are available online.
Exclusive: Visit www.UltimateScholarshipBook.com and enter code GL34312 for updates on this award.

(344) • Gravure Publishing Council Scholarship

Gravure Education Foundation
1200-A Scottsville Road
Rochester, NY 14624
Phone: 315-589-8879
Fax: 585-436-7689
Email: lwshatch@gaa.org
http://www.gaa.org
Purpose: To support undergraduate students to help them enter the printing industry.
Eligibility: Applicants must major in printing, graphic arts or graphic communications and be at least a junior at the time the scholarship is awarded. Applicants should be interested in promoting gravure as the preferred method in high-quality printing.

Target applicants: College students. Adult students.
Minimum GPA: 3.0
Amount: $1,500.
Number of awards: 1.
Deadline: May 31.
How to apply: Applications are available online.
Exclusive: Visit www.UltimateScholarshipBook.com and enter code GR34412 for updates on this award.

(345) • Harlequin Dance Scholarship

American Harlequin Corporation
Dance Scholarship Program
1531 Glen Avenue
Moorestown, NJ 08057
Phone: 800-642-6440
Fax: 856-231-4403
Email: dance@harlequinfloors.com
http://www.harlequinfloors.com
Purpose: To aid dance students.
Eligibility: Applicants must be U.S. or Canadian citizens between the ages of 15 and 21. They must be enrolled at a public or private dance school. Selection is made through a random drawing.
Target applicants: High school students. College students.
Amount: Varies.
Number of awards: Varies.
Deadline: November 1.
How to apply: Applications are available online. An application form is required.
Exclusive: Visit www.UltimateScholarshipBook.com and enter code AM34512 for updates on this award.

(346) • Harvie Jordan Scholarship

American Translators Association
225 Reinekers Lane
Suite 590
Alexandria, VA 22314
Phone: 703-683-6100
Fax: 703-683-6122
Email: ata@atanet.org
http://www.atanet.org
Purpose: To support members of the Spanish Language Division of the American Translators Association.
Eligibility: Applicants must have been ATA Spanish Language Division members for at least two years. They must also be able to show that they have made important contributions to translation and interpretation.
Target applicants: College students. Graduate school students. Adult students.
Amount: Paid registration to ATA Conference.
Number of awards: Varies.
Deadline: September 17.
How to apply: Applications are available online.
Exclusive: Visit www.UltimateScholarshipBook.com and enter code AM34612 for updates on this award.

(347) • Henry Luce Foundation/ACLS Dissertation Fellowships in American Art

American Council of Learned Societies (ACLS)
633 Third Avenue
New York, NY 10017-6795
Phone: 212-697-1505
Fax: 212-949-8058
Email: sfisher@acls.org
http://www.contemplativemind.org/
Purpose: To support Ph.D. candidates working on art history dissertations.
Eligibility: Applicants must be Ph.D. candidates in an art history department in the U.S. who are working on dissertations about American visual arts history. All the Ph.D. requirements should be met except the dissertation before taking the fellowship. Applicants should submit an application, a proposal, a bibliography, illustrations (optional), a publications list (optional), three reference letters and an official transcript of graduate record. The fellowship lasts for a year.
Target applicants: Graduate school students. Adult students.
Amount: $25,000.
Number of awards: 10.
Deadline: November 10.
How to apply: Applications are available online.
Exclusive: Visit www.UltimateScholarshipBook.com and enter code AM34712 for updates on this award.

(348) • IACI/NUI Visiting Fellowship in Irish Studies

Irish-American Cultural Institute (IACI)
AN FORAS CULTUIR GAEL-MHEIRCHEANACH
1 Lackawanna Place
Morristown, NJ 07960
Phone: 973-605-1991
Fax: 973-605-8875
http://www.iaci-usa.org
Purpose: To award fellowships to Irish studies scholars to spend one semester at the University of Ireland-Galway.
Eligibility: Applicants must provide a description of how the fellowship will be used and a curriculum vitae with a list of publications.
Target applicants: Graduate school students. Adult students.
Amount: Varies.
Number of awards: Varies.
Deadline: December 31.
How to apply: Application is available online.
Exclusive: Visit www.UltimateScholarshipBook.com and enter code IR34812 for updates on this award.

(349) • IDSA Undergraduate Scholarships

Industrial Designers Society of America
45195 Business Court
Suite 250
Dulles, VA 20166
Phone: 703-707-6000
Fax: 703-787-8501
Email: idsa@idsa.org
http://www.idsa.org
Purpose: To help industrial design students in their final year of schooling.
Eligibility: Applicants must be full-time students enrolled in an IDSA-listed program in their next-to-last year of the program, have a minimum 3.0 GPA, be members of an IDSA Student Chapter and be U.S. citizens or residents. Applicants must submit a letter of intent, 20 visual examples of their work and a transcript. Awards are based solely on the excellence of the submitted works.
Target applicants: College students. Adult students.
Minimum GPA: 3.0
Amount: $1,500.

Number of awards: 1.
Deadline: May 30.
How to apply: Applications are available online.
Exclusive: Visit www.UltimateScholarshipBook.com and enter code IN34912 for updates on this award.

---

(350) • Illustrators of the Future

L. Ron Hubbard
P.O. Box 3190
Los Angeles, CA 90078
Phone: 323-466-3310
Email: contests@authorservicesinc.com
http://www.writersofthefuture.com
Purpose: To discover deserving amateur aspiring illustrators.
Eligibility: Applicants must not have published more than three black-and-white story illustrations or more than one color painting in national media. Applicants must also submit three original illustrations done in a black-and-white medium in three different themes.
Target applicants: High school students. College students. Graduate school students. Adult students.
Amount: $500-$5,000.
Number of awards: 3 awards are given quarterly with a grand prize awarded annually.
Deadline: December 31, March 31, June 30, September 30.
How to apply: There is no application form.
Exclusive: Visit www.UltimateScholarshipBook.com and enter code L.35012 for updates on this award.

---

(351) • International Scholarships

American Institute for Foreign Study
AIFS College Division
River Plaza
9 W. Broad Street
Stamford, CT 06902
Phone: 800-727-2437
Fax: 203-399-5597
Email: info@aifs.com
http://www.aifsabroad.com
Purpose: To promote international understanding through study abroad.
Eligibility: Applicants must be currently enrolled college undergraduates with a minimum 3.0 GPA who show leadership potential and are involved in extra-curricular activities centered on multicultural or international issues. Applicants must submit a 1,000-word essay on how study abroad will change their lives.
Target applicants: College students. Adult students.
Minimum GPA: 3.0
Amount: $1,000.
Number of awards: 40.
Deadline: April 15 for fall semester and October 1 for spring semester.
How to apply: Applications are available online.
Exclusive: Visit www.UltimateScholarshipBook.com and enter code AM35112 for updates on this award.

---

(352) • International Trumpet Guild Conference Scholarship

International Trumpet Guild
John Irish, Department of Music
Angelo State University
ASU Station #10906
San Angelo, TX 76909
Email: confscholarships@trumpetguild.org
http://www.trumpetguild.org
Purpose: To improve the artistic level of trumpet players.
Eligibility: Applicants must be students and record audition songs onto a tape or CD. There are different age group categories, and each category has its own performance requirements. Applicants must be ITG members.
Target applicants: Junior high students or younger. High school students. College students. Graduate school students. Adult students.
Amount: Varies.
Number of awards: Varies.
Deadline: February 15.
How to apply: Applications are available online.
Exclusive: Visit www.UltimateScholarshipBook.com and enter code IN35212 for updates on this award.

---

(353) • Irene Ryan Acting Scholarships

John F. Kennedy Center for the Performing Arts
2700 F Street NW
Washington, DC 20566
Phone: 800-444-1324
http://www.kennedy-center.org/education/actf/actfira.html
Purpose: To aid outstanding student performers.
Eligibility: Applicants must be undergraduate or graduate students who have appeared in a participating or associate production of the Kennedy Center American College Theater Festival. Students must be nominated by their schools and perform an audition in each round of the competition in which they participate.
Target applicants: College students. Graduate school students. Adult students.
Amount: Up to $2,500.
Number of awards: 19.
Deadline: Varies.
How to apply: Applications are available from your sponsor.
Exclusive: Visit www.UltimateScholarshipBook.com and enter code JO35312 for updates on this award.

---

(354) • Jeanne S. Chall Research Fellowship

International Reading Association
The Jeanne S. Chall Research Fellowship
Division of Research and Policy
800 Barksdale Road, P.O. Box 8139
Newark, DE 19714
Phone: 302-731-1600
Fax: 302-731-1057
http://www.reading.org
Purpose: To support dissertation research in reading.
Eligibility: Applicants must be doctoral students planning or beginning their dissertation on one of the following topics in the field of reading: beginning reading, readability, reading difficulty, stages of reading development, the relation of vocabulary to reading and diagnosing and teaching adults with limited reading ability. Applicants must also be members of the International Reading Association.
Target applicants: Graduate school students. Adult students.
Amount: $6,000.
Number of awards: 1.
Deadline: November 1.
How to apply: Applications are available online.
Exclusive: Visit www.UltimateScholarshipBook.com and enter code IN35412 for updates on this award.

(355) • Joel Polsky Academic Achievement Award

American Society of Interior Designers (ASID) Educational Foundation Inc.
608 Massachusetts Avenue NE
Washington, DC 20002-6006
Phone: 202-546-3480
Fax: 202-546-3240
http://www.asid.org

Purpose: To recognize an interior design student's project.

Eligibility: Applicants must be undergraduate or graduate students in interior design and should submit entry forms and projects such as research papers or doctoral and master's theses that focus on interior design topics. The projects are judged on content, breadth of material, coverage of the topic, innovative subject matter, bibliography and references. The society may exhibit any entry for two years.

Target applicants: College students. Graduate school students. Adult students.

Amount: $1,000.

Number of awards: 1.

Deadline: March 1.

How to apply: Applications are available online.

Exclusive: Visit www.UltimateScholarshipBook.com and enter code AM35512 for updates on this award.

(356) • Johansen International Competition for Young String Players

Friday Morning Music Club Inc.
801 K Street NW
Washington, DC 20001
Phone: 202-333-2075
Email: johanesncomp@fmmc.org
http://www.fmmc.org

Purpose: To support young instrumentalists.

Eligibility: Applicants must be students of violin, viola or cello between the ages of 13 and 17 at the time of competition. Students must not be under professional management and must perform five pieces for the competition. Note: We do not recommend applying to scholarships that charge application fees. However, some scholarships of this type charge fees and are included for completeness.

Target applicants: Junior high students or younger. High school students.

Amount: $5,000-$10,000.

Number of awards: 9.

Deadline: December 1.

How to apply: Applications are available online. An application form, repertoire list, audition CD, release forms, education and experience page and $75 application fee are required.

Exclusive: Visit www.UltimateScholarshipBook.com and enter code FR35612 for updates on this award.

(357) • John Lennon Scholarship Competition

BMI Foundation Inc.
320 W. 57th Street
New York, NY 10019
Phone: 212-586-2000
Email: info@bmifoundation.org
http://www.bmifoundation.org

Purpose: Established in 1997 by Yoko Ono in conjunction with the BMI Foundation, the John Lennon Scholarship recognizes the talent of young songwriters.

Eligibility: Applicants must be age 15 to 25 and write an original song to be reviewed by a prestigious panel of judges. Entries are to be submitted by music schools, universities, youth orchestras and the Music Educators National Conference (MENC).

Target applicants: Junior high students or younger. High school students. College students. Graduate school students.

Amount: $5,000-$10,000.

Number of awards: 3.

Deadline: January 31.

How to apply: Please see the website for a full list of eligible organizations that may submit entries.

Exclusive: Visit www.UltimateScholarshipBook.com and enter code BM35712 for updates on this award.

(358) • John O. Crane Memorial Fellowship

Institute of Current World Affairs
Steven Butler, Executive Director
4545 42nd Street NW
Suite 311
Washington, DC 20016
Phone: 202-364-4068
Fax: 202-364-0498
Email: apply@icwa.org
http://www.icwa.org

Purpose: To promote independent study abroad in Central Europe, Eastern Europe and the Middle East.

Eligibility: Applicants must be under the age of 36 and must have strong, credible ties to American society. They must propose an independent research project that would be conducted in Central Europe, Eastern Europe or the Middle East and be proficient in a native language that is commonly spoken in the proposed research site. Selection is based on the overall strength of the application.

Target applicants: High school students. College students. Graduate school students. Adult students.

Amount: Varies.

Number of awards: Varies.

Deadline: Varies.

How to apply: Application instructions are available online. A letter of interest and resume are required for the initial phase of the application process.

Exclusive: Visit www.UltimateScholarshipBook.com and enter code IN35812 for updates on this award.

(359) • JTG Scholarship in Scientific and Technical Translation or Interpretation

American Translators Association
225 Reinekers Lane
Suite 590
Alexandria, VA 22314
Phone: 703-683-6100
Fax: 703-683-6122
Email: ata@atanet.org
http://www.atanet.org

Purpose: To support students in the fields of translation and interpretation.

Eligibility: Applicants must be enrolled or planning to enroll in a graduate or undergraduate degree program for either scientific and technical translation or interpretation. Students must be attending school full-time, and they must have completed one year of post-secondary schooling. Applicants should also have at least a 3.0 overall GPA and a 3.5 GPA in translation or interpretation courses.

Target applicants: College students. Graduate school students. Adult students.
Minimum GPA: 3.0
Amount: $2,500.
Number of awards: 1.
Deadline: June 6.
How to apply: Applications are available online.
Exclusive: Visit www.UltimateScholarshipBook.com and enter code AM35912 for updates on this award.

(360) • Julius and Esther Stulberg International String Competition

Julius and Esther Stulberg Competition Inc.
359 S Kalamazoo Mall #14
Kalamazoo, MI 49007
Phone: 269-343-2776
Email: stulbergcomp@yahoo.com
http://www.stulberg.org
Purpose: To support young instrumentalists.
Eligibility: Applicants must be students of violin, viola, cello or double bass, be 19 years of age or younger as of January 1 of the year of competition and perform a Bach piece and a solo for the competition.
Target applicants: Junior high students or younger. High school students.
Amount: $500-$5,000.
Number of awards: 4.
Deadline: December 17.
How to apply: Applications are available online. An application form, proof of age and audition CD are required.
Exclusive: Visit www.UltimateScholarshipBook.com and enter code JU36012 for updates on this award.

(361) • Junior Competition

Gina Bachauer International Piano Foundation
138 W. Broadway, Suite 220
Salt Lake City, UT 84101
Phone: 801-297-4250
Fax: 801-521-9202
Email: info@bachauer.com
http://www.bachauer.com
Purpose: To reward top piano prodigies, ages 11 to 13.
Eligibility: Applicants must perform at this competition in Salt Lake City, Utah. Students are provided with housing but must provide own transportation to and from Salt Lake City. Applicants must perform a 20-minute program of solo music and a 30-minute program of solo music.
Target applicants: Junior high students or younger.
Amount: Up to $7,000.
Number of awards: 6.
Deadline: The competition is June 18-23.
How to apply: Applications are available online.
Exclusive: Visit www.UltimateScholarshipBook.com and enter code GI36112 for updates on this award.

(362) • Junior Composers Award

National Federation of Music Clubs Junior Composers Award
Karen Greenhalgh
8261 San Juan Range Road
Littleton, CO 80127
Phone: 317-882-4003
Fax: 317-882-4019
Email: kgreenhalgh3@aol.com
http://www.nfmc-music.org
Purpose: To support young composers.
Eligibility: There are four age classes: 9 and under; 10-12; 13-15 and 16-18. Applicants must be members of the National Federation of Music Clubs. Selection is based on content and musicianship. There is a $1.25 entry fee plus state entry fee. Note: We do not recommend applying to scholarships that charge application fees. However, some scholarships of this type charge fees and are included for completeness.
Target applicants: Junior high students or younger. High school students.
Amount: $50-$200.
Number of awards: Varies.
Deadline: February 1.
How to apply: Applications are available online.
Exclusive: Visit www.UltimateScholarshipBook.com and enter code NA36212 for updates on this award.

(363) • Junior Fellowships

Dumbarton Oaks
1703 32nd Street NW
Washington, DC 20007
Phone: 202-339-6401
Fax: 202-339-6419
Email: dumbartonoaks@doaks.org
http://www.doaks.org
Purpose: To provide fellowships to scholars engaged in Byzantine studies, Pre-Columbian studies and garden and landscape studies.
Eligibility: Applicants at the time of application should have fulfilled all preliminary requirements for a Ph.D. and be willing to work on a dissertation or final project at Dumbarton Oaks under the direction of a faculty member at their own university. The fellowships are in the following areas: Byzantine Studies (including related aspects of late Roman, early Christian, western medieval, Slavic and Near Eastern Studies), Pre-Columbian Studies (of Mexico, Central America and Andean South America) and garden and landscape studies. Fellowships are based on demonstrated scholarly ability and preparation of the candidate (including knowledge of the required languages) and value of the study or project and its relevance to Dumbarton Oaks.
Target applicants: Graduate school students. Adult students.
Amount: $22,110.
Number of awards: Varies.
Deadline: November 1.
How to apply: Applicants must submit ten complete, collated sets of: application letter, proposal and personal and professional data. They must also submit an official transcript and three recommendation letters, with one from the faculty advisor.
Exclusive: Visit www.UltimateScholarshipBook.com and enter code DU36312 for updates on this award.

(364) • King Olav V Norwegian-American Heritage Fund

Sons of Norway Foundation
1455 West Lake Street
Minneapolis, MN 55408
Phone: 800-945-8851
Fax: 612-827-0658
Email: foundation@sofn.com
http://www.sofn.com

Purpose: To promote educational exchange between Norway and North America.
Eligibility: Applicants must be Americans, 18 years or older, who would like to further their interest in Norwegian heritage or in modern Norway at an institution of higher learning. The fund also welcomes applications from Norwegians who desire to further their studies in North America. Selection is based on grade point average, participation in school and community activities, work experience, education and career goals and personal and school references.
Target applicants: High school students. College students. Adult students.
Amount: $1,000-$1,500.
Number of awards: Varies.
Deadline: March 1.
How to apply: Applications are available online.
Exclusive: Visit www.UltimateScholarshipBook.com and enter code SO36412 for updates on this award.

(365) • KOR Memorial Scholarship

Klingon Language Institute
P.O. Box 634
Flourtown, PA 19031
http://www.kli.org/scholarship
Purpose: To encourage language study.
Eligibility: Applicants must be full-time undergraduate or graduate students pursuing a degree in the field of language study. They must be nominated by the chair, head or dean of their department. Nominating faculty must submit a nominating letter, two additional faculty letters of recommendation and a personal statement and resume from the nominee. Knowledge of Klingon is not required.
Target applicants: College students. Graduate school students. Adult students.
Amount: $500.
Number of awards: 1.
Deadline: June 1.
How to apply: There is no application form.
Exclusive: Visit www.UltimateScholarshipBook.com and enter code KL36512 for updates on this award.

(366) • Lions International Peace Poster Contest

Lions Club International
300 W. 22nd Street
Oak Brook, IL 60523-8842
Phone: 630-571-5466
Email: pr@lionsclubs.org
http://www.lionsclubs.org
Purpose: To award creative youngsters with cash prizes for outstanding poster designs.
Eligibility: Students must be 11, 12 or 13 years old as of the deadline and must be sponsored by their local Lions club. Entries will be judged at the local, district, multiple district and international levels. Posters will be evaluated on originality, artistic merit and expression of the assigned theme.
Target applicants: Junior high students or younger.
Amount: $500-$2,500.
Number of awards: 24.
Deadline: November 15.
How to apply: Applications are available from your local Lion's Club.
Exclusive: Visit www.UltimateScholarshipBook.com and enter code LI36612 for updates on this award.

(367) • Lotte Lenya Competition for Singers

Kurt Weill Foundation for Music
7 East 20th Street
3rd Floor
New York, NY 10003
Phone: 212-505-5240
Fax: 212-353-9663
Email: kwfinfo@dwf.org
http://www.kwf.org
Purpose: To recognize excellence in music theater performance.
Eligibility: Applicants must be between 19 and 32 years old and attend a regional competition, performing four selections. If contestants are unable to participate in any of the scheduled regional auditions, they may instead submit a videotape or DVD, which must contain all four of the required repertoire selections. Finalists will be chosen, based on vocal beauty and technique, interpretation, acting, repertoire variety and presence.
Target applicants: High school students. College students. Graduate school students. Adult students.
Amount: $500-$15,000 plus travel stipend.
Number of awards: Varies.
Deadline: January 31.
How to apply: Applications are available online.
Exclusive: Visit www.UltimateScholarshipBook.com and enter code KU36712 for updates on this award.

(368) • Mabelle Wilhelmina Boldt Scholarship

American Society of Interior Designers (ASID) Educational Foundation Inc.
608 Massachusetts Avenue NE
Washington, DC 20002-6006
Phone: 202-546-3480
Fax: 202-546-3240
http://www.asid.org
Purpose: To help interior designers continue their education.
Eligibility: Applicants must be enrolled in or have applied for admission to a graduate-level interior design program at a degree-granting institution. Students must have been active designers for at least five years before returning to graduate school. The scholarship is based on academic and creative accomplishment. Applicants must submit undergraduate transcripts, a statement and a letter of recommendation. Preference is given to students with a focus on design research. ASID may publish some of the research.
Target applicants: Graduate school students. Adult students.
Amount: $2,000.
Number of awards: Varies.
Deadline: March 1.
How to apply: Applications are available online.
Exclusive: Visit www.UltimateScholarshipBook.com and enter code AM36812 for updates on this award.

(369) • Metropolitan Opera National Council Auditions

Metropolitan Opera
Lincoln Center
New York, NY 10023
Phone: 212-870-4515
Fax: 212-870-7648
Email: ncouncil@metopera.org
http://www.metoperafamily.org/metopera/auditions/national

Purpose: To recruit young talent for the Metropolitan Opera.
Eligibility: Applicants must be U.S. or Canadian citizens, residents of at least one year or students in U.S. or Canadian institutions of higher learning. Applicants must also be 20 to 30 years of age, have musical training and background and demonstrate operatic potential. They must be able to sing in more than one language. Applicants must audition with five arias. Note: We do not recommend applying to scholarships that charge application fees. However, some scholarships of this type charge fees and are included for completeness.
Target applicants: High school students. College students. Graduate school students. Adult students.
Amount: $1,500-$15,000.
Number of awards: Varies.
Deadline: Varies.
How to apply: Applications are available online. An application form, proof of age, proof of residency/college enrollment (foreign applicants only) and $30 application fee are required.
Exclusive: Visit www.UltimateScholarshipBook.com and enter code ME36912 for updates on this award.

---

(370) · Morton Gould Young Composer Award

ASCAP Foundation
One Lincoln Plaza
New York, NY 10023
Phone: 212-621-6219
http://www.ascapfoundation.org
Purpose: To encourage young composers early in their careers.
Eligibility: Applicants must be composers who have not turned 30 before January 1 of the current year. They must be U.S. citizens or permanent residents or enrolled students with a student visa. Applicants must submit an original composition.
Target applicants: Junior high students or younger. High school students. College students. Graduate school students. Adult students.
Amount: Varies.
Number of awards: Varies.
Deadline: March 1.
How to apply: Applications are available online.
Exclusive: Visit www.UltimateScholarshipBook.com and enter code AS37012 for updates on this award.

---

(371) · NAMTA Foundation Art Scholarships

NAMTA Foundation for the Visual Arts
15806 Brookway Drive
Suite 300
Huntersville, NC 28078
Phone: 800-746-2682
Fax: 704-892-6247
Email: foundation@namta.org
http://www.namtafoundation.org
Purpose: To support visual arts majors.
Eligibility: Applicants must be graduating high school seniors or current college students and major in painting, drawing, sketching, sculpture or some other form of visual art. Selection is based on artistic talent and potential, interest and enthusiasm for the fine arts. Extracurricular activities, GPA and financial need are also considered.
Target applicants: High school students. College students. Adult students.
Amount: Varies.
Number of awards: Varies.
Deadline: March 1.
How to apply: Applications are available online. An application form, essay and two to three work samples are required.
Exclusive: Visit www.UltimateScholarshipBook.com and enter code NA37112 for updates on this award.

---

(372) · National High School Poetry Contest/ Easterday Poetry Award

Live Poets Society
P.O. Box 8841
Turnersville, NJ 08012
Email: lpsnj@comcast.net
http://www.highschoolpoetrycontest.com
Purpose: To provide a venue for young poets to be recognized.
Eligibility: Applicants must be U.S. high school students. Submitted poems must be 20 lines or less, in English, unpublished and not simultaneously submitted to any other competition. Applicants may only submit one poem during any 90-day span and must include a self-addressed, stamped envelope with each mailed entry, or applicants may submit their poems online. Submissions are accepted year-round.
Target applicants: High school students.
Amount: $100-$1,000 + publication.
Number of awards: 12.
Deadline: Varies.
How to apply: There is no application form.
Exclusive: Visit www.UltimateScholarshipBook.com and enter code LI37212 for updates on this award.

---

(373) · National Italian American Foundation Scholarship

National Italian American Foundation
1860 19th Street NW
Washington, DC 20009
Phone: 202-387-0600
Fax: 202-387-0800
Email: scholarships@niaf.org
http://www.niaf.org
Purpose: To support Italian American students and students of any ethnic background studying Italian language or studies.
Eligibility: Applicants must either be Italian American students who demonstrate outstanding academic achievement or be students from any ethnic background majoring or minoring in Italian language, Italian studies, Italian American studies or a related field and demonstrate outstanding academic achievement. Applicants must also plan to be or currently be enrolled in an accredited institution of higher education, have a minimum 3.5 GPA and be U.S. citizens or permanent residents.
Target applicants: High school students. College students. Adult students.
Minimum GPA: 3.5
Amount: $2,000-$12,000.
Number of awards: Varies.
Deadline: March 5.
How to apply: Applications are available online.
Exclusive: Visit www.UltimateScholarshipBook.com and enter code NA37312 for updates on this award.

---

(374) · National Junior Classical League (NJCL) Scholarships

National Junior Classical League
1122 Oak Street North
Fargo, ND 58102

Phone: 513-529-7741
Fax: 513-529-7742
Email: administrator@njcl.org
http://www.njcl.org
Purpose: To support students studying the classics.
Eligibility: Applicants must be NJCL members in good standing, entering college the upcoming year, and studying the classics. Special consideration is given to those planning to teach Latin, Greek or classical humanities. Selection is based on financial need, JCL service, academics and recommendations.
Target applicants: High school students.
Amount: $1,200-$2,500.
Number of awards: Varies.
Deadline: May 1.
How to apply: Applications are available online or by written request.
Exclusive: Visit www.UltimateScholarshipBook.com and enter code NA37412 for updates on this award.

(375) · National Latin Exam Scholarship

National Latin Exam
University of Mary Washington
1301 College Avenue
Fredericksburg, VA 22401
Phone: 888-378-7721
Email: nle@umw.edu
http://www.nle.org
Purpose: To reward students for their Latin proficiency.
Eligibility: Applicants must be gold medal winners in Latin III-IV Prose, III-IV Poetry or Latin V-VI on the National Latin Exam. Applicants must be high school seniors who agree to take at least one Latin or classical Greek each semester during their first year of college. A classics in translation course does not count.
Target applicants: High school students.
Amount: $1,000.
Number of awards: 21.
Scholarship may be renewable.
Deadline: September 15.
How to apply: Applications are mailed to eligible students. Renewal applications are available online.
Exclusive: Visit www.UltimateScholarshipBook.com and enter code NA37512 for updates on this award.

(376) · National Peace Essay Contest

United States Institute of Peace
1200 17th Street, NW
Suite 200
Washington, DC 20036
Phone: 202-457-1700
Email: essay_contest@usip.org
http://www.usip.org
Purpose: To expand educational opportunities for young Americans.
Eligibility: Applicants must be in grades 9 through 12 and home schooled students or students who are U.S. citizens attending high schools overseas. Applicants need the sponsorship of any school, school club, youth group, community group or religious organization. Selection is based on the quality of the research, analysis, form, style and mechanics of the essay.
Target applicants: High school students.
Amount: $5,000-$10,000.
Number of awards: 56.
Deadline: February 1.
How to apply: Applications are available online.
Exclusive: Visit www.UltimateScholarshipBook.com and enter code UN37612 for updates on this award.

(377) · National Sculpture Society Scholarship

National Sculpture Society
237 Park Avenue
Ground Floor
New York, NY 10017
Phone: 212-764-5645
Email: nss1893@aol.com
http://www.nationalsculpture.org
Purpose: To award scholarships to students of figurative or representative sculpture.
Eligibility: Applicants must provide brief biographies and an explanation of their background in sculpture, two recommendation letters and photographs of their sculpture work. Students must also demonstrate financial need.
Target applicants: College students. Adult students.
Amount: $2,000.
Number of awards: Varies.
Deadline: June 2.
How to apply: Follow the application guidelines listed on the website.
Exclusive: Visit www.UltimateScholarshipBook.com and enter code NA37712 for updates on this award.

(378) · National Security Education Program David L. Boren Undergraduate Scholarships

Institute of International Education
1400 K Street NW
Washington, DC 20005
Phone: 202-326-7672
Fax: 202-326-7835
Email: boren@iie.org
http://www.iie.org
Purpose: To provide an opportunity for undergraduate students to study abroad in certain countries that are vital to U.S. security interests.
Eligibility: Applicants must be U.S. undergraduate students who have a strong interest in working for the U.S. federal government after graduation. They must intend to study abroad in one of several countries that have been overlooked traditionally by students wishing to travel overseas for academic purposes. They must be able to demonstrate how their studies abroad would contribute to U.S. national security interests. Preference will be given to students who can commit to a full academic year of study abroad. Selection is based on the overall strength of the application.
Target applicants: College students. Adult students.
Amount: Up to $20,000.
Number of awards: Varies.
Deadline: February 10.
How to apply: Applications are available online. An application form and supporting materials are required.
Exclusive: Visit www.UltimateScholarshipBook.com and enter code IN37812 for updates on this award.

(379) · National Ten Minute Play Contest

Actors Theatre of Louisville
National Ten Minute Play Contest
316 W. Main Street
Louisville, KY 40202-4218

Phone: 502-584-1265
http://www.actorstheatre.org
Purpose: To identify emerging playwrights.
Eligibility: Each playwright may only submit one script no more than 10 pages in length that has not been previously submitted. Applicants must be U.S. citizens or permanent residents.
Target applicants: Junior high students or younger. High school students. College students. Graduate school students. Adult students.
Amount: $1,000.
Number of awards: Varies.
Deadline: November 1.
How to apply: No application is necessary.
Exclusive: Visit www.UltimateScholarshipBook.com and enter code AC37912 for updates on this award.

(380) • NFMC Claire Ulrich Whitehurst Piano Award

National Federation of Music Clubs Claire Ulrich Whitehurst Piano Award
Claire-Frances Whitehurst
3360 SW 18th Street
Miami, FL 33145-1853
Phone: 305-445-2128
Fax: 317-638-0503
Email: info@nfmc-music.org
http://www.nfmc-music.org
Purpose: To support young piano players.
Eligibility: Applicants must be high school sophomores, juniors or seniors under age 18 and members of the National Federation of Music Clubs and must submit taped piano solo performances. There is a $10 entry fee. Note: We do not recommend applying to scholarships that charge application fees. However, some scholarships of this type charge fees and are included for completeness.
Target applicants: High school students.
Amount: $500.
Number of awards: 1.
Deadline: February 1 on even numbered years.
How to apply: Applications are available online.
Exclusive: Visit www.UltimateScholarshipBook.com and enter code NA38012 for updates on this award.

(381) • NFMC Lynn Freeman Olson Composition Awards

National Federation of Music Clubs Olson Awards
James Schnars
6550 Shoreline Drive
Suite 7505
St. Petersburg, FL 33708
Phone: 317-638-4003
Fax: 317-638-0503
Email: info@nfmc-music.org
http://www.nfmc-music.org
Purpose: To support student composers.
Eligibility: Applicants must be at least in grade 7 and no older than age 25. Three awards are given, one for each category: intermediate (grades 7 to 9), high school (grades 10 to 12) and advanced (high school graduates through age 25). Applicants must be members of the National Federation of Music Clubs and must submit an original piano composition to be judged. This biennial award is given in odd numbered years.
Target applicants: Junior high students or younger. High school students. College students.
Amount: $500-$1,500.
Number of awards: 3.
Deadline: March 1.
How to apply: Applications are available online.
Exclusive: Visit www.UltimateScholarshipBook.com and enter code NA38112 for updates on this award.

(382) • NFMC Wendell Irish Viola Award

National Federation of Music Clubs (AR)
Dr. George Keck
421 Cherry Street
Arkadelphia, AR 71923
Phone: 317-638-4003
Fax: 317-638-0503
Email: keckg@obu.edu
http://www.nfmc-music.org
Purpose: To recognize musically talented students.
Eligibility: Applicants must be between the ages of 12 and 18 and must be Individual Junior Special members or Active Junior Club members of the National Federation of Music Clubs. Applicants must enter in their state of residence by submitting a taped performance.
Target applicants: Junior high students or younger. High school students.
Amount: $500.
Number of awards: 5.
Deadline: February 1.
How to apply: Applications are available online.
Exclusive: Visit www.UltimateScholarshipBook.com and enter code NA38212 for updates on this award.

(383) • Nido Qubein Scholarship

National Speakers Association
1500 S. Priest Drive
Attn: Scholarship Committee
Tempe, AZ 85281
Phone: 480-968-2552
Fax: 480-968-0911
http://www.nsaspeaker.org
Purpose: To encourage study in the field of professional speaking.
Eligibility: Applicants must be full-time students majoring or minoring in speech. Selection is based on application, essay, recommendation and college transcript.
Target applicants: College students. Graduate school students. Adult students.
Amount: $5,000.
Number of awards: 4.
Deadline: June 1.
How to apply: Applications are available online or by written request.
Exclusive: Visit www.UltimateScholarshipBook.com and enter code NA38312 for updates on this award.

(384) • Northwest Perspectives Essay Contest

Oregon Quarterly Magazine
204 Alder Building
5528 University of Oregon
Eugene, OR 97403
Phone: 541-346-5047
Email: quarterly@uoregon.edu
http://www.oregonquarterly.com
Purpose: To aid those who have written the best essays on a topic that is related to the Northwest region.

Eligibility: Entrants must be current undergraduate or graduate students, or they must be nonfiction writers who 1) have never won first place in the contest; 2) have not had any featured articles published in the Oregon Quarterly in the past calendar year; 3) are not employees of the Oregon Quarterly or University of Oregon Advancement and 4) are not family members of Oregon Quarterly or University of Oregon Advancement employees. Entrants must submit an essay on a topic that pertains to the Northwest region. Selection is based on the overall strength of the essay.
Target applicants: College students. Graduate school students. Adult students.
Amount: Up to $750.
Number of awards: 6.
Deadline: January 15.
How to apply: Entry instructions are available online. A cover letter and essay are required.
Exclusive: Visit www.UltimateScholarshipBook.com and enter code OR38412 for updates on this award.

---

(385) · Optimist International Essay Contest

Optimist International
4494 Lindell Boulevard
St. Louis, MO 63108
Phone: 314-371-6000
Fax: 314-371-6006
Email: programs@optimist.org
http://www.optimist.org
Purpose: To reward students based on their essay-writing skills.
Eligibility: Applicants must be under 19 years of age as of December 31 of the current school year and application must be made through a local Optimist Club. The essay topic is, "I want to make a difference because..." Applicants compete at the club, district and international level. District winners receive a $650 scholarship, and three international winners receive prizes up to $6,000. Scoring is based on organization, vocabulary and style, grammar and punctuation, neatness and adherence to the contest rules.
Target applicants: High school students.
Amount: $650-$6,000.
Number of awards: Varies.
Deadline: February 28.
How to apply: Contact your local Optimist Club.
Exclusive: Visit www.UltimateScholarshipBook.com and enter code OP38512 for updates on this award.

---

(386) · Patriot's Pen Youth Essay Contest

Veterans of Foreign Wars
406 W. 34th Street
Kansas City, MO 64111
Phone: 816-968-1117
Fax: 816-968-1149
Email: kharmer@vfw.org
http://www.vfw.org
Purpose: To give students in grades 6 through 8 an opportunity to write essays that express their views on democracy.
Eligibility: Applicants must be enrolled as a 6th, 7th or 8th grader in a public, private or parochial school in the U.S., its territories or possessions. Home-schooled students and dependents of U.S. military or civilian personnel in overseas schools may also apply. Foreign exchange students and former applicants who placed in the national finals are ineligible. Students must submit essays based on an annual theme to their local VFW posts. If an essay is picked to advance, the entry is judged at the District (regional) level, then the Department (state) level and finally at the National level. Essays are judged 30 percent on knowledge of the theme, 35 percent on development of the theme and 35 percent on clarity.
Target applicants: Junior high students or younger.
Amount: Up to $10,000.
Number of awards: Varies.
Deadline: November 1.
How to apply: Applications are available online or by contacting the local VFW office. Entries must be turned into the local VFW office. Contact information for these offices can be found online or by calling the VFW National Programs headquarters at 816-968-1117.
Exclusive: Visit www.UltimateScholarshipBook.com and enter code VE38612 for updates on this award.

---

(387) · Platt Family Scholarship Prize Essay Contest

The Lincoln Forum
c/o Don McCue, Curator of the Lincoln Memorial Shrine
125 West Vine Street
92373, CA 92373
Phone: 909-798-7632
Email: archives@akspl.org
http://www.thelincolnforum.org
Purpose: To reward students who have written the best essays on a topic related to Abraham Lincoln.
Eligibility: Applicants must be full-time undergraduate students who are enrolled at a U.S. college or university during the spring term of the contest entry year. They must submit an essay on a sponsor-determined topic that is related to Abraham Lincoln. Selection is based on the overall strength of the essay.
Target applicants: College students. Adult students.
Amount: $250-$1,000.
Number of awards: 3.
Deadline: August 31.
How to apply: Entry instructions are available online. An essay is required.
Exclusive: Visit www.UltimateScholarshipBook.com and enter code TH38712 for updates on this award.

---

(388) · Playwright Discovery Award

VSA Arts
818 Connecticut Avenue NW
Suite 600
Washington, DC 20006
Phone: 800-933-8721
Fax: 202-429-0868
Email: info@vsarts.org
http://www.vsarts.org
Purpose: To award promising young writers with scholarship funds and a chance to have one of their scripts professionally produced at the John F. Kennedy Center for the Performing Arts.
Eligibility: Applicants must be students in grades 6-12. Applicants are to create an original one-act script of less than 40 pages that documents the experience of living with a disability. Applicants themselves need not be disabled, but the script must address the issue. Selected scripts will be performed for middle school, high school, and adult audiences. First and second place winners will have their plays performed at the JFK Performing Arts Center.
Target applicants: Junior high students or younger. High school students.
Amount: Varies.

Number of awards: Varies.
Deadline: Varies.
How to apply: Applications are available online.
Exclusive: Visit www.UltimateScholarshipBook.com and enter code VS38812 for updates on this award.

(389) • Poster Contest for High School Students

Christophers
12 E. 48th Street
New York, NY 10017
http://www.christophers.org
Purpose: To reward students for interpreting a given theme through poster art.
Eligibility: Entrants must be high school students. Students must work individually to create posters of original content. Posters are judged by a panel based on overall impact, expression of the year's theme, artistic merit and originality.
Target applicants: High school students.
Amount: $250-$1,000.
Number of awards: 8.
Deadline: January 23.
How to apply: Applications are available online.
Exclusive: Visit www.UltimateScholarshipBook.com and enter code CH38912 for updates on this award.

(390) • Princess Grace Awards

Princess Grace Awards
150 E. 58th Street
21st Floor
New York, NY 10155
Phone: 212-317-1470
Fax: 212-317-1473
Email: grants@pgfusa.org
http://www.pgfusa.com
Purpose: To assist emerging young artists in theater, dance and film to realize their career goals.
Eligibility: Applicants must submit an example of their work in the category in which they apply: theatre, dance, choreography, film or playwriting. Theatre and dance applicants require the sponsorship of a professional company or school, one nominee per institution. Awards are based on the artistic quality of the artist's work, potential for future excellence and activities.
Target applicants: High school students. College students. Adult students.
Amount: Up to $25,000.
Number of awards: Varies.
Deadline: Varies.
How to apply: Applications are available online.
Exclusive: Visit www.UltimateScholarshipBook.com and enter code PR39012 for updates on this award.

(391) • Print and Graphics Scholarship

Graphic Arts Information Network
Print and Graphics Scholarship Foundation
Scholarship Competition
200 Deer Run Road
Sewickley, PA 15143
Phone: 412-741-6860
Fax: 412-741-2311
Email: pgsf@gatf.org
http://www.gain.org
Purpose: To provide financial assistance for postsecondary education to students interested in graphic communications careers.
Eligibility: Applicants must be high school seniors or high school graduates who have not started college yet, or college students enrolled in a two- or four-year college program. Applicants must be full-time students, be interested in a career in graphic communications and able to maintain a 3.0 GPA.
Target applicants: High school students. College students. Adult students.
Minimum GPA: 3.0
Amount: Varies.
Number of awards: 200+.
Scholarship may be renewable.
Deadline: March 1 for high school and April 1 for college.
How to apply: Applications are available online.
Exclusive: Visit www.UltimateScholarshipBook.com and enter code GR39112 for updates on this award.

(392) • Prize in Ethics Essay Contest

Elie Wiesel Foundation for Humanity
555 Madison Avenue, 20th Floor
New York, NY 10022
Phone: 212-490-7788
Fax: 212-490-6006
Email: info@eliewieselfoundation.org
http://www.eliewieselfoundation.org
Purpose: To promote the thought and discussion of ethics and their place in education.
Eligibility: Applicants must be registered full-time juniors and seniors at accredited colleges and universities in the U.S. Students must write an essay dealing with ethics and have a faculty sponsor review their essay and sign the entry form.
Target applicants: College students. Adult students.
Amount: $500-$5,000.
Number of awards: 5.
Deadline: December 6.
How to apply: Applications are available online.
Exclusive: Visit www.UltimateScholarshipBook.com and enter code EL39212 for updates on this award.

(393) • Project on Nuclear Issues Essay Contest

Center for Strategic and International Studies
Project on Nuclear Issues
1800 K Street, NW
Washington, DC 20006
Phone: 202-887-0200
Fax: 202-775-3199
Email: jward@csis.org
http://www.csis.org
Purpose: To reward those who have written the best essays on a topic related to nuclear weapons.
Eligibility: Applicants must be current undergraduates, graduate students or recent college graduates. They must submit an essay on some facet of nuclear weapons policy or strategy. Selection is based on the overall strength of the essay.
Target applicants: College students. Graduate school students. Adult students.
Amount: $1,500-$5,000.
Number of awards: 4.
Deadline: August 31.

How to apply: Application instructions are available online. A cover letter and essay are required.
Exclusive: Visit www.UltimateScholarshipBook.com and enter code CE39312 for updates on this award.

(394) • Red Vines Drawing Contest

American Licorice Company
2796 NW Clearwater Drive
Bend, OR 97701
http://www.redvines.com
Purpose: To recognize outstanding drawing ability.
Eligibility: Applicants must be U.S. legal residents. They must be at least six years old. They must submit an original drawing for consideration. Selection is based on artistic ability.
Target applicants: Junior high students or younger. High school students. College students. Graduate school students. Adult students.
Amount: Up to $2,500.
Number of awards: 9.
Deadline: September 30.
How to apply: Entry forms are available online. An entry form and drawing are required.
Exclusive: Visit www.UltimateScholarshipBook.com and enter code AM39412 for updates on this award.

(395) • Rotary International Ambassadorial Scholarship Program

Rotary International
One Rotary Center
1560 Sherman Avenue
Evanston, IL 60201
Phone: 847-866-3000
Fax: 847-328-8554
Email: scholarshipinquiries@rotaryintl.org
http://www.rotary.org
Purpose: To further international understanding and friendly relations among people of different countries.
Eligibility: Applicants must be citizens of a country in which there are Rotary clubs and have completed at least two years of college-level coursework or equivalent professional experience before starting their scholarship studies. Initial applications are made through local clubs. Students must be proficient in the language of the proposed host country.
Target applicants: College students. Graduate school students. Adult students.
Amount: Varies.
Number of awards: Varies.
Deadline: As early as March for club deadlines.
How to apply: Applications are available through your local Rotary club or online.
Exclusive: Visit www.UltimateScholarshipBook.com and enter code RO39512 for updates on this award.

(396) • Ruth Lilly Poetry Fellowship

Poetry Magazine
444 N. Michigan Avenue
Suite 1850
Chicago, IL 60611-4034
Phone: 312-787-7070
Fax: 312-787-6650
Email: mail@poetryfoundation.org
http://www.poetryfoundation.org/foundation/prizes_fellowship.html
Purpose: To encourage the study of writing and poetry.
Eligibility: Applicants must be U.S. residents between the ages of 21 and 31. They must be currently enrolled undergraduate or graduate students majoring in English or creative writing.
Target applicants: College students. Graduate school students. Adult students.
Amount: $15,000.
Number of awards: Varies.
Deadline: April 1.
How to apply: Applications are available online. An essay and a poetry submission are required.
Exclusive: Visit www.UltimateScholarshipBook.com and enter code PO39612 for updates on this award.

(397) • Sadler's Wells Global Dance Contest

Sadler's Wells
Phone: 020 7863 8198
Fax: 020 7863 8199
Email: info@globaldancecontest.com
http://www.globaldancecontest.com
Purpose: To support outstanding dancers and choreographers.
Eligibility: Applicants must be 18 years of age or older or over the age of majority if it is higher than 18 in their country. They must submit a dance video to YouTube and register for the contest.
Target applicants: High school students. College students. Graduate school students. Adult students.
Amount: $2,980.
Number of awards: 1.
Deadline: June 30.
How to apply: Applications are available online. A registration form and YouTube video are required.
Exclusive: Visit www.UltimateScholarshipBook.com and enter code SA39712 for updates on this award.

(398) • Scholarship Program for Young Pianists

Chopin Foundation of the United States, Inc.
1440 79th Street Causeway
Suite 117
Miami, FL 33141
Phone: 305-868-0624
Fax: 305-865-5150
Email: info@chopin.org
http://www.chopin.org
Purpose: To support pianists to prepare and qualify for the American National Chopin Piano Competition.
Eligibility: The program is available to any qualified American pianists age 14 to 17 who are enrolled in secondary or undergraduate institutions as full-time students. Applicants also must study music and major in piano. They must submit applications, statements of career goals, two references, audio tapes and $25 fee. Note: We do not recommend applying to scholarships that charge application fees. However, some scholarships of this type charge fees and are included for completeness.
Target applicants: High school students. College students.
Amount: $1,000.
Number of awards: Up to 10.
Scholarship may be renewable.
Deadline: April 15.
How to apply: Applications are available online.
Exclusive: Visit www.UltimateScholarshipBook.com and enter code CH39812 for updates on this award.

(399) · Scholarships to Oslo International Summer School

Sons of Norway Foundation
1455 West Lake Street
Minneapolis, MN 55408
Phone: 800-945-8851
Fax: 612-827-0658
Email: foundation@sofn.com
http://www.sofn.com

Purpose: To give financial support to students who attend Oslo International Summer School.

Eligibility: Applicants who are admitted to Oslo International Summer School and who are Sons of Norway members or children or grandchildren of current members are eligible. Membership must be in effect for one calendar year prior to application. Selection is based on financial need, essay, GPA and letters of recommendation. Extra consideration is given to students who are members of Sons of Norway.

Target applicants: College students. Graduate school students. Adult students.

Amount: $1,500.

Number of awards: 2.

Deadline: March 1.

How to apply: Applications are available online.

Exclusive: Visit www.UltimateScholarshipBook.com and enter code SO39912 for updates on this award.

(400) · Senior Fellowship Program

National Gallery of Art
2000B South Club Drive
Landover, MD 20785
Phone: 202-842-6482
Fax: 202-789-3026
http://www.nga.gov/resources/casva.htm

Purpose: To award fellowships to scholars in the visual arts.

Eligibility: Applicants should have held the Ph.D. for five years or more or possess an equivalent record of professional accomplishment at the time of application. They must submit application forms, proposals, copies of publications and three letters of recommendation. Fellowships are for full-time research, and scholars are expected to reside in Washington and to participate in the activities of the Center. One Paul Mellon Fellowship, one Frese Senior Fellowship and four to six Ailsa Mellon Bruce and Samuel H. Kress Senior Fellowships will be awarded for the academic year. The Paul Mellon and Ailsa Mellon Bruce Senior Fellowships support research in the history, theory and criticism of the visual arts of any geographical area and of any period. The Samuel H. Kress Senior Fellowships support research on European art before the early nineteenth century. The Frese Senior Fellowship is for study in the history, theory and criticism of sculpture, prints and drawings or decorative arts of any geographical area and of any period. Applications are also accepted from scholars in other disciplines whose work is related.

Target applicants: Graduate school students. Adult students.

Amount: Up to $50,000.

Number of awards: 5-7.

Deadline: October 15.

How to apply: Applications are available online.

Exclusive: Visit www.UltimateScholarshipBook.com and enter code NA40012 for updates on this award.

(401) · Short-Term Travel Grants (STG)

International Research and Exchanges Board (IREX)
2121 K Street NW
Suite 700
Washington, DC 20037
Phone: 202-628-8188
Fax: 202-628-8189
Email: irex@irex.org
http://www.irex.org

Purpose: To provide travel grants for U.S. postdoctoral scholars and holders of other graduate degrees to travel to Europe and Eurasia.

Eligibility: Applicants must be U.S. citizens or permanent residents for at least three consecutive years before applying for the grant and must hold a Ph.D. or other terminal degree. The grant is for up to eight weeks for independent research projects. Projects must contribute to the knowledge of political, economic or cultural development of the region and how that knowledge is relevant to U.S. foreign policy.

Target applicants: Graduate school students. Adult students.

Amount: Varies.

Number of awards: Varies.

Deadline: February 2.

How to apply: Applications are available online.

Exclusive: Visit www.UltimateScholarshipBook.com and enter code IN40112 for updates on this award.

(402) · Signet Classic Student Scholarship Essay Contest

Penguin Group (USA)
Academic Marketing Department
Signet Classic Student Scholarship
375 Hudson Street
New York, NY 10014
http://us.penguingroup.com/static/html/services-academic/essayhome.html

Purpose: To reward high school students for their essays on literature.

Eligibility: Applicants must be high school juniors or seniors or equivalent home schooled students and write an essay on one of four selected topics based on a piece of literature. Each English teacher may only submit one junior and one senior essay. Selection is based on style, content, grammar and originality.

Target applicants: High school students.

Amount: $1,000.

Number of awards: 5.

Deadline: April 14.

How to apply: English teachers submit entries.

Exclusive: Visit www.UltimateScholarshipBook.com and enter code PE40212 for updates on this award.

(403) · Sinfonia Foundation Scholarship

Sinfonia Foundation
Scholarship Committee
10600 Old State Road
Evansville, IN 47711-1399
Phone: 800-473-2649 x110
Email: sef@sinfonia.org
http://www.sinfonia.org/SEF/

Purpose: To assist the collegiate members and chapters of Sinfonia.

Eligibility: Applicants must be in college for at least two semesters with good academic standing and submit references and an essay.

Target applicants: College students. Adult students.

Amount: $1,500-$2,500.
Number of awards: 2.
Deadline: February 1.
How to apply: Applications are available online.
Exclusive: Visit www.UltimateScholarshipBook.com and enter code SI40312 for updates on this award.

(404) • Sorantin Competition

San Angelo Symphony
Sorantin Award
P.O. Box 5922
San Angelo, TX 76902
Phone: 325-658-5877
Fax: 325-653-1045
Email: assistant@sanangelosymphony.org
http://www.sanangelosymphony.org
Purpose: To promote musical performances.
Eligibility: There are two divisions of the competition: piano and strings. A winner and a runner-up are selected in each division, and an overall winner is selected to perform with the San Angelo Symphony and will receive an extra $3,000. Applicants cannot have reached their 28th birthday by November 15. There is a $60 application fee. Note: We do not recommend applying to scholarships that charge application fees. However, some scholarships of this type charge fees and are included for completeness.
Target applicants: Junior high students or younger. High school students. College students. Graduate school students. Adult students.
Amount: $1,000-$3,000.
Number of awards: Varies.
Deadline: October 9.
How to apply: Applications are available online.
Exclusive: Visit www.UltimateScholarshipBook.com and enter code SA40412 for updates on this award.

(405) • Stacey Scholarship Fund

John F. and Anna Lee Stacey Scholarship Fund
1700 N.E. 63rd Street
Oklahoma City, OK 73111
Phone: 405-478-2250
Fax: 405-478-4714
Email: emuno@nationalcowboymuseum.org
http://www.cowboyhalloffame.org
Purpose: To educate young men and women who aim to enter the art profession.
Eligibility: Applicants must be between the ages of 18 and 35 and must submit no more than 10 35mm slides of their painting or drawing work for judging along with a letter outlining the applicant's ambitions and plans. Letters of recommendation will also be taken into account during selection.
Target applicants: High school students. College students. Graduate school students. Adult students.
Amount: $5,000.
Number of awards: Varies.
Deadline: February 1.
How to apply: Applications are available online.
Exclusive: Visit www.UltimateScholarshipBook.com and enter code JO40512 for updates on this award.

(406) • Stella Blum Research Grant

Costume Society of America (CSA)
Ann Wass
5903 60th Avenue
Riverdale, MD 20737
Phone: 800-272-9447
Fax: 908-359-7619
Email: national.office@costumesocietyamerica.com
http://www.costumesocietyamerica.com
Purpose: To support a CSA student member working in the field of North American costume.
Eligibility: Applicants must be accepted into an undergraduate or graduate degree program at an accredited university for the time during which the grant would apply, conduct a research project in the area of North American costume and be members of the Costume Society of America (CSA) in good standing. Applications are judged according to significance of topic, feasibility, time frame, methodology, bibliography, budget, applicant's qualifications and how the research might further the field of costumes.
Target applicants: High school students. College students. Graduate school students. Adult students.
Amount: $2,000 plus a travel component of up to $500 to attend National Symposium.
Number of awards: 1.
Deadline: May 1.
How to apply: Applications are available by email or phone.
Exclusive: Visit www.UltimateScholarshipBook.com and enter code CO40612 for updates on this award.

(407) • Stillman-Kelley Awards

National Federation of Music Clubs Stillman-Kelley Award
Sue Breuer
4404 Travis Country
Circle B4
Austin, TX 78735
Phone: 512-892-5633
http://www.nfmc-music.org
Purpose: To support young musicians and composers.
Eligibility: Applicants must be instrumentalists under the age of 17 and be members of the National Federation of Music Clubs. This award rotates by region with the Northeastern and Southeastern regions in even years and Central and Western regions in odd years.
Target applicants: High school students.
Amount: $500-$1,000.
Number of awards: 2.
Deadline: February 1.
How to apply: Applications are available online.
Exclusive: Visit www.UltimateScholarshipBook.com and enter code NA40712 for updates on this award.

(408) • Student Academy Awards

Academy of Motion Picture Arts and Sciences
8949 Wilshire Boulevard
Beverly Hills, CA 90211
Phone: 310-247-3000
Email: rmiller@oscars.org
http://www.oscars.org
Purpose: To support filmmakers with no previous professional experience.

Eligibility: Applicants must be full-time students at an accredited U.S. college, university, film school or art school. Films must be made as a part of a school curriculum in the categories of alternative, animation, documentary or narrative. Selection is based on originality, entertainment, production quality and resourcefulness. Past winners include Spike Lee, Trey Parker, Bob Saget and Oscar winners John Lasseter and Robert Zemeckis.
Target applicants: College students. Graduate school students. Adult students.
Amount: Varies.
Number of awards: Varies.
Deadline: April 1.
How to apply: Applications are available online.
Exclusive: Visit www.UltimateScholarshipBook.com and enter code AC40812 for updates on this award.

(409) • Student Design Competition

International Housewares Association
6400 Shafer Court, Suite 650
Rosemont, IL 60018
Phone: 847-292-4200
Fax: 847-292-4211
http://www.housewares.org
Purpose: To honor and encourage young, up-and-coming designers to enter careers in the housewares industry.
Eligibility: Applicants must be enrolled as an undergraduate or graduate student at an IDSA-affiliated college or university.
Target applicants: College students. Graduate school students. Adult students.
Amount: Varies.
Number of awards: Varies.
Deadline: December 29.
How to apply: Applications are available online.
Exclusive: Visit www.UltimateScholarshipBook.com and enter code IN40912 for updates on this award.

(410) • Student Translation Award

American Translators Association
225 Reinekers Lane
Suite 590
Alexandria, VA 22314
Phone: 703-683-6100
Fax: 703-683-6122
Email: ata@atanet.org
http://www.atanet.org
Purpose: To encourage translation projects by students.
Eligibility: Applicants must be graduate or undergraduate students or a group of students attending an accredited U.S. college or university. The project should have post-grant results such as a publication, conference presentation or teaching material. Computer-assisted translations, dissertations and theses are not eligible, and students who are already published translators are not eligible. Translations must be from a foreign language into English. Preference is given to students who have been or are currently enrolled in translator training programs. There is a limit of one entry per student. Applicants should submit entry forms, statements of purpose, letter of recommendation, translation sample with corresponding source-language text, proof of permission to publish from copyright holder and sample outline or other material demonstrating the nature of the work (if the project is not a translation).
Target applicants: College students. Graduate school students. Adult students.
Amount: $500.
Number of awards: 1.
Deadline: June 30.
How to apply: Applications are available online.
Exclusive: Visit www.UltimateScholarshipBook.com and enter code AM41012 for updates on this award.

(411) • Swackhamer Peace Essay Contest

Nuclear Age Peace Foundation
1187 Coast Village Road
PMB 121, Suite 1
Santa Barbara, CA 93108-2794
Phone: 805-965-3443
Fax: 805-568-0466
http://www.wagingpeace.org
Purpose: To encourage high school students to create a video on world peace.
Eligibility: Students must be in any high school in the world and submit a video on the provided topic. Selection is based on analysis of the subject matter, originality, development of point of view, insight, clarity of expression, organization and grammar.
Target applicants: High school students.
Amount: Varies.
Number of awards: 3.
Deadline: June 1.
How to apply: Applications are available online.
Exclusive: Visit www.UltimateScholarshipBook.com and enter code NU41112 for updates on this award.

(412) • Taylor/Blakeslee University Fellowships

Council for the Advancement of Science Writing (CASW)
P.O. Box 910
Hedgesville, WV 25427
Phone: 304-754-6786
Email: diane@nasw.org
http://www.casw.org
Purpose: To help graduate students in science writing.
Eligibility: Applicants must be U.S. citizens who are enrolled in U.S. graduate-level science writing programs.
Target applicants: Graduate school students. Adult students.
Amount: $5,000.
Number of awards: Varies.
Deadline: July 1.
How to apply: Contact the organization for more information.
Exclusive: Visit www.UltimateScholarshipBook.com and enter code CO41212 for updates on this award.

(413) • Thelma A. Robinson Award in Ballet

National Federation of Music Clubs (Coral Gables, FL)
Anne Cruxent
5530 Lajeune Road
Coral Gables, FL 33146
Phone: 330-638-4003
Fax: 317-638-0503
Email: acruxent@bellsouth.net
http://www.nfmc-music.org
Purpose: To support students who are ballet dancers.
Eligibility: Applicants must be between the ages of 13 and 16. There is no entry fee, but applicants must be members of the NFMC.

Target applicants: Junior high students or younger. High school students.
Amount: $2,500.
Number of awards: 1.
Deadline: October 1.
How to apply: Applications are available online.
Exclusive: Visit www.UltimateScholarshipBook.com and enter code NA41312 for updates on this award.

---

(414) • Thespian Scholarships

Educational Theatre Association
2343 Auburn Avenue
Cincinnati, OH 45219
Phone: 513-421-3900
http://www.edta.org
Purpose: To support student thespians.
Eligibility: Applicants must be seniors in high school, active members of the International Thespian Society and planning to major or minor in communicative arts. Most of the scholarships require an audition or tech portfolio.
Target applicants: High school students.
Amount: $4,500.
Number of awards: Varies.
Deadline: February 1-May 3.
How to apply: Applications are available online.
Exclusive: Visit www.UltimateScholarshipBook.com and enter code ED41412 for updates on this award.

---

(415) • Translation Prize

American-Scandinavian Foundation
58 Park Avenue
New York, NY 10016
Phone: 212-879-9779
Email: grants@amscan.org
http://www.amscan.org
Purpose: To encourage the English translation of Scandinavian literature.
Eligibility: The award is given to the best English translation of poetry, fiction, drama or literary prose written by a Scandinavian author in Danish, Finnish, Icelandic, Norwegian or Swedish after 1800. Translations may not previously have been published in the English language.
Target applicants: Junior high students or younger. High school students. College students. Graduate school students. Adult students.
Amount: $2,000.
Number of awards: Varies.
Scholarship may be renewable.
Deadline: June 1.
How to apply: There is no application form. Please see website for submission details.
Exclusive: Visit www.UltimateScholarshipBook.com and enter code AM41512 for updates on this award.

---

(416) • Tuition Scholarship Program

Thomas Pniewski, Director of Cultural Affairs
Kosciuszko Foundation
15 East 65th Street
New York, NY 10021-6595
Phone: 212-734-2130 x214
Fax: 212-628-4552
Email: tompkf@aol.com
http://www.thekf.org/kf/about/about_us/
Purpose: To provide funding to qualified students for full-time graduate studies in the United States and several graduate programs in Poland.
Eligibility: Applicants must be U.S. citizens or permanent residents of Polish descent, beginning or continuing graduate students and have a minimum 3.0 GPA. U.S. citizens who are majoring in Polish studies are also eligible. Selection is based on academic performance, achievements, motivation, interest in Polish subjects or involvement in the Polish community and financial need.
Target applicants: College students. Graduate school students. Adult students.
Minimum GPA: 3.0
Amount: $1,000-$7,000.
Number of awards: Varies.
Scholarship may be renewable.
Deadline: January 5.
How to apply: Applications are available online.
Exclusive: Visit www.UltimateScholarshipBook.com and enter code TH41612 for updates on this award.

---

(417) • U.S. Department of Education Fulbright-Hays Project Abroad Scholarship for Programs in China

Council on International Educational Exchange
7 Custom House Street, 3rd Floor
Portland, ME 04101
Phone: 800-40-STUDY
Fax: 207-553-7699
Email: scholarships@ciee.org
http://www.ciee.org
Purpose: To assist students who are participating in the Chinese language programs offered by the Council Study Centers.
Eligibility: Applicants must participate in the Council Study Centers Chinese language programs at Beijing, Shanghai, Nanjing, or Taipei, have completed two years of college level Mandarin Chinese, be a U.S. citizen or U.S. permanent resident, be a junior, senior, or graduate student who plans to pursue further studies or a career related to China, demonstrate high merit and demonstrate financial need.
Target applicants: College students. Graduate school students. Adult students.
Amount: $1,000-$8,000.
Number of awards: Varies.
Deadline: April 1 or November 1.
How to apply: Applications are available online.
Exclusive: Visit www.UltimateScholarshipBook.com and enter code CO41712 for updates on this award.

---

(418) • Ukulele Festival Hawaii's College Scholarship Program

Ukulele Festival Hawaii
c/o Roy Sakuma Productions, Inc.
3555 Harding Avenue, Suite 1
Honolulu, HI 96816
Phone: 808-732-3739
Email: info@roysakuma.net
http://www.roysakuma.net/ukulelefestival
Purpose: To support students who play the ukulele.
Eligibility: Applicants must be Hawaii high school seniors in good standing. They must plan to attend a four-year college or university in the fall following graduation.
Target applicants: High school students.
Amount: $1,000.

Number of awards: Varies.
Deadline: March 31.
How to apply: Applications are available from Roy Sakuma Productions. An application form is required.
Exclusive: Visit www.UltimateScholarshipBook.com and enter code UK41812 for updates on this award.

(419) • Undergraduate Scholarships

Sigma Alpha Iota Philanthropies
Director, Undergraduate Scholarships
One Tunnel Road
Asheville, NC 28805
Phone: 828-251-0606
Fax: 828-251-0644
Email: jkpete@cox.net
http://www.sai-national.org
Purpose: To assist members of the Sigma Alpha Iota organization who have demonstrated outstanding leadership abilities, musical talent and scholastic achievement.
Eligibility: Applicants must be active members of at least one year of the Sigma Alpha Iota organization, be in good standing and demonstrate financial need.
Target applicants: College students. Adult students.
Amount: $1,500-$2,000.
Number of awards: 15.
Deadline: March 15.
How to apply: Applications are available online.
Exclusive: Visit www.UltimateScholarshipBook.com and enter code SI41912 for updates on this award.

(420) • Urban Outreach Grants

American String Teachers Association (ASTA)
4153 Chain Bridge Road
Fairfax, VA 22030
Phone: 703-279-2113
Fax: 703-279-2114
Email: asta@astaweb.com
http://www.astaweb.com
Purpose: To help economically disadvantaged urban school children study stringed instruments.
Eligibility: Applicants must be economically disadvantaged urban school children through grade 12 who want to study stringed instruments. There are two projects, individual and group. Funds given by the Urban Outreach Program must be matched by state and/or local sources. Project coordinator(s) must be active members of ASTA. Applicants should submit an application signed by the state chapter president, project description and proposed budget.
Target applicants: Junior high students or younger. High school students.
Amount: $850.
Number of awards: Varies.
Deadline: June 1.
How to apply: Applications are available online.
Exclusive: Visit www.UltimateScholarshipBook.com and enter code AM42012 for updates on this award.

(421) • Visiting Senior Fellowship Program

National Gallery of Art
2000B South Club Drive
Landover, MD 20785
Phone: 202-842-6482
Fax: 202-789-3026
http://www.nga.gov/resources/casva.htm
Purpose: To award fellowships to scholars in visual arts.
Eligibility: Applicants must have held their Ph.D. for five years or more or who possess an equivalent record of professional accomplishment at the time of application. Applications are considered for research in the history, theory and criticism of the visual arts of any geographical area and of any period. Applicants must submit application forms, proposals, copies of a publication and two letters of recommendation. Fellowships are for full-time research, and scholars are expected to reside in Washington and to participate in the activities of the Center. Applications are also accepted from scholars in other disciplines whose work is related. The Center awards up to twelve short-term Paul Mellon and Ailsa Mellon Bruce Visiting Senior Fellowships. The deadlines are March 21 for the fellowship from September to February and September 21 for March through August.
Target applicants: Graduate school students. Adult students.
Amount: $6,000-$8,000 plus photography allowance.
Number of awards: Up to 12.
Scholarship may be renewable.
Deadline: September 21 and March 21.
How to apply: Applications are available online.
Exclusive: Visit www.UltimateScholarshipBook.com and enter code NA42112 for updates on this award.

(422) • Werner B. Thiele Memorial Scholarship

Gravure Education Foundation
1200-A Scottsville Road
Rochester, NY 14624
Phone: 315-589-8879
Fax: 585-436-7689
Email: lwshatch@gaa.org
http://www.gaa.org
Purpose: To award scholarships to college juniors and seniors majoring in printing, graphic arts or graphic communications.
Eligibility: Applicants must be enrolled full-time at one of the GEF Learning Resource Centers: Arizona State University, California Polytechnic State University, Clemson University, Murray State, Rochester Institute of Technology, University of Wisconsin - Stout or Western Michigan University.
Target applicants: College students. Adult students.
Minimum GPA: 3.0
Amount: $1,000.
Number of awards: 1.
Deadline: May 31.
How to apply: Applications are available online or by mail.
Exclusive: Visit www.UltimateScholarshipBook.com and enter code GR42212 for updates on this award.

(423) • Women Band Directors International College Scholarships

Women Band Directors International
Diane Gorzycki
WBDI Scholarship Chair
7424 Whistlestop Drive
Austin, TX 78749
Email: dgorzycki@austin.rr.com
http://www.womenbanddirectors.org
Purpose: To support future female band directors.

Eligibility: Applicants must be studying instrumental music with the intention of becoming a band director. One scholarship will be available to all-level college and graduate students, while the other three are designated for undergraduate upperclassmen.
Target applicants: College students. Graduate school students. Adult students.
Amount: $300-$500.
Number of awards: 11.
Deadline: December 1.
How to apply: Applications are available online.
Exclusive: Visit www.UltimateScholarshipBook.com and enter code WO42312 for updates on this award.

(424) • Working Abroad Grant

InterExchange Inc.
161 Sixth Avenue
New York, NY 10013
Phone: 212-924-0446
Fax: 212-924-0575
Email: grants@interexchange.org
http://www.interexchange.org/content/1/en/Home.html
Purpose: To further international understanding and promote cultural awareness by supporting young Americans in working abroad.
Eligibility: Applicants must be accepted to any InterExchange Working Abroad program except for language schools. They must also be U.S. citizens or permanent residents age 18 to 28.
Target applicants: High school students. College students. Graduate school students. Adult students.
Amount: $1,500.
Number of awards: Varies.
Deadline: 8 weeks prior to program start date.
How to apply: Applications are available online.
Exclusive: Visit www.UltimateScholarshipBook.com and enter code IN42412 for updates on this award.

(425) • Worldstudio Foundation Scholarship Program

Worldstudio Foundation
200 Varick Street
Suite 507
New York, NY 10014
Phone: 212-807-1990
Fax: 212-807-1799
Email: scholarshipcoordinator@worldstudio.org
http://www.worldstudio.org
Purpose: To support art and design students who need financial assistance.
Eligibility: Applicants must be full-time undergraduate or graduate students of fine or commercial art, design or architecture. They must have a GPA of at least 2.0 and demonstrate financial need. Applicants must be U.S. citizens or permanent residents. Minority students will be given special consideration.
Target applicants: High school students. College students. Graduate school students. Adult students.
Minimum GPA: 2.0
Amount: $500-$5,000.
Number of awards: Varies.
Deadline: April 2.
How to apply: Applications are available online.
Exclusive: Visit www.UltimateScholarshipBook.com and enter code WO42512 for updates on this award.

(426) • Writing Awards

Scholastic
557 Broadway
New York, NY 10012
Phone: 212-343-6100
Fax: 212-389-3939
Email: a&wgeneralinfo@scholastic.com
http://www.artandwriting.org
Purpose: To reward creative young writers.
Eligibility: Applicants must be in grades 7 through 12 in U.S. or Canadian schools and must submit writing pieces or portfolios in one of the following categories: dramatic script, general writing portfolio, humor, journalism, nonfiction portfolio, novel, personal essay/memoir, poetry, science fiction/fantasy, short story and short short story.
Target applicants: Junior high students or younger. High school students.
Amount: Up to $10,000.
Number of awards: Varies.
Deadline: Varies based on location; November through January.
How to apply: Applications are available online.
Exclusive: Visit www.UltimateScholarshipBook.com and enter code SC42612 for updates on this award.

(427) • Young American Creative Patriotic Art Awards Program

Ladies Auxiliary VFW
406 West 34th Street
10th Floor
Kansas City, MO 64111
Phone: 816-561-8655 x19
Fax: 816-931-4753
Email: jmillick@ladiesauxvfw.org
http://www.ladiesauxvfw.org
Purpose: To encourage patriotic art.
Eligibility: Applicants must be high school students in the same state as the sponsoring Ladies Auxiliary. They must submit one piece of patriotic art on paper or canvas. Art must have been completed during the current school year and must be accompanied by a teacher's signature. Applicants must participate in a local Auxiliary competition before advancing to the national level.
Target applicants: High school students.
Amount: $5,000-$10,000.
Number of awards: 8.
Deadline: March 31.
How to apply: Applications are available online.
Exclusive: Visit www.UltimateScholarshipBook.com and enter code LA42712 for updates on this award.

(428) • Young Jazz Composer Award

ASCAP Foundation
One Lincoln Plaza
New York, NY 10023
Phone: 212-621-6219
http://www.ascapfoundation.org
Purpose: To recognize the talent of young jazz composers.
Eligibility: Applicants must be under the age of 30 and U.S. citizens or permanent residents. They must submit one original composition, including a score and performance, if possible.
Target applicants: Junior high students or younger. High school students. College students. Graduate school students. Adult students.

Amount: Varies.
Number of awards: Varies.
Deadline: December 1.
How to apply: Applications are available online.
Exclusive: Visit www.UltimateScholarshipBook.com and enter code AS42812 for updates on this award.

(429) • YoungArts Program

National Foundation for Advancement in the Arts
444 Brickell Avenue
P-14
Miami, FL 33131
Phone: 800-970-ARTS
Fax: 305-377-1149
Email: info@nfaa.org
http://www.nfaa.org
Purpose: To reward talented young individuals in the arts.
Eligibility: Applicants must be either high school seniors or 17 or 18 years old by December 1 of the year of application. Students must be U.S. citizens or permanent residents. The disciplines included are cinematic arts, dance, jazz, music, photography, theater, visual arts, voice and writing. Those applying in the discipline of jazz music may be registered aliens. There is a nonrefundable fee. Note: We do not recommend applying to scholarships that charge application fees. However, some scholarships of this type charge fees and are included for completeness.
Target applicants: High school students.
Amount: $100-$10,000.
Number of awards: Varies.
Deadline: October 14.
How to apply: Applications are available online.
Exclusive: Visit www.UltimateScholarshipBook.com and enter code NA42912 for updates on this award.

(430) • Youth Free Expression Network Film Contest

National Coalition Against Censorship (NCAC)
275 Seventh Avenue
15th Floor
New York, NY 10001
Phone: 212-807-6222
Fax: 212-807-6245
Email: ncac@ncac.org
http://www.ncac.org
Purpose: To reward students who create films on a given topic related to censorship.
Eligibility: Students must be 19 years or younger. Films must be four minutes or less in a variety of genres including documentary, music video and experimental. Top three winners receive cash stipends.
Target applicants: Junior high students or younger. High school students. College students.
Amount: Up to $1,000.
Number of awards: 3.
Deadline: August 14.
How to apply: Applications are available online.
Exclusive: Visit www.UltimateScholarshipBook.com and enter code NA43012 for updates on this award.

SOCIAL SCIENCES

(431) • A. Harry Passow Classroom Teacher Scholarship

National Association for Gifted Children
1707 L Street NW
Suite 550
Chair, Awards Committee
Washington, DC 20036
Phone: 202-785-4268
Fax: 202-785-4248
Email: nagc@nagc.org
http://www.nagc.org
Purpose: To award excellent teachers of gifted students of grades K-12.
Eligibility: Applicants must be teachers of gifted students of grades K-12 and be continuing their education. Applicants must also have been members of NAGC for at least one year. Selection is based on commitment to teaching as shown by reviews from students, parents, principal and peers and admission into a graduate or certification program in gifted education.
Target applicants: Graduate school students. Adult students.
Amount: Varies.
Number of awards: Varies.
Deadline: April 19.
How to apply: Applications are available online.
Exclusive: Visit www.UltimateScholarshipBook.com and enter code NA43112 for updates on this award.

(432) • AAF Student ADDY Awards

American Advertising Foundation
1101 Vermont Avenue NW, Suite 500
Washington, DC 20005
Phone: 800-999-2231
Email: ctucker@aaf.org
http://www.studentaddys.com
Purpose: To support students interested in advertising.
Eligibility: Applicants must be enrolled in an accredited U.S. institution of higher learning full- or part-time. Students must submit an advertising project created for the competition or from a previous unpaid project or competition. Work must have been created while the applicant was a student or intern but not employed in advertising. Note: We do not recommend applying to scholarships that charge application fees. However, some scholarships of this type charge fees and are included for completeness.
Target applicants: College students. Adult students.
Amount: $1,000.
Number of awards: Varies.
Deadline: Varies.
How to apply: Applications available online and must be submitted to your local club or district. A list of local clubs and districts is online. An application form, project and $20 application fee are required.
Exclusive: Visit www.UltimateScholarshipBook.com and enter code AM43212 for updates on this award.

(433) • AALL Educational Scholarships

American Association of Law Libraries
105 W. Adams
Suite 3300
Chicago, IL 60604
Phone: 312-939-4764
Fax: 312-431-1097
Email: scholarships@aall.org
http://www.aallnet.org
Purpose: To encourage students to pursue careers as law librarians.
Eligibility: There are five levels of awards: 1. Library Degree for Law School Graduates, awarded to a law school graduate with law library experience pursuing a degree at an accredited library school. 2. Library School Graduates Attending Law School, awarded to a library school graduate pursuing a degree at an accredited law school who has law library experience and no more than 36 semester credit hours left before obtaining the law degree. 3. Library Degree for Non-Law School Graduates, awarded to a college graduate with law library experience who is seeking a degree involving law librarianship courses at an accredited library school. 4. Library School Graduates Seeking A Non-Law Degree, awarded to library school graduates who are seeking degrees in fields other than law. 5. Law Librarians in Continuing Education Courses, awarded to law librarians with a degree from an accredited library or law school who are continuing their education. Preference is given to AALL members, but a non-member can apply. All applicants must intend to have careers as law librarians. There must be financial need for awards 1-4.
Target applicants: Graduate school students. Adult students.
Amount: Varies.
Number of awards: Varies.
Scholarship may be renewable.
Deadline: April 1.
How to apply: Applications are available online, by mail with a self-addressed, stamped envelope, by fax, by phone or by email.
Exclusive: Visit www.UltimateScholarshipBook.com and enter code AM43312 for updates on this award.

(434) • ABCTE Teach and Inspire Scholarship Program

American Board for Certification of Teacher Excellence
1225 19th Street NW
Suite 400
Washington, DC 20036
Phone: 877-669-2228
Fax: 202-261-2638
http://www.abcte.org
Purpose: To aid students planning to enroll in the ABCTE teacher certification program.
Eligibility: Applicants must be U.S. citizens or permanent residents. They must hold a bachelor's degree and must have at least 15 credit hours in the teaching subject of interest. Recent graduates (those who have earned their degrees within the past three years) either must have a degree in the teaching subject of interest or must have relevant work experience. The following teaching subjects qualify for this scholarship: English (grades 6-12), special education (grades K-6), general science (grades 5-9), physics (grades 6-12), chemistry (grades 6-12), biology (grades 6-12) or mathematics (grades 6-12). Those who already hold a renewable teaching license are ineligible for this award. Applicants must be willing to commit to teaching in a high-need district in Florida, Mississippi or South Carolina for a period of three years. Selection is based on the overall strength of the application.
Target applicants: College students. Adult students.
Amount: Full tuition plus $1,000 stipend.
Number of awards: Varies.
Deadline: Multiple deadlines throughout year.
How to apply: Applications are available online. An application form, personal essays, transcripts and one recommendation form are required.
Exclusive: Visit www.UltimateScholarshipBook.com and enter code AM43412 for updates on this award.

(435) · Abe Schechter Graduate Scholarship

Radio Television Digital News Association
4121 Plank Road #512
Fredericksburg, VA 22407
Phone: 202-659-6510
Fax: 202-223-4007
Email: staceys@rtdna.org
http://www.rtdna.org
Purpose: To honor professional achievements in electronic journalism.
Eligibility: Applicants must be full-time or incoming graduate students. Applicants may be enrolled in any major as long as their career intent is television or radio news. Applicants may only apply for one RTNDA scholarship.
Target applicants: Graduate school students. Adult students.
Amount: $2,000.
Number of awards: 1.
Deadline: May 10.
How to apply: Applications are available online.
Exclusive: Visit www.UltimateScholarshipBook.com and enter code RA43512 for updates on this award.

(436) · Above and Beyond Scholarship

California School Library Association
950 Glenn Drive, Suite 150
Folsom, CA 95630
Phone: 916-447-2684
Fax: 916-447-2695
Email: csla@pacbell.net
http://www.csla.net/
Purpose: To support library media teachers pursuing advanced degrees or National Board Certification.
Eligibility: Applicants must be professional members of the California School Library Association and California residents intending to continue working in California in the school library profession after completing their additional education. Students must submit a 500-word essay describing their professional goals and how an advanced degree or certification applies to those goals and three letters of recommendation.
Target applicants: Graduate school students. Adult students.
Amount: $1,000.
Number of awards: Varies.
Deadline: May 30.
How to apply: Applications are available online.
Exclusive: Visit www.UltimateScholarshipBook.com and enter code CA43612 for updates on this award.

(437) · Academic Scholarship for High School Seniors

National Restaurant Association Educational Foundation
175 W. Jackson Boulevard
Suite 1500
Chicago, IL 60604-2702
Phone: 800-765-2122
Fax: 312-715-1010
Email: scholars@naref.org
http://www.nraef.org
Purpose: To support students majoring in food services.
Eligibility: Applicants must have been accepted into an accredited restaurant or food service related program, have had at least 250 hours of restaurant or food service-related work experience, submit a letter of recommendation and have a minimum 2.75 GPA.
Target applicants: High school students.
Minimum GPA: 2.75
Amount: Varies.
Number of awards: Varies.
Deadline: August 18.
How to apply: Applications are available online.
Exclusive: Visit www.UltimateScholarshipBook.com and enter code NA43712 for updates on this award.

(438) · Academic Scholarship For Undergraduate College Students

National Restaurant Association Educational Foundation
175 W. Jackson Boulevard
Suite 1500
Chicago, IL 60604-2702
Phone: 800-765-2122
Fax: 312-715-1010
Email: scholars@naref.org
http://www.nraef.org
Purpose: To assist restaurant and food service students.
Eligibility: Applicants must be currently majoring in a restaurant or foodservice program and submit a transcript, proof of restaurant or foodservice-related work experience of a minimum of 750 hours and a letter of recommendation.
Target applicants: College students. Adult students.
Minimum GPA: 2.75
Amount: $2,500.
Number of awards: Varies.
Deadline: March 31.
How to apply: Applications are available online.
Exclusive: Visit www.UltimateScholarshipBook.com and enter code NA43812 for updates on this award.

(439) · Achievement Award

National Council of Teachers of English
1111 W. Kenyon Road
Urbana, IL 61801
Phone: 217-328-3870
Fax: 217-328-9645
Email: aa@ncte.org
http://www.ncte.org
Purpose: To recognize outstanding student writers.
Eligibility: Applicants must be current high school juniors who will graduate the following school year, and they must be nominated for the award by their high school English department. Nominees must provide two writing samples: one timed response to a prompt written under the supervision of a teacher and one sample of their best work.
Target applicants: High school students.
Amount: Certificate.
Number of awards: Varies.
Deadline: February 15.
How to apply: Applications are available online. However, students must be nominated by their high school English departments.
Exclusive: Visit www.UltimateScholarshipBook.com and enter code NA43912 for updates on this award.

(440) · ACLS Digital Innovation Fellowships

American Council of Learned Societies (ACLS)
633 Third Avenue
New York, NY 10017-6795
Phone: 212-697-1505

Fax: 212-949-8058
Email: sfishcr@acls.org
http://www.contemplativemind.org/
Purpose: To support humanities scholars who work on digital projects.
Eligibility: Applicants must be scholars in the humanities fields and have Ph.D. degrees. An application, a proposal, a project plan, a budget plan, a bibliography, a publications list, three reference letters and one institutional statement are required. In addition to the stipend, there are also funds for project costs. The fellowship should last an academic year.
Target applicants: Graduate school students. Adult students.
Amount: Up to $85,000.
Number of awards: Up to 6.
Deadline: September 29.
How to apply: Applications are available online.
Exclusive: Visit www.UltimateScholarshipBook.com and enter code AM44012 for updates on this award.

(441) • ACLS Fellowships

American Council of Learned Societies (ACLS)
633 Third Avenue
New York, NY 10017-6795
Phone: 212-697-1505
Fax: 212-949-8058
Email: sfisher@acls.org
http://www.contemplativemind.org/
Purpose: To support a scholar in the study of humanities.
Eligibility: Applicants must have a Ph.D. degree and at least a three year period since their last supported research. An application, a proposal, bibliography, publications list and two reference letters are required. The award levels are based on the position of the applicant: professor and equivalent, associate professor and equivalent and assistant professor and equivalent. The ACLS fellowships include ACLS/SSRC/NEH International and Area Studies Fellowships and ACLS/New York Public Library Fellowships.
Target applicants: Graduate school students. Adult students.
Amount: Up to $60,000.
Number of awards: Varies.
Deadline: September 29.
How to apply: Applications are available online.
Exclusive: Visit www.UltimateScholarshipBook.com and enter code AM44112 for updates on this award.

(442) • ACOR-CAORC Fellowships

American Center of Oriental Research (ACOR)
656 Beacon Street, 5th Floor
Boston, MA 02215
Phone: 617-353-6571
Fax: 617-353-6575
Email: acor@bu.edu
http://www.bu.edu/acor
Purpose: To assist master's and pre-doctoral students conducting research in Jordan.
Eligibility: Applicants must be U.S. citizen graduate students researching topics involving scholarship in Near Eastern studies. Recipients are required to engage in scholarly and cultural activities while residing at the American Center of Oriental Research (ACOR) in Jordan. The fellowships last from two to six months. The award includes room and board at ACOR, transportation, a stipend and research funds.
Target applicants: Graduate school students. Adult students.
Amount: Up to $29,400.
Number of awards: At least 2.
Deadline: February 1.
How to apply: Applications are available online.
Exclusive: Visit www.UltimateScholarshipBook.com and enter code AM44212 for updates on this award.

(443) • Adelle and Erwin Tomash Fellowship in the History of Information Processing

Charles Babbage Institute
Center for the History of Information Processing
211 Andersen Library, University of Minnesota
222 - 21st Avenue South
Minneapolis, MN 55455
Phone: 612-624-5050
Email: yostx003@tc.umn.edu
http://www.cbi.umn.edu
Purpose: To support a graduate student who is researching the history of computing.
Eligibility: Applicants must be graduate students who have completed all doctoral degree requirements except the research and writing of the dissertation. Students must submit a curriculum vitae and a five-page statement and justification of the research program.
Target applicants: Graduate school students. Adult students.
Amount: $14,000.
Number of awards: 1.
Deadline: January 15.
How to apply: Visit the website for more information.
Exclusive: Visit www.UltimateScholarshipBook.com and enter code CH44312 for updates on this award.

(444) • Adult Students in Scholastic Transition (ASIST)

Executive Women International (EWI)
515 South 700 East
Suite 2A
Salt Lake City, UT 84102
Phone: 801-355-2800
Fax: 801-355-2852
Email: ewi@ewiconnect.com
http://www.executivewomen.org
Purpose: To assist adult students who face major life transitions.
Eligibility: Applicants may be single parents, individuals just entering the workforce or displaced workers.
Target applicants: College students. Adult students.
Amount: Varies.
Number of awards: Varies.
Deadline: Varies by Chapter.
How to apply: Contact your local EWI chapter.
Exclusive: Visit www.UltimateScholarshipBook.com and enter code EX44412 for updates on this award.

(445) • Affirmative Action Scholarship

Special Libraries Association
331 S. Patrick Street
Alexandria, VA 22314
Phone: 703-647-4900
Fax: 703-647-4901
Email: sla@sla.org
http://www.sla.org
Purpose: To support minority students who show an interest in special librarianship.

Eligibility: Applicants must be college seniors or graduates who are members of a minority group admitted by a recognized library school or information science program and demonstrate financial need. Preference is given to SLA members and those who show an interest in special library work. Applicants must submit an essay on their contribution to special librarianship.
Target applicants: College students. Graduate school students. Adult students.
Amount: $6,000.
Number of awards: 1.
Deadline: January 1 through September 30.
How to apply: Applications are available online.
Exclusive: Visit www.UltimateScholarshipBook.com and enter code SP44512 for updates on this award.

(446) • AGA Scholarships

Association of Government Accountants (AGA)
2208 Mount Vernon Avenue
Alexandria, VA 22301-1314
Phone: 800-242-7211
Email: rortiz@agacgfm.org
http://www.agacgfm.org

Purpose: To support public financial management students.
Eligibility: Applicants for full-time or part-time scholarships must be an AGA member or family member (spouse, child or grandchild), and scholarships must be used for full-time or part-time undergraduate study in a financial management academic area such as accounting, auditing, budgeting, economics, finance, electronic data processing, information resources management or public administration. Essays and transcripts are required. There are two categories for high school students/ graduates and undergraduates/graduates. The Academic Scholarships are based on academic achievement and the student's potential for making a contribution to public financial management. A reference letter from an AGA member and from another professional such as a professor, guidance counselor or employer is required. Applicants to the Community Service Scholarships do not have to be AGA members, must be pursuing a degree in a financial management academic discipline and must be actively involved in community service projects. The awards are based on community service and accomplishments. A letter of recommendation from a community service organization and from another professional are required.
Target applicants: High school students. College students. Graduate school students. Adult students.
Minimum GPA: 2.5
Amount: $1,000.
Number of awards: 9.
Deadline: March 31.
How to apply: Applications are available online.
Exclusive: Visit www.UltimateScholarshipBook.com and enter code AS44612 for updates on this award.

(447) • AICPA/Accountemps Student Scholarship

American Institute of Certified Public Accountants
Academic and Career Development Division
220 Leigh Farm Road
Durham, NC 27707
Phone: 919-402-4014
Fax: 919-412-4705
Email: educat@aicpa.org
http://www.aicpa.org

Purpose: To aid AICPA Student Affiliate members who are pursuing higher education in information systems, accounting or finance.
Eligibility: Applicants must be U.S. citizens or permanent residents who are full-time students at an accredited U.S. college or university. They must be majoring in accounting, finance or information systems and must have completed at least 30 semester or 45 quarter hours of study, including six or more semester hours in accounting. They must have a GPA of 3.0 or higher. Current Certified Public Accountants (CPAs) are ineligible. Selection is based on academic merit, leadership skills and professional potential.
Target applicants: College students. Graduate school students. Adult students.
Minimum GPA: 3.0
Amount: $2,500.
Number of awards: 5.
Deadline: April 1.
How to apply: Applications are available online. An application form, official transcript, course schedule, standardized test score report (graduate students only), personal essay and two letters of recommendation are required.
Exclusive: Visit www.UltimateScholarshipBook.com and enter code AM44712 for updates on this award.

(448) • Al Neuharth Free Spirit Scholarship and Conference Program

Freedom Forum
1101 Wilson Boulevard
Arlington, VA 22209
Phone: 703-284-2814
Fax: 703-284-3529
Email: freespirit@freedomforum.org
http://www.freedomforum.org/freespirit

Purpose: To provide assistance to students who meet the criteria of being a "free spirit."
Eligibility: Applicants must be high school seniors who plan to pursue a career in journalism and who are "free spirits," defined as those who "dream, dare and do."
Target applicants: High school students.
Amount: Varies.
Number of awards: Varies.
Deadline: October 15.
How to apply: Applications are available online.
Exclusive: Visit www.UltimateScholarshipBook.com and enter code FR44812 for updates on this award.

(449) • American Bar Association Essay and Writing Competitions

American Bar Association
321 North Clark Street
Chicago, IL 60610
Phone: 312-988-5415
Email: legalosf@abanet.org
http://www.abanet.org/lsd/

Purpose: To support and recognize achievement among law students.
Eligibility: The American Bar Association (ABA) sponsors a variety of essay and writing competitions for ABA student members. Each competition is centered on a specific legal topic. Topics include affordable housing and community, community development law, law and aging, antitrust, business law, criminal justice, dispute resolution, entertainment and sports law, family law, health care, labor and employment, liability,

education, public contracts, real estate, tort and insurance and children. Selection is based on the strength of the essay.
Target applicants: Graduate school students. Adult students.
Amount: Varies.
Number of awards: Varies.
Deadline: Varies.
How to apply: Applications are available online. Application requirements vary by competition.
Exclusive: Visit www.UltimateScholarshipBook.com and enter code AM44912 for updates on this award.

(450) · American Bar Association-Bar/Bri Scholarships

BAR/BRI Bar Review
ABA Scholarship Committee
111 W. Jackson Boulevard
Chicago, IL 60604
Email: abalsd@abanet.org
http://www.barbri.com/wps/portal/barbri/home
Purpose: To defer the cost of study for graduating law students who must take the BAR/BRI exam.
Eligibility: Applicants must be ABA Law Student Division members who will be December or May graduates and will use the award toward their BAR/BRI tuition. Scholarships will vary in amount depending upon the applicant's financial condition and the size of the applicant pool.
Target applicants: Graduate school students. Adult students.
Amount: Varies.
Number of awards: Varies.
Deadline: November 30.
How to apply: Applications are available online.
Exclusive: Visit www.UltimateScholarshipBook.com and enter code BA45012 for updates on this award.

(451) · American Express Scholarship Competition

American Hotel and Lodging Educational Foundation (AH&LEF)
1201 New York Avenue NW
Suite 600
Washington, DC 20005-3931
Phone: 202-289-3188
Fax: 202-289-3199
Email: chammond@ahlef.org
http://www.ahlef.org
Purpose: To provide financial assistance to students pursuing a degree in hospitality management.
Eligibility: Applicants must be enrolled in an accredited undergraduate program resulting in a degree in hospitality management. Students or their parents must be employed in the lodging industry by an American Hotel and Lodging Association member facility.
Target applicants: College students. Adult students.
Amount: Up to $2,000.
Number of awards: Varies.
Deadline: June 15.
How to apply: Applications are available online.
Exclusive: Visit www.UltimateScholarshipBook.com and enter code AM45112 for updates on this award.

(452) · American Society of Travel Agents (ASTA) American Express Travel Undergraduate Scholarship

Tourism Cares
275 Turnpike Street
Suite 307
Canton, MA 02021
Phone: 781-821-5990
Fax: 781-821-8949
Email: carolynv@tourismcares.org
http://www.tourismcares.org
Purpose: To aid rising undergraduate freshmen who are planning to pursue higher education in travel, tourism and hospitality.
Eligibility: Applicants must be permanent residents of the U.S. who are graduating high school seniors at a school that has an Academy of Hospitality and Tourism (AOHT) program. They must have a GPA of 3.0 or higher on a four-point scale and be accepted at an accredited postsecondary institution located in the U.S. or Canada. They must be planning to study travel, tourism or hospitality. Selection is based on the overall strength of the application.
Target applicants: High school students.
Minimum GPA: 3.0
Amount: $1,000.
Number of awards: 1.
Deadline: April 15.
How to apply: Applications are available online. An application form, resume, proof of residency, official transcript, proof of college acceptance, personal essay and two recommendation letters are required.
Exclusive: Visit www.UltimateScholarshipBook.com and enter code TO45212 for updates on this award.

(453) · American Society of Travel Agents (ASTA) Arnold Rigby Graduate Scholarship

Tourism Cares
275 Turnpike Street
Suite 307
Canton, MA 02021
Phone: 781-821-5990
Fax: 781-821-8949
Email: carolynv@tourismcares.org
http://www.tourismcares.org
Purpose: To assist those who are studying hospitality, travel and tourism at the graduate level.
Eligibility: Applicants must be permanent residents of the U.S. or Canada and must be entering or returning graduate students who are enrolled at an accredited U.S. or Canadian four-year postsecondary institution. They must be studying hospitality, tourism or travel and must have a GPA of 3.0 or higher on a four-point scale. Selection is based on the overall strength of the application.
Target applicants: Graduate school students. Adult students.
Minimum GPA: 3.0
Amount: $2,500.
Number of awards: 2.
Deadline: April 15.
How to apply: Applications are available online. An application form, proof of residency, a resume, an official transcript, a personal essay and two letters of recommendation are required.
Exclusive: Visit www.UltimateScholarshipBook.com and enter code TO45312 for updates on this award.

(454) · American Society of Travel Agents (ASTA) Avis Budget Group Graduate Scholarship

Tourism Cares
275 Turnpike Street
Suite 307
Canton, MA 02021

Phone: 781-821-5990
Fax: 781-821-8949
Email: carolynv@tourismcares.org
http://www.tourismcares.org

Purpose: To aid those who are studying hospitality, travel and tourism at the graduate level.

Eligibility: Applicants must be permanent residents of the U.S. or Canada and be graduate students who are enrolled or have been accepted at an accredited postsecondary institution located in one of those two countries. They must be studying a hospitality-, tourism- or travel-related subject and have a GPA of 3.0 or higher on a four-point scale. Selection is based on the student's proven commitment to the tourism and hospitality industries.

Target applicants: College students. Graduate school students. Adult students.

Minimum GPA: 3.0

Amount: $2,000.

Number of awards: 1.

Deadline: April 15.

How to apply: Applications are available online. An application form, proof of permanent residency, resume, two recommendation letters, official transcript and personal essay are required.

Exclusive: Visit www.UltimateScholarshipBook.com and enter code TO45412 for updates on this award.

(455) • American Society of Travel Agents (ASTA) David J. Hallissey Memorial Undergraduate or Graduate Internship

Tourism Cares
275 Turnpike Street
Suite 307
Canton, MA 02021
Phone: 781-821-5990
Fax: 781-821-8949
Email: carolynv@tourismcares.org
http://www.tourismcares.org

Purpose: To aid travel, tourism and hospitality students who have an interest in marketing research.

Eligibility: Applicants may be permanent residents of any country but must be enrolled at an accredited four-year U.S. postsecondary institution. They must be entering or returning graduate students or rising undergraduate sophomores, juniors or seniors. They must be studying tourism, travel or hospitality with an interest in marketing research as it relates to marketing and must have strong interpersonal skills and strong written and verbal communication skills. They must have a GPA of 3.0 or higher on a four-point scale. Applicants must have knowledge of Microsoft Excel software. Selection is based on the overall strength of the application.

Target applicants: College students. Graduate school students. Adult students.

Minimum GPA: 3.0

Amount: $2,000.

Number of awards: 1.

Deadline: April 15.

How to apply: Applications are available online. An application form, proof of residency, a resume, an official transcript, a personal essay and one letter of recommendation are required.

Exclusive: Visit www.UltimateScholarshipBook.com and enter code TO45512 for updates on this award.

(456) • American Society of Travel Agents (ASTA) Healy Graduate Scholarship

Tourism Cares
275 Turnpike Street
Suite 307
Canton, MA 02021
Phone: 781-821-5990
Fax: 781-821-8949
Email: carolynv@tourismcares.org
http://www.tourismcares.org

Purpose: To aid those who are studying hospitality, tourism and travel at the graduate level.

Eligibility: Applicants must be permanent residents of the U.S. and must be entering or returning graduate students who are enrolled at an accredited U.S. four-year institution. They must be studying hospitality, tourism or travel and have a GPA of 3.0 or higher on a four-point scale. Selection is based on the student's proven commitment to the hospitality and tourism industries.

Target applicants: College students. Graduate school students. Adult students.

Minimum GPA: 3.0

Amount: $1,000.

Number of awards: 1.

Deadline: April 15.

How to apply: Applications are available online. An application form, resume, proof of residency, a personal essay, an official transcript and two letters of recommendation are required.

Exclusive: Visit www.UltimateScholarshipBook.com and enter code TO45612 for updates on this award.

(457) • American Society of Travel Agents (ASTA) Holland America Line Graduate Research Scholarship

Tourism Cares
275 Turnpike Street
Suite 307
Canton, MA 02021
Phone: 781-821-5990
Fax: 781-821-8949
Email: carolynv@tourismcares.org
http://www.tourismcares.org

Purpose: To aid graduate students who are conducting tourism-related research.

Eligibility: Applicants may be permanent residents of any country but must be accepted or enrolled as graduate students at an accredited U.S. or Canadian four-year postsecondary institution. They must be conducting tourism-related research and must have a GPA of 3.0 or higher on a four-point scale. Selection is based on the overall strength of the research project.

Target applicants: College students. Graduate school students. Adult students.

Minimum GPA: 3.0

Amount: $4,000.

Number of awards: 1.

Deadline: April 15.

How to apply: Applications are available online. An application form, one letter of recommendation, a resume, a research proposal, a personal essay and an official transcript are required.

Exclusive: Visit www.UltimateScholarshipBook.com and enter code TO45712 for updates on this award.

(458) • American Society of Travel Agents (ASTA) Joseph R. Stone Graduate Scholarship

Tourism Cares
275 Turnpike Street
Suite 307
Canton, MA 02021
Phone: 781-821-5990
Fax: 781-821-8949
Email: carolynv@tourismcares.org
http://www.tourismcares.org

Purpose: To aid those who are studying travel, tourism and hospitality at the graduate level.

Eligibility: Applicants must be permanent residents of the U.S. or Canada and be entering or returning graduate students at an accredited U.S. or Canadian four-year institution. They must be studying travel, tourism or hospitality and must have a GPA of 3.0 or higher on a four-point scale. Selection is based on the overall strength of the application.

Target applicants: College students. Graduate school students. Adult students.

Minimum GPA: 3.0

Amount: $2,500.

Number of awards: 3.

Deadline: April 15.

How to apply: Applications are available online. An application form, proof of residency, a resume, an official transcript, two letters of recommendation and a personal essay are required.

Exclusive: Visit www.UltimateScholarshipBook.com and enter code TO45812 for updates on this award.

(459) • American Society of Travel Agents (ASTA) Tourism Cares-Contiki Vacations Undergraduate Scholarship

Tourism Cares
275 Turnpike Street
Suite 307
Canton, MA 02021
Phone: 781-821-5990
Fax: 781-821-8949
Email: carolynv@tourismcares.org
http://www.tourismcares.org

Purpose: To aid those who are studying travel, tourism and hospitality at the undergraduate level.

Eligibility: Applicants must be permanent residents of the U.S. who are enrolled at an accredited U.S. two-year or four-year postsecondary institution. They must be entering the second year of a two-year program or entering the third or fourth year of a four-year program. By May of the application year, they must have completed 30 credits or more if in a two-year program or 60 credits or more if in a four-year program. They must be studying hospitality, tourism or travel and have a GPA of 3.0 or higher on a four-point scale. Contiki Vacations employees and their family members are ineligible. Selection is based on the overall strength of the application.

Target applicants: College students. Adult students.

Minimum GPA: 3.0

Amount: $1,500.

Number of awards: 1.

Deadline: April 15.

How to apply: Applications are available online. An application form, a resume, proof of residency, two recommendation letters, an official transcript and a personal essay are required.

Exclusive: Visit www.UltimateScholarshipBook.com and enter code TO45912 for updates on this award.

(460) • Annual Logistics Scholarship Competition

International Society of Logistics
Chairman, Scholarships Review Committee
Logistics Education Foundation
8100 Professional Place, Suite 111
Hyattsville, MD 20785
Phone: 301-459-8446
Fax: 301-459-1522
Email: solehq@sole.org
http://www.sole.org

Purpose: The organization is dedicated to upgrading the quality and availability of logistics education.

Eligibility: Applicants must be pursuing a bachelor's or master's degree in logistics or a logistics-related major and be full-time students with a full-time course load. Applicants' intention to pursue a logistics-related career, scholastic achievements and current and potential contributions to the logistics profession are considered.

Target applicants: College students. Graduate school students. Adult students.

Amount: $1,000.

Number of awards: Varies.

Deadline: May 15.

How to apply: Applications are available online.

Exclusive: Visit www.UltimateScholarshipBook.com and enter code IN46012 for updates on this award.

(461) • APF/COGDOP Graduate Research Scholarships

American Psychological Association Foundation
750 First Street NE
Washington, DC 20002
Phone: 800-374-2721
http://www.apa.org/apf

Purpose: To assist graduate psychology students.

Eligibility: Applicants must attend a school whose psychology department is a member in good standing of Council of Graduate Departments of Psychology (COGDOP). Applicants are nominated by their schools' departments with no more than three nominees at each school.

Target applicants: Graduate school students. Adult students.

Amount: $1,000-$5,000.

Number of awards: 13.

Deadline: June 30.

How to apply: Applicants must be nominated.

Exclusive: Visit www.UltimateScholarshipBook.com and enter code AM46112 for updates on this award.

(462) • APF/TOPSS Scholars Essay Competition

American Psychological Association Foundation
750 First Street NE
Washington, DC 20002
Phone: 800-374-2721
http://www.apa.org/apf

Purpose: To assist students who are studying psychology.

Eligibility: Applicants must be high school students who have been or are presently enrolled in a psychology course and must write an essay answering a question from the APA. A Teachers of Psychology in

Secondary Schools (TOPSS) member must sponsor all candidates, and each school may submit no more than ten papers.
Target applicants: High school students.
Amount: $1,000.
Number of awards: 3.
Deadline: March 1.
How to apply: Submission information is available online.
Exclusive: Visit www.UltimateScholarshipBook.com and enter code AM46212 for updates on this award.

(463) · Arc Welding Awards

James F. Lincoln Arc Welding Foundation
Secretary
P.O. Box 17188
Cleveland, OH 44117-9949
http://www.jflf.org
Purpose: To award prizes for arc welding projects made by the applicant or a group of applicants.
Eligibility: Projects may fit into one of the following categories: home, recreational or artistic equipment; shop tool, machine or mechanical device; a structure; agricultural equipment or a repair. Applicants must submit a paper about the creation of the project and be enrolled in a shop class. Applicants must also be enrolled in high school, adult evening classes, two-year/community college, vocational school, apprentice program, trade school, in-plant training or technical school and may not be college students enrolled in a bachelor's or master's program.
Target applicants: High school students. College students. Adult students.
Amount: Up to $1,000.
Number of awards: 95.
Deadline: June 1.
How to apply: Applications are available online.
Exclusive: Visit www.UltimateScholarshipBook.com and enter code JA46312 for updates on this award.

(464) · ARIT Fellowships for Research in Turkey

American Research Institute in Turkey (ARIT)
3260 South Street
Philadelphia, PA 19104-6324
Phone: 215-898-3474
Fax: 215-898-0657
Email: leinwand@sas.upenn.edu
http://ccat.sas.upenn.edu/ARIT
Purpose: To support scholars in their research in Turkey.
Eligibility: Applicants must be scholars or advanced graduate students involved in research on ancient, medieval or modern times in Turkey, in any field of the humanities and social sciences. Student applicants must have completed all requirements for the doctorate except the dissertation before beginning any ARIT-sponsored research. Non-U.S. applicants must be connected to an educational institution in the U.S. or Canada. Applicants should submit applications, three letters of recommendation and graduate transcripts.
Target applicants: Graduate school students. Adult students.
Amount: Varies.
Number of awards: Varies.
Deadline: November 1.
How to apply: Applications are available online.
Exclusive: Visit www.UltimateScholarshipBook.com and enter code AM46412 for updates on this award.

(465) · ARRL Scholarship Honoring Senator Barry Goldwater, K7UGA

American Radio Relay League Foundation
225 Main Street
Newington, CT 06111
Phone: 860-594-0397
Fax: 860-594-0259
Email: foundation@arrl.org
http://www.arrlf.org
Purpose: To assist ham radio operators in furthering their educations.
Eligibility: Applicants must have at least a novice ham radio license, be studying for a bachelor's or graduate degree and attend a regionally-accredited institute.
Target applicants: High school students. College students. Graduate school students. Adult students.
Amount: $5,000.
Number of awards: 1.
Deadline: February 1.
How to apply: Applications are available online.
Exclusive: Visit www.UltimateScholarshipBook.com and enter code AM46512 for updates on this award.

(466) · Association of Equipment Management Professionals Foundation Scholarships

Association of Equipment Management Professionals (AEMP)
P.O. Box 1368
Glenwood Springs, CO 81602
Phone: 970-384-0510
Fax: 970-384-0512
Email: stan@aemp.org
http://www.aemp.org
Purpose: To support students interested in the field of heavy equipment management.
Eligibility: Applicants must have a GPA of 2.0 or higher. Scholarship recipients must maintain a 3.0 or higher GPA in their studies. Preference is given to students who are motivated, responsible and have the potential for great achievement.
Target applicants: High school students. College students. Adult students.
Minimum GPA: 2.0
Amount: Up to $2,000.
Number of awards: Varies.
Deadline: May 1.
How to apply: Applications are available online. An application form, transcript and two letters of recommendation are required.
Exclusive: Visit www.UltimateScholarshipBook.com and enter code AS46612 for updates on this award.

(467) · BEA National Scholarships in Broadcasting

Broadcast Education Association
1771 North Street NW
Washington, DC 20036
Phone: 888-380-7222
Email: beainfo@beaweb.org
http://www.beaweb.org
Purpose: To honor broadcasters and the broadcast industry.
Eligibility: Applicants must be college juniors or seniors or graduate students at BEA member universities, students pursuing freshman and sophomore instruction only or students who have already completed BEA two-year programs at a four-year college.

Target applicants: College students. Graduate school students. Adult students.
Amount: Varies.
Number of awards: Varies.
Deadline: October 12.
How to apply: Applications are available online.
Exclusive: Visit www.UltimateScholarshipBook.com and enter code BR46712 for updates on this award.

(468) • Beat the GMAT Scholarship

Beat the GMAT
Email: scholarship@beatthegmat.com
http://www.beatthegmat.com
Purpose: To support students who are members of the Beat the GMAT discussion forum.
Eligibility: Applicants must be in their final year of college or have completed college and must plan to go to business school. They must have a PayPal account to receive winnings. Two essays are required.
Target applicants: College students. Adult students.
Amount: $500 plus non-cash prizes.
Number of awards: 5.
Deadline: May 8.
How to apply: Applications are available online. Contact information, two references, two essays, a photo and bio are required. Applications must be sent via email.
Exclusive: Visit www.UltimateScholarshipBook.com and enter code BE46812 for updates on this award.

(469) • Begun Scholarship

California Library Association
4030 Lennane Drive
Sacramento, CA 95834
Phone: 916-779-4573
Fax: 916-419-2874
Email: info@cla-net.org
http://www.cla-net.org
Purpose: To assist California library or information sciences graduate students at California schools.
Eligibility: Applicants must be California graduate students attending an American Library Association accredited school and have completed core coursework toward a master's of library and science or information studies degree. Recipients must also plan to become a children's or young adult librarian in a California public library and to join the California Library Association if not already a member.
Target applicants: Graduate school students. Adult students.
Amount: $3,000.
Number of awards: 1.
Deadline: July 15.
How to apply: Applications are available online.
Exclusive: Visit www.UltimateScholarshipBook.com and enter code CA46912 for updates on this award.

(470) • Betsy Plank/PRSSA Scholarship

Public Relations Student Society of America
33 Maiden Lane
11th Floor
New York, NY 10038
Phone: 212-460-1474
Fax: 212-995-0757
Email: prssa@prsa.org
http://www.prssa.org
Purpose: To assist public relations students.
Eligibility: Applicants must be PRSSA members enrolled in an undergraduate public relations program and be college juniors or seniors. One eligible student may be nominated from each PRSSA chapter. Selection is based on academic achievement, leadership, experience and commitment to public relations. Applicants need to include a 300-word statement of commitment to public relations.
Target applicants: College students. Adult students.
Amount: $1,500-$2,000.
Number of awards: 3.
Deadline: June 6.
How to apply: Applications are available online.
Exclusive: Visit www.UltimateScholarshipBook.com and enter code PU47012 for updates on this award.

(471) • Bill Salerno, W2ONV, Memorial Scholarship

American Radio Relay League Foundation
225 Main Street
Newington, CT 06111
Phone: 860-594-0397
Fax: 860-594-0259
Email: foundation@arrl.org
http://www.arrlf.org
Purpose: To provide financial assistance to amateur radio operators with high academic achievement.
Eligibility: Applicants must hold an active Amateur Radio License of any class and attend an accredited four-year college or university. They must have a GPA of 3.7 or higher, and their household income may not exceed $100,000 per year. They must not have previously received the Salerno Scholarship.
Target applicants: High school students. College students. Adult students.
Minimum GPA: 3.7
Amount: $1,000.
Number of awards: 2.
Deadline: February 1.
How to apply: Applications are available online.
Exclusive: Visit www.UltimateScholarshipBook.com and enter code AM47112 for updates on this award.

(472) • Bob East Scholarship

National Press Photographers Foundation Bob East Scholarship
Chuck Fadely
The Miami Herald
One Herald Plaza
Miami, FL 33132
Phone: 305-376-2015
http://www.nppa.org
Purpose: To encourage newcomers in photojournalism.
Eligibility: Applicants must either be an undergraduate in the first three and one half years of college or be planning to pursue postgraduate work.
Target applicants: College students. Graduate school students. Adult students.
Amount: $2,000.
Number of awards: 1.
Deadline: Varies.
How to apply: Applications are available online.
Exclusive: Visit www.UltimateScholarshipBook.com and enter code NA47212 for updates on this award.

(473) • Bodie McDowell Scholarship

Outdoor Writers Association of America
121 Hickory Street
Suite 1
Missoula, MT 59801
Phone: 406-728-7434
Fax: 406-728-7445
Email: krhoades@owaa.org
http://www.owaa.org

Purpose: To support students in outdoor communications fields.

Eligibility: Applicants must be students of outdoor communications fields including print, film, art or broadcasting and must be either undergraduate students entering their junior or senior year or graduate students.

Target applicants: College students. Graduate school students. Adult students.

Amount: $1,000-$5,000.

Number of awards: 3 or more.

Deadline: Varies.

How to apply: Applicants are available online.

Exclusive: Visit www.UltimateScholarshipBook.com and enter code OU47312 for updates on this award.

(474) • Bound to Stay Bound Books Scholarship

Association for Library Service to Children
50 E. Huron Street
Chicago, IL 60611
Phone: 800-545-2433
Fax: 312-944-7671
Email: alsc@ala.org
http://www.ala.org/alsc

Purpose: To support students pursuing their MLS degrees.

Eligibility: Applicants must intend to pursue an MLS or advanced degree, plan to work in children's librarianship and be U.S. or Canadian citizens. Selection is based on academic excellence, leadership and a desire to work with children in any type of library.

Target applicants: College students. Graduate school students. Adult students.

Amount: $7,000.

Number of awards: 4.

Deadline: March 1.

How to apply: Applications are available online.

Exclusive: Visit www.UltimateScholarshipBook.com and enter code AS47412 for updates on this award.

(475) • BSA Research Fellowship

Bibliographical Society of America
P.O. Box 1537
Lenox Hill Station
New York, NY 10021
Phone: 212-452-2710
Email: bsa@bibsocamer.org
http://www.bibsocamer.org

Purpose: To provide financial assistance to those pursuing bibliographical studies.

Eligibility: Applicants must submit proposals for studying books as historical evidence or an examination of the history of book trades or publishing history.

Target applicants: College students. Graduate school students. Adult students.

Amount: $2,000.

Number of awards: Varies.

Deadline: Varies.

How to apply: Applications are available online.

Exclusive: Visit www.UltimateScholarshipBook.com and enter code BI47512 for updates on this award.

(476) • CaGIS Scholarships

American Congress on Surveying and Mapping (ACSM)
6 Montgomery Village Avenue
Suite 403
Gaithersburg, MD 20879
Phone: 240-632-9716
Fax: 240-632-1321
Email: ilse.genovese@acsm.net
http://www.acsm.net

Purpose: To support excellence in cartography or GIScience.

Eligibility: Applicants must be enrolled full-time in a four-year undergraduate or graduate degree program in cartography or geographic information science. Prior scholarship winners may apply. Applicants are judged on their records, statements, letters of recommendation and professional activities.

Target applicants: College students. Graduate school students. Adult students.

Amount: $500-$1,000.

Number of awards: 2.

Scholarship may be renewable.

Deadline: January 15.

How to apply: Applications are available online.

Exclusive: Visit www.UltimateScholarshipBook.com and enter code AM47612 for updates on this award.

(477) • California - Hawaii Elks Association Vocational Grants

California-Hawaii Elks Association
5450 E. Lamona Avenue
Fresno, CA 93727-2224
Phone: 559-222-8071
Fax: 559-222-8073
http://www.chea-elks.org

Purpose: To provide assistance to those pursuing vocational/technical education.

Eligibility: Applicants must be U.S. citizens and California or Hawaii residents. They must plan to pursue a vocational or technical course of study above and supplemental to high school or preparatory school. A high school diploma or equivalent is not required. Students planning to transfer into a bachelor's degree program upon completion of vocational studies are not eligible.

Target applicants: High school students. College students. Adult students.

Amount: $1,000.

Number of awards: 58.

Scholarship may be renewable.

Deadline: 3 months after application is issued.

How to apply: Applications are available online.

Exclusive: Visit www.UltimateScholarshipBook.com and enter code CA47712 for updates on this award.

(478) • Carole J. Streeter, KB9JBR Scholarship

American Radio Relay League Foundation
225 Main Street
Newington, CT 06111
Phone: 860-594-0397
Fax: 860-594-0259
Email: foundation@arrl.org
http://www.arrlf.org

Purpose: To support students who are involved in amateur radio.
Eligibility: Applicants must have an amateur radio license of Technician Class or higher. Preference will be given to applicants with Morse Code proficiency and those studying health and healing arts.
Target applicants: High school students. College students. Adult students.
Amount: $750.
Number of awards: 1.
Deadline: February 1.
How to apply: Applications are available online.
Exclusive: Visit www.UltimateScholarshipBook.com and enter code AM47812 for updates on this award.

(479) • Carole Simpson Scholarship

Radio Television Digital News Association
4121 Plank Road #512
Fredericksburg, VA 22407
Phone: 202-659-6510
Fax: 202-223-4007
Email: staceys@rtdna.org
http://www.rtdna.org

Purpose: To honor professional achievements in electronic journalism.
Eligibility: Applicants must be full-time college sophomores or higher with at least one full academic year remaining. Applicants may be enrolled in any major as long as their career intent is television or radio news. Applicants may only apply for one RTNDA scholarship. Preference is given to students of color.
Target applicants: College students. Adult students.
Amount: $2,000.
Number of awards: 1.
Deadline: May 10.
How to apply: Applications are available online.
Exclusive: Visit www.UltimateScholarshipBook.com and enter code RA47912 for updates on this award.

(480) • Chain des Rotisseurs Scholarship

American Academy of Chefs
180 Center Place Way
St. Augustine, FL 32095
Phone: 800-624-9458
Fax: 904-825-4758
Email: educate@acfchefs.net
http://www.acfchefs.org

Purpose: To assist students attending culinary programs.
Eligibility: Applicants must be enrolled in an accredited post-secondary school of culinary arts or AAC-approved post-secondary culinary training program, be excellent students and have completed at least one grading period. Applicants should submit applications, two recommendation letters, financial aid release forms, transcripts and signed photo releases. Selection is based on application, financial need, references and transcript.
Target applicants: College students. Adult students.
Amount: Varies.
Number of awards: Varies.
Deadline: May 1 or September 1.
How to apply: Applications are available online.
Exclusive: Visit www.UltimateScholarshipBook.com and enter code AM48012 for updates on this award.

(481) • Charles A. Ryskamp Research Fellowships

American Council of Learned Societies (ACLS)
633 Third Avenue
New York, NY 10017-6795
Phone: 212-697-1505
Fax: 212-949-8058
Email: sfisher@acls.org
http://www.contemplativemind.org/

Purpose: To support scholars researching the humanities field.
Eligibility: The fellowships are for advanced assistant professors and untenured associate professors. By the application deadline, the applicants should have finished their institution's last reappointment review before tenure review, and their tenure review is not finished. The applicants should have a Ph.D. or equivalent and be in a tenure-track position at degree-granting U.S. institutions during the fellowship. Previous supported research leaves do not affect eligibility. The application process involves the application, proposal, bibliography, publications list and four reference letters.
Target applicants: Graduate school students. Adult students.
Amount: Up to $80,722.
Number of awards: Up to 12.
Deadline: September 29.
How to apply: Applications are available online.
Exclusive: Visit www.UltimateScholarshipBook.com and enter code AM48112 for updates on this award.

(482) • Charles and Lucille King Family Foundation Scholarship

Charles and Lucille King Family Foundation
366 Madison Avenue
10th Floor
New York, NY 10017
Phone: 212-682-2913
Email: info@kingfoundation.org
http://www.kingfoundation.org

Purpose: To assist film and television students.
Eligibility: Applicants must be undergraduate juniors or seniors and demonstrate academic ability, financial need and professional potential. Applicants must also major in film and television. Applicants must submit applications, personal statements, three recommendation letters and transcripts.
Target applicants: College students. Adult students.
Amount: Up to $2,500.
Number of awards: Varies.
Scholarship may be renewable.
Deadline: April 15.
How to apply: Applications are available online or by written request between September 1 and April 1.
Exclusive: Visit www.UltimateScholarshipBook.com and enter code CH48212 for updates on this award.

(483) · Charles Clarke Cordle Memorial Scholarship

American Radio Relay League Foundation
225 Main Street
Newington, CT 06111
Phone: 860-594-0397
Fax: 860-594-0259
Email: foundation@arrl.org
http://www.arrlf.org

Purpose: To assist ham radio operators in furthering their educations.
Eligibility: Applicants must have any class of ham radio license, have a minimum 2.5 GPA and be residents of and attend school in Georgia or Alabama.
Target applicants: High school students. College students. Graduate school students. Adult students.
Minimum GPA: 2.5
Amount: $1,000.
Number of awards: 1.
Deadline: February 1.
How to apply: Applications are available online but may not be completed electronically. All completed applications must be mailed.
Exclusive: Visit www.UltimateScholarshipBook.com and enter code AM48312 for updates on this award.

(484) · Charles N. Fisher Memorial Scholarship

American Radio Relay League Foundation
225 Main Street
Newington, CT 06111
Phone: 860-594-0397
Fax: 860-594-0259
Email: foundation@arrl.org
http://www.arrlf.org

Purpose: To assist ham radio operators in furthering their educations.
Eligibility: Applicants must have any class of ham radio license, be residents of the ARRL Southwestern Division (Arizona, Los Angeles, Orange County, San Diego or Santa Barbara), attend a regionally-accredited college or university and study electronics, communications or a related field.
Target applicants: College students. Graduate school students. Adult students.
Amount: $1,000.
Number of awards: 1.
Deadline: February 1.
How to apply: Applications are available online. Completed applications must be submitted by mail, not electronically.
Exclusive: Visit www.UltimateScholarshipBook.com and enter code AM48412 for updates on this award.

(485) · Chicago FM Club Scholarships

American Radio Relay League Foundation
225 Main Street
Newington, CT 06111
Phone: 860-594-0397
Fax: 860-594-0259
Email: foundation@arrl.org
http://www.arrlf.org

Purpose: To assist ham radio operators in furthering their educations.
Eligibility: Applicants must have at least a technician ham radio license, be residents of the FCC Ninth Call District (Illinois, Indiana or Wisconsin) and be students at an accredited post-secondary two- or four-year college or trade school.
Target applicants: College students. Adult students.
Amount: $500.
Number of awards: Varies.
Deadline: February 1.
How to apply: Applications are available online but must be sent in by mail.
Exclusive: Visit www.UltimateScholarshipBook.com and enter code AM48512 for updates on this award.

(486) · Chuck Reville, K3FT Memorial Scholarship

Foundation for Amateur Radio, Inc.
FAR Scholarships
P.O. Box 911
Columbia, MD 21044
Phone: 410-552-2652
Fax: 410-981-5146
Email: dave.prestel@gmail.com
http://www.farweb.org

Purpose: To support licensed amateur radio enthusiasts who are pursuing bachelor's degrees in engineering or any of the physical sciences.
Eligibility: Applicants must be licensed amateur radio enthusiasts who are enrolled full-time in a bachelor's degree program in engineering or physical science. Selection is based on the overall strength of the application.
Target applicants: College students. Adult students.
Amount: $1,000.
Number of awards: Varies.
Deadline: March 31.
How to apply: Applications are available online. An application form is required.
Exclusive: Visit www.UltimateScholarshipBook.com and enter code FO48612 for updates on this award.

(487) · CLA Reference Services Press Fellowship

California Library Association
4030 Lennane Drive
Sacramento, CA 95834
Phone: 916-779-4573
Fax: 916-419-2874
Email: info@cla-net.org
http://www.cla-net.org

Purpose: To support college seniors and graduates pursuing master's degrees in library science.
Eligibility: Applicants must either be California residents enrolled in a master's program at an American Library Association-approved library school in any state or residents of any state enrolled in an ALA-approved library school master's program in California. Recipients are expected to pursue a career in reference or information service librarianship and take at least three classes about reference or information service.
Target applicants: College students. Graduate school students. Adult students.
Amount: $3,000.
Number of awards: 1.
Deadline: June 15.
How to apply: Applications are available online.
Exclusive: Visit www.UltimateScholarshipBook.com and enter code CA48712 for updates on this award.

(488) • CLA Scholarship for Minority Students in Memory of Edna Yelland

California Library Association
4030 Lennane Drive
Sacramento, CA 95834
Phone: 916-779-4573
Fax: 916-419-2874
Email: info@cla-net.org
http://www.cla-net.org

Purpose: To assist minority California graduate students who are pursuing degrees in library or information science.
Eligibility: Applicants must be California residents, be American Indian, African American, Mexican American, Latino, Asian American, Pacific Islander or Filipino and be accepted into or enrolled in an American Library Association accredited state library school. The award is based on financial need, and an interview is required.
Target applicants: Graduate school students. Adult students.
Amount: $2,500.
Number of awards: 3.
Deadline: May 31.
How to apply: Applications are available online.
Exclusive: Visit www.UltimateScholarshipBook.com and enter code CA48812 for updates on this award.

(489) • Clifford H. "Ted" Rees, Jr. Scholarship

Air-Conditioning, Heating and Refrigeration Institute
Clifford H. "Ted" Rees, Jr. Scholarship Foundation
2111 Wilson Boulevard
Suite 500
Arlington, VA 22201
Phone: 703-524-8800
Fax: 703-528-3816
Email: ahri@ahrinet.org
http://www.ahrinet.org

Purpose: To support students preparing for careers in heating, ventilation, air-conditioning and refrigeration (HVACR) technology.
Eligibility: Applicants must be U.S. citizens, nationals or resident aliens intending to become U.S. citizens. They must be enrolled in an accredited HVACR technician training program and have plans to become entry-level commercial refrigeration technicians, residential air-conditioning and heating technicians or light commercial air-conditioning and heating technicians after graduation. Selection is based on stated career goals and commitment to pursuing entry-level work in the HVACR field.
Target applicants: College students. Adult students.
Amount: Up to $2,000.
Number of awards: 15.
Deadline: July 1.
How to apply: Applications are available online. An application form, two recommendation letters, personal statement and copy of alien registration card (if applicable) are required.
Exclusive: Visit www.UltimateScholarshipBook.com and enter code AI48912 for updates on this award.

(490) • CNF Professional Growth Scholarship

Child Nutrition Foundation
Scholarship Committee
700 S. Washington Street, Suite 300
Alexandria, VA 22314
Phone: 703-739-3900
Email: jcurtis@schoolnutrition.org
http://www.schoolnutrition.org

Purpose: To support the continuing education of School Nutrition Association members.
Eligibility: Applicants must be members of the School Nutrition Association for at least one year who are enrolled in an undergraduate or graduate program in a school foodservice related field.
Target applicants: College students. Graduate school students. Adult students.
Amount: Varies.
Number of awards: Varies.
Scholarship may be renewable.
Deadline: April 1.
How to apply: Applications are available online.
Exclusive: Visit www.UltimateScholarshipBook.com and enter code CH49012 for updates on this award.

(491) • College Photographer of the Year

National Press Photographers Foundation College Photographer of the Year
David Rees
CPOY Director, School of Journalism, The University of Missouri
106 Lee Hills Hall
Columbus, MO 65211
Phone: 573-882-4442
Fax: 919-383-7261
Email: jourdlr@showme.missouri.edu
http://www.nppa.org

Purpose: To award outstanding student work in photojournalism and provide a forum for student photographers to gauge their skills.
Eligibility: Applicants must be currently enrolled in a full-time four-year college or university, provide a portfolio and demonstrate financial need. Applicants can apply to as many NPPA scholarships as desired, but only one award will be granted per student.
Target applicants: College students. Adult students.
Amount: $500-$1,000.
Number of awards: 2.
Deadline: October 1.
How to apply: Applications are available by written or email request.
Exclusive: Visit www.UltimateScholarshipBook.com and enter code NA49112 for updates on this award.

(492) • College/University Excellence of Scholarship Awards

National Council for Geographic Education
Jacksonville State University
206-A Martin Hall
700 Pelham Road North
Jacksonville, AL 36265-1602
Phone: 256-782-5293
Fax: 256-782-5336
Email: ncge@jsu.edu
http://www.ncge.org

Purpose: To recognize senior geography majors.
Eligibility: Every college or university geography department in North America may submit the name of its outstanding graduating senior geography majors. The students receive certificates.
Target applicants: College students. Adult students.
Amount: Varies.
Number of awards: Varies.
Deadline: May 15.

How to apply: Nomination materials are described online.
Exclusive: Visit www.UltimateScholarshipBook.com and enter code NA49212 for updates on this award.

(493) • Contemplative Practice Fellowship Program

American Council of Learned Societies (ACLS)
633 Third Avenue
New York, NY 10017-6795
Phone: 212-697-1505
Fax: 212-949-8058
Email: sfisher@acls.org
http://www.contemplativemind.org/
Purpose: To support scholars interested in contemplative practices.
Eligibility: There are two awards, Contemplative Practice Fellowships and Contemplative Program Development Fellowships. The first is for $10,000, and the second is for $20,000. Applicants for the Contemplative Practice Fellowships must be scholars who are full-time faculty members at accredited U.S. academic institutions who want to integrate contemplative practices into their courses. Preferred applicants will have experience with contemplative practice. The fellowship is for a summer or semester. The Contemplative Program Development Fellowships is for scholars who are full-time faculty members and faculty-status administrators at accredited U.S. academic institutions who want to develop academic courses involving contemplative studies. The fellowship lasts for an academic year.
Target applicants: Graduate school students. Adult students.
Amount: $10,000 and $20,000.
Number of awards: Varies.
Deadline: November 10.
How to apply: Applications are available online.
Exclusive: Visit www.UltimateScholarshipBook.com and enter code AM49312 for updates on this award.

(494) • CPAexcel Scholarship

CPAexcel
http://www.cpaexcel.com/students/scholarship.html
Purpose: To assist students who are taking accounting courses.
Eligibility: Applicants must be full-time or part-time college juniors or seniors or graduate students who are taking at least one accounting course. Selection is based on a random drawing.
Target applicants: College students. Graduate school students. Adult students.
Amount: $5,000.
Number of awards: 1.
Deadline: November 30.
How to apply: Applications are available online.
Exclusive: Visit www.UltimateScholarshipBook.com and enter code CP49412 for updates on this award.

(495) • Darrel Hess Community College Geography Scholarship

Association of American Geographers (AAG) Hess Scholarship
1710 Sixteenth Street NW
Washington, DC 20009-3198
Phone: 202-234-1450
Fax: 202-234-2744
Email: grantsawards@aag.org
http://www.aag.org
Purpose: To support geography majors.
Eligibility: Applicants must be currently enrolled at a U.S. community college, junior college, city college or similar two-year educational institution, have completed at least two transfer courses in geography and plan to transfer to a four-year institution as a geography major. The award is based on academic excellence and promise. Applications, personal statements, two recommendation letters and transcripts are required.
Target applicants: College students. Adult students.
Amount: $1,000.
Number of awards: 2.
Deadline: December 31.
How to apply: Applications are available online.
Exclusive: Visit www.UltimateScholarshipBook.com and enter code AS49512 for updates on this award.

(496) • David S. Barr Awards

Newspaper Guild - CWA
501 3rd Street NW
6th Floor
Washington, DC 20001-2797
Phone: 202-434-7177
Fax: 202-434-1472
Email: guild@cwa-union.org
http://www.newsguild.org
Purpose: To support student journalists.
Eligibility: Applicants must be high school or post-secondary students at any type of institution and have published or broadcast a work in the previous year that helped to correct an injustice or promote justice and fairness. No more than one entry per applicant may be submitted.
Target applicants: High school students. College students. Graduate school students. Adult students.
Amount: $500-$1,500.
Number of awards: 2.
Deadline: January 28.
How to apply: Applications are available online. An application form, five copies of submitted work and brief summary of work are required.
Exclusive: Visit www.UltimateScholarshipBook.com and enter code NE49612 for updates on this award.

(497) • Dayton Amateur Radio Association Scholarship

American Radio Relay League Foundation
225 Main Street
Newington, CT 06111
Phone: 860-594-0397
Fax: 860-594-0259
Email: foundation@arrl.org
http://www.arrlf.org
Purpose: To provide financial assistance to students who are amateur radio operators.
Eligibility: Applicants must be accepted or enrolled at an accredited four-year institution of higher learning. They must possess an Amateur Radio License of any class.
Target applicants: High school students. College students. Adult students.
Amount: $1,000.
Number of awards: 4.
Deadline: February 1.
How to apply: Applications are available online.
Exclusive: Visit www.UltimateScholarshipBook.com and enter code AM49712 for updates on this award.

(498) • Distinguished Service Award for Students

Society for Technical Communication
Manager of the Distinguished Community Awards Committee
7107 Paradise Park Bend
Richmond , TX 77469
Phone: 703-522-4114
Email: stc@stc.org
http://www.stc.org

Purpose: To assist students who are pursuing degrees in an area of technical communication.

Eligibility: Applicants must be full-time undergraduate or graduate students who have completed at least one year of post-secondary education and who have at least one full year of academic work remaining to complete their degree programs. Students must also be in the field of communication of information about technical subjects and be student members of the STC. Applicants must be nominated by student chapters.

Target applicants: College students. Graduate school students. Adult students.

Amount: $1,000.

Number of awards: 7.

Deadline: October 30.

How to apply: Applications are available online.

Exclusive: Visit www.UltimateScholarshipBook.com and enter code SO49812 for updates on this award.

(499) • Distinguished Student Scholar Award

Pi Lambda Theta
P.O. Box 6626
Bloomington, IN 47407
Phone: 800-487-3411
Fax: 812-339-3462
Email: office@pilambda.org
http://www.pilambda.org

Purpose: To recognize education majors with leadership potential and a dedication to education.

Eligibility: Applicants must be education majors of at least sophomore level who demonstrate leadership skills and a strong dedication to education. They must be nominated for the scholarship by an instructor or supervisor. Applicants must have a GPA of at least 3.5 and demonstrate significant contributions to local or national education efforts. This scholarship is only available in odd years.

Target applicants: College students. Adult students.

Minimum GPA: 3.5

Amount: $500.

Number of awards: Varies.

Deadline: February 10.

How to apply: Applications are available online.

Exclusive: Visit www.UltimateScholarshipBook.com and enter code PI49912 for updates on this award.

(500) • DJNF Summer Internships

Dow Jones Newspaper Fund
P.O. Box 300
Princeton, NJ 08543-0300
Phone: 609-452-2820
Fax: 609-520-5804
Email: djnf@dowjones.com
https://www.newspaperfund.org/PageText/Prg_HomePages.aspx?Page_ID=Prg_CollegeIntern

Purpose: To assist student journalists.

Eligibility: Applicants must be college students interested in pursuing journalism careers and paid summer internships. The three programs have their own requirements. Applicants to the Multimedia, News and Sports Editing Programs must be juniors, seniors or graduate students and must take a pre-qualifying copy editing exam. Candidates must submit the application form, a resume, a transcript and a 500-word essay. Applicants for the Business Reporting Internship Program must be sophomores, juniors, seniors or graduate students. Candidates should submit application forms, resumes, three to five recent clips, a transcript and 500-word essay. They must also take the business reporting test.

Target applicants: College students. Graduate school students. Adult students.

Amount: $1,000.

Number of awards: Up to 100.

Deadline: November 2.

How to apply: Applications are available online.

Exclusive: Visit www.UltimateScholarshipBook.com and enter code DO50012 for updates on this award.

(501) • Donald Groves Fund

American Numismatic Society
75 Varick Street
Floor 11
New York, NY 10013
Phone: 212-571-4470
Fax: 212-571-4479
Email: info@numismatics.org
http://www.numismatics.org

Purpose: To support publication in the field of early American numismatics, which involves materials created no later than 1800.

Eligibility: Funding is available for travel, research and publication costs. Applicants must submit an outline of the proposed research, research methods, funding amount requested and how the funds will be used.

Target applicants: Graduate school students. Adult students.

Amount: Varies.

Number of awards: Varies.

Deadline: Varies.

How to apply: Application instructions are available online. Applications should be mailed to the ANS, Attn.: Secretary of the Society.

Exclusive: Visit www.UltimateScholarshipBook.com and enter code AM50112 for updates on this award.

(502) • Donald Riebhoff Memorial Scholarship

American Radio Relay League Foundation
225 Main Street
Newington, CT 06111
Phone: 860-594-0397
Fax: 860-594-0259
Email: foundation@arrl.org
http://www.arrlf.org

Purpose: To assist ham radio operators in furthering their educations.

Eligibility: Applicants must have at least a technician ham radio license, be undergraduate or graduate students in international studies at an accredited post-secondary institution and be members of ARRL.

Target applicants: College students. Graduate school students. Adult students.

Amount: $1,000.

Number of awards: 1.

Deadline: February 1.

How to apply: Applications are available online. Completed applications must be mailed in. They cannot be completed electronically.

Exclusive: Visit www.UltimateScholarshipBook.com and enter code AM50212 for updates on this award.

(503) • Dr. Aura-Lee A. and James Hobbs Pittenger American History Scholarship

National Society Daughters of the American Revolution
Committee Services Office
Attn.: Scholarships
1776 D Street NW
Washington, DC 20006-5303
Phone: 202-628-1776
http://www.dar.org
Purpose: To promote the study of American history and government.
Eligibility: Applicants must be high school seniors planning to major in American history and American government. The award is up to $2,000 each year for up to four years. All applicants must obtain a letter of sponsorship from their local DAR chapter. However, affiliation with DAR is not required.
Target applicants: High school students.
Amount: $2,000.
Number of awards: Varies.
Scholarship may be renewable.
Deadline: February 15.
How to apply: Applications are available by written request with a self-addressed, stamped envelope.
Exclusive: Visit www.UltimateScholarshipBook.com and enter code NA50312 for updates on this award.

(504) • Dr. James L. Lawson Memorial Scholarship

American Radio Relay League Foundation
225 Main Street
Newington, CT 06111
Phone: 860-594-0397
Fax: 860-594-0259
Email: foundation@arrl.org
http://www.arrlf.org
Purpose: To assist ham radio operators in furthering their educations.
Eligibility: Applicants must have at least a general ham radio license, be residents of and attend post-secondary institutions in the New England states (Connecticut, Maine, Massachusetts, New Hampshire, Rhode Island or Vermont) or New York state and be pursuing a bachelor's or graduate degree in electronics, communications or a related field.
Target applicants: College students. Graduate school students. Adult students.
Amount: $500.
Number of awards: 1.
Deadline: February 1.
How to apply: Applications are available online but cannot be completed electronically. All applications must be mailed.
Exclusive: Visit www.UltimateScholarshipBook.com and enter code AM50412 for updates on this award.

(505) • Earl I. Anderson Scholarship

American Radio Relay League Foundation
225 Main Street
Newington, CT 06111
Phone: 860-594-0397
Fax: 860-594-0259
Email: foundation@arrl.org
http://www.arrlf.org
Purpose: To assist ham radio operators with furthering their educations.
Eligibility: Applicants must have some form of ham radio operating license, be residents of Florida, Illinois, Indiana or Michigan, major in electronic engineering or a related technical field and be ARRL members.
Target applicants: College students. Graduate school students. Adult students.
Amount: $1,250.
Number of awards: 3.
Deadline: February 1.
How to apply: Applications are available online. Completed applications must be submitted by mail.
Exclusive: Visit www.UltimateScholarshipBook.com and enter code AM50512 for updates on this award.

(506) • Ecolab Scholarship Competition

American Hotel and Lodging Educational Foundation (AH&LEF)
1201 New York Avenue NW
Suite 600
Washington, DC 20005-3931
Phone: 202-289-3188
Fax: 202-289-3199
Email: chammond@ahlef.org
http://www.ahlef.org
Purpose: To provide scholarships for students who intend to earn a degree in hospitality management.
Eligibility: Applicants must be enrolled or intend to enroll full-time in a two- or four-year U.S. college or university.
Target applicants: High school students. College students. Adult students.
Amount: Up to $2,000.
Number of awards: 14.
Deadline: May 1.
How to apply: Applications are available online.
Exclusive: Visit www.UltimateScholarshipBook.com and enter code AM50612 for updates on this award.

(507) • Ed Bradley Scholarship

Radio Television Digital News Association
4121 Plank Road #512
Fredericksburg, VA 22407
Phone: 202-659-6510
Fax: 202-223-4007
Email: staceys@rtdna.org
http://www.rtdna.org
Purpose: To honor professional achievements in electronic journalism.
Eligibility: Applicants must be full-time college sophomores or higher with at least one full academic year remaining. Applicants may be enrolled in any major as long as their career intent is television or radio news. Applicants may only apply for one RTNDA scholarship. Preference will be given to undergraduate students of color.
Target applicants: College students. Adult students.
Amount: $10,000.
Number of awards: 1.
Deadline: May 10.
How to apply: Applications are available online.
Exclusive: Visit www.UltimateScholarshipBook.com and enter code RA50712 for updates on this award.

(508) • Edmond A. Metzger Scholarship

American Radio Relay League Foundation
225 Main Street
Newington, CT 06111
Phone: 860-594-0397
Fax: 860-594-0259
Email: foundation@arrl.org
http://www.arrlf.org

Purpose: To assist ham radio operators in furthering their educations.
Eligibility: Applicants must have at least a novice ham radio license, be undergraduate or graduate students in electrical engineering, be residents of and attend schools in the ARRL Central Division (Illinois, Indiana or Wisconsin) and be members of ARRL.
Target applicants: College students. Graduate school students. Adult students.
Amount: $500.
Number of awards: 1.
Deadline: February 1.
How to apply: Applications are available online. Completed applications must be mailed in. They cannot be completed electronically.
Exclusive: Visit www.UltimateScholarshipBook.com and enter code AM50812 for updates on this award.

(509) • Edmund S. Muskie Graduate Fellowship Program

International Research and Exchanges Board (IREX)
2121 K Street NW
Suite 700
Washington, DC 20037
Phone: 202-628-8188
Fax: 202-628-8189
Email: irex@irex.org
http://www.irex.org

Purpose: To provide fellowships to encourage graduate students and professionals from Eurasia to study in the United States.
Eligibility: Applicants must hold an undergraduate degree and be a citizen, national or permanent resident of Armenia, Azerbaijan, Belarus, Georgia, Kazakhstan, Kyrgyzstan, Moldova, Russian Federation, Tajikistan, Turkmenistan, Ukraine or Uzbekistan. Students must also be able to obtain and retain a U.S. J-1 visa. Applicants must be in one of the following fields of study: business administration, economics, education, environmental management, international affairs, journalism/mass communication, law, library/information science, public administration, public health or public policy.
Target applicants: Graduate school students. Adult students.
Amount: Varies.
Number of awards: Varies.
Deadline: Varies.
Exclusive: Visit www.UltimateScholarshipBook.com and enter code IN50912 for updates on this award.

(510) • Edward J. Nell Memorial Scholarships in Journalism

Quill and Scroll Society
University of Iowa School of Journalism and Mass Communications
100 Adler Journalism Building
Iowa City, IA 52242
Phone: 319-335-3457
Fax: 319-335-3989
Email: quill-scroll@uiowa.edu
http://www.uiowa.edu/~quill-sc/

Purpose: To aid high school journalists seeking to improve their skills and techniques.
Eligibility: Applicants to the Nell Scholarship must have been national winners in the Yearbook Excellence Contest or the International Writing/Photography Contest.
Target applicants: High school students.
Amount: Varies.
Number of awards: Varies.
Deadline: May 10.
How to apply: Applications are available online.
Exclusive: Visit www.UltimateScholarshipBook.com and enter code QU51012 for updates on this award.

(511) • Electronic Document Systems Foundation Scholarship Awards

Electronic Document Systems Foundation
1845 Precinct Line Road, Suite 212
Hurst, TX 76054
Phone: 817-849-1145
Fax: 817-849-1185
Email: info@edsf.org
http://www.edsf.org

Purpose: To support students interested in pursuing careers in document management and communication.
Eligibility: Applicants must be full-time students interested in a career in the preparation, production or distribution of documents. Possible areas of study include marketing, graphic arts, e-commerce, imaging science, printing, web authoring, electronic publishing, computer science, telecommunications or business. For most scholarships, applicants must be junior, senior or graduate students; however opportunities exist for students at all levels, including those attending two-year colleges. Specific scholarships are available for U.S. and Canadian citizens.
Target applicants: College students. Graduate school students. Adult students.
Amount: $500-$5,000.
Number of awards: Varies.
Deadline: May 1.
How to apply: Applications are available online.
Exclusive: Visit www.UltimateScholarshipBook.com and enter code EL51112 for updates on this award.

(512) • Enid Hall Griswold Memorial Scholarship

National Society Daughters of the American Revolution
Committee Services Office
Attn.: Scholarships
1776 D Street NW
Washington, DC 20006-5303
Phone: 202-628-1776
http://www.dar.org

Purpose: To assist college students pursuing studies in political science, history, government or economics.
Eligibility: Applicants must be college juniors or seniors majoring in political science, history, government or economics. All applicants must obtain a letter of sponsorship from their local DAR chapter. However, affiliation with DAR is not required.
Target applicants: College students. Adult students.
Amount: $1,000.
Number of awards: 1.
Deadline: February 15.

How to apply: Applications are available by written request with a self-addressed, stamped envelope.
Exclusive: Visit www.UltimateScholarshipBook.com and enter code NA51212 for updates on this award.

(513) · Esther R. Sawyer Research Award

Institute of Internal Auditors Research Foundation
247 Maitland Avenue
Altamonte Springs, FL 32701-4201
Phone: 407-937-1100
Fax: 407-937-1101
Email: research@theiia.org
http://www.theiia.org
Purpose: To award internal auditing students.
Eligibility: Applicants should be accepted to or currently enrolled in a graduate program in internal auditing at an IIA-endorsed school or have taken internal auditing undergraduate courses at an IIA-endorsed school and be enrolled in any graduate program in internal auditing or business. An original manuscript on a topic related to modern internal auditing is required. The award is based on the topic, value to the audit profession, originality and the quality of writing.
Target applicants: College students. Graduate school students. Adult students.
Amount: $5,000.
Number of awards: 1.
Deadline: March 1.
How to apply: Application materials are described online.
Exclusive: Visit www.UltimateScholarshipBook.com and enter code IN51312 for updates on this award.

(514) · Eugene Gene Sallee, W4YFR Memorial Scholarship

American Radio Relay League Foundation
225 Main Street
Newington, CT 06111
Phone: 860-594-0397
Fax: 860-594-0259
Email: foundation@arrl.org
http://www.arrlf.org
Purpose: To support students who are involved in amateur radio.
Eligibility: Applicants must have an FCC amateur radio license at the level of Technician Plus or higher. Students must have at least a 3.0 GPA.
Target applicants: High school students. College students. Adult students.
Minimum GPA: 3.0
Amount: $500.
Number of awards: 1.
Deadline: February 1.
How to apply: Applications are available online.
Exclusive: Visit www.UltimateScholarshipBook.com and enter code AM51412 for updates on this award.

(515) · Executive Women International Scholarship Program

Executive Women International (EWI)
515 South 700 East
Suite 2A
Salt Lake City, UT 84102
Phone: 801-355-2800
Fax: 801-355-2852
Email: ewi@ewiconnect.com
http://www.executivewomen.org
Purpose: To assist high school students in achieving their higher education goals.
Eligibility: Applicants must be high school juniors who plan to pursue four-year degrees at accredited colleges or universities. Selection is based on application materials, communication skills, academic record, extracurricular activities and leadership.
Target applicants: High school students.
Amount: $500-$10,000.
Number of awards: Varies.
Deadline: April.
How to apply: Applications are available by request from the applicant's local Executive Women International chapter. An application form and supporting documents are required.
Exclusive: Visit www.UltimateScholarshipBook.com and enter code EX51512 for updates on this award.

(516) · Fisher Broadcasting Scholarships for Minorities

Fisher Communications Inc.
100 4th Avenue N.
Suite 440
Seattle, WA 98109
Phone: 206-404-7000
Email: info@fsci.com
http://www.fsci.com
Purpose: To attract minority students into careers in broadcasting.
Eligibility: Applicants must be college sophomores enrolled in a broadcast, marketing or journalism curriculum at a college or vocational-technical school, be of non-white origin, and have a minimum 2.5 GPA. Residents outside of Washington, Oregon, Idaho, Montana and must apply scholarship funds to colleges in those states. Residents of those states may apply scholarship awards to out-of-state schools.
Target applicants: College students. Adult students.
Minimum GPA: 2.5
Amount: Varies.
Number of awards: Varies.
Deadline: April 30.
How to apply: Applications are available online.
Exclusive: Visit www.UltimateScholarshipBook.com and enter code FI51612 for updates on this award.

(517) · Florence C. and Robert H. Lister Fellowship

Crow Canyon Archeological Center
23390 Road K
Cortez, CO 81321-9908
Phone: 800-422-8975
Email: schoolprograms@crowcanyon.org
http://www.crowcanyon.org
Purpose: To assist graduate students in the archeology of American Indian cultures of the Southwest.
Eligibility: Applicants must be enrolled in a North American Ph.D. program and have projects based on archaeological, ethnoarchaeological or paleoenvironmental research in the southwestern United States and northern Mexico. The award is offered every other year.
Target applicants: Graduate school students. Adult students.
Amount: $7,000.
Number of awards: 1.
Deadline: Varies.
How to apply: Applications are available online.

Exclusive: Visit www.UltimateScholarshipBook.com and enter code CR51712 for updates on this award.

(518) • FOWA Scholarship for Outdoor Communicators

Florida Outdoor Writers Association
24 NW 33rd Court
Suite A
Gainesville, FL 32706
Phone: 352-284-1763
Email: execdir@fowa.org
http://www.fowa.org

Purpose: To aid students who plan to enter the field of outdoor communications.

Eligibility: Applicants must be students at Florida colleges or universities or students from any school whose applications are endorsed by a FOWA member or faculty advisor. They must have a career goal that entails communicating love and appreciation of hunting, fishing and other outdoor activities. Selection is based on essay, faculty advisor or FOWA member endorsement, scholastic merit and extracurricular activities. Preference is given to journalism and communications majors.

Target applicants: High school students. College students. Adult students.

Amount: $500-$1,000.

Number of awards: Varies.

Deadline: May 3.

How to apply: Applications are available online. A cover page, essay, resume and letter of endorsement are required. Other supporting materials will be considered.

Exclusive: Visit www.UltimateScholarshipBook.com and enter code FL51812 for updates on this award.

(519) • Frances M. Schwartz Fellowship

American Numismatic Society
75 Varick Street
Floor 11
New York, NY 10013
Phone: 212-571-4470
Fax: 212-571-4479
Email: info@numismatics.org
http://www.numismatics.org

Purpose: To award fellowships in support of the study of numismatics and museum methodology at the American Numismatic Society.

Eligibility: Applicants must hold a B.A. or equivalent.

Target applicants: Graduate school students. Adult students.

Amount: Up to $2,000.

Number of awards: Varies.

Deadline: March 1.

How to apply: Applications are available online or by mail.

Exclusive: Visit www.UltimateScholarshipBook.com and enter code AM51912 for updates on this award.

(520) • Francis Walton Memorial Scholarship

American Radio Relay League Foundation
225 Main Street
Newington, CT 06111
Phone: 860-594-0397
Fax: 860-594-0259
Email: foundation@arrl.org
http://www.arrlf.org

Purpose: To assist ham radio operators in furthering their educations.

Eligibility: Applicants must have at least five words per minute certification, be residents of the ARRL Central Division (Illinois, Indiana or Wisconsin) and pursue a bachelor's or graduate degree at a regionally-accredited institution.

Target applicants: High school students. College students. Graduate school students. Adult students.

Amount: $500.

Number of awards: Varies.

Deadline: February 1.

How to apply: Applications are available online but must be mailed in.

Exclusive: Visit www.UltimateScholarshipBook.com and enter code AM52012 for updates on this award.

(521) • Francis X. Crowley Scholarship

New England Water Works Association
125 Hopping Brook Road
Holliston, MA 01746
Phone: 508-893-7979
Email: tmacelhaney@preloadinc.com
http://www.newwa.org

Purpose: To support civil engineering, environmental engineering and business management students.

Eligibility: Applicants must be New England Water Works Association student members. They must be enrolled in a postsecondary degree program in civil engineering, environmental engineering or business management. Selection is based on the overall strength of the application.

Target applicants: College students. Adult students.

Amount: $3,000.

Number of awards: 1.

Deadline: April 1.

How to apply: Applications are available online. An application form, a personal essay, an official transcript and one recommendation letter are required.

Exclusive: Visit www.UltimateScholarshipBook.com and enter code NE52112 for updates on this award.

(522) • Frank M. Coda Scholarship

American Society of Heating, Refrigerating and Air-Conditioning Engineers
1791 Tullie Circle, NE
Atlanta, GA 30329
Phone: 404-636-8400
Fax: 404-321-5478
Email: lbenedict@ashrae.org
http://www.ashrae.org

Purpose: To support undergraduate students who are preparing for careers in the heating, ventilation, air-conditioning and refrigeration industry.

Eligibility: Applicants must be current or entering full-time undergraduates enrolled in a bachelor's of science, bachelor's of engineering or pre-engineering degree program in preparation for a career in HVACR. They must attend a school that has an ASHRAE student branch, is accredited by ABET or is accredited by a non-USA agency that has signed a Memorandum of Understanding with ABET or the Washington Accord. They must be in the top 30 percent of their class and must have a GPA of 3.0 or higher on a four-point scale. Selection is based on the overall strength of the application.

Target applicants: High school students. College students. Adult students.

Minimum GPA: 3.0

Amount: $5,000.
Number of awards: 1.
Scholarship may be renewable.
Deadline: December 1.
How to apply: Applications are available online. An application form, official college transcript (or proof of enrollment for rising freshmen) and two letters of reference are required.
Exclusive: Visit www.UltimateScholarshipBook.com and enter code AM52212 for updates on this award.

---

(523) • Frank Sarli Memorial Scholarship

National Court Reporters Association
8224 Old Courthouse Road
Vienna, VA 22182-3808
Phone: 800-272-6272
Email: dgaede@ncrahq.org
http://www.ncraonline.org
Purpose: To support the court reporting profession.
Eligibility: Applicants must be in good academic standing at an approved court-reporting program, be members of the NCRA and have a minimum 3.5 GPA.
Target applicants: College students. Adult students.
Minimum GPA: 3.5
Amount: $2,000.
Number of awards: 1.
Deadline: May 14.
How to apply: Applications are available online.
Exclusive: Visit www.UltimateScholarshipBook.com and enter code NA52312 for updates on this award.

---

(524) • Fred R. McDaniel Memorial Scholarship

American Radio Relay League Foundation
225 Main Street
Newington, CT 06111
Phone: 860-594-0397
Fax: 860-594-0259
Email: foundation@arrl.org
http://www.arrlf.org
Purpose: To assist ham radio operators in furthering their educations.
Eligibility: Applicants must have at least a general ham radio license, be residents of and attend a post-secondary institution in the FCC Fifth Call District (Texas, Oklahoma, Arkansas, Louisiana, Mississippi or New Mexico) and be studying for a bachelor's or graduate degree in electronics, communications or a related field. Preference is given to applicants with a 3.0 GPA or higher.
Target applicants: College students. Graduate school students. Adult students.
Amount: $500.
Number of awards: 1.
Deadline: February 1.
How to apply: Applications are available online but must be sent in by mail.
Exclusive: Visit www.UltimateScholarshipBook.com and enter code AM52412 for updates on this award.

---

(525) • Frederic G. Melcher Scholarship

Association for Library Service to Children
50 E. Huron Street
Chicago, IL 60611
Phone: 800-545-2433
Fax: 312-944-7671
Email: alsc@ala.org
http://www.ala.org/alsc
Purpose: To support students who want to become children's librarians.
Eligibility: Applicants must intend to pursue an MLS degree, plan to work in children's librarianship and be U.S. or Canadian citizens. Selection is based on academic excellence, leadership and desire to work with children in any type of library.
Target applicants: College students. Graduate school students. Adult students.
Amount: $6,000.
Number of awards: 2.
Deadline: March 1.
How to apply: Applications are available online.
Exclusive: Visit www.UltimateScholarshipBook.com and enter code AS52512 for updates on this award.

---

(526) • Frederick Burkhardt Residential Fellowships for Recently Tenured Scholars

American Council of Learned Societies (ACLS)
633 Third Avenue
New York, NY 10017-6795
Phone: 212-697-1505
Fax: 212-949-8058
Email: sfisher@acls.org
http://www.contemplativemind.org/
Purpose: To support scholars researching in the humanities field.
Eligibility: Applicants must be recently tenured humanists and must be employed in tenured positions at U.S. degree-granting institutions during the fellowship. An application, a proposal, a bibliography, a publications list, three reference letters and one institutional statement are required. Previous supported research leaves does not affect eligibility.
Target applicants: Graduate school students. Adult students.
Amount: $75,000.
Number of awards: Up to 9.
Deadline: September 29.
How to apply: Applications are available online.
Exclusive: Visit www.UltimateScholarshipBook.com and enter code AM52612 for updates on this award.

---

(527) • FSF Scholarship Program

Funeral Service Foundation
13625 Bishop's Drive
Brookfield, WI 53005
Phone: 877-402-5900
Fax: 262-789-6977
Email: kbuenger@funeralservicefoundation.org
http://www.funeralservicefoundation.org
Purpose: To provide financial assistance for higher education to those working in fields related to funeral service.
Eligibility: Applicants must be undergraduate students enrolled in funeral science programs.
Target applicants: College students. Adult students.
Amount: $1,000-$2,500.
Number of awards: Varies.
Deadline: March.
How to apply: Applications are available online.
Exclusive: Visit www.UltimateScholarshipBook.com and enter code FU52712 for updates on this award.

(528) • Fund for American Studies Internships

Fund for American Studies
1706 New Hampshire Avenue NW
Washington, DC 20009
Phone: 800-741-6964
Email: admissions@tfas.org
http://www.dcinternships.org

Purpose: To provide scholarships for students attending one of the Fund's internship programs.

Eligibility: There are programs in comparative political and economic systems, political journalism, business and government, philanthropy and international institutes. Each program includes classes, an internship and special events. Students take classes at Georgetown University and live in downtown Washington, DC. Summer and school-year programs are available.

Target applicants: College students. Adult students.

Amount: Varies.

Number of awards: Varies.

Deadline: Varies.

How to apply: Applications are available online.

Exclusive: Visit www.UltimateScholarshipBook.com and enter code FU52812 for updates on this award.

(529) • Future Teacher Scholarship

Journalism Education Association Future Teacher Scholarship
Kansas State University
103 Kedzie Hall
Manhattan, KS 66506
Phone: 330-672-8297
Email: cbowen@kent.edu
http://www.jea.org

Purpose: To provide scholarships for upper-level or master's students who intend to teach scholastic journalism.

Eligibility: Applicants must be education majors focusing on learning to teach scholastic journalism at the secondary school level.

Target applicants: College students. Graduate school students. Adult students.

Amount: $1,000.

Number of awards: Up to 3.

Deadline: October 15.

How to apply: Application information is available online.

Exclusive: Visit www.UltimateScholarshipBook.com and enter code JO52912 for updates on this award.

(530) • Gamma Theta Upsilon-Geographical Honor Society

Gamma Theta Upsilon
Dr. Donald Zeigler
Old Dominion University
1181 University Drive
Virginia Beach, VA 23453
http://www.gammathetaupsilon.org

Purpose: To support geography knowledge and awareness by awarding monetary assistance to college and graduate students.

Eligibility: Applicants must be initiated through a Gamma Theta Upsilon chapter.

Target applicants: College students. Graduate school students. Adult students.

Amount: $1,000.

Number of awards: 5.

Deadline: June 1.

How to apply: Applications are available online.

Exclusive: Visit www.UltimateScholarshipBook.com and enter code GA53012 for updates on this award.

(531) • Gary Wagner, K3OMI Scholarship

American Radio Relay League Foundation
225 Main Street
Newington, CT 06111
Phone: 860-594-0397
Fax: 860-594-0259
Email: foundation@arrl.org
http://www.arrlf.org

Purpose: To support engineering students who are involved in amateur radio.

Eligibility: Applicants must have an amateur radio license of Novice Class or higher. Students may be pursuing a bachelor's degree in any field of engineering. They must be residents of one of the following states: North Carolina, Virginia, West Virginia, Maryland or Tennessee. Preference will be given to students with financial need.

Target applicants: High school students. College students. Adult students.

Amount: $1,000.

Number of awards: 1.

Deadline: February 1.

How to apply: Applications are available online.

Exclusive: Visit www.UltimateScholarshipBook.com and enter code AM53112 for updates on this award.

(532) • Gary Yoshimura Scholarship

Public Relations Student Society of America
33 Maiden Lane
11th Floor
New York, NY 10038
Phone: 212-460-1474
Fax: 212-995-0757
Email: prssa@prsa.org
http://www.prssa.org

Purpose: To assist public relations students.

Eligibility: Applicants must be PRSSA members with a minimum 3.0 GPA in the pursuit of higher education in the public relations field. Applicants must submit an essay on personal or professional challenges and a statement on financial need.

Target applicants: College students. Graduate school students. Adult students.

Minimum GPA: 3.0

Amount: $2,400.

Number of awards: 1.

Deadline: January 31.

How to apply: Applications are available online.

Exclusive: Visit www.UltimateScholarshipBook.com and enter code PU53212 for updates on this award.

(533) • GED Jump Start Scholarship

Child Nutrition Foundation
Scholarship Committee
700 S. Washington Street, Suite 300
Alexandria, VA 22314
Phone: 703-739-3900
Email: jcurtis@schoolnutrition.org

http://www.schoolnutrition.org
Purpose: To support School Nutrition Association members in earning a GED.
Eligibility: Applicants must be School Nutrition Association members who do not currently have a GED or high school diploma and plan on earning a GED within a year of receiving the scholarship.
Target applicants: College students. Adult students.
Amount: $200.
Number of awards: Varies.
Deadline: Applications are accepted throughout the year.
How to apply: Applications are available online.
Exclusive: Visit www.UltimateScholarshipBook.com and enter code CH53312 for updates on this award.

(534) • General Fund Scholarships

American Radio Relay League Foundation
225 Main Street
Newington, CT 06111
Phone: 860-594-0397
Fax: 860-594-0259
Email: foundation@arrl.org
http://www.arrlf.org
Purpose: To assist ham radio operators in furthering their educations.
Eligibility: Applicants must have any level of ham radio license.
Target applicants: High school students. College students. Graduate school students. Adult students.
Amount: $2,000.
Number of awards: Varies.
Deadline: February 1.
How to apply: Applications are available online. Completed applications must be submitted by mail.
Exclusive: Visit www.UltimateScholarshipBook.com and enter code AM53412 for updates on this award.

(535) • George A. Strait Minority Scholarship

American Association of Law Libraries
105 W. Adams
Suite 3300
Chicago, IL 60604
Phone: 312-939-4764
Fax: 312-431-1097
Email: scholarships@aall.org
http://www.aallnet.org
Purpose: To encourage minorities to enter careers as law librarians.
Eligibility: Applicants must be a member of a minority group as defined by U.S. government rules, degree candidates in an accredited library or law school, and intend to pursue a career as law librarians. Law library experience is preferred. Applicants must also have financial need and have at least one quarter or semester left after the scholarship is given.
Target applicants: Graduate school students. Adult students.
Amount: Varies.
Number of awards: Varies.
Scholarship may be renewable.
Deadline: April 1.
How to apply: Applications are available online, by mail with a self-addressed, stamped envelope, by fax, by phone or by email.
Exclusive: Visit www.UltimateScholarshipBook.com and enter code AM53512 for updates on this award.

(536) • George and Viola Hoffman Award

Association of American Geographers (AAG) Hoffman Award
Frostburg State University
101 Braddock Road
c/o George White
Frostburg, MD 21532-2303
Phone: 301-687-4000
Email: gwhite@frostburg.edu
http://www.aag.org
Purpose: To support graduate research in Eastern Europe.
Eligibility: Applicants must research toward a master's thesis or doctoral dissertation on a geographical subject in Eastern Europe which includes the countries of East Central and Southeast Europe from Poland south to Romania, Bulgaria and the successor states of the former Yugoslavia. The research topics may be historical or contemporary, systematic or regional, limited to a small area or comparative. Applicants must submit applications including a statement of the research topic, research methods, field of study, schedule and bibliography. Applicants should also submit a letter describing professional achievements and the goals and a letter of support from a sponsoring faculty member.
Target applicants: Graduate school students. Adult students.
Amount: $350-$500.
Number of awards: Varies.
Deadline: December 31.
How to apply: Application materials are described online.
Exclusive: Visit www.UltimateScholarshipBook.com and enter code AS53612 for updates on this award.

(537) • George M. Brooker Collegiate Scholarship for Minorities

Institute of Real Estate Management
IREM Foundation Administrator
430 N. Michigan Avenue
Chicago, IL 60611
Phone: 800-837-0706
Fax: 800-338-4736
http://www.irem.org
Purpose: To increase minority participation in the real estate industry.
Eligibility: Applicants must be minorities, be U.S. citizens, declare a major in real estate or a related field, have a minimum 3.0 GPA in the major and have completed two courses in real estate or plan to finish them. Applicants must submit a 500-word essay explaining their reason for pursuing a real estate career. Applicants must also submit three general letters of recommendation and a letter of recommendation from a local IREM chapter officer.
Target applicants: College students. Graduate school students. Adult students.
Minimum GPA: 3.0
Amount: $2,500-$5,000.
Number of awards: Varies.
Deadline: From the 15th to the end of the month every month except for October, November, and December.
How to apply: Applications are available online.
Exclusive: Visit www.UltimateScholarshipBook.com and enter code IN53712 for updates on this award.

(538) • Giles Sutherland Rich Memorial Scholarship

Federal Circuit Bar Association
1620 I Street NW
Suite 900
Washington, DC 20006

Phone: 202-466-3923
Fax: 202-833-1061
http://www.fedcirbar.org
Purpose: To support promising law students who demonstrate financial need.
Eligibility: Applicants must be undergraduate or graduate law students who demonstrate academic ability and financial need. They must submit a one-page statement describing their financial need, their interest in law and their qualifications for the award. Applicants must also submit a transcript and curriculum vitae.
Target applicants: College students. Graduate school students. Adult students.
Amount: $10,000.
Number of awards: 1.
Deadline: April 30.
How to apply: There is no application form.
Exclusive: Visit www.UltimateScholarshipBook.com and enter code FE53812 for updates on this award.

(539) · Golden Gate Restaurant Association Scholarship

Golden Gate Restaurant Association
Scholarship Foundation
120 Montgomery Street, Suite 1280
San Francisco, CA 94104
Phone: 415-781-5348
Fax: 415-781-3925
Email: ggra@ggra.org
http://www.ggra.org
Purpose: To provide scholarships for college students who wish to pursue a career in the restaurant/food service industry.
Eligibility: Applicants must be California residents at time of application submission and pursue a major in food service.
Target applicants: High school students. College students. Adult students.
Amount: Up to $6,500.
Number of awards: Varies.
Deadline: April 30.
How to apply: Applications are available online or by mail.
Exclusive: Visit www.UltimateScholarshipBook.com and enter code GO53912 for updates on this award.

(540) · Grades 7-12 Excellence of Scholarship Awards

National Council for Geographic Education
Jacksonville State University
206-A Martin Hall
700 Pelham Road North
Jacksonville, AL 36265-1602
Phone: 256-782-5293
Fax: 256-782-5336
Email: ncge@jsu.edu
http://www.ncge.org
Purpose: To recognize outstanding geography students.
Eligibility: Nominators must be NCGE members who teach grades 7-12 geography courses and who nominate students in their classes. Only one student in each section or class may be nominated.
Target applicants: Junior high students or younger. High school students.
Amount: Varies.
Number of awards: Varies.
Deadline: May 15.
How to apply: Nominating materials are described online.
Exclusive: Visit www.UltimateScholarshipBook.com and enter code NA54012 for updates on this award.

(541) · Harrell Family Fellowship

American Center of Oriental Research (ACOR)
656 Beacon Street, 5th Floor
Boston, MA 02215
Phone: 617-353-6571
Fax: 617-353-6575
Email: acor@bu.edu
http://www.bu.edu/acor
Purpose: To assist a graduate student with expenses on an archaeological project in Jordan.
Eligibility: Applicants must be graduate students in a program approved by a recognized academic review body. The funds must be used for archaeological or related research.
Target applicants: Graduate school students. Adult students.
Amount: $1,800.
Number of awards: 1.
Deadline: February 1.
How to apply: Applications are available online.
Exclusive: Visit www.UltimateScholarshipBook.com and enter code AM54112 for updates on this award.

(542) · Harry S. Truman Research Grant

Harry S. Truman Library Institute for National and International Affairs
Grants Administrator
500 W. U.S. Highway 24
Independence, MO 64050
Phone: 816-268-8248
Fax: 816-268-8299
Email: lisa.sullivan@nara.gov
http://www.trumanlibrary.org
Purpose: To promote the Truman Library as a center for research.
Eligibility: Graduate students and post-doctoral scholars are most encouraged to apply, but others completing advanced research will be considered. Preference is given to research dealing with enduring public policy and foreign policy issues that have a high chance of being published or otherwise shared publicly. Applicants can receive up to two research grants in a five-year period. Grant winners must submit a report at the end of their studies.
Target applicants: Graduate school students. Adult students.
Amount: Up to $2,500.
Number of awards: Varies.
Deadline: April 1 and October 1.
How to apply: Applications are available online.
Exclusive: Visit www.UltimateScholarshipBook.com and enter code HA54212 for updates on this award.

(543) · Harry S. Truman Undergraduate Student Grant

Harry S. Truman Library Institute for National and International Affairs
Grants Administrator
500 W. U.S. Highway 24
Independence, MO 64050
Phone: 816-268-8248

Fax: 816-268-8299
Email: lisa.sullivan@nara.gov
http://www.trumanlibrary.org
Purpose: To promote the Truman Library as a center for research.
Eligibility: Applicants must be writing a senior thesis on an aspect of the life and career of Harry S. Truman or public and foreign policy issues that were prominent during the Truman years, describe in writing the proposed project and show how using the Truman Library for research will help their future development. Grant winners must submit a written report on their research.
Target applicants: College students. Adult students.
Amount: Up to $2,500.
Number of awards: Varies.
Deadline: April 1 and October 1.
How to apply: There is no application form.
Exclusive: Visit www.UltimateScholarshipBook.com and enter code HA54312 for updates on this award.

(544) • Hawaii Association of Broadcasters Scholarship

Hawaii Association of Broadcasters Inc.
P.O. Box 22112
Honolulu, HI 96823-2112
Phone: 808-599-1455
Fax: 808-599-7784
Email: stephanieuyeda@hawaii.rr.com
http://www.hawaiibroadcasters.com
Purpose: To support students pursuing careers in broadcasting.
Eligibility: Applicants must be high school seniors or undergraduate students and attend an accredited two- or four-year college, university or broadcast school in the U.S. full-time. Students must also have a 2.75 GPA or higher and intend to work in the broadcast industry in Hawaii upon completion of their education.
Target applicants: High school students. College students. Adult students.
Minimum GPA: 2.75
Amount: Varies.
Number of awards: Varies.
Deadline: Varies.
How to apply: Applications are available online. An application form, letter of recommendation and transcript are required.
Exclusive: Visit www.UltimateScholarshipBook.com and enter code HA54412 for updates on this award.

(545) • Henry Belin du Pont Dissertation Fellowship

Hagley Museum and Library
Center for the History of Business, Technology and Society
P.O. Box 3630
Wilmington, DE 19807-0630
Phone: 302-655-2400
Fax: 302-658-3188
http://www.hagley.org
Purpose: To provide four-month fellowships for doctoral students performing dissertation research.
Eligibility: Applicants must be doctoral students who have completed all course work and are performing dissertation research. Research topics should involve historical questions and should relate to the collections in the Hagley Library. Fellows will receive housing, office space, a computer and Internet access. A presentation is required at the end of the residence period.
Target applicants: Graduate school students. Adult students.
Amount: $6,000.
Number of awards: Varies.
Deadline: November 15.
How to apply: Applications are available online. For more information contact Dr. Roger Horowitz at rhorowitz@hagley.org.
Exclusive: Visit www.UltimateScholarshipBook.com and enter code HA54512 for updates on this award.

(546) • Herbert Hoover Presidential Library Association Travel Grant Program

Herbert Hoover Presidential Library Association
P.O. Box 696
West Branch, IA 52358
Phone: 800-828-0475
Fax: 319-643-2391
Email: scholarship@hooverassociation.org
http://www.hooverassociation.org
Purpose: To provide financial aid to individuals to research at the Herbert Hoover Presidential Library in West Branch, Iowa.
Eligibility: Applicants must be current graduate students, post-doctoral scholars or independent researchers. Applicants must also ensure that the library's contents will meet their research needs before applying.
Target applicants: Graduate school students. Adult students.
Amount: $500-$1,500.
Number of awards: Varies.
Deadline: March 1.
How to apply: Applications are available online.
Exclusive: Visit www.UltimateScholarshipBook.com and enter code HE54612 for updates on this award.

(547) • Holocaust Remembrance Project Essay Contest

Holland and Knight Charitable Foundation
P.O. Box 2877
Tampa, FL 33601
Phone: 866-HK-CARES
Email: holocaust@hklaw.com
http://holocaust.hklaw.com
Purpose: To reward high school students who write essays about the Holocaust.
Eligibility: Applicants must be age 19 and under who are currently enrolled as high school students in grades 9 to 12 (including home-schooled students), high school seniors or students who are enrolled in a high school equivalency program and be residents of either the United States or Mexico or United States citizens living abroad. Applicants should submit essays about the Holocaust and entry forms. Every essay must include works cited, a reference page or a bibliography. First place winners will receive free trips to Washington, DC.
Target applicants: High school students.
Amount: $5,000.
Number of awards: Varies.
Deadline: April 2.
How to apply: Essays may be submitted online.
Exclusive: Visit www.UltimateScholarshipBook.com and enter code HO54712 for updates on this award.

(548) • Horace Mann Scholarship

Horace Mann Insurance Companies
1 Horace Mann Plaza
Springfield, IL 62715

Phone: 800-999-1030
http://www.horacemann.com
Purpose: To help public and private K-12 educators.
Eligibility: Applicants must be an educator currently employed by a U.S. public or private school and planning to enter a two- or four-year college or university. Applicants must also have at least two or more years of teaching experience. Selection is based on an essay and school and community activities. The program is not open to residents of Hawaii, New Jersey and New York.
Target applicants: College students. Adult students.
Amount: $1,000-$5,000.
Number of awards: 35.
Deadline: March 1.
How to apply: Applications are available online.
Exclusive: Visit www.UltimateScholarshipBook.com and enter code HO54812 for updates on this award.

(549) · Horace Samuel and Marion Galbraith Merrill Travel Grants in Twentieth-Century American Political History

Organization of American Historians
112 N. Bryan Avenue
P.O. Box 5457
Bloomington, IN 47408
Phone: 812-855-9852
Fax: 812-855-0696
Email: awards@oah.org
http://www.oah.org
Purpose: Named after a University of Maryland political historian and his wife, the Horace Samuel and Marion Galbraith Merrill Travel Grants seek to perpetuate the couple's desire to assist fledgling scholars and authors.
Eligibility: The award provides stipends, access to research collections and opportunities to interview current and former public figures in Washington, DC. Only applications from current OAH members are accepted.
Target applicants: Junior high students or younger. High school students. College students. Graduate school students. Adult students.
Amount: $500-$3,000.
Number of awards: Varies.
Deadline: December 1.
How to apply: A copy of a completed submission package (clearly labeled "Merrill Travel Grants") must be mailed directly to each selector. The required contents of the package and the names and addresses of the selectors are available online.
Exclusive: Visit www.UltimateScholarshipBook.com and enter code OR54912 for updates on this award.

(550) · HORIZONS Foundation Scholarship

Women In Defense
HORIZONS Foundation
c/o National Defense Industrial Association
2111 Wilson Boulevard, Suite 400
Arlington, VA 22201
Phone: 703-247-2552
Fax: 703-527-6945
Email: jcasey@ndia.org
http://wid.ndia.org
Purpose: To encourage women to pursue careers related to the national security interests of the United States and to provide development opportunities to women already working in national security fields.
Eligibility: Applicants must be full- or part-time female students at an accredited university or college and must have reached at least junior level status. Applicants must also demonstrate an interest in a career related to national security and defense, have a minimum GPA of 3.25 and demonstrate financial need. Preference is given to students in security studies, military history, government relations, engineering, computer science, physics, mathematics, business, law, international relations, political science or economics.
Target applicants: College students. Graduate school students. Adult students.
Minimum GPA: 3.25
Amount: Varies.
Number of awards: Varies.
Deadline: July 1.
How to apply: Applications are available online.
Exclusive: Visit www.UltimateScholarshipBook.com and enter code WO55012 for updates on this award.

(551) · HSMAI Foundation Scholarship

Hospitality Sales and Marketing Association International (HSMAI)
1760 Old Meadow Road, #500
McLean, VA 22102
Phone: 703-506-2010
Email: info@hsmai.org
http://www.hsmai.org
Purpose: To assist students pursuing a career in hospitality sales and marketing.
Eligibility: Applicants must be full-time or part-time undergraduate or graduate students pursuing a career in hospitality sales and marketing. Amounts of scholarships vary from year to year.
Target applicants: College students. Graduate school students. Adult students.
Amount: $500-$2,000.
Number of awards: Varies.
Deadline: June 15.
How to apply: Applications are available online.
Exclusive: Visit www.UltimateScholarshipBook.com and enter code HO55112 for updates on this award.

(552) · Huntington Fellowships

Huntington Library, Art Collections and Botanical Gardens
1151 Oxford Road
San Marino, CA 91108
Phone: 626-405-2194
Fax: 626-449-5703
Email: cpowell@huntington.org
http://www.huntington.org
Purpose: To provide fellowships to doctoral students and recipients in British and American history, literature, art history and the history of science and medicine.
Eligibility: Applicants must have a Ph.D. or equivalent or be doctoral candidates at the dissertation stage. Cover sheets, project descriptions, curriculum vitae and three letters of recommendation are required.
Target applicants: Graduate school students. Adult students.
Amount: $2,500-$50,000.
Number of awards: More than 100.
Deadline: December 15.
How to apply: Application materials are described online.
Exclusive: Visit www.UltimateScholarshipBook.com and enter code HU55212 for updates on this award.

(553) • Huntington-British Academy Fellowships for Study in Great Britain

Huntington Library, Art Collections and Botanical Gardens
1151 Oxford Road
San Marino, CA 91108
Phone: 626-405-2194
Fax: 626-449-5703
Email: cpowell@huntington.org
http://www.huntington.org

Purpose: To offer scholars exchange fellowships to research British and American history, literature, art history and the history of science and medicine.
Eligibility: Applicants must have a Ph.D. or equivalent. Applicants must submit cover sheets, project descriptions, curriculum vitae and three letters of recommendation.
Target applicants: Graduate school students. Adult students.
Amount: Varies.
Number of awards: Varies.
Deadline: December 15.
How to apply: There is no application form, and application materials are described online.
Exclusive: Visit www.UltimateScholarshipBook.com and enter code HU55312 for updates on this award.

(554) • IEHA Scholarship

International Executive Housekeepers Association (IEHA) Education Foundation
1001 Eastwind Drive, Suite 301
Westerville, OH 43081-3361
Phone: 800-200-6342
Fax: 614-895-1248
Email: excel@ieha.org
http://www.ieha.org

Purpose: To support IEHA members who are pursuing undergraduate or associate's degrees or IEHA certification.
Eligibility: Applicants must submit a 2,000-word manuscript about an issue in the housekeeping industry. The winning manuscript will be selected by a panel of judges and published.
Target applicants: College students. Adult students.
Amount: Up to $800.
Number of awards: Varies.
Deadline: January 10.
How to apply: Applications are available online.
Exclusive: Visit www.UltimateScholarshipBook.com and enter code IN55412 for updates on this award.

(555) • IFEC Scholarships Award

International Foodservice Editorial Council (IFEC)
P.O. Box 491
Hyde Park, NY 12538
Phone: 845-229-6973
Email: ifec@ifeconline.com
http://www.ifeconline.com

Purpose: To assist students interested in foodservice combined with communication arts.
Eligibility: Applicants must be enrolled at a post-secondary, degree-granting educational institution and must demonstrate training, skill and interest in the foodservice industry and communication arts. Eligible majors from foodservice and communications areas include culinary arts, hotel/restaurant/hospitality management, dietetics, nutrition, food science/technology, journalism, public relations, mass communication, English, broadcast journalism, marketing, photography, graphic arts and related studies.
Target applicants: College students. Graduate school students. Adult students.
Amount: $500-$4,000.
Number of awards: 4-9.
Deadline: March 15.
How to apply: Applications are available online.
Exclusive: Visit www.UltimateScholarshipBook.com and enter code IN55512 for updates on this award.

(556) • IFSEA Worthy Goal Scholarship

International Food Service Executives Association
Joseph Quagliano
8824 Stancrest Drive
Las Vegas, NV 89134
Phone: 502-589-3602
http://www.ifsea.com

Purpose: To help students receive food service management training beyond the high school level.
Eligibility: Applicants must be enrolled or accepted at a college as a full-time student in a food service related major. Students must provide a financial statement, personal statement, list of work experience and professional activities, transcripts, recommendations and a statement describing how the scholarship would help them reach their goals.
Target applicants: High school students. College students. Graduate school students. Adult students.
Amount: $250-$1,500.
Number of awards: Varies.
Scholarship may be renewable.
Deadline: February 1.
How to apply: Applications are available online.
Exclusive: Visit www.UltimateScholarshipBook.com and enter code IN55612 for updates on this award.

(557) • IMA Memorial Education Fund Scholarship

Institute of Management Accountants (IMA)
10 Paragon Drive
Montvale, NJ 07645-1760
Phone: 800-638-4427
Email: students@imanet.org
http://www.imanet.org

Purpose: To support students in fields related to management accounting.
Eligibility: Applicants must be full- and part-time undergraduate and graduate students, be IMA student members and declare which four- or five-year management accounting, financial management or information technology related program they plan to pursue as a career or list a related field. Candidates should submit applications, resumes, transcripts, two recommendations and statements. Advanced degree students must pass one part of the CMA/CFM certification.
Target applicants: College students. Graduate school students. Adult students.
Minimum GPA: 2.8
Amount: $2,500.
Number of awards: Varies.
Deadline: February 15.
How to apply: Applications are available online.
Exclusive: Visit www.UltimateScholarshipBook.com and enter code IN55712 for updates on this award.

(558) • Imagine America Scholarship

Imagine America Foundation
1101 Connecticut Avenue NW
Suite 901
Washington, DC 20036
Phone: 202-336-6800
Fax: 202-408-8102
Email: scholarships@imagine-america.org
http://www.imagine-america.org

Purpose: To help high school seniors pursue a postsecondary career education.

Eligibility: Applicants must have a minimum 2.5 high school GPA, demonstrate financial need and have demonstrated community service during their senior year.

Target applicants: High school students.

Minimum GPA: 2.5

Amount: $1,000.

Number of awards: Varies.

Deadline: December 31.

How to apply: Applications are available online.

Exclusive: Visit www.UltimateScholarshipBook.com and enter code IM55812 for updates on this award.

(559) • International Order of Alhambra Scholarship

International Order of Alhambra
4200 Leeds Avenue
Baltimore, MD 21229
Phone: 410-242-0660
Fax: 410-536-5729
Email: hq@orderalhambra.org
http://www.orderalhambra.org

Purpose: To provide financial assistance to undergraduate students who wish to become special education teachers or to those who give care to the permanently disabled.

Eligibility: One of the purposes of the organization is to provide assistance, education and residences to the developmentally disabled.

Target applicants: High school students. College students. Adult students.

Amount: Varies.

Number of awards: Varies.

Deadline: Varies.

How to apply: Contact the organization for more information.

Exclusive: Visit www.UltimateScholarshipBook.com and enter code IN55912 for updates on this award.

(560) • IRARC Memorial Joseph P. Rubino WA4MMD Scholarship

American Radio Relay League Foundation
225 Main Street
Newington, CT 06111
Phone: 860-594-0397
Fax: 860-594-0259
Email: foundation@arrl.org
http://www.arrlf.org

Purpose: To provide financial assistance to amateur radio operators who are seeking an undergraduate degree or electronic technician certification.

Eligibility: Applicants must hold an active Amateur Radio License in any class and be studying at an accredited institution. They must have a minimum GPA of 2.5. Preference is given to Florida residents, particularly those from Brevard County and those with need and lower GPAs.

Target applicants: High school students. College students. Adult students.

Minimum GPA: 2.5

Amount: $750.

Number of awards: Varies.

Deadline: February 1.

How to apply: Applications are available online.

Exclusive: Visit www.UltimateScholarshipBook.com and enter code AM56012 for updates on this award.

(561) • ISFA College Scholarship

Insurance Scholarship Foundation of America
14286-19 Beach Boulevard
Suite 353
Jacksonville, FL 32250
Phone: 904-821-7188
Email: foundation@inssfa.org
http://www.inssfa.org

Purpose: To promote studies in the insurance industry.

Eligibility: Applicants must major in insurance, risk management or actuarial science, have completed two insurance or risk management-related courses, currently attending a college or university and be completing or have completed the second year of college, have a minimum 3.0 GPA and be a NAIW Student Member.

Target applicants: College students. Graduate school students. Adult students.

Minimum GPA: 3.0

Amount: $500-$5,000.

Number of awards: Varies.

Deadline: January 15.

How to apply: Applications are available online.

Exclusive: Visit www.UltimateScholarshipBook.com and enter code IN56112 for updates on this award.

(562) • J. Franklin Jameson Fellowship in American History

American Historical Association
400 A Street SE
Washington, DC 20003
Phone: 202-544-2422
Fax: 202-544-8307
Email: info@historians.org
http://www.historians.org

Purpose: To support one semester of scholarly research in the Library of Congress collections.

Eligibility: Applicants must hold a Ph.D. or equivalent, must have earned the degree within the past seven years and may not have published a book-length historical work. Projects should focus on American history.

Target applicants: Graduate school students. Adult students.

Amount: $5,000.

Number of awards: Varies.

Deadline: March 15.

How to apply: Application instructions are available online.

Exclusive: Visit www.UltimateScholarshipBook.com and enter code AM56212 for updates on this award.

(563) • Jack Kinnaman Scholarship

National Education Association
NEA-Retired, Room 410
1201 16th Street NW
Washington, DC 20036
Phone: 202-822-7149
http://www.nea.org

Purpose: To honor the memory of NEA-retired vice president and former advisory council member Jack Kinnaman.

Eligibility: Applicants must be NEA student members, major in education and have a minimum 2.5 GPA. An essay describing activities in NEA, a brief paragraph describing financial need, two letters of recommendation and a copy of the most recent transcript are required.

Target applicants: College students. Adult students.

Minimum GPA: 2.5

Amount: Varies.

Number of awards: 1.

Deadline: April 15.

How to apply: Applications are available online.

Exclusive: Visit www.UltimateScholarshipBook.com and enter code NA56312 for updates on this award.

(564) • James A. Turner, Jr. Memorial Scholarship

American Welding Society Foundation
550 NW LeJeune Road
Miami, FL 33126
Phone: 800-443-9353
Email: info@aws.org
http://www.aws.org

Purpose: To aid those interested in a management career in welding store operations or distributorship.

Eligibility: Applicants must be full-time students pursuing a four-year bachelor's of business degree, plan to enter management careers in welding store operations or distributorship, be high school graduates at least 18 years of age and be employed a minimum of 10 hours per week at a welding distributorship. Preference is given to members of the American Welding Society.

Target applicants: College students. Adult students.

Amount: $3,500.

Number of awards: 1.

Deadline: February 15.

How to apply: Applications are available online.

Exclusive: Visit www.UltimateScholarshipBook.com and enter code AM56412 for updates on this award.

(565) • James F. Connolly LexisNexis Academic and Library Solutions Scholarship

American Association of Law Libraries
105 W. Adams
Suite 3300
Chicago, IL 60604
Phone: 312-939-4764
Fax: 312-431-1097
Email: scholarships@aall.org
http://www.aallnet.org

Purpose: To support a librarian interested in becoming a law librarian.

Eligibility: Preference will be given to librarians who are interested in government documents. Applicants must be library school graduates with experience working in a law library who intend to obtain a degree at an accredited law school and have careers as law librarians. Applicants should have no more than 36 semester credit hours left before qualifying for the degree and should have financial need.

Target applicants: Graduate school students. Adult students.

Amount: Varies.

Number of awards: 1.

Scholarship may be renewable.

Deadline: April 1.

How to apply: Applications are available online, by mail with a self-addressed, stamped envelope, by fax, by phone and by email.

Exclusive: Visit www.UltimateScholarshipBook.com and enter code AM56512 for updates on this award.

(566) • James J. Hill Research Grants

James J. Hill Research Library
80 W. Fourth Street
Saint Paul, MN 55102
Phone: 651-265-5500
Email: manuscripts@jjhill.org
http://www.jjhill.org

Purpose: To assist scholars whose research requires them to use the business information manuscript collections at the Hill Library.

Eligibility: Applicants must be college or university professors, independent scholars or Ph.D. candidates who are working on their dissertations. Applications must include a research proposal, projected budget and three letters of recommendation.

Target applicants: Graduate school students. Adult students.

Amount: $2,000.

Number of awards: Varies.

Deadline: November 1.

How to apply: Applications are available by email, phone or online at http://www.jjhill.org/History/grant_program.html.

Exclusive: Visit www.UltimateScholarshipBook.com and enter code JA56612 for updates on this award.

(567) • Jane M. Klausman Women in Business Scholarship Fund

Zonta International
1211 West 22nd Street
Oak Brook, IL 60523
Phone: 630-928-1400
Fax: 630-928-1559
Email: zontaintl@zonta.org
http://www.zonta.org

Purpose: To help female business management majors overcome gender barriers.

Eligibility: Applicants must be eligible to enter their junior or senior year in an undergraduate degree program at an accredited institution when funds are received. Applicants must also have an outstanding academic record in their college career, and they must show intent to complete a business program.

Target applicants: College students. Adult students.

Amount: $1,000-$5,000.

Number of awards: Varies.

Deadline: July 1.

How to apply: Applications are available online or from your local Zonta Club.

Exclusive: Visit www.UltimateScholarshipBook.com and enter code ZO56712 for updates on this award.

(568) • Japan-IMF Scholarship Program for Advanced Studies

Institute of International Education
1400 K Street NW
Washington, DC 20005
Phone: 202-326-7672
Fax: 202-326-7835
Email: boren@iie.org
http://www.iie.org

Purpose: To support Japanese nationals pursuing a Ph.D. in macroeconomics and related fields.
Eligibility: Applicants must be admitted to a school outside of Japan that has a strong doctoral program in macroeconomics. This scholarship covers all reasonable expenses for two years of graduate study. Scholarship recipients must receive no other scholarships or earn income while receiving the scholarship. They are also expected to apply for employment with IMF upon completion of their degrees.
Target applicants: College students. Adult students.
Amount: Tuition plus travel expenses and paid internship.
Number of awards: Up to 7.
Scholarship may be renewable.
Deadline: January 31.
How to apply: Applications are available online. An application form, personal statement, transcript, GRE and TOEFL or IELTS scores, copy of application to doctoral program and two letters of reference are required.
Exclusive: Visit www.UltimateScholarshipBook.com and enter code IN56812 for updates on this award.

(569) • Jean Cebik Memorial Scholarship

American Radio Relay League Foundation
225 Main Street
Newington, CT 06111
Phone: 860-594-0397
Fax: 860-594-0259
Email: foundation@arrl.org
http://www.arrlf.org

Purpose: To provide scholarship assistance to amateur radio operators.
Eligibility: Applicants must hold a Technician Class Amateur Radio License or higher, and they must be attending a four-year college or university.
Target applicants: High school students. College students. Adult students.
Amount: $1,000.
Number of awards: 1.
Deadline: February 1.
How to apply: Applications are available online.
Exclusive: Visit www.UltimateScholarshipBook.com and enter code AM56912 for updates on this award.

(570) • Jennifer C. Groot Fellowship

American Center of Oriental Research (ACOR)
656 Beacon Street, 5th Floor
Boston, MA 02215
Phone: 617-353-6571
Fax: 617-353-6575
Email: acor@bu.edu
http://www.bu.edu/acor

Purpose: To assist students with expenses on an archaeological project.
Eligibility: Applicants must be undergraduate or graduate students with little or no archaeological field experience and be U.S. or Canadian citizens. Recipients will travel to Jordan for the project.
Target applicants: College students. Graduate school students. Adult students.
Amount: $1,800.
Number of awards: At least 2.
Deadline: February 1.
How to apply: Applications are available online but must be submitted by mail.
Exclusive: Visit www.UltimateScholarshipBook.com and enter code AM57012 for updates on this award.

(571) • Jessica King Scholarship

Association for International Practical Training (AIPT)
10400 Little Patuxent Parkway
Suite 250
Columbia, MD 21044-3519
Phone: 410-997-2200
Fax: 410-992-3924
Email: aipt@aipt.org
http://www.aipt.org

Purpose: To help students in the international hospitality field.
Eligibility: Applicants must be between 18 and 35 years old, have a degree in the hospitality industry or be currently employed for at least one year in the hospitality industry and be fluent in the host country's language. Applicants must also have been offered an overseas position and be participating in an AIPT-sponsored program. The scholarship is based on merit.
Target applicants: College students. Graduate school students. Adult students.
Amount: $2,000.
Number of awards: Varies.
Deadline: Accepted year round.
How to apply: Applications are available by email.
Exclusive: Visit www.UltimateScholarshipBook.com and enter code AS57112 for updates on this award.

(572) • Joe Francis Haircare Scholarship Program

Joe Francis Haircare Scholarship Foundation
P.O. Box 50625
Minneapolis, MN 55405
Phone: 651-769-1757
Fax: 651-459-8371
http://www.joefrancis.com

Purpose: To provide barber and cosmetology students with financial aid.
Eligibility: Applicants must be sponsored by one of the following: a fully accredited, recognized barber or cosmetology school, a licensed salon owner or manager, a full-service distributor or a member of the International Chain Association, Beauty and Barber Supply Institute, Cosmetology Advancement Foundation or National Cosmetology Association. Applicants must be actively enrolled in cosmetology school or planning to enroll during or after the award month of August. Judging is based on financial need, motivation and character.
Target applicants: High school students. College students. Adult students.
Amount: $1,000.
Number of awards: 20.
Deadline: June 1.
How to apply: Applications are available online.

Exclusive: Visit www.UltimateScholarshipBook.com and enter code JO57212 for updates on this award.

(573) • Joe Perdue Scholarship

Club Foundation
1733 King Street
Alexandria, VA 22314
Phone: 703-739-9500
Fax: 703-739-0124
Email: schaverr@clubfoundation.org
http://www.clubfoundation.org

Purpose: To support students pursuing careers in private club management.
Eligibility: Applicants must be pursuing managerial careers in the private club industry, have completed their freshman year of college, have a minimum 2.5 GPA and be enrolled full-time for the following year. An essay and letters of recommendation are also required.
Target applicants: College students. Adult students.
Minimum GPA: 2.5
Amount: Varies.
Number of awards: Varies.
Deadline: May 1.
How to apply: Applications are available online.
Exclusive: Visit www.UltimateScholarshipBook.com and enter code CL57312 for updates on this award.

(574) • John Bayliss Broadcast Foundation Scholarships

John Bayliss Broadcast Foundation
171 17th Street
Pacific Grove, CA 93950
Phone: 212-424-6410
Email: cbutrum@baylissfoundation.org
http://www.baylissfoundation.org

Purpose: This scholarship helps students who are pursuing careers in radio.
Eligibility: Applicants must be attending an institution of higher learning in the U.S., be entering their junior or senior year and have a GPA of 3.0 or higher. Students must be working toward a career in the radio industry. Preference is given to students with a history of radio-related activities and those pursuing careers in commercial radio.
Target applicants: College students. Adult students.
Minimum GPA: 3.0
Amount: $5,000.
Number of awards: Varies.
Deadline: Varies.
How to apply: Applications are available online. An application form, resume, transcript, essay and three letters of recommendation are required.
Exclusive: Visit www.UltimateScholarshipBook.com and enter code JO57412 for updates on this award.

(575) • John F. Kennedy Profile in Courage Essay Contest

John F. Kennedy Library Foundation
Columbia Point
Boston, MA 02125
Phone: 617-514-1649
Email: profiles@nara.gov
http://www.jfkcontest.org

Purpose: To encourage students to research and write about politics and John F. Kennedy.
Eligibility: Applicants must be in grades 9 through 12 in public or private schools or be home-schooled and write an essay about the political courage of a U.S. elected official who served during or after 1956. Essays must have source citations. Applicants must register online before sending essays and have a nominating teacher review the essay. The winner and teacher will be invited to the Kennedy Library to accept the award, and the winner's teacher will receive a grant. Essays are judged on content (55 percent) and presentation (45 percent).
Target applicants: High school students.
Amount: $500-$10,000.
Number of awards: Up to 7.
Deadline: January 7.
How to apply: Applications are available online. A registration form and essay are required.
Exclusive: Visit www.UltimateScholarshipBook.com and enter code JO57512 for updates on this award.

(576) • John R. Johnson Memorial Scholarship Endowment

American Association of Law Libraries
105 W. Adams
Suite 3300
Chicago, IL 60604
Phone: 312-939-4764
Fax: 312-431-1097
Email: scholarships@aall.org
http://www.aallnet.org

Purpose: To encourage current and future law librarians in memory of John Johnson, a prominent law librarian.
Eligibility: Applicants who apply for any of the AALL Educational Scholarships become automatically eligible to receive this award. No separate application is necessary. Applicants must intend to have careers as law librarians. Preference is given to AALL members, but a non-member may apply.
Target applicants: Graduate school students. Adult students.
Amount: Varies.
Number of awards: Varies.
Scholarship may be renewable.
Deadline: April 1.
How to apply: Applications are available online, by mail with a self-addressed, stamped envelope, by fax, by phone or by email.
Exclusive: Visit www.UltimateScholarshipBook.com and enter code AM57612 for updates on this award.

(577) • Joseph S. Rumbaugh Historical Oration Contest

National Society of the Sons of the American Revolution
1000 S. Fourth Street
Louisville, KY 40203
Phone: 502-589-1776
Email: contests@sar.org
http://www.sar.org

Purpose: To encourage students to learn more about the Revolutionary War and its impact on modern America.
Eligibility: Applicants must prepare a speech of five to six minutes on some aspect of the Revolutionary War. The contest is open to high school sophomores, juniors and seniors at public, private and parochial high schools, as well as home-schooled students. Eligibility for the national contest is determined by contests on the state and local level.

Target applicants: High school students.
Amount: $200-$3,000.
Number of awards: Varies.
Deadline: June 4.
How to apply: Applications are available from local chapters of Sons of the American Revolution.
Exclusive: Visit www.UltimateScholarshipBook.com and enter code NA57712 for updates on this award.

(578) • Junior Fellowships

American Institute of Indian Studies
1130 E. 59th Street
Chicago, IL 60637
Phone: 773-702-8638
Email: aiis@uchicago.edu
http://www.indiastudies.org
Purpose: To support doctoral candidates at U.S. universities who wish to travel to India to conduct dissertation research on Indian aspects of their academic discipline.
Eligibility: Applicants must be doctoral candidates at a U.S. university. Junior fellows are affiliated with Indian universities and research mentors. Awards may last up to 11 months.
Target applicants: Graduate school students. Adult students.
Amount: Varies.
Number of awards: Varies.
Deadline: July 1.
How to apply: Applications are available by mail or email.
Exclusive: Visit www.UltimateScholarshipBook.com and enter code AM57812 for updates on this award.

(579) • K2TEO Martin J. Green, Sr. Memorial Scholarship

American Radio Relay League Foundation
225 Main Street
Newington, CT 06111
Phone: 860-594-0397
Fax: 860-594-0259
Email: foundation@arrl.org
http://www.arrlf.org
Purpose: To provide financial assistance to students who are amateur radio operators.
Eligibility: Applicants must hold a general class or higher amateur radio license. Preference is given to students from ham families.
Target applicants: High school students. College students. Graduate school students. Adult students.
Amount: $1,000.
Number of awards: 1.
Deadline: February 1.
How to apply: Applications are available online.
Exclusive: Visit www.UltimateScholarshipBook.com and enter code AM57912 for updates on this award.

(580) • Ken Kashiwahara Scholarship

Radio Television Digital News Association
4121 Plank Road #512
Fredericksburg, VA 22407
Phone: 202-659-6510
Fax: 202-223-4007
Email: staceys@rtdna.org
http://www.rtdna.org
Purpose: To honor professional achievements in electronic journalism.
Eligibility: Applicants must be full-time college sophomores or higher with at least one full academic year remaining. Applicants may be enrolled in any major as long as their career intent is television or radio news. Applicants may only apply for one RTNDA scholarship. Preference is given to students of color.
Target applicants: College students. Adult students.
Amount: $2,500.
Number of awards: 1.
Deadline: May 10.
How to apply: Applications are available online.
Exclusive: Visit www.UltimateScholarshipBook.com and enter code RA58012 for updates on this award.

(581) • Kit C. King Graduate Scholarship Fund

National Press Photographers Association Kit C. King Graduate Scholarship Fund
Scott R. Sines
Managing Editor, Memphis Commercial-Appeal
495 Union Avenue
Memphis, TN 38103
Phone: 901-529-5843
Email: sines@commercialappeal.com
http://www.nppa.org
Purpose: To support photojournalism students.
Eligibility: Applicants must provide a portfolio, be pursuing an advanced degree in journalism with an emphasis in photojournalism and demonstrate financial need. Applicants can apply to as many NPPA scholarships as desired, but only one award will be granted per student.
Target applicants: Graduate school students. Adult students.
Amount: $2,000.
Number of awards: 1.
Deadline: Varies.
How to apply: Applications are available online.
Exclusive: Visit www.UltimateScholarshipBook.com and enter code NA58112 for updates on this award.

(582) • L. Phil Wicker Scholarship

American Radio Relay League Foundation
225 Main Street
Newington, CT 06111
Phone: 860-594-0397
Fax: 860-594-0259
Email: foundation@arrl.org
http://www.arrlf.org
Purpose: To assist ham radio operators in furthering their educations.
Eligibility: Applicants must have at least a general ham radio license, be residents of and attending school in the ARRL Roanoke Division (North Carolina, South Carolina, Virginia, West Virginia) and be undergraduate or graduate students in electronics, communications or another related field.
Target applicants: College students. Graduate school students. Adult students.
Amount: $1,000.
Number of awards: 1.
Deadline: February 1.
How to apply: Applications are available online. Completed applications must be submitted by mail.
Exclusive: Visit www.UltimateScholarshipBook.com and enter code AM58212 for updates on this award.

(583) · Laurel Fund

Educational Foundation for Women in Accounting
P.O. Box 1925
Southeastern, PA 19399
Phone: 610-407-9229
Fax: 610-644-3713
Email: info@efwa.org
http://www.efwa.org

Purpose: To provide scholarships to women pursuing advanced degrees in accounting.
Eligibility: This award is available to women pursuing a Ph.D. in accounting. The awardees are selected based on scholarship, service and financial need. Applicants must have completed their comprehensive exams before the previous fall semester.
Target applicants: Graduate school students. Adult students.
Amount: Up to $5,000.
Number of awards: Varies.
Deadline: May 30.
How to apply: Applications are available online.
Exclusive: Visit www.UltimateScholarshipBook.com and enter code ED58312 for updates on this award.

(584) · Lawrence G. Foster Award for Excellence in Public Relations

Public Relations Student Society of America
33 Maiden Lane
11th Floor
New York, NY 10038
Phone: 212-460-1474
Fax: 212-995-0757
Email: prssa@prsa.org
http://www.prssa.org

Purpose: To assist public relations students.
Eligibility: Applicants must be undergraduate students majoring in public relations who are committed to careers in public relations. Applicants must submit an essay on what excellence in public relations is and how they plan to achieve excellence in their own careers.
Target applicants: College students. Adult students.
Amount: $1,500.
Number of awards: 1.
Deadline: June 6.
How to apply: Applications are available online.
Exclusive: Visit www.UltimateScholarshipBook.com and enter code PU58412 for updates on this award.

(585) · Learning and Leadership Grants

NEA Foundation
1201 16th Street NW
Suite 416
Washington, DC 20036
Phone: 202-822-7840
Fax: 202-822-7779
Email: info-neafoundation@list.nea.org
http://www.neafoundation.org

Purpose: To support public school teachers, public education support professionals and faculty or staff in public institutions of higher education in professional development experiences such as summer institutes or action research.
Eligibility: Applicants must be current public school teachers in grades K-12, public school education support professionals or faculty and staff at public higher education institutions. The professional development must improve practice, curriculum and student achievement. Funds may be used for fees, travel expenses, books or materials. There is also a grant for groups for $5,000.
Target applicants: Graduate school students. Adult students.
Amount: $2,000.
Number of awards: Varies.
Deadline: February 1, June 1, October 15.
How to apply: Applications are available online. Applications may be submitted at any time and are reviewed three times each year on February 1, June 1 and October 15.
Exclusive: Visit www.UltimateScholarshipBook.com and enter code NE58512 for updates on this award.

(586) · Legal Opportunity Scholarship Fund

American Bar Association
321 North Clark Street
Chicago, IL 60610
Phone: 312-988-5415
Email: legalosf@abanet.org
http://www.abanet.org/lsd/

Purpose: To assist first-year law school students.
Eligibility: Applicants must be U.S. citizens or permanent residents. They must be entering the first year of law school during the year of application. They must have a cumulative undergraduate GPA of 2.5 or higher. Selection is based on the overall strength of the application.
Target applicants: College students. Graduate school students. Adult students.
Minimum GPA: 2.5
Amount: $5,000.
Number of awards: Varies.
Scholarship may be renewable.
Deadline: March 1.
How to apply: Applications are available online. An application form, personal statement, two recommendation letters and a transcript are required.
Exclusive: Visit www.UltimateScholarshipBook.com and enter code AM58612 for updates on this award.

(587) · Litherland Scholarship

International Technology Education Association
Foundation for Technology Education
1914 Association Drive, Suite 201
Reston, VA 20191
Phone: 703-860-2100
Fax: 703-860-0353
Email: bmongold@iteaconnect.org
http://www.iteaconnect.org

Purpose: To provide scholarships for undergraduate students pursuing a career in teaching technology.
Eligibility: Applicants must be members of ITEA, be full-time undergraduate students majoring in technology education teacher preparation and have a minimum 2.5 GPA.
Target applicants: College students. Adult students.
Minimum GPA: 2.5
Amount: $1,000.
Number of awards: Varies.
Deadline: December 1.
How to apply: Application information is available online.
Exclusive: Visit www.UltimateScholarshipBook.com and enter code IN58712 for updates on this award.

(588) • Lou and Carole Prato Sports Reporting Scholarship

Radio Television Digital News Association
4121 Plank Road #512
Fredericksburg, VA 22407
Phone: 202-659-6510
Fax: 202-223-4007
Email: staceys@rtdna.org
http://www.rtdna.org

Purpose: To provide monetary assistance to a student pursuing a career as a sports reporter for radio or television.
Eligibility: Applicants must be full-time college sophomores or higher with at least one full academic year remaining. Applicants may be enrolled in any major but must have a career goal of becoming a sports reporter for television or radio. Applicants may only apply for one RTNDA scholarship.
Target applicants: College students. Adult students.
Amount: $1,000.
Number of awards: 1.
Deadline: May 10.
How to apply: Applications are available online.
Exclusive: Visit www.UltimateScholarshipBook.com and enter code RA58812 for updates on this award.

(589) • Lou Hochberg Awards

Orgone Biophysical Research Laboratory
P.O. Box 1148
Ashland, OR 97520
Phone: 541-522-0118
Fax: 541-522-0118
Email: info@orgonelab.org
http://www.orgonelab.org

Purpose: The Orgone Biophysical Research Lab offers a number of awards to students, scholars and journalists through a program set up by Louis Hochberg, a social worker who was dedicated to the sociological discoveries of Wilhelm Reich.
Eligibility: The Lou Hochberg Awards are given to winning theses and dissertations, university and college essays, high school essays and published articles that focus on Reich's sociological work. There are categories for students, scholars or journalists beginning at high school age through adulthood. A suggested list of topics and a bibliography is available online.
Target applicants: High school students. College students. Graduate school students. Adult students.
Amount: $500-$1,500.
Number of awards: 5.
Deadline: May 15 and December 15.
How to apply: Each award has a specific set of instructions for submitting a package for consideration. Guidelines are listed online.
Exclusive: Visit www.UltimateScholarshipBook.com and enter code OR58912 for updates on this award.

(590) • Luci S. Williams Houston Scholarship

Bay Area Black Journalists Association
1714 Franklin Street #100-260
Oakland, CA 94612
Phone: 510-464-1000
Email: info@babja.org
http://babja.org

Purpose: To support aspiring photojournalists.
Eligibility: Applicants must be studying photojournalism and may be enrolled at any institution of higher learning nationwide.
Target applicants: College students. Adult students.
Amount: $2,500.
Number of awards: 1.
Deadline: June 15.
How to apply: Applications are available online. An application form, transcript, resume, work samples, three letters of recommendation and an essay are required.
Exclusive: Visit www.UltimateScholarshipBook.com and enter code BA59012 for updates on this award.

(591) • Lyndon B. Johnson Foundation Grants-in-Aid Research

Lyndon B. Johnson Foundation
2313 Red River Street
Austin, TX 78705
Phone: 512-478-7829
Fax: 512-478-9104
Email: webmaster@lbjlib.utexas.edu
http://www.lbjlibrary.org/

Purpose: To assist with the travel and room-and-board expenses of those wishing to conduct research at the Lyndon B. Johnson Foundation Library.
Eligibility: Applicants must first contact the library to determine if their topic is appropriate for study at the facility. Applicants must also calculate the estimated amount of the grant before making a request.
Target applicants: College students. Adult students.
Amount: $500-$2,500.
Number of awards: Varies.
Deadline: March 15 and September 15.
How to apply: Applications are available online.
Exclusive: Visit www.UltimateScholarshipBook.com and enter code LY59112 for updates on this award.

(592) • Maley / FTE Scholarship

International Technology Education Association
Foundation for Technology Education
1914 Association Drive, Suite 201
Reston, VA 20191
Phone: 703-860-2100
Fax: 703-860-0353
Email: bmongold@iteaconnect.org
http://www.iteaconnect.org

Purpose: To support technology education teachers.
Eligibility: Applicants must be members of ITEA and plan to pursue or continue graduate study. Candidates must provide their plans for graduate study, description of need, college transcript and three recommendation letters.
Target applicants: College students. Graduate school students. Adult students.
Amount: $1,000.
Number of awards: Varies.
Deadline: December 1.
How to apply: Application information is available online.
Exclusive: Visit www.UltimateScholarshipBook.com and enter code IN59212 for updates on this award.

(593) • Marsh College Scholarship

Insurance Scholarship Foundation of America
14286-19 Beach Boulevard
Suite 353
Jacksonville, FL 32250
Phone: 904-821-7188
Email: foundation@inssfa.org
http://www.inssfa.org

Purpose: To aid actuarial science, risk management and insurance students.

Eligibility: Applicants must be undergraduate or graduate students who are majoring or minoring in actuarial science, risk management or insurance. They must be seeking a bachelor's, master's or doctoral degree, have completed at least one year of college and have completed at least two three-credit courses in actuarial science, risk management or insurance. They must have a GPA of 3.0 or higher on a four-point scale. Selection is based on the overall strength of the application.

Target applicants: College students. Graduate school students. Adult students.

Minimum GPA: 3.0

Amount: $500-$5,000.

Number of awards: Varies.

Deadline: January 15.

How to apply: Applications are available online. An application form and supporting materials are required.

Exclusive: Visit www.UltimateScholarshipBook.com and enter code IN59312 for updates on this award.

(594) • Mary Lou Brown Scholarship

American Radio Relay League Foundation
225 Main Street
Newington, CT 06111
Phone: 860-594-0397
Fax: 860-594-0259
Email: foundation@arrl.org
http://www.arrlf.org

Purpose: To assist ham radio operators with furthering their educations.

Eligibility: Applicants must have at least a general ham radio license, be residents of the ARRL Northwest Division (Alaska, Idaho, Montana, Oregon or Washington), be working for a bachelor's or graduate degree, have a minimum 3.0 GPA and have demonstrated interest in promoting the Amateur Radio Service.

Target applicants: High school students. College students. Graduate school students. Adult students.

Minimum GPA: 3.0

Amount: $2,500.

Number of awards: Varies.

Deadline: February 1.

How to apply: Applications are available online. Completed applications must be submitted by mail.

Exclusive: Visit www.UltimateScholarshipBook.com and enter code AM59412 for updates on this award.

(595) • Minorities and Women Educational Scholarship

Appraisal Institute
550 W. Van Buren Street
Suite 1000
Chicago, IL 60607
Phone: 312-335-4100
Fax: 312-335-4400
Email: wwoodburn@appraisalinstitute.org
http://www.appraisalinstitute.org

Purpose: To assist minority and women college students in pursuing degrees in real estate appraisal or related fields.

Eligibility: Applicants must be women or American Indians, Alaska Natives, Asians, African Americans, Hispanics or Latinos, Native Hawaiians or other Pacific Islanders. Applicants must be full- or part-time students enrolled in real estate courses and working toward a degree, have a minimum 2.5 GPA and demonstrate financial need.

Target applicants: College students. Adult students.

Minimum GPA: 2.5

Amount: $1,000.

Number of awards: Varies.

Deadline: April 15.

How to apply: Applications are available online.

Exclusive: Visit www.UltimateScholarshipBook.com and enter code AP59512 for updates on this award.

(596) • Minority Fellowship Program

American Sociological Association Minority Fellowship Program
1430 K Street NW
Suite 600
Washington, DC 20005
Phone: 202-383-9005
Fax: 202-638-0882
Email: minority.affairs@asanet.org
http://www.asanet.org

Purpose: To provide pre-doctoral graduate education for sociology students.

Eligibility: Applicants may be new or continuing graduate students in sociology who are enrolled in a program that grants the Ph.D. Students must be members of an underrepresented minority group in the U.S.: African American, Latino, Asian/Pacific Islander or American Indians/Alaska Natives. Applicants must also be U.S. citizens, non-citizen nationals of the U.S. or have been lawfully admitted to the U.S. for permanent residence. The fellowship is awarded for 12 months and typically renewable for up to three years in total. Tuition and fees are arranged with the home department. MFP Fellows are selected each year by the MFP Advisory Panel, a rotating, appointed group of senior scholars in sociology. Fellows can be involved in any area of sociological research, though particular MFP award lines devoted to drug abuse research may be possible contingent on funding.

Target applicants: Graduate school students. Adult students.

Amount: $15,000.

Number of awards: Varies.

Deadline: January 31.

How to apply: Applications are available online.

Exclusive: Visit www.UltimateScholarshipBook.com and enter code AM59612 for updates on this award.

(597) • Minority Scholarship Program

Fredrikson and Byron, P.A.
200 S. Sixth Street
Suite 4000
Minneapolis, MN 55402-1425
Phone: 612-492-7000
Fax: 612-492-7077
Email: market@fredlaw.com
http://www.fredlaw.com

Purpose: To provide opportunities for law students from diverse backgrounds.
Eligibility: In addition to the financial award, scholarship winners are also invited to serve as summer associates at the firm. An application form, two recommendations, a writing sample, a current law school transcript, an undergraduate transcript and a resume are required.
Target applicants: Graduate school students. Adult students.
Amount: $10,000.
Number of awards: 1.
Deadline: March 31.
How to apply: Applications are available online.
Exclusive: Visit www.UltimateScholarshipBook.com and enter code FR59712 for updates on this award.

(598) · MLA Scholarship

Medical Library Association
65 East Wacker Place
Suite 1900
Chicago, IL 60601-7246
Phone: 800-545-2433 x4276
Fax: 312-419-8950
Email: spectrum@ala.org
http://www.mlanet.org
Purpose: To aid a student with finishing their education at an ALA-accredited library school.
Eligibility: Applicants must be either entering or less than half-way through an accredited graduate school program in a field relevant to library science and be U.S. or Canadian citizens or permanent residents.
Target applicants: Graduate school students. Adult students.
Amount: Up to $5,000.
Number of awards: 1.
Deadline: December 1.
How to apply: Applications are available online.
Exclusive: Visit www.UltimateScholarshipBook.com and enter code ME59812 for updates on this award.

(599) · MLA Scholarship for Minority Students

Medical Library Association
65 East Wacker Place
Suite 1900
Chicago, IL 60601-7246
Phone: 800-545-2433 x4276
Fax: 312-419-8950
Email: spectrum@ala.org
http://www.mlanet.org
Purpose: To aid minority students entering or currently attending graduate library school.
Eligibility: Applicants must be African-American, Hispanic, Asian, Native American or Pacific Islander and entering or currently attending an ALA-accredited library school and be no more than halfway through the program. Applicants must also be citizens or permanent residents of the United States or Canada.
Target applicants: Graduate school students. Adult students.
Amount: $5,000.
Number of awards: 1.
Deadline: December 1.
How to apply: Applications are available online.
Exclusive: Visit www.UltimateScholarshipBook.com and enter code ME59912 for updates on this award.

(600) · MLA/NLM Spectrum Scholarship

Medical Library Association
65 East Wacker Place
Suite 1900
Chicago, IL 60601-7246
Phone: 800-545-2433 x4276
Fax: 312-419-8950
Email: spectrum@ala.org
http://www.mlanet.org
Purpose: To aid minority students in becoming health sciences information professionals.
Eligibility: Applicants must be American Indian/Alaska Native, Asian, Black/African American, Hispanic/Latino or Native Hawaiian/Other Pacific Islander students attending accredited library schools who are studying fields relevant to library science and who plan to enter the health sciences information field.
Target applicants: College students. Graduate school students. Adult students.
Amount: $3,250.
Number of awards: 2.
Deadline: March 1.
How to apply: Applications are available online.
Exclusive: Visit www.UltimateScholarshipBook.com and enter code ME60012 for updates on this award.

(601) · NACA East Coast Graduate Student Scholarship

National Association for Campus Activities
13 Harbison Way
Columbia, SC 29212
Phone: 803-732-6222
Fax: 803-749-1047
Email: info@naca.org
http://www.naca.org
Purpose: To provide assistance to graduate students who are attending a college or university on the East Coast.
Eligibility: Applicants must be enrolled in master's or doctorate degree programs in student personnel services or a related area. Applicants must be attending a graduate school in Washington DC, Delaware, Maryland, New Jersey, New York or Eastern Pennsylvania, be involved in campus activities and plan to pursue a career in campus activities.
Target applicants: Graduate school students. Adult students.
Amount: Varies.
Number of awards: 2.
Deadline: May 30.
How to apply: Applications are available online.
Exclusive: Visit www.UltimateScholarshipBook.com and enter code NA60112 for updates on this award.

(602) · Nancy Curry Scholarship

Child Nutrition Foundation
Scholarship Committee
700 S. Washington Street, Suite 300
Alexandria, VA 22314
Phone: 703-739-3900
Email: jcurtis@schoolnutrition.org
http://www.schoolnutrition.org
Purpose: To support students wishing to enter the school foodservice industry.

Eligibility: Applicants or the parents of applicants must be School Nutrition Association members for at least one year and be enrolled in a school foodservice-related program at an educational institution.
Target applicants: High school students. College students. Graduate school students. Adult students.
Amount: Varies.
Number of awards: Varies.
Deadline: April 1.
How to apply: Applications are available online.
Exclusive: Visit www.UltimateScholarshipBook.com and enter code CH60212 for updates on this award.

(603) • Naomi Berber Memorial Scholarship

Print and Graphics Scholarship Foundation
Attn.: Bernie Eckert
200 Deer Run Road
Sewickley, PA 15143-2600
http://www.gain.net
Purpose: To support students interested in careers in printing and graphic communication.
Eligibility: Applicants must be high school seniors, graduates or students at two- or four-year colleges. They must be full-time students and maintain a GPA of 3.0 or higher.
Target applicants: High school students. College students. Adult students.
Minimum GPA: 3.0
Amount: Varies.
Number of awards: Varies.
Deadline: March 1 for high school students and April 1 for college students.
How to apply: Applications are available online. An application form, transcript, two letters of recommendation, course of study and self-addressed stamped envelope are required.
Exclusive: Visit www.UltimateScholarshipBook.com and enter code PR60312 for updates on this award.

(604) • Nation Institute/I.F. Stone Award for Student Journalism

Nation Institute
116 E 16th Street
8th Floor
New York, NY 10003
Phone: 212-822-0250
Fax: 212-253-5356
http://www.nationinstitute.org/awards
Purpose: To support student journalists.
Eligibility: Applicants must be enrolled in a U.S. college or university and submit articles written outside of regular coursework within the year prior to the application deadline. Selection is based on the article's exhibition of commitment to human rights, concern for truth-telling, interest in topics ignored by mainstream media, investigative zeal and progressive politics.
Target applicants: College students. Adult students.
Amount: $1,000.
Number of awards: 1.
Deadline: Varies.
How to apply: No application form is necessary.
Exclusive: Visit www.UltimateScholarshipBook.com and enter code NA60412 for updates on this award.

(605) • National D-Day Museum Online Essay Contest

National D-Day Museum Foundation
945 Magazine Street
New Orleans, LA 70130
Phone: 504-527-6012
Fax: 504-527-6088
Email: info@nationalww2museum.org
http://www.ddaymuseum.org
Purpose: To increase awareness of World War II by giving students the opportunity to compete in an essay contest.
Eligibility: Applicants must be high school students in the United States, its territories or its military bases. They must prepare an essay of up to 1,000 words based on a topic specified by the sponsor and related to World War II. Only the first 500 valid essays will be accepted.
Target applicants: High school students.
Amount: $500-$1,000.
Number of awards: 3.
Deadline: March 26.
How to apply: Applications are available online. An essay and contact information are required.
Exclusive: Visit www.UltimateScholarshipBook.com and enter code NA60512 for updates on this award.

(606) • National Defense Transportation Association, St. Louis Area Chapter Scholarship

National Defense Transportation Association-Scott St. Louis Chapter
Attention: Scholarship Committee
P.O. Box 25486
Scott Air Force Base, IL 62225-0486
http://www.ndtascottstlouis.org
Purpose: To promote careers in business, transportation logistics and physical distribution.
Eligibility: Preference is given to students majoring in business, transportation logistics and physical distribution or a related field. High school students must live in Illinois or Missouri. College students must attend school in Colorado, Iowa, Illinois, Indiana, Kansas, Michigan, Minnesota, Missouri, Montana, North Dakota, Nebraska, South Dakota, Wisconsin or Wyoming.
Target applicants: High school students. College students. Adult students.
Amount: $2,000-$3,500.
Number of awards: 6.
Deadline: March 1.
How to apply: Applications are available online.
Exclusive: Visit www.UltimateScholarshipBook.com and enter code NA60612 for updates on this award.

(607) • National History Day Contest

National History Day
0119 Cecil Hall
University of Maryland
College Park, MD 20742
Phone: 301-314-9739
Fax: 301-314-9767
Email: info@nhd.org
http://www.nationalhistoryday.org
Purpose: To reward students for their scholarship, initiative and cooperation.
Eligibility: Applicants must be in grades 6-12 and prepare throughout the school year history presentations based on an annual theme. Around

February or March students compete in district History Day contests. District winners then prepare for the state contests, held usually in April or May. Those winners advance to the national contest held in June at the University of Maryland.
Target applicants: Junior high students or younger. High school students.
Amount: Varies.
Number of awards: Varies.
Deadline: Varies.
How to apply: Applications are available online.
Exclusive: Visit www.UltimateScholarshipBook.com and enter code NA60712 for updates on this award.

(608) · National Scholarship Program

American Board of Funeral Service Education
Scholarship Committee
3414 Ashland Avenue, Suite G
St. Joseph, MO 64506
Phone: 816-233-3747
Fax: 816-233-3793
http://www.abfse.org
Purpose: To assist students enrolled in funeral service or mortuary science programs.
Eligibility: Applicants must be undergraduate students who have completed at least one semester or quarter of study in funeral service or mortuary science education at an accredited school and have at least one term remaining in their study. Applicants must be U.S. citizens.
Target applicants: College students. Adult students.
Amount: $500-$2,500.
Number of awards: Varies.
Deadline: March 1 or September 1.
How to apply: Applications are available online.
Exclusive: Visit www.UltimateScholarshipBook.com and enter code AM60812 for updates on this award.

(609) · National Society of Hispanic MBAs Scholarship

National Society of Hispanic MBAs
1303 Walnut Hill Lane Suite 100
Irving, TX 75038
Phone: 877-467-4622
Fax: 214-596-9325
Email: scholarships@nshmba.org
http://www.nshmba.org
Purpose: To provide financial support to Hispanic students pursuing an MBA.
Eligibility: Applicants must be U.S. citizens or legal permanent residents of Hispanic heritage (defined as having at least one parent of full Hispanic heritage or both parents of half-Hispanic heritage). Students must be members of the NSHMBA, but they may enroll at a special application rate. Applicants must be enrolled or planning to enroll in master's programs in business or management at an accredited college or university. Scholarships are based on academic achievement, work experience, personal statement, community service, recommendations and financial need.
Target applicants: College students. Graduate school students. Adult students.
Amount: $2,500-$10,000.
Number of awards: Varies.
Deadline: April 30.
How to apply: Applications are available online.
Exclusive: Visit www.UltimateScholarshipBook.com and enter code NA60912 for updates on this award.

(610) · National Tour Association (NTA) Dr. Tom Anderson Graduate Scholarship

Tourism Cares
275 Turnpike Street
Suite 307
Canton, MA 02021
Phone: 781-821-5990
Fax: 781-821-8949
Email: carolynv@tourismcares.org
http://www.tourismcares.org
Purpose: To aid those who are studying travel, hospitality or tourism at the graduate level.
Eligibility: Applicants must be permanent residents of the U.S. or Canada and must be entering or returning graduate students who are enrolled at an accredited U.S. or Canadian four-year institution. They must be studying hospitality, tourism or travel and must have a GPA of 3.0 or higher on a four-point scale. Selection is based on the overall strength of the application.
Target applicants: College students. Graduate school students. Adult students.
Minimum GPA: 3.0
Amount: $1,000.
Number of awards: 1.
Deadline: April 15.
How to apply: Applications are available online. An application form, proof of residency, resume, two letters of recommendation, personal essay and official transcript are required.
Exclusive: Visit www.UltimateScholarshipBook.com and enter code TO61012 for updates on this award.

(611) · National Tour Association (NTA) Eric Friedheim Graduate Scholarship

Tourism Cares
275 Turnpike Street
Suite 307
Canton, MA 02021
Phone: 781-821-5990
Fax: 781-821-8949
Email: carolynv@tourismcares.org
http://www.tourismcares.org
Purpose: To assist graduate students who are studying hospitality, travel and tourism.
Eligibility: Applicants must be U.S. permanent residents who are entering or returning full-time graduate students at an accredited U.S. four-year college or university. They must be studying hospitality, travel or tourism and must have a GPA of 3.0 or higher on a four-point scale. Selection is based on the overall strength of the application.
Target applicants: Graduate school students. Adult students.
Minimum GPA: 3.0
Amount: $1,000.
Number of awards: 1.
Deadline: April 15.
How to apply: Applications are available online. An application form, a personal essay, a resume, proof of residency, two recommendation letters and an official transcript are required.
Exclusive: Visit www.UltimateScholarshipBook.com and enter code TO61112 for updates on this award.

(612) • National Tour Association (NTA) Luray Caverns Graduate Research Scholarship

Tourism Cares
275 Turnpike Street
Suite 307
Canton, MA 02021
Phone: 781-821-5990
Fax: 781-821-8949
Email: carolynv@tourismcares.org
http://www.tourismcares.org

Purpose: To aid graduate students who are conducting tourism-related research.

Eligibility: Applicants can be permanent residents of any country but must be enrolled at an accredited U.S. or Canadian four-year postsecondary institution. They must be entering or returning graduate students who are conducting research that focuses on tourism. They must have a proven commitment to the tourism industry, and must have a GPA of 3.0 or higher on a four-point scale. Selection is based on the strength of the research project.

Target applicants: College students. Graduate school students. Adult students.

Minimum GPA: 3.0

Amount: $3,000.

Number of awards: 1.

Deadline: April 15.

How to apply: Applications are available online. An application form, proof of residency, a personal essay, a resume, a research proposal, an official transcript and one letter of recommendation are required.

Exclusive: Visit www.UltimateScholarshipBook.com and enter code TO61212 for updates on this award.

(613) • National Tour Association (NTA) New Horizons-Kathy LeTarte Undergraduate Scholarship

Tourism Cares
275 Turnpike Street
Suite 307
Canton, MA 02021
Phone: 781-821-5990
Fax: 781-821-8949
Email: carolynv@tourismcares.org
http://www.tourismcares.org

Purpose: To aid Michigan residents who are studying travel, tourism and hospitality at the undergraduate level.

Eligibility: Applicants must be permanent residents of Michigan and must be enrolled at an accredited U.S. or Canadian four-year postsecondary institution. They must be rising undergraduate juniors or seniors who are studying travel, tourism or hospitality. They must have 60 or more credits completed by May of the application year and must have a GPA of 3.0 or higher on a four-point scale. Selection is based on the overall strength of the application.

Target applicants: College students. Adult students.

Minimum GPA: 3.0

Amount: $1,000.

Number of awards: 1.

Deadline: April 15.

How to apply: Applications are available online. An application form, personal essay, official transcript, proof of Michigan residency, resume and two letters of recommendation are required.

Exclusive: Visit www.UltimateScholarshipBook.com and enter code TO61312 for updates on this award.

(614) • National Tour Association (NTA) Rene Campbell-Ruth McKinney Undergraduate Scholarship

Tourism Cares
275 Turnpike Street
Suite 307
Canton, MA 02021
Phone: 781-821-5990
Fax: 781-821-8949
Email: carolynv@tourismcares.org
http://www.tourismcares.org

Purpose: To assist residents of North Carolina who are pursuing undergraduate degrees in tourism, travel or hospitality.

Eligibility: Applicants must be permanent residents of North Carolina and must be full-time rising undergraduate juniors or seniors at an accredited four-year college or university located in the U.S. or Canada. They must be studying hospitality, tourism or travel, have completed 60 credits or more by May of the application year and have a GPA of 3.0 or higher on a four-point scale. Selection is based on the overall strength of the application.

Target applicants: College students. Adult students.

Minimum GPA: 3.0

Amount: $1,000.

Number of awards: 1.

Deadline: April 15.

How to apply: Applications are available online. An application form, resume, proof of North Carolina residency, personal essay, two letters of recommendation and official transcript are required.

Exclusive: Visit www.UltimateScholarshipBook.com and enter code TO61412 for updates on this award.

(615) • National Tour Association (NTA) Travel Leaders Graduate Scholarship

Tourism Cares
275 Turnpike Street
Suite 307
Canton, MA 02021
Phone: 781-821-5990
Fax: 781-821-8949
Email: carolynv@tourismcares.org
http://www.tourismcares.org

Purpose: To assist graduate students who are studying hospitality, travel and tourism.

Eligibility: Applicants may be permanent residents of any country but must be entering or returning graduate students at an accredited U.S. or Canadian four-year college or university. They must be full-time students who are studying hospitality, travel or tourism and must have a GPA of 3.0 or higher on a four-point scale. Selection is based on the overall strength of the application.

Target applicants: College students. Graduate school students. Adult students.

Minimum GPA: 3.0

Amount: $1,000.

Number of awards: 3.

Deadline: April 15.

How to apply: Applications are available online. An application form, proof of residency, a personal essay, two letters of recommendation, an official transcript and a resume are required.

Exclusive: Visit www.UltimateScholarshipBook.com and enter code TO61512 for updates on this award.

(616) · National Tour Association (NTA) Yellow Ribbon Undergraduate or Graduate Scholarship

Tourism Cares
275 Turnpike Street
Suite 307
Canton, MA 02021
Phone: 781-821-5990
Fax: 781-821-8949
Email: carolynv@tourismcares.org
http://www.tourismcares.org

Purpose: To aid hospitality, travel and tourism students who have physical or sensory disabilities.

Eligibility: Applicants must be permanent residents of the U.S. or Canada and be full-time students who have a sensory or physical disability. They must be entering or returning undergraduate or graduate students who are enrolled at an accredited U.S. or Canadian postsecondary institution and must be studying tourism, travel or hospitality. They must have a GPA of 2.5 or higher on a four-point scale. Selection is based on the overall strength of the application.

Target applicants: High school students. College students. Graduate school students. Adult students.

Minimum GPA: 2.5

Amount: $5,000.

Number of awards: 1.

Deadline: April 15.

How to apply: Applications are available online. An application form, proof of residency, proof of disability, resume, two letters of recommendation, official transcript and personal essay are required.

Exclusive: Visit www.UltimateScholarshipBook.com and enter code TO61612 for updates on this award.

(617) · National Tour Association State Scholarship

Tourism Cares
275 Turnpike Street
Suite 307
Canton, MA 02021
Phone: 781-821-5990
Fax: 781-821-8949
Email: carolynv@tourismcares.org
http://www.tourismcares.org

Purpose: To assist undergraduate and graduate students who are studying travel and tourism.

Eligibility: Applicants must be in their junior or senior year of undergraduate study or entering or returning year of graduate study at an accredited four-year college or university in the U.S. or Canada and enrolled in a travel and tourism-related program. They must have a GPA of 3.0 or higher.

Target applicants: College students. Graduate school students. Adult students.

Minimum GPA: 3.0

Amount: $1,000.

Number of awards: 11.

Deadline: April 15.

How to apply: Applications are available online. In addition to the application form, a resume, recommendation letter, essay and transcript are required.

Exclusive: Visit www.UltimateScholarshipBook.com and enter code TO61712 for updates on this award.

(618) · National Washington Crossing Foundation Scholarship

Washington Crossing Foundation
P.O. Box 503
Levittown, PA 19058
Phone: 215-949-8841
Fax: 215-949-8843
Email: info@gwcf.org
http://www.gwcf.org

Purpose: To support students who are planning careers in government service.

Eligibility: Students must be in their senior year of high school. Applicants must submit an essay and a letter of recommendation.

Target applicants: High school students.

Amount: $500-$5,000.

Number of awards: Varies.

Scholarship may be renewable.

Deadline: January 15.

How to apply: Applications are available online.

Exclusive: Visit www.UltimateScholarshipBook.com and enter code WA61812 for updates on this award.

(619) · NCCPAP Scholarship

National Conference of CPA Practitioners NCCPAP Scholarship
Attention: Scholarship Committee
22 Jericho Turnpike, Suite 110
Mineola, NY 11501
Phone: 888-488-5400
Email: lanak.nccpap@verizon.net
http://www.nccpap.org

Purpose: To assist future certified public accountants.

Eligibility: Applicants must be graduating high school seniors with a minimum GPA of 3.3 planning to become certified public accountants. They must be full-time students applying to or accepted at a two- or four-year college.

Target applicants: High school students.

Minimum GPA: 3.3

Amount: $1,000.

Number of awards: Varies.

Deadline: December 15.

How to apply: Applications are available online.

Exclusive: Visit www.UltimateScholarshipBook.com and enter code NA61912 for updates on this award.

(620) · NCDXF Scholarship

American Radio Relay League Foundation
225 Main Street
Newington, CT 06111
Phone: 860-594-0397
Fax: 860-594-0259
Email: foundation@arrl.org
http://www.arrlf.org

Purpose: To provide financial assistance to amateur radio operators with interest in DXing.

Eligibility: Applicants must hold a Technician Class or higher Amateur Radio License and demonstrate activity and interest in DXing. They must attend a junior college, trade school or four-year college or university in the United States.

Target applicants: High school students. College students. Adult students.

Amount: $1,500.
Number of awards: 2.
Deadline: February 1.
How to apply: Applications are available online.
Exclusive: Visit www.UltimateScholarshipBook.com and enter code AM62012 for updates on this award.

(621) • NCGE and Nystrom Geography Award

National Council for Geographic Education
Jacksonville State University
206-A Martin Hall
700 Pelham Road North
Jacksonville, AL 36265-1602
Phone: 256-782-5293
Fax: 256-782-5336
Email: ncge@jsu.edu
http://www.ncge.org
Purpose: To award K-12 teachers for exemplary annual meeting materials presentations.
Eligibility: Applicants must be K-12 teachers (or group of teachers) who submit descriptions of classroom presentations that they have created. The presentation must show current trends in geographic education and display an original approach to teaching geography. Formats may include lessons, simulations, workshops or other learning activities. Winners of a NCGE scholarship award are required to present their lessons during the NCGE meeting in order to receive the scholarship. Applicants must submit the Call for Proposal, NCGE Scholarship application, abstracts, three letters of recommendation, lesson plan, proof of use of the lesson in the classroom, presenter registration form and registration.
Target applicants: Graduate school students. Adult students.
Amount: $1,500.
Number of awards: Varies.
Deadline: April 13.
How to apply: Applications are available online.
Exclusive: Visit www.UltimateScholarshipBook.com and enter code NA62112 for updates on this award.

(622) • Nell Bryant Robinson Scholarship

Phi Upsilon Omicron Inc.
National Office
P.O. Box 329
Fairmont, WV 26555
Phone: 304-368-0612
Email: info@phiu.org
http://www.phiu.org
Purpose: To aid Phi Upsilon Omicron members who are pursuing bachelor's degrees in family and consumer sciences.
Eligibility: Preference is given to applicants who are majoring in food and nutrition or dietetics. Selection is based on the overall strength of the application.
Target applicants: College students. Adult students.
Amount: $500-$4,000.
Number of awards: Varies.
Deadline: February 1.
How to apply: Applications are available online. An application form, official transcript, personal statement and three recommendation letters are required.
Exclusive: Visit www.UltimateScholarshipBook.com and enter code PH62212 for updates on this award.

(623) • NEMAL Electronics Scholarship

American Radio Relay League Foundation
225 Main Street
Newington, CT 06111
Phone: 860-594-0397
Fax: 860-594-0259
Email: foundation@arrl.org
http://www.arrlf.org
Purpose: To provide scholarship assistance to amateur radio operators from the Southeast United States who are studying electronics and communications.
Eligibility: Applicants must possess a General Class or higher Amateur Radio License and attend an accredited college or university. They must demonstrate financial need and have a GPA of 3.0 or higher. Preference is given to residents of the Southeastern United States and those who participate in community service or civic volunteer organizations.
Target applicants: High school students. College students. Adult students.
Minimum GPA: 3.0
Amount: $1,000.
Number of awards: 1.
Deadline: February 1.
How to apply: Applications are available online.
Exclusive: Visit www.UltimateScholarshipBook.com and enter code AM62312 for updates on this award.

(624) • Nettie Dracup Memorial Scholarship

American Congress on Surveying and Mapping (ACSM)
6 Montgomery Village Avenue
Suite 403
Gaithersburg, MD 20879
Phone: 240-632-9716
Fax: 240-632-1321
Email: ilse.genovese@acsm.net
http://www.acsm.net
Purpose: To aid geodetic surveying students.
Eligibility: Applicants must be U.S. citizens who are undergraduate students enrolled in an accredited degree program in geodetic surveying. They must be members of the American Congress on Surveying and Mapping (ACSM). Selection is based on the applicant's academic achievement, personal statement, recommendations and professional activities.
Target applicants: College students. Adult students.
Amount: $2,000.
Number of awards: 2.
Deadline: November 2.
How to apply: Applications are available online. An application form, official transcript, personal statement, three recommendation letters and proof of ACSM membership are required.
Exclusive: Visit www.UltimateScholarshipBook.com and enter code AM62412 for updates on this award.

(625) • New England FEMARA Scholarships

American Radio Relay League Foundation
225 Main Street
Newington, CT 06111
Phone: 860-594-0397
Fax: 860-594-0259
Email: foundation@arrl.org
http://www.arrlf.org

Purpose: To assist ham radio operators in furthering their educations.
Eligibility: Applicants must have at least a technician ham radio license and be residents of the New England States (Connecticut, Maine, Massachusetts, New Hampshire, Rhode Island or Vermont).
Target applicants: High school students. College students. Graduate school students. Adult students.
Amount: $1,000.
Number of awards: Varies.
Deadline: February 1.
How to apply: Applications are available online. Completed applications must be mailed in. They cannot be completed electronically.
Exclusive: Visit www.UltimateScholarshipBook.com and enter code AM62512 for updates on this award.

(626) • NFMC Gretchen Van Roy Music Education Scholarship

National Federation of Music Clubs (FL)
Rose M. Suggs
1000 Applewood Drive Apt. 188
Roswell , GA 30076
Phone: 678-997-8556
Fax: 317-638-0503
Email: rose331s@bellsouth.net
http://www.nfmc-music.org
Purpose: To support students majoring in music education.
Eligibility: Applicants must be college juniors majoring in music education and must be affiliated with the National Federation of Music Clubs. There is no application fee to apply.
Target applicants: College students. Adult students.
Amount: $1,000.
Number of awards: 1.
Deadline: April 1.
How to apply: Applications are available online.
Exclusive: Visit www.UltimateScholarshipBook.com and enter code NA62612 for updates on this award.

(627) • NPPF Television News Scholarship

National Press Photographers Foundation Television News Scholarship
Ed Dooks
5 Mohawk Dr
Lexington, MA 02421-6217
Phone: 781-861-6062
Email: dooks@verizon.net
http://www.nppa.org
Purpose: To support students with television news photojournalism potential but with little opportunity and great need.
Eligibility: Applicants must be full-time juniors or seniors at a four-year college or university, provide a portfolio and demonstrate financial need. Applicants must also have courses in TV news photojournalism and continue in this program towards a bachelor's degree. Applicants can apply to as many NPPA scholarships as desired, but only one award will be granted per student.
Target applicants: College students. Adult students.
Amount: $2,000.
Number of awards: Varies.
Deadline: Varies.
How to apply: Applications are available online.
Exclusive: Visit www.UltimateScholarshipBook.com and enter code NA62712 for updates on this award.

(628) • NSA Scholarship Foundation

National Society of Accountants Scholarship Program
Scholarship America
One Scholarship Way
P.O. Box 297
Saint Peter, MN 56082
Phone: 507-931-1682
http://www.nsacct.org
Purpose: To support students entering the accounting profession.
Eligibility: Applicants must be undergraduate students majoring in accounting with a minimum 3.0 GPA and be U.S. or Canadian citizens.
Target applicants: College students. Adult students.
Minimum GPA: 3.0
Amount: $500-$2,000.
Number of awards: 32.
Deadline: March 10.
How to apply: Applications are available online.
Exclusive: Visit www.UltimateScholarshipBook.com and enter code NA62812 for updates on this award.

(629) • NTA Arnold Rigby Graduate Scholarship

Tourism Cares
275 Turnpike Street
Suite 307
Canton, MA 02021
Phone: 781-821-5990
Fax: 781-821-8949
Email: carolynv@tourismcares.org
http://www.tourismcares.org
Purpose: To aid those who are studying travel, tourism and hospitality at the graduate level.
Eligibility: Applicants must be permanent residents of the U.S. or Canada and be enrolled at an accredited, four-year postsecondary institution located in the U.S. or Canada. They must be entering or returning graduate students who are studying hospitality, tourism or travel and must have a GPA of 3.0 or higher on a four-point scale. Selection is based on the overall strength of the application.
Target applicants: College students. Graduate school students. Adult students.
Minimum GPA: 3.0
Amount: $1,000.
Number of awards: 1.
Deadline: April 15.
How to apply: Applications are available online. An application form, a personal essay, a resume, an official transcript, two letters of recommendation and proof of residency are required.
Exclusive: Visit www.UltimateScholarshipBook.com and enter code TO62912 for updates on this award.

(630) • NTA Dave Herren Memorial Undergraduate or Graduate Scholarship

Tourism Cares
275 Turnpike Street
Suite 307
Canton, MA 02021
Phone: 781-821-5990
Fax: 781-821-8949
Email: carolynv@tourismcares.org
http://www.tourismcares.org

Purpose: To aid those who are pursuing higher education in travel, tourism and hospitality.
Eligibility: Applicants must be permanent residents of the U.S. and be enrolled at an accredited U.S. four-year postsecondary institution. They must be studying travel, tourism or hospitality and be entering or returning graduate students or rising undergraduate juniors or seniors. They must have a GPA of 3.0 or higher on a four-point scale. Undergraduate applicants must have completed 60 or more credits by May of the application year. Selection is based on the overall strength of the application.
Target applicants: College students. Graduate school students. Adult students.
Minimum GPA: 3.0
Amount: $1,000.
Number of awards: 1.
Deadline: April 15.
How to apply: Applications are available online. An application form, personal essay, proof of residency, a resume, an official transcript and two letters of recommendation are required.
Exclusive: Visit www.UltimateScholarshipBook.com and enter code TO63012 for updates on this award.

(631) • NTA Mayflower Tours Patrick Murphy Undergraduate or Graduate Internship

Tourism Cares
275 Turnpike Street
Suite 307
Canton, MA 02021
Phone: 781-821-5990
Fax: 781-821-8949
Email: carolynv@tourismcares.org
http://www.tourismcares.org
Purpose: To aid travel and tourism students who have an interest in political science.
Eligibility: Applicants may be permanent residents of any country but must be enrolled at an accredited U.S. four-year college or university. They must be entering or returning graduate students or rising undergraduate sophomores, juniors or seniors. They must be pursuing a degree in travel and tourism with an interest in political science. Applicants must have strong interpersonal skills and strong oral and written communication skills. They must have a GPA of 3.0 or higher on a four-point scale. Selection is based on the overall strength of the application.
Target applicants: College students. Graduate school students. Adult students.
Minimum GPA: 3.0
Amount: $2,000.
Number of awards: 1.
Deadline: April 15.
How to apply: Applications are available online. An application form, a resume, proof of residency, one letter of recommendation, a personal essay and an official transcript are required.
Exclusive: Visit www.UltimateScholarshipBook.com and enter code TO63112 for updates on this award.

(632) • Optimist International Oratorical Contest

Optimist International
4494 Lindell Boulevard
St. Louis, MO 63108
Phone: 314-371-6000
Fax: 314-371-6006
Email: programs@optimist.org
http://www.optimist.org
Purpose: To reward students based on their oratorical performance.
Eligibility: Applicants must be students in the U.S., Canada or Caribbean under the age of 16 as of December 31st of the entry year. Selection is based on an oratorical contest.
Target applicants: Junior high students or younger. High school students.
Amount: $1,000-$2,500.
Number of awards: 2-3.
Deadline: Late March and June 15.
How to apply: Contact your local Optimist Club.
Exclusive: Visit www.UltimateScholarshipBook.com and enter code OP63212 for updates on this award.

(633) • Otto M. Stanfield Legal Scholarship

Unitarian Universalist Association
25 Beacon Street
Boston, MA 02108
Phone: 617-742-2100
Email: info@uua.org
http://www.uua.org
Purpose: To help Unitarian Universalist students entering or attending law school.
Eligibility: Applicants should be planning to attend or currently attending law school at the graduate level. The award is based on activity with Unitarian Universalism and financial need. Applicants should submit transcripts and recommendations.
Target applicants: Graduate school students. Adult students.
Amount: Varies.
Number of awards: Varies.
Deadline: February 15.
How to apply: Applications are available online.
Exclusive: Visit www.UltimateScholarshipBook.com and enter code UN63312 for updates on this award.

(634) • Overseas Press Club Foundation Scholarships/ Internships

Overseas Press Club Foundation
40 W. 45 Street
New York, NY 10036
Phone: 201-493-9087
Fax: 201-612-9915
Email: foundation@opcofamerica.org
http://www.overseaspressclubfoundation.org
Purpose: To encourage undergraduate and graduate students attending American colleges and universities to pursue careers as foreign correspondents.
Eligibility: Scholarships are open to undergraduate and graduate students with an interest in a career as a foreign correspondent. Eligible students must be attending American colleges or universities.
Target applicants: College students. Graduate school students. Adult students.
Amount: $2,000.
Number of awards: 12.
Deadline: December 1.
How to apply: Applications are available online.
Exclusive: Visit www.UltimateScholarshipBook.com and enter code OV63412 for updates on this award.

(635) • Padgett Foundation Scholarship Program

Padgett Business Services Foundation
160 Hawthorne Park
Athens, GA 30606
Phone: 800-723-4388
Fax: 800-548-1040
Email: scholarship@smallbizpros.com
http://www.smallbizpros.com

Purpose: To support the education of the children of small business owners.
Eligibility: Applicants must be high school seniors planning to attend an accredited post-secondary school. They must be the children or dependents of a small business owner, defined as employing fewer than 20 people, who owns at least a 10 percent share of the company and is active in day-to-day operations.
Target applicants: High school students.
Amount: $500-$3,500.
Number of awards: Varies.
Deadline: March 1.
How to apply: Applications are available online.
Exclusive: Visit www.UltimateScholarshipBook.com and enter code PA63512 for updates on this award.

(636) • Parsons Brinckerhoff –Golden Apple Scholarship

Conference of Minority Transportation Officials
818 18th Street NW, Suite 850
Washington, DC 20006
Phone: 202-530-0551
Fax: 202-530-0617
Email: comto@comto.org
http://www.comto.org

Purpose: To support students who are pursuing careers in transportation in the fields of communications, marketing or finance.
Eligibility: Applicants must be graduating high school students who have been members of COMTO for at least one year. They must have at least a 2.0 GPA and be accepted into a college or technical school program.
Target applicants: High school students.
Minimum GPA: 2.0
Amount: $2,500.
Number of awards: Varies.
Deadline: April 16.
How to apply: Applications are available online.
Exclusive: Visit www.UltimateScholarshipBook.com and enter code CO63612 for updates on this award.

(637) • Paul and Helen L. Grauer Scholarship

American Radio Relay League Foundation
225 Main Street
Newington, CT 06111
Phone: 860-594-0397
Fax: 860-594-0259
Email: foundation@arrl.org
http://www.arrlf.org

Purpose: To assist ham radio operators in furthering their educations.
Eligibility: Applicants must have at least a novice ham radio license, be residents and attend school in the ARRL Midwest Division (Iowa, Kansas, Missouri or Nebraska) and be undergraduate or graduate students in electronics, communications or another related field.
Target applicants: College students. Graduate school students. Adult students.
Amount: $1,000.
Number of awards: 1.
Deadline: February 1.
How to apply: Applications are available online. Completed applications must be submitted by mail.
Exclusive: Visit www.UltimateScholarshipBook.com and enter code AM63712 for updates on this award.

(638) • Perry F. Hadlock Memorial Scholarship

American Radio Relay League Foundation
225 Main Street
Newington, CT 06111
Phone: 860-594-0397
Fax: 860-594-0259
Email: foundation@arrl.org
http://www.arrlf.org

Purpose: To assist students who are involved in amateur radio and seeking a bachelor's degree or higher in a technology-related field.
Eligibility: Applicants must hold Technician Class Amateur Radio License or higher in the ARRL Atlantic or Hudson Division. They must be seeking a bachelor's degree or higher in a technology related field with preference given to electrical and electronics engineering students.
Target applicants: High school students. College students. Graduate school students. Adult students.
Amount: $2,000.
Number of awards: 1.
Deadline: February 1.
How to apply: Applications are available online.
Exclusive: Visit www.UltimateScholarshipBook.com and enter code AM63812 for updates on this award.

(639) • Persina Scholarship for Diversity in Journalism

National Press Club
529 14th Street
13th Floor
Washington, DC 20045
Phone: 202-662-7500
http://www.press.org

Purpose: To support promising future journalists.
Eligibility: Applicants must be high school seniors, have a GPA of 3.0 or higher and plan to enter college the year after graduation.
Target applicants: High school students.
Minimum GPA: 3.0
Amount: $2,000 plus $500 book stipend.
Number of awards: 1.
Deadline: March 1.
How to apply: Applications are available online. An application form, essay, transcript, copy of FAFSA, letter of acceptance or proof of college application, three letters of recommendation and up to five work samples are required.
Exclusive: Visit www.UltimateScholarshipBook.com and enter code NA63912 for updates on this award.

(640) • PHD ARA Scholarship

American Radio Relay League Foundation
225 Main Street
Newington, CT 06111
Phone: 860-594-0397

Fax: 860-594-0259
Email: foundation@arrl.org
http://www.arrlf.org
Purpose: To assist ham radio operators in furthering their educations.
Eligibility: Applicants must have any class of ham radio license, be residents of the ARRL Midwest Division (Iowa, Kansas, Missouri, Nebraska) and be studying journalism, computer science or electronic engineering. Applicants may also be the children of deceased amateur radio operators.
Target applicants: College students. Graduate school students. Adult students.
Amount: $1,000.
Number of awards: 1.
Deadline: February 1.
How to apply: Applications are available online but may not be completed electronically. All completed applications must be mailed.
Exclusive: Visit www.UltimateScholarshipBook.com and enter code AM64012 for updates on this award.

(641) • Pi Sigma Alpha Washington Internship Scholarships

Pi Sigma Alpha
The Washington Center
2301 M Street NW, Fifth Floor
Washington, DC 20037-1427
Email: info@twc.edu
http://www.apsanet.org/~psa/
Purpose: To provide Pi Sigma Alpha members with scholarships to participate in summer or fall term internships in Washington, DC.
Eligibility: Applicants must belong to Pi Sigma Alpha and be nominated by their local chapter. The award is for a political science internship is based on academic achievement and service to the organization.
Target applicants: College students. Graduate school students. Adult students.
Amount: $2,000.
Number of awards: 3.
Deadline: May 1.
How to apply: Applications are available online.
Exclusive: Visit www.UltimateScholarshipBook.com and enter code PI64112 for updates on this award.

(642) • Pierre and Patricia Bikai Fellowship

American Center of Oriental Research (ACOR)
656 Beacon Street, 5th Floor
Boston, MA 02215
Phone: 617-353-6571
Fax: 617-353-6575
Email: acor@bu.edu
http://www.bu.edu/acor
Purpose: To help graduate students in an archaeological project at the American Center of Oriental Research.
Eligibility: Applicants must be graduate students. The fellowship includes room and board at ACOR and $600 a month and may be combined with the Harrell and Groot fellowships. The fellowship does not support field work or travel. Recipients must live at the ACOR center in Jordan from June of one year to May of the next.
Target applicants: Graduate school students. Adult students.
Amount: $600 monthly stipend plus room and board.
Number of awards: Varies.
Deadline: February 1.
How to apply: Applications are available online.
Exclusive: Visit www.UltimateScholarshipBook.com and enter code AM64212 for updates on this award.

(643) • Predoctoral Fellowships for Historians of American Art to Travel Abroad

National Gallery of Art
2000B South Club Drive
Landover, MD 20785
Phone: 202-842-6482
Fax: 202-789-3026
http://www.nga.gov/resources/casva.htm
Purpose: To award fellowships to doctoral students in art history who are studying aspects of art and architecture of the United States, including native and pre-Revolutionary America.
Eligibility: Applicants must be nominated by the chair of a graduate department of art history or other appropriate department. Each department may support two candidates. Applicants should submit proposals, itineraries, a curriculum vitae, two letters of support from professors and an additional letter of nomination from the chair. The fellowship is for a period of six to eight weeks of continuous travel abroad in areas such as Africa, Asia, South America or Europe to sites of historical and cultural interest. The travel fellowship is intended to encourage art-historical experience beyond the applicant's major field not for the advancement of a dissertation. Preference is given to those who have had little opportunity for professional travel abroad.
Target applicants: Graduate school students. Adult students.
Amount: Up to $4,500.
Number of awards: Up to 6.
Deadline: February 15.
How to apply: Application materials are described online.
Exclusive: Visit www.UltimateScholarshipBook.com and enter code NA64312 for updates on this award.

(644) • Professional Scholarships

Insurance Scholarship Foundation of America
14286-19 Beach Boulevard
Suite 353
Jacksonville, FL 32250
Phone: 904-821-7188
Email: foundation@inssfa.org
http://www.inssfa.org
Purpose: To promote excellence in the insurance industry by helping in the education of its employees.
Eligibility: Applicants must have been employed in the industry for at least three years, be an NAIW member for a minimum of three years, have the CPIW/M designation, have demonstrated active involvement in NAIW leadership activities and be engaged in a course of study designed to improve knowledge and skills in performing employment responsibilities.
Target applicants: College students. Graduate school students. Adult students.
Amount: $50-$2,000.
Number of awards: Varies.
Deadline: August 15.
How to apply: Applications are available online.
Exclusive: Visit www.UltimateScholarshipBook.com and enter code IN64412 for updates on this award.

(645) • Professor Sidney Gross Memorial Award

Public Relations Student Society of America
33 Maiden Lane
11th Floor
New York, NY 10038
Phone: 212-460-1474
Fax: 212-995-0757
Email: prssa@prsa.org
http://www.prssa.org
Purpose: To assist public relations undergraduate students.
Eligibility: Applicants must be undergraduate students who demonstrate superior understanding of ethical principles in public relations. Applicants need to write a response to a given scenario and must be members of the PRSSA.
Target applicants: College students. Adult students.
Amount: $1,000.
Number of awards: Varies.
Deadline: Varies.
How to apply: Applications are available online.
Exclusive: Visit www.UltimateScholarshipBook.com and enter code PU64512 for updates on this award.

(646) • Project Vote Smart National Internship Program

Project Vote Smart
Internship Coordinator
1 Common Ground
Philipsburg, MT 59858
Phone: 406-859-8683
Fax: 406-859-8680
Email: intern@votesmart.org
http://www.votesmart.org
Purpose: To encourage students and recent college graduates to develop an interest in voter education.
Eligibility: Applicants must be current college students in good standing or recent college graduates. They must be able to approach voter education work with a non-partisan attitude and be willing to commit to a ten-week internship. Selection is based on the overall strength of the application.
Target applicants: College students. Adult students.
Amount: Varies.
Number of awards: Varies.
Deadline: Varies.
How to apply: Applications are available online. An application form, resume, cover letter and three references are required.
Exclusive: Visit www.UltimateScholarshipBook.com and enter code PR64612 for updates on this award.

(647) • ProStart National Certificate of Achievement Scholarship

National Restaurant Association Educational Foundation
175 W. Jackson Boulevard
Suite 1500
Chicago, IL 60604-2702
Phone: 800-765-2122
Fax: 312-715-1010
Email: scholars@naref.org
http://www.nraef.org
Purpose: To support students who have been recognized in the HBA/ProStart School-to-Career Initiative.
Eligibility: Applicants must be graduating high school seniors and must have received the ProStart national Certificate of Achievement from participation in the HBA/ProStart School-to-Career Initiative. Applicants must also submit a copy of the National Restaurant Association Educational Foundation's ProStart National Certificate of Achievement, GPA and acceptance into a culinary and/or restaurant/foodservice management related program.
Target applicants: High school students.
Minimum GPA: 2.75
Amount: Starting at $2,500.
Number of awards: Varies.
Deadline: August 18.
How to apply: Applications are available online.
Exclusive: Visit www.UltimateScholarshipBook.com and enter code NA64712 for updates on this award.

(648) • Ray and Gertrude Marshall Scholarship

American Culinary Federation
180 Center Place Way
St. Augustine, FL 32095
Phone: 800-624-9458
Fax: 904-825-4758
Email: acf@acfchefs.net
http://www.acfchefs.org
Purpose: To assist students in culinary programs.
Eligibility: Applicants must be ACF junior members enrolled in a post-secondary culinary arts program or an ACF apprenticeship program and must have completed at least one grading period. Selection is based on financial need, GPA, recommendations and work experience.
Target applicants: College students. Adult students.
Amount: $500-$1,000.
Number of awards: Varies.
Deadline: May 1 and September 1.
How to apply: Applications are available online or by written request.
Exclusive: Visit www.UltimateScholarshipBook.com and enter code AM64812 for updates on this award.

(649) • Ray, NRP and Katie, WKTE Pautz Scholarship

American Radio Relay League Foundation
225 Main Street
Newington, CT 06111
Phone: 860-594-0397
Fax: 860-594-0259
Email: foundation@arrl.org
http://www.arrlf.org
Purpose: To provide financial assistance to amateur radio operators from the ARRL Midwest Division.
Eligibility: Applicants must be ARRL members with a General Class or higher Amateur Radio License. They must be residents of Iowa, Kansas, Missouri or Nebraska and should major in electronics, computer science or a related field at a four-year institution.
Target applicants: High school students. College students. Adult students.
Amount: $500-$1,000.
Number of awards: 1.
Deadline: February 1.
How to apply: Applications are available online.
Exclusive: Visit www.UltimateScholarshipBook.com and enter code AM64912 for updates on this award.

(650) • Reid Blackburn Scholarship

National Press Photographers Foundation Blackburn Scholarship
Fay Blackburn
The Columbian
P.O. Box 180
Vancouver, WA 98666
Phone: 360-759-8027
Fax: 919-383-7261
Email: fay.blackburn@columbian.com
http://www.nppa.org

Purpose: To support photojournalism students.
Eligibility: Applicants must have completed one year at a full-time four-year college or university, provide a portfolio, demonstrate financial need and must have courses in photojournalism and have at least half a year of undergraduate study left. Applicants can apply to as many NPPA scholarships as desired, but only one award will be granted per student.
Target applicants: College students. Adult students.
Amount: $2,000.
Number of awards: Varies.
Deadline: Varies.
How to apply: Applications are available online.
Exclusive: Visit www.UltimateScholarshipBook.com and enter code NA65012 for updates on this award.

(651) • Richard W. Bendicksen Memorial Scholarship

American Radio Relay League Foundation
225 Main Street
Newington, CT 06111
Phone: 860-594-0397
Fax: 860-594-0259
Email: foundation@arrl.org
http://www.arrlf.org

Purpose: To provide financial assistance to amateur radio operators.
Eligibility: Applicants must hold an active amateur radio license of any class, and they must be attending a four-year institution of higher learning.
Target applicants: High school students. College students. Adult students.
Amount: $1,000.
Number of awards: 1.
Deadline: February 1.
How to apply: Applications are available online.
Exclusive: Visit www.UltimateScholarshipBook.com and enter code AM65112 for updates on this award.

(652) • Ritchie-Jennings Memorial Scholarship

Association of Certified Fraud Examiners
Scholarships Program Coordinator
The Gregor Building
716 West Avenue
Austin, TX 78701
Phone: 512-478-9000
Fax: 512-478-9297
Email: memberservices@acfe.com
http://www.acfe.com

Purpose: To support the college education of accounting, business, finance and criminal justice students who may become Certified Fraud Examiners in the future.
Eligibility: Applicants must be full-time undergraduate or graduate students with a declared major or minor in criminal justice, accounting, business or finance. Students must submit three letters of recommendation, with at least one from a Certified Fraud Examiner or local CFE Chapter and must write an essay on why they deserve the scholarship and how fraud awareness will help their career.
Target applicants: College students. Graduate school students. Adult students.
Amount: $1,000-$10,000.
Number of awards: 30.
Deadline: January 21.
How to apply: Applications are available online.
Exclusive: Visit www.UltimateScholarshipBook.com and enter code AS65212 for updates on this award.

(653) • Scholarship in Book Production and Publishing

Bookbuilders West
1032 Irving Street #602
San Francisco, CA 94122-2200
http://www.bookbuilders.org

Purpose: To support students pursuing careers in publishing.
Eligibility: Applicants must be enrolled in a college, university or technical school in Alaska, Arizona, California, Colorado, Hawaii, Idaho, Montana, Nevada, New Mexico, Oregon, Utah, Washington or Wyoming and have a GPA of 2.0 or higher.
Target applicants: College students. Adult students.
Minimum GPA: 2.0
Amount: $1,000.
Number of awards: Varies.
Deadline: May 24.
How to apply: Applications are available from your school's publishing department. An application form, letter from faculty member and student book project are required.
Exclusive: Visit www.UltimateScholarshipBook.com and enter code BO65312 for updates on this award.

(654) • Schwan's Food Service Scholarship

Child Nutrition Foundation
Scholarship Committee
700 S. Washington Street, Suite 300
Alexandria, VA 22314
Phone: 703-739-3900
Email: jcurtis@schoolnutrition.org
http://www.schoolnutrition.org

Purpose: To support those entering the school foodservice industry.
Eligibility: Applicants or parents of applicants must be School Nutrition Association members for at least one year and be pursuing a field of study related to school foodservice.
Target applicants: High school students. College students. Graduate school students. Adult students.
Amount: Up to $1,000.
Number of awards: Varies.
Scholarship may be renewable.
Deadline: April 1.
How to apply: Applications are available online.
Exclusive: Visit www.UltimateScholarshipBook.com and enter code CH65412 for updates on this award.

(655) • Scripps Howard Top Ten Scholarship

Scripps Howard Foundation
Top Ten Scholarship
P.O. Box 5380

Cincinnati, OH 45201
Phone: 513-977-3035
Fax: 513-977-3800
Email: vlmartin@scripps.com
http://www.scripps.com
Purpose: To recognize the top journalism students in the country.
Eligibility: Applicants are nominated by their college and must be full-time college students entering their junior or senior year and studying journalism. Selection is based on academic achievement, commitment to a career journalism and essay.
Target applicants: College students. Adult students.
Amount: $10,000.
Number of awards: 10.
Deadline: May 15.
How to apply: Applications are available by request.
Exclusive: Visit www.UltimateScholarshipBook.com and enter code SC65512 for updates on this award.

(656) • Seth Horen, K1LOM Memorial Scholarship

American Radio Relay League Foundation
225 Main Street
Newington, CT 06111
Phone: 860-594-0397
Fax: 860-594-0259
Email: foundation@arrl.org
http://www.arrlf.org
Purpose: To provide scholarship assistance to active amateur radio operators.
Eligibility: Applicants must hold an active Amateur Radio License in any class and must be attending a four-year institution of higher learning.
Target applicants: High school students. College students. Adult students.
Amount: $500.
Number of awards: 1.
Deadline: February 1.
How to apply: Applications are available online.
Exclusive: Visit www.UltimateScholarshipBook.com and enter code AM65612 for updates on this award.

(657) • Shell/CAPT Process Technology Scholarship

Center for the Advancement of Process Technology
1200 Amburn Road
Texas City, TX 77591
Phone: 409-938-1211
Fax: 409-938-1285
Email: sturnbough@com.edu
http://www.captech.org
Purpose: To aid students who are preparing for careers in chemical, mechanical or physical process technology.
Eligibility: Applicants must be U.S. citizens or authorized to work full-time in the U.S. They must be enrolled in or planning to enroll in a two-year degree program in electrical technology, mechanical technology, process technology, compression technology, industrial maintenance technology, petroleum technology or instrumentation technology. They must have a GPA of 2.5 or better. Selection is based on the overall strength of the application.
Target applicants: High school students. College students. Adult students.
Minimum GPA: 2.5
Amount: Up to $2,200.
Number of awards: Varies.
Scholarship may be renewable.
Deadline: May 14.
How to apply: Applications are available online. An application form, official transcript and two recommendation letters are required.
Exclusive: Visit www.UltimateScholarshipBook.com and enter code CE65712 for updates on this award.

(658) • Shields-Gillespie Scholarship

American Orff-Schulwerk Association (AOSA)
P.O. Box 391089
Cleveland, OH 44139-8089
Phone: 440-543-5366
Email: info@aosa.org
http://www.aosa.org
Purpose: To assist pre-K and kindergarten teachers with program funding, including instruments and training.
Eligibility: Applicants must be a member of AOSA. Applicants must be U.S. citizens or have lived in the United States for the past five years. Programs should focus on music/movement learning.
Target applicants: College students. Graduate school students. Adult students.
Amount: Varies.
Number of awards: Varies.
Deadline: January 25.
How to apply: Applications are available online for AOSA members.
Exclusive: Visit www.UltimateScholarshipBook.com and enter code AM65812 for updates on this award.

(659) • SLA Scholarship

Special Libraries Association
331 S. Patrick Street
Alexandria, VA 22314
Phone: 703-647-4900
Fax: 703-647-4901
Email: sla@sla.org
http://www.sla.org
Purpose: To support students who wish to pursue careers in special librarianship.
Eligibility: Applicants must be college graduates or college seniors with an interest in special librarianship who are admitted by a recognized library school or information science program and demonstrate financial need. Preference is given to SLA members and those who show an interest in special library work.
Target applicants: College students. Graduate school students. Adult students.
Amount: $6,000.
Number of awards: Up to 3.
Deadline: January 1 through September 30.
How to apply: Applications are available online.
Exclusive: Visit www.UltimateScholarshipBook.com and enter code SP65912 for updates on this award.

(660) • Specialty Equipment Market Association (SEMA) Memorial Scholarship

Specialty Equipment Market Association
1575 S. Valley Vista Drive
Diamond Bar, CA 91765
Phone: 909-396-0289
Fax: 909-860-0184

Email: education@sema.org
http://www.sema.org
Purpose: To support the education of students pursuing careers in the automotive aftermarket.
Eligibility: Applicants must show financial need, have a minimum 2.5 GPA and pursue a career in the automotive aftermarket or related field.
Target applicants: College students. Adult students.
Minimum GPA: 2.5
Amount: $1,000-$4,000.
Number of awards: Varies.
Deadline: April 16.
How to apply: Applications are available online.
Exclusive: Visit www.UltimateScholarshipBook.com and enter code SP66012 for updates on this award.

---

(661) • SPS Future Teacher Scholarship

Society of Physics Students
One Physics Ellipse
College Park, MD 20740
Phone: 301-209-3007
Fax: 301-209-0839
Email: sps@aip.org
http://www.spsnational.org/programs/scholarships/
Purpose: To provide scholarships to physics majors who are participating in a teacher education program and who intend to pursue a career in physics education.
Eligibility: Applicants must be members of SPS and intend to pursue a career in teaching physics. Students must be undergraduate physics majors, at least in their junior year of study at the time of application.
Target applicants: College students. Adult students.
Amount: $2,000.
Number of awards: 1.
Deadline: February 15.
How to apply: Applications are available online or from chapter advisors.
Exclusive: Visit www.UltimateScholarshipBook.com and enter code SO66112 for updates on this award.

---

(662) • SSPI Scholarship Program

Society of Satellite Professionals International (SSPI)
Tamara Bond
55 Broad Street
14th Floor
New York, NY 10004
Phone: 212-809-5199
Fax: 212-825-0075
Email: rbell@sspi.org
http://www.sspi.org
Purpose: To help high school and university graduates with undergraduate and post-graduate study in satellite-related disciplines.
Eligibility: Applicants must be high school seniors, undergraduate or graduate students who are members of SSPI (membership is free) studying satellite-related technologies, policies or applications. Some scholarships have requirements such as interests, financial need, residency, gender, race or GPA. The award is based on commitment to education and careers in the satellite fields, academic and leadership achievement, potential for contribution to the satellite communications industry and a scientific, engineering, research, business or creative submission.
Target applicants: High school students. College students. Graduate school students. Adult students.
Amount: $5,000.
Number of awards: Varies.
Deadline: April 30.
How to apply: Applications are available online.
Exclusive: Visit www.UltimateScholarshipBook.com and enter code SO66212 for updates on this award.

---

(663) • Steven Hymans Extended Stay Scholarship

American Hotel and Lodging Educational Foundation (AH&LEF)
1201 New York Avenue NW
Suite 600
Washington, DC 20005-3931
Phone: 202-289-3188
Fax: 202-289-3199
Email: chammond@ahlef.org
http://www.ahlef.org
Purpose: To provide scholarships to help educate students on the needs of extended stay visitors in the lodging industry.
Eligibility: Applicants must be undergraduate students who have experience working at an extended stay facility and must pursue a career in that segment of the lodging industry.
Target applicants: College students. Adult students.
Amount: Up to $3,000.
Number of awards: Varies.
Deadline: May 1.
How to apply: Applications are available online.
Exclusive: Visit www.UltimateScholarshipBook.com and enter code AM66312 for updates on this award.

---

(664) • Stuart Cameron and Margaret McLeod Memorial Scholarship

Institute of Management Accountants (IMA)
10 Paragon Drive
Montvale, NJ 07645-1760
Phone: 800-638-4427
Email: students@imanet.org
http://www.imanet.org
Purpose: To help management accounting students.
Eligibility: Applicants must be full- and part-time undergraduate and graduate students, be IMA student members and declare which four- or five-year management accounting, financial management or information technology related program they plan to pursue as a career or list a related field. Candidates should submit applications, resumes, transcripts, two recommendations and statements. Advanced degree students must pass one part of the CMA/CFM certification.
Target applicants: College students. Graduate school students. Adult students.
Minimum GPA: 2.8
Amount: $5,000.
Number of awards: 1.
Deadline: February 15.
How to apply: Applications are available online.
Exclusive: Visit www.UltimateScholarshipBook.com and enter code IN66412 for updates on this award.

---

(665) • Student Achievement Grants

NEA Foundation
1201 16th Street NW
Suite 416
Washington, DC 20036
Phone: 202-822-7840

Fax: 202-822-7779
Email: info-neafoundation@list.nea.org
http://www.neafoundation.org
Purpose: To promote the academic achievement of students in U.S. public schools and public higher education institutions by providing funds for teachers.
Eligibility: Applicants must be current public school teachers in PreK-12, public school education support professionals or faculty or staff at public higher education institutions. Preference is given to those who work with economically disadvantaged students and NEA members. The grants may be used for materials, supplies, equipment, transportation, software or scholars-in-residence and in some cases professional development. The work should "engage students in critical thinking and problem solving that deepens their knowledge of standards-based subject matter."
Target applicants: Graduate school students. Adult students.
Amount: $5,000.
Number of awards: Varies.
Deadline: February 1, June 1, October 15.
How to apply: Applications are available online and may be submitted at any time. Applications are reviewed three times each year on February 1, June 1 and October 15.
Exclusive: Visit www.UltimateScholarshipBook.com and enter code NE66512 for updates on this award.

(666) · Student Journalist Investigative Reporting Award

Journalism Education Association
Kansas State University
103 Kedzie Hall
Manhattan, KS 66506
Phone: 785-532-5532
Fax: 785-532-5563
Email: jea@spub.ksu.edu
http://www.jea.org
Purpose: To present awards to secondary school students who have made a difference in their own lives, the lives of others or their community or school through journalism.
Eligibility: Applicants must have a teacher who is a member of JEA. Submitted works must have been published within the past two years.
Target applicants: High school students.
Amount: $1,000.
Number of awards: 1.
Deadline: March 1.
How to apply: Applications are available online.
Exclusive: Visit www.UltimateScholarshipBook.com and enter code JO66612 for updates on this award.

(667) · Student with a Disability Scholarship

American Speech-Language-Hearing Foundation
2200 Research Boulevard
Rockville, MD 20850
Phone: 301-296-8700
Email: foundation@asha.org
http://www.ashfoundation.org
Purpose: To support a graduate student with a disability studying communication sciences and disorders.
Eligibility: Master's degree candidates must be in programs accredited by the Council on Academic Accreditation for Audiology and Speech Pathology, but doctoral programs do not have to be accredited. The applicants should submit a transcript, essay, reference form and statement of good standing; be recommended by a faculty or workplace committee and have not received scholarships from the ASHA Foundation. Students must attend their programs full-time.
Target applicants: Graduate school students. Adult students.
Amount: $4,000.
Number of awards: 1.
Deadline: Varies.
How to apply: Applications are available online.
Exclusive: Visit www.UltimateScholarshipBook.com and enter code AM66712 for updates on this award.

(668) · Summer Fellowship Program

American Institute for Economic Research
P.O. Box 1000
Attn.: Susan Gillette, Assistant to the President
Great Barrington, MA 01230
Phone: 413-528-1216
Fax: 413-528-0103
Email: fellowship@aier.org
http://www.aier.org
Purpose: To provide summer fellowships for college seniors entering a doctoral program in economics or economics-related studies.
Eligibility: Applicants must be college seniors who will enter a doctoral program in economics or an affiliated program.
Target applicants: College students. Adult students.
Amount: Room and board plus $500 stipend.
Number of awards: Varies.
Deadline: Varies.
How to apply: Applications are available online.
Exclusive: Visit www.UltimateScholarshipBook.com and enter code AM66812 for updates on this award.

(669) · Teacher Education Scholarship Fund

American Montessori Society
281 Park Avenue South
New York, NY 10010
Phone: 212-358-1250
Fax: 212-358-1256
Email: info@amshq.org
http://www.amshq.org
Purpose: To support future Montessori teachers.
Eligibility: Applicants must be accepted into but not yet attending an AMS teacher education program. Financial need, the applicant's personal statement and letters of recommendation are considered.
Target applicants: High school students. College students. Adult students.
Amount: Varies.
Number of awards: Varies.
Scholarship may be renewable.
Deadline: May 1.
How to apply: Applications are available online.
Exclusive: Visit www.UltimateScholarshipBook.com and enter code AM66912 for updates on this award.

(670) · Teacher of the Year Award

Veterans of Foreign Wars Teacher of the Year Award
406 W. 34th Street
Kansas City, MO 64111
Phone: 816-968-1117
Fax: 816-968-1149

Email: tbeauchamp@vfw.org
http://www.vfw.org
Purpose: To salute the nation's top elementary, junior high and high school teachers who educate their students about citizenship and American history and traditions.
Eligibility: Applicants must be current classroom teachers who teach at least half of the school day in a classroom environment, grades K-12. Previous winners from the state or national levels are not eligible. Fellow teachers, supervisors or other interested individuals who are not related to the nominee may send in nominations; no self-nominations will be accepted.
Target applicants: Graduate school students. Adult students.
Amount: $1,000.
Number of awards: 3.
Deadline: November 1.
How to apply: Applications are available online but initial nominations must be sent to the local VFW office. Visit the website for more information.
Exclusive: Visit www.UltimateScholarshipBook.com and enter code VE67012 for updates on this award.

(671) • Thomas H. Steel Fellowship Fund

Pride Law Fund
P.O. Box 2602
San Francisco, CA 94104
Email: info@pridelawfund.org
http://www.pridelawfund.org
Purpose: To support law students with a project that serves the lesbian, gay, bisexual and transgendered community.
Eligibility: Applicants must be students in their last year of law school or lawyers within three years of graduating from law school. The award is based on the quality and scope of the project, proposal, public service activities and relation to the LGBT community. Applicants should submit applications, resumes, project descriptions, two reference letters, budget, timetable and law school transcript.
Target applicants: Graduate school students. Adult students.
Amount: Up to $35,000.
Number of awards: 1.
Deadline: April 1.
How to apply: Applications are available online.
Exclusive: Visit www.UltimateScholarshipBook.com and enter code PR67112 for updates on this award.

(672) • TLMI Four Year Colleges/Full-Time Students Scholarship

Tag and Label Manufacturers Institute Inc.
40 Shuman Boulevard, Suite 295
Naperville, IL 60563
Phone: 630-357-9222
Fax: 630-357-0192
http://www.tlmi.com
Purpose: To assist upper-level students planning to pursue a career in tag and label manufacturing.
Eligibility: Applicants must demonstrate an interest in the tag and label manufacturing industry while taking appropriate courses at an accredited four-year college. They must be full-time sophomores or juniors with a GPA of at least 3.0. Applicants must submit a personal statement and three letters of recommendation attesting to their character.
Target applicants: College students. Adult students.
Minimum GPA: 3.0
Amount: $5,000.
Number of awards: 6.
Deadline: March 31.
How to apply: Applications are available online and by phone.
Exclusive: Visit www.UltimateScholarshipBook.com and enter code TA67212 for updates on this award.

(673) • Tobin Sorenson Physical Education Scholarship

Pi Lambda Theta
P.O. Box 6626
Bloomington, IN 47407
Phone: 800-487-3411
Fax: 812-339-3462
Email: office@pilambda.org
http://www.pilambda.org
Purpose: To support future K-12 physical education teachers.
Eligibility: Applicants must be pursuing a career as a physical education teacher, adapted physical education teacher, coach, recreational therapist, dance therapist or related profession at the K-12 level. They must be at least college sophomores with a GPA of 3.5 or higher. Applicants must also demonstrate leadership abilities and involvement in extracurricular activities related to their chosen profession. This scholarship is only awarded in odd years.
Target applicants: College students. Adult students.
Minimum GPA: 3.5
Amount: $1,000.
Number of awards: 1.
Deadline: February 10.
How to apply: Applications are available online.
Exclusive: Visit www.UltimateScholarshipBook.com and enter code PI67312 for updates on this award.

(674) • Tom and Judith Comstock Scholarship

American Radio Relay League Foundation
225 Main Street
Newington, CT 06111
Phone: 860-594-0397
Fax: 860-594-0259
Email: foundation@arrl.org
http://www.arrlf.org
Purpose: To assist ham radio operators in furthering their educations.
Eligibility: Applicants must have any class of ham radio license, be residents of Texas or Oklahoma and be high school seniors accepted at a two- or four-year college or university.
Target applicants: High school students.
Amount: $2,000.
Number of awards: 1.
Deadline: February 1.
How to apply: Applications are available online but may not be completed electronically. All completed applications must be mailed.
Exclusive: Visit www.UltimateScholarshipBook.com and enter code AM67412 for updates on this award.

(675) • Tourism Cares Sustainable Tourism Scholarship

Tourism Cares
275 Turnpike Street
Suite 307
Canton, MA 02021
Phone: 781-821-5990
Fax: 781-821-8949

Email: carolynv@tourismcares.org
http://www.tourismcares.org
Purpose: To promote sustainable tourism and to assist graduate students who are studying tourism.
Eligibility: Applicants must be enrolled in a tourism program at the graduate level at an accredited college or university in any country and have a GPA of 3.0 or higher. Students in developing countries are encouraged to apply.
Target applicants: Graduate school students. Adult students.
Minimum GPA: 3.0
Amount: $1,000.
Number of awards: 1.
Deadline: April 15.
How to apply: Applications are available online.
Exclusive: Visit www.UltimateScholarshipBook.com and enter code TO67512 for updates on this award.

(676) • Transatlantic Fellows Program

German Marshall Fund of the United States
1744 R Street NW
Washington, DC 20009
Phone: 202-683-2650
Fax: 202-265-1662
Email: info@gmfus.org
http://www.gmfus.org
Purpose: To research topics of foreign policy, international security, trade and economic development and immigration.
Eligibility: Fellowships are by invitation from GMF and are issued to senior policy-practitioners, journalists, academics and businesspeople. Fellows work in residence in Washington, DC and Brussels, Belgium.
Target applicants: Graduate school students. Adult students.
Amount: Varies.
Number of awards: Varies.
Deadline: Varies.
How to apply: Contact John K. Glenn at the organization for more information.
Exclusive: Visit www.UltimateScholarshipBook.com and enter code GE67612 for updates on this award.

(677) • Undergraduate Scholarship

International Technology Education Association
Foundation for Technology Education
1914 Association Drive, Suite 201
Reston, VA 20191
Phone: 703-860-2100
Fax: 703-860-0353
Email: bmongold@iteaconnect.org
http://www.iteaconnect.org
Purpose: To support undergraduate students majoring in technology education teacher preparation.
Eligibility: Applicants must be members of ITEA, be full-time undergraduate students and have a minimum 2.5 GPA.
Target applicants: College students. Adult students.
Minimum GPA: 2.5
Amount: $1,000.
Number of awards: 1.
Deadline: December 1.
How to apply: Application information is available online.
Exclusive: Visit www.UltimateScholarshipBook.com and enter code IN67712 for updates on this award.

(678) • Undergraduate Scholarships

Radio Television Digital News Association
4121 Plank Road #512
Fredericksburg, VA 22407
Phone: 202-659-6510
Fax: 202-223-4007
Email: staceys@rtdna.org
http://www.rtdna.org
Purpose: To honor professional achievements in electronic journalism.
Eligibility: Applicants must be full-time college sophomores or higher with at least one full academic year remaining. Applicants may be enrolled in any major as long as their career intent is television or radio news. Applicants may only apply for one RTNDA scholarship.
Target applicants: College students. Adult students.
Amount: $10,000.
Number of awards: 8.
Deadline: May 10.
How to apply: Applications are available online.
Exclusive: Visit www.UltimateScholarshipBook.com and enter code RA67812 for updates on this award.

(679) • United States Senate Youth Program

William Randolph Hearst Foundation
90 New Montgomery Street, Suite 1212
San Francisco, CA 94105
Phone: 800-841-7048 x 4540
Fax: 415-243-0760
Email: ussyp@hearstfdn.org
http://www.hearstfdn.org/ussyp/
Purpose: To expose students to their government in action.
Eligibility: Applicants must be high school juniors or seniors in an elected position at school or in civic or educational offices. USSYP brings the highest level officials from each branch of government together with a group of 104 high school student delegates for an intensive week-long educational program held in Washington, DC.
Target applicants: High school students.
Amount: $5,000.
Number of awards: 104.
Deadline: Varies by state.
How to apply: To apply, contact your high school principal, counselor or state selection contact. State selection contact information is located on the home page of the website.
Exclusive: Visit www.UltimateScholarshipBook.com and enter code WI67912 for updates on this award.

(680) • Wesley-Logan Prize

American Historical Association
400 A Street SE
Washington, DC 20003
Phone: 202-544-2422
Fax: 202-544-8307
Email: info@historians.org
http://www.historians.org
Purpose: To award a prize to a scholarly/literary book focusing on the history of dispersion, relocation, settlement or adjustment of people from Africa; or on their return to that continent.
Eligibility: Books must have been published between May 1 of the previous year and April 30 of the entry year. Entries are mailed directly to committee members.

Target applicants: Junior high students or younger. High school students. College students. Graduate school students. Adult students.
Amount: Varies.
Number of awards: Varies.
Deadline: May 15.
How to apply: Application information is available on approximately March 30.
Exclusive: Visit www.UltimateScholarshipBook.com and enter code AM68012 for updates on this award.

---

(681) • William B. Ruggles Right to Work Scholarship

National Institute for Labor Relations Research (NILRR)
William B. Ruggles Scholarship Selection Committee
5211 Port Royal Road, Suite 510
Springfield, VA 22151
Phone: 703-321-9606
Fax: 703-321-7342
Email: research@nilrr.org
http://www.nilrr.org
Purpose: To support students who are dedicated to high journalistic standards.
Eligibility: Applicants must be undergraduate or graduate students majoring in journalism and demonstrate an understanding of the principles of voluntary unionism and the economic and social problems of compulsory unionism.
Target applicants: College students. Graduate school students. Adult students.
Amount: $2,000.
Number of awards: 1.
Deadline: December 31.
How to apply: Applications are available online.
Exclusive: Visit www.UltimateScholarshipBook.com and enter code NA68112 for updates on this award.

---

(682) • William R. Goldfarb Memorial Scholarship

American Radio Relay League Foundation
225 Main Street
Newington, CT 06111
Phone: 860-594-0397
Fax: 860-594-0259
Email: foundation@arrl.org
http://www.arrlf.org
Purpose: To provide financial assistance to high school seniors who are amateur radio operators and are seeking a bachelor's degree in business, computers, medical, nursing, engineering or science.
Eligibility: Applicants must have demonstrated financial need and be planning to attend a regionally accredited institution of higher learning.
Target applicants: High school students.
Amount: Up to $10,000.
Number of awards: 1.
Deadline: February 1.
How to apply: Applications are available online.
Exclusive: Visit www.UltimateScholarshipBook.com and enter code AM68212 for updates on this award.

---

(683) • William S. Bullinger Scholarship

Federal Circuit Bar Association
1620 I Street NW
Suite 900
Washington, DC 20006
Phone: 202-466-3923
Fax: 202-833-1061
http://www.fedcirbar.org
Purpose: To support financially needy but academically promising law students.
Eligibility: Applicants must be undergraduate or graduate law student who demonstrate financial need and academic promise. They must submit a one-page statement describing their financial circumstances, their interest in law and their qualifications for the scholarship along with transcripts and a curriculum vitae. Applicants will be considered for the William S. Bullinger Scholarship when applying for the Giles Sutherland Rich Memorial Scholarship.
Target applicants: College students. Graduate school students. Adult students.
Amount: $5,000.
Number of awards: 1.
Deadline: April 15.
How to apply: There is no application form.
Exclusive: Visit www.UltimateScholarshipBook.com and enter code FE68312 for updates on this award.

---

(684) • Women in Geographic Education Scholarship

National Council for Geographic Education
Jacksonville State University
206-A Martin Hall
700 Pelham Road North
Jacksonville, AL 36265-1602
Phone: 256-782-5293
Fax: 256-782-5336
Email: ncge@jsu.edu
http://www.ncge.org
Purpose: To aid undergraduate or graduate women planning careers in geographic education.
Eligibility: Applicants must be enrolled in a program leading to a career in geographic education, submit an essay on the provided topic and have an overall GPA of 3.0 and a geography GPA of 3.5. The winner receives an additional $300 travel stipend if she attends the NCGE Annual Meeting.
Target applicants: College students. Graduate school students. Adult students.
Minimum GPA: 3.0
Amount: $500.
Number of awards: 1.
Deadline: June 30.
How to apply: Applications are available online.
Exclusive: Visit www.UltimateScholarshipBook.com and enter code NA68412 for updates on this award.

---

(685) • Women in Need Scholarship

Educational Foundation for Women in Accounting
P.O. Box 1925
Southeastern, PA 19399
Phone: 610-407-9229
Fax: 610-644-3713
Email: info@efwa.org
http://www.efwa.org
Purpose: This scholarship was established to provide financial assistance to female reentry students who are pursuing degrees in accounting.
Eligibility: Applicants must be female students pursuing a degree in accounting. This award is directed toward incoming, current or

reentering juniors. Selection criteria include commitment to the study of accounting, accounting aptitude, established goals and financial need.
Target applicants: College students. Adult students.
Amount: Up to $2,000.
Number of awards: 1.
Scholarship may be renewable.
Deadline: April 30.
How to apply: Applications are available online.
Exclusive: Visit www.UltimateScholarshipBook.com and enter code ED68512 for updates on this award.

(686) • Women in Transition Scholarship

Educational Foundation for Women in Accounting
P.O. Box 1925
Southeastern, PA 19399
Phone: 610-407-9229
Fax: 610-644-3713
Email: info@efwa.org
http://www.efwa.org
Purpose: This scholarship was established to provide financial assistance to female reentry students who are pursuing degrees in accounting.
Eligibility: Applicants must be female students pursuing a degree in accounting. The award is directed toward incoming, current or reentering freshmen. Selection criteria include commitment to the study of accounting, aptitude, and financial need.
Target applicants: High school students. College students. Adult students.
Amount: Up to $4,000.
Number of awards: 1.
Scholarship may be renewable.
Deadline: April 30.
How to apply: Applications are available online.
Exclusive: Visit www.UltimateScholarshipBook.com and enter code ED68612 for updates on this award.

(687) • Yasme Foundation Scholarship

American Radio Relay League Foundation
225 Main Street
Newington, CT 06111
Phone: 860-594-0397
Fax: 860-594-0259
Email: foundation@arrl.org
http://www.arrlf.org
Purpose: To support science and engineering students who are involved in amateur radio.
Eligibility: Applicants must have an active amateur radio license. Students must be enrolled in a four-year college or university. Preference will be given to students in the top 10 percent of their class and those who have participated in community service and local amateur radio clubs.
Target applicants: High school students. College students. Adult students.
Amount: $2,000.
Number of awards: Varies.
Scholarship may be renewable.
Deadline: February 1.
How to apply: Applications are available online.
Exclusive: Visit www.UltimateScholarshipBook.com and enter code AM68712 for updates on this award.

(688) • Yoshiyama Young Entrepreneurs Program

Hitachi Foundation
1215 17th Street NW
Washington, DC 20036
Phone: 202-457-0588
Fax: 202-296-1098
http://www.hitachifoundation.org
Purpose: To recognize student entrepreneurs.
Eligibility: Applicants must be at least 18 years old and must have been 29 years old or younger when their business began generating revenue. The applicant's business must be one to five years old, have generated revenue for at least one year and help create opportunities for low-income Americans. Selection is based on the applicant's motivation and vision and knowledge of low-wealth individuals and the potential of the business.
Target applicants: College students. Graduate school students. Adult students.
Amount: Up to $50,000 over two years.
Number of awards: Varies.
Deadline: March.
How to apply: Applications are available online.
Exclusive: Visit www.UltimateScholarshipBook.com and enter code HI68812 for updates on this award.

(689) • Youth Scholarship

Society of Broadcast Engineers
9102 N. Meridian Street
Suite 150
Indianapolis, IN 46260
Phone: 317-846-9000
Fax: 317-846-9120
Email: mclappe@sbe.org
http://www.sbe.org
Purpose: To help students who plan to pursue a career in the technical aspects of broadcasting.
Eligibility: Applicants must be graduating high school seniors who plan to enroll in a technical school, college or university and should pursue studies leading to a career in broadcasting engineering or a related field. Preference is given to members of SBE, but any student may apply. Applicants should submit applications, transcripts, biographies and statements. Recipients must write a paper about broadcast engineering.
Target applicants: High school students.
Amount: $1,000-$3,000.
Number of awards: Up to 3.
Deadline: July 1.
How to apply: Applications are available online.
Exclusive: Visit www.UltimateScholarshipBook.com and enter code SO68912 for updates on this award.

(690) • Zachary Taylor Stevens Memorial Scholarship

American Radio Relay League Foundation
225 Main Street
Newington, CT 06111
Phone: 860-594-0397
Fax: 860-594-0259
Email: foundation@arrl.org
http://www.arrlf.org
Purpose: To support students who are involved in amateur radio.
Eligibility: Applicants must have an amateur radio license of Technician Class or higher. Preference will be given to students residing in call areas

in Michigan, Ohio and West Virginia. Students may be enrolled in a two-year or four-year college or technical school.
Target applicants: High school students. College students. Adult students.
Amount: $750.
Number of awards: 1.
Deadline: February 1.
How to apply: Applications are available online.
Exclusive: Visit www.UltimateScholarshipBook.com and enter code AM69012 for updates on this award.

SCIENCES

(691) • A.O. Putnam Memorial Scholarship

Institute of Industrial Engineers
3577 Parkway Lane
Suite 200
Norcross, GA 30092
Phone: 800-494-0460
Fax: 770-441-3295
Email: bcameron@iienet.org
http://www.iienet2.org

Purpose: To help undergraduate Institute members who plan to pursue careers in management consulting.

Eligibility: Applicants must be undergraduate students enrolled in a college in the United States, Canada or Mexico with an accredited industrial engineering program, major in industrial engineering and be active members. Preference is given to students who plan to work in management consulting. Students may not apply directly for this scholarship and must be nominated. The award is based on academic ability, character, leadership, potential service to the industrial engineering profession and financial need.

Target applicants: College students. Adult students.
Minimum GPA: 3.4
Amount: $700.
Number of awards: 1.
Deadline: February 1.
How to apply: Nomination forms are available online.
Exclusive: Visit www.UltimateScholarshipBook.com and enter code IN69112 for updates on this award.

(692) • AAAE Foundation Scholarship

American Association of Airport Executives
601 Madison Street, Ste. 400
Alexandria, VA 22314
Phone: 703-824-0500
Fax: 703-820-1395
Email: member.services@aaae.org
http://www.aaae.org

Purpose: To support students of aviation.

Eligibility: Applicants must be enrolled in an aviation program with at least junior standing and at least a 3.0 GPA. Eligibility is unrelated to membership in AAAE. Winners are selected based on academic records, financial need, participation in school and community activities, work experience and a personal statement. Applicants must recommended by their school.

Target applicants: College students. Adult students.
Minimum GPA: 3.0
Amount: $1,000.
Number of awards: 10.
Deadline: March 31.
How to apply: To obtain an application, contact the scholarship or financial aid office at the college you attend. Scholarship information is usually mailed to universities and colleges in early January.
Exclusive: Visit www.UltimateScholarshipBook.com and enter code AM69212 for updates on this award.

(693) • AACE International Competitive Scholarships

Association for the Advancement of Cost Engineering
Attn: Staff Director - Education
209 Prairie Avenue
Suite 100
Morgantown, WV 26501-5934
http://www.aacei.org

Purpose: To aid students enrolled in programs related to cost engineering and cost management.

Eligibility: Applicants must be full-time students enrolled in one of the following programs: agricultural engineering, architectural engineering, building construction, business administration, chemical engineering, civil engineering, industrial engineering, manufacturing engineering, mechanical engineering, mining engineering, electrical engineering or quantity surveying. Those who are in their final year of undergraduate study must be accepted to attend a graduate program full-time in the next academic year. Selection is based on academic performance (35 percent), extracurricular activities (35 percent) and essay (30 percent).

Target applicants: College students. Graduate school students. Adult students.
Amount: $2,000-$8,000.
Number of awards: Varies.
Deadline: February 15.
How to apply: Applications are available online. An application form and essay are required.
Exclusive: Visit www.UltimateScholarshipBook.com and enter code AS69312 for updates on this award.

(694) • AACT National Candy Technologists John Kitt Memorial Scholarship Program

American Association of Candy Technologists
175 Rock Road
Glen Rock, NJ 07452
Phone: 201-652-2655
Fax: 201-652-3419
Email: aactinfo@gomc.com
http://www.aactcandy.org

Purpose: To aid students with a demonstrated interested in confectionery technology.

Eligibility: Applicants must be rising college sophomores, juniors or seniors at an accredited four-year college or university in North America. They must major in food science, chemical science, biological science or a related area. A GPA of 3.0 or higher is required.

Target applicants: College students. Adult students.
Minimum GPA: 3.0
Amount: $5,000.
Number of awards: 1.
Deadline: April 16.
How to apply: Applications are available online. An application form, list of academic, work and other activities, list of honors and awards, statement of goals and transcript are required.
Exclusive: Visit www.UltimateScholarshipBook.com and enter code AM69412 for updates on this award.

(695) • AAGS Joseph F. Dracup Scholarship Award

American Congress on Surveying and Mapping (ACSM)
6 Montgomery Village Avenue
Suite 403
Gaithersburg, MD 20879
Phone: 240-632-9716
Fax: 240-632-1321
Email: ilse.genovese@acsm.net
http://www.acsm.net

Purpose: To aid ACSM members who are enrolled in a four-year degree program in surveying or a closely related subject.

Eligibility: Applicants must be members of the American Congress on Surveying and Mapping (ACSM). Preference will be given to students whose coursework is significantly focused on geodetic surveying. Students who will be graduating before December of the award disbursement year are ineligible. Selection is based on academic merit, personal statement, recommendations, professional involvement and financial need.
Target applicants: College students. Adult students.
Amount: $2,000.
Number of awards: Varies.
Scholarship may be renewable.
Deadline: November 2.
How to apply: Applications are available online. An application form, personal statement, official transcript, three recommendation letters and proof of ACSM membership are required.
Exclusive: Visit www.UltimateScholarshipBook.com and enter code AM69512 for updates on this award.

(696) • AATCC Materials Design Competition

American Association of Textile Chemists and Colorists
One Davis Drive
Research Triangle Park, NC 27709-2215
Phone: 919-549-3544
Email: creech@aatcc.org
http://www.aatcc.org
Purpose: To promote innovative product development.
Eligibility: Applicants may be undergraduate or graduate students and must complete a materials design project in one of the following focus areas: industrial/technical and sports materials; medical, biomedical/protective materials and devices or smart/electronic/optoelectronic and nano-materials. They must submit an entry form by February 13, and the finished project must be submitted by April 15.
Target applicants: College students. Graduate school students. Adult students.
Amount: $500-$1,000.
Number of awards: 6.
Deadline: February 13.
How to apply: Applications are available online. An entry form, text proposal and electronic or digital poster board of the proposal are required.
Exclusive: Visit www.UltimateScholarshipBook.com and enter code AM69612 for updates on this award.

(697) • Abel Wolman Fellowship

American Water Works Association
6666 W. Quincy Avenue
Denver, CO 80235-3098
Phone: 303-347-6201
Fax: 303-795-7603
Email: lmoody@awwa.org
http://www.awwa.org
Purpose: To support doctoral students pursuing advanced training and research in the field of water supply and treatment.
Eligibility: Applicants must obtain a Ph.D. within two years of the award, must be citizens of the U.S., Canada or Mexico and should submit applications, transcripts, GRE scores, three recommendation letters, course of study and description of the dissertation research study and how it pertains to water supply and treatment. The award is based on academics, the connection between the research and water supply and treatment and the applicant's research skills.
Target applicants: Graduate school students. Adult students.
Amount: Up to $25,000.
Number of awards: 1.
Scholarship may be renewable.
Deadline: January 18.
How to apply: Applications are available online.
Exclusive: Visit www.UltimateScholarshipBook.com and enter code AM69712 for updates on this award.

(698) • Academic Achievement Award

American Water Works Association
6666 W. Quincy Avenue
Denver, CO 80235-3098
Phone: 303-347-6201
Fax: 303-795-7603
Email: lmoody@awwa.org
http://www.awwa.org
Purpose: To recognize contributions to the field of public water supply.
Eligibility: Master's theses and doctoral dissertations that are relevant to the water supply industry are eligible. Unbound manuscripts must be the work of a single author and be submitted during the competition year in which they were submitted for the degree. Students may major in any area as long as the research is directly related to the drinking water supply industry. In addition to the application, students must submit a one-page abstract of the manuscript and a letter of endorsement from the major professor or department chair. The doctoral dissertation awards are $3,000 and $1,500. The master's thesis awards are $3,000 and $1,500.
Target applicants: Graduate school students. Adult students.
Amount: $1,500-$3,000.
Number of awards: 4.
Deadline: October 1.
How to apply: Applications are available online.
Exclusive: Visit www.UltimateScholarshipBook.com and enter code AM69812 for updates on this award.

(699) • Academic Study Award

American Association of Occupational Health Nurses (AAOHN) Foundation
2920 Brandywine Road
Suite 100
Atlanta, GA 30341
Phone: 770-455-7757
Fax: 770-455-7271
Email: ann@aaohn.org
https://www.aaohn.org/
Purpose: To provide further education for occupational and environmental health professionals.
Eligibility: Applicants must be registered nurses enrolled full- or part-time in a nationally accredited school of nursing baccalaureate program with an interest in occupational and environmental health or be registered nurses enrolled full- or part-time in a graduate program that has application to occupational and environmental health. Applicants should submit a narrative and letters of recommendation.
Target applicants: College students. Graduate school students. Adult students.
Amount: $3,500.
Number of awards: 4.
Scholarship may be renewable.
Deadline: December 1.
How to apply: Applications are available online.
Exclusive: Visit www.UltimateScholarshipBook.com and enter code AM69912 for updates on this award.

(700) • ACEC New York Scholarship Program

American Council of Engineering Companies of New York
6 Airline Drive
Albany, NY 12205
Phone: 518-452-8611
Fax: 518-452-1710
http://www.acecny.org/scholar.html

Purpose: To support students who plan to become consulting engineers.
Eligibility: Applicants must be in their third year of study in a four-year program or their fourth year of study in a five-year program at an engineering school in New York State. They must major in mechanical engineering, electrical engineering, structural engineering, civil engineering, environmental engineering, chemical engineering, engineering technology or surveying. They must plan to make New York State their home and/or career area. Selection is based on work experience (25 percent), college activities and recommendations (15 percent), essay (30 percent) and GPA (30 percent).
Target applicants: College students. Adult students.
Amount: $7,500.
Number of awards: At least 9.
Deadline: December 18.
How to apply: Applications are available online. An application form, essay, transcript and two recommendations are required.
Exclusive: Visit www.UltimateScholarshipBook.com and enter code AM70012 for updates on this award.

(701) • ACI Student Fellowship Program

American Concrete Institute Student Fellowship Program
38800 Country Club Drive
Farmington Hills, MI 48331
Phone: 248-848-3816
Fax: 248-848-3801
Email: scholarships@concrete.org
http://www.concrete.org

Purpose: To encourage careers in the concrete field.
Eligibility: Applicants must be full-time undergraduate or graduate students nominated by a faculty member who is also a member of the ACI. Students must be studying engineering, construction management or another relevant field. Applicants may live anywhere in the world, but actual study must take place in the U.S. or Canada. Finalists for a fellowship must attend an ACI convention for an interview. In addition to the monetary award, the scholarship also includes conference fees, mentoring and a potential internship.
Target applicants: College students. Graduate school students. Adult students.
Amount: $10,000.
Number of awards: Varies.
Scholarship may be renewable.
Deadline: October 30.
How to apply: Applicants must be nominated by ACI-member faculty in order to receive an application.
Exclusive: Visit www.UltimateScholarshipBook.com and enter code AM70112 for updates on this award.

(702) • ACI-James Instruments Student Award for Research on NDT of Concrete

American Concrete Institute ACI-James Instruments Student Award
F. Dirk Heidbrink
Wiss Janney, Elstner Associates, Inc
330 Pfingsten Road
Northbrook, IL 60062
Phone: 248-848-3700
Fax: 248-848-3701
Email: fheidbrink@wje.com
http://www.aci-int.org

Purpose: To recognize outstanding research in the area of concrete and concrete materials using NDT methods.
Eligibility: Applicants must submit an original research paper on a topic related to the nondestructive testing (NDT) of concrete. The research must have been done by applicants while enrolled either as an undergraduate or a graduate student in an accredited institution of higher education.
Target applicants: College students. Graduate school students. Adult students.
Amount: $800.
Number of awards: 1.
Deadline: December 4.
How to apply: There is no application form. Papers must be submitted by mail.
Exclusive: Visit www.UltimateScholarshipBook.com and enter code AM70212 for updates on this award.

(703) • ACI-NA Airport Commissioner's Scholarships

Airports Council International-North America
1775 K Street, NW
Suite 500
Washington, DC 20006
Phone: 888-424-7767
Fax: 202-331-1362
http://www.aci-na.org

Purpose: To assist students who plan careers in airport management or administration.
Eligibility: Applicants must be enrolled in an undergraduate or graduate program in airport management or airport operations. Applicants must attend an accredited school in the U.S. or Canada and have a GPA of at least 3.0.
Target applicants: High school students. College students. Graduate school students. Adult students.
Minimum GPA: 3.0
Amount: Up to $2,500.
Number of awards: Up to 6.
Deadline: April 15 (spring) and December 15 (fall).
How to apply: Applications are available online.
Exclusive: Visit www.UltimateScholarshipBook.com and enter code AI70312 for updates on this award.

(704) • ACIL Scholarship

American Council of Independent Laboratories
1629 K Street NW, Suite 400
Washington, DC 20006-1633
Phone: 202-887-5872
Fax: 202-887-0021
Email: jallen@acil.org
http://www.acil.org

Purpose: To encourage students to enter the laboratory testing community.
Eligibility: Applicants must be college juniors or higher attending a four-year university or graduate school program and must major in physics, chemistry, engineering, geology, biology or environmental science. In addition to the applications, applicants should submit resumes, two

recommendation letters, transcripts and any information about other scholarships received.
Target applicants: College students. Graduate school students. Adult students.
Amount: Up to $4,000.
Number of awards: Varies.
Deadline: April 9.
How to apply: Applications are available online.
Exclusive: Visit www.UltimateScholarshipBook.com and enter code AM70412 for updates on this award.

(705) • ACSM - AAGS - NSPS Scholarships

American Congress on Surveying and Mapping (ACSM)
6 Montgomery Village Avenue
Suite 403
Gaithersburg, MD 20879
Phone: 240-632-9716
Fax: 240-632-1321
Email: ilse.genovese@acsm.net
http://www.acsm.net
Purpose: To award excellent surveying and mapping students.
Eligibility: There are several different types of awards. The first is for students enrolled in two-year degree programs in surveying technology. The second is for students enrolled in or accepted to a graduate program in geodetic surveying or geodesy. The third is for students enrolled in four-year degree programs in surveying (or in related areas such as geomatics or surveying engineering). The last type is for students enrolled in a two-year or four-year surveying (and closely related) degree program, either full or part-time. All awards are based on academic record, statement, recommendation letters and professional activities.
Target applicants: College students. Graduate school students. Adult students.
Amount: $500-$2,500.
Number of awards: 15.
Deadline: November 2.
How to apply: Applications are available online.
Exclusive: Visit www.UltimateScholarshipBook.com and enter code AM70512 for updates on this award.

(706) • ADAF Student Scholarship

American Dietetic Association Foundation
120 South Riverside Plaza
Suite 2000
Chicago, IL 60606-6995
Phone: 800-877-1600
Email: education@eatright.org
http://www.eatright.org
Purpose: To encourage students in a dietetic program.
Eligibility: Applicants should be American Dietetic Association members and enrolled in their junior or senior year of a baccalaureate or coordinated program in dietetics or the second year of study in a dietetic technician program, a dietetic internship program or a graduate program. One application form is used for all ADAF scholarships.
Target applicants: College students. Graduate school students. Adult students.
Amount: $500-$3,000.
Number of awards: Varies.
Deadline: Varies.
How to apply: Applications are available online.
Exclusive: Visit www.UltimateScholarshipBook.com and enter code AM70612 for updates on this award.

(707) • Adams Scholarship Grant

American Society of Agricultural Engineers Foundation
Administrator
Scholarship Fund
2950 Niles Road
St. Joseph, MI 49085
Phone: 269-429-0300
Fax: 269-429-3852
http://www.asae.org
Purpose: To aid undergraduate students with an interest in agricultural machinery product design and development.
Eligibility: Applicants must be biological or agricultural engineering majors in eligible accredited programs in the U.S. or Canada. Applicants must also have completed at least one year of undergraduate study and have at least one year of undergraduate study remaining, have a minimum 2.5 GPA, have an interest in agricultural machinery product design and development and demonstrate financial need.
Target applicants: College students. Adult students.
Minimum GPA: 2.5
Amount: $1,000.
Number of awards: 1.
Deadline: March 17.
How to apply: Application is by formal letter.
Exclusive: Visit www.UltimateScholarshipBook.com and enter code AM70712 for updates on this award.

(708) • ADDC Education Trust Scholarship

Desk and Derrick Educational Trust
5153 E 51st Street, Suite 107
Tulsa, OK 74135
Phone: 918-622-1749
Fax: 918-622-1675
Email: adotulsa@swbell.net
http://www.addc.org
Purpose: To promote studies in the energy industry.
Eligibility: Applicants must be U.S. or Canadian citizens, have completed two years of undergraduate study, have a minimum 3.0 GPA and demonstrate financial need. Students must be pursuing a degree in a field related to the petroleum, energy or allied industries and plan to work full-time in the petroleum, energy or allied industry or research alternative fuels such as coal, electric, solar, wind hydroelectric, nuclear or ethanol.
Target applicants: College students. Adult students.
Minimum GPA: 3.0
Amount: Varies.
Number of awards: Varies.
Deadline: April 1.
How to apply: Applications are available online.
Exclusive: Visit www.UltimateScholarshipBook.com and enter code DE70812 for updates on this award.

(709) • ADEA/Sigma Phi Alpha Linda Devore Scholarship

American Dental Education Association
1400 K Street NW
Suite 1100
Washington, DC 20005
Phone: 202-289-7201
Fax: 202-289-7204
Email: morganm@adea.org

http://www.adea.org
Purpose: To aid allied dental education students.
Eligibility: Applicants must be members of the American Dental Education Association (ADEA) and be enrolled in a dental hygiene, dental education or public health degree program. They must be in good academic standing and demonstrate leadership in dental education or health care. Selection is based on the overall strength of the application.
Target applicants: College students. Graduate school students. Adult students.
Amount: $1,000.
Number of awards: 1.
Deadline: November 1.
How to apply: Applications are available online. An application form, an official transcript, a personal statement and two reference letters are required.
Exclusive: Visit www.UltimateScholarshipBook.com and enter code AM70912 for updates on this award.

(710) • ADHA Institute Scholarship Program

American Dental Hygienists' Association (ADHA) Institute for Oral Health
Scholarship Award Program
444 North Michigan Avenue
Suite 3400
Chicago, IL 60611
Phone: 312-440-8900
Email: institute@adha.net
http://www.adha.org/ioh
Purpose: To assist students pursuing a career in dental hygiene.
Eligibility: Applicants should be enrolled full-time (unless applying for a part-time scholarship) in an accredited dental hygiene program in the U.S., be finishing their first year and have a minimum 3.0 GPA. Undergraduate students should be active members of the Student American Dental Hygienists' Association or the American Dental Hygienists Association. Graduate students should be active members of the Student American Dental Hygienists' Association or the American Dental Hygienists Association, have a valid dental hygiene license and a bachelor's degree. There should be financial need of at least $1,500, with the exception of the merit-based scholarships.
Target applicants: College students. Graduate school students. Adult students.
Minimum GPA: 3.0
Amount: $1,000-$2,000.
Number of awards: Varies.
Deadline: February 1.
How to apply: Applications are available online.
Exclusive: Visit www.UltimateScholarshipBook.com and enter code AM71012 for updates on this award.

(711) • AFCEA General John A. Wickham Scholarships

Armed Forces Communications and Electronics Association (AFCEA)
4400 Fair Lakes Court
Fairfax, VA 22033
Phone: 703-631-6149
Fax: 703-631-4693
http://www.afcea.org
Purpose: Monetary assistance for college is awarded to sophomores and juniors who are studying electrical, computer, chemical or aerospace engineering, computer science, physics or mathematics.
Eligibility: Applicants must be full-time college sophomores or juniors in accredited four-year U.S. colleges or universities, be U.S. citizens, be working toward a degree in electrical, computer, chemical or aerospace engineering, computer science, physics or mathematics and have a minimum 3.5 GPA. Applicants do not need to be affiliated with the U.S. military.
Target applicants: College students. Adult students.
Minimum GPA: 3.5
Amount: $2,000.
Number of awards: Varies.
Deadline: May 1.
How to apply: Applications are available online.
Exclusive: Visit www.UltimateScholarshipBook.com and enter code AR71112 for updates on this award.

(712) • AFCEA Ralph W. Shrader Diversity Scholarships

Armed Forces Communications and Electronics Association (AFCEA)
4400 Fair Lakes Court
Fairfax, VA 22033
Phone: 703-631-6149
Fax: 703-631-4693
http://www.afcea.org
Purpose: Monetary assistance is awarded to graduate students studying electrical, computer, chemical or aerospace engineering, mathematics, physics, computer science, computer technology, electronics, communications technology or engineering or information management systems.
Eligibility: Applicants must be U.S. citizens, full-time postgraduate students working toward a master's degree in electrical, computer, chemical or aerospace engineering, mathematics, physics, computer science, computer technology, electronics, communications technology, communications engineering or information management at an accredited U.S. university. Distance learning or online programs will not qualify. Primary consideration will be given for demonstrated excellence. Applicants do not need to be affiliated with the U.S. military.
Target applicants: Graduate school students. Adult students.
Amount: $3,000.
Number of awards: Varies.
Deadline: February 15.
How to apply: Applications are available online.
Exclusive: Visit www.UltimateScholarshipBook.com and enter code AR71212 for updates on this award.

(713) • AFCEA Scholarship for Working Professionals

Armed Forces Communications and Electronics Association (AFCEA)
4400 Fair Lakes Court
Fairfax, VA 22033
Phone: 703-631-6149
Fax: 703-631-4693
http://www.afcea.org
Purpose: To aid science and technology professionals who are pursuing undergraduate and graduate degrees.
Eligibility: Applicants must be U.S. citizens, be currently employed in the science or technology field and be graduate students or undergraduate sophomores, juniors or seniors. They must be enrolled part-time at an accredited U.S. postsecondary institution and be studying computer science, aerospace engineering, electrical engineering, chemical engineering, systems engineering, mathematics, physics, computer information systems, technical management or a related subject. They

must have a GPA of 3.0 or higher. Selection is based on the overall strength of the application.
Target applicants: College students. Graduate school students. Adult students.
Minimum GPA: 3.0
Amount: $2,000.
Number of awards: Varies.
Deadline: September 1.
How to apply: Applications are available online. An application form, official transcript and two recommendation letters are required.
Exclusive: Visit www.UltimateScholarshipBook.com and enter code AR71312 for updates on this award.

(714) • AFFIRM University Scholarship

Association for Federal Information Resources Management (AFFIRM)
P.O. Box 2848
Alexandria, VA 22301
Phone: 703-549-1160
Fax: 703-995-4890
Email: info@affirm.org
http://www.affirm.org
Purpose: To aid financially needy undergraduate students who are majoring in information technology (IT) or a related discipline at a participating college.
Eligibility: Students must be college juniors or seniors at one of the following schools: Carnegie Mellon University, George Mason University, George Washington University, LaSalle University, Syracuse University or the University of Maryland-University College. Applicants must be pursuing a degree in information technology (IT) or a related subject, must be enrolled full-time (12+ credits) and must have a cumulative GPA of 3.0 or more. Selection is based on academic merit, an academic letter of recommendation and financial need.
Target applicants: College students. Adult students.
Minimum GPA: 3.0
Amount: Varies.
Number of awards: Varies.
Deadline: Varies.
How to apply: Applications are available through each partner university's financial aid office. An application form and one recommendation letter is required.
Exclusive: Visit www.UltimateScholarshipBook.com and enter code AS71412 for updates on this award.

(715) • AfterCollege / AACN Nursing Scholarship Fund

American Association of Colleges of Nursing
One Dupont Circle NW
Suite 350
Washington, DC 20036
Phone: 202-463-6930
Fax: 202-785-8320
Email: anniea@aacn.nche.edu
http://www.aacn.nche.edu
Purpose: To assist students pursuing careers in nursing.
Eligibility: Applicants must be enrolled in a bachelor's, master's or doctoral program in nursing at an AACN member institution and have a minimum 3.25 GPA.
Target applicants: College students. Graduate school students. Adult students.
Minimum GPA: 3.25
Amount: $2,500.
Number of awards: 8 per year.
Deadline: January 31, April 30, July 31 and October 31.
How to apply: Applications are available online. Winners are announced within 60 days of each deadline.
Exclusive: Visit www.UltimateScholarshipBook.com and enter code AM71512 for updates on this award.

(716) • AGC Graduate Scholarships

Associated General Contractors of America
333 John Carlyle Street
Suite 200
Alexandria, VA 22314
Phone: 703-837-5342
Fax: 703-837-5402
Email: sladef@agc.org
http://www.agc.org
Purpose: Monetary assistance is awarded to college seniors pursuing graduate degrees that will lead to careers in construction or civil engineering.
Eligibility: Applicants must be college seniors enrolled in an undergraduate construction or civil engineering degree program or college graduates with a degree in construction or civil engineering. Applicants must also be enrolled or planning to enroll full-time in a graduate level construction or civil engineering degree program.
Target applicants: College students. Graduate school students. Adult students.
Amount: $7,500.
Number of awards: 2.
Deadline: November 1.
How to apply: Applications are available online.
Exclusive: Visit www.UltimateScholarshipBook.com and enter code AS71612 for updates on this award.

(717) • AGC Undergraduate Scholarships

Associated General Contractors of America
333 John Carlyle Street
Suite 200
Alexandria, VA 22314
Phone: 703-837-5342
Fax: 703-837-5402
Email: sladef@agc.org
http://www.agc.org
Purpose: To assist students pursuing studies that lead to a career in construction or civil engineering.
Eligibility: Applicants must be sophomores or juniors enrolled in or planning to enroll in ABET- or ACCE-accredited construction or civil engineering programs at four- or five-year colleges.
Target applicants: College students. Adult students.
Amount: $2,500.
Number of awards: Over 100.
Scholarship may be renewable.
Deadline: November 1.
How to apply: Applications are available online.
Exclusive: Visit www.UltimateScholarshipBook.com and enter code AS71712 for updates on this award.

(718) • AHIMA Foundation Merit Scholarships

American Health Information Management Association (AHIMA) Foundation

233 N. Michigan Avenue, 21st Floor
Chicago, IL 60601-5800
Phone: 312-233-1175
Email: info@ahimafoundation.org
http://www.ahimafoundation.org
Purpose: To provide merit scholarships to those enrolled in degree programs pursuing health information technology or health information administration.
Eligibility: Applicants must be members of AHIMA, have a minimum 3.0 GPA on a 4.0 scale, have at least six hours completed in health information management (HIM) or health information technology (HIT), have at least one semester remaining in their course of study and be taking at least six hours per semester in pursuit of the degree. The degrees eligible are AA degrees, BA/BS degrees and those who are credentialed and pursing a master's degree. Scholarships are also available for HIM professionals pursuing graduate degrees in the health information field.
Target applicants: College students. Graduate school students. Adult students.
Minimum GPA: 3.0
Amount: $2,500.
Number of awards: Up to 100.
Deadline: April 28.
How to apply: Applications are available online.
Exclusive: Visit www.UltimateScholarshipBook.com and enter code AM71812 for updates on this award.

(719) • AIA/AAF Minority / Disadvantaged Scholarship

American Architectural Foundation
1799 New York Avenue NW
Washington, DC 20006
Phone: 202-626-7318
Fax: 202-626-7420
Email: info@archfoundation.org
http://www.soanefoundation.com/fellowship.html
Purpose: To provide scholarships for students who intend to study architecture and who could not otherwise afford to enter a degree-seeking program.
Eligibility: Applicants must be high school seniors or college freshmen who intend to study architecture in an NAAB-accredited program. Transfer students from technical schools or community colleges who wish to attend an NAAB-accredited program are also eligible.
Target applicants: High school students. College students. Adult students.
Amount: $1,000-$2,500.
Number of awards: Up to 20.
Scholarship may be renewable.
Deadline: March 26.
How to apply: Applications are available by email. An application form and a recommendation letter are required.
Exclusive: Visit www.UltimateScholarshipBook.com and enter code AM71912 for updates on this award.

(720) • AIAA Foundation Undergraduate Scholarship Program

American Institute of Aeronautics and Astronautics
1801 Alexander Bell Drive
Suite 500
Reston, VA 20191-4344
Phone: 800-639-AIAA
Fax: 703-264-7551
Email: stephenb@aiaa.org
http://www.aiaa.org
Purpose: AIAA advances the arts, sciences and technology of aeronautics and astronautics.
Eligibility: Applicants must be enrolled in an accredited college or university and have completed at least one semester or quarter of college work with a minimum 3.3 GPA. Applicants must plan to enter a career in science or engineering related to the technical activities of the AIAA. Applicants do not have to be AIAA student members to apply but must join before accepting scholarships. Selection is based on scholarship, career goals, recommendations and extracurricular activities.
Target applicants: College students. Adult students.
Minimum GPA: 3.3
Amount: $2,000-$2,500.
Number of awards: 30.
Scholarship may be renewable.
Deadline: January 31.
How to apply: Applications are available online.
Exclusive: Visit www.UltimateScholarshipBook.com and enter code AM72012 for updates on this award.

(721) • Air Traffic Control Association Scholarship Program

Air Traffic Control Association
1101 King Street
Suite 300
Alexandria, VA 22134
Phone: 703-299-2430
Fax: 703-299-2437
Email: info@atca.org
http://www.atca.org
Purpose: To assist students enrolled in aviation-related courses and full-time air traffic control employees and their children.
Eligibility: Applicants must be enrolled or accepted into an accredited college or university and have coursework leading to a bachelor's or graduate degree related to an aviation related career, be full-time aviation employees pursuing advanced study in air traffic control or aviation or be the children of air traffic control specialists.
Target applicants: High school students. College students. Graduate school students. Adult students.
Amount: Varies.
Number of awards: Varies.
Deadline: May 1.
How to apply: Applications are available online.
Exclusive: Visit www.UltimateScholarshipBook.com and enter code AI72112 for updates on this award.

(722) • AIST Benjamin F. Fairless Scholarship (AIME)

Iron and Steel Society
Attn.: Lori Wharrey
AIST Foundation
186 Thorn Hill Road
Warrendale, PA 15086
Phone: 724-776-6040 x621
Fax: 724-776-1880
Email: lwharrey@aist.org
http://www.aistfoundation.org
Purpose: To honor the memory of Benjamin F. Fairless, former Chairman of the Board of U.S. Steel Corporation.

Eligibility: Applicants must be enrolled full-time in an accredited university in North America and majoring in engineering, metallurgy or materials science. Applicants must also have a GPA of 3.0 or higher and plan to pursue a career in the iron and steel industry.
Target applicants: College students. Graduate school students. Adult students.
Minimum GPA: 3.0
Amount: $2,000.
Number of awards: 3.
Deadline: March 4.
How to apply: Applications are available online.
Exclusive: Visit www.UltimateScholarshipBook.com and enter code IR72212 for updates on this award.

(723) • AIST Ronald E. Lincoln Memorial Scholarship

Iron and Steel Society
Attn.: Lori Wharrey
AIST Foundation
186 Thorn Hill Road
Warrendale, PA 15086
Phone: 724-776-6040 x621
Fax: 724-776-1880
Email: lwharrey@aist.org
http://www.aistfoundation.org
Purpose: To honor the memory of Ronald Lincoln and to reward students who demonstrate leadership and innovation.
Eligibility: Applicants must be enrolled full-time in an accredited university in North America and majoring in engineering, metallurgy or materials science. Applicants must also have a GPA of 3.0 or higher and plan to pursue a career in the iron and steel industry.
Target applicants: College students. Adult students.
Minimum GPA: 3.0
Amount: $3,000.
Number of awards: 2.
Deadline: March 4.
How to apply: Applications are available online.
Exclusive: Visit www.UltimateScholarshipBook.com and enter code IR72312 for updates on this award.

(724) • AIST William E. Schwabe Memorial Scholarship

Iron and Steel Society
Attn.: Lori Wharrey
AIST Foundation
186 Thorn Hill Road
Warrendale, PA 15086
Phone: 724-776-6040 x621
Fax: 724-776-1880
Email: lwharrey@aist.org
http://www.aistfoundation.org
Purpose: To honor the memory of William E. Schwabe, steelmaking pioneer.
Eligibility: Applicants must be enrolled full-time in an accredited university in North America and majoring in engineering, metallurgy or materials science. Applicants must also have a GPA of 3.0 or higher and plan to pursue a career in the iron and steel industry.
Target applicants: College students. Adult students.
Minimum GPA: 3.0
Amount: $3,000.
Number of awards: 1.
Deadline: March 4.
How to apply: Applications are available online.
Exclusive: Visit www.UltimateScholarshipBook.com and enter code IR72412 for updates on this award.

(725) • AIST Willy Korf Memorial Fund

Iron and Steel Society
Attn.: Lori Wharrey
AIST Foundation
186 Thorn Hill Road
Warrendale, PA 15086
Phone: 724-776-6040 x621
Fax: 724-776-1880
Email: lwharrey@aist.org
http://www.aistfoundation.org
Purpose: To honor the memory of the late Willy Korf, the founder of the Korf Group and to assist students who plan to enter the fields of engineering, metallurgy or materials science in the iron and steel industry.
Eligibility: Applicants must be enrolled full-time in an accredited university in North America and majoring in engineering, metallurgy or materials science. Applicants must also have a GPA of 3.0 or higher and plan to pursue a career in the iron and steel industry.
Target applicants: College students. Adult students.
Minimum GPA: 3.0
Amount: $3,000.
Number of awards: 3.
Deadline: March 4.
How to apply: Applications are available online.
Exclusive: Visit www.UltimateScholarshipBook.com and enter code IR72512 for updates on this award.

(726) • Alice T. Schafer Prize

Association for Women in Mathematics
4114 Computer and Space Sciences Building
University of Maryland
College Park, MD 20742
Phone: 301-405-7892
Fax: 301-314-9074
Email: awm@math.umd.edu
http://www.awm-math.org
Purpose: To support female students who are studying mathematics.
Eligibility: Nominees must be female college undergraduates and either be U.S. citizens or have a school address in the U.S. Selection is based on performance in advanced mathematics courses and special programs, interest in mathematics, ability to conduct independent work and performance in mathematical competitions at the local or national level.
Target applicants: College students. Adult students.
Amount: Varies.
Number of awards: 1-2.
Deadline: October 1.
How to apply: Applicants must be nominated.
Exclusive: Visit www.UltimateScholarshipBook.com and enter code AS72612 for updates on this award.

(727) • Alice W. Rooke Scholarship

National Society Daughters of the American Revolution
Committee Services Office
Attn.: Scholarships
1776 D Street NW
Washington, DC 20006-5303
Phone: 202-628-1776
http://www.dar.org

Purpose: To assist students in becoming medical doctors.
Eligibility: Applicants must be accepted into or enrolled in a graduate course of study to become a medical doctor. All applicants must obtain a letter of sponsorship from their local DAR chapter. However, affiliation with DAR is not required.
Target applicants: Graduate school students. Adult students.
Amount: Up to $5,000.
Number of awards: Varies.
Scholarship may be renewable.
Deadline: April 15.
How to apply: Applications are available by written request with a self-addressed, stamped envelope.
Exclusive: Visit www.UltimateScholarshipBook.com and enter code NA72712 for updates on this award.

---

(728) • Allied Dental Health Scholarships

American Dental Association Foundation
211 East Chicago Avenue
Chicago, IL 60611
Phone: 312-440-2763
Fax: 312-440-3526
Email: famularor@ada.org
http://www.ada.org
Purpose: To encourage students to pursue careers in dental hygiene, dental assisting, dentistry and dental laboratory technology.
Eligibility: Applicants must be either in their final year of study in an accredited dental hygiene program, entering students in an accredited dental assisting program or in their final year of study in an accredited dental laboratory technician program. Selection is based on minimum financial need of $1,000, academic achievement, a biographical sketch and references. A minimum 3.0 GPA is required. Only two scholarship applications per school are allowed, so schools may set their own in-school application deadlines that are earlier.
Target applicants: College students. Graduate school students. Adult students.
Minimum GPA: 3.0
Amount: $1,000.
Number of awards: 30.
Deadline: June 11.
How to apply: Applications are available from dental school officials.
Exclusive: Visit www.UltimateScholarshipBook.com and enter code AM72812 for updates on this award.

---

(729) • Alpha Mu Tau Fraternity Scholarships

American Society for Clinical Laboratory Science
6701 Democracy Boulevard, Suite 300
Bethesda, MD 20817
Phone: 301-657-2768
Fax: 301-657-2909
Email: ascls@ascls.org
http://www.ascls.org
Purpose: To support new professionals in the clinical laboratory sciences.
Eligibility: Applicants must be undergraduate students entering or in their last year of study in an NAACLS-accredited program in Clinical Laboratory Science/Medical Technology or Clinical Laboratory Technician/Medical Laboratory Technician. Applicants must be a U.S. citizen or a permanent resident of the U.S.
Target applicants: College students. Adult students.
Amount: Up to $1,500.
Number of awards: Varies.
Deadline: April 1.
How to apply: Applications are available online.
Exclusive: Visit www.UltimateScholarshipBook.com and enter code AM72912 for updates on this award.

---

(730) • AMBUCS Scholars

AMBUCS
P.O. Box 5127
High Point, NC 27262
Phone: 800-838-1845
Fax: 336-852-6830
Email: janiceb@ambucs.org
http://www.ambucs.org
Purpose: To provide more opportunities for the disabled by encouraging students to become therapists.
Eligibility: Applicants must be undergraduate juniors or seniors or graduate students pursuing their master's or doctoral degrees and must have been accepted into an accredited program in physical therapy, occupational therapy, speech language pathology or hearing audiology. Assistant programs are ineligible. Selection is based on financial need, U.S. citizenship, community service, academic achievement, character and career plans.
Target applicants: College students. Graduate school students. Adult students.
Amount: $500-$6,000.
Number of awards: Varies.
Deadline: April 15.
How to apply: Applications are available online.
Exclusive: Visit www.UltimateScholarshipBook.com and enter code AM73012 for updates on this award.

---

(731) • Amelia Earhart Fellowships

Zonta International
1211 West 22nd Street
Oak Brook, IL 60523
Phone: 630-928-1400
Fax: 630-928-1559
Email: zontaintl@zonta.org
http://www.zonta.org
Purpose: To support women in science and engineering.
Eligibility: Applicants must be pursuing graduate PhD/doctoral degrees in aerospace-related sciences and aerospace-related engineering.
Target applicants: Graduate school students. Adult students.
Amount: Up to $10,000.
Number of awards: 35.
Deadline: November 15.
Exclusive: Visit www.UltimateScholarshipBook.com and enter code ZO73112 for updates on this award.

---

(732) • American Architectural Foundation and Sir John Soane's Museum Foundation Traveling Fellowship

American Architectural Foundation
1799 New York Avenue NW
Washington, DC 20006
Phone: 202-626-7318
Fax: 202-626-7420
Email: info@archfoundation.org
http://www.soanefoundation.com/fellowship.html

Purpose: To provide scholarships enabling graduate students to travel to England and to study the work of Sir John Soane (or Sir John Soane's Museum and its collections).
Eligibility: Applicants must be enrolled in graduate programs focusing on the history of art, architecture, decorative arts or interior design.
Target applicants: Graduate school students. Adult students.
Amount: $5,000.
Number of awards: 1.
Deadline: March 1.
How to apply: Applications are available online.
Exclusive: Visit www.UltimateScholarshipBook.com and enter code AM73212 for updates on this award.

(733) • American Quarter Horse Foundation Scholarship

American Quarter Horse Foundation
Scholarship Program
2601 East Interstate 40
Amarillo, TX 79104
Phone: 806-378-5029
Fax: 806-376-1005
Email: foundation@aqha.org
http://www.aqha.com
Purpose: To encourage future Quarter Horse industry professionals.
Eligibility: Applicants must demonstrate involvement in equine-related activities and be members of American Quarter Horse Association (AQHA) or American Quarter Horse Youth Association (AQHYA) for a minimum of up to three years, depending on the scholarship. Selection is based on financial need, academic achievement, equine involvement, references and career plans. A transcript and three references are required for all scholarships. All other requirements vary by scholarship.
Target applicants: High school students. College students. Graduate school students. Adult students.
Amount: Varies.
Number of awards: Varies.
Scholarship may be renewable.
Deadline: December 1.
How to apply: Applications are available online.
Exclusive: Visit www.UltimateScholarshipBook.com and enter code AM73312 for updates on this award.

(734) • AMS / Industry / Government Graduate Fellowships

American Meteorological Society
Fellowship and Scholarship Department
45 Beacon Street
Boston, MA 02108-3693
Phone: 617-227-2426 x246
Fax: 617-742-8718
Email: dsampson@ametsoc.org
http://www.ametsoc.org/AMS/
Purpose: To attract students to prepare for careers in the meteorological, oceanic and hydrologic fields.
Eligibility: Applicants must be entering their first year of graduate study the following year and plan to pursue advanced degrees in the atmospheric and related oceanic and hydrologic sciences. Awards are based on undergraduate performance. References, transcripts and GRE scores may be sent under separate cover. References can be sent to dfernand@ametsoc.org.
Target applicants: College students. Adult students.
Minimum GPA: 3.25
Amount: $22,000.
Number of awards: Varies.
Deadline: February 5.
How to apply: Applications are available online.
Exclusive: Visit www.UltimateScholarshipBook.com and enter code AM73412 for updates on this award.

(735) • AMS Graduate Fellowship in the History of Science

American Meteorological Society
Fellowship and Scholarship Department
45 Beacon Street
Boston, MA 02108-3693
Phone: 617-227-2426 x246
Fax: 617-742-8718
Email: dsampson@ametsoc.org
http://www.ametsoc.org/AMS/
Purpose: To support students writing dissertations on the history of atmospheric or related oceanic or hydrologic sciences.
Eligibility: Applicants must be graduate students who plan to write dissertations on the history of atmospheric or related oceanic or hydrologic sciences. Students must submit a cover letter with vitae, official transcripts, a typed description of the dissertation topic and three letters of recommendation.
Target applicants: Graduate school students. Adult students.
Amount: $15,000.
Number of awards: Varies.
Deadline: February 11.
How to apply: Submit materials to address listed.
Exclusive: Visit www.UltimateScholarshipBook.com and enter code AM73512 for updates on this award.

(736) • AMS Undergraduate Scholarships

American Meteorological Society
Fellowship and Scholarship Department
45 Beacon Street
Boston, MA 02108-3693
Phone: 617-227-2426 x246
Fax: 617-742-8718
Email: dsampson@ametsoc.org
http://www.ametsoc.org/AMS/
Purpose: To encourage undergraduate students to pursue careers in the atmospheric and related oceanic and hydrologic sciences.
Eligibility: Applicants must be full-time students majoring in the atmospheric or related oceanic or hydrologic science and entering their final undergraduate year, show intent to make the atmospheric or related sciences their career and have a minimum 3.25 GPA. For the Schroeder scholarship, applicants must demonstrate financial need. For the Murphy scholarship, applicants must demonstrate interest in weather forecasting through curricular or extracurricular activities and for the Crow scholarship, applicants must demonstrate interest in applied meteorology. The Glahn scholarship will be awarded to a student with a strong interest in statistical meteorology.
Target applicants: College students. Adult students.
Minimum GPA: 3.25
Amount: Varies.
Number of awards: Varies.
Deadline: February 11.
How to apply: Applications are available online.
Exclusive: Visit www.UltimateScholarshipBook.com and enter code AM73612 for updates on this award.

(737) · AMS/Industry Minority Scholarships

American Meteorological Society
Fellowship and Scholarship Department
45 Beacon Street
Boston, MA 02108-3693
Phone: 617-227-2426 x246
Fax: 617-742-8718
Email: dsampson@ametsoc.org
http://www.ametsoc.org/AMS/

Purpose: To support minority students who have been traditionally underrepresented in the sciences, especially Hispanic, Native American and African American students.

Eligibility: Applicants must be minority students who will be entering their freshman year of college in the following fall and must plan to pursue degrees in the atmospheric or related oceanic and hydrologic sciences. Applicants must submit applications, transcripts, recommendation letters and SAT or equivalent scores. Original materials should be mailed to the closest AMS Local Chapter listed at the bottom of the application, and copies should be mailed to headquarters.

Target applicants: High school students.
Amount: $3,000.
Number of awards: Varies.
Scholarship may be renewable.
Deadline: February 11.
How to apply: Applications are available online.
Exclusive: Visit www.UltimateScholarshipBook.com and enter code AM73712 for updates on this award.

(738) · AMT Student Scholarship

American Medical Technologists
10700 W. Higgins Road
Rosemont, IL 60018
Phone: 800-275-1268
Fax: 847-823-0458
http://www.amt1.com

Purpose: To provide financial assistance to students interested in medical technology careers.

Eligibility: Applicants must be high school graduates or current seniors planning to attend an accredited institution to pursue an American Medical Technologists-certified career, which includes medical laboratory technology, medical assisting, dental assisting, phlebotomy and office laboratory technician.

Target applicants: High school students.
Amount: $500.
Number of awards: 5.
Deadline: April 1.
How to apply: Applications are available online.
Exclusive: Visit www.UltimateScholarshipBook.com and enter code AM73812 for updates on this award.

(739) · Amtrol Inc. Scholarship

American Ground Water Trust
16 Centre Street
Concord, NH 03301
Phone: 603-228-5444
Fax: 603-228-6557
http://www.agwt.org

Purpose: To provide scholarships for high school seniors to pursue a career in a ground water-related field.

Eligibility: Applicants must be high school seniors with intentions to pursue a career in ground water management or a related field. Students must be entering their freshman year at a four-year accredited institution. Prior research or experience with the field is required.

Target applicants: High school students.
Minimum GPA: 3.0
Amount: $1,000.
Number of awards: Varies.
Deadline: June 1.
How to apply: Applications are available online.
Exclusive: Visit www.UltimateScholarshipBook.com and enter code AM73912 for updates on this award.

(740) · Angus Foundation Scholarship

American Foundation
3201 Frederick Avenue
St. Joseph, MO 64506
Phone: 816-383-5100
Fax: 816-233-9703
Email: angus@angus.org
http://www.angusfoundation.org

Purpose: To provide scholarships to youth active in the Angus breed.

Eligibility: Applicants must have been members of the National Junior Angus Association and must be junior, regular or life members of the American Angus Association at the time of application. Applicants must be high school seniors or enrolled in a junior college, four-year college or other accredited institution of post-secondary education in an undergraduate program and have a minimum 2.0 GPA. Students may not have reached their 25th birthday by January 1 of the year of application.

Target applicants: High school students. College students.
Minimum GPA: 2.0
Amount: $1,000-$5,000.
Number of awards: 52.
Deadline: May 1.
How to apply: Applications are available online or by written request.
Exclusive: Visit www.UltimateScholarshipBook.com and enter code AM74012 for updates on this award.

(741) · Annie's Sustainable Agriculture Scholarships

Annie's Homegrown Inc.
564 Gateway Drive
Napa, CA 94558
Phone: 800-288-1089
Email: scholarships@annies.com
http://www.annies.com

Purpose: To aid undergraduate and graduate students preparing for careers in sustainable foods and organic agriculture.

Eligibility: Applicants must be full-time undergraduate or graduate students attending an institution of higher learning located in the United States. They must be in the process of completing a significant amount of coursework in sustainable agriculture. Selection is based on the overall strength of the application.

Target applicants: High school students. College students. Graduate school students. Adult students.
Amount: $2,500-$10,000.
Number of awards: Varies.
Deadline: Varies.

How to apply: Applications are available online. An application form, personal statement, transcript and two letters of recommendation are required.
Exclusive: Visit www.UltimateScholarshipBook.com and enter code AN74112 for updates on this award.

(742) · Annual NBNA Scholarships

National Black Nurses Association
8630 Fenton Street
Suite 330
Silver Spring, MD 20910
Phone: 800-575-6298
Fax: 301-589-3223
Email: nbna@erols.com
http://www.nbna.org
Purpose: To promote excellence in education and in continuing education programs for African American nurses and allied health professionals.
Eligibility: Applicants must be African Americans currently enrolled in a nursing program and be in good academic standing, be members of the NBNA, be members of a local chapter and have at least a full year of school remaining. Applicants must submit with their application an essay, references, an official transcript and evidence of participation in student nurse activities and involvement in the African American community.
Target applicants: College students. Adult students.
Amount: $500-$2,000.
Number of awards: Varies.
Deadline: April 15.
How to apply: Applications are available online.
Exclusive: Visit www.UltimateScholarshipBook.com and enter code NA74212 for updates on this award.

(743) · ANS Graduate Scholarship

American Nuclear Society
555 North Kensington Avenue
La Grange Park, IL 60526
Phone: 800-323-3044
Fax: 708-352-0499
Email: hr@ans.org
http://www.ans.org
Purpose: To assist full-time graduate students who are pursuing advanced degrees in a nuclear-related field.
Eligibility: Applicants must be full-time students at an accredited graduate school in a program leading to an advanced degree in nuclear science, nuclear engineering or a nuclear-related field. There are also individual graduate scholarships. Applicants should submit applications, transcripts, recommendation letter and three reference forms.
Target applicants: Graduate school students. Adult students.
Amount: Varies.
Number of awards: Up to 29.
Deadline: February 1.
How to apply: Applications are available online.
Exclusive: Visit www.UltimateScholarshipBook.com and enter code AM74312 for updates on this award.

(744) · ANS Incoming Freshman Scholarships

American Nuclear Society
555 North Kensington Avenue
La Grange Park, IL 60526
Phone: 800-323-3044
Fax: 708-352-0499
Email: hr@ans.org
http://www.ans.org
Purpose: To aid high school seniors who are planning to major in nuclear engineering at the undergraduate level.
Eligibility: Applicants must be graduating high school seniors who have been accepted at an accredited postsecondary institution. They must have plans to major in nuclear engineering. Selection is based on academic merit, personal essay and recommendations.
Target applicants: High school students.
Amount: $1,000.
Number of awards: Up to 4.
Deadline: April 1.
How to apply: Applications are available online. An application form, personal essay, two letters of recommendation and an official transcript are required.
Exclusive: Visit www.UltimateScholarshipBook.com and enter code AM74412 for updates on this award.

(745) · ANS Undergraduate Scholarship

American Nuclear Society
555 North Kensington Avenue
La Grange Park, IL 60526
Phone: 800-323-3044
Fax: 708-352-0499
Email: hr@ans.org
http://www.ans.org
Purpose: To assist undergraduate students who are pursuing careers in the field of nuclear science.
Eligibility: Applicants must be at least sophomores or students who have completed two or more years and will be entering as juniors or seniors in an accredited university and must be enrolled in a program leading to a degree in nuclear science, nuclear engineering or a nuclear-related field. Applicants should submit applications, transcripts, recommendation letter and three reference forms. There are individual undergraduate scholarships for students who have completed two or more years in a course of study leading to a degree in nuclear science, nuclear engineering or a nuclear-related field.
Target applicants: College students. Adult students.
Amount: Varies.
Number of awards: Up to 37.
Deadline: February 1.
How to apply: Applications are available online.
Exclusive: Visit www.UltimateScholarshipBook.com and enter code AM74512 for updates on this award.

(746) · Antoinette Lierman Medlin Scholarship

Geological Society of America
Program Officer
Grants, Awards and Recognition
P.O. Box 9140
Boulder, CO 80301-9140
Phone: 303-357-1028
Fax: 303-357-1070
Email: awards@geosociety.org
http://www.geosociety.org
Purpose: To assist full-time students involved in research in coal geology.
Eligibility: Applicants must be full-time students who are conducting research in coal geology pertaining to origin, occurrence, geologic characteristics or economic implications.

Target applicants: Graduate school students. Adult students.
Amount: $1,500-$2,000.
Number of awards: 2.
Deadline: February 15.
How to apply: No application is necessary. Students must send a cover letter, proposal and letter of recommendation.
Exclusive: Visit www.UltimateScholarshipBook.com and enter code GE74612 for updates on this award.

(747) • AOC Scholarships

Association of Old Crows
1000 N. Payne Street
Suite 300
Alexandria, VA 22314-1652
Phone: 703-549-1600
Fax: 703-549-2589
Email: richetti@crows.org
http://www.crows.org
Purpose: To encourage students interested in strong defense capability emphasizing electronic warfare and information operations.
Eligibility: Applicants should consult their AOC chapters for scholarship guidelines.
Target applicants: College students. Graduate school students. Adult students.
Amount: Varies.
Number of awards: Varies.
Deadline: Varies.
How to apply: Applications are available online.
Exclusive: Visit www.UltimateScholarshipBook.com and enter code AS74712 for updates on this award.

(748) • AORN Foundation Scholarship Program

Association of Perioperative Registered Nurses
2170 S. Parker Road
Suite 300
Denver, CO 80231
Phone: 800-755-2676
Email: sstokes@aorn.org
http://www.aorn.org
Purpose: To encourage the education of nurses and future nurses.
Eligibility: Applicants must be current nursing students or AORN members accepted to an accredited program and have a minimum 3.0 GPA. Applicants must also demonstrate financial need.
Target applicants: College students. Graduate school students. Adult students.
Minimum GPA: 3.0
Amount: Varies.
Number of awards: Varies.
Deadline: June 15.
How to apply: Applications are available online.
Exclusive: Visit www.UltimateScholarshipBook.com and enter code AS74812 for updates on this award.

(749) • AOS Master's Scholarship Program

American Orchid Society
16700 AOS Lane
Delray Beach, FL 33446-4351
Phone: 561-404-2000
Fax: 561-404-2045
Email: theaos@aos.org
http://www.aos.org
Purpose: To provide a two-year scholarship for completing a master's thesis on orchid education, orchidology or a related topic.
Eligibility: Applicants must be enrolled in a master's program at an accredited institution. The thesis project must focus on orchid education, applied science or orchid biology. The scholarship is limited to two consecutive years.
Target applicants: Graduate school students. Adult students.
Amount: $5,000.
Number of awards: Varies.
Scholarship may be renewable.
Deadline: Varies.
How to apply: Applications are available online.
Exclusive: Visit www.UltimateScholarshipBook.com and enter code AM74912 for updates on this award.

(750) • Appaloosa Youth Association Art Contest

Appaloosa Horse Club
Appaloosa Youth Foundation Scholarship Committee
2720 W. Pullman Road
Moscow, ID 83843
Phone: 208-882-5578
Fax: 208-882-8150
Email: acaap@appaloosa.com
http://www.appaloosa.com
Purpose: To allow students to showcase their artistic talents with Appaloosa-themed projects.
Eligibility: Applicants age 18 and under should submit drawings, paintings and hand-built ceramics or sculptures with the Appaloosa theme. There are two age divisions: 13 and under and 14 to 18. Awards are based on originality, creativity and the theme.
Target applicants: Junior high students or younger. High school students.
Amount: Varies.
Number of awards: 3.
Deadline: May 1.
How to apply: Applications are available online.
Exclusive: Visit www.UltimateScholarshipBook.com and enter code AP75012 for updates on this award.

(751) • Appaloosa Youth Association Essay Contest

Appaloosa Horse Club
Appaloosa Youth Foundation Scholarship Committee
2720 W. Pullman Road
Moscow, ID 83843
Phone: 208-882-5578
Fax: 208-882-8150
Email: acaap@appaloosa.com
http://www.appaloosa.com
Purpose: To reward students for essays that demonstrate their love of the Appaloosa breed.
Eligibility: Applicants must be 18 and under and should submit entry forms and essays on the provided themes. There are two age divisions: 13 and under and 14 to 18. Awards are based on originality and accuracy.
Target applicants: Junior high students or younger. High school students.
Amount: Varies.
Number of awards: Varies.
Deadline: May 1.
How to apply: Applications are available online.

Exclusive: Visit www.UltimateScholarshipBook.com and enter code AP75112 for updates on this award.

(752) • Appaloosa Youth Association Speech Contest

Appaloosa Horse Club
Appaloosa Youth Foundation Scholarship Committee
2720 W. Pullman Road
Moscow, ID 83843
Phone: 208-882-5578
Fax: 208-882-8150
Email: acaap@appaloosa.com
http://www.appaloosa.com

Purpose: To reward students for their speeches on Appaloosa.
Eligibility: Applicants should be 18 and under and can enter two divisions: a speech on a pre-determined topic or an impromptu speech. Age groups are 13 and under and 14 to 18. The speech is given at the World Championship Appaloosa Youth World Show.
Target applicants: Junior high students or younger. High school students.
Amount: $250.
Number of awards: Varies.
Deadline: June 1.
How to apply: Applications are available online.
Exclusive: Visit www.UltimateScholarshipBook.com and enter code AP75212 for updates on this award.

(753) • Apprentice Ecologist Initiative Youth Scholarship Program

Nicodemus Wilderness Project
P.O. Box 40712
Albuquerque, NM 87196
Email: mail@wildernessproject.org
http://www.wildernessproject.org

Purpose: To aid ecologically-minded youth.
Eligibility: Applicants must be students who are between the ages of 13 and 21. They must devise and complete an environmental conservation project then write an essay describing the experience. Selection is based on the quality of the project and essay.
Target applicants: Junior high students or younger. High school students. College students.
Amount: $850.
Number of awards: 3.
Deadline: December 31.
How to apply: Application instructions are available online. An essay and a project photo are required.
Exclusive: Visit www.UltimateScholarshipBook.com and enter code NI75312 for updates on this award.

(754) • APS Minority Scholarship

American Physical Society
One Physics Ellipse
College Park, MD 20740-3844
Phone: 301-209-3200
Fax: 301-209-0865
Email: wilson@aps.org
http://www.aps.org

Purpose: To assist minorities studying physics.
Eligibility: Applicants must be African-American, Hispanic American or Native American U.S. citizens or permanent residents who plan to or are majoring in physics. Applicants must be high school seniors, college freshmen or college sophomores.
Target applicants: High school students. College students. Adult students.
Amount: Varies.
Number of awards: Varies.
Scholarship may be renewable.
Deadline: February 1.
How to apply: Applications are available online.
Exclusive: Visit www.UltimateScholarshipBook.com and enter code AM75412 for updates on this award.

(755) • ARM Undergraduate Student Fellowships

Academia Resource Management
535 E 4500 S, Suite D120
Salt Lake City, UT 84107-2988
Phone: 801-273-8911
Fax: 801-277-5632
Email: info@armanagement.org
http://www.armanagement.org

Purpose: To support scientific and technological study in non-academic settings under the guidance of mentors at sponsoring facilities.
Eligibility: Applicants must plan to be science or technology interns or fellows at national laboratories and sponsoring institutions and be undergraduates in any accredited institution within six months of the start of their award. The award is based on academic performance, career goals, recommendations and compatibility with the host facility. Applications, a recommendation letter and transcripts are required. Applicants do not need to be enrolled in an ARM member institution to apply.
Target applicants: College students. Adult students.
Amount: Varies.
Number of awards: Varies.
Deadline: February 15.
How to apply: Applications are available online.
Exclusive: Visit www.UltimateScholarshipBook.com and enter code AC75512 for updates on this award.

(756) • ASAE Foundation Scholarship

American Society of Agricultural Engineers Foundation
Administrator
Scholarship Fund
2950 Niles Road
St. Joseph, MI 49085
Phone: 269-429-0300
Fax: 269-429-3852
http://www.asae.org

Purpose: To assist student members of ASAE.
Eligibility: Applicants must have completed at least one year of undergraduate study and have at least one year of undergraduate study remaining, major in agricultural or biological engineering at an eligible accredited degree program in the U.S. or Canada, have a minimum 2.5 GPA and demonstrate financial need.
Target applicants: College students. Adult students.
Minimum GPA: 2.5
Amount: $1,000.
Number of awards: 1.
Deadline: March 17.
How to apply: Application is by formal letter.
Exclusive: Visit www.UltimateScholarshipBook.com and enter code AM75612 for updates on this award.

(757) • ASCA/AISC Student Design Competition

Association of Collegiate Schools of Architecture
1735 New York Avenue NW
Washington, DC 20006
Phone: 202-765-2324
Fax: 202-628-0448
http://www.acsa-arch.org/competitions/home.aspx
Purpose: To encourage innovation in architecture.
Eligibility: Applicants must be architecture students at ACSA member schools in the United States, Canada or Mexico and be college juniors, seniors or graduate students. Students must submit a design project on one of the association's featured themes, and they must work under the direction of a faculty sponsor.
Target applicants: College students. Graduate school students. Adult students.
Amount: Up to $2,500.
Number of awards: 6.
Deadline: February 8.
How to apply: Applications are available online.
Exclusive: Visit www.UltimateScholarshipBook.com and enter code AS75712 for updates on this award.

(758) • ASDSO Dam Safety Scholarships

Association of State Dam Safety Officials
450 Old Vine Street
2nd Floor
Lexington, KY 40507
Phone: 859-257-5140
Fax: 859-323-1958
Email: info@damsafety.org
http://www.damsafety.org
Purpose: To increase awareness of careers in dam safety.
Eligibility: Applicants must be full-time seniors in an accredited civil engineering program or a related field and show an interest in a career related to dam design, construction or operation. Students must have a minimum 2.5 GPA for the first two years of college, be recommended by their academic advisor and write an essay on what ASDSO is and why dam safety is important. Financial need is considered.
Target applicants: College students. Adult students.
Minimum GPA: 2.5
Amount: Up to $10,000.
Number of awards: Varies.
Deadline: March 31.
How to apply: Applications are available online.
Exclusive: Visit www.UltimateScholarshipBook.com and enter code AS75812 for updates on this award.

(759) • ASEV Scholarships

American Society for Enology and Viticulture
P.O. Box 1855
Davis, CA 95617-1855
Phone: 530-753-3142
Fax: 530-753-3318
Email: society@asev.org
http://www.asev.org
Purpose: To support those seeking a degree in enology, viticulture or in a curriculum focusing on a science basic to the wine and grape industry.
Eligibility: Applicants must be undergraduate or graduate students enrolled in or accepted into a full-time accredited four-year university program, must reside in North America (Canada, Mexico or the U.S.) and must be at least juniors for the upcoming academic year. Applicants must be enrolled in a major or in a graduate group concentrating on enology or viticulture or in a curriculum with a focus on a science basic to the wine and grape industry. The application, transcripts and two letters of recommendation are required.
Target applicants: College students. Graduate school students. Adult students.
Minimum GPA: 3.0 for undergraduate students and 3.2 for graduate students
Amount: Varies.
Number of awards: Varies.
Deadline: March 1.
How to apply: Applications are available online, by phone or by email.
Exclusive: Visit www.UltimateScholarshipBook.com and enter code AM75912 for updates on this award.

(760) • ASF Olin Fellowships

Atlantic Salmon Federation
P.O. Box 807
Calais, ME 04619-0807
Phone: 506-529-1033
Fax: 506-529-4438
Email: asfweb@nbnet.nb.ca
http://www.asf.ca
Purpose: To help fund projects that focus on solving problems in Atlantic salmon biology, management and conservation.
Eligibility: Applicants must be studying or actively engaged in salmon management or research. The award is open to U.S. and Canadian applicants.
Target applicants: College students. Graduate school students. Adult students.
Amount: $1,000-$3,000.
Number of awards: Varies.
Deadline: March 15.
How to apply: Applications are available by mail.
Exclusive: Visit www.UltimateScholarshipBook.com and enter code AT76012 for updates on this award.

(761) • ASHA Youth Scholarships

American Saddlebred Horse Association Foundation
4083 Iron Works Parkway
Lexington, KY 40511
Phone: 859-259-2742 x343
Fax: 859-259-1628
http://www.saddlebred.com
Purpose: To help youths involved with Saddlebreds.
Eligibility: This award is based on academic excellence, financial need, extracurricular activities, community service, involvement with American Saddlebred horses and personal references. An interview may be part of the selection process. Applicants should write an essay about school experiences, special interests, hobbies and American Saddlebred Horse Association activities. Scholarships are given only to high school seniors or recent graduates.
Target applicants: High school students.
Amount: $2,500-$5,000.
Number of awards: 6.
Deadline: April 30.
How to apply: Applications are available online.
Exclusive: Visit www.UltimateScholarshipBook.com and enter code AM76112 for updates on this award.

(762) • ASHRAE Scholarship Program

American Society of Heating, Refrigerating and Air-Conditioning Engineers
1791 Tullie Circle, NE
Atlanta, GA 30329
Phone: 404-636-8400
Fax: 404-321-5478
Email: lbenedict@ashrae.org
http://www.ashrae.org

Purpose: To encourage heating, ventilating, air conditioning and refrigeration education.

Eligibility: Applicants must be full-time undergraduates majoring in engineering or engineering technology or graduate students in a related course of study approved by the Accreditation Board for Engineering and Technology (ABET) or another accrediting agency recognized by ASHRAE with a minimum 3.0 GPA. Selection is based on financial need, leadership, character and potential contribution to the heating, ventilating, air conditioning or refrigeration profession. Applicants must also submit recommendations from instructors.

Target applicants: College students. Graduate school students. Adult students.

Minimum GPA: 3.0

Amount: $3,000-$10,000.

Number of awards: Varies.

Deadline: December 1.

How to apply: Applications are available online.

Exclusive: Visit www.UltimateScholarshipBook.com and enter code AM76212 for updates on this award.

(763) • ASM Foundation Scholarship Awards

ASM International Foundation
9639 Kinsman Road
Materials Park, OH 44073
Phone: 440-338-5151
Fax: 440-338-4634
Email: asmif@asminternational.org
http://asmcommunity.asminternational.org/portal/site/www/Foundation

Purpose: To support undergraduates studying metallurgy or materials science engineering.

Eligibility: Applicants must be student members of ASM International, major in metallurgy or materials science engineering and be juniors or seniors at a North American university that has a bachelor's degree program in science and engineering. Applications, personal statements, transcripts, two recommendation forms and photographs are required. The award is based on academics, interest in the metallurgy/materials engineering field and character.

Target applicants: College students. Adult students.

Amount: Varies.

Number of awards: 37.

Deadline: May 1.

How to apply: Applications are available online.

Exclusive: Visit www.UltimateScholarshipBook.com and enter code AS76312 for updates on this award.

(764) • ASM Outstanding Scholars Awards

ASM International Foundation
9639 Kinsman Road
Materials Park, OH 44073
Phone: 440-338-5151
Fax: 440-338-4634
Email: asmif@asminternational.org
http://asmcommunity.asminternational.org/portal/site/www/Foundation

Purpose: To recognize distinguished scholars in metallurgy or materials science engineering.

Eligibility: Applicants must be student members of ASM International, major in metallurgy or materials science engineering and be juniors or seniors at a North American university that has a bachelor's degree program in science and engineering. Applications, personal statements, transcripts, two recommendation forms and photographs are required. The award is based on academics, interest in the metallurgy/materials engineering field and personal character.

Target applicants: College students. Adult students.

Amount: $2,000.

Number of awards: 3.

Deadline: May 1.

How to apply: Applications are available online.

Exclusive: Visit www.UltimateScholarshipBook.com and enter code AS76412 for updates on this award.

(765) • ASME Foundation Scholarships

American Society of Mechanical Engineers (ASME)
Three Park Avenue
New York, NY 10016
Phone: 800-843-2763
Fax: 973-882-1717
Email: infocentral@asme.org
http://www.asme.org

Purpose: To aid ASME student members who are enrolled in an undergraduate mechanical engineering, mechanical engineering technology or related degree program.

Eligibility: Applicants must be current ASME student members who are currently enrolled in (or have been accepted into) an ABET-accredited (or similarly accredited) undergraduate degree program in mechanical engineering, mechanical engineering technology or a subject related to one of these. They must be rising or current sophomores, juniors or seniors. Selection is based on academic achievement and professional potential in engineering.

Target applicants: College students. Adult students.

Amount: $1,500.

Number of awards: Up to 17.

Deadline: March 1.

How to apply: Applications are available online through an electronic application system. Current ASME membership, submittal of application through the online system, a transcript and recommendation letters are required.

Exclusive: Visit www.UltimateScholarshipBook.com and enter code AM76512 for updates on this award.

(766) • ASME Foundation-ASME Auxiliary FIRST Clarke Scholarship

American Society of Mechanical Engineers (ASME)
Three Park Avenue
New York, NY 10016
Phone: 800-843-2763
Fax: 973-882-1717
Email: infocentral@asme.org
http://www.asme.org

Purpose: To help FIRST Robotics team members who are interested in pursuing a career in mechanical engineering or mechanical engineering technology.
Eligibility: Applicants must be high school seniors who are FIRST Robotics team members. They must be nominated for the award by an ASME member, an ASME Auxiliary member or a student ASME member who is also involved with FIRST. Students must plan to enroll in an ABET-accredited or similarly accredited mechanical engineering or mechanical engineering technology degree program. They must be able to begin undergraduate studies no later than the fall following graduation from high school. Selection is based on the overall strength of the application.
Target applicants: High school students.
Amount: $5,000.
Number of awards: 5.
Deadline: March 15.
How to apply: Applications are available online. An application form, nomination letter, resume or transcript and financial data worksheet are required.
Exclusive: Visit www.UltimateScholarshipBook.com and enter code AM76612 for updates on this award.

(767) • ASNE Scholarship Program

American Society of Naval Engineers
1452 Duke Street
Alexandria, VA 22314-3458
Phone: 703-836-6727
Fax: 703-836-7491
Email: dwoodbury@navalengineers.org
http://www.navalengineers.org
Purpose: To encourage college students to enter the field of naval engineering and to provide support to naval engineers pursuing advanced education.
Eligibility: Applications must be for the last year of a full-time or co-op undergraduate program or for one year of full-time graduate study for a designated engineering or physical science degree at an accredited school. Applicants must be U.S. citizens pursuing careers in naval engineering. Graduate student applicants must be members of ASNE. An applicant's academic record, work history, professional promise and interest, extracurricular activities and recommendations are considered. Financial need may be considered.
Target applicants: College students. Graduate school students. Adult students.
Amount: $3,000-$4,000.
Number of awards: Varies.
Deadline: February 15.
How to apply: Applications are available online or by written request.
Exclusive: Visit www.UltimateScholarshipBook.com and enter code AM76712 for updates on this award.

(768) • ASNT Fellowship

American Society for Nondestructive Testing
1711 Arlingate Lane
P.O. Box 28518
Columbus, OH 43228
Phone: 800-222-2768
Fax: 614-274-6899
Email: sthomas@asnt.org
http://www.asnt.org
Purpose: To fund research in nondestructive testing.
Eligibility: The award is given to an educational institution accredited by ABET to fund research in nondestructive testing (NDT) at the postgraduate level. One proposal per faculty member will be considered annually. Applicants should submit research proposal, program of study, description of facilities, budget, background on faculty advisor and background on graduate student.
Target applicants: Graduate school students. Adult students.
Amount: Up to $15,000.
Number of awards: Up to 5.
Deadline: October 15.
How to apply: Applications are available online.
Exclusive: Visit www.UltimateScholarshipBook.com and enter code AM76812 for updates on this award.

(769) • Association for Women in Science (AWIS) Educational Awards

Association for Women in Science
1442 Duke Street
Alexandria, VA 22314
Phone: 202-326-8940
Fax: 202-326-8960
Email: awisedfd@awis.org
http://www.awis.org
Purpose: To assist female students who plan to study science.
Eligibility: For the undergraduate scholarship, applicants must be in their second or third year of college and expect to major in science or a related field. For the graduate scholarship, students must have been admitted to candidacy for the Ph.D. in a life or physical science or engineering program. Selection is based on academic achievement, the importance of the research question addressed, quality of the research, reference letters and the applicant's potential for future contributions to science and related fields.
Target applicants: College students. Adult students.
Amount: $500 and $1,000.
Number of awards: 15-20.
Deadline: Varies.
How to apply: Applications are available online.
Exclusive: Visit www.UltimateScholarshipBook.com and enter code AS76912 for updates on this award.

(770) • Association for Women in Science Predoctoral Awards

Association for Women in Science
1442 Duke Street
Alexandria, VA 22314
Phone: 202-326-8940
Fax: 202-326-8960
Email: awisedfd@awis.org
http://www.awis.org
Purpose: To recognize female students enrolled in a behavioral, life, physical or social science or engineering program leading to a Ph.D. degree.
Eligibility: Three of the awards have limitations for students in certain fields and one is reserved for a student who interrupted her education for at least three years to raise a family. Awards are given based on academic achievement, the importance of the research question addressed, the quality of the research and the applicant's potential for future contributions to science or engineering.
Target applicants: Graduate school students. Adult students.
Amount: $1,000.
Number of awards: 5-10.

Deadline: January 29.
How to apply: Applications are available online.
Exclusive: Visit www.UltimateScholarshipBook.com and enter code AS77012 for updates on this award.

(771) • Association of Federal Communications Consulting Engineers Scholarships

Association of Federal Communications Consulting Engineers
P.O. Box 19333
Washington, DC 20036
Phone: 703-780-4824
Email: secretary@afcce.org
http://www.afcce.org

Purpose: To aid full-time undergraduate students attending an accredited college or university in pursuit of a degree in a telecommunications-related subject.
Eligibility: Applicants must be full-time (12+ units per semester) undergraduate students at an accredited postsecondary institution. They must be rising juniors or above and must be enrolled in a subject that is related to the radio communications consulting engineering field. They must have or acquire an AFCCE member who will act as a sponsor. Selection is based on the overall strength of the application.
Target applicants: College students. Adult students.
Amount: Varies.
Number of awards: Varies.
Deadline: Varies.
How to apply: Applications are available online. An application form, transcript, personal statement and sponsorship by an AFCCE member are required.
Exclusive: Visit www.UltimateScholarshipBook.com and enter code AS77112 for updates on this award.

(772) • Association of Food and Drug Officials Scholarship Award

Association of Food and Drug Officials
2550 Kingston Road
Suite 311
York, PA 17402
Phone: 717-757-2888
Fax: 717-755-8089
Email: afdo@afdo.org
http://www.afdo.org

Purpose: To support college students who are studying food, drug or consumer product safety.
Eligibility: Applicants must be in their third or fourth year of college at an accredited institution and demonstrate a desire to work in a career of research, regulatory work, quality control or teaching in an area related to food, drug or consumer product safety. Applicants must also have demonstrated leadership capabilities, a minimum 3.0 GPA and submit two letters of recommendation from faculty.
Target applicants: College students. Adult students.
Minimum GPA: 3.0
Amount: $1,500.
Number of awards: 3.
Deadline: February 1.
How to apply: Applications are available online.
Exclusive: Visit www.UltimateScholarshipBook.com and enter code AS77212 for updates on this award.

(773) • ASTM International Katherine and Bryant Mather Scholarship

ASTM International
100 Barr Harbor Drive
P.O. Box C700
West Conshohocken, PA 19428
Phone: 610-832-9500
Email: awards@astm.org
http://www.astm.org

Purpose: To aid students who are enrolled in degree programs that are related to the cement and concrete technology industry.
Eligibility: Applicants must be full-time undergraduate sophomores, undergraduate juniors, undergraduate seniors or graduate students. They must be enrolled in a degree program that is related to cement construction or concrete materials technology at an accredited institution of higher learning. Selection is based on the overall strength of the application.
Target applicants: College students. Graduate school students. Adult students.
Amount: $7,500.
Number of awards: Varies.
Scholarship may be renewable.
Deadline: April 30.
How to apply: Applications are available online. An application form, one reference letter, an official transcript and a personal statement are required.
Exclusive: Visit www.UltimateScholarshipBook.com and enter code AS77312 for updates on this award.

(774) • Astronaut Scholarship

Astronaut Scholarship Foundation
6225 Vectorspace Boulevard
Titusville, FL 32780
Phone: 321-269-6101
Fax: 321-264-9176
Email: linnleblanc@astronautscholarship.org
http://www.astronautscholarship.org

Purpose: To ensure the United States' continued leadership in science by assisting promising physical science and engineering students.
Eligibility: Applicants must be sophomore, junior or senior undergraduate or graduate students in physical science or engineering at Clemson University, Georgia Institute of Technology, Harvey Mudd College, Miami University, North Carolina A&T State University, North Carolina State University, North Dakota State University, Pennsylvania State University, Purdue University, Syracuse University, Texas A&M University, Tufts University, University of Central Florida, University of Colorado, University of Kentucky, University of Minnesota, University of Michigan, University of Oklahoma, University of Washington or Washington University and must be nominated by faculty or staff. Applicants may not directly apply for the scholarship. Students must have excellent grades and have performed research or lab work in their field.
Target applicants: College students. Graduate school students. Adult students.
Amount: $10,000.
Number of awards: One per school.
Deadline: Varies.
How to apply: Applicants must be nominated.
Exclusive: Visit www.UltimateScholarshipBook.com and enter code AS77412 for updates on this award.

(775) • AUA Foundation Research Scholars Program

American Foundation for Urologic Disease Inc.
1000 Corporate Boulevard
Linthicum, MD 21090
Phone: 410-689-3750
Fax: 410-689-3850
Email: grants@auafoundation.org
http://www.urologyhealth.org
Purpose: To help young men and women who intend to pursue careers in urologic research.
Eligibility: Applicants must be researchers who conduct their research in the U.S. or Canada. Funding is provided for post-doctoral research only.
Target applicants: Graduate school students. Adult students.
Amount: Varies.
Number of awards: Up to 12.
Deadline: July 26.
How to apply: Applications are available online.
Exclusive: Visit www.UltimateScholarshipBook.com and enter code AM77512 for updates on this award.

(776) • Automotive Hall of Fame Scholarships

Automotive Hall of Fame
Award and Scholarship Programs
21400 Oakwood Boulevard
Dearborn, MI 48124
Phone: 313-240-4000
Fax: 313-240-8641
http://www.automotivehalloffame.org
Purpose: To assist students interested in automotive careers.
Eligibility: Applicants must be interested in automotive careers. Other requirements vary depending on the specific scholarship.
Target applicants: High school students. College students. Adult students.
Amount: Varies.
Number of awards: Varies.
Deadline: June 1.
How to apply: Applications are available online or by sending a self-addressed, stamped envelope.
Exclusive: Visit www.UltimateScholarshipBook.com and enter code AU77612 for updates on this award.

(777) • Aviation Distributors and Manufacturers Association Scholarship Program

Aviation Distributors and Manufacturers Association
100 North 20th Street
4th Floor
Philadelphia, PA 19103
Phone: 215-564-3484
Fax: 215-963-9784
Email: adma@fernley.com
http://www.adma.org
Purpose: To help students who are planning to pursue careers in aviation.
Eligibility: Applicants must be third- or fourth-year students enrolled at an accredited four-year institution of higher learning and working towards the Bachelor of Science (BS) in aviation management or professional piloting, or must be second-year A&P mechanic students enrolled in an accredited two-year program. They must have a minimum GPA of 3.0. Selection is based on academic achievement, recommendation letters, extracurricular activities, leadership skills and financial need.
Target applicants: College students. Adult students.
Minimum GPA: 3.0
Amount: Varies.
Number of awards: Varies.
Deadline: March 27.
How to apply: Applications are available online. An application form, two recommendation letters, a transcript and a personal statement are required.
Exclusive: Visit www.UltimateScholarshipBook.com and enter code AV77712 for updates on this award.

(778) • Aviation Insurance Association Scholarship

Aviation Insurance Association
400 Admiral Boulevard
Kansas City, MO 64106
Phone: 816-221-8488
Fax: 816-472-7765
Email: mandie@robstan.com
http://www.aiaweb.org
Purpose: To help upper division undergraduate aviation students.
Eligibility: Applicants must be enrolled in an undergraduate program in aviation at a school that is a member of the University Aviation Association (UAA). They must have completed at least 45 units of coursework in their degree program, 15 or more of which must be for aviation courses. They must have a GPA of 2.5 or higher.
Target applicants: College students. Adult students.
Minimum GPA: 2.5
Amount: $5,000.
Number of awards: 1.
Deadline: February 28.
How to apply: Applications are available online. Five sets of the following items are required: application form, personal statement, transcript, one letter of recommendation and any FAA certificates (if applicable).
Exclusive: Visit www.UltimateScholarshipBook.com and enter code AV77812 for updates on this award.

(779) • AWM Biographies Contest

Association for Women in Mathematics
4114 Computer and Space Sciences Building
University of Maryland
College Park, MD 20742
Phone: 301-405-7892
Fax: 301-314-9074
Email: awm@math.umd.edu
http://www.awm-math.org
Purpose: To increase awareness of women's contributions to the mathematical sciences.
Eligibility: Applicants must interview a woman working in a mathematical career and write an essay based on the interview. Applicants may be from the sixth grade to graduate students.
Target applicants: Junior high students or younger. High school students. College students. Adult students.
Amount: Varies.
Number of awards: At least 3.
Deadline: February 27.
How to apply: Applications are available online and must be submitted online.
Exclusive: Visit www.UltimateScholarshipBook.com and enter code AS77912 for updates on this award.

(780) • Bachelor's Scholarships

Oncology Nursing Society
ONS Foundation
125 Enterprise Drive
Pittsburgh, PA 15275-1214
Phone: 412-859-6100
Fax: 412-859-6163
Email: foundation@ons.org
http://www.ons.org

Purpose: To improve oncology nursing by assisting RNs in furthering their education.

Eligibility: Applicants who are registered nurses must have a current license to practice as an RN, have more than a high school diploma and be currently enrolled in an undergraduate nursing degree program in a school of nursing recognized by the National League for Nursing or the Commission on Collegiate Nursing Education. Applicants who are not registered nurses must be currently enrolled in an undergraduate nursing degree program in a school of nursing recognized by the National League for Nursing or the Commission on Collegiate Nursing Education. Non-RN applicants must be in the nursing component of the program and must have an interest in and commitment to oncology nursing. At least one Bachelor Scholarship is available to a non-RN applicant living in Ohio and West Virginia. There is a $5 application fee. Note: We do not recommend applying to scholarships that charge application fees. However, some scholarships of this type charge fees and are included for completeness.

Target applicants: College students. Adult students.

Amount: $2,000.

Number of awards: Varies.

Deadline: February 1.

How to apply: Applications are available online or by email request.

Exclusive: Visit www.UltimateScholarshipBook.com and enter code ON78012 for updates on this award.

(781) • Baroid Scholarship

American Ground Water Trust
16 Centre Street
Concord, NH 03301
Phone: 603-228-5444
Fax: 603-228-6557
http://www.agwt.org

Purpose: To support high school seniors intending to pursue a career in a ground water-related field.

Eligibility: Applicants must be high school seniors entering an accredited four-year college or university and intending to pursue a career in a ground water-related field.

Target applicants: High school students.

Minimum GPA: 3.0

Amount: $1,000.

Number of awards: Varies.

Deadline: June 1.

How to apply: Applications are available online.

Exclusive: Visit www.UltimateScholarshipBook.com and enter code AM78112 for updates on this award.

(782) • Barry M. Goldwater Scholarship and Excellence in Education Program

Barry M. Goldwater Scholarship and Excellence in Education Foundation
6225 Brandon Avenue, Suite 315
Springfield, VA 22150
Phone: 703-756-6012
Fax: 703-756-6015
Email: goldwater@act.org
http://www.act.org/goldwater/

Purpose: To assist college students who pursue studies that lead to careers as scientists, mathematicians and engineers.

Eligibility: Applicants must be full-time college sophomores or juniors, U.S. citizens or resident aliens, have a minimum "B" GPA and be in the upper fourth of their class. Award must be used during the junior or senior year of college. Selection is based on potential and intent to pursue careers in mathematics, the natural sciences or engineering.

Target applicants: College students. Adult students.

Minimum GPA: 3.0

Amount: Up to $7,500.

Number of awards: Up to 300.

Deadline: January 27.

How to apply: Institutions nominate college sophomores or juniors. Applicants may not apply directly to the foundation.

Exclusive: Visit www.UltimateScholarshipBook.com and enter code BA78212 for updates on this award.

(783) • Battery Division Student Research Award

Electrochemical Society
65 South Main Street, Building D
Pennington, NJ 08534-2839
Phone: 609-737-1902
Fax: 609-737-2743
Email: awards@electrochem.org
http://www.electrochem.org

Purpose: To recognize young engineers and scientists in the field of electrochemical power sources.

Eligibility: Applicants must be accepted or enrolled in a college or university and must submit transcripts, an outline of the proposed research project, a description of how the project is related to the field of electrochemical power sources, a record of achievements in industrial work and a letter of recommendation from the research supervisor. Awards are based on academic performance, past research, proposed research and the recommendation.

Target applicants: High school students. College students. Graduate school students. Adult students.

Amount: $1,000.

Number of awards: Varies.

Deadline: March 15.

How to apply: Application materials are described online.

Exclusive: Visit www.UltimateScholarshipBook.com and enter code EL78312 for updates on this award.

(784) • Beef Industry Scholarship

National Cattlemen's Foundation
9110 East Nichols Avenue
Suite 300
Centennial, CO 80112
Phone: 303-694-0305
Fax: 303-770-7745
Email: ncf@beef.org
http://www.nationalcattlemensfoundation.org

Purpose: To aid students who are preparing for careers in the beef industry.

Eligibility: Applicants must be graduating high school seniors or college undergraduates, and they must have plans to be enrolled full-time in a two-year or four-year undergraduate program during the upcoming academic year. They must be enrolled in a beef industry-related program of study and have a demonstrated interest in pursuing a career in the beef industry through previous coursework taken, internships completed or other life experiences. They or their families must be members of the National Cattlemen's Beef Association. Selection is based on the strength of the essay, letter of intent and reference letters.
Target applicants: High school students. College students. Adult students.
Amount: $1,500.
Number of awards: 10.
Scholarship may be renewable.
Deadline: December 1.
How to apply: Applications are available online. An application form, letter of intent, personal essay and two reference letters are required.
Exclusive: Visit www.UltimateScholarshipBook.com and enter code NA78412 for updates on this award.

(785) • Behavioral Sciences Student Fellowship

Epilepsy Foundation
8301 Professional Place
Landover, MD 20785
Phone: 301-459-3700
Email: researchwebsupport@efa.org
http://www.epilepsyfoundation.org
Purpose: To encourage students to pursue careers in epilepsy research or practice settings.
Eligibility: Applicants must be undergraduate or graduate students in the behavioral sciences, have an epilepsy-related study, have a qualified mentor who can supervise the project and have an interest in careers in epilepsy research or practice settings. The project must be in the U.S. and should not be for dissertation research. The award is based on the quality of the project, relevance to epilepsy, interest in epilepsy and the quality of the proposed lab or facility. Applicants must submit three recommendation letters, statement of intent, biographical sketch and research plan.
Target applicants: College students. Graduate school students. Adult students.
Amount: $3,000.
Number of awards: Varies.
Deadline: March 15.
How to apply: Application materials are described online.
Exclusive: Visit www.UltimateScholarshipBook.com and enter code EP78512 for updates on this award.

(786) • Benjamin Willard Niebel Scholarship

Institute of Industrial Engineers
3577 Parkway Lane
Suite 200
Norcross, GA 30092
Phone: 800-494-0460
Fax: 770-441-3295
Email: bcameron@iienet.org
http://www.iienet2.org
Purpose: To award students majoring in industrial engineering.
Eligibility: Applicants must be full-time undergraduate or graduate students enrolled in a college in the United States, Canada or Mexico with an accredited industrial engineering program, major in industrial engineering and be active members. Students may not apply directly for this scholarship and must be nominated. The award is based on academic ability, character, leadership, potential service to the industrial engineering profession and financial need.
Target applicants: College students. Graduate school students. Adult students.
Minimum GPA: 3.4
Amount: $2,000.
Number of awards: 2.
Deadline: February 1.
How to apply: Nomination forms are available online.
Exclusive: Visit www.UltimateScholarshipBook.com and enter code IN78612 for updates on this award.

(787) • Berna Lou Cartwright Scholarship

American Society of Mechanical Engineers (ASME)
Three Park Avenue
New York, NY 10016
Phone: 800-843-2763
Fax: 973-882-1717
Email: infocentral@asme.org
http://www.asme.org
Purpose: To aid U.S. mechanical engineering majors.
Eligibility: Applicants must be U.S. citizens who are entering the final year of an ABET-accredited undergraduate degree program in mechanical engineering. Selection is based on academic achievement, character, participation in the American Society of Mechanical Engineers (if applicable) and financial need.
Target applicants: College students. Adult students.
Amount: $2,000.
Number of awards: 1.
Deadline: March 15.
How to apply: Applications are available online. An application form, official transcript and three recommendation letters are required.
Exclusive: Visit www.UltimateScholarshipBook.com and enter code AM78712 for updates on this award.

(788) • Bill Kane Scholarship, Undergraduate

American Association for Health Education
1900 Association Drive
Reston, VA 20191
Phone: 703-476-3437
Fax: 703-476-6638
Email: aahe@aahperd.org
http://www.aahperd.org/aahe
Purpose: To support health education students.
Eligibility: Applicants must be full-time undergraduate health majors in their sophomore, junior or senior years. They must have a GPA of at least 3.25 and write an essay about what they hope to accomplish as a health educator.
Target applicants: College students. Adult students.
Minimum GPA: 3.25
Amount: $1,000.
Number of awards: 1.
Deadline: November 15.
How to apply: Applications are available online.
Exclusive: Visit www.UltimateScholarshipBook.com and enter code AM78812 for updates on this award.

(789) • Black and Veatch Scholarships

Black and Veatch
11401 Lamar Avenue
Overland Park, KS 66211
Phone: 913-458-2000
Fax: 913-458-2934
http://www.rmel.org/

Purpose: To assist students at select universities, technical schools and engineering colleges.

Eligibility: Black and Veatch is an engineering, consulting and construction company that specializes in infrastructure development in energy, water, information and government markets. For information on eligibility, please contact the endowment or financial aid office at your university, engineering college or technical school.

Target applicants: College students. Adult students.

Amount: Varies.

Number of awards: Varies.

Deadline: Varies.

How to apply: Contact the financial aid office for application information.

Exclusive: Visit www.UltimateScholarshipBook.com and enter code BL78912 for updates on this award.

(790) • BMW/SAE Engineering Scholarship

Society of Automotive Engineers International
400 Commonwealth Drive
Warrendale, PA 15096
Phone: 724-776-4841
Fax: 724-776-0790
Email: scholarships@sae.org
http://www.sae.org

Purpose: To support engineering students with high potential.

Eligibility: Applicants must be U.S. citizens with a GPA of 3.75 or higher. They must rank in the 90th percentile in math and critical reading on the SAT or ACT and must pursue an engineering or related degree through an ABET-accredited program.

Target applicants: College students. Adult students.

Minimum GPA: 3.75

Amount: $1,500.

Number of awards: 1.

Scholarship may be renewable.

Deadline: January 15.

How to apply: Applications are available online. An application form, transcript and SAT/ACT scores are required.

Exclusive: Visit www.UltimateScholarshipBook.com and enter code SO79012 for updates on this award.

(791) • Brian Jenneman Memorial Scholarship

Community Foundation of Louisville
Waterfront Plaza
325 West Main Street
Suite 1110
Louisville, KY 40202
Phone: 502-585-4649
Fax: 502-587-7484
Email: gails@cflouisville.org
http://www.cflouisville.org

Purpose: To help U.S. students who are training to become paramedics.

Eligibility: Applicants must be 18 years of age or older and must be accepted into a certified paramedic training program. They must be U.S. residents and must be in a training program based in the U.S. Selection is based on commitment to the paramedic profession and to public service.

Target applicants: High school students.

Amount: Up to $1,500.

Number of awards: 4.

Scholarship may be renewable.

Deadline: July 15.

How to apply: Applications are available online. An application form, official transcript and three recommendation forms are required.

Exclusive: Visit www.UltimateScholarshipBook.com and enter code CO79112 for updates on this award.

(792) • BSN Scholarship

Association of Rehabilitation Nurses
4700 W. Lake Avenue
Glenview, IL 60025
Phone: 800-229-7530
Fax: 888-458-0456
Email: gelliott@connect2amc.com
http://www.rehabnurse.org

Purpose: To help nurses pursuing a bachelor's of science in nursing.

Eligibility: Applicants must be members of and involved in ARN, enrolled in a bachelor's of science in nursing (BSN) program, have completed at least one course, be currently practicing rehabilitation nursing and have a minimum of two years' experience in rehabilitation nursing. Applications, transcripts, a summary of professional and educational goals and achievements and two recommendation letters are required. Applications should be submitted by fax or email.

Target applicants: College students. Adult students.

Amount: $1,000.

Number of awards: Varies.

Deadline: June 1.

How to apply: Applications are available online.

Exclusive: Visit www.UltimateScholarshipBook.com and enter code AS79212 for updates on this award.

(793) • Bud Glover Memorial Scholarship

Aircraft Electronics Association
4217 South Hocker
Independence, MO 64055
Phone: 816-373-6565
Fax: 816-478-3100
Email: info@aea.net
http://www.aea.net

Purpose: To support students who wish to pursue a career in avionics and aircraft repair.

Eligibility: Applicants must be high school seniors or college students who plan to or are attending an accredited school in an avionics or aircraft repair program.

Target applicants: High school students. College students. Adult students.

Amount: $1,000.

Number of awards: 1.

Deadline: February 15.

How to apply: Applications are available by contacting the organization for more information.

Exclusive: Visit www.UltimateScholarshipBook.com and enter code AI79312 for updates on this award.

(794) • Buick Achievers Scholarship Program

General Motors (GM) Foundation
300 Renaissance Center
MC 482-C27-D76
Detroit, MI 48265
http://www.buickachievers.com

Purpose: To recognize and reward college-bound students who excel both in the classroom and in the community.

Eligibility: Applicants must be high school seniors or high school graduates entering college for the first time. Students must plan to enroll in full-time undergraduate study at an accredited four-year college or university and must be U.S. citizens and have permanent residence in the United States. Applicants should plan to major in a course of study that focuses on science, technology, engineering or math. Some design, marketing, accounting, finance and business majors are also eligible. Scholarship applicants should demonstrate an interest in pursuing a career in the automotive or related industries using these areas of study. Other criteria for selecting winners will include: financial need, participation and leadership in community and school activities, work experience, educational and career goals and unusual circumstances. Also, being a first-generation college student, female, minority, military veteran or a dependent of military personnel, while not required, may weigh in the selection process.

Target applicants: High school students. College students. Adult students.

Amount: Up to $25,000.

Number of awards: 100.

Scholarship may be renewable.

Deadline: March 31.

How to apply: Applications are available online.

Exclusive: Visit www.UltimateScholarshipBook.com and enter code GE79412 for updates on this award.

(795) • C.B. Gambrell Undergraduate Scholarship

Institute of Industrial Engineers
3577 Parkway Lane
Suite 200
Norcross, GA 30092
Phone: 800-494-0460
Fax: 770-441-3295
Email: bcameron@iienet.org
http://www.iienet2.org

Purpose: To help undergraduate industrial engineering students from the U.S.

Eligibility: Applicants must be full-time undergraduate students who have completed their freshman year in an accredited industrial engineering program, major in industrial engineering and be active members of the Institute of Industrial Engineers. Students may not apply directly for this scholarship and must be nominated. The award is based on academic ability, character, leadership, potential service to the industrial engineering profession and financial need.

Target applicants: College students. Adult students.

Minimum GPA: 3.4

Amount: $600.

Number of awards: 1.

Deadline: February 1.

How to apply: Nomination forms are available online.

Exclusive: Visit www.UltimateScholarshipBook.com and enter code IN79512 for updates on this award.

(796) • Cadbury Adams Community Outreach Scholarships

American Dental Hygienists' Association (ADHA) Institute for Oral Health
Scholarship Award Program
444 North Michigan Avenue
Suite 3400
Chicago, IL 60611
Phone: 312-440-8900
Email: institute@adha.net
http://www.adha.org/ioh

Purpose: To reward students committed to improving oral health in their communities.

Eligibility: Applicants must have completed one year in an accredited dental hygiene program and demonstrate financial need of at least $1,500. They must also demonstrate through an essay a commitment to improving oral health in their communities. Applicants must be active SADHA or ADHA members and submit a goals statement.

Target applicants: College students. Adult students.

Amount: $1,000-$2,000.

Number of awards: Varies.

Deadline: February 1.

How to apply: Applications are available online.

Exclusive: Visit www.UltimateScholarshipBook.com and enter code AM79612 for updates on this award.

(797) • Campus Safety Health and Environmental Management Association Scholarship

National Safety Council
CSHEMA, Scholarship Committee
CSHEMA Division, National Safety Council
12100 Sunset Hills Road ,Suite 130
Reston , VA 20190-3221
Phone: 703-234-4141
Fax: 703-435-4390
Email: info@cshema.org
http://www.cshema.org/

Purpose: To encourage the study of safety.

Eligibility: Applicants must be full-time undergraduate or graduate students with at least one year left in their degree program. Applicants must also write an essay about health, safety or environmental issues relevant to the university or college campus.

Target applicants: College students. Adult students.

Amount: $2,000.

Number of awards: 1.

Deadline: March 31.

How to apply: Applications are available online.

Exclusive: Visit www.UltimateScholarshipBook.com and enter code NA79712 for updates on this award.

(798) • Canadian Section Student Award

Electrochemical Society
65 South Main Street, Building D
Pennington, NJ 08534-2839
Phone: 609-737-1902
Fax: 609-737-2743
Email: awards@electrochem.org
http://www.electrochem.org

Purpose: To support a student at a Canadian university who is pursuing an advanced degree related to electrochemical science and technology and/or solid state science and technology.
Eligibility: Applicants must be nominated in writing by a university faculty member of a Canadian university. Nominations must then be supported by letters of recommendation from personnel at the university, in industry or in government. The nomination should have a student curriculum vitae, a letter of recommendation from the nominating professor and a brief outline of the proposed and completed research project written by the student.
Target applicants: Graduate school students. Adult students.
Amount: $1,500.
Number of awards: 1.
Deadline: February 28.
How to apply: Application materials are described online.
Exclusive: Visit www.UltimateScholarshipBook.com and enter code EL79812 for updates on this award.

(799) • Careers in Agriculture Scholarship Program

Winfield Solutions LLC
MS 5850
1080 County Road F West
Shoreview, MN 55126
Phone: 800-426-8109
Email: info@winfieldsolutionsllc.com
http://www.agrisolutionsinfo.com
Purpose: To aid high school seniors who are interested in pursuing a career in agriculture.
Eligibility: Applicants must be high school seniors who plan to enroll in a two-year or four-year degree program related to agriculture in the fall following graduation. Dependents of employees of Winfield Solutions LLC or Land O' Lakes Inc. are ineligible. Selection is based on academic achievement, proven leadership in agriculture and professional interest in the field of agriculture.
Target applicants: High school students.
Amount: $1,000.
Number of awards: 20.
Deadline: February 1.
How to apply: Applications are available online. An application form, two character evaluations, a transcript and a personal essay are required.
Exclusive: Visit www.UltimateScholarshipBook.com and enter code WI79912 for updates on this award.

(800) • Caroline E. Holt Nursing Scholarship

National Society Daughters of the American Revolution
Committee Services Office
Attn.: Scholarships
1776 D Street NW
Washington, DC 20006-5303
Phone: 202-628-1776
http://www.dar.org
Purpose: To support students who are studying to become nurses.
Eligibility: Applicants must demonstrate financial need and attend an accredited school of nursing. All applicants must obtain a letter of sponsorship from their local DAR chapter. However, no affiliation with DAR is necessary.
Target applicants: High school students. College students. Adult students.
Amount: $1,000.
Number of awards: Varies.
Deadline: February 15.
How to apply: Applications are available by written request and must include a self-addressed, stamped envelope.
Exclusive: Visit www.UltimateScholarshipBook.com and enter code NA80012 for updates on this award.

(801) • Carville M. Akehurst Memorial Scholarship

American Nursery and Landscape Association
Horticultural Research Institute
1000 Vermont Avenue NW
Suite 300
Washington, DC 20005
Phone: 202-789-5980 x3014
Fax: 202-789-1893
Email: tjodon@anla.org
http://www.anla.org
Purpose: To provide scholarships for undergraduate and graduate students who plan to pursue careers in horticulture.
Eligibility: Applicants must be enrolled full-time in a landscaping or horticultural program at a two- or four-year accredited institution and be residents of Maryland, Virginia or West Virginia.
Target applicants: College students. Graduate school students. Adult students.
Minimum GPA: 2.7
Amount: $2,000.
Number of awards: 1.
Scholarship may be renewable.
Deadline: Varies.
How to apply: Applications are available online.
Exclusive: Visit www.UltimateScholarshipBook.com and enter code AM80112 for updates on this award.

(802) • Cedarcrest Farms Scholarship

American Jersey Cattle Association
6486 East Main Street
Reynoldsburg, OH 43068
Phone: 614-861-3636
Fax: 614-861-8040
Email: info@usjersey.com
http://www.usjersey.com
Purpose: To aid American Jersey Cattle Association members studying dairy product marketing, large animal veterinary practice, dairy manufacturing or dairy production.
Eligibility: Applicants must be AJCA members studying dairy manufacturing, dairy product marketing, dairy production or large animal veterinary practice at the undergraduate or graduate level. They must have a GPA of 2.5 or above and must plan to pursue a career in agriculture. Selection is based on the overall strength of the application.
Target applicants: College students. Graduate school students. Adult students.
Minimum GPA: 2.5
Amount: Varies.
Number of awards: Varies.
Deadline: July 1.
How to apply: Applications are available online. An application form, transcript and up to two letters of recommendation are required.
Exclusive: Visit www.UltimateScholarshipBook.com and enter code AM80212 for updates on this award.

(803) · Centex Homes "Build Your Future" Scholarship

National Housing Endowment
1201 15th Street NW
Washington, DC 20005
Phone: 800-368-5242
Fax: 202-266-8177
Email: nhe@nahb.com
http://www.nationalhousingendowment.org
Purpose: To aid U.S. students who plan to pursue careers in the building industry.
Eligibility: Applicants must be U.S. undergraduate freshmen, sophomores or juniors who are enrolled full-time in a housing-related degree program (construction, civil engineering, architecture, building trades or management, etc.). They must have at least one full academic year remaining in their course of study and maintain an overall GPA of at least 2.5 and major GPA of at least 3.0. Preference will be given to applicants who demonstrate financial need or who are members of a building industry-related service or professional organization, especially the National Association of Home Builders. Selection is based on financial need, academic achievement, GPA, work experience, extracurricular activities and professional goals.
Target applicants: College students. Adult students.
Minimum GPA: 2.5
Amount: Varies.
Number of awards: Varies.
Scholarship may be renewable.
Deadline: March 4.
How to apply: Applications are available online. An application form, a transcript, two recommendation letters, a list of degree requirements, a personal essay and a statement of financial status are required.
Exclusive: Visit www.UltimateScholarshipBook.com and enter code NA80312 for updates on this award.

(804) · Charlie Wells Memorial Aviation Scholarships

Charlie Wells Memorial Scholarship Fund
P.O. Box 262
Springfield, IL 62705
Email: rog@wellsscholarship.com
http://www.wellsscholarship.com
Purpose: To support students wishing to pursue careers in aviation.
Eligibility: Applicants must be a resident of the U.S. or a U.S. territory, and they must be full-time students enrolled in an aviation-related academic program. Selection is based on the overall strength of the application.
Target applicants: College students. Adult students.
Amount: Varies.
Number of awards: Varies.
Deadline: April 30.
How to apply: Applications are available online. An application form, two recommendation letters and a transcript are required.
Exclusive: Visit www.UltimateScholarshipBook.com and enter code CH80412 for updates on this award.

(805) · Charlotte McGuire Scholarship

American Holistic Nurses' Association
P.O. Box 2130
Flagstaff, AZ 86003-2130
Phone: 800-278-2462 x10
Fax: 928-526-2752
Email: info@ahna.org
http://www.ahna.org
Purpose: To provide scholarships to nurses in undergraduate or graduate nursing programs or other graduate programs related to holistic nursing.
Eligibility: Applicants must be pursuing an education in holistic nursing and be members of the AHNA.
Target applicants: College students. Graduate school students. Adult students.
Minimum GPA: 3.0
Amount: Varies.
Number of awards: Varies.
Deadline: March 15.
How to apply: Applications are available online or from AHNA Headquarters.
Exclusive: Visit www.UltimateScholarshipBook.com and enter code AM80512 for updates on this award.

(806) · Charlotte Woods Memorial Scholarship

Transportation Clubs International Scholarships
Attn.: Bill Blair
Zimmer Worldwide Logistics
15710 JFK Boulevard
Houston, TX 77032
Phone: 877-858-8627
Email: bblair@zimmerworldwide.com
http://www.transportationclubsinternational.com
Purpose: To support students who want to enter the transportation industry.
Eligibility: Applicants must be enrolled in an accredited institution of higher learning in a vocational or degree program in the fields of transportation logistics or traffic management and must be TCI members or dependents of members. The awards are based upon scholastic ability, potential, professional interest and character. Financial need is also considered.
Target applicants: College students. Adult students.
Amount: Varies.
Number of awards: Varies.
Deadline: May 31.
How to apply: Applications are available online.
Exclusive: Visit www.UltimateScholarshipBook.com and enter code TR80612 for updates on this award.

(807) · Clinical Research Pre-Doctoral Fellowship

American Nurses Association (ANA)
8515 Georgia Avenue, Suite 400
Attn.: Janet Jackson, Program Manager
Silver Spring, MD 20910-3492
Phone: 301-628-5247
Fax: 301-628-5349
http://www.nursingworld.org
Purpose: To provide stipends and tuition assistance to nurses studying minority psychiatric-mental health and substance abuse.
Eligibility: Applicants must be members of the ANA, have their master's degree and plan to pursue doctoral degrees. Fellowships may last from three to five years.
Target applicants: Graduate school students. Adult students.
Amount: Varies.
Number of awards: Varies.
Deadline: March 1.
How to apply: Applications available online.
Exclusive: Visit www.UltimateScholarshipBook.com and enter code AM80712 for updates on this award.

(808) • Colgate "Bright Smiles, Bright Futures" Minority Scholarships

American Dental Hygienists' Association (ADHA) Institute for Oral Health
Scholarship Award Program
444 North Michigan Avenue
Suite 3400
Chicago, IL 60611
Phone: 312-440-8900
Email: institute@adha.net
http://www.adha.org/ioh

Purpose: To support members of groups underrepresented in dental hygiene programs.

Eligibility: Applicants must have completed one year of an accredited dental hygiene curriculum and be a member of a group that is underrepresented in the field of dental hygiene. Examples of eligible groups include African-American, Hispanic, Asian, Native American and male students. Applicants must also demonstrate financial need of at least $1,500, be active members of SADHA or ADHA and submit a goals statement.

Target applicants: College students. Adult students.

Amount: $1,000-$2,000.

Number of awards: Varies.

Deadline: February 1.

How to apply: Applications are available online.

Exclusive: Visit www.UltimateScholarshipBook.com and enter code AM80812 for updates on this award.

(809) • Collegiate Inventors Competition

National Inventors Hall of Fame
221 S. Broadway
Akron, OH 44308-1505
Phone: 330-849-6887
Email: collegiate@invent.org
http://www.invent.org

Purpose: To encourage college students in science, engineering, mathematics, technology and creative invention and to stimulate interest in technology and economic leadership.

Eligibility: Applicants must have been full-time college or university students during part of the 12-month period prior to the entry date. Up to four students may work as a team, and at least one student must meet the full-time criteria. Judging is based on originality and inventiveness, as well as the invention's potential value to society.

Target applicants: College students. Graduate school students. Adult students.

Amount: Up to $15,000.

Number of awards: Varies.

Deadline: Varies.

How to apply: Applications are available online.

Exclusive: Visit www.UltimateScholarshipBook.com and enter code NA80912 for updates on this award.

(810) • Composites Division/Harold Giles Scholarship

Society of Plastics Engineers
13 Church Hill Road
Newtown, CT 06470
Phone: 203-775-0471
Fax: 203-775-8490
Email: info@4spe.org
http://www.4spe.org

Purpose: To aid undergraduate and graduate students who have an interest in the plastics industry.

Eligibility: Applicants must have an interest in the plastics industry, major in or take courses leading to a career in the plastics industry and be in good academic standing. Financial need is considered.

Target applicants: College students. Graduate school students. Adult students.

Amount: $1,000.

Number of awards: 1.

Deadline: February 15.

How to apply: Applications are available online.

Exclusive: Visit www.UltimateScholarshipBook.com and enter code SO81012 for updates on this award.

(811) • Congressional Black Caucus Spouses Cheerios Brand Health Initiative Scholarship

Congressional Black Caucus Foundation
1720 Massachusetts Avenue NW
Washington, DC 20036
Phone: 202-263-2800
Fax: 202-775-0773
Email: info@cbcfinc.org
http://www.cbcfinc.org

Purpose: To support minority students who are studying health-related fields.

Eligibility: Applicants do NOT need to be African American. Students must attend school or reside in a district represented by a Congressional Black Caucus member. Students must have at least a 2.5 GPA, and they must be enrolled or accepted into a full-time undergraduate degree program. Applicants must show leadership qualities and community service participation.

Target applicants: High school students. College students. Adult students.

Minimum GPA: 2.5

Amount: Varies.

Number of awards: Varies.

Deadline: June 1.

How to apply: Applications are available online.

Exclusive: Visit www.UltimateScholarshipBook.com and enter code CO81112 for updates on this award.

(812) • Continuing Education Award

American Association of Occupational Health Nurses (AAOHN) Foundation
2920 Brandywine Road
Suite 100
Atlanta, GA 30341
Phone: 770-455-7757
Fax: 770-455-7271
Email: ann@aaohn.org
https://www.aaohn.org/

Purpose: To support the continuing education of occupational and environmental health professionals.

Eligibility: Applicants must be employed in the field of occupational and environmental health nursing and demonstrate an interest in occupational and environmental health. A narrative, a letter of support from the employer and material describing the continuing education activity are required. This scholarship is for continuing education activities not tuition for an academic program.

Target applicants: Graduate school students. Adult students.

Amount: $1,500.

Number of awards: 13.
Deadline: December 1.
How to apply: Applications are available online.
Exclusive: Visit www.UltimateScholarshipBook.com and enter code AM81212 for updates on this award.

(813) • Corrosion Division Morris Cohen Graduate Student Award

Electrochemical Society
65 South Main Street, Building D
Pennington, NJ 08534-2839
Phone: 609-737-1902
Fax: 609-737-2743
Email: awards@electrochem.org
http://www.electrochem.org
Purpose: To recognize graduate research in corrosion science and/or engineering.
Eligibility: Applicants must be graduate students who have completed all the requirements for their degrees within two years prior to the nomination deadline. Nomination may be made by the applicant's research supervisor or someone familiar with the applicant's research work. A summary of the applicant's master's or Ph.D. research work, reports, memberships and involvement with scientific societies, awards, an academic record and reprints of publications are required.
Target applicants: Graduate school students. Adult students.
Amount: $1,000 plus travel expenses.
Number of awards: 1.
Deadline: December 15.
How to apply: Application materials are listed online.
Exclusive: Visit www.UltimateScholarshipBook.com and enter code EL81312 for updates on this award.

(814) • D.W. Simpson Actuarial Science Scholarship

D.W. Simpson and Company
1800 Larchmont Avenue
Chicago, IL 60613
Phone: 800-837-8338
Fax: 312-951-8386
Email: actuaries@dwsimpson.com
http://www.dwsimpson.com/scholar.html
Purpose: To assist college students interested in an actuarial science career.
Eligibility: Eligible students must be college seniors majoring in actuarial science who are eligible to work in the U.S. and have taken and passed a minimum of one actuarial examination.
Target applicants: College students. Adult students.
Minimum GPA: 3.0
Amount: $1,000.
Number of awards: 2.
Deadline: April 30 and October 31.
How to apply: Applications are available online.
Exclusive: Visit www.UltimateScholarshipBook.com and enter code D.81412 for updates on this award.

(815) • Dade-Behring / Coordinating Council on the Clinical Laboratory Workforce Scholarship

American Society for Clinical Laboratory Science
6701 Democracy Boulevard, Suite 300
Bethesda, MD 20817
Phone: 301-657-2768
Fax: 301-657-2909
Email: ascls@ascls.org
http://www.ascls.org
Purpose: To assist students in the second year of a Clinical Laboratory Technician (CLT/MLT) program.
Eligibility: Applicants must be currently enrolled in a NAACLS-accredited Clinical Laboratory Technician (CLT/MLT) program and planning to complete their final year of study by the end of the following August. Applicants must have a GPA of at least 2.5.
Target applicants: College students. Adult students.
Minimum GPA: 2.5
Amount: $1,000.
Number of awards: 50.
Deadline: August 1 through November 1.
How to apply: Applications are available online.
Exclusive: Visit www.UltimateScholarshipBook.com and enter code AM81512 for updates on this award.

(816) • Dairy Student Recognition Program

National Dairy Shrine
P.O. Box 1
Maribel, WI 54227
Phone: 920-863-6333
Fax: 920-863-8328
Email: info@dairyshrine.org
http://www.dairyshrine.org
Purpose: To recognize graduating college seniors planning careers related to dairy.
Eligibility: Applicants must be U.S. citizens planning to enter the fields such as dairy production agriculture, marketing, agricultural law, business, veterinary medicine or environmental science. Selection is based on leadership skills, academic achievement and interest in dairy cattle.
Target applicants: College students. Adult students.
Amount: Up to $1,500.
Number of awards: Varies up to 7.
Deadline: May 1.
How to apply: Applications are available online, and two applicants per college or university are accepted each year.
Exclusive: Visit www.UltimateScholarshipBook.com and enter code NA81612 for updates on this award.

(817) • Dan L. Meisinger Sr. Memorial Learn to Fly Scholarship

National Air Transportation Foundation Meisinger Scholarship
4226 King Street
Alexandria, VA 22302
Phone: 703-845-9000
Fax: 703-845-8176
http://www.nata.aero
Purpose: To provide an annual flight training scholarship.
Eligibility: Applicants must be enrolled in an aviation program with a B or better GPA and be a resident of Kansas, Missouri or Illinois. Students should be recommended by an aviation professional; independent applications are also considered.
Target applicants: College students. Graduate school students. Adult students.
Minimum GPA: 3.0
Amount: $2,500.

Number of awards: Varies.
Deadline: Last Friday in November.
How to apply: Applications are available online.
Exclusive: Visit www.UltimateScholarshipBook.com and enter code NA81712 for updates on this award.

(818) • Darling International Inc. FFA Scholarship

National FFA Organization
P.O. Box 68960
6060 FFA Drive
Indianapolis, IN 46268-0960
Phone: 317-802-6060
Fax: 317-802-6051
Email: scholarships@ffa.org
http://www.ffa.org/
Purpose: To assist students of land grant colleges in Colorado, Iowa, Illinois, Indiana, Kansas, Nebraska and Wisconsin in obtaining a degree in agriculture.
Eligibility: Applicants must be current FFA members and high school seniors or college students planning to enroll or currently enrolled full-time. Students only need to complete the online application one time to be considered for all FFA-administered scholarships. The application requires information about the student's activities and a 1,000-word essay. Awards may be used for books, supplies, tuition, fees and room and board.
Target applicants: College students. Adult students.
Amount: $2,000.
Number of awards: 1.
Deadline: February 15.
How to apply: Applications are available online.
Exclusive: Visit www.UltimateScholarshipBook.com and enter code NA81812 for updates on this award.

(819) • David Alan Quick Scholarship

EAA Aviation Center
P.O. Box 2683
Oshkosh, WI 54903
Phone: 877-806-8902
Fax: 920-426-6865
Email: scholarships@eaa.org
http://www.youngeagles.org
Purpose: To support students in aerospace or aeronautical engineering.
Eligibility: Applicants must be in their junior or senior year at an accredited college or university pursuing a degree in aerospace or aeronautical engineering. Applicants must be involved in school and community activities as well as aviation and be EAA members or be recommended by an EAA member.
Target applicants: College students. Adult students.
Amount: $500.
Number of awards: 1.
Scholarship may be renewable.
Deadline: February 28.
How to apply: Applications are available online.
Exclusive: Visit www.UltimateScholarshipBook.com and enter code EA81912 for updates on this award.

(820) • David Arver Memorial Scholarship

Aircraft Electronics Association
4217 South Hocker
Independence, MO 64055
Phone: 816-373-6565
Fax: 816-478-3100
Email: info@aea.net
http://www.aea.net
Purpose: To support students who wish to pursue a career in avionics or aircraft repair.
Eligibility: Applicants must be high school seniors or college students who plan to or are attending an accredited school in an avionics or aircraft repair program.
Target applicants: High school students. College students. Adult students.
Amount: Varies.
Number of awards: 1.
Deadline: February 15.
How to apply: Applications are available by contacting the organization for more information.
Exclusive: Visit www.UltimateScholarshipBook.com and enter code AI82012 for updates on this award.

(821) • David S. Bruce Awards for Excellence in Undergraduate Research

American Physiological Society
Education Office
9650 Rockville Pike
Bethesda, MD 20814-3991
Phone: 301-634-7787
Fax: 301-634-7241
Email: education@the-aps.org
http://www.the-aps.org
Purpose: To award undergraduate students for excellence in experimental biology research.
Eligibility: Applicants must be enrolled as an undergraduate at time of application and at time of meeting. Students must be first authors of the abstract and must be working with an APS member who will confirm the authorship. Applicants must submit a one-page paper discussing research and career plans and an abstract to be reviewed by a committee at the annual Experimental Biology meeting.
Target applicants: College students. Adult students.
Amount: $500.
Number of awards: Varies.
Deadline: November 4 (EB abstract) and January 11 (application).
How to apply: Applications are available online.
Exclusive: Visit www.UltimateScholarshipBook.com and enter code AM82112 for updates on this award.

(822) • Delta Faucet Company Scholarships

Plumbing-Heating-Cooling Contractors–National Association
P.O. Box 6808
180 South Washington Street
Falls Church, VA 22046
Phone: 800-533-7694
Fax: 703-237-7442
Email: scholarships@naphcc.org
http://www.phccweb.org
Purpose: To elevate the technical and business competence of the plumbing-heating-cooling (p-h-c) industry by awarding scholarships to students who are enrolled in a p-h-c-related major.
Eligibility: Applicants must be students who are currently enrolled or plan to be enrolled in a p-h-c-related major at an accredited four-year college or university or two-year technical college, community college or trade school. Apprentice program students must also be working full-

time for a licensed plumbing or HVAC contractor who is a member of the PHCC. Two $2,500 scholarships are awarded to students who are enrolled in either a PHCC-approved apprentice program or a full-time certificate or degree program at an accredited two-year community college, technical college or trade school. Four $2,500 scholarships are awarded to students who are enrolled in an undergraduate degree program at an accredited four-year college or university.
Target applicants: High school students. College students. Adult students.
Amount: $2,500.
Number of awards: Up to 6.
Deadline: May 1.
How to apply: Applications are available online, by email or by phone.
Exclusive: Visit www.UltimateScholarshipBook.com and enter code PL82212 for updates on this award.

(823) • Denny Lydic Scholarship

Transportation Clubs International Scholarships
Attn.: Bill Blair
Zimmer Worldwide Logistics
15710 JFK Boulevard
Houston, TX 77032
Phone: 877-858-8627
Email: bblair@zimmerworldwide.com
http://www.transportationclubsinternational.com
Purpose: To support students in the field of transportation.
Eligibility: Applicants must be enrolled in an accredited institution of higher learning in a vocational or degree program in the fields of transportation, logistics or traffic management. The awards are based upon scholastic ability, potential, professional interest and character. Financial need is also considered.
Target applicants: College students. Adult students.
Amount: Varies.
Number of awards: Varies.
Deadline: May 31.
How to apply: Applications are available online.
Exclusive: Visit www.UltimateScholarshipBook.com and enter code TR82312 for updates on this award.

(824) • Dental Student Scholarship

American Dental Association Foundation
211 East Chicago Avenue
Chicago, IL 60611
Phone: 312-440-2763
Fax: 312-440-3526
Email: famularor@ada.org
http://www.ada.org
Purpose: To encourage students to pursue careers in dental hygiene, dental assisting, dentistry and dental laboratory technology.
Eligibility: Applicants must be full-time entering second-year students in an accredited dental program and demonstrate a minimum financial need of $2,500. Applicants must submit applications, two reference forms, and biographies. Selection is based on financial need, academic achievement, biographical sketch and references. A minimum 3.0 GPA is required. Only two scholarship applications are allowed per school, so schools may set their own in-school application deadlines that are earlier.
Target applicants: College students. Graduate school students. Adult students.
Minimum GPA: 3.0
Amount: $1,000.
Number of awards: Varies.
Deadline: June 11.
How to apply: Applications are available from dental school officials.
Exclusive: Visit www.UltimateScholarshipBook.com and enter code AM82412 for updates on this award.

(825) • Department of Homeland Security Undergraduate Scholarships

Oak Ridge Institute for Science and Education
P.O. Box 117
Oak Ridge, TN 37831-0117
Phone: 865-576-3146
Fax: 865-241-2923
Email: dhsed@orau.org
http://www.orau.gov/dhsed/
Purpose: To support students studying in fields relevant to homeland security.
Eligibility: Applicants must be U.S. citizens who have not yet earned a bachelor's degree and must have a cumulative GPA of 3.3 or higher. They must major in a homeland security science, technology, engineering or mathematics field with coursework or research relevant to homeland security. Full-time students must be in their second year of college attendance, and part-time students must have completed at least 45 but no more than 60 semester hours. Applicants may not have any commitments that would prevent them from attending school full-time, attending the fall DHS HS-STEM Career Development Conference and participating full-time in a 10-week internship in the summer following awarding of the scholarship or completing the homeland security service requirement following completion of their degrees.
Target applicants: College students. Adult students.
Minimum GPA: 3.3
Amount: Tuition plus stipend.
Number of awards: Varies.
Scholarship may be renewable.
Deadline: January 5.
How to apply: Applications are available online. An application form, two reference reports, transcript, copy of birth certificate and essays are required.
Exclusive: Visit www.UltimateScholarshipBook.com and enter code OA82512 for updates on this award.

(826) • DMI Milk Marketing Scholarship

National Dairy Shrine
P.O. Box 1
Maribel, WI 54227
Phone: 920-863-6333
Fax: 920-863-8328
Email: info@dairyshrine.org
http://www.dairyshrine.org
Purpose: To encourage students to pursue careers in the marketing of dairy foods.
Eligibility: Applicants must be second, third or fourth year college students at two- or four-year universities, have a minimum 2.5 GPA and major in dairy science, animal science, agricultural communications, agricultural education, general agriculture or food and nutrition.
Target applicants: College students. Adult students.
Minimum GPA: 2.5
Amount: $1,000-$1,500.
Number of awards: 6-8.
Deadline: May 1.
How to apply: Applications are available online.

Exclusive: Visit www.UltimateScholarshipBook.com and enter code NA82612 for updates on this award.

(827) • Doctoral Scholars Forgivable Loan Program

Society of Automotive Engineers International
400 Commonwealth Drive
Warrendale, PA 15096
Phone: 724-776-4841
Fax: 724-776-0790
Email: scholarships@sae.org
http://www.sae.org

Purpose: To provide funding to assist promising engineering graduate students to pursue careers in teaching at the college level.
Eligibility: Applicants must hold an undergraduate degree from an engineering program and have been admitted to a doctoral program with the purpose of teaching engineering at the college level. Selection is based on scholastic achievement, desire to teach, interest in mobility technology and support of the SAE Collegiate Chapter Faculty advisor.
Target applicants: Graduate school students. Adult students.
Amount: $5,000.
Number of awards: 1-2.
Scholarship may be renewable.
Deadline: February 15.
How to apply: Applications are available online.
Exclusive: Visit www.UltimateScholarshipBook.com and enter code SO82712 for updates on this award.

(828) • Dolores E. Fisher Award

Mel Fisher Maritime Heritage Society and Museum
200 Greene Street
Key West, FL 33040
Phone: 305-294-2633
Email: office@melfisher.org
http://www.melfisher.org

Purpose: To aid female students who are interested in pursuing ocean- or marine-related careers.
Eligibility: Applicants must be female students between the ages of 16 and 30. They must have plans to pursue a career in a marine- or ocean-related field. Selection is based on the personal essay and stated career goals.
Target applicants: High school students. College students. Graduate school students. Adult students.
Amount: $1,000.
Number of awards: 1.
Deadline: Varies.
How to apply: Applications are available online. An application form, personal essay, three recommendation letters and a statement of career goals are required.
Exclusive: Visit www.UltimateScholarshipBook.com and enter code ME82812 for updates on this award.

(829) • Don King Student Fellowship

Huntington's Disease Society of America
505 Eighth Avenue, Suite 902
New York, NY 10018
Phone: 800-345-4372
Fax: 212-239-3430
Email: rgraze@hdsa.org
http://www.hdsa.org

Purpose: To sponsor Huntington's Disease research.
Eligibility: Applicants must be current undergraduate life science or pre-medical students or first-year medical students attending accredited institutions in the United States where HDSA sponsors HD research. Recipients will conduct full-time research for 10 weeks. A letter of support and a project plan are required. The award is based on academic achievement, scientific merit of the project and the relevancy to HD.
Target applicants: College students. Graduate school students. Adult students.
Amount: $3,000.
Number of awards: Varies.
Deadline: May 1.
How to apply: Applications are available by email, by mail or online.
Exclusive: Visit www.UltimateScholarshipBook.com and enter code HU82912 for updates on this award.

(830) • Donald Burnside Memorial Scholarship

AOPA Air Safety Foundation
421 Aviation Way
Frederick, MD 21701
Phone: 301-695-2000
Fax: 301-695-2375
Email: aopahq@aopa.org
http://www.aopa.org

Purpose: To assist students in non-engineering aviation programs.
Eligibility: Applicants must be college juniors or seniors and have at least one semester or quarter to be completed, have a minimum 3.25 GPA and be enrolled in a baccalaureate level, non-engineering aviation degree program at a four-year institution. Applicants must also submit an essay on a topic provided on the website.
Target applicants: College students. Adult students.
Minimum GPA: 3.25
Amount: $1,000.
Number of awards: 1.
Deadline: March 31.
How to apply: Applications are available online.
Exclusive: Visit www.UltimateScholarshipBook.com and enter code AO83012 for updates on this award.

(831) • Donald F. and Mildred Topp Othmer Foundation

American Institute of Chemical Engineers - (AIChE)
3 Park Avenue
New York, NY 10016
Phone: 212-591-7634
Fax: 212-591-8890
Email: awards@aiche.org
http://www.aiche.org

Purpose: To support AIChE student members.
Eligibility: Applicants must be members of an AIChE Student Chapter or Chemical Engineering Club. Applicants must be nominated by their student chapter advisors. Awards are presented on the basis of academic achievement and involvement in student chapter activities.
Target applicants: College students. Graduate school students. Adult students.
Amount: $1,000.
Number of awards: 15.
Deadline: July 1.
How to apply: Applications are available online.
Exclusive: Visit www.UltimateScholarshipBook.com and enter code AM83112 for updates on this award.

(832) · Dorothy Budnek Memorial Scholarship

Association for Radiologic and Imaging Nursing
7794 Grow Drive
Pensacola, FL 32514
Phone: 866-486-2762
Fax: 850-484-8762
Email: arin@dancyamc.com
http://www.arinursing.org

Purpose: To help ARNA members continue their nursing education.
Eligibility: Applicants must be active members of the American Radiological Nurses Association for three years, have a current nursing license and be enrolled in an approved academic program. Students should submit the application, a statement of purpose, two recommendation letters, a transcript which shows a minimum 2.5 GPA, a statement of financial support and a copy of the nursing license.
Target applicants: Graduate school students. Adult students.
Minimum GPA: 2.5
Amount: $600.
Number of awards: 1.
Deadline: December 1.
How to apply: Applications are available online.
Exclusive: Visit www.UltimateScholarshipBook.com and enter code AS83212 for updates on this award.

(833) · Dorothy M. and Earl S. Hoffman Award

American Vacuum Society
120 Wall Street, 32nd Floor
New York, NY 10005-3993
Phone: 212-248-0200
Fax: 212-248-0245
Email: angela@avs.org
http://www.avs.org

Purpose: To recognize excellence in continuing graduate studies in the sciences and technologies related to AVS.
Eligibility: Applicants must be graduate students in an accredited academic institution. An application, summary of research, letters of recommendation and transcript are required. The award is based on achievement in research and academic record. The top five student nominees are invited to present talks on their research to the trustees at the international symposium. The trustees then select one recipient for the Dorothy M. and Earl S. Hoffman Award. The award covers travel expenses to the symposium.
Target applicants: Graduate school students. Adult students.
Amount: Varies.
Number of awards: 1.
Deadline: Varies.
How to apply: Applications are available online.
Exclusive: Visit www.UltimateScholarshipBook.com and enter code AM83312 for updates on this award.

(834) · Dr. Alfred C. Fones Scholarship

American Dental Hygienists' Association (ADHA) Institute for Oral Health
Scholarship Award Program
444 North Michigan Avenue
Suite 3400
Chicago, IL 60611
Phone: 312-440-8900
Email: institute@adha.net
http://www.adha.org/ioh

Purpose: To provide support to dental hygiene educators.
Eligibility: Applicants must be undergraduate or graduate students planning to become a teacher of dental hygienists and submit a goals statement. They must also be active members of SADHA or ADHA and demonstrate financial need of at least $1,500.
Target applicants: College students. Graduate school students. Adult students.
Amount: $1,000-$2,000.
Number of awards: 1.
Deadline: February 1.
How to apply: Applications are available online.
Exclusive: Visit www.UltimateScholarshipBook.com and enter code AM83412 for updates on this award.

(835) · Dr. Harold Hillenbrand Scholarship

American Dental Hygienists' Association (ADHA) Institute for Oral Health
Scholarship Award Program
444 North Michigan Avenue
Suite 3400
Chicago, IL 60611
Phone: 312-440-8900
Email: institute@adha.net
http://www.adha.org/ioh

Purpose: To support outstanding dental hygiene students.
Eligibility: Applicants must have completed one year of an accredited dental hygiene program with a GPA of at least 3.5. They must demonstrate excellence in both academics and clinical performance. Applicants must also demonstrate financial need of at least $1,500, be active members of SADHA or ADHA and submit a goals statement.
Target applicants: College students. Adult students.
Minimum GPA: 3.5
Amount: $1,000-$2,000.
Number of awards: 1.
Deadline: February 1.
How to apply: Applications are available online.
Exclusive: Visit www.UltimateScholarshipBook.com and enter code AM83512 for updates on this award.

(836) · DuPont Challenge Science Essay Award

DuPont
The DuPont Challenge
Science Essay Awards Program, c/o General Learning Communications
900 Skokie Boulevard, Suite 200
Northbrook, IL 60062
Phone: 847-205-3000
http://thechallenge.dupont.com

Purpose: To promote interest in scientific studies.
Eligibility: Applicants must be full-time students between grades 7 and 12 in a U.S. or Canadian school and write a 700- to 1,000-word essay about a scientific or technological development that interests them.
Target applicants: Junior high students or younger. High school students.
Amount: $200-$5,000.
Number of awards: Varies.
Deadline: January 31.
How to apply: Applications are available online.
Exclusive: Visit www.UltimateScholarshipBook.com and enter code DU83612 for updates on this award.

(837) • Dutch and Ginger Arver Scholarship

Aircraft Electronics Association
4217 South Hocker
Independence, MO 64055
Phone: 816-373-6565
Fax: 816-478-3100
Email: info@aea.net
http://www.aea.net

Purpose: To support students who wish to pursue a career in avionics or aircraft repair.

Eligibility: Applicants must be high school seniors or college students who plan to or are attending an accredited school in avionics or aircraft repair.

Target applicants: High school students. College students. Adult students.

Amount: Varies.

Number of awards: 1.

Deadline: February 15.

How to apply: Applications are available by contacting the organization for more information.

Exclusive: Visit www.UltimateScholarshipBook.com and enter code AI83712 for updates on this award.

(838) • Dwight D. Gardner Scholarship

Institute of Industrial Engineers
3577 Parkway Lane
Suite 200
Norcross, GA 30092
Phone: 800-494-0460
Fax: 770-441-3295
Email: bcameron@iienet.org
http://www.iienet2.org

Purpose: To award undergraduate members of the Institute of Industrial Engineers.

Eligibility: Applicants must be undergraduate students enrolled in a college in the United States, Canada or Mexico with an accredited industrial engineering program, major in industrial engineering and be active members. Students may not apply directly for this scholarship and must be nominated. The award is based on academic ability, character, leadership, potential service to the industrial engineering profession and financial need.

Target applicants: College students. Adult students.

Minimum GPA: 3.4

Amount: $3,000.

Number of awards: 3.

Deadline: February 1.

How to apply: Nomination forms are available online.

Exclusive: Visit www.UltimateScholarshipBook.com and enter code IN83812 for updates on this award.

(839) • E.J. Sierieja Memorial Fellowship

Institute of Industrial Engineers
3577 Parkway Lane
Suite 200
Norcross, GA 30092
Phone: 800-494-0460
Fax: 770-441-3295
Email: bcameron@iienet.org
http://www.iienet2.org

Purpose: To award graduate students pursuing advanced studies in the area of transportation.

Eligibility: Applicants must be full-time graduate students, majoring in transportation and active members. Students may not apply directly for this scholarship and must be nominated. The award is based on academic ability, character, leadership, potential service to the industrial engineering profession and financial need. Preference is given to students focusing on rail transportation.

Target applicants: Graduate school students. Adult students.

Minimum GPA: 3.4

Amount: $700.

Number of awards: 1.

Deadline: February 1.

How to apply: Nomination forms are available online.

Exclusive: Visit www.UltimateScholarshipBook.com and enter code IN83912 for updates on this award.

(840) • East Asia and Pacific Summer Institutes

National Science Foundation East Asia and Pacific Summer Institutes
1818 N Street NW
Suite T-50
Washington, DC 20036
Phone: 866-501-2922
Email: eapsi@asee.org
http://www.nsfsi.org

Purpose: To develop globally-engaged U.S. scientists and engineers knowledgeable about the Asian and Pacific regions.

Eligibility: Applicants must be U.S. graduate students enrolled in a research-oriented master's or Ph.D. program or college graduates enrolled in a joint bachelor's/master's program at a U.S. institution. Students must pursue studies in science and engineering research. The award provides summer research experience in Australia, China, Japan, Korea, New Zealand, Singapore or Taiwan, a $5,000 stipend, round-trip airfare, living expenses and orientation in Washington, DC.

Target applicants: Graduate school students. Adult students.

Amount: $5,000, airfare and living expenses.

Number of awards: 210.

Deadline: December.

How to apply: Applications are available online. A cover sheet, application form, project summary, project description, biographical sketch, two letters of recommendation and supplementary documents listed on the website are required.

Exclusive: Visit www.UltimateScholarshipBook.com and enter code NA84012 for updates on this award.

(841) • Eight and Forty Lung and Respiratory Nursing Scholarship Fund

American Legion
Attn.: Americanism and Children and Youth Division
P.O. Box 1055
Indianapolis, IN 46206
Phone: 317-630-1249
Fax: 317-630-1369
Email: acy@legion.org
http://www.legion.org

Purpose: To assist registered nurses.

Eligibility: Applicants must plan to be employed full-time in hospitals, clinics or health departments in a position related to lung and respiratory control.

Target applicants: College students. Graduate school students. Adult students.

Amount: $3,000.
Number of awards: Varies.
Deadline: May 15.
How to apply: Applications are available by written request.
Exclusive: Visit www.UltimateScholarshipBook.com and enter code AM84112 for updates on this award.

(842) · Eileen J. Garrett Scholarship

Parapsychology Foundation
P.O. Box 1562
New York, NY 10021-0043
Phone: 212-628-1550
Fax: 212-628-1559
Email: office@parapsychology.org
http://www.parapsychology.org
Purpose: To aid a student attending an accredited school in the academic study of parapsychology.
Eligibility: Applicants must be college undergraduates or graduate students and include a sample of writings on parapsychology, three references and application form.
Target applicants: College students. Graduate school students. Adult students.
Amount: $3,000.
Number of awards: 1.
Deadline: July 15.
How to apply: Applications are available online or by email.
Exclusive: Visit www.UltimateScholarshipBook.com and enter code PA84212 for updates on this award.

(843) · Elson T. Killam Memorial Scholarship

New England Water Works Association
125 Hopping Brook Road
Holliston, MA 01746
Phone: 508-893-7979
Email: tmacelhaney@preloadinc.com
http://www.newwa.org
Purpose: To support civil and environmental engineering students who are members of the New England Water Works Association.
Eligibility: Applicants must be enrolled in a civil or environmental engineering degree program and must be members of NEWWA. Selection is based on the overall strength of the application.
Target applicants: College students. Adult students.
Amount: $1,500.
Number of awards: 1.
Deadline: April 1.
How to apply: Applications are available online. An application form, official transcript and one recommendation letter are required.
Exclusive: Visit www.UltimateScholarshipBook.com and enter code NE84312 for updates on this award.

(844) · ENA Foundation Undergraduate Scholarship

Emergency Nurses Association
915 Lee Street
Des Plaines, IL 60016
Phone: 847-460-4100
Fax: 847-460-4004
Email: foundation@ena.org
http://www.ena.org
Purpose: To promote research and education in emergency care.
Eligibility: Applicants must be nurses pursuing baccalaureate degrees in nursing and must have been ENA members for at least 12 months before applying. Selection is based on application, statement of goals, references and transcript.
Target applicants: College students. Adult students.
Amount: $2,000-$5,000.
Number of awards: 8.
Deadline: June 1.
How to apply: Applications are available online.
Exclusive: Visit www.UltimateScholarshipBook.com and enter code EM84412 for updates on this award.

(845) · Engineering Undergraduate Award

American Society for Nondestructive Testing
1711 Arlingate Lane
P.O. Box 28518
Columbus, OH 43228
Phone: 800-222-2768
Fax: 614-274-6899
Email: sthomas@asnt.org
http://www.asnt.org
Purpose: To support students studying nondestructive testing.
Eligibility: Applicants must be undergraduate students enrolled in an engineering program of an accredited university and specialize in nondestructive testing (NDT). A nominating letter, transcript, three letters of recommendation and an essay describing the role of NDT/NDE in their career are required.
Target applicants: College students. Adult students.
Amount: $3,000.
Number of awards: Up to 3.
Deadline: December 15.
How to apply: Applications are available online.
Exclusive: Visit www.UltimateScholarshipBook.com and enter code AM84512 for updates on this award.

(846) · Eugene S. Kropf Scholarship

University Aviation Association Eugene S. Kropf Scholarship
Kevin R. Kuhlmann, Professor of Aviation and Aerospace Science
Metropolitan State College of Denver
Campus Box 30, P.O. Box 173362
Denver, CO 80217
Phone: 334-844-2434
Fax: 334-844-2432
http://www.uaa.aero
Purpose: To support students studying an aviation-related curriculum.
Eligibility: Applicants must be U.S. citizens enrolled in an aviation-related curriculum of a two-year or a four-year degree at a UAA member college or university. Students must have a 3.0 GPA and write a 250-word paper on how they can improve aviation education.
Target applicants: College students. Adult students.
Minimum GPA: 3.0
Amount: $500.
Number of awards: 1.
Deadline: May 31.
How to apply: Applications are available online.
Exclusive: Visit www.UltimateScholarshipBook.com and enter code UN84612 for updates on this award.

(847) • F.W. Beichley Scholarship

American Society of Mechanical Engineers (ASME)
Three Park Avenue
New York, NY 10016
Phone: 800-843-2763
Fax: 973-882-1717
Email: infocentral@asme.org
http://www.asme.org

Purpose: To support mechanical engineering students.

Eligibility: Applicants must be ASME student members enrolled in an eligible accredited mechanical engineering baccalaureate program. Selection is based on leadership, scholastic ability, potential contribution to the mechanical engineering profession and financial need. The scholarship is only applicable for study in the junior or senior year.

Target applicants: College students. Adult students.
Amount: $2,500.
Number of awards: 1.
Deadline: March 1.
How to apply: Applications are available online.
Exclusive: Visit www.UltimateScholarshipBook.com and enter code AM84712 for updates on this award.

(848) • Fellowship Award

Damon Runyon Cancer Research Foundation
675 Third Avenue, 25th Floor
New York, NY 10017
Phone: 212-455-0520
Fax: 212-455-0529
Email: awards@drcrf.org
http://www.drcrf.org

Purpose: To support the training of postdoctoral scientists as they start their research careers.

Eligibility: Applicants must have completed one or more of the following degrees or its equivalent: M.D., Ph.D., M.D./Ph.D., D.D.S. or D.V.M. Applicants should submit an application cover sheet, sponsor's biographical sketch, CV, degree certificate, letter, research proposal, summary of research form, up to three reprints of work and four letters of reference. This is a three-year award with various deadlines and funding. The research must be conducted at a university, hospital or research institution. International candidates may apply to do their research only in the United States.

Target applicants: Graduate school students. Adult students.
Amount: $50,000-$60,000.
Number of awards: Varies.
Deadline: March 15.
How to apply: Applications are available online.
Exclusive: Visit www.UltimateScholarshipBook.com and enter code DA84812 for updates on this award.

(849) • Fellowship in Aerospace History

American Historical Association
400 A Street SE
Washington, DC 20003
Phone: 202-544-2422
Fax: 202-544-8307
Email: info@historians.org
http://www.historians.org

Purpose: To provide funding for an academic research project related to aerospace history.

Eligibility: Applicants must possess a doctorate degree in history or a related field or be enrolled in a doctorate program (all coursework completed). One fellow will be appointed for one academic year. The fellow will be expected to write a report and present a paper or lecture on the research at the end of the term.

Target applicants: Graduate school students. Adult students.
Amount: $20,000.
Number of awards: 1.
Deadline: March 1.
How to apply: Applications are available online.
Exclusive: Visit www.UltimateScholarshipBook.com and enter code AM84912 for updates on this award.

(850) • Ferrous Metallurgy Education Today (FeMET)

Iron and Steel Society
Attn.: Lori Wharrey
AIST Foundation
186 Thorn Hill Road
Warrendale, PA 15086
Phone: 724-776-6040 x621
Fax: 724-776-1880
Email: lwharrey@aist.org
http://www.aistfoundation.org

Purpose: To increase the number of metallurgy and materials science students in North America and to encourage them to pursue careers in the iron and steel industry.

Eligibility: Applicants must be college juniors who are majoring in metallurgy or materials science at a North American University, and they must show interest in the iron and steel industry. Applicants must also have a minimum GPA of 3.0 and be eligible for and commit to a paid summer internship at a North American steel company.

Target applicants: College students. Adult students.
Minimum GPA: 3.0
Amount: $5,000.
Number of awards: 10.
Scholarship may be renewable.
Deadline: March 5.
How to apply: Applications are available online.
Exclusive: Visit www.UltimateScholarshipBook.com and enter code IR85012 for updates on this award.

(851) • Foundation for Neonatal Research and Education Scholarships

Foundation for Neonatal Research and Education
200 East Holly Avenue
Box 56
Pitman, NJ 08071
Phone: 856-256-2343
Fax: 856-589-7463
Email: fnre@ajj.com
http://www.inurse.com/fnre

Purpose: To aid practicing neonatal nurses who are pursuing additional education through an undergraduate or graduate degree program in nursing.

Eligibility: Applicants must be accepted into a Bachelor of Science in Nursing (BSN) program (current Registered Nurses), a Master of Science in Nursing (MSN) program for advanced practice in neonatal nursing, a doctoral degree program in nursing or a Master's or post-Master's nursing degree program in Business Management or Nursing Administration. They must have a GPA of 3.0 or more and must be actively involved in neonatal nursing at the professional level. They cannot have received

a grant or scholarship from the FNRE within the past five years, and they cannot be current members of the FNRE Scholarship Committee or Board. Selection is based on the overall strength of the application.
Target applicants: College students. Graduate school students. Adult students.
Minimum GPA: 3.0
Amount: Varies.
Number of awards: Varies.
Deadline: May 1.
How to apply: Applications are available online. An application form, resume, enrollment verification letter, personal statement, three evaluation letters and a transcript are required.
Exclusive: Visit www.UltimateScholarshipBook.com and enter code FO85112 for updates on this award.

(852) • Foundation for Surgical Technology Advanced Education/Medical Mission Scholarship

Association of Surgical Technologists
6 W. Dry Creek Circle
Littleton, CO 80120
Phone: 800-637-7433
Fax: 303-694-9169
Email: kludwig@ast.org
http://www.ast.org
Purpose: To help practitioners with continuing education or medical missionary work.
Eligibility: Applicants must be active AST members, document the educational program or mission program and provide two recommendation letters.
Target applicants: College students. Graduate school students. Adult students.
Amount: Varies.
Number of awards: Varies.
Deadline: December 31.
How to apply: Applications are available online.
Exclusive: Visit www.UltimateScholarshipBook.com and enter code AS85212 for updates on this award.

(853) • Foundation for Surgical Technology Scholarships

Association of Surgical Technologists
6 W. Dry Creek Circle
Littleton, CO 80120
Phone: 800-637-7433
Fax: 303-694-9169
Email: kludwig@ast.org
http://www.ast.org
Purpose: To support the continuing education of surgical technology students.
Eligibility: Applicants should be enrolled in accredited surgical technology programs and be eligible to sit for the Certified Surgical Technologist examination sponsored by the National Board of Surgical Technology and Surgical Assisting. Applications, transcripts, a minimum 3.0 GPA, essays and recommendation letters are required.
Target applicants: College students. Adult students.
Minimum GPA: 3.0
Amount: Up to $2,000.
Number of awards: 15.
Deadline: March 1.
How to apply: Applications are available online.
Exclusive: Visit www.UltimateScholarshipBook.com and enter code AS85312 for updates on this award.

(854) • Foundation for Surgical Technology Student Scholarship

Association of Surgical Technologists
6 W. Dry Creek Circle
Littleton, CO 80120
Phone: 800-637-7433
Fax: 303-694-9169
Email: kludwig@ast.org
http://www.ast.org
Purpose: To help surgical technology students in CAAHEP-accredited surgical technology programs.
Eligibility: Applicants must be currently enrolled in a surgical technology program accredited by the Commission on Accreditation of Allied Health Education Programs (CAAHEP). Applicants must also demonstrate academic achievement and financial need. Applications, transcripts and an instructor evaluation are required.
Target applicants: College students. Adult students.
Amount: Varies.
Number of awards: Varies.
Deadline: March 1.
How to apply: Applications are available online.
Exclusive: Visit www.UltimateScholarshipBook.com and enter code AS85412 for updates on this award.

(855) • Foundation of the National Student Nurses' Association Career Mobility Scholarships

National Student Nurses' Association
45 Main Street
Suite 606
Brooklyn, NY 11201
Phone: 718-210-0705
Fax: 718-797-1186
Email: nsna@nsna.org
http://www.nsna.org
Purpose: To aid nursing and pre-nursing students who are enrolled in LPN to RN, RN to BSN and RN to MSN programs.
Eligibility: Applicants must be nursing or pre-nursing students who are pursuing LPN to RN, RN to BSN or RN to MSN degrees. Selection is based on the overall strength of the application.
Target applicants: College students. Graduate school students. Adult students.
Amount: $2,000.
Number of awards: Varies.
Deadline: January 13.
How to apply: Applications are available online. An application form and supporting documents are required.
Exclusive: Visit www.UltimateScholarshipBook.com and enter code NA85512 for updates on this award.

(856) • Foundation of the National Student Nurses' Association Specialty Scholarship

National Student Nurses' Association
45 Main Street
Suite 606
Brooklyn, NY 11201
Phone: 718-210-0705

Fax: 718-797-1186
Email: nsna@nsna.org
http://www.nsna.org
Purpose: To aid nursing students who are planning to pursue careers in specialized areas.
Eligibility: Applicants must be nursing students who are interested in a specialized area of nursing practice. Selection is based on the overall strength of the application.
Target applicants: College students. Adult students.
Amount: $2,000.
Number of awards: Varies.
Deadline: January 13.
How to apply: Applications are available online. An application form and supporting materials are required.
Exclusive: Visit www.UltimateScholarshipBook.com and enter code NA85612 for updates on this award.

(857) • Frank and Brennie Morgan Prize for Outstanding Research in Mathematics by an Undergraduate Student

American Mathematical Society and Mathematical Association of America
Dr. Martha J. Siegel, MAA Secretary
Mathematics Department, Towson University
339 YR, 8000 York Road
Towson, MD 21252
Phone: 410-704-2980
Email: siegel@towson.edu
http://www.ams.org
Purpose: Awarded to an undergraduate student (or students who have collaborated) for research in the field of mathematics.
Eligibility: Applicants must be undergraduate students at colleges or universities in the United States or its possessions, Canada and Mexico. Students must be nominated.
Target applicants: College students. Adult students.
Amount: $1,200.
Number of awards: 1.
Deadline: July 15.
How to apply: Nomination information is available by email. Questions should be directed to Dr. Martha J. Siegel at the address above. Nominations and submissions should be sent to: Morgan Prize Committee, c/o Robert J. Daverman, American Mathematical Society, 312D Ayres Hall, University of Tennessee, Knoxville, TN 37996.
Exclusive: Visit www.UltimateScholarshipBook.com and enter code AM85712 for updates on this award.

(858) • Frank and Dorothy Miller ASME Auxiliary Scholarships

American Society of Mechanical Engineers (ASME)
Three Park Avenue
New York, NY 10016
Phone: 800-843-2763
Fax: 973-882-1717
Email: infocentral@asme.org
http://www.asme.org
Purpose: To support U.S. mechanical engineering and mechanical engineering technology undergraduates.
Eligibility: Applicants must be U.S. citizens and residents of North America. They must be rising undergraduate sophomores, juniors or seniors who are enrolled in an ABET-accredited (or equivalent) mechanical engineering, mechanical engineering technology or related program at a U.S. postsecondary institution. They must be ASME student members who are in good standing. Selection is based on leadership, integrity and potential contribution to the field of mechanical engineering.
Target applicants: College students. Adult students.
Amount: $2,000.
Number of awards: Up to 2.
Deadline: March 1.
How to apply: The application form is available through ASME's online scholarship application system. This form, an official transcript, a personal statement and up to two recommendation letters are required.
Exclusive: Visit www.UltimateScholarshipBook.com and enter code AM85812 for updates on this award.

(859) • Frank Lanza Memorial Scholarship

Phi Theta Kappa Honor Society
1625 Eastover Drive
Jackson, MS 39211
Phone: 601-984-3504
Fax: 601-984-3548
Email: scholarship.programs@ptk.org
http://www.ptk.org
Purpose: To aid financially needy students who are pursuing associate's degrees in emergency medical services, registered nursing or respiratory care.
Eligibility: Applicants must be enrolled in an associate's degree program in respiratory care, emergency medical services or registered nursing at a regionally accredited community college. They must have completed 50 percent or more of their degree programs, have a GPA of 3.0 or higher on a four-point scale and be enrolled for six or more credit hours per semester. They must have a college record that is free of disciplinary action and must not have a criminal record. Selection is based on financial need.
Target applicants: College students. Adult students.
Minimum GPA: 3.0
Amount: $1,000.
Number of awards: Up to 25.
Deadline: October 15.
How to apply: Applications are available online. An application form, Student Aid Report and supporting materials are required.
Exclusive: Visit www.UltimateScholarshipBook.com and enter code PH85912 for updates on this award.

(860) • Fred M. Young, Sr./SAE Engineering Scholarship

Society of Automotive Engineers International
400 Commonwealth Drive
Warrendale, PA 15096
Phone: 724-776-4841
Fax: 724-776-0790
Email: scholarships@sae.org
http://www.sae.org
Purpose: To support high school seniors who are planning to study engineering at the undergraduate level.
Eligibility: Applicants must be U.S. citizens and must be high school seniors. They must have SAT or ACT scores that rank in the 90th percentile and must have a GPA of 3.75 or higher on a four-point scale. They must plan to enroll in an ABET-accredited undergraduate engineering program. Selection is based on the overall strength of the application.

Target applicants: High school students.
Minimum GPA: 3.75
Amount: $1,000.
Number of awards: 1.
Scholarship may be renewable.
Deadline: January 15.
How to apply: Applications are available online. An application form, official transcript and standardized test scores are required.
Exclusive: Visit www.UltimateScholarshipBook.com and enter code SO86012 for updates on this award.

(861) • Freshman and Sophomore Scholarships

Institute of Food Technologists (IFT)
525 W. Van Buren
Suite 1000
Chicago, IL 60607
Phone: 312-782-8424
Email: ejplummer@ift.org
http://www.ift.org
Purpose: To help young food scientists who plan to work in industry, government and academia.
Eligibility: Applicants for the freshman scholarships must be academically outstanding high school graduates or seniors who will enter college for the first time in an approved program in food science/technology. The deadline for the freshman scholarships is February 15. Applicants for the sophomore scholarships must be academically outstanding college freshman with a minimum 2.5 GPA in an approved program in food science/technology. The deadline for the sophomore scholarships is March 1. All candidates must submit applications, transcripts and a recommendation.
Target applicants: High school students. College students. Adult students.
Minimum GPA: 2.5
Amount: $1,000.
Number of awards: 31.
Deadline: February 15 for freshmen, March 1 for sophomores.
How to apply: Applications are available online.
Exclusive: Visit www.UltimateScholarshipBook.com and enter code IN86112 for updates on this award.

(862) • Freshman Undergraduate Scholarship

American Meteorological Society
Fellowship and Scholarship Department
45 Beacon Street
Boston, MA 02108-3693
Phone: 617-227-2426 x246
Fax: 617-742-8718
Email: dsampson@ametsoc.org
http://www.ametsoc.org/AMS/
Purpose: To encourage high school students to pursue careers in the atmospheric and related oceanic and hydrologic sciences.
Eligibility: Applicants must enter as full-time freshmen the following fall and major in the atmospheric or related oceanic and hydrologic sciences. Applicants should submit applications, transcripts, recommendation letter and SAT or equivalent scores.
Target applicants: High school students.
Amount: $2,500.
Number of awards: Varies.
Scholarship may be renewable.
Deadline: February 11.
How to apply: Applications are available online.
Exclusive: Visit www.UltimateScholarshipBook.com and enter code AM86212 for updates on this award.

(863) • Future Engineers Scholarship

Kelly Engineering Resources
999 West Big Beaver Road
Troy, MI 48084
Phone: 248-362-4444
Email: kfirst@kellyservices.com
http://www.kellyengineering.us
Purpose: To support engineering students.
Eligibility: Applicants must be U.S. citizens, resident aliens or U.S. nationals. They must be full-time undergraduate students who are enrolled in or who have been accepted into the school of engineering at their postsecondary institution. Students must have junior or senior standing and have a GPA of 3.0 or higher on a four-point scale. Selection is based on academic achievement and professional commitment to the field of engineering.
Target applicants: College students. Adult students.
Minimum GPA: 3.0
Amount: $5,000.
Number of awards: 1.
Deadline: October 15.
How to apply: Applications are available online. An application form, personal essay, transcript and two letters of recommendation are required.
Exclusive: Visit www.UltimateScholarshipBook.com and enter code KE86312 for updates on this award.

(864) • Gabe A. Hartl Scholarship

Air Traffic Control Association
1101 King Street
Suite 300
Alexandria, VA 22134
Phone: 703-299-2430
Fax: 703-299-2437
Email: info@atca.org
http://www.atca.org
Purpose: To support air traffic control students.
Eligibility: Applicants must be enrolled in or plan to be enrolled in a two- to four-year postsecondary program in air traffic control as a part-time or full-time student. The program must be approved by the Federal Aviation Administration as a college training initiative supporter. They must have 30 or more semester hours (or 45 or more quarter hours) remaining in their program of study at the time of submitting the application. Selection is based on the overall strength of the application.
Target applicants: High school students. College students. Adult students.
Amount: Varies.
Number of awards: Varies.
Deadline: May 1.
How to apply: Applications are available online. An application form, official transcript, two letters of recommendation and essay response are required.
Exclusive: Visit www.UltimateScholarshipBook.com and enter code AI86412 for updates on this award.

(865) • Gaige Fund Award

American Society of Ichthyologists and Herpetologists
Maureen Donnelly, Secretary
Department of Biological Sciences, Florida International University

11200 SW 8th Street
Miami, FL 33199
Phone: 305-348-1235
Fax: 305-348-1986
Email: asih@fiu.edu
http://www.asih.org
Purpose: To support young herpetologists.
Eligibility: Applicants must be members of ASIH and studying for an advanced degree. The award may be used for museum or laboratory study, travel, fieldwork or other activities that will enhance their careers and their contributions to the science of herpetology. Both merit and need will be considered.
Target applicants: Graduate school students. Adult students.
Amount: $400-$1,000.
Number of awards: Varies.
Deadline: March 1.
How to apply: Applications are available by email or written request.
Exclusive: Visit www.UltimateScholarshipBook.com and enter code AM86512 for updates on this award.

---

(866) • Garland Duncan Scholarships

American Society of Mechanical Engineers (ASME)
Three Park Avenue
New York, NY 10016
Phone: 800-843-2763
Fax: 973-882-1717
Email: infocentral@asme.org
http://www.asme.org
Purpose: To support mechanical engineering students.
Eligibility: Applicants must be ASME student members, be enrolled in an eligible accredited mechanical engineering baccalaureate program, have strong academic performance and be college juniors or seniors. Selection is based on character, integrity, leadership, scholastic ability, potential contribution to the mechanical engineering profession and financial need.
Target applicants: College students. Adult students.
Amount: $4,500.
Number of awards: 2.
Deadline: March 1.
How to apply: Applications are available online.
Exclusive: Visit www.UltimateScholarshipBook.com and enter code AM86612 for updates on this award.

---

(867) • Garmin Scholarship

Aircraft Electronics Association
4217 South Hocker
Independence, MO 64055
Phone: 816-373-6565
Fax: 816-478-3100
Email: info@aea.net
http://www.aea.net
Purpose: To support students who wish to pursue a career in avionics and aircraft repair.
Eligibility: Applicants must be high school seniors or college students who plan to or are attending an accredited school in an avionics or aircraft repair program.
Target applicants: High school students. College students. Adult students.
Amount: Varies.
Number of awards: 1.
Deadline: February 15.
How to apply: Applications are available online.
Exclusive: Visit www.UltimateScholarshipBook.com and enter code AI86712 for updates on this award.

---

(868) • Gary Kiteley Executive Director Scholarship

University Aviation Association (UAA)
David NewMyer
College of Applied Sciences and Arts, Southern Illinois University Carbondale
1365 Douglas Drive, Room 126
Carbondale , IL 62901-6623
Phone: 618-453-8898
Fax: 618-453-7286
Email: newmyer@siu.edu
http://www.uaa.aero
Purpose: To support aviation students at UAA institutions.
Eligibility: Applicants must be enrolled at a UAA member college or university in an aviation-related curriculum and be a UAA student member. Fifteen hours in an associate degree program or 30 hours in a bachelor's degree program should have been completed.
Target applicants: College students. Adult students.
Minimum GPA: 3.0
Amount: $500.
Number of awards: 1.
Deadline: Varies.
How to apply: Applications are available online.
Exclusive: Visit www.UltimateScholarshipBook.com and enter code UN86812 for updates on this award.

---

(869) • GAT Wings to the Future Management Scholarship

Women in Aviation, International
Morningstar Airport
3647 State Route 503 South
West Alexandria, OH 45381
Phone: 937-839-4647
Fax: 937-839-4645
Email: dwallace@wai.org
http://www.wai.org
Purpose: To support female aviation business and management students.
Eligibility: Applicants must be female members of Women in Aviation, International. They must be enrolled full-time in an accredited postsecondary program in aviation business or aviation management and must have a GPA of 3.0 or higher. Selection is based on the overall strength of the application.
Target applicants: College students. Adult students.
Minimum GPA: 3.0
Amount: $2,500.
Number of awards: 1.
Deadline: November 20.
How to apply: Applications are available online. An application form, personal essay, resume, three recommendation letters and copies of all medical and aviation certificates (if applicable) are required.
Exclusive: Visit www.UltimateScholarshipBook.com and enter code WO86912 for updates on this award.

---

(870) • GBT Student Support Program

National Radio Astronomy Observatory (NRAO)
NRAO Headquarters

520 Edgemont Road
Charlottesville, VA 22903
Phone: 434-296-0211
Fax: 434-296-0278
Email: info@nrao.edu
http://www.nrao.edu
Purpose: To support student research at the Robert C. Byrd Green Bank Telescope (GBT).
Eligibility: GBT is the largest fully steerable single aperture antenna. Students begin the application process by completing a preliminary funding proposal form. If the proposal is accepted, they will be informed of further requirements.
Target applicants: College students. Graduate school students. Adult students.
Amount: Up to $35,000.
Number of awards: Varies.
Deadline: Varies.
How to apply: Applications are available online.
Exclusive: Visit www.UltimateScholarshipBook.com and enter code NA87012 for updates on this award.

(871) • GCSAA Scholars Competition

Golf Course Superintendents Association of America
GCSAA Career Development Department
1421 Research Park Drive
Lawrence, KS 66049
Phone: 800-472-7878
Fax: 785-832-3643
Email: mbrhelp@gcsaa.org
http://www.gcsaa.org
Purpose: To support students preparing for careers in golf course management.
Eligibility: Applicants must be GCSAA members who are undergraduate students enrolled in an accredited degree program in turf management or a closely related subject. They must have completed at least 24 semester credits or one year of full-time study in their degree program. Selection is based on academic excellence, career potential, recommendations, work history and extracurricular activities.
Target applicants: College students. Adult students.
Amount: Up to $6,000.
Number of awards: Varies.
Deadline: June 1.
How to apply: Applications are available online. An application form, personal essay, transcripts and reports from the applicant's academic advisor and golf course superintendent are required.
Exclusive: Visit www.UltimateScholarshipBook.com and enter code GO87112 for updates on this award.

(872) • GCSAA Student Essay Contest

Golf Course Superintendents Association of America
GCSAA Career Development Department
1421 Research Park Drive
Lawrence, KS 66049
Phone: 800-472-7878
Fax: 785-832-3643
Email: mbrhelp@gcsaa.org
http://www.gcsaa.org
Purpose: To support students pursuing degrees in golf course management.
Eligibility: Applicants must be undergraduate or graduate students pursuing degrees in turfgrass science, agronomy or any other golf course management-related field. Applicants must be members of GCSAA and write an essay on golf course management.
Target applicants: College students. Graduate school students. Adult students.
Amount: $1,000-$2,000.
Number of awards: Up to 3.
Deadline: March 31.
How to apply: Applications are available by contacting Pam Smith, 800-472-7878 x3678.
Exclusive: Visit www.UltimateScholarshipBook.com and enter code GO87212 for updates on this award.

(873) • General James H. Doolittle Scholarship

Communities Foundation of Texas
5500 Caruth Haven Lane
Dallas, TX 75225
Phone: 214-750-4222
Email: info@cftexas.org
http://www.cftexas.org
Purpose: To support aeronautical engineering and aerospace science students.
Eligibility: Applicants must be undergraduate juniors, undergraduate seniors or graduate students enrolled in a degree program in aerospace science or aeronautical engineering. Students do NOT need to be Texas residents. Selection is based on the overall strength of the application.
Target applicants: College students. Graduate school students. Adult students.
Amount: Up to $5,000.
Number of awards: Varies.
Deadline: May 7.
How to apply: Applications are available online. An application form and supporting documents are required.
Exclusive: Visit www.UltimateScholarshipBook.com and enter code CO87312 for updates on this award.

(874) • GeoEye Award

American Society for Photogrammetry and Remote Sensing (ASPRS)
The Imaging and Geospatial Information Society
5410 Grosvenor Lane
Suite 210
Bethesda, MD 20814
Phone: 301-493-0290 x101
Fax: 301-493-0208
Email: scholarships@asprs.org
http://www.asprs.org
Purpose: To support remote sensing education and stimulate the development of applications of high-resolution digital satellite imagery for applied research by undergraduate or graduate students.
Eligibility: Applicants must be full-time undergraduate or graduate students at an accredited college or university with proper image processing facilities. Selection is based on the application, letters of recommendation and a brief two-page proposal. The structure for the proposal can be found on the website. This award consists of high resolution digital satellite imagery valued at up to $2,000.
Target applicants: College students. Graduate school students. Adult students.
Amount: Imagery award.
Number of awards: 1-3.
Deadline: December 1.
How to apply: Applications are available online.

Exclusive: Visit www.UltimateScholarshipBook.com and enter code AM87412 for updates on this award.

(875) • George A. Hall / Harold F. Mayfield Award

Wilson Ornithological Society
Dr. Robert B. Payne
Museum of Zoology, University of Michigan
1109 Gedes Avenue
Ann Arbor, MI 48109
Email: rbpayne@umich.edu
http://www.wilsonsociety.org
Purpose: To assist those who are conducting avian research.
Eligibility: Applicants must be independent researchers without access to funds available at colleges, universities or government agencies and must be non-professionals currently conducting avian research. Applicants must also be willing to present their research results at an annual meeting of the Wilson Ornithological Society.
Target applicants: High school students. College students. Graduate school students. Adult students.
Amount: $1,000.
Number of awards: 1.
Deadline: February 1.
How to apply: Applications are available online.
Exclusive: Visit www.UltimateScholarshipBook.com and enter code WI87512 for updates on this award.

(876) • George A. Roberts Scholarships

ASM International Foundation
9639 Kinsman Road
Materials Park, OH 44073
Phone: 440-338-5151
Fax: 440-338-4634
Email: asmif@asminternational.org
http://asmcommunity.asminternational.org/portal/site/www/Foundation
Purpose: To help students interested in the metallurgy or materials engineering field.
Eligibility: Applicants must be student members of ASM International, plan to major in metallurgy or materials science engineering and be juniors or seniors at a North American university that has a bachelor's degree program in science and engineering. Applications, personal statements, transcripts, two recommendation forms, photographs and financial aid officers' contact information are required. The award is based on academics, interest in the field, character and financial need.
Target applicants: College students. Adult students.
Amount: $6,000.
Number of awards: Up to 7.
Deadline: May 1.
How to apply: Applications are available online.
Exclusive: Visit www.UltimateScholarshipBook.com and enter code AS87612 for updates on this award.

(877) • Gertrude Cox Scholarship For Women In Statistics

American Statistical Association
Dr. Amita Manatunga, Gertrude Cox Scholarship Committee Chair
Department of Biostatistics, Emory University
1518 Clifton Road NE #374
Atlanta, GA 30322
Phone: 404-727-1309
Fax: 404-727-1370
Email: amanatu@sph.emory.edu
http://www.amstat.org
Purpose: To encourage women to pursue education for careers in statistics.
Eligibility: Applicants must be women who are full-time students in a graduate-level statistics programs.
Target applicants: Graduate school students. Adult students.
Amount: $2,000.
Number of awards: Varies.
Deadline: April 1.
How to apply: Applications are available online.
Exclusive: Visit www.UltimateScholarshipBook.com and enter code AM87712 for updates on this award.

(878) • Gilbreth Memorial Fellowship

Institute of Industrial Engineers
3577 Parkway Lane
Suite 200
Norcross, GA 30092
Phone: 800-494-0460
Fax: 770-441-3295
Email: bcameron@iienet.org
http://www.iienet2.org
Purpose: To support graduate student Institute members.
Eligibility: Applicants must be graduate students at an institution in the United States, Canada or Mexico, majoring in industrial engineering or its equivalent and active members. Students may not apply directly for this scholarship and must be nominated. The award is based on academic ability, character, leadership, potential service to the industrial engineering profession and financial need.
Target applicants: Graduate school students. Adult students.
Minimum GPA: 3.4
Amount: $3,000.
Number of awards: 2.
Deadline: February 1.
How to apply: Nomination forms are available online.
Exclusive: Visit www.UltimateScholarshipBook.com and enter code IN87812 for updates on this award.

(879) • Giuliano Mazzetti Scholarship

Society of Manufacturing Engineers Education Foundation
One SME Drive
P.O. Box 930
Dearborn, MI 48121
Phone: 313-425-3300
Fax: 313-425-3411
Email: foundation@sme.org
http://www.smeef.org
Purpose: To support undergraduate students of manufacturing engineering and technology.
Eligibility: Applicants must be full-time undergraduate students who have completed 30 or more credit hours at a postsecondary institution located in the United States or Canada. They must be studying manufacturing engineering, technology or a related subject and must have plans to pursue a career in one of these same fields. Students must have a GPA of 3.0 or more on a four-point scale. Selection is based on the overall strength of the application.
Target applicants: College students. Adult students.
Minimum GPA: 3.0
Amount: At least $1,000.

Number of awards: Varies.
Deadline: February 1.
How to apply: Applications are available online. An application form, personal statement, resume, transcript and two recommendation letters are required.
Exclusive: Visit www.UltimateScholarshipBook.com and enter code SO87912 for updates on this award.

(880) · Gladys Anderson Emerson Scholarship

Iota Sigma Pi (ISP) ND
Professor Kathryn A. Thomasson, Iota Sigma Pi Director for Student Awards
University of North Dakota, Department of Chemistry
P.O. Box 9024
Grand Forks, ND 58202-9024
Phone: 701-777-3199
Fax: 701-777-2331
Email: kthomasson@chem.und.edu
http://www.iotasigmapi.info
Purpose: To award achievement in the fields of chemistry and biochemistry by women.
Eligibility: Applicants must have attained junior status at an accredited college or university, be female and be nominated by a member of Iota Sigma Pi.
Target applicants: College students. Graduate school students. Adult students.
Amount: $2,000.
Number of awards: Up to 2.
Deadline: February 15.
How to apply: Applications are available online.
Exclusive: Visit www.UltimateScholarshipBook.com and enter code IO88012 for updates on this award.

(881) · Graduate Fellowships

Institute of Food Technologists (IFT)
525 W. Van Buren
Suite 1000
Chicago, IL 60607
Phone: 312-782-8424
Email: ejplummer@ift.org
http://www.ift.org
Purpose: To award graduate students researching food science or technology.
Eligibility: Applicants should be graduate students pursuing an M.S. and/or Ph.D. at the time the fellowship becomes effective and should research an area of food science or technology. Applications, transcripts and three recommendation letters are required.
Target applicants: Graduate school students. Adult students.
Amount: $1,000-$5,000.
Number of awards: Varies.
Deadline: February 19.
How to apply: Applications are available online.
Exclusive: Visit www.UltimateScholarshipBook.com and enter code IN88112 for updates on this award.

(882) · Graduate Research Award (GRA)

American Vacuum Society
120 Wall Street, 32nd Floor
New York, NY 10005-3993
Phone: 212-248-0200
Fax: 212-248-0245
Email: angela@avs.org
http://www.avs.org
Purpose: To support graduate studies in the sciences and technologies related to the AVS.
Eligibility: Applicants must be graduate students in an accredited academic institution. Awards are based on research and academic record. The awards cover travel expenses to the international symposium. Applicants should submit applications, recommendation letters, research summaries and transcripts.
Target applicants: Graduate school students. Adult students.
Amount: Varies.
Number of awards: Varies.
Deadline: May 5.
How to apply: Applications are available online.
Exclusive: Visit www.UltimateScholarshipBook.com and enter code AM88212 for updates on this award.

(883) · Graduate Research Fellowship Program

National Science Foundation Graduate Research Fellowship Operations Center
Suite T-50
1818 N Street, NW
Washington, DC 20036
Phone: 866-NSF-GRFP
Email: info@nsfgrfp.org
http://www.fastlane.nsf.gov/grfp/
Purpose: To assist science and engineering graduate students.
Eligibility: Applicants must be full-time students who have completed no more than 12 months of graduate study and be U.S. citizens, U.S. nationals or permanent residents. The fields of study are interdisciplinary, computer and information science and engineering, mathematical sciences, geosciences, psychology, social sciences, life sciences, chemistry, physics and astronomy and engineering.
Target applicants: Graduate school students. Adult students.
Amount: $40,500 and $1,000 travel allowance.
Number of awards: 1,000.
Deadline: November 2-12.
How to apply: Applications are available online. An online application form, official transcript and three letters of reference submitted electronically are required.
Exclusive: Visit www.UltimateScholarshipBook.com and enter code NA88312 for updates on this award.

(884) · Graduate Scholarships Program

Society of Naval Architects and Marine Engineers
601 Pavonia Avenue
Jersey City, NJ 07306
Phone: 201-798-4800
Fax: 201-798-4975
Email: efaustino@sname.org
http://www.sname.org
Purpose: To aid students who are pursuing a master's degree in a subject that is related to the marine industry.
Eligibility: Applicants must be members of the Society of Naval Architects and Marine Engineers (SNAME). They must be working towards a master's degree in ocean engineering, marine engineering, naval architecture or another marine-related subject. Students who will be receiving their degree before October 1 of the application year are ineligible. Selection is based on the overall strength of the application.
Target applicants: Graduate school students. Adult students.

Amount: Up to $20,000.
Number of awards: Varies.
Deadline: February 1.
How to apply: Applications are available online. An application form, transcript, standardized test scores and three recommendation letters are required.
Exclusive: Visit www.UltimateScholarshipBook.com and enter code SO88412 for updates on this award.

(885) · Graduate Student Research Grants

Geological Society of America
Program Officer
Grants, Awards and Recognition
P.O. Box 9140
Boulder, CO 80301-9140
Phone: 303-357-1028
Fax: 303-357-1070
Email: awards@geosociety.org
http://www.geosociety.org
Purpose: To support thesis and dissertation research for graduate students in geological science.
Eligibility: Applicants must currently be enrolled in a geological science graduate program at an institution in the United States, Canada, Mexico or Central America. Applicants must also be members of the Geological Society of America (GSA).
Target applicants: Graduate school students. Adult students.
Amount: Varies.
Number of awards: Varies.
Deadline: February 1.
How to apply: Applications are available online.
Exclusive: Visit www.UltimateScholarshipBook.com and enter code GE88512 for updates on this award.

(886) · Graduate Student Scholarship

American Speech-Language-Hearing Foundation
2200 Research Boulevard
Rockville, MD 20850
Phone: 301-296-8700
Email: foundation@asha.org
http://www.ashfoundation.org
Purpose: To support graduate students in communication sciences and disorders.
Eligibility: Applicants must be full-time graduate students in U.S. communication sciences and disorders programs. Master's degree candidates must be in programs accredited by the Council on Academic Accreditation for Audiology and Speech Pathology, but doctoral programs do not have to be accredited. Transcripts, an essay, a reference form and a statement of good standing are required.
Target applicants: Graduate school students. Adult students.
Amount: $4,000.
Number of awards: Up to 7.
Deadline: Varies.
How to apply: Applications are available online.
Exclusive: Visit www.UltimateScholarshipBook.com and enter code AM88612 for updates on this award.

(887) · Graduate Summer Student Research Assistantship

National Radio Astronomy Observatory (NRAO)
NRAO Headquarters
520 Edgemont Road
Charlottesville, VA 22903
Phone: 434-296-0211
Fax: 434-296-0278
Email: info@nrao.edu
http://www.nrao.edu
Purpose: To allow graduate students to perform astronomical research at National Radio Astronomy Observatory (NRAO) sites.
Eligibility: Applicants must be first- or second-year graduate students interested in astronomical research. Recipients work on-site for 10 to 12 weeks, beginning in late May or early June.
Target applicants: Graduate school students. Adult students.
Amount: Up to $652 per week stipend plus travel expenses.
Number of awards: Varies.
Deadline: February 1.
How to apply: Applications are available online.
Exclusive: Visit www.UltimateScholarshipBook.com and enter code NA88712 for updates on this award.

(888) · Green Mountain Water Environment Association Scholarship

Vermont Student Assistance Corporation
10 East Allen Street
P.O. Box 2000
Winooski, VT 05404
Phone: 800-882-4166
Fax: 802-654-3765
Email: info@vsac.org
http://www.vsac.org
Purpose: To aid students pursuing higher education in an environment-related subject.
Eligibility: Applicants must be full-time undergraduate students enrolled in an accredited institution of higher learning that is eligible for federal Title IV funding. They must be studying a subject related to environmental studies and must have a GPA of 3.0 or higher. Students must be active in community service and must demonstrate financial need. Selection is based on the overall strength of the application.
Target applicants: College students. Adult students.
Minimum GPA: 3.0
Amount: $1,000.
Number of awards: 1.
Deadline: March 5.
How to apply: Applications are available online. An application form, personal essay, official transcript and one letter of recommendation are required.
Exclusive: Visit www.UltimateScholarshipBook.com and enter code VE88812 for updates on this award.

(889) · Grotto Scholarships

DeMolay Foundation
10200 NW Ambassador Drive
Kansas City, MO 64153
Phone: 800-336-6529
Fax: 816-891-9062
Email: demolay@demolay.org
http://www.demolay.org
Purpose: To assist medical students.
Eligibility: Applicants must be enrolled in a dental, medical or pre-medical program at an accredited institution but do not need to be active members of DeMolay. Students should complete an application and submit it to the DeMolay Service and Leadership Center.

Target applicants: College students. Graduate school students. Adult students.
Amount: $1,500.
Number of awards: 4.
Deadline: April 1.
How to apply: Applications are available online.
Exclusive: Visit www.UltimateScholarshipBook.com and enter code DE88912 for updates on this award.

(890) • H.P. Milligan Aviation Scholarship

EAA Aviation Center
P.O. Box 2683
Oshkosh, WI 54903
Phone: 877-806-8902
Fax: 920-426-6865
Email: scholarships@eaa.org
http://www.youngeagles.org
Purpose: To support excellence among individuals studying aviation.
Eligibility: Applicants must be enrolled in an accredited college, aviation academy or technical school pursuing a course of study focusing on aviation. Applicants must also be involved in school and community activities as well as aviation and be an EAA member or be recommended by an EAA member.
Target applicants: High school students. College students. Adult students.
Amount: $500.
Number of awards: 1.
Scholarship may be renewable.
Deadline: February 28.
How to apply: Applications are available online.
Exclusive: Visit www.UltimateScholarshipBook.com and enter code EA89012 for updates on this award.

(891) • Hansen Scholarship

EAA Aviation Center
P.O. Box 2683
Oshkosh, WI 54903
Phone: 877-806-8902
Fax: 920-426-6865
Email: scholarships@eaa.org
http://www.youngeagles.org
Purpose: To support excellence among individuals studying the technologies and the skills needed in the field of aviation.
Eligibility: Applicants must be enrolled in an accredited college or university pursuing a degree in aerospace engineering or aeronautical engineering and must be involved in school and community activities as well as aviation. Applicants must be in good academic standing. Financial need will be considered. Applicants must also be EAA members or be recommended by an EAA member.
Target applicants: College students. Graduate school students. Adult students.
Amount: $1,000.
Number of awards: Varies.
Scholarship may be renewable.
Deadline: February 28.
How to apply: Applications are available online.
Exclusive: Visit www.UltimateScholarshipBook.com and enter code EA89112 for updates on this award.

(892) • Harness Tracks of America Scholarship Fund

Harness Tracks of America
4640 E. Sunrise, Suite 200
Tucson, AZ 85718
Phone: 520-529-2525
Fax: 520-529-3235
Email: info@harnesstracks.com
http://www.harnesstracks.com
Purpose: To provide assistance to students who are involved in the harness racing industry.
Eligibility: Applicants must have a parent or parents involved in harness racing or must be active in the business. Applicants must also demonstrate active merit or financial need.
Target applicants: Junior high students or younger. High school students. College students. Adult students.
Amount: $5,000.
Number of awards: 5.
Deadline: May 15.
How to apply: Applications are available by telephone.
Exclusive: Visit www.UltimateScholarshipBook.com and enter code HA89212 for updates on this award.

(893) • Harold and Inge Marcus Scholarship

Institute of Industrial Engineers
3577 Parkway Lane
Suite 200
Norcross, GA 30092
Phone: 800-494-0460
Fax: 770-441-3295
Email: bcameron@iienet.org
http://www.iienet2.org
Purpose: To aid industrial engineering students who are members of the Institute of Industrial Engineers (IIE).
Eligibility: Applicants must be undergraduate or graduate industrial engineering students who have been formally nominated for the award by their industrial engineering department heads. They must be full-time students who are active IIE members in good standing and must have an undergraduate GPA of 3.4 or higher on a four-point scale. Selection is based on academic achievement, integrity, financial need and potential contribution to the industrial engineering field.
Target applicants: College students. Adult students.
Minimum GPA: 3.4
Amount: $1,000.
Number of awards: 1.
Deadline: February 1.
How to apply: Applications will be mailed to those who have been formally nominated by their department heads. A formal nomination, an application packet and supporting documents are required.
Exclusive: Visit www.UltimateScholarshipBook.com and enter code IN89312 for updates on this award.

(894) • Harold Bettinger Scholarship

American Floral Endowment
1601 Duke Street
Alexandria, VA 22314
Phone: 703-838-5211
Fax: 703-838-5212
Email: afe@endowment.org
http://www.endowment.org

Purpose: To aid current horticulture students who are planning to pursue careers in a horticulture-related business.
Eligibility: Applicants must be U.S. or Canadian citizens or residents. They must be graduate students or rising undergraduate sophomores, juniors or seniors. They must have a GPA of 2.0 or higher. They must be horticulture students who are pursuing a major or minor in business or marketing, and must have plans to pursue a career in the horticulture business field. Selection is based on the overall strength of the application.
Target applicants: College students. Graduate school students. Adult students.
Minimum GPA: 2.0
Amount: Varies.
Number of awards: Varies.
Deadline: May 1.
How to apply: Applications are available online. An application form, two letters of recommendation, a personal statement and a transcript are required.
Exclusive: Visit www.UltimateScholarshipBook.com and enter code AM89412 for updates on this award.

(895) • Harry J. Harwick Scholarship

Medical Group Management Association
104 Inverness Terrace East
Englewood, CO 80112
Phone: 877-275-6462
Email: acmpe@mgma.com
http://www.mgma.com
Purpose: To aid undergraduate and graduate students of public health, health care management, health care administration and related areas of medical practice management.
Eligibility: Applicants must be enrolled in an undergraduate or graduate degree program in public health, health care management, health care administration or a related medical practice management subject. Undergraduates must be enrolled in a program that is a member of the Association of University Programs in Health Administration (AUPHA), and graduate students must be enrolled in a program that has been accredited by the Commission on Accreditation of Healthcare Management Education (CAHME). Selection is based on the overall strength of the application.
Target applicants: College students. Graduate school students. Adult students.
Amount: Varies.
Number of awards: Varies.
Deadline: May 1.
How to apply: Applications are available online. An application form and supporting documents are required.
Exclusive: Visit www.UltimateScholarshipBook.com and enter code ME89512 for updates on this award.

(896) • Health Careers Scholarship

International Order of the King's Daughters and Sons
Director
P.O. Box 1040
Chautauqua, NY 14722
http://www.iokds.org
Purpose: To assist students interested in pursuing health careers.
Eligibility: Applicants must be full-time students pursuing a career in medicine, dentistry, nursing, pharmacy, physical or occupational therapy or medical technologies. R.N. students and those pursuing an M.D. or D.D.S must have completed at least one year of schooling at an accredited institution. All others must be entering at least their third year of school. Pre-med students are not eligible. Applicants must be U.S. or Canadian citizens.
Target applicants: College students. Graduate school students. Adult students.
Amount: $1,000.
Number of awards: Varies.
Deadline: April 1.
How to apply: Applications are available by sending a self-addressed, stamped legal size envelope.
Exclusive: Visit www.UltimateScholarshipBook.com and enter code IN89612 for updates on this award.

(897) • Health Resources and Services Administration-Bureau of Health Professions Scholarships for Disadvantaged Students

United States Public Health Service
Health Resources and Services Administration
5600 Fishers Lane
Rockville, MD 20857
http://bhpr.hrsa.gov/dsa
Purpose: To support students from disadvantaged backgrounds who are pursuing health-related careers.
Eligibility: Applicants must be full-time students, be from a disadvantaged background, demonstrate financial need and be studying in a health field, including medicine, nursing, veterinary medicine, dentistry, pharmacy and others. They must be U.S. citizens, nationals or permanent residents. All other criteria are set by individual schools.
Target applicants: High school students. College students. Graduate school students. Adult students.
Amount: Up to the full cost of schooling plus living allowance.
Number of awards: Varies.
Deadline: Varies.
How to apply: Applications are available from participating schools.
Exclusive: Visit www.UltimateScholarshipBook.com and enter code UN89712 for updates on this award.

(898) • Health Sciences Student Fellowship

Epilepsy Foundation
8301 Professional Place
Landover, MD 20785
Phone: 301-459-3700
Email: researchwebsupport@efa.org
http://www.epilepsyfoundation.org
Purpose: To encourage students to pursue careers in epilepsy in either research or practice settings.
Eligibility: Applicants must be enrolled in medical school, a doctoral program or other graduate program; have an epilepsy-related study; have a qualified mentor who can supervise the project and have access to a lab or clinic to conduct the project. The project must be in the U.S. and should not be for dissertation research. The award is based on the quality of the project, relevance of the project to epilepsy, applicant's interest in epilepsy, applicant's qualifications and the quality of the lab or clinic. Applicants should submit three recommendation letters, statement of intent, biographical sketch and research plan.
Target applicants: Graduate school students. Adult students.
Amount: $3,000.
Number of awards: Varies.
Deadline: March 15.
How to apply: Applications are available online.

Exclusive: Visit www.UltimateScholarshipBook.com and enter code EP89812 for updates on this award.

(899) • Henry Adams Scholarship

American Society of Heating, Refrigerating and Air-Conditioning Engineers
1791 Tullie Circle, NE
Atlanta, GA 30329
Phone: 404-636-8400
Fax: 404-321-5478
Email: lbenedict@ashrae.org
http://www.ashrae.org

Purpose: To aid undergraduate engineering students who are preparing for careers in the heating, ventilation, air-conditioning and refrigeration (HVACR) industry.
Eligibility: Applicants must be undergraduate engineering or pre-engineering students. They must be enrolled in or accepted into an ABET-accredited school, a school that is accredited by a non-U.S. agency that has entered into a Memorandum of Understanding agreement with ABET or a school that hosts a recognized student branch of the American Society of Heating, Refrigerating and Air-Conditioning Engineers (ASHRAE). The applicant's program of study must offer adequate preparation for a career in the HVACR industry. Applicants must have a GPA of 3.0 or higher and must be ranked in the top 30 percent of their class. Selection is based on the overall strength of the application.
Target applicants: College students. Adult students.
Minimum GPA: 3.0
Amount: $3,000.
Number of awards: 1.
Scholarship may be renewable.
Deadline: December 1.
How to apply: Applications are available online. An application form, official transcript and one recommendation letter are required.
Exclusive: Visit www.UltimateScholarshipBook.com and enter code AM89912 for updates on this award.

(900) • Henry Hecaen and Manfred Meier Neuropsychology Scholarships

American Psychological Association Foundation
750 First Street NE
Washington, DC 20002
Phone: 800-374-2721
http://www.apa.org/apf

Purpose: To assist neuropsychology graduate students.
Eligibility: Applicants must demonstrate need and demonstrate potential for a promising career in the field of neuropsychology. Applicants should also submit a letter that documents their scholarly and research accomplishments, financial need and how the award will be used.
Target applicants: Graduate school students. Adult students.
Amount: $2,500.
Number of awards: 2.
Deadline: June 1.
How to apply: There is no official application.
Exclusive: Visit www.UltimateScholarshipBook.com and enter code AM90012 for updates on this award.

(901) • Herbert Levy Memorial Scholarship

Society of Physics Students
One Physics Ellipse
College Park, MD 20740
Phone: 301-209-3007
Fax: 301-209-0839
Email: sps@aip.org
http://www.spsnational.org/programs/scholarships/

Purpose: To provide financial assistance for physics students in any year of undergraduate study.
Eligibility: Applicants must be physics majors, be members of SPS and demonstrate scholarly achievement and financial need.
Target applicants: College students. Adult students.
Amount: $2,000.
Number of awards: 1.
Deadline: February 15.
How to apply: Applications are available online or from SPS Chapter Advisors.
Exclusive: Visit www.UltimateScholarshipBook.com and enter code SO90112 for updates on this award.

(902) • Hertz Foundation's Graduate Fellowship Award

Fannie and John Hertz Foundation
2456 Research Drive
Livermore, CA 94550-3850
Phone: 925-373-1642
Fax: 925-373-6329
Email: askhertz@hertzfoundation.org
http://www.hertzfoundation.com

Purpose: To help graduate students in the applied physical and engineering sciences.
Eligibility: Applicants must be college seniors planning to pursue or graduate students currently pursuing a Ph.D. in the applied physical and engineering sciences or modern biology which applies the physical sciences. Successful applicants must attend one of the foundation's approved schools. The award is based on merit, creativity and potential for research.
Target applicants: College students. Graduate school students. Adult students.
Amount: Valued at $240,000 over 5 years.
Number of awards: 15.
Scholarship may be renewable.
Deadline: October 28.
How to apply: Applications are available online, by phone or by email.
Exclusive: Visit www.UltimateScholarshipBook.com and enter code FA90212 for updates on this award.

(903) • HHMI-NIH Research Scholars (Cloister Program)

Howard Hughes Medical Institute Research Scholars
1 Cloister Court, Building 60
Bethesda, MD 20814-1460
Phone: 800-424-9924
Email: research_scholars@hhmi.org
http://www.hhmi.org/research/cloister/

Purpose: To award fellowships to medical students.
Eligibility: Applicants must be enrolled in a U.S. medical school or dental school but not in M.D./Ph.D., D.D.S./Ph.D. or Ph.D. programs or have an M.D. or Ph.D. in lab-based biological sciences. Recipients will conduct research at the National Institutes of Health in Bethesda, MD. Research experience is not required. Applicants should submit research areas of interest, personal statements, professional activities,

awards, publications (optional), letters of reference, undergraduate and medical or dental school transcripts and MCAT or DAT scores.
Target applicants: Graduate school students. Adult students.
Amount: $27,000 plus books, travel and educational expenses.
Number of awards: 42.
Deadline: January 10.
How to apply: Applications are available online.
Exclusive: Visit www.UltimateScholarshipBook.com and enter code HO90312 for updates on this award.

(904) • HIMSS Foundation Scholarship

Healthcare Information and Management Systems Society
230 E. Ohio Street, Suite 500
Chicago, IL 60611-3269
Phone: 312-664-4467
Fax: 312-664-6143
http://www.himss.org
Purpose: To provide scholarships based on academic achievement and leadership in the field of healthcare information and management systems.
Eligibility: Applicants must be members of HIMSS and study healthcare information and management systems. Scholarships are also available from individual chapters listed on the HIMSS website.
Target applicants: College students. Adult students.
Amount: $5,000.
Number of awards: 7.
Deadline: Varies.
How to apply: Application details are available online.
Exclusive: Visit www.UltimateScholarshipBook.com and enter code HE90412 for updates on this award.

(905) • Holly Cornell Scholarship

American Water Works Association
6666 W. Quincy Avenue
Denver, CO 80235-3098
Phone: 303-347-6201
Fax: 303-795-7603
Email: lmoody@awwa.org
http://www.awwa.org
Purpose: To support female and/or minority master's students pursuing advanced training in the field of water supply and treatment.
Eligibility: Applicants must be females and/or minorities who have been accepted to or are current master's degree students in engineering. Applications, transcripts, GRE scores, three recommendation letters, statements and course of study are required. The award is based on academics and leadership.
Target applicants: Graduate school students. Adult students.
Amount: $5,000.
Number of awards: 1.
Deadline: January 15.
How to apply: Applications are available online.
Exclusive: Visit www.UltimateScholarshipBook.com and enter code AM90512 for updates on this award.

(906) • Hooper Memorial Scholarship

Transportation Clubs International Scholarships
Attn.: Bill Blair
Zimmer Worldwide Logistics
15710 JFK Boulevard
Houston, TX 77032
Phone: 877-858-8627
Email: bblair@zimmerworldwide.com
http://www.transportationclubsinternational.com
Purpose: To support students who want to enter the transportation industry.
Eligibility: Applicants must be enrolled in an accredited institution of higher learning in a vocational or degree program in the fields of transportation logistics or traffic management. The awards are based upon scholastic ability, potential, professional interest and character. Financial need is also considered.
Target applicants: College students. Adult students.
Amount: Varies.
Number of awards: Varies.
Deadline: May 31.
How to apply: Applications are available online.
Exclusive: Visit www.UltimateScholarshipBook.com and enter code TR90612 for updates on this award.

(907) • HSA Research Grants

Herb Society of America
Attn.: Research Grant
9019 Kirtland Chardon Road
Kirtland, OH 44094
Phone: 440-256-0514
Fax: 440-256-0541
Email: herbs@herbsociety.org
http://www.herbsociety.org
Purpose: To educate about herbs and contribute to the fields of horticulture, science, literature, history, art and/or economics.
Eligibility: Applicants must have a proposed program of scientific, academic or artistic investigation of herbal plants. Applicants must describe their research needs in 500 words or less and include a proposed budget with specific budget items listed. This grant may not be used in combination with funding from another source and may not be used to pay for salaries, tuition or private garden development.
Target applicants: College students. Graduate school students. Adult students.
Amount: Up to $5,000.
Number of awards: Varies by year.
Deadline: January 31.
How to apply: Applications are available online or by written request.
Exclusive: Visit www.UltimateScholarshipBook.com and enter code HE90712 for updates on this award.

(908) • IEEE Presidents' Scholarship

Institute of Electrical and Electronics Engineers (IEEE)
445 Hoes Lane
Piscataway, NJ 08854
Phone: 732-562-3860
Email: supportieee@ieee.org
http://www.ieee.org/scholarships
Purpose: To award a student for a project relevant to electrical engineering, electronics engineering, computer science or other IEEE fields of interest.
Eligibility: Applicants must be student members who use engineering, science and computing to solve a problem. Students may compete individually or as a team.
Target applicants: High school students.
Amount: $10,000.
Number of awards: Varies.
Scholarship may be renewable.

Deadline: May 8.
How to apply: Contact the organization for more information.
Exclusive: Visit www.UltimateScholarshipBook.com and enter code IN90812 for updates on this award.

(909) • IIE Council of Fellows Undergraduate Scholarship

Institute of Industrial Engineers
3577 Parkway Lane
Suite 200
Norcross, GA 30092
Phone: 800-494-0460
Fax: 770-441-3295
Email: bcameron@iienet.org
http://www.iienet2.org
Purpose: To support undergraduate student members.
Eligibility: Applicants must be full-time undergraduate students enrolled in a college in the United States, Canada or Mexico with an accredited industrial engineering program, major in industrial engineering and be active members. Students may apply directly for this scholarship and do not need to be nominated. The award is based on academic ability, character, leadership, potential service to the industrial engineering profession and financial need.
Target applicants: College students. Adult students.
Minimum GPA: 3.4
Amount: Varies.
Number of awards: Varies.
Deadline: February 1.
How to apply: Applications are available online.
Exclusive: Visit www.UltimateScholarshipBook.com and enter code IN90912 for updates on this award.

(910) • Industrial Electrolysis and Electrochemical Engineering Division H.H. Dow Memorial Student Award

Electrochemical Society
65 South Main Street, Building D
Pennington, NJ 08534-2839
Phone: 609-737-1902
Fax: 609-737-2743
Email: awards@electrochem.org
http://www.electrochem.org
Purpose: To recognize young engineers and scientists in the fields of electrochemical engineering and applied electrochemistry.
Eligibility: Applicants must be accepted to or enrolled in a graduate program. The application requires transcripts, a description of the research project, a description of how the project relates to electrochemical engineering or applied electrochemistry, a biography, a resume or curriculum vitae and a letter of recommendation from the research supervisor. The award is based on academic performance, research and the recommendation.
Target applicants: Graduate school students. Adult students.
Amount: $1,000.
Number of awards: Varies.
Deadline: September 15.
How to apply: Application materials are described online.
Exclusive: Visit www.UltimateScholarshipBook.com and enter code EL91012 for updates on this award.

(911) • Industrial Electrolysis and Electrochemical Engineering Division Student Achievement Awards

Electrochemical Society
65 South Main Street, Building D
Pennington, NJ 08534-2839
Phone: 609-737-1902
Fax: 609-737-2743
Email: awards@electrochem.org
http://www.electrochem.org
Purpose: To recognize young engineers and scientists in electrochemical engineering and to encourage the recipients to enter careers in the field.
Eligibility: Applicants must be accepted by or enrolled in a college or university and propose a research project. The application must include transcripts, research outline, statement describing how the project relates to electrochemical engineering, record of industrial work and letter of recommendation from the research supervisor. The award is based on academic performance, research and the recommendation.
Target applicants: High school students. College students. Graduate school students. Adult students.
Amount: $1,000.
Number of awards: Varies.
Deadline: September 15.
How to apply: Application materials are described online.
Exclusive: Visit www.UltimateScholarshipBook.com and enter code EL91112 for updates on this award.

(912) • Injection Molding Division Scholarship

Society of Plastics Engineers
13 Church Hill Road
Newtown, CT 06470
Phone: 203-775-0471
Fax: 203-775-8490
Email: info@4spe.org
http://www.4spe.org
Purpose: To aid students who have employment or academic experience in injection molding.
Eligibility: Applicants must be full-time undergraduate or graduate students who are in good academic standing. They must have experience in injection molding through courses taken, research conducted or formal employment. They must have an interest in the plastics/polymer industry and must have taken courses that would prepare them for a career in this field. Selection is based on academic merit and financial need.
Target applicants: College students. Graduate school students. Adult students.
Amount: $3,000.
Number of awards: 1.
Deadline: February 15.
How to apply: Applications are available online. An application form, three recommendation letters, transcripts, a personal statement, a list of extracurricular activities and honors and employment history are required.
Exclusive: Visit www.UltimateScholarshipBook.com and enter code SO91212 for updates on this award.

(913) • Intel Science Talent Search

Intel Corporation and Science Service
Society for Science and the Public
1719 North Street NW
Washington, DC 20036

Phone: 202-785-2255
Fax: 202-785-1243
Email: sciedu@sciserv.org
http://www.societyforscience.org/sts/
Purpose: To recognize excellence in science among the nation's youth and encourage the exploration of science.
Eligibility: Applicants must be high school seniors in the U.S., Puerto Rico, Guam, Virgin Islands, American Samoa, Wake or Midway Islands or the Marianas. U.S. citizens attending foreign schools are also eligible. Applicants must complete college entrance exams and complete individual research projects and provide a report on the research.
Target applicants: High school students.
Amount: $1,000-$100,000.
Number of awards: 300.
Deadline: November 17.
How to apply: Applications are available by request.
Exclusive: Visit www.UltimateScholarshipBook.com and enter code IN91312 for updates on this award.

(914) • International Gas Turbine Institute Scholarship

American Society of Mechanical Engineers (ASME)
Three Park Avenue
New York, NY 10016
Phone: 800-843-2763
Fax: 973-882-1717
Email: infocentral@asme.org
http://www.asme.org
Purpose: To aid American Society of Mechanical Engineers (ASME) student members who are interested in the gas turbine industry.
Eligibility: Applicants must be student members of ASME who are in good standing. They must be enrolled in an accredited undergraduate or graduate degree program in mechanical engineering or aerospace engineering. They must be interested in the turbomachinery, gas turbine or propulsion industry. Preference will be given to those who have employment or research experience in one of the aforementioned industries. Selection is based on academic achievement and demonstrated interest in the gas turbine industry.
Target applicants: College students. Graduate school students. Adult students.
Amount: $4,000.
Number of awards: 1.
Deadline: March 15.
How to apply: Applications may be completed online. An electronic application form, official transcript, personal statement and one to two recommendation letters are required.
Exclusive: Visit www.UltimateScholarshipBook.com and enter code AM91412 for updates on this award.

(915) • International Student Scholarship

American Speech-Language-Hearing Foundation
2200 Research Boulevard
Rockville, MD 20850
Phone: 301-296-8700
Email: foundation@asha.org
http://www.ashfoundation.org
Purpose: To support an international graduate student in communication sciences and disorders.
Eligibility: Applicants must be full-time students in the U.S. Master's degree candidates must be in programs accredited by the Council on Academic Accreditation for Audiology and Speech Pathology, but doctoral programs do not have to be accredited. The applicants should submit transcripts, an essay and a reference form.
Target applicants: Graduate school students. Adult students.
Amount: $4,000.
Number of awards: Varies.
Deadline: Varies.
How to apply: Applications are available online.
Exclusive: Visit www.UltimateScholarshipBook.com and enter code AM91512 for updates on this award.

(916) • Irene and Daisy MacGregor Memorial Scholarship

National Society Daughters of the American Revolution
Committee Services Office
Attn.: Scholarships
1776 D Street NW
Washington, DC 20006-5303
Phone: 202-628-1776
http://www.dar.org
Purpose: To assist students in becoming medical doctors.
Eligibility: Applicants must be accepted into or enrolled in a graduate course of study to become a medical doctor. Those pursuing study in psychiatric nursing at the graduate level at a medical school may also apply, and preference is given to females. All applicants must obtain a letter of sponsorship from their local DAR chapter. However, affiliation with DAR is not required.
Target applicants: Graduate school students. Adult students.
Amount: Up to $5,000.
Number of awards: Varies.
Scholarship may be renewable.
Deadline: April 15.
How to apply: Applications are available by written request with a self-addressed, stamped envelope.
Exclusive: Visit www.UltimateScholarshipBook.com and enter code NA91612 for updates on this award.

(917) • Irene E. Newman Scholarship

American Dental Hygienists' Association (ADHA) Institute for Oral Health
Scholarship Award Program
444 North Michigan Avenue
Suite 3400
Chicago, IL 60611
Phone: 312-440-8900
Email: institute@adha.net
http://www.adha.org/ioh
Purpose: To support students interested in public health or community dental health.
Eligibility: Applicants must be undergraduate or graduate students interested in public health or community dental health. They must also demonstrate financial need of at least $1,500, submit a goals statement and be active members of SADHA or ADHA.
Target applicants: College students. Graduate school students. Adult students.
Amount: $1,000-$2,000.
Number of awards: 1.
Deadline: February 1.
How to apply: Applications are available online.
Exclusive: Visit www.UltimateScholarshipBook.com and enter code AM91712 for updates on this award.

(918) • IRF Fellowship Program

International Road Federation
Madison Place
500 Montgomery Street, 5th Floor
Alexandria, VA 22314
Phone: 703-535-1001
Fax: 703-535-1007
Email: info@internationalroadfederation.org
http://www.irfnet.org

Purpose: To provide fellowships in support of graduate study in a transportation-related field.
Eligibility: Applicants must demonstrate potential leadership in the highway industry in financing, administration, planning, design, construction, operations or maintenance. They must also have three to 15 years of work experience in transportation, a bachelor's of science degree (or equivalent) in a transportation-related discipline and a commitment to full-time study for a minimum of nine months.
Target applicants: Graduate school students. Adult students.
Amount: Varies.
Number of awards: Varies.
Deadline: Varies.
How to apply: More information is available online.
Exclusive: Visit www.UltimateScholarshipBook.com and enter code IN91812 for updates on this award.

(919) • ISS Scholarship Foundation

Iron and Steel Society
Attn.: Lori Wharrey
AIST Foundation
186 Thorn Hill Road
Warrendale, PA 15086
Phone: 724-776-6040 x621
Fax: 724-776-1880
Email: lwharrey@aist.org
http://www.aistfoundation.org

Purpose: To attract talented and dedicated students to careers within the iron and steel and steel-related industries.
Eligibility: Applicants must be full-time college juniors or seniors majoring in metallurgy, metallurgical engineering or materials science. Other related majors are considered with a letter from the academic adviser. Applicants must have a minimum 3.0 GPA in the major or a minimum 3.25 GPA if they are undeclared and be ISS student members or submit an application for membership with the scholarship application.
Target applicants: College students. Adult students.
Minimum GPA: 3.0
Amount: $2,000.
Number of awards: 5.
Deadline: March 4.
How to apply: Applications are available online.
Exclusive: Visit www.UltimateScholarshipBook.com and enter code IR91912 for updates on this award.

(920) • Jack Horkheimer Award

Astronomical League
7241 Jarboe
Kansas City, MO 64114
Phone: 816-444-4878
Email: carroll-iorg@kc.rr.com
http://www.astroleague.org

Purpose: To assist young Astronomical League members.
Eligibility: Applicants must be Astronomical League members under the age of 19 on the date of the application. The award is based on involvement in the organization.
Target applicants: Junior high students or younger. High school students.
Amount: $1,000 plus travel expenses and telescope.
Number of awards: Varies.
Deadline: March 31.
How to apply: Applications are available online.
Exclusive: Visit www.UltimateScholarshipBook.com and enter code AS92012 for updates on this award.

(921) • Jane Delano Student Nurse Scholarship

American Red Cross
National Headquarters
2025 E Street NW
Washington, DC 20006
Phone: 202-303-5000
Email: littlefieldv@usa.redcross.org
http://www.redcross.org

Purpose: To aid Red Cross volunteers who are attending nursing school.
Eligibility: Applicants must be enrolled in an accredited nursing school and be in good academic standing. They must have volunteered with a Red Cross unit at least once within the past five years and have completed at least one academic year of college at the time of application. Selection is based on the overall strength of the application.
Target applicants: College students. Graduate school students. Adult students.
Amount: $3,000.
Number of awards: 3.
Deadline: July 1.
How to apply: Applications are available online. An application form, a personal essay, an endorsement from a Red Cross unit and an endorsement from the student's nursing school dean or chair are required.
Exclusive: Visit www.UltimateScholarshipBook.com and enter code AM92112 for updates on this award.

(922) • Jean Theodore Lacordaire Prize

Coleopterists Society
Anthony I. Cognato, Chair
Texas A & M University
College Station, TX 77845-2475
Phone: 979-458-0404
Email: a.cognato@tamu.edu
http://www.coleopsoc.org

Purpose: To recognize the work of coleopterists.
Eligibility: Applicants must be graduate students whose papers are nominated for the competition. The papers must be about coleoptera (beetle) systematics or biology published in a journal or book. Self-nominations are not accepted.
Target applicants: Graduate school students. Adult students.
Amount: $300.
Number of awards: 1.
Deadline: March 1.
How to apply: Application materials are described online.
Exclusive: Visit www.UltimateScholarshipBook.com and enter code CO92212 for updates on this award.

(923) • Jimmy A. Young Memorial Education Recognition Award

American Association for Respiratory Care
9425 North MacArthur Boulevard
Suite 100
Irving, TX 75063-4706
Phone: 972-243-2272
Fax: 972-484-2720
Email: info@aarc.org
http://www.aarc.org

Purpose: To recognize outstanding minority students in respiratory care education programs.
Eligibility: Applicants must be enrolled in an accredited respiratory care education program and have a minimum 3.0 GPA. Students must submit an original paper on respiratory care. Preference is given to minority students.
Target applicants: College students. Graduate school students. Adult students.
Minimum GPA: 3.0
Amount: Up to $1,000.
Number of awards: 1.
Deadline: June 15.
How to apply: Applications are available online.
Exclusive: Visit www.UltimateScholarshipBook.com and enter code AM92312 for updates on this award.

(924) • John and Elsa Gracik Scholarships

American Society of Mechanical Engineers (ASME)
Three Park Avenue
New York, NY 10016
Phone: 800-843-2763
Fax: 973-882-1717
Email: infocentral@asme.org
http://www.asme.org

Purpose: To support mechanical engineering students.
Eligibility: Applicants must be ASME student members, enrolled in an eligible accredited mechanical engineering baccalaureate program and be U.S. citizens. Selection is based on scholastic ability, financial need, character, leadership and potential contribution to the mechanical engineering profession.
Target applicants: College students. Adult students.
Amount: $1,600.
Number of awards: 18.
Deadline: March 1.
How to apply: Applications are available online.
Exclusive: Visit www.UltimateScholarshipBook.com and enter code AM92412 for updates on this award.

(925) • John and Muriel Landis Scholarship

American Nuclear Society
555 North Kensington Avenue
La Grange Park, IL 60526
Phone: 800-323-3044
Fax: 708-352-0499
Email: hr@ans.org
http://www.ans.org

Purpose: To assist disadvantaged students to seek careers in a nuclear-related field.
Eligibility: Applicants must be undergraduate or graduate students enrolled or planning to enroll in a U.S. college or university who are also planning a career in nuclear science, nuclear engineering or another nuclear-related field. High school seniors may apply. Students must have greater than average financial need. Applicants must submit applications, transcripts, sponsor forms and three reference forms.
Target applicants: High school students. College students. Graduate school students. Adult students.
Amount: Varies.
Number of awards: Up to 8.
Deadline: February 1.
How to apply: Applications are available online.
Exclusive: Visit www.UltimateScholarshipBook.com and enter code AM92512 for updates on this award.

(926) • John Culver Wooddy Scholarships

Actuarial Foundation
475 North Martingale Road
Suite 600
Schaumburg, IL 60173
Phone: 847-706-3535
Fax: 847-706-3599
Email: scholarships@actfnd.org
http://www.actuarialfoundation.org

Purpose: To assist students who plan to become actuaries.
Eligibility: Applicants must be undergraduate students who will receive their degrees by August 31 of the year following the application deadline. Students must be in the top quartile of their class and have completed a minimum of one actuarial examination. A recommendation from a professor is required. Only one applicant per school is permitted. Preference is given to applicants who have demonstrated leadership ability in extracurricular activities.
Target applicants: College students. Adult students.
Amount: $2,000.
Number of awards: Varies.
Deadline: June 24.
How to apply: Applications are available online.
Exclusive: Visit www.UltimateScholarshipBook.com and enter code AC92612 for updates on this award.

(927) • John Henry Comstock Graduate Student Awards

Entomological Society of America
10001 Derekwood Lane
Suite 100
Lanham, MD 20706
Phone: 301-731-4535
Fax: 301-731-4538
Email: esa@entsoc.org
http://www.entsoc.org

Purpose: To encourage graduate students interested in entomology to attend the Annual Meeting of the Entomological Society of America.
Eligibility: Applicants must be graduate students and members of the ESA. Each ESA branch has its own eligibility requirements, so an interested student must contact their Branch Secretary-Treasurer for more information.
Target applicants: Graduate school students. Adult students.
Amount: Travel expenses plus $100.
Number of awards: 6.
Deadline: August 15.
How to apply: Applications are available online.
Exclusive: Visit www.UltimateScholarshipBook.com and enter code EN92712 for updates on this award.

(928) • John J. McKetta Scholarship

American Institute of Chemical Engineers - (AIChE)
3 Park Avenue
New York, NY 10016
Phone: 212-591-7634
Fax: 212-591-8890
Email: awards@aiche.org
http://www.aiche.org

Purpose: To support chemical engineering students.

Eligibility: Applicants must be chemical engineering incoming undergraduate juniors or seniors and be planning a career in the chemical engineering process industries. Applicants must also have a minimum 3.0 GPA and be attending an ABET accredited school in the U.S., Canada or Mexico. Selection is based on an essay outlining career goals, leadership in an AIChE student chapter or other university sponsored activity and letters of recommendation. Preference is given to members of AIChE.

Target applicants: College students. Adult students.

Minimum GPA: 3.0

Amount: $5,000.

Number of awards: 1.

Deadline: July 1.

How to apply: Applications are available online.

Exclusive: Visit www.UltimateScholarshipBook.com and enter code AM92812 for updates on this award.

(929) • John L. Imhoff Scholarship

Institute of Industrial Engineers
3577 Parkway Lane
Suite 200
Norcross, GA 30092
Phone: 800-494-0460
Fax: 770-441-3295
Email: bcameron@iienet.org
http://www.iienet2.org

Purpose: To award a student who has contributed to the development of the industrial engineering profession through international understanding.

Eligibility: Applicants must be pursuing a B.S., master's or doctorate degree in an accredited IE program and have at least two years of school remaining. Students may not apply directly for this scholarship and must be nominated. An essay describing the candidate's international contributions to industrial engineering and three references are required. IIE membership is not required.

Target applicants: College students. Graduate school students. Adult students.

Minimum GPA: 3.4

Amount: $1,000.

Number of awards: 1.

Deadline: February 1.

How to apply: More information is available online.

Exclusive: Visit www.UltimateScholarshipBook.com and enter code IN92912 for updates on this award.

(930) • John M. Haniak Scholarship

ASM International Foundation
9639 Kinsman Road
Materials Park, OH 44073
Phone: 440-338-5151
Fax: 440-338-4634
Email: asmif@asminternational.org
http://asmcommunity.asminternational.org/portal/site/www/Foundation

Purpose: To aid undergraduate materials science and engineering (MSE) students.

Eligibility: Applicants must be Material Advantage student members of ASM International. They must be rising juniors or seniors enrolled in an undergraduate materials science and engineering program at an accredited school located in North America. Applicants must be attending a school that has an accredited science and engineering program that confers a bachelor's degree. Selection is based on academic achievement and financial need.

Target applicants: College students. Adult students.

Amount: $1,500.

Number of awards: 1.

Scholarship may be renewable.

Deadline: May 1.

How to apply: Applications are available online. An application form, personal essay, up to two recommendation letters, a transcript and an applicant photo are required.

Exclusive: Visit www.UltimateScholarshipBook.com and enter code AS93012 for updates on this award.

(931) • John Mabry Forestry Scholarship

Railway Tie Association
115 Commerce Drive
Suite C
Fayetteville, GA 30214
Phone: 770-460-5553
Fax: 770-460-5573
Email: ties@rta.org
http://www.rta.org

Purpose: To aid forestry school students.

Eligibility: Applicants must be enrolled in an accredited forestry program at an postsecondary institution. They must be in the second year of a two-year technical school program or in the third or fourth year of a four-year college or university program. Students who are in the final year of their program must remain enrolled for the entirety of the academic year. Selection is based on academic merit, leadership ability, stated career goals and financial need.

Target applicants: College students. Adult students.

Amount: $1,500.

Number of awards: 2.

Deadline: June 30.

How to apply: Applications are available online. An application form and supporting documents are required.

Exclusive: Visit www.UltimateScholarshipBook.com and enter code RA93112 for updates on this award.

(932) • John S.W. Fargher Scholarship

Institute of Industrial Engineers
3577 Parkway Lane
Suite 200
Norcross, GA 30092
Phone: 800-494-0460
Fax: 770-441-3295
Email: bcameron@iienet.org
http://www.iienet2.org

Purpose: To award graduate students in industrial engineering who have demonstrated leadership.

Eligibility: Applicants must be full-time graduate students with at least one full year left who are enrolled in a college in the United States

with an accredited industrial engineering program. Candidates must also major in industrial engineering or engineering management and be active members who have demonstrated leadership in industrial engineering-related activities. Students may not apply directly for this scholarship and must be nominated.
Target applicants: Graduate school students. Adult students.
Minimum GPA: 3.0
Amount: $1,000.
Number of awards: 1.
Deadline: September 1.
How to apply: More information is available online.
Exclusive: Visit www.UltimateScholarshipBook.com and enter code IN93212 for updates on this award.

(933) · John V. Wehausen Graduate Scholarship

Society of Naval Architects and Marine Engineers
601 Pavonia Avenue
Jersey City, NJ 07306
Phone: 201-798-4800
Fax: 201-798-4975
Email: efaustino@sname.org
http://www.sname.org
Purpose: To aid students who are seeking a master's degree in a marine-related subject.
Eligibility: Applicants must be members of the Society of Naval Architects and Marine Engineers (SNAME) or another respected marine society. They must be pursuing a master's degree in naval architecture, ocean engineering, marine engineering or another marine-related subject. Students who will be completing their degree before April 15 of the award disbursement year are ineligible. Selection is based on the overall strength of the application.
Target applicants: Graduate school students. Adult students.
Amount: Up to $6,000.
Number of awards: Varies.
Deadline: February 1.
How to apply: Applications are available online. An application form, transcript and three reference letters are required.
Exclusive: Visit www.UltimateScholarshipBook.com and enter code SO93312 for updates on this award.

(934) · John Wright Memorial Scholarship

Tree Research and Education Endowment Fund
552 S. Washington Street
Suite 109
Naperville, IL 60540
Phone: 630-369-8300
Fax: 630-369-8382
Email: treefund@treefund.org
http://www.treefund.org
Purpose: To help undergraduate and technical college students pursuing careers in commercial arboriculture.
Eligibility: Applicants must be high school seniors entering college or community college or returning college students seeking a first bachelor's degree or associate's degree while attending an accredited U.S. college or university. All applicants must plan to enter the arboriculture industry and have a minimum 3.0 GPA. Consideration will be given for honorably discharged veterans and present members of the U.S. Armed Forces, Reserves and National Guard.
Target applicants: High school students. College students. Adult students.
Minimum GPA: 3.0
Amount: $2,000.
Number of awards: 1.
Deadline: June 15.
How to apply: Applications are available online.
Exclusive: Visit www.UltimateScholarshipBook.com and enter code TR93412 for updates on this award.

(935) · Johnny Davis Memorial Scholarship

Aircraft Electronics Association
4217 South Hocker
Independence, MO 64055
Phone: 816-373-6565
Fax: 816-478-3100
Email: info@aea.net
http://www.aea.net
Purpose: To support students of avionics and aircraft repair.
Eligibility: Applicants must be high school seniors or college students who plan to or are attending an accredited school in an avionics or aircraft repair program.
Target applicants: High school students. College students. Adult students.
Amount: Varies.
Number of awards: 1.
Deadline: February 15.
How to apply: Applications are available by contacting the organization for more information.
Exclusive: Visit www.UltimateScholarshipBook.com and enter code AI93512 for updates on this award.

(936) · Johnson & Johnson Scholarships

American Dental Hygienists' Association (ADHA) Institute for Oral Health
Scholarship Award Program
444 North Michigan Avenue
Suite 3400
Chicago, IL 60611
Phone: 312-440-8900
Email: institute@adha.net
http://www.adha.org/ioh
Purpose: To aid dental hygiene students.
Eligibility: Applicants must be enrolled full-time in an accredited certificate, associate's degree or bachelor's degree program in dental hygiene in the U.S. They must have completed at least one year of the certificate or degree program and be active members of the American Dental Hygienists' Association (ADHA) or the Student American Dental Hygienists' Association (SADHA). They must demonstrate financial need of $1,500 or more and have a GPA of 3.5 or higher on a four-point scale. Selection is based on academic merit and financial need.
Target applicants: College students. Adult students.
Minimum GPA: 3.5
Amount: $1,000.
Number of awards: Varies.
Deadline: February 1.
How to apply: Applications are available online. An application form, personal statement, faculty evaluation, program director verification and financial needs form are required.
Exclusive: Visit www.UltimateScholarshipBook.com and enter code AM93612 for updates on this award.

(937) • Joseph C. Johnson Memorial Grant

American Society of Certified Engineering Technicians (ASCET)
P.O. Box 1536
Brandon, MS 39043
Phone: 601-824-8991
Email: general-manager@ascet.org
http://www.ascet.org

Purpose: To support engineering technology students.

Eligibility: Applicants must have a minimum 3.0 GPA, be U.S. citizens or legal residents of the country in which they are currently living, be either a student, certified, regular, registered or associate member of the American Society of Certified Engineering Technicians (ASCET) and be full- or part-time students in an engineering technology program. Students in a two-year program should apply in the first year to receive the grant for their second year. Students in a four-year program who apply in the third year may receive the grant for their fourth year. Applicants must show financial need and submit three letters of recommendation.

Target applicants: College students. Adult students.
Minimum GPA: 3.0
Amount: $750.
Number of awards: 1.
Deadline: April 1.
How to apply: Applications are available online.
Exclusive: Visit www.UltimateScholarshipBook.com and enter code AM93712 for updates on this award.

(938) • Joseph Frasca Excellence in Aviation Scholarship

University Aviation Association (UAA)
David NewMyer
College of Applied Sciences and Arts, Southern Illinois University Carbondale
1365 Douglas Drive, Room 126
Carbondale , IL 62901-6623
Phone: 618-453-8898
Fax: 618-453-7286
Email: newmyer@siu.edu
http://www.uaa.aero

Purpose: To encourage students to reach the highest level of achievement in their aviation studies.

Eligibility: Applicants must be juniors or seniors enrolled at a UAA member college or university with at least a 3.0 GPA. Students must demonstrate excellence in all areas related to aviation and have FAA certification in either aviation maintenance or flight. Applicants must be a member of at least one aviation organization and be involved in aviation activities that demonstrate interest in and enthusiasm for aviation.

Target applicants: College students. Adult students.
Minimum GPA: 3.0
Amount: $1,000.
Number of awards: 2.
Deadline: April 12.
How to apply: Applications are available online.
Exclusive: Visit www.UltimateScholarshipBook.com and enter code UN93812 for updates on this award.

(939) • Joseph M. Parish Memorial Grant

American Society of Certified Engineering Technicians (ASCET)
P.O. Box 1536
Brandon, MS 39043
Phone: 601-824-8991
Email: general-manager@ascet.org
http://www.ascet.org

Purpose: To help engineering technology students.

Eligibility: Applicants must have a minimum 3.0 GPA, be U.S. citizens or legal residents of the country in which they are currently living, be student members of the American Society of Certified Engineering Technicians (ASCET) and be full-time students in an engineering technology program. Applicants in a two-year program should apply in the first year to receive the grant for their second year. Students in a four-year program who apply in the third year may receive the grant for their fourth year. Applicants must show financial need. Students pursuing a BS degree in engineering are not eligible for this grant.

Target applicants: College students. Adult students.
Minimum GPA: 3.0
Amount: $500.
Number of awards: 1.
Scholarship may be renewable.
Deadline: April 1.
How to apply: Applications are available online.
Exclusive: Visit www.UltimateScholarshipBook.com and enter code AM93912 for updates on this award.

(940) • Junior and Senior Scholarships

Institute of Food Technologists (IFT)
525 W. Van Buren
Suite 1000
Chicago, IL 60607
Phone: 312-782-8424
Email: ejplummer@ift.org
http://www.ift.org

Purpose: To encourage undergraduate students in food science or technology.

Eligibility: Applicants must be college sophomores, juniors or seniors pursuing an approved program in food science or food technology. Applications, transcripts and a recommendation letter are required.

Target applicants: College students. Adult students.
Amount: $500-$5,000.
Number of awards: Varies.
Deadline: February 19.
How to apply: Applications are available online.
Exclusive: Visit www.UltimateScholarshipBook.com and enter code IN94012 for updates on this award.

(941) • Junior Scholarship Program

American Kennel Club
260 Madison Avenue
New York, NY 10016
Phone: 212-696-8200
http://www.akc.org

Purpose: To assist students who are involved with AKC purebred dogs.

Eligibility: Applicants must be under age 18 with an AKC registered purebred dog. Selection is based on involvement with AKC registered dogs, academic achievement and financial need. The scholarship program awards a total of $150,000 annually.

Target applicants: Junior high students or younger. High school students.
Amount: Varies.
Number of awards: Varies.
Deadline: February 18.

How to apply: Applications are available online.
Exclusive: Visit www.UltimateScholarshipBook.com and enter code AM94112 for updates on this award.

(942) • K. K. Wang Scholarship

Society of Plastics Engineers
13 Church Hill Road
Newtown, CT 06470
Phone: 203-775-0471
Fax: 203-775-8490
Email: info@4spe.org
http://www.4spe.org
Purpose: To aid students who have injection molding and computer-aided engineering (CAE) experience.
Eligibility: Applicants must be enrolled full-time at an institution of higher learning. They must have academic or professional experience in computer-aided engineering (CAE) and injection molding. Applicants must have taken courses related to plastics and must have a professional interest in the plastics/polymer industry. Selection is based on the overall strength of the application.
Target applicants: College students. Adult students.
Amount: $2,000.
Number of awards: 1.
Deadline: February 15.
How to apply: Applications are available online. An application form, three recommendation letters, transcripts, a personal statement, a list of extracurricular activities and a resume are required.
Exclusive: Visit www.UltimateScholarshipBook.com and enter code SO94212 for updates on this award.

(943) • Karen O'Neil Memorial Scholarship

Emergency Nurses Association
915 Lee Street
Des Plaines, IL 60016
Phone: 847-460-4100
Fax: 847-460-4004
Email: foundation@ena.org
http://www.ena.org
Purpose: To promote advanced degrees in emergency nursing.
Eligibility: Applicants must be nurses pursuing an advanced degree and must have been ENA members for at least 12 months before applying.
Target applicants: Graduate school students. Adult students.
Amount: $3,000.
Number of awards: 1.
Deadline: June 1.
How to apply: Applications are available online.
Exclusive: Visit www.UltimateScholarshipBook.com and enter code EM94312 for updates on this award.

(944) • Kenneth Andrew Roe Scholarship

American Society of Mechanical Engineers (ASME)
Three Park Avenue
New York, NY 10016
Phone: 800-843-2763
Fax: 973-882-1717
Email: infocentral@asme.org
http://www.asme.org
Purpose: To support students who are studying mechanical engineering.
Eligibility: Applicants must be ASME student members, be enrolled in an ABET accredited mechanical engineering baccalaureate program, be North American residents and be U.S. citizens. Applicants must also be juniors or seniors in college with strong academic performance, character and integrity.
Target applicants: College students. Adult students.
Amount: $10,000.
Number of awards: 1.
Deadline: March 1.
How to apply: Applications are available online.
Exclusive: Visit www.UltimateScholarshipBook.com and enter code AM94412 for updates on this award.

(945) • Klussendorf Scholarship

National Dairy Shrine
P.O. Box 1
Maribel, WI 54227
Phone: 920-863-6333
Fax: 920-863-8328
Email: info@dairyshrine.org
http://www.dairyshrine.org
Purpose: To honor students in dairy husbandry fields.
Eligibility: Applicants must be first, second or third year college students at two- or four-year universities, must major in a dairy husbandry field and plan to enter the dairy field.
Target applicants: College students. Adult students.
Amount: $2,000.
Number of awards: 2.
Deadline: May 1.
How to apply: Applications are available online.
Exclusive: Visit www.UltimateScholarshipBook.com and enter code NA94512 for updates on this award.

(946) • Larry Williams Photography and AYA Photo Contest

Appaloosa Horse Club
Appaloosa Youth Foundation Scholarship Committee
2720 W. Pullman Road
Moscow, ID 83843
Phone: 208-882-5578
Fax: 208-882-8150
Email: acaap@appaloosa.com
http://www.appaloosa.com
Purpose: To support students who express their love of the Appaloosa through photography.
Eligibility: Applicants must submit multiple photographs in three divisions: 13 and under, 14 to 18 and 4H/FFA youths 18 and under.
Target applicants: Junior high students or younger. High school students.
Amount: $100.
Number of awards: 9.
Deadline: May 1.
How to apply: Applications are available online.
Exclusive: Visit www.UltimateScholarshipBook.com and enter code AP94612 for updates on this award.

(947) • Larson Aquatic Research Support (LARS)

American Water Works Association
6666 W. Quincy Avenue
Denver, CO 80235-3098
Phone: 303-347-6201
Fax: 303-795-7603

Email: lmoody@awwa.org
http://www.awwa.org
Purpose: To support doctoral and master's students interested in careers in the fields of corrosion control, treatment and distribution of domestic and industrial water supplies, aquatic chemistry and/or environmental chemistry.
Eligibility: Applicants must pursue an advanced (master's or doctoral) degree at an institution of higher education located in Canada, Guam, Puerto Rico, Mexico or the U.S. Applications, resumes, transcripts, GRE scores, three recommendation letters and a course of study are required. Master's students also must submit a statement of educational plans and career objectives or a research plan. Ph.D. students must submit research plans. The master's grant is $5,000, and the doctoral grant is $7,000. The award is based on academics and leadership.
Target applicants: Graduate school students. Adult students.
Amount: $5,000-$7,000.
Number of awards: 2.
Deadline: January 18.
How to apply: Applications are available online.
Exclusive: Visit www.UltimateScholarshipBook.com and enter code AM94712 for updates on this award.

(948) • Lawrence E. and Thelma J. Norrie Memorial Scholarship

Foundation for Amateur Radio, Inc.
FAR Scholarships
P.O. Box 911
Columbia, MD 21044
Phone: 410-552-2652
Fax: 410-981-5146
Email: dave.prestel@gmail.com
http://www.farweb.org
Purpose: To aid amateur radio licensees who are pursuing or planning to pursue postsecondary education.
Eligibility: Applicants must be U.S. residents, hold a valid amateur radio license and be enrolled in or accepted at an accredited postsecondary institution for full-time study. Preference will be given to applicants who are enrolled in a bachelor's, master's or doctoral degree program in science or engineering. Preference will also be given to undergraduate juniors, undergraduate seniors and graduate students. Selection is based on the overall strength of the application.
Target applicants: College students. Graduate school students. Adult students.
Amount: $2,500.
Number of awards: Varies.
Deadline: March 31.
How to apply: Applications are available online. An application form and references are required.
Exclusive: Visit www.UltimateScholarshipBook.com and enter code FO94812 for updates on this award.

(949) • Lawrence Ginocchio Aviation Scholarship

National Business Aviation Association
1200 18th Street NW
Suite 400
Washington, DC 20036
Phone: 202-783-9250
Fax: 202-331-8364
Email: info@nbaa.org
http://www.nbaa.org
Purpose: To aid undergraduate aviation students of integrity.
Eligibility: Applicants must be undergraduate sophomores, juniors or seniors who are enrolled at a school that is a National Business Aviation Association (NBAA)/University Aviation Association (UAA) member institution. They must have a GPA of 3.0 or higher on a four-point scale. Applicants must demonstrate personal qualities of honor, selflessness and helping others through business aviation activities. Selection is based on the overall strength of the application.
Target applicants: College students. Adult students.
Minimum GPA: 3.0
Amount: $5,000.
Number of awards: 5.
Deadline: July 31.
How to apply: Applications are available online. An application form, resume, official transcript, personal essay and two recommendation letters are required.
Exclusive: Visit www.UltimateScholarshipBook.com and enter code NA94912 for updates on this award.

(950) • Lee S. Evans Scholarship

National Housing Endowment
1201 15th Street NW
Washington, DC 20005
Phone: 800-368-5242
Fax: 202-266-8177
Email: nhe@nahb.com
http://www.nationalhousingendowment.org
Purpose: To aid students who are preparing for careers in residential construction management.
Eligibility: Applicants must be full-time undergraduate or graduate students. They must have completed at least one semester of college coursework at the time of applying for the scholarship and must have at least one year remaining in their programs of study at the time of award disbursement; fifth-year seniors are ineligible. Applicants must have a demonstrated interest in pursuing a career in the residential construction industry. Preference will be given to current student members of the National Association of Home Builders (NAHB) and to applicants who are enrolled in a four-year degree program that focuses on construction management. Selection is based on academic merit, recommendations, extracurricular activities, work experience and financial need.
Target applicants: College students. Graduate school students. Adult students.
Amount: Up to $5,000.
Number of awards: Varies.
Scholarship may be renewable.
Deadline: October 30.
How to apply: Applications are available online. An application form, an official transcript, a degree program outline and two letters of recommendation are required.
Exclusive: Visit www.UltimateScholarshipBook.com and enter code NA95012 for updates on this award.

(951) • Lee Tarbox Memorial Scholarship

Aircraft Electronics Association
4217 South Hocker
Independence, MO 64055
Phone: 816-373-6565
Fax: 816-478-3100
Email: info@aea.net
http://www.aea.net
Purpose: To support students of avionics and aircraft repair.

Eligibility: Applicants must be high school seniors or college students who plan to or are attending an accredited school in an avionics or aircraft repair program.
Target applicants: High school students. College students. Adult students.
Amount: Varies.
Number of awards: 1.
Deadline: February 15.
How to apply: Applications are available by contacting the organization for more information.
Exclusive: Visit www.UltimateScholarshipBook.com and enter code AI95112 for updates on this award.

(952) • Len Assante Scholarship Fund

National Ground Water Association
601 Dempsey Road
Westerville, OH 43081-8978
Phone: 800-551-7379
Fax: 614-898-7786
Email: ngwa@ngwa.org
http://www.ngwa.org
Purpose: To support students in fields related to the ground water industry.
Eligibility: Applicants must be high school graduates or college students with a minimum 2.5 GPA who are studying fields related to the ground water industry including geology, hydrology, hydrogeology, environmental sciences or microbiology or well drilling two-year associate degree programs.
Target applicants: High school students. College students. Adult students.
Minimum GPA: 2.5
Amount: Varies.
Number of awards: Varies.
Deadline: January 15.
How to apply: Applications are available by mail or e-mail.
Exclusive: Visit www.UltimateScholarshipBook.com and enter code NA95212 for updates on this award.

(953) • Lewis C. Hoffman Scholarship

American Ceramic Society
600 North Cleveland Avenue
Suite 210
Westerville, OH 43082
Phone: 866-721-3322
Fax: 301-206-9789
Email: customerservice@ceramics.org
http://www.ceramics.org
Purpose: To support undergraduate ceramics and materials science and engineering students.
Eligibility: Applicants must be undergraduates who will have completed 70 or more semester credits (or quarter credit equivalent) at the time of award disbursement. Selection is based on essay response, GPA, recommendation letter, extracurricular involvements and standardized test scores (if available).
Target applicants: College students. Adult students.
Amount: $2,000.
Number of awards: 1.
Deadline: August 5.
How to apply: This scholarship does not require an application form. The applicant's essay response, a recommendation letter and a list of extracurricular activities are required.
Exclusive: Visit www.UltimateScholarshipBook.com and enter code AM95312 for updates on this award.

(954) • Liberty Mutual Safety Research Fellowship Program

American Society of Safety Engineers
1800 East Oakton Street
Des Plaines, IL 60018
Phone: 847-699-2929
Fax: 847-768-3434
Email: mgoranson@asse.org
http://www.asse.org
Purpose: To award research fellowships to promote safety research.
Eligibility: Applicants must be U.S. citizens and either have their Ph.D. or be working toward a masters or Ph.D. Preference is given to applicants working within an ABET-accredited safety program. The selection committee prefers applied safety/health research with a broad appeal and gives special consideration to ASSE members. Recipients must spend four to six weeks during the summer at the Liberty Mutual Research Center, in Hopkinton, MA, and write an article on their research or an outline for a grant proposal to continue the research.
Target applicants: Graduate school students. Adult students.
Amount: Up to $9,500 stipend.
Number of awards: Varies.
Deadline: February 1.
How to apply: Applications are available online.
Exclusive: Visit www.UltimateScholarshipBook.com and enter code AM95412 for updates on this award.

(955) • Light Metals Division Scholarship

The Minerals, Metals and Materials Society
184 Thorn Hill Road
Warrendale, PA 15086
Phone: 724-776-9000
Fax: 724-776-3770
Email: students@tms.org
http://www.tms.org
Purpose: To aid undergraduate students who are majoring in metallurgical engineering or materials science and engineering.
Eligibility: Applicants must be full-time undergraduate sophomores or juniors who are enrolled in a degree program in metallurgical engineering or materials science and engineering. They must be student members of TMS, The Minerals, Metals and Materials Society. Selection is based on academic merit, extracurricular activities, recommendations and personal statement.
Target applicants: College students. Adult students.
Amount: $4,000.
Number of awards: 3.
Deadline: March 15.
How to apply: Applications are available online. An application form, transcript, personal statement and three recommendation letters are required.
Exclusive: Visit www.UltimateScholarshipBook.com and enter code TH95512 for updates on this award.

(956) • Lisa Zaken Award For Excellence

Institute of Industrial Engineers
3577 Parkway Lane
Suite 200
Norcross, GA 30092

Phone: 800-494-0460
Fax: 770-441-3295
Email: bcameron@iienet.org
http://www.iienet2.org
Purpose: To award excellence in scholarly activities and leadership related to the industrial engineering profession on campus.
Eligibility: Applicants must be undergraduate or graduate students with at least one year remaining, major in industrial engineering and be active members who have been leaders in IIE. Students may not apply directly for this scholarship and must be nominated. The award is based on academic ability and leadership related to industrial engineering.
Target applicants: College students. Graduate school students. Adult students.
Minimum GPA: 3.0
Amount: $700.
Number of awards: 1.
Deadline: February 1.
How to apply: Nomination forms are available online.
Exclusive: Visit www.UltimateScholarshipBook.com and enter code IN95612 for updates on this award.

(957) • Lockheed Martin/HENAAC Scholars Program

Great Minds in STEM (HENAAC)
3900 Whiteside Street
Los Angeles, CA 90063
Phone: 323-262-0997
Fax: 323-262-0946
Email: jcano@greatmindsinstem.org
http://www.greatmindsinstem.org
Purpose: To aid computer science and engineering students.
Eligibility: Applicants must be U.S. citizens or permanent residents and full-time students who are majoring in computer science or aerospace, electrical, mechanical, software or systems engineering. They must have a GPA of 3.0 or higher. Applicants are not required to be Hispanic but must demonstrate strong leadership and involvement in the Hispanic community. Selection is based on the overall strength of the application.
Target applicants: College students. Graduate school students. Adult students.
Minimum GPA: 3.0
Amount: Varies.
Number of awards: Varies.
Scholarship may be renewable.
Deadline: April 30.
How to apply: Applications are available online. An application form, official transcript, recommendation letters, personal essay and resume are required.
Exclusive: Visit www.UltimateScholarshipBook.com and enter code GR95712 for updates on this award.

(958) • Lois Britt Pork Industry Memorial Scholarship Program

National Pork Producers Council
122 C Street, NW
Suite 875
Washington, DC 20001
Phone: 202-347-3600
Fax: 202-347-5265
Email: wrigleyj@nppc.org
http://www.nppc.org
Purpose: To support students who are preparing for careers in the pork industry.
Eligibility: Applicants must be undergraduates enrolled in either a two-year swine program or a four-year college of agriculture. They must be interested in pursuing a career in the pork industry. Selection is based on the strength of the personal essay.
Target applicants: College students. Adult students.
Amount: $2,500.
Number of awards: 4.
Deadline: January 15.
How to apply: Applications are available online. An information sheet, cover letter, personal essay and two reference letters are required.
Exclusive: Visit www.UltimateScholarshipBook.com and enter code NA95812 for updates on this award.

(959) • Long-Term Member Sponsored Scholarship

Society of Automotive Engineers International
400 Commonwealth Drive
Warrendale, PA 15096
Phone: 724-776-4841
Fax: 724-776-0790
Email: scholarships@sae.org
http://www.sae.org
Purpose: This scholarship recognizes outstanding SAE student members who actively support SAE and its activities.
Eligibility: Applicants must be college juniors and student members of SAE, major in engineering and actively support SAE and its programs. The scholarship will be awarded purely on the basis of the student's support for SAE and its programs.
Target applicants: College students. Adult students.
Amount: $1,000.
Number of awards: Varies.
Deadline: February 15.
How to apply: Applications are available online.
Exclusive: Visit www.UltimateScholarshipBook.com and enter code SO95912 for updates on this award.

(960) • Louis Agassiz Fuertes Award

Wilson Ornithological Society
Dr. Robert B. Payne
Museum of Zoology, University of Michigan
1109 Gedes Avenue
Ann Arbor, MI 48109
Email: rbpayne@umich.edu
http://www.wilsonsociety.org
Purpose: To support ornithologists' research.
Eligibility: Applicants must be students or young professionals doing avian research. Applicants must be willing to report their research results at an annual meeting of the Wilson Ornithological Society.
Target applicants: High school students. College students. Graduate school students. Adult students.
Amount: $2,500.
Number of awards: Up to 2.
Deadline: February 1.
How to apply: Applications are available online.
Exclusive: Visit www.UltimateScholarshipBook.com and enter code WI96012 for updates on this award.

(961) • Lowell Gaylor Memorial Scholarship

Aircraft Electronics Association
4217 South Hocker
Independence, MO 64055

Phone: 816-373-6565
Fax: 816-478-3100
Email: info@aea.net
http://www.aea.net
Purpose: To support students of avionics and aircraft repair.
Eligibility: Applicants must be high school seniors or college students who plan to or are attending an accredited school in an avionics or aircraft repair program.
Target applicants: High school students. College students. Adult students.
Amount: Varies.
Number of awards: 1.
Deadline: February 15.
How to apply: Applications are available by contacting the organization for more information.
Exclusive: Visit www.UltimateScholarshipBook.com and enter code AI96112 for updates on this award.

(962) • Lowell H. and Dorothy Loving Undergraduate Scholarship

American Congress on Surveying and Mapping (ACSM)
6 Montgomery Village Avenue
Suite 403
Gaithersburg, MD 20879
Phone: 240-632-9716
Fax: 240-632-1321
Email: ilse.genovese@acsm.net
http://www.acsm.net
Purpose: To aid undergraduate surveying and mapping students.
Eligibility: Applicants must be members of the American Congress on Surveying and Mapping (ACSM). They must be undergraduate juniors or seniors who are enrolled in a surveying and mapping degree program at a four-year institution located in the U.S. They must have a plan of study that includes coursework in two or more of the following areas: spatial measurement system analysis and design; land surveying; photogrammetry and remote sensing or geometric geodesy. Selection is based on academic merit, personal statement, recommendation letters, professional involvement and financial need.
Target applicants: College students. Adult students.
Amount: $2,500.
Number of awards: 1.
Scholarship may be renewable.
Deadline: November 2.
How to apply: Applications are available online. An application form, personal statement, proof of ACSM membership, three letters of recommendation and an official transcript are required.
Exclusive: Visit www.UltimateScholarshipBook.com and enter code AM96212 for updates on this award.

(963) • Lucille and Charles A. Wert Scholarship

ASM International Foundation
9639 Kinsman Road
Materials Park, OH 44073
Phone: 440-338-5151
Fax: 440-338-4634
Email: asmif@asminternational.org
http://asmcommunity.asminternational.org/portal/site/www/Foundation
Purpose: To aid undergraduate Material Advantage student members who demonstrate financial need.
Eligibility: Applicants must be rising undergraduate juniors or seniors who are attending a North American college or university. They must be Material Advantage student members. Preference will be given to those who are enrolled in an accredited bachelor's degree program in metallurgy or materials science engineering; applicants with related majors are eligible only if they have completed a significant amount of coursework in one of the aforementioned subjects. Applicants must demonstrate financial need. Selection is based on academic merit, proven career interest in the field and personal values.
Target applicants: College students. Adult students.
Amount: Up to $10,000.
Number of awards: 1.
Scholarship may be renewable.
Deadline: May 1.
How to apply: Applications are available online. An application form, personal statement, up to two recommendations and applicant photo are required.
Exclusive: Visit www.UltimateScholarshipBook.com and enter code AS96312 for updates on this award.

(964) • Lydia's Professional Uniform/AACN Excellence in Academics Nursing Scholarship

American Association of Colleges of Nursing
One Dupont Circle NW
Suite 350
Washington, DC 20036
Phone: 202-463-6930
Fax: 202-785-8320
Email: anniea@aacn.nche.edu
http://www.aacn.nche.edu
Purpose: To support undergraduate nursing students.
Eligibility: Applicants must be full-time nursing students in their junior year of a bachelor's of science (BSN) program with a minimum 3.5 GPA. The application form and an essay about their career aspirations and financial need are required.
Target applicants: College students. Adult students.
Minimum GPA: 3.5
Amount: $2,500.
Number of awards: 2.
Deadline: August 1 and November 1.
How to apply: Applications are available online and may be returned by fax or email.
Exclusive: Visit www.UltimateScholarshipBook.com and enter code AM96412 for updates on this award.

(965) • Madeline Pickett (Halbert) Cogswell Nursing Scholarship

National Society Daughters of the American Revolution
Committee Services Office
Attn.: Scholarships
1776 D Street NW
Washington, DC 20006-5303
Phone: 202-628-1776
http://www.dar.org
Purpose: To support nursing students.
Eligibility: Applicants must desire to attend or be attending an accredited school of nursing. Students must be members, descendants of members or eligible for membership in NSDAR. The DAR member number must be submitted on the application.
Target applicants: High school students. College students. Adult students.

Amount: $1,000.
Number of awards: Varies.
Deadline: February 15.
How to apply: Applications are available by written request with a self-addressed, stamped envelope.
Exclusive: Visit www.UltimateScholarshipBook.com and enter code NA96512 for updates on this award.

(966) · Margaret E. Swanson Scholarship

American Dental Hygienists' Association (ADHA) Institute for Oral Health
Scholarship Award Program
444 North Michigan Avenue
Suite 3400
Chicago, IL 60611
Phone: 312-440-8900
Email: institute@adha.net
http://www.adha.org/ioh
Purpose: To provide support to dental hygiene students who show leadership potential.
Eligibility: Applicants must have completed one year of an accredited dental hygiene program, pursuing a certificate or associates degree in the field. They must show evidence of organizational leadership potential. Applicants must also demonstrate financial need of at least $1,500, be active members of SADHA or ADHA and submit a goals statement.
Target applicants: College students. Adult students.
Amount: $1,000-$2,000.
Number of awards: 1.
Deadline: February 1.
How to apply: Applications are available online.
Exclusive: Visit www.UltimateScholarshipBook.com and enter code AM96612 for updates on this award.

(967) · Marliave Fund

Association of Engineering Geologists Foundation Marliave Fund
Paul Santi, Department of Geology and Geological Engineering
Colorado School of Mines
Berthoud Hall
Golden, CO 80401
Phone: 303-273-3108
Email: psanti@mines.edu
http://www.aegfoundation.org
Purpose: To reward outstanding students in engineering geology and geological engineering.
Eligibility: Applicants must be seniors or graduate students in a college or university program directly applicable to geological engineering and be members of the Association of Engineering Geologists.
Target applicants: College students. Graduate school students. Adult students.
Amount: Varies.
Number of awards: 1.
Deadline: February 1.
How to apply: Applications are available online or by written request.
Exclusive: Visit www.UltimateScholarshipBook.com and enter code AS96712 for updates on this award.

(968) · Marshall E. McCullough Scholarship

National Dairy Shrine
P.O. Box 1
Maribel, WI 54227
Phone: 920-863-6333
Fax: 920-863-8328
Email: info@dairyshrine.org
http://www.dairyshrine.org
Purpose: To support students who plan careers in agricultural-related communications.
Eligibility: Applicants must be high school seniors planning to enter a four-year university with intent to major in the dairy or animal sciences with a communications emphasis or agricultural journalism with a dairy or animal science emphasis, and they must intend to work in the dairy industry following graduation.
Target applicants: High school students.
Amount: $1,500 and $2,500.
Number of awards: 2.
Deadline: May 1.
How to apply: Applications are available online.
Exclusive: Visit www.UltimateScholarshipBook.com and enter code NA96812 for updates on this award.

(969) · Marvin Mundel Memorial Scholarship

Institute of Industrial Engineers
3577 Parkway Lane
Suite 200
Norcross, GA 30092
Phone: 800-494-0460
Fax: 770-441-3295
Email: bcameron@iienet.org
http://www.iienet2.org
Purpose: To assist undergraduate engineering students with an interest in work measurement and methods engineering.
Eligibility: Applicants must be full-time undergraduate students enrolled in a college in the United States, Canada or Mexico with an accredited industrial engineering program, major in industrial engineering and be active members. Students may not apply directly for this scholarship and must be nominated. The award is based on academic ability, character, leadership, potential service to the industrial engineering profession and financial need. Preference is given to students with a demonstrated interest in work measurement and methods engineering.
Target applicants: College students. Adult students.
Minimum GPA: 3.4
Amount: $1,000.
Number of awards: 2.
Deadline: February 1.
How to apply: Nomination forms are available online.
Exclusive: Visit www.UltimateScholarshipBook.com and enter code IN96912 for updates on this award.

(970) · Mary Opal Wolanin Scholarship

National Gerontological Nursing Association (NGNA)
7794 Grow Drive
Pensacola, FL 32514
Phone: 800-723-0560
Fax: 850-484-8762
Email: ngna@puetzamc.com
http://www.ngna.org
Purpose: To award gerontology and geriatric nursing undergraduate and graduate students.
Eligibility: For the undergraduate scholarship, applicants must be full- or part-time nursing students in an accredited U.S. school of nursing and must plan to work in a gerontology or geriatric setting. For the graduate scholarship, applicants must be nursing students with a

major in gerontology or geriatric nursing at an accredited U.S. nursing program and carry a minimum of six credits. Applicants must submit two recommendation letters, transcripts, professional/educational statements and financial statements.
Target applicants: College students. Graduate school students. Adult students.
Minimum GPA: 3.0
Amount: $500.
Number of awards: 2.
Deadline: July 1.
How to apply: Applications are available online.
Exclusive: Visit www.UltimateScholarshipBook.com and enter code NA97012 for updates on this award.

(971) • Mary Rhein Memorial Scholarship

Mu Alpha Theta
c/o University of Oklahoma
601 Elm Avenue
Room 1102
Norman, OK 73019
Phone: 405-325-4489
Fax: 405-325-7184
Email: matheta@ou.edu
http://www.mualphatheta.org
Purpose: To aid graduating high school seniors who are active Mu Alpha Theta members.
Eligibility: Applicants must be graduating high school seniors who are outstanding mathematics students. They must be active Mu Alpha Theta members who have been of service in the area of mathematics and who have participated in local, regional or national mathematics competitions. Applicants must have plans to pursue a mathematics-related career. Selection is based on the overall strength of the application.
Target applicants: High school students.
Amount: $5,000.
Number of awards: 1.
Deadline: March 1.
How to apply: Applications are available online. An application form, student essay, official transcript and three recommendation letters are required.
Exclusive: Visit www.UltimateScholarshipBook.com and enter code MU97112 for updates on this award.

(972) • Masonic-Range Science Scholarship

Society for Range Management (SRM)
10030 W. 27th Avenue
Wheat Ridge, CO 80215-6601
Phone: 303-986-3309
Fax: 303-986-3892
Email: vtrujillo@rangelands.org
http://www.rangelands.org
Purpose: To help a high school senior, college freshman or college sophomore majoring in range science or a closely related field.
Eligibility: Applicants must be sponsored by a member of the Society for Range Management (SRM), the National Association of Conservation Districts (NACD) or the Soil and Water Conservation Society (SWCS). Applicants must also submit an application form, transcript, SAT or ACT scores and two letters of reference.
Target applicants: High school students. College students. Adult students.
Amount: Varies.
Number of awards: Varies.
Deadline: January 8.
How to apply: Applications are available online.
Exclusive: Visit www.UltimateScholarshipBook.com and enter code SO97212 for updates on this award.

(973) • Materials Processing and Manufacturing Division Scholarship

The Minerals, Metals and Materials Society
184 Thorn Hill Road
Warrendale, PA 15086
Phone: 724-776-9000
Fax: 724-776-3770
Email: students@tms.org
http://www.tms.org
Purpose: To aid undergraduate student members of TMS who are majoring in metallurgical engineering or materials science and engineering.
Eligibility: Applicants must be full-time undergraduate sophomores or juniors whose studies must be focused on the integration of process control technology into manufacturing, materials technology research or the manufacturing process. Selection is based on academic merit, personal statement, recommendations, leadership skills, extracurricular activities and coursework relevance.
Target applicants: College students. Adult students.
Amount: $2,500.
Number of awards: 2.
Deadline: March 15.
How to apply: Applications are available online. An application form, personal statement, three recommendation letters and a transcript are required.
Exclusive: Visit www.UltimateScholarshipBook.com and enter code TH97312 for updates on this award.

(974) • Mattie J.T. Stepanek Caregiving Scholarship

Rosalynn Carter Institute for Caregiving
800 GSW Drive
Georgia Southwestern State University
Americus, GA 31709
Phone: 229-928-1234
Fax: 229-931-2663
http://www.rosalynncarter.org
Purpose: To aid caregivers who are seeking to enhance their caregiving skills through higher education.
Eligibility: Applicants must be family, professional or paraprofessional caregivers. They must be enrolled in or planning to enroll in college coursework that will provide them with additional skills that they can use in their caregiving activities. Selection is based on the overall strength of the application.
Target applicants: High school students. College students. Graduate school students. Adult students.
Amount: $2,500.
Number of awards: 4.
Deadline: Varies.
How to apply: Applications are available online. An application form and supporting materials are required.
Exclusive: Visit www.UltimateScholarshipBook.com and enter code RO97412 for updates on this award.

(975) • McAllister Memorial Scholarship

AOPA Air Safety Foundation
421 Aviation Way
Frederick, MD 21701
Phone: 301-695-2000
Fax: 301-695-2375
Email: aopahq@aopa.org
http://www.aopa.org

Purpose: To assist students in non-engineering aviation programs.
Eligibility: Applicants must be college juniors or seniors and have at least one semester or quarter to be completed, have a minimum 3.25 GPA and be enrolled in a baccalaureate level, non-engineering aviation degree program at a four-year institution. Applicants must also submit an essay on a topic posted on the website.
Target applicants: College students. Adult students.
Minimum GPA: 3.25
Amount: $1,000.
Number of awards: 1.
Deadline: March 31.
How to apply: Applications are available online.
Exclusive: Visit www.UltimateScholarshipBook.com and enter code AO97512 for updates on this award.

(976) • McNeil Rural Health Scholarship

National Association of Pediatric Nurse Practitioners (NAPNAP)
20 Brace Road
Suite 200
Cherry Hill, NJ 08034-2634
Phone: 856-857-9700
Fax: 856-857-1600
Email: info@napnap.org
http://www.napnap.org

Purpose: To improve pediatric health care provided by pediatric nurse practitioners.
Eligibility: Applicants must be enrolled in a full-time master's degree PNP program, plan to work in a rural area for two years after graduating, be a registered nurse with one year of pediatrics experience (other experience may be considered), have financial need and be a NAPNAP member. An application and RN license are required.
Target applicants: Graduate school students. Adult students.
Minimum GPA: 3.0
Amount: $10,000-$20,000.
Number of awards: 2.
Deadline: June 30.
How to apply: Applications are available online.
Exclusive: Visit www.UltimateScholarshipBook.com and enter code NA97612 for updates on this award.

(977) • Medical Student Summer Research Training in Aging Program

American Federation for Aging Research (AFAR)
70 West 40th Street, 11th Floor
New York, NY 10018
Phone: 212-703-9977
Fax: 212-997-0330
Email: grants@afar.org
http://www.afar.org

Purpose: To support early medical students who demonstrate an interest in geriatric medicine or age-related research with an opportunity to serve under top experts in the field.
Eligibility: Applicants must be osteopathic or allopathic students who have completed at least one year of medical school at a U.S. institution. Students must have a faculty sponsor from their home institution. The program lasts 8 to 12 weeks, and monthly stipends are provided.
Target applicants: Graduate school students. Adult students.
Amount: $1,748 monthly stipend.
Number of awards: Varies.
Deadline: January 31.
How to apply: Applications are available online.
Exclusive: Visit www.UltimateScholarshipBook.com and enter code AM97712 for updates on this award.

(978) • Medtronic Physio-Control Advanced Nursing Practice Scholarship

Emergency Nurses Association
915 Lee Street
Des Plaines, IL 60016
Phone: 847-460-4100
Fax: 847-460-4004
Email: foundation@ena.org
http://www.ena.org

Purpose: Monetary assistance for an advanced degree is awarded to an emergency nurse. Priority is given to those pursuing careers in cardiac nursing.
Eligibility: Applicants must be nurses pursuing advanced clinical practice degrees to become clinical nurse specialists or nurse practitioners. Preference is given to applicants focusing on cardiac nursing. Applicants must have been ENA members for at least 12 months before applying.
Target applicants: Graduate school students. Adult students.
Amount: $3,000.
Number of awards: 1.
Deadline: June 1.
How to apply: Applications are available online.
Exclusive: Visit www.UltimateScholarshipBook.com and enter code EM97812 for updates on this award.

(979) • Melvin R. Green Scholarships

American Society of Mechanical Engineers (ASME)
Three Park Avenue
New York, NY 10016
Phone: 800-843-2763
Fax: 973-882-1717
Email: infocentral@asme.org
http://www.asme.org

Purpose: To support mechanical engineering students.
Eligibility: Applicants must have outstanding character and integrity, be ASME student members, be enrolled in an eligible accredited mechanical engineering baccalaureate program, be college juniors or seniors and have strong academic performance.
Target applicants: College students. Adult students.
Amount: $4,000.
Number of awards: 2.
Deadline: March 1.
How to apply: Applications are available online.
Exclusive: Visit www.UltimateScholarshipBook.com and enter code AM97912 for updates on this award.

(980) • Members-at-Large Reentry Award

Iota Sigma Pi (ISP)
Dr. Joanne Bedlek-Anslow, MAL Coordinator
Camden High School, Science
1022 Ehrenclou Drive
Camden, SC 29020
http://www.iotasigmapi.info

Purpose: To recognize potential achievement in chemistry and related fields for a woman undergraduate or graduate student who has been absent from academia for at least three years.
Eligibility: Applicants must be female undergraduate or graduate students at an accredited four-year institution and be nominated by a faculty member or an Iota Sigma Pi member.
Target applicants: College students. Graduate school students. Adult students.
Amount: $1,500.
Number of awards: 1.
Deadline: April 1.
How to apply: Application information is available online.
Exclusive: Visit www.UltimateScholarshipBook.com and enter code IO98012 for updates on this award.

(981) • MGMA Midwest Section Scholarship

Medical Group Management Association
104 Inverness Terrace East
Englewood, CO 80112
Phone: 877-275-6462
Email: acmpe@mgma.com
http://www.mgma.com

Purpose: To aid MGMA Midwest Section members who are pursuing higher education in a subject that is related to medical practice management.
Eligibility: Applicants must be members of the Medical Group Management Association (MGMA). They must be residents of one of the MGMA Midwest Section states, namely Illinois, Indiana, Iowa, Michigan, Minnesota, Nebraska, North Dakota, Ohio, South Dakota or Wisconsin. They must be undergraduate or graduate students who are enrolled in a degree program that is related to medical practice management (such as public health, business administration or health care administration). Selection is based on the overall strength of the application.
Target applicants: College students. Graduate school students. Adult students.
Amount: Varies.
Number of awards: Varies.
Deadline: May 1.
How to apply: Applications are available online. An application form and supporting materials are required.
Exclusive: Visit www.UltimateScholarshipBook.com and enter code ME98112 for updates on this award.

(982) • MGMA Western Section Scholarship

Medical Group Management Association
104 Inverness Terrace East
Englewood, CO 80112
Phone: 877-275-6462
Email: acmpe@mgma.com
http://www.mgma.com

Purpose: To aid MGMA Western Section members who are pursuing higher education in subjects that are related to medical practice management.
Eligibility: Applicants must be residents of one of the MGMA Western Section states, namely Alaska, Arizona, California, Colorado, Hawaii, Idaho, Montana, Nevada, New Mexico, Oregon, Utah, Washington or Wyoming. They must be undergraduate or graduate students who are enrolled in a degree program relating to medical practice management (such as public health, business administration or health care administration). Selection is based on the overall strength of the application.
Target applicants: College students. Graduate school students. Adult students.
Amount: Varies.
Number of awards: Varies.
Deadline: May 1.
How to apply: Applications are available online. An application form and supporting materials are required.
Exclusive: Visit www.UltimateScholarshipBook.com and enter code ME98212 for updates on this award.

(983) • Michael Dunaway Scholarship

American Society of Extra-Corporeal Technology (AmSECT)
2209 Dickens Road
P.O. Box 11086
Richmond, VA 23230-1086
Phone: 804-565-6363
Fax: 804-282-0090
Email: patelpump@sbcglobal.net
http://www.amsect.org

Purpose: To support those studying perfusion.
Eligibility: Applicants must be current student members of AmSECT, be in a CAAHEP accredited perfusion education program, have finished 25 percent of the coursework, have a minimum 2.75 GPA and submit an application, essay and a transcript.
Target applicants: College students. Graduate school students. Adult students.
Minimum GPA: 2.75
Amount: $1,000.
Number of awards: Varies.
Deadline: December 15.
How to apply: Applications are available online.
Exclusive: Visit www.UltimateScholarshipBook.com and enter code AM98312 for updates on this award.

(984) • Michael Kidger Memorial Scholarship

International Society for Optical Engineering
P.O. Box 10
Bellingham, WA 98227-0010
Phone: 360-685-5452
Fax: 360-647-1445
Email: scholarships@spie.org
http://www.spie.org

Purpose: To support students in the optical design field.
Eligibility: Applicants must be in the optical design field and must have one year remaining of their studies. Students must submit a summary of their academic background and interest in optical design and two letters of recommendation.
Target applicants: College students. Adult students.
Amount: $5,000.
Number of awards: 1.

Deadline: March 31.
How to apply: Applications are available online.
Exclusive: Visit www.UltimateScholarshipBook.com and enter code IN98412 for updates on this award.

---

(985) · Microsoft Tuition Scholarships

Microsoft Corporation
One Microsoft Way
Redmond, WA 98052-8303
Phone: 800-642-7676
Fax: 425-936-7329
Email: scholars@microsoft.com
http://www.microsoft.com/college/

Purpose: Offering more than a half-million dollars in scholarships, Microsoft is looking for undergraduates who display an interest in the software industry and are committed to leadership.
Eligibility: Applicants must be in a full-time undergraduate program related to computer science. Recipients will have to complete salaried internships in Redmond, Washington. There are special scholarships for women, minorities and disabled students.
Target applicants: College students. Adult students.
Minimum GPA: 3.0
Amount: Up to full tuition.
Number of awards: Varies.
Deadline: February 1.
How to apply: Application requirements are online.
Exclusive: Visit www.UltimateScholarshipBook.com and enter code MI98512 for updates on this award.

---

(986) · Mid-Continent Instrument Scholarship

Aircraft Electronics Association
4217 South Hocker
Independence, MO 64055
Phone: 816-373-6565
Fax: 816-478-3100
Email: info@aea.net
http://www.aea.net

Purpose: To support students who wish to pursue a career in avionics or aircraft repair.
Eligibility: Applicants must be high school seniors or college students who plan to or are attending an accredited school in an avionics or aircraft repair program.
Target applicants: High school students. College students. Adult students.
Amount: Varies.
Number of awards: 1.
Deadline: February 15.
How to apply: Applications are available by contacting the organization for more information.
Exclusive: Visit www.UltimateScholarshipBook.com and enter code AI98612 for updates on this award.

---

(987) · Milton F. Lunch Research Fellowship

National Society of Professional Engineers
1420 King Street
Alexandria, VA 22314-2794
Phone: 703-684-2885
Fax: 703-836-4875
Email: memserv@nspe.org
http://www.nspe.org

Purpose: To honor the memory of Milton F. Lunch, who was the NSPE's general counsel for 40 years.
Eligibility: Students must be U.S. citizens and be pursuing a career in engineering, architecture, construction or law and be enrolled in an undergraduate or graduate program in one of those fields. Undergraduate students must be rising seniors and have a minimum GPA of 3.0 on a 4.0 scale.
Target applicants: College students. Graduate school students. Adult students.
Minimum GPA: 3.0
Amount: $8,000 stipend.
Number of awards: 1.
Deadline: January 28.
How to apply: Applications are available online.
Exclusive: Visit www.UltimateScholarshipBook.com and enter code NA98712 for updates on this award.

---

(988) · Minority Dental Student Scholarship

American Dental Association Foundation
211 East Chicago Avenue
Chicago, IL 60611
Phone: 312-440-2763
Fax: 312-440-3526
Email: famularor@ada.org
http://www.ada.org

Purpose: To encourage minority students to pursue careers in dental hygiene, dental assisting, dentistry and dental laboratory technology.
Eligibility: Applicants must be African American, Hispanic or Native American full-time students entering their second year in an accredited dental program and must demonstrate a minimum financial need of $2,500. Applicants must submit applications, two reference forms, enrollment letters and biographies. Selection is based on financial need, academic achievement, biographical sketch and references. A minimum 3.0 GPA is required. Only two scholarship applications per school are allowed, so schools may set their own in-school application deadlines that are earlier.
Target applicants: College students. Adult students.
Minimum GPA: 3.0
Amount: $1,000.
Number of awards: Varies.
Deadline: June 11.
How to apply: Applications are available from dental school officials.
Exclusive: Visit www.UltimateScholarshipBook.com and enter code AM98812 for updates on this award.

---

(989) · Minority Student Scholarship

American Speech-Language-Hearing Foundation
2200 Research Boulevard
Rockville, MD 20850
Phone: 301-296-8700
Email: foundation@asha.org
http://www.ashfoundation.org

Purpose: To support a minority graduate student in communication sciences and disorders.
Eligibility: Applicants should be full-time minority graduate students. Master's degree candidates must be in programs accredited by the Council on Academic Accreditation for Audiology and Speech Pathology, but doctoral programs do not have to be accredited. Transcripts, an essay and a reference form are required.
Target applicants: Graduate school students. Adult students.
Amount: $4,000.

Number of awards: Varies.
Deadline: Varies.
How to apply: Applications are available online.
Exclusive: Visit www.UltimateScholarshipBook.com and enter code AM98912 for updates on this award.

(990) • Monsanto Company/The National Association of Farm Broadcasters Commitment to Agriculture Scholarship

National FFA Organization
P.O. Box 68960
6060 FFA Drive
Indianapolis, IN 46268-0960
Phone: 317-802-6060
Fax: 317-802-6051
Email: scholarships@ffa.org
http://www.ffa.org/
Purpose: To support students whose families are involved in production agriculture.
Eligibility: Applicants must be high school seniors or college students planning to enroll or currently enrolled full-time. Students must have a minimum SAT score of 1320 or ACT score of 18, and they must be pursuing degrees in areas related to agriculture. Students only need to complete the online application one time to be considered for all FFA-administered scholarships. The application requires information about the students' activities and a 1,000-word essay. Awards may be used for books, supplies, tuition, fees and room and board. Applicants may be members or non-members of the FFA.
Target applicants: High school students. College students. Adult students.
Amount: $1,500.
Number of awards: 100.
Deadline: February 15.
How to apply: Applications are available online.
Exclusive: Visit www.UltimateScholarshipBook.com and enter code NA99012 for updates on this award.

(991) • Morton B. Duggan, Jr. Memorial Education Recognition Award

American Association for Respiratory Care
9425 North MacArthur Boulevard
Suite 100
Irving, TX 75063-4706
Phone: 972-243-2272
Fax: 972-484-2720
Email: info@aarc.org
http://www.aarc.org
Purpose: To recognize outstanding students in respiratory care education programs.
Eligibility: Applicants must be enrolled in an accredited respiratory care education program and have a minimum 3.0 GPA. Students must submit an original paper on respiratory care. Preference is given to residents of Georgia and South Carolina.
Target applicants: College students. Graduate school students. Adult students.
Minimum GPA: 3.0
Amount: Up to $1,000.
Number of awards: 1.
Deadline: June 15.
How to apply: Applications are available online.
Exclusive: Visit www.UltimateScholarshipBook.com and enter code AM99112 for updates on this award.

(992) • Myrtle and Earl Walker Scholarship

Society of Manufacturing Engineers Education Foundation
One SME Drive
P.O. Box 930
Dearborn, MI 48121
Phone: 313-425-3300
Fax: 313-425-3411
Email: foundation@sme.org
http://www.smeef.org
Purpose: To help manufacturing engineering and technology undergraduates.
Eligibility: Applicants must be full-time undergraduate students who are studying manufacturing engineering or technology at an accredited postsecondary institution located in the U.S. or Canada. They must have a GPA of 3.0 or higher on a four-point scale and must have completed 15 or more credit hours. They must have plans to pursue a career in manufacturing engineering or technology. Selection is based on the overall strength of the application.
Target applicants: College students. Adult students.
Minimum GPA: 3.0
Amount: Varies.
Number of awards: Varies.
Deadline: February 1.
How to apply: Applications are available online. An application form, personal statement, resume, transcript and two recommendation letters are required.
Exclusive: Visit www.UltimateScholarshipBook.com and enter code SO99212 for updates on this award.

(993) • NAMEPA Scholarship Program

National Association of Multicultural Engineering Program Advocates
341 N. Maitland Avenue
Suite 130
Maitland, FL 32751
Phone: 407-647-8839
Fax: 407-629-2502
Email: namepa@namepa.org
http://www.namepa.org
Purpose: To support minority students to become engineers.
Eligibility: Applicants must be African American, Latino and American Indian high school seniors admitted at a college or university as an engineering major with a minimum 2.7 GPA and minimum ACT score of 25 or minimum SAT score of 1000. Applicants must attend a NAMEPA member institution. Transfer students are also eligible. Selection is based on coursework in high school, course distribution, activities, a one-page narrative and recommendations.
Target applicants: High school students.
Minimum GPA: 2.7
Amount: $1,000.
Number of awards: Varies.
Deadline: May 15.
How to apply: Applications are available online.
Exclusive: Visit www.UltimateScholarshipBook.com and enter code NA99312 for updates on this award.

(994) • Naomi Brack Student Scholarship

National Organization for Associate Degree Nursing
7794 Grow Drive
Pensacola, FL 32514
Phone: 850-484-6948
Fax: 850-484-8762
Email: richelle.torres@dancyamc.com
http://www.noadn.org
Purpose: To aid associate's degree nursing (ADN) students.
Eligibility: Applicants must be currently enrolled in an associate's degree program in nursing at a state-approved institution. They must have a GPA of 3.0 or more on a four-point scale and must be active in their school's student nursing association. Selection is based on the overall strength of the application.
Target applicants: College students. Adult students.
Minimum GPA: 3.0
Amount: $1,000.
Number of awards: Varies.
Deadline: September 1.
How to apply: Applications are available online. An application form, personal statement, transcript, nomination form and two letters of recommendation are required.
Exclusive: Visit www.UltimateScholarshipBook.com and enter code NA99412 for updates on this award.

(995) • NAPA Research and Education Foundation Scholarship

National Asphalt Pavement Association
5100 Forbes Boulevard
Lanham, MD 20706
Phone: 888-468-6499
Fax: 301-731-4621
http://www.hotmix.org
Purpose: To aid engineering and construction students who are interested in hot mix asphalt technology.
Eligibility: Applicants must be U.S. citizens who are enrolled full-time at an accredited postsecondary institution. They must be majoring in construction management, civil engineering or construction engineering. The applicant's school must offer at least one course on hot mix asphalt (HMA) technology. Selection is based on academic achievement, leadership potential, extracurricular involvements and stated career goals.
Target applicants: College students. Graduate school students. Adult students.
Amount: Varies.
Number of awards: Varies.
Scholarship may be renewable.
Deadline: Varies.
How to apply: Applications may be requested from the student's state National Asphalt Pavement Association representative. An application form and supporting materials are required.
Exclusive: Visit www.UltimateScholarshipBook.com and enter code NA99512 for updates on this award.

(996) • National Aviation Explorer Scholarships

Explorers Learning for Life
P.O. Box 152079
Irving, TX 75015
Phone: 972-580-2433
Fax: 972-580-2137
Email: pchestnu@lflmail.org
http://www.learningforlife.org/exploring
Purpose: To support students who are pursuing careers in the aviation industry.
Eligibility: Students must be active members of an Aviation Explorer post. Applicants must submit an essay and three letters of recommendation.
Target applicants: Junior high students or younger. High school students. College students. Adult students.
Amount: $3,000-$10,000.
Number of awards: 10.
Deadline: March 31.
How to apply: Applications are available online.
Exclusive: Visit www.UltimateScholarshipBook.com and enter code EX99612 for updates on this award.

(997) • National Dairy Shrine/Iager Dairy Scholarship

National Dairy Shrine
P.O. Box 1
Maribel, WI 54227
Phone: 920-863-6333
Fax: 920-863-8328
Email: info@dairyshrine.org
http://www.dairyshrine.org
Purpose: To aid dairy and animal science students who are planning for careers in the dairy industry.
Eligibility: Applicants must be entering the second year of a two-year agricultural college program in dairy or animal science. They must have a GPA of 2.5 or higher on a four-point scale. Selection is based on academic merit, leadership skills and professional commitment to the dairy industry.
Target applicants: College students. Adult students.
Minimum GPA: 2.5
Amount: $1,000.
Number of awards: 1.
Deadline: May 1.
How to apply: Applications are available online. An application form, official transcript, personal essay and two recommendation letters are required.
Exclusive: Visit www.UltimateScholarshipBook.com and enter code NA99712 for updates on this award.

(998) • National FFA College and Vocational/ Technical School Scholarship Program

National FFA Organization
P.O. Box 68960
6060 FFA Drive
Indianapolis, IN 46268-0960
Phone: 317-802-6060
Fax: 317-802-6051
Email: scholarships@ffa.org
http://www.ffa.org/
Purpose: The scholarship program supports FFA members and agriculture.
Eligibility: FFA awards more than $2 million in scholarships. The programs have various eligibility requirements and award amounts. Applicants must be U.S. citizens and high school seniors or current college students. For some awards, students must be FFA members.
Target applicants: High school students. College students. Adult students.
Amount: Varies.
Number of awards: Varies.

Scholarship may be renewable.
Deadline: February 15.
How to apply: Applications are available online or from your local FFA advisor.
Exclusive: Visit www.UltimateScholarshipBook.com and enter code NA99812 for updates on this award.

(999) • National Foliage Foundation General Scholarships

National Foliage Foundation
1533 Park Center Drive
Orlando, FL 32835
Phone: 800-375-3642
Fax: 407-295-1619
Email: info@nationalfoliagefoundation.org
http://www.nationalfoliagefoundation.org
Purpose: To aid horticulture students who are interested in pursuing careers in foliage growing and marketing.
Eligibility: Applicants must be graduating high school seniors or full-time undergraduate or graduate students. They must be enrolled in or planning to enroll in a horticulture or related degree program and must have a GPA of 2.5 or higher. They must be interested in pursuing a career in foliage marketing or growing. Selection is based on the overall strength of the application.
Target applicants: High school students. College students. Graduate school students. Adult students.
Minimum GPA: 2.5
Amount: Varies.
Number of awards: Varies.
Scholarship may be renewable.
Deadline: January 15.
How to apply: Applications are available online. An application form, transcript, two recommendation letters and a personal essay are required.
Exclusive: Visit www.UltimateScholarshipBook.com and enter code NA99912 for updates on this award.

(1000) • National Garden Clubs Scholarship

National Garden Clubs Inc.
4401 Magnolia Avenue
St. Louis, MO 63110
Phone: 314-776-7574
Fax: 314-776-5108
Email: headquarters@gardenclub.org
http://www.gardenclub.org
Purpose: To promote the study of horticulture and related fields.
Eligibility: Applicants must be full-time juniors, seniors, graduate students or sophomores applying for the junior year and major in one of the following fields: agriculture education, horticulture, floriculture, landscape design, botany, biology, plant pathology/science, forestry, agronomy, environmental concerns, economics, environmental conservation, city planning, wildlife science, habitat or forest/systems ecology, land management or related areas.
Target applicants: College students. Graduate school students. Adult students.
Minimum GPA: 3.25
Amount: $3,500.
Number of awards: 35.
Deadline: March 1.
How to apply: Applications are available online and must be mailed to the applicants' state Garden Club scholarship chairman.
Exclusive: Visit www.UltimateScholarshipBook.com and enter code NA100012 for updates on this award.

(1001) • National Network for Environmental Management Studies Fellowship Program

Environmental Protection Agency
NNEMS Fellowship Program
Environmental Education Division
1200 Pennsylvania Avenue
Washington, DC 20460
Phone: 800-358-8769
Email: carolyn.pitera@ttemi.com
http://www.epa.gov/education/students.html
Purpose: To provide students with research opportunities, to increase public awareness of environmental issues and to encourage students to pursue careers in environmental protection.
Eligibility: Applicants must be undergraduate or graduate students, be U.S. citizens or legal residents, be enrolled in an academic program directly related to pollution control, have a minimum 3.0 GPA, have completed four courses relating to the environmental field and submit a research project proposal.
Target applicants: College students. Graduate school students. Adult students.
Minimum GPA: 3.0
Amount: Varies.
Number of awards: Varies.
Deadline: March 4.
How to apply: Applications are available online.
Exclusive: Visit www.UltimateScholarshipBook.com and enter code EN100112 for updates on this award.

(1002) • National Potato Council Scholarship

National Potato Council
1300 L Street NW #910
Washington, DC 20005
Phone: 202-682-9456
Fax: 202-682-0333
http://www.nationalpotatocouncil.org
Purpose: To aid students pursuing studies that support the potato industry.
Eligibility: Applicants must be graduate agribusiness students. Selection is based on academic achievement, leadership abilities and potato-related areas of graduate study (such as agricultural engineering, agronomy, crop and soil sciences, entomology, food sciences, horticulture and plant pathology).
Target applicants: Graduate school students. Adult students.
Amount: $5,000.
Number of awards: 1.
Deadline: June 15.
How to apply: Applications are available online. An application form, essay, transcripts, list of activities and two references are required.
Exclusive: Visit www.UltimateScholarshipBook.com and enter code NA100212 for updates on this award.

(1003) • National Science and Mathematics Access to Retain Talent Grant

Federal Student Aid
U.S. Department of Education
400 Maryland Avenue, SW
Washington, DC 20202

Phone: 800-433-3243
http://studentaid.ed.gov
Purpose: To assist students who are majoring in physical, life or computer sciences, mathematics, technology, engineering or a foreign language that is critical to national security in continuing their educations.
Eligibility: Applicants must be U.S. citizens who are Pell Grant recipients, enrolled full-time in a physical, life or computer science, engineering, mathematics, technology or critical foreign language program at a four-year institution and have a college GPA of 3.0 or higher in the coursework required for the major. Students must be at least college sophomores, and the award may be used for the third and fourth year of undergraduate study.
Target applicants: College students. Adult students.
Minimum GPA: 3.0
Amount: Up to $4,000.
Number of awards: Varies.
Deadline: Varies.
How to apply: Applications are available from your financial aid office.
Exclusive: Visit www.UltimateScholarshipBook.com and enter code FE100312 for updates on this award.

(1004) • National Student Design Competition

American Institute of Chemical Engineers - (AIChE)
3 Park Avenue
New York, NY 10016
Phone: 212-591-7634
Fax: 212-591-8890
Email: awards@aiche.org
http://www.aiche.org
Purpose: To test chemical engineering students' skills in calculation and evaluation of technical data and economic factors.
Eligibility: Applicants must be members of an AIChE student chapter.
Target applicants: College students. Graduate school students. Adult students.
Amount: $200-$500.
Number of awards: 3.
Deadline: June 4.
How to apply: Applications are available online.
Exclusive: Visit www.UltimateScholarshipBook.com and enter code AM100412 for updates on this award.

(1005) • National Student Nurses' Association Scholarship

National Student Nurses' Association
45 Main Street
Suite 606
Brooklyn, NY 11201
Phone: 718-210-0705
Fax: 718-797-1186
Email: nsna@nsna.org
http://www.nsna.org
Purpose: To promote interest in the nursing field.
Eligibility: Applicants must be currently enrolled in a state-approved school of nursing or pre-nursing in associate degree, baccalaureate, diploma, doctorate or master's programs.
Target applicants: College students. Graduate school students. Adult students.
Amount: $1,000-$2,500.
Number of awards: Varies.
Deadline: January 14.
How to apply: Applications are available online.
Exclusive: Visit www.UltimateScholarshipBook.com and enter code NA100512 for updates on this award.

(1006) • National Wildlife Federation Ecology Fellowship

National Wildlife Federation
11100 Wildlife Center Drive
Reston, VA 20190-5362
Phone: 800-822-9919
http://www.nwf.org
Purpose: The fellowship program provides funding for campus ecology projects.
Eligibility: Applicants must create a plan for a campus ecology program, working with a project advisor and verifier. All Campus Ecology fellows are required to attend a training program.
Target applicants: College students. Graduate school students. Adult students.
Amount: Varies.
Number of awards: Varies.
Deadline: Varies.
How to apply: Applications are available online.
Exclusive: Visit www.UltimateScholarshipBook.com and enter code NA100612 for updates on this award.

(1007) • National Young Astronomer Award

Astronomical League
7241 Jarboe
Kansas City, MO 64114
Phone: 816-444-4878
Email: carroll-iorg@kc.rr.com
http://www.astroleague.org
Purpose: To support young astronomers.
Eligibility: Applicants must be 14 to 19 years old, not yet enrolled in college at the award deadline and do not have to be members of an astronomy club or of the Astronomical League. International students of the same age are eligible if they are enrolled in a U.S. secondary school on the application deadline. The application consists of the application form, summary of astronomy related activities and optional exhibits.
Target applicants: Junior high students or younger. High school students.
Amount: Varies.
Number of awards: 3.
Deadline: January 31.
How to apply: Applications are available online.
Exclusive: Visit www.UltimateScholarshipBook.com and enter code AS100712 for updates on this award.

(1008) • NAWIC Founders' Undergraduate Scholarship

National Association of Women in Construction
327 South Adams Street
Fort Worth, TX 76104
Phone: 800-552-3506
Fax: 817-877-0324
Email: nawic@nawic.org
http://www.nawic.org
Purpose: To aid undergraduates who are preparing for careers in construction.
Eligibility: Applicants must be full-time, degree-seeking undergraduates who are studying a construction-related subject at a postsecondary

institution located in the U.S. or Canada. Students do NOT need to be female. They must have a cumulative GPA of 3.0 or higher and have plans to pursue a career in a construction-related field. Selection is based on stated career goals, extracurricular activities, work experience, academic achievement and financial need.
Target applicants: College students. Adult students.
Minimum GPA: 3.0
Amount: Up to $2,000.
Number of awards: Varies.
Scholarship may be renewable.
Deadline: March 15.
How to apply: Applications are available online. An application form, transcript, employment history, extracurricular activities list and personal statement are required.
Exclusive: Visit www.UltimateScholarshipBook.com and enter code NA100812 for updates on this award.

(1009) • NBRC/AMP Gareth B. Gish, MS, RRT Memorial and William F. Miller, MD Postgraduate Education Recognition Awards

American Association for Respiratory Care
9425 North MacArthur Boulevard
Suite 100
Irving, TX 75063-4706
Phone: 972-243-2272
Fax: 972-484-2720
Email: info@aarc.org
http://www.aarc.org
Purpose: To aid qualified respiratory therapists in pursuing advanced degrees.
Eligibility: Applicants must be respiratory therapists who have been accepted into an advanced degree program of a fully accredited school. Application must be accompanied by an original essay describing how the award will aid in achieving an advanced degree and future goals in health care. A minimum 3.0 GPA is required.
Target applicants: College students. Graduate school students. Adult students.
Minimum GPA: 3.0
Amount: Up to $1,500.
Number of awards: 2.
Deadline: June 15.
How to apply: Applications are available online.
Exclusive: Visit www.UltimateScholarshipBook.com and enter code AM100912 for updates on this award.

(1010) • NBRC/AMP William W. Burgin, Jr. MD and Robert M. Lawrence, MD Education Recognition Awards

American Association for Respiratory Care
9425 North MacArthur Boulevard
Suite 100
Irving, TX 75063-4706
Phone: 972-243-2272
Fax: 972-484-2720
Email: info@aarc.org
http://www.aarc.org
Purpose: To recognize outstanding students in respiratory care education programs.
Eligibility: Applicants must be enrolled in an accredited respiratory care education program as a second-year student pursuing an associate's degree or as a junior or senior pursuing a bachelor's degree. In addition to an original paper dealing with respiratory care, applicants must submit an original essay describing how this award will help them reach their degrees and their future goals in the field of health care.
Target applicants: College students. Adult students.
Amount: Up to $2,500.
Number of awards: 2.
Deadline: June 15.
How to apply: Applications are available online.
Exclusive: Visit www.UltimateScholarshipBook.com and enter code AM101012 for updates on this award.

(1011) • NCAPA Endowment Grant

North Carolina Academy of Physician Assistants
1121 Slater Road
Durham, NC 27703
Phone: 800-352-2271
Fax: 919-479-9726
Email: ncapa@ncapa.org
https://www.netforumondemand.com/eWeb/StartPage.aspx?Site=NCAPA
Purpose: To aid physician assistant school students.
Eligibility: Applicants must be current student members of the North Carolina Academy of Physician Assistants (NCAPA). They must be rising second- or third-year students in an accredited physician assistant degree program. Selection is based on the overall strength of the application.
Target applicants: College students. Graduate school students. Adult students.
Amount: Varies.
Number of awards: Varies.
Deadline: June 10.
How to apply: Applications are available online. An application form, financial aid statement, personal essay and official transcript.
Exclusive: Visit www.UltimateScholarshipBook.com and enter code NO101112 for updates on this award.

(1012) • NCPA Foundation Presidential Scholarship

National Community Pharmacists Association
NCPA Foundation
100 Daingerfield Road
Alexandria, VA 22314
Phone: 703-683-8200
Fax: 703-683-3619
Email: info@ncpanet.org
http://www.ncpanet.org
Purpose: To support students who plan to enter the pharmaceutical field.
Eligibility: Applicants must be student members of NCPA and enrolled in a U.S. school or college of pharmacy full-time. Selection is based on academic achievement and leadership.
Target applicants: College students. Graduate school students. Adult students.
Amount: $2,000.
Number of awards: Varies.
Deadline: April 15.
How to apply: Applications are available online.
Exclusive: Visit www.UltimateScholarshipBook.com and enter code NA101212 for updates on this award.

(1013) • NDPRB Undergraduate Scholarship Program

National Dairy Promotion and Research Board
c/o Jolene Griffin
Dairy Management Inc.
10255 West Higgins Road, Suite 900
Rosemont, IL 60018
Phone: 847-627-3320
Email: jolene.griffin@rosedmi.com
http://www.dairycheckoff.com

Purpose: To aid undergraduates who are studying a dairy-related subject.
Eligibility: Applicants must be rising undergraduate sophomores, juniors or seniors. They must be majoring in a subject that emphasizes dairy (such as agriculture education, business, communications, economics, food science, journalism, marketing or public relations). Applicants must plan to pursue a career in the dairy industry. Selection is based on stated career goals, academic excellence, dairy-related coursework completed, leadership and integrity.
Target applicants: College students. Adult students.
Amount: $1,500.
Number of awards: Up to 19.
Scholarship may be renewable.
Deadline: May 31.
How to apply: Applications are available online. An application form, personal statement, one recommendation letter and an official transcript are required.
Exclusive: Visit www.UltimateScholarshipBook.com and enter code NA101312 for updates on this award.

(1014) • NDSEG Fellowship Program

Department of Defense, American Society for Engineering Education
1818 N Street NW
Suite 600
Washington, DC 20036
Phone: 202-331-3546
Fax: 202-265-8504
Email: ndseg@asee.org
http://ndseg.asee.org

Purpose: To award fellowships to those in science and engineering.
Eligibility: Applicants must pursue a doctoral degree in an area of Department of Defense interest: aeronautical and astronautical engineering, biosciences, chemical engineering, chemistry, civil engineering, cognitive, neural, and behavioral sciences, computer and computational sciences, electrical engineering, geosciences, materials science and engineering, mathematics, mechanical engineering, naval architecture and ocean engineering, oceanography and physics. Applicants must have completed no more than one academic year of graduate study as a part-time or full-time student or be in their final year of undergraduate studies. The award is based on academic achievement, personal statements, recommendations and Graduate Record Examination scores. Fellowships may be used only at U.S. institutions of higher education offering doctoral degrees.
Target applicants: College students. Graduate school students. Adult students.
Amount: $30,500-$31,500.
Number of awards: 200.
Scholarship may be renewable.
Deadline: December 17.
How to apply: Applications are available online.
Exclusive: Visit www.UltimateScholarshipBook.com and enter code DE101412 for updates on this award.

(1015) • Need-Based Scholarship Program

National Medical Fellowships Inc.
5 Hanover Square
15th Floor
New York, NY 10004
Phone: 212-483-8880
Email: info@nmfonline.org
http://www.nmfonline.org

Purpose: To help first- and second-year minority medical students.
Eligibility: Applicants must be African American, Mexican American, Native American, Alaska Native, Native Hawaiian or mainland Puerto Rican students accepted by accredited U.S. medical schools for M.D. or D.O. degrees. Select programs are open to third-year students. Applications, transcripts, recommendation letters and financial documents are required.
Target applicants: Graduate school students. Adult students.
Amount: $10,000.
Number of awards: Varies.
Deadline: August 31.
How to apply: Applications are available online, by mail and from the medical schools.
Exclusive: Visit www.UltimateScholarshipBook.com and enter code NA101512 for updates on this award.

(1016) • NEHA/AAS Scholarship Awards

National Environmental Health Association and the American Academy of Sanitarians
NEHA/AAS Scholarship
Scholarship Coordinator
720 S. Colorado Boulevard, Suite 1000-N
Denver, CO 80246
Phone: 303-756-9090
Fax: 303-691-9490
Email: cdimmitt@neha.org
http://www.neha.org

Purpose: To support students planning careers in environmental health.
Eligibility: Applicants must be either undergraduate or graduate students. The undergraduate scholarships are to be used during the junior or senior year at an Environmental Health Accreditation Council (EHAC) or NEHA member school. The graduate scholarship is available to applicants who are enrolled in a graduate program of studies in environmental health sciences and/or public health.
Target applicants: College students. Graduate school students. Adult students.
Amount: Varies.
Number of awards: Varies.
Scholarship may be renewable.
Deadline: February 1.
How to apply: Applications are available online.
Exclusive: Visit www.UltimateScholarshipBook.com and enter code NA101612 for updates on this award.

(1017) • Nellie Yeoh Whetten Award

American Vacuum Society
120 Wall Street, 32nd Floor
New York, NY 10005-3993
Phone: 212-248-0200
Fax: 212-248-0245
Email: angela@avs.org
http://www.avs.org

Purpose: To support women in graduate studies in the sciences and technologies related to AVS.
Eligibility: Applicants must be female graduate students in an accredited academic institution and must send an application, report on candidate form, two letters of recommendation and college and graduate school transcripts.
Target applicants: Graduate school students. Adult students.
Amount: Varies.
Number of awards: Varies.
Deadline: May 5.
How to apply: Applications are available online.
Exclusive: Visit www.UltimateScholarshipBook.com and enter code AM101712 for updates on this award.

(1018) · Neuroscience Research Prize

American Academy of Neurology
1080 Montreal Avenue
Saint Paul, MN 55116
Phone: 651-695-2704
Fax: 651-695-2791
Email: ejackson@aan.com
http://www.aan.com
Purpose: To encourage high school students of scientific aptitude to explore the field of neuroscience.
Eligibility: Applicants must be U.S. high school students. They must have completed an original, independent laboratory research project on a subject that is related to the brain or nervous system. Selection is based on creativity, the strength of the applicant's research report and relevance of the research project to neuroscience.
Target applicants: High school students.
Amount: $1,000.
Number of awards: 4.
Deadline: November 1.
How to apply: Applications are available online. An application form and research report are required.
Exclusive: Visit www.UltimateScholarshipBook.com and enter code AM101812 for updates on this award.

(1019) · New Century Scholars Program

American Speech-Language-Hearing Foundation
2200 Research Boulevard
Rockville, MD 20850
Phone: 301-296-8700
Email: foundation@asha.org
http://www.ashfoundation.org
Purpose: To support graduate students and researchers who are studying communication sciences and disorders.
Eligibility: Students applying for the scholarship must be enrolled in a research or teaching doctoral program to obtain a Ph.D. or its equivalent. Researchers applying for the grant must have teacher-investigator careers, either in an academic environment or in external research institutions.
Target applicants: Graduate school students. Adult students.
Amount: Up to $10,000.
Number of awards: Varies.
Deadline: Varies.
How to apply: Applications are available online.
Exclusive: Visit www.UltimateScholarshipBook.com and enter code AM101912 for updates on this award.

(1020) · New Look Laser Tattoo Removal Semiannual Scholarship

New Look Laser Tattoo Removal
c/o Nicole Carter, Scholarship Coordinator
1770 St. James Place
Suite 105
Houston, TX 77056
Phone: 713-783-2000
Email: scholarship@newlookhouston.com
http://www.newlookhouston.com
Purpose: To aid students who are preparing for careers in engineering, nursing, medicine, natural sciences or applied sciences.
Eligibility: Applicants must be U.S. citizens or permanent residents who are enrolled or planning to enroll at an accredited college or university. They must be studying or planning to study engineering, medicine, nursing, natural sciences or applied sciences. They must have a GPA of 3.0 or higher. Selection is based on the overall strength of the application.
Target applicants: High school students. College students. Adult students.
Minimum GPA: 3.0
Amount: $1,000.
Number of awards: 1.
Deadline: June 30 and November 30.
How to apply: Application instructions are available online. A cover sheet, writing project and transcript are required.
Exclusive: Visit www.UltimateScholarshipBook.com and enter code NE102012 for updates on this award.

(1021) · NFMC Dorothy Dann Bullock Music Therapy Award and the NFMC Ruth B. Robertson Music Therapy Award

National Federation of Music Clubs Bullock and Robertson Awards
Anita Louise Steele
Gilden School of Music
Ohio University
Athens, OH 45701
Phone: 740-593-4249
Fax: 317-638-0503
Email: steelea@ohio.edu
http://www.nfmc-music.org
Purpose: To assist students who plan to enter careers in music therapy.
Eligibility: Applicants must be college students majoring in music therapy in schools approved by the National Association of Music Therapists and AMTA. Selection is based on musical talent, skills and training with an emphasis on piano ability in accompanying and sight reading. Other selection criteria are self-reliance, leadership, ability to work with groups and dedication to music therapy as a career. Applicants must be members of the National Federation of Music Clubs.
Target applicants: College students. Graduate school students. Adult students.
Amount: $400-$1,250.
Number of awards: Varies.
Deadline: March 1.
How to apply: Applications are available online.
Exclusive: Visit www.UltimateScholarshipBook.com and enter code NA102112 for updates on this award.

(1022) · NHSC Scholarship

National Health Service Corps
U.S. Department of Health and Human Services

200 Independence Avenue SW
Washington, DC 20201
Phone: 800-221-9393
Email: callcenter@hrsa.gov
http://nhsc.bhpr.hrsa.gov
Purpose: To aid students committed to providing health care in communities of great need.
Eligibility: Applicants must be enrolled or accepted into allopathic or osteopathic medical schools, family nurse practitioner programs, nurse-midwifery programs, physician assistant programs or dental school. Upon completion of training, scholars must choose practice sites in federally designated health professional shortage areas for one year for each year of support received.
Target applicants: College students. Graduate school students. Adult students.
Amount: Full tuition and fees plus $1,289 stipend.
Number of awards: 200.
Scholarship may be renewable.
Deadline: Varies.
How to apply: Applications are available by telephone request.
Exclusive: Visit www.UltimateScholarshipBook.com and enter code NA102212 for updates on this award.

(1023) • NIH Undergraduate Scholarship Program

U.S. Department of Health and Human Services National Institutes of Health
2 Center Drive
Room 2E30
MSC 0230
Bethesda, MD 20892
Phone: 800-528-7689
Fax: 301-480-3123
Email: ugsp@nih.gov
https://ugsp.nih.gov/home.asp?m=00
Purpose: To offer competitive scholarships to students who are committed to careers in biomedical, behavioral and social science health-related research.
Eligibility: Applicants must be enrolled or accepted for enrollment as full-time students at an accredited undergraduate institution, have an underprivileged background and have a minimum 3.5 GPA or be within the top 5 percent of their class. Applicants must also show a commitment to pursuing careers in biomedical, behavioral and social science research at the NIH.
Target applicants: College students. Adult students.
Minimum GPA: 3.5
Amount: $20,000.
Number of awards: Varies.
Scholarship may be renewable.
Deadline: February 28.
How to apply: Applications are available online.
Exclusive: Visit www.UltimateScholarshipBook.com and enter code U.102312 for updates on this award.

(1024) • NIH Undergraduate Scholarship Program for Students from Disadvantaged Backgrounds

National Institutes of Health
Office of Loan Repayment and Scholarship
2 Center Drive
MSC 0230
Bethesda, MD 20892-0230
Phone: 800-528-7689
Fax: 301-480-3123
Email: ugsp@nih.gov
https://ugsp.nih.gov/home.asp?m=00
Purpose: To develop new health-related researchers and to give disadvantaged students research opportunities that they might not have otherwise.
Eligibility: Applicants must be planning a career in biomedical, behavioral or social science health-related research, have financial need, have a minimum 3.5 GPA or be within the top 5 percent of their class and attend an accredited school. For every year that students receive the scholarship, they must attend a summer training program and work for one year at the NIH.
Target applicants: High school students. College students. Adult students.
Minimum GPA: 3.5
Amount: Up to $20,000.
Number of awards: Varies.
Scholarship may be renewable.
Deadline: February 28.
How to apply: Applications are available online.
Exclusive: Visit www.UltimateScholarshipBook.com and enter code NA102412 for updates on this award.

(1025) • NPCA Educational Foundation Scholarships

National Precast Concrete Association (NPCA)
1320 City Center Drive
Suite 200
Carmel, IN 46032
Phone: 800-366-7731
Fax: 317-571-0041
http://www.precast.org/splash/
Purpose: To aid students who are preparing for careers in the precast concrete industry.
Eligibility: Applicants must be high school seniors or undergraduate students who are enrolled in or planning to enroll in a program of study that is related to the building, construction or precast concrete industries. Selection is based on the overall strength of the application.
Target applicants: High school students. College students. Adult students.
Amount: Up to $2,200.
Number of awards: Varies.
Scholarship may be renewable.
Deadline: December 31.
How to apply: Applications are available online. An application form, transcript and two letters of recommendation are required.
Exclusive: Visit www.UltimateScholarshipBook.com and enter code NA102512 for updates on this award.

(1026) • NPFDA Scholarships

National Poultry and Food Distributors Association
2014 Osborne Road
St. Marys, GA 31558
Phone: 770-535-9901
Fax: 770-535-7385
Email: info@npfda.org
http://www.npfda.org
Purpose: To aid undergraduates who are enrolled in poultry- or agriculture-related degree programs.
Eligibility: Applicants must be rising undergraduate juniors or seniors who are full-time students at a U.S. postsecondary institution. They

must be pursuing a poultry- or agriculture-related program of study. Selection is based on the overall strength of the application.
Target applicants: College students. Adult students.
Amount: Up to $2,000.
Number of awards: Varies.
Deadline: May 31.
How to apply: Applications are available online. An application form, official transcript, personal statement and one letter of recommendation are required.
Exclusive: Visit www.UltimateScholarshipBook.com and enter code NA102612 for updates on this award.

(1027) • Nurse Candidate Program

Navy Medicine Manpower, Personnel, Training and Education Command
8901 Wisconsin Avenue
Building 1, Tower 13, Room 13132
Bethesda, MD 20889
Phone: 301-295-1217
Fax: 301-295-6865
Email: oh@med.navy.mil
http://www.med.navy.mil/sites/navmedmpte/Pages/default.aspx
Purpose: To aid students who are pursuing the bachelor of science in nursing (BSN).
Eligibility: Applicants must be U.S. citizens and be full-time students who have completed two or more years of a four-year bachelor of science in nursing (BSN) degree program at an accredited college or university. They must meet the Navy's physical fitness requirements. Recipients of this award will be required to fulfill an active duty service obligation of up to five years as an officer in the Navy Nurse Corps. Selection is based on the overall strength of the application.
Target applicants: College students. Adult students.
Amount: Up to $10,000.
Number of awards: Varies.
Scholarship may be renewable.
Deadline: Varies.
How to apply: Applications may be obtained by contacting a Navy recruiting officer. An application form and supporting materials are required.
Exclusive: Visit www.UltimateScholarshipBook.com and enter code NA102712 for updates on this award.

(1028) • Nurseries Foundation Award

Oregon Association of Nurseries
29751 SW Town Center Loop West
Wilsonville, OR 97070
Phone: 800-342-6401
Fax: 503-682-5099
Email: info@oan.org
http://www.oan.org
Purpose: To aid horticulture students.
Eligibility: Applicants must be majoring in horticulture. Selection is based on the overall strength of the application.
Target applicants: College students. Adult students.
Amount: $1,000.
Number of awards: 1.
Deadline: April 1.
How to apply: Applications are available online. An application form, official transcript and three recommendation letters are required.
Exclusive: Visit www.UltimateScholarshipBook.com and enter code OR102812 for updates on this award.

(1029) • Nursing Scholarship

CampusRN
2464 Massachusetts Avenue
Suite 210
Cambridge, MA 02140
Phone: 617-661-2613
Fax: 617-661-2620
Email: scholarships@campuscareercenter.com
http://www.campusrn.com/scholarships/scholarships.asp
Purpose: To provide financial assistance for nursing students from all fifty states.
Eligibility: Applicants must be nursing students at schools that have registered in the scholarship program by linking to the CampusRN website. An essay is required. Finalists may be asked to submit awards, letters of recommendation and other materials upon selection.
Target applicants: College students. Graduate school students. Adult students.
Amount: $2,500.
Number of awards: 6.
Deadline: April 1.
How to apply: Applications are available online.
Exclusive: Visit www.UltimateScholarshipBook.com and enter code CA102912 for updates on this award.

(1030) • Old Guard Oral Presentation Competition

American Society of Mechanical Engineers (ASME)
Three Park Avenue
New York, NY 10016
Phone: 800-843-2763
Fax: 973-882-1717
Email: infocentral@asme.org
http://www.asme.org
Purpose: To support the professional development of student members of the American Society of Mechanical Engineers (ASME).
Eligibility: Applicants must be certified as ASME student members in good standing. They must be undergraduate engineering students who have been chosen by their student section or academic department head to participate. Applicants must do a 20-minute oral presentation on a relevant engineering topic. Selection is based on presentation content, organization, delivery, effectiveness and discussion.
Target applicants: College students. Adult students.
Amount: Up to $2,000.
Number of awards: Varies.
Deadline: Varies.
How to apply: Entry forms are available online. An entry form and oral presentation are required.
Exclusive: Visit www.UltimateScholarshipBook.com and enter code AM103012 for updates on this award.

(1031) • Operations and Power Division Scholarship

American Nuclear Society
555 North Kensington Avenue
La Grange Park, IL 60526
Phone: 800-323-3044
Fax: 708-352-0499
Email: hr@ans.org
http://www.ans.org
Purpose: To aid nuclear science and nuclear engineering students.
Eligibility: Applicants must be U.S. citizens or permanent residents and be student members of the American Nuclear Society (ANS). They must be undergraduate or graduate students who have completed two

or more years of study toward a four-year degree in nuclear science or nuclear engineering. Students must be enrolled at an accredited U.S. postsecondary institution. Selection is based on academic merit.
Target applicants: College students. Adult students.
Amount: Varies.
Number of awards: Varies.
Deadline: February 1.
How to apply: Applications are available online. An application form, transcript and three references are required.
Exclusive: Visit www.UltimateScholarshipBook.com and enter code AM103112 for updates on this award.

(1032) • Oral-B Laboratories Dental Hygiene Scholarships

American Dental Hygienists' Association (ADHA) Institute for Oral Health
Scholarship Award Program
444 North Michigan Avenue
Suite 3400
Chicago, IL 60611
Phone: 312-440-8900
Email: institute@adha.net
http://www.adha.org/ioh
Purpose: To provide support to dental hygiene students who are committed to academic excellence, research and education.
Eligibility: Applicants must be pursuing a baccalaureate degree in dental hygiene with a GPA of at least 3.5 and show dedication to professional excellence, scholarship, quality research and dental hygiene education. They must demonstrate financial need of at least $1,500, be active members of SADHA or ADHA and submit a goals statement.
Target applicants: College students. Adult students.
Minimum GPA: 3.5
Amount: $1,000.
Number of awards: Varies.
Deadline: February 1.
How to apply: Applications are available online.
Exclusive: Visit www.UltimateScholarshipBook.com and enter code AM103212 for updates on this award.

(1033) • Outstanding Undergraduate Researchers Award Program

Computing Research Association
1100 17th Street NW
Suite 507
Washington, DC 20036
Phone: 202-234-2111
Fax: 202-667-1066
Email: info@cra.org
http://www.cra.org
Purpose: To support undergraduates who have completed outstanding research in the field of computing.
Eligibility: Applicants must be undergraduates at a North American college or university and must have conducted some type of computing research. Nominations from two faculty members and a recommendation from the chair of the applicant's home department are also required. Preference is given to undergraduate seniors. Selection is based on the quality of computing research, academic achievement and community involvement.
Target applicants: College students. Adult students.
Amount: $1,000.
Number of awards: 2.
Deadline: Varies.
How to apply: Information on how to apply for this award may be requested by writing to awards@cra.org. A recommendation from the chair of the applicant's home department and nominations from two faculty members are required.
Exclusive: Visit www.UltimateScholarshipBook.com and enter code CO103312 for updates on this award.

(1034) • Parsons Brinckerhoff – Engineering Scholarship

Conference of Minority Transportation Officials
818 18th Street NW, Suite 850
Washington, DC 20006
Phone: 202-530-0551
Fax: 202-530-0617
Email: comto@comto.org
http://www.comto.org
Purpose: To support COMTO members who are studying engineering.
Eligibility: Applicants must be undergraduate students who have been COMTO members for at least one year. They must have at least a 3.0 GPA.
Target applicants: College students. Adult students.
Minimum GPA: 3.0
Amount: $5,000.
Number of awards: Varies.
Deadline: April 16.
How to apply: Applications are available online.
Exclusive: Visit www.UltimateScholarshipBook.com and enter code CO103412 for updates on this award.

(1035) • Paul A. Stewart Awards

Wilson Ornithological Society
Dr. Robert B. Payne
Museum of Zoology, University of Michigan
1109 Gedes Avenue
Ann Arbor, MI 48109
Email: rbpayne@umich.edu
http://www.wilsonsociety.org
Purpose: To promote bird research.
Eligibility: Applicants' proposals should, but are not required to, cover the area of the study of bird movements based on banding, using the analysis and recovery of banded birds, with an emphasis on economic ornithology. Applicants must be willing to present their research results at an annual meeting of the Wilson Ornithological Society.
Target applicants: Junior high students or younger. High school students. College students. Graduate school students. Adult students.
Amount: $500.
Number of awards: Up to 8.
Deadline: February 1.
How to apply: Applications are available online.
Exclusive: Visit www.UltimateScholarshipBook.com and enter code WI103512 for updates on this award.

(1036) • Paul Cole Scholarship Award

Society of Nuclear Medicine
Development Office
1850 Samuel Morse Drive
Reston, VA 20190
Phone: 703-708-9000
Fax: 703-708-9020

Email: grantinfo@snm.org
http://www.snm.org
Purpose: To promote excellence in healthcare through the support of education and research in nuclear medicine technology.
Eligibility: Applicants must have a minimum 2.5 GPA and be high school seniors or college undergraduates enrolled in or accepted by accredited institutions and be in the nuclear medicine technology field.
Target applicants: High school students. College students. Adult students.
Minimum GPA: 2.5
Amount: $500-$1,000.
Number of awards: 28.
Deadline: January 14.
How to apply: Applications are available online.
Exclusive: Visit www.UltimateScholarshipBook.com and enter code SO103612 for updates on this award.

(1037) • Paul H. Robbins, P.E., Honorary Scholarship

National Society of Professional Engineers
1420 King Street
Alexandria, VA 22314-2794
Phone: 703-684-2885
Fax: 703-836-4875
Email: memserv@nspe.org
http://www.nspe.org
Purpose: To aid students in engineering.
Eligibility: Applicants must be members of NSPE, current engineering undergraduate students entering their junior year only and enrolled in ABET-accredited engineering programs that participate in the NSPE Professional Engineers in Education (PEE) Sustaining University Program (SUP).
Target applicants: College students. Adult students.
Amount: $5,000.
Number of awards: 1.
Scholarship may be renewable.
Deadline: March 1.
How to apply: Applications are available online.
Exclusive: Visit www.UltimateScholarshipBook.com and enter code NA103712 for updates on this award.

(1038) • Payzer Scholarship

EAA Aviation Center
P.O. Box 2683
Oshkosh, WI 54903
Phone: 877-806-8902
Fax: 920-426-6865
Email: scholarships@eaa.org
http://www.youngeagles.org
Purpose: To support students interested in technical careers.
Eligibility: Applicants must be accepted or enrolled in an accredited college or university with an emphasis on technical information and must intend to pursue a career in engineering, mathematics or the physical or biological sciences. Applicants must also be involved in school and community activities as well as aviation and be members of EAA.
Target applicants: High school students. College students. Graduate school students. Adult students.
Amount: $5,000.
Number of awards: 1.
Deadline: February 28.
How to apply: Applications are available online.
Exclusive: Visit www.UltimateScholarshipBook.com and enter code EA103812 for updates on this award.

(1039) • Peggy Dixon Two-Year Scholarship

Society of Physics Students
One Physics Ellipse
College Park, MD 20740
Phone: 301-209-3007
Fax: 301-209-0839
Email: sps@aip.org
http://www.spsnational.org/programs/scholarships/
Purpose: To help students seeking a bachelor's degree in physics to transition from a two-year to a four-year program.
Eligibility: Applicants must be members of SPS. Students must have finished at least one semester or quarter of the introductory physics sequence and must be registered in the appropriate subsequent physics classes.
Target applicants: College students. Adult students.
Amount: $2,000.
Number of awards: 1.
Deadline: February 15.
How to apply: Applications are available online or from chapter advisors.
Exclusive: Visit www.UltimateScholarshipBook.com and enter code SO103912 for updates on this award.

(1040) • Perennial Plant Association Scholarship

Perennial Plant Association
3383 Schirtzinger Road
Hilliard, OH 43026
Phone: 614-771-8431
Fax: 614-876-5238
Email: ppa@perennialplant.org
http://www.perennialplant.org
Purpose: To aid undergraduates who are studying horticulture or a related subject.
Eligibility: Applicants must be enrolled in a two- or four-year degree program while majoring or minoring in horticulture or a related subject. They must have a GPA of 3.0 or higher on a four-point scale. Previous recipients of this scholarship are not eligible. Preference will be given to applicants who are planning to pursue careers in perennials. Selection is based on the overall strength of the application.
Target applicants: College students. Adult students.
Minimum GPA: 3.0
Amount: $1,000.
Number of awards: 5.
Deadline: March 1.
How to apply: Applications are available online. An application form, official transcript, personal statement and three recommendation letters are required.
Exclusive: Visit www.UltimateScholarshipBook.com and enter code PE104012 for updates on this award.

(1041) • Petroleum Division College Scholarships

ASME International Petroleum Technology Institute
Attn: Student Scholarship Program
11757 Katy Freeway
Suite 865
Houston, TX 77079
Phone: 281-493-3491
Fax: 281-493-3493

Email: torkayc@asme.org
http://www.asme ipti.org
Purpose: To aid undergraduate engineering students who are members of the American Society of Mechanical Engineers (ASME).
Eligibility: Applicants must be ASME student members who are enrolled in an ABET-accredited undergraduate degree program in engineering. They must have an overall GPA of 2.5 or higher on a four-point scale. Selection is based on the overall strength of the application.
Target applicants: College students. Adult students.
Minimum GPA: 2.5
Amount: $2,000.
Number of awards: 5.
Deadline: May 27.
How to apply: Applications are available online. An application form, official transcript, personal statement and one recommendation letter are required.
Exclusive: Visit www.UltimateScholarshipBook.com and enter code AS104112 for updates on this award.

(1042) • Petroleum Division High School Scholarships

ASME International Petroleum Technology Institute
Attn: Student Scholarship Program
11757 Katy Freeway
Suite 865
Houston, TX 77079
Phone: 281-493-3491
Fax: 281-493-3493
Email: torkayc@asme.org
http://www.asme-ipti.org
Purpose: To aid high school seniors who are planning to major in engineering.
Eligibility: Applicants must have a pre-declared major of engineering listed on their college applications and a GPA of 3.0 or higher on a four-point scale. Selection is based on the overall strength of the application.
Target applicants: High school students.
Minimum GPA: 3.0
Amount: $1,000.
Number of awards: 2.
Deadline: May 27.
How to apply: Applications are available online. An application form, personal essay, official transcript and one letter of recommendation are required.
Exclusive: Visit www.UltimateScholarshipBook.com and enter code AS104212 for updates on this award.

(1043) • PHCC Educational Foundation Scholarship

Plumbing-Heating-Cooling Contractors–National Association
P.O. Box 6808
180 South Washington Street
Falls Church, VA 22046
Phone: 800-533-7694
Fax: 703-237-7442
Email: scholarships@naphcc.org
http://www.phccweb.org
Purpose: To elevate the technical and business competence of the plumbing-heating-cooling (p-h-c) industry by awarding scholarships to students who are enrolled in a p-h-c-related major.
Eligibility: Applicants must be currently enrolled or plan to enroll in a p-h-c-related major at an accredited four-year college or university or two-year technical college, community college or trade school. Students enrolled in an approved apprentice program must also be working full-time for a licensed plumbing or HVACR contractor who is a member of the PHCC.
Target applicants: High school students. College students. Adult students.
Amount: $1,500-$5,000.
Number of awards: Up to 23.
Deadline: May 1.
How to apply: Applications are available online or by email.
Exclusive: Visit www.UltimateScholarshipBook.com and enter code PL104312 for updates on this award.

(1044) • Phoebe Pember Memorial Scholarship

United Daughters of the Confederacy
328 North Boulevard
Richmond, VA 23220
Phone: 804-355-1636
Fax: 804-353-1396
Email: hqudc@rcn.com
http://www.hqudc.org
Purpose: To aid Confederate descendants who are undergraduate nursing students.
Eligibility: Applicants must be the direct descendant of an eligible Confederate. They must be enrolled in an undergraduate degree program in nursing at an accredited U.S. college or university and have a GPA of 3.0 or higher on a four-point scale. Selection is based on the overall strength of the application.
Target applicants: College students. Adult students.
Minimum GPA: 3.0
Amount: Varies.
Number of awards: Varies.
Scholarship may be renewable.
Deadline: Varies.
How to apply: Applications are available online. An application form, personal statement, official transcript, one letter of recommendation, endorsement from sponsoring UDC Chapter, applicant photo and proof of Confederate ancestry are required.
Exclusive: Visit www.UltimateScholarshipBook.com and enter code UN104412 for updates on this award.

(1045) • Physician Assistant Foundation Scholarship

Physician Assistant Foundation
PA Foundation Scholarship Committee
950 North Washington Street
Alexandria, VA 22314-1552
Phone: 703-519-5686
Fax: 703-684-1924
Email: aapa@aapa.org
http://www.aapa.org
Purpose: To support physician assistants.
Eligibility: Applicants must be American Academy of Physician Assistants (AAPA) members and currently enrolled in the professional phase of a PA training program at an ARC-PA-accredited physician assistant program. Students are judged on the basis of financial need, community and professional involvement, goals and academic performance.
Target applicants: College students. Adult students.
Amount: Varies.
Number of awards: Varies.
Deadline: January 15.
How to apply: Applications are available online.

Exclusive: Visit www.UltimateScholarshipBook.com and enter code PH104512 for updates on this award.

(1046) · Pioneers of Flight

National Air Transportation Foundation
Pioneers of Flight Scholarship Program, Attn.: Professor Gregory Schwab, Chair
Department of Aerospace Technology, TC 216
Indiana State University
Terre Haute, IN 47809
Email: aeschwab@isugw.indstate.edu
http://www.nata.aero
Purpose: To assist students pursuing general aviation as a career.
Eligibility: Applicants must be full-time students at an accredited four-year institution, be sophomores or juniors at the time of application and plan to pursue a career in aviation.
Target applicants: College students. Adult students.
Minimum GPA: 3.0
Amount: $1,000.
Number of awards: 2.
Deadline: Last Friday in December.
How to apply: Applications are available online.
Exclusive: Visit www.UltimateScholarshipBook.com and enter code NA104612 for updates on this award.

(1047) · Plastics Pioneers Association Scholarships

Society of Plastics Engineers
13 Church Hill Road
Newtown, CT 06470
Phone: 203-775-0471
Fax: 203-775-8490
Email: info@4spe.org
http://www.4spe.org
Purpose: To aid students who are planning for careers in plastics technology and engineering.
Eligibility: Applicants must be full-time undergraduate students who intend to pursue careers as plastics technicians or engineers. Selection is based on the overall strength of the application.
Target applicants: College students. Adult students.
Amount: $3,000.
Number of awards: Varies.
Deadline: February 15.
How to apply: Applications are available online. An application form, three recommendation letters, a transcript and personal statement are required.
Exclusive: Visit www.UltimateScholarshipBook.com and enter code SO104712 for updates on this award.

(1048) · Polymer Modifiers and Additives Division Scholarships

Society of Plastics Engineers
13 Church Hill Road
Newtown, CT 06470
Phone: 203-775-0471
Fax: 203-775-8490
Email: info@4spe.org
http://www.4spe.org
Purpose: To aid students who have an interest in the plastics industry.
Eligibility: Applicants must have an interest in the plastics industry, major in or take courses leading to a career in the plastics industry and be in good academic standing. Financial need is considered.
Target applicants: College students. Adult students.
Amount: $4,000.
Number of awards: 4.
Deadline: February 15.
How to apply: Applications are available online.
Exclusive: Visit www.UltimateScholarshipBook.com and enter code SO104812 for updates on this award.

(1049) · PPQ William F. Helms Student Scholarship

U.S. Department of Agriculture
Animal and Plant Health Inspection Service
1400 Independence Avenue SW
Room 1133, South Building
Washington, DC 20250
Phone: 202-720-6312
Fax: 202-720-2365
Email: sophia.l.kirby@usda.gov
http://www.aphis.usda.gov
Purpose: To support students who are pursuing higher education studies in agriculture or the biological sciences.
Eligibility: Applicants must be U.S. citizens who are undergraduate sophomores or juniors at an accredited U.S. college or university. They must be studying a subject in agriculture or the biological sciences and have a GPA of 2.5 or higher. Selection is based on the overall strength of the application.
Target applicants: College students. Adult students.
Minimum GPA: 2.5
Amount: Up to $10,000.
Number of awards: Varies.
Scholarship may be renewable.
Deadline: March 1.
How to apply: Applications are available by request from the U.S. Department of Agriculture. An application form, personal statement, transcript, three recommendation letters and documentation of U.S. military service (if applicable) are required.
Exclusive: Visit www.UltimateScholarshipBook.com and enter code U.104912 for updates on this award.

(1050) · Pratt & Whitney Golden Eagle Award

Tuskegee Airmen Scholarship Foundation
P.O. Box 83395
Los Angeles, CA 90045
Phone: 310-215-3985
Email: arnoldwarrior@msn.com
http://www.taisf.org/scholar.htm
Purpose: To aid students who intend to pursue careers in aviation, aerospace engineering, aerospace research or engineering technology.
Eligibility: Applicants must be high school seniors who have a GPA of 3.0 or higher on a four-point scale. They must have a demonstrated interest in pursuing a career in aerospace research, aerospace engineering, aviation or engineering technology. Selection is based on academic merit, extracurricular activities, character and financial need.
Target applicants: High school students.
Minimum GPA: 3.0
Amount: $5,000.
Number of awards: 1.
Scholarship may be renewable.
Deadline: January 15.

How to apply: Applications are available by request from the student's local Tuskegee Airmen chapter. An application form, two essays and family income verification are required.
Exclusive: Visit www.UltimateScholarshipBook.com and enter code TU105012 for updates on this award.

(1051) • Predoctoral Research Training Fellowship

Epilepsy Foundation
8301 Professional Place
Landover, MD 20785
Phone: 301-459-3700
Email: researchwebsupport@efa.org
http://www.epilepsyfoundation.org
Purpose: To support pre-doctoral students with dissertation research relating to epilepsy.
Eligibility: Applicants must be full-time graduate students pursuing a Ph.D. degree in neuroscience, physiology, pharmacology, psychology, biochemistry, genetics, nursing, pharmacy or other related areas; have a dissertation research project; have a qualified mentor who can supervise the project and have access to resources to conduct the project. The project must be in the U.S. and its territories. The award is based on the quality of the dissertation project, relevance to epilepsy, the applicant's qualifications, the mentor's qualifications and the quality of the proposed environment.
Target applicants: Graduate school students. Adult students.
Amount: $20,000.
Number of awards: Varies.
Deadline: August 31.
How to apply: Applicants must submit three recommendation letters including one from the mentor, a statement of intent, a biographical sketch, a cover sheet form, a lay summary, transcripts and a research plan.
Exclusive: Visit www.UltimateScholarshipBook.com and enter code EP105112 for updates on this award.

(1052) • Presidents Scholarship of the Institute of Industrial Engineers

Institute of Industrial Engineers
3577 Parkway Lane
Suite 200
Norcross, GA 30092
Phone: 800-494-0460
Fax: 770-441-3295
Email: bcameron@iienet.org
http://www.iienet2.org
Purpose: To support undergraduate industrial engineering students.
Eligibility: Applicants must be active student members of the Institute of Industrial Engineers (IIE). They must be full-time undergraduates enrolled in an industrial engineering degree program and have a GPA of 3.4 or higher on a four-point scale. They must have demonstrated leadership skills. Applicants must be nominated by their academic department heads. Selection is based on professional leadership potential, character, financial need and academic merit.
Target applicants: College students. Adult students.
Minimum GPA: 3.4
Amount: $1,000.
Number of awards: 1.
Deadline: November 15.
How to apply: Nomination forms are available online. A nomination form completed by the applicant's academic department head is required.
Exclusive: Visit www.UltimateScholarshipBook.com and enter code IN105212 for updates on this award.

(1053) • Professional Engineers In Government (PEG)

National Society of Professional Engineers
1420 King Street
Alexandria, VA 22314-2794
Phone: 703-684-2885
Fax: 703-836-4875
Email: memserv@nspe.org
http://www.nspe.org
Purpose: To aid students in engineering.
Eligibility: Applicants must be graduate students pursuing an MBA, master's degree in public administration or master's degree in engineering management and must also be engineering interns or licensed professional engineers. Selection is based on undergraduate GPA, GRE or GMAT score, professional activities, community activities, two recommendation letters, essay and membership. Preference is given to government employees.
Target applicants: Graduate school students. Adult students.
Amount: $2,500.
Number of awards: 1.
Deadline: March 15.
How to apply: Applications are available online.
Exclusive: Visit www.UltimateScholarshipBook.com and enter code NA105312 for updates on this award.

(1054) • Professional Engineers In Industry (PEI) Scholarship

National Society of Professional Engineers
1420 King Street
Alexandria, VA 22314-2794
Phone: 703-684-2885
Fax: 703-836-4875
Email: memserv@nspe.org
http://www.nspe.org
Purpose: To aid students in engineering.
Eligibility: Applicants must be undergraduate sophomores, juniors or seniors or graduate students with a minimum 2.5 GPA who are sponsored by a NSPE/PEI member and enrolled in an accredited engineering program. Preference is given to relatives or dependents of NSPE members.
Target applicants: College students. Graduate school students. Adult students.
Minimum GPA: 2.5
Amount: $2,500.
Number of awards: 1.
Deadline: April 1.
How to apply: Applications are available online.
Exclusive: Visit www.UltimateScholarshipBook.com and enter code NA105412 for updates on this award.

(1055) • Promise of Nursing Regional Scholarship Program

National Student Nurses' Association
45 Main Street
Suite 606
Brooklyn, NY 11201
Phone: 718-210-0705
Fax: 718-797-1186
Email: nsna@nsna.org
http://www.nsna.org

Purpose: To aid nursing students who are attending school in certain regions of the U.S.
Eligibility: Applicants must be U.S. citizens, permanent residents or resident aliens. They must be enrolled in a nursing degree program at a school located in Georgia (graduate students only), Louisiana, Maryland, Massachusetts, Mississippi, New Jersey (graduate students only), Oregon, Pennsylvania, Tennessee, Washington, certain areas in California, certain areas in Texas or certain areas in Florida. Selection is based on academic merit, involvement in community health and financial need. Note: We do not recommend applying to scholarships that charge application fees. However, some scholarships of this type charge fees and are included for completeness.
Target applicants: College students. Graduate school students. Adult students.
Amount: Varies.
Number of awards: Varies.
Deadline: January 14.
How to apply: Applications are available online. An application form, official transcript and other supporting materials are required. $10 processing fee.
Exclusive: Visit www.UltimateScholarshipBook.com and enter code NA105512 for updates on this award.

(1056) • Proton Energy Scholarship Program

Proton Energy
10 Technology Drive
Wallingford, CT 06492
Phone: 203-678-2000
Email: scholarshipinfo@protonenergy.com
http://www.protonenergyscholarship.com/about.asp
Purpose: To assist students who show promise in the field of science or technology.
Eligibility: Applicants must be high school seniors who demonstrate outstanding achievement, excellence and promise in the field of science or technology and who plan to pursue higher education in this field. Students must also be U.S. citizens or permanent residents and declare a science- or technology-related major. Selection is based on academic performance, ability and promise; commitment to a career in a science- or technology-related field; strength of application; demonstrated leadership, work ethic and community involvement and financial need.
Target applicants: High school students.
Amount: $500-$100,000.
Number of awards: Varies.
Scholarship may be renewable.
Deadline: February 11.
How to apply: Applications are available online. Both an online and paper application packet must be submitted.
Exclusive: Visit www.UltimateScholarshipBook.com and enter code PR105612 for updates on this award.

(1057) • Rain Bird Scholarship

Landscape Architecture Foundation
818 18th Street NW
Suite 810
Washington, DC 20006
Phone: 202-331-7070
Fax: 202-331-7079
Email: scholarships@lafoundation.org
http://www.asla.org/
Purpose: To recognize outstanding landscape architecture students.
Eligibility: Applicants must be college juniors or fourth- or fifth-year seniors who are landscape architecture, horticulture or irrigation science students who have a demonstrated commitment to the landscape architecture profession and exhibit financial need. Applications can only be sent by email.
Target applicants: College students. Adult students.
Amount: $2,500.
Number of awards: 1.
Deadline: February 15.
How to apply: Applicants should follow the guidelines.
Exclusive: Visit www.UltimateScholarshipBook.com and enter code LA105712 for updates on this award.

(1058) • Ralph K. Hillquist Honorary SAE Scholarship

Society of Automotive Engineers International
400 Commonwealth Drive
Warrendale, PA 15096
Phone: 724-776-4841
Fax: 724-776-0790
Email: scholarships@sae.org
http://www.sae.org
Purpose: To aid mechanical and automotive engineering students.
Eligibility: Applicants must be U.S. citizens and full-time undergraduate juniors who are enrolled in an ABET-accredited mechanical or automotive engineering degree program at a U.S. college or university. They must have a GPA of 3.0 or higher. Preference will be given to applicants who have completed coursework in noise and vibration (e.g. physics, statics, vibration or dynamics). Selection is based on academic merit, leadership and special studies in noise and vibration.
Target applicants: College students. Adult students.
Minimum GPA: 3.0
Amount: $1,000.
Number of awards: 1.
Deadline: January 15.
How to apply: Applications are available online. An application form, official transcript and standardized test scores are required.
Exclusive: Visit www.UltimateScholarshipBook.com and enter code SO105812 for updates on this award.

(1059) • Raney Fund Award

American Society of Ichthyologists and Herpetologists
Maureen Donnelly, Secretary
Department of Biological Sciences, Florida International University
11200 SW 8th Street
Miami, FL 33199
Phone: 305-348-1235
Fax: 305-348-1986
Email: asih@fiu.edu
http://www.asih.org
Purpose: To support young ichthyologists.
Eligibility: Applicants should be members of ASIH and should be enrolled for an advanced degree, although those with developing careers may receive the award under exceptional circumstances. Awards may be used for museums or laboratory study, travel, fieldwork or other activities that will enhance their professional careers and their contributions to the science of ichthyology. Scholarships are awarded on the basis of merit and need.
Target applicants: Graduate school students. Adult students.
Amount: $400-$1,000.
Number of awards: Varies.
Deadline: March 1.

How to apply: Applications are available by email or written request.
Exclusive: Visit www.UltimateScholarshipBook.com and enter code AM105912 for updates on this award.

(1060) • Raymond Davis Scholarship

Society for Imaging Science and Technology
7003 Kilworth Lane
Springfield, VA 22151
Phone: 703-642-9090
Fax: 703-642-9094
Email: info@imaging.org
http://www.imaging.org
Purpose: To support students who are studying imaging science and technology.
Eligibility: Applicants must be full-time graduate or undergraduate students studying photographic or imaging engineering or science who have completed or will complete two academic years of college before the term of the scholarship.
Target applicants: College students. Graduate school students. Adult students.
Amount: $1,000.
Number of awards: Varies.
Deadline: October 1.
How to apply: Applications are available online.
Exclusive: Visit www.UltimateScholarshipBook.com and enter code SO106012 for updates on this award.

(1061) • Research Award

American Ornithologists' Union
Avian Ecology Lab
Archbold Biological Station
123 Main Drive
Venus, FL 33960
Phone: 863-465-2571
Email: rbowman@archbold-station.org
http://www.aou.org
Purpose: To provide research funding for members of the American Ornithologists Union.
Eligibility: Applicants must be members of the AOU and must submit proposals for research projects on avian biology, avian systematics, paleo-ornithology, biogeography, neotropical biology or ornithology.
Target applicants: College students. Graduate school students. Adult students.
Amount: Up to $2,500.
Number of awards: Varies.
Deadline: February 1.
How to apply: The submission procedure and tips for writing a proposal are described on the website.
Exclusive: Visit www.UltimateScholarshipBook.com and enter code AM106112 for updates on this award.

(1062) • Research Training Fellowships for Medical Students (Medical Fellows Program)

Howard Hughes Medical Institute
4000 Jones Bridge Road
Chevy Chase, MD 20815-6789
Phone: 800-448-4882
Fax: 301-215-8888
Email: fellows@hhmi.org
http://www.hhmi.org
Purpose: To support a year of full-time biomedical research training for medical and dental students.
Eligibility: Applicants must be enrolled in a U.S. medical school or dental school, and the fellowship research may be conducted at an academic or nonprofit institution in the United States or abroad if the fellow's mentor is affiliated with a U.S. institution. The research should focus on biological processes or disease mechanisms. The fellowship is based on the applicant's ability, potential research career as a physician/scientist and training. Applicants must submit research plans, personal statements, letters of reference, transcripts and MCAT or DAT scores.
Target applicants: Graduate school students. Adult students.
Amount: $40,500.
Number of awards: Varies.
Deadline: January 11.
How to apply: Applications are available online.
Exclusive: Visit www.UltimateScholarshipBook.com and enter code HO106212 for updates on this award.

(1063) • Reuben Trane Scholarship

American Society of Heating, Refrigerating and Air-Conditioning Engineers
1791 Tullie Circle, NE
Atlanta, GA 30329
Phone: 404-636-8400
Fax: 404-321-5478
Email: lbenedict@ashrae.org
http://www.ashrae.org
Purpose: To support engineering undergraduates who are preparing for careers in the heating, ventilation, air-conditioning and refrigeration (HVACR) industry.
Eligibility: Applicants must be attending a school that houses a student branch of the American Society of Heating, Refrigerating and Air-Conditioning Engineers (ASHRAE), is ABET-accredited (U.S. institutions) or is ABET-affiliated (international institutions). Applicants must be undergraduate students who are enrolled in an engineering or pre-engineering curriculum that provides adequate preparation for a career in the HVACR industry. They must have a GPA of 3.0 or higher on a four-point scale or must be in the top 30 percent of their class. Selection is based on the overall strength of the application.
Target applicants: College students. Adult students.
Minimum GPA: 3.0
Amount: $10,000.
Number of awards: 4.
Scholarship may be renewable.
Deadline: December 1.
How to apply: Applications are available online. The application form, official transcript, one letter of recommendation and the evaluation form from an ASHRAE student branch interview (if applicable) are required.
Exclusive: Visit www.UltimateScholarshipBook.com and enter code AM106312 for updates on this award.

(1064) • Richard J. Stull Student Essay Competition in Healthcare Management

American College of Healthcare Executives
One North Franklin Street
Suite 1700
Chicago, IL 60606
Phone: 312-424-2800
Fax: 312-424-0023
Email: rmorton@ache.org
http://www.ache.org

Purpose: To support future healthcare executives.
Eligibility: Applicants must be undergraduate or graduate students enrolled in a healthcare administration degree program at a U.S. or Canadian postsecondary institution that is an American College of Healthcare Executives (ACHE) Higher Education network participant. They must be ACHE student associates or active affiliates. Submitted essays cannot have been published before and must be the sole creation of the applicant. Residents and other postgraduate students are ineligible. Selection is based on relevance of subject matter, creativity, practical applicability of subject matter and clarity.
Target applicants: College students. Graduate school students. Adult students.
Amount: Up to $4,000.
Number of awards: 6.
Deadline: December 10.
How to apply: Essay submission guidelines are available online. An essay is required.
Exclusive: Visit www.UltimateScholarshipBook.com and enter code AM106412 for updates on this award.

(1065) • Richard Jensen Scholarship

National Alliance of Independent Crop Consultants
349 East Nolley Drive
Collierville, TN 38017
Phone: 901-861-0511
Fax: 901-861-0512
Email: jonesnaicc@aol.com
http://www.naicc.org
Purpose: To aid undergraduate students of crop production.
Eligibility: Applicants must be undergraduate juniors who are majoring in an agricultural subject that is related to crop production (such as agronomy, horticulture, weed science, soil sciences, entomology or plant pathology). Selection is based on the overall strength of the application.
Target applicants: College students. Adult students.
Amount: $2,000.
Number of awards: 1.
Deadline: September 15.
How to apply: Applications are available online. An application form, transcript, proof of enrollment and two reference letters are required.
Exclusive: Visit www.UltimateScholarshipBook.com and enter code NA106512 for updates on this award.

(1066) • Richard L. Davis, FACMPE - Managers Scholarship

Medical Group Management Association
104 Inverness Terrace East
Englewood, CO 80112
Phone: 877-275-6462
Email: acmpe@mgma.com
http://www.mgma.com
Purpose: To aid medical practice management professionals who are college students.
Eligibility: Applicants must be current medical practice management professionals who are enrolled in an undergraduate or graduate degree program that is related to medical practice management. Selection is based on the overall strength of the application.
Target applicants: College students. Graduate school students. Adult students.
Amount: Varies.
Number of awards: Varies.
Deadline: May 1.
How to apply: Applications are available online. An application form and supporting materials are required.
Exclusive: Visit www.UltimateScholarshipBook.com and enter code ME106612 for updates on this award.

(1067) • Richard L. Davis, FACMPE/Barbara B. Watson, FACMPE - National Scholarship

Medical Group Management Association
104 Inverness Terrace East
Englewood, CO 80112
Phone: 877-275-6462
Email: acmpe@mgma.com
http://www.mgma.com
Purpose: To aid medical practice management students.
Eligibility: Applicants must be undergraduate or graduate students who are enrolled in a degree program that is related to medical practice management (such as healthcare administration, public health or business administration). Selection is based on the overall strength of the application.
Target applicants: College students. Graduate school students. Adult students.
Amount: Varies.
Number of awards: Varies.
Deadline: May 1.
How to apply: Applications are available online. An application form and supporting materials are required.
Exclusive: Visit www.UltimateScholarshipBook.com and enter code ME106712 for updates on this award.

(1068) • Richard Lee Vernon Aviation Scholarship

EAA Aviation Center
P.O. Box 2683
Oshkosh, WI 54903
Phone: 877-806-8902
Fax: 920-426-6865
Email: scholarships@eaa.org
http://www.youngeagles.org
Purpose: To support students pursuing training leading to a professional aviation occupations.
Eligibility: Applicants must be accepted to an accredited college, university or aviation technical school pursuing a course of study focusing on aviation. Applicants must also be involved in school and community activities as well as aviation. Recipient must show need for financial support.
Target applicants: High school students.
Amount: $500.
Number of awards: 1.
Deadline: February 28.
How to apply: Applications are available online.
Exclusive: Visit www.UltimateScholarshipBook.com and enter code EA106812 for updates on this award.

(1069) • Robert B. Oliver ASNT Scholarship

American Society for Nondestructive Testing
1711 Arlingate Lane
P.O. Box 28518
Columbus, OH 43228
Phone: 800-222-2768
Fax: 614-274-6899
Email: sthomas@asnt.org

http://www.asnt.org
Purpose: To support students in nondestructive testing.
Eligibility: Applicants must be undergraduate students enrolled in an engineering program of an accredited university and specialize in nondestructive testing (NDT). A nominating letter, transcript, three letters of recommendation and an essay describing the role of NDT/NDE in their career are required. The award is based on creativity, content, format and readability and the student's involvement in a research project.
Target applicants: College students. Adult students.
Amount: $2,500.
Number of awards: Up to 3.
Deadline: February 15.
How to apply: Applications are available online.
Exclusive: Visit www.UltimateScholarshipBook.com and enter code AM106912 for updates on this award.

(1070) · Robert E. Altenhofen Memorial Scholarship

American Society for Photogrammetry and Remote Sensing (ASPRS)
The Imaging and Geospatial Information Society
5410 Grosvenor Lane
Suite 210
Bethesda, MD 20814
Phone: 301-493-0290 x101
Fax: 301-493-0208
Email: scholarships@asprs.org
http://www.asprs.org
Purpose: To encourage and commend college students who display ability in the theoretical aspects of photogrammetry.
Eligibility: Applicants must be undergraduate or graduate students and submit several pieces with their applications including: a two-page statement regarding plans for continuing studies in theoretical photogrammetry, papers, research reports or other items written by the applicants and academic transcripts. Recipients are required to submit a report on the work they accomplish during the award period.
Target applicants: College students. Graduate school students. Adult students.
Amount: $2,000.
Number of awards: 1.
Deadline: December 1.
How to apply: Applications are available online.
Exclusive: Visit www.UltimateScholarshipBook.com and enter code AM107012 for updates on this award.

(1071) · Robert E. Dougherty Educational Foundation Scholarship Award

Composite Panel Association
Robert E. Dougherty Educational Foundation
19465 Deerfield Avenue
Suite 306
Leesburg, VA 20176
Phone: 703-724-1128
Fax: 703-724-1588
Email: arodriguez@cpamail.org
http://www.pbmdf.com
Purpose: To aid students who are preparing for careers in the composite panel field.
Eligibility: Applicants must be nominated for this award by a Robert E. Dougherty Educational Foundation member company or member institution. They must be North American citizens and be graduate students or rising undergraduate juniors or seniors who are studying industrial engineering, mechanical engineering, chemistry, forest products, wood science or wood technology. Selection is based on the overall strength of the application.
Target applicants: College students. Graduate school students. Adult students.
Amount: $5,000.
Number of awards: 5.
Scholarship may be renewable.
Deadline: March 1.
How to apply: Applications are available online. An application form, official transcript and academic adviser appraisal are required.
Exclusive: Visit www.UltimateScholarshipBook.com and enter code CO107112 for updates on this award.

(1072) · Robert E. Thunen Memorial Scholarships

Illuminating Engineering Society of North America
1514 Gibbons Drive
Alameda, CA 94501
Phone: 510-864-0204
Fax: 510-864-8511
Email: mrcatisbac@aol.com
http://www.iesna.org
Purpose: To help students who plan to pursue illumination as a career.
Eligibility: Applicants must be full-time junior, senior or graduate students in an accredited four-year college in Northern California, Nevada, Oregon or Washington who plan to pursue illumination as a career. The application, statement of purpose and at least three letters of recommendation are required. Students should review the IESNA Lighting Handbook to see the available fields of study.
Target applicants: College students. Graduate school students. Adult students.
Amount: $2,500.
Number of awards: 2.
Deadline: April 1.
How to apply: Applications are available by mail and email.
Exclusive: Visit www.UltimateScholarshipBook.com and enter code IL107212 for updates on this award.

(1073) · Rubber Division Undergraduate Scholarship

American Chemical Society
1155 Sixteenth Street, NW
Washington, DC 20036
Phone: 800-227-5558
Fax: 614-447-3713
Email: crobinson@rubber.org
http://www.acs.org
Purpose: To aid undergraduate students who are majoring in subjects related to the rubber industry.
Eligibility: Applicants must be rising undergraduate juniors or seniors. They must be majoring in chemistry, chemical engineering, polymer science, mechanical engineering, physics or any other subject that is related to the rubber industry. Selection is based on the overall strength of the application.
Target applicants: College students. Adult students.
Amount: $5,000.
Number of awards: 3.
Deadline: Varies.
How to apply: Applications are available online. An application form and supporting materials are required.
Exclusive: Visit www.UltimateScholarshipBook.com and enter code AM107312 for updates on this award.

(1074) • Russell and Sigurd Varian Award

American Vacuum Society
120 Wall Street, 32nd Floor
New York, NY 10005-3993
Phone: 212-248-0200
Fax: 212-248-0245
Email: angela@avs.org
http://www.avs.org
Purpose: To support continuing graduate studies in the sciences and technologies related to AVS.
Eligibility: Applicants must be graduate students in an accredited academic institution. Five finalists are invited to present talks on their research to the trustees at the international symposium. The trustees then select one student to receive the award, which also covers travel expenses. Applicants should submit applications, research summaries, letters of recommendations and transcripts.
Target applicants: Graduate school students. Adult students.
Amount: Varies.
Number of awards: 1.
Deadline: Varies.
How to apply: Applications are available online.
Exclusive: Visit www.UltimateScholarshipBook.com and enter code AM107412 for updates on this award.

(1075) • Ruth Abernathy Presidential Scholarship

American Alliance for Health, Physical Education, Recreation and Dance
1900 Association Drive
Reston, VA 20191
Phone: 800-213-7193
Email: dcallis@aahperd.org
http://www.aahperd.org
Purpose: To honor deserving students in the areas of health, physical education, recreation and dance.
Eligibility: Applicants must be members of the American Alliance for Health, Physical Education, Recreation and Dance (AAHPERD), but they may join when applying and must major in health, physical education, recreation or dance. Undergraduate applicants must have a minimum 3.5 GPA and have junior or senior status when applying. Graduate applicants must have a minimum 3.5 GPA and have completed one semester of full-time study. Selection is based on scholastic achievement, leadership, community service and character.
Target applicants: College students. Graduate school students. Adult students.
Minimum GPA: 3.5
Amount: $1,250-$1,750.
Number of awards: 5.
Deadline: October 15.
How to apply: Applications are available online.
Exclusive: Visit www.UltimateScholarshipBook.com and enter code AM107512 for updates on this award.

(1076) • SAE Engineering Scholarships

Society of Automotive Engineers International
400 Commonwealth Drive
Warrendale, PA 15096
Phone: 724-776-4841
Fax: 724-776-0790
Email: scholarships@sae.org
http://www.sae.org
Purpose: To offer a number of scholarships to qualified students who are interested in the study of engineering and related sciences.
Eligibility: Applicants must be high school seniors and intend to enroll in an engineering or related science program and meet minimum grade point averages and SAT/ACT scores. There are several corporate sponsored scholarships available. There is a $5 fee. Note: We do not recommend applying to scholarships that charge application fees. However, some scholarships of this type charge fees and are included for completeness.
Target applicants: High school students.
Amount: Varies.
Number of awards: Varies.
Scholarship may be renewable.
Deadline: Varies.
How to apply: Applications are available online.
Exclusive: Visit www.UltimateScholarshipBook.com and enter code SO107612 for updates on this award.

(1077) • Schonstedt Scholarship in Surveying

American Congress on Surveying and Mapping (ACSM)
6 Montgomery Village Avenue
Suite 403
Gaithersburg, MD 20879
Phone: 240-632-9716
Fax: 240-632-1321
Email: ilse.genovese@acsm.net
http://www.acsm.net
Purpose: To aid surveying students.
Eligibility: Applicants must be members of the American Congress on Surveying and Mapping (ACSM). They must be enrolled in a four-year surveying degree program. Preference will be given to applicants with junior or senior standing. Selection is based on academic merit, personal statement, references and extracurricular activities.
Target applicants: College students. Adult students.
Amount: $1,500.
Number of awards: 2.
Scholarship may be renewable.
Deadline: December 17.
How to apply: Applications are available online. An application form, proof of ASCM membership, official transcript, personal statement and three reference letters are required.
Exclusive: Visit www.UltimateScholarshipBook.com and enter code AM107712 for updates on this award.

(1078) • Scotts Company Scholars Program

Golf Course Superintendents Association of America
GCSAA Career Development Department
1421 Research Park Drive
Lawrence, KS 66049
Phone: 800-472-7878
Fax: 785-832-3643
Email: mbrhelp@gcsaa.org
http://www.gcsaa.org
Purpose: To offer monetary assistance for postsecondary education to a students from diverse cultural and socioeconomic backgrounds.
Eligibility: Applicants must be graduating high school seniors or college freshmen, sophomores or juniors who have been accepted at a two-year or longer program and must be pursuing a career in the green industry.
Target applicants: High school students. College students. Adult students.
Amount: $500-$2,500.

Number of awards: 7.
Deadline: March 1.
How to apply: Applications are available by contacting Pam Smith, 800-472-7878 x3678.
Exclusive: Visit www.UltimateScholarshipBook.com and enter code GO107812 for updates on this award.

(1079) • SEE Education Foundation Scholarships

International Society of Explosives Engineers
30325 Bainbridge Road
Cleveland, OH 44139
Phone: 440-349-4400
Fax: 440-349-3788
http://www.isee.org
Purpose: To aid students who are preparing for careers in the commercial explosives industry.
Eligibility: Applicants must be enrolled in an accredited degree program that provides adequate training for a career in the commercial explosives industry. They must have completed at least one year of their degree program and must demonstrate financial need. Employees of the International Society of Explosives Engineers (ISEE) and their relatives are ineligible. Selection is based on the overall strength of the application.
Target applicants: College students. Graduate school students. Adult students.
Amount: Varies.
Number of awards: Varies.
Deadline: May 1.
How to apply: Applications are available online. An application form, goal statement, income information, two letters of reference and an official transcript are required.
Exclusive: Visit www.UltimateScholarshipBook.com and enter code IN107912 for updates on this award.

(1080) • Sertoma Communicative Disorders Scholarship

Sertoma International
1912 E. Meyer Boulevard
Kansas City, MO 64132
Phone: 816-333-8300
Fax: 816-333-4320
Email: infosertoma@sertomahq.org
http://www.sertoma.org
Purpose: To fund graduate students of audiology and speech-language pathology.
Eligibility: Applicants must be citizens of the U.S. Applicants must also be accepted into a graduate level program in speech language pathology and/or audiology at a college in the U.S. recognized by ASHA's Council and have a minimum 3.2 overall GPA in all undergraduate and graduate-level courses.
Target applicants: College students. Graduate school students. Adult students.
Minimum GPA: 3.2
Amount: $1,000.
Number of awards: Varies.
Deadline: March 30.
How to apply: Applications are available online.
Exclusive: Visit www.UltimateScholarshipBook.com and enter code SE108012 for updates on this award.

(1081) • Sharps Scholarship Program

Sharps Compliance Inc.
9220 Kirby Drive
Suite 500
Houston, TX 77054
Phone: 800-772-5657
Email: scholarship@sharpsinc.com
http://www.sharpsinc.com
Purpose: To reward health care students who have written the best essays on the topic of accidental needle-stick injuries.
Eligibility: Applicants must be U.S. or Canadian citizens. They must be enrolled or planning to enroll at an accredited college or university during the fall or spring term following the application deadline. They must be studying or planning to study a health care-related subject and must submit a 1,250- to 1,500-word essay on the topic of how to prevent accidental needle-stick injuries. Selection is based on the overall strength of the essay.
Target applicants: High school students. College students. Adult students.
Amount: $750-$1,500.
Number of awards: 3.
Deadline: April 30.
How to apply: Application instructions are available online. An entry form and essay are required.
Exclusive: Visit www.UltimateScholarshipBook.com and enter code SH108112 for updates on this award.

(1082) • Shaw-Worth Memorial Scholarship

Humane Society of the United States
New England Regional Office
P.O. Box 619
Jacksonville, VT 05342
Phone: 802-368-2790
Fax: 802-368-2756
Email: nero@hsus.org
http://www.hsus.org
Purpose: To recognize a New England high school senior who has made a meaningful contribution to animal protection over a significant period of time.
Eligibility: Applicants must be high school seniors in a New England public, private, parochial or vocational school. Awards are based on the work the applicants have done on behalf of animals, such as inspiring leadership in animal protection organizations or presentations on humane topics. Neither scholastic standing nor financial need is considered. No application is required, only a narrative about the applicants' achievements in animal protection.
Target applicants: High school students.
Amount: $1,500.
Number of awards: 1.
Deadline: March 15.
How to apply: Submit materials to the address listed.
Exclusive: Visit www.UltimateScholarshipBook.com and enter code HU108212 for updates on this award.

(1083) • Shlemon Awards

Geological Society of America
Program Officer
Grants, Awards and Recognition
P.O. Box 9140
Boulder, CO 80301-9140

Phone: 303-357-1028
Fax: 303-357-1070
Email: awards@geosociety.org
http://www.geosociety.org
Purpose: To assist graduate students in conducting research in engineering geology.
Eligibility: Applicants must be members of the Geological Society of America's Engineering Geology Division, and they must be conducting research at the master's or doctoral level.
Target applicants: Graduate school students. Adult students.
Amount: $1,000.
Number of awards: 2.
Deadline: March 15.
How to apply: Applications are available online.
Exclusive: Visit www.UltimateScholarshipBook.com and enter code GE108312 for updates on this award.

(1084) · Siemens Competition in Math, Science and Technology

Siemens Foundation
170 Wood Avenue South
Iselin, NJ 08330
Phone: 877-822-5233
Fax: 732-603-5890
Email: foundation.us@siemens.com
http://www.siemens-foundation.org
Purpose: To provide high school students with an opportunity to meet other students interested in math, science and technology and to provide monetary assistance with college expenses.
Eligibility: Students must submit research reports either individually or in teams of two or three members. Individual applicants must be high school seniors. Team project applicants must be high school students but do not need to be seniors. Projects may be scientific research, technological inventions or mathematical theories.
Target applicants: High school students.
Amount: $1,000-$100,000.
Number of awards: Varies.
Deadline: October 1.
How to apply: Applications are available online.
Exclusive: Visit www.UltimateScholarshipBook.com and enter code SI108412 for updates on this award.

(1085) · Sigma Phi Alpha Undergraduate Scholarship

American Dental Hygienists' Association (ADHA) Institute for Oral Health
Scholarship Award Program
444 North Michigan Avenue
Suite 3400
Chicago, IL 60611
Phone: 312-440-8900
Email: institute@adha.net
http://www.adha.org/ioh
Purpose: To aid outstanding Sigma Phi Alpha Dental Hygiene Honor Society students.
Eligibility: Applicants must be members of the Sigma Phi Alpha Dental Hygiene Honor Society who are enrolled in a certificate, associate's degree or bachelor's degree program in dental hygiene at a school that has an active chapter of Sigma Phi Alpha. They must have a major GPA of 3.5 or higher. Selection is based on the overall strength of the application.
Target applicants: College students. Adult students.
Minimum GPA: 3.5
Amount: Varies.
Number of awards: Varies.
Deadline: February 1.
How to apply: Applications are available online. An application form and supporting materials are required.
Exclusive: Visit www.UltimateScholarshipBook.com and enter code AM108512 for updates on this award.

(1086) · Small Cash Grant Program

American Society of Certified Engineering Technicians (ASCET)
P.O. Box 1536
Brandon, MS 39043
Phone: 601-824-8991
Email: general-manager@ascet.org
http://www.ascet.org
Purpose: To help engineering technology students.
Eligibility: Applicants must be a student, certified, regular, registered or associate member of the American Society of Certified Engineering Technicians (ASCET) or be high school seniors in the last five months of the academic year who will be enrolled in an engineering technology curriculum no later than six months following the selection for the award. Students must have passing grades in their present curriculum and submit transcripts and a recommendation letter.
Target applicants: High school students. College students. Adult students.
Amount: $400.
Number of awards: Varies.
Deadline: April 1.
How to apply: Applications are available online.
Exclusive: Visit www.UltimateScholarshipBook.com and enter code AM108612 for updates on this award.

(1087) · Society of Exploration Geophysicists (SEG) Scholarship

Society of Exploration Geophysicists
Scholarship Committee
SEG Foundation
P.O. Box 702740
Tulsa, OK 74170-2740
Phone: 918-497-5500
Fax: 918-497-5560
Email: scholarships@seg.org
http://www.seg.org
Purpose: To fund individuals who are involved or interested in the field of geophysics.
Eligibility: Applicants must intend to pursue a career in exploration geophysics. Applicants must also be one of the following: A high school student with above average grades planning to enter college the next fall term, an undergraduate whose grades are above average or a graduate student pursuing a career in exploration geophysics in operations, teaching or research.
Target applicants: High school students. College students. Graduate school students. Adult students.
Amount: $500-$14,000.
Number of awards: Varies.
Scholarship may be renewable.
Deadline: March 1.
How to apply: Applications are available online or by written request.
Exclusive: Visit www.UltimateScholarshipBook.com and enter code SO108712 for updates on this award.

(1088) • Society of Manufacturing Engineers Directors Scholarship

Society of Manufacturing Engineers Education Foundation
One SME Drive
P.O. Box 930
Dearborn, MI 48121
Phone: 313-425-3300
Fax: 313-425-3411
Email: foundation@sme.org
http://www.smeef.org
Purpose: To aid undergraduate manufacturing engineering students.
Eligibility: Applicants must be full-time undergraduates who are enrolled at an accredited U.S. or Canadian postsecondary institution. They must be majoring in manufacturing engineering or a related subject and have completed at least 30 college credit hours. They must have a GPA of 3.5 or higher on a four-point scale and must have plans to pursue a career in manufacturing. Preference will be given to those with proven leadership skills. Selection is based on the overall strength of the application.
Target applicants: College students. Adult students.
Minimum GPA: 3.5
Amount: Varies.
Number of awards: Varies.
Deadline: February 1.
How to apply: Applications are available online. An application form and supporting materials are required.
Exclusive: Visit www.UltimateScholarshipBook.com and enter code SO108812 for updates on this award.

(1089) • Society of Naval Architects and Marine Engineers Undergraduate Scholarships

Society of Naval Architects and Marine Engineers
601 Pavonia Avenue
Jersey City, NJ 07306
Phone: 201-798-4800
Fax: 201-798-4975
Email: efaustino@sname.org
http://www.sname.org
Purpose: To assist college juniors and seniors who are studying marine industry fields.
Eligibility: Applicants must be U.S. or Canadian college juniors and seniors who are members of the SNAME and are working towards degrees in naval architecture, marine engineering, ocean engineering or marine industry related areas fields.
Target applicants: College students. Adult students.
Amount: $2,000.
Number of awards: Varies.
Scholarship may be renewable.
Deadline: June 15.
How to apply: Applications are available by email.
Exclusive: Visit www.UltimateScholarshipBook.com and enter code SO108912 for updates on this award.

(1090) • Society of Plastics Engineers (SPE) General Scholarships

Society of Plastics Engineers
13 Church Hill Road
Newtown, CT 06470
Phone: 203-775-0471
Fax: 203-775-8490
Email: info@4spe.org
http://www.4spe.org
Purpose: To aid students who have demonstrated or expressed an interest in the plastics industry.
Eligibility: Applicants must have a demonstrated or expressed interest in the plastics industry and be majoring in or taking courses that would lead to a career in the plastics industry. Applicants must be in good academic standing. Financial need is considered for most scholarships.
Target applicants: College students. Adult students.
Amount: Up to $4,000.
Number of awards: Varies.
Scholarship may be renewable.
Deadline: February 15.
How to apply: Applications are available online.
Exclusive: Visit www.UltimateScholarshipBook.com and enter code SO109012 for updates on this award.

(1091) • Southwest Park and Recreation Training Institute Student Scholarships

Southwest Park and Recreation Training Institute
P.O. Box 330154
Fort Worth, TX 76163
Phone: 817-292-8974
Fax: 817-361-8515
Email: lampe@swprti.org
http://www.swprti.org
Purpose: To aid students who are preparing for careers in parks and recreation.
Eligibility: Applicants must be graduate students or undergraduate sophomores, juniors or seniors. They must be majoring in recreation, recreation administration, park administration, landscape architecture or a related subject and have a GPA of 2.0 or higher on a four-point scale. Selection is based on the overall strength of the application.
Target applicants: College students. Graduate school students. Adult students.
Minimum GPA: 2.0
Amount: $1,000.
Number of awards: 3.
Deadline: October 31.
How to apply: Applications are available online. An application form and supporting materials are required.
Exclusive: Visit www.UltimateScholarshipBook.com and enter code SO109112 for updates on this award.

(1092) • SPIE Student Scholarships

International Society for Optical Engineering
P.O. Box 10
Bellingham, WA 98227-0010
Phone: 360-685-5452
Fax: 360-647-1445
Email: scholarships@spie.org
http://www.spie.org
Purpose: To promote students who have the potential to contribute to the field of optics.
Eligibility: Applicants must be high school, undergraduate or graduate students enrolled full-time in programs in the field of optics, optical science and engineering. Students must be members of SPIE, although they may submit a membership application along with the scholarship application. Applicants must also submit two sealed letters of reference.
Target applicants: High school students. College students. Adult students.

Amount: $1,000-$11,000.
Number of awards: Varies.
Deadline: January 15.
How to apply: Applications are available online.
Exclusive: Visit www.UltimateScholarshipBook.com and enter code IN109212 for updates on this award.

(1093) • Spring Meadow Nursery Scholarship

American Nursery and Landscape Association
Horticultural Research Institute
1000 Vermont Avenue NW
Suite 300
Washington, DC 20005
Phone: 202-789-5980 x3014
Fax: 202-789-1893
Email: tjodon@anla.org
http://www.anla.org
Purpose: To help students obtain a degree in horticulture.
Eligibility: Applicants must be enrolled full-time in an undergraduate or graduate landscape horticultural or related program at a two- or four-year accredited institution. Preference is given to those who plan to pursue a career in horticulture.
Target applicants: College students. Graduate school students. Adult students.
Minimum GPA: 2.25
Amount: $1,500.
Number of awards: Varies.
Scholarship may be renewable.
Deadline: April 1.
How to apply: Applications are available online.
Exclusive: Visit www.UltimateScholarshipBook.com and enter code AM109312 for updates on this award.

(1094) • SPS Leadership Scholarships

Society of Physics Students
One Physics Ellipse
College Park, MD 20740
Phone: 301-209-3007
Fax: 301-209-0839
Email: sps@aip.org
http://www.spsnational.org/programs/scholarships/
Purpose: To further the study of physics.
Eligibility: Applicants must be undergraduates at least in their junior year, physics majors and active members of SPS.
Target applicants: College students. Adult students.
Amount: $2,000-$5,000.
Number of awards: Varies.
Deadline: February 15.
How to apply: Applications are available online and from SPS Chapter Advisors.
Exclusive: Visit www.UltimateScholarshipBook.com and enter code SO109412 for updates on this award.

(1095) • Stan Beck Fellowship

Entomological Society of America
10001 Derekwood Lane
Suite 100
Lanham, MD 20706
Phone: 301-731-4535
Fax: 301-731-4538
Email: esa@entsoc.org
http://www.entsoc.org
Purpose: To support college or graduate students in entomology.
Eligibility: Applicants must be undergraduate or graduate students in entomology who demonstrate need based on physical limitations or economic, minority or environmental conditions.
Target applicants: College students. Graduate school students. Adult students.
Amount: Varies.
Number of awards: 1.
Deadline: July 1.
How to apply: Applications are available online.
Exclusive: Visit www.UltimateScholarshipBook.com and enter code EN109512 for updates on this award.

(1096) • STEEL Engineering Education Link Initiative

Iron and Steel Society
Attn.: Lori Wharrey
AIST Foundation
186 Thorn Hill Road
Warrendale, PA 15086
Phone: 724-776-6040 x621
Fax: 724-776-1880
Email: lwharrey@aist.org
http://www.aistfoundation.org
Purpose: To increase the number of students studying engineering and pursuing careers in the iron and steel industry.
Eligibility: Applicants must be juniors in an accredited North American university with a minimum GPA of 3.0, and they must demonstrate interest in the iron and steel industry. They must also be eligible for and commit to a summer internship at a steel company in the country in which they are studying.
Target applicants: College students. Adult students.
Minimum GPA: 3.0
Amount: $5,000.
Number of awards: 10.
Scholarship may be renewable.
Deadline: March 5.
How to apply: Applications are available online. Questions about this specific scholarship may be directed to blakshmi@steel.org or 202-452-7143.
Exclusive: Visit www.UltimateScholarshipBook.com and enter code IR109612 for updates on this award.

(1097) • Stew Tweed Fisheries and Aquaculture Scholarship Fund

New Jersey Marine Sciences Consortium/New Jersey Sea Grant
Sandy Hook Field Station - Building #22
Fort Hancock, NJ 07732
Phone: 732-872-1300
Email: msamuel@ngmsc.org
http://www.njmsc.org
Purpose: To aid students interested in fisheries and aquaculture.
Eligibility: Applicants must be U.S. citizens and New Jersey residents who are high school seniors or undergraduate or graduate college students. They must pursue studies or participate in an outstanding research or technology project focusing on fisheries or aquaculture. A minimum GPA of 3.0 is required.
Target applicants: High school students. College students. Graduate school students. Adult students.
Minimum GPA: 3.0

Amount: $1,000-$1,500.
Number of awards: 2.
Deadline: Varies.
How to apply: Applications are available online. An application form, two letters of recommendation and transcript are required.
Exclusive: Visit www.UltimateScholarshipBook.com and enter code NE109712 for updates on this award.

(1098) • Stoye and Storer Awards

American Society of Ichthyologists and Herpetologists
Maureen Donnelly, Secretary
Department of Biological Sciences, Florida International University
11200 SW 8th Street
Miami, FL 33199
Phone: 305-348-1235
Fax: 305-348-1986
Email: asih@fiu.edu
http://www.asih.org
Purpose: To recognize the best oral and poster presentations in categories related to ichthyology and herpetology.
Eligibility: Applicants must be the sole authors and presenters of their projects, be members of ASIH, be full-time students or have completed a thesis or dissertation defense during the previous 12 months. Presentations are judged by introduction, methods, data analysis and interpretation, conclusions, presentation and visual aids.
Target applicants: College students. Graduate school students. Adult students.
Amount: Varies.
Number of awards: Varies.
Deadline: Varies.
How to apply: Applications are available by request.
Exclusive: Visit www.UltimateScholarshipBook.com and enter code AM109812 for updates on this award.

(1099) • Structural Metals Division Scholarship

The Minerals, Metals and Materials Society
184 Thorn Hill Road
Warrendale, PA 15086
Phone: 724-776-9000
Fax: 724-776-3770
Email: students@tms.org
http://www.tms.org
Purpose: To aid metallurgical and materials science engineering students.
Eligibility: Applicants must be student members of The Minerals, Metals and Materials Society (TMS), be full-time undergraduate sophomores or juniors and be majoring in metallurgical or materials science engineering. Their studies must concentrate on the science and engineering of load-bearing materials. Selection is based on the overall strength of the application.
Target applicants: College students. Adult students.
Amount: $2,500.
Number of awards: 2.
Deadline: March 15.
How to apply: Applications are available online. An application form, personal statement, transcript and three recommendation letters are required.
Exclusive: Visit www.UltimateScholarshipBook.com and enter code TH109912 for updates on this award.

(1100) • Student Design Competition

Society of American Registered Architects
P.O. Box 280
Newport, TN 37822
Phone: 888-385-7272
Fax: 423-487-0365
Email: cathiemoscato@sara-national.org
http://www.sara-national.org
Purpose: To support architecture students.
Eligibility: Applicants may be attending accredited architectural schools, be undergraduate students in a bachelor's of arts or a bachelor's of science in an architecture program or be graduate students in a master's of architecture program in pursuit of a first professional degree. Students must secure the sponsorship of a faculty member.
Target applicants: College students. Graduate school students. Adult students.
Amount: $500-$6,000.
Number of awards: 3.
Deadline: September 1 for registration form.
How to apply: Applications are available online or by written request.
Exclusive: Visit www.UltimateScholarshipBook.com and enter code SO110012 for updates on this award.

(1101) • Student Poster Session Awards

Electrochemical Society
65 South Main Street, Building D
Pennington, NJ 08534-2839
Phone: 609-737-1902
Fax: 609-737-2743
Email: awards@electrochem.org
http://www.electrochem.org
Purpose: To award students for work related to fields of interest to ECS.
Eligibility: Applicants must be pursuing degrees at any college or university and prepare an abstract on work performed. The applicants must also prepare a poster to present at the society meeting where they will be judged. Two awards are in the categories of electrochemical science and technology and solid-state science and technology.
Target applicants: College students. Graduate school students. Adult students.
Amount: $250.
Number of awards: 2.
Deadline: Varies.
How to apply: Application materials are described online.
Exclusive: Visit www.UltimateScholarshipBook.com and enter code EL110112 for updates on this award.

(1102) • Student Research Fellowship Award

Crohn's and Colitis Foundation of America Inc.
386 Park Avenue South
17th floor
New York, NY 10016
Phone: 800-932-2423
Email: info@ccfa.org
http://www.ccfa.org
Purpose: To stimulate interest in research careers in inflammatory bowel disease by providing salary support for research projects.
Eligibility: Applicants must be undergraduate, graduate or medical students not yet engaged in thesis research. Students must attend an accredited North American school and conduct their research with a

mentor. The planned research project must last at least 10 weeks and must be relevant to IBD.
Target applicants: College students. Graduate school students. Adult students.
Amount: $2,500.
Number of awards: Up to 16.
Deadline: March 15.
How to apply: Applications are available online.
Exclusive: Visit www.UltimateScholarshipBook.com and enter code CR110212 for updates on this award.

(1103) · Student Research Scholarships

Bat Conservation International
Scholarship Program
P.O. Box 162603
Austin, TX 78716
Phone: 512-327-9721
Fax: 512-327-9724
Email: grants@batcon.org
http://www.batcon.org
Purpose: To support students who will contribute to our knowledge about bats.
Eligibility: Applicants must be graduate students and submit a research proposal that addresses a specific area of bat conservation. The application form provides several potential research topics.
Target applicants: Graduate school students. Adult students.
Amount: $1,000-$5,000.
Number of awards: Varies.
Deadline: December 15.
How to apply: Applications are available online.
Exclusive: Visit www.UltimateScholarshipBook.com and enter code BA110312 for updates on this award.

(1104) · Student Travel Contingency Grants

International Society for Optical Engineering
P.O. Box 10
Bellingham, WA 98227-0010
Phone: 360-685-5452
Fax: 360-647-1445
Email: scholarships@spie.org
http://www.spie.org
Purpose: To assist students who need support to travel to present at a SPIE meeting.
Eligibility: Applicants must be presenting an accepted paper at a SPIE-sponsored meeting and not have any other way of supporting their travel. Applicants must be full-time students who are not full-time employees in industry, government or academia. The students must also submit a letter of recommendation and a written statement of support from the chair of the SPIE-sponsored meeting.
Target applicants: College students. Graduate school students. Adult students.
Amount: $500-$750.
Number of awards: Varies.
Deadline: 10 weeks prior to the start of meeting.
How to apply: Applications are available online.
Exclusive: Visit www.UltimateScholarshipBook.com and enter code IN110412 for updates on this award.

(1105) · Tafford Uniforms Nursing Scholarship Program

Tafford Uniforms
1370 Welsh Road
North Wales, PA 19454
Phone: 800-697-3321
http://www.tafford.com
Purpose: To aid nursing students.
Eligibility: Applicants must be enrolled in an accredited licensed practical nurse (LPN), licensed vocational nurse (LVN), associate's degree in nursing (ADN), bachelor of science in nursing (BSN) or master's of science in nursing (MSN) degree program. Selection is based on the overall strength of the application.
Target applicants: College students. Graduate school students. Adult students.
Amount: Varies.
Number of awards: Varies.
Deadline: Varies.
How to apply: Applications are available online. An application form and supporting materials are required.
Exclusive: Visit www.UltimateScholarshipBook.com and enter code TA110512 for updates on this award.

(1106) · Tau Beta Pi/Society of Automotive Engineers Engineering Scholarship

Society of Automotive Engineers International
400 Commonwealth Drive
Warrendale, PA 15096
Phone: 724-776-4841
Fax: 724-776-0790
Email: scholarships@sae.org
http://www.sae.org
Purpose: To aid future college students who are planning to major in engineering.
Eligibility: Applicants must be U.S. citizens, be graduating high school seniors and have plans to major in engineering at an ABET-accredited institution. They must have a GPA of 3.75 or higher and must have SAT or ACT scores that rank in the 90th percentile. Selection is based on the overall strength of the application.
Target applicants: High school students.
Minimum GPA: 3.75
Amount: $1,000.
Number of awards: 6.
Deadline: January 15.
How to apply: Applications are available online. An application form, official transcript and standardized test scores are required.
Exclusive: Visit www.UltimateScholarshipBook.com and enter code SO110612 for updates on this award.

(1107) · Ted Neward Scholarship

Society of Plastics Engineers
13 Church Hill Road
Newtown, CT 06470
Phone: 203-775-0471
Fax: 203-775-8490
Email: info@4spe.org
http://www.4spe.org
Purpose: To aid students who have an interest in the plastics industry.
Eligibility: Applicants must be U.S. citizens, have an interest in the plastics industry, major in or take courses leading to a career in the plastics industry and be in good academic standing. Financial need is considered.

Target applicants: College students. Graduate school students. Adult students.
Amount: $3,000.
Number of awards: 3.
Deadline: February 15.
How to apply: Applications are available online.
Exclusive: Visit www.UltimateScholarshipBook.com and enter code SO110712 for updates on this award.

(1108) · The Father James B. Macelwane Annual Awards in Meteorology

American Meteorological Society
Fellowship and Scholarship Department
45 Beacon Street
Boston, MA 02108-3693
Phone: 617-227-2426 x246
Fax: 617-742-8718
Email: dsampson@ametsoc.org
http://www.ametsoc.org/AMS/
Purpose: To encourage interest in meteorology among college students.
Eligibility: Applicants must be enrolled as undergraduates and submit an original student paper on an aspect of atmospheric science. No more than two students from any one institution may enter papers in any one contest, and there is no application form needed.
Target applicants: College students. Graduate school students. Adult students.
Amount: $1,000.
Number of awards: 1.
Deadline: June 11.
How to apply: Submit materials to address listed.
Exclusive: Visit www.UltimateScholarshipBook.com and enter code AM110812 for updates on this award.

(1109) · Thermoforming Division Memorial Scholarships

Society of Plastics Engineers
13 Church Hill Road
Newtown, CT 06470
Phone: 203-775-0471
Fax: 203-775-8490
Email: info@4spe.org
http://www.4spe.org
Purpose: To aid students who have an interest in the plastics industry.
Eligibility: Applicants must have a 3.0 GPA and an interest in the plastics industry, major in or take courses leading to a career in the plastics industry and be in good academic standing. Applicants must have experience in the thermoforming industry, such as courses taken, research conducted or jobs held.
Target applicants: College students. Graduate school students. Adult students.
Minimum GPA: 3.0
Amount: Up to $5,000.
Number of awards: Varies.
Deadline: February 15.
How to apply: Applications are available online.
Exclusive: Visit www.UltimateScholarshipBook.com and enter code SO110912 for updates on this award.

(1110) · Thermoplastic Elastomers Special Interest Group Scholarship

Society of Plastics Engineers
13 Church Hill Road
Newtown, CT 06470
Phone: 203-775-0471
Fax: 203-775-8490
Email: info@4spe.org
http://www.4spe.org
Purpose: To aid students who have a demonstrated interest in thermoplastic elastomers.
Eligibility: Applicants must be full-time undergraduate or graduate students who have a proven interest in thermoplastic elastomers. This interest must be shown by relevant jobs held, internships completed, coursework completed or research undertaken. Selection is based on the overall strength of the application.
Target applicants: College students. Graduate school students. Adult students.
Amount: $2,500.
Number of awards: 1.
Deadline: February 15.
How to apply: Applications are available online. An application form, official transcript, three references and a personal statement are required.
Exclusive: Visit www.UltimateScholarshipBook.com and enter code SO111012 for updates on this award.

(1111) · Thermoplastic Materials and Foams Division Scholarship

Society of Plastics Engineers
13 Church Hill Road
Newtown, CT 06470
Phone: 203-775-0471
Fax: 203-775-8490
Email: info@4spe.org
http://www.4spe.org
Purpose: To aid undergraduate students who have a demonstrated interest in thermoplastic materials and foams.
Eligibility: Applicants must be full-time undergraduate students who are interested in thermoplastic materials and foams. This interest must be shown by relevant internship experiences, jobs held, coursework completed or research undertaken. Selection is based on the overall strength of the application.
Target applicants: College students. Adult students.
Amount: $2,500.
Number of awards: 1.
Deadline: February 15.
How to apply: Applications are available online. An application form, three references, transcript and personal statement are required.
Exclusive: Visit www.UltimateScholarshipBook.com and enter code SO111112 for updates on this award.

(1112) · Thermoset Division/James I. MacKenzie Memorial Scholarship

Society of Plastics Engineers
13 Church Hill Road
Newtown, CT 06470
Phone: 203-775-0471
Fax: 203-775-8490
Email: info@4spe.org
http://www.4spe.org

Purpose: To aid students who have an interest in the plastics industry and have experience in the thermoset industry.
Eligibility: Applicants must have an interest in the plastics industry and major in or take courses leading to a career in the plastics industry. Applicants must also have experience in the thermoset industry, such as courses taken, research conducted or jobs held.
Target applicants: College students. Adult students.
Amount: $1,500.
Number of awards: 2.
Deadline: February 15.
How to apply: Applications are available online.
Exclusive: Visit www.UltimateScholarshipBook.com and enter code SO111212 for updates on this award.

(1113) • Thomas E. Powers/Detroit Section Scholarship

Society of Plastics Engineers
13 Church Hill Road
Newtown, CT 06470
Phone: 203-775-0471
Fax: 203-775-8490
Email: info@4spe.org
http://www.4spe.org
Purpose: To aid undergraduate students who are interested in the plastics industry.
Eligibility: Applicants must be full-time undergraduate students in good academic standing who have completed coursework in or are majoring in a subject that relates to the plastics industry (such as engineering, polymer science, physics or chemistry). Selection is based on the overall strength of the application.
Target applicants: College students. Adult students.
Amount: $4,000.
Number of awards: 1.
Deadline: February 15.
How to apply: Applications are available online. An application form, personal statement, transcript and three recommendation letters are required.
Exclusive: Visit www.UltimateScholarshipBook.com and enter code SO111312 for updates on this award.

(1114) • Thomas M. Stetson Scholarship

American Ground Water Trust
16 Centre Street
Concord, NH 03301
Phone: 603-228-5444
Fax: 603-228-6557
http://www.agwt.org
Purpose: To provide scholarships for high school seniors pursuing careers in a ground water-related field.
Eligibility: Applicants must be high school seniors with intentions to pursue a career in ground water-related field. Applicants must attend a college or university located west of the Mississippi River.
Target applicants: High school students.
Minimum GPA: 3.0
Amount: $1,500.
Number of awards: 1.
Deadline: June 1.
How to apply: Applications are available online.
Exclusive: Visit www.UltimateScholarshipBook.com and enter code AM111412 for updates on this award.

(1115) • Thomas R. Camp Scholarship

American Water Works Association
6666 W. Quincy Avenue
Denver, CO 80235-3098
Phone: 303-347-6201
Fax: 303-795-7603
Email: lmoody@awwa.org
http://www.awwa.org
Purpose: To support students conducting applied research in the drinking water field.
Eligibility: Applicants must pursue graduate degrees at an institution of higher education in Canada, Guam, Puerto Rico, Mexico or the U.S. This is awarded to doctoral students in even years and master's students in odd years. Applicants must submit applications, resumes, transcripts, GRE scores, three recommendation letters, statements and research plans. The award is based on academics and leadership.
Target applicants: Graduate school students. Adult students.
Amount: $5,000.
Number of awards: 1.
Deadline: January 15.
How to apply: Applications are available online.
Exclusive: Visit www.UltimateScholarshipBook.com and enter code AM111512 for updates on this award.

(1116) • Thompson Delmar Learning Student Scholarship

Association of Surgical Technologists
6 W. Dry Creek Circle
Littleton, CO 80120
Phone: 800-637-7433
Fax: 303-694-9169
Email: kludwig@ast.org
http://www.ast.org
Purpose: To support surgical technology students.
Eligibility: The award is based on academic achievement and writing skills. Applicants must plan to attend or currently attend a CAAHEP-accredited program. Applications and progress reports are required.
Target applicants: College students. Adult students.
Minimum GPA: 2.5
Amount: $1,500.
Number of awards: 1.
Deadline: March 1.
How to apply: Applications are available online.
Exclusive: Visit www.UltimateScholarshipBook.com and enter code AS111612 for updates on this award.

(1117) • Tilford Fund

Association of Engineering Geologists Foundation Tilford Fund
NRT Scholarship Committee
70 Forest Lane
Placitas, NM 87043
http://www.aegfoundation.org
Purpose: To provide financial assistance for field studies in engineering geology.
Eligibility: Applicants must be members of the Association of Engineering Geologists who are college or graduate students. Applicants are chosen on the basis of scholarship, ability, participation and potential for contributions to the profession.
Target applicants: College students. Graduate school students. Adult students.

Amount: Varies.
Number of awards: at least 2.
Deadline: February 1.
How to apply: Applications are available online.
Exclusive: Visit www.UltimateScholarshipBook.com and enter code AS111712 for updates on this award.

(1118) · Timothy Bigelow and Palmer W. Bigelow, Jr. Scholarship

American Nursery and Landscape Association
Horticultural Research Institute
1000 Vermont Avenue NW
Suite 300
Washington, DC 20005
Phone: 202-789-5980 x3014
Fax: 202-789-1893
Email: tjodon@anla.org
http://www.anla.org
Purpose: To help students from New England who want to pursue a career in horticulture.
Eligibility: Applicants must be seniors in a two-year course and have finished the first year, juniors in a four-year course and have finished the first two years or be graduate students. Undergraduates must have a minimum 2.25 GPA and graduate students a minimum 3.0 GPA. Students must be from Connecticut, Maine, Massachusetts, New Hampshire, Rhode Island or Vermont. Preference will be given to applicants who have financial need and who plan to work in the nursery industry after graduation, including starting a business.
Target applicants: College students. Graduate school students. Adult students.
Minimum GPA: 2.25
Amount: $2,000.
Number of awards: Varies.
Deadline: Varies.
How to apply: Applications are available online or by mail.
Exclusive: Visit www.UltimateScholarshipBook.com and enter code AM111812 for updates on this award.

(1119) · TMC/SAE Donald D. Dawson Technical Scholarship

Society of Automotive Engineers International
400 Commonwealth Drive
Warrendale, PA 15096
Phone: 724-776-4841
Fax: 724-776-0790
Email: scholarships@sae.org
http://www.sae.org
Purpose: To aid current and future engineering students.
Eligibility: Applicants must be U.S. citizens, be high school seniors or current undergraduate students and be enrolled in or planning to enroll in an ABET-accredited engineering degree program. They must have a GPA of 3.25 or higher and an SAT I math score of 600 or higher and a critical reading score of 550 or higher or must have an ACT composite score of 27 or higher. Selection is based on the overall strength of the application.
Target applicants: High school students. College students. Adult students.
Minimum GPA: 3.25
Amount: $1,500.
Number of awards: Varies.
Scholarship may be renewable.
Deadline: January 15.
How to apply: Applications are available online. An application form, personal essay, official transcript and standardized test scores are required.
Exclusive: Visit www.UltimateScholarshipBook.com and enter code SO111912 for updates on this award.

(1120) · TMS Best Paper Contest

The Minerals, Metals and Materials Society
184 Thorn Hill Road
Warrendale, PA 15086
Phone: 724-776-9000
Fax: 724-776-3770
Email: students@tms.org
http://www.tms.org
Purpose: To support the professional development of metallurgy and materials science students.
Eligibility: Applicants must be student members of The Minerals, Metals and Materials Society (TMS). They must prepare and submit a technical essay on a topic that is related to metallurgy or materials science. Selection is based on originality and the quality of research.
Target applicants: College students. Graduate school students. Adult students.
Amount: Up to $1,000.
Number of awards: 4.
Deadline: May 1.
How to apply: Submission guidelines are available online. A technical essay, cover sheet and faculty endorsement are required.
Exclusive: Visit www.UltimateScholarshipBook.com and enter code TH112012 for updates on this award.

(1121) · TMS Technical Division Student Poster Contest

The Minerals, Metals and Materials Society
184 Thorn Hill Road
Warrendale, PA 15086
Phone: 724-776-9000
Fax: 724-776-3770
Email: students@tms.org
http://www.tms.org
Purpose: To aid student members of the Minerals, Metals and Materials Society.
Eligibility: Applicants must be student members of the Minerals, Metals and Materials Society (TMS), be full-time undergraduate or graduate students and create a poster that addresses a topic that would be of interest for one of the five technical divisions of TMS. Selection is based on the overall strength of the poster.
Target applicants: College students. Graduate school students. Adult students.
Amount: Up to $1,000.
Number of awards: 10.
Deadline: Varies.
How to apply: Applications are available online. An application form and poster are required.
Exclusive: Visit www.UltimateScholarshipBook.com and enter code TH112112 for updates on this award.

(1122) · TMS/International Symposium of Superalloys Scholarships

The Minerals, Metals and Materials Society
184 Thorn Hill Road
Warrendale, PA 15086

Phone: 724-776-9000
Fax: 724-776-3770
Email: students@tms.org
http://www.tms.org
Purpose: To aid metallurgical engineering and materials science and engineering students.
Eligibility: Applicants must be student members of the Minerals, Metals and Materials Society (TMS) and be full-time undergraduate or graduate students majoring in metallurgical engineering or materials science and engineering. They must have a demonstrated interest in the high-temperature, high-performance materials used in the gas turbine industry. Selection is based on academic merit, extracurricular activities, relevant coursework completed and recommendation letters.
Target applicants: College students. Graduate school students. Adult students.
Amount: $2,000.
Number of awards: 2.
Deadline: March 15.
How to apply: Applications are available online. An application form, transcript, personal essay and three recommendation letters are required.
Exclusive: Visit www.UltimateScholarshipBook.com and enter code TH112212 for updates on this award.

(1123) • Transoft Solutions Inc. AOTC (Ahead of the Curve) Scholarship

Institute of Transportation Engineers
1627 Eye Street NW
Suite 600
Washington, DC 20006
Phone: 202-785-0060
Fax: 202-785-0609
Email: ite_staff@ite.org
http://www.ite.org
Purpose: To aid students who are majoring in transportation or traffic engineering.
Eligibility: Applicants must be undergraduate, graduate or doctoral students who are majoring in transportation engineering or traffic engineering. They must be attending an accredited postsecondary institution located in the U.S. or Canada. Selection is based on academic merit, personal essay and recommendations.
Target applicants: College students. Graduate school students. Adult students.
Amount: $2,000.
Number of awards: 1.
Deadline: April 1.
How to apply: Applications are available online. An application form, personal essay, resume, official transcript and three references are required.
Exclusive: Visit www.UltimateScholarshipBook.com and enter code IN112312 for updates on this award.

(1124) • Travel Grants

Geological Society of America
Program Officer
Grants, Awards and Recognition
P.O. Box 9140
Boulder, CO 80301-9140
Phone: 303-357-1028
Fax: 303-357-1070
Email: awards@geosociety.org
http://www.geosociety.org
Purpose: To provide undergraduate and graduate students with grants to travel to GSA section meetings and to the GSA annual meeting.
Eligibility: Applicants must be members of GSA. Each regional section has its own application process.
Target applicants: College students. Graduate school students. Adult students.
Amount: Varies.
Number of awards: Varies.
Deadline: Varies.
How to apply: Application information for each region is available online.
Exclusive: Visit www.UltimateScholarshipBook.com and enter code GE112412 for updates on this award.

(1125) • Trimmer Foundation Student Scholarships

Associated Builders and Contractors
Trimmer Education Foundation
4250 N. Fairfax Drive
9th Floor
Arlington, VA 22203
Phone: 703-812-2000
Email: studentchapters@abc.org
http://www.abc.org
Purpose: To assist students in construction-related degree programs.
Eligibility: Applicants must be enrolled in a construction-related program and must be current active members in the student chapter program or be employed by an ABC firm.
Target applicants: College students. Adult students.
Minimum GPA: 2.85
Amount: $5,000.
Number of awards: Varies.
Deadline: May 21.
How to apply: Applications are available by email request.
Exclusive: Visit www.UltimateScholarshipBook.com and enter code AS112512 for updates on this award.

(1126) • Tylenol Scholarship

Tylenol
Phone: 877-895-3665
http://www.tylenol.com
Purpose: Each year Tylenol gives away $250,000 in scholarships to college and graduate students pursuing careers in healthcare.
Eligibility: Applicants must major or intend to major in a health care-related area.
Target applicants: College students. Graduate school students. Adult students.
Amount: $5,000-$10,000.
Number of awards: 40.
Deadline: May 14.
How to apply: Applications are available online.
Exclusive: Visit www.UltimateScholarshipBook.com and enter code TY112612 for updates on this award.

(1127) • UAA Janice K. Barden Aviation Scholarship

National Business Aviation Association
1200 18th Street NW
Suite 400
Washington, DC 20036
Phone: 202-783-9250
Fax: 202-331-8364

Email: info@nbaa.org
http://www.nbaa.org
Purpose: To aid aviation students attending a University Aviation Association (UAA) or National Business Aviation Association (NBAA) member school.
Eligibility: Applicants must be U.S. citizens who are studying a subject that is related to aviation. Selection is based on the overall strength of the application.
Target applicants: College students. Adult students.
Amount: $1,000.
Number of awards: 5.
Deadline: November 1.
How to apply: Applications are available online. An application form, personal essay, transcript, resume and one recommendation letter are required.
Exclusive: Visit www.UltimateScholarshipBook.com and enter code NA112712 for updates on this award.

(1128) · Undergraduate Award for Excellence in Chemistry

Iota Sigma Pi (ISP) ND
Professor Kathryn A. Thomasson, Iota Sigma Pi Director for Student Awards
University of North Dakota, Department of Chemistry
P.O. Box 9024
Grand Forks, ND 58202-9024
Phone: 701-777-3199
Fax: 701-777-2331
Email: kthomasson@chem.und.edu
http://www.iotasigmapi.info
Purpose: To award female undergraduate students for excellence in the field of chemistry study.
Eligibility: Applicants must be female senior chemistry students at an accredited four-year college or university and be nominated by a member of the faculty.
Target applicants: College students. Adult students.
Amount: $500.
Number of awards: 1.
Deadline: February 15.
How to apply: Applications are available online.
Exclusive: Visit www.UltimateScholarshipBook.com and enter code IO112812 for updates on this award.

(1129) · Undergraduate Scholarship

Entomological Society of America
10001 Derekwood Lane
Suite 100
Lanham, MD 20706
Phone: 301-731-4535
Fax: 301-731-4538
Email: esa@entsoc.org
http://www.entsoc.org
Purpose: To help students enter the field of entomology.
Eligibility: Applicants must have been enrolled in the previous fall as undergraduate students in entomology, zoology, biology or a related science at a college or university and must have accumulated a minimum of 30 credits at the time the award is presented in August. Students must have completed at least one course in entomology or a project in entomology.
Target applicants: College students. Adult students.
Amount: $2,000.
Number of awards: 1.
Deadline: July 1.
How to apply: Applications are available online.
Exclusive: Visit www.UltimateScholarshipBook.com and enter code EN112912 for updates on this award.

(1130) · Undergraduate Scholarship and Construction Crafts Scholarship

National Association of Women in Construction
327 South Adams Street
Fort Worth, TX 76104
Phone: 800-552-3506
Fax: 817-877-0324
Email: nawic@nawic.org
http://www.nawic.org
Purpose: To offer financial aid to women pursuing construction-related degrees.
Eligibility: Applicants must be currently enrolled in a construction-related degree program as full-time students, have at least one term of study remaining in a course of study leading to a degree or an associate degree in a construction-related field, desire a career in a construction-related field and have a minimum 3.0 GPA.
Target applicants: College students. Adult students.
Minimum GPA: 3.0
Amount: $1,000-$2,000.
Number of awards: Varies.
Deadline: March 15.
How to apply: Applications are available online.
Exclusive: Visit www.UltimateScholarshipBook.com and enter code NA113012 for updates on this award.

(1131) · Undergraduate Student Research Grants

Geological Society of America
Program Officer
Grants, Awards and Recognition
P.O. Box 9140
Boulder, CO 80301-9140
Phone: 303-357-1028
Fax: 303-357-1070
Email: awards@geosociety.org
http://www.geosociety.org
Purpose: To provide research grants to undergraduate students studying geology who are members of GSA.
Eligibility: Applicants must be members of GSA and attend school in one of the following GSA sections: Northeastern, North-Central or Southeastern. Each section has a separate application process.
Target applicants: High school students. College students. Adult students.
Amount: Varies.
Number of awards: Varies.
Deadline: Varies.
How to apply: Application instructions for each region are available online.
Exclusive: Visit www.UltimateScholarshipBook.com and enter code GE113112 for updates on this award.

(1132) • Undergraduate Student Summer Research Fellowships

American Physiological Society
Education Office
9650 Rockville Pike
Bethesda, MD 20814-3991
Phone: 301-634-7787
Fax: 301-634-7241
Email: education@the-aps.org
http://www.the-aps.org

Purpose: To support full-time summer study for undergraduate students in the laboratory of an established researcher.

Eligibility: Applicants must be enrolled in an undergraduate program, and faculty sponsor must be an active member of APS. Fellowships are awarded to students pursuing a career as a basic research scientist.

Target applicants: College students. Adult students.

Amount: $4,000 stipend plus up to $1,300 travel expenses.

Number of awards: Up to 24.

Deadline: February 1.

How to apply: Applications are available online.

Exclusive: Visit www.UltimateScholarshipBook.com and enter code AM113212 for updates on this award.

(1133) • Undergraduate Summer Student Research Assistantship

National Radio Astronomy Observatory (NRAO)
NRAO Headquarters
520 Edgemont Road
Charlottesville, VA 22903
Phone: 434-296-0211
Fax: 434-296-0278
Email: info@nrao.edu
http://www.nrao.edu

Purpose: To allow students to perform astronomical research at National Radio Astronomy Observatory (NRAO) sites.

Eligibility: Depending on the specific program, applicants must be either undergraduates or graduating college seniors. Recipients work on-site for 10 to 12 weeks, beginning in late May or early June.

Target applicants: College students. Adult students.

Amount: Up to $652 per week stipend plus travel expenses.

Number of awards: Varies.

Deadline: February 1.

How to apply: Applications are available online.

Exclusive: Visit www.UltimateScholarshipBook.com and enter code NA113312 for updates on this award.

(1134) • United Parcel Service Scholarship for Female Students

Institute of Industrial Engineers
3577 Parkway Lane
Suite 200
Norcross, GA 30092
Phone: 800-494-0460
Fax: 770-441-3295
Email: bcameron@iienet.org
http://www.iienet2.org

Purpose: To help female undergraduate engineering member students.

Eligibility: Applicants must be full-time female students at an institution in the United States, Canada or Mexico with an accredited industrial engineering program, majoring in industrial engineering or its equivalent and active members. Students may not apply directly for this scholarship and must be nominated. The award is based on academic ability, character, leadership, potential service to the industrial engineering profession and financial need.

Target applicants: College students. Adult students.

Minimum GPA: 3.4

Amount: $4,000.

Number of awards: 1.

Deadline: February 1.

How to apply: Nomination forms are available online.

Exclusive: Visit www.UltimateScholarshipBook.com and enter code IN113412 for updates on this award.

(1135) • United States Steel Corporation Scholarship

Society of Women Engineers
120 South LaSalle Street
Suite 1515
Chicago, IL 60603
Phone: 877-793-4636
Email: scholarshipapplication@swe.org
http://www.swe.org

Purpose: To aid female undergraduates who are majoring in engineering and computer science.

Eligibility: Applicants must be U.S. citizens and be rising undergraduate juniors who are majoring in computer science or engineering. They must have a GPA of 3.0 or higher on a four-point scale. Selection is based on the overall strength of the application.

Target applicants: College students. Adult students.

Minimum GPA: 3.0

Amount: $5,000.

Number of awards: 5.

Deadline: Varies.

How to apply: Applications are available online. An application form and supporting materials are required.

Exclusive: Visit www.UltimateScholarshipBook.com and enter code SO113512 for updates on this award.

(1136) • USDA/1890 National Scholars Program

U.S. Department of Agriculture
Animal and Plant Health Inspection Service
1400 Independence Avenue SW
Room 1133, South Building
Washington, DC 20250
Phone: 202-720-6312
Fax: 202-720-2365
Email: sophia.l.kirby@usda.gov
http://www.aphis.usda.gov

Purpose: To aid students who are planning to study agriculture or a related subject in college.

Eligibility: Applicants must be U.S. citizens and be entering undergraduate freshmen who have a high school diploma or a GED. They must have a GPA of 3.0 or higher and have a combined critical reading/math SAT score of 1,000 or higher or a composite ACT score of 21 or higher. They must plan to enroll at an 1890 Land Grant institution and have plans to major in agriculture; agriculture business/management; agriculture economics; agricultural engineering/mechanics; agricultural productions and technology; agronomy or crop science; animal science; botany; farm and range management; fish, game, or wildlife management; food services/technology; forestry and related services; home economics/nutrition/human development; horticulture;

natural resources management; soil conservation/soil science or other related disciplines (e.g., biological sciences, pre-veterinary medicine, or computer science). They must also have proven leadership skills and must have experience with community service. Selection is based on the overall strength of the application.
Target applicants: High school students.
Minimum GPA: 3.0
Amount: Varies.
Number of awards: Varies.
Deadline: Varies.
How to apply: Applications are available by request from the Civil Rights Enforcement and Compliance section of the Animal and Plant Health Inspection Service branch of the USDA. An application form and supporting materials are required.
Exclusive: Visit www.UltimateScholarshipBook.com and enter code U.113612 for updates on this award.

(1137) • Vertical Flight Foundation Engineering Scholarships

Vertical Flight Foundation
217 N. Washington Street
Alexandria, VA 22314
Phone: 703-684-6777
Fax: 703-739-9279
Email: staff@vtol.org
http://www.vtol.org
Purpose: The Vertical Flight Foundation was founded to support the education in rotorcraft and vertical-takeoff-and-landing aircraft engineering.
Eligibility: Applicants must be full-time students at accredited schools of engineering and submit a transcript with an academic endorsement from a professor or dean. Applicants need not be members of AHS.
Target applicants: College students. Graduate school students. Adult students.
Amount: $1,000-$4,000.
Number of awards: Varies.
Deadline: February 1.
How to apply: Applications are available online.
Exclusive: Visit www.UltimateScholarshipBook.com and enter code VE113712 for updates on this award.

(1138) • Vinyl Plastics Division Scholarship

Society of Plastics Engineers
13 Church Hill Road
Newtown, CT 06470
Phone: 203-775-0471
Fax: 203-775-8490
Email: info@4spe.org
http://www.4spe.org
Purpose: To aid students who plan to enter the vinyl plastics industry.
Eligibility: Applicants must be undergraduate students pursuing a career in the plastics industry and be in good academic standing. Preference is given to applicants with experience in the vinyl industry. Financial need is considered.
Target applicants: College students. Adult students.
Amount: $3,000.
Number of awards: 1.
Deadline: February 15.
How to apply: Applications are available online.
Exclusive: Visit www.UltimateScholarshipBook.com and enter code SO113812 for updates on this award.

(1139) • VIP Women in Technology Scholarship

Visionary Integration Professionals
80 Iron Point Circle
Suite 100
Folsom, CA 95630
Phone: 916-985-9625
Fax: 916-985-9632
Email: wits@vipconsulting.com
http://www.vipconsulting.com
Purpose: To aid female students who are preparing for careers in information technology or a related subject.
Eligibility: Applicants must be attending or accepted at a two- or four-year postsecondary institution located in the U.S. They must be planning to pursue a career in information technology or a related field. Selection is based on academic merit, a personal essay and extracurricular activities.
Target applicants: High school students. College students. Adult students.
Amount: Up to $2,500.
Number of awards: Varies.
Deadline: March 15.
How to apply: Applications are available online. An application form, official transcript, personal essay and list of extracurricular activities are required.
Exclusive: Visit www.UltimateScholarshipBook.com and enter code VI113912 for updates on this award.

(1140) • William A. Fischer Memorial Scholarship

American Society for Photogrammetry and Remote Sensing (ASPRS)
The Imaging and Geospatial Information Society
5410 Grosvenor Lane
Suite 210
Bethesda, MD 20814
Phone: 301-493-0290 x101
Fax: 301-493-0208
Email: scholarships@asprs.org
http://www.asprs.org
Purpose: To support graduate study in new uses of remote sensing data or techniques that relate to the natural, cultural or agricultural resources of the Earth.
Eligibility: Applicants must be prospective or current graduate students and submit letters of recommendation, a two-page statement detailing educational and career plans for continuing studies in remote sensing applications and transcripts. It is also recommended that applicants submit technical papers, research reports or other items that indicate their capabilities. Recipients must submit a report of their work during the award period.
Target applicants: Graduate school students. Adult students.
Amount: $2,000.
Number of awards: 1.
Deadline: December 1.
How to apply: Applications are available online.
Exclusive: Visit www.UltimateScholarshipBook.com and enter code AM114012 for updates on this award.

(1141) • William Park Woodside Founder's Scholarship

ASM International Foundation
9639 Kinsman Road
Materials Park, OH 44073
Phone: 440-338-5151
Fax: 440-338-4634

Email: asmif@asminternational.org
http://asmcommunity.asminternational.org/portal/site/www/
Foundation
Purpose: To support students who follow the spirit of ASM International.
Eligibility: Applicants must be student members of ASM International, major in metallurgy or materials science engineering and be juniors or seniors at a North American university that has a bachelor's degree program in science and engineering. Applications, personal statements, transcripts, two recommendation forms, photographs and financial aid officers' contact information are required. The award is based on academics, interest in the metallurgy/materials engineering field, character and financial need. The award is for one year of full tuition up to $10,000.
Target applicants: College students. Adult students.
Amount: $10,000.
Number of awards: 1.
Deadline: May 1.
How to apply: Applications are available online.
Exclusive: Visit www.UltimateScholarshipBook.com and enter code AS114112 for updates on this award.

(1142) · William R. Kimel, P.E., Engineering Scholarship

National Society of Professional Engineers
1420 King Street
Alexandria, VA 22314-2794
Phone: 703-684-2885
Fax: 703-836-4875
Email: memserv@nspe.org
http://www.nspe.org
Purpose: To assist engineering students from Kansas and Missouri in paying for their education.
Eligibility: Applicants must be permanent residents of and enrolled in an accredited undergraduate engineering program in Kansas or Missouri. Applications are only considered from students in their junior year.
Target applicants: College students. Adult students.
Amount: $2,500.
Number of awards: 1.
Deadline: March 1.
How to apply: Applications are available online.
Exclusive: Visit www.UltimateScholarshipBook.com and enter code NA114212 for updates on this award.

(1143) · Women's Scholarship

National Strength and Conditioning Association (NSCA) Foundation
1885 Bob Johnson Drive
Colorado Springs, CO 80906
Phone: 800-815-6826
Fax: 719-632-6367
Email: nsca@nsca-lift.org
http://www.nsca-lift.org
Purpose: To encourage women to enter the field of strength and conditioning.
Eligibility: Applicants should be women age 17 and older who have been accepted by an accredited institution for a graduate degree in strength and conditioning. Applicants must be NSCA members and plan to pursue careers in strength and conditioning. A cover letter of application, application form, resume, transcript, three letters of recommendation and essay are required. The award is based on grades, strength and conditioning experience, NSCA involvement, awards, community involvement, essay and recommendations.
Target applicants: Graduate school students. Adult students.
Amount: $1,500.
Number of awards: Varies.
Deadline: March 15.
How to apply: Application materials are described online.
Exclusive: Visit www.UltimateScholarshipBook.com and enter code NA114312 for updates on this award.

(1144) · Yanmar/SAE Scholarship

Society of Automotive Engineers International
400 Commonwealth Drive
Warrendale, PA 15096
Phone: 724-776-4841
Fax: 724-776-0790
Email: scholarships@sae.org
http://www.sae.org
Purpose: This scholarship is sponsored by the SAE Foundation and the Yanmar Diesel America Corporation.
Eligibility: Applicants must be entering their senior year of undergraduate engineering or enrolled in a postgraduate engineering or related science program. Applicants must also pursue a course of study or research related to the conservation of energy in transportation, agriculture and construction and power generation.
Target applicants: College students. Graduate school students. Adult students.
Amount: $1,000.
Number of awards: 1.
Scholarship may be renewable.
Deadline: February 15.
How to apply: Applications are available online.
Exclusive: Visit www.UltimateScholarshipBook.com and enter code SO114412 for updates on this award.

(1145) · Young Naturalist Awards

American Museum of Natural History
Central Park West at 79th Street
New York, NY 10024
Phone: 212-769-5100
Email: yna@amnh.org
http://www.amnh.org
Purpose: The Young Naturalist Awards is an inquiry-based research competition that challenges students in grades 7 to 12 to complete an investigation of the natural world. It encourages students to explore an area of science that interests them, typically in life science, Earth science, ecology or astronomy.
Eligibility: Applicants must be students in grade 7 through 12 who are currently enrolled in a public, private, parochial or home school in the United States, Canada, U.S. territories or in a U.S.-sponsored school abroad. Each essay is judged primarily on its scientific merits.
Target applicants: Junior high students or younger. High school students.
Amount: Up to $2,500.
Number of awards: 12.
Deadline: March 1.
How to apply: Applications are available online.
Exclusive: Visit www.UltimateScholarshipBook.com and enter code AM114512 for updates on this award.

(1146) • Youth Activity Grant

Explorers Club
46 E. 70th Street
New York, NY 10021
Phone: 212-628-8383
Fax: 212-288-4449
Email: youth@explorers.org
http://www.explorers.org

Purpose: To provide grants for high school and college students to research the natural sciences through field research.

Eligibility: Applicants must provide a three-page explanation of their project, be high school or college students and be U.S. residents. The grants allow students to conduct field research in the natural sciences under the supervision of a qualified scientist or institution.

Target applicants: High school students. College students. Adult students.

Amount: $500-$5,000.

Number of awards: Varies.

Deadline: December 15.

How to apply: Applications are available online.

Exclusive: Visit www.UltimateScholarshipBook.com and enter code EX114612 for updates on this award.

(1147) • Youth Incentive Award

Coleopterists Society
Dr. David G. Furth, Entomology, NHB, MRC 165
P.O. Box 37012
Smithsonian institution
Washington, DC 20013-7012
Phone: 202-633-0990
Fax: 202-786-2894
Email: furthd@si.edu
http://www.coleopsoc.org

Purpose: To recognize young people studying beetles.

Eligibility: Applicants should be coleopterists in grades 7-12 and submit individual proposals such as field collecting trips to conduct beetle species inventories or diversity studies, attending workshops or visiting entomology or natural history museums for training and projects on beetles, studying beetle biology, etc. Students are strongly encouraged to find an adult advisor (i.e., teacher, youth group leader, parent) to provide guidance in the proposal development, but the proposal must be written by the applicant. The Coleopterists Society can help establish contacts between applicants and professional coleopterists. The award is based on creativity, educational benefit to the applicant, scientific merit, feasibility and budget. There are two winners: one for grades 7-9 and one for grades 10-12.

Target applicants: Junior high students or younger. High school students.

Amount: Varies.

Number of awards: 2.

Deadline: November 15.

How to apply: Applications are available online.

Exclusive: Visit www.UltimateScholarshipBook.com and enter code CO114712 for updates on this award.

(1148) • Youth Program

Appaloosa Horse Club
Appaloosa Youth Foundation Scholarship Committee
2720 W. Pullman Road
Moscow, ID 83843
Phone: 208-882-5578
Fax: 208-882-8150
Email: acaap@appaloosa.com
http://www.appaloosa.com

Purpose: To reward student members of the Appaloosa Youth Association or the Appaloosa Horse Club who are pursuing higher education.

Eligibility: Applicants must be members of the Appaloosa Youth Association or the Appaloosa Horse Club and must attend or plan to attend an institute of higher learning.

Target applicants: High school students. College students. Graduate school students. Adult students.

Minimum GPA: 2.5

Amount: $1,000-$2,000.

Number of awards: Varies.

Scholarship may be renewable.

Deadline: June 1.

How to apply: Applications are available online.

Exclusive: Visit www.UltimateScholarshipBook.com and enter code AP114812 for updates on this award.

STATE OF RESIDENCE

(1149) · AAS Scholarship

T.E.A.C.H. Early Childhood OHIO
OCCRRA
6660 Doubletree Avenue
Suite 11
Columbus, OH 43229
Phone: 614-396-5959
Fax: 614-396-5960
Email: teach@occrra.org
http://teach.occrra.org

Purpose: To aid Ohio child care center employees who are pursuing an associate's degree in early childhood education.

Eligibility: Applicants must be employed at an Ohio child care center that has been given a one-, two- or three-star rating through the Step Up to Quality initiative. They must have held their position at the center for at least a year and must work there for 30 or more hours per week. They must earn less than $15 per hour and be enrolled in or planning to enroll in an associate's degree program in early childhood education. Scholarship recipients must agree to stay with the program for at least one year after winning the award. Selection is based on the overall strength of the application.

Target applicants: High school students. College students. Adult students.

Amount: Varies.

Number of awards: Varies.

Deadline: Varies.

How to apply: Applications are available online. An application form, recent pay stub, one recommendation letter, copy of center license and FAFSA information are required.

Exclusive: Visit www.UltimateScholarshipBook.com and enter code T.114912 for updates on this award.

(1150) · ABC Stores Jumpstart Scholarship

Hawaii Community Foundation - Scholarships
1164 Bishop Street, Suite 800
Honolulu, HI 96813
Phone: 888-731-3863
Fax: 808-521-6286
Email: scholarships@hcf-hawaii.org
http://www.hawaiicommunityfoundation.org

Purpose: To support employees of ABC Stores and their dependents.

Eligibility: Applicants must reside in Nevada, Hawaii, Guam or Saipan. Students must have at least a 2.7 GPA.

Target applicants: High school students. College students. Adult students.

Minimum GPA: 2.7

Amount: Varies.

Number of awards: Varies.

Deadline: March 1.

How to apply: To apply, register online, complete the online application and select the scholarships to which you wish to apply. In addition, mail the supporting materials: printed confirmation page from the online application, personal statement, copy of Student Aid Report (SAR) available at www.fafsa.ed.gov and official transcript.

Exclusive: Visit www.UltimateScholarshipBook.com and enter code HA115012 for updates on this award.

(1151) · Academic Challenge Scholarship

Arkansas Department of Higher Education
114 East Capitol
Little Rock, AR 72201-3818
Phone: 501-371-2050
Fax: 501-371-2001
Email: finaid@adhe.arknet.edu
http://www.adhe.edu/Pages/home.aspx

Purpose: To encourage Arkansas high school graduates to enroll in Arkansas colleges and universities.

Eligibility: Applicants must be graduating Arkansas high school seniors who meet academic minimum standards and income requirements.

Target applicants: High school students.

Minimum GPA: 2.25

Amount: $2,500-$5,000.

Number of awards: Varies.

Scholarship may be renewable.

Deadline: Varies.

How to apply: Applications are available through your high school counselor.

Exclusive: Visit www.UltimateScholarshipBook.com and enter code AR115112 for updates on this award.

(1152) · Academic Excellence Scholarship

State of Wisconsin Higher Educational Aids Board
P.O. Box 7885
Madison, WI 53707
Phone: 608-267-2206
Fax: 608-267-2808
Email: heabmail@wisconsin.gov
http://heab.state.wi.us

Purpose: To assist outstanding Wisconsin students who are planning to attend college in Wisconsin.

Eligibility: Applicants must be high school seniors who plan to enroll full-time at an eligible Wisconsin college or university. The award is given to the student with the highest GPA in each public and private Wisconsin high school.

Target applicants: High school students.

Amount: $2,250.

Number of awards: Varies.

Deadline: March 1.

How to apply: No application is required. Each high school designates the student who has the highest GPA of the graduating high school class.

Exclusive: Visit www.UltimateScholarshipBook.com and enter code ST115212 for updates on this award.

(1153) · Academic Scholars Program

Oklahoma State Regents for Higher Education
655 Research Parkway
Suite 200
Oklahoma City, OK 73104
Phone: 405-225-9100
Email: llangston@osrhe.edu
http://www.okhighered.org

Purpose: To assist students in attending Oklahoma colleges and universities.

Eligibility: Applicants can qualify for the program by being Oklahoma or out-of-state students who are named National Merit Scholars, National Merit Finalists or U.S. Presidential Scholars; by being Oklahoma residents who score above the 99.5 percentile on the SAT

or ACT or by being nominated by an Oklahoma public college or institution. Applicants must attend an Oklahoma college or university. Selection is based on academic merit.
Target applicants: High school students.
Amount: Varies.
Number of awards: Varies.
Scholarship may be renewable.
Deadline: Varies.
How to apply: Applications are available from the applicant's high school guidance counselor, by telephone request and online. An application form and supporting documents are required.
Exclusive: Visit www.UltimateScholarshipBook.com and enter code OK115312 for updates on this award.

(1154) • Access College Early Scholarship

Nebraska Coordinating Commission for Postsecondary Education
P.O. Box 95005
Lincoln, NE 68509
Phone: 402-471-2847
Fax: 402-471-2886
http://www.ccpe.state.ne.us
Purpose: To support Nebraska high school students who are enrolled in early college courses.
Eligibility: Applicants must demonstrate financial need through proof of participation in government aid programs or documentation of recent family hardships. They may be in any year of high school.
Target applicants: High school students.
Amount: Full tuition and fees.
Number of awards: Varies.
Scholarship may be renewable.
Deadline: Varies.
How to apply: Applications are available online.
Exclusive: Visit www.UltimateScholarshipBook.com and enter code NE115412 for updates on this award.

(1155) • Access to Better Learning and Education Grant Program

Florida Department of Education
Office of Student Financial Assistance
1940 N. Monroe Street
Suite 70
Tallahassee, FL 32303-4759
Phone: 888-827-2004
Fax: 850-245-9667
Email: osfa@fldoe.org
http://www.floridastudentfinancialaid.org
Purpose: To help undergraduate students from Florida who want to attend Florida private colleges or universities.
Eligibility: Applicants must be Florida residents for at least a year and first-time undergraduate students enrolled in degree programs (except theology or divinity degrees). Applicants must meet Florida's general state aid eligibility requirements. Participating institutions determine application procedures, deadlines and student eligibility.
Target applicants: High school students. College students. Adult students.
Amount: $986.
Number of awards: Varies.
Scholarship may be renewable.
Deadline: Varies.
How to apply: Contact the financial aid office at eligible Florida colleges and universities.
Exclusive: Visit www.UltimateScholarshipBook.com and enter code FL115512 for updates on this award.

(1156) • ACEC Colorado Scholarship Program

American Council of Engineering Companies of Colorado
800 Grant Street
Suite 100
Denver, CO 80203
Phone: 303-832-2200
Fax: 303-832-0400
Email: acec@acec-co.org
http://www.acec-co.org
Purpose: To support engineering students.
Eligibility: Applicants must be full-time students pursuing a bachelor's degree in engineering or surveying at an accredited college or university in Colorado. They must be entering their junior, senior or fifth year. Selection is based on GPA (28 percent), essay (25 percent), work experience (20 percent), recommendation (17 percent) and extracurricular activities (10 percent).
Target applicants: College students. Adult students.
Amount: Varies.
Number of awards: Varies.
Deadline: January 26.
How to apply: Applications are available online. An application form, transcript, essay and recommendation are required.
Exclusive: Visit www.UltimateScholarshipBook.com and enter code AM115612 for updates on this award.

(1157) • Ada Mucklestone Memorial Scholarship

American Legion Auxiliary, Department of Illinois
2720 E. Lincoln
Bloomington, IL 61704
Phone: 309-663-9366
Email: webmaster@illegion.org
http://illegion.org/index.shtml
Purpose: To provide financial aid to students who are children, grandchildren or great-grandchildren of veterans who are eligible for membership in the American Legion.
Eligibility: Students must be residents of Illinois who are in their senior year of high school or who have graduated but have not previously attended college. They must be children, grandchildren, or great-grandchildren of Armed Forces veterans who served during American Legion eligibility dates.
Target applicants: High school students.
Amount: $1,000.
Number of awards: Varies.
Deadline: March 15.
How to apply: Applications are available by mail.
Exclusive: Visit www.UltimateScholarshipBook.com and enter code AM115712 for updates on this award.

(1158) • Adobe Systems Computer Science Scholarships

Society of Women Engineers
120 South LaSalle Street
Suite 1515
Chicago, IL 60603
Phone: 877-793-4636
Email: scholarshipapplication@swe.org

http://www.swe.org
Purpose: To support female engineering students.
Eligibility: Applicants must be in their junior or senior year of an accredited engineering program. They must be U.S. citizens. A minimum GPA of 3.0 is required. Preference is given to students attending schools in the San Francisco Bay area.
Target applicants: College students. Adult students.
Minimum GPA: 3.0
Amount: $1,500-$2,000.
Number of awards: 2.
Deadline: February 15.
How to apply: Applications are available online. An application form, transcript and reference are required.
Exclusive: Visit www.UltimateScholarshipBook.com and enter code SO115812 for updates on this award.

(1159) • AFS Twin City Memorial Scholarship

Foundry Educational Foundation
1695 North Penny Lane
Schaumburg, IL 60173
Phone: 847-490-9200
Fax: 847-890-6270
Email: info@fefinc.org
http://www.fefinc.org
Purpose: To aid students from Minnesota, western Wisconsin and northern Iowa who are attending a Foundry Education Foundation (FEF) member school.
Eligibility: Applicants must be residents of Minnesota, western Wisconsin or northern Iowa. Preference will be given to students who are completing coursework in a foundry-related subject. Selection is based on the overall strength of the application.
Target applicants: College students. Adult students.
Amount: Varies.
Number of awards: Varies.
Deadline: October 8.
How to apply: Applications are available online. An application form and supporting materials are required.
Exclusive: Visit www.UltimateScholarshipBook.com and enter code FO115912 for updates on this award.

(1160) • AFS Wisconsin Past President Scholarship

Foundry Educational Foundation
1695 North Penny Lane
Schaumburg, IL 60173
Phone: 847-490-9200
Fax: 847-890-6270
Email: info@fefinc.org
http://www.fefinc.org
Purpose: To aid Wisconsin-area students who wish to pursue careers in the cast metal industry.
Eligibility: Students must be enrolled at an Foundry Educational Foundation (FEF) member school, a school located in Wisconsin or a school located in a state that is adjacent to Wisconsin. They also must have previous work experience, preferably in the cast metal industry. Selection is based on the student's academic record, his or her residential proximity to the AFS Wisconsin Chapter area, the proximity of the student's school to the AFS Wisconsin Chapter area, relevance of the student's degree program to the cast metal industry and relevant work experience.
Target applicants: High school students. College students. Adult students.
Amount: Varies.
Number of awards: Varies.
Deadline: December 15.
How to apply: Applications are available online. A completed FEF profile and supporting documents are required.
Exclusive: Visit www.UltimateScholarshipBook.com and enter code FO116012 for updates on this award.

(1161) • AGC of Massachusetts Scholarships

Associated General Contractors of Massachusetts
888 Worcester Street
Suite 40
Wellesley, MA 02482
Phone: 781-235-2680
Fax: 781-235-6020
Email: fristoe@agcmass.org
http://www.agcmass.org
Purpose: To aid Massachusetts residents who are college sophomores, juniors or seniors and who are enrolled in degree programs related to construction or civil engineering.
Eligibility: Applicants must be undergraduate sophomores or above at an accredited college or university. They must be legal residents of Massachusetts (though they may attend school outside of the state) and must be enrolled in a degree program related to construction or civil engineering. Selection is based on financial need and the overall strength of the application.
Target applicants: College students. Adult students.
Amount: $2,500-$7,500.
Number of awards: Over 100.
Scholarship may be renewable.
Deadline: November 1.
How to apply: Applications are available online. An application form and an official transcript are required.
Exclusive: Visit www.UltimateScholarshipBook.com and enter code AS116112 for updates on this award.

(1162) • Agnes M. Lindsay Scholarship

Massachusetts Department of Higher Education
Office of Student Financial Assistance
454 Broadway
Suite 200
Revere, MA 02151
Phone: 617-727-9420
Fax: 617-727-0667
Email: osfa@osfa.mass.edu
http://www.osfa.mass.edu/default.asp
Purpose: To provide assistance to Massachusetts students who are from rural parts of the state, demonstrate financial need and attend a Massachusetts public institution of higher education.
Eligibility: Applicants must be permanent Massachusetts residents for at least one year before the beginning of the academic year. Applicants must also be enrolled full-time in an undergraduate program and maintain satisfactory academic progress.
Target applicants: College students. Adult students.
Amount: Varies.
Number of awards: Varies.
Deadline: Varies.
How to apply: Applications are available by phone.
Exclusive: Visit www.UltimateScholarshipBook.com and enter code MA116212 for updates on this award.

(1163) • AIAA Alabama-Mississippi Section Engineering Scholarship

American Institute of Aeronautics and Astronautics-Alabama-Mississippi Section
P.O. Box 7208
Huntsville, AL 35807
Phone: 800-639-2422
Fax: 703-264-7551
http://www.al-ms-aiaa.org

Purpose: To support Alabama and Mississippi students who plan to prepare for careers in aeronautics and astronautics.
Eligibility: Applicants must be graduating high school seniors who are residents of Alabama or Mississippi. They must plan to attend an ABET-accredited university in Alabama or Mississippi and intend to major in an area of science or engineering that provides adequate preparation for a career in the aerospace industry. Selection is based on the overall strength of the student's application.
Target applicants: High school students.
Amount: $500-$1,500.
Number of awards: 3.
Deadline: May 21.
How to apply: Applications are available online. An application form, an essay and a transcript are required.
Exclusive: Visit www.UltimateScholarshipBook.com and enter code AM116312 for updates on this award.

(1164) • Aid for Part-Time Study

New York State Higher Education Services Corporation (HESC)
99 Washington Avenue
Albany, NY 12255
Phone: 888-697-4372
Email: hescwebmail@hesc.org
http://www.hesc.com/content.nsf/

Purpose: To assist part-time undergraduate students at New York State institutions.
Eligibility: Applicants must meet income eligibility requirements, be enrolled for at least 3 but less than 12 semester hours per semester or at least 4 but less than 8 semester hours per quarter in an eligible undergraduate program, be New York State residents and be U.S. citizens or eligible noncitizens. Tuition charges must exceed $100 per year, and once payments begin, students must maintain a C average.
Target applicants: High school students. College students. Adult students.
Amount: Up to $2,000.
Number of awards: Varies.
Scholarship may be renewable.
Deadline: Varies.
How to apply: Contact the financial aid office to receive an APTS application.
Exclusive: Visit www.UltimateScholarshipBook.com and enter code NE116412 for updates on this award.

(1165) • Alabama Concrete Industries Association Scholarships

Alabama Concrete Industries Association
2000 Southbridge Parkway
Suite 600
Birmingham, AL 35209
Phone: 205-908-4327
Email: dgreen@natcem.com
http://www.alconcrete.org

Purpose: To support students studying fields related to the concrete industry.
Eligibility: Applicants must be high school seniors, be accepted into an engineering college and pursue a degree in civil or structural engineering, architecture or studies related to the concrete construction/materials industry or attend a trade/technical school with course work related to the concrete construction industry or the concrete or masonry trades. They must be Alabama residents with a 2.5 or higher GPA.
Target applicants: High school students.
Minimum GPA: 2.5
Amount: $8,000.
Number of awards: 2.
Scholarship may be renewable.
Deadline: November 30.
How to apply: Applications are available from your school's guidance office. An application form, letter of recommendation and essay are required.
Exclusive: Visit www.UltimateScholarshipBook.com and enter code AL116512 for updates on this award.

(1166) • Alabama Student Grant Program

State of Alabama
Commission on Higher Education
100 N. Union Street
P.O. Box 302000
Montgomery, AL 36130-2000
Phone: 334-242-1998
Fax: 334-242-0268
http://www.ache.state.al.us

Purpose: To assist Alabama residents planning to attend colleges in the state.
Eligibility: Applicants must be Alabama residents attending or planning to attend Birmingham-Southern College, Concordia College, Faulkner University, Huntingdon College, Judson College, Miles College, Oakwood College, Samford University, Selma University, Southeastern Bible College, Southern Vocational College, Spring Hill College, Stillman College or the University of Mobile.
Target applicants: High school students. College students. Adult students.
Amount: Up to $1,200.
Number of awards: Varies.
Deadline: Varies.
How to apply: Contact the college financial aid office.
Exclusive: Visit www.UltimateScholarshipBook.com and enter code ST116612 for updates on this award.

(1167) • Alan Johnston Memorial Scholarship

Los Alamos National Laboratory Foundation
1302 Calle de la Merced
Suite A
Espanola, NM 87532
Phone: 505-753-8890
Fax: 505-753-8915
Email: info@lanlfoundation.org
http://www.lanlfoundation.org

Purpose: To support undergraduate students from Northern New Mexico.
Eligibility: Students must have at least a 3.25 GPA, and they must have either an SAT score of at least 1350 or an ACT score of at least 19. Applicants must submit an essay and two letters of recommendation.

Target applicants: High school students. College students. Adult students.
Minimum GPA: 3.25
Amount: $1,000.
Number of awards: Varies.
Deadline: January 18.
How to apply: Applications are available online.
Exclusive: Visit www.UltimateScholarshipBook.com and enter code LO116712 for updates on this award.

(1168) • Albert E. and Florence W. Newton Nursing Scholarship

Rhode Island Foundation
One Union Station
Providence, RI 02903
Phone: 401-274-4564
Fax: 401-331-8085
Email: lmonahan@rifoundation.org
http://www.rifoundation.org
Purpose: To aid undergraduate nursing students.
Eligibility: Applicants must be undergraduate students seeking a diploma or degree in nursing. They must demonstrate financial need. Preference will be given to Rhode Island residents. Selection is based on academic merit and financial need.
Target applicants: College students. Adult students.
Amount: $500-$2,000.
Number of awards: Varies.
Scholarship may be renewable.
Deadline: April 16.
How to apply: Applications are available online. An application form and supporting materials are required.
Exclusive: Visit www.UltimateScholarshipBook.com and enter code RH116812 for updates on this award.

(1169) • Albert H. Hix. W8AH Memorial Scholarship

American Radio Relay League Foundation
225 Main Street
Newington, CT 06111
Phone: 860-594-0397
Fax: 860-594-0259
Email: foundation@arrl.org
http://www.arrlf.org
Purpose: To provide scholarship assistance to amateur radio operators who are from the West Virginia Section or Roanoke Division or who are attending school in the West Virginia section.
Eligibility: Applicants must hold a General Class or higher Amateur Radio License and have a GPA of 3.0 or higher.
Target applicants: High school students. College students. Adult students.
Minimum GPA: 3.0
Amount: $500.
Number of awards: 1.
Deadline: February 1.
How to apply: Applications are available online.
Exclusive: Visit www.UltimateScholarshipBook.com and enter code AM116912 for updates on this award.

(1170) • Albert M. Lappin Scholarship

American Legion, Department of Kansas
1314 SW Topeka Boulevard
Topeka, KS 66612
Phone: 785-232-9315
Fax: 785-232-1399
http://www.ksamlegion.org
Purpose: To assist the education of needy and worthy children of American Legion and American Legion Auxiliary members.
Eligibility: Applicants must be high school seniors or college freshmen or sophomores who are average or better students. They must be the son or daughter of a veteran and enrolling or enrolled in a post-secondary school in Kansas. A parent must have been a member of the Kansas American Legion or American Legion Auxiliary for the previous three years. In addition, the children of deceased parents are eligible if the parent was a paid member at the time of death. Applicants must submit a 1040 income statement, documentation of parent's veteran status, three letters of recommendation with only one from a teacher, an essay on the topic of "Why I Want to Go to College" and a high school transcript. Applicants must maintain a C average in college and verify enrollment at the start of each semester.
Target applicants: High school students. College students. Adult students.
Amount: $1,000.
Number of awards: 1.
Deadline: February 15.
How to apply: Applications are available online.
Exclusive: Visit www.UltimateScholarshipBook.com and enter code AM117012 for updates on this award.

(1171) • Albert Yanni Scholarship Program

West Virginia Department of Education
Building 6, Room 243
1900 Kanawha Boulevard E.
Charleston, WV 25305
Phone: 304-558-3897
Email: gcoulson@access.k12.wv.us
http://wvde.state.wv.us
Purpose: To provide incentives and encouragement for career and technical students to pursue higher education.
Eligibility: Applicants must be public high school seniors in West Virginia who rank in the top quarter of their class or have an unweighted GPA of 3.0 or higher. They must have completed four or more units in a single technical concentration, have no final semester grades below a C and plan to pursue higher education in a career field related to their technical concentration.
Target applicants: High school students.
Minimum GPA: 3.0
Amount: $2,000.
Number of awards: Up to 20.
Deadline: March 31.
How to apply: Applications are available online.
Exclusive: Visit www.UltimateScholarshipBook.com and enter code WE117112 for updates on this award.

(1172) • Albuquerque ARC/Toby Cross Scholarship

American Radio Relay League Foundation
225 Main Street
Newington, CT 06111
Phone: 860-594-0397
Fax: 860-594-0259

Email: foundation@arrl.org
http://www.arrlf.org
Purpose: To provide financial assistance to amateur radio operators.
Eligibility: Applicants must be New Mexico residents who hold an amateur radio license. They should be candidates for undergraduate degrees.
Target applicants: High school students. College students. Adult students.
Amount: $500.
Number of awards: 1.
Deadline: February 1.
How to apply: Applications are available online.
Exclusive: Visit www.UltimateScholarshipBook.com and enter code AM117212 for updates on this award.

(1173) • Alert Scholarship

Alert Magazine
P.O. Box 4833
Boise, ID 83711
Phone: 208-375-7911
Fax: 208-376-0770
http://www.alertmagazine.org
Purpose: To promote the prevention of drug and alcohol abuse.
Eligibility: Scholarships are awarded for the best editorials on the prevention of drug and alcohol abuse. Winning editorials will be published in Alert Magazine. Applicants must be high school students between the ages of 18 and 19 and residents of Colorado, Idaho, Montana, North Dakota, South Dakota, Washington or Wyoming.
Target applicants: High school students.
Minimum GPA: 2.5
Amount: $500.
Number of awards: Varies.
Deadline: Ongoing.
How to apply: No application necessary.
Exclusive: Visit www.UltimateScholarshipBook.com and enter code AL117312 for updates on this award.

(1174) • All Iowa Opportunity Scholarship

Iowa College Student Aid Commission
200 10th Street, 4th Floor
Des Moines, IA 50309
Phone: 515-242-3344
Fax: 515-242-3388
Email: info@iowacollegeaid.org
http://www.iowacollegeaid.org
Purpose: To recognize Iowa's top students.
Eligibility: Applicants must be Iowa residents who have a minimum 2.5 GPA and demonstrate financial need. Awards may only be used at eligible Iowa institutions. Selection is based on class rank and standardized test scores.
Target applicants: High school students.
Minimum GPA: 2.5
Amount: Up to full tuition.
Number of awards: Varies.
Deadline: March 1.
How to apply: Applications are available online.
Exclusive: Visit www.UltimateScholarshipBook.com and enter code IO117412 for updates on this award.

(1175) • Allan Eldin and Agnes Sutorik Geiger Scholarship Fund

Hawaii Community Foundation - Scholarships
1164 Bishop Street, Suite 800
Honolulu, HI 96813
Phone: 888-731-3863
Fax: 808-521-6286
Email: scholarships@hcf-hawaii.org
http://www.hawaiicommunityfoundation.org
Purpose: To support Hawaii students who are pursuing degrees in veterinary science.
Eligibility: Students must have at least a 3.0 GPA.
Target applicants: High school students. College students. Adult students.
Minimum GPA: 3.0
Amount: Varies.
Number of awards: Varies.
Deadline: March 1.
How to apply: To apply, register online, complete the online application and select the scholarships to which you wish to apply. In addition, mail the supporting materials: printed confirmation page from the online application, personal statement, copy of Student Aid Report (SAR) available at www.fafsa.ed.gov and official transcript.
Exclusive: Visit www.UltimateScholarshipBook.com and enter code HA117512 for updates on this award.

(1176) • Allen W. Plumb Scholarship

New Hampshire Land Surveyors Foundation
77 Main Street
P.O. Box 689
Raymond, NH 03077
Phone: 603-895-4822
Fax: 603-462-0343
Email: info@nhlsa.org
http://www.nhlsa.org
Purpose: To aid college forestry majors who are New Hampshire residents and who plan to pursue careers in land surveying.
Eligibility: Applicants must be college sophomores, juniors or seniors who are residents of New Hampshire. They must be enrolled in a forestry program at a two-year or four-year institution, and they must intend to become professional land surveyors. Selection is based on academic achievement in any surveying coursework that the student has completed.
Target applicants: College students. Adult students.
Amount: $2,000.
Number of awards: Varies.
Deadline: November 5.
How to apply: Applications are available online. An application form, a transcript, an essay and three letters of recommendation are required.
Exclusive: Visit www.UltimateScholarshipBook.com and enter code NE117612 for updates on this award.

(1177) • Allied Health Care Professional Scholarship Program

Illinois Department of Public Health
535 W. Jefferson Street
Springfield, IL 62761
Phone: 217-782-4977
Fax: 217-782-3987
Email: dph.mailus@illinois.gov

http://www.idph.state.il.us
Purpose: To encourage more nurse practitioners, physician assistants and certified nurse midwives to set up practices in rural areas of Illinois.
Eligibility: Applicants must be accepted to or currently enrolled in an accredited Illinois school to become a nurse practitioner, physician assistant or certified nurse midwife. Students must demonstrate financial need, and they may be full-time or part-time students as long as part-time students are enrolled for at least a third of the hours required to be a full-time student. Scholarship recipients agree to set up their practice in designated shortage areas after graduation.
Target applicants: High school students. College students. Graduate school students. Adult students.
Amount: $7,500.
Number of awards: Varies.
Scholarship may be renewable.
Deadline: June 30.
How to apply: Applications are available online.
Exclusive: Visit www.UltimateScholarshipBook.com and enter code IL117712 for updates on this award.

(1178) · Allied Healthcare Scholarship Program

California Health and Welfare Agency - Office of Statewide Health Planning and Development
Health Professions Education Foundation
818 K Street, Room 210
Sacramento, CA 95814
Phone: 916-324-6500
Fax: 916-324-6585
Email: hpef@oshpd.state.ca.us
http://www.healthprofessions.ca.gov
Purpose: To increase the number of allied healthcare professional working in medically underserved areas of California.
Eligibility: Applicants must be enrolled in a California community college or university and be studying one of the following programs: medical imaging, occupational therapy, physical therapy, respiratory care, social work, pharmacy and diagnostic medical sonography, pharmacy technician, medical laboratory technologist, surgical technician or ultrasound technician. Those selected will complete a one-year service contract or work volunteer hours in a medically underserved area of California. Financial need, work experience, academic achievement and community involvement are considered. Preference is given to those who expect to graduate within two years of application.
Target applicants: College students. Graduate school students. Adult students.
Amount: Up to $4,000.
Number of awards: Varies.
Scholarship may be renewable.
Deadline: September 11.
How to apply: Applications are available online.
Exclusive: Visit www.UltimateScholarshipBook.com and enter code CA117812 for updates on this award.

(1179) · Alma White - Delta Kappa Gamma Scholarship

Hawaii Community Foundation - Scholarships
1164 Bishop Street, Suite 800
Honolulu, HI 96813
Phone: 888-731-3863
Fax: 808-521-6286
Email: scholarships@hcf-hawaii.org
http://www.hawaiicommunityfoundation.org
Purpose: To support students in Hawaii who are planning careers in teaching.
Eligibility: Applicants must be majoring in education. Students must be a college junior, college senior or graduate student.
Target applicants: College students. Graduate school students. Adult students.
Amount: Varies.
Number of awards: Varies.
Deadline: March 1.
How to apply: To apply, register online, complete the online application and select the scholarships to which you wish to apply. In addition, mail the supporting materials: printed confirmation page from the online application, personal statement, copy of Student Aid Report (SAR) available at www.fafsa.ed.gov and official transcript.
Exclusive: Visit www.UltimateScholarshipBook.com and enter code HA117912 for updates on this award.

(1180) · Alpha Gamma Rho 4-H Scholarship

Michigan 4-H Youth Development
Children, Youth, Families and Communities
Michigan State University Extension
160 Agriculture Hall
East Lansing, MI 48824
Phone: 517-432-7575
Fax: 517-355-6748
Email: msue4h@msu.edu
http://web1.msue.msu.edu/cyf/youth/index.html
Purpose: To help entering and current Michigan State University students who have participated in 4-H and who are majoring in a subject that is related to the food, fiber and life sciences industry.
Eligibility: Applicants must be high school seniors or college freshmen, sophomores or juniors who are or who plan to enroll at Michigan State University. They must have at least one year of participation in 4-H, and they must pursue degrees in subjects related to the food, fiber and life sciences industry. Selection is based on 4-H achievements, academic success and leadership experience.
Target applicants: High school students. College students. Adult students.
Amount: $400.
Number of awards: 1.
Deadline: December 1.
How to apply: Applications are available online. An application form, essay and one recommendation letter are required.
Exclusive: Visit www.UltimateScholarshipBook.com and enter code MI118012 for updates on this award.

(1181) · Alpha Omichron #2520 Chapter President's Honorarium

Epsilon Sigma Alpha Foundation
P.O. Box 270517
Fort Collins, CO 80527
Phone: 970-223-2824
Fax: 970-223-4456
Email: kloyd@knoxy.net
http://www.esaintl.com/esaf
Purpose: To provide funds for the education of Maricopa County, Arizona residents.
Eligibility: Applicants may pursue any major at any school in the United States. Selection of applicants is based on character, leadership, service, financial need and scholastic ability, each having equal bearing.

Target applicants: High school students. College students. Adult students.
Amount: $500.
Number of awards: 1.
Deadline: February 1.
How to apply: Applications are available online.
Exclusive: Visit www.UltimateScholarshipBook.com and enter code EP118112 for updates on this award.

(1182) • Alpha Upsilon #1884 - Oregon Scholarship

Epsilon Sigma Alpha Foundation
P.O. Box 270517
Fort Collins, CO 80527
Phone: 970-223-2824
Fax: 970-223-4456
Email: kloyd@knoxy.net
http://www.esaintl.com/esaf
Purpose: To provide financial assistance to residents of Hillsboro, Oregon.
Eligibility: Applicants may attend any school and pursue any major. Selection of applicants is based equally on character, leadership, service, financial need and scholastic ability.
Target applicants: High school students. College students. Adult students.
Amount: $1,000.
Number of awards: 1.
Deadline: February 1.
How to apply: Applications are available online.
Exclusive: Visit www.UltimateScholarshipBook.com and enter code EP118212 for updates on this award.

(1183) • American Association of Japanese University Women Scholarship Program

American Association of Japanese University Women
Masako Mera
445 Surfview Drive
Pacific Palisades, CA 90272
Phone: 310-230-7860
Email: scholarship@aajuw.org
http://www.aajuw.org
Purpose: To support female students who demonstrate leadership and facilitate cultural relationships.
Eligibility: Applicants must be starting their junior or senior year in college or be in graduate school at a California school. They must be able to attend the awards ceremony in Los Angeles at their own expense. Students must also submit an essay showing how their studies will contribute to leadership or to the relationship between the United States and Japan.
Target applicants: College students. Graduate school students. Adult students.
Amount: $1,500.
Number of awards: 2.
Deadline: October 31.
How to apply: Applications are available online.
Exclusive: Visit www.UltimateScholarshipBook.com and enter code AM118312 for updates on this award.

(1184) • American Council of Engineering Companies of New Jersey Member Organization Scholarship

American Council of Engineering Companies of New Jersey
66 Morris Avenue
Springfield, NJ 07081
Phone: 973-564-5848
Fax: 973-564-7480
Email: barbara@cecnj.org
http://www.cecnj.org
Purpose: To help students who are enrolled in engineering or accredited land surveying degree programs.
Eligibility: Applicants must be rising undergraduate juniors or above enrolled in an ABET-accredited bachelor's degree program in engineering, a master's degree program in engineering, a doctoral degree program in engineering or an accredited land surveying program. Master's students must either be enrolled in an ABET-accredited program or must hold a bachelor's degree in engineering from an ABET-accredited school. Doctoral students must hold either an ABET-accredited bachelor's degree or an ABET-accredited master's degree in engineering. They must be U.S. citizens. Selection is based on GPA, personal essay, recommendation letter, work experience and extracurricular involvement.
Target applicants: College students. Graduate school students. Adult students.
Amount: Varies.
Number of awards: 3.
Deadline: November 20.
How to apply: Applications are available online. An application form, a personal essay, an official transcript and one recommendation form are required.
Exclusive: Visit www.UltimateScholarshipBook.com and enter code AM118412 for updates on this award.

(1185) • American Council of Engineering Companies of South Dakota Scholarship

American Council of Engineering Companies of South Dakota
P.O. Box 398
Rapid City, SD 57709
Phone: 605-394-6674
Email: contact@cecsd.org
http://www.cecsd.org
Purpose: To assist South Dakota college undergraduates who are studying engineering.
Eligibility: Applicants must be rising undergraduate juniors, seniors or fifth-year students enrolled in a civil, electrical or mechanical engineering program. They must be enrolled at a South Dakota school and must be interested in pursuing a career in consulting engineering. Selection is based on GPA, recommendation form, personal essay, work experience, extracurricular activities and community involvement.
Target applicants: College students. Adult students.
Amount: $1,000.
Number of awards: 1.
Scholarship may be renewable.
Deadline: December 31.
How to apply: Applications are available online. An application form, a personal essay and one recommendation form are required.
Exclusive: Visit www.UltimateScholarshipBook.com and enter code AM118512 for updates on this award.

(1186) • American Essay Contest Scholarship

American Legion Auxiliary, Department of Illinois
2720 E. Lincoln
Bloomington, IL 61704
Phone: 309-663-9366
Email: webmaster@illegion.org
http://illegion.org/index.shtml

Purpose: To award outstanding 500-word essays written on assigned topics.
Eligibility: Applicants must be enrolled in an Illinois school in grades eight to twelve.
Target applicants: Junior high students or younger. High school students.
Amount: $100-$1,200.
Number of awards: Varies.
Deadline: February 4.
How to apply: Application information is available by contacting the local American Legion Unit or Auxiliary.
Exclusive: Visit www.UltimateScholarshipBook.com and enter code AM118612 for updates on this award.

(1187) • American Indian Endowed Scholarship

Washington Higher Education Coordinating Board
917 Lakeridge Way
P.O. Box 43430
Olympia, WA 98504
Phone: 360-753-7850
Fax: 360-753-6243
Email: info@hecb.wa.gov
http://www.hecb.wa.gov

Purpose: To help students who have ties to the Native American community and have financial need pay for higher education.
Eligibility: Applicants must have financial need according to a completed Free Application for Federal Student Aid (FAFSA), be residents of Washington state and enroll full-time as an undergraduate or graduate in an eligible program.
Target applicants: High school students. College students. Graduate school students. Adult students.
Amount: $500-$2,000.
Number of awards: Approximately 15.
Scholarship may be renewable.
Deadline: February 1.
How to apply: Applications are available online.
Exclusive: Visit www.UltimateScholarshipBook.com and enter code WA118712 for updates on this award.

(1188) • American Institute of Graphic Arts (AIGA) Honolulu Chapter Scholarship Fund

Hawaii Community Foundation - Scholarships
1164 Bishop Street, Suite 800
Honolulu, HI 96813
Phone: 888-731-3863
Fax: 808-521-6286
Email: scholarships@hcf-hawaii.org
http://www.hawaiicommunityfoundation.org

Purpose: To support students who are majoring in graphic design, visual communication or commercial arts.
Eligibility: Students must be residents of Hawaii.
Target applicants: High school students. College students. Adult students.
Amount: Varies.
Number of awards: Varies.
Deadline: March 1.
How to apply: To apply, register online, complete the online application and select the scholarships to which you wish to apply. In addition, mail the supporting materials: printed confirmation page from the online application, personal statement, copy of Student Aid Report (SAR) available at www.fafsa.ed.gov and official transcript.
Exclusive: Visit www.UltimateScholarshipBook.com and enter code HA118812 for updates on this award.

(1189) • American Justice Essay Scholarship

Washington State Trial Lawyers Association
1809 7th Avenue #1500
Seattle, WA 98101-1328
Phone: 206-464-1011
Fax: 206-464-0703
Email: wstla@wstla.org
http://www.wstla.org

Purpose: To promote awareness of the role that the civil justice system plays in society through an essay contest.
Eligibility: Applicants must be attending high school in the state of Washington and must subsequently attend college in order to receive the scholarship. Essays must be four to five pages and be on the given topic on advocacy in the American justice system.
Target applicants: High school students.
Amount: $1,000-$3,000.
Number of awards: 3.
Deadline: March 18.
How to apply: Applications are available online.
Exclusive: Visit www.UltimateScholarshipBook.com and enter code WA118912 for updates on this award.

(1190) • American Legion Auxiliary, Department of California $1,000 Scholarships

American Legion Auxiliary, Department of California
401 Van Ness Avenue
Room 113
San Francisco, CA 94102
Phone: 415-861-5092
Fax: 415-861-8365
Email: calegionaux@calegionaux.org
http://www.calegionaux.org

Purpose: To provide support to the children of U.S. Armed Forces members.
Eligibility: One of applicant's parents must have served in the U.S. Armed Forces during an eligible period. Applicants must be California resident high school seniors or graduates who have had to postpone school due to health or financial reasons and plan to attend a California college or university. Applicants must also demonstrate financial need.
Target applicants: High school students. College students. Adult students.
Amount: $1,000.
Number of awards: 4.
Deadline: March 16.
How to apply: Applications are available online.
Exclusive: Visit www.UltimateScholarshipBook.com and enter code AM119012 for updates on this award.

(1191) • American Legion Auxiliary, Department of California $2,000 Scholarships

American Legion Auxiliary, Department of California
401 Van Ness Avenue
Room 113
San Francisco, CA 94102
Phone: 415-861-5092
Fax: 415-861-8365
Email: calegionaux@calegionaux.org
http://www.calegionaux.org

Purpose: To provide support to children of U.S. Armed Forces members.
Eligibility: One of applicant's parents must have served in the U.S. Armed Forces during an eligible period. Applicants must attend a California college or university, be California resident high school seniors or graduates who have not begun college because of illness or need and demonstrate need.
Target applicants: High school students. College students. Adult students.
Amount: $2,000.
Number of awards: 1.
Deadline: March 16.
How to apply: Applications are available online.
Exclusive: Visit www.UltimateScholarshipBook.com and enter code AM119112 for updates on this award.

(1192) • American Legion Auxiliary, Department of California $500 Scholarships

American Legion Auxiliary, Department of California
401 Van Ness Avenue
Room 113
San Francisco, CA 94102
Phone: 415-861-5092
Fax: 415-861-8365
Email: calegionaux@calegionaux.org
http://www.calegionaux.org

Purpose: To provide support to the children of U.S. Armed Forces members.
Eligibility: One of applicant's parents must have served in the U.S. Armed Forces during an eligible period. Applicants must be California resident high school seniors or graduates who have had to postpone school due to health or financial reasons and plan to attend a California college or university. Applicants must also demonstrate financial need.
Target applicants: High school students. College students. Adult students.
Amount: $500.
Number of awards: 3.
Deadline: March 16.
How to apply: Applications are available online.
Exclusive: Visit www.UltimateScholarshipBook.com and enter code AM119212 for updates on this award.

(1193) • American Legion Department of Arkansas High School Oratorical Scholarship Program

American Legion, Department of Arkansas
Department Oratorical Chairman, Roger Lacy
P.O. Box 3280
Little Rock, AR 72203
Phone: 501-375-1104
Fax: 501-375-4236
Email: alegion@swbell.net
http://www.arlegion.org/Oratorical.html

Purpose: To enhance high school students' experience with and understanding of the U.S. Constitution. The contest will help develop students' leadership skills and civic appreciation, as well as the ability to deliver thoughtful, insightful orations regarding U.S. citizenship and its inherent responsibilities.
Eligibility: Applicants must be high school students under the age of 20 who are U.S. citizens or legal residents and residents of the state. Students first give an oration within their state and winners compete at the national level. The oration must be related to the Constitution of the United States focusing on the duties and obligations citizens have to the government. It must be in English and be between eight and ten minutes. There is also an assigned topic which is posted on the website, and it should be between three and five minutes.
Target applicants: High school students.
Amount: $2,000.
Number of awards: 3.
Deadline: December 15.
How to apply: Applications are available online.
Exclusive: Visit www.UltimateScholarshipBook.com and enter code AM119312 for updates on this award.

(1194) • American Legion Department of Florida General Scholarship

American Legion, Department of Florida
P.O. Box 547859
Orlando, FL 32854
Phone: 407-295-2631
Fax: 407-299-0901
http://www.floridalegion.org

Purpose: To support descendents of American Legion members and deceased veterans.
Eligibility: Applicants must be direct descendents of American Legion Department of Florida members in good standing or deceased U.S. veterans who would have been eligible for membership. They must be seniors at accredited Florida high schools who plan to pursue undergraduate study upon graduation. Funds must be used within four years of graduation, excluding active military service.
Target applicants: High school students.
Amount: Varies.
Number of awards: Varies.
Deadline: March 1.
How to apply: Applications are available online. An application form and copy of documentation of veteran's service are required.
Exclusive: Visit www.UltimateScholarshipBook.com and enter code AM119412 for updates on this award.

(1195) • American Savings Bank Scholarship Program

Hawaii Community Foundation - Scholarships
1164 Bishop Street, Suite 800
Honolulu, HI 96813
Phone: 888-731-3863
Fax: 808-521-6286
Email: scholarships@hcf-hawaii.org
http://www.hawaiicommunityfoundation.org

Purpose: To assist Hawaii high school graduates with college expenses at state schools.
Eligibility: Applicants must be entering college freshmen and demonstrate scholastic aptitude, leadership, financial need and character. Four scholarships are awarded, one for the University of Hawaii College System, one for Chaminade University of Honolulu, one for Brigham Young University-Hawaii Campus and one for Hawaii Pacific University.

Applicants must be full-time students and must have a minimum 3.0 GPA. The award is renewable and includes an offer of a paid internship.
Target applicants: High school students.
Minimum GPA: 3.0
Amount: $5,000.
Number of awards: 4.
Scholarship may be renewable.
Deadline: March 1.
How to apply: Applications are available at any American Savings Branch.
Exclusive: Visit www.UltimateScholarshipBook.com and enter code HA119512 for updates on this award.

(1196) • American Society of Travel Agents (ASTA) Pacific Northwest Chapter-William Hunt Undergraduate Scholarship

Tourism Cares
275 Turnpike Street
Suite 307
Canton, MA 02021
Phone: 781-821-5990
Fax: 781-821-8949
Email: carolynv@tourismcares.org
http://www.tourismcares.org
Purpose: To aid Alaska, Idaho, Montana, Oregon and Washington residents who are studying travel, tourism and hospitality at the undergraduate level.
Eligibility: Applicants must be permanent residents of Montana, Alaska, Oregon, Idaho or Washington and must be undergraduate students who are enrolled at an accredited postsecondary institution located in the U.S. or Canada. They must be entering the second year of a two-year program or entering the third or fourth year of a four-year program. By May of the application year, they must have completed 30 or more credits if in a two-year program or 60 or more credits if in a four-year program. They must be studying hospitality, tourism or travel and have a GPA of 3.0 or higher on a four-point scale. Selection is based on the overall strength of the application.
Target applicants: College students. Adult students.
Minimum GPA: 3.0
Amount: $1,500.
Number of awards: 2.
Deadline: April 15.
How to apply: Applications are available online. An application form, personal essay, proof of residency, a resume, an official transcript and two letters of recommendation are required.
Exclusive: Visit www.UltimateScholarshipBook.com and enter code TO119612 for updates on this award.

(1197) • Americanism and Government Test Program

American Legion, Department of Wisconsin
2930 American Legion Drive
P.O. Box 388
Portage, WI 53901
Phone: 608-745-1090
Fax: 608-745-0179
Email: info@wilegion.org
http://www.wilegion.org
Purpose: To award outstanding performance on the Americanism and Government Test, a 50-question examination based on state and federal government and history.
Eligibility: Participants must be enrolled in a Wisconsin high school and in their sophomore, junior or senior year.
Target applicants: High school students.
Amount: $250-$500.
Number of awards: 32.
Deadline: Varies.
How to apply: Application information is available by contacting your local principal, teacher or guidance counselor.
Exclusive: Visit www.UltimateScholarshipBook.com and enter code AM119712 for updates on this award.

(1198) • Angie M. Houtz Memorial Fund Scholarship

Angie M. Houtz Memorial Fund
P.O. Box 634
Olney, MD 20830-0634
Email: angiefund@yahoo.com
http://www.theangiefund.com/
Purpose: To honor the memory of Angie Houtz, victim of the September 11, 2001 attack on the Pentagon.
Eligibility: Applicants must attend or be accepted to attend a public college in Maryland full-time. They must have an unweighted GPA of 3.0 or higher and have participated in at least 200 hours of community service. They cannot be related to a member of the scholarship fund's board of directors.
Target applicants: High school students. College students. Adult students.
Minimum GPA: 3.0
Amount: $3,000.
Number of awards: At least 1.
Deadline: April 1.
How to apply: Applications are available online.
Exclusive: Visit www.UltimateScholarshipBook.com and enter code AN119812 for updates on this award.

(1199) • Ann Arbor AWC Scholarship for Women in Computing

Association for Women in Computing-Ann Arbor Chapter
P.O. Box 1864
Ann Arbor, MI 48106
Email: students@awc-aa.org
http://www.awc-aa.org
Purpose: To aid Michigan women pursuing education for careers in computing.
Eligibility: Applicants must be female Michigan residents who are studying to prepare for or further their careers in technology and computing at an accredited institution of higher learning. They must be U.S. citizens or permanent residents. Degree-seeking candidates must have at least two semesters of coursework remaining before completion of their educational programs. Applicants seeking a computer certification must apply the scholarship to tuition or course fees only. Selection is based on the strength of essay responses and on the level of involvement in the computing community.
Target applicants: High school students. College students. Adult students.
Amount: Varies.
Number of awards: Varies.
Deadline: April 30.
How to apply: Applications are available online. An application form, three personal essays, a resume and two letters of recommendation are required.

Exclusive: Visit www.UltimateScholarshipBook.com and enter code AS119912 for updates on this award.

(1200) • Antonio Cirino Memorial Art Education Fellowship

Rhode Island Foundation
One Union Station
Providence, RI 02903
Phone: 401-274-4564
Fax: 401-331-8085
Email: lmonahan@rifoundation.org
http://www.rifoundation.org
Purpose: To support Rhode Island students who are pursuing careers in art education.
Eligibility: Applicants must demonstrate an interest in learning about and practicing art. Preference will be given to visual artists. Students must be enrolled or planning to enroll in a master's or doctoral program that will lead to a career in art education.
Target applicants: Graduate school students. Adult students.
Amount: $2,000-$10,000.
Number of awards: Varies.
Scholarship may be renewable.
Deadline: June 15.
How to apply: Applications are available online.
Exclusive: Visit www.UltimateScholarshipBook.com and enter code RH120012 for updates on this award.

(1201) • Archibald Rutledge Scholarship Program

South Carolina State Department of Education
1429 Senate Street
Room 701-A
Columbia, SC 29201
Phone: 803-734-8116
http://ed.sc.gov
Purpose: To support students who exhibit academic and artistic excellence.
Eligibility: Applicants must be high school seniors in South Carolina public schools, have attended South Carolina public schools for the past two consecutive years and be U.S. citizens. There are four categories: creative writing, drama, music and visual arts. For the creative writing category, a sonnet, lyric or narrative poem no longer than one page must be submitted. For the drama category, an original, short, one-act play with a performing time of 20 to 45 minutes must be submitted. For the music category, an original composition of three to five minutes must be submitted. For the visual arts category, an original visual composition must be submitted. Compositions are judged on creativity, originality and quality of expression and content.
Target applicants: High school students.
Amount: $2,000.
Number of awards: 5.
Deadline: February 4.
How to apply: Applications are available online. An application form, composition and process folio are required.
Exclusive: Visit www.UltimateScholarshipBook.com and enter code SO120112 for updates on this award.

(1202) • Arizona BPW Foundation Annual Scholarships

Arizona Business and Professional Women's Foundation
P.O. Box 32596
Phoenix, AZ 85064
http://www.arizonabpwfoundation.com/scholarships.html
Purpose: To provide education assistance to women.
Eligibility: Applicants must be women who are returning to school to broaden their job prospects at a community college in Arizona. They must provide a career goal statement, financial need statement, most recent transcript, most recent income tax return and two letters of recommendation.
Target applicants: College students. Adult students.
Amount: Varies.
Number of awards: Varies.
Deadline: March 1.
How to apply: Applications are available online.
Exclusive: Visit www.UltimateScholarshipBook.com and enter code AR120212 for updates on this award.

(1203) • Arizona Chapter MOAA Educational Scholarships

Military Officers Association of American-Arizona Chapter
4333 W. Echo Lane
Glendale, AZ 85302
Phone: 623-931-1546
Email: terrytassin@cox.net
http://www.azchaptermoaa.org
Purpose: To provide educational assistance to JROTC graduates.
Eligibility: Applicants must be in the next-to-last year of a JROTC program. They must be in good academic standing and demonstrate loyalty and potential for military leadership. They must attend a high school sponsored by the Arizona Chapter of MOAA.
Target applicants: High school students.
Amount: Varies.
Number of awards: Varies.
Deadline: Varies.
How to apply: Applications are available online.
Exclusive: Visit www.UltimateScholarshipBook.com and enter code MI120312 for updates on this award.

(1204) • Arizona Network of Executive Women in Hospitality Scholarship Awards

Network of Executive Women in Hospitality, Arizona
930 E. Canyon Way
Chandler, AZ 85249
Phone: 800-593-6394
Fax: 800-693-6394
Email: trusha1979@yahoo.com
http://www.newh.org
Purpose: To support Arizona students wishing to enter the hospitality industry.
Eligibility: Applicants must be enrolled in a degree or certification program for which they have completed half of the requirements. They must plan to pursue a career in the hospitality industry including hotel/restaurant management, culinary/foodservice, architecture or interior design. Financial need and a 3.0 or higher GPA are required.
Target applicants: College students. Adult students.
Minimum GPA: 3.0
Amount: Varies.
Number of awards: Varies.
Deadline: October 1.
How to apply: Applications are available online. An application form, essay, transcript and letters of recommendation are required.

Exclusive: Visit www.UltimateScholarshipBook.com and enter code NE120412 for updates on this award.

(1205) · Arizona Non-Traditional Education for Women Scholarships

Arizona Business and Professional Women's Foundation
P.O. Box 32596
Phoenix, AZ 85064
http://www.arizonabpwfoundation.com/scholarships.html
Purpose: To provide assistance for women pursuing male-dominated career paths.
Eligibility: Applicants must be returning to school to pursue a career in an occupation in which 25 percent or fewer of the jobs are held by women. They must attend an institution of higher learning in the state of Arizona and be 20 years of age or older.
Target applicants: College students. Adult students.
Amount: Varies.
Number of awards: Varies.
Deadline: March 1.
How to apply: Applications are available online.
Exclusive: Visit www.UltimateScholarshipBook.com and enter code AR120512 for updates on this award.

(1206) · Arizona Private Postsecondary Education Student Financial Assistance Program (PFAP)

Arizona Commission for Postsecondary Education
2020 N. Central Avenue, Suite 550
Phoenix, AZ 85004
Phone: 602-258-2435
Fax: 602-258-2483
Email: judi@azhighered.org
http://www.azhighered.org
Purpose: To assist Arizona students earning baccalaureate degrees at private postsecondary schools.
Eligibility: Applicants must be residents of Arizona attending a licensed and accredited private postsecondary institution.
Target applicants: College students. Adult students.
Amount: Up to $4,000.
Number of awards: Varies.
Scholarship may be renewable.
Deadline: Varies.
How to apply: Applications are available through your school's financial aid office.
Exclusive: Visit www.UltimateScholarshipBook.com and enter code AR120612 for updates on this award.

(1207) · Arkansas Game and Fish Commission Conservation Scholarship

Arkansas Game and Fish Commission
2 Natural Resources Drive
Little Rock, AR 72205
Phone: 800-364-4263
http://www.agfc.com
Purpose: To aid Arkansas students preparing for careers in natural resources conservation.
Eligibility: Applicants must be Arkansas residents who are high school seniors or undergraduate-level college students. They must have a GPA of 2.5 or above and must be planning to pursue a career in natural resources conservation. They cannot have received full scholarship or grant funding from another source. Selection is based on the standardized scoring of each application as a whole.
Target applicants: High school students. College students. Adult students.
Minimum GPA: 2.5
Amount: $2,000-$3,000.
Number of awards: Varies.
Scholarship may be renewable.
Deadline: June 10.
How to apply: Applications are available online. An application form, personal statement, essay, official transcript, three personal references, one recommendation letter, photograph and statement of intent to pursue a four-year degree (for those currently attending a two-year institution) are required.
Exclusive: Visit www.UltimateScholarshipBook.com and enter code AR120712 for updates on this award.

(1208) · Arkansas Public Health Association Annual Scholarships for Arkansas Students in a Public Health Field

Arkansas Public Health Association
P.O. Box 250327
Little Rock, AR 72225
http://www.arkpublichealth.org
Purpose: To help financially needy Arkansas students who are pursuing higher education in the field of public health.
Eligibility: Applicants must be Arkansas residents who are high school seniors, high school graduates, GED holders or college sophomores or above at the undergraduate level. They must have a GPA of 2.5 or more and must demonstrate financial need. They must be enrolled at or have plans to enroll at a vocational school, technical school, two-year college or four-year college or university. Students must be interested in pursuing a career in public health. Selection is based on GPA, professional public health goals, previous involvement in the health care field and financial need.
Target applicants: High school students. College students. Adult students.
Minimum GPA: 2.5
Amount: $500-$1,000.
Number of awards: Varies.
Deadline: March 16.
How to apply: Applications are available online. An application form, official transcripts, explanation of financial need, personal statement and two letters of recommendation are required.
Exclusive: Visit www.UltimateScholarshipBook.com and enter code AR120812 for updates on this award.

(1209) · Arkansas Service Memorial Fund

Arkansas Community Foundation
1400 W. Markham
Suite 206
Little Rock, AR 72201
Phone: 888-220-2723
Fax: 501-372-1166
Email: arcf@arcf.org
http://www.arcf.org
Purpose: To provide financial assistance for students with a parent who died in service to his or her community, state or nation.
Eligibility: Applicants must be Arkansas residents who plan to attend an institution of higher learning in the state. Scholarships are awarded by local Arkansas Community Foundation chapters.

Target applicants: High school students. College students. Adult students.
Amount: Varies.
Number of awards: Varies.
Deadline: Varies.
How to apply: Applications are available online.
Exclusive: Visit www.UltimateScholarshipBook.com and enter code AR120912 for updates on this award.

(1210) • Art Scholarship

Liberty Graphics
P.O. Box 5
44 Main Street
Liberty, ME 04949
Phone: 207-589-4596
Fax: 207-589-4415
Email: jay@lgtees.com
http://www.lgtees.com
Purpose: To encourage exploration and expression through traditional visual mediums.
Eligibility: Applicants must be seniors at a Maine high school and be legal residents of Maine. Students must submit artwork, usually with a theme of Maine and the outdoors.
Target applicants: High school students.
Amount: $1,000.
Number of awards: 1.
Deadline: April 15.
How to apply: Applications are available from your high school guidance counselor or on the Liberty Graphics website beginning in late February or early March of each year.
Exclusive: Visit www.UltimateScholarshipBook.com and enter code LI121012 for updates on this award.

(1211) • Aspire Award

Tennessee Student Assistance Corporation
404 James Robertson Parkway
Suite 1510, Parkway Towers
Nashville, TN 37243
Phone: 800-342-1663
Fax: 615-741-6101
Email: tsac.aidinfo@tn.gov
http://www.tn.gov/CollegePays/
Purpose: To provide supplemental support to recipients of the Tennessee HOPE Scholarship.
Eligibility: Applicants must be entering freshmen with a minimum ACT score of 21, minimum SAT score of 980 or minimum 3.0 GPA. Home-schooled applicants must have a minimum ACT score of 21 or SAT score of 980. GED applicants must have a minimum GED score of 525 and minimum ACT score of 21 or SAT score of 980. Independent students or the parents of dependent students must have an adjusted gross income under $36,000.
Target applicants: High school students.
Minimum GPA: 3.0
Amount: $1,500.
Number of awards: Varies.
Deadline: September 1 and February 1.
How to apply: Applications are available through completion of the FAFSA.
Exclusive: Visit www.UltimateScholarshipBook.com and enter code TE121112 for updates on this award.

(1212) • Associate Degree Nursing Scholarship Program

California Health and Welfare Agency - Office of Statewide Health Planning and Development
Health Professions Education Foundation
818 K Street, Room 210
Sacramento, CA 95814
Phone: 916-324-6500
Fax: 916-324-6585
Email: hpef@oshpd.state.ca.us
http://www.healthprofessions.ca.gov
Purpose: To increase the number of registered nurses working in medically underserved areas of California.
Eligibility: Applicants must be California residents enrolled in an associate degree nursing program at a California school, agree to pursue a bachelor's degree in nursing within five years and be fluent in a language other than English. Financial need, work experience, community involvement and academic achievement are considered. Preference is given to those who will graduate within two years and to those who plan to remain in a medically underserved area past the service time required. Recipients must sign a two-year service contract to work in a medically underserved area as an RN.
Target applicants: College students. Adult students.
Amount: Up to $10,000.
Number of awards: Varies.
Scholarship may be renewable.
Deadline: September 11.
How to apply: Applications are available online.
Exclusive: Visit www.UltimateScholarshipBook.com and enter code CA121212 for updates on this award.

(1213) • Associated General Contractors of Connecticut Scholarships

Connecticut Construction Industries Association
912 Silas Deane Highway
Wethersfield, CT 06109
Phone: 860-529-6855
Fax: 860-563-0616
Email: ccia-info@ctconstruction.org
http://www.ctconstruction.org
Purpose: To aid students planning to pursue careers in civil engineering or building and construction technology.
Eligibility: Applicants must be high school seniors who intend to enroll in a four-year civil engineering or construction technology program or who plan to complete a construction program at a two-year institution before entering a four-year institution. They must be U.S. citizens or legal residents and must be interested in a career in construction. Selection is based on academic achievement, level of interest in a construction career, work experience, evaluation forms, extracurricular activities and financial need.
Target applicants: High school students.
Amount: $2,500.
Number of awards: Varies.
Deadline: March 31.
How to apply: Applications are available online. An application form, two personal evaluation forms, one faculty evaluation form and an official transcript are required.
Exclusive: Visit www.UltimateScholarshipBook.com and enter code CO121312 for updates on this award.

(1214) • Associated General Contractors of Minnesota Scholarships

Associated General Contractors of Minnesota
Capitol Office Building
525 Park Street
Suite #110
St. Paul, MN 55103-2186
Phone: 800-552-7670
Fax: 651-632-8928
Email: jsanem@agcmn.org
http://www.agcmn.org

Purpose: To support outstanding students in Minnesota.
Eligibility: Applicants must attend a Minnesota institution of higher learning with a concentration in construction or construction-related courses. Applications are judged equally on academic performance, career objectives, financial need, personal information and application clarity.
Target applicants: College students. Adult students.
Amount: Varies.
Number of awards: Varies.
Deadline: January 3 and May 15.
How to apply: Applications are available online. An application form, personal statement, academic core plan, career objectives and recent color photo are required.
Exclusive: Visit www.UltimateScholarshipBook.com and enter code AS121412 for updates on this award.

(1215) • Associated General Contractors of Vermont Scholarships

Associated General Contractors of Vermont
P.O. Box 750
Montpelier, VT 05601
Phone: 802-223-2374
Fax: 802-223-1809
Email: info@agctv.org
http://www.agcvt.org

Purpose: To aid financially needy students who are pursuing education or further training in a construction-related field.
Eligibility: Applicants must be receiving education or further training in a construction-related field and must demonstrate financial need. Selection is based on the overall strength of the application.
Target applicants: High school students. College students. Adult students.
Amount: $1,000.
Number of awards: 3.
Deadline: April 10.
How to apply: Application documents are available online. Two recommendation letters, an explanation of financial status and a personal essay are required.
Exclusive: Visit www.UltimateScholarshipBook.com and enter code AS121512 for updates on this award.

(1216) • Atlanta Network of Executive Women in Hospitality Scholarship Awards

Network of Executive Women in Hospitality, Atlanta
141 New Street #234
Decatur, GA 30030
Phone: 404-377-1778
Email: ryan@kaidatl.com
http://www.newh.org

Purpose: To support Atlanta students pursuing careers in the hospitality industry.
Eligibility: Applicants must be enrolled in an accredited degree or certification program in which they have completed half the requirements in a hospitality-related area including hotel/restaurant management, culinary/foodservice, architecture or interior design. They must demonstrate financial need and have a GPA of 3.0 or higher.
Target applicants: College students. Adult students.
Minimum GPA: 3.0
Amount: Varies.
Number of awards: Varies.
Deadline: Varies.
How to apply: Applications are available online. An application form, essay, transcript, project that reflects skills and letters of recommendation are required.
Exclusive: Visit www.UltimateScholarshipBook.com and enter code NE121612 for updates on this award.

(1217) • Atlanta Press Club Journalism Scholarship Award

Atlanta Press Club Inc.
34 Broad Street
18th Floor
Atlanta, GA 30303
Phone: 404-577-7377
Fax: 404-223-3706
Email: info@atlpressclub.org
http://www.atlpressclub.org

Purpose: To aid students pursuing careers in journalism.
Eligibility: Applicants must be college juniors or seniors working toward a career in news at a Georgia college or university. They should be able to provide samples of published or broadcast work.
Target applicants: College students. Adult students.
Amount: $1,500.
Number of awards: 4.
Deadline: February 25.
How to apply: Applications are available online. An application form, samples of published or broadcast work, transcript, essay and letter of reference are required.
Exclusive: Visit www.UltimateScholarshipBook.com and enter code AT121712 for updates on this award.

(1218) • AWA Scholarships

Association for Women in Architecture
22815 Frampton Avenue
Torrance, CA 90501-5304
Phone: 310-534-8466
Fax: 310-257-6885
Email: scholarship@awa-la.org
http://www.awa-la.org

Purpose: To support women studying architecture.
Eligibility: Applicants must be female residents of California or attend a California school and must be enrolled in one of the following majors: architecture, landscape architecture, urban and/or land planning, interior design, environmental design, architectural rendering and illustrating, civil, electrical, mechanical or structural engineering. Applicants must also have completed a minimum of 18 units in their major by the application due date. The award is based on grades, personal statement, financial need, recommendations and submitted materials. Applicants must be able to go to Los Angeles for interviews. Applications, two recommendation letters, transcripts, financial statements, personal statements and self-addressed stamped envelopes are required.

Target applicants: College students. Graduate school students. Adult students.
Amount: $1,000.
Number of awards: 5.
Deadline: April 15.
How to apply: Applications are available online.
Exclusive: Visit www.UltimateScholarshipBook.com and enter code AS121812 for updates on this award.

(1219) • AWC Seattle Professional Chapter Scholarships

Association for Women in Communications - Seattle Professional Chapter
Scholarship Chair
P.O. Box 472
Mountlake Terrace, WA 98043
Phone: 206-654-2929
Email: awcseattle@verizon.net
http://www.seattleawc.org
Purpose: To support students of communications.
Eligibility: Applicants must be Washington State residents who are college juniors, seniors or graduate students at Washington State four-year colleges. Students must major in print and broadcast journalism, television and radio production, film advertising, public relations, marketing, graphic design, multimedia design, photography or technical communication. Selection is based on demonstrated excellence in communications, contributions toward communications, scholastic achievement, financial need and work samples.
Target applicants: College students. Graduate school students. Adult students.
Amount: Varies.
Number of awards: 2.
Deadline: April 30.
How to apply: Applications are available online. An application form, cover letter, transcript, resume and two work samples are required.
Exclusive: Visit www.UltimateScholarshipBook.com and enter code AS121912 for updates on this award.

(1220) • Bach Organ and Keyboard Music Scholarship

Rhode Island Foundation
One Union Station
Providence, RI 02903
Phone: 401-274-4564
Fax: 401-331-8085
Email: lmonahan@rifoundation.org
http://www.rifoundation.org
Purpose: To support music majors who are studying keyboard instruments.
Eligibility: Applicants must be residents of the state of Rhode Island. Students must be currently enrolled in a college music program, and they must show financial need.
Target applicants: High school students. College students. Graduate school students. Adult students.
Amount: $800-$1,000.
Number of awards: Varies.
Deadline: June 1.
How to apply: Applications are available online.
Exclusive: Visit www.UltimateScholarshipBook.com and enter code RH122012 for updates on this award.

(1221) • Bachelor of Science Nursing Scholarship Program

California Health and Welfare Agency - Office of Statewide Health Planning and Development
Health Professions Education Foundation
818 K Street, Room 210
Sacramento, CA 95814
Phone: 916-324-6500
Fax: 916-324-6585
Email: hpef@oshpd.state.ca.us
http://www.healthprofessions.ca.gov
Purpose: To increase the number of professional nurses practicing in medically underserved areas of California by assisting nursing students attending California schools.
Eligibility: Applicants must be attending a California undergraduate nursing program and be fluent in a language other than English. Financial need, work experience, academic achievement and community involvement are considered. A two-year service agreement to work in a medically underserved area of California is required. Preference is given to those who expect to graduate within two years and to those who plan to remain in a medically underserved area after the service agreement has expired.
Target applicants: College students. Adult students.
Amount: Up to $13,000.
Number of awards: Varies.
Scholarship may be renewable.
Deadline: September 11.
How to apply: Applications are available online.
Exclusive: Visit www.UltimateScholarshipBook.com and enter code CA122112 for updates on this award.

(1222) • Banatao Filipino American Education Fund

Asian Pacific Fund
225 Bush Street
Suite 590
San Francisco, CA 94104
Phone: 415-433-6859
Fax: 415-433-2425
Email: scholarship@asianpacificfund.org
http://www.asianpacificfund.org
Purpose: To help school students of Filipino heritage in pursuing a college education.
Eligibility: Applicants for the college scholarship should be high school seniors of at least half Filipino heritage with a GPA of at least a "B" who will enroll at four-year colleges or universities and plan to major in engineering, computer science or physical sciences (health professionals, such as doctors and nurses not included). Each scholarship is renewable up to three years based on satisfactory academic performance in a full-time undergraduate program. Awards are for undergraduate study only and are based on potential, motivation and financial need. Applicants must be residents of one of the following counties: Alameda, Contra Costa, Marin, Merced, Monterey, Napa, Sacramento, San Francisco, San Joaquin, San Mateo, Santa Clara, Santa Cruz, Solano, Sonoma or Stanislaus. Applicants for the college prep scholarship must be high school juniors of at least half Filipino heritage with a GPA of 2.7 who plan to attend four-year colleges or universities and are interested in SAT preparation and college admissions counseling. Students should have an interest in engineering, math or science and be residents of one of the the following counties: Alameda, Contra Costa, Marin, Napa, San Francisco, San Joaquin, San Mateo, Santa Clara, Solano or Sonoma.
Target applicants: High school students.

Minimum GPA: 2.7
Amount: $5,000.
Number of awards: 5.
Scholarship may be renewable.
Deadline: March 31.
How to apply: Application are available online.
Exclusive: Visit www.UltimateScholarshipBook.com and enter code AS122212 for updates on this award.

(1223) • Bank of America Achievement Awards

Bank of America Foundation
Department 3246
P.O. Box 37000
San Francisco, CA 94137
Phone: 800-218-9946
http://www.bankofamerica.com/foundation/index.cfm?template=fd_ca
Purpose: To provide educational assistance to California students.
Eligibility: Applicants must be high school seniors from the state of California. A committee at each high school nominates outstanding students in the categories of applied arts and trades, fine arts, liberal arts and science and mathematics. Scholastic ability, awards and participation in school and community activities are considered.
Target applicants: High school students.
Amount: $500-$2,000.
Number of awards: Varies.
Deadline: Varies.
How to apply: Participants must be nominated by their schools.
Exclusive: Visit www.UltimateScholarshipBook.com and enter code BA122312 for updates on this award.

(1224) • Barking Foundation Grants and Scholarships

Barking Foundation
P.O. Box 855
Bangor, ME 04401
Phone: 207-990-2910
Fax: 207-990-2975
Email: info@barkingfoundation.org
http://www.barkingfoundation.org
Purpose: To financially assist residents of Maine with their post-secondary education goals.
Eligibility: Applicants must be residents of Maine and have demonstrated financial need. There is no minimum GPA requirement for first-time applicants, but to reapply, recipients must have a minimum 3.0 GPA.
Target applicants: College students. Adult students.
Amount: $3,000.
Number of awards: 50.
Scholarship may be renewable.
Deadline: February 19.
How to apply: Printable applications are available online, but applications must be mailed.
Exclusive: Visit www.UltimateScholarshipBook.com and enter code BA122412 for updates on this award.

(1225) • Ben W. Fortson, Jr., Scholarship

Surveying and Mapping Society of Georgia
P.O. Box 778
Douglasville, GA 30133
Phone: 770-947-1767
Fax: 770-947-1725
Email: ginger_samsog@bellsouth.net
http://www.samsog.org
Purpose: To help Georgia undergraduate land surveying students.
Eligibility: Applicants must be Georgia residents enrolled in an undergraduate land surveying program of study at an accredited institution of higher learning. They must have completed at least 20 percent of their program requirements before receiving any scholarship monies awarded. Students must also maintain a 2.4 overall GPA and 2.7 GPA in surveying courses. Preference is given to full-time students seeking a bachelor's degree. Selection is based on the overall strength of the application.
Target applicants: College students. Adult students.
Minimum GPA: 2.4
Amount: Varies.
Number of awards: Varies.
Deadline: Varies.
How to apply: Applications are available online. An application form and transcript are required.
Exclusive: Visit www.UltimateScholarshipBook.com and enter code SU122512 for updates on this award.

(1226) • Benjamin C. Blackburn Scholarship

Friends of the Frelinghuysen Arboretum
P.O. Box 1295
Morristown, NJ 07960
Phone: 973-326-7601
Email: webmaster@arboretumfriends.org
http://www.arboretumfriends.org
Purpose: To help New Jersey students who are planning for careers in agronomy, botany, environmental science, floriculture, horticulture, landscape design or plant science.
Eligibility: Applicants must be New Jersey residents. They must have earned at least 24 credits towards a degree in floriculture, landscape design, agronomy, plant science, environmental science, botany or horticulture at an accredited college or university. They must have plans to pursue a career in one of these fields after graduation. They must have a GPA of 3.0 or higher. If awarded the scholarship, the recipient will be expected to to give a 10-minute speech on his or her horticultural interests and goals at the Arboretum's annual meeting. Selection is based on the overall strength of the application.
Target applicants: College students. Adult students.
Minimum GPA: 3.0
Amount: Up to $1,250.
Number of awards: 2.
Deadline: March 31.
How to apply: Applications are available online. An application form, personal essay, transcript, a list of the courses that currently are being taken and four letters of recommendation are required.
Exclusive: Visit www.UltimateScholarshipBook.com and enter code FR122612 for updates on this award.

(1227) • Benjamin Franklin/Edith Green Scholarship

Oregon Student Assistance Commission
1500 Valley River Drive
Suite 100
Eugene, OR 97401
Phone: 541-687-7400
Fax: 541-687-7414
Email: awardinfo@osac.state.or.us
http://www.osac.state.or.us

Purpose: To assist Oregon high school students who are planning to attend a public four-year postsecondary institution in Oregon.
Eligibility: Applicants must be U.S. citizens or legal residents. They must be Oregon residents, be graduating high school seniors and have a GPA of 3.45 to 3.55. Applicants who owe a refund on an educational grant or who have defaulted on an educational loan are ineligible. Selection is based on financial need.
Target applicants: High school students.
Minimum GPA: 3.4
Amount: Varies.
Number of awards: Varies.
Deadline: March 1.
How to apply: Applications are available online. An application form, supporting materials and FAFSA completion are required.
Exclusive: Visit www.UltimateScholarshipBook.com and enter code OR122712 for updates on this award.

(1228) · BI-LO/SpiritFest Scholarship

Eray Promotions
342 Crepe Myrtle Drive
Greer, SC 29651
http://www.eraypromotions.com
Purpose: To recognize academic excellence and leadership qualities of minority students.
Eligibility: Applicants must be minority high school seniors with a minimum 3.0 GPA. Applicants must complete an application which including a 300 word autobiography which highlights volunteer activities, leadership experience, extracurricular activities, work experience, honors and special awards. Three letters of recommendation and an official transcript must also be submitted.
Target applicants: High school students.
Minimum GPA: 3.0
Amount: $1,500.
Number of awards: 2.
Deadline: August 1.
How to apply: Applications are available online.
Exclusive: Visit www.UltimateScholarshipBook.com and enter code ER122812 for updates on this award.

(1229) · Big 33 Scholarship Foundation Scholarships

Big 33 Scholarship Foundation
P.O. Box 213
511 Bridge Street
New Cumberland, PA 17070
Phone: 717-774-3303
Fax: 717-774-1749
Email: info@big33.org
http://www.big33.org
Purpose: To provide need-based scholarships to high school seniors with well-rounded educational and extracurricular success.
Eligibility: Applicants must be high school seniors enrolled in a public or accredited private school in Ohio or Pennsylvania. Students must have at least a 2.0 grade point average from their sophomore and junior year and be planning to continue education beyond high school at a technical school or accredited higher education institution.
Target applicants: High school students.
Minimum GPA: 2.0
Amount: Varies.
Number of awards: Varies.
Deadline: February 12.
How to apply: Applications are available online.
Exclusive: Visit www.UltimateScholarshipBook.com and enter code BI122912 for updates on this award.

(1230) · Big Y Scholarship Programs

Big Y
Scholarship Committee
P.O. Box 7840
Springfield, MA 01102-7840
Phone: 413-504-4047
http://www.bigy.com
Purpose: To reward students in the Big Y market area and those affiliated with Big Y.
Eligibility: Applicants must either be Big Y employees or their dependents or must reside or attend school in Western or Central Massachusetts, Norfolk County, Massachusetts or Connecticut. The scholarships are available to high school seniors, undergraduates, graduates, community college students and adult students. Applicants should submit transcripts, college entrance exams scores and two recommendation letters. Big Y employees must submit one recommendation from their supervisor. Selection is based on achievements, awards, community involvement, leadership positions and class rank. Eight scholarships are available specifically for dependents of law enforcement officers and firefighters.
Target applicants: High school students. College students. Graduate school students. Adult students.
Amount: Varies.
Number of awards: 300.
Deadline: February 1.
How to apply: Applications are available at any Big Y location from October through January each year. Applications are also available at guidance offices of schools within Big Y's market area.
Exclusive: Visit www.UltimateScholarshipBook.com and enter code BI123012 for updates on this award.

(1231) · BioOhio Annual Scholarship

BioOhio
1275 Kinnear Road
Columbus, OH 43212
Phone: 614-675-3686
Fax: 614-675-3687
Email: mschutte@bioohio.com
http://www.bioohio.com
Purpose: To aid Ohio students who are interested in pursuing higher education in a bioscience-related subject.
Eligibility: Applicants must be Ohio residents. They must be high school seniors who are planning to study a bioscience-related subject at an Ohio college or university. Selection is based on the overall strength of the application.
Target applicants: High school students.
Amount: $1,250.
Number of awards: 4.
Deadline: March 19.
How to apply: Applications are available online. An application form, personal essay, transcript, two recommendation letters, a list of extracurricular activities and standardized test scores are required.

Exclusive: Visit www.UltimateScholarshipBook.com and enter code BI123112 for updates on this award.

(1232) • Blossom Kalama Evans Memorial Scholarship Fund

Hawaii Community Foundation - Scholarships
1164 Bishop Street, Suite 800
Honolulu, HI 96813
Phone: 888-731-3863
Fax: 808-521-6286
Email: scholarships@hcf-hawaii.org
http://www.hawaiicommunityfoundation.org
Purpose: To support students who are dedicated to serving the native Hawaiian community.
Eligibility: Applicants must be of Hawaiian ancestry, and they must be a college junior, college senior or graduate student.
Target applicants: College students. Graduate school students. Adult students.
Amount: Varies.
Number of awards: Varies.
Deadline: March 1.
How to apply: To apply, register online, complete the online application and select the scholarships to which you wish to apply. In addition, mail the supporting materials: printed confirmation page from the online application, personal statement, copy of Student Aid Report (SAR) available at www.fafsa.ed.gov and official transcript.
Exclusive: Visit www.UltimateScholarshipBook.com and enter code HA123212 for updates on this award.

(1233) • Bluewolf Technology Scholarship

Bluewolf
220 Fifth Avenue
15th Floor
New York, NY 10001
Phone: 866-455-9653
Fax: 646-336-6438
http://www.bluewolf.com
Purpose: To help promising students who are interested in technology careers.
Eligibility: Applicants must be seniors at New York City public schools. They must have a GPA of 3.0 or higher and demonstrate an aptitude for computer science and/or technology. They must demonstrate financial need.
Target applicants: High school students.
Minimum GPA: 3.0
Amount: $2,000.
Number of awards: 2.
Deadline: July 31.
How to apply: Applications are available online. An application form, essay, up to two letters of reference, transcript and SAT/ACT scores are required.
Exclusive: Visit www.UltimateScholarshipBook.com and enter code BL123312 for updates on this award.

(1234) • BNSF Leadership Scholarship

BNSF Foundation
c/o ISTS
200 Crutchfield Avenue
Nashville, TN 37210
Phone: 615-320-3149
Fax: 615-320-3151
Email: info@appplyists.com
https://aim.applyists.net/BNSFLeadership
Purpose: To assist Wyoming and New Mexico high school seniors.
Eligibility: Applicants must be residents of Wyoming or New Mexico and must complete the online application. Each state will be divided geographically into four quadrants, and the top two finalists selected from each quadrant based on the online application will be invited to an awards dinner in May. The top finalist in each quadrant of the state will receive $2,500 in scholarships per year over a four-year period for a total of $10,000. The runner-up in each quadrant will receive a one-time $2,500 scholarship. Selection is based on the online application, a 500-word essay on leadership, academic records and school and community activities.
Target applicants: High school students.
Amount: $2,500-$10,000.
Number of awards: 16.
Scholarship may be renewable.
Deadline: April 1.
How to apply: Applications are available online.
Exclusive: Visit www.UltimateScholarshipBook.com and enter code BN123412 for updates on this award.

(1235) • Board of Governors' Medical Scholarship-Loan Program

College Foundation of North Carolina
P.O. Box 41966
Raleigh, NC 27629
Phone: 888-234-6400
Fax: 919-821-3139
Email: programinformation@cfnc.org
http://www.cfnc.org
Purpose: To assist medical students at North Carolina institutions who have financial need and want to practice medicine in the state.
Eligibility: Applicants must be accepted to the Duke University School of Medicine, Brody School of Medicine at East Carolina University, The University of North Carolina at Chapel Hill School of Medicine or the Wake Forest University School of Medicine. They must be residents of North Carolina.
Target applicants: Graduate school students. Adult students.
Amount: $5,000 yearly plus tuition, mandatory fees and a laptop.
Number of awards: Varies.
Scholarship may be renewable.
Deadline: May 15.
How to apply: Applications are available from your school's financial aid office.
Exclusive: Visit www.UltimateScholarshipBook.com and enter code CO123512 for updates on this award.

(1236) • Bob Eddy Scholarship Program

Society of Professional Journalists-Connecticut Professional Chapter
71 Kenwood Avenue
Fairfield, CT 06824
Phone: 212-683-5700 x364
Email: destock@ctspj.org
http://www.ctspj.org
Purpose: To support students interested in journalism careers.
Eligibility: Applicants must be rising college juniors or seniors at a four-year college and Connecticut residents or students of Connecticut

schools. They should be able to submit samples of work that shows interest and competency in journalism.
Target applicants: College students. Adult students.
Amount: $250-$2,000.
Number of awards: 4.
Deadline: April 7.
How to apply: Applications are available online. An application form, transcript, essay and writing samples, tapes or related work in any media are required.
Exclusive: Visit www.UltimateScholarshipBook.com and enter code SO123612 for updates on this award.

(1237) · Bob Stevens Memorial Scholarship

Garden State Scholastic Press Foundation
840 Bear Tavern Road
Suite 305
West Trenton, NJ 08628-1019
Email: scholarship@gsspa.org
http://www.gsspa.org
Purpose: To support high school journalism students.
Eligibility: Applicants must be graduating New Jersey high school seniors who are nominated by a GSSPA member, have a GPA of 3.0 or higher and have participated in high school journalism for at least two years.
Target applicants: High school students.
Minimum GPA: 3.0
Amount: $1,500.
Number of awards: 1.
Deadline: February 15.
How to apply: Applications are available online. An application form, transcript, three or four letters of recommendation and portfolio with work samples are required.
Exclusive: Visit www.UltimateScholarshipBook.com and enter code GA123712 for updates on this award.

(1238) · Boettcher Foundation Scholarship

Boettcher Foundation
600 Seventeenth Street
Suite 2210 South
Denver, CO 80202-5422
Phone: 800-323-9640
Email: scholarships@boettcherfoundation.org
http://www.boettcherfoundation.org
Purpose: To recognize high school seniors who plan to make contributions to the people in the state of Colorado.
Eligibility: Applicants must be high school seniors and current, legal residents of the state of Colorado who will graduate in the top 5 percent of their class. Applicants must have a composite score of 27 on the ACT or 1200 on the SAT. They should submit applications, essays, transcripts and standardized test scores. Selection is based on academic merit, demonstration of leadership skills, community service and character.
Target applicants: High school students.
Amount: Full tuition plus $2,800 stipend.
Number of awards: 40.
Scholarship may be renewable.
Deadline: November 1.
How to apply: Contact high school counselors for more information.
Exclusive: Visit www.UltimateScholarshipBook.com and enter code BO123812 for updates on this award.

(1239) · Bohdan "Bo" Kolinsky Memorial Scholarship

Connecticut Sports Writers Alliance
P.O. Box 70
Unionville, CT 06085-0070
Phone: 860-677-0087
Email: rbrtbarton@aol.com
http://www.ctsportswriters.org
Purpose: To aid aspiring sports journalists.
Eligibility: Applicants must be Connecticut high school seniors, be admitted to an accredited four-year college and plan to pursue studies leading to a career in sports journalism. Winners may apply for grants for succeeding years of undergraduate study as long as they make satisfactory progress, but no student may receive more than $6,500 in funds.
Target applicants: High school students.
Amount: At least $1,000.
Number of awards: 1.
Scholarship may be renewable.
Deadline: February 7.
How to apply: Applications are available online. An application form, essay, summary of academic and employment history, evidence of good academic standing, letter of recommendation and three samples of published work are required.
Exclusive: Visit www.UltimateScholarshipBook.com and enter code CO123912 for updates on this award.

(1240) · Booz Allen Hawaii Scholarship Fund

Hawaii Community Foundation - Scholarships
1164 Bishop Street, Suite 800
Honolulu, HI 96813
Phone: 888-731-3863
Fax: 808-521-6286
Email: scholarships@hcf-hawaii.org
http://www.hawaiicommunityfoundation.org
Purpose: To support undergraduate students in Hawaii.
Eligibility: Students must be residents of Hawaii or dependents of military members stationed there. Applicants must be attending or planning to attend a four-year college or university. Students must have at least a 3.0 GPA.
Target applicants: High school students. College students. Adult students.
Minimum GPA: 3.0
Amount: Varies.
Number of awards: Varies.
Deadline: March 1.
How to apply: To apply, register online, complete the online application and select the scholarships to which you wish to apply. In addition, mail the supporting materials: printed confirmation page from the online application, personal statement, copy of Student Aid Report (SAR) available at www.fafsa.ed.gov and official transcript.
Exclusive: Visit www.UltimateScholarshipBook.com and enter code HA124012 for updates on this award.

(1241) · Boy Scout Scholarship

American Legion, Department of Illinois
P.O. Box 2910
Bloomington, IL 61702
Phone: 309-663-0361
Fax: 309-663-5783
http://www.illegion.org

Purpose: To award a member of the Boy Scouts with a one-year scholarship.
Eligibility: Applicants must be graduating seniors in high school, Senior Boy Scouts or Explorers and residents of Illinois. Students must write an essay on Americanism and/or Boy Scout programs.
Target applicants: High school students.
Amount: $200-$700.
Number of awards: 3.
Deadline: Varies.
How to apply: Application information is available by contacting your local Boy Scout office or American Legion Scout Chairman.
Exclusive: Visit www.UltimateScholarshipBook.com and enter code AM124112 for updates on this award.

(1242) • Buena M. Chesshir Scholarship

Virginia Business and Professional Women's Foundation
P.O. Box 4842
McLean, VA 22103-4842
Phone: 800-525-3729
Email: bpwfoundation@act.org
http://www.vabpwfoundation.org
Purpose: To support adult women in Virginia who are planning to continue their education.
Eligibility: Applicants must be at least 25 years of age, and they must have a definite plan to use their education for advancement in the workplace. Students must be officially accepted at a Virginia college, and they must complete a bachelor's or master's degree within two years. Applicants must provide three letters of recommendation. Awards are based on financial need, educational goals and academic achievement.
Target applicants: College students. Graduate school students. Adult students.
Amount: $500-$1,000.
Number of awards: Varies.
Scholarship may be renewable.
Deadline: April 1.
How to apply: Applications are available online.
Exclusive: Visit www.UltimateScholarshipBook.com and enter code VI124212 for updates on this award.

(1243) • Business and Professional Women of Kentucky Foundation Grant

Kentucky Federation of Business and Professional Women
200 Compton Drive
Frankfort, KY 40601
Phone: 606-451-6654
Email: joanne.story@kctcs.edu
http://www.bpw-ky.org/foundation.shtml
Purpose: To promote economic self-sufficiency for Kentucky women.
Eligibility: Applicants must be Kentucky residents who are at least 18 years of age. They must be employed or planning a career in the Kentucky workforce and attending an institution of higher learning. Individuals may receive a grant no more than once every 24 months. Deadlines are April 30 and October 31 of each year.
Target applicants: High school students. College students. Adult students.
Amount: Varies.
Number of awards: Varies.
Deadline: April 30 and October 31.
How to apply: Applications are available online.
Exclusive: Visit www.UltimateScholarshipBook.com and enter code KE124312 for updates on this award.

(1244) • Business and Professional Women/Maine Continuing Education Scholarship

Business and Professional Women/Maine Futurama Foundation
103 County Road
Oakland, ME 04963
Email: webmaster@bpwmaine.org
http://www.bpwmaine.org/files/index.php?id=10
Purpose: To provide financial assistance to female students.
Eligibility: Applicants must be Maine residents who have completed at least one year of college or will have done so by the end of the spring semester following application. They must be in good standing or on an approved leave of absence of one year or less at their educational institution. Financial need is required, and the student must have a definite plan to complete the program in which she is enrolled.
Target applicants: College students. Adult students.
Amount: $1,200.
Number of awards: Varies.
Deadline: April 20.
How to apply: Applications are available online.
Exclusive: Visit www.UltimateScholarshipBook.com and enter code BU124412 for updates on this award.

(1245) • Cal Grant A

California Student Aid Commission
P.O. Box 419026
Rancho Cordova, CA 95741-9026
Phone: 888-224-7268
Fax: 916-464-8002
Email: studentsupport@csac.ca.gov
http://www.csac.ca.gov
Purpose: To assist California students in obtaining higher education.
Eligibility: Applicants must be California residents who are attending or plan to attend an eligible California college or university pursuing at least two years of coursework. They must enroll for no less than half time and meet program income requirements. They may not have already earned a bachelor's degree or higher, and they must not be in default on a student loan or owe a grant repayment without having made satisfactory arrangements for repayment. Students with a GPA of 3.0 or higher who meet all requirements will receive an entitlement award, and students with a GPA of at least 2.4 may apply for a competitive award.
Target applicants: High school students. College students. Adult students.
Minimum GPA: 2.4
Amount: Up to $10,302.
Number of awards: Varies.
Scholarship may be renewable.
Deadline: March 2.
How to apply: Application materials are available online. A FAFSA and a GPA verification form are required.
Exclusive: Visit www.UltimateScholarshipBook.com and enter code CA124512 for updates on this award.

(1246) • Cal Grant B

California Student Aid Commission
P.O. Box 419026
Rancho Cordova, CA 95741-9026
Phone: 888-224-7268
Fax: 916-464-8002
Email: studentsupport@csac.ca.gov
http://www.csac.ca.gov

Purpose: To provide living expense, tuition and fee assistance for low-income students.
Eligibility: Applicants must be California residents with financial need for attendance at an eligible California college or university. They must enroll for at least half time. A minimum GPA of 2.0 is required. Students who meet financial and eligibility requirements will receive a Cal Grant B entitlement award. Other eligible students can apply for a Cal Grant B competitive award. Competitive award selection is based on family income, education level of parents, GPA, time out of high school and special considerations.
Target applicants: High school students. College students. Adult students.
Minimum GPA: 2.0
Amount: Up to full tuition.
Number of awards: Varies.
Scholarship may be renewable.
Deadline: March 2.
How to apply: Application materials are available online. A FAFSA and a GPA verification form are required.
Exclusive: Visit www.UltimateScholarshipBook.com and enter code CA124612 for updates on this award.

(1247) · Cal Grant C

California Student Aid Commission
P.O. Box 419026
Rancho Cordova, CA 95741-9026
Phone: 888-224-7268
Fax: 916-464-8002
Email: studentsupport@csac.ca.gov
http://www.csac.ca.gov
Purpose: To aid students participating in occupational and vocational programs.
Eligibility: Applicants must be California residents. They must enroll in a vocational program at a California community college, independent college or vocational school that is at least four months long. Funds may be received for up to two years. Eligible students will receive an application by mail from the California Student Aid Commission in mid-April.
Target applicants: High school students. College students. Adult students.
Amount: Varies.
Number of awards: Varies.
Scholarship may be renewable.
Deadline: May 15.
How to apply: Applications are available by mail. A FAFSA and an application form are required.
Exclusive: Visit www.UltimateScholarshipBook.com and enter code CA124712 for updates on this award.

(1248) · Cal Grant Entitlement Award

California Student Aid Commission
P.O. Box 419026
Rancho Cordova, CA 95741-9026
Phone: 888-224-7268
Fax: 916-464-8002
Email: studentsupport@csac.ca.gov
http://www.csac.ca.gov
Purpose: To support California resident students.
Eligibility: Applicants must complete the Free Application for Federal Student Aid (FAFSA) and file a verified grade point average with the California Student Aid Commission. Students must be California residents, be U.S. citizens or eligible noncitizens, meet U.S. Selective Service requirements, attend an eligible California postsecondary institution, be enrolled at least half-time, maintain satisfactory academic progress and not be in default on any student loan. Cal Grant A Entitlement Awards are for undergraduate institutions of not less than two academic years. Cal Grant B Entitlement Awards are for low-income students for living and transportation expenses, supplies and books at institutions of not less than one year. Cal Grant C Awards are for occupational or vocational programs. Cal Grant T Awards are for teacher credential candidates.
Target applicants: High school students. College students. Adult students.
Amount: Varies.
Number of awards: Varies.
Deadline: March 2.
How to apply: Applications are available by request.
Exclusive: Visit www.UltimateScholarshipBook.com and enter code CA124812 for updates on this award.

(1249) · California - Hawaii Elks Major Project Undergraduate Scholarship Program for Students with Disabilities

California-Hawaii Elks Association
5450 E. Lamona Avenue
Fresno, CA 93727-2224
Phone: 559-222-8071
Fax: 559-222-8073
http://www.chea-elks.org
Purpose: To provide education assistance for students with disabilities.
Eligibility: Applicants must be U.S. citizens and California or Hawaii residents who have a physical, neurological, visual or hearing impairment or a speech/language disorder. They must be high school seniors or graduates or have passed the GED or California High School Proficiency Examination.
Target applicants: High school students.
Amount: $1,000-$2,000.
Number of awards: 20-30.
Scholarship may be renewable.
Deadline: March 15.
How to apply: Applications are available online.
Exclusive: Visit www.UltimateScholarshipBook.com and enter code CA124912 for updates on this award.

(1250) · California Community Foundation Scholarships

California Community Foundation
445 S. Figueroa Street, Suite 3400
Los Angeles, CA 90071-1638
Phone: 213-413-4130
Fax: 213-622-2979
Email: csalazar@ccf-la.org
http://www.calfund.org
Purpose: To assist California residents attending college or graduate school.
Eligibility: The fund has about $2 million which is disbursed through a variety of scholarships for California residents pursuing higher education through undergraduate or graduate work in or out of state. There are scholarships for students pursuing specific majors, with specific personal, academic or leadership qualities and that honor family members or colleagues.

Target applicants: High school students. College students. Graduate school students. Adult students.
Amount: Varies.
Number of awards: Varies.
Scholarship may be renewable.
Deadline: Varies.
How to apply: Please contact your financial aid office for more information.
Exclusive: Visit www.UltimateScholarshipBook.com and enter code CA125012 for updates on this award.

(1251) • California Council of the Blind Scholarships

California Council of the Blind
578 B Street
Hayward, CA 94541
Phone: 510-537-7877
Fax: 510-537-7830
Email: ccotb@ccbnet.org
http://www.ccbnet.org
Purpose: To assist blind California residents for college, graduate or vocational studies.
Eligibility: Applicants must be legally blind residents of California attending an accredited college, university or vocational school full-time or with at least 12 units per term. The school does not have to be in California. Proof of blindness is required. A letter from the local chapter's president or member recommending the applicant is helpful. Award money can't be spent on food, clothing or shelter.
Target applicants: College students. Graduate school students. Adult students.
Amount: Varies.
Number of awards: Varies.
Scholarship may be renewable.
Deadline: June 15.
How to apply: Applications are available online.
Exclusive: Visit www.UltimateScholarshipBook.com and enter code CA125112 for updates on this award.

(1252) • California Fee Waiver Program for Children of Veterans

California Department of Veterans Affairs
1227 O Street
Sacramento, CA 95814
Phone: 800-952-5626
http://www.cdva.ca.gov
Purpose: To provide educational assistance for dependents of veterans.
Eligibility: Applicants must be the children, spouses, unmarried surviving spouses or registered domestic partners of veterans who are deceased or totally disabled due to service-related causes. The veteran must have served during a qualifying war period, and the child must be under 27 years of age (30 if the child is a veteran). There is no age limit for spouses or domestic partners. Children of veterans who have a service-connected disability, had one at the time of death or died of service-related causes may qualify if their income is at or below the national poverty level. In this case, there is no age limit.
Target applicants: High school students. College students. Adult students.
Amount: Tuition.
Number of awards: Varies.
Scholarship may be renewable.
Deadline: Varies.
How to apply: Applications are available online.
Exclusive: Visit www.UltimateScholarshipBook.com and enter code CA125212 for updates on this award.

(1253) • California Fee Waiver Program for Dependents of Deceased or Disabled National Guard Members

California Department of Veterans Affairs
1227 O Street
Sacramento, CA 95814
Phone: 800-952-5626
http://www.cdva.ca.gov
Purpose: To provide education assistance to dependents of deceased or disabled National Guard members.
Eligibility: Applicants must be dependents or surviving spouses or domestic partners of California National Guard members who were killed or permanently disabled during active duty in service to the state. Spouses or domestic partners must not have remarried or terminated the relationship.
Target applicants: High school students. College students. Adult students.
Amount: Tuition.
Number of awards: Varies.
Scholarship may be renewable.
Deadline: Varies.
How to apply: Applications are available online.
Exclusive: Visit www.UltimateScholarshipBook.com and enter code CA125312 for updates on this award.

(1254) • California Fee Waiver Program for Recipients of the Medal of Honor and Their Children

California Department of Veterans Affairs
1227 O Street
Sacramento, CA 95814
Phone: 800-952-5626
http://www.cdva.ca.gov
Purpose: To provide financial assistance for Medal of Honor recipients and their families.
Eligibility: Applicants must be Medal of Honor recipients, their children or dependents of a Registered Domestic Partner. Children must meet age, income and residency requirements. This award is only applicable toward undergraduate studies.
Target applicants: High school students. College students. Adult students.
Amount: Tuition.
Number of awards: Varies.
Scholarship may be renewable.
Deadline: Varies.
How to apply: Applications are available online.
Exclusive: Visit www.UltimateScholarshipBook.com and enter code CA125412 for updates on this award.

(1255) • California Hall of Fame Dreamers Challenge

The California Museum
c/o California Hall of Fame Dreamers Challenge
1020 O Street
Sacramento, CA 95814
Phone: 916-654-5688
Fax: 916-653-0314
Email: satkinson@sos.ca.gov
http://www.californiamuseum.org

Purpose: To aid artistic college-bound students in California.
Eligibility: Applicants must be graduating high school seniors who are attending a public, private or home school in California. They must submit an artistic or creative work that describes how they would like to change the world. Selection is based on the creativity and originality of the work submitted.
Target applicants: High school students.
Amount: $5,000.
Number of awards: 2.
Deadline: October 15.
How to apply: Entry forms are available online. An entry form, artistic work and personal essay are required.
Exclusive: Visit www.UltimateScholarshipBook.com and enter code TH125512 for updates on this award.

(1256) • California Interscholastic Federation (CIF) Scholar-Athlete of the Year

California Interscholastic Federation (CIF)
CIF State Office
Attn.: CIF Scholar-Athlete of the Year
1320 Harbor Bay Parkway, Suite 140
Alameda, CA 94502
Phone: 510-521-4447
Fax: 510-521-4449
Email: info@cifstate.org
http://www.cifstate.org
Purpose: To recognize high school student-athletes with exemplary academic and athletic careers and personal standards.
Eligibility: Applicants must be high school seniors with a minimum 3.7 GPA, demonstrate outstanding athletic performance in a minimum of two years of varsity play in California and exhibit character, trustworthiness, respect, responsibility, fairness, caring and citizenship.
Target applicants: High school students.
Minimum GPA: 3.7
Amount: 2,000-5,000.
Number of awards: 20.
Deadline: February 11.
How to apply: Applications are available by request.
Exclusive: Visit www.UltimateScholarshipBook.com and enter code CA125612 for updates on this award.

(1257) • California Law Enforcement Personnel Dependents Grant Program

California Student Aid Commission
P.O. Box 419026
Rancho Cordova, CA 95741-9026
Phone: 888-224-7268
Fax: 916-464-8002
Email: studentsupport@csac.ca.gov
http://www.csac.ca.gov
Purpose: To provide assistance for the families of deceased or disabled law enforcement personnel.
Eligibility: Applicants must be spouses or children of California peace officers, Department of Corrections or Youth Authority employees or full-time firefighters who were killed or totally disabled due to accident or injury in the line of duty. They must enroll at an accredited California community college, college or university for a minimum of six units. Financial need is required. Awards match the amount of a Cal Grant award.
Target applicants: High school students. College students. Adult students.
Amount: $100-$11,259.
Number of awards: Varies.
Scholarship may be renewable.
Deadline: Rolling.
How to apply: Applications are available by mail or phone. An application form, copy of FAFSA Student Aid Report and documentation of the law enforcement personnel's death or injury are required.
Exclusive: Visit www.UltimateScholarshipBook.com and enter code CA125712 for updates on this award.

(1258) • California Masonic Foundation Scholarship

California Masonic Foundation
1111 California Street
San Francisco, CA 94108-2284
Phone: 415-776-7000
Email: foundation@californiamasons.org
http://www.freemason.org
Purpose: To aid students in pursuit of a higher education.
Eligibility: Applicants must be U.S. citizens, be California residents for at least one year, be current high school seniors with a minimum 3.0 GPA, plan to attend an accredited two- or four-year college or university full-time and demonstrate financial need. There are a number of awards based on residence, career goals and general selection criteria.
Target applicants: High school students.
Minimum GPA: 3.0
Amount: $6,000-$40,000.
Number of awards: Varies.
Scholarship may be renewable.
Deadline: February 15.
How to apply: Applications are available online.
Exclusive: Visit www.UltimateScholarshipBook.com and enter code CA125812 for updates on this award.

(1259) • California Oratorical Contest

American Legion, Department of California
401 Van Ness Avenue, Room 117
San Francisco, CA 94102
Phone: 415-431-2400
Fax: 415-255-1571
Email: calegion@pacific.net
http://www.calegion.org
Purpose: To enhance high school students' experience with and understanding of the U.S. Constitution. The contest will help develop students' leadership skills and civic appreciation, as well as the ability to deliver thoughtful, insightful orations regarding U.S. citizenship and its inherent responsibilities.
Eligibility: Applicants must be high school students under the age of 20 who are U.S. citizens or legal residents and residents of the state. Students first give an oration within their state and winners compete at the national level. The oration must be related to the Constitution of the United States focusing on the duties and obligations citizens have to the government. It must be in English and be between eight and ten minutes. There is also an assigned topic which is posted on the website, and it should be between three and five minutes.
Target applicants: Junior high students or younger. High school students.
Amount: Up to $2,700.
Number of awards: Varies.
Deadline: February 15.
How to apply: Applications are available by email.

Exclusive: Visit www.UltimateScholarshipBook.com and enter code AM125912 for updates on this award.

(1260) • California Restaurant Association Educational Foundation Scholarship for High School Seniors

California Restaurant Association
621 Capitol Mall
Suite 2000
Sacramento, CA 95814
Phone: 800-765-4842
Fax: 916-447-6182
Email: membership@calrest.org
http://www.calrest.org
Purpose: To aid students with restaurant work experience.
Eligibility: Applicants must be high school seniors who are California residents and U.S. citizens or permanent residents and be enrolled in at least nine credit hours at an accredited institution of higher learning and have a GPA of 2.75 or higher. Students must plan to enroll in two consecutive semesters and have at least 250 hours of work experience in the restaurant industry.
Target applicants: High school students.
Minimum GPA: 2.75
Amount: Varies.
Number of awards: Varies.
Deadline: April 15.
How to apply: Applications are available online. An application form, essay, copy of curriculum, transcript, proof of work experience and one to three letters of recommendation are required.
Exclusive: Visit www.UltimateScholarshipBook.com and enter code CA126012 for updates on this award.

(1261) • California Restaurant Association Educational Foundation Scholarships for Undergraduate Students

California Restaurant Association
621 Capitol Mall
Suite 2000
Sacramento, CA 95814
Phone: 800-765-4842
Fax: 916-447-6182
Email: membership@calrest.org
http://www.calrest.org
Purpose: To support students with restaurant work experience.
Eligibility: Applicants must be California residents, U.S. citizens or permanent residents and undergraduate students who are enrolled in at least nine credit hours at an accredited institution of higher learning. A GPA of 2.75 or higher is required. Applicants must enroll in two consecutive semesters and have completed at least one grading term of a postsecondary program. Rising sophomores must have 400 hours of restaurant work experience, and those beyond the sophomore year must have 550 hours of experience.
Target applicants: College students. Adult students.
Minimum GPA: 2.75
Amount: Varies.
Number of awards: Varies.
Deadline: March 31.
How to apply: Applications are available online. An application form, essay, copy of curriculum, transcript, proof of work experience and one to three letters of recommendation are required.
Exclusive: Visit www.UltimateScholarshipBook.com and enter code CA126112 for updates on this award.

(1262) • California State Fair Academic Achievers Scholarships

California State Fair
P.O. Box 15649
Sacramento, CA 95852
Phone: 916-263-3636
Email: koneil@calexpo.com
http://www.bigfun.org
Purpose: To reward and motivate well-rounded, high-achieving California students.
Eligibility: Applicants must be enrolled or plan to enroll in a four-year accredited California institution of higher learning. They must have a GPA of 3.0 or higher and have a valid California ID.
Target applicants: High school students. College students. Adult students.
Minimum GPA: 3.0
Amount: Up to $5,000.
Number of awards: 24.
Deadline: March 12.
How to apply: Applications are available online.
Exclusive: Visit www.UltimateScholarshipBook.com and enter code CA126212 for updates on this award.

(1263) • California State PTA Scholarship

California State PTA
930 Georgia Street
Los Angeles, CA 90015-1322
Phone: 213-620-1100
Fax: 213-620-1411
http://www.capta.org
Purpose: To support high school seniors who have contributed to the community.
Eligibility: Applicants must attend a public California high school, be high school seniors who have served their school and community and be members of the PTA.
Target applicants: High school students.
Amount: $500.
Number of awards: Varies.
Deadline: February 1.
How to apply: Applications are available online.
Exclusive: Visit www.UltimateScholarshipBook.com and enter code CA126312 for updates on this award.

(1264) • California Wine Grape Growers Foundation Scholarships

California Association of Wine Grape Growers
601 University Avenue
Suite 135
Sacramento, CA 95825
Phone: 916-924-5370
Email: info@cawg.org
http://www.cwggf.org
Purpose: To support children of California vineyard workers.
Eligibility: Applicants must be high school seniors who are children of vineyard workers who were employed during one of the two seasons prior to application. Waivers are available for children of wine grape

growers based on financial need. Applicants must plan to attend any campus of the University of California or California State University systems, or any California community college. Selection criteria include financial need, scholastic ability, community involvement, leadership and/or work history and determination to succeed.
Target applicants: High school students.
Amount: $2,000-$8,000.
Number of awards: At least 6.
Deadline: April 4.
How to apply: Applications are available online. An application form, transcript, letter of recommendation and two-page essay are required. SAT or ACT scores are required for students applying for a four-year scholarship.
Exclusive: Visit www.UltimateScholarshipBook.com and enter code CA126412 for updates on this award.

(1265) • Californians For Disability Rights Foundation Scholarship

Californians for Disability Rights
1722 J Street
Suite 2
Sacramento, CA 95814
Phone: 916-447-2237
Fax: 916-447-7324
http://cdr-foundation.blogspot.com/
Purpose: To aid disabled individuals who want to improve the lives of others with disabilities in obtaining higher education.
Eligibility: Applicants must have a verified physical, mental or learning disability that severely limits at least one major life activity. They must be admitted to or enrolled in an accredited California college or university. Selection is based equally on demonstrated leadership and essay.
Target applicants: High school students. College students. Adult students.
Amount: $500.
Number of awards: Varies.
Deadline: March 2.
How to apply: Applications are available online. An application form, verification of disability, letter of recommendation, proof of college enrollment or acceptance and essay are required.
Exclusive: Visit www.UltimateScholarshipBook.com and enter code CA126512 for updates on this award.

(1266) • Candon, Todd and Seabolt Scholarship Fund

Hawaii Community Foundation - Scholarships
1164 Bishop Street, Suite 800
Honolulu, HI 96813
Phone: 888-731-3863
Fax: 808-521-6286
Email: scholarships@hcf-hawaii.org
http://www.hawaiicommunityfoundation.org
Purpose: To support Hawaii students who are majoring in accounting or finance.
Eligibility: Students must be in their junior or senior year of college with at least a 2.7 GPA.
Target applicants: College students. Adult students.
Minimum GPA: 2.7
Amount: Varies.
Number of awards: Varies.
Deadline: March 1.
How to apply: To apply, register online, complete the online application and select the scholarships to which you wish to apply. In addition, mail the supporting materials: printed confirmation page from the online application, personal statement, copy of Student Aid Report (SAR) available at www.fafsa.ed.gov and official transcript.
Exclusive: Visit www.UltimateScholarshipBook.com and enter code HA126612 for updates on this award.

(1267) • Caped General Excellence Scholarship

California Association for Postsecondary Education and Disability
71423 Biskra Road
Rancho Mirage, CA 92270
Phone: 760-346-8206
Fax: 760-340-5275
Email: bjaworski@csub.edu
http://www.caped.net
Purpose: To provide financial assistance to high achievers in academics, community and campus life.
Eligibility: Applicants must have a verifiable disability and demonstrate financial need. A minimum GPA of 2.5 is required for undergraduates and a minimum GPA of 3.0 for graduate students. Applicants must be taking at least six semester units or four quarter units at a public or private California institution of higher learning.
Target applicants: College students. Graduate school students. Adult students.
Minimum GPA: 2.5
Amount: $1,500.
Number of awards: 1.
Deadline: September 19.
How to apply: Applications are available online.
Exclusive: Visit www.UltimateScholarshipBook.com and enter code CA126712 for updates on this award.

(1268) • Capitol Scholarship

Connecticut Department of Higher Education
61 Woodland Street
Hartford, CT 06105-2326
Phone: 860-947-1855
Fax: 860-947-1838
Email: byrd@ctdhe.org
http://www.ctdhe.org
Purpose: To assist Connecticut student residents.
Eligibility: Applicants must be Connecticut residents who are U.S. citizens or permanent resident aliens and high school seniors or graduates in the top 20 percent of their class or with a minimum SAT score of 1800. The award must be used at a Connecticut college or at colleges in states that have reciprocity agreements and is based on financial need.
Target applicants: High school students. College students. Adult students.
Amount: $500-$3,000.
Number of awards: Varies.
Deadline: February 15.
How to apply: Applications are available online.
Exclusive: Visit www.UltimateScholarshipBook.com and enter code CO126812 for updates on this award.

(1269) • CAPPS Scholarship Program

California Association of Private Postsecondary Schools
400 Capitol Mall
Suite 1560
Sacramento, CA 95814
Phone: 916-447-5500

Email: info@cappsonline.org
http://www.cappsonline.org
Purpose: To allow private postsecondary schools to offer tuition scholarships to students.
Eligibility: Applicants must be legal California residents who have fulfilled the admission requirements for the school that is pledging their CAPPS scholarship. Application is restricted to high school and adult students only. Recipients are chosen on the basis of application date and each individual school's judging standards.
Target applicants: High school students.
Amount: $5,000.
Number of awards: 4.
Deadline: August 31.
How to apply: Applications are available online.
Exclusive: Visit www.UltimateScholarshipBook.com and enter code CA126912 for updates on this award.

(1270) • Career Advancement Program Tuition Waiver

Massachusetts Department of Higher Education
Office of Student Financial Assistance
454 Broadway
Suite 200
Revere, MA 02151
Phone: 617-727-9420
Fax: 617-727-0667
Email: osfa@osfa.mass.edu
http://www.osfa.mass.edu/default.asp
Purpose: To support Massachusetts public school teachers in the first three years of teaching.
Eligibility: Applicants must pass all three parts of the Massachusetts Teachers Test. They must be teaching at a Massachusetts public school in the same year that the award is used and they must be residents of the state. Applicants must also enroll in graduate courses at one of the nine Massachusetts State College campuses or the University of Massachusetts.
Target applicants: Graduate school students. Adult students.
Amount: Up to $900 ($300 per course).
Number of awards: Varies.
Scholarship may be renewable.
Deadline: Varies.
How to apply: Applications are available at college financial aid offices.
Exclusive: Visit www.UltimateScholarshipBook.com and enter code MA127012 for updates on this award.

(1271) • Career Aid for Technical Students Program

New Hampshire Charitable Foundation
37 Pleasant Street
Concord, NH 03301-4005
Phone: 603-225-6641
Fax: 603-225-1700
Email: info@nhcf.org
http://www.nhcf.org/Page.aspx?pid=183
Purpose: To aid students who need training beyond high school to meet their career goals.
Eligibility: Applicants must be New Hampshire residents who are dependent students under the age of 24. They must plan to enroll at least half-time in an accredited vocational or technical program that does not lead to a bachelor's degree. They must apply for federal financial aid and demonstrate financial need.
Target applicants: High school students. College students.
Amount: $1,000-$3,500.
Number of awards: Varies.
Deadline: June 1.
How to apply: Applications are available online. Application form, transcript, evaluation form and financial statement are required.
Exclusive: Visit www.UltimateScholarshipBook.com and enter code NE127112 for updates on this award.

(1272) • Career Colleges and Schools of Texas Scholarship Program

Career Colleges and Schools of Texas
P.O. Box 11539
Austin, TX 78711
Phone: 866-909-2278
Email: scholars@careerscholarships.org
http://www.colleges-schools.org
Purpose: To help Texas high school seniors who want to attend trade or technical schools in the state.
Eligibility: Participating institutions, which are listed on the website, provide scholarships to students who choose to enroll at their schools. Since each school has its own guidelines, applicants should contact a particular school for more information.
Target applicants: High school students.
Amount: $1,000.
Number of awards: Varies.
Deadline: Varies.
How to apply: Applicants should contact their high school counselors or participating schools.
Exclusive: Visit www.UltimateScholarshipBook.com and enter code CA127212 for updates on this award.

(1273) • Cargill Community Scholarship Program

National FFA Organization
P.O. Box 68960
6060 FFA Drive
Indianapolis, IN 46268-0960
Phone: 317-802-6060
Fax: 317-802-6051
Email: scholarships@ffa.org
http://www.ffa.org/
Purpose: To provide financial assistance for well-rounded high school students.
Eligibility: Applicants must be pursuing a two- or four-year degree. They must live near a Cargill or Cargill joint venture facility, and their applications must be signed by a local Cargill employee. Academic achievement, leadership and community service are required. Cargill has locations in Arkansas; Colorado; the Gulf Area communities of Alabama, Louisiana and Texas; Illinois; Indiana; Iowa; Kansas; Minnesota; Missouri; Nebraska; North Dakota; Ohio; South Dakota; Texas and Wisconsin.
Target applicants: High school students.
Amount: $1,000.
Number of awards: 350.
Deadline: February 15.
How to apply: Applications are available online.
Exclusive: Visit www.UltimateScholarshipBook.com and enter code NA127312 for updates on this award.

(1274) • Carl W. Christiansen Scholarship

Rhode Island Society of Certified Public Accountants
45 Royal Little Drive
Providence, RI 02904
Phone: 401-331-5720
Fax: 401-454-5780
Email: rmancini@riscpa.org
http://www.riscpa.org

Purpose: To support Rhode Island students who are pursuing careers in public accounting.
Eligibility: Students must have at least a 3.0 GPA. Applicants must submit a short essay and a letter of recommendation.
Target applicants: College students. Adult students.
Minimum GPA: 3.0
Amount: Varies.
Number of awards: Varies.
Deadline: January 15.
How to apply: Applications are available online.
Exclusive: Visit www.UltimateScholarshipBook.com and enter code RH127412 for updates on this award.

(1275) • Carolina Rice Scholarship Program

Carolina Rice
c/o Riviana Foods Inc.
P.O. Box 2636
Houston, TX 77252
Phone: 808-226-9522
Fax: 713-942-1826
http://www.carolinarice.com/scholarship

Purpose: To assist students in metropolitan areas in obtaining higher education.
Eligibility: Applicants must be high school seniors in New York/New Jersey, Chicago, Miami Dade and Broward Counties, Los Angeles and Orange County,or San Francisco/San Jose. They must submit essays on how a college education will help them achieve their goals.
Target applicants: High school students.
Amount: $2,000.
Number of awards: 5.
Deadline: February 15.
How to apply: Applications are available online.
Exclusive: Visit www.UltimateScholarshipBook.com and enter code CA127512 for updates on this award.

(1276) • Carpenter Scholarship

Club Zion
221 Chester Avenue
Bakersfield, CA 93301
Phone: 661-631-2582
Email: contact@clubzion.com
http://www.clubzion.com

Purpose: To assist Christian students who are interested in a trade career.
Eligibility: Applicants must live in the Kern County, California area and have dedicated their lives to Christ. They must have a GPA of 3.0 or higher and be involved in a local church. Two letters of recommendation, SAT scores and high school transcripts are required. Winners must complete one hour of ministry service or volunteer work each week.
Target applicants: High school students.
Minimum GPA: 3.0
Amount: Varies.
Number of awards: Varies.
Deadline: Varies.
How to apply: Applications are available from Club Zion.
Exclusive: Visit www.UltimateScholarshipBook.com and enter code CL127612 for updates on this award.

(1277) • Cash Grant Program

Massachusetts Department of Higher Education
Office of Student Financial Assistance
454 Broadway
Suite 200
Revere, MA 02151
Phone: 617-727-9420
Fax: 617-727-0667
Email: osfa@osfa.mass.edu
http://www.osfa.mass.edu/default.asp

Purpose: To help needy students pay college or university fees and non-state-supported tuition.
Eligibility: Students must be permanent residents of Massachusetts for at least one year before the academic year for which the grant is awarded. Students must also demonstrate financial need, be enrolled in at least three credits per semester in an eligible undergraduate program and not have previously earned a bachelor's degree or higher.
Target applicants: High school students. College students. Adult students.
Amount: Up to full tuition.
Number of awards: Varies.
Scholarship may be renewable.
Deadline: Varies.
How to apply: Applications are available from your financial aid office.
Exclusive: Visit www.UltimateScholarshipBook.com and enter code MA127712 for updates on this award.

(1278) • Castle & Cooke George W.Y. Yim Scholarship Fund

Hawaii Community Foundation - Scholarships
1164 Bishop Street, Suite 800
Honolulu, HI 96813
Phone: 888-731-3863
Fax: 808-521-6286
Email: scholarships@hcf-hawaii.org
http://www.hawaiicommunityfoundation.org

Purpose: To support the dependents of Castle and Cooke employees.
Eligibility: Employees must have had at least one year of service with an affiliated company of Castle and Cooke Hawaii. Students must have at least a 3.0 GPA.
Target applicants: High school students. College students. Adult students.
Minimum GPA: 3.0
Amount: Varies.
Number of awards: Varies.
Deadline: March 1.
How to apply: To apply, register online, complete the online application and select the scholarships to which you wish to apply. In addition, mail the supporting materials: printed confirmation page from the online application, personal statement, copy of Student Aid Report (SAR) available at www.fafsa.ed.gov and official transcript.
Exclusive: Visit www.UltimateScholarshipBook.com and enter code HA127812 for updates on this award.

(1279) • Categorical Tuition Waiver

Massachusetts Department of Higher Education
Office of Student Financial Assistance
454 Broadway
Suite 200
Revere, MA 02151
Phone: 617-727-9420
Fax: 617-727-0667
Email: osfa@osfa.mass.edu
http://www.osfa.mass.edu/default.asp

Purpose: To provide financial support to Massachusetts students who would otherwise not be able to afford higher education.
Eligibility: Applicants must be residents of the state of Massachusetts for at least one year prior to the beginning of the academic year in which the scholarship is used. They also must be members of one of the following groups of people: veterans or active members of the armed forces, Native Americans, senior citizens or clients of either the Massachusetts Rehabilitation Commission or Commission for the Blind. Students must be enrolled in at least three credits per semester in a state undergraduate or certificate program, and they must remain in satisfactory academic standing.
Target applicants: High school students. College students. Adult students.
Amount: Up to full tuition.
Number of awards: Varies.
Deadline: Varies.
How to apply: Applications are available at college financial aid offices.
Exclusive: Visit www.UltimateScholarshipBook.com and enter code MA127912 for updates on this award.

(1280) • Cayetano Foundation Scholarships

Hawaii Community Foundation - Scholarships
1164 Bishop Street, Suite 800
Honolulu, HI 96813
Phone: 888-731-3863
Fax: 808-521-6286
Email: scholarships@hcf-hawaii.org
http://www.hawaiicommunityfoundation.org

Purpose: To support exceptional Hawaii students.
Eligibility: Applicants must be upcoming high school graduates in Hawaii. They must have a GPA of 3.5 or higher. Preference is given to students who have overcome financial and social obstacles and to the students with the greatest financial need.
Target applicants: High school students.
Minimum GPA: 3.5
Amount: Varies.
Number of awards: Varies.
Deadline: February 18.
How to apply: Applications are available online. An application form, personal statement, copy of FAFSA Student Aid Report, transcript, two letters of recommendation and an essay are required.
Exclusive: Visit www.UltimateScholarshipBook.com and enter code HA128012 for updates on this award.

(1281) • CCNMA Scholarships

California Chicano News Media Association
USC Annenberg School of Journalism
727 W. 27th Street, Room 201
Los Angeles, CA 90007-3212
Phone: 213-821-0075
Fax: 213-743-1838
Email: ccnmainfo@ccnma.org
http://www.ccnma.org

Purpose: To support Latino students with career goals in journalism.
Eligibility: Applicants must be Latino and either California residents or be attending California schools. While the student's degree does not have to be in journalism, they must demonstrate plans to pursue a career in journalism. An interview and autobiographical essay are required. Awards are based also on financial need, academic achievement and a civic responsibility.
Target applicants: High school students. College students. Graduate school students. Adult students.
Amount: $1,000.
Number of awards: Varies.
Deadline: April 3.
How to apply: Applications are available online.
Exclusive: Visit www.UltimateScholarshipBook.com and enter code CA128112 for updates on this award.

(1282) • Center for the Arts Scholarship Foundation of Broward Scholarship

Florida State Thespian Society
Michael J. Higgins, State Director
Douglas Anderson School of the Arts
2445 San Diego Road
Jacksonville, FL 32207
Phone: 813-417-6520
Fax: 904-645-5900
http://www.flthespian.com

Purpose: To support future actors.
Eligibility: Applicants must be Florida high school seniors who have actively participated in a district competition in the Florida State Thespian Society and are fully qualified to attend the state competition and be members of the International Thespian Society. Students must intend to pursue a career in theatre, demonstrate potential to do so and have a minimum GPA of 3.0, SAT score of 1280 or ACT score of 26. Applicants must audition for the award. Those auditioning in musical theatre must have a letter of recommendation. Note: We do not recommend applying to scholarships that charge application fees. However, some scholarships of this type charge fees and are included for completeness.
Target applicants: High school students.
Minimum GPA: 3.0
Amount: $1,000.
Number of awards: 1.
Deadline: Varies.
How to apply: Applications are available from the Florida State Thespian Society. An application form, $10 application fee and letter of recommendation (for musical theatre only) are required.
Exclusive: Visit www.UltimateScholarshipBook.com and enter code FL128212 for updates on this award.

(1283) • Central Arizona DX Association Scholarship

American Radio Relay League Foundation
225 Main Street
Newington, CT 06111
Phone: 860-594-0397
Fax: 860-594-0259
Email: foundation@arrl.org
http://www.arrlf.org

Purpose: To provide scholarship assistance to amateur radio operators from Arizona.
Eligibility: Applicants must be Arizona residents with a Technician Class or higher Amateur Radio License. They must have a GPA of 3.2 or higher. Graduating high school seniors receive preference over current college students.
Target applicants: High school students. College students. Adult students.
Minimum GPA: 3.2
Amount: $1,000.
Number of awards: 1.
Deadline: February 1.
How to apply: Applications are available online.
Exclusive: Visit www.UltimateScholarshipBook.com and enter code AM128312 for updates on this award.

(1284) • CESDA Diversity Scholarship

Colorado Educational Services and Development Association
P.O. Box 40214
Denver, CO 80204
Phone: 303-352-3231
Email: melissa.quinteros@ccd.edu
http://www.cesda.org
Purpose: To provide financial assistance for disadvantaged students.
Eligibility: Applicants must be either first generation college students, members of underrepresented ethnic or racial minorities or show financial need. They must be Colorado residents who are high school seniors at the time of application. Students must have a GPA of 2.8 or higher and enroll in a two- or four-year Colorado college or university in the fall following graduation. They must take at least six credit hours to qualify.
Target applicants: High school students.
Minimum GPA: 2.8
Amount: $1,000.
Number of awards: Varies.
Deadline: March 15.
How to apply: Applications are available online.
Exclusive: Visit www.UltimateScholarshipBook.com and enter code CO128412 for updates on this award.

(1285) • CEW Scholarships

Center for the Education of Women
330 E. Liberty
Ann Arbor, MI 48104-2289
Phone: 734-998-7080
Fax: 734-998-6203
http://www.umich.edu/~cew
Purpose: To support women who are returning to college after an interruption.
Eligibility: Applicants must be women who are returning to school after an interruption of at least 48 consecutive months or a total of 50 months excluding interruptions of less than 8 months. Candidates must be working toward a clear educational goal at any University of Michigan campus. Preference is given to women wishing to study in non-traditional fields such as mathematics, physical sciences and engineering.
Target applicants: Graduate school students. Adult students.
Amount: $1,000-$8,000.
Number of awards: Approximately 40.
Deadline: Varies.
How to apply: Applications are available online.
Exclusive: Visit www.UltimateScholarshipBook.com and enter code CE128512 for updates on this award.

(1286) • CHAHRM Scholarship

Colorado Healthcare Association for Human Resource Management
c/o Gini Adams, Director of Employee and Public Relations
Yuma District Hospital
1000 West 8th Avenue
Yuma, CO 80759
Phone: 970-848-4602
http://www.chahrm.org
Purpose: To aid students enrolled in a healthcare or human resources degree program.
Eligibility: Applicants must be in the final year of study for a degree in a healthcare- or human resources-related subject at an accredited technical college or university. They must have a GPA of 3.0 or higher. Selection is based on academic merit, stated career goals, work history, extracurricular activities and references.
Target applicants: College students. Adult students.
Minimum GPA: 3.0
Amount: $1,000.
Number of awards: Varies.
Deadline: September 25.
How to apply: Applications are available online. An application form, a transcript, a personal essay and a faculty advisor reference are required.
Exclusive: Visit www.UltimateScholarshipBook.com and enter code CO128612 for updates on this award.

(1287) • Charles Dubose Scholarship

Connecticut Architecture Foundation
370 James Street
Suite 402
New Haven, CT 06513
Phone: 203-865-2195
Fax: 203-562-5378
http://www.aiact.org
Purpose: To assist architecture students.
Eligibility: Applicants must have completed two years of an NAAB accredited architecture program leading to a bachelor's degree as of June 30 of the year of application. Students enrolled in non-accredited programs who have been accepted to an NAAB accredited master's degree program, as well as those currently enrolled in such a program, are also eligible. Applicants must be full-time students. Preference is given to students at the University of Pennsylvania, Georgia Institute of Technology and Fontainebleau summer program and to Connecticut residents.
Target applicants: College students. Graduate school students. Adult students.
Amount: $1,200-$5,000.
Number of awards: Varies.
Deadline: April 22.
How to apply: Applications are available online. An application form, statement of goals, resume, financial aid information sheet, two letters of reference and submission of a favorite project are required.
Exclusive: Visit www.UltimateScholarshipBook.com and enter code CO128712 for updates on this award.

(1288) • Charles Gallagher Student Financial Assistance Program

Missouri Student Assistance Resource Services (MOSTARS)
Missouri Department of Higher Education
3515 Amazonas Drive
Jefferson City, MO 65109
Phone: 800-473-6757
Fax: 573-751-6635
http://www.dhe.mo.gov

Purpose: To provide need-based grants for Missouri citizens to access Missouri postsecondary education.
Eligibility: Applicants must be U.S. citizens or eligible noncitizens, Missouri residents who are full-time undergraduates at an approved Missouri postsecondary schools and working toward their first baccalaureate degree. Applicants must demonstrate financial need.
Target applicants: High school students. College students. Adult students.
Amount: Varies.
Number of awards: Varies.
Scholarship may be renewable.
Deadline: April 1.
How to apply: Complete the Free Application for Federal Student Aid (FAFSA) by April 1 of the upcoming academic year.
Exclusive: Visit www.UltimateScholarshipBook.com and enter code MI128812 for updates on this award.

(1289) • Charles McDaniel Teacher Scholarship

Georgia Student Finance Commission
2082 East Exchange Place
Tucker, GA 30084
Phone: 800-505-4732
Fax: 770-724-9089
Email: support@gacollege411.org
http://www.gacollege411.org

Purpose: To support students in Georgia pursuing a degree in teaching.
Eligibility: Applicants must be full-time juniors or seniors at a public Georgia college or university. They must be admitted to their school's college or department of education and have a GPA of 3.25 or higher. Applicants must be legal residents of Georgia, have graduated from a Georgia high school, be U.S. citizens or permanent resident aliens, be in compliance with Selective Service requirements and not be in default on student financial aid. Eligible colleges and universities can nominate one student each year.
Target applicants: College students. Adult students.
Minimum GPA: 3.25
Amount: $1,000.
Number of awards: 3.
Deadline: July 15.
How to apply: Applications are available online and from college education departments.
Exclusive: Visit www.UltimateScholarshipBook.com and enter code GE128912 for updates on this award.

(1290) • Charles R. Hemenway Memorial Scholarship

University of Hawaii
Student Services Center Room 413
2600 Campus Road
Honolulu, HI 96822
Phone: 808-956-4642
Email: seed@hawaii.edu
http://www2.honolulu.hawaii.edu/

Purpose: To assist residents of Hawaii with college education expenses.
Eligibility: Applicants must demonstrate financial need and be Hawaii residents. Applicants must also be enrolled at least half-time at any of the campuses of the University of Hawaii. Selection is based on character and "qualities of good citizenship."
Target applicants: High school students. College students. Adult students.
Minimum GPA: 2.0
Amount: $500.
Number of awards: Varies.
Scholarship may be renewable.
Deadline: June 18.
How to apply: Applications are available online.
Exclusive: Visit www.UltimateScholarshipBook.com and enter code UN129012 for updates on this award.

(1291) • Charles W. and Annette Hill Scholarship

American Legion, Department of Kansas
1314 SW Topeka Boulevard
Topeka, KS 66612
Phone: 785-232-9315
Fax: 785-232-1399
http://www.ksamlegion.org

Purpose: To provide financial assistance to needy and worthy children of members of the American Legion.
Eligibility: Applicants must be descendents of an American Legion member with a GPA of at least 3.0. Special consideration will be given to students studying science, engineering or business administration. Applicants must submit three letters of recommendation, with only one from a teacher, an essay on "Why I Want to Go to College," a high school transcript, documentation of parent's veteran status and a 1040 income statement. Applicants must maintain a 3.0 GPA in college and verify enrollment at the start of each semester.
Target applicants: High school students. College students. Adult students.
Minimum GPA: 3.0
Amount: $1,000.
Number of awards: 1.
Deadline: February 15.
How to apply: Applications are available online.
Exclusive: Visit www.UltimateScholarshipBook.com and enter code AM129112 for updates on this award.

(1292) • Charles W. Riley Fire and Emergency Medical Services Tuition Reimbursement Program

Maryland Higher Education Commission
Office of Student Financial Assistance
839 Bestgate Road, Suite 400
Annapolis, MD 21401
Phone: 800-974-1024
Fax: 410-260-3200
Email: osfamail@mhec.state.md.us
http://www.mhec.state.md.us

Purpose: To support Maryland students who are majoring and working in firefighting or emergency medical services fields.
Eligibility: Applicants must be active firefighters, ambulance or rescue squad members living and serving in the state of Maryland. Students must attend a Maryland college majoring in fire service technology or emergency medical technology. They must continue to serve throughout college and for one year after graduating.

Target applicants: College students. Graduate school students. Adult students.
Amount: Varies.
Number of awards: Varies.
Scholarship may be renewable.
Deadline: July 1.
How to apply: Applications are available online.
Exclusive: Visit www.UltimateScholarshipBook.com and enter code MA129212 for updates on this award.

(1293) • Cheryl A. Ruggiero Scholarship

Rhode Island Society of Certified Public Accountants
45 Royal Little Drive
Providence, RI 02904
Phone: 401-331-5720
Fax: 401-454-5780
Email: rmancini@riscpa.org
http://www.riscpa.org
Purpose: To support female students who are pursuing careers in public accounting.
Eligibility: Students must be residents of the state of Rhode Island, and they must have at least a 3.0 GPA. Applicants must submit a short essay and a letter of recommendation.
Target applicants: College students. Adult students.
Minimum GPA: 3.0
Amount: Varies.
Number of awards: Varies.
Deadline: January 15.
How to apply: Applications are available online.
Exclusive: Visit www.UltimateScholarshipBook.com and enter code RH129312 for updates on this award.

(1294) • Chesapeake Urology Associates Scholarship

Central Scholarship Bureau
1700 Reisterstown Road
Suite 220
Baltimore, MD 21208-2903
Phone: 410-415-5558
Fax: 410-415-5501
Email: info@centralsb.org
http://www.centralsb.org
Purpose: To assist full-time Maryland undergraduate students pursuing a degree in pre-medicine, pre-nursing and ancillary health fields.
Eligibility: Applicants must be U.S. citizens or permanent residents, have a minimum 2.0 GPA and meet specified income requirements. The awards are based on commitment to the medical field, financial need and academic excellence. An application form, budget form, school bill, transcript, Student Aid Report, school financial aid award letter and essay are required.
Target applicants: High school students. College students. Adult students.
Minimum GPA: 2.0
Amount: Up to $5,000.
Number of awards: Varies.
Deadline: May 10.
How to apply: Applications are available online.
Exclusive: Visit www.UltimateScholarshipBook.com and enter code CE129412 for updates on this award.

(1295) • Chicago Scholars Award

Chicago Scholars Foundation
333 W. Wacker Drive, 33rd Floor
Chicago, IL 60606
Phone: 312-917-6868
Fax: 312-917-7806
Email: chischolars@nuveen.com
http://www.chicagoscholars.org
Purpose: To recognize high school juniors in the Chicago area who have overcome considerable obstacles to succeed in high school and attend college.
Eligibility: One award is presented to one junior from each Chicago high school graduating class. Applicants must be nominated by their high school and be Chicago residents or attend a Chicago high school and have a minimum 3.5 GPA. Applicants' financial need is also a consideration.
Target applicants: High school students.
Minimum GPA: 3.5
Amount: Varies.
Number of awards: Varies.
Deadline: February 28.
How to apply: Applicants must be nominated by their high schools.
Exclusive: Visit www.UltimateScholarshipBook.com and enter code CH129512 for updates on this award.

(1296) • Chicana/Latina Foundation Scholarship

Chicana/Latina Foundation Scholarship Program
1419 Burlingame Avenue, Suite N
Burlingame, CA 94010
Phone: 650-373-1084
Fax: 650-373-1090
Email: info@chicanalatina.org
http://www.chicanalatina.org
Purpose: To assist Latina students in completing their educations.
Eligibility: Applicants must be Chicana/Latina women who have lived in the Northern California counties for at least two years and are attending school at an accredited institution in the same region. Undergraduate applicants must be full-time students who have completed at least 15 semester units and earned a 2.5 GPA. Applicants must demonstrate leadership and community involvement and agree to volunteer at least five years in support of the Chicana/Latina Foundation if they receive the scholarship.
Target applicants: College students. Graduate school students. Adult students.
Minimum GPA: 2.5
Amount: $1,500.
Number of awards: 30.
Deadline: Varies.
How to apply: Applications are available online.
Exclusive: Visit www.UltimateScholarshipBook.com and enter code CH129612 for updates on this award.

(1297) • Child Care Provider Scholarship

Maryland Higher Education Commission
Office of Student Financial Assistance
839 Bestgate Road, Suite 400
Annapolis, MD 21401
Phone: 800-974-1024
Fax: 410-260-3200
Email: osfamail@mhec.state.md.us

http://www.mhec.state.md.us
Purpose: To encourage and support students to enter the field of childhood development or early childhood education.
Eligibility: Applicants and their parents must be legal residents of the state of Maryland. Applicants must enroll at a two- or four-year Maryland college or university as a full-time or part-time degree-seeking undergraduate. Applicants must enter a child development program or an early childhood education program. Applicants must also sign a promissory note agreeing to provide child care services in Maryland at the rate of one year for each year of the award.
Target applicants: High school students. College students. Adult students.
Amount: $1,000-$2,000.
Number of awards: Varies.
Scholarship may be renewable.
Deadline: June 15.
How to apply: Complete and file a Child Care Provider Scholarship application.
Exclusive: Visit www.UltimateScholarshipBook.com and enter code MA129712 for updates on this award.

(1298) • Children and Youth Scholarships

American Legion, Department of Maine
21 College Avenue
Waterville, ME 04901
Phone: 207-873-3229
Email: legionme@me.acadia.net
http://www.mainelegion.org
Purpose: To provide financial support to Maine students.
Eligibility: Applicants must be high school seniors or college students attending or planning to attend an accredited college or vocational school. Applicants must also demonstrate financial need and include two letters of recommendation and a personal statement.
Target applicants: High school students. College students. Adult students.
Amount: $500.
Number of awards: 7.
Deadline: May 1.
How to apply: Applications are available online.
Exclusive: Visit www.UltimateScholarshipBook.com and enter code AM129812 for updates on this award.

(1299) • Chiropractic Education Assistance Scholarship

Oklahoma State Regents for Higher Education
655 Research Parkway
Suite 200
Oklahoma City, OK 73104
Phone: 405-225-9100
Email: llangston@osrhe.edu
http://www.okhighered.org
Purpose: To provide financial assistance to Oklahoma students who are studying chiropractic at out-of-state institutions.
Eligibility: Applicants must have been Oklahoma residents for at least five years and be enrolled in or accepted to an accredited chiropractic school. They must maintain a minimum GPA of 3.0.
Target applicants: High school students. College students. Graduate school students. Adult students.
Minimum GPA: 3.0
Amount: Up to $6,000.
Number of awards: Varies.
Scholarship may be renewable.
Deadline: End of May.
How to apply: Applications are available from your institution.
Exclusive: Visit www.UltimateScholarshipBook.com and enter code OK129912 for updates on this award.

(1300) • Chittenden Bank Scholarship

Vermont Student Assistance Corporation
10 East Allen Street
P.O. Box 2000
Winooski, VT 05404
Phone: 800-882-4166
Fax: 802-654-3765
Email: info@vsac.org
http://www.vsac.org
Purpose: To provide financial assistance to Vermont students.
Eligibility: Applicants must be high school or college students attending or planning to attend an accredited Vermont college or university that is approved for Title IV funding. They must demonstrate academic achievement, financial need and school or community involvement.
Target applicants: High school students. College students. Adult students.
Amount: $2,500.
Number of awards: 2.
Deadline: March 4.
How to apply: Applications are available online.
Exclusive: Visit www.UltimateScholarshipBook.com and enter code VE130012 for updates on this award.

(1301) • Christa McAuliffe Scholarship

Tennessee Student Assistance Corporation
404 James Robertson Parkway
Suite 1510, Parkway Towers
Nashville, TN 37243
Phone: 800-342-1663
Fax: 615-741-6101
Email: tsac.aidinfo@tn.gov
http://www.tn.gov/CollegePays/
Purpose: To support Tennessee students who are pursuing careers in teaching.
Eligibility: Applicants must be in the second semester of their junior year in a teaching program at a Tennessee college, and they must be enrolled full-time. Students must have at least a 3.5 GPA and an SAT or ACT score that is at least as high as the national average. They must not have any defaulted state or federal student loans. Recipients must agree to teach in a Tennessee elementary or secondary school for a period of time upon graduation.
Target applicants: College students. Adult students.
Minimum GPA: 3.5
Amount: $500.
Number of awards: Varies.
Deadline: April 1.
How to apply: Applications are available online.
Exclusive: Visit www.UltimateScholarshipBook.com and enter code TE130112 for updates on this award.

(1302) · Christian A. Herter Memorial Scholarship Program

Massachusetts Department of Higher Education
Office of Student Financial Assistance
454 Broadway
Suite 200
Revere, MA 02151
Phone: 617-727-9420
Fax: 617-727-0667
Email: osfa@osfa.mass.edu
http://www.osfa.mass.edu/default.asp

Purpose: To provide educational opportunities to Massachusetts students who demonstrate academic promise and a desire to attend post-secondary institutions.
Eligibility: Applicants must be enrolled in a public or private secondary school in the Commonwealth of Massachusetts and be legal residents of the state. Applicants must have a cumulative grade point average of 2.5 and exhibit difficult personal circumstances, high financial need and strong academic promise to continue education beyond the secondary level.
Target applicants: High school students.
Minimum GPA: 2.5
Amount: Up to $15,000.
Number of awards: Varies.
Scholarship may be renewable.
Deadline: April 1.
How to apply: Applications are available online.
Exclusive: Visit www.UltimateScholarshipBook.com and enter code MA130212 for updates on this award.

(1303) · Chuck Fulgham Scholarship

Dallas Foundation
900 Jackson Street
Suite 705
Dallas, TX 75202
Phone: 214-741-9898
Email: rlasseter@dallasfoundation.org
http://www.dallasfoundation.org

Purpose: To support average students.
Eligibility: Applicants must be Texas residents who are adult graduates of literacy programs or high school graduates or GED holders with a GPA of 3.0 or lower who are interested in the humanities. Students must be accepted to or enrolled in an accredited institution of higher learning and demonstrate financial need. Preference is given to Dallas county residents and students who have participated in sports.
Target applicants: High school students. College students. Adult students.
Amount: Up to $2,500.
Number of awards: Varies.
Deadline: April 1.
How to apply: Applications are available online. An application form, transcript or GED certificate, copy of FAFSA or Student Aid Report, essay, list of activities and work experience and letter of recommendation are required.
Exclusive: Visit www.UltimateScholarshipBook.com and enter code DA130312 for updates on this award.

(1304) · Churchill Family Scholarship

Maine Community Foundation
245 Main Street
Ellsworth, ME 04605
Phone: 207-667-9735
Fax: 207-667-0447
Email: jwarren@mainecf.org
http://www.mainecf.org

Purpose: To support students in vocal music education or performance.
Eligibility: Students must be female high school seniors in Maine and planning to major in vocal music education or performance.
Target applicants: High school students.
Amount: Varies.
Number of awards: Varies.
Deadline: Varies.
How to apply: Applications are available in January on the Maine Community Foundation website or by contacting Musica de Filia.
Exclusive: Visit www.UltimateScholarshipBook.com and enter code MA130412 for updates on this award.

(1305) · Cindy Kolb Memorial Scholarship

California Association for Postsecondary Education and Disability
71423 Biskra Road
Rancho Mirage, CA 92270
Phone: 760-346-8206
Fax: 760-340-5275
Email: bjaworski@csub.edu
http://www.caped.net

Purpose: To provide financial assistance for students with disabilities.
Eligibility: Applicants must have a verifiable disability. They must be students at a four-year institution of higher learning in California with a GPA of at least 2.5 if an undergraduate or 3.0 if a graduate student. A letter of recommendation, a letter of application and documentation of the student's disability is required.
Target applicants: College students. Graduate school students. Adult students.
Minimum GPA: 2.5
Amount: $1,000.
Number of awards: 1.
Deadline: September 19.
How to apply: Applications are available online.
Exclusive: Visit www.UltimateScholarshipBook.com and enter code CA130512 for updates on this award.

(1306) · Clair A. Hill Scholarship

Association of California Water Agencies
910 K Street
Suite 100
Sacramento, CA 95814
Phone: 916-441-4545
Fax: 916-325-4849
Email: acwabox@acwa.com
http://www.acwa.com

Purpose: To support California undergraduates pursuing degrees in a water resources-related subject.
Eligibility: Applicants must be California residents who are rising juniors or seniors at a participating postsecondary institution located in California. They must be pursuing an undergraduate degree in a water resources-related subject and be full-time students enrolled for the entirety of the upcoming school year. Selection is based on professional commitment to the water resources field, academic achievement and financial need.
Target applicants: College students. Adult students.
Amount: $5,000.
Number of awards: 1.

Deadline: February 1.
How to apply: Applications are available online. An application form, personal essay, transcript and two to three letters of recommendation are required.
Exclusive: Visit www.UltimateScholarshipBook.com and enter code AS130612 for updates on this award.

(1307) · Clanseer and Anna Johnson Scholarships

Community Foundation of New Jersey
P.O. Box 338
Morristown, NJ 07963-0338
Phone: 973-267-5533
Fax: 973-267-2903
Email: fkrueger@cfnj.org
http://www.cfnj.org
Purpose: To provide education assistance for disadvantaged African American students.
Eligibility: Applicants must have been born in the United States and be New Jersey residents. They must have an A or B average in science and math-related subjects and maintain above average grades overall. Financial need and merit are considered. Scholarship winners are asked to perform at least ten hours of community service each week for a year following graduation.
Target applicants: High school students.
Amount: $6,000.
Number of awards: 4.
Deadline: April 1.
How to apply: Applications are available online.
Exclusive: Visit www.UltimateScholarshipBook.com and enter code CO130712 for updates on this award.

(1308) · Clem Judd, Jr., Memorial Scholarship

Hawaii Hotel and Lodging Association
2250 Kalakaua Avenue
Suite 404-4
Honolulu, HI 96815
http://www.hawaiihotels.org
Purpose: To help Hawaiian residents majoring in hotel management.
Eligibility: Applicants must have a minimum 3.0 GPA, be able to prove Hawaiian ancestry and be enrolled full-time at a U.S. university or college.
Target applicants: High school students. College students. Adult students.
Minimum GPA: 3.0
Amount: $1,000-$2,500.
Number of awards: 1.
Deadline: July 1.
How to apply: Applications are available by written request beginning February 1.
Exclusive: Visit www.UltimateScholarshipBook.com and enter code HA130812 for updates on this award.

(1309) · Clete Roberts Memorial Journalism Scholarship Award

Associated Press Television and Radio Association
c/o Roberta Gonzales
CBS 5 TV
855 Battery Street
San Francisco, CA 94111
http://www.aptra.org
Purpose: To aid students pursuing careers in broadcast journalism.
Eligibility: Applicants must be current students at California, Nevada or Hawaii colleges or universities and be able to provide tapes or other samples of work related to broadcast journalism.
Target applicants: College students. Adult students.
Amount: $1,500.
Number of awards: Varies.
Deadline: December 31.
How to apply: Applications are available online. An application form and work samples are required.
Exclusive: Visit www.UltimateScholarshipBook.com and enter code AS130912 for updates on this award.

(1310) · Collaborative Teachers Tuition Waiver

Massachusetts Department of Higher Education
Office of Student Financial Assistance
454 Broadway
Suite 200
Revere, MA 02151
Phone: 617-727-9420
Fax: 617-727-0667
Email: osfa@osfa.mass.edu
http://www.osfa.mass.edu/default.asp
Purpose: To provide graduate school tuition waivers for Massachusetts teachers who become student teacher mentors.
Eligibility: Applicants must be public school teachers living and working in the state of Massachusetts. They must also agree to mentor a student teacher from a state college or university in their own classroom, and they must be planning to attend graduate school at one of the nine campuses of Massachusetts State College or the University of Massachusetts.
Target applicants: Graduate school students. Adult students.
Amount: Varies.
Number of awards: Varies.
Scholarship may be renewable.
Deadline: Varies.
How to apply: Applications are available at college financial aid offices.
Exclusive: Visit www.UltimateScholarshipBook.com and enter code MA131012 for updates on this award.

(1311) · College Access Program

Kentucky Higher Education Assistance Authority
P.O. Box 798
Frankfort, KY 40602
Phone: 800-928-8926
Email: blane@kheaa.com
http://www.kheaa.com
Purpose: To aid Kentucky students with financial need.
Eligibility: Applicants must be Kentucky residents, be enrolled at least half-time in undergraduate academic programs and have an Expected Family Contribution (EFC) based on the FAFSA of lower than approximately $3,850.
Target applicants: College students. Adult students.
Amount: Up to $1,900.
Number of awards: Varies.
Deadline: Varies.
How to apply: Complete the Free Application for Federal Student Aid (FAFSA).
Exclusive: Visit www.UltimateScholarshipBook.com and enter code KE131112 for updates on this award.

(1312) • College Affordability Grant

New Mexico Higher Education Department
2048 Galisteo Street
Santa Fe, NM 87505
Phone: 800-279-9777
Fax: 505-476-8454
Email: heather.romero@state.nm.us
http://hed.state.nm.us

Purpose: To support New Mexico residents who are attending public colleges in the state.
Eligibility: Applicants must demonstrate financial need, and they cannot have any other state grants or scholarships. Students must be enrolled in at least six credit hours per semester.
Target applicants: High school students. College students. Adult students.
Amount: Up to $1,000.
Number of awards: Varies.
Scholarship may be renewable.
Deadline: Varies.
How to apply: Applications are available at college financial aid offices.
Exclusive: Visit www.UltimateScholarshipBook.com and enter code NE131212 for updates on this award.

(1313) • College Scholarship Assistance Program

State Council of Higher Education for Virginia
101 N. 14th Street
James Monroe Building
Richmond, VA 23219
Phone: 804-225-2600
Fax: 804-225-2604
Email: communications@schev.edu
http://www.schev.edu

Purpose: To assist Virginia students who have extreme financial need.
Eligibility: Applicants must be U.S. citizens or eligible non-citizens and Virginia residents. They must be enrolled or planning to enroll at least half-time at a public, postsecondary institution or an eligible private, nonprofit four-year institution in Virginia. They must have an Expected Family Contribution (EFC) of less than half of the cost of attendance. Applicants who have earned an associate's or bachelor's degree previously are ineligible. Selection is based on financial need.
Target applicants: High school students. College students. Adult students.
Amount: $400-$5,000.
Number of awards: Varies.
Scholarship may be renewable.
Deadline: Varies.
How to apply: Application is made by completing the FAFSA and completing the Tuition Assistance Grant Program application form (private college attendees only).
Exclusive: Visit www.UltimateScholarshipBook.com and enter code ST131312 for updates on this award.

(1314) • CollegeBoundfund Academic Promise Scholarship

Rhode Island Higher Education Assistance Authority
560 Jefferson Boulevard
Warwick, RI 02886
Phone: 401-736-1100
Fax: 401-732-3541
Email: scholarships@riheaa.org
http://www.riheaa.org

Purpose: To assist outstanding Rhode Island high school students.
Eligibility: Applicants must be graduating Rhode Island high school seniors who plan to attend a postsecondary institution full-time and demonstrate academic achievement and financial need.
Target applicants: High school students.
Amount: Up to $10,000.
Number of awards: Varies.
Scholarship may be renewable.
Deadline: March 1.
How to apply: Complete the Free Application for Federal Student Aid (FAFSA).
Exclusive: Visit www.UltimateScholarshipBook.com and enter code RH131412 for updates on this award.

(1315) • Collegiate Scholarship

Texas 4-H Youth Development Foundation
7607 Eastmark Drive, Suite 101
College Station, TX 77840
Phone: 979-845-1213
Fax: 979-845-6495
Email: texas4hfoundation@ag.tamu.edu
http://texas4-h.tamu.edu/

Purpose: To support undergraduate students in Texas.
Eligibility: Applicants must have actively participated in a 4-H program during their high school years. They must be currently enrolled full-time with at least a 2.7 GPA. Recipients must have completed at least 30 credit hours by the time scholarship payments begin. Awards are based on financial need, academic achievement and 4-H experience.
Target applicants: College students. Adult students.
Minimum GPA: 2.7
Amount: Varies.
Number of awards: Varies.
Deadline: Varies.
How to apply: Applications are available online.
Exclusive: Visit www.UltimateScholarshipBook.com and enter code TE131512 for updates on this award.

(1316) • Colorado Business and Professional Women Education Foundation

Colorado Federation of Business and Professional Women
P.O. Box 1189
Boulder, CO 80306-1189
Phone: 303-443-2573
Email: office@cbpwef.org
http://www.cbpwef.org

Purpose: To provide education assistance for adult women.
Eligibility: Applicants must be women who are 25 years of age or older, United States citizens and Colorado residents for at least 12 months prior to the application deadline. They must be enrolled in or attending an accredited Colorado college, university or vocational training institution. Deadlines for application are May 31 for the fall semester and October 31 for the spring semester.
Target applicants: College students. Adult students.
Amount: Varies.
Number of awards: Varies.
Deadline: May 31 and October 31.
How to apply: Applications are available online.
Exclusive: Visit www.UltimateScholarshipBook.com and enter code CO131612 for updates on this award.

(1317) • Colorado Masons Benevolent Fund Scholarships

Colorado Masons Benevolent Fund Association
1130 Panorama Drive
Colorado Springs, CO 80904
Email: scholarships@coloradomasons.org
http://www.coloradofreemasons.org/index.html

Purpose: To help Colorado students.

Eligibility: Applicants must be graduating seniors from a Colorado public high school planning to attend a Colorado postsecondary institution. Selection is based on leadership, maturity, need and scholastic ability without reference to race, creed, color, sex or Masonic relationship.

Target applicants: High school students.

Amount: Up to $7,000.

Number of awards: Varies.

Scholarship may be renewable.

Deadline: Varies.

How to apply: Contact your high school counselor.

Exclusive: Visit www.UltimateScholarshipBook.com and enter code CO131712 for updates on this award.

(1318) • Colorado Nurses Association Nightingale Scholarship

Colorado Nurses Foundation
7400 East Arapahoe Road
Suite 211
Centennial, CO 80112
Phone: 303-694-4728
Fax: 303-694-4869
Email: mail@cnfound.org
http://www.cnfound.org/

Purpose: To aid Colorado nursing students who are Colorado Nurses Association or Colorado Student Nurse Association members.

Eligibility: Students must be Colorado residents who are Colorado Nurses Association or Colorado Student Nurses Association members. They must be second-year ASN students; third- or fourth-year BSN students; RNs enrolled at a school of nursing at any postsecondary level; currently practicing RNs enrolled in a doctoral nursing program or Doctor of Nursing Practice (DNP) students. Undergraduates must have a GPA of 3.25 or above, and graduate students must have a GPA of 3.5 or above. Applicants must have plans to practice nursing in the state of Colorado after graduation. Selection is based on stated career goals, GPA, financial need, participation in community and professional organizations and commitment to practicing nursing in Colorado.

Target applicants: College students. Graduate school students. Adult students.

Minimum GPA: 3.25 for undergraduate students and 3.5 for graduate students

Amount: $1,000-$2,500.

Number of awards: Varies.

Deadline: Varies.

How to apply: Applications are available online. An application form, statement of financial need, personal essay, two recommendations, resume, transcript and copy of CNA or CSNA membership card are required.

Exclusive: Visit www.UltimateScholarshipBook.com and enter code CO131812 for updates on this award.

(1319) • Colorado Oratorical Contest

American Legion, Department of Colorado
7465 E. 1st Avenue, Suite D
Denver, CO 80230
Phone: 303-366-5201
Fax: 303-366-7618
Email: garylbarnett@comcast.net
http://www.coloradolegion.org

Purpose: To enhance high school students' experience with and understanding of the U.S. Constitution. The contest will help develop students' leadership skills and civic appreciation, as well as the ability to deliver thoughtful, insightful orations regarding U.S. citizenship and its inherent responsibilities.

Eligibility: Applicants must be high school students under the age of 20 who are U.S. citizens or legal residents and residents of the state. Students first give an oration within their state and winners compete at the national level. The oration must be related to the Constitution of the United States focusing on the duties and obligations citizens have to the government. It must be in English and be between eight and ten minutes. There is also an assigned topic which is posted on the website, and it should be between three and five minutes.

Target applicants: Junior high students or younger. High school students.

Amount: $500-$4,000.

Number of awards: Varies.

Deadline: Varies.

How to apply: Applications are available online.

Exclusive: Visit www.UltimateScholarshipBook.com and enter code AM131912 for updates on this award.

(1320) • Colorado State Thespians Scholarships

Colorado State Thespians
200 S. Dexter Street
Denver, CO 80246-1055
Phone: 720-972-4501
Email: info@cothespians.com
http://www.cothespians.com

Purpose: To help students who participate in theatre.

Eligibility: Applicants must be high school seniors, have a minimum 2.75 GPA, plan to attend one of 30 participating universities, colleges or conservatories from across the nation and major in theatre. Students must perform an audition in acting, musical theatre or dance or prepare a portfolio of their expertise in technical theatre to present on the designated audition day in Denver, Colorado. Admission and additional scholarships may be offered by the colleges based on the audition. Note: We do not recommend applying to scholarships that charge application fees. However, some scholarships of this type charge fees and are included for completeness.

Target applicants: High school students.

Minimum GPA: 2.75

Amount: $1,000.

Number of awards: 3.

Deadline: November 1.

How to apply: Applications are available online. An application form, photo and $35 application fee are required.

Exclusive: Visit www.UltimateScholarshipBook.com and enter code CO132012 for updates on this award.

(1321) • Colorado Student Aid Program

Colorado Commission on Higher Education
1380 Lawrence Street
Suite 1200
Denver, CO 80204
Phone: 303-866-2723
Fax: 303-866-4266
Email: cche@state.co.us
http://www.state.co.us/cche

Purpose: To assist Colorado student residents.

Eligibility: Applicants must be Colorado residents who plan to enroll or are enrolled in eligible programs at eligible Colorado postsecondary institutions. Applicants must make satisfactory academic progress and have not defaulted in educational loans or grants. Awards are need-based and merit-based and are made by institutions to students.

Target applicants: High school students. College students. Adult students.

Amount: Varies.

Number of awards: Varies.

Deadline: Varies.

How to apply: Contact your financial aid office.

Exclusive: Visit www.UltimateScholarshipBook.com and enter code CO132112 for updates on this award.

(1322) • Commonwealth "Good Citizen" Scholarships

Association of Independent Colleges and Universities of Pennsylvania
101 N. Front Street
Harrisburg, PA 17101
Phone: 717-232-8649
Fax: 717-233-8574
Email: duck@aicup.org
http://www.aicup.org

Purpose: To provide financial assistance for students who have demonstrated good citizenship.

Eligibility: Applicants must have demonstrated a commitment to community service and creativity in shaping volunteer activities. They must be full-time current or upcoming undergraduate students at an AICUP member college or university. A two-page essay is required.

Target applicants: High school students. College students. Adult students.

Amount: Varies.

Number of awards: Varies.

Deadline: Varies.

How to apply: Applications are available from financial aid offices of qualifying institutions.

Exclusive: Visit www.UltimateScholarshipBook.com and enter code AS132212 for updates on this award.

(1323) • Community Banker Association of Illinois Annual Scholarship Program

Community Banker Association of Illinois
901 Community Drive
Springfield, IL 62703-5184
Phone: 800-736-2224
Email: bobbiw@cbai.com
http://www.cbai.com

Purpose: To assist Illinois high school seniors.

Eligibility: Applicants must write essays and be sponsored by a participating CBAI member bank. There is an essay topic related to community banking, and the short essays are judged on understanding of community banking philosophy, accurate information, clear and concise sentences, logical organization, proper grammar, correct punctuation and spelling and conclusion/summary.

Target applicants: High school students.

Amount: Up to $4,000.

Number of awards: 13.

Deadline: February 7.

How to apply: A list of participating banks and more information is available by email.

Exclusive: Visit www.UltimateScholarshipBook.com and enter code CO132312 for updates on this award.

(1324) • Community Foundation of Middle Tennessee Fine Arts and Music Scholarship

Community Foundation of Middle Tennessee
3833 Cleghorn Avenue #400
Nashville, TN 37215-2519
Phone: 888-540-5200
Email: mail@cfmt.org
http://www.cfmt.org

Purpose: To aid students in pursuing careers in visual arts and music.

Eligibility: Applicants must be current students at an accredited college or university, take at least six credit hours and be enrolled in a bachelor's of fine art, bachelor's of studio art, master's of fine art or bachelor's or master's in music program. Art students must major in painting, drawing, sculpture, ceramics, photography or printmaking. Preference for music scholarships is given to those studying acoustic mandolin or acoustic guitar. A minimum GPA of 3.0 is required.

Target applicants: College students. Graduate school students. Adult students.

Minimum GPA: 3.0

Amount: Varies.

Number of awards: Varies.

Deadline: March 15.

How to apply: Applications are available online. An application form, transcript, essay, Student Aid Report and two appraisal forms are required.

Exclusive: Visit www.UltimateScholarshipBook.com and enter code CO132412 for updates on this award.

(1325) • Community Scholarship Fund

Hawaii Community Foundation - Scholarships
1164 Bishop Street, Suite 800
Honolulu, HI 96813
Phone: 888-731-3863
Fax: 808-521-6286
Email: scholarships@hcf-hawaii.org
http://www.hawaiicommunityfoundation.org

Purpose: To assist college and graduate students majoring in arts, education, humanities or social science.

Eligibility: Applicants must demonstrate accomplishment, motivation, initiative, vision and intention to work in Hawaii and major in the arts, architecture, education, humanities or social science.

Target applicants: High school students. College students. Graduate school students. Adult students.

Amount: Varies.

Number of awards: Varies.

Deadline: March 1.

How to apply: To apply, register online, complete the online application and select the scholarships to which you wish to apply. In addition, mail the supporting materials: printed confirmation page from the online

application, personal statement, copy of Student Aid Report (SAR) available at www.fafsa.ed.gov and official transcript.
Exclusive: Visit www.UltimateScholarshipBook.com and enter code HA132512 for updates on this award.

(1326) • Competitive Scholarships

New Mexico Higher Education Department
2048 Galisteo Street
Santa Fe, NM 87505
Phone: 800-279-9777
Fax: 505-476-8454
Email: heather.romero@state.nm.us
http://hed.state.nm.us
Purpose: To provide a financial incentive for exceptional out-of-state students to attend college in New Mexico.
Eligibility: Applicants must be non-residents of the state of New Mexico, and they must be willing to enroll full-time in a public four-year university in New Mexico. Students applying to Eastern New Mexico University, New Mexico Highlands University, New Mexico Institute of Mining and Technology or Western New Mexico University must have one of the following combinations: a GPA of at least 3.0 and an ACT score of at least 23, or a GPA of at least 3.5 and an ACT of at least 20. Students applying to the University of New Mexico or New Mexico State University must have either an ACT score of 26 and a GPA of 3.0 or an ACT score of 23 and a GPA of 3.5.
Target applicants: High school students. College students. Adult students.
Minimum GPA: 3.0
Amount: $100.
Number of awards: Varies.
Scholarship may be renewable.
Deadline: Varies.
How to apply: Applications are available at college financial aid offices.
Exclusive: Visit www.UltimateScholarshipBook.com and enter code NE132612 for updates on this award.

(1327) • Connecticut Aid for Public College Students

Connecticut Department of Higher Education
61 Woodland Street
Hartford, CT 06105-2326
Phone: 860-947-1855
Fax: 860-947-1838
Email: byrd@ctdhe.org
http://www.ctdhe.org
Purpose: To assist Connecticut student residents.
Eligibility: Applicants must be Connecticut residents attending a public Connecticut college or university. The award is based on financial need.
Target applicants: High school students. College students. Adult students.
Amount: Up to amount of unmet financial need.
Number of awards: Varies.
Deadline: Varies.
How to apply: Apply through your college financial aid office.
Exclusive: Visit www.UltimateScholarshipBook.com and enter code CO132712 for updates on this award.

(1328) • Connecticut ASLA Student Scholarship

American Society of Landscape Architects
370 James Street
4th Floor
New Haven, CT 06513
Phone: 800-878-1474
Email: executivedirector@ctasla.org
http://www.ctasla.org
Purpose: To support students who are studying landscape architecture or environmental education.
Eligibility: Applicants must be Connecticut residents and be enrolled in an accredited post-secondary landscape architecture or environmental education program. Both undergraduate and graduate students may apply.
Target applicants: College students. Graduate school students. Adult students.
Amount: $2,500.
Number of awards: Varies.
Deadline: March 15.
How to apply: Applications are available online. An application form, transcript, personal statement and letter of recommendation are required.
Exclusive: Visit www.UltimateScholarshipBook.com and enter code AM132812 for updates on this award.

(1329) • Connecticut Association of Land Surveyors Memorial Scholarship Fund

Connecticut Association of Land Surveyors Inc.
78 Beaver Road
Wethersfield, CT 06109
Phone: 860-563-1990
Fax: 860-529-9700
Email: kathy@ctsurveyor.com
http://www.ctsurveyor.com
Purpose: To support Connecticut students who are preparing for careers in land surveying.
Eligibility: Applicants must be Connecticut residents who are enrolled in or who have been accepted into a postsecondary academic program in surveying or a related subject (geography, engineering or science). They must have plans to pursue a career in land surveying and must demonstrate interest in the field through previous work experience or other activities. Selection is based on the overall strength of the application.
Target applicants: High school students. College students. Adult students.
Amount: Varies.
Number of awards: Varies.
Deadline: June 1.
How to apply: Applications are available online. A resume, transcript and statement of qualifications are required.
Exclusive: Visit www.UltimateScholarshipBook.com and enter code CO132912 for updates on this award.

(1330) • Connecticut Building Congress Scholarships

Connecticut Building Congress
P.O. Box 743
Enfield, CT 06083
Phone: 860-228-1387
Fax: 860-741-8809
Email: cbc@cbc-ct.org
http://www.cbc-ct.org
Purpose: To aid students pursuing degrees in construction fields.
Eligibility: Applicants must be graduating seniors at Connecticut high schools and Connecticut residents. Students must be entering associate, bachelor's or master's degree programs in architecture, engineering,

construction management, surveying, planning or another construction-related course of study.
Target applicants: High school students.
Amount: $500-$2,000.
Number of awards: Varies.
Scholarship may be renewable.
Deadline: March 30.
How to apply: Applications are available online. An application form, essay, transcript and FAFSA Student Aid Report are required.
Exclusive: Visit www.UltimateScholarshipBook.com and enter code CO133012 for updates on this award.

(1331) · Connecticut Chapter Air and Waste Management Association Scholarship

Air and Waste Management Association-Connecticut Chapter
c/o Dana Lowes
TRC
21 Griffin Road
Windsor, CT 06082
Phone: 860-257-0767
Email: ryarmac@sci-techinc.com
http://www.awmanewengland.org/connecticut_chapter.htm
Purpose: To aid Connecticut students who are preparing for careers in air and waste management or other environmental areas.
Eligibility: Applicants must be Connecticut residents who have been accepted at or are enrolled at a postsecondary institution full-time. They must be studying or have plans to study a science or engineering subject that is related to air and waste management or a related environmental subject, and they must intend to pursue careers in one of these areas. Selection is based on academic achievement, stated career goals, extracurricular involvements and letters of recommendation.
Target applicants: High school students. College students. Adult students.
Amount: Up to $1,000.
Number of awards: Varies.
Scholarship may be renewable.
Deadline: First business day after April 15.
How to apply: Applications are available online. An application form, transcript, resume, two letters of recommendation and plan of study statement are required.
Exclusive: Visit www.UltimateScholarshipBook.com and enter code AI133112 for updates on this award.

(1332) · Connecticut Dunkin' Donuts Franchisee Scholarship Program

Connecticut Association of Schools
30 Realty Drive
Cheshire, CT 06410
Phone: 203-250-1111
Fax: 203-250-1345
http://www.casciac.org
Purpose: To provide financial assistance for well-rounded students.
Eligibility: Applicants must be high school seniors and Connecticut residents who excel in academics, demonstrate leadership and participate in school and community activities. They must plan to enroll at least half-time in a bachelor's degree, associate degree or certificate program at an accredited institution of higher learning.
Target applicants: High school students.
Amount: $1,000.
Number of awards: 100.
Deadline: April 15.
How to apply: Applications are available from Dunkin' Donuts stores and high school guidance offices beginning March 1 of each year.
Exclusive: Visit www.UltimateScholarshipBook.com and enter code CO133212 for updates on this award.

(1333) · Connecticut Independent College Student Grant Program

Connecticut Department of Higher Education
61 Woodland Street
Hartford, CT 06105-2326
Phone: 860-947-1855
Fax: 860-947-1838
Email: byrd@ctdhe.org
http://www.ctdhe.org
Purpose: To assist Connecticut student residents.
Eligibility: Applicants must be Connecticut residents attending an independent Connecticut college or university. Awards are based on financial need.
Target applicants: High school students. College students. Adult students.
Amount: Up to $8,341.
Number of awards: Varies.
Deadline: Varies.
How to apply: Apply through your college financial aid office.
Exclusive: Visit www.UltimateScholarshipBook.com and enter code CO133312 for updates on this award.

(1334) · Connecticut League for Nursing Scholarship

Connecticut League for Nursing
51 North Main Street
Suite 3D
Southington, CT 06489
Phone: 860-276-9621
Email: lisa@ctleaguefornursing.org
http://www.ctleaguefornursing.org/
Purpose: To aid Connecticut residents who are enrolled in a CLN supporting member nursing education program at an accredited postsecondary institution located in Connecticut.
Eligibility: Applicants must be Connecticut residents who are attending a postsecondary institution located in Connecticut. They must be enrolled in a nursing education program at a CLN supporting member school. Students must have completed the first year of a diploma program, the first year of an ASN program, the third year of a BSN program, everything but the senior year of an RN to BSN program or at least 18 hours of a graduate program in nursing. Selection is based on academic achievement, professional potential and financial need.
Target applicants: College students. Graduate school students. Adult students.
Amount: Varies.
Number of awards: Varies.
Deadline: October 9.
How to apply: Applications are available online. An application form, verification of student status (for BSN and graduate students only), faculty reference and an official transcript are required.
Exclusive: Visit www.UltimateScholarshipBook.com and enter code CO133412 for updates on this award.

(1335) • Connecticut National Guard Foundation Scholarship Program

Connecticut National Guard Foundation Inc.
State Armory
360 Broad Street
Hartford, CT 06105-3795
Phone: 860-241-1550
Fax: 860-293-2929
Email: scholarship.committee@ctngfoundation.org
http://www.ctngfoundation.org

Purpose: To provide assistance to National Guard members and their families.
Eligibility: Applicants must be Connecticut National Guard members or their sons, daughters or spouses. They must be enrolled in or plan to enroll in an accredited degree or technical program. Selection criteria include achievement and citizenship.
Target applicants: High school students. College students. Adult students.
Amount: $1,000-$3,000.
Number of awards: 6.
Deadline: March 15.
How to apply: Applications are available online. An application form, two letters of recommendation, a list of extracurricular activities and accomplishments, transcript including GPA and a personal statement are required.
Exclusive: Visit www.UltimateScholarshipBook.com and enter code CO133512 for updates on this award.

(1336) • Continuing/Re-entry Students Scholarship

American Legion Auxiliary, Department of California
401 Van Ness Avenue
Room 113
San Francisco, CA 94102
Phone: 415-861-5092
Fax: 415-861-8365
Email: calegionaux@calegionaux.org
http://www.calegionaux.org

Purpose: To provide support to children of U.S. Armed Forces members.
Eligibility: One of applicant's parents must have served in the U.S. Armed Forces during an eligible period. Applicants must be California residents planning to attend a California college or university and must be continuing or re-entry college students.
Target applicants: College students. Adult students.
Amount: $500-$1,000.
Number of awards: 5.
Deadline: March 16.
How to apply: Applications are available online.
Exclusive: Visit www.UltimateScholarshipBook.com and enter code AM133612 for updates on this award.

(1337) • Cora Aguda Manayan Fund

Hawaii Community Foundation - Scholarships
1164 Bishop Street, Suite 800
Honolulu, HI 96813
Phone: 888-731-3863
Fax: 808-521-6286
Email: scholarships@hcf-hawaii.org
http://www.hawaiicommunityfoundation.org

Purpose: To support Hawaii students of Filipino ancestry who are dedicated to helping others.
Eligibility: Students must be majoring in a health-related field. Preference may be given to students who are attending school in Hawaii.
Target applicants: High school students. College students. Adult students.
Amount: Varies.
Number of awards: Varies.
Deadline: March 1.
How to apply: To apply, register online, complete the online application and select the scholarships to which you wish to apply. In addition, mail the supporting materials: printed confirmation page from the online application, personal statement, copy of Student Aid Report (SAR) available at www.fafsa.ed.gov and official transcript.
Exclusive: Visit www.UltimateScholarshipBook.com and enter code HA133712 for updates on this award.

(1338) • COSA Youth Development Program Scholarships

Confederation of Oregon School Administrators
707 13th Street SE
Suite 100
Salem, OR 97301
Phone: 503-581-3141
Fax: 503-581-9840
Email: sera@cosa.k12.or.us
http://www.cosa.k12.or.us

Purpose: To provide financial assistance for Oregon students.
Eligibility: Applicants must be students at an Oregon public high school who are active in their communities and schools. They must have a GPA of 3.5 or higher and plan to attend an Oregon college or university. A field of study must be chosen. An endorsement from a COSA member is required, and the student must enroll in college the fall after high school graduation.
Target applicants: High school students.
Minimum GPA: 3.5
Amount: $1,000.
Number of awards: 12.
Deadline: February 25.
How to apply: Applications are available online, from your high school guidance counselor and the COSA office. An application form, one-page autobiography, letter of recommendation from a COSA member and transcript are required.
Exclusive: Visit www.UltimateScholarshipBook.com and enter code CO133812 for updates on this award.

(1339) • Costco Wholesale Scholarships

Independent Colleges of Washington
600 Stewart Street, Suite 600
Seattle, WA 98101
Phone: 206-623-4494
Fax: 206-625-9621
Email: info@icwashington.org
http://www.icwashington.org

Purpose: To assist minority students with financial need who are attending an independent college of Washington.
Eligibility: Applicants must demonstrate financial need and be a member of an underrepresented minority population. Students at Pacific Lutheran University, Seattle Pacific University, St. Martin's University, University of Puget Sound, Walla Walla University, Whitman College and Whitworth University are eligible.
Target applicants: College students. Adult students.
Amount: Varies.

Number of awards: Varies.
Deadline: Varies.
How to apply: No application is necessary. Each college or university selects recipients from eligible students.
Exclusive: Visit www.UltimateScholarshipBook.com and enter code IN133912 for updates on this award.

(1340) • Critical Needs Teacher Program

Mississippi Office of Student Financial Aid
3825 Ridgewood Road
Jackson, MS 39211
Phone: 800-327-2980
Fax: 601-432-6527
Email: sfa@ihl.state.ms.us
http://www.ihl.state.ms.us
Purpose: To increase the supply of teachers for public schools in Mississippi.
Eligibility: Applicants must be enrolled as full-time students in programs leading to an 'A' level teaching license and must have a college GPA of 2.5 or higher. Applicants must be admitted to an eligible Mississippi institution at the time of application. Applicants must also agree to the service obligation, which calls for one year of service in a Mississippi public school district located in a critical teacher shortage area for each year the scholarship is received.
Target applicants: College students. Graduate school students. Adult students.
Minimum GPA: 2.5
Amount: Full tuition.
Number of awards: Varies.
Scholarship may be renewable.
Deadline: March 31.
How to apply: Contact the Mississippi Office of Student Financial Aid for an application.
Exclusive: Visit www.UltimateScholarshipBook.com and enter code MI134012 for updates on this award.

(1341) • Critical Teacher Shortage Loan Forgiveness Program

Florida Department of Education
Office of Student Financial Assistance
1940 N. Monroe Street
Suite 70
Tallahassee, FL 32303-4759
Phone: 888-827-2004
Fax: 850-245-9667
Email: osfa@fldoe.org
http://www.floridastudentfinancialaid.org
Purpose: To help Florida public school teachers with loans.
Eligibility: Applicants should be teaching in the critical shortage area full-time at least 90 days of the school year under contract at a publicly funded Florida school, and they should have valid Florida teacher's certificates (temporary or professional) or Florida Department of Health licenses (temporary or permanent) in the same critical shortage area as teaching. Applicants must apply by the end of the first year of having both the critical shortage position and the critical shortage certificate or license. This program helps repay undergraduate and graduate educational loans that led to certification in a critical teacher shortage subject area, and the loans must have paid for courses before becoming a certified teacher. Applicants should submit applications and transcripts. A list of critical teacher shortage areas is online.
Target applicants: College students. Graduate school students. Adult students.
Amount: up to $10,000.
Number of awards: Varies.
Scholarship may be renewable.
Deadline: July 15.
How to apply: Applications are available online.
Exclusive: Visit www.UltimateScholarshipBook.com and enter code FL134112 for updates on this award.

(1342) • Critical Teacher Shortage Tuition Reimbursement Program

Florida Department of Education
Office of Student Financial Assistance
1940 N. Monroe Street
Suite 70
Tallahassee, FL 32303-4759
Phone: 888-827-2004
Fax: 850-245-9667
Email: osfa@fldoe.org
http://www.floridastudentfinancialaid.org
Purpose: To help Florida full-time publicly-funded school employees get teacher's certification at a grade level and in a subject area designated as a critical teacher shortage subject area.
Eligibility: Applicants must have valid Florida Teacher's Certificates (temporary or professional) or Florida Department of Health Licenses (temporary or permanent) and be enrolled in undergraduate or graduate courses.
Target applicants: College students. Graduate school students. Adult students.
Minimum GPA: 3.0
Amount: Varies.
Number of awards: Varies.
Deadline: September 15.
How to apply: Applications are available online.
Exclusive: Visit www.UltimateScholarshipBook.com and enter code FL134212 for updates on this award.

(1343) • Crumley Roberts - Crib to College Scholarship

Crumley Roberts, Attorneys at Law
Stephen M. Keaney, Director of Community Relations
2400 Freeman Mill Road
Suite 300
Greensboro, NC 27406
Phone: 336-333-0044
Email: smkeaney@crumleyroberts.com
http://www.crumleyroberts.com
Purpose: To help North Carolina high school seniors who have performed community service.
Eligibility: Applicants must plan to attend four-year colleges or universities. Transcripts, three recommendation letters, applications and essays are required. Winners also receive laptop computers. No phone calls, please.
Target applicants: High school students.
Minimum GPA: 3.0
Amount: $1,000.
Number of awards: 6.
Deadline: February 1.
How to apply: Applications are available online.
Exclusive: Visit www.UltimateScholarshipBook.com and enter code CR134312 for updates on this award.

(1344) • CTA César E. Chávez Memorial Education Awards Program

California Teachers Association (CTA)
CTA Human Rights Department
P.O. Box 921
Burlingame, CA 94011-0921
Phone: 650-697-1400
Fax: 650-552-5001
http://www.cta.org

Purpose: To honor César Chávez by rewarding students and teachers who follow his vision and guiding principles.
Eligibility: A student or group of up to five students must submit an essay or visual piece under the supervision of a teacher or professor who is a member of the CTA. Students may be in kindergarten through high school or in community college. All works must focus on topics such as non-violence and their relationship to Chávez's legacy. Visit the website for a complete list of topics and specific essay and visual arts submission requirements.
Target applicants: Junior high students or younger. High school students. College students. Adult students.
Amount: $1,000.
Number of awards: Varies.
Deadline: Varies.
How to apply: Applications are available online.
Exclusive: Visit www.UltimateScholarshipBook.com and enter code CA134412 for updates on this award.

(1345) • CTAHPERD Gibson-Laemel Scholarship

Connecticut Association of Health, Physical Education, Recreation and Dance
c/o Janice Skene, CTAHPERD Scholarship Chair
Eastbury School
1389 Neipsic Road
Glastonbury, CT 06033
Phone: 860-652-7858
Email: skenej@glastonburyus.org
http://www.ctahperd.org

Purpose: To support students majoring in areas related to physical education.
Eligibility: Applicants must be Connecticut students who have declared a major in health, physical education, recreation or dance. Students must be college juniors or seniors, maintain a GPA of 2.7 or higher and be CTAHPERD members.
Target applicants: College students. Adult students.
Minimum GPA: 2.7
Amount: $1,000.
Number of awards: Varies.
Deadline: May 1.
How to apply: Applications are available online. An application form, personal statement, transcript and two letters of recommendation are required.
Exclusive: Visit www.UltimateScholarshipBook.com and enter code CO134512 for updates on this award.

(1346) • Dana Christmas Scholarship for Heroism

New Jersey Higher Education Student Assistance Authority
P.O. Box 540
Trenton, NJ 08625
Phone: 800-792-8670
Email: clientservices@hesaa.org
http://www.hesaa.org

Purpose: To support New Jersey students who have carried out heroic acts.
Eligibility: Applicants must have been 21 years old or younger and residents of the state of New Jersey during the time of their heroic act.
Target applicants: Junior high students or younger. High school students. College students. Adult students.
Amount: Up to $10,000.
Number of awards: Up to 5.
Deadline: October 15.
How to apply: Applications are available online.
Exclusive: Visit www.UltimateScholarshipBook.com and enter code NE134612 for updates on this award.

(1347) • Daniel Cardillo Charitable Fund

Maine Community Foundation
245 Main Street
Ellsworth, ME 04605
Phone: 207-667-9735
Fax: 207-667-0447
Email: jwarren@mainecf.org
http://www.mainecf.org

Purpose: To provide financial support for young people to pursue their extracurricular interests.
Eligibility: Students must be passionately committed to an activity outside of school, and they must show financial need for further pursuit of that activity. Applicants should also be able to show that they care deeply about other people.
Target applicants: High school students.
Amount: Varies.
Number of awards: Varies.
Deadline: May 1.
How to apply: Applications are available online.
Exclusive: Visit www.UltimateScholarshipBook.com and enter code MA134712 for updates on this award.

(1348) • Daniel E. Lambert Memorial Scholarship

American Legion, Department of Maine
21 College Avenue
Waterville, ME 04901
Phone: 207-873-3229
Email: legionme@me.acadia.net
http://www.mainelegion.org

Purpose: To support the descendents of veterans who demonstrate financial need and who are residents of Maine.
Eligibility: Applicants must be enrolled in an accredited college or vocational technical school and be U.S. citizens. A parent or grandparent must be a veteran, verified by a copy of military discharge papers with the application. Applicants must have good character and believe in the American way of life.
Target applicants: College students. Adult students.
Amount: $1,000.
Number of awards: Up to 2.
Deadline: May 1.
How to apply: Applications are available online.
Exclusive: Visit www.UltimateScholarshipBook.com and enter code AM134812 for updates on this award.

(1349) • David Ehrhardt Founders Memorial Scholarship

Mississippi Thespians
1000 Gerard Avenue
Quincy, IL 62305
http://www.mississippithespians.com

Purpose: To support students who are members of Mississippi Thespians.

Eligibility: Applicants must be high school seniors who have been accepted to and plan to enroll in a two- or four-year accredited institution of higher learning. They must be Mississippi Thespians members in good standing who have been active for at least four years.

Target applicants: High school students.

Amount: $1,000.

Number of awards: 1.

Deadline: June 6.

How to apply: Applications are available online. An application form, three- to five-page essay and three letters of recommendation are required.

Exclusive: Visit www.UltimateScholarshipBook.com and enter code MI134912 for updates on this award.

(1350) • David L. Stashower Visionary Scholarships

Liggett Stashower Inc.
1228 Euclid Avenue
Cleveland, OH 44115
Phone: 216-348-8500
Email: info@liggett.com
http://www.liggett.com

Purpose: To aid students who are majoring in communications and related fields.

Eligibility: Applicants must be rising college seniors who are majoring in advertising, graphic design, public relations or communications and attend a recognized Ohio college or university. Selection is based on academic achievement, faculty recommendations and supporting documents.

Target applicants: College students. Adult students.

Amount: $2,000.

Number of awards: 2.

Deadline: April 16.

How to apply: Applications are available online. An application form, personal statement, transcript and letter of recommendation are required.

Exclusive: Visit www.UltimateScholarshipBook.com and enter code LI135012 for updates on this award.

(1351) • David W. Misek, N8NPX Memorial Scholarship

American Radio Relay League Foundation
225 Main Street
Newington, CT 06111
Phone: 860-594-0397
Fax: 860-594-0259
Email: foundation@arrl.org
http://www.arrlf.org

Purpose: To provide financial assistance to amateur radio operators from Ohio.

Eligibility: Applicants must hold a Technician Class or higher Amateur Radio License and attend or plan to attend a four-year college or university. They must be current residents of Greene, Montgomery, Champaign, Darke, Preble, Miami, Clark, Butler or Warren County, Ohio.

Target applicants: High school students. College students. Adult students.

Amount: $1,500.

Number of awards: Up to 3.

Deadline: February 1.

How to apply: Applications are available online.

Exclusive: Visit www.UltimateScholarshipBook.com and enter code AM135112 for updates on this award.

(1352) • DC Tuition Assistance Grant Program

Government of the District of Columbia
DC Tuition Assistance Grant Program
441 4th Street NW, Suite 350 North
Washington, DC 20001
Phone: 877-485-6751
http://osse.dc.gov

Purpose: To provide financial assistance to students in the District of Columbia who wish to attend either a public university in a different state or a historically Black college or university.

Eligibility: Applicants must be residents who have lived in the District of Columbia for at least 12 months prior to the beginning of their freshman year of college. Applicants must also either plan to or be currently enrolled at least half-time in an undergraduate or certificate program.

Target applicants: High school students. College students.

Amount: Up to $10,000.

Number of awards: Varies.

Scholarship may be renewable.

Deadline: June 30.

How to apply: Applications are available online.

Exclusive: Visit www.UltimateScholarshipBook.com and enter code GO135212 for updates on this award.

(1353) • Delaware Community Foundation Youth Opportunity Scholarships

Delaware Community Foundation
Community Service Building
100 West 10th Street, Suite 115
P.O. Box 1636
Wilmington, DE 19899
Phone: 302-571-8004
Fax: 302-571-1553
Email: rgentsch@delcf.org
http://www.delcf.org

Purpose: To aid students who have been affected by chronic illness.

Eligibility: Applicants must have experienced a chronic illness that lasted at least six months and has hindered their ability to pursue education. They must be students or former students in the state of Delaware. Preference is given to those who are or were enrolled in the First State School or any of its branches.

Target applicants: High school students. College students. Adult students.

Amount: Varies.

Number of awards: Varies.

Deadline: April 1.

How to apply: Applications are available online. An application form and two letters of recommendation are required.

Exclusive: Visit www.UltimateScholarshipBook.com and enter code DE135312 for updates on this award.

(1354) • Delaware Diamond State Scholarship

Delaware Higher Education Commission
Carvel State Office Building
5th Floor
820 North French Street
Wilmington, DE 19801-3509
Phone: 800-292-7935
Fax: 302-577-6765
Email: dhec@doe.k12.de.us
http://www.doe.k12.de.us/infosuites/students_family/dhec/
Purpose: To support academically-talented Delaware student residents.
Eligibility: Applicants must be residents of Delaware, U.S. citizens or eligible non-citizens, high school seniors who rank in the upper quarter of their class and score a minimum of 1200 on the SAT and enroll as full-time students in a degree program at a regionally accredited college.
Target applicants: High school students.
Amount: $1,250.
Number of awards: 50.
Scholarship may be renewable.
Deadline: March 24.
How to apply: Applications are available online.
Exclusive: Visit www.UltimateScholarshipBook.com and enter code DE135412 for updates on this award.

(1355) • Delaware Educational Benefits for Children of Deceased Veterans and Others

Delaware Higher Education Commission
Carvel State Office Building
5th Floor
820 North French Street
Wilmington, DE 19801-3509
Phone: 800-292-7935
Fax: 302-577-6765
Email: dhec@doe.k12.de.us
http://www.doe.k12.de.us/infosuites/students_family/dhec/
Purpose: To assist children of deceased veterans.
Eligibility: Applicants must be U.S. citizens or eligible non-citizens who have been Delaware residents for at least three years prior to application. They must be the child of an armed forces member who died from a service-related cause, is/was a prisoner of war or has been declared missing in action; a state police officer whose death was service-related or a Department of Transportation employee who worked on the state highway system whose death was job-related. Applicants must be 16 to 24 years of age. Priority is given to students attending a Delaware public college, followed by students attending Delaware private colleges and those attending out-of-state institutions. Those attending private or out-of-state colleges must pursue majors that are not offered by Delaware public colleges.
Target applicants: High school students. College students.
Amount: Varies.
Number of awards: Varies.
Scholarship may be renewable.
Deadline: 4 weeks prior to the start of classes.
How to apply: Applications are available online. An application form is required.
Exclusive: Visit www.UltimateScholarshipBook.com and enter code DE135512 for updates on this award.

(1356) • Delaware Governor's Workforce Development Grant

Delaware Higher Education Commission
Carvel State Office Building
5th Floor
820 North French Street
Wilmington, DE 19801-3509
Phone: 800-292-7935
Fax: 302-577-6765
Email: dhec@doe.k12.de.us
http://www.doe.k12.de.us/infosuites/students_family/dhec/
Purpose: To assist students who are also working in Delaware.
Eligibility: Applicants must be residents of Delaware and U.S. citizens or eligible non-citizens who are 18 or older. Applicants must meet income requirements. Students must attend a participating school in Delaware on a part-time basis and be employed in Delaware full-time with a small employer, part-time or through temporary employment. Applicants must be employed by an eligible employer who contributes to the Blue Collar Training Fund Program. Academic progress is monitored.
Target applicants: College students. Adult students.
Amount: Up to $2,000.
Number of awards: Varies.
Scholarship may be renewable.
Deadline: End of free drop/add period each semester.
How to apply: Applications are available online.
Exclusive: Visit www.UltimateScholarshipBook.com and enter code DE135612 for updates on this award.

(1357) • Delaware Scholarship Incentive Program

Delaware Higher Education Commission
Carvel State Office Building
5th Floor
820 North French Street
Wilmington, DE 19801-3509
Phone: 800-292-7935
Fax: 302-577-6765
Email: dhec@doe.k12.de.us
http://www.doe.k12.de.us/infosuites/students_family/dhec/
Purpose: To assist Delaware student residents.
Eligibility: Applicants must be legal residents of Delaware and U.S. citizens or eligible non-citizens who are enrolled full-time at a regionally-accredited undergraduate institution in Delaware or Pennsylvania. Other undergraduate and graduate students will be considered if their major is not available at a public college in Delaware. Students must demonstrate substantial financial need and have a minimum 2.5 GPA. Applicants must also submit the Free Application for Federal Student Aid (FAFSA).
Target applicants: High school students. College students. Graduate school students. Adult students.
Minimum GPA: 2.5
Amount: $700-$2,220.
Number of awards: Varies.
Deadline: April 15.
How to apply: Delaware residents are automatically considered for the scholarship when their FAFSA form is received.
Exclusive: Visit www.UltimateScholarshipBook.com and enter code DE135712 for updates on this award.

(1358) • Delaware Solid Waste Authority John P. "Pat" Healy Scholarship

Delaware Higher Education Commission
Carvel State Office Building
5th Floor
820 North French Street
Wilmington, DE 19801-3509
Phone: 800-292-7935
Fax: 302-577-6765
Email: dhec@doe.k12.de.us
http://www.doe.k12.de.us/infosuites/students_family/dhec/

Purpose: To aid Delaware students who are preparing for careers in environmental engineering or environmental science.
Eligibility: Applicants must be Delaware residents, U.S. citizens or eligible non-citizens and full-time students. They must be high school seniors, undergraduate freshmen or undergraduate sophomores majoring in or planning to major in environmental sciences or environmental engineering at a Delaware college or university. They also must complete a Free Application for Federal Student Aid (FAFSA) form for the upcoming school year. Selection is based on academic achievement, leadership skills, extracurricular involvement and financial need.
Target applicants: High school students. College students. Adult students.
Amount: $2,000.
Number of awards: Varies.
Scholarship may be renewable.
Deadline: March 12.
How to apply: Applications are available online. An application form, personal essay, transcript and FAFSA are required.
Exclusive: Visit www.UltimateScholarshipBook.com and enter code DE135812 for updates on this award.

(1359) • Delegate Scholarship

Maryland Higher Education Commission
Office of Student Financial Assistance
839 Bestgate Road, Suite 400
Annapolis, MD 21401
Phone: 800-974-1024
Fax: 410-260-3200
Email: osfamail@mhec.state.md.us
http://www.mhec.state.md.us

Purpose: To assist Maryland undergraduate and graduate students who can demonstrate financial need.
Eligibility: Applicants must be legal residents of the state of Maryland and complete the Free Application for Federal Student Aid (FAFSA). They must show financial need if the Office of Student Financial Assistance (OFSA) makes the award for the applicant's delegate. Applicants must be or must plan to be degree-seeking students at a Maryland institution. Selection is based on the overall strength of the application.
Target applicants: High school students. College students. Graduate school students. Adult students.
Amount: At least $200.
Number of awards: Varies.
Scholarship may be renewable.
Deadline: March 1.
How to apply: Complete and file the Free Application for Federal Student Aid (FAFSA). Contact delegate's office for specific application forms. The Office of Student Financial Assistance (OSFA) can provide a list of all state legislators. An application form and supporting documents are required.
Exclusive: Visit www.UltimateScholarshipBook.com and enter code MA135912 for updates on this award.

(1360) • Delta Sigma Theta Washington Alumnae Chapter Scholarships

Delta Sigma Theta Sorority, Inc.-Washington DC Alumnae Chapter
P.O. Box 90202
Washington, DC 20090-0202
Email: washdcalum@yahoo.com
http://www.wdcac.org

Purpose: To aid Washington, DC residents.
Eligibility: Applicants must be Washington, DC residents who are attending Washington, DC public or private high schools. They must be graduating seniors at the time of application and must have taken the SAT or ACT.
Target applicants: High school students.
Amount: $1,000-$3,000.
Number of awards: Varies.
Deadline: March 31.
How to apply: Applications are available online. An application form, copy of ACT or SAT scores, proof of family income, two letters of recommendation, autobiographic sketch and transcript with GPA are required.
Exclusive: Visit www.UltimateScholarshipBook.com and enter code DE136012 for updates on this award.

(1361) • Denise Bertucci Memorial Scholarship

Jaycees of Wisconsin Foundation Inc.
P.O. Box 1547
Appleton, WI 54912
Phone: 920-954-2573
http://www.wijaycees.org/foundation.html

Purpose: To support non-traditional students in Wisconsin.
Eligibility: Applicants must be 21 years of age or older, have returned to school after at least two years off and have completed at least two semesters since returning to school. Students must attend a Wisconsin college or university full-time and pursue a two-year or longer undergraduate program. A GPA of 3.0 or higher is required.
Target applicants: College students. Adult students.
Minimum GPA: 3.0
Amount: $500.
Number of awards: 1.
Deadline: Varies.
How to apply: Applications are available from your school's financial aid office. An application form, transcript and three letters of recommendation are required.
Exclusive: Visit www.UltimateScholarshipBook.com and enter code JA136112 for updates on this award.

(1362) • Dependent Children Scholarship

Tennessee Student Assistance Corporation
404 James Robertson Parkway
Suite 1510, Parkway Towers
Nashville, TN 37243
Phone: 800-342-1663
Fax: 615-741-6101
Email: tsac.aidinfo@tn.gov
http://www.tn.gov/CollegePays/

Purpose: To support the dependents of injured law enforcement officers, firemen and emergency medical service workers.

Eligibility: Applicants must be enrolled or accepted at a Tennessee college for full-time undergraduate study. Students must provide evidence that a parent or caregiver was killed or completely and permanently disabled while performing job duties.
Target applicants: High school students. College students. Adult students.
Amount: Varies.
Number of awards: Varies.
Scholarship may be renewable.
Deadline: July 15.
How to apply: Applications are available online.
Exclusive: Visit www.UltimateScholarshipBook.com and enter code TE136212 for updates on this award.

(1363) • Derivative Duo Scholarship

Pride Foundation
1122 East Pike Street
PMB 1001
Seattle, WA 98122
Phone: 800-735-7287
Email: anthony@pridefoundation.org
http://www.pridefoundation.org
Purpose: To support lesbian, gay, bisexual, transgender or straight ally Washington students who are pursuing higher education in mental health or human services.
Eligibility: Applicants must be lesbian, gay, bisexual, transgender or straight ally residents of the state of Washington and must be studying a mental health or human services subject at the postsecondary level. Selection is based on the overall strength of the application and financial need.
Target applicants: College students. Adult students.
Amount: Varies.
Number of awards: Varies.
Deadline: January 31.
How to apply: Applications are to be completed through an electronic submittal system online. The online application, statement of financial need and letter of recommendation are required.
Exclusive: Visit www.UltimateScholarshipBook.com and enter code PR136312 for updates on this award.

(1364) • Des Moines Symphony Alliance College/ Emerging Professional Division Young Artist Competition

Des Moines Symphony Alliance
221 Walnut Street
Des Moines, IA 50309
Phone: 515-280-4000
Fax: 515-280-4005
Email: info@dmsymphony.org
http://www.dmsymphony.org
Purpose: To support college musicians.
Eligibility: Applicants must play piano or a standard orchestra instrument and be Iowa residents or students at an Iowa college or university who have not reached their 25th birthdays at the time of competition. Participants must perform a standard concerto in its entirety from memory. Note: We do not recommend applying to scholarships that charge application fees. However, some scholarships of this type charge fees and are included for completeness.
Target applicants: College students.
Amount: Up to $1,000.
Number of awards: 3.
Deadline: December 7.
How to apply: Applications are available online. An application form, $30 application fee and CD recording of the concerto to be performed are required.
Exclusive: Visit www.UltimateScholarshipBook.com and enter code DE136412 for updates on this award.

(1365) • Distinguished Scholar Award

Maryland Higher Education Commission
Office of Student Financial Assistance
839 Bestgate Road, Suite 400
Annapolis, MD 21401
Phone: 800-974-1024
Fax: 410-260-3200
Email: osfamail@mhec.state.md.us
http://www.mhec.state.md.us
Purpose: To aid outstanding Maryland students.
Eligibility: Applicants (and the parents of applicants who are dependents) must be Maryland residents. They must be high school juniors who have plans to attend a Maryland two-year, four-year or private career school after graduation. High schools may nominate students of academic achievement or artistic talent. Finalists in the National Merit Scholarship and National Achievement Scholarship programs automatically receive the award when they attend college in Maryland. Applicants must have plans to enroll as full-time, degree-seeking students. Selection is based on merit.
Target applicants: High school students.
Amount: $3,000.
Number of awards: Varies.
Scholarship may be renewable.
Deadline: February.
How to apply: Applications may be obtained from your high school guidance counselor. An application form and supporting documents are required.
Exclusive: Visit www.UltimateScholarshipBook.com and enter code MA136512 for updates on this award.

(1366) • Distinguished Scholar Community College Transfer Program

Maryland Higher Education Commission
Office of Student Financial Assistance
839 Bestgate Road, Suite 400
Annapolis, MD 21401
Phone: 800-974-1024
Fax: 410-260-3200
Email: osfamail@mhec.state.md.us
http://www.mhec.state.md.us
Purpose: To provide financial support for Maryland community college students transferring to four-year Maryland colleges.
Eligibility: Applicants must have 60 credit hours completed at a Maryland community college with a grade point average of at least 3.0. Students must apply for the scholarship within one year of graduating from community college, and afterwards they must attend a Maryland four-year college as a full-time student.
Target applicants: College students. Adult students.
Minimum GPA: 3.0
Amount: $3,000.
Number of awards: Varies.
Scholarship may be renewable.
Deadline: March 25.
How to apply: Applications are available online.

Exclusive: Visit www.UltimateScholarshipBook.com and enter code MA136612 for updates on this award.

(1367) • District of Columbia Tuition Assistance Grant

DC Tuition Assistance Grant Office
441 4th Street NW
Suite 450 North
Washington, DC 20001
Phone: 202-727-2824
http://www.tuitiongrant.dc.gov
Purpose: To make attending out-of-state, private and Historically Black schools more affordable for DC residents.
Eligibility: Applicants must be residents of Washington, DC for at least 12 months before the start of their freshman year of college, high school graduates or GED recipients, enrolled at least half-time at an eligible institution and be 24 years of age or younger. Applicants must maintain satisfactory academic progress, not have defaulted on student loans, have registered with the Selective Service, be U.S. citizens or permanent residents, have not already received a B.A. or B.S. and have not been incarcerated.
Target applicants: High school students. College students.
Amount: $2,500-$10,000.
Number of awards: Varies.
Scholarship may be renewable.
Deadline: June 30.
How to apply: Applications are available online.
Exclusive: Visit www.UltimateScholarshipBook.com and enter code DC136712 for updates on this award.

(1368) • Dominique Lisa Pandolfo Scholarship

Community Foundation of New Jersey
P.O. Box 338
Morristown, NJ 07963-0338
Phone: 973-267-5533
Fax: 973-267-2903
Email: fkrueger@cfnj.org
http://www.cfnj.org
Purpose: To help young women achieve their goals and be successful.
Eligibility: Applicants must be females who have been nominated by the Dominique Lisa Pandolfo Scholarship Committee. They must exhibit outstanding character, potential, merit, personality and leadership qualities, and they must demonstrate financial need. Applicants must be New Jersey residents.
Target applicants: High school students.
Amount: $5,000.
Number of awards: 1.
Deadline: April 1.
How to apply: Applications are available online.
Exclusive: Visit www.UltimateScholarshipBook.com and enter code CO136812 for updates on this award.

(1369) • Don't Mess with Texas Scholarship

Don't Mess with Texas
c/o EnviroMedia
1717 West 6th Street, Suite 400
Austin, TX 78703
Phone: 512-476-4368
Email: scholarship@dontmesswithtexas.org
http://www.dontmesswithtexas.org
Purpose: To support students concerned about litter.
Eligibility: Student must be a Texas high school senior who wants to attend a two- or four-year college or university in Texas. To apply for the scholarship, students must complete the application and one or two essays and submit two letters of recommendation (one from a school-related source and the other from a non-school related source).
Target applicants: High school students.
Amount: $1,000-$3,000.
Number of awards: 3.
Deadline: April 4.
How to apply: Applications are available online.
Exclusive: Visit www.UltimateScholarshipBook.com and enter code DO136912 for updates on this award.

(1370) • Doris and Clarence Glick Classical Music Scholarship

Hawaii Community Foundation - Scholarships
1164 Bishop Street, Suite 800
Honolulu, HI 96813
Phone: 888-731-3863
Fax: 808-521-6286
Email: scholarships@hcf-hawaii.org
http://www.hawaiicommunityfoundation.org
Purpose: To provide financial assistance for Hawaii students of classical music.
Eligibility: Applicants must be majoring in music with an emphasis on classical music. They must have a GPA of 2.7 or higher, and they must describe their program of study as it relates to classical music in their personal statement.
Target applicants: High school students. College students. Adult students.
Minimum GPA: 2.7
Amount: Varies.
Number of awards: Varies.
Deadline: March 1.
How to apply: To apply, register online, complete the online application and select the scholarships to which you wish to apply. In addition, mail the supporting materials: printed confirmation page from the online application, personal statement, copy of Student Aid Report (SAR) available at www.fafsa.ed.gov and official transcript.
Exclusive: Visit www.UltimateScholarshipBook.com and enter code HA137012 for updates on this award.

(1371) • Dorothy Campbell Memorial Scholarship

Oregon Student Assistance Commission
1500 Valley River Drive
Suite 100
Eugene, OR 97401
Phone: 541-687-7400
Fax: 541-687-7414
Email: awardinfo@osac.state.or.us
http://www.osac.state.or.us
Purpose: To assist female Oregon high school students who have an interest in golf.
Eligibility: Applicants must be U.S. citizens or legal residents, Oregon residents and graduating high school seniors. They must have a GPA of 2.75 or higher and must have plans to attend a four-year Oregon college or university. Applicants must not owe a refund on an educational grant and must not be in default of an educational loan. Preference is given to applicants who are members of a high school golf team (if available). Selection is based on financial need.
Target applicants: High school students.

Minimum GPA: 2.75
Amount: Varies.
Number of awards: Varies.
Scholarship may be renewable.
Deadline: March 1.
How to apply: Applications are available online. An application form, personal essay, supporting materials and completion of the FAFSA are required.
Exclusive: Visit www.UltimateScholarshipBook.com and enter code OR137112 for updates on this award.

(1372) • Dorothy D. Greer Journalist of the Year Scholarship Competition

Colorado High School Press Association
CSU Student Media
Lory Student Center Box 13
Fort Collins, CO 80523
Phone: 303-594-8589
Email: chspa@comcast.net
http://www.chspaonline.org
Purpose: To support outstanding young journalists.
Eligibility: Applicants must be Colorado high school seniors whose schools are members of the Colorado High School Press Association. Students must have worked on their yearbook or newspaper for at least two years. A GPA of 3.0 or higher is required. Selection criteria include neatness (10 percent), quality of work (40 percent), personal statement (20 percent), letters of recommendation (20 percent) and grades (10 percent).
Target applicants: High school students.
Minimum GPA: 3.0
Amount: Up to $2,000.
Number of awards: 1.
Deadline: February 15.
How to apply: Applications are available online. An application form, personal statement, transcript, three to four letters of recommendation, samples of published work and action photo are required.
Exclusive: Visit www.UltimateScholarshipBook.com and enter code CO137212 for updates on this award.

(1373) • Dottie Martin Teachers Scholarship

North Carolina Federation of Republican Women
Joyce Glass, Chairman
4413 Driftwood Drive
Clemmons, NC 27012
Phone: 336-766-0067
Email: fglass@triad.rr.com
http://www.ncfederationofrepublicanwomen.org
Purpose: To support education students.
Eligibility: Applicants must be current college students planning to enter the field of education. The scholarship committee is especially interested in students who want to go into the fields of child guidance and counseling to make a difference in the lives of North Carolina children. Applicants must include an essay addressing their reasons for applying, career goals; plans for teaching in North Carolina, a description of their financial situation, why they should receive the scholarship and information on their personal values.
Target applicants: College students. Graduate school students. Adult students.
Amount: $500.
Number of awards: 1.
Deadline: June 1.
How to apply: Applications are available online.
Exclusive: Visit www.UltimateScholarshipBook.com and enter code NO137312 for updates on this award.

(1374) • Douvas Memorial Scholarship

Wyoming Department of Education
2300 Capitol Avenue
Hathaway Building, 2nd Floor
Cheyenne, WY 82002
Phone: 307-777-7673
Fax: 307-777-6234
Email: webmaster@educ.state.ky.us
http://www.k12.wy.us
Purpose: To assist first generation Americans in obtaining higher education.
Eligibility: Applicants must have been born in the United States but have parents who were born outside the country. They must be high school seniors or between the ages of 18 and 22, and they must be Wyoming residents. They must attend a Wyoming community college or the University of Wyoming.
Target applicants: High school students. College students.
Amount: $500.
Number of awards: 1.
Deadline: April 29.
How to apply: Applications are available online.
Exclusive: Visit www.UltimateScholarshipBook.com and enter code WY137412 for updates on this award.

(1375) • Downeast Feline Fund

Maine Community Foundation
245 Main Street
Ellsworth, ME 04605
Phone: 207-667-9735
Fax: 207-667-0447
Email: jwarren@mainecf.org
http://www.mainecf.org
Purpose: To provide support to students from Maine who are pursuing veterinary education.
Eligibility: Applicants must be graduates of Maine high schools. They must be currently enrolled in a school of veterinary medicine. Preference will be given to students who are in their third or fourth year of school.
Target applicants: College students. Adult students.
Amount: Varies.
Number of awards: Varies.
Deadline: Varies.
How to apply: Applications are available online.
Exclusive: Visit www.UltimateScholarshipBook.com and enter code MA137512 for updates on this award.

(1376) • Dr. Alvin and Monica Saake Foundation Scholarship

Hawaii Community Foundation - Scholarships
1164 Bishop Street, Suite 800
Honolulu, HI 96813
Phone: 888-731-3863
Fax: 808-521-6286
Email: scholarships@hcf-hawaii.org
http://www.hawaiicommunityfoundation.org
Purpose: To provide assistance for Hawaii students who are majoring in sports medicine and related fields.

Eligibility: Applicants must plan to attend an accredited college or university full-time, major in kinesiology, sports medicine, physical therapy, occupational therapy or a related field. They must have a minimum GPA of 2.7 and be college juniors, college seniors or graduate students.
Target applicants: College students. Graduate school students. Adult students.
Minimum GPA: 2.7
Amount: Varies.
Number of awards: Varies.
Deadline: March 1.
How to apply: To apply, register online, complete the online application and select the scholarships to which you wish to apply. In addition, mail the supporting materials: printed confirmation page from the online application, personal statement, copy of Student Aid Report (SAR) available at www.fafsa.ed.gov and official transcript.
Exclusive: Visit www.UltimateScholarshipBook.com and enter code HA137612 for updates on this award.

(1377) • Dr. and Mrs. Arthur F. Sullivan Fund

Connecticut Community Foundation Center for Philanthropy
43 Field Street
Waterbury, CT 06702
Phone: 203-753-1315
Fax: 203-756-3054
Email: info@conncf.org
http://www.conncf.org
Purpose: To provide financial assistance to students who are entering or enrolled in medical school.
Eligibility: Applicants must be accepted to or enrolled in medical school. They must reside in the Connecticut Community Foundation's service area and demonstrate exemplary academic achievement.
Target applicants: College students. Graduate school students. Adult students.
Amount: Approximately $500.
Number of awards: Varies.
Deadline: March 1.
How to apply: Applications are available online.
Exclusive: Visit www.UltimateScholarshipBook.com and enter code CO137712 for updates on this award.

(1378) • Dr. Donald L. Moak Scholarship

Alabama Bankers Association
534 Adams Avenue
Montgomery, AL 36104
Phone: 334-834-1890
Fax: 334-834-4443
Email: info@alabamabankers.org
http://www.alabamabankers.org
Purpose: To provide educational assistance for the children of bankers.
Eligibility: Applicants must be Alabama residents with a parent who is employed full-time at an Alabama bank. They must be high school seniors at the time of application and plan to enroll in a college or university full-time. SAT or ACT scores are required, but there is no minimum score to be considered.
Target applicants: High school students.
Amount: $1,000.
Number of awards: 1.
Deadline: April 1.
How to apply: Applications are available online.
Exclusive: Visit www.UltimateScholarshipBook.com and enter code AL137812 for updates on this award.

(1379) • Dr. Hans and Clara Zimmerman Foundation Education Scholarship

Hawaii Community Foundation - Scholarships
1164 Bishop Street, Suite 800
Honolulu, HI 96813
Phone: 888-731-3863
Fax: 808-521-6286
Email: scholarships@hcf-hawaii.org
http://www.hawaiicommunityfoundation.org
Purpose: To provide financial assistance to Hawaii students who want to study education.
Eligibility: Applicants major in education with an emphasis in teaching. They must have a GPA of 2.8 or higher, demonstrate good character and be full-time students. Preference is given to students of Hawaiian ethnicity and to students with at least two years of teaching experience. Applicants must discuss their teaching philosophies in their personal statement.
Target applicants: High school students. College students. Graduate school students. Adult students.
Minimum GPA: 2.8
Amount: Varies.
Number of awards: Varies.
Deadline: March 1.
How to apply: To apply, register online, complete the online application and select the scholarships to which you wish to apply. In addition, mail the supporting materials: printed confirmation page from the online application, personal statement, copy of Student Aid Report (SAR) available at www.fafsa.ed.gov and official transcript.
Exclusive: Visit www.UltimateScholarshipBook.com and enter code HA137912 for updates on this award.

(1380) • Dr. Hans and Clara Zimmerman Foundation Health Scholarships

Hawaii Community Foundation - Scholarships
1164 Bishop Street, Suite 800
Honolulu, HI 96813
Phone: 888-731-3863
Fax: 808-521-6286
Email: scholarships@hcf-hawaii.org
http://www.hawaiicommunityfoundation.org
Purpose: To provide financial assistance to Hawaii students who want to study in health fields.
Eligibility: Applicants must plan to major in a health-related field other than sports medicine, non-clinical psychology or social work at a U.S. college or university. They must be full-time college juniors, college seniors or graduate students, and they must have a GPA of 3.0 or higher.
Target applicants: College students. Graduate school students. Adult students.
Minimum GPA: 3.0
Amount: Varies.
Number of awards: Varies.
Deadline: March 1.
How to apply: To apply, register online, complete the online application and select the scholarships to which you wish to apply. In addition, mail the supporting materials: printed confirmation page from the online application, personal statement, copy of Student Aid Report (SAR) available at www.fafsa.ed.gov and official transcript.
Exclusive: Visit www.UltimateScholarshipBook.com and enter code HA138012 for updates on this award.

(1381) • Dr. Robert W. Sims Memorial Scholarship

Florida Association of Educational Data Systems
c/o Ms. Marsha Cole, FAEDS Scholarship Chairperson
Duval County Public Schools
3047 Boulevard Center Drive, Team Center B, 2nd Floor
Jacksonville, FL 32207
Phone: 904-348-5730
Fax: 904-348-5737
Email: colem@duvalschools.org
http://www.faeds.org
Purpose: To aid Florida computer science and information technology students.
Eligibility: Applicants must be U.S. citizens and residents of Florida. They must be enrolled in or plan to enroll in a postsecondary degree program in computer science, information technology or a related subject at an accredited school in Florida. They must be full-time students and must have a GPA of 2.5 or higher. Selection is based on the overall strength of the application.
Target applicants: High school students. College students. Adult students.
Minimum GPA: 2.5
Amount: $3,000.
Number of awards: Varies.
Deadline: February 15.
How to apply: Applications are available online. An application form, official transcript, resume, three recommendation letters, a degree program description and a personal essay are required.
Exclusive: Visit www.UltimateScholarshipBook.com and enter code FL138112 for updates on this award.

(1382) • Dr. William S. Boyd Scholarship

Chiropractic Association of Louisiana
10636 Timberlake Drive
Baton Rouge, LA 70810
Phone: 225-769-5560
http://www.cal-online.org
Purpose: To aid Louisiana chiropractic students.
Eligibility: Applicants must be Louisiana residents who are juniors or seniors at a CCE-accredited chiropractic college located in Louisiana. They must have a GPA of 2.75 or higher and must intend to work in Louisiana after graduation. Selection is based on the overall strength of the application.
Target applicants: College students. Adult students.
Minimum GPA: 2.75
Amount: Varies.
Number of awards: At least 1.
Deadline: June 30.
How to apply: Applications are available by request from the CAL. An application form, three letters of recommendation and an endorsement from a current member of the CAL are required.
Exclusive: Visit www.UltimateScholarshipBook.com and enter code CH138212 for updates on this award.

(1383) • DSS Tuition Waiver For Foster Care Children

Massachusetts Department of Higher Education
Office of Student Financial Assistance
454 Broadway
Suite 200
Revere, MA 02151
Phone: 617-727-9420
Fax: 617-727-0667
Email: osfa@osfa.mass.edu
http://www.osfa.mass.edu/default.asp
Purpose: To provide financial support to Massachusetts foster children who are pursuing higher education.
Eligibility: Applicants must be current or former foster children who were placed in Massachusetts state custody for at least 12 months due to a Care and Protection Petition. They must not have been adopted or returned home, and they must be 24 years old or younger. Students must be enrolled as full-time undergraduates at a state-supported school.
Target applicants: High school students. College students. Adult students.
Amount: Full tuition for eligible courses.
Number of awards: Varies.
Deadline: Varies.
How to apply: Applications are available at college financial aid offices.
Exclusive: Visit www.UltimateScholarshipBook.com and enter code MA138312 for updates on this award.

(1384) • Dunn Fellowship Program and Marzullo Internship Program

Governor's Office of the State of Illinois
Dunn Fellowship Program and Marzullo Internship Program
503 William G. Stratton Building
Springfield, IL 62706
Phone: 217-524-1381
http://www.illinois.gov/gov/intopportunities.htm
Purpose: To provide college graduates with an opportunity to experience daily operations in state government for one year.
Eligibility: Fellows must possess a bachelor's degree, and Vito Marzullo interns must be Illinois residents. Fellows will be assigned to various posts in the Governor's office or in an office under the Governor's jurisdiction.
Target applicants: College students. Adult students.
Amount: $31,332 plus benefits.
Number of awards: Varies.
Deadline: Varies.
How to apply: Applications are available online or by mail.
Exclusive: Visit www.UltimateScholarshipBook.com and enter code GO138412 for updates on this award.

(1385) • E. Lanier (Lanny) Finch Scholarship

Georgia Association of Broadcasters Inc.
8010 Roswell Road
Suite 150
Atlanta, GA 30350
Phone: 770-395-7200
Fax: 770-395-7235
http://www.gab.org
Purpose: To support students interested in broadcasting careers.
Eligibility: Applicants must be Georgia residents and full-time students at an accredited college or university. Students must be rising juniors or seniors pursuing degrees in some aspect of the broadcasting industry. Selection is based on scholastic records, extracurricular activities, community involvement and leadership potential.
Target applicants: College students. Adult students.
Amount: $1,500.
Number of awards: Up to 4.
Deadline: April 30.
How to apply: Applications are available online. An application form, transcript and answers to essay questions are required.

Exclusive: Visit www.UltimateScholarshipBook.com and enter code GE138512 for updates on this award.

(1386) • E.E. Black Scholarship Fund

Hawaii Community Foundation - Scholarships
1164 Bishop Street, Suite 800
Honolulu, HI 96813
Phone: 888-731-3863
Fax: 808-521-6286
Email: scholarships@hcf-hawaii.org
http://www.hawaiicommunityfoundation.org

Purpose: To provide financial assistance to dependents of Tesoro Hawaii employees.
Eligibility: Applicants must be dependents of Tesoro Hawaii employees or the company's subsidiaries. They must be full-time undergraduate students, and they must maintain a GPA of 3.0 or higher.
Target applicants: High school students. College students. Adult students.
Minimum GPA: 3.0
Amount: Varies.
Number of awards: Varies.
Deadline: March 1.
How to apply: To apply, register online, complete the online application and select the scholarships to which you wish to apply. In addition, mail the supporting materials: printed confirmation page from the online application, personal statement, copy of Student Aid Report (SAR) available at www.fafsa.ed.gov and official transcript.
Exclusive: Visit www.UltimateScholarshipBook.com and enter code HA138612 for updates on this award.

(1387) • E.H. Marth Food and Environmental Scholarship

Wisconsin Association for Food Protection
P.O. Box 329
Sun Prairie, WI 53590
Phone: 608-833-6181
Email: kglass@wisc.edu
http://www.wafp-wi.org

Purpose: To support students who are preparing for careers that are related to food or environmental sanitation.
Eligibility: Applicants must be Wisconsin residents who are enrolled at or have been accepted into a postsecondary institution that is either located in the state of Wisconsin or that has a reciprocal enrollment agreement with Wisconsin. They must be or plan to be enrolled full-time in an undergraduate academic program that is related to food science, environmental sanitation or dairy science. Selection is based on the overall strength of the application.
Target applicants: High school students. College students. Adult students.
Amount: $1,500.
Number of awards: 1.
Scholarship may be renewable.
Deadline: July 1.
How to apply: Applications are available online. An application form, official transcript and letter of recommendation are required.
Exclusive: Visit www.UltimateScholarshipBook.com and enter code WI138712 for updates on this award.

(1388) • Eagle Scout of the Year

American Legion, Department of Wisconsin
2930 American Legion Drive
P.O. Box 388
Portage, WI 53901
Phone: 608-745-1090
Fax: 608-745-0179
Email: info@wilegion.org
http://www.wilegion.org

Purpose: To award outstanding service as an Eagle Scout at the state level.
Eligibility: Applicants must demonstrate outstanding service in community, church and school and must be at least 15 years of age, in high school and either members of a troop chartered by the American Legion/Auxiliary or sons or grandsons of members of the American Legion/Auxiliary. Students must have received the Eagle Scout Award as well as the Boy Scout religious emblem. Scholarships may be used to attend a state-accredited college, university or other school above the high school level.
Target applicants: High school students.
Amount: $2,500-$10,000.
Number of awards: 4.
Deadline: Varies.
How to apply: Applications are available from the local Legion Post or from the Wisconsin American Legion Headquarters.
Exclusive: Visit www.UltimateScholarshipBook.com and enter code AM138812 for updates on this award.

(1389) • Early Childhood Educators Scholarship

Massachusetts Department of Higher Education
Office of Student Financial Assistance
454 Broadway
Suite 200
Revere, MA 02151
Phone: 617-727-9420
Fax: 617-727-0667
Email: osfa@osfa.mass.edu
http://www.osfa.mass.edu/default.asp

Purpose: To support the education of Massachusetts teachers employed in early childhood settings.
Eligibility: Applicants must be legal residents of Massachusetts who have worked as early childhood educators in the state for at least one year prior to receiving the scholarship. They must continue working in the profession while enrolled in school and upon completion of the degree. Students must be enrolled in Early Childhood Education or a related undergraduate program, and they cannot have any previously earned bachelor's degrees.
Target applicants: College students. Adult students.
Amount: up to $28,800.
Number of awards: Varies.
Scholarship may be renewable.
Deadline: June 1.
How to apply: Applications are available online.
Exclusive: Visit www.UltimateScholarshipBook.com and enter code MA138912 for updates on this award.

(1390) • Early College for ME

Early College for ME
Maine Community College System
323 State Street
Augusta, ME 04330-7131

Phone: 207-767-5210 x4115
Email: info@mccs.me.edu
http://www.earlycollege.me.edu
Purpose: To help high school students who are undecided about college.
Eligibility: Applicants must be in their junior year at one of the 74 Maine high schools participating in the program. The list of schools is online at http://www.earlycollege.me.edu/participating.html. Students must be Maine residents for at least one year prior to entering the first year of college and must have not yet made plans for college and yet be capable of succeeding at a community college. High schools may also take financial need into consideration when selecting students for the program as well as whether or not the student is the first one to attend college in their family. The program provides community college courses in the senior year of high school, as available, as well as financial aid for a one-year or two-year degree program at a Maine community college.
Target applicants: High school students.
Amount: Up to $2,000.
Number of awards: Varies.
Deadline: Varies, set by each school.
How to apply: Speak with your guidance counselor at your high school about entering the program.
Exclusive: Visit www.UltimateScholarshipBook.com and enter code EA139012 for updates on this award.

(1391) · Ed and Charlotte Rodgers Scholarships

Alabama Road Builders Association Inc.
630 Adams Avenue
Montgomery, AL 36104
Phone: 800-239-5828
Fax: 334-265-4931
http://www.alrba.org
Purpose: To support financially needy civil engineering students.
Eligibility: Applicants must be full-time civil engineering students who have completed their first year of college. They must be in good standing academically, have a good GPA and demonstrate financial need. Selection is based on leadership skills, awards received and extracurricular involvements.
Target applicants: College students. Adult students.
Amount: Varies.
Number of awards: Varies.
Deadline: April 1.
How to apply: Applications are available online. An application form, a recent photo and a personal essay are required.
Exclusive: Visit www.UltimateScholarshipBook.com and enter code AL139112 for updates on this award.

(1392) · Edmund F. Maxwell Foundation Scholarship

Edmund F. Maxwell Foundation
P.O. Box 22537
Seattle, WA 98122-0537
Email: admin@maxwell.org
http://www.maxwell.org
Purpose: The scholarship is intended to assist high-achieving students who follow the ideals of Edmund F. Maxwell: ability, aptitude and citizenship.
Eligibility: Applicants must be from Western Washington and plan to attend an accredited independent school that is primarily not tax-funded. Students must submit a FAFSA form and demonstrate financial need.
Target applicants: High school students.
Amount: Up to $5,000.
Number of awards: Varies.
Scholarship may be renewable.
Deadline: April 30.
How to apply: Applications are available online at http://www.maxwell.org/app.html.
Exclusive: Visit www.UltimateScholarshipBook.com and enter code ED139212 for updates on this award.

(1393) · Educational Excellence Scholarship

Kentucky Higher Education Assistance Authority
P.O. Box 798
Frankfort, KY 40602
Phone: 800-928-8926
Email: blane@kheaa.com
http://www,kheaa.com
Purpose: To reward outstanding Kentucky high school students.
Eligibility: Applicants must have a minimum 2.5 GPA, be graduating from eligible Kentucky high schools and meet high school graduation requirements. The scholarship amount is based on high school GPA and ACT composite score.
Target applicants: High school students.
Minimum GPA: 2.5
Amount: Varies.
Number of awards: Varies.
Scholarship may be renewable.
Deadline: Varies.
How to apply: High schools send eligible students' GPAs to the Kentucky Department of Education. There is no application for this award.
Exclusive: Visit www.UltimateScholarshipBook.com and enter code KE139312 for updates on this award.

(1394) · Educational Opportunity Fund (EOF) Grant

New Jersey Commission on Higher Education
P.O. Box 542
Trenton, NJ 08625
Phone: 609-292-4310
Fax: 609-292-7225
Email: meverett@che.state.nj.us
http://www.state.nj.us/highereducation
Purpose: To support underprivileged students in New Jersey.
Eligibility: Applicants must be able to show financial need and a background of family poverty, and they cannot exceed the established maximum income. They must be enrolled full-time in one of the participating public or private colleges in New Jersey, and they must have been residents of the state for at least 12 months prior to enrollment. Students pursuing a bachelor's degree cannot have any prior baccalaureate degrees, and students pursuing a two-year degree cannot have any previous associate's degrees. Applicants must not major in theology or divinity.
Target applicants: High school students. College students. Adult students.
Amount: $200-$2,500.
Number of awards: Varies.
Scholarship may be renewable.
Deadline: Varies.
How to apply: Applications are available from campus EOF directors.
Exclusive: Visit www.UltimateScholarshipBook.com and enter code NE139412 for updates on this award.

(1395) • Educational Rewards Grant

Massachusetts Department of Higher Education
Office of Student Financial Assistance
454 Broadway
Suite 200
Revere, MA 02151
Phone: 617-727-9420
Fax: 617-727-0667
Email: osfa@osfa.mass.edu
http://www.osfa.mass.edu/default.asp
Purpose: To assist dislocated or incumbent workers in getting the education they need to gain employment in high-demand occupations.
Eligibility: Students must be dislocated workers, or their income must be at or below 200 percent of poverty level. Students must also be enrolled in an eligible program at an eligible institution, and they must be U.S. citizens and Massachusetts residents.
Target applicants: College students. Adult students.
Amount: $200-$3,000.
Number of awards: Varies.
Deadline: Varies.
How to apply: Applications are available online. Applicants must also complete the Free Application for Federal Student Aid.
Exclusive: Visit www.UltimateScholarshipBook.com and enter code MA139512 for updates on this award.

(1396) • Edward J. Bloustein Distinguished Scholars

New Jersey Higher Education Student Assistance Authority
P.O. Box 540
Trenton, NJ 08625
Phone: 800-792-8670
Email: clientservices@hesaa.org
http://www.hesaa.org
Purpose: To support the highest achieving New Jersey students.
Eligibility: Applicants must be high school seniors who are New Jersey residents, be ranked in the top 10 percent of their classes, have a minimum SAT score of 1260 and plan to attend an institution of higher education. Juniors who are ranked first, second or third in their class at the end of the year may also apply. Applicants who attend high schools in the state's urban and economically distressed areas, who rank in the top 10 percent of their class and who have a minimum 3.0 GPA may also be selected through funding from the Urban Scholars Program.
Target applicants: High school students.
Amount: Up to $1,000.
Number of awards: Varies.
Scholarship may be renewable.
Deadline: October 1 and March 1.
How to apply: Applicants are nominated by their high schools and must complete and submit the Free Application for Federal Student Aid (FAFSA).
Exclusive: Visit www.UltimateScholarshipBook.com and enter code NE139612 for updates on this award.

(1397) • Edward L. Simeth Scholarships

Tool, Die and Machining Association of Wisconsin
W175 N11117 Stonewood Drive
Suite 204
Germantown, WI 53022
Phone: 262-532-2440
Fax: 262-532-2430
Email: info@tdmaw.org
http://www.tdmaw.org
Purpose: To support Wisconsin students who are enrolled in a machine tool operations or tool and die training program at an accredited technical school.
Eligibility: Applicants must be Wisconsin residents, and they must have a high school diploma or GED. They must have completed at least one semester at an accredited technical school located in Wisconsin. Students must be enrolled in a machine tool operations or tool and die program, taking 12 credits or more per semester. They must have a GPA of 3.0 or higher. Selection is based on the overall strength of the application.
Target applicants: College students. Adult students.
Minimum GPA: 3.0
Amount: Up to $500.
Number of awards: Varies.
Scholarship may be renewable.
Deadline: January 15 and June 15.
How to apply: Applications are available online. An application form, an official transcript and two references are required.
Exclusive: Visit www.UltimateScholarshipBook.com and enter code TO139712 for updates on this award.

(1398) • Edward Payson and Bernice Piilani Irwin Scholarship

Hawaii Community Foundation - Scholarships
1164 Bishop Street, Suite 800
Honolulu, HI 96813
Phone: 888-731-3863
Fax: 808-521-6286
Email: scholarships@hcf-hawaii.org
http://www.hawaiicommunityfoundation.org
Purpose: To provide financial assistance to Hawaii students who are pursuing careers in journalism.
Eligibility: Applicants must be college juniors, college seniors or graduate students majoring in journalism or communications. They must have a GPA of 2.7 or higher.
Target applicants: College students. Graduate school students. Adult students.
Minimum GPA: 2.7
Amount: Varies.
Number of awards: Varies.
Deadline: March 1.
How to apply: To apply, register online, complete the online application and select the scholarships to which you wish to apply. In addition, mail the supporting materials: printed confirmation page from the online application, personal statement, copy of Student Aid Report (SAR) available at www.fafsa.ed.gov and official transcript.
Exclusive: Visit www.UltimateScholarshipBook.com and enter code HA139812 for updates on this award.

(1399) • Eizo and Toyo Sakumoto Trust Scholarship

Hawaii Community Foundation - Scholarships
1164 Bishop Street, Suite 800
Honolulu, HI 96813
Phone: 888-731-3863
Fax: 808-521-6286
Email: scholarships@hcf-hawaii.org
http://www.hawaiicommunityfoundation.org
Purpose: To assist Hawaiian students of Japanese ancestry.
Eligibility: Applicants must be Hawaii residents of primarily Japanese ancestry who were born in the state and plan to attend a college or university in Hawaii. They must have a GPA of 3.5 or higher.

Target applicants: High school students. College students. Adult students.
Minimum GPA: 3.5
Amount: Varies.
Number of awards: Varies.
Deadline: March 1.
How to apply: To apply, register online, complete the online application and select the scholarships to which you wish to apply. In addition, mail the supporting materials: printed confirmation page from the online application, personal statement, copy of Student Aid Report (SAR) available at www.fafsa.ed.gov and official transcript.
Exclusive: Visit www.UltimateScholarshipBook.com and enter code HA139912 for updates on this award.

(1400) • Eldon Roesler Scholarship

Wisconsin Agri-Service Association Inc.
6000 Gisholt Drive
Suite 208
Madison, WI 53713
Phone: 608-223-1111
Fax: 608-223-1147
Email: info@wasa.org
http://www.wasa.org
Purpose: To aid Wisconsin students who are preparing for careers in agriculture.
Eligibility: Applicants must be Wisconsin residents who have completed at least one year of undergraduate study at a Wisconsin postsecondary institution. They must be enrolled in or plan to pursue a career in an agriculture-related subject and must have a GPA of 2.75 or higher. Preference is given to the children of WASA members and the children of WASA company employees. Selection is based on academic achievement, leadership skills and financial need.
Target applicants: College students. Adult students.
Minimum GPA: 2.75
Amount: $1,000.
Number of awards: 4.
Deadline: April 30.
How to apply: Applications are available online. An application form, two letters of reference, a transcript and a personal essay are required.
Exclusive: Visit www.UltimateScholarshipBook.com and enter code WI140012 for updates on this award.

(1401) • Ellison Onizuka Memorial Scholarship Fund

Hawaii Community Foundation - Scholarships
1164 Bishop Street, Suite 800
Honolulu, HI 96813
Phone: 888-731-3863
Fax: 808-521-6286
Email: scholarships@hcf-hawaii.org
http://www.hawaiicommunityfoundation.org
Purpose: To provide financial assistance to Hawaii students who plan to major in aerospace engineering.
Eligibility: Applicants must be graduating high school in the year of application and plan to pursue a degree in aerospace engineering or a related field. Students must have a GPA of 2.7, and their transcripts must list their SAT scores.
Target applicants: High school students.
Minimum GPA: 2.7
Amount: Varies.
Number of awards: Varies.
Deadline: March 1.
How to apply: To apply, register online, complete the online application and select the scholarships to which you wish to apply. In addition, mail the supporting materials: printed confirmation page from the online application, two letters of recommendation, personal statement, copy of Student Aid Report (SAR) available at www.fafsa.ed.gov and official transcript. The personal statement must describe participation in extracurricular activities, clubs and community service.
Exclusive: Visit www.UltimateScholarshipBook.com and enter code HA140112 for updates on this award.

(1402) • Emily M. Hewitt Memorial Scholarship

Calaveras Big Trees Association
P.O. Box 1196
Arnold, CA 95223
Phone: 209-795-3840
Fax: 209-795-6680
Email: info@bigtrees.org
http://www.bigtrees.org
Purpose: To support students who are committed to communicate a love of nature and an understanding of need to practice conservation.
Eligibility: Applicants must be enrolled full-time in an accredited California post-secondary educational institution and must have career goals that are related to communicating and interpreting nature's wonder. Students pursuing degrees in environmental protection, forestry, wildlife and fisheries biology, parks and recreation, park management, environmental law and public policy, environmental art and California history are encouraged to apply. Selection is based on dedication to the ideals of the scholarship and financial need.
Target applicants: College students. Adult students.
Amount: $1,000.
Number of awards: 1.
Deadline: April 15.
How to apply: Student must submit a statement of personal and career goals, a resume (and portfolio if applicable) and transcripts of all college work completed to date. On the cover page, include your name, address, phone number and college major.
Exclusive: Visit www.UltimateScholarshipBook.com and enter code CA140212 for updates on this award.

(1403) • Engineering and Land Surveying Scholarships

Consulting Engineers and Land Surveyors of California
1303 J Street
Suite 450
Sacramento, CA 95814
Phone: 916-441-7991
Fax: 916-441-6312
http://www.celsoc.org
Purpose: To help undergraduate and graduate students studying engineering or land surveying at California schools.
Eligibility: Applicants must be entering their third or fourth year (or fifth year of a five-year program) of undergraduate study for the upper division scholarships, or be entering or continuing graduate study for the graduate scholarships. Undergraduate students must be enrolled full-time and working toward a degree at an accredited engineering or land surveying program. Graduate students must be enrolled at least half time and working toward a degree at an accredited engineering or land surveying program. Students must submit application folders, including 500-word essays, transcripts, and recommendation forms.

Target applicants: College students. Graduate school students. Adult students.
Minimum GPA: 3.2
Amount: $1,000-$7,500.
Number of awards: Varies.
Deadline: January 3.
How to apply: Applications are available online.
Exclusive: Visit www.UltimateScholarshipBook.com and enter code CO140312 for updates on this award.

(1404) · Engineers Foundation of Ohio General Fund Scholarship

Engineers Foundation of Ohio
400 South Fifth Street
Suite 300
Columbus, OH 28315
Phone: 614-223-1177
Fax: 614-223-1131
Email: efo@ohioengineer.com
http://www.ohioengineer.com
Purpose: To aid Ohio engineering students.
Eligibility: Applicants must be U.S. citizens and residents of Ohio. They must be rising juniors or seniors enrolled full-time in an ABET-accredited engineering program that leads to the bachelor of science or its equivalent. They must have a GPA of 3.0 or higher on a 4-point scale. Selection is based on academic achievement, extracurricular involvements and financial need.
Target applicants: College students. Adult students.
Minimum GPA: 3.0
Amount: $1,000.
Number of awards: 1.
Deadline: December 15.
How to apply: Applications are available online. An application form, personal essay, faculty evaluation and transcript are required.
Exclusive: Visit www.UltimateScholarshipBook.com and enter code EN140412 for updates on this award.

(1405) · Engineers Foundation of Wisconsin College Freshmen Scholarships

Wisconsin Society of Professional Engineers
7044 South 13th Street
Oak Creek, WI 53154
Phone: 414-908-4950
Fax: 414-768-8001
Email: customercare@wspe.org
http://www.wspe.org
Purpose: To aid Wisconsin high school seniors who are planning to pursue education and careers in engineering.
Eligibility: Applicants must be current high school seniors who are U.S. citizens and Wisconsin residents. They must plan to enroll in an undergraduate engineering program at an ABET-accredited school and must intend to pursue careers in engineering after graduating. They must have a GPA of 3.0 or more and an ACT composite score of at least 24. Selection is based on GPA, ACT score, class rank, extracurricular involvement, honors, personal essay and any AP or college-level courses taken.
Target applicants: High school students.
Minimum GPA: 3.0
Amount: $1,000.
Number of awards: Varies.
Deadline: December 21.
How to apply: Applications are available online. An application form, transcript and personal essay are required.
Exclusive: Visit www.UltimateScholarshipBook.com and enter code WI140512 for updates on this award.

(1406) · Epsilon Sigma Alpha

College Foundation of North Carolina
P.O. Box 41966
Raleigh, NC 27629
Phone: 888-234-6400
Fax: 919-821-3139
Email: programinformation@cfnc.org
http://www.cfnc.org
Purpose: To provide financial assistance to students who want to work with exceptional children.
Eligibility: Applicants must be enrolled in an accredited college or university, either at the undergraduate level or as a North Carolina teacher seeking training, and must be training to work with special needs children up to the age of 21 in an educational setting. They must agree to teach at a North Carolina public school for at least one year after graduation.
Target applicants: College students. Graduate school students. Adult students.
Amount: $500-$2,500.
Number of awards: Varies.
Deadline: April 1.
How to apply: Applications are available online.
Exclusive: Visit www.UltimateScholarshipBook.com and enter code CO140612 for updates on this award.

(1407) · Esther Kanagawa Memorial Art Scholarship

Hawaii Community Foundation - Scholarships
1164 Bishop Street, Suite 800
Honolulu, HI 96813
Phone: 888-731-3863
Fax: 808-521-6286
Email: scholarships@hcf-hawaii.org
http://www.hawaiicommunityfoundation.org
Purpose: To provide financial assistance to Hawaii students who are majoring in fine arts.
Eligibility: Applicants must major in fine arts at an accredited college or university. They must have a GPA of 2.7 or higher and demonstrate financial need and good character.
Target applicants: High school students. College students. Adult students.
Minimum GPA: 2.7
Amount: Varies.
Number of awards: Varies.
Deadline: March 1.
How to apply: To apply, register online, complete the online application and select the scholarships to which you wish to apply. In addition, mail the supporting materials: printed confirmation page from the online application, personal statement, copy of Student Aid Report (SAR) available at www.fafsa.ed.gov and official transcript.
Exclusive: Visit www.UltimateScholarshipBook.com and enter code HA140712 for updates on this award.

(1408) • Ethics in Business Scholarship Program

Florida Department of Education
Office of Student Financial Assistance
1940 N. Monroe Street
Suite 70
Tallahassee, FL 32303-4759
Phone: 888-827-2004
Fax: 850-245-9667
Email: osfa@fldoe.org
http://www.floridastudentfinancialaid.org

Purpose: To help undergraduate college students who enroll at community colleges and eligible private Florida colleges or universities.
Eligibility: Applicants should contact financial aid offices at participating institutions for more information. Participating institutions determine deadlines, award amounts and eligibility.
Target applicants: High school students. College students. Adult students.
Amount: Varies.
Number of awards: Varies.
Deadline: Varies.
How to apply: Contact financial aid offices at participating institutions.
Exclusive: Visit www.UltimateScholarshipBook.com and enter code FL140812 for updates on this award.

(1409) • Excel Staffing Companies Scholarships for Excellence in Continuing Education

Albuquerque Community Foundation (ACF)
P.O. Box 36960
Albuquerque, NM 87176
Phone: 505-883-6240
Email: foundation@albuquerquefoundation.org
http://www.albuquerquefoundation.org

Purpose: To assist individuals who demonstrate a commitment to achieving a career goal.
Eligibility: Applicants must be at least 21 years old and be Albuquerque area residents. Applicants must also work a minimum of 30 hours a week, have a 3.0 minimum GPA and be in need of financial assistance to obtain a goal.
Target applicants: College students. Graduate school students. Adult students.
Minimum GPA: 3.0
Amount: $500-$1,000.
Number of awards: Up to 4.
Scholarship may be renewable.
Deadline: July 1.
How to apply: Applications are available online.
Exclusive: Visit www.UltimateScholarshipBook.com and enter code AL140912 for updates on this award.

(1410) • Excellence in Service Award

Florida's Office of Campus Volunteers
Florida Campus Compact
325 John Knox Road
Building F, Suite 210
Tallahassee, FL 32303
Phone: 850-488-7782
Fax: 850-922-2928
Email: info@floridacompact.org
http://www.floridacompact.org

Purpose: To reward students who perform outstanding acts of service in their communities.
Eligibility: Applicants must be full-time undergraduate students at an accredited public or private institution of higher education within the state of Florida.
Target applicants: College students. Adult students.
Amount: $500.
Number of awards: 3-6.
Deadline: January 11.
How to apply: Applications are available online.
Exclusive: Visit www.UltimateScholarshipBook.com and enter code FL141012 for updates on this award.

(1411) • Exceptional Circumstances Scholarships

Workforce Safety and Insurance
P.O. Box 5585
Bismarck, ND 58506-5585
Phone: 701-328-3828
Fax: 701-328-3820
Email: ndwsi@nd.gov
http://www.workforcesafety.com/workers/typesofbenefits.asp

Purpose: To provide financial assistance to injured North Dakota workers.
Eligibility: Applicants must be workers who have been injured on the job and would benefit from the funds due to exceptional circumstances. They must have completed the WSI rehabilitation process, and there must be no outstanding litigation on a rehabilitation plan. Applicants must reapply each year and maintain a satisfactory GPA in order to continue to receive funds.
Target applicants: High school students. College students. Adult students.
Amount: Up to $10,000.
Number of awards: Varies.
Scholarship may be renewable.
Deadline: Varies.
How to apply: Applications are available by phone.
Exclusive: Visit www.UltimateScholarshipBook.com and enter code WO141112 for updates on this award.

(1412) • Exemption from Tuition Fees for Dependents of Kentucky Veterans

Kentucky Department of Veterans Affairs
Attn.: Tuition Waiver Coordinator
321 W. Main Street
Suite 390
Louisville, KY 40202
Phone: 502-595-4447
Email: barbaraa.hale@ky.gov
http://veterans.ky.gov

Purpose: To support the families of Kentucky veterans.
Eligibility: Applicants must be children, stepchildren, adopted children, spouses or unremarried widows or widowers of qualifying Kentucky veterans. The veteran must have died on active duty or as a result of a service-connected disability, be 100 percent disabled from service, be totally disabled with wartime service or be deceased and have served during wartime. Children of veterans must be 26 years of age or younger.
Target applicants: High school students. College students. Adult students.
Amount: Full tuition.
Number of awards: Varies.
Deadline: Varies.

How to apply: Applications are available online. An application form, birth or marriage certificate, veteran's discharge certificate, death certificate or disability award letter and evidence of Kentucky residency are required.
Exclusive: Visit www.UltimateScholarshipBook.com and enter code KE141212 for updates on this award.

(1413) • F. Koehnen Ltd. Scholarship Fund

Hawaii Community Foundation - Scholarships
1164 Bishop Street, Suite 800
Honolulu, HI 96813
Phone: 888-731-3863
Fax: 808-521-6286
Email: scholarships@hcf-hawaii.org
http://www.hawaiicommunityfoundation.org
Purpose: To provide financial assistance to students whose parents or grandparents are employed in Hawaiian retail establishments.
Eligibility: Applicants must be Hawaii high school graduates with a GPA of 2.5 or higher. They must be children or grandchildren of retail employees on the island of Hawaii.
Target applicants: High school students.
Minimum GPA: 2.5
Amount: Varies.
Number of awards: Varies.
Deadline: March 1.
How to apply: To apply, register online, complete the online application and select the scholarships to which you wish to apply. In addition, mail the supporting materials: printed confirmation page from the online application, personal statement, copy of Student Aid Report (SAR) available at www.fafsa.ed.gov and official transcript.
Exclusive: Visit www.UltimateScholarshipBook.com and enter code HA141312 for updates on this award.

(1414) • Family District 1 Scholarships

American Hellenic Education Progressive Association
1909 Q Street NW
Suite 500
Washington, DC 20009
Phone: 202-232-6300
Fax: 202-232-2140
Email: ahepa@ahepa.org
http://www.ahepa.org
Purpose: To provide financial assistance for those pursuing higher education.
Eligibility: Applicants must be graduating seniors, high school graduates or current undergraduate or graduate students who plan to attend a college or university full-time during the calendar year of application. They must be residents of Alabama, Georgia, Mississippi, South Carolina, Tennessee or Florida.
Target applicants: High school students. College students. Graduate school students. Adult students.
Amount: Varies.
Number of awards: varies.
Deadline: March 31.
How to apply: Applications are available online. The current application must be used and must be sent by certified mail and return receipt requested.
Exclusive: Visit www.UltimateScholarshipBook.com and enter code AM141412 for updates on this award.

(1415) • Federal Chafee Educational and Training Grant

Oregon Student Assistance Commission
1500 Valley River Drive
Suite 100
Eugene, OR 97401
Phone: 541-687-7400
Fax: 541-687-7414
Email: awardinfo@osac.state.or.us
http://www.osac.state.or.us
Purpose: To provide financial assistance to students who have been in foster care.
Eligibility: Applicants must be in foster care or have been in foster care for at least six months after their 14th birthday or be adopted from the foster care system after age 16. Funding is provided on a first come, first served basis. The deadlines are: August 1 for the fall term, November 1 for the winter term, February 1 for the spring term and May 1 for the summer term.
Target applicants: High school students. College students. Graduate school students.
Amount: Up to $3,000.
Number of awards: Varies.
Scholarship may be renewable.
Deadline: August 1, November 1, February 1, May 1.
How to apply: Applications are available online.
Exclusive: Visit www.UltimateScholarshipBook.com and enter code OR141512 for updates on this award.

(1416) • Fellowship on Women and Public Policy

Center for Women in Government and Civil Society
University at Albany, SUNY
135 Western Avenue
Draper Hall 302
Albany, NY 12222
Phone: 518-442-3900
Fax: 518-442-3877
http://www.cwig.albany.edu
Purpose: To encourage New York state graduate students to pursue jobs in public policy.
Eligibility: Students must be enrolled in a graduate program at an accredited college or university in New York and have completed at least 12 credits before applying but not be scheduled to graduate before the internship. Applicants must demonstrate an interest in improving the status of women and underrepresented populations.
Target applicants: Graduate school students. Adult students.
Amount: $9,000 stipend and tuition assistance.
Number of awards: Varies.
Deadline: September 30, although applications will be considered throughout the fall.
How to apply: Applications are available online.
Exclusive: Visit www.UltimateScholarshipBook.com and enter code CE141612 for updates on this award.

(1417) • Filipino Nurses' Organization of Hawaii Scholarship

Hawaii Community Foundation - Scholarships
1164 Bishop Street, Suite 800
Honolulu, HI 96813
Phone: 888-731-3863
Fax: 808-521-6286

Email: scholarships@hcf-hawaii.org
http://www.hawaiicommunityfoundation.org
Purpose: To assist Filipino students who are seeking degrees in nursing.
Eligibility: Applicants must be Hawaii residents who are of Filipino descent. They must be full-time students.
Target applicants: High school students. College students. Adult students.
Minimum GPA: 2.7
Amount: Varies.
Number of awards: Varies.
Deadline: February 18.
How to apply: To apply, register online, complete the online application and select the scholarships to which you wish to apply. In addition, mail the supporting materials: printed confirmation page from the online application, personal statement, copy of Student Aid Report (SAR) available at www.fafsa.ed.gov and official transcript.
Exclusive: Visit www.UltimateScholarshipBook.com and enter code HA141712 for updates on this award.

(1418) • Financial Women International Scholarship

Hawaii Community Foundation - Scholarships
1164 Bishop Street, Suite 800
Honolulu, HI 96813
Phone: 888-731-3863
Fax: 808-521-6286
Email: scholarships@hcf-hawaii.org
http://www.hawaiicommunityfoundation.org
Purpose: To provide financial assistance to female business majors in Hawaii.
Eligibility: Applicants must be college juniors, college seniors or graduate students. They must have a minimum GPA of 3.5.
Target applicants: College students. Graduate school students. Adult students.
Minimum GPA: 3.5
Amount: Varies.
Number of awards: Varies.
Deadline: March 1.
How to apply: To apply, register online, complete the online application and select the scholarships to which you wish to apply. In addition, mail the supporting materials: printed confirmation page from the online application, personal statement, copy of Student Aid Report (SAR) available at www.fafsa.ed.gov and official transcript.
Exclusive: Visit www.UltimateScholarshipBook.com and enter code HA141812 for updates on this award.

(1419) • First Generation Matching Grant Program

Florida Department of Education
Office of Student Financial Assistance
1940 N. Monroe Street
Suite 70
Tallahassee, FL 32303-4759
Phone: 888-827-2004
Fax: 850-245-9667
Email: osfa@fldoe.org
http://www.floridastudentfinancialaid.org
Purpose: To help Florida undergraduate students with financial need who are enrolled in state universities and whose parents have not earned bachelor's degrees.
Eligibility: Applicants must submit applications and the Free Application for Federal Student Aid (FAFSA). Each university determines its own deadline.
Target applicants: High school students. College students. Adult students.
Amount: Varies.
Number of awards: Varies.
Deadline: Varies.
How to apply: Applications are at the financial aid offices of state universities.
Exclusive: Visit www.UltimateScholarshipBook.com and enter code FL141912 for updates on this award.

(1420) • First in Family Scholarship

J. Craig and Page T. Smith Scholarship Foundation
505 20th Street N
Suite 1800
Birmingham, AL 35203
Phone: 205-250-6669
Email: ahrian@smithscholarships.com
http://www.smithscholarships.com
Purpose: To provide assistance for students who face financial, physical or emotional challenges and who have participated in volunteer work or assisted their families.
Eligibility: Applicants must be seniors at an Alabama high school and plan to attend an Alabama four-year college the following fall. Students must also write two essays about their future plans and their community service or family assistance endeavors and provide three letters of recommendation.
Target applicants: High school students.
Amount: Varies.
Number of awards: Varies.
Deadline: Varies.
How to apply: Applications are available online or by mail.
Exclusive: Visit www.UltimateScholarshipBook.com and enter code J.142012 for updates on this award.

(1421) • First Lieutenant Michael L. Lewis, Jr. Memorial Fund Scholarship

American Legion Auxiliary, Department of New York
112 State Street
Suite 1310
Albany, NY 12207
Phone: 518-463-1162
Fax: 518-449-5406
Email: alanyterry@nycap.rr.com
http://www.deptny.org/Scholarships.htm
Purpose: To support New York American Legion Auxiliary members.
Eligibility: Applicants must be New York Auxiliary members in good standing. One scholarship is awarded to a Junior Member who is a high school senior or graduate, and another will be awarded to a Senior Member who plans to continue his or her education. If there are no senior applications, both scholarships will be awarded to Junior Members. Selection is based equally on character, Americanism, leadership and scholarship and is made by a committee of three impartial judges.
Target applicants: High school students. College students. Adult students.
Amount: Varies.
Number of awards: 2.
Deadline: March 25.
How to apply: Applications are available online. An application form, copy of Auxiliary membership card, essay, statement of extracurricular and other activities and transcript are required. High school seniors must also submit a letter of acceptance from the college they plan to attend.

Exclusive: Visit www.UltimateScholarshipBook.com and enter code AM142112 for updates on this award.

(1422) • First State Manufactured Housing Association Scholarship

Delaware Higher Education Commission
Carvel State Office Building
5th Floor
820 North French Street
Wilmington, DE 19801-3509
Phone: 800-292-7935
Fax: 302-577-6765
Email: dhec@doe.k12.de.us
http://www.doe.k12.de.us/infosuites/students_family/dhec/

Purpose: To provide assistance to residents of manufactured homes.

Eligibility: Applicants must be legal residents of Delaware. They may be high school seniors or former graduates seeking higher education. They must have lived in a manufactured home for at least one year prior to application. They may enroll in any accredited program full- or part-time. Selection criteria include scholastic achievement, financial need, essay and recommendations.

Target applicants: High school students. College students. Adult students.

Amount: Up to $2,000.

Number of awards: 2.

Deadline: April 8.

How to apply: Applications are available online. An application form, essay, FAFSA and transcript are required.

Exclusive: Visit www.UltimateScholarshipBook.com and enter code DE142212 for updates on this award.

(1423) • Florida Association of Postsecondary Schools and Colleges (FAPSC) Scholarship Program

Florida Association of Postsecondary Schools and Colleges
150 S. Monroe Street, Suite 303
Tallahassee, FL 32301
Phone: 850-577-3139
Fax: 850-577-3133
Email: mail@fapsc.org
http://www.fapsc.org

Purpose: To aid Florida students.

Eligibility: Applicants must be high school seniors or recent GED recipients in the state of Florida. They must have a GPA of 2.0 or higher and must attend a participating career college or school.

Target applicants: High school students.

Minimum GPA: 2.0

Amount: Up to full tuition.

Number of awards: Varies.

Deadline: March 11.

How to apply: Applications are available online. An application form, transcript and essay are required.

Exclusive: Visit www.UltimateScholarshipBook.com and enter code FL142312 for updates on this award.

(1424) • Florida Association of Postsecondary Schools and Colleges Scholarship Program

Florida Association of Postsecondary Schools and Colleges
150 S. Monroe Street, Suite 303
Tallahassee, FL 32301
Phone: 850-577-3139
Fax: 850-577-3133
Email: mail@fapsc.org
http://www.fapsc.org

Purpose: To provide full and partial-tuition scholarships to Florida students planning to attend a private Florida career school or college.

Eligibility: Applicants must either be graduating from high school or receiving a GED in Florida and have a 2.0 or higher GPA.

Target applicants: High school students.

Minimum GPA: 2.0

Amount: Up to Full Tuition.

Number of awards: Varies.

Deadline: March 11.

How to apply: Applications are available from guidance counselors and participating FAPSC schools.

Exclusive: Visit www.UltimateScholarshipBook.com and enter code FL142412 for updates on this award.

(1425) • Florida Bright Futures Scholarship Program

Florida Department of Education
Office of Student Financial Assistance
1940 N. Monroe Street
Suite 70
Tallahassee, FL 32303-4759
Phone: 888-827-2004
Fax: 850-245-9667
Email: osfa@fldoe.org
http://www.floridastudentfinancialaid.org

Purpose: Lottery-funded scholarships are awarded to Florida high school seniors as reward for academic achievements and to assist with postsecondary education.

Eligibility: Applicants must earn a Florida high school diploma or equivalent, have not been found guilty or pled no contest to a felony charge and meet the award's academic requirements. Applicants must also be Florida residents, U.S. citizens or eligible noncitizens and be accepted by and enrolled in an eligible Florida public or private college or vocational school at least quarter time. Application must be completed during the senior year of high school.

Target applicants: High school students.

Amount: Varies.

Number of awards: Varies.

Deadline: High school graduation.

How to apply: Apply by completing the Florida Financial Aid Application. The application is available online at www.floridastudentfinancialaid.org or from your high school guidance counselor.

Exclusive: Visit www.UltimateScholarshipBook.com and enter code FL142512 for updates on this award.

(1426) • Florida Engineering Society University Scholarships

Florida Engineering Society
P.O. Box 750
Tallahassee, FL 32302
Phone: 850-224-7121
Fax: 850-222-4349
Email: fes@fleng.org
http://www.fleng.org

Purpose: To support students who are enrolled in an undergraduate engineering degree program at a Florida university.

Eligibility: Applicants must be rising juniors or seniors enrolled in an undergraduate engineering program at a Florida university. They must

have a GPA of 3.0 or higher, and they must be U.S. citizens or residents of Florida. Selection is based on the overall strength of the application.
Target applicants: College students. Adult students.
Minimum GPA: 3.0
Amount: Varies.
Number of awards: 5.
Deadline: February 15.
How to apply: Applications are available online. An application form, a transcript and one recommendation letter are required.
Exclusive: Visit www.UltimateScholarshipBook.com and enter code FL142612 for updates on this award.

(1427) • Florida Engineers in Construction Scholarship

Florida Engineers in Construction
125 South Gadsden Street
Tallahassee, FL 32301
Phone: 850-224-7121
Fax: 850-222-4349
Email: fes@fleng.org
http://www.fleng.org
Purpose: To aid Florida engineering majors who are interested in careers in construction.
Eligibility: Applicants must be undergraduate juniors or seniors enrolled in an accredited degree program in engineering at a Florida university. They must have a GPA of at least 3.0 on a 4.0 scale and must have plans to pursue a career in construction. Selection is based on the overall strength of the application.
Target applicants: College students. Adult students.
Minimum GPA: 3.0
Amount: $1,000.
Number of awards: 1.
Deadline: February 15.
How to apply: Applications are available online. An application form, a transcript and one letter of recommendation are required.
Exclusive: Visit www.UltimateScholarshipBook.com and enter code FL142712 for updates on this award.

(1428) • Florida Oratorical Contest

American Legion, Department of Florida
P.O. Box 547859
Orlando, FL 32854
Phone: 407-295-2631
Fax: 407-299-0901
http://www.floridalegion.org
Purpose: To enhance high school students' experience with and understanding of the U.S. Constitution. The contest will help develop students' leadership skills and civic appreciation, as well as the ability to deliver thoughtful, insightful orations regarding U.S. citizenship and its inherent responsibilities.
Eligibility: Applicants must be high school students under the age of 20 who are U.S. citizens or legal residents and residents of the state. Students first give an oration within their state and winners compete at the national level. The oration must be related to the Constitution of the United States focusing on the duties and obligations citizens have to the government. It must be in English and be between eight and ten minutes. There is also an assigned topic which is posted on the website, and it should be between three and five minutes.
Target applicants: Junior high students or younger. High school students.
Amount: $500-$18,000.
Number of awards: Varies.
Deadline: Varies.
How to apply: Applications are available by contacting the local American Legion Post.
Exclusive: Visit www.UltimateScholarshipBook.com and enter code AM142812 for updates on this award.

(1429) • Florida Student Assistance Grant Program

Florida Department of Education
Office of Student Financial Assistance
1940 N. Monroe Street
Suite 70
Tallahassee, FL 32303-4759
Phone: 888-827-2004
Fax: 850-245-9667
Email: osfa@fldoe.org
http://www.floridastudentfinancialaid.org
Purpose: To help degree-seeking, Florida resident, undergraduate students who have financial need and who are enrolled in participating postsecondary institutions.
Eligibility: There are three student financial aid programs: The Florida Public Student Assistance Grant is for students who attend state universities and public community colleges. The Florida Private Student Assistance Grant is for students who attend eligible private, non-profit, four-year colleges and universities. The Florida Postsecondary Student Assistance Grant is for students who attend eligible degree-granting private colleges and universities that are ineligible under the Florida Private Student Assistance Grant. High school students in the top 20 percent of their classes receive priority funding.
Target applicants: High school students. College students. Adult students.
Amount: $200-$2,069.
Number of awards: Varies.
Scholarship may be renewable.
Deadline: Each school determines its own deadline.
How to apply: Applicants must submit the Free Application for Federal Student Aid (FAFSA).
Exclusive: Visit www.UltimateScholarshipBook.com and enter code FL142912 for updates on this award.

(1430) • Ford Opportunity Scholarship

Oregon Student Assistance Commission
1500 Valley River Drive
Suite 100
Eugene, OR 97401
Phone: 541-687-7400
Fax: 541-687-7414
Email: awardinfo@osac.state.or.us
http://www.osac.state.or.us
Purpose: To assist Oregon undergraduate students who are single parents.
Eligibility: Applicants must be U.S. citizens or legal residents, high school graduates or GED recipients and Oregon residents who are single heads of household with custody of one or more dependent children. They must be supporting their child(ren) without the aid of a domestic partner. Applicants must have a minimum 3.0 GPA or 2650 GED score and must be attending or planning to attend a non-profit Oregon college or community college on a full-time basis by fall of the application year. Applicants who owe an educational loan grant or who have defaulted student loans are ineligible, as are those who already hold a bachelor's degree. Selection is based on financial need.

Target applicants: High school students. College students. Adult students.
Minimum GPA: 3.0
Amount: Varies.
Number of awards: Varies.
Deadline: March 1.
How to apply: Applications are available online. An application form, proof of GPA or GED score and completion of the FAFSA are required.
Exclusive: Visit www.UltimateScholarshipBook.com and enter code OR143012 for updates on this award.

(1431) • Ford Scholars Scholarship

Oregon Student Assistance Commission
1500 Valley River Drive
Suite 100
Eugene, OR 97401
Phone: 541-687-7400
Fax: 541-687-7414
Email: awardinfo@osac.state.or.us
http://www.osac.state.or.us
Purpose: To assist Oregon students who plan to pursue a bachelor's degree.
Eligibility: Applicants must be U.S. citizens or legal residents. They must be Oregon residents who are high school graduates, GED recipients or community college students who will be transferring to an Oregon four-year college with junior standing during the fall of the application year. They must have a GPA of 3.0 or higher or a GED score of 2650 or higher, have plans to earn a bachelor's degree at a non-profit Oregon institution and be enrolled as a full-time student no later than the fall of the application year. They must owe no educational grant refund money and must have no defaulted student loans. Applicants who have earned a bachelor's degree previously are ineligible. Selection is based on financial need.
Target applicants: High school students. College students. Adult students.
Minimum GPA: 3.0
Amount: Varies.
Number of awards: Varies.
Scholarship may be renewable.
Deadline: March 1.
How to apply: Applications are available online. An application form, proof of GPA or GED score and completion of the FAFSA are required.
Exclusive: Visit www.UltimateScholarshipBook.com and enter code OR143112 for updates on this award.

(1432) • Foster Child Grant Program

Massachusetts Department of Higher Education
Office of Student Financial Assistance
454 Broadway
Suite 200
Revere, MA 02151
Phone: 617-727-9420
Fax: 617-727-0667
Email: osfa@osfa.mass.edu
http://www.osfa.mass.edu/default.asp
Purpose: To assist children who have lived in foster homes in obtaining higher education.
Eligibility: Applicants must be placed in the custody of the Department of Social Services and be permanent residents of the state of Massachusetts. Students must also be 24 years of age or younger and apply for financial aid.
Target applicants: High school students. College students. Graduate school students.
Amount: Up to $6,000.
Number of awards: Varies.
Scholarship may be renewable.
Deadline: Varies.
How to apply: Applications are available by phone from the Massachusetts Office of Student Financial Assistance or from your social worker.
Exclusive: Visit www.UltimateScholarshipBook.com and enter code MA143212 for updates on this award.

(1433) • Frances A. Mays Scholarship Award

Virginia Association for Health, Physical Education, Recreation and Dance
7812 Falling Hill Terrace
Chesterfield, VA 23832
Phone: 804-304-1768
Fax: 804-608-0486
Email: info@vahperd.org
http://www.vahperd.org
Purpose: To aid students majoring in fields related to physical education.
Eligibility: Applicants must be seniors at Virginia colleges or universities pursuing a degree in health, physical education, recreation or dance and be members of VAHPERD and AAHPERD. Students must have an overall GPA of 2.8 or higher and a major GPA of 3.0 or higher and demonstrate high ideals, good scholarship and professional ethics. Applicants must be nominated by their schools.
Target applicants: College students. Adult students.
Minimum GPA: 2.8
Amount: Varies.
Number of awards: 1.
Deadline: October 1.
How to apply: Applications are available from your university's VAHPERD representative. An application form and letter of reference are required.
Exclusive: Visit www.UltimateScholarshipBook.com and enter code VI143312 for updates on this award.

(1434) • Frank del Olmo Memorial Scholarship

California Chicano News Media Association
USC Annenberg School of Journalism
727 W. 27th Street, Room 201
Los Angeles, CA 90007-3212
Phone: 213-821-0075
Fax: 213-743-1838
Email: ccnmainfo@ccnma.org
http://www.ccnma.org
Purpose: To assist California Latino college students who demonstrate a desire to pursue a career in journalism.
Eligibility: Applicants must be Latino, be either California residents or attending California schools and have an interest in pursuing a journalism career. An interview is required. Financial need, academic achievement and community involvement are also considered.
Target applicants: High school students. College students. Adult students.
Amount: $500-$1,000.
Number of awards: Varies.
Deadline: April 2.
How to apply: Applications are available online.

Exclusive: Visit www.UltimateScholarshipBook.com and enter code CA143412 for updates on this award.

(1435) • Frank O'Bannon Grant Program

State Student Assistance Commission of Indiana
150 W. Market Street
Suite 500
Indianapolis, IN 46204
Phone: 888-528-4719
Fax: 317-232-3260
Email: grants@ssaci.state.in.us
http://www.in.gov/ssaci

Purpose: To aid Indiana students in attending eligible postsecondary schools.
Eligibility: Applicants must be high school graduates and attend or plan to attend eligible Indiana colleges or universities full-time.
Target applicants: High school students. College students. Adult students.
Amount: Varies.
Number of awards: Varies.
Deadline: March 10.
How to apply: Complete the Free Application for Federal Student Aid (FAFSA).
Exclusive: Visit www.UltimateScholarshipBook.com and enter code ST143512 for updates on this award.

(1436) • Frank Woods Memorial Scholarship

University of California 4-H Youth Development Program
University of California-Davis
DANR Building
One Shields Avenue
Davis, CA 95616
Phone: 530-754-8518
Email: fourhstateofc@ucdavis.edu
http://www.ca4h.org

Purpose: To support students pursuing higher education in agriculture or a related field.
Eligibility: Applicants must have been enrolled in the California 4-H Youth Development program at the time of their high school graduation. They must be enrolled or plan to enroll full-time at a postsecondary institution and must be between the ages of 16 and 25 at the time of submitting the application. They must be studying or planning to study an agriculture-related subject and must have a GPA of 2.8 or higher. Selection is based on leadership skills, civic awareness and the impact that 4-H involvement has had on the applicant's life.
Target applicants: High school students. College students.
Minimum GPA: 2.8
Amount: $1,000.
Number of awards: 1.
Scholarship may be renewable.
Deadline: April 30.
How to apply: Applications are available online. An application cover page, personal essay, resume and enrollment verification or college transcript are required.
Exclusive: Visit www.UltimateScholarshipBook.com and enter code UN143612 for updates on this award.

(1437) • Freehold Soil Conservation District Scholarship

Freehold Soil Conservation District
4000 Kozloski Road
P.O. Box 5033
Freehold, NJ 07728
Phone: 732-683-8500
Fax: 732-683-9140
Email: info@freeholdscd.org
http://www.freeholdscd.org

Purpose: To support college juniors and seniors majoring in the conservation of natural resources.
Eligibility: Applicants must be residents of Middlesex or Monmouth County, New Jersey, entering the junior or senior year in the fall. Students must major in an area related to conservation of natural resources such as agriculture; forestry; conservation; environmental or soil science; environmental studies, education or policy; resource management or geology.
Target applicants: College students. Adult students.
Amount: $2,000.
Number of awards: 3.
Deadline: Varies.
How to apply: Applications are available online.
Exclusive: Visit www.UltimateScholarshipBook.com and enter code FR143712 for updates on this award.

(1438) • Fresh Start Scholarship

Fresh Start Scholarship Foundation
P.O. Box 7784
Wilmington, DE 19803
Phone: 302-656-4411
Fax: 610-347-0438
Email: fsscholar@comcast.net
http://www.wwb.org/freshstart.html

Purpose: To help women who are returning to school.
Eligibility: Applicants should be women at least 20 years old with financial need who have a high school diploma or G.E.D., have had at least a two year break in education either after finishing high school or during college studies and are enrolled in a Delaware college in a two- or four-year degree program at the undergraduate level. Applicants should have at least a C average if already in college.
Target applicants: College students. Adult students.
Amount: Varies.
Number of awards: Varies.
Deadline: May 31.
How to apply: Applications are available online or by mail and include a personal statement. A social service agency or college representative should recommend applicants.
Exclusive: Visit www.UltimateScholarshipBook.com and enter code FR143812 for updates on this award.

(1439) • Friends of Senator Jack Perry Migrant Scholarship

Genesco Migrant Center
27 Lackawanna Avenue
Mount Morris, NY 14510
Phone: 800-245-5681
http://www.migrant.net

Purpose: To aid migrant farm workers.

Eligibility: Applicants must have past or present eligibility for Migrant Education services in New York State. Preference is given to seniors in New York State high schools and high school seniors outside the state who have a history of movement to New York State, but college students are also considered. Applicants must be accepted at a post-secondary institution of higher learning, preferably in New York State. Financial need is required.
Target applicants: High school students. College students. Adult students.
Amount: Varies.
Number of awards: Varies.
Deadline: Varies.
How to apply: Applications are available by mail or phone.
Exclusive: Visit www.UltimateScholarshipBook.com and enter code GE143912 for updates on this award.

(1440) • Futurama Foundation Career Advancement Scholarship

Business and Professional Women/Maine Futurama Foundation
103 County Road
Oakland, ME 04963
Email: webmaster@bpwmaine.org
http://www.bpwmaine.org/files/index.php?id=10
Purpose: To provide financial assistance for women who want to advance their careers.
Eligibility: Applicants must be female Maine residents who are age 30 or older. They must need financial assistance to improve their skills or complete education for career advancement. They must have a definite plan to use their training to improve their chances of advancement, train for a new career or to enter or reenter the job market.
Target applicants: College students. Adult students.
Amount: $1,200.
Number of awards: 1.
Deadline: April 20.
How to apply: Applications are available from your local BPW chapter or your financial aid office.
Exclusive: Visit www.UltimateScholarshipBook.com and enter code BU144012 for updates on this award.

(1441) • Future Teachers Scholarship

Oklahoma State Regents for Higher Education
655 Research Parkway
Suite 200
Oklahoma City, OK 73104
Phone: 405-225-9100
Email: llangston@osrhe.edu
http://www.okhighered.org
Purpose: To encourage students to become teachers in critical teacher shortage areas in Oklahoma public schools.
Eligibility: Applicants must be residents of Oklahoma who have been nominated by their institution on the basis of rank in the top 15 percent of high school class, rank in the top 15 percent of students in SAT or ACT scores, admission to an education program at an accredited Oklahoma institution or high academic achievement in undergraduate coursework. Applicants must maintain a GPA of 2.5 or higher and agree to teach in a shortage area in an Oklahoma public school for at least three years after graduation and licensure.
Target applicants: High school students. College students. Adult students.
Minimum GPA: 2.5
Amount: Up to $1,500.
Number of awards: Varies.
Deadline: Varies.
How to apply: Applications are submitted by the nominating institution.
Exclusive: Visit www.UltimateScholarshipBook.com and enter code OK144112 for updates on this award.

(1442) • Gallo Blue Chip Scholarship

Harness Horse Youth Foundation
16575 Carey Road
Westfield, IN 46074
Phone: 317-867-5877
Fax: 317-867-5896
Email: ellen@hhyf.org
http://www.hhyf.org
Purpose: To support the children of horse trainers and caretakers.
Eligibility: Applicants must have been raised or currently reside in New Jersey or New York. Students must be at least in their senior year of high school, and they cannot be pursuing a graduate degree. Selection is based on financial need and academic achievements.
Target applicants: High school students. College students. Adult students.
Amount: Varies.
Number of awards: Varies.
Deadline: April 30.
How to apply: Applications are available online.
Exclusive: Visit www.UltimateScholarshipBook.com and enter code HA144212 for updates on this award.

(1443) • Garden Club of Ohio Inc. Scholarships

Garden Club of Ohio Inc.
State Scholarship Chairman
Ms. Cleopatra Lehman
1658 17th Street
Cuyahoga Falls, OH 44223
Phone: 330-928-8897
Email: clehman6@neo.rr.com
http://www.gardenclubofohio.org
Purpose: To support Ohio students pursuing higher education in subjects related to plant science, environmental science, horticulture, floriculture, city planning and wildlife.
Eligibility: Applicants must be residents of Ohio and must be enrolled in a postsecondary degree program related to environmental science, plant science, horticulture, floriculture, city planning or wildlife. They must be rising undergraduate juniors, undergraduate seniors or graduate students and have a GPA of 3.0 or higher. Selection is based on the overall strength of the application.
Target applicants: College students. Graduate school students. Adult students.
Minimum GPA: 3.0
Amount: Varies.
Number of awards: Varies.
Deadline: March 1.
How to apply: Applications are available online. An application form, transcript, personal statement, financial aid statement and three letters of recommendation are required.
Exclusive: Visit www.UltimateScholarshipBook.com and enter code GA144312 for updates on this award.

(1444) • GEAR UP ALASKA Scholarship Program

Alaska Commission on Postsecondary Education
3030 Vintage Boulevard
Juneau, AK 99801
Phone: 800-441-2962
Fax: 907-465-5316
Email: customer_service@acpe.state.ak.us
http://alaskadvantage.state.ak.us
Purpose: To provide financial aid to students in Alaska.
Eligibility: Applicants must be students under the age of 22 who have participated in GEAR UP Programs in 6th, 7th and 8th grade and who have met GEAR UP academic requirements. Students must be seniors at an Alaskan high school or have received a diploma or GED from an Alaskan high school. Applicants must complete the Free Application for Federal Student Aid (FAFSA) and then submit the Student Aid Report (SAR) and federal income tax forms with their application. The award is based on financial need.
Target applicants: High school students. College students.
Amount: up to $28,000.
Number of awards: Varies.
Scholarship may be renewable.
Deadline: May 31.
How to apply: Applications are available by contacting the scholarship coordinator.
Exclusive: Visit www.UltimateScholarshipBook.com and enter code AL144412 for updates on this award.

(1445) • GEAR UP Summer Scholarship

State Student Assistance Commission of Indiana
150 W. Market Street
Suite 500
Indianapolis, IN 46204
Phone: 888-528-4719
Fax: 317-232-3260
Email: grants@ssaci.state.in.us
http://www.in.gov/ssaci
Purpose: To support Indiana students who are planning to enroll in summer courses.
Eligibility: Applicants must be high school seniors or college freshmen, and they must be enrolled or planning to enroll full-time at an Indiana college. Students must be eligible for the 21st Century Scholars Program. Scholarship funds may be used for college preparatory courses, prerequisites or degree requirements.
Target applicants: High school students. College students. Adult students.
Amount: $1,500.
Number of awards: Varies.
Deadline: May 31.
How to apply: Applications are available by mail. Completing the FAFSA is required.
Exclusive: Visit www.UltimateScholarshipBook.com and enter code ST144512 for updates on this award.

(1446) • General Assembly Merit Scholarship

Tennessee Student Assistance Corporation
404 James Robertson Parkway
Suite 1510, Parkway Towers
Nashville, TN 37243
Phone: 800-342-1663
Fax: 615-741-6101
Email: tsac.aidinfo@tn.gov
http://www.tn.gov/CollegePays/
Purpose: To provide supplemental support to recipients of the Tennessee HOPE Scholarship.
Eligibility: Students graduating from public schools or category 1, 2, and 3 private schools must have at least a 3.75 GPA and either a 29 on the ACT or a 1280 on the SAT. Home-schooled or non-category 1, 2, or 3 private school students must complete at least 12 college credit hours while in high school, and they must have at least a 3.0 GPA in those courses. Recipients of the Aspire Award are not eligible.
Target applicants: High school students. College students. Adult students.
Minimum GPA: 3.75
Amount: $1,000.
Number of awards: Varies.
Deadline: Varies.
How to apply: Applications are available through completion of the FAFSA.
Exclusive: Visit www.UltimateScholarshipBook.com and enter code TE144612 for updates on this award.

(1447) • General Assembly Scholarship

Illinois Student Assistance Commission
1755 Lake Cook Road
Deerfield, IL 60015
Phone: 800-899-4722
Fax: 847-831-8549
Email: collegezone@isac.org
http://www.collegezone.com
Purpose: To assist Illinois students.
Eligibility: Applicants must be Illinois high school students planning to attend a state-supported university. They must contact their State Senator and State Representative to be considered for the award, and they must live within the legislative district of that Senator or Representative.
Target applicants: High school students.
Amount: Full tuition for one to four years.
Number of awards: 1-4 per district.
Scholarship may be renewable.
Deadline: Varies.
How to apply: Applications are available from your State Senator and State Representative.
Exclusive: Visit www.UltimateScholarshipBook.com and enter code IL144712 for updates on this award.

(1448) • George Mason Business Scholarship Fund

Hawaii Community Foundation - Scholarships
1164 Bishop Street, Suite 800
Honolulu, HI 96813
Phone: 888-731-3863
Fax: 808-521-6286
Email: scholarships@hcf-hawaii.org
http://www.hawaiicommunityfoundation.org
Purpose: To assist Hawaii students who are majoring in business administration.
Eligibility: Applicants must be seniors at a Hawaiian college or university and have a GPA of 3.0 or higher. They must discuss why they have chosen to pursue a business career and how they expect to make a difference in the business world in their personal statement.
Target applicants: College students. Adult students.
Minimum GPA: 3.0
Amount: Varies.

Number of awards: Varies.
Deadline: March 1.
How to apply: To apply, register online, complete the online application and select the scholarships to which you wish to apply. In addition, mail the supporting materials: printed confirmation page from the online application, personal statement, copy of Student Aid Report (SAR) available at www.fafsa.ed.gov and official transcript.
Exclusive: Visit www.UltimateScholarshipBook.com and enter code HA144812 for updates on this award.

(1449) • George V. Soule Scholarship

Ruffed Grouse Society of Maine
P.O. Box 111
Hampden, ME 04444
Email: rgs@srdcorp.com
http://www.ruffedgrousemaine.com
Purpose: To aid Maine students who are preparing for careers in a wildlife conservation-related field.
Eligibility: Applicants must be residents of Maine who are enrolled in or plan to enroll in a postsecondary program in wildlife conservation, forest management, conservation law enforcement or a related subject. They must have attended a secondary school located in the state of Maine and have a GPA of 3.0 or higher. Selection is based on the overall strength of the application.
Target applicants: High school students. College students. Adult students.
Minimum GPA: 3.0
Amount: $3,000.
Number of awards: Up to 2.
Deadline: April 8.
How to apply: Applications are available online. An application form, personal essay, two to three recommendation letters and a transcript are required.
Exclusive: Visit www.UltimateScholarshipBook.com and enter code RU144912 for updates on this award.

(1450) • Georgia Oratorical Contest

American Legion, Department of Georgia
3035 Mt. Zion Road
Stockbridge, GA 30281
Phone: 678-289-8883
Fax: 678-289-8885
Email: amerlegga@bellsouth.net
http://www.galegion.org
Purpose: To enhance high school students' experience with and understanding of the U.S. Constitution. The contest will help develop students' leadership skills and civic appreciation, as well as the ability to deliver thoughtful, insightful orations regarding U.S. citizenship and its inherent responsibilities.
Eligibility: Applicants must be high school students under the age of 20 who are U.S. citizens or legal residents and residents of the state. Students first give an oration within their state and winners compete at the national level. The oration must be related to the Constitution of the United States focusing on the duties and obligations citizens have to the government. It must be in English and be between eight and ten minutes. There is also an assigned topic which is posted on the website, and it should be between three and five minutes.
Target applicants: Junior high students or younger. High school students.
Amount: Up to $3,150.
Number of awards: Varies.
Deadline: Varies according to Local Post.
How to apply: Applications are available by contacting the local American Legion Post.
Exclusive: Visit www.UltimateScholarshipBook.com and enter code AM145012 for updates on this award.

(1451) • Georgia Press Educational Foundation Scholarships

Georgia Press Educational Foundation, Inc.
Georgia Press Building
30266 Mercer University Drive
Suite 200
Atlanta, GA 30343-4137
Phone: 770-454-6776
Fax: 770-454-6778
Email: mail@gapress.org
http://www.gapress.org
Purpose: To aid students interested in newspaper journalism.
Eligibility: Applicants must be high school seniors or undergraduate students who have been Georgia residents for three years, or their parents must have been Georgia residents for two years. Students must attend a Georgia college or university, demonstrate financial need and be recommended by a counselor, principal, professor or Georgia Press Association member.
Target applicants: High school students. College students. Adult students.
Amount: $1,000.
Number of awards: Varies.
Deadline: February 1.
How to apply: Applications are available online. An application form, transcript, copy of SAT scores, copy of tax return, anticipated budget, school photograph and letter of recommendation are required.
Exclusive: Visit www.UltimateScholarshipBook.com and enter code GE145112 for updates on this award.

(1452) • Georgia Thespians Achievement Scholarships

Georgia Thespians
2280 Remington Court
Marietta, GA 30066
Phone: 678-936-6022
Email: gailg.jones@hallco.org
http://www.gathespians.org
Purpose: To support outstanding thespians.
Eligibility: Applicants must be Georgia high school students and perform an audition in one of the following categories: acting, technical theatre, singing or theatre education.
Target applicants: Junior high students or younger. High school students.
Amount: $2,000.
Number of awards: 11.
Deadline: January 8.
How to apply: Applications are available online. An application form and resume of thespian troupe experience are required.
Exclusive: Visit www.UltimateScholarshipBook.com and enter code GE145212 for updates on this award.

(1453) • Georgia Tuition Equalization Grant

Georgia Student Finance Commission
2082 East Exchange Place
Tucker, GA 30084
Phone: 800-505-4732
Fax: 770-724-9089
Email: support@gacollege411.org
http://www.gacollege411.org
Purpose: To support Georgia resident students.
Eligibility: Applicants must be full-time students at eligible private colleges or universities in Georgia or in out-of-state four-year public colleges within 50 miles of students' residences and be U.S. citizens.
Target applicants: College students. Adult students.
Amount: $200 per quarter, $300 per semester.
Number of awards: Varies.
Scholarship may be renewable.
Deadline: Varies.
How to apply: Applications are available online.
Exclusive: Visit www.UltimateScholarshipBook.com and enter code GE145312 for updates on this award.

(1454) • Get Ready for Math and Science Conditional Scholarship Program

Washington Higher Education Coordinating Board
917 Lakeridge Way
P.O. Box 43430
Olympia, WA 98504
Phone: 360-753-7850
Fax: 360-753-6243
Email: info@hecb.wa.gov
http://www.hecb.wa.gov
Purpose: To assist high achievers in math and science in obtaining a degree in a qualified math or science program.
Eligibility: Applicants must be Washington students who achieve a level 4 on the math or science section of the tenth grade WASL or score above the 95th percentile in math on the SAT or ACT and come from a family with income at or below 125 percent of the state's median family income for two years prior to application. They must begin college within one year of high school graduation, make satisfactory academic progress and enter in a qualifying math or science program by the end of the first term of their junior year. They must also make a commitment to work in a qualifying math or science occupation within the state for at least three years.
Target applicants: High school students.
Amount: Up to full tuition.
Number of awards: Varies.
Scholarship may be renewable.
Deadline: Varies.
How to apply: Applications are available from the College Success Foundation by phone at 877-655-4097.
Exclusive: Visit www.UltimateScholarshipBook.com and enter code WA145412 for updates on this award.

(1455) • GET-IT Student Scholarship

Michigan Council of Women in Technology Foundation
Attn.: Scholarship Committee
19011 Norwich Road
Livonia, MI 48152
Fax: 248-281-5391
Email: info@mcwt.org
http://www.mcwtf.org
Purpose: To aid female information technology students.
Eligibility: Applicants must be high school seniors, Michigan residents and U.S. citizens who are involved in the GET-IT program and have a GPA of 2.5 or higher. There is more information about starting a GET-IT program at your school on the MCWTF website. Students must enroll in a degree program in information systems, business applications, computer science, computer engineering, software engineering or information security.
Target applicants: High school students.
Minimum GPA: 2.5
Amount: $1,000.
Number of awards: Varies.
Scholarship may be renewable.
Deadline: January 31.
How to apply: Applications are available online. An application form, transcript and two letters of recommendation are required.
Exclusive: Visit www.UltimateScholarshipBook.com and enter code MI145512 for updates on this award.

(1456) • Gilbert Matching Student Grant

Massachusetts Department of Higher Education
Office of Student Financial Assistance
454 Broadway
Suite 200
Revere, MA 02151
Phone: 617-727-9420
Fax: 617-727-0667
Email: osfa@osfa.mass.edu
http://www.osfa.mass.edu/default.asp
Purpose: To assist needy students in attending private institutions of higher education or nursing schools.
Eligibility: Students must be permanent residents of Massachusetts, demonstrate financial need, maintain satisfactory academic progress and attend an eligible Massachusetts institution. Applicants must not have earned a bachelor's or professional degree, nor a first diploma from a hospital or professional nursing program.
Target applicants: High school students. College students. Adult students.
Amount: $200-$2,500.
Number of awards: Varies.
Scholarship may be renewable.
Deadline: Varies.
How to apply: Applications are available from your school's financial aid office.
Exclusive: Visit www.UltimateScholarshipBook.com and enter code MA145612 for updates on this award.

(1457) • GlaxoSmithKlein Opportunity Scholarship

Triangle Community Foundation
324 Blackwell Street
Suite 1220
Durham, NC 27701
Phone: 919-474-8370
Fax: 919-941-9208
Email: libby@trianglecf.org
http://www.trianglecf.org
Purpose: To assist residents of Durham, Orange or Wake County, North Carolina who have overcome significant adversity.
Eligibility: Applicants must be U.S. citizens who have held this status for at least one year, and they must be residents of Durham, Orange or

Wake County who have lived there for at least one year. They must be enrolled at or planning to enroll at a North Carolina community college or public university. They must be eligible for in-state tuition. Only those who have overcome significant adversity should apply. Selection is based on the applicant's desire for self-improvement and potential for success.
Target applicants: High school students. College students. Adult students.
Amount: Up to $5,000.
Number of awards: Varies.
Scholarship may be renewable.
Deadline: March 15.
How to apply: Applications are available online. An application form, personal essay, official transcript and one letter of recommendation are required.
Exclusive: Visit www.UltimateScholarshipBook.com and enter code TR145712 for updates on this award.

(1458) • Glenn B. Hudson Memorial Scholarship

Central Ohio Golf Course Superintendents Association
c/o Sean Magginis
492 South Chillicothe Street
Plain City, OH 43064
Phone: 614-645-3211
http://www.cogcsa.org
Purpose: To aid Ohio turfgrass management students.
Eligibility: Applicants must be Ohio turfgrass management students who are enrolled in a program requiring 20 credits or more of study. The program of study must include at least 10 credits of coursework in turfgrass management. Students must have a cumulative GPA of 2.5 or higher and a major GPA of 2.75 or higher. Selection is based on academic merit, professional commitment to golf course management and financial need.
Target applicants: College students. Adult students.
Minimum GPA: 2.5
Amount: $3,000.
Number of awards: 1.
Deadline: May 2.
How to apply: Applications are available online. An application form, transcript, personal statement and two recommendation letters are required.
Exclusive: Visit www.UltimateScholarshipBook.com and enter code CE145812 for updates on this award.

(1459) • Golden Apple Scholars of Illinois (Illinois Scholars Program)

Illinois Department of Public Health
535 W. Jefferson Street
Springfield, IL 62761
Phone: 217-782-4977
Fax: 217-782-3987
Email: dph.mailus@illinois.gov
http://www.idph.state.il.us
Purpose: To offer scholarships to promising students pursuing teaching degrees.
Eligibility: Applicants must be Illinois high school seniors or college sophomores at one of the 53 partner universities in Illinois who are interested in teaching. There are a limited number of spots for college sophomores, and all college students must be nominated by a university liaison. Students must commit to teaching in an Illinois school of need for five years after graduation.
Target applicants: High school students. College students. Adult students.
Amount: Financial assistance for four years at one of 53 colleges in Illinois.
Number of awards: Varies.
Scholarship may be renewable.
Deadline: December 1.
How to apply: Applications are available by calling 312-407-0433, extension 105.
Exclusive: Visit www.UltimateScholarshipBook.com and enter code IL145912 for updates on this award.

(1460) • Golden LEAF Scholars Program - Two-Year Colleges

College Foundation of North Carolina
P.O. Box 41966
Raleigh, NC 27629
Phone: 888-234-6400
Fax: 919-821-3139
Email: programinformation@cfnc.org
http://www.cfnc.org
Purpose: To provide need-based financial assistance to North Carolina community college students.
Eligibility: Applicants must be residents of one of the 73 eligible counties and meet specific income requirements as evidenced by FAFSA information (for curriculum students) or the federal TRIO formula (for occupational education students). Degree-seeking students must be enrolled at least half-time.
Target applicants: High school students. College students. Adult students.
Amount: Up to $750 per semester.
Number of awards: Varies.
Scholarship may be renewable.
Deadline: Varies.
How to apply: Applications are available online.
Exclusive: Visit www.UltimateScholarshipBook.com and enter code CO146012 for updates on this award.

(1461) • Good Eats Scholarship Fund

Hawaii Community Foundation - Scholarships
1164 Bishop Street, Suite 800
Honolulu, HI 96813
Phone: 888-731-3863
Fax: 808-521-6286
Email: scholarships@hcf-hawaii.org
http://www.hawaiicommunityfoundation.org
Purpose: To provide financial assistance to Hawaii students pursuing degrees in agriculture and culinary arts, and to encourage them to return to Hawaii upon graduation.
Eligibility: Applicants must be Hawaii residents who plan to study culinary arts or agriculture at a college or university in the continental United States. They must have a GPA of 2.7 or higher and demonstrate interest in food production and preparation through their school or community activities.
Target applicants: High school students. College students. Adult students.
Minimum GPA: 2.7
Amount: Varies.
Number of awards: Varies.
Deadline: March 1.

How to apply: To apply, register online, complete the online application and select the scholarships to which you wish to apply. In addition, mail the supporting materials: printed confirmation page from the online application, personal statement, copy of Student Aid Report (SAR) available at www.fafsa.ed.gov and official transcript.
Exclusive: Visit www.UltimateScholarshipBook.com and enter code HA146112 for updates on this award.

(1462) • Gorgas Scholarship Competition

Alabama Academy of Science
c/o Dr. Ellen Buckner
4064 HAHN Building, College of Nursing
University of South Alabama
Mobile, AL 36688
Email: ebuckner@usouthal.edu
http://www.gorgasscholar.org
Purpose: To aid Alabama residents who are planning to pursue higher education in science.
Eligibility: Applicants must be Alabama residents who are rising undergraduate freshman and have completed a scientific research project and an accompanying report of no more than 20 pages. They must have completed all college entrance requirements by October 1 of the year of application submission. Selection is based on the quality of the scientific research paper that is submitted as part of the application.
Target applicants: High school students.
Amount: Up to $4,000.
Number of awards: 5.
Deadline: January 7.
How to apply: Applications are available online. An entry form, research paper, official transcript, one letter of recommendation and additional research-related documentation are required.
Exclusive: Visit www.UltimateScholarshipBook.com and enter code AL146212 for updates on this award.

(1463) • Governor's Coalition For Youth with Disabilities Scholarships

Governor's Coalition for Youth with Disabilities
P.O. Box 2485
Hartford, CT 06146-2485
Email: info@gcyd.org
http://www.gycd.org
Purpose: To support students with disabilities.
Eligibility: Applicants must be graduating high school seniors who are Connecticut residents. They must have a disability according to the Individuals with Disabilities Act or Section 504 of the Rehabilitation Act of 1973. They must plan to pursue post-secondary education, show promise for success and demonstrate responsibility and good character.
Target applicants: High school students.
Amount: Up to full tuition.
Number of awards: Varies.
Scholarship may be renewable.
Deadline: February 4.
How to apply: Applications are available online or from your high school guidance office. An application form and essay are required, and transcripts, letters of recommendation and resumes will be considered.
Exclusive: Visit www.UltimateScholarshipBook.com and enter code GO146312 for updates on this award.

(1464) • Governor's Cup Scholarship

Idaho State Board of Education
P.O. Box 83720
Boise, ID 83720
Phone: 208-334-2270
Fax: 208-334-2632
Email: dkelly@osbe.state.id.us
http://www.boardofed.idaho.gov
Purpose: Monetary assistance is provided to Idaho resident high school seniors planning to attend state colleges.
Eligibility: Applicants must be Idaho high school seniors planning to attend Idaho colleges or universities full-time and have a minimum 2.8 GPA. Public service is a significant factor.
Target applicants: High school students.
Minimum GPA: 2.8
Amount: $3,000.
Number of awards: 12.
Scholarship may be renewable.
Deadline: January 15.
How to apply: Applications are available online.
Exclusive: Visit www.UltimateScholarshipBook.com and enter code ID146412 for updates on this award.

(1465) • Governor's Postsecondary Merit Scholarship

Montana Guaranteed Student Loan Program
P.O. Box 203101
Helena, MT 59620
Phone: 800-537-7508
Fax: 406-444-1869
http://www.mgslp.state.mt.us
Purpose: To assist Montana residents in getting a college education in the state and to reduce the amount of student debt so that more students can remain in the state after graduation.
Eligibility: Students must be residents of Montana who have been accepted to an eligible institution of higher learning in the state. Students must also have a minimum GPA of 3.0, SAT score of 20 or higher or SAT score of 1380, and be enrolled in a certificate, associate or bachelor's degree program.
Target applicants: High school students.
Minimum GPA: 3.0
Amount: Varies.
Number of awards: Varies.
Deadline: March 1.
How to apply: Applications are available online.
Exclusive: Visit www.UltimateScholarshipBook.com and enter code MO146512 for updates on this award.

(1466) • Governor's Scholars Program

Arkansas Department of Higher Education
114 East Capitol
Little Rock, AR 72201-3818
Phone: 501-371-2050
Fax: 501-371-2001
Email: finaid@adhe.arknet.edu
http://www.adhe.edu/Pages/home.aspx
Purpose: To assist outstanding Arkansas high school graduates to encourage them to attend postsecondary schools in Arkansas.
Eligibility: Applicants must be Arkansas graduating high school seniors who will attend an Arkansas college or university. Selection is based on academic achievement, test scores and leadership. A minimum

ACT score of 27, SAT score of 1220 or 3.5 GPA in academic courses is required.
Target applicants: High school students.
Minimum GPA: 3.5
Amount: Up to $4,000.
Number of awards: Varies.
Scholarship may be renewable.
Deadline: February 1.
How to apply: Applications are available through your high school counselor and online.
Exclusive: Visit www.UltimateScholarshipBook.com and enter code AR146612 for updates on this award.

(1467) • Governor's Scholarship Program

Georgia Student Finance Commission
2082 East Exchange Place
Tucker, GA 30084
Phone: 800-505-4732
Fax: 770-724-9089
Email: support@gacollege411.org
http://www.gacollege411.org
Purpose: To aid graduating Georgia high school seniors attend Georgia colleges or universities.
Eligibility: Applicants must be selected by the Georgia Department of Education or be a valedictorian, salutatorian or STAR student and enroll full-time as an undergraduate at a Georgia institution. A minimum 3.0 GPA is required for renewal.
Target applicants: High school students.
Amount: $900 average.
Number of awards: Varies.
Scholarship may be renewable.
Deadline: Last day of classes or exams for the academic period.
How to apply: Applications are available online.
Exclusive: Visit www.UltimateScholarshipBook.com and enter code GE146712 for updates on this award.

(1468) • Graduate and Professional Scholarship Program

Maryland Higher Education Commission
Office of Student Financial Assistance
839 Bestgate Road, Suite 400
Annapolis, MD 21401
Phone: 800-974-1024
Fax: 410-260-3200
Email: osfamail@mhec.state.md.us
http://www.mhec.state.md.us
Purpose: To assist Maryland graduate and professional school students.
Eligibility: Applicants must be U.S. citizens or eligible non-citizens and legal residents of the state of Maryland. They must be degree-seeking graduate or professional students in nursing, veterinary medicine, law, social work, medicine, dentistry or pharmacology. They must be enrolled at one of the following schools: University of Maryland; Baltimore (UMB) Schools of Medicine, Dentistry, Law, Pharmacy, or Social Work; University of Baltimore School of Law; The Johns Hopkins University School of Medicine; The Virginia-Maryland Regional College of Veterinary Medicine or an eligible Maryland institution that grants a graduate degree in nursing, social work or pharmacology (first professional degree only). Selection is based on financial need.
Target applicants: Graduate school students. Adult students.
Amount: $1,000-$5,000.
Number of awards: Varies.
Scholarship may be renewable.
Deadline: Varies.
How to apply: Application is made by completing the FAFSA and contacting the student's financial aid office.
Exclusive: Visit www.UltimateScholarshipBook.com and enter code MA146812 for updates on this award.

(1469) • Graduate and Undergraduate Assistance Program

State Council of Higher Education for Virginia
101 N. 14th Street
James Monroe Building
Richmond, VA 23219
Phone: 804-225-2600
Fax: 804-225-2604
Email: communications@schev.edu
http://www.schev.edu
Purpose: To assist students in attending Virginia schools.
Eligibility: Applicants must be admitted to an eligible Virginia college or university and demonstrate academic excellence. Applicants do not need to be Virginia residents.
Target applicants: High school students. College students. Graduate school students. Adult students.
Amount: Varies.
Number of awards: Varies.
Deadline: Varies.
How to apply: Contact your financial aid office.
Exclusive: Visit www.UltimateScholarshipBook.com and enter code ST146912 for updates on this award.

(1470) • Graduate Tuition Waiver

Massachusetts Department of Higher Education
Office of Student Financial Assistance
454 Broadway
Suite 200
Revere, MA 02151
Phone: 617-727-9420
Fax: 617-727-0667
Email: osfa@osfa.mass.edu
http://www.osfa.mass.edu/default.asp
Purpose: To provide financial support to Massachusetts graduate students.
Eligibility: Students must be enrolled in graduate level courses at a Massachusetts public school that is not a community college. Applicants must not owe any refunds on previously received financial aid, and they must not have defaulted on any government loans.
Target applicants: Graduate school students. Adult students.
Amount: Varies.
Number of awards: Varies.
Deadline: Varies.
How to apply: Applications are available at college financial aid offices.
Exclusive: Visit www.UltimateScholarshipBook.com and enter code MA147012 for updates on this award.

(1471) • Grand Rapids Chapter Construction Specifications Institute Scholarship

Construction Specifications Institute - Grand Rapids Chapter
P.O. Box 2826
Grand Rapids, MI 49501

http://www.csigrandrapids.org
Purpose: To aid students interested in construction careers.
Eligibility: Applicants must plan to be enrolled in an accredited Michigan college, university or trade school in the upcoming academic year and pursue a course of study related to the construction industry. Selection is based on scholastic ability, references, writing ability and how applicant will benefit from scholarship. CSI membership or relation to a CSI member is also considered.
Target applicants: High school students. College students. Adult students.
Amount: Varies.
Number of awards: Varies.
Deadline: April 15.
How to apply: Applications are available online. An application form, essay and three letters of reference are required.
Exclusive: Visit www.UltimateScholarshipBook.com and enter code CO147112 for updates on this award.

(1472) • Granite State Scholars Program

New Hampshire Postsecondary Education Commission
3 Barrell Court
Suite 300
Concord, NH 03301
Phone: 603-271-2555 x352
Fax: 603-271-2696
Email: jknapp@pec.state.nh.us
http://www.state.nh.us/postsecondary
Purpose: To support Granite State Scholars in New Hampshire.
Eligibility: Students must have been designated as Granite State Scholars in high school. Students become Scholars by being ranked in the top 10 percent of their class and having a combined SAT I score of 1200 or more (math and reading comprehension) or an equivalent ACT score. They must be pursuing an undergraduate degree at a public school in New Hampshire, and they must have no previous bachelor's degrees. Applicants must also show financial need.
Target applicants: High school students. College students. Adult students.
Amount: Varies.
Number of awards: Varies.
Deadline: Varies.
How to apply: Applications are available at college financial aid offices.
Exclusive: Visit www.UltimateScholarshipBook.com and enter code NE147212 for updates on this award.

(1473) • Granville P. Meade Scholarship

Virginia Department of Education
P.O. Box 2120
Richmond, VA 23218
Phone: 804-225-3349
Fax: 804-371-2456
Email: joseph.wharff@doe.virginia.gov
http://www.pen.k12.va.us
Purpose: To support graduating high school seniors in Virginia.
Eligibility: Students must have been born in Virginia, and they must plan to attend a public or private Virginia school. They must demonstrate financial need, academic achievement, extracurricular activities and good character. Recipients must maintain a 2.5 GPA.
Target applicants: High school students.
Minimum GPA: 2.5
Amount: $2,000.
Number of awards: Varies.
Scholarship may be renewable.
Deadline: March 7.
How to apply: Applications are available online.
Exclusive: Visit www.UltimateScholarshipBook.com and enter code VI147312 for updates on this award.

(1474) • Greater Kanawha Valley Foundation Scholarship Program

Greater Kanawha Valley Foundation
1600 Huntington Square
900 Lee Street, East
Charleston, WV 25301
Phone: 304-346-3620
Fax: 304-346-3640
Email: tgkvf@tgkvf.org
http://www.tgkvf.org
Purpose: To provide financial assistance to prospective college students from the state of West Virginia.
Eligibility: Applicants must be residents of West Virginia, be full-time students (12 hours) and demonstrate good moral character. Many awards are available, and each individual award may have additional eligibility requirements. Applicants must have a minimum 2.5 GPA and an ACT score of at least 20.
Target applicants: High school students. College students. Adult students.
Minimum GPA: 2.5
Amount: Varies.
Number of awards: 90.
Scholarship may be renewable.
Deadline: January 15.
How to apply: Applications are available online at http://www.tgkvf.org/scholar.htm.
Exclusive: Visit www.UltimateScholarshipBook.com and enter code GR147412 for updates on this award.

(1475) • Greater Pittsburgh Golf Course Superintendents Association Scholarship

Greater Pittsburgh Golf Course Superintendents Association
2993 Amy Drive
South Park, PA 15129
Phone: 412-714-8707
Fax: 412-650-8155
Email: gpgcsa@comcast.net
http://www.gpgcsa.org
Purpose: To aid students preparing for careers in turf grass management.
Eligibility: Applicants must be full-time students enrolled in a postsecondary program emphasizing turf grass management. They must have a GPA of 2.0 or higher. Selection is based on the overall strength of the application.
Target applicants: College students. Adult students.
Minimum GPA: 2.0
Amount: $1,000.
Number of awards: 2.
Deadline: July 31.
How to apply: Applications are available online. An application form, transcript, personal statement and two recommendation letters are required.
Exclusive: Visit www.UltimateScholarshipBook.com and enter code GR147512 for updates on this award.

(1476) • Greenhouse Scholars Scholarship

Greenhouse Scholars
Attn: Amy Vreeland
1011 Walnut Street
2nd Floor
Boulder, CO 80302
Phone: 303-460-1735
Fax: 303-464-7796
Email: avreeland@greenhousescholars.org
http://www.greenhousescholars.org

Purpose: To provide financial assistance to high-performing, under-resourced students who are leaders and contributors to their communities.

Eligibility: Applicants must be high school seniors who plan to attend a four-year college or university. They must be U.S. citizens who reside and attend school in Colorado. They must have an unweighted GPA of 3.5 or higher, and they must demonstrate leadership, perseverance and financial need. Their household income must be $70,000 a year or less. Winners must participate in an internship and the company's Whole Person program.

Target applicants: High school students.
Minimum GPA: 3.5
Amount: Up to $5,000.
Number of awards: Varies.
Scholarship may be renewable.
Deadline: January 20.
How to apply: Applications are available online.
Exclusive: Visit www.UltimateScholarshipBook.com and enter code GR147612 for updates on this award.

(1477) • Growing Up Asian in America

Asian Pacific Fund
225 Bush Street
Suite 590
San Francisco, CA 94104
Phone: 415-433-6859
Fax: 415-433-2425
Email: scholarship@asianpacificfund.org
http://www.asianpacificfund.org

Purpose: To celebrate Asian heritage.

Eligibility: Applicants do NOT need to be Asian American. Students must be K-12 students in the nine counties of the San Francisco Bay Area and must submit entries in the art and essay categories. There is a theme for each year's competition.

Target applicants: Junior high students or younger. High school students.
Amount: $1,000-$2,000.
Number of awards: Varies.
Deadline: Varies.
How to apply: Applications are available at schools and libraries.
Exclusive: Visit www.UltimateScholarshipBook.com and enter code AS147712 for updates on this award.

(1478) • Guardian Scholarships

Workforce Safety and Insurance
P.O. Box 5585
Bismarck, ND 58506-5585
Phone: 701-328-3828
Fax: 701-328-3820
Email: ndwsi@nd.gov
http://www.workforcesafety.com/workers/typesofbenefits.asp

Purpose: To provide financial assistance to the families of North Dakota workers who lost their lives due to work-related injuries.

Eligibility: Applicants must be spouses or dependent children of workers who died as a result of work-related injuries. Upon approval, they may receive funds for up to five years if they reapply each year and maintain a satisfactory GPA.

Target applicants: High school students. College students. Adult students.
Amount: Up to $4,000.
Number of awards: Varies.
Scholarship may be renewable.
Deadline: Varies.
How to apply: Applications are available by phone.
Exclusive: Visit www.UltimateScholarshipBook.com and enter code WO147812 for updates on this award.

(1479) • Guy M. Wilson Scholarship

American Legion, Department of Michigan
212 N. Verlinden Avenue, Ste. A
Lansing, MI 48915
Phone: 517-371-4720 x11
Fax: 517-371-2401
Email: programs@michiganlegion.org
http://www.michiganlegion.org

Purpose: To aid students who are the sons or daughters of veterans who plan to attend a Michigan college.

Eligibility: Applicants must be residents of Michigan who are planning to attend a Michigan college or university and who are the sons or daughters of veterans. Students must have a minimum GPA of 2.5 and must have demonstrated financial need. Applicants must provide proof of a parent's military service record and an indication of their abilities to fulfill their goals and intentions. They should send scholarship information to their county district committee person.

Target applicants: High school students.
Minimum GPA: 2.5
Amount: $500.
Number of awards: Varies.
Deadline: January 17.
How to apply: Applications are available online.
Exclusive: Visit www.UltimateScholarshipBook.com and enter code AM147912 for updates on this award.

(1480) • Guy P. Gannett Scholarship

Maine Community Foundation
245 Main Street
Ellsworth, ME 04605
Phone: 207-667-9735
Fax: 207-667-0447
Email: jwarren@mainecf.org
http://www.mainecf.org

Purpose: To provide renewable financial support to students in Maine who are majoring in journalism or a related field.

Eligibility: Students must be graduates of Maine high schools or home-schooled in Maine. Applicants are considered for the award based on their interest in journalism, financial need and academic achievement. They must also continue to demonstrate an interest in journalism in college.

Target applicants: High school students. College students. Graduate school students. Adult students.
Amount: Varies.

Number of awards: Varies.
Scholarship may be renewable.
Deadline: May 1.
How to apply: Applications are available online in January or by contacting the Maine Community Foundation.
Exclusive: Visit www.UltimateScholarshipBook.com and enter code MA148012 for updates on this award.

(1481) • H-E-B Pharmacy Scholarship

University Interscholastic League
1701 Manor Road
Austin, TX 78722
Phone: 512-471-5883
Fax: 512-232-7311
Email: bbaxendale@mail.utexas.edu
http://www.uil.utexas.edu
Purpose: To aid University Interscholastic League academic meet participants who are planning to enter the pharmacy profession in a location serviced by an H-E-B Pharmacy.
Eligibility: Applicants must have participated in a University Interscholastic League academic meet during high school in one of the following categories: mathematics, accounting, calculator applications, number sense, spelling and vocabulary, journalism, ready writing, speech, debate, literary criticism, current issues and events, debate, one-act play, social studies, science, computer science or computer applications. Preference is given to those applicants who have plans to pursue a pharmacy career in an area served by an H-E-B Pharmacy. Selection is based on the overall strength of the application.
Target applicants: High school students.
Amount: $1,000.
Number of awards: Varies.
Deadline: June 1.
How to apply: Applications are available online. An application form, official transcript, one recommendation letter and copies of parents' federal tax forms are required.
Exclusive: Visit www.UltimateScholarshipBook.com and enter code UN148112 for updates on this award.

(1482) • H.M. Muffly Memorial Scholarship

Colorado Nurses Foundation
7400 East Arapahoe Road
Suite 211
Centennial, CO 80112
Phone: 303-694-4728
Fax: 303-694-4869
Email: mail@cnfound.org
http://www.cnfound.org/
Purpose: To aid nursing students working towards bachelor's, master's or doctoral degrees.
Eligibility: Applicants must be Colorado residents who are planning to practice nursing in Colorado. They must be juniors or seniors working towards the Bachelor of Science in Nursing (BSN); Registered Nurses (RNs) pursuing the bachelor's degree or higher in a school of nursing; practicing RNs pursuing a doctoral degree in nursing; or second- or third-year Doctor of Nursing Practice (DNP) students. Undergraduates must have a GPA of 3.25 or higher, and graduate students must have a GPA of 3.5 or higher. Selection is based on GPA, financial need, recommendations, community involvement and commitment to professional practice in Colorado.
Target applicants: College students. Graduate school students. Adult students.
Minimum GPA: 3.25 for undergraduate students and 3.5 for graduate students
Amount: $1,500.
Number of awards: 1.
Deadline: October 31.
How to apply: Applications are available online. An application form, schedule of classes, two recommendation letters, financial need statement, transcript and personal essay are required.
Exclusive: Visit www.UltimateScholarshipBook.com and enter code CO148212 for updates on this award.

(1483) • HACE ComEd Latino Scholarship

Hispanic Alliance for Career Enhancement
100 South Wacker Drive
Suite 700
Chicago, IL 60606
Phone: 312-435-0498
Fax: 312-435-1494
Email: info@hace-usa.org
http://www.hace-usa.org
Purpose: To aid Latino Illinois residents who are pursuing postsecondary education in selected subjects.
Eligibility: Applicants must be undergraduate freshmen, sophomores, juniors or seniors studying one of the following subjects: math, computer science, accounting, physics, engineering, chemistry, business, business administration, business management, communications, media relations or pre-law studies. They must have documented community service involvement and must have a GPA of 3.0 or higher. Selection is based on the overall strength of the application.
Target applicants: College students. Adult students.
Minimum GPA: 3.0
Amount: $2,500.
Number of awards: 5.
Deadline: September 10.
How to apply: Applications are available by request via email to rocio@hace-usa.org. An application form and supporting documents are required.
Exclusive: Visit www.UltimateScholarshipBook.com and enter code HI148312 for updates on this award.

(1484) • Harriet Hayes Austin Memorial Scholarship for Nursing

Topeka Community Foundation
5431 SW 29th Street
Suite 300
Topeka, KS 66614
Phone: 785-272-4804
Fax: 785-272-4644
Email: matalone@topekacommunityfoundation.org
http://www.topekacommunityfoundation.org
Purpose: To aid students who are pursuing the Bachelor of Science in Nursing (BSN) degree at an accredited postsecondary institution located in Kansas.
Eligibility: Applicants must be U.S. citizens who are enrolled in or who plan to enroll in a BSN program at an accredited school located in Kansas. They must demonstrate financial need. Preference is given to Kansas residents. Selection is based on the overall strength of the application.
Target applicants: High school students. College students. Adult students.
Amount: $1,000.

Number of awards: 5.
Deadline: February 2.
How to apply: Applications are available online. An application form, official transcript, one letter of recommendation, personal statements, financial analysis form and proof of U.S. citizenship are required.
Exclusive: Visit www.UltimateScholarshipBook.com and enter code TO148412 for updates on this award.

(1485) • Harry Alan Gregg Foundation Grants

Harry Alan Gregg Foundation Grants
1 Verney Drive
Greenfield, NH 03047
Phone: 603-547-3311
Fax: 603-547-3232
http://www.crotchedmountain.org
Purpose: To provide financial assistance for the disabled.
Eligibility: Applicants must be New Hampshire residents with physical, intellectual or emotional disabilities or their families. Funds may be used for a variety of purposes but must benefit the person with a disability. Selection is based on need. Applications are reviewed four times a year, with deadlines in March, June, September and December.
Target applicants: High school students. College students. Graduate school students. Adult students.
Amount: $200-$400.
Number of awards: Varies.
Deadline: March, June, September and December.
How to apply: Applications are available online. Documentation of the expense must be provided before payment will be made.
Exclusive: Visit www.UltimateScholarshipBook.com and enter code HA148512 for updates on this award.

(1486) • Harry Barfield KBA Scholarship Program

Kentucky Broadcasters Association
101 Enterprise Drive
Frankfort, KY 40601
Phone: 888-843-5221
Email: cnath1@email.uky.edu
http://www.kba.org
Purpose: To aid aspiring young broadcasters.
Eligibility: Applicants must be attending a college or university in Kentucky and major or plan to major in broadcasting or telecommunications. Preference is given to second semester sophomores, and funds are awarded in the junior year and renewable for the senior year.
Target applicants: College students. Adult students.
Amount: $2,500.
Number of awards: Up to 4.
Deadline: April 24.
How to apply: Applications are available online. An application form, transcript, essay, list of extracurricular activities and letter of recommendation are required.
Exclusive: Visit www.UltimateScholarshipBook.com and enter code KE148612 for updates on this award.

(1487) • Hattie Tedrow Memorial Fund Scholarship

American Legion, Department of North Dakota
405 W. Maine Avenue, Suite 4A
P.O. Box 5057
West Fargo, ND 58078
Phone: 701-293-3120
Fax: 701-293-9951
Email: adjutant@ndlegion.org
http://www.ndlegion.org
Purpose: To support descendants of veterans.
Eligibility: Applicants must be high school seniors, North Dakota residents and U.S. citizens. They must be direct descendants of veterans with honorable service in the U.S. military.
Target applicants: High school students.
Amount: Varies.
Number of awards: Varies.
Deadline: April 15.
How to apply: Applications are available by mail. An application form, essay and proof of veteran's military service are required.
Exclusive: Visit www.UltimateScholarshipBook.com and enter code AM148712 for updates on this award.

(1488) • Hawaii Community Foundation Scholarships

Hawaii Community Foundation - Scholarships
1164 Bishop Street, Suite 800
Honolulu, HI 96813
Phone: 888-731-3863
Fax: 808-521-6286
Email: scholarships@hcf-hawaii.org
http://www.hawaiicommunityfoundation.org
Purpose: To help Hawaii residents who show financial need.
Eligibility: The Hawaii Community Foundation Scholarship Program has over 120 different scholarship funds covering areas such as vocational education, those in foster care, ethnicity, religion and major. Applicants must be Hawaii residents who plan to attend nonprofit two- or four-year colleges as either full-time undergraduate or graduate students. Applicants must also have academic achievement and good moral character. A personal statement, Student Aid Report, transcript, recommendation letter and essay may be required depending on the specific scholarship.
Target applicants: High school students. College students. Graduate school students. Adult students.
Minimum GPA: 2.7
Amount: Varies.
Number of awards: Varies.
Deadline: March 1.
How to apply: Applications are available online.
Exclusive: Visit www.UltimateScholarshipBook.com and enter code HA148812 for updates on this award.

(1489) • Hawaii Society of Certified Public Accountants Scholarship Fund

Hawaii Community Foundation - Scholarships
1164 Bishop Street, Suite 800
Honolulu, HI 96813
Phone: 888-731-3863
Fax: 808-521-6286
Email: scholarships@hcf-hawaii.org
http://www.hawaiicommunityfoundation.org
Purpose: To provide financial assistance for those pursuing degrees in accounting.
Eligibility: Applicants must be college juniors, college seniors or graduate students attending an accredited four-year Hawaii institution of higher learning with a major or concentration in accounting. They must have a minimum GPA of 3.0.
Target applicants: College students. Graduate school students. Adult students.

Minimum GPA: 3.0
Amount: Varies.
Number of awards: Varies.
Deadline: March 1.
How to apply: To apply, register online, complete the online application and select the scholarships to which you wish to apply. In addition, mail the supporting materials: printed confirmation page from the online application, personal statement, copy of Student Aid Report (SAR) available at www.fafsa.ed.gov and official transcript.
Exclusive: Visit www.UltimateScholarshipBook.com and enter code HA148912 for updates on this award.

(1490) · Hawaii Veterans Memorial Fund Scholarship

Hawaii Community Foundation - Scholarships
1164 Bishop Street, Suite 800
Honolulu, HI 96813
Phone: 888-731-3863
Fax: 808-521-6286
Email: scholarships@hcf-hawaii.org
http://www.hawaiicommunityfoundation.org
Purpose: To provide financial assistance for Hawaii graduate students.
Eligibility: Applicants must be pursuing graduate studies at a U.S. college or university. They must have a GPA of 3.5 or higher. An additional award is available for students with high academic achievement, excellent character and an interest in contributing to professional and community service activities in Hawaii. Applicants do not need to be veterans or the children of veterans.
Target applicants: College students. Graduate school students. Adult students.
Minimum GPA: 3.5
Amount: Varies.
Number of awards: Varies.
Deadline: March 1.
How to apply: To apply, register online, complete the online application and select the scholarships to which you wish to apply. In addition, mail the supporting materials: printed confirmation page from the online application, personal statement, copy of Student Aid Report (SAR) available at www.fafsa.ed.gov and official transcript.
Exclusive: Visit www.UltimateScholarshipBook.com and enter code HA149012 for updates on this award.

(1491) · Health Professional Loan Repayment

Washington Higher Education Coordinating Board
917 Lakeridge Way
P.O. Box 43430
Olympia, WA 98504
Phone: 360-753-7850
Fax: 360-753-6243
Email: info@hecb.wa.gov
http://www.hecb.wa.gov
Purpose: To attract health professionals to work in shortage areas in Washington state.
Eligibility: Applicants must be employed, or be under contract to be employed, at an eligible site, provide proof of eligible student debt, provide primary care and sign a contract to serve for at least three years. Eligible professions are physician, physician assistant or nurse practitioner, licensed nurse, midwife, pharmacist, dentist or dental hygienist.
Target applicants: College students. Graduate school students. Adult students.
Amount: Up to $25,000.
Number of awards: Varies.
Scholarship may be renewable.
Deadline: April 30.
How to apply: Applications are available online.
Exclusive: Visit www.UltimateScholarshipBook.com and enter code WA149112 for updates on this award.

(1492) · Health Professional Scholarship

Washington Higher Education Coordinating Board
917 Lakeridge Way
P.O. Box 43430
Olympia, WA 98504
Phone: 360-753-7850
Fax: 360-753-6243
Email: info@hecb.wa.gov
http://www.hecb.wa.gov
Purpose: To attract health professionals to work in shortage areas in Washington state.
Eligibility: Applicants must be training for primary care health professions, be U.S. citizens, have completed all applicable prerequisite coursework and sign a Promissory Note that states that they will serve for at least three years in a shortage area in Washington state. They must not be in default on a student loan.
Target applicants: College students. Graduate school students. Adult students.
Amount: Varies.
Number of awards: Varies.
Scholarship may be renewable.
Deadline: April 30.
How to apply: Applications are available online.
Exclusive: Visit www.UltimateScholarshipBook.com and enter code WA149212 for updates on this award.

(1493) · Health Professions Education Scholarship Program

California Health and Welfare Agency - Office of Statewide Health Planning and Development
Health Professions Education Foundation
818 K Street, Room 210
Sacramento, CA 95814
Phone: 916-324-6500
Fax: 916-324-6585
Email: hpef@oshpd.state.ca.us
http://www.healthprofessions.ca.gov
Purpose: To increase medical care to underserved areas of California by assisting residents who are studying to become dentists, dental hygienists, nurse practitioners, certified midwives and physician assistants.
Eligibility: Applicants must be California residents who have been accepted by or are enrolled in an accredited California program. Financial need, work experience and career goals are considered, and preference is given to applicants who plan to remain in a medically underserved area past the service time. Those selected must sign a two-year service agreement to work in a medically underserved area of California.
Target applicants: College students. Graduate school students. Adult students.
Amount: Up to $10,000.
Number of awards: Varies.
Scholarship may be renewable.
Deadline: March 24.
How to apply: Applications are available online.

Exclusive: Visit www.UltimateScholarshipBook.com and enter code CA149312 for updates on this award.

(1494) • Health Research and Educational Trust Health Career Scholarships

New Jersey Hospital Association
760 Alexander Road
P.O. Box 1
Princeton, NJ 08543
Phone: 609-275-4000
Fax: 609-275-4113
Email: research@njha.com
http://www.njha.com

Purpose: To aid New Jersey students enrolled in certain healthcare-related degree programs.

Eligibility: Applicants must be New Jersey residents. They must be undergraduate juniors, undergraduate seniors or graduate students enrolled in a nursing, allied health professions, healthcare administration or hospital administration degree program. Applicants must have a GPA of 3.0 or higher and must demonstrate financial need. Selection is based on the quality of the personal essay submitted as part of the application.

Target applicants: College students. Graduate school students. Adult students.

Minimum GPA: 3.0

Amount: Varies.

Number of awards: Varies.

Deadline: July 31.

How to apply: Application instructions are available online. Applicant contact information, a personal essay, an official transcript and proof of financial need are required.

Exclusive: Visit www.UltimateScholarshipBook.com and enter code NE149412 for updates on this award.

(1495) • Henry A. Zuberano Scholarship

Hawaii Community Foundation - Scholarships
1164 Bishop Street, Suite 800
Honolulu, HI 96813
Phone: 888-731-3863
Fax: 808-521-6286
Email: scholarships@hcf-hawaii.org
http://www.hawaiicommunityfoundation.org

Purpose: To assist Hawaii students who are majoring in political science, international relations, international business or public administration.

Eligibility: Applicants must have a GPA of 2.7 or higher.

Target applicants: High school students. College students. Adult students.

Minimum GPA: 2.7

Amount: Varies.

Number of awards: Varies.

Deadline: March 1.

How to apply: To apply, register online, complete the online application and select the scholarships to which you wish to apply. In addition, mail the supporting materials: printed confirmation page from the online application, personal statement, copy of Student Aid Report (SAR) available at www.fafsa.ed.gov and official transcript.

Exclusive: Visit www.UltimateScholarshipBook.com and enter code HA149512 for updates on this award.

(1496) • Henry Sachs Foundation Scholarship

Henry Sachs Foundation
90 S. Cascade Avenue
Suite 1410
Colorado Springs, CO 80903
Phone: 719-633-2353
Email: info@sachsfoundation.org
http://www.sachsfoundation.org

Purpose: To aid African-American high school students in Colorado to obtain a college education.

Eligibility: Applicants must be African-American residents of Colorado for at least five years. Applicants must be either seniors in high school or have graduated in the last three years but are not currently attending college. Awards are based on high school grade point average and financial need. If selected, applicants must attend a personal interview in order to receive the grant money.

Target applicants: High school students.

Amount: $5,000.

Number of awards: 50.

Scholarship may be renewable.

Deadline: March 31.

How to apply: Applications are available online.

Exclusive: Visit www.UltimateScholarshipBook.com and enter code HE149612 for updates on this award.

(1497) • Herbert Hoover Uncommon Student Award

Herbert Hoover Presidential Library Association
P.O. Box 696
West Branch, IA 52358
Phone: 800-828-0475
Fax: 319-643-2391
Email: scholarship@hooverassociation.org
http://www.hooverassociation.org

Purpose: To honor Herbert Hoover by rewarding students who live up to his ideal of the "uncommon man."

Eligibility: Applicants must be juniors in an Iowa high school or be homeschooled. Students must submit a project proposal and two letters of recommendation. Recipients must attend a weekend program during the summer and are expected to complete the proposed project. Grades, essays and test scores are not considered.

Target applicants: High school students.

Amount: $750-$5,000.

Number of awards: Approximately 15.

Deadline: March 31.

How to apply: Applications are available online.

Exclusive: Visit www.UltimateScholarshipBook.com and enter code HE149712 for updates on this award.

(1498) • Herff Jones Scholarship

University Interscholastic League
1701 Manor Road
Austin, TX 78722
Phone: 512-471-5883
Fax: 512-232-7311
Email: bbaxendale@mail.utexas.edu
http://www.uil.utexas.edu

Purpose: To support high school yearbook staff.

Eligibility: Applicants must be graduating high school seniors in Texas, have a 3.0 or higher GPA and plan to major or minor in a

communications-related field. Students must also have been involved in journalism during high school.
Target applicants: High school students.
Minimum GPA: 3.0
Amount: $1,200.
Number of awards: 1.
Deadline: March 22.
How to apply: Applications are available online. An application form, letter of recommendation and three to five samples of student journalism work are required.
Exclusive: Visit www.UltimateScholarshipBook.com and enter code UN149812 for updates on this award.

(1499) • Herman J. Smith Scholarship

National Housing Endowment
1201 15th Street NW
Washington, DC 20005
Phone: 800-368-5242
Fax: 202-266-8177
Email: nhe@nahb.com
http://www.nationalhousingendowment.org
Purpose: To aid students who are planning for careers in mortgage finance or the construction industry.
Eligibility: Applicants must be full-time undergraduate or graduate students attending an accredited four-year institution. They must have at least one more year of study to complete after the date of award disbursement; fifth-year seniors are ineligible for this award. They must be majoring in and planning to pursue a career in mortgage finance, construction management or another construction-related subject. Preference is given to Texas residents, students who attend school in Texas and current members of their school's National Association of Home Builders student chapter. Selection is based on academic merit, recommendations, work experience, extracurricular activities, career goals and financial need.
Target applicants: College students. Graduate school students. Adult students.
Amount: Up to $2,000.
Number of awards: Varies.
Scholarship may be renewable.
Deadline: May 3.
How to apply: Applications are available online. An application form, course schedule, official transcripts and three recommendation letters are required.
Exclusive: Visit www.UltimateScholarshipBook.com and enter code NA149912 for updates on this award.

(1500) • HFMA Connecticut Chapter Scholarships

Healthcare Financial Management Association-Connecticut Chapter
c/o Cassandra Mitchell, Scholarship Committee Chairperson
John Dempsey Hospital Finance Department
263 Farmington Avenue
Farmington, CT 06030
Phone: 860-679-2916
Fax: 860-679-3071
Email: mitchellc@uchc.edu
http://www.cthfma.org
Purpose: To aid students pursuing higher education in a healthcare or financial management subject.
Eligibility: Applicants must be matriculated students attending an accredited college or university located in Connecticut; matriculated students attending a non-Connecticut school who are also the spouse or child of an HFMA Connecticut Chapter member; matriculated students who are Connecticut residents and who commute to an accredited school that is located in an HFMA Region 1 state or matriculated students who are permanent healthcare industry employees working in the state of Connecticut. They must be studying or planning to study financial management or a healthcare subject. Selection is based on the strength of the applicant's essay.
Target applicants: High school students. College students. Graduate school students. Adult students.
Amount: Up to $4,000.
Number of awards: Varies.
Deadline: August 14.
How to apply: Applications are available online. An application form, essay, references and verification of enrollment are required.
Exclusive: Visit www.UltimateScholarshipBook.com and enter code HE150012 for updates on this award.

(1501) • Hideko and Zenzo Matsuyama Scholarship Fund

Hawaii Community Foundation - Scholarships
1164 Bishop Street, Suite 800
Honolulu, HI 96813
Phone: 888-731-3863
Fax: 808-521-6286
Email: scholarships@hcf-hawaii.org
http://www.hawaiicommunityfoundation.org
Purpose: To provide financial assistance for high school graduates who are seeking higher education.
Eligibility: Applicants must be graduates of Hawaiian high schools or GED recipients who plan to attend a college or university in Hawaii or the continental U.S. full-time. They must have a GPA of 3.0 or higher. Preference may be given to individuals of Japanese descent who were born in Hawaii.
Target applicants: College students. Adult students.
Minimum GPA: 3.0
Amount: Varies.
Number of awards: Varies.
Deadline: March 1.
How to apply: To apply, register online, complete the online application and select the scholarships to which you wish to apply. In addition, mail the supporting materials: printed confirmation page from the online application, personal statement, copy of Student Aid Report (SAR) available at www.fafsa.ed.gov and official transcript.
Exclusive: Visit www.UltimateScholarshipBook.com and enter code HA150112 for updates on this award.

(1502) • High Plains Journal/KJLA Scholarship

Kansas Livestock Association
6301 SW 37th Street
Topeka, KS 66614-5129
Email: jenni@kla.org
http://www.kla.org/scholarapp.htm
Purpose: To support students interested in agricultural communications.
Eligibility: Applicants must attend a Kansas university, major in agricultural communications or a related field and be planning a career in agricultural writing or publications.
Target applicants: College students. Adult students.
Amount: Varies.
Number of awards: Varies.
Deadline: Varies.

How to apply: Applications are available online. An application form, two letters of recommendation, transcript and information about communications employment or internship experience are required.
Exclusive: Visit www.UltimateScholarshipBook.com and enter code KA150212 for updates on this award.

(1503) • High Technology Scholar/Intern Tuition Waiver

Massachusetts Department of Higher Education
Office of Student Financial Assistance
454 Broadway
Suite 200
Revere, MA 02151
Phone: 617-727-9420
Fax: 617-727-0667
Email: osfa@osfa.mass.edu
http://www.osfa.mass.edu/default.asp
Purpose: To provide financial aid and internship connections to computer technology and engineering students in Massachusetts.
Eligibility: Students must be enrolled in an undergraduate program at a Massachusetts public college and must not have previously earned a bachelor's degree. Applicants must have approval from the company or organization that is funding the scholarship. Students must not owe refunds on any previous financial aid or have any defaulted government loans.
Target applicants: High school students. College students. Adult students.
Amount: Up to full tuition.
Number of awards: Varies.
Deadline: Varies.
How to apply: Applications are available at college financial aid offices.
Exclusive: Visit www.UltimateScholarshipBook.com and enter code MA150312 for updates on this award.

(1504) • Higher Education Academic Scholarship Program (Bright Flight)

Missouri Student Assistance Resource Services (MOSTARS)
Missouri Department of Higher Education
3515 Amazonas Drive
Jefferson City, MO 65109
Phone: 800-473-6757
Fax: 573-751-6635
http://www.dhe.mo.gov
Purpose: This merit-based program encourages top-ranked high school seniors to attend approved Missouri postsecondary schools.
Eligibility: Applicants must be U.S. citizens or eligible noncitizens, Missouri residents and have an ACT or SAT score within the top 3 percent of all Missouri students taking those tests. Applicants must be high school seniors who enroll as first-time, full-time students at an approved Missouri postsecondary school.
Target applicants: High school students.
Amount: Up to $3,000.
Number of awards: Varies.
Scholarship may be renewable.
Deadline: July 31.
How to apply: For an application contact your high school counselor or MOSTARS.
Exclusive: Visit www.UltimateScholarshipBook.com and enter code MI150412 for updates on this award.

(1505) • Higher Education Adult Part-Time Student (HEAPS) Grant Program

West Virginia Higher Education Policy Commission
1018 Kanawha Boulevard, East
Suite 700
Charleston, WV 25301
Phone: 304-558-2101
Fax: 304-558-5719
Email: financialaiddirector@hepc.wvnet.edu
http://www.hepc.wvnet.edu
Purpose: To assist adult West Virginia students.
Eligibility: Applicants must be West Virginia residents, be U.S. citizens or permanent residents, be enrolled or accepted for enrollment in an undergraduate institution on a part-time basis and demonstrate financial need.
Target applicants: College students. Adult students.
Amount: Varies.
Number of awards: Varies.
Scholarship may be renewable.
Deadline: Deadline of individual institution.
How to apply: Complete the Free Application for Federal Student Aid (FAFSA).
Exclusive: Visit www.UltimateScholarshipBook.com and enter code WE150512 for updates on this award.

(1506) • Higher Education Legislative Plan (HELP)

Mississippi Office of Student Financial Aid
3825 Ridgewood Road
Jackson, MS 39211
Phone: 800-327-2980
Fax: 601-432-6527
Email: sfa@ihl.state.ms.us
http://www.ihl.state.ms.us
Purpose: To assist financially needy Mississippi students afford tuition.
Eligibility: Applicants must be U.S. citizens or eligible noncitizens, Mississippi residents and have a minimum college GPA of 2.5 and have graduated from high school within the past two years. Applicants must be attending an eligible Mississippi institution, must have a minimum ACT score of 20 and must document an average gross income of $36,000 or less over the prior two years, and must have the results of a processed Student Aid Report (SAR). Students who file the Free Application for Federal Student Aid (FAFSA) will receive a SAR report.
Target applicants: High school students. College students. Adult students.
Minimum GPA: 2.5
Amount: Full Tuition.
Number of awards: Varies.
Scholarship may be renewable.
Deadline: March 31.
How to apply: Contact the Mississippi Office of Student Financial Aid for an application.
Exclusive: Visit www.UltimateScholarshipBook.com and enter code MI150612 for updates on this award.

(1507) • Ho'omaka Hou Scholarship

Hawaii Community Foundation - Scholarships
1164 Bishop Street, Suite 800
Honolulu, HI 96813
Phone: 888-731-3863
Fax: 808-521-6286

Email: scholarships@hcf-hawaii.org
http://www.hawaiicommunityfoundation.org
Purpose: To support students who have overcome substance abuse or other difficulties in their lives.
Eligibility: Applicants must show financial need. Students must attend college or technical school in Hawaii.
Target applicants: High school students. College students. Adult students.
Amount: $2,000.
Number of awards: 16.
Deadline: March 1.
How to apply: Applications are available online. In addition, mail the supporting materials: personal statement, one letter of recommendation, copy of Student Aid Report (SAR) available at www.fafsa.ed.gov and official transcript.
Exclusive: Visit www.UltimateScholarshipBook.com and enter code HA150712 for updates on this award.

(1508) • Hobble (LPN) Nursing Scholarship

American Legion, Department of Kansas
1314 SW Topeka Boulevard
Topeka, KS 66612
Phone: 785-232-9315
Fax: 785-232-1399
http://www.ksamlegion.org
Purpose: To assist future Kansas nurses.
Eligibility: Applicants must be Kansas residents attending an accredited Kansas school to receive a degree in Licensed Practical Nursing (LPN) and planning to practice their career in Kansas. Applicants must also demonstrate financial need and be 18 before taking the Kansas State Board examination.
Target applicants: High school students. College students. Adult students.
Amount: $300.
Number of awards: Varies.
Deadline: Varies.
How to apply: Applications are available online and may be requested from Department Headquarters.
Exclusive: Visit www.UltimateScholarshipBook.com and enter code AM150812 for updates on this award.

(1509) • HomeStreet Bank Scholarships

Independent Colleges of Washington
600 Stewart Street, Suite 600
Seattle, WA 98101
Phone: 206-623-4494
Fax: 206-625-9621
Email: info@icwashington.org
http://www.icwashington.org
Purpose: To provide assistance to students with financial need and who are attending an independent college of Washington.
Eligibility: Recipients should have low or moderate income and be in good academic standing with their college or university. Students attending Gonzaga University, Heritage University, Pacific Lutheran University, Saint Martin's University, Seattle Pacific University, Seattle University, University of Puget Sound, Walla Walla University, Whitman College or Whitworth University are eligible.
Target applicants: College students. Adult students.
Amount: $1,000.
Number of awards: 10.
Deadline: Varies.
How to apply: No application is required. Recipients are selected by their school's financial aid office.
Exclusive: Visit www.UltimateScholarshipBook.com and enter code IN150912 for updates on this award.

(1510) • Honors Award

Louisiana Office of Student Financial Assistance
P.O. Box 91202
Baton Rouge, LA 70821-9202
Phone: 800-259-5626 x1012
Fax: 225-922-0790
Email: custserv@osfa.la.gov
http://www.osfa.state.la.us
Purpose: To aid Louisiana student residents.
Eligibility: Applicants must be Louisiana residents and U.S. citizens, apply during their senior year in high school, use the award at a Louisiana college or university, have a minimum 3.0 GPA and have a minimum ACT score of 27 or equivalent SAT I score.
Target applicants: High school students.
Minimum GPA: 3.0
Amount: Full tuition plus $800 stipend.
Number of awards: Varies.
Scholarship may be renewable.
Deadline: July 1.
How to apply: The application is the Free Application for Federal Student Aid (FAFSA). ACT or SAT I scores must also be reported.
Exclusive: Visit www.UltimateScholarshipBook.com and enter code LO151012 for updates on this award.

(1511) • Hope Community College Transfer Scholarship

Maryland Higher Education Commission
Office of Student Financial Assistance
839 Bestgate Road, Suite 400
Annapolis, MD 21401
Phone: 800-974-1024
Fax: 410-260-3200
Email: osfamail@mhec.state.md.us
http://www.mhec.state.md.us
Purpose: To help Maryland community college students who want to transfer into a four-year Maryland college or university.
Eligibility: Applicants must be U.S. citizens or eligible noncitizens and current Maryland community college students who will have completed at least 60 credits or who will have earned an associate's degree by the end of the semester in which they will transfer to a Maryland four-year institution.
Target applicants: College students. Adult students.
Amount: Varies.
Number of awards: Varies.
Scholarship may be renewable.
Deadline: January 1-March 1.
How to apply: Complete and file the Free Application for Federal Student Aid (FAFSA), and complete and file the HOPE Community College Transfer Scholarship application.
Exclusive: Visit www.UltimateScholarshipBook.com and enter code MA151112 for updates on this award.

(1512) • HOPE Scholarship Program

Georgia Student Finance Commission
2082 East Exchange Place
Tucker, GA 30084
Phone: 800-505-4732
Fax: 770-724-9089
Email: support@gacollege411.org
http://www.gacollege411.org
Purpose: To support students attending Georgia institutions.
Eligibility: Applicants must have graduated from high school and be attending or planning to attend college in Georgia.
Target applicants: High school students. College students. Adult students.
Amount: Tuition for public schools, up to $1,750 per semester at private schools.
Number of awards: Varies.
Scholarship may be renewable.
Deadline: Varies.
How to apply: Applications are available online.
Exclusive: Visit www.UltimateScholarshipBook.com and enter code GE151212 for updates on this award.

(1513) • Howard P. Rawlings Educational Assistance (EA) Grant

Maryland Higher Education Commission
Office of Student Financial Assistance
839 Bestgate Road, Suite 400
Annapolis, MD 21401
Phone: 800-974-1024
Fax: 410-260-3200
Email: osfamail@mhec.state.md.us
http://www.mhec.state.md.us
Purpose: To help Maryland students who demonstrate financial need.
Eligibility: Applicants (and their parents, if applicants are dependents) must be residents of the state of Maryland. They must be high school seniors or undergraduate students and must be or plan to become full-time, degree-seeking students. They must complete the Free Application for Federal Student Aid (FAFSA) and must demonstrate financial need. Selection is based on financial need.
Target applicants: High school students. College students. Adult students.
Amount: Varies.
Number of awards: Varies.
Scholarship may be renewable.
Deadline: March 1.
How to apply: To apply, applicants must fill out and submit the FAFSA.
Exclusive: Visit www.UltimateScholarshipBook.com and enter code MA151312 for updates on this award.

(1514) • Howard P. Rawlings Guaranteed Access (GA) Grant

Maryland Higher Education Commission
Office of Student Financial Assistance
839 Bestgate Road, Suite 400
Annapolis, MD 21401
Phone: 800-974-1024
Fax: 410-260-3200
Email: osfamail@mhec.state.md.us
http://www.mhec.state.md.us
Purpose: To help Maryland students with financial need afford college.
Eligibility: Applicants and their parents must both be legal residents of the state of Maryland. Applicants must be U.S. citizens or eligible noncitizens, complete the Free Application for Federal Student Aid (FAFSA) and the Guaranteed Access (GA) Grant application. Applicants and families must also meet the established income limits to qualify.
Target applicants: High school students.
Amount: $400-$13,700.
Number of awards: Varies.
Scholarship may be renewable.
Deadline: March 1.
How to apply: Complete the FAFSA.
Exclusive: Visit www.UltimateScholarshipBook.com and enter code MA151412 for updates on this award.

(1515) • Hugh A. Smith Scholarship Fund

American Legion, Department of Kansas
1314 SW Topeka Boulevard
Topeka, KS 66612
Phone: 785-232-9315
Fax: 785-232-1399
http://www.ksamlegion.org
Purpose: To provide assistance to needy and worthy children of American Legion and American Legion Auxiliary members.
Eligibility: Applicants must be average or better students who are high school seniors or college freshmen or sophomores enrolling or enrolled in a post-secondary school in Kansas. They must be the son or daughter of a veteran, and a parent must have been a member of the Kansas American Legion or American Legion Auxiliary for the past three years. The children of deceased parents are also eligible if the parent was a paid member at the time of death. Applicants must submit three letters of recommendation, including one from a teacher, an essay on "Why I Want to Go to College," high school transcript, a 1040 income statement and documentation of parent's veteran status.
Target applicants: High school students. College students. Adult students.
Amount: $500.
Number of awards: 1.
Deadline: February 15.
How to apply: Applications are available online.
Exclusive: Visit www.UltimateScholarshipBook.com and enter code AM151512 for updates on this award.

(1516) • Ichiro and Masako Hirata Scholarship

Hawaii Community Foundation - Scholarships
1164 Bishop Street, Suite 800
Honolulu, HI 96813
Phone: 888-731-3863
Fax: 808-521-6286
Email: scholarships@hcf-hawaii.org
http://www.hawaiicommunityfoundation.org
Purpose: To provide financial assistance to Hawaii students who are pursuing degrees in education.
Eligibility: Applicants must be majoring or concentrating in education. They must be college juniors, college seniors or graduate students and have a GPA of 3.0 or higher.
Target applicants: College students. Graduate school students. Adult students.
Minimum GPA: 3.0
Amount: Varies.
Number of awards: Varies.
Deadline: March 1.

How to apply: To apply, register online, complete the online application and select the scholarships to which you wish to apply. In addition, mail the supporting materials: printed confirmation page from the online application, personal statement, copy of Student Aid Report (SAR) available at www.fafsa.ed.gov and official transcript.
Exclusive: Visit www.UltimateScholarshipBook.com and enter code HA151612 for updates on this award.

(1517) • ICW Boeing Company Scholarship

Independent Colleges of Washington
600 Stewart Street, Suite 600
Seattle, WA 98101
Phone: 206-623-4494
Fax: 206-625-9621
Email: info@icwashington.org
http://www.icwashington.org
Purpose: To assist students attending independent Washington colleges.
Eligibility: Applicants must be enrolled at an ICW member institution at the time of the award and be involved with community service. A GPA of 3.25 is required.
Target applicants: High school students. College students. Adult students.
Minimum GPA: 3.25
Amount: Up to $2,500.
Number of awards: 1.
Deadline: March 13.
How to apply: Applications are available online. An application form, resume, essay, letter of recommendation and transcript are required.
Exclusive: Visit www.UltimateScholarshipBook.com and enter code IN151712 for updates on this award.

(1518) • ICW/Boyer Scholarship

Independent Colleges of Washington
600 Stewart Street, Suite 600
Seattle, WA 98101
Phone: 206-623-4494
Fax: 206-625-9621
Email: info@icwashington.org
http://www.icwashington.org
Purpose: To reward students who are making contributions to their campus community.
Eligibility: Recipients must be attending an ICW college or university. Recipients are selected by their colleges. Students attending Gonzaga University, Heritage University, Pacific Lutheran University, Saint Martin's University, Seattle Pacific University, Seattle University, University of Puget Sound, Walla Walla University, Whitman College or Whitworth University are eligible.
Target applicants: College students. Adult students.
Amount: $1,000.
Number of awards: 10.
Deadline: March 12.
How to apply: No application is required.
Exclusive: Visit www.UltimateScholarshipBook.com and enter code IN151812 for updates on this award.

(1519) • Idaho Promise Category A Scholarship

Idaho State Board of Education
P.O. Box 83720
Boise, ID 83720
Phone: 208-334-2270
Fax: 208-334-2632
Email: dkelly@osbe.state.id.us
http://www.boardofed.idaho.gov
Purpose: To support outstanding Idaho high school seniors.
Eligibility: Applicants must be Idaho residents, be graduating seniors of Idaho high schools and enroll full-time at an eligible Idaho college or university. Academic applicants must also be in the top 10 percent of their graduating class, have a minimum 3.5 GPA and a minimum ACT score of 28. Professional-technical applicants must have a minimum 2.8 GPA and take the COMPASS test.
Target applicants: High school students.
Minimum GPA: 2.8
Amount: $3,000.
Number of awards: 25.
Scholarship may be renewable.
Deadline: January 15.
How to apply: Contact your high school guidance counselor.
Exclusive: Visit www.UltimateScholarshipBook.com and enter code ID151912 for updates on this award.

(1520) • Idaho Promise Category B Scholarship

Idaho State Board of Education
P.O. Box 83720
Boise, ID 83720
Phone: 208-334-2270
Fax: 208-334-2632
Email: dkelly@osbe.state.id.us
http://www.boardofed.idaho.gov
Purpose: Monetary assistance is provided to Idaho resident high school students for freshman expenses at Idaho colleges or universities.
Eligibility: Applicants must have graduated from an Idaho high school, be entering freshmen at an eligible Idaho college or university, be residents of Idaho and have a minimum 3.0 GPA or minimum ACT score of 20. Applicants must also be younger than 22 years old and complete at least 12 credits per semester with a minimum 2.5 GPA to remain eligible for renewal.
Target applicants: High school students. College students.
Minimum GPA: 3.0
Amount: Up to $1,200.
Number of awards: Varies.
Scholarship may be renewable.
Deadline: Varies.
How to apply: Contact eligible college or university financial aid office.
Exclusive: Visit www.UltimateScholarshipBook.com and enter code ID152012 for updates on this award.

(1521) • Idaho State Broadcasters Association Scholarships

Idaho State Broadcasters Association
270 N 27th Street
Suite B
Boise, ID 83702-4741
Phone: 208-345-3072
Fax: 208-343-8046
Email: isba@qwestoffice.net
http://www.idahobroadcasters.org
Purpose: To aid students planning careers in broadcasting.
Eligibility: Applicants must be enrolled full-time in an Idaho college or university, have exhibited superior potential in activities or courses related to broadcasting and be respected among their peer groups. Students

must have a GPA of 2.0 or higher in the first two years of college and a GPA of 2.5 in the last two years.
Target applicants: College students. Adult students.
Minimum GPA: 2.0
Amount: $1,000.
Number of awards: At least 2.
Deadline: March 15.
How to apply: Applications are available online. An application form, letter of recommendation, transcript and essay are required.
Exclusive: Visit www.UltimateScholarshipBook.com and enter code ID152112 for updates on this award.

(1522) • Illinois American Legion Scholarship Program

American Legion Auxiliary, Department of Illinois
2720 E. Lincoln
Bloomington, IL 61704
Phone: 309-663-9366
Email: webmaster@illegion.org
http://illegion.org/index.shtml
Purpose: To award scholarships to graduating students enrolled in Illinois high schools.
Eligibility: Applicants must be children or grandchildren of American Legion Illinois members and must be in their senior year of high school. Awards may be used to further education at an accredited college, university or technical school.
Target applicants: High school students.
Amount: $1,000.
Number of awards: Varies.
Deadline: March 15.
How to apply: Application information is available by contacting the American Legion, Department of Illinois.
Exclusive: Visit www.UltimateScholarshipBook.com and enter code AM152212 for updates on this award.

(1523) • Illinois AMVETS Junior ROTC Scholarship

Illinois AMVETS Service Foundation
AMVETS Department of Illinois
2200 South Sixth Street
Springfield, IL 62703
Phone: 217-528-4713
Fax: 217-528-9896
Email: crystal@ilamvets.org
http://www.ilamvets.org
Purpose: To provide financial assistance for college to high school ROTC members.
Eligibility: Applicants must be Illinois high school seniors who are participating in a Junior ROTC program and have taken the SAT or ACT.
Target applicants: High school students.
Amount: $3,000.
Number of awards: Varies.
Deadline: March 1.
How to apply: Applications are available online.
Exclusive: Visit www.UltimateScholarshipBook.com and enter code IL152312 for updates on this award.

(1524) • Illinois AMVETS Ladies Auxiliary Memorial Scholarship

Illinois AMVETS Service Foundation
AMVETS Department of Illinois
2200 South Sixth Street
Springfield, IL 62703
Phone: 217-528-4713
Fax: 217-528-9896
Email: crystal@ilamvets.org
http://www.ilamvets.org
Purpose: To provide financial assistance to children and grandchildren of U.S. veterans and members of the military.
Eligibility: Applicants must be Illinois high school seniors who have taken the SAT or ACT, and they must be the children or grandchildren of veterans who were honorably discharged after September 15, 1940 or who are currently serving in the military.
Target applicants: High school students.
Amount: $500.
Number of awards: Varies.
Deadline: March 1.
How to apply: Applications are available online.
Exclusive: Visit www.UltimateScholarshipBook.com and enter code IL152412 for updates on this award.

(1525) • Illinois AMVETS Ladies Auxiliary Worchid Scholarship

Illinois AMVETS Service Foundation
AMVETS Department of Illinois
2200 South Sixth Street
Springfield, IL 62703
Phone: 217-528-4713
Fax: 217-528-9896
Email: crystal@ilamvets.org
http://www.ilamvets.org
Purpose: To provide financial assistance for students whose parents are U.S. veterans.
Eligibility: Applicants must be Illinois high school seniors whose mother or father is a U.S. veteran who was honorably discharged after September 15, 1940. They must also have taken the SAT or ACT.
Target applicants: High school students.
Amount: $500.
Number of awards: Varies.
Deadline: March 1.
How to apply: Applications are available online.
Exclusive: Visit www.UltimateScholarshipBook.com and enter code IL152512 for updates on this award.

(1526) • Illinois AMVETS Sad Sacks Nursing Scholarship

Illinois AMVETS Service Foundation
AMVETS Department of Illinois
2200 South Sixth Street
Springfield, IL 62703
Phone: 217-528-4713
Fax: 217-528-9896
Email: crystal@ilamvets.org
http://www.ilamvets.org
Purpose: To assist Illinois students who are pursuing a career in nursing.
Eligibility: Applicants must be Illinois high school seniors who have been accepted into a nursing program or students who are already attending nursing school in Illinois. They must have financial need and a satisfactory academic record, character and activity record. Dependents of deceased or disabled veterans receive priority.
Target applicants: High school students. College students. Adult students.

Amount: Varies.
Number of awards: Varies.
Deadline: March 1.
How to apply: Applications are available online.
Exclusive: Visit www.UltimateScholarshipBook.com and enter code IL152612 for updates on this award.

(1527) • Illinois AMVETS Service Foundation Scholarship

Illinois AMVETS Service Foundation
AMVETS Department of Illinois
2200 South Sixth Street
Springfield, IL 62703
Phone: 217-528-4713
Fax: 217-528-9896
Email: crystal@ilamvets.org
http://www.ilamvets.org
Purpose: To help Illinois students pay for college.
Eligibility: Applicants musts be Illinois high school seniors who have taken the SAT or ACT. Preference is given to students who are the children or grandchildren of Illinois veterans.
Target applicants: High school students.
Amount: $3,000.
Number of awards: Varies.
Deadline: March 1.
How to apply: Applications are available online.
Exclusive: Visit www.UltimateScholarshipBook.com and enter code IL152712 for updates on this award.

(1528) • Illinois AMVETS Trade School Scholarship

Illinois AMVETS Service Foundation
AMVETS Department of Illinois
2200 South Sixth Street
Springfield, IL 62703
Phone: 217-528-4713
Fax: 217-528-9896
Email: crystal@ilamvets.org
http://www.ilamvets.org
Purpose: To provide financial assistance to Illinois students who plan to attend a trade school.
Eligibility: Applicants must be seniors at an Illinois high school who have been accepted into a trade school program. Students must submit a copy of their acceptance letter with the application form. Preference is given to students who are the children or grandchildren of veterans.
Target applicants: High school students.
Amount: $3,000.
Number of awards: Varies.
Deadline: March 1.
How to apply: Applications are available online.
Exclusive: Visit www.UltimateScholarshipBook.com and enter code IL152812 for updates on this award.

(1529) • Illinois Association for Health, Physical Education, Recreation and Dance Scholarships

Illinois Association for Health, Physical Education, Recreation and Dance
P.O. Box 1326
Jacksonville, IL 62651
Phone: 217-245-6413
Fax: 217-245-5261
Email: iahperd@iahperd.org
http://www.iahperd.org
Purpose: To support physical education students.
Eligibility: Applicants must be full-time undergraduate students at colleges or universities in Illinois and must major in health, physical education, recreation or dance. Students must have been members of IAHPERD since December 1 of the previous year and may receive this award no more than twice.
Target applicants: College students. Adult students.
Amount: $1,000.
Number of awards: 5.
Scholarship may be renewable.
Deadline: May 15.
How to apply: Applications are available online. An application form, cover letter, resume, essay, transcript and two letters of recommendation are required.
Exclusive: Visit www.UltimateScholarshipBook.com and enter code IL152912 for updates on this award.

(1530) • Illinois Department of Children and Family Services Scholarship Program

Illinois Department of Children and Family Services
406 E. Monroe Street
Springfield, IL 62701
Phone: 217-557-5805
http://www.state.il.us/dcfs
Purpose: To support students who have been under the guardianship of the Department of Children and Family Services.
Eligibility: Applicants must be between 16 and 21 years of age as of the application deadline and have a diploma from an accredited high school or a GED by the end of the current school year. Students must be in the Subsidized Guardianship Program, or the department must have court-ordered legal guardianship or have had legal guardianship for the applicant before adoption was finalized. Recipients must attend an Illinois state community college or university.
Target applicants: High school students. College students.
Amount: Up to full tuition plus $471 monthly stipend.
Number of awards: Varies.
Scholarship may be renewable.
Deadline: March 31.
How to apply: Applications are available online. An application form, transcript or copy of GED, SAT or ACT scores, three letters of recommendation and a college transcript (if applicable) are required.
Exclusive: Visit www.UltimateScholarshipBook.com and enter code IL153012 for updates on this award.

(1531) • Illinois Excellence in Agriculture Scholarship

Office of the Illinois State Treasurer
Division of Economic Opportunity
300 West Jefferson Street
Springfield, IL 62702
Phone: 217-557-6436
Fax: 217-557-6439
Email: webmaster@treasurer.state.il.us
http://www.treasurer.il.gov/programs/cultivate-illinois/scholarships.aspx
Purpose: To aid Illinois students planning to study an agriculture-related subject in college.

Eligibility: Applicants must be Illinois residents and high school seniors who are accepted into an accredited postsecondary institution located in Illinois. They must have plans to major in and to pursue careers in an agriculture-related subject. Applicants must have a GPA of 2.75 or higher. Selection is based on the overall strength of the application.
Target applicants: High school students.
Minimum GPA: 2.75
Amount: $2,500.
Number of awards: 10.
Deadline: May 14.
How to apply: Applications are available online. An application form, personal essay, statement of goals, official transcript and two letters of recommendation are required.
Exclusive: Visit www.UltimateScholarshipBook.com and enter code OF153112 for updates on this award.

(1532) • Illinois Future Teacher Corps (IFTC) Program

Illinois Student Assistance Commission
1755 Lake Cook Road
Deerfield, IL 60015
Phone: 800-899-4722
Fax: 847-831-8549
Email: collegezone@isac.org
http://www.collegezone.com
Purpose: To assist talented and financially needy students who are interested in pursuing a career in education.
Eligibility: Applicants must be Illinois residents who are U.S. citizens or eligible non-citizens. They must be enrolled as a junior or above in an approved teacher education program and maintain at least a 2.5 GPA. Applicants must submit a FAFSA form, comply with Selective Service requirements and not be in default on any student loans. Applicants are not eligible to receive the scholarship in the same year as receiving a Minority Teachers of Illinois (MTI) Scholarship or Illinois Special Education Teacher Tuition Waiver (SETTW). Scholarship recipients agree to teach in Illinois after graduating.
Target applicants: College students. Graduate school students. Adult students.
Minimum GPA: 2.5
Amount: $5,000-$15,000.
Number of awards: Varies.
Scholarship may be renewable.
Deadline: March 1, but applications received after this date will be considered as funding allows.
How to apply: Applications are available online.
Exclusive: Visit www.UltimateScholarshipBook.com and enter code IL153212 for updates on this award.

(1533) • Illinois Hospital Research and Educational Foundation Scholarship

Illinois Hospital Research and Educational Foundation
1151 East Warrenville Road
P.O. Box 3015
Naperville, IL 60566
Phone: 630-276-5498
Email: rlemberis@ihastaff.org
http://www.ihatoday.org
Purpose: To aid Illinois students enrolled in hospital-related healthcare certificate and degree programs.
Eligibility: Applicants must be Illinois residents. They must be either enrolled in or accepted into a hospital-related healthcare degree or certificate program, excluding any programs having a general education curriculum (such as pre-medicine programs). Applicants must have at least one year remaining in their program of study. They should have a GPA of 3.5 on a four-point scale in order to be competitive for this award. Selection is based on academic merit and financial need.
Target applicants: High school students. College students. Adult students.
Amount: $1,000.
Number of awards: Varies.
Deadline: April 15.
How to apply: Applications are available online. An application form, official transcript, two letters of recommendation, personal statement and proof of acceptance into a qualifying degree program (for rising freshmen only) are required.
Exclusive: Visit www.UltimateScholarshipBook.com and enter code IL153312 for updates on this award.

(1534) • Illinois Oratorical Contest

American Legion Auxiliary, Department of Illinois
2720 E. Lincoln
Bloomington, IL 61704
Phone: 309-663-9366
Email: webmaster@illegion.org
http://illegion.org/index.shtml
Purpose: To enhance high school students' experience with and understanding of the U.S. Constitution. The contest will help develop students' leadership skills and civic appreciation, as well as the ability to deliver thoughtful, insightful orations regarding U.S. citizenship and its inherent responsibilities.
Eligibility: Applicants must be high school students under the age of 20 who are U.S. citizens or legal residents and residents of the state. Students first give an oration within their state and winners compete at the national level. The oration must be related to the Constitution of the United States focusing on the duties and obligations citizens have to the government. It must be in English and be between eight and ten minutes. There is also an assigned topic which is posted on the website, and it should be between three and five minutes.
Target applicants: High school students.
Amount: Up to $2,000.
Number of awards: 11.
Deadline: February 4.
How to apply: Application information is available by contacting the local American Legion Post or Illinois Department Headquarters.
Exclusive: Visit www.UltimateScholarshipBook.com and enter code AM153412 for updates on this award.

(1535) • Incentive Program for Aspiring Teachers

Massachusetts Department of Higher Education
Office of Student Financial Assistance
454 Broadway
Suite 200
Revere, MA 02151
Phone: 617-727-9420
Fax: 617-727-0667
Email: osfa@osfa.mass.edu
http://www.osfa.mass.edu/default.asp
Purpose: To provide financial support for Massachusetts college students who are studying to become teachers.
Eligibility: Applicants must be in their third or fourth year at a public college in the state of Massachusetts, and they must be enrolled in a field with teacher shortages. They must have a 3.0 GPA in general education courses, and they must remain in satisfactory academic standing while

receiving the scholarship. Students must agree to work in a public school in Massachusetts for two years after earning a bachelor's degree.
Target applicants: College students. Adult students.
Minimum GPA: 3.0
Amount: Full Tuition.
Number of awards: Varies.
Scholarship may be renewable.
Deadline: Varies.
How to apply: Applications are available at college financial aid offices.
Exclusive: Visit www.UltimateScholarshipBook.com and enter code MA153512 for updates on this award.

(1536) · Independence Excavating 50th Anniversary Scholarship

Associated General Contractors of Ohio
1755 Northwest Boulevard
Columbus, OH 43212
Phone: 614-486-6446
Fax: 614-486-6498
Email: web@agcohio.com
http://www.agcohio.com
Purpose: To aid students who are preparing for construction-related careers at postsecondary institutions located in Michigan, Ohio, Pennsylvania and West Virginia.
Eligibility: Applicants must be U.S. citizens. They must be in at least the second year of study in a two-year, four-year or five-year undergraduate degree program that is related to construction. They must be enrolled at a postsecondary institution located in West Virginia, Pennsylvania, Ohio or Michigan and have a GPA of 2.5 or higher. Applicants must have plans to work in the construction industry. Selection is based on the overall strength of the application.
Target applicants: College students. Adult students.
Minimum GPA: 2.5
Amount: Varies.
Number of awards: 1.
Deadline: June 15.
How to apply: Applications are available online. An application form, transcript and personal essay are required.
Exclusive: Visit www.UltimateScholarshipBook.com and enter code AS153612 for updates on this award.

(1537) · Independent Living Act (Foster Care Tuition Waiver)

Oklahoma State Regents for Higher Education
655 Research Parkway
Suite 200
Oklahoma City, OK 73104
Phone: 405-225-9100
Email: llangston@osrhe.edu
http://www.okhighered.org
Purpose: To assist students who have been in foster care in obtaining higher education.
Eligibility: Applicants must be residents of Oklahoma who have graduated within the past three years from an accredited high school in or bordering Oklahoma or have received their GED. They must be 21 years of age or younger and have been in DHS custody for at least nine months between ages 16 and 18. They must be enrolled in a public institution or in certain programs at technology centers.
Target applicants: High school students. College students.
Amount: Tuition.
Number of awards: Varies.
Scholarship may be renewable.
Deadline: Varies.
How to apply: Contact by phone or email for more information on how to apply.
Exclusive: Visit www.UltimateScholarshipBook.com and enter code OK153712 for updates on this award.

(1538) · Indiana Broadcasters Association College Scholarships

Indiana Broadcasters Association
3003 E 98th Street
Suite 161
Indianapolis, IN 46280
Phone: 800-342-6276
Fax: 317-573-0895
Email: indba@aol.com
http://www.indianabroadcasters.org
Purpose: To support student broadcasters.
Eligibility: Applicants must be Indiana residents and current college students with a 3.0 or higher GPA. Students must be actively participating in a college broadcast facility or working for a commercial broadcast facility and be attending an IBA member institution that has a radio/TV facility on campus and/or offers majors in telecommunications or broadcast journalism.
Target applicants: College students. Adult students.
Minimum GPA: 3.0
Amount: Varies.
Number of awards: Varies.
Deadline: March 5.
How to apply: Applications are available online. An application form, essay and transcript request form are required.
Exclusive: Visit www.UltimateScholarshipBook.com and enter code IN153812 for updates on this award.

(1539) · Indiana Oratorical Contest

American Legion, Department of Indiana
777 N. Meridian Street
Indianapolis, IN 46204
Phone: 317-630-1300
http://www.indlegion.org
Purpose: To enhance high school students' experience with and understanding of the U.S. Constitution. The contest will help develop students' leadership skills and civic appreciation, as well as the ability to deliver thoughtful, insightful orations regarding U.S. citizenship and its inherent responsibilities.
Eligibility: Applicants must be high school students under the age of 20 who are U.S. citizens or legal residents and residents of the state. Students first give an oration within their state and winners compete at the national level. The oration must be related to the Constitution of the United States focusing on the duties and obligations citizens have to the government. It must be in English and be between eight and ten minutes. There is also an assigned topic which is posted on the website, and it should be between three and five minutes.
Target applicants: High school students.
Amount: $1,000-$3,400.
Number of awards: Varies.
Deadline: December 10.
How to apply: Application information is available from the local American Legion Post and online.

Exclusive: Visit www.UltimateScholarshipBook.com and enter code AM153912 for updates on this award.

(1540) · Ione M. Allen Music Scholarship

Center for Scholarship Administration
Wachovia Accounts
4320-G Wade Hampton Boulevard
Taylors, SC 29687
Phone: 866-608-0001
Email: wachoviascholars@bellsouth.net
https://www.csascholars.org/index.php

Purpose: To provide financial assistance to Western North Carolina students who are interested in music.
Eligibility: Applicants must be residents of Buncombe, Cherokee, Clay, Graham, Haywood, Henderson, Jackson, Macon, Madison, Polk, Swain or Transylvania County, North Carolina. They must possess musical talent and attend an accredited conservatory or other institution with a recognized music department. All applicants must be interviewed and present a performance.
Target applicants: High school students.
Amount: Varies.
Number of awards: Varies.
Scholarship may be renewable.
Deadline: January 24.
How to apply: Applications are available online.
Exclusive: Visit www.UltimateScholarshipBook.com and enter code CE154012 for updates on this award.

(1541) · Iowa Grants

Iowa College Student Aid Commission
200 10th Street, 4th Floor
Des Moines, IA 50309
Phone: 515-242-3344
Fax: 515-242-3388
Email: info@iowacollegeaid.org
http://www.iowacollegeaid.org

Purpose: To assist needy Iowa students.
Eligibility: Applicants must be enrolled in or planning to enroll at least part-time in an undergraduate program at eligible Iowa colleges, universities and community colleges and be U.S. citizens. Selection is based on need, with priority given to the neediest applicants.
Target applicants: High school students. College students. Adult students.
Amount: Up to $1,000.
Number of awards: Varies.
Scholarship may be renewable.
Deadline: As soon as possible after January 1.
How to apply: Complete the Free Application for Federal Student Aid (FAFSA).
Exclusive: Visit www.UltimateScholarshipBook.com and enter code IO154112 for updates on this award.

(1542) · Iowa Newspaper Association Scholarships

Iowa Newspaper Association
319 E 5th Street
Des Moines, IA 50309
Phone: 515-244-2145
Fax: 515-244-4855
Email: ina@inanews.com
http://www.inanews.com

Purpose: To support students preparing for careers in the newspaper industry.
Eligibility: Applicants must be Iowa residents who are high school seniors or current college students and must attend an in-state college or university. Students must plan to work in the newspaper industry in Iowa upon completion of their degrees.
Target applicants: High school students. College students. Adult students.
Amount: $500-$1,000.
Number of awards: Varies.
Deadline: February 12.
How to apply: Applications are available online. An application form, two letters of reference, personal statement and two writing samples are required.
Exclusive: Visit www.UltimateScholarshipBook.com and enter code IO154212 for updates on this award.

(1543) · Iowa Oratorical Contest

American Legion, Department of Iowa
720 Lyon Street
Des Moines, IA 50309
Phone: 800-365-8387
Fax: 515-282-7583
Email: programs@ialegion.org
http://www.ialegion.org

Purpose: To enhance high school students' experience with and understanding of the U.S. Constitution. The contest will help develop students' leadership skills and civic appreciation, as well as the ability to deliver thoughtful, insightful orations regarding U.S. citizenship and its inherent responsibilities.
Eligibility: Applicants must be high school students under the age of 20 who are U.S. citizens or legal residents and residents of the state. Students first give an oration within their state and winners compete at the national level. The oration must be related to the Constitution of the United States focusing on the duties and obligations citizens have to the government. It must be in English and be between eight and ten minutes. There is also an assigned topic which is posted on the website, and it should be between three and five minutes.
Target applicants: High school students.
Amount: Up to $3,500.
Number of awards: Varies.
Deadline: February 13.
How to apply: Applications are available online.
Exclusive: Visit www.UltimateScholarshipBook.com and enter code AM154312 for updates on this award.

(1544) · Iowa Physician Assistant Society Scholarship

Iowa Physician Assistant Society
525 SW 5th Street
Suite A
Des Moines, IA 50309
Phone: 515-282-8192
Fax: 515-282-9117
Email: info@iapasociety.org
http://www.iapasociety.org

Purpose: To aid Iowa students who are enrolled in a physician assistant degree program.
Eligibility: Applicants must be enrolled in an approved Physician Assistant (PA) degree program at a postsecondary institution located in Iowa. They must have had an outstanding undergraduate academic record, strong leadership skills and a well-developed knowledge of the

role of the professional physician assistant. Selection is based on academic merit, demonstrated leadership ability, commitment to the field of physician assisting, extracurricular activities and professional awareness.
Target applicants: College students. Adult students.
Amount: $1,000.
Number of awards: 2.
Deadline: September 5.
How to apply: Applications are available online. An application form, transcript and personal statement are required.
Exclusive: Visit www.UltimateScholarshipBook.com and enter code IO154412 for updates on this award.

(1545) • Iowa Pork Foundation President's Scholarship

Iowa Pork Producers Association
1636 NW 114th Street
P.O. Box 71009
Clive, IA 50325
Phone: 800-372-7675
Fax: 515-225-0563
Email: info@iowapork.org
http://www.iowapork.org
Purpose: To aid Iowa agriculture students who are interested in the pork industry.
Eligibility: Applicants must be Iowa residents who are enrolled at or who plan to enroll at a two-year or four-year postsecondary institution located in Iowa. They must be majoring in or have plans to major in an agriculture-related undergraduate program that focuses on swine production. They must maintain a GPA of 2.5 or higher. Selection is based on the overall strength of the application.
Target applicants: High school students. College students. Adult students.
Minimum GPA: 2.5
Amount: $1,000.
Number of awards: 4.
Scholarship may be renewable.
Deadline: April 30.
How to apply: Applications are available online. An application form, two recommendation letters and a transcript are required.
Exclusive: Visit www.UltimateScholarshipBook.com and enter code IO154512 for updates on this award.

(1546) • Iowa Scholarship for the Arts

Iowa Arts Council
600 E. Locust
Des Moines, IA 50319-0290
Phone: 515-281-6412
Fax: 515-242-6498
http://www.iowaartscouncil.org
Purpose: To aid outstanding young artists.
Eligibility: Applicants must be Iowa residents and graduating high school seniors and show proven artistic ability in dance, literature, music, theatre, traditional arts or visual arts. Students must be accepted full-time to an accredited Iowa college or university and must major in one of the aforementioned areas.
Target applicants: High school students.
Amount: $1,000.
Number of awards: Varies.
Deadline: February 1.
How to apply: Applications are available online. An application form, two letters of recommendation and an essay are required.
Exclusive: Visit www.UltimateScholarshipBook.com and enter code IO154612 for updates on this award.

(1547) • Iowa Thespian Chapter Board Senior Scholarships

Iowa Thespian Chapter
604 Belmont Road
Bettendorf, IA 52722
Phone: 563-332-5151
Fax: 563-823-1950
Email: myattw@pleasval.k12.ia.us
http://www.iowathespians.org
Purpose: To aid promising young thespians.
Eligibility: Applicants must be Iowa high school seniors and have an overall GPA of 2.0 or higher with a GPA of 3.0 or higher in arts-related classes. Students must be members of the International Thespian Society in good standing. Applicants must plan to major or minor in theatre, film, radio and television, broadcasting, music or dance. Applicants must also perform an audition at the Iowa Thespian Festival in the performance, technical or theatre educator category.
Target applicants: High school students.
Minimum GPA: 2.0
Amount: $1,000.
Number of awards: 3.
Deadline: Varies.
How to apply: Applications are available from the Iowa Thespian Society. An application form and resume are required.
Exclusive: Visit www.UltimateScholarshipBook.com and enter code IO154712 for updates on this award.

(1548) • Iowa Tuition Grants

Iowa College Student Aid Commission
200 10th Street, 4th Floor
Des Moines, IA 50309
Phone: 515-242-3344
Fax: 515-242-3388
Email: info@iowacollegeaid.org
http://www.iowacollegeaid.org
Purpose: To help students attend Iowa's independent colleges and universities.
Eligibility: Applicants must be enrolled in or planning to enroll at least part-time in an eligible Iowa college or university and demonstrate financial need. Priority is given to the neediest applicants.
Target applicants: High school students. College students. Adult students.
Amount: Up to $14,260.
Number of awards: Varies.
Scholarship may be renewable.
Deadline: May 1.
How to apply: Complete the Free Application for Federal Student Aid (FAFSA).
Exclusive: Visit www.UltimateScholarshipBook.com and enter code IO154812 for updates on this award.

(1549) • Iowa Vocational-Technical Tuition Grants

Iowa College Student Aid Commission
200 10th Street, 4th Floor
Des Moines, IA 50309
Phone: 515-242-3344

Fax: 515-242-3388
Email: info@iowacollegeaid.org
http://www.iowacollegeaid.org
Purpose: To aid those Iowa residents enrolled in vocational-technical programs at community colleges.
Eligibility: Applicants must be enrolled in or planning to enroll in a career education or option course of at least 12 weeks duration at an Iowa area community college and be U.S. citizens or permanent residents.
Target applicants: High school students. College students. Adult students.
Amount: Up to $2,400.
Number of awards: Varies.
Scholarship may be renewable.
Deadline: July 1.
How to apply: Complete the Free Application for Federal Student Aid (FAFSA).
Exclusive: Visit www.UltimateScholarshipBook.com and enter code IO154912 for updates on this award.

(1550) • Irvine W. Cook WA0CGS Scholarship

American Radio Relay League Foundation
225 Main Street
Newington, CT 06111
Phone: 860-594-0397
Fax: 860-594-0259
Email: foundation@arrl.org
http://www.arrlf.org
Purpose: To provide scholarship assistance to Kansas residents who are amateur radio operators.
Eligibility: Applicants must be residents of Kansas and holders of an active amateur radio license of any class. Preference is given to students who are studying electronics, communications or a related subject at the baccalaureate level or higher.
Target applicants: College students. Graduate school students. Adult students.
Amount: $1,000.
Number of awards: 1.
Deadline: February 1.
How to apply: Applications are available online.
Exclusive: Visit www.UltimateScholarshipBook.com and enter code AM155012 for updates on this award.

(1551) • Ivomec Generations of Excellence Internship and Scholarship Program

Texas CattleWomen
Lampasas, TX 76550
Phone: 512-556-9149
Email: juliemurnin@cattledesign.com
http://www.txcattlewomen.org
Purpose: To aid Texas students who are preparing for careers in the beef industry.
Eligibility: Applicants must be permanent residents of Texas and be graduate students or rising undergraduate juniors or seniors who are enrolled at a Texas college or university. They must be majoring in agriculture or a related subject, must have a background in beef cattle and have a GPA of 2.5 or higher. Selection is based on the overall strength of the application.
Target applicants: College students. Graduate school students. Adult students.
Minimum GPA: 2.5
Amount: $1,000.
Number of awards: Varies.
Deadline: May 1.
How to apply: Applications are available online. An application form and supporting materials are required.
Exclusive: Visit www.UltimateScholarshipBook.com and enter code TE155112 for updates on this award.

(1552) • J.A. Knowles Memorial Scholarship

United Methodist Church
Office of Loans and Scholarships
P.O. BOX 340007
Nashville, TN 37203-0007
Phone: 615-340-7344
Fax: 615-340-7367
Email: umscholar@gbhem.org
http://www.gbhem.org
Purpose: To support Texas Methodist college students.
Eligibility: Applicants must be enrolled full-time at any accredited college or graduate school in Texas and active members of the Methodist church in Texas for at least one year before applying for the scholarship. Students must have at least a 2.5 GPA and be U.S. citizens or permanent residents.
Target applicants: High school students. College students. Graduate school students. Adult students.
Minimum GPA: 2.5
Amount: Varies.
Number of awards: Varies.
Deadline: April 15-May 1.
How to apply: Applications are available online in January.
Exclusive: Visit www.UltimateScholarshipBook.com and enter code UN155212 for updates on this award.

(1553) • J.D. Edsal Advertising Scholarship/Women's Advertising Club Scholarship

Rhode Island Foundation
One Union Station
Providence, RI 02903
Phone: 401-274-4564
Fax: 401-331-8085
Email: lmonahan@rifoundation.org
http://www.rifoundation.org
Purpose: To support undergraduate students who are planning to work in advertising.
Eligibility: Applicants must be residents of Rhode Island. They must be majoring in advertising, public relations, graphic design, marketing, film, television or broadcast production. Students must be at least in their sophomore year of college, and they must be attending school full-time. Applicants must show financial need and a commitment to an advertising career.
Target applicants: College students. Adult students.
Amount: $500-$1,000.
Number of awards: 1.
Deadline: April 30.
How to apply: Applications are available online.
Exclusive: Visit www.UltimateScholarshipBook.com and enter code RH155312 for updates on this award.

(1554) • J.R. Popalisky Scholarship

American Water Works Association - Missouri Section
Chester A. Bender, P.E., Scholarship Committee Chair

c/o Ponzer Youngquist, P.A.
227 East Dennis Avenue
Olathe, KS 66061
Phone: 913-782-0541
Email: cbender@pyengineers.com
http://www.awwa-mo.org
Purpose: To aid Missouri students whose coursework is related to the water supply industry.
Eligibility: Applicants must be U.S. citizens who are enrolled at an accredited college or university located in Missouri. They must have completed coursework in subjects relating to the water supply industry (such as environmental engineering, civil engineering or environmental science). Students who are receiving funding from an employer are ineligible. Selection is based on coursework relevance, GPA, financial need, recommendations, personal essay and extracurricular activities.
Target applicants: College students. Adult students.
Amount: $1,000.
Number of awards: Varies.
Deadline: March 24.
How to apply: Applications are available online. An application form, personal essay and a financial analysis form are required.
Exclusive: Visit www.UltimateScholarshipBook.com and enter code AM155412 for updates on this award.

(1555) • Jack E. Barger, Sr. Memorial Nursing Scholarship

Nursing Foundation of Pennsylvania
2578 Interstate Drive
Suite 101
Harrisburg, PA 17110
Phone: 717-827-4369
Fax: 717-657-3796
Email: nfp@panurses.org
http://www.panurses.org
Purpose: To aid Pennsylvania nursing undergraduates who are serving in the military, are veterans, are military spouses, are veterans' spouses or who are the children of active duty military or veterans.
Eligibility: Candidates must be residents of Pennsylvania and must be enrolled in an undergraduate nursing program at an institution located in Pennsylvania. They must be active duty military, veterans, military spouses, veterans' spouses or the children of active duty military or veterans. Candidates are nominated for this award by the deans and department heads in the school of nursing at their institutions. Selection of award recipients will be determined by lottery.
Target applicants: College students. Adult students.
Amount: $1,000.
Number of awards: 6.
Deadline: April 24.
How to apply: Candidates are not required to submit an application for this award. Instead, the dean or department head of the candidate's school must submit a formal nomination to the scholarship committee.
Exclusive: Visit www.UltimateScholarshipBook.com and enter code NU155512 for updates on this award.

(1556) • Jack F. Tolbert Memorial Student Grant Program

Maryland Higher Education Commission
Office of Student Financial Assistance
839 Bestgate Road, Suite 400
Annapolis, MD 21401
Phone: 800-974-1024
Fax: 410-260-3200
Email: osfamail@mhec.state.md.us
http://www.mhec.state.md.us
Purpose: To assist students who are attending or planning to attend a private career school.
Eligibility: Students and their parents if they are dependents must be residents of Maryland. Applicants must also enroll at an approved private career school in the state for at least 18 hours per week.
Target applicants: High school students. College students. Adult students.
Amount: Up to $500.
Number of awards: Varies.
Scholarship may be renewable.
Deadline: March 1.
How to apply: Students apply by completing the Free Application for Federal Student Aid (FAFSA) and turning it in to the financial aid office of the career school they will attend.
Exclusive: Visit www.UltimateScholarshipBook.com and enter code MA155612 for updates on this award.

(1557) • James F. and Doris M. Barton Scholarship

American Quarter Horse Foundation
Scholarship Program
2601 East Interstate 40
Amarillo, TX 79104
Phone: 806-378-5029
Fax: 806-376-1005
Email: foundation@aqha.org
http://www.aqha.com
Purpose: To aid New York students who are current members of the Empire State Youth Quarter Horse Association and either the American Quarter Horse Association or the American Quarter Horse Youth Association.
Eligibility: Applicants must be New York residents who are members of the Empire State Youth Quarter Horse Association (ESYQHA). They also must be members of either the American Quarter Horse Association (AQHA) or the American Quarter Horse Youth Association (AQHYA). They must be enrolled in or planning to enroll in a two- or four-year degree program at an accredited postsecondary institution. Applicants must have a GPA of 3.0 or higher. Selection is based on the overall strength of the application.
Target applicants: High school students. College students. Adult students.
Minimum GPA: 3.0
Amount: $5,000.
Number of awards: Varies.
Deadline: December 1.
How to apply: Applications are available online. An application form, Student Aid Report (SAR), transcript, two recommendations, proof of residency and proof of association membership are required.
Exclusive: Visit www.UltimateScholarshipBook.com and enter code AM155712 for updates on this award.

(1558) • James F. Davis Memorial Scholarship

National Foliage Foundation
1533 Park Center Drive
Orlando, FL 32835
Phone: 800-375-3642
Fax: 407-295-1619
Email: info@nationalfoliagefoundation.org
http://www.nationalfoliagefoundation.org

Purpose: To aid students pursuing higher education in horticulture or a related discipline in Florida.
Eligibility: Applicants must be rising freshmen or undergraduates at an accredited postsecondary institution located in Florida. They must be full-time students who are enrolled in or who are planning to enroll in a degree program in horticulture or a related subject. They must have a GPA of 2.0 or higher. Selection is based on the overall strength of the application.
Target applicants: High school students. College students. Adult students.
Minimum GPA: 2.0
Amount: Varies.
Number of awards: Varies.
Scholarship may be renewable.
Deadline: January 15.
How to apply: Applications are available online. An application form, transcript, personal essay and two letters of recommendation are required.
Exclusive: Visit www.UltimateScholarshipBook.com and enter code NA155812 for updates on this award.

(1559) • James J. Burns and C.A. Haynes Scholarship

Rhode Island Foundation
One Union Station
Providence, RI 02903
Phone: 401-274-4564
Fax: 401-331-8085
Email: lmonahan@rifoundation.org
http://www.rifoundation.org
Purpose: To support students who are planning to work in the textile industry.
Eligibility: Students must be currently enrolled in a textile program. They must demonstrate financial need or academic excellence. Preference will be given to students whose parents are members of the National Association of Textile Supervisors.
Target applicants: High school students. College students. Graduate school students. Adult students.
Amount: $1,000.
Number of awards: Varies.
Deadline: June 1.
How to apply: Applications are available online.
Exclusive: Visit www.UltimateScholarshipBook.com and enter code RH155912 for updates on this award.

(1560) • James L. Shriver Scholarship

Community Foundation of Western Massachusetts
1500 Main Street
P.O. Box 15769
Springfield, MA 01115
Phone: 413-732-2858
Fax: 413-733-8565
Email: scholar@communityfoundation.org
http://www.communityfoundation.org
Purpose: To help students from western Massachusetts to pursue technical careers.
Eligibility: Applicants must attend a U.S. college or university part-time or full-time. Application forms, transcripts and Student Aid Reports are required. Selection is based on financial need and academic merit.
Target applicants: High school students. College students. Graduate school students. Adult students.
Amount: Varies.
Number of awards: Varies.
Deadline: March 31.
How to apply: Applications are available online and by phone.
Exclusive: Visit www.UltimateScholarshipBook.com and enter code CO156012 for updates on this award.

(1561) • James V. Day Scholarship

American Legion, Department of Maine
21 College Avenue
Waterville, ME 04901
Phone: 207-873-3229
Email: legionme@me.acadia.net
http://www.mainelegion.org
Purpose: To provide financial assistance to the children or grandchildren of American Legion, Department of Maine members.
Eligibility: Applicants must be U.S. citizens, residents of Maine and graduating high school seniors. They must be enrolled in an accredited college or vocational technical school and provide evidence of financial need. Applicants must demonstrate good character and a belief in the American way of life.
Target applicants: High school students.
Amount: $500.
Number of awards: Up to 2.
Deadline: May 1.
How to apply: Applications are available online.
Exclusive: Visit www.UltimateScholarshipBook.com and enter code AM156112 for updates on this award.

(1562) • James W. Colgan Loan

Community Foundation of Western Massachusetts
1500 Main Street
P.O. Box 15769
Springfield, MA 01115
Phone: 413-732-2858
Fax: 413-733-8565
Email: scholar@communityfoundation.org
http://www.communityfoundation.org
Purpose: To provide interest-free educational loans for students who have lived in Massachusetts for the past five years.
Eligibility: Applicants must be part-time or full-time undergraduate or graduate students. Students should provide application forms, transcripts and Student Aid Reports. Recipients will begin repaying the loan three months after graduation, and no interest is charged as long as the monthly payments are made on time.
Target applicants: High school students. College students. Graduate school students. Adult students.
Amount: Varies.
Number of awards: Varies.
Deadline: March 31.
How to apply: Applications are available online and by phone.
Exclusive: Visit www.UltimateScholarshipBook.com and enter code CO156212 for updates on this award.

(1563) • James. F. Byrnes Scholarships

James F. Byrnes Foundation
P.O. Box 6781
Columbia, SC 29260-6781
Phone: 803-254-9325
Fax: 803-254-9354
Email: Info@byrnesscholars.org

http://www.byrnesscholars.org
Purpose: To support South Carolina students with deceased parents.
Eligibility: Applicants must be residents of South Carolina whose parent or parents are deceased and must attend or plan to attend a four-year college or university.
Target applicants: High school students. College students. Adult students.
Minimum GPA: 2.5
Amount: $3,250.
Number of awards: Varies.
Scholarship may be renewable.
Deadline: February 15.
How to apply: Applications are available online.
Exclusive: Visit www.UltimateScholarshipBook.com and enter code JA156312 for updates on this award.

(1564) • Janelle Downing Memorial 4-H Scholarship

Missouri 4-H Foundation
Center for Youth Development
8th Floor Clark Hall
Columbia, MO 65211
Phone: 573-882-9360
Fax: 573-884-4225
Email: lemmonc@missouri.edu
http://mo4h.missouri.edu
Purpose: To aid present and former Missouri 4-H members who are preparing for careers in veterinary medicine and animal science.
Eligibility: Applicants must be Missouri residents who are present or former members of 4-H and who are rising undergraduate freshmen who are planning to major in veterinary medicine, pre-veterinary medicine or animal science. They must have a GPA of 3.0 or higher on a four-point scale. Preference will be given to those who will be enrolling at the University of Missouri College of Agriculture as freshmen. Selection is based on 4-H achievements, stated career goals and financial need.
Target applicants: High school students.
Minimum GPA: 3.0
Amount: $1,000.
Number of awards: 1.
Deadline: April 1.
How to apply: Applications are available online. An application form, transcript, financial information and essay are required.
Exclusive: Visit www.UltimateScholarshipBook.com and enter code MI156412 for updates on this award.

(1565) • Jean Lee/Jeff Marvin Collegiate Scholarships

Indiana Association for Health, Physical Education, Recreation and Dance
2007 Wilno Drive
Marion, IN 46952
Phone: 765-664-8319
Email: hatch@cometck.com
http://www.indiana-ahperd.org
Purpose: To aid students pursuing degrees in physical education-related fields.
Eligibility: Applicants must be attending an Indiana college or university and be upcoming juniors or seniors who are majoring in health education, physical education, recreation, dance education or allied areas.
Target applicants: College students. Adult students.
Amount: $1,000.
Number of awards: 4.
Deadline: December 1.
How to apply: Applications are available online. An application form, goals statement, statement of need, list of activities during college attendance, philosophy statement and two letters of recommendation are required.
Exclusive: Visit www.UltimateScholarshipBook.com and enter code IN156512 for updates on this award.

(1566) • Jeff Krosnoff Scholarship

Jeff Krosnoff Scholarship Fund
P.O. Box 8585
La Crescenta, CA 91214
Email: jtheisinger@charter.net
http://www.krosnoffscholarship.com/Scholarship.htm
Purpose: To support California high school seniors who plan to enter four-year colleges.
Eligibility: Applicants must have an excellent academic record with a cumulative high school GPA of at least 3.0. Students must submit a transcript and a two- to four-page essay. The essay is given the greatest weight in the selection process.
Target applicants: High school students.
Minimum GPA: 3.0
Amount: $10,000.
Number of awards: 1.
Deadline: January 11.
How to apply: Applications are available online.
Exclusive: Visit www.UltimateScholarshipBook.com and enter code JE156612 for updates on this award.

(1567) • Jennet Colliflower Nursing Scholarship

Dade Community Foundation
200 South Biscayne Boulevard
Suite 505
Miami, FL 33131
Phone: 305-371-2711
Fax: 305-371-5342
Email: claudianna.williams@dadecommunityfoundation.org
http://www.dadecommunityfoundation.org
Purpose: To aid Florida nursing students.
Eligibility: Applicants must be Florida residents who are rising undergraduate juniors or seniors. They must be enrolled full-time in a nursing degree program at a Florida postsecondary institution. Selection is based on academic merit, stated career goals, extracurricular involvement, volunteer experience and financial need.
Target applicants: College students. Adult students.
Amount: $1,000.
Number of awards: 2.
Deadline: May 8.
How to apply: Applications are available online. An application form, official transcript, one letter of recommendation and personal essay are required.
Exclusive: Visit www.UltimateScholarshipBook.com and enter code DA156712 for updates on this award.

(1568) • Jennings and Beulah Haggerty Scholarship

Lincoln Community Foundation
215 Centennial Mall South, Suite 100
Lincoln, NE 68508
Phone: 402-474-2345
Fax: 402-476-8532

Email: lcf@lcf.org
http://www.lcf.org
Purpose: To support high school seniors in Lincoln, Nebraska.
Eligibility: Students must rank in the top 1/3 of their high school class. Applicants must have financial need, and they must apply for financial aid at their chosen school before contacting the Lincoln Community Foundation.
Target applicants: High school students.
Amount: $500-$2,000.
Number of awards: Varies.
Deadline: July 1.
How to apply: Applications are available online.
Exclusive: Visit www.UltimateScholarshipBook.com and enter code LI156812 for updates on this award.

(1569) • Jere W. Thompson, Jr. Scholarship

Dallas Foundation
900 Jackson Street
Suite 705
Dallas, TX 75202
Phone: 214-741-9898
Email: rlasseter@dallasfoundation.org
http://www.dallasfoundation.org
Purpose: To aid Texas civil engineering and construction engineering undergraduates.
Eligibility: Applicants must be rising undergraduate juniors enrolled full-time at a Texas postsecondary institution. They must be majoring in civil engineering or construction engineering and must demonstrate financial need. Selection is based on the overall strength of the application.
Target applicants: College students. Adult students.
Amount: Up to $2,000.
Number of awards: Varies.
Scholarship may be renewable.
Deadline: April 1.
How to apply: Applications are available online. An application form, financial information survey, a copy of the applicant's FAFSA form, an official transcript, personal statement and one to three recommendation letters are required.
Exclusive: Visit www.UltimateScholarshipBook.com and enter code DA156912 for updates on this award.

(1570) • Jerome B. Steinbach Scholarship

Oregon Student Assistance Commission
1500 Valley River Drive
Suite 100
Eugene, OR 97401
Phone: 541-687-7400
Fax: 541-687-7414
Email: awardinfo@osac.state.or.us
http://www.osac.state.or.us
Purpose: To assist Oregon undergraduate students.
Eligibility: Applicants must be natural-born U.S. citizens and Oregon residents. They must be rising undergraduate sophomores, juniors or seniors at an accredited U.S. postsecondary institution and have a GPA of 3.5 or higher. U.S. Bank employees and their relatives are ineligible. Selection is based on financial need.
Target applicants: College students. Adult students.
Minimum GPA: 3.5
Amount: Varies.
Number of awards: Varies.
Scholarship may be renewable.
Deadline: Varies.
How to apply: Applications are available online. A completed FAFSA, application form and supporting documents are required.
Exclusive: Visit www.UltimateScholarshipBook.com and enter code OR157012 for updates on this award.

(1571) • Jewish Vocational Service Scholarship Fund

Jewish Vocational Service
6505 Wilshire Boulevard
Suite 200
Los Angeles, CA 90048
Phone: 323-761-8888
Fax: 323-761-8575
Email: scholarship@jvsla.org
http://www.jvsla.org
Purpose: To assist Los Angeles-area Jewish students.
Eligibility: Applicants must be U.S. citizens or permanent legal residents and permanent and legal residents of Los Angeles county. Students must also plan to attend full-time an approved U.S. college or vocational school and maintain a minimum 2.7 GPA. Selection is based primarily on financial need as well as Jewish community involvement and community service.
Target applicants: High school students.
Minimum GPA: 2.7
Amount: $1,000-$5,000.
Number of awards: Varies.
Deadline: March 11.
How to apply: Applications are available online.
Exclusive: Visit www.UltimateScholarshipBook.com and enter code JE157112 for updates on this award.

(1572) • Jimmy Rane Foundation Scholarships

Jimmy Rane Foundation
P.O. Box 40
Abbeville, AL 36310
Phone: 866-763-4228
Email: jimmyrane@act.org
http://www.jimmyranefoundation.org
Purpose: To support students who are planning to pursue undergraduate degrees.
Eligibility: Applicants must be high school seniors who are residents of North Carolina, South Carolina, Georgia, Alabama, Oklahoma, Missouri, Nebraska, Arkansas, Tennessee, Louisiana, Mississippi, Florida or Texas.
Target applicants: High school students.
Minimum GPA: 3.0
Amount: Varies.
Number of awards: Varies.
Deadline: February 18.
How to apply: Applications are available online.
Exclusive: Visit www.UltimateScholarshipBook.com and enter code JI157212 for updates on this award.

(1573) • Joe Foss, An American Hero Scholarship

Sioux Falls Area Community Foundation
300 N. Phillips Avenue, Suite 102
Sioux Falls, SD 57104
Phone: 605-336-7055
Email: pgale@sfacf.org

http://www.sfacf.org
Purpose: To support high school seniors who have strong values, courage and patriotism.
Eligibility: Applicants must have at least a 3.5 GPA and an ACT score of 21 or above. Students must reside in South Dakota.
Target applicants: High school students.
Minimum GPA: 3.5
Amount: $1,000.
Number of awards: Varies.
Deadline: March 15.
How to apply: Applications are available online.
Exclusive: Visit www.UltimateScholarshipBook.com and enter code SI157312 for updates on this award.

(1574) · Joe J. Welker Memorial Scholarship

Delaware Engineering Society Scholarship Program
c/o Delaware Higher Education Commission
Carvel State Office Building
820 North French Street
Wilmington, DE 19801
http://www.desonline.us
Purpose: To aid Delaware high school seniors who are planning to enroll in an ABET-accredited engineering program in the fall following graduation.
Eligibility: Applicants must be graduating high school seniors who either are attending a school located in Delaware or are Delaware residents. They must have plans to enroll in an ABET-accredited engineering program in the fall following high school graduation. They must have a minimum SAT critical reading score of 500, a minimum SAT math score of 600 and a minimum SAT writing score of 500. Selection is based on the overall strength of the application.
Target applicants: High school students.
Amount: Up to $2,000.
Number of awards: Varies.
Deadline: December 8.
How to apply: Applications are available online. An application form, official transcript, personal essay, SAT scores and two letters of recommendation are required.
Exclusive: Visit www.UltimateScholarshipBook.com and enter code DE157412 for updates on this award.

(1575) · Joel Abromson Memorial Scholarship

EqualityMaine
P.O. Box 1951
1 Pleasant Street, 2nd Floor
Portland, ME 04104
Phone: 207-761-3732
Fax: 207-761-3752
Email: info@equalitymaine.org
http://www.equalitymaine.org
Purpose: To promote equality for students regardless of their sexual orientation and gender expression through an essay contest.
Eligibility: Applicants must be Maine high school seniors, and they must be accepted to an institution of higher learning.
Target applicants: High school students.
Amount: $1,000.
Number of awards: Varies.
Deadline: April 15.
How to apply: Students may apply by sending a cover letter, essay, two letters of recommendation and a copy of their college acceptance letter to EqualityMaine.
Exclusive: Visit www.UltimateScholarshipBook.com and enter code EQ157512 for updates on this award.

(1576) · Joel Garcia Memorial Scholarship

California Chicano News Media Association
USC Annenberg School of Journalism
727 W. 27th Street, Room 201
Los Angeles, CA 90007-3212
Phone: 213-821-0075
Fax: 213-743-1838
Email: ccnmainfo@ccnma.org
http://www.ccnma.org
Purpose: To support Latino students studying journalism who are California residents or are attending California schools.
Eligibility: Applicants must be Latino and either attending California schools or be California residents attending out-of-state schools. Students must show an interest in journalism (broadcast, print, photo or online) and demonstrate financial need and academic achievement.
Target applicants: High school students. College students. Adult students.
Amount: $500-$1,000.
Number of awards: Varies.
Deadline: April 2.
How to apply: Applications are available online, by email, by mail or by phone.
Exclusive: Visit www.UltimateScholarshipBook.com and enter code CA157612 for updates on this award.

(1577) · Johanna Drew Cluney Fund

Hawaii Community Foundation - Scholarships
1164 Bishop Street, Suite 800
Honolulu, HI 96813
Phone: 888-731-3863
Fax: 808-521-6286
Email: scholarships@hcf-hawaii.org
http://www.hawaiicommunityfoundation.org
Purpose: To aid students pursuing vocational education.
Eligibility: Applicants must be Hawaii residents who are enrolled full-time in vocational degree programs at a University of Hawaii school. They must be first-time degree seekers who plan to enter the workforce upon graduation. Deadlines are July 1 and October 1.
Target applicants: College students. Adult students.
Amount: Varies.
Number of awards: Varies.
Deadline: July 1.
How to apply: Applications are available online. An application form, personal statement and letter of recommendation are required.
Exclusive: Visit www.UltimateScholarshipBook.com and enter code HA157712 for updates on this award.

(1578) · John and Abigail Adams Scholarship

Massachusetts Department of Higher Education
Office of Student Financial Assistance
454 Broadway
Suite 200
Revere, MA 02151
Phone: 617-727-9420
Fax: 617-727-0667
Email: osfa@osfa.mass.edu
http://www.osfa.mass.edu/default.asp

Purpose: To attract high-performing high school seniors to Massachusetts public institutions of higher education and to reward previous achievements.
Eligibility: Applicants must be permanent residents of Massachusetts, score in the Advanced category in one category of the 10th grade MCAS test and in the Proficient or Advanced category in the other and have a combined MCAS score in the top 25 percent of their school district. Scholarship winners must maintain a 3.0 or higher GPA for continued eligibility.
Target applicants: High school students.
Amount: Full Tuition.
Number of awards: Varies.
Scholarship may be renewable.
Deadline: Varies.
How to apply: No application is necessary, but students must complete the Free Application for Federal Student Aid.
Exclusive: Visit www.UltimateScholarshipBook.com and enter code MA157812 for updates on this award.

(1579) • John and Anne Clifton Scholarship

Hawaii Community Foundation - Scholarships
1164 Bishop Street, Suite 800
Honolulu, HI 96813
Phone: 888-731-3863
Fax: 808-521-6286
Email: scholarships@hcf-hawaii.org
http://www.hawaiicommunityfoundation.org
Purpose: To assist students pursuing vocational degrees.
Eligibility: Applicants must be enrolled in a vocational program at a University of Hawaii school.
Target applicants: High school students. College students. Adult students.
Amount: Varies.
Number of awards: Varies.
Deadline: July 1.
How to apply: Applications are available online beginning in early March.
Exclusive: Visit www.UltimateScholarshipBook.com and enter code HA157912 for updates on this award.

(1580) • John Blanchard Memorial Scholarship

California School Library Association
950 Glenn Drive, Suite 150
Folsom, CA 95630
Phone: 916-447-2684
Fax: 916-447-2695
Email: csla@pacbell.net
http://www.csla.net/
Purpose: To assist a school library paraprofessional in becoming a certified school library media teacher.
Eligibility: Applicants must be members of the California School Library Association who are currently working or have worked in the last three years in a classified library position. Candidates must be currently enrolled in a degree program for certification as a library media teacher and California residents planning to work in California after completing their programs. Three letters of recommendation are required.
Target applicants: College students. Graduate school students. Adult students.
Amount: $1,000.
Number of awards: 1.
Deadline: May 30.
How to apply: Applications are available online.
Exclusive: Visit www.UltimateScholarshipBook.com and enter code CA158012 for updates on this award.

(1581) • John D. and Virginia Riesch Scholarship

Wisconsin Medical Society Foundation
330 East Lakeside Street
Madison, WI 53715
Phone: 866-442-3800
Fax: 608-442-3851
Email: mary.oleson@wismed.org
http://www.wisconsinmedicalsociety.org/foundation
Purpose: To aid students who are training to become physicians or nurses.
Eligibility: Applicants must be U.S. citizens. They must be full-time students enrolled in a medical school or nursing degree program at an accredited Wisconsin college or university. Rising undergraduate freshmen, undergraduate medical students and nursing students enrolled in a less than two-year program are ineligible. Preference will be given to Wisconsin residents and to applicants who are planning to practice in Wisconsin. Selection is based on academic merit, personal qualities, recommendations and financial need.
Target applicants: College students. Graduate school students. Adult students.
Amount: Varies.
Number of awards: Varies.
Deadline: April 1.
How to apply: Applications are available online. An application form, personal statement, transcript and two recommendation letters are required.
Exclusive: Visit www.UltimateScholarshipBook.com and enter code WI158112 for updates on this award.

(1582) • John Dawe Dental Education Fund

Hawaii Community Foundation - Scholarships
1164 Bishop Street, Suite 800
Honolulu, HI 96813
Phone: 888-731-3863
Fax: 808-521-6286
Email: scholarships@hcf-hawaii.org
http://www.hawaiicommunityfoundation.org
Purpose: To provide financial assistance to Hawaii students pursuing careers in dental professions.
Eligibility: Applicants must be enrolled full-time in a school of dentistry, dental hygiene or dental assisting. They must have a GPA of 2.7 or higher. Two letters of recommendation and a letter from the applicant's school confirming enrollment in the dentistry or dental hygiene program are required.
Target applicants: High school students. College students. Graduate school students. Adult students.
Minimum GPA: 2.7
Amount: Varies.
Number of awards: Varies.
Deadline: March 1.
How to apply: To apply, register online, complete the online application and select the scholarships to which you wish to apply. In addition, mail the supporting materials: printed confirmation page from the online application, personal statement, copy of Student Aid Report (SAR) available at www.fafsa.ed.gov and official transcript.
Exclusive: Visit www.UltimateScholarshipBook.com and enter code HA158212 for updates on this award.

(1583) • John R. Lillard VAOC Scholarship

Virginia Department of Aviation
5702 Gulfstream Road
Richmond, VA 23250
Phone: 804-236-3624
Fax: 804-236-3635
Email: director@doav.virginia.gov
http://www.doav.virginia.gov

Purpose: To aid Virginia high school seniors who are planning for careers in aviation.

Eligibility: Applicants must be Virginia high school seniors who have an unweighted GPA of 3.75 or higher. They must be accepted into or enrolled in an aviation-related program at an accredited postsecondary institution and must have plans to pursue a career in aviation. Selection is based on academic merit, personal essay, leadership skills and financial need.

Target applicants: High school students.
Minimum GPA: 3.75
Amount: $3,000.
Number of awards: Varies.
Deadline: February 18.

How to apply: Applications are available online. An application form, personal essay, official transcript, verification of college acceptance or enrollment, list of extracurricular activities and up to three recommendation letters are required.

Exclusive: Visit www.UltimateScholarshipBook.com and enter code VI158312 for updates on this award.

(1584) • John Schwartz Scholarship

American Institute of Wine and Food - Pacific Northwest Chapter
213-37 39th Avenue
Box 216
Bayside, NY 11361
Phone: 800-274-2493
Email: bsteinmetz100@hotmail.com
http://www.aiwf.org

Purpose: To aid students pursuing culinary degrees.

Eligibility: Applicants must have been Washington State residents for at least two years, be enrolled in a Washington State accredited culinary or winemaking arts program and have a GPA of 3.0 or higher.

Target applicants: College students. Adult students.
Minimum GPA: 3.0
Amount: $1,500.
Number of awards: 4.
Deadline: Varies.

How to apply: Applications are available from your school's culinary or winemaking arts department. An application form, resume and references are required.

Exclusive: Visit www.UltimateScholarshipBook.com and enter code AM158412 for updates on this award.

(1585) • John W. Rogers Memorial Scholarship

Missouri Bankers Foundation
P.O. Box 57
207 East Capitol Avenue
Jefferson City, MO 65101
Phone: 573-636-8151
Fax: 573-634-2754
http://www.mobankers.com/content.aspx?id=8814

Purpose: To aid high school seniors who are planning to pursue higher education in agriculture or a banking-related subject.

Eligibility: Applicants must be graduating high school seniors who have plans to major in agriculture or a banking-related subject at the postsecondary level. Preference will be given to applicants who are planning to attend the University of Missouri-Columbia. Selection is based on the overall strength of the application.

Target applicants: High school students.
Amount: $500.
Number of awards: Varies.
Deadline: March 26.

How to apply: Applications are available online. An application form, official transcript, ACT scores, a list of extracurricular activities and two recommendation letters are required.

Exclusive: Visit www.UltimateScholarshipBook.com and enter code MI158512 for updates on this award.

(1586) • Joint Admissions Tuition Advantage Program Waiver

Massachusetts Department of Higher Education
Office of Student Financial Assistance
454 Broadway
Suite 200
Revere, MA 02151
Phone: 617-727-9420
Fax: 617-727-0667
Email: osfa@osfa.mass.edu
http://www.osfa.mass.edu/default.asp

Purpose: To encourage community college graduates to enter into a four-year program by awarding a tuition waiver equal to 33 percent of the resident tuition rate at a state college or participating university.

Eligibility: Applicants must be enrolled in a state college or university and have completed an associate degree at a public community college within the prior calendar year as a participant in the Joint Admissions Program with a minimum GPA of 3.0.

Target applicants: College students. Adult students.
Minimum GPA: 3.0
Amount: Up to 33 percent of state tuition.
Number of awards: Varies.
Scholarship may be renewable.
Deadline: Varies.

How to apply: Contact the financial aid office at the institution attending or planning to attend for application forms and deadlines.

Exclusive: Visit www.UltimateScholarshipBook.com and enter code MA158612 for updates on this award.

(1587) • Jose Marti Scholarship Challenge Grant

Florida Department of Education
Office of Student Financial Assistance
1940 N. Monroe Street
Suite 70
Tallahassee, FL 32303-4759
Phone: 888-827-2004
Fax: 850-245-9667
Email: osfa@fldoe.org
http://www.floridastudentfinancialaid.org

Purpose: To help Florida students in need who are of Hispanic origin.

Eligibility: Applicants must have been born in or have a natural parent who was born in either Mexico or Spain, or a Hispanic country of the Caribbean, Central or South America, regardless of race. Students must plan to attend Florida public or eligible private institutions as

undergraduate or graduate students, but graduating high school seniors get preference.
Target applicants: High school students. College students. Graduate school students. Adult students.
Minimum GPA: 3.0
Amount: $2,000.
Number of awards: Varies.
Scholarship may be renewable.
Deadline: April 1.
How to apply: Applicants must submit the initial student Florida Financial Aid Application by April 1 and the Free Application for Federal Student Aid (FAFSA) by May 15.
Exclusive: Visit www.UltimateScholarshipBook.com and enter code FL158712 for updates on this award.

(1588) • Joseph A. Murphy Scholarship

New England Water Works Association
125 Hopping Brook Road
Holliston, MA 01746
Phone: 508-893-7979
Email: tmacelhaney@preloadinc.com
http://www.newwa.org
Purpose: To aid NEWWA student members who are majoring in civil engineering, environmental engineering, business or a related subject.
Eligibility: Applicants must be student members of the New England Water Works Association (NEWWA). They must be majoring in environmental engineering, civil engineering, business or a related subject. Selection is based on the overall strength of the application.
Target applicants: College students. Adult students.
Amount: $1,500.
Number of awards: 1.
Deadline: April 1.
How to apply: Applications are available online. An application form, official transcript and one letter of recommendation are required.
Exclusive: Visit www.UltimateScholarshipBook.com and enter code NE158812 for updates on this award.

(1589) • Joseph Shinoda Memorial Scholarship

Joseph Shinoda Memorial Scholarship Foundation Inc.
c/o Barbara A. McCaleb
Executive Secretary
234 Via La Paz
San Luis Obispo, CA 93401
http://www.shinodascholarship.org
Purpose: To aid students who are preparing for careers in commercial floriculture.
Eligibility: Applicants must be enrolled at an accredited four-year institution in the U.S. or at a community college located in California and be rising undergraduate sophomores, juniors or seniors. They must be majoring in a floriculture-related subject and be planning to pursue a career in domestic floriculture in the U.S. after graduation. Selection is based on academic merit, character, work experience and financial need.
Target applicants: College students. Adult students.
Amount: Up to $5,000.
Number of awards: Varies.
Deadline: March 30.
How to apply: Applications are available online. An application form, an official transcript and two letters of recommendation are required.
Exclusive: Visit www.UltimateScholarshipBook.com and enter code JO158912 for updates on this award.

(1590) • Joseph W. Mayo ALS Scholarship

Maine Community Foundation
245 Main Street
Ellsworth, ME 04605
Phone: 207-667-9735
Fax: 207-667-0447
Email: jwarren@mainecf.org
http://www.mainecf.org
Purpose: To support students who are related to or caring for Amyotrophic Lateral Sclerosis (ALS)/Lou Gehrig's Disease patients.
Eligibility: Students must currently be attending a post-secondary school. While their current school may be in any state, they must have graduated from a Maine high school or received a GED in Maine. Applicants should also be related to an ALS patient in one of the following ways: children, stepchildren, grandchildren, spouses, domestic partners or primary caregivers.
Target applicants: College students. Adult students.
Amount: Varies.
Number of awards: Varies.
Deadline: May 1.
How to apply: Applications are available online.
Exclusive: Visit www.UltimateScholarshipBook.com and enter code MA159012 for updates on this award.

(1591) • Judge William F. Cooper Scholarship

Center for Scholarship Administration
Wachovia Accounts
4320-G Wade Hampton Boulevard
Taylors, SC 29687
Phone: 866-608-0001
Email: wachoviascholars@bellsouth.net
https://www.csascholars.org/index.php
Purpose: To provide financial assistance to female students from Georgia who plan to attend college in South Carolina.
Eligibility: Applicants must be high school seniors who have financial need. Students must have an acceptable GPA and plan to study in any field except law, theology or medicine. Nursing is acceptable.
Target applicants: High school students.
Amount: Varies.
Number of awards: Varies.
Scholarship may be renewable.
Deadline: March 15.
How to apply: Applications are available online.
Exclusive: Visit www.UltimateScholarshipBook.com and enter code CE159112 for updates on this award.

(1592) • Juliette M. Atherton Scholarship - Seminary Studies

Hawaii Community Foundation - Scholarships
1164 Bishop Street, Suite 800
Honolulu, HI 96813
Phone: 888-731-3863
Fax: 808-521-6286
Email: scholarships@hcf-hawaii.org
http://www.hawaiicommunityfoundation.org
Purpose: To support Hawaii students who plan to be ordained in the Protestant faith.
Eligibility: Students must be attending a graduate school of theology.
Target applicants: Graduate school students. Adult students.
Amount: Varies.

Number of awards: Varies.
Deadline: March 1.
How to apply: To apply, register online, complete the online application and select the scholarships to which you wish to apply. In addition, mail the supporting materials: printed confirmation page from the online application, personal statement, copy of Student Aid Report (SAR) available at www.fafsa.ed.gov and official transcript.
Exclusive: Visit www.UltimateScholarshipBook.com and enter code HA159212 for updates on this award.

(1593) • KAB Broadcast Scholarship Program

Kansas Association of Broadcasters
2709 SW 29th Street
Topeka, KS 66614
Phone: 785-235-1307
Fax: 785-233-3052
Email: info@kab.net
http://www.kab.net
Purpose: To support future broadcasters.
Eligibility: Applicants must be Kansas residents and be attending a Kansas college or university the fall semester after application. Those attending four-year institutions must be entering the junior or senior year, and those attending two-year institutions must be entering their sophomore year. Students must enroll in a broadcast or related curriculum for at least 12 hours. A GPA of 2.5 or greater is required.
Target applicants: College students. Adult students.
Minimum GPA: 2.5
Amount: Varies.
Number of awards: Varies.
Deadline: May 1.
How to apply: Applications are available online. An application form, essay and up to three letters of recommendation are required.
Exclusive: Visit www.UltimateScholarshipBook.com and enter code KA159312 for updates on this award.

(1594) • Kansas Agricultural Aviation Association Scholarship

Kansas Agricultural Aviation Association
P.O. Box 12010
Wichita, KS 67277
Phone: 316-617-5680
Fax: 316-945-2330
http://www.ksagaviation.org
Purpose: To aid Kansas students who are pursuing higher education in Kansas.
Eligibility: Applicants must be Kansas residents who are enrolled at or planning to enroll at a Kansas postsecondary institution. They must be recommended for the award by a member of the Kansas Agricultural Aviation Association (KAAA) and must demonstrate financial need. Preference will be given to students who are majoring in or planning to major in agriculture, agricultural business, aviation or engineering. Selection is based on academic merit and financial need.
Target applicants: High school students. College students. Adult students.
Amount: $1,000.
Number of awards: Varies.
Deadline: March 15.
How to apply: Applications are available online. An application form, transcript, financial need statement and two recommendation letters are required.
Exclusive: Visit www.UltimateScholarshipBook.com and enter code KA159412 for updates on this award.

(1595) • Kansas City IFMA Scholarship

International Facility Management Association - Kansas City Chapter
P.O. Box 412591
Kansas City, MO 64141
Phone: 816-329.5009
Email: info@kcifma.com
http://www.kcifma.com
Purpose: To aid Kansas and Missouri students who are planning for careers in facility management.
Eligibility: Applicants must be full-time undergraduates, full-time graduate students or part-time graduate students enrolled at a postsecondary institution located in Kansas or Missouri. They must be majoring in a subject that is related to facility management (such as business operations, construction science, interior design, environmental design, architecture or engineering). Selection is based on stated career goals, GPA, recommendations, extracurricular activities and applicant interview.
Target applicants: College students. Graduate school students. Adult students.
Amount: Varies.
Number of awards: Varies.
Deadline: March 19.
How to apply: Applications are available online. An application form, letter of professional intent, two letters of recommendation and an official transcript are required.
Exclusive: Visit www.UltimateScholarshipBook.com and enter code IN159512 for updates on this award.

(1596) • Kansas Comprehensive Grants

Kansas Board of Regents
Curtis State Office Building
Suite 520
1000 SW Jackson Street
Topeka, KS 66612
Phone: 785-296-3421
Fax: 785-296-0983
Email: dlindeman@ksbor.org
http://www.kansasregents.org
Purpose: To help needy Kansas students attend Kansas colleges and universities.
Eligibility: Applicants must be enrolled full-time at an eligible Kansas institution. Selection is based on financial need.
Target applicants: College students. Adult students.
Amount: $100-$3,500.
Number of awards: Varies.
Deadline: April 1.
How to apply: Complete the Free Application for Federal Student Aid (FAFSA).
Exclusive: Visit www.UltimateScholarshipBook.com and enter code KA159612 for updates on this award.

(1597) • Kansas Ethnic Minority Scholarship

Kansas Board of Regents
Curtis State Office Building
Suite 520
1000 SW Jackson Street
Topeka, KS 66612

Phone: 785-296-3421
Fax: 785-296-0983
Email: dlindeman@ksbor.org
http://www.kansasregents.org
Purpose: To aid outstanding Kansas minority students with financial need.
Eligibility: Applicants must be African American, Native Indian or Alaskan Native, Asian or Pacific Islander or Hispanic. Priority is given to graduating high school seniors. Applicants must have one of the following: a minimum ACT score of 21 or SAT score of 816, a minimum 3.0 GPA, a top 33 percent ranking in their high school class, completion of Kansas Scholars Curriculum, selection by National Merit Corporation or selection by College Board as a Hispanic Scholar.
Target applicants: High school students. College students. Adult students.
Minimum GPA: 3.0
Amount: $1,850.
Number of awards: Varies.
Scholarship may be renewable.
Deadline: April.
How to apply: Applications are available online.
Exclusive: Visit www.UltimateScholarshipBook.com and enter code KA159712 for updates on this award.

(1598) • Kansas Nutrition Council Scholarship

Kansas Nutrition Council
Barbara Beier, Awards and Scholarship Committee Chair
Shawnee County Health Agency
1615 SW 8th Street
Topeka, KS 66606
Phone: 785-368-2155
Email: barbara.beier@snco.us
http://www.sne.org/KansasNutritionCouncil.htm
Purpose: To aid Kansas students who are pursuing higher education in nutrition, family and consumer sciences or a related subject.
Eligibility: Applicants must be Kansas residents who are rising undergraduate juniors, rising undergraduate seniors or graduate students enrolled at a college or university located in Kansas. They must be majoring in nutrition, dietetics, family and consumer sciences or a related subject. Selection is based on the overall strength of the application.
Target applicants: College students. Graduate school students. Adult students.
Amount: $1,000.
Number of awards: 1.
Deadline: March 1.
How to apply: Applications are available online. An application form, personal essay, two recommendation letters and an official transcript are required.
Exclusive: Visit www.UltimateScholarshipBook.com and enter code KA159812 for updates on this award.

(1599) • Kansas Oratorical Contest

American Legion, Department of Kansas
1314 SW Topeka Boulevard
Topeka, KS 66612
Phone: 785-232-9315
Fax: 785-232-1399
http://www.ksamlegion.org
Purpose: To enhance high school students' experience with and understanding of the U.S. Constitution. The contest will help develop students' leadership skills and civic appreciation, as well as the ability to deliver thoughtful, insightful orations regarding U.S. citizenship and its inherent responsibilities.
Eligibility: Applicants must be high school students under the age of 20 who are U.S. citizens or legal residents and residents of the state. Students first give an oration within their state and winners compete at the national level. The oration must be related to the Constitution of the United States focusing on the duties and obligations citizens have to the government. It must be in English and be between eight and ten minutes. There is also an assigned topic which is posted on the website, and it should be between three and five minutes.
Target applicants: High school students.
Amount: $150-$1,500.
Number of awards: Varies.
Deadline: January 15.
How to apply: Applications are available from schools and local American Legion Posts.
Exclusive: Visit www.UltimateScholarshipBook.com and enter code AM159912 for updates on this award.

(1600) • Karen B. Lewis Career Education Scholarship

Virginia Business and Professional Women's Foundation
P.O. Box 4842
McLean, VA 22103-4842
Phone: 800-525-3729
Email: bpwfoundation@act.org
http://www.vabpwfoundation.org
Purpose: To support female students who are enrolled in technical schools or career training programs.
Eligibility: Applicants must be at least 18 years of age and be accepted into an accredited training program in the state of Virginia. Students must complete their course of study within two years. Applicants must show financial need and have concrete plans to use their training for advancement in business, industry or trade occupations.
Target applicants: High school students. College students. Adult students.
Amount: $500-$1,000.
Number of awards: Varies.
Deadline: April 1.
How to apply: Applications are available online.
Exclusive: Visit www.UltimateScholarshipBook.com and enter code VI160012 for updates on this award.

(1601) • Katherine H. Dilley Scholarship Fund

Arizona State Society Daughters of the American Revolution
Email: ranaholc@netzero.net
http://www.rootsweb.ancestry.com/~azsocdar/
Purpose: To aid students who are planning for careers in occupational therapy or physical therapy.
Eligibility: Applicants must be enrolled in or planning to enroll in a degree program in occupational therapy or physical therapy at an accredited institution of higher learning. Selection is based on the overall strength of the application.
Target applicants: High school students. College students. Graduate school students. Adult students.
Amount: Varies.
Number of awards: Varies.
Scholarship may be renewable.
Deadline: February 1.
How to apply: Applications are available by request. A letter of application, financial aid form, official transcript and two letters of recommendation are required.

Exclusive: Visit www.UltimateScholarshipBook.com and enter code AR160112 for updates on this award.

(1602) • Kathryn D. Sullivan Science and Engineering Fellowship

South Carolina Space Grant Consortium
Department of Geology and Environmental Sciences
College of Charleston
66 George Street
Charleston, SC 29424
Phone: 843-953-5463
Fax: 843-953-5446
Email: scozzarot@cofc.edu
http://www.cofc.edu

Purpose: To aid rising undergraduate seniors who are studying the natural sciences, technology or engineering.
Eligibility: Applicants must be U.S. citizens and must be sponsored by a faculty member. Selection is based on recommendation letters, academic merit, faculty sponsorship and stated academic goals and interests in science, technology and engineering.
Target applicants: College students. Adult students.
Amount: $7,000.
Number of awards: 1.
Deadline: February 4.
How to apply: Applications are available online. An application form, personal essay, two recommendation letters, a transcript and a resume are required.
Exclusive: Visit www.UltimateScholarshipBook.com and enter code SO160212 for updates on this award.

(1603) • Kentucky Tuition Grant

Kentucky Higher Education Assistance Authority
P.O. Box 798
Frankfort, KY 40602
Phone: 800-928-8926
Email: blane@kheaa.com
http://www.kheaa.com

Purpose: To provide grants to Kentucky residents to attend the Commonwealth's independent colleges.
Eligibility: Applicants must be full-time students enrolled at eligible private institutions. Students must not be enrolled in divinity, theology or religious education degree programs. This is a need-based program.
Target applicants: College students. Adult students.
Amount: $200-$2,964.
Number of awards: Varies.
Deadline: Varies.
How to apply: Complete the Free Application for Federal Student Aid (FAFSA).
Exclusive: Visit www.UltimateScholarshipBook.com and enter code KE160312 for updates on this award.

(1604) • Kentucky Veterans Tuition Waiver Program

Kentucky Department of Veterans Affairs
Attn.: Tuition Waiver Coordinator
321 W. Main Street
Suite 390
Louisville, KY 40202
Phone: 502-595-4447
Email: barbaraa.hale@ky.gov
http://veterans.ky.gov

Purpose: To assist the families of Kentucky veterans in obtaining higher education.
Eligibility: Applicants must be children, stepchildren, adopted children, spouses or unremarried widows/widowers of Kentucky veterans and must be age 26 or younger. The veteran must have died in active duty or as a result of a service-connected disability, have a service-connected 100 percent disability, or have served during wartime and be totally disabled or have died for any reason.
Target applicants: High school students. College students. Adult students.
Amount: Full Tuition Waiver.
Number of awards: Varies.
Scholarship may be renewable.
Deadline: Varies.
How to apply: Applications are available online.
Exclusive: Visit www.UltimateScholarshipBook.com and enter code KE160412 for updates on this award.

(1605) • Kids' Chance of Arizona Scholarships

Kids' Chance of Arizona
P.O. Box 36753
Phoenix, AZ 85067-6753
Phone: 602-253-4360
http://www.azkidschance.org/

Purpose: To provide financial assistance to children of Arizona workers who have been killed or injured on the job.
Eligibility: Applicants must be children of parents who were permanently or catastrophically injured or killed in an employment-related accident. They must be Arizona residents, and the parent's death or injury must have caused a major decrease in the family's income.
Target applicants: High school students. College students.
Amount: Varies.
Number of awards: Varies.
Deadline: Varies.
How to apply: Applications are available online.
Exclusive: Visit www.UltimateScholarshipBook.com and enter code KI160512 for updates on this award.

(1606) • Kids' Chance of Indiana Scholarship Program

Kids' Chance of Indiana Inc.
721 East Broadway
Fortville, IN 46040
Phone: 317-485-0043 x123
Email: president@kidschancein.org
http://www.kidschancein.org

Purpose: To assist children of Indiana workers who have been injured or killed on the job in obtaining higher education.
Eligibility: Applicants must be children of Indiana workers who were fatally or catastrophically injured in a work-related accident or as a result of an occupational disease that is compensable by the state's workers' compensation board. They must be 16 to 25 years of age.
Target applicants: High school students. College students.
Amount: $500-$3,000.
Number of awards: Varies.
Deadline: Varies.
How to apply: Applications are available online.
Exclusive: Visit www.UltimateScholarshipBook.com and enter code KI160612 for updates on this award.

(1607) • Kids' Chance of Louisiana Scholarships

Louisiana Bar Foundation
601 St. Charles Avenue
Third Floor
New Orleans, LA 70130
Phone: 504-561-1046
Fax: 504-566-1926
Email: kidschance@raisingthebar.org
http://www.raisingthebar.org

Purpose: To assist students whose parents were killed or injured on the job.
Eligibility: Applicants must be dependents of workers who died or were permanently disabled in a compensable work-related accident in Louisiana. They must be Louisiana residents 16 to 25 years of age, maintain a C average or higher and demonstrate financial need. Applicants must plan to work toward an associate's or bachelor's degree, certificate or license at an accredited Louisiana institution of higher learning.
Target applicants: High school students. College students.
Minimum GPA: 2.0
Amount: $500-$3,000.
Number of awards: Varies.
Deadline: February 28.
How to apply: Applications are available online.
Exclusive: Visit www.UltimateScholarshipBook.com and enter code LO160712 for updates on this award.

(1608) • Kids' Chance of Maryland Scholarships

Kids' Chance of Maryland
P.O. Box 20262
Baltimore, MD 21284
Phone: 410-832-4702
Fax: 410-832-4726
Email: info@kidschance-md.org
http://www.kidschance-md.org

Purpose: To provide financial assistance to children whose parents were killed or seriously injured on the job.
Eligibility: Applicants must be children of parents who were permanently or catastrophically injured or killed in an employment-related accident. They must be Maryland residents 16 to 25 years of age, and the parent's death or injury must have caused a major decrease in the family's income.
Target applicants: High school students. College students.
Amount: Up to Full Tuition.
Number of awards: Varies.
Deadline: Varies.
How to apply: Applications are available online.
Exclusive: Visit www.UltimateScholarshipBook.com and enter code KI160812 for updates on this award.

(1609) • Kids' Chance of Missouri Scholarships

Kids' Chance Inc. of Missouri
P.O. Box 410384
St. Louis, MO 63141
Phone: 314-997-3390
Email: susgrp@charter.net
http://www.mokidschance.org

Purpose: To assist children whose parents have been injured or killed in work related accidents.
Eligibility: Applicants must be Missouri students whose parent has died or sustained a serious injury in a work-related accident that is compensable under Missouri Workers' Compensation Law. They must demonstrate financial need.
Target applicants: High school students. College students. Adult students.
Amount: Up to tuition, books, supplies, housing, meals and other expenses.
Number of awards: Varies.
Scholarship may be renewable.
Deadline: April 30.
How to apply: Applications are available online. A transcript, two letters of recommendation, a brief narrative of the parent's accident, last year's tax returns and documentation of the parent's injury or death are required.
Exclusive: Visit www.UltimateScholarshipBook.com and enter code KI160912 for updates on this award.

(1610) • Kids' Chance of North Carolina Scholarships

Kids' Chance of North Carolina Inc.
P.O. Box 470426
Charlotte, NC 28247-0426
Phone: 704-264-9111
Email: info@kidschancenc.org
http://www.kidschancenc.org

Purpose: To provide financial assistance to North Carolina students whose parents were seriously injured or died on the job.
Eligibility: Applicants must be students between the ages of 16 and 25 whose parents were killed or injured as a result of a compensable work-related injury or illness. The parent's death or injury must have resulted in a major decrease in family income.
Target applicants: High school students. College students.
Amount: Up to $5,000.
Number of awards: Varies.
Deadline: Varies.
How to apply: Applications are available online.
Exclusive: Visit www.UltimateScholarshipBook.com and enter code KI161012 for updates on this award.

(1611) • Kids' Chance of Pennsylvania Scholarships

Kids' Chance of Pennsylvania
P.O. Box 543
Pottstown, PA 19464
Phone: 484-945-2104
Fax: 610-970-7520
Email: info@kidschanceofpa.org
http://www.kidschanceofpa.org

Purpose: To provide financial assistance to students with parents who have been killed or catastrophically injured due to work-related accidents or illnesses.
Eligibility: Applicants must be Pennsylvania students whose parent was killed or seriously injured in a compensable work-related accident. They must be 16 to 25 years of age and be accepted to an accredited institution of higher learning.
Target applicants: High school students. College students.
Amount: Up to $5,000.
Number of awards: Varies.
Deadline: April 15.
How to apply: Applications are available online.
Exclusive: Visit www.UltimateScholarshipBook.com and enter code KI161112 for updates on this award.

(1612) • Kids' Chance of Washington Scholarships

Kids' Chance of Washington
P.O. Box 185
Olympia, WA 98507-0185
Phone: 800-572-5762
Fax: 360-943-2333
Email: debbie@wscff.org
http://www.kidschancewa.com

Purpose: To provide financial assistance to children and spouses of Washington workers who have been killed or injured on the job.
Eligibility: Applicants must be children or spouses of Washington workers who have died or been seriously injured due to a work-related injury. They must also have financial need.
Target applicants: High school students. College students. Adult students.
Amount: Varies.
Number of awards: Varies.
Deadline: Varies.
How to apply: Applications are available online.
Exclusive: Visit www.UltimateScholarshipBook.com and enter code KI161212 for updates on this award.

(1613) • Kids' Chance of West Virginia Scholarships

Greater Kanawha Valley Foundation
1600 Huntington Square
900 Lee Street, East
Charleston, WV 25301
Phone: 304-346-3620
Fax: 304-346-3640
Email: tgkvf@tgkvf.org
http://www.tgkvf.org

Purpose: To provide financial assistance to children of workers who were disabled or fatally injured on the job.
Eligibility: Applicants must be children between the ages of 16 and 25 whose parent was permanently and totally disabled or fatally injured in a compensable work-related accident in West Virginia. Academic performance, leadership and contributions to school and community are considered.
Target applicants: High school students. College students.
Amount: $1,000.
Number of awards: Varies.
Deadline: January 15.
How to apply: Applications are available online.
Exclusive: Visit www.UltimateScholarshipBook.com and enter code GR161312 for updates on this award.

(1614) • Kilbourn-Sawyer Memorial Scholarship

Vermont Student Assistance Corporation
10 East Allen Street
P.O. Box 2000
Winooski, VT 05404
Phone: 800-882-4166
Fax: 802-654-3765
Email: info@vsac.org
http://www.vsac.org

Purpose: To aid Vermont students who are planning to pursue higher education in a construction-related field.
Eligibility: Applicants must be Vermont residents, U.S. citizens or eligible non-citizens and graduating high school seniors. They must demonstrate academic achievement and financial need and plan to pursue higher education in construction or engineering at an institution that has been approved for federal Title IV funding. Selection is based on personal essays, academic merit, recommendation letter and financial need.
Target applicants: High school students.
Amount: $2,000.
Number of awards: 1.
Deadline: March 5.
How to apply: Applications are available online. An application form, official transcript, academic certification form, two personal essays and one recommendation letter are required.
Exclusive: Visit www.UltimateScholarshipBook.com and enter code VE161412 for updates on this award.

(1615) • Kimber Richter Family Scholarship

Community Foundation of Western Massachusetts
1500 Main Street
P.O. Box 15769
Springfield, MA 01115
Phone: 413-732-2858
Fax: 413-733-8565
Email: scholar@communityfoundation.org
http://www.communityfoundation.org

Purpose: To help students of the Baha'i faith from western Massachusetts.
Eligibility: Applicants must attend a U.S. college or university part-time or full-time. Application forms, transcripts and Student Aid Reports are required. Selection is based on financial need and academic merit.
Target applicants: High school students. College students. Graduate school students. Adult students.
Amount: Varies.
Number of awards: Varies.
Deadline: March 31.
How to apply: Applications are available online and by phone.
Exclusive: Visit www.UltimateScholarshipBook.com and enter code CO161512 for updates on this award.

(1616) • Kittie M. Fairey Educational Fund Scholarships

Kittie M. Fairey Educational Fund Scholarship Program
4320-G Wade Hampton Boulevard
Taylors, SC 29687
Phone: 866-608-0001
Email: sandralee41@bellsouth.net
https://www.csascholars.org/index.php

Purpose: To help South Carolina high school seniors who want to attend colleges or universities in the state.
Eligibility: Applicants must be high school seniors with a minimum combined SAT score of 900 who plan to be full-time students pursuing a bachelor's of arts or bachelor's of science degree. Selection is based on academic merit and financial need, and the applicants' parents' adjusted gross income must not exceed $40,000. A transcript, recommendation letter, essay and parents' tax documents are required. Employees of Wachovia Bank are not eligible.
Target applicants: High school students.
Minimum GPA: 3.0
Amount: Up to one-half tuition and room and board.
Number of awards: Varies.
Scholarship may be renewable.
Deadline: November 15.
How to apply: Applications are available online.

Exclusive: Visit www.UltimateScholarshipBook.com and enter code KI161612 for updates on this award.

(1617) • Kohl Excellence Scholarships

Herb Kohl Educational Foundation Inc.
P.O. Box 7841
Madison, WI 53707
Phone: 608-266-1098
Email: john.johnson@dpi.state.wi.us
http://www.kohleducation.org/students

Purpose: To assist Wisconsin students in obtaining higher education.
Eligibility: Applicants must be Wisconsin residents who are graduating high school in the year of application. They must be in good standing with their schools and demonstrate the potential for success in postsecondary education. Deadlines vary by school but are generally the second week of November.
Target applicants: High school students.
Amount: $1,000.
Number of awards: 100.
Deadline: November.
How to apply: Applications are available online starting in October of each year and from Wisconsin high schools in mid-September. Three letters of recommendation are required.
Exclusive: Visit www.UltimateScholarshipBook.com and enter code HE161712 for updates on this award.

(1618) • L.G. Wells Scholarship

Confederation of Oregon School Administrators
707 13th Street SE
Suite 100
Salem, OR 97301
Phone: 503-581-3141
Fax: 503-581-9840
Email: sera@cosa.k12.or.us
http://www.cosa.k12.or.us

Purpose: To aid Oregon students who are planning to pursue undergraduate studies at an Oregon college or university.
Eligibility: Applicants must be graduating seniors at an Oregon public high school, have a GPA of 3.5 or higher and be active participants in extracurricular and community-related activities. They must have plans to attend an Oregon institution of higher learning and must plan to begin postsecondary studies during the fall following high school graduation. They must demonstrate financial need or must have plans to major in education or engineering. Applicants must be formally endorsed by a member of the Confederation of Oregon School Administrators (COSA). Selection is based on the overall strength of the application.
Target applicants: High school students.
Minimum GPA: 3.5
Amount: $1,000.
Number of awards: 3.
Deadline: February 25.
How to apply: Applications are available online. An application form, endorsement from a COSA member, personal statement and transcript are required.
Exclusive: Visit www.UltimateScholarshipBook.com and enter code CO161812 for updates on this award.

(1619) • La Plaza Scholarship Fund

Central Indiana Community Foundation
615 North Alabama Street
Suite 119
Indianapolis, IN 46204-1498
Phone: 317-634-2423
Fax: 317-684-0943
http://www.cicf.org

Purpose: To provide financial assistance to Indiana residents who are self-motivated and have financial need.
Eligibility: Applicants must be high school seniors who have demonstrated financial need and self-motivation. They must have a GPA of 2.7 or higher and plan to attend an Indiana college or university. Preference is given to Hispanic students and to those attending four-year degree programs.
Target applicants: High school students.
Minimum GPA: 2.7
Amount: Varies.
Number of awards: Varies.
Deadline: March 5.
How to apply: Applications are available online.
Exclusive: Visit www.UltimateScholarshipBook.com and enter code CE161912 for updates on this award.

(1620) • Laheenae Rebecca Hart Gay Scholarship

Hawaii Community Foundation - Scholarships
1164 Bishop Street, Suite 800
Honolulu, HI 96813
Phone: 888-731-3863
Fax: 808-521-6286
Email: scholarships@hcf-hawaii.org
http://www.hawaiicommunityfoundation.org

Purpose: To support Hawaii students who are pursuing degrees in art.
Eligibility: Students may major in any art field except performing arts, film arts or culinary arts.
Target applicants: High school students. College students. Adult students.
Amount: Varies.
Number of awards: Varies.
Deadline: March 1.
How to apply: To apply, register online, complete the online application and select the scholarships to which you wish to apply. In addition, mail the supporting materials: printed confirmation page from the online application, personal statement, copy of Student Aid Report (SAR) available at www.fafsa.ed.gov and official transcript.
Exclusive: Visit www.UltimateScholarshipBook.com and enter code HA162012 for updates on this award.

(1621) • Lambeth Family Scholarship

Seattle Foundation
1200 Fifth Avenue
Suite 1300
Seattle, WA 98101-3151
Phone: 206-622-2294
Fax: 206-622-7673
Email: info@seattlefoundation.org
http://www.seattlefoundation.org

Purpose: To aid students who are pursuing higher education in computer science, the natural sciences, business, mathematics or engineering.

Eligibility: Applicants must be enrolled in a degree-granting program in business, computer science, engineering, mathematics or the natural sciences. Selection is based on the overall strength of the application.
Target applicants: High school students.
Amount: $3,000.
Number of awards: 8.
Deadline: March 1.
How to apply: Applications are available online. An application form and supporting documents are required.
Exclusive: Visit www.UltimateScholarshipBook.com and enter code SE162112 for updates on this award.

(1622) • Lapiz Family Scholarship

Asian Pacific Fund
225 Bush Street
Suite 590
San Francisco, CA 94104
Phone: 415-433-6859
Fax: 415-433-2425
Email: scholarship@asianpacificfund.org
http://www.asianpacificfund.org
Purpose: To support students from farm working backgrounds who attend the University of California.
Eligibility: Applicants must be full-time undergraduate students at University of California (preference given to students at UC Davis and UC Santa Cruz), be farm workers or the children of farm or migrant workers and have a minimum 3.0 GPA. The award is based on merit and financial need. Applicants should submit applications, transcripts, essays, resumes and Student Aid Reports.
Target applicants: College students. Adult students.
Minimum GPA: 3.0
Amount: $1,000.
Number of awards: 2.
Deadline: March 31.
How to apply: Applications are available online.
Exclusive: Visit www.UltimateScholarshipBook.com and enter code AS162212 for updates on this award.

(1623) • Laptop/Printer Grant

Michigan Council of Women in Technology Foundation
Attn.: Scholarship Committee
19011 Norwich Road
Livonia, MI 48152
Fax: 248-281-5391
Email: info@mcwt.org
http://www.mcwtf.org
Purpose: To help female students who need computers.
Eligibility: Applicants must be Michigan residents who are pursuing degrees in information systems, business applications, computer science, computer engineering, software engineering or information security and need a laptop to achieve their goals. Students must have a GPA of 2.8 or higher. Selection criteria include GPA, essay, technology-related activities, letters of recommendation, community service and completeness of application.
Target applicants: High school students. College students. Graduate school students. Adult students.
Minimum GPA: 2.8
Amount: Up to $2,000.
Number of awards: 3.
Deadline: January 31.
How to apply: Applications are available online. An application form, transcript and letter of recommendation are required.
Exclusive: Visit www.UltimateScholarshipBook.com and enter code MI162312 for updates on this award.

(1624) • Last Dollar Grant

CollegeBound Foundation
Scholarship, Research and Retention Services
300 Water Street
Suite 300
Baltimore, MD 21202
Phone: 410-783-2905
Fax: 410-727-5786
Email: info@collegeboundfoundation.org
http://www.collegeboundfoundation.org
Purpose: To help Baltimore City public high school graduates who will attend Maryland colleges.
Eligibility: Applicants must be new graduates of Baltimore City public high schools, have family income of no more than $75,000 per year and contribute at least 15 percent of their college costs through self-help. Students must attend Bowie State University, Coppin State University, Frostburg State University, Morgan State University, St. Mary's College of Maryland, Towson University, University of Maryland College Park, University of Maryland Eastern Shore or Villa Julie College. Applicants must also attend the Transition to College Workshop and the Annual Scholars' Luncheon and other program events scheduled throughout the year. The Student Aid Report, college acceptance letters, financial aid award letter and transcript are required. The grant is given to students whose Expected Family Contribution and financial aid package are less than the cost to attend college. The award is renewable up to five years.
Target applicants: High school students.
Amount: $3,000.
Number of awards: Varies.
Scholarship may be renewable.
Deadline: March 1.
How to apply: Applications are available online.
Exclusive: Visit www.UltimateScholarshipBook.com and enter code CO162412 for updates on this award.

(1625) • Latinos for Dental Careers Scholarship

California Dental Association
1201 K Street
Suite 1511
Phone: 800-232-7645
Email: foundationinfo@cda.org
http://www.cdafoundation.org
Purpose: To aid California dental school students of Latino descent.
Eligibility: Applicants must be enrolled in or accepted into a California dental school as full-time students. They must be of Latino descent and must be preparing for a career as a dentist or dental hygienist. Selection is based on the overall strength of the application.
Target applicants: High school students. College students. Graduate school students. Adult students.
Amount: Up to $1,000.
Number of awards: Varies.
Scholarship may be renewable.
Deadline: April 30.
How to apply: Applications are available online. An application form and supporting materials are required.
Exclusive: Visit www.UltimateScholarshipBook.com and enter code CA162512 for updates on this award.

(1626) • Laura N. Dowsett Fund

Hawaii Community Foundation - Scholarships
1164 Bishop Street, Suite 800
Honolulu, HI 96813
Phone: 888-731-3863
Fax: 808-521-6286
Email: scholarships@hcf-hawaii.org
http://www.hawaiicommunityfoundation.org

Purpose: To support Hawaii students who are majoring in occupational therapy.
Eligibility: Applicants must be college juniors, college seniors or graduate students.
Target applicants: College students. Graduate school students. Adult students.
Amount: Varies.
Number of awards: Varies.
Deadline: March 1.
How to apply: To apply, register online, complete the online application and select the scholarships to which you wish to apply. In addition, mail the supporting materials: printed confirmation page from the online application, personal statement, copy of Student Aid Report (SAR) available at www.fafsa.ed.gov and official transcript.
Exclusive: Visit www.UltimateScholarshipBook.com and enter code HA162612 for updates on this award.

(1627) • Law Enforcement Officer Memorial Scholarship

New Jersey Higher Education Student Assistance Authority
P.O. Box 540
Trenton, NJ 08625
Phone: 800-792-8670
Email: clientservices@hesaa.org
http://www.hesaa.org

Purpose: To support the dependent children of New Jersey law enforcement officers who were killed in active duty.
Eligibility: Students must be enrolled full-time in an undergraduate program at an approved New Jersey college.
Target applicants: High school students. College students. Adult students.
Amount: Varies.
Number of awards: Varies.
Scholarship may be renewable.
Deadline: October 1.
How to apply: Applications are available online.
Exclusive: Visit www.UltimateScholarshipBook.com and enter code NE162712 for updates on this award.

(1628) • Leadership for Diversity Scholarship

California School Library Association
950 Glenn Drive, Suite 150
Folsom, CA 95630
Phone: 916-447-2684
Fax: 916-447-2695
Email: csla@pacbell.net
http://www.csla.net/

Purpose: To encourage diversity in the library media teacher profession.
Eligibility: Applicants must be members of a traditionally underrepresented group attending or planning to attend an accredited library media teacher credential program and plan to work in California for three years after completing the program. Applicants must provide a 250-word statement about their qualifications, career goals, financial situation and commitment to supporting multicultural students and two letters of reference.
Target applicants: High school students. College students. Graduate school students. Adult students.
Amount: $1,500.
Number of awards: 1.
Deadline: April 30.
How to apply: Applications are available online.
Exclusive: Visit www.UltimateScholarshipBook.com and enter code CA162812 for updates on this award.

(1629) • Leadership Scholarship

Los Alamos National Laboratory Foundation
1302 Calle de la Merced
Suite A
Espanola, NM 87532
Phone: 505-753-8890
Fax: 505-753-8915
Email: info@lanlfoundation.org
http://www.lanlfoundation.org

Purpose: To support students from Northern New Mexico who have demonstrated leadership skills in their homes, schools and communities.
Eligibility: Students must have at least a 3.25 GPA, and they must have either an SAT score of at least 1350 or an ACT score of at least 19. Applicants must submit an essay and two letters of recommendation.
Target applicants: High school students. College students. Adult students.
Minimum GPA: 3.25
Amount: $2,500.
Number of awards: Varies.
Scholarship may be renewable.
Deadline: January 18.
How to apply: Applications are available online.
Exclusive: Visit www.UltimateScholarshipBook.com and enter code LO162912 for updates on this award.

(1630) • LEAF Scholarships

California Landscape Contractors Association
1491 River Park Drive
Suite 100
Sacramento, CA 95815
Phone: 916-830-2780
Fax: 916-830-2788
Email: web_admin@clca.org
http://www.clca.org

Purpose: To support ornamental horticulture students.
Eligibility: Applicants must attend an accredited California community college or state university and take a minimum of six credits.
Target applicants: College students. Adult students.
Amount: Varies.
Number of awards: Up to 20.
Deadline: April 15.
How to apply: Applications are available online. An application form, transcript and three letters of reference are required.
Exclusive: Visit www.UltimateScholarshipBook.com and enter code CA163012 for updates on this award.

(1631) • Lebanese American Heritage Club Scholarships

Lebanese American Heritage Club
4337 Maple Road
Dearborn, MI 48126
Phone: 313-846-8480
Fax: 313-846-2710
Email: lahc@lahc.org
http://www.lahc.org/scholarship/eligibility

Purpose: To encourage members of the Lebanese American community to become involved with regional and national media.

Eligibility: Applicants must U.S. citizens and Michigan residents, be of Arab descent and have a GPA of 3.0 or higher (3.5 for graduate students). They must maintain full-time status. Special consideration is given to students majoring in mass communications, political science and related fields, those enrolled or planning to attend institutions that contribute to the Arab American Scholarship Fund and those who did not receive the scholarship in the preceding year.

Target applicants: High school students. College students. Graduate school students. Adult students.

Minimum GPA: 3.0 for undergraduate applicants and 3.5 for graduate applicants

Amount: $1,000.

Number of awards: Varies.

Deadline: April 6.

How to apply: Applications are available online.

Exclusive: Visit www.UltimateScholarshipBook.com and enter code LE163112 for updates on this award.

(1632) • Lee-Jackson Foundation Scholarship

Lee-Jackson Foundation
P.O. Box 8121
Charlottesville, VA 22906
Phone: 434-977-1861
http://www.lee-jackson.org

Purpose: To honor the memories of Robert E. Lee and Thomas J. "Stonewall" Jackson and provide scholarships to Virginia students.

Eligibility: Applicants must be juniors, seniors or the equivalent in a Virginia public high school, private high school or homeschooling program and be residents of Virginia who plan to attend an accredited four-year college or university in the U.S. as full-time students. Financial need is not a basis for selection. Applicants must write an essay that demonstrates an appreciation for the character and virtues of Generals Robert E. Lee and Thomas "Stonewall" Jackson.

Target applicants: High school students.

Amount: $1,000-$10,000.

Number of awards: 27.

Deadline: Mid-December.

How to apply: Applications are available online and must be submitted to your school principal or guidance counselor by your school's deadline, which is typically mid-December.

Exclusive: Visit www.UltimateScholarshipBook.com and enter code LE163212 for updates on this award.

(1633) • Legacy Inc. Environmental Education Scholarship

Legacy Inc.
P.O. Box 3813
Montgomery, AL 36109
Phone: 334-270-5921
Fax: 334-270-5527
Email: info@legacyenved.org
http://www.legacyenved.org

Purpose: To aid Alabama students who are planning for careers in the environmental field.

Eligibility: Applicants must be Alabama residents who are rising undergraduate juniors, rising undergraduate seniors or graduate students enrolled at an Alabama postsecondary institution. They must have plans to pursue a career in an environment-related field. Selection is based on the overall strength of the application.

Target applicants: College students. Graduate school students. Adult students.

Amount: Up to $2,000.

Number of awards: Varies.

Deadline: May 1.

How to apply: Applications are available online. An application form, transcript and three recommendation letters are required.

Exclusive: Visit www.UltimateScholarshipBook.com and enter code LE163312 for updates on this award.

(1634) • Legacy of Learning Scholarships

Workers Compensation Fund
392 East 6400 South
Murray, UT 84107
Phone: 801-288-8060
Fax: 801-284-8983
Email: pjones@wcfgroup.com
http://www.wcfgroup.com

Purpose: To provide financial assistance to dependents of Utah workers killed in on-the-job accidents.

Eligibility: Applicants must be the spouse or child of a worker who died in an industrial accident that is compensable through the Workers Compensation Fund. Transcript with SAT or ACT scores and two letters of recommendation are required.

Target applicants: High school students. College students. Adult students.

Amount: Up to $1,500.

Number of awards: Varies.

Deadline: July 1.

How to apply: Applications are available online.

Exclusive: Visit www.UltimateScholarshipBook.com and enter code WO163412 for updates on this award.

(1635) • Legislative Endowment Scholarships

New Mexico Higher Education Department
2048 Galisteo Street
Santa Fe, NM 87505
Phone: 800-279-9777
Fax: 505-476-8454
Email: heather.romero@state.nm.us
http://hed.state.nm.us

Purpose: To support New Mexico undergraduate students with financial need attend postsecondary institutions in New Mexico.

Eligibility: Applicants must be undergraduate students who are New Mexico residents and attending public postsecondary institutions at least half-time in the state. Preference is given to adult students and transfer students from two-year New Mexico public postsecondary institutions to four-year institutions.

Target applicants: College students. Adult students.

Amount: $1,000-$2,500.

Number of awards: Varies.

Deadline: Varies.
How to apply: Contact your financial aid office and complete the Free Application for Federal Student Aid (FAFSA).
Exclusive: Visit www.UltimateScholarshipBook.com and enter code NE163512 for updates on this award.

(1636) · Legislative Essay Scholarship

Delaware Higher Education Commission
Carvel State Office Building
5th Floor
820 North French Street
Wilmington, DE 19801-3509
Phone: 800-292-7935
Fax: 302-577-6765
Email: dhec@doe.k12.de.us
http://www.doe.k12.de.us/infosuites/students_family/dhec/
Purpose: To reward Delaware high school seniors who submit winning essays.
Eligibility: Applicants must be seniors in public or private schools or in home school programs who plan to enroll full-time at nonprofit, regionally accredited colleges. Applicants should submit essays on a topic listed on the website.
Target applicants: High school students.
Amount: $1,000-$10,000.
Number of awards: Up to 62.
Deadline: November 30.
How to apply: Applications are available online.
Exclusive: Visit www.UltimateScholarshipBook.com and enter code DE163612 for updates on this award.

(1637) · Legislative for Future Excellence (LIFE) Scholarship Program

South Carolina Commission on Higher Education
1333 Main Street
Suite 200
Columbia, SC 29201
Phone: 803-737-2260
Fax: 803-737-2297
Email: shubbard@che.sc.gov
http://www.che400.state.sc.us
Purpose: Monetary assistance is provided to South Carolina resident students pursuing higher education.
Eligibility: Applicants must graduate from a high school in South Carolina or outside of South Carolina if parent is a legal resident of South Carolina, attend an eligible South Carolina public or private college full-time and be a resident of South Carolina. Entering freshmen must meet two of the following: have a minimum 3.0 GPA, a minimum SAT score of 1100 or ACT score of 24 or graduate in the top 30 percent of their class.
Target applicants: High school students. College students. Adult students.
Minimum GPA: 3.0
Amount: $4,700.
Number of awards: Varies.
Scholarship may be renewable.
Deadline: Varies.
How to apply: Your college will determine your eligibility based on your high school transcript. There is no application form.
Exclusive: Visit www.UltimateScholarshipBook.com and enter code SO163712 for updates on this award.

(1638) · Legislative Lottery Scholarships

New Mexico Higher Education Department
2048 Galisteo Street
Santa Fe, NM 87505
Phone: 800-279-9777
Fax: 505-476-8454
Email: heather.romero@state.nm.us
http://hed.state.nm.us
Purpose: To support graduating New Mexico high school seniors with financial need.
Eligibility: Applicants must be graduating high school seniors in New Mexico, enroll full-time at an eligible New Mexico public college or university and maintain a minimum 2.5 GPA during the first college semester.
Target applicants: High school students.
Amount: Full tuition.
Number of awards: Varies.
Scholarship may be renewable.
Deadline: Varies.
How to apply: Contact your financial aid office.
Exclusive: Visit www.UltimateScholarshipBook.com and enter code NE163812 for updates on this award.

(1639) · Leo Bourassa Scholarship

Virginia Lakes and Watersheds Association
4229 Lafayette Center Drive
Suite 1850
Chantilly, VA 20151
Phone: 757-671-6222
Email: shelly.frie@gmail.com
http://www.vlwa.org/
Purpose: To acknowledge students for their accomplishments in the field of water resources.
Eligibility: Applicants must be Virginia residents and students in good standing at an accredited college or university in the state. They must complete at least two semesters of undergraduate study by the award date. They must also be full-time undergraduate or full- or part-time graduate students enrolled in curricula related to water resources.
Target applicants: College students. Graduate school students. Adult students.
Amount: $2,500.
Number of awards: 2.
Deadline: May 31.
How to apply: Applications are available online.
Exclusive: Visit www.UltimateScholarshipBook.com and enter code VI163912 for updates on this award.

(1640) · Leslie Moore - Baltimore and Howard County Scholarship

CollegeBound Foundation
Scholarship, Research and Retention Services
300 Water Street
Suite 300
Baltimore, MD 21202
Phone: 410-783-2905
Fax: 410-727-5786
Email: info@collegeboundfoundation.org

http://www.collegeboundfoundation.org
Purpose: To help Baltimore and Howard County public high school seniors who have performed community service.
Eligibility: Applicants must be accepted to community colleges, universities or technical schools. A transcript, essay, two recommendation letters and college acceptance letters are required, and finalists should be available for interviews. One award is for a Baltimore county public high school senior, and the other award is for a Howard county public high school senior.
Target applicants: High school students.
Minimum GPA: 2.0
Amount: $2,500.
Number of awards: 2.
Scholarship may be renewable.
Deadline: March 1.
How to apply: Applications are available online.
Exclusive: Visit www.UltimateScholarshipBook.com and enter code CO164012 for updates on this award.

(1641) • Lessans Family Scholarship

Central Scholarship Bureau
1700 Reisterstown Road
Suite 220
Baltimore, MD 21208-2903
Phone: 410-415-5558
Fax: 410-415-5501
Email: info@centralsb.org
http://www.centralsb.org
Purpose: To assist undergraduate Jewish students in Maryland.
Eligibility: Applicants must have already applied for a Central Scholarship Bureau interest-free loan for the current year, be enrolled at an accredited college, university or vocational school, have a certain income level and apply for financial aid and, if offered, accept a subsidized Stafford loan. An application form, budget form, copy of school bills, transcript, Student Aid Report, school financial aid award letter and essay are required. Selection is based on need and merit.
Target applicants: High school students. College students. Adult students.
Minimum GPA: 3.0
Amount: Varies.
Number of awards: Varies.
Scholarship may be renewable.
Deadline: May 10.
How to apply: Applications are available online.
Exclusive: Visit www.UltimateScholarshipBook.com and enter code CE164112 for updates on this award.

(1642) • Leveraged Incentive Grant Program

New Hampshire Postsecondary Education Commission
3 Barrell Court
Suite 300
Concord, NH 03301
Phone: 603-271-2555 x352
Fax: 603-271-2696
Email: jknapp@pec.state.nh.us
http://www.state.nh.us/postsecondary
Purpose: To provide financial assistance based on merit and need to undergraduate students at New Hampshire institutions of higher learning.
Eligibility: Applicants must be residents of New Hampshire, demonstrate financial need and merit and be full-time sophomore, junior or senior students at an accredited undergraduate institution.
Target applicants: College students. Adult students.
Amount: Up to $7,500.
Number of awards: Varies.
Deadline: Varies.
How to apply: Applications are available from your financial aid office.
Exclusive: Visit www.UltimateScholarshipBook.com and enter code NE164212 for updates on this award.

(1643) • Leveraging Educational Assistance Partnership (LEAP)

Louisiana Office of Student Financial Assistance
P.O. Box 91202
Baton Rouge, LA 70821-9202
Phone: 800-259-5626 x1012
Fax: 225-922-0790
Email: custserv@osfa.la.gov
http://www.osfa.state.la.us
Purpose: To provide need-based grants to academically qualified Louisiana students.
Eligibility: Students must be U.S. citizens or eligible noncitizens and residents of Louisiana, earn a high school diploma with a minimum 2.0 GPA or GED score minimum and meet the selection criteria of their particular college. All applicants must have substantial financial need as demonstrated on the Free Application for Federal Student Aid (FAFSA) form.
Target applicants: High school students. College students. Adult students.
Minimum GPA: 2.0
Amount: $200-$2,000.
Number of awards: Varies.
Scholarship may be renewable.
Deadline: July 1.
How to apply: Contact your school's financial aid office for specific information about their LEAP program.
Exclusive: Visit www.UltimateScholarshipBook.com and enter code LO164312 for updates on this award.

(1644) • Leveraging Educational Assistance Partnership (LEAP)

Arizona Commission for Postsecondary Education
2020 N. Central Avenue, Suite 550
Phoenix, AZ 85004
Phone: 602-258-2435
Fax: 602-258-2483
Email: judi@azhighered.org
http://www.azhighered.org
Purpose: State and federal agencies have partnered together to provide awards to Arizona college and graduate students attending Arizona schools.
Eligibility: Applicants must be Arizona residents attending participating Arizona postsecondary institutions full-time or half-time as undergraduate or graduate students. The award is based on financial need.
Target applicants: High school students. College students. Graduate school students. Adult students.
Amount: $100-$2,500.
Number of awards: Varies.
Deadline: Varies.

How to apply: Apply through your financial aid office.
Exclusive: Visit www.UltimateScholarshipBook.com and enter code AR164412 for updates on this award.

(1645) • Leveraging Educational Assistance Partnership (LEAP) Grant

Georgia Student Finance Commission
2082 East Exchange Place
Tucker, GA 30084
Phone: 800-505-4732
Fax: 770-724-9089
Email: support@gacollege411.org
http://www.gacollege411.org
Purpose: To aid residents of Georgia with substantial financial need in attending postsecondary institutions in Georgia.
Eligibility: Applicants must demonstrate substantial financial need, be eligible to receive the Pell Grant and be enrolled at a Georgia college, university or technical college at least half-time. Applicants must also complete and submit the Free Application for Federal Student Aid (FAFSA) and for renewal must maintain satisfactory academic progress.
Target applicants: College students. Adult students.
Amount: Up to $2,000.
Number of awards: Varies.
Scholarship may be renewable.
Deadline: Varies.
How to apply: Applications are available by telephone request.
Exclusive: Visit www.UltimateScholarshipBook.com and enter code GE164512 for updates on this award.

(1646) • Leveraging Educational Assistance Partnership (LEAP) Grant

Utah Higher Education Assistance Authority
P.O. Box 145112
Salt Lake City, UT 84114
Phone: 877-336-7378
Fax: 801-366-8430
Email: uheaa@utahsbr.edu
http://www.uheaa.org
Purpose: To assist Utah college students.
Eligibility: Applicants must be enrolled at a participating Utah postsecondary institution. They must demonstrate financial need according to federal guidelines. Other eligibility requirements differ by campus. Selection is based on financial need.
Target applicants: High school students. College students. Adult students.
Amount: Up to $2,500.
Number of awards: Varies.
Deadline: Varies.
How to apply: Application is made by completing the FAFSA.
Exclusive: Visit www.UltimateScholarshipBook.com and enter code UT164612 for updates on this award.

(1647) • Leveraging Educational Assistance State Partnership Program (LEAP)

Idaho State Board of Education
P.O. Box 83720
Boise, ID 83720
Phone: 208-334-2270
Fax: 208-334-2632
Email: dkelly@osbe.state.id.us
http://www.boardofed.idaho.gov
Purpose: To aid students attending Idaho colleges or universities regardless of their states of residence.
Eligibility: Applicants must demonstrate financial need, attend eligible public or private colleges or universities in Idaho and take a minimum of six credits. Applicants may be residents of any state.
Target applicants: College students. Adult students.
Amount: Up to $5,000.
Number of awards: Varies.
Scholarship may be renewable.
Deadline: Varies.
How to apply: Contact your financial aid office.
Exclusive: Visit www.UltimateScholarshipBook.com and enter code ID164712 for updates on this award.

(1648) • Library Media Teacher Scholarship

California School Library Association Paraprofessional Scholarship
1001 26th Street
Sacramento, CA 95816
Phone: 916-447-2684
Fax: 916-447-2695
Email: csla@pacbell.net
http://www.csla.net/
Purpose: To encourage students who plan to become library media teachers.
Eligibility: Applicants must be currently enrolled in a school library media credential program or master's degree program. Candidates must be residents of the California School Library Association Southern Section region and must provide three letters of recommendation.
Target applicants: College students. Graduate school students. Adult students.
Amount: $1,000.
Number of awards: Varies.
Deadline: February 15.
How to apply: Applications are available online.
Exclusive: Visit www.UltimateScholarshipBook.com and enter code CA164812 for updates on this award.

(1649) • Licensed Vocational Nurse to Associate Degree Nursing Scholarship

Health Professions Education Foundation
400 R Street
Suite 460
Sacramento, CA 95811
Phone: 916-326-3640
Fax: 916-324-6585
Email: stran@oshpd.ca.gov
http://www.oshpd.ca.gov
Purpose: To aid licensed vocational nurses in California who are pursuing an associate's degree in nursing.
Eligibility: Applicants must be licensed vocational nurses (LVNs) who are enrolled in or have been accepted into an accredited associate's degree in nursing (ADN) program in the state of California. They must be attending or planning to attend school at least part-time (six or more credits per semester) and must commit to two years of nursing practice in an underserved area of California after graduation. Selection is based on the overall strength of the application.
Target applicants: College students. Adult students.
Amount: Up to $8,000.
Number of awards: Varies.

Deadline: September 11.
How to apply: Applications are available online. An application form, official transcript, personal statement, financial information, two recommendation letters and proof of vocational nurse licensure are required.
Exclusive: Visit www.UltimateScholarshipBook.com and enter code HE164912 for updates on this award.

(1650) • Lillie and Noel Fitzgerald Memorial Scholarship

New Jersey State Nurses Association
Institute for Nursing
1479 Pennington Road
Trenton, NJ 08618
Phone: 609-883-5335
Fax: 609-883-5343
Email: sandy@njsna.org
http://www.njsna.org
Purpose: To aid New Jersey nursing students.
Eligibility: Applicants must be New Jersey residents enrolled in or applying for admission into a nursing diploma or degree program at a New Jersey postsecondary institution. Registered Nurse applicants must be members of the New Jersey State Nurses Association (NJSNA). Selection is based on leadership, GPA and financial need.
Target applicants: High school students. College students. Graduate school students. Adult students.
Amount: Varies.
Number of awards: Varies.
Deadline: January 15.
How to apply: Applications are available online. An application form, transcript, financial information, reference letter, personal statement and resume (for RNs only) are required.
Exclusive: Visit www.UltimateScholarshipBook.com and enter code NE165012 for updates on this award.

(1651) • Lilly Endowment Community Scholarship Program

Independent Colleges of Indiana
3135 N. Meridian Street
Indianapolis, IN 46208-4717
Phone: 317-236-6090
Fax: 317-236-6086
Email: info@icindiana.org
http://www.icindiana.org/lecsp/lilly.asp
Purpose: To raise the level of education in Indiana.
Eligibility: Applicants must be Indiana high school seniors who have been accepted into a full-time bachelor's degree program at an accredited public or private institution of higher learning in Indiana.
Target applicants: High school students.
Amount: Full Tuition.
Number of awards: Varies.
Scholarship may be renewable.
Deadline: Varies.
How to apply: Applications are available online and from local Indiana Community Foundations.
Exclusive: Visit www.UltimateScholarshipBook.com and enter code IN165112 for updates on this award.

(1652) • Lilly Lorénzen Scholarship

American Swedish Institute
2600 Park Avenue
Minneapolis, MN 55407
Phone: 612-870-3355
Fax: 612-871-8682
Email: karink@americanswedishinst.org
http://www.americanswedishinst.org
Purpose: To assist Minnesota residents who wish to carry out scholarly or creative studies in Sweden.
Eligibility: Applicants must speak Swedish and have a desire to contribute to American-Swedish cultural exchange. They must plan to carry out studies in Sweden and have demonstrable achievement in their chosen field of study. Students must provide a college transcript or statement of professional and community achievement.
Target applicants: College students. Graduate school students. Adult students.
Amount: $1,000.
Number of awards: 1.
Deadline: May 1.
How to apply: Applications are available online.
Exclusive: Visit www.UltimateScholarshipBook.com and enter code AM165212 for updates on this award.

(1653) • Lily and Catello Sorrentino Memorial Scholarship

Rhode Island Foundation
One Union Station
Providence, RI 02903
Phone: 401-274-4564
Fax: 401-331-8085
Email: lmonahan@rifoundation.org
http://www.rifoundation.org
Purpose: To assist adult students who are continuing their undergraduate studies at colleges or universities in Rhode Island.
Eligibility: Applicants must be residents of Rhode Island, be over 25 years of age and attend a non-parochial college or university in the state.
Target applicants: College students. Adult students.
Amount: $500-$1,000.
Number of awards: Varies.
Deadline: May 14.
How to apply: Applications are available online.
Exclusive: Visit www.UltimateScholarshipBook.com and enter code RH165312 for updates on this award.

(1654) • Linda Craig Memorial Scholarship Presented by St. Vincent Sports Medicine

Pacers Foundation
125 S. Pennsylvania Street
Indianapolis, IN 46204
Phone: 317-917-2864
Fax: 317-917-2599
Email: foundation@pacers.com
http://www.nba.com/pacers/news/Foundation_Index.html
Purpose: To support Indiana students interested in sports medicine, physical therapy and related fields.
Eligibility: Applicants must U.S. citizens who have completed at least four semesters of an undergraduate program majoring in medicine, sports medicine, physical therapy or a related area. They must have a GPA of at least 3.0 and demonstrate outstanding character, integrity

and leadership. Applicants may not have received a full scholarship from any other organization.
Target applicants: College students. Adult students.
Minimum GPA: 3.0
Amount: Varies.
Number of awards: Varies.
Deadline: July 1.
How to apply: Applications are available online.
Exclusive: Visit www.UltimateScholarshipBook.com and enter code PA165412 for updates on this award.

(1655) · Lisa Sechrist Memorial Foundation Scholarship

Lisa Sechrist Memorial Foundation
8500 Executive Park Avenue
Suite 300
Fairfax, VA 22031
http://www.lisasechrist.com/scholarship.html
Purpose: To honor the memory of Lisa Sechrist by assisting young women in obtaining a college education.
Eligibility: Applicants must be Virginia high school seniors in the process of applying to an accredited college, university or technical school or who have already been accepted. Members of honor societies and those who participate in sports or other extracurricular activities will receive special consideration. Selection is based on need, integrity, merit and academic potential.
Target applicants: High school students.
Amount: Up to $2,500.
Number of awards: 1.
Deadline: March 31.
How to apply: Applications are available online.
Exclusive: Visit www.UltimateScholarshipBook.com and enter code LI165512 for updates on this award.

(1656) · Loan Assistance Repayment Program Primary Care Services

Maryland Higher Education Commission
Office of Student Financial Assistance
839 Bestgate Road, Suite 400
Annapolis, MD 21401
Phone: 800-974-1024
Fax: 410-260-3200
Email: osfamail@mhec.state.md.us
http://www.mhec.state.md.us
Purpose: To support primary care physicians and medical residents.
Eligibility: Medical resident applicants must be graduates of a Maryland college, and they must have at least one year remaining in a primary care residency program. Physician applicants must have a valid primary care license and currently work in an underserved area of Maryland. All applicants must have outstanding loans on which they have not defaulted. Specialization in one of the following fields is required: general internal medicine, family practice medicine, general pediatrics, obstetrics/gynecology or gynecology. Applicants must agree to work in an underserved area of Maryland for two to four years after winning the scholarship and completing their residency.
Target applicants: Graduate school students. Adult students.
Amount: $25,000-$30,000.
Number of awards: Varies.
Scholarship may be renewable.
Deadline: August 16.
How to apply: Applications are available from the Department of Health and Mental Hygiene.
Exclusive: Visit www.UltimateScholarshipBook.com and enter code MA165612 for updates on this award.

(1657) · Lois Livingston McMillen Memorial Fund

Connecticut Community Foundation Center for Philanthropy
43 Field Street
Waterbury, CT 06702
Phone: 203-753-1315
Fax: 203-756-3054
Email: info@conncf.org
http://www.conncf.org
Purpose: To provide financial assistance to women who are studying or plan to study art, especially painting or design.
Eligibility: Applicants must be women who plan to study art at an accredited college or university, or in an artist-in-residence program. They must also live in the Connecticut Community Foundation's service area.
Target applicants: High school students. College students. Adult students.
Amount: $500-$4,000.
Number of awards: Varies.
Deadline: March 15.
How to apply: Applications are available online.
Exclusive: Visit www.UltimateScholarshipBook.com and enter code CO165712 for updates on this award.

(1658) · Lori Rhett Memorial Scholarship

National Association for Campus Activities
13 Harbison Way
Columbia, SC 29212
Phone: 803-732-6222
Fax: 803-749-1047
Email: info@naca.org
http://www.naca.org
Purpose: The scholarship recognizes the achievements of student leaders who are undergraduate or graduate students.
Eligibility: Applicants must hold a significant campus leadership position and demonstrate significant leadership skills and abilities. Students must also be making significant contributions through on- or off-campus volunteering and must attend school in Alaska, Idaho, Montana, Oregon or Washington.
Target applicants: College students. Graduate school students. Adult students.
Minimum GPA: 2.5
Amount: Varies.
Number of awards: 1.
Deadline: June 30.
How to apply: Applications are available online.
Exclusive: Visit www.UltimateScholarshipBook.com and enter code NA165812 for updates on this award.

(1659) · Los Alamos Employees' Scholarship

Los Alamos National Laboratory Foundation
1302 Calle de la Merced
Suite A
Espanola, NM 87532
Phone: 505-753-8890
Fax: 505-753-8915

Email: info@lanlfoundation.org
http://www.lanlfoundation.org
Purpose: To provide financial assistance for students in northern New Mexico who plan to pursue undergraduate degrees in fields of study that will benefit the community.
Eligibility: Selection is based on academic performance, including the pursuit in high school of a rigorous course of study, GPA and standardized test scores, varied extracurricular and community service activities, strong critical thinking skills and career goals that are relevant to the needs of the northern New Mexico community. Some consideration is also given to financial need, ethnic diversity and equally representing all the regions of northern New Mexico. Applicants must have a minimum 3.25 GPA and either minimum score of 19 on the ACT or 930 on the SAT (Math and Critical Reading).
Target applicants: College students. Adult students.
Minimum GPA: 3.25
Amount: Varies.
Number of awards: Varies.
Scholarship may be renewable.
Deadline: January 18.
How to apply: Applications are available online.
Exclusive: Visit www.UltimateScholarshipBook.com and enter code LO165912 for updates on this award.

(1660) • Los Alamos National Laboratory Foundation

Los Alamos National Laboratory Foundation
1302 Calle de la Merced
Suite A
Espanola, NM 87532
Phone: 505-753-8890
Fax: 505-753-8915
Email: info@lanlfoundation.org
http://www.lanlfoundation.org
Purpose: To assist Northern New Mexico students in obtaining higher education.
Eligibility: Applicants must be permanent residents of the counties of Los Alamos, Mora, Rio Arriba, San Miguel, Sandoval, Santa Fe or Taos, New Mexico. Several scholarships are available, some open to all and some based on area of study.
Target applicants: High school students. College students. Adult students.
Amount: Up to $7,500.
Number of awards: Varies.
Scholarship may be renewable.
Deadline: January 18.
How to apply: Applications are available online.
Exclusive: Visit www.UltimateScholarshipBook.com and enter code LO166012 for updates on this award.

(1661) • Lottery Tuition Assistance Program

South Carolina Board for Technical and Comprehensive Education
1333 Main Street
Suite 200
Columbia, SC 29201
Phone: 803-737-2260
Fax: 803-737-2297
Email: mmdowell@che.sc.gov
http://www.che400.state.sc.us
Purpose: To assist South Carolina residents attending a two-year public or independent institution of higher learning.
Eligibility: Applicants must complete the Free Application for Federal Student Aid (FAFSA), be residents of South Carolina and be enrolled a minimum of six credit hours at a technical college.
Target applicants: High school students. College students. Adult students.
Amount: $900 per term.
Number of awards: Varies.
Deadline: Varies.
How to apply: Applications are available by telephone request.
Exclusive: Visit www.UltimateScholarshipBook.com and enter code SO166112 for updates on this award.

(1662) • Louis B. Russell, Jr. Memorial Scholarship

Indiana State Teachers Association
150 W. Market Street
Indianapolis, IN 46204
Phone: 800-382-4037
Email: dboyd@ista-in.org
http://www.ista-in.org/dynamic.aspx?id=162
Purpose: To provide financial assistance to ethnic minorities who are seeking vocational or technical education.
Eligibility: Applicants must be ethnic minority high school seniors who plan to pursue education in the area of industrial arts, vocational education or technical education at an accredited college or university.
Target applicants: High school students.
Amount: $1,000.
Number of awards: 1.
Scholarship may be renewable.
Deadline: March 1.
How to apply: Applications are available online.
Exclusive: Visit www.UltimateScholarshipBook.com and enter code IN166212 for updates on this award.

(1663) • Louisiana Go Grant

Louisiana Office of Student Financial Assistance
P.O. Box 91202
Baton Rouge, LA 70821-9202
Phone: 800-259-5626 x1012
Fax: 225-922-0790
Email: custserv@osfa.la.gov
http://www.osfa.state.la.us
Purpose: To help students from moderate and low income families afford a college education.
Eligibility: Applicants must be Louisiana residents who have been admitted and enrolled in an undergraduate program at a Louisiana public or private college or university. They must be first time freshmen or adult students who have not been enrolled in credit bearing courses for at least one academic year. Financial need is required.
Target applicants: High school students. College students. Adult students.
Amount: Up to $2,000.
Number of awards: Varies.
Deadline: Varies.
How to apply: All eligible students who have filed a Free Application for Federal Student Aid are considered for this grant.
Exclusive: Visit www.UltimateScholarshipBook.com and enter code LO166312 for updates on this award.

(1664) • Louisiana Memorial Scholarship

American Radio Relay League Foundation
225 Main Street
Newington, CT 06111
Phone: 860-594-0397
Fax: 860-594-0259
Email: foundation@arrl.org
http://www.arrlf.org

Purpose: To provide financial assistance to Louisiana students who are amateur radio operators.
Eligibility: Applicants must hold a Technician Class or higher Amateur Radio License and either be Louisiana residents or attend school in Louisiana. They must have a GPA of 3.0 or higher. Only students who are accepted to or enrolled in a four-year college or university are eligible.
Target applicants: High school students. College students. Adult students.
Minimum GPA: 3.0
Amount: $750.
Number of awards: 1.
Deadline: February 1.
How to apply: Applications are available online.
Exclusive: Visit www.UltimateScholarshipBook.com and enter code AM166412 for updates on this award.

(1665) • Louisiana-Mississippi GCSA Turf Scholar Competition

Louisiana-Mississippi Golf Course Superintendents Association
P. O. Box 80047
Starkville, MS 39759
Phone: 866-656-4272
Fax: 866-656-4272
Email: lmgcsa@earthlink.net
http://www.lmgcsa.com

Purpose: To aid undergraduate golf course management students.
Eligibility: Applicants must be undergraduate students who are enrolled in an accredited two- to five-year degree program in golf course management or a related subject. They must have completed at least one year (24 credit hours) of the degree program. Selection is based on academic merit, level of professional preparation and career potential.
Target applicants: College students. Adult students.
Amount: Varies.
Number of awards: Varies.
Deadline: June 1.
How to apply: Applications are available online. An application form, transcripts, personal statement, golf course superintendent evaluation and academic advisor evaluation are required.
Exclusive: Visit www.UltimateScholarshipBook.com and enter code LO166512 for updates on this award.

(1666) • Luso-American Education Foundation General Fund Scholarship

Luso-American Education Foundation
P.O. Box 2967
Dublin, CA 94568
Phone: 925-828-3883
Fax: 925-828-3883
Email: odom@luso-american.org
http://www.luso-american.org

Purpose: To provide educational opportunities for Portuguese students.
Eligibility: Applicants must be residents of California and high school students who are of Portuguese descent with a GPA of 3.5 or higher, or who are taking classes in the Portuguese language with a GPA of 3.0 or higher. They must be enrolled in a college, university, trade or business school and have taken the SAT or ACT. Two letters of recommendation are required.
Target applicants: High school students.
Minimum GPA: 3.0
Amount: $500-$1,500.
Number of awards: 13-17.
Deadline: March 1.
How to apply: Applications are available by phone, fax, mail or email.
Exclusive: Visit www.UltimateScholarshipBook.com and enter code LU166612 for updates on this award.

(1667) • Lynn M. Smith Memorial Scholarship

California Association for Postsecondary Education and Disability
71423 Biskra Road
Rancho Mirage, CA 92270
Phone: 760-346-8206
Fax: 760-340-5275
Email: bjaworski@csub.edu
http://www.caped.net

Purpose: To provide financial assistance to community college students with disabilities in California.
Eligibility: Applicants must have a verifiable disability and demonstrate financial need. They must be currently enrolled in a community college and pursuing a vocational career path.
Target applicants: College students. Adult students.
Amount: $1,000.
Number of awards: 1.
Deadline: September 19.
How to apply: Applications are available online.
Exclusive: Visit www.UltimateScholarshipBook.com and enter code CA166712 for updates on this award.

(1668) • M. Josephine O'Neil Arts Award

Delta Kappa Gamma Society International Lambda State Organization
c/o Linda McDonnell
3201 Newell Drive
Granite City, IL 62040-5160
Phone: 618-452-3201
Email: llmcdonell@excite.com
http://www.deltakappagamma.org/IL

Purpose: To support outstanding female artists.
Eligibility: Applicants must be Illinois residents and be sophomores at an accredited community college or current or upcoming juniors at an accredited four-year college or university. Students must demonstrate outstanding accomplishment in music, visual arts, dance, theater or the literary arts.
Target applicants: College students. Adult students.
Amount: $6,000.
Number of awards: Varies.
Deadline: February 1.
How to apply: Applications are available online. An application form, transcript, evidence of accomplishment in the arts (such as reviews, awards, etc.) and an artwork sample are required.
Exclusive: Visit www.UltimateScholarshipBook.com and enter code DE166812 for updates on this award.

(1669) • M.E. Amstutz Memorial Award

Illinois Society of Professional Engineers
100 East Washington Street
Springfield, IL 62701
Phone: 217-544-7424
Fax: 217-528-6545
Email: info@illinoisengineer.com
http://www.ilspe.com

Purpose: To aid Illinois undergraduate engineering students.
Eligibility: Applicants must be undergraduate juniors or seniors who are enrolled in an ABET-accredited engineering degree program at an Illinois college or university. They must have a B average or better in engineering coursework and must demonstrate financial need. Selection is based on academic merit, financial need, extracurricular activities and personal essay.
Target applicants: College students. Adult students.
Minimum GPA: 3.0
Amount: $1,500.
Number of awards: 1.
Deadline: March 31.
How to apply: Applications are available online. An application form, official transcript, two reference letters and personal essay are required.
Exclusive: Visit www.UltimateScholarshipBook.com and enter code IL166912 for updates on this award.

(1670) • Mabel Mayforth Scholarship

Federated Garden Clubs of Vermont Inc.
c/o Jen Hanlon, Scholarship Chair
676 Arthur John Road
Island Pond, VT 05846
Phone: 877-876-4273
http://vermontfgcv.com/index.php

Purpose: To support students who are studying in fields related to plants.
Eligibility: Applicants must be Vermont residents who are college juniors, seniors or graduate students and must major in horticulture, floriculture, landscape, design, conservation, forestry, agronomy, plant pathology or biology with emphasis on plants, ecology or allied subjects. They must be full-time students at an accredited institution with a GPA of 3.0 or higher. Previous winners may reapply.
Target applicants: College students. Graduate school students. Adult students.
Minimum GPA: 3.0
Amount: Up to $1,000.
Number of awards: 1.
Deadline: March 1.
How to apply: Applications are available online. An application form, list of extracurricular activities, letter of application, transcript and three letters of recommendation are required.
Exclusive: Visit www.UltimateScholarshipBook.com and enter code FE167012 for updates on this award.

(1671) • Mackinac Scholarship

American Society of Civil Engineers-Michigan Section
ASCE Scholarships
P.O. Box 15276
Lansing, MI 48901
Phone: 734-459-3231
Email: lak1204@sbcglobal.net
http://sections.asce.org/michigan

Purpose: To aid Michigan civil engineering students.
Eligibility: Applicants must be U.S. citizens and Michigan residents. They must be rising undergraduate juniors or seniors who are enrolled full-time in an ABET-accredited civil engineering degree program. They must have a GPA of 2.5 or higher on a four-point scale. Selection is based on academic achievement, personal qualities and financial need.
Target applicants: College students. Adult students.
Minimum GPA: 2.5
Amount: $6,000.
Number of awards: 1.
Deadline: May 25.
How to apply: Applications are available online. An application form and an official transcript are required.
Exclusive: Visit www.UltimateScholarshipBook.com and enter code AM167112 for updates on this award.

(1672) • Maine BPW Continuing Education Scholarship

Business and Professional Women/Maine Futurama Foundation
103 County Road
Oakland, ME 04963
Email: webmaster@bpwmaine.org
http://www.bpwmaine.org/files/index.php?id=10

Purpose: To provide financial assistance to Maine women who are already attending an institution of higher learning.
Eligibility: Applicants must be female Maine residents who are currently attending a college or training program.
Target applicants: College students. Graduate school students. Adult students.
Amount: $1,200.
Number of awards: Varies.
Deadline: April 20.
How to apply: Applications are available from your local BPW chapter.
Exclusive: Visit www.UltimateScholarshipBook.com and enter code BU167212 for updates on this award.

(1673) • Maine Chapter No. 276 Scholarship

National Association of Women in Construction - Maine Chapter
P.O. Box 366
Hallowell, ME 04347
Phone: 207-623-4685
Email: nawicmaine@aol.com
http://www.nawicmaine.org

Purpose: To aid Maine students who are planning for careers in construction-related fields.
Eligibility: Applicants must be Maine residents who are graduating high school seniors. They must have plans to pursue higher education in a construction-related subject in preparation for a construction-related career. Selection is based on academic merit and financial need.
Target applicants: High school students.
Amount: $500-$1,000.
Number of awards: Varies.
Scholarship may be renewable.
Deadline: May 1.
How to apply: Applications are available online. An application form, transcript and two recommendation letters are required.
Exclusive: Visit www.UltimateScholarshipBook.com and enter code NA167312 for updates on this award.

(1674) · Maine Community Foundation Scholarship Program

Maine Community Foundation
245 Main Street
Ellsworth, ME 04605
Phone: 207-667-9735
Fax: 207-667-0447
Email: jwarren@mainecf.org
http://www.mainecf.org

Purpose: To provide financial assistance to Maine students.

Eligibility: There are a number of scholarships in this program for Maine traditional and adult students to attend private high schools, undergraduate colleges or graduate schools. Many are limited to residents of a specific county or graduates of a certain high school.

Target applicants: High school students. College students. Graduate school students. Adult students.

Amount: Varies.

Number of awards: Varies.

Deadline: Varies.

How to apply: Applications are available online.

Exclusive: Visit www.UltimateScholarshipBook.com and enter code MA167412 for updates on this award.

(1675) · Maine Demolay and Pine Tree Youth Foundation Scholarships

Maine Demolay and Pine Tree Youth Foundation
P.O. Box 816
Bangor, ME 04402
Phone: 207-773-5184
Email: grandlodge@mainemason.org
http://www.pinetreeyouth.org

Purpose: To support Maine high school seniors.

Eligibility: Applicants must submit a short essay. Students must demonstrate financial need.

Target applicants: High school students.

Amount: Varies.

Number of awards: Varies.

Deadline: March 20.

How to apply: Applications are available online.

Exclusive: Visit www.UltimateScholarshipBook.com and enter code MA167512 for updates on this award.

(1676) · Maine Innkeepers Association Hospitality Scholarships

Maine Innkeepers Association
304 US Route 1
Freeport, ME 04032
Phone: 207-865-6100
Fax: 207-865-6120
Email: info@maineinns.com
http://www.maineinns.com

Purpose: To support students enrolled in hospitality-related programs.

Eligibility: Applicants must be Maine residents and accepted to an accredited institution of higher learning with specialties in hotel administration or culinary sciences. Students must plan to begin a career in hospitality upon completion of their degrees.

Target applicants: High school students. College students. Adult students.

Amount: $500-$2,000.

Number of awards: Varies.

Deadline: April 9.

How to apply: Applications are available from the Maine Innkeepers Association.

Exclusive: Visit www.UltimateScholarshipBook.com and enter code MA167612 for updates on this award.

(1677) · Maine Legislative Memorial Scholarship Fund

Maine Education Services
131 Presumpscot Street
Portland, ME 04103
Phone: 800-922-6352
Fax: 207-791-3616
Email: info@mesfoundation.com
http://www.mesfoundation.com

Purpose: To support Maine students who are planning to attend or currently attend college in Maine.

Eligibility: Students must be accepted to or enrolled in a Maine college, technical school or graduate school. Applicants must be able to show academic excellence, community service or employment and financial need.

Target applicants: High school students. College students. Graduate school students. Adult students.

Amount: $1,000.

Number of awards: 16.

Deadline: April 16.

How to apply: Applications are available online.

Exclusive: Visit www.UltimateScholarshipBook.com and enter code MA167712 for updates on this award.

(1678) · Maine Masonic Aid for Continuing Education

Maine Education Services
131 Presumpscot Street
Portland, ME 04103
Phone: 800-922-6352
Fax: 207-791-3616
Email: info@mesfoundation.com
http://www.mesfoundation.com

Purpose: To assist adults who are pursuing higher education in Maine.

Eligibility: Applicants must qualify for independent student status for the purposes of federal financial aid. They must demonstrate financial need as well as a commitment to community service and intent to complete their educational plans.

Target applicants: College students. Adult students.

Amount: $1,000.

Number of awards: 12.

Deadline: April 16.

How to apply: Applications are available online.

Exclusive: Visit www.UltimateScholarshipBook.com and enter code MA167812 for updates on this award.

(1679) · Maine Metal Products Association Scholarship

Maine Education Services
131 Presumpscot Street
Portland, ME 04103
Phone: 800-922-6352
Fax: 207-791-3616
Email: info@mesfoundation.com
http://www.mesfoundation.com

Purpose: To support outstanding students who are planning to study metal working trades in college or technical school.
Eligibility: Students must be residents of the state of Maine, and they must be accepted or enrolled in a Maine post secondary school. They must be in school full-time with a C average. Applicants should also have plans to study one of the following metal working fields: mechanical engineering, machine tool technology, sheet metal fabrication, welding or metals industry CADCAM.
Target applicants: High school students. College students. Adult students.
Minimum GPA: 2.0
Amount: Varies.
Number of awards: Varies.
Deadline: April 16.
How to apply: Applications are available online.
Exclusive: Visit www.UltimateScholarshipBook.com and enter code MA167912 for updates on this award.

(1680) • Maine Oratorical Contest

American Legion, Department of Maine
21 College Avenue
Waterville, ME 04901
Phone: 207-873-3229
Email: legionme@me.acadia.net
http://www.mainelegion.org
Purpose: To enhance high school students' experience with and understanding of the U.S. Constitution. The contest will help develop students' leadership skills and civic appreciation, as well as the ability to deliver thoughtful, insightful orations regarding U.S. citizenship and its inherent responsibilities.
Eligibility: Applicants must be high school students under the age of 20 who are U.S. citizens or legal residents and residents of the state. Students first give an oration within their state and winners compete at the national level. The oration must be related to the Constitution of the United States focusing on the duties and obligations citizens have to the government. It must be in English and be between eight and ten minutes. There is also an assigned topic which is posted on the website, and it should be between three and five minutes.
Target applicants: High school students.
Amount: $1,500-$18,000.
Number of awards: Varies.
Deadline: Varies.
How to apply: Application information is available by contacting the local American Legion Post.
Exclusive: Visit www.UltimateScholarshipBook.com and enter code AM168012 for updates on this award.

(1681) • Maine State Chamber of Commerce Scholarship

Maine Education Services
131 Presumpscot Street
Portland, ME 04103
Phone: 800-922-6352
Fax: 207-791-3616
Email: info@mesfoundation.com
http://www.mesfoundation.com
Purpose: To provide support to high school seniors who plan to study education or business and to adult students who are currently studying education.
Eligibility: Applicants must be currently attending a Maine high school in order to be eligible for the high school award, and preference may be given to students who are planning to attend Maine colleges. Preference will also be given to students who are planning to major in fields related to education or business. Students applying for the adult award must have independent status and must be studying education at a two-year college.
Target applicants: High school students. College students. Adult students.
Amount: $1,500.
Number of awards: 3.
Deadline: April 16.
How to apply: Applications are available online.
Exclusive: Visit www.UltimateScholarshipBook.com and enter code MA168112 for updates on this award.

(1682) • Maine State Grant Program

Maine Education Assistance Division
Finance Authority of Maine (FAME)
5 Community Drive
P.O. Box 949
Augusta, ME 04332
Phone: 800-228-3734
Fax: 207-623-0095
Email: education@famemaine.com
http://www.famemaine.com
Purpose: To support Maine undergraduate students who have financial need.
Eligibility: Applicants must be U.S. citizens or eligible non-citizens, be Maine residents and submit the Free Application for Federal Student Aid (FAFSA) by May 1. They must have an Expected Family Contribution (EFC) of $4,100 or less. Selection is based on financial need.
Target applicants: High school students. College students. Adult students.
Amount: $250-$1,250.
Number of awards: Varies.
Scholarship may be renewable.
Deadline: May 1.
How to apply: Application is made by completing the FAFSA.
Exclusive: Visit www.UltimateScholarshipBook.com and enter code MA168212 for updates on this award.

(1683) • Maine State Society Foundation Scholarship

Maine State Society Foundation of Washington, DC
3678 Bay Drive
Edgewater, MD 21037
Phone: 703-237-1031
Email: joanmbeach@aol.com
http://www.mainestatesociety.org
Purpose: To provide financial assistance to Maine students.
Eligibility: Applicants must be full-time students who are at least sophomores and must attend an accredited, non-profit college or university located in Maine.
Target applicants: College students.
Minimum GPA: 3.0
Amount: $1,000.
Number of awards: Varies.
Deadline: April 1.
How to apply: Applications are available by mail and online.
Exclusive: Visit www.UltimateScholarshipBook.com and enter code MA168312 for updates on this award.

(1684) • Maine Veterans Dependents Educational Benefits

Bureau of Veterans' Services
117 State House Station
Augusta, ME 04333-0117
Phone: 207-626-4464
Fax: 207-626-4471
Email: mainebvs@maine.gov
http://www.maine.gov/dvem/bvs/index.htm

Purpose: To provide the opportunity for dependents of veterans to obtain higher education.

Eligibility: Applicants must be children whose mother or father is or was a veteran in the state of Maine. They must be at least 16 years old and be high school graduates. They must be pursuing a college degree. Benefits must be awarded prior to the dependent's 22nd birthday, unless he or she is serving in the U.S. Armed Forces, in which case they may be awarded until his or her 26th birthday.

Target applicants: High school students. College students. Adult students.

Amount: Full tuition.

Number of awards: Varies.

Scholarship may be renewable.

Deadline: Varies.

How to apply: Applications are available online.

Exclusive: Visit www.UltimateScholarshipBook.com and enter code BU168412 for updates on this award.

(1685) • Maine Vietnam Veterans Scholarship

Maine Community Foundation
245 Main Street
Ellsworth, ME 04605
Phone: 207-667-9735
Fax: 207-667-0447
Email: jwarren@mainecf.org
http://www.mainecf.org

Purpose: To support Vietnam veterans from Maine and their descendants.

Eligibility: Applicants must either have served in the United States Armed Forces in Vietnam or be descendants of someone who served in Vietnam. In some cases, children of U.S. Armed Forces veterans in general may qualify.

Target applicants: High school students. College students. Graduate school students. Adult students.

Amount: Varies.

Number of awards: Varies.

Deadline: May 1.

How to apply: Applications are available at high school guidance offices or online.

Exclusive: Visit www.UltimateScholarshipBook.com and enter code MA168512 for updates on this award.

(1686) • Mainely Character Scholarship

Mainely Character
P.O. Box 11131
Portland, ME 04103
Email: info@mainelycharacter.org
http://www.mainelycharacter.org

Purpose: To reward Maine students who demonstrate good character and positive self-development.

Eligibility: Applicants must be Maine residents who plan to attend a Title IV eligible institution of higher learning for the first time in the fall following application. They should display the characteristics of courage, integrity, responsibility and concern. A 500-word essay is required.

Target applicants: High school students.

Amount: $5,000.

Number of awards: 1.

Deadline: March 1.

How to apply: Applications are available online.

Exclusive: Visit www.UltimateScholarshipBook.com and enter code MA168612 for updates on this award.

(1687) • Malcolm Baldrige Scholarship

Connecticut Community Foundation Center for Philanthropy
43 Field Street
Waterbury, CT 06702
Phone: 203-753-1315
Fax: 203-756-3054
Email: info@conncf.org
http://www.conncf.org

Purpose: To provide financial assistance to students in international business, trade or manufacturing.

Eligibility: Applicants must be Connecticut students who are entering or currently attending a Connecticut college or university, and they must demonstrate exemplary academic achievement. International business students must be fluent in or be formally studying a foreign language.

Target applicants: High school students. College students. Adult students.

Amount: $2,000-$4,000.

Number of awards: Varies.

Deadline: March 15.

How to apply: Applications are available online.

Exclusive: Visit www.UltimateScholarshipBook.com and enter code CO168712 for updates on this award.

(1688) • Mamoru and Aiko Takitani Foundation Scholarship

Mamoru and Aiko Takitani Foundation
P.O. Box 10687
Honolulu, HI 96816
Email: info@takitanifoundation.org
http://www.takitani.org

Purpose: To assist Hawaii resident students with business school, technical school, community college or four-year college expenses.

Eligibility: Applicants must be graduating high school seniors and Hawaii residents. Applicants must also demonstrate scholastic achievement, participation in activities and have been accepted into an accredited institution. Community service and financial need are also considered.

Target applicants: High school students.

Amount: $1,000-$10,000.

Number of awards: Varies.

Deadline: February 9.

How to apply: Contact your high school guidance counselor.

Exclusive: Visit www.UltimateScholarshipBook.com and enter code MA168812 for updates on this award.

(1689) • Margaret A. Pemberton Scholarship

Black Nurses Association of Greater Washington, DC Area Inc.
P.O. Box 55285
Washington, DC 20040
Phone: 202-291-8866
Email: contactus@bnaofgwdca.org
http://www.bnaofgwdca.org

Purpose: To aid Washington, DC students who are planning to pursue higher education in nursing.

Eligibility: Applicants must be U.S. citizens, be graduating seniors who are students at a Washington, DC high school and be accepted into a National League for Nursing bachelor's degree program at a U.S. postsecondary institution. They must have a GPA of 2.8 or higher and must demonstrate financial need. Selection is based on the overall strength of the application.

Target applicants: High school students.

Minimum GPA: 2.8

Amount: Up to $2,000.

Number of awards: 1-2.

Deadline: April 15.

How to apply: Applications are available online. An application form, personal statement, official transcript, copy of college acceptance letter and two recommendation letters are required.

Exclusive: Visit www.UltimateScholarshipBook.com and enter code BL168912 for updates on this award.

(1690) • Margaret A. Stafford Nursing Scholarship

Delaware Community Foundation
Community Service Building
100 West 10th Street, Suite 115
P.O. Box 1636
Wilmington, DE 19899
Phone: 302-571-8004
Fax: 302-571-1553
Email: rgentsch@delcf.org
http://www.delcf.org

Purpose: To aid Delaware students who are pursuing higher education in nursing.

Eligibility: Applicants must be Delaware residents who are enrolled in or who have been accepted into a nursing degree program at an accredited college or university. Selection is based on the overall strength of the application.

Target applicants: High school students. College students. Adult students.

Amount: Varies.

Number of awards: Varies.

Deadline: April 1.

How to apply: Applications are available online. An application form, transcript, personal statement and two recommendation letters are required.

Exclusive: Visit www.UltimateScholarshipBook.com and enter code DE169012 for updates on this award.

(1691) • Margaret Raley New York State Migrant Scholarship

BOCES Geneseo Migrant Center
27 Lackawanna Avenue
Mt. Morris, NY 14510
Phone: 800-245-5681
Fax: 585-658-7969
Email: info@migrant.net
http://www.migrant.net

Purpose: To recognize the educational achievement of migrant farmworker students with a history of migration to and/or within New York State.

Eligibility: Applicants must be migrants who are high school seniors and have plans to attend a post-secondary institution or other advanced training. Applicants must also have a history of migration to and/or within New York State. Recipients are selected on the basis of demonstrated commitment to educational goals, participation in school/MEOP-related activities, participation in community-related activities, demonstration of good citizenship qualities, presentation of high mobility and the overcoming of unusual odds or need.

Target applicants: High school students.

Amount: $500.

Number of awards: Varies.

Deadline: April 19.

How to apply: Applications are available online.

Exclusive: Visit www.UltimateScholarshipBook.com and enter code BO169112 for updates on this award.

(1692) • Marguerite Ross Barnett Memorial Scholarship

Missouri Student Assistance Resource Services (MOSTARS)
Missouri Department of Higher Education
3515 Amazonas Drive
Jefferson City, MO 65109
Phone: 800-473-6757
Fax: 573-751-6635
http://www.dhe.mo.gov

Purpose: This scholarship was established for students who are employed while attending school part-time.

Eligibility: Applicants must be U.S. citizens or eligible noncitizens, Missouri residents and enrolled at least half-time but less than full-time at a participating Missouri college or university. Applicants must also be employed for at least 20 hours per week and be able to demonstrate financial need.

Target applicants: High school students. College students. Adult students.

Amount: Tuition for 6-9 credit hours.

Number of awards: Varies.

Scholarship may be renewable.

Deadline: August 1.

How to apply: Applications are available online.

Exclusive: Visit www.UltimateScholarshipBook.com and enter code MI169212 for updates on this award.

(1693) • MARILN Professional Scholarship Award

Massachusetts/Rhode Island League for Nursing
1 Thompson Square
Charlestown, MA 02129
Phone: 617-242-3009
Email: mariln@verizon.net
http://www.nln.org

Purpose: To aid Massachusetts and Rhode Island practical nursing students.

Eligibility: Applicants must be Massachusetts or Rhode Island residents and have lived in Massachusetts or Rhode Island for at least four years before having entered that practical nursing program. They must be full-time students who have completed four months of their program of study. Selection is based on stated career goals and professional potential.

Target applicants: College students. Adult students.
Amount: Varies.
Number of awards: Varies.
Deadline: February 28.
How to apply: Applications are available online. An application form, official transcript, personal essay and two recommendation letters are required.
Exclusive: Visit www.UltimateScholarshipBook.com and enter code MA169312 for updates on this award.

(1694) • Marion Maccarrell Scott Scholarship

Hawaii Community Foundation - Scholarships
1164 Bishop Street, Suite 800
Honolulu, HI 96813
Phone: 888-731-3863
Fax: 808-521-6286
Email: scholarships@hcf-hawaii.org
http://www.hawaiicommunityfoundation.org
Purpose: To support graduating high school students in Hawaii who are committed to world peace.
Eligibility: Applicants must have attended a public high school in Hawaii, and they must plan to attend college on the U.S. mainland. Students must have at least a 2.8 GPA.
Target applicants: High school students.
Minimum GPA: 2.8
Amount: Varies.
Number of awards: Varies.
Deadline: March 1.
How to apply: To apply, register online, complete the online application and select the scholarships to which you wish to apply. In addition, mail the supporting materials: printed confirmation page from the online application, personal statement, essay, copy of Student Aid Report (SAR) available at www.fafsa.ed.gov and official transcript.
Exclusive: Visit www.UltimateScholarshipBook.com and enter code HA169412 for updates on this award.

(1695) • Marlin R. Scarborough Memorial Scholarship

South Dakota Board of Regents
306 East Capitol Ave, Suite 200
Pierre, SD 57501-2545
Phone: 605-773-3455
Fax: 605-773-5320
Email: info@sdbor.edu
http://www.sdbor.edu
Purpose: To support undergraduate students in South Dakota.
Eligibility: Applicants must submit an essay detailing their leadership qualities, academic achievements and community service. Students must attend a public South Dakota university with at least a 3.5 GPA, and they must be in their junior year at the time they receive the scholarship funding.
Target applicants: College students. Adult students.
Minimum GPA: 3.5
Amount: $1,000.
Number of awards: 1.
Deadline: Varies.
How to apply: Applications are available online.
Exclusive: Visit www.UltimateScholarshipBook.com and enter code SO169512 for updates on this award.

(1696) • Marvin L. Zuidema Scholarship Award

American Society of Civil Engineers-Michigan Section
ASCE Scholarships
P.O. Box 15276
Lansing, MI 48901
Phone: 734-459-3231
Email: lak1204@sbcglobal.net
http://sections.asce.org/michigan
Purpose: To aid American Society of Civil Engineers (ASCE) student members in Michigan who have contributed meaningfully to student civil engineering activities.
Eligibility: Applicants must be U.S. citizens, Michigan residents and rising juniors or seniors who are enrolled full-time in an ABET-accredited civil engineering degree program. They must have a GPA of 2.5 or higher on a four-point scale and have made a notable contribution to civil engineering student activities. Selection is based on academic merit.
Target applicants: College students. Adult students.
Minimum GPA: 2.5
Amount: $1,500.
Number of awards: 1.
Deadline: May 25.
How to apply: Applications are available online. An application form and an official transcript are required.
Exclusive: Visit www.UltimateScholarshipBook.com and enter code AM169612 for updates on this award.

(1697) • Mary Anne Williams Scholarship

Virginia Division, United Daughters of the Confederacy
c/o Mrs. Jean Frawner
6501 Norman Bridge Road
Hanover, VA 23069
Email: 2vp@vaudc.org
http://www.vaudc.org
Purpose: To aid Virginia pre-medical and engineering students who are lineal descendants of Confederate veterans.
Eligibility: Applicants must be Virginia residents who are lineal descendants of a worthy Confederate veteran. They must be undergraduate or graduate students who are majoring in pre-medicine or engineering at a Virginia postsecondary institution. They must have a GPA of 3.0 or higher on a four-point scale. Applicants must demonstrate financial need. Selection is based on academic achievement and financial need.
Target applicants: College students. Graduate school students. Adult students.
Minimum GPA: 3.0
Amount: Varies.
Number of awards: 1.
Scholarship may be renewable.
Deadline: April 30.
How to apply: Applications are available by request. An application form, proof of Confederate ancestry, a recent applicant photo, an official transcript, two recommendation letters, a personal statement and an endorsement from a Virginia Division UDC chapter are required.
Exclusive: Visit www.UltimateScholarshipBook.com and enter code VI169712 for updates on this award.

(1698) • Mary Benevento/CTAHPERD Scholarship

Connecticut Association of Health, Physical Education, Recreation and Dance
c/o Janice Skene, CTAHPERD Scholarship Chair

Eastbury School
1389 Neipsic Road
Glastonbury, CT 06033
Phone: 860-652-7858
Email: skenej@glastonburyus.org
http://www.ctahperd.org
Purpose: To aid Connecticut students who are planning to pursue higher education in school health teaching, physical education, recreation or dance.
Eligibility: Applicants must be U.S. citizens and Connecticut residents. They must be high school seniors who are planning to pursue a bachelor's degree in school health teaching, physical education, recreation or dance at an accredited Connecticut postsecondary institution. Selection is based on academic merit, professional potential and character.
Target applicants: High school students.
Amount: $1,000.
Number of awards: Varies.
Deadline: April 1.
How to apply: Applications are available online. An application form, transcript, personal statement and one letter of recommendation are required.
Exclusive: Visit www.UltimateScholarshipBook.com and enter code CO169812 for updates on this award.

(1699) • Mary Eileen Dixey Scholarship

American Occupational Therapy Foundation
4720 Montgomery Lane
P.O. Box 31220
Bethesda, MD 20824
Phone: 301-652-6611
Fax: 301-656-3620
Email: jcooper@aotf.org
http://www.aotf.org
Purpose: To aid New Hampshire occupational therapy students.
Eligibility: Applicants must be New Hampshire residents who are members of the American Occupational Therapy Association (AOTA). They must be enrolled full-time in an accredited occupational therapy program at the associate's or master's degree level in the state of New Hampshire. Master's level students must be enrolled in a first professional degree program and must have completed at least one year of study to be eligible. Selection is based on the overall strength of the application.
Target applicants: College students. Graduate school students. Adult students.
Amount: $2,000.
Number of awards: 1.
Deadline: December 2.
How to apply: Applications are available online. An application form, two personal references and a program director statement are required.
Exclusive: Visit www.UltimateScholarshipBook.com and enter code AM169912 for updates on this award.

(1700) • Mary Graham Lasley Scholarship Competition

Symphony Orchestra League of Alexandria
2121 Eisenhower Avenue
Suite 608
Alexandria, VA 22314
Phone: 703-548-0885
Fax: 703-548-0985
http://www.alexsym.org/lasley.shtml
Purpose: To support performing artists.
Eligibility: Applicants must be full-time undergraduate or graduate music students who are Virginia, Maryland or Washington, DC residents or students at colleges, universities or conservatories in Virginia, Maryland or Washington DC. Students must be 25 years of age or younger. Prior first place winners may not reenter. Note: We do not recommend applying to scholarships that charge application fees. However, some scholarships of this type charge fees and are included for completeness.
Target applicants: College students. Graduate school students.
Amount: $1,000-$2,000.
Number of awards: Up to 3.
Deadline: March 10.
How to apply: Applications are available online. An application form, resume and $25 entry fee are required.
Exclusive: Visit www.UltimateScholarshipBook.com and enter code SY170012 for updates on this award.

(1701) • Mary Karele Milligan Scholarship

Czech Cultural Center
4920 San Jacinto
Houston, TX 77004
Phone: 713-528-2060
Fax: 713-528-2017
Email: czech@czechcenter.org
http://www.czechcenter.org
Purpose: To provide financial assistance to children of Czech descent.
Eligibility: Applicants must have at least one Czech parent and be full-time undergraduate degree candidates to a four-year college or university. They must either be Texas residents or sons or daughters of members of the Czech Cultural Center Houston.
Target applicants: High school students.
Amount: $1,000.
Number of awards: 3.
Scholarship may be renewable.
Deadline: March 12.
How to apply: Applications are available online.
Exclusive: Visit www.UltimateScholarshipBook.com and enter code CZ170112 for updates on this award.

(1702) • Mary Macon McGuire Educational Grant

Virginia Federation of Women's Clubs
P.O. Box 8750
Richmond, VA 23226
Phone: 800-699-8392
Fax: 804-288-0341
Email: headquarters@gfwcvirginia.org
http://www.gfwcvirginia.org
Purpose: To support Virginia women who are returning to school in order to better support their families.
Eligibility: Students must submit an essay and three letters of recommendation. Applicants must show financial need.
Target applicants: College students. Adult students.
Amount: $2,500.
Number of awards: 2.
Deadline: March 15.
How to apply: Applications are available online.
Exclusive: Visit www.UltimateScholarshipBook.com and enter code VI170212 for updates on this award.

(1703) · Mary McLeod Bethune Scholarship Program

Florida Department of Education
Office of Student Financial Assistance
1940 N. Monroe Street
Suite 70
Tallahassee, FL 32303-4759
Phone: 888-827-2004
Fax: 850-245-9667
Email: osfa@fldoe.org
http://www.floridastudentfinancialaid.org

Purpose: To help Florida-resident undergraduate students who attend or plan to attend Bethune-Coleman College, Edward Waters College, Florida A&M University or Florida Memorial University.
Eligibility: Applicants must show financial need as determined by the school and meet the application procedures and deadlines of the participating schools.
Target applicants: High school students. College students. Adult students.
Minimum GPA: 3.0
Amount: $3,000.
Number of awards: Varies.
Scholarship may be renewable.
Deadline: Varies.
How to apply: Applications may be obtained from the participating schools' financial aid offices.
Exclusive: Visit www.UltimateScholarshipBook.com and enter code FL170312 for updates on this award.

(1704) · Mary Rubin and Benjamin M. Rubin Scholarship Fund

Central Scholarship Bureau
1700 Reisterstown Road
Suite 220
Baltimore, MD 21208-2903
Phone: 410-415-5558
Fax: 410-415-5501
Email: info@centralsb.org
http://www.centralsb.org

Purpose: To help women from Maryland who plan to attend an accredited school.
Eligibility: Applicants must have been out of high school for at least a year and be permanent residents of Maryland. Selection is based on academic achievement, extracurricular activities and financial need. A transcript, recommendation, Student Aid Report (SAR), school financial aid letter, budget form and essay are required.
Target applicants: College students. Graduate school students. Adult students.
Minimum GPA: 3.0
Amount: $2,500.
Number of awards: Varies.
Deadline: May 10.
How to apply: Applications are available online.
Exclusive: Visit www.UltimateScholarshipBook.com and enter code CE170412 for updates on this award.

(1705) · Maryann K. Murtha Memorial Scholarship

American Legion Auxiliary, Department of New York
112 State Street
Suite 1310
Albany, NY 12207
Phone: 518-463-1162
Fax: 518-449-5406
Email: alanyterry@nycap.rr.com
http://www.deptny.org/Scholarships.htm

Purpose: To provide financial assistance to students whose parents, grandparents or great-grandparents served in the Armed Forces during wartime.
Eligibility: Applicants must be children, grandchildren or great-grandchildren of Armed Forces veterans who served during World War I, World War II, the Korean Conflict, the Vietnam War, Grenada/Lebanon, Panama or the Persian Gulf. Students must be high school seniors, U.S. citizens and New York State residents.
Target applicants: High school students.
Amount: $1,000.
Number of awards: 1.
Deadline: March 1.
How to apply: Applications are available online.
Exclusive: Visit www.UltimateScholarshipBook.com and enter code AM170512 for updates on this award.

(1706) · Masonic Scholarship Program

Grand Lodge of Iowa, A.F. and A.M.
Scholarship Selection Committee
P.O. Box 279
Cedar Rapids, Iowa 52406-0279
Phone: 319-365-1438
Fax: 319-365-1439
Email: scholarships@gl-iowa.org
http://www.gl-iowa.org

Purpose: To reward high school seniors from Iowa public high schools for academics and leadership skills.
Eligibility: Applicants must be pursuing a post-secondary education in any state at an institution which provides a two-year or four-year college program or vocational training. They do not need to have a Masonic connection. Selection is based on academic record, communication skills and financial need, but the most important is service to school and community with an emphasis on leadership roles. Finalists will be asked to appear before the committee for personal interviews.
Target applicants: High school students.
Amount: $2,000.
Number of awards: 60.
Deadline: February 1.
How to apply: Applications are available online or from guidance departments at Iowa public high schools.
Exclusive: Visit www.UltimateScholarshipBook.com and enter code GR170612 for updates on this award.

(1707) · Massachusetts Community Colleges Access Grant

Massachusetts Community Colleges
Old South Building
294 Washington Street
Mezzanine #18
Boston, MA 02108
Phone: 617-542-2911
Email: jshamon@mcceo.mass.edu
http://www.masscc.org

Purpose: To make a Massachusetts community college education accessible for all.
Eligibility: Applicants must be pursuing an associate degree at a Massachusetts community college. Students whose household income

is $36,000 per year or less are eligible to receive funds to cover full tuition and fees.
Target applicants: High school students. College students. Adult students.
Amount: Up to full tuition.
Number of awards: Varies.
Deadline: Varies.
How to apply: Applications are available from Massachusetts community college financial aid offices.
Exclusive: Visit www.UltimateScholarshipBook.com and enter code MA170712 for updates on this award.

(1708) • Massachusetts Department of Social Services Adopted Children Tuition Waiver

Massachusetts Department of Higher Education
Office of Student Financial Assistance
454 Broadway
Suite 200
Revere, MA 02151
Phone: 617-727-9420
Fax: 617-727-0667
Email: osfa@osfa.mass.edu
http://www.osfa.mass.edu/default.asp
Purpose: To aid Massachusetts adoptees who are pursuing higher education at a public institution in Massachusetts.
Eligibility: Applicants must be U.S. citizens or eligible non-citizens who are Massachusetts residents. They must be age 24 or younger and must have been adopted through the Massachusetts Department of Social Services (DSS) by eligible Massachusetts residents. They must be enrolled in undergraduate courses at a public Massachusetts college or university. MD courses at the University of Massachusetts Medical Center are ineligible for funding. Applicants cannot have earned a baccalaureate degree previously. Selection is based on the overall strength of the application.
Target applicants: High school students. College students.
Amount: Full Tuition Waiver.
Number of awards: Varies.
Scholarship may be renewable.
Deadline: Varies.
How to apply: Applications instructions are available by request from the applicant's financial aid office or from the Massachusetts Office of Student Financial Assistance.
Exclusive: Visit www.UltimateScholarshipBook.com and enter code MA170812 for updates on this award.

(1709) • Massachusetts Part-Time Grant

Massachusetts Department of Higher Education
Office of Student Financial Assistance
454 Broadway
Suite 200
Revere, MA 02151
Phone: 617-727-9420
Fax: 617-727-0667
Email: osfa@osfa.mass.edu
http://www.osfa.mass.edu/default.asp
Purpose: To aid Massachusetts part-time undergraduate students.
Eligibility: Applicants must U.S. citizens or eligible non-citizens who have been Massachusetts residents for at least one year. They must be enrolled in an undergraduate degree or certificate program on a part-time basis (6 to 11 credits per semester) at a Massachusetts postsecondary institution. They must not owe refund money on an educational grant or have any defaulted student loans. Applicants who have earned a bachelor's or professional degree previously are ineligible.
Target applicants: High school students. College students. Adult students.
Amount: At least $200.
Number of awards: Varies.
Scholarship may be renewable.
Deadline: Varies.
How to apply: Application is made by completing the FAFSA and then contacting your financial aid office.
Exclusive: Visit www.UltimateScholarshipBook.com and enter code MA170912 for updates on this award.

(1710) • Massachusetts Student Broadcaster Scholarship

Massachusetts Broadcasters Association
43 Riverside Avenue
PMB 401
Medford, MA 02155
http://www.massbroadcasters.org/students/index.cfm
Purpose: To support student broadcasters.
Eligibility: Applicants must be Massachusetts residents who are enrolled or plan to enroll in an accredited institution of higher learning that offers degrees in television and radio broadcasting. Students must meet their school's definition of a full-time student. Selection is based on financial need, academic merit, community service, extracurricular activities and work experience.
Target applicants: High school students. College students. Adult students.
Amount: Varies.
Number of awards: Varies.
Deadline: Varies.
How to apply: Applications are available online. An application form, transcript and financial statement are required.
Exclusive: Visit www.UltimateScholarshipBook.com and enter code MA171012 for updates on this award.

(1711) • MASSGrant

Massachusetts Department of Higher Education
Office of Student Financial Assistance
454 Broadway
Suite 200
Revere, MA 02151
Phone: 617-727-9420
Fax: 617-727-0667
Email: osfa@osfa.mass.edu
http://www.osfa.mass.edu/default.asp
Purpose: To provide need-based financial assistance to undergraduate students who reside in Massachusetts and who are enrolled in and pursuing a program of higher education.
Eligibility: Applicants must be permanent legal residents of Massachusetts and have an Expected Family Contribution (EFC) between $0 and $3,800. Applicants must be enrolled as full-time students in a certificate, associate or bachelor's degree program and not have received a prior bachelor's degree or its equivalent.
Target applicants: High school students. College students. Adult students.
Amount: Varies.
Number of awards: Varies.
Scholarship may be renewable.
Deadline: May 1.

How to apply: Complete and submit the Free Application for Federal Student Aid (FAFSA).
Exclusive: Visit www.UltimateScholarshipBook.com and enter code MA171112 for updates on this award.

(1712) • Math and Science Teaching Incentive Scholarships

New York State Higher Education Services Corporation (HESC)
99 Washington Avenue
Albany, NY 12255
Phone: 888-697-4372
Email: hescwebmail@hesc.org
http://www.hesc.com/content.nsf/
Purpose: To support students in New York who are planning careers in math or science secondary education.
Eligibility: Applicants must have at least a 2.5 GPA. Recipients must agree to work for at least five years after graduation as a secondary school science or math teacher in the state of New York.
Target applicants: College students. Adult students.
Minimum GPA: 2.5
Amount: Up to full tuition.
Number of awards: Varies.
Scholarship may be renewable.
Deadline: Varies.
How to apply: Applications are available online.
Exclusive: Visit www.UltimateScholarshipBook.com and enter code NE171212 for updates on this award.

(1713) • Mathematics and Science Teachers Scholarship Program

Massachusetts Department of Higher Education
Office of Student Financial Assistance
454 Broadway
Suite 200
Revere, MA 02151
Phone: 617-727-9420
Fax: 617-727-0667
Email: osfa@osfa.mass.edu
http://www.osfa.mass.edu/default.asp
Purpose: To provide support to Massachusetts teachers who are currently teaching math or science and need required schooling to satisfy certification requirements.
Eligibility: Applicants must be currently teaching math or science at a Massachusetts public K-12 school, and they must continue to be employed in that capacity throughout the completion of the degree. Students must be enrolled in an undergraduate or graduate degree program for certification in math or science. They must sign an agreement to continue teaching one of these subjects in Massachusetts for a specified length of time after completion of the degree program.
Target applicants: College students. Graduate school students. Adult students.
Amount: Up to full tuition for three courses per semester.
Number of awards: Varies.
Scholarship may be renewable.
Deadline: October 15.
How to apply: Applications are available online.
Exclusive: Visit www.UltimateScholarshipBook.com and enter code MA171312 for updates on this award.

(1714) • Matters of Life and Death Scholarship Writing Contest

Compassion and Choices of Northern California
3701 Sacramento Street, #439
San Francisco, CA 94118
Phone: 866-825-8967
Email: admin@compassionandchoicesnca.org
http://www.compassionandchoicesnca.org
Purpose: To expose students to the issues surrounding aid in dying and to financially assist college-bound scholars.
Eligibility: Applicants must be high school juniors or seniors in the state of California during the school year of application. They must plan to attend an institution of higher learning upon graduation. A 1,000 word essay is required on a topic related to aid-in-dying.
Target applicants: High school students.
Amount: Up to $1,000.
Number of awards: 3.
Deadline: June 1.
How to apply: No application form is required, please visit the website for the essay prompt (www.compassionandchoicesnca.org/essay.php). Applicants must send an essay with a cover letter that includes their name, address, phone number, email address, school name and grade level. Email your entries to admin@compassionandchoicesnca.org and in the subject line, write: Your Last Name, Your First Name. Or you may mail your entries to: Matters of Life and Death Scholarship Writing Contest at the address listed.
Exclusive: Visit www.UltimateScholarshipBook.com and enter code CO171412 for updates on this award.

(1715) • McCurry Foundation Scholarship

McCurry Foundation Inc.
Scholarship Selection Committee
11645 Beach Boulevard, Suite 200
Jacksonville, FL 32246
http://www.mccurryfoundation.org
Purpose: To provide assistance to college students who have demonstrated leadership, a responsible work ethic and academic excellence.
Eligibility: Applicants must be public high school seniors who have demonstrated leadership, a responsible work ethic, community involvement, service, and academic excellence with a GPA of at least 3.0. Students must demonstrate financial need,with a maximum family income of $75,000. Preference is given to students from Clay, Duval, Nassau and St. Johns Counties in Florida and from Glynn County in Georgia.
Target applicants: High school students.
Minimum GPA: 3.0
Amount: Varies.
Number of awards: Varies.
Scholarship may be renewable.
Deadline: February 15.
How to apply: Applications are available online.
Exclusive: Visit www.UltimateScholarshipBook.com and enter code MC171512 for updates on this award.

(1716) • McGraw Foundation Emergency Financial Aid Award

Associated Colleges of Illinois
20 North Wacker Drive
Suite 1456
Chicago, IL 60606

Phone: 312-263-2391
Fax: 213-263-3424
Email: aci@acifund.org
https://www.acigrantsadministration.org/Scholarships/
Purpose: To aid undergraduates students who are in need of emergency financial assistance.
Eligibility: Applicants must be full-time undergraduate students who are from middle-income families. They must be experiencing a personal financial emergency, must be ineligible for other sources of emergency aid and cannot be receiving any such aid from any other source. Applicants must have tried to secure part-time employment. Selection is based on financial need.
Target applicants: College students. Adult students.
Amount: $2,500.
Number of awards: 20.
Deadline: Varies.
How to apply: Applications are available online. An application form and a personal essay are required.
Exclusive: Visit www.UltimateScholarshipBook.com and enter code AS171612 for updates on this award.

(1717) • Medallion Fund

New Hampshire Charitable Foundation
37 Pleasant Street
Concord, NH 03301-4005
Phone: 603-225-6641
Fax: 603-225-1700
Email: info@nhcf.org
http://www.nhcf.org/Page.aspx?pid=183
Purpose: To improve the skilled workforce in areas of need in New Hampshire.
Eligibility: Applicants must be enrolling in an accredited vocational or technical program that does not lead to a bachelor's or advanced degree. They must be legal residents of New Hampshire and intend to work in a vocational or technical career when their schooling is complete. Preference is given to those who plan to go into the manufacturing trade sector or have little or no other opportunities for training or education.
Target applicants: High school students. College students. Adult students.
Amount: Varies.
Number of awards: Varies.
Deadline: Rolling.
How to apply: Applications are available online.
Exclusive: Visit www.UltimateScholarshipBook.com and enter code NE171712 for updates on this award.

(1718) • Medical Student Scholarship Program

Illinois Department of Public Health
535 W. Jefferson Street
Springfield, IL 62761
Phone: 217-782-4977
Fax: 217-782-3987
Email: dph.mailus@illinois.gov
http://www.idph.state.il.us
Purpose: To increase the number of medical professionals in rural areas of Illinois.
Eligibility: Applicants must be Illinois residents enrolled in an Illinois allopathic or osteopathic medical school. Students must be planning to practice in one or more of the following medical fields: family practice, general internal medicine, general pediatrics or obstetrics/gynecology. Applicants must show evidence of financial need. Scholarship recipients agree to set up practice in an area designated as having a shortage of primary care providers.
Target applicants: Graduate school students. Adult students.
Amount: Varies.
Number of awards: Varies.
Scholarship may be renewable.
Deadline: May 15.
How to apply: Applications are available online.
Exclusive: Visit www.UltimateScholarshipBook.com and enter code IL171812 for updates on this award.

(1719) • MEFA UPlan Prepaid Tuition Waiver Program

Massachusetts Educational Financing Authority
125 Summer Street
Suite 300
Boston, MA 02110
Phone: 800-449-6332
Fax: 617-261-9765
Email: info@mefa.org
http://www.mefa.org
Purpose: To provide financial aid in the form of tuition waivers to Massachusetts students who prepay their tuition at lower rates.
Eligibility: Applicants must be planning to attend a school in the state of Massachusetts which participates in the UPlan program.
Target applicants: Junior high students or younger. High school students. College students. Adult students.
Amount: Varies.
Number of awards: Varies.
Scholarship may be renewable.
Deadline: Varies.
How to apply: Applications are available online.
Exclusive: Visit www.UltimateScholarshipBook.com and enter code MA171912 for updates on this award.

(1720) • Mel Ferris Scholarship Program

California Architectural Foundation
1303 J Street
Suite 200
Sacramento, CA 95814
Phone: 916-448-9082
Email: mharperbarton@aiacc.org
http://www.aiacc.org
Purpose: To support architecture students.
Eligibility: Applicants must be students in good standing at Academy of Art University, California College of the Arts, Cal Poly Pomona, Cal Poly San Luis Obispo, New School of Art and Architecture, SCI-ARC, UCLA, UC Berkeley, USC or Woodbury University. Graduate students may apply if they are studying architecture for the first time in graduate school. Selection is based on school and community service (10 percent), academics (20 percent), financial need (20 percent) and portfolio (50 percent).
Target applicants: College students. Graduate school students. Adult students.
Amount: $500-$5,000.
Number of awards: 6.
Deadline: February 14.
How to apply: Applications are available online. An application form, statement of goals, statement of financial need, statement of community service, transcript and graphics illustrating best work are required.
Exclusive: Visit www.UltimateScholarshipBook.com and enter code CA172012 for updates on this award.

(1721) • Mellinger Scholarships

Edward Arthur Mellinger Educational Foundation Inc.
1025 E. Broadway
P.O. Box 770
Monmouth, IL 61462
Phone: 309-734-2419
Fax: 309-734-4435
Email: info@mellinger.org
http://www.mellinger.org

Purpose: The E. A. Mellinger Foundation supports education as a memorial to its namesake.
Eligibility: Applicants must live in Western Illinois or Eastern Iowa, submit the FAFSA form and demonstrate financial need and attend an accredited university. Awards are based on academic achievement. Part-time students are also eligible for scholarships, and loans are also available to graduate students.
Target applicants: High school students. College students. Adult students.
Amount: $300-$1,500.
Number of awards: Varies.
Scholarship may be renewable.
Deadline: May 1.
How to apply: Applications are available by mail or online. Application forms are only available from February 1 to May 1 each year.
Exclusive: Visit www.UltimateScholarshipBook.com and enter code ED172112 for updates on this award.

(1722) • Memorial Scholarships

New York State Higher Education Services Corporation (HESC)
99 Washington Avenue
Albany, NY 12255
Phone: 888-697-4372
Email: hescwebmail@hesc.org
http://www.hesc.com/content.nsf/

Purpose: To support the spouses and dependents of deceased firefighters, volunteer firefighters, police officers, peace officers and EMS workers from the state of New York.
Eligibility: Applicants must be full-time undergraduate students, and they may attend any public or private school in the state of New York.
Target applicants: College students. Adult students.
Amount: Up to full tuition plus room and board.
Number of awards: Varies.
Scholarship may be renewable.
Deadline: Varies.
How to apply: Applications are available online.
Exclusive: Visit www.UltimateScholarshipBook.com and enter code NE172212 for updates on this award.

(1723) • Mexican Scholarship Fund

Central Indiana Community Foundation
615 North Alabama Street
Suite 119
Indianapolis, IN 46204-1498
Phone: 317-634-2423
Fax: 317-684-0943
http://www.cicf.org

Purpose: To provide financial assistance to Indiana residents of Mexican descent.
Eligibility: Applicants must have a minimum GPA of 3.3, demonstrate academic promise and demonstrate financial need. Preference is given to students of Mexican descent. Awards may be used for tuition, required fees or room and board.
Target applicants: High school students.
Minimum GPA: 3.3
Amount: Varies.
Number of awards: Varies.
Deadline: March 5.
How to apply: Applications are available online.
Exclusive: Visit www.UltimateScholarshipBook.com and enter code CE172312 for updates on this award.

(1724) • Michael Curry Summer Internship Program

Governor's Office of the State of Illinois Michael Curry Summer Internship Program
107 William G. Stratton Building
Springfield, IL 62706
Phone: 217-782-5189
http://www.illinois.gov/GOV/internships.htm

Purpose: To provide internships for college juniors, seniors or graduate students.
Eligibility: Applicants must be Illinois residents. Recipients work full-time in an agency under the jurisdiction of the Governor for 10 weeks during the summer.
Target applicants: College students. Graduate school students. Adult students.
Amount: $3,000 stipend.
Number of awards: Varies.
Deadline: Varies.
How to apply: Applications are available online or by mail.
Exclusive: Visit www.UltimateScholarshipBook.com and enter code GO172412 for updates on this award.

(1725) • Michigan Competitive Scholarship

Michigan Tuition Grant Program
Office of Scholarships and Grants
P.O. Box 30462
Lansing, MI 48909
Phone: 888-447-2687
Email: osg@michigan.gov
http://www.michigan.gov/osg

Purpose: To assist students who plan to attend a Michigan public or private college.
Eligibility: Applicants must be Michigan residents since July 1 of the previous calendar year and have received a qualifying score on the ACT and a minimum 2.0 GPA. Applicants must also demonstrate financial need and be enrolled in an approved Michigan college or university. Applicants cannot be pursuing a degree in theology, divinity or religious education. This award is based on both financial need and academic merit.
Target applicants: High school students. College students. Adult students.
Minimum GPA: 2.0
Amount: $510-$1,610.
Number of awards: Varies.
Scholarship may be renewable.
Deadline: March 1.
How to apply: File a Free Application for Federal Student Aid (FAFSA).
Exclusive: Visit www.UltimateScholarshipBook.com and enter code MI172512 for updates on this award.

(1726) • Michigan Department of Treasury

Michigan Department of Treasury
P.O. Box 30462
Lansing, MI 48909
Phone: 888-447-2687
Email: osg@michigan.gov
http://www.michigan.gov

Purpose: To remind Michigan families of the importance of saving for higher education.

Eligibility: Applicants must be Michigan residents who are in the 12th grade or below and do not already have four years paid of the Michigan Education Trust prepaid tuition plan. An adult must enter on the student's behalf. The award pays for one semester of free tuition.

Target applicants: Junior high students or younger. High school students.

Amount: One semester of tuition.

Number of awards: 1.

Deadline: August 31.

How to apply: Applications are available online.

Exclusive: Visit www.UltimateScholarshipBook.com and enter code MI172612 for updates on this award.

(1727) • Michigan Merit Award

Michigan Tuition Grant Program
Office of Scholarships and Grants
P.O. Box 30462
Lansing, MI 48909
Phone: 888-447-2687
Email: osg@michigan.gov
http://www.michigan.gov/osg

Purpose: To support Michigan students who have demonstrated academic merit.

Eligibility: Applicants must graduate from high school or obtain a GED in Michigan or be a Michigan resident who graduated from an out-of-state high school. Students must take the following MEAP tests prior to high school graduation: writing, reading, mathematics and science. They should score level 1 or level 2 on all four of the tests. Alternatively, students may use qualifying scores from the SAT, ACT or the WorkKeys test.

Target applicants: High school students.

Amount: Up to $3,000.

Number of awards: Varies.

Deadline: November 15.

How to apply: Applications are available online.

Exclusive: Visit www.UltimateScholarshipBook.com and enter code MI172712 for updates on this award.

(1728) • Michigan Oratorical Contest

American Legion, Department of Michigan
212 N. Verlinden Avenue, Ste. A
Lansing, MI 48915
Phone: 517-371-4720 x11
Fax: 517-371-2401
Email: programs@michiganlegion.org
http://www.michiganlegion.org

Purpose: To enhance high school students' experience with and understanding of the U.S. Constitution. The contest will help develop students' leadership skills and civic appreciation, as well as the ability to deliver thoughtful, insightful orations regarding U.S. citizenship and its inherent responsibilities.

Eligibility: Applicants must be high school students under the age of 20 who are U.S. citizens or legal residents and residents of the state. Students first give an oration within their state and winners compete at the national level. The oration must be related to the Constitution of the United States focusing on the duties and obligations citizens have to the government. It must be in English and be between eight and ten minutes. There is also an assigned topic which is posted on the website, and it should be between three and five minutes.

Target applicants: High school students.

Amount: Up to $1,500.

Number of awards: Varies.

Deadline: January 3.

How to apply: Application information is available online under the link "Forms and Applications."

Exclusive: Visit www.UltimateScholarshipBook.com and enter code AM172812 for updates on this award.

(1729) • Michigan Police Officer and Fire Fighters Survivor Tuition

Michigan Commission on Law Enforcement Standards
714 S. Harrison Road
East Lansing, MI 48823
Phone: 517-332-2521
http://www.michigan.gov/msp

Purpose: To assist spouses and children of police officers and firefighters who were killed in the line of duty.

Eligibility: Applicants must be the spouse or child of a deceased Michigan sheriff, deputy, village or township marshal, state, city, village or township officer or a fire department member who was responsible for extinguishing fires. The death must have been the direct result of an injury incurred in the line of duty. The applicant must be a Michigan resident whose family income is less than 400 percent of the federal poverty level, excluding death benefits from the deceased officer or firefighter. If the applicant is the child of the officer or firefighter, the child must have been under the age of 21 at the time of death.

Target applicants: High school students. College students. Adult students.

Amount: Tuition.

Number of awards: Varies.

Scholarship may be renewable.

Deadline: Varies.

How to apply: Applications are available online.

Exclusive: Visit www.UltimateScholarshipBook.com and enter code MI172912 for updates on this award.

(1730) • Michigan Tuition Grant

Michigan Tuition Grant Program
Office of Scholarships and Grants
P.O. Box 30462
Lansing, MI 48909
Phone: 888-447-2687
Email: osg@michigan.gov
http://www.michigan.gov/osg

Purpose: To assist Michigan students who are pursuing higher education in Michigan.

Eligibility: Applicants must be U.S. citizens, permanent residents or approved refugees. They must be Michigan residents who have lived there since at least July 1 of the previous calendar year and must be undergraduate students who are attending an approved Michigan college or university at least part-time. They must demonstrate financial need and not be in default on a federal student loan. Applicants who

are pursuing degrees in divinity, theology or religious education are ineligible. Selection is based on financial need.
Target applicants: College students. Adult students.
Amount: Up to $1,512.
Number of awards: Varies.
Scholarship may be renewable.
Deadline: Varies.
How to apply: Application is made by filing the FAFSA.
Exclusive: Visit www.UltimateScholarshipBook.com and enter code MI173012 for updates on this award.

(1731) • Michigan Tuition Incentive Program

Michigan Department of Treasury
P.O. Box 30462
Lansing, MI 48909
Phone: 888-447-2687
Email: osg@michigan.gov
http://www.michigan.gov
Purpose: To encourage Michigan students to complete high school and seek higher education.
Eligibility: Applicants must be upcoming high school graduates or GED recipients under the age of 20 and also must have received Medicaid for 24 months in a 36 month period after their 12th birthday. Qualifying students will receive an acceptance form, which must be returned to the Office of Scholarships and Grants to become eligible. The program covers tuition and mandatory fees for students pursuing an associate degree and up to $2,000 for studies from the sophomore to graduate level.
Target applicants: High school students.
Amount: Up to full tuition.
Number of awards: Varies.
Scholarship may be renewable.
Deadline: Varies.
How to apply: Applications are available from the Michigan Department of Human Services.
Exclusive: Visit www.UltimateScholarshipBook.com and enter code MI173112 for updates on this award.

(1732) • Middle School Essay Contest

American Legion, Department of Virginia
1708 Commonwealth Avenue
Richmond, VA 23230
Phone: 804-353-6606
Fax: 804-358-1940
http://www.valegion.org
Purpose: To promote citizenship in young Virginia students.
Eligibility: Applicants must write an essay on an assigned topic. The essay should be written at the student's desk during school time and will be evaluated based on originality, sincerity and the student's ability to communicate meaning.
Target applicants: Junior high students or younger.
Amount: $100-$500.
Number of awards: Varies.
Deadline: March 1.
How to apply: Applications are available online and from sponsoring Posts.
Exclusive: Visit www.UltimateScholarshipBook.com and enter code AM173212 for updates on this award.

(1733) • Midwest Student Exchange Program

Midwest Higher Education Compact
1300 S. Second Street
Suite 130
Minneapolis, MN 55454-1079
Phone: 612-626-1602
Fax: 612-626-8290
Email: jenniferd@mhec.org
http://msep.mhec.org
Purpose: The program aims to make attending out-of-state schools more affordable for students in member states.
Eligibility: Applicants must currently live in Indiana, Kansas, Michigan, Minnesota, Missouri, Nebraska, North Dakota or Wisconsin and wish to attend a participating school in one of these states outside their own. Other eligibility requirements vary depending on the state and school.
Target applicants: High school students. College students. Graduate school students. Adult students.
Amount: $500-$3,000.
Number of awards: Varies.
Scholarship may be renewable.
Deadline: Varies.
How to apply: Students must clearly mark that they are an MSEP student when applying to the school of their choice.
Exclusive: Visit www.UltimateScholarshipBook.com and enter code MI173312 for updates on this award.

(1734) • Mildred R. Knoles Opportunity Scholarship

American Legion Auxiliary, Department of Illinois
2720 E. Lincoln
Bloomington, IL 61704
Phone: 309-663-9366
Email: webmaster@illegion.org
http://illegion.org/index.shtml
Purpose: To provide financial assistance to Illinois veterans and their descendants.
Eligibility: Applicants must be veterans who served during eligibility dates or their children, grandchildren or great-grandchildren. They must be residents of Illinois and be in need of financial assistance.
Target applicants: High school students. College students. Adult students.
Amount: $800-$1,000.
Number of awards: Varies.
Deadline: Varies.
How to apply: Applications are available from your local American Legion Auxiliary.
Exclusive: Visit www.UltimateScholarshipBook.com and enter code AM173412 for updates on this award.

(1735) • Mildred Towle Scholarship - Study Abroad

Hawaii Community Foundation - Scholarships
1164 Bishop Street, Suite 800
Honolulu, HI 96813
Phone: 888-731-3863
Fax: 808-521-6286
Email: scholarships@hcf-hawaii.org
http://www.hawaiicommunityfoundation.org
Purpose: To support Hawaii students who plan to study abroad.
Eligibility: Applicants must study abroad as a junior, senior or graduate student. Students must have at least a 3.0 GPA.
Target applicants: College students. Graduate school students. Adult students.

Minimum GPA: 3.0
Amount: Varies.
Number of awards: Varies.
Deadline: March 1.
How to apply: To apply, register online, complete the online application and select the scholarships to which you wish to apply. In addition, mail the supporting materials: printed confirmation page from the online application, personal statement, copy of Student Aid Report (SAR) available at www.fafsa.ed.gov and official transcript.
Exclusive: Visit www.UltimateScholarshipBook.com and enter code HA173512 for updates on this award.

(1736) • Mildred Towle Scholarship for African-Americans

Hawaii Community Foundation - Scholarships
1164 Bishop Street, Suite 800
Honolulu, HI 96813
Phone: 888-731-3863
Fax: 808-521-6286
Email: scholarships@hcf-hawaii.org
http://www.hawaiicommunityfoundation.org
Purpose: To support African American students who are attending colleges in Hawaii.
Eligibility: Students must have at least a 3.0 GPA.
Target applicants: High school students. College students. Adult students.
Minimum GPA: 3.0
Amount: Varies.
Number of awards: Varies.
Deadline: March 1.
How to apply: To apply, register online, complete the online application and select the scholarships to which you wish to apply. In addition, mail the supporting materials: printed confirmation page from the online application, personal statement, copy of Student Aid Report (SAR) available at www.fafsa.ed.gov and official transcript.
Exclusive: Visit www.UltimateScholarshipBook.com and enter code HA173612 for updates on this award.

(1737) • Military Service Recognition Scholarship

New York State Higher Education Services Corporation (HESC)
99 Washington Avenue
Albany, NY 12255
Phone: 888-697-4372
Email: hescwebmail@hesc.org
http://www.hesc.com/content.nsf/
Purpose: To support the dependents and spouses of injured or deceased military personnel from the state of New York.
Eligibility: Military personnel must have been injured on or after August 2, 1990, and they must have been New York state residents at the time of the injury.
Target applicants: High school students. College students. Adult students.
Amount: Up to full tuition plus living expenses.
Number of awards: Varies.
Scholarship may be renewable.
Deadline: Varies.
How to apply: Applications are available online.
Exclusive: Visit www.UltimateScholarshipBook.com and enter code NE173712 for updates on this award.

(1738) • Milton Fisher Scholarship for Innovation and Creativity

Community Foundation for Greater New Haven
70 Audubon Street
New Haven, CT 06510-9755
Phone: 203-777-2386
Fax: 203-787-6584
Email: contactus@cfgnh.org
http://www.rbffoundation.org/scholarship.html
Purpose: To reward and encourage innovative problem solving.
Eligibility: Applicants must be high school juniors or seniors or must be entering or in the first year of an undergraduate degree program. They must be Connecticut or New York City residents or students who attend or plan to attend a Connecticut or New York City institution of higher learning.
Target applicants: High school students. College students. Adult students.
Amount: $1,000-$5,000.
Number of awards: 3-5.
Deadline: April 18.
How to apply: Applications are available online.
Exclusive: Visit www.UltimateScholarshipBook.com and enter code CO173812 for updates on this award.

(1739) • Minnesota Academic Excellence Scholarship

Minnesota Office of Higher Education Services
1450 Energy Park Drive
Suite 350
Saint Paul, MN 55108
Phone: 651-642-0567
Fax: 651-642-0675
Email: ginny.dodds@state.mn.us
http://www.mheso.state.mn.us
Purpose: To help students who have demonstrated outstanding ability, achievement and potential in selected areas of study.
Eligibility: Applicants must be Minnesota residents who have been admitted to a full-time program in an approved Minnesota college or university. Applicants must have demonstrated achievement in one of the following subjects: English or creative writing, fine arts, foreign language, math, science or social science.
Target applicants: High school students. College students. Adult students.
Amount: Up to full tuition.
Number of awards: Varies.
Scholarship may be renewable.
Deadline: Varies.
How to apply: For information about the status of this program, applicants should contact the schools they wish to attend.
Exclusive: Visit www.UltimateScholarshipBook.com and enter code MI173912 for updates on this award.

(1740) • Minnesota Indian Scholarship Program

Minnesota Office of Higher Education Services
1450 Energy Park Drive
Suite 350
Saint Paul, MN 55108
Phone: 651-642-0567
Fax: 651-642-0675
Email: ginny.dodds@state.mn.us

http://www.mheso.state.mn.us
Purpose: To provide money to help Native American students pay for higher education.
Eligibility: Applicants must be at least one-fourth Native American, Minnesota residents and members of a federally recognized Indian tribe. Applicants must be a high school graduate or posses a GED and have been accepted by an approved college, university or vocational school in Minnesota.
Target applicants: College students. Graduate school students. Adult students.
Amount: Up to $6,000.
Number of awards: Varies.
Scholarship may be renewable.
Deadline: July 1.
How to apply: This award is administered by the Minnesota Department of Children, Families, and Learning (CFL), and must be approved by the Minnesota Indian Scholarship Committee. To receive an application, contact your local tribal education office.
Exclusive: Visit www.UltimateScholarshipBook.com and enter code MI174012 for updates on this award.

(1741) • Minnesota Oratorical Contest

American Legion, Department of Minnesota
Third Floor, Veterans Service Building
20 W. 12th Street, Room 300A
St. Paul, MN 55155
Phone: 651-291-1800
Fax: 651-291-1057
Email: department@mnlegion.org
http://www.mnlegion.org
Purpose: To enhance high school students' experience with and understanding of the U.S. Constitution. The contest will help develop students' leadership skills and civic appreciation, as well as the ability to deliver thoughtful, insightful orations regarding U.S. citizenship and its inherent responsibilities.
Eligibility: Applicants must be high school students under the age of 20 who are U.S. citizens or legal residents and residents of the state. Students first give an oration within their state and winners compete at the national level. The oration must be related to the Constitution of the United States focusing on the duties and obligations citizens have to the government. It must be in English and be between eight and ten minutes. There is also an assigned topic which is posted on the website, and it should be between three and five minutes.
Target applicants: High school students.
Amount: Up to $1,200.
Number of awards: 4.
Deadline: January 28.
How to apply: Application information is available by email.
Exclusive: Visit www.UltimateScholarshipBook.com and enter code AM174112 for updates on this award.

(1742) • Minnesota State Grant

Minnesota Office of Higher Education Services
1450 Energy Park Drive
Suite 350
Saint Paul, MN 55108
Phone: 651-642-0567
Fax: 651-642-0675
Email: ginny.dodds@state.mn.us
http://www.mheso.state.mn.us
Purpose: To aid Minnesota students who are pursuing higher education in Minnesota.
Eligibility: Applicants must be U.S. citizens or permanent residents who are Minnesota residents. They must be high school graduates, GED recipients or at least 17 years old by the end of the academic year. They must be enrolled in a diploma, certificate or degree program for at least three credits at an eligible Minnesota school. Applicants who are in default of a federal or state SELF student loan are ineligible, as are those who owe the Office of Higher Education for the overpayment of a state grant. They cannot have earned a baccalaureate degree previously or be more than 30 days past due on child support payments. Selection is based on financial need.
Target applicants: High school students. College students. Adult students.
Amount: Up to $9,059.
Number of awards: Varies.
Scholarship may be renewable.
Deadline: Varies.
How to apply: Application is made by filing the FAFSA.
Exclusive: Visit www.UltimateScholarshipBook.com and enter code MI174212 for updates on this award.

(1743) • Minority and At-Risk Scholarship

Idaho State Board of Education
P.O. Box 83720
Boise, ID 83720
Phone: 208-334-2270
Fax: 208-334-2632
Email: dkelly@osbe.state.id.us
http://www.boardofed.idaho.gov
Purpose: To aid students who are "at-risk" of not being able to be college educated due to cultural, economic or physical circumstances.
Eligibility: Applicants must have graduated from an Idaho high school, and meet three of the following criteria: be a first-generation college student, be disabled, be a migrant farm worker or the dependent of one, demonstrate significant financial need or be a member of an ethnic minority underrepresented in Idaho higher education. Applicants must also attend an eligible Idaho college or university.
Target applicants: College students. Adult students.
Amount: Up to $3,000.
Number of awards: Varies.
Scholarship may be renewable.
Deadline: Varies.
How to apply: Applications are available by telephone request.
Exclusive: Visit www.UltimateScholarshipBook.com and enter code ID174312 for updates on this award.

(1744) • Minority Teacher/Special Education Services Scholarship

State Student Assistance Commission of Indiana
150 W. Market Street
Suite 500
Indianapolis, IN 46204
Phone: 888-528-4719
Fax: 317-232-3260
Email: grants@ssaci.state.in.us
http://www.in.gov/ssaci
Purpose: To support students in Indiana who are pursuing degrees in teaching, special education, physical therapy or occupational therapy.
Eligibility: Applicants must be enrolled or planning to enroll in college full-time. Students must have at least a 2.0 GPA, and financial need may

be considered. Preference will be given to black and Hispanic students. Students must agree to work in the state of Indiana for a period of time after graduation.
Target applicants: High school students. College students. Adult students.
Minimum GPA: 2.0
Amount: Up to $4,000.
Number of awards: Varies.
Scholarship may be renewable.
Deadline: Varies.
How to apply: Applications are available online.
Exclusive: Visit www.UltimateScholarshipBook.com and enter code ST174412 for updates on this award.

(1745) • Mississippi Association of Broadcasters Scholarship Program

Mississippi Association of Broadcasters
855 S Pear Orchard Road
Suite 403
Ridgeland, MI 39157
Phone: 601-957-9121
http://www.msbroadcasters.org
Purpose: To support students involved in broadcasting.
Eligibility: Applicants must be Mississippi residents and be enrolled in an accredited broadcast curriculum at a Mississippi two- or four-year college.
Target applicants: College students. Adult students.
Amount: Up to $4,000.
Number of awards: Varies.
Deadline: May 1.
How to apply: Applications are available online. An application form, essay and up to three letters of recommendation are required.
Exclusive: Visit www.UltimateScholarshipBook.com and enter code MI174512 for updates on this award.

(1746) • Mississippi Educational Assistance for MIA/POW Dependents

Mississippi State Veterans Affairs Board
P.O. Box 5947
Pearl, MS 39288-5947
Phone: 601-576-4850
Fax: 601-576-4868
Email: grice@vab.state.ms.us
http://www.vab.state.ms.us
Purpose: To provide educational assistance to children of veterans reported as POW or MIA.
Eligibility: Applicants must be dependents of armed service members from or stationed in Mississippi who have been prisoners of war or missing in action. The scholarship will pay tuition for up to eight semesters at an accredited institution of higher learning.
Target applicants: High school students. College students. Adult students.
Amount: Tuition.
Number of awards: Varies.
Deadline: Varies.
How to apply: Applications are available from Mississippi Veterans Affairs offices.
Exclusive: Visit www.UltimateScholarshipBook.com and enter code MI174612 for updates on this award.

(1747) • Mississippi Eminent Scholars Grant (MESG)

Mississippi Office of Student Financial Aid
3825 Ridgewood Road
Jackson, MS 39211
Phone: 800-327-2980
Fax: 601-432-6527
Email: sfa@ihl.state.ms.us
http://www.ihl.state.ms.us
Purpose: To recognize academically high performing Mississippi students.
Eligibility: Applicants must be U.S. citizens or eligible noncitizens and current legal residents of Mississippi who are enrolled as full-time, 'first-time-in-college' undergraduates. Applicants must have a high school GPA of 3.5 and a minimum ACT of 29. National Merit/National Achievement semifinalists with a 3.5 grade-point average qualify without the test score.
Target applicants: High school students.
Minimum GPA: 3.5
Amount: Varies.
Number of awards: Varies.
Scholarship may be renewable.
Deadline: September.
How to apply: Applicants must complete an MTAG/MESG application and either a FAFSA or a Statement of Certification (a waiver for completing the FAFSA).
Exclusive: Visit www.UltimateScholarshipBook.com and enter code MI174712 for updates on this award.

(1748) • Mississippi Scholarship

American Radio Relay League Foundation
225 Main Street
Newington, CT 06111
Phone: 860-594-0397
Fax: 860-594-0259
Email: foundation@arrl.org
http://www.arrlf.org
Purpose: To provide financial assistance to Mississippi students who are amateur radio operators and are studying electronics or communications.
Eligibility: Applicants must be licensed amateur radio operators and residents of Mississippi who attend an institution of higher learning in Mississippi. They must be seeking a bachelor's degree or higher in electronics, communication or a related field, and they must be under 30 years old.
Target applicants: High school students. College students. Graduate school students. Adult students.
Amount: $500.
Number of awards: 1.
Deadline: February 1.
How to apply: Applications are available online.
Exclusive: Visit www.UltimateScholarshipBook.com and enter code AM174812 for updates on this award.

(1749) • Mississippi Tuition Assistance Grant (MTAG)

Mississippi Office of Student Financial Aid
3825 Ridgewood Road
Jackson, MS 39211
Phone: 800-327-2980
Fax: 601-432-6527
Email: sfa@ihl.state.ms.us
http://www.ihl.state.ms.us
Purpose: To assist financially needy Mississippi students afford tuition.

Eligibility: Applicants must be current legal residents of Mississippi who are enrolled as full-time undergraduates. Applicants must have a high school grade-point average of 2.5 and a minimum ACT of 15.
Target applicants: High school students. College students. Adult students.
Minimum GPA: 2.5
Amount: Varies.
Number of awards: Varies.
Scholarship may be renewable.
Deadline: September.
How to apply: Applicants must complete an MTAG/MESG application and either a FAFSA or a Statement of Certification (a waiver for completing the FAFSA).
Exclusive: Visit www.UltimateScholarshipBook.com and enter code MI174912 for updates on this award.

(1750) • Missouri College Guarantee Program

Missouri Student Assistance Resource Services (MOSTARS)
Missouri Department of Higher Education
3515 Amazonas Drive
Jefferson City, MO 65109
Phone: 800-473-6757
Fax: 573-751-6635
http://www.dhe.mo.gov
Purpose: To assist Missouri students who have demonstrated financial need and high school or college academic achievement.
Eligibility: Applicants must be U.S. citizens or eligible noncitizens, Missouri residents and have a high school GPA of 2.5 and an ACT score of 20 or an SAT I score of 950. Applicants must have participated in high school extracurricular activities and be enrolled full-time at a participating Missouri college or university.
Target applicants: High school students. College students. Adult students.
Minimum GPA: 2.5
Amount: Varies.
Number of awards: Varies.
Scholarship may be renewable.
Deadline: April 1.
How to apply: Complete the Free Application for Federal Student Aid (FAFSA) and have achieved the required ACT or SAT score and the other high school eligibility requirements by April 1.
Exclusive: Visit www.UltimateScholarshipBook.com and enter code MI175012 for updates on this award.

(1751) • Missouri Oratorical Contest

American Legion, Department of Missouri
P.O. Box 179
Jefferson City, MO 65102
Phone: 800-846-9023
Fax: 573-893-2980
Email: bmayberry@missourilegion.org
http://www.missourilegion.org/
Purpose: To enhance high school students' experience with and understanding of the U.S. Constitution. The contest will help develop students' leadership skills and civic appreciation, as well as the ability to deliver thoughtful, insightful orations regarding U.S. citizenship and its inherent responsibilities.
Eligibility: Applicants must be high school students under the age of 20 who are U.S. citizens or legal residents and residents of the state. Students first give an oration within their state and winners compete at the national level. The oration must be related to the Constitution of the United States focusing on the duties and obligations citizens have to the government. It must be in English and be between eight and ten minutes. There is also an assigned topic which is posted on the website, and it should be between three and five minutes.
Target applicants: High school students.
Amount: $1,400-$18,000.
Number of awards: Varies.
Deadline: November 30.
How to apply: Application information is available by email.
Exclusive: Visit www.UltimateScholarshipBook.com and enter code AM175112 for updates on this award.

(1752) • Missouri State Thespian Scholarships

Missouri State Thespians
Attn.: Debbie Corbin
1426 E Highway 176
Spokane, MO 65754
Email: info@mo-thespians.com
http://www.mo-thespians.com
Purpose: To support young Missouri thespians.
Eligibility: Applicants must be high school seniors, International Thespians members and delegates to the conference. Students must have a GPA of 2.5 or higher and audition in the category of performance, technical or theatre education.
Target applicants: High school students.
Minimum GPA: 2.5
Amount: Varies.
Number of awards: 9.
Deadline: December 1.
How to apply: Applications are available online. An application form is required.
Exclusive: Visit www.UltimateScholarshipBook.com and enter code MI175212 for updates on this award.

(1753) • Monetary Award Program (MAP)

Illinois Department of Public Health
535 W. Jefferson Street
Springfield, IL 62761
Phone: 217-782-4977
Fax: 217-782-3987
Email: dph.mailus@illinois.gov
http://www.idph.state.il.us
Purpose: To provide grants to eligible Illinois undergraduate students.
Eligibility: Applicants must be residents of Illinois, enrolled at a MAP-approved Illinois institution and carry a minimum of three hours per term. Applicants must also demonstrate financial need and maintain satisfactory academic progress.
Target applicants: High school students. College students. Adult students.
Amount: Varies.
Number of awards: Varies.
Scholarship may be renewable.
Deadline: As soon as possible after January 1.
How to apply: Complete the Free Application for Federal Student Aid (FAFSA).
Exclusive: Visit www.UltimateScholarshipBook.com and enter code IL175312 for updates on this award.

(1754) • Montana Cattlewomen Scholarship

Montana CattleWomen, Inc.
420 N. California
Helena, MT 59601
Phone: 406-442-3420
Fax: 406-449-5105
Email: pam@mtbeef.org
http://www.montanacattlewomen.org

Purpose: To support a Montana university or college student whose major field of study benefits the livestock industry.

Eligibility: Applicants must be from Montana and currently enrolled as a sophomore or higher in an accredited university or college in Montana. Students must have a cumulative grade point average of 2.7 or more and demonstrate a need for financial assistance. Selection is based on demonstrated need and student's potential to benefit the livestock industry. Preference is given to students from an agriculture background and/or members or children of members of Montana CattleWomen.

Target applicants: College students. Adult students.

Minimum GPA: 2.7

Amount: $1,000.

Number of awards: 1.

Deadline: March 15.

How to apply: Application instructions are available online. A personal resume, academic resume, high school and college transcripts, essay, applicant photo, photo of family living situation and three recommendation letters are required.

Exclusive: Visit www.UltimateScholarshipBook.com and enter code MO175412 for updates on this award.

(1755) • Montana Higher Education Grant

Student Assistance Foundation of Montana
2500 Broadway
Helena, MT 59601
Phone: 406-495-7800
Fax: 406-495-7880
Email: customerservice@safmt.org
http://www.safmt.org

Purpose: To assist Montana students who have exceptional financial need.

Eligibility: Applicants must be Montana residents who have exceptional financial need. Grants are awarded through individual colleges and universities. Selection is based on financial need.

Target applicants: High school students. College students. Adult students.

Amount: $500.

Number of awards: Varies.

Scholarship may be renewable.

Deadline: Varies.

How to apply: Application is made by completing the Free Application for Federal Student Aid (FAFSA).

Exclusive: Visit www.UltimateScholarshipBook.com and enter code ST175512 for updates on this award.

(1756) • Montana Tuition Assistance Program/Baker Grant

Student Assistance Foundation of Montana
2500 Broadway
Helena, MT 59601
Phone: 406-495-7800
Fax: 406-495-7880
Email: customerservice@safmt.org
http://www.safmt.org

Purpose: To aid Montana students who are pursuing higher education.

Eligibility: Applicants must be residents of Montana. They must have earnings greater than 500 times the federal minimum wage and have an Expected Family Contribution (EFC) that is less than the maximum federal Pell Grant plus $2,500. Selection is based on financial need.

Target applicants: High school students. College students. Adult students.

Amount: $100-$2,000.

Number of awards: Varies.

Deadline: Varies.

How to apply: Application instructions are available by request from the applicant's college financial aid office.

Exclusive: Visit www.UltimateScholarshipBook.com and enter code ST175612 for updates on this award.

(1757) • Montana University System Honor Scholarship

Montana Guaranteed Student Loan Program
P.O. Box 203101
Helena, MT 59620
Phone: 800-537-7508
Fax: 406-444-1869
http://www.mgslp.state.mt.us

Purpose: To reward Montana high school seniors with outstanding academic achievement.

Eligibility: Applicants must have a 3.4 or higher GPA, meet specific college preparatory requirements and have been enrolled in an accredited Montana high school for at least three years prior to graduation, including their senior year. Applicants must also be accepted to and attend a Montana public university or community college.

Target applicants: High school students.

Minimum GPA: 3.4

Amount: Varies.

Number of awards: Up to 200.

Scholarship may be renewable.

Deadline: February 15.

How to apply: Applications are available from your high school guidance counselor.

Exclusive: Visit www.UltimateScholarshipBook.com and enter code MO175712 for updates on this award.

(1758) • MSPE Harry R. Ball, P.E. Grant

Michigan Society of Professional Engineers
215 North Walnut Street
P.O. Box 15276
Lansing, MI 48901
Phone: 517-487-9388
Fax: 517-487-0635
Email: mspe@michiganspe.org
http://www.michiganspe.org

Purpose: To aid Michigan students who are planning to pursue an undergraduate degree in engineering.

Eligibility: Applicants must be U.S. citizens, residents of Michigan and high school seniors. They must be accepted at an ABET-accredited college or university in Michigan and must have plans to pursue a degree in engineering. Students must have a GPA of 3.0 or higher for both the 10th and 11th grade years and a minimum composite ACT score of 26 or higher. Selection is based on GPA, ACT score, personal essay, extracurricular activities, any college-level coursework completed and honors received.

Target applicants: High school students.
Minimum GPA: 3.0
Amount: $2,000.
Number of awards: 1.
Deadline: Third Monday in February.
How to apply: Applications are available online. An application form, personal essay and official transcript are required.
Exclusive: Visit www.UltimateScholarshipBook.com and enter code MI175812 for updates on this award.

(1759) • MSPE Kenneth B. Fishbeck, P.E., Memorial Grant

Michigan Society of Professional Engineers
215 North Walnut Street
P.O. Box 15276
Lansing, MI 48901
Phone: 517-487-9388
Fax: 517-487-0635
Email: mspe@michiganspe.org
http://www.michiganspe.org
Purpose: To aid Michigan students who are planning to pursue higher education in engineering.
Eligibility: Applicants must be high school seniors who are Michigan residents and U.S. citizens. They must have a GPA of 3.0 or higher for the sophomore and junior years of high school and a composite ACT score of 26 or higher. Students must be accepted into a Michigan institution of higher learning that has an ABET-accredited engineering degree program. Selection is based on personal essay, awards and recognitions, GPA, ACT scores and any college-level coursework that has been completed.
Target applicants: High school students.
Minimum GPA: 3.0
Amount: $1,000.
Number of awards: 1.
Deadline: Third Monday in February.
How to apply: Applications are available online. An application form, transcript, personal essay and ACT score report are required.
Exclusive: Visit www.UltimateScholarshipBook.com and enter code MI175912 for updates on this award.

(1760) • Music Committee Scholarship

American Legion, Department of Kansas
1314 SW Topeka Boulevard
Topeka, KS 66612
Phone: 785-232-9315
Fax: 785-232-1399
http://www.ksamlegion.org
Purpose: To support Kansas students who have distinguished themselves in the field of music.
Eligibility: Applicants must be Kansas residents who are currently high school seniors or college freshmen or sophomores. They must have a proven talent and background in music and be planning to major or minor in music at an approved Kansas post-secondary institution. Applicants must also be average or better students. Three letters of recommendation, with only one from a music teacher, a 1040 income statement, a high school transcript and a statement describing why they are applying for the scholarship are required. The scholarship will be awarded in two installments; recipients must maintain a C average to receive the second installment.
Target applicants: High school students. College students. Adult students.
Amount: $1,000.
Number of awards: 1.
Deadline: February 15.
How to apply: Applications are available online.
Exclusive: Visit www.UltimateScholarshipBook.com and enter code AM176012 for updates on this award.

(1761) • NACA East Coast Undergraduate Scholarship for Student Leaders

National Association for Campus Activities
13 Harbison Way
Columbia, SC 29212
Phone: 803-732-6222
Fax: 803-749-1047
Email: info@naca.org
http://www.naca.org
Purpose: To provide financial assistance to East Coast student leaders.
Eligibility: Students must hold a significant campus leadership position, demonstrate significant leadership skills and abilities and make significant contributions through on- or off-campus volunteering. Students must attend school in Delaware, New Jersey, Maryland, New York, Eastern Pennsylvania or Washington, DC.
Target applicants: College students. Adult students.
Minimum GPA: 2.5
Amount: Varies.
Number of awards: 2.
Deadline: March 31.
How to apply: Applications are available online.
Exclusive: Visit www.UltimateScholarshipBook.com and enter code NA176112 for updates on this award.

(1762) • NACA Southeast Region Student Leader Scholarship

National Association for Campus Activities
13 Harbison Way
Columbia, SC 29212
Phone: 803-732-6222
Fax: 803-749-1047
Email: info@naca.org
http://www.naca.org
Purpose: To provide financial assistance to Southeast student leaders.
Eligibility: Students must hold a significant campus leadership position, demonstrate significant leadership skills and abilities and make significant contributions through on- or off-campus volunteering. Students must attend school in Alabama, Florida, Georgia, Mississippi, North Carolina, South Carolina, Tennessee, Virginia or Puerto Rico.
Target applicants: College students. Adult students.
Amount: Varies.
Number of awards: Up to 4.
Deadline: March 31.
How to apply: Applications are available online.
Exclusive: Visit www.UltimateScholarshipBook.com and enter code NA176212 for updates on this award.

(1763) • NADCA Indiana Chapter 25 Scholarship

Foundry Educational Foundation
1695 North Penny Lane
Schaumburg, IL 60173
Phone: 847-490-9200

Fax: 847-890-6270
Email: info@fefinc.org
http://www.fefinc.org
Purpose: To aid Indiana region students who have a demonstrated interest in the die cast and cast metal industries.
Eligibility: Applicants must be residents of Indiana or of a state that is adjacent to Indiana. They must be enrolled at an Indiana school or at a Foundry Educational Foundation (FEF) member school located in a state that is adjacent to Indiana. They must have prior work experience in manufacturing, the die casting industry or the cast metal industry. Preference will be given to applicants who are studying a subject that is related to the die casting industry. Selection is based on the overall strength of the application.
Target applicants: High school students. College students. Adult students.
Amount: Varies.
Number of awards: Varies.
Deadline: June 1.
How to apply: Applications are available online. An application form and supporting documents are required.
Exclusive: Visit www.UltimateScholarshipBook.com and enter code FO176312 for updates on this award.

(1764) • Nancy Penn Lyons Scholarship Fund

Community Foundation for Greater Atlanta Inc.
50 Hurt Plaza
Suite 449
Atlanta, GA 30303
Phone: 404-688-5525
Fax: 404-688-3060
Email: info@cfgreateratlanta.org
http://www.cfgreateratlanta.org
Purpose: To provide assistance to needy students who have been accepted to prestigious or out-of-state universities.
Eligibility: Applicants must be graduating high school seniors who have been Georgia residents for at least one year. They must have an ACT score of 22 or higher or an SAT composite score of 1000 or higher and a GPA of 3.0 or greater. They must have participated in community service and have financial need, and they must not be attending a public institution in the state of Georgia.
Target applicants: High school students.
Minimum GPA: 3.0
Amount: $5,000.
Number of awards: 5.
Scholarship may be renewable.
Deadline: March 15.
How to apply: Applications are available online.
Exclusive: Visit www.UltimateScholarshipBook.com and enter code CO176412 for updates on this award.

(1765) • Nathaniel Alston Student Achievement Scholarship

Pennsylvania Society of Physician Assistants
P.O. Box 128
Greensburg, PA 15601
Phone: 724-836-6411
Fax: 724-836-4449
Email: hohpac@windstream.net
http://www.pspa.net
Purpose: To aid outstanding physician assistant students attending school in Pennsylvania.
Eligibility: Applicants must be current students in good standing who are enrolled in an accredited physician assistant program in the state of Pennsylvania. They must be current Pennsylvania Society of Physician Assistants (PSPA) members who demonstrate outstanding leadership and participation in their schools and communities. Selection is based on the overall strength of the application.
Target applicants: College students. Graduate school students. Adult students.
Amount: $1,000.
Number of awards: 6.
Deadline: June 30.
How to apply: Applications are available online. An application form and personal essay are required.
Exclusive: Visit www.UltimateScholarshipBook.com and enter code PE176512 for updates on this award.

(1766) • National Tour Association (NTA) La Macchia Family Undergraduate Scholarship

Tourism Cares
275 Turnpike Street
Suite 307
Canton, MA 02021
Phone: 781-821-5990
Fax: 781-821-8949
Email: carolynv@tourismcares.org
http://www.tourismcares.org
Purpose: To aid those who are studying hospitality, tourism or travel at the undergraduate level in Wisconsin.
Eligibility: Applicants must be permanent residents of the U.S., full-time students and rising undergraduate juniors or seniors who are enrolled at an accredited four-year institution located in Wisconsin. They must be studying tourism, travel or hospitality and have a GPA of 3.0 or higher on a four-point scale. Applicants must have completed 60 or more credits by May of the application year. Selection is based on the overall strength of the application.
Target applicants: College students. Adult students.
Minimum GPA: 3.0
Amount: $1,000.
Number of awards: 1.
Deadline: April 15.
How to apply: Applications are available online. An application form, proof of residency, resume, two letters of recommendation, official transcript and personal essay are required.
Exclusive: Visit www.UltimateScholarshipBook.com and enter code TO176612 for updates on this award.

(1767) • NAWIC Granite State Chapter Scholarships

National Association of Women in Construction-Granite State Chapter #218
c/o Bayview Construction Corp.
170 West Road
Suite #10
Portsmouth, NH 03801
Phone: 603-659-4442
Email: callamethyst@earthlink.net
http://www.nawicnh.com
Purpose: To aid New Hampshire students who are preparing for careers in the field of construction.
Eligibility: Applicants must be New Hampshire residents who are entering the second, third or fourth year of an undergraduate program in a construction-related subject. They must have a GPA of 2.0 or higher. Selection is based on the overall strength of the application.

Target applicants: College students. Adult students.
Minimum GPA: 2.0
Amount: Varies.
Number of awards: Varies.
Deadline: April 1.
How to apply: Instructions for how to apply are available online. A personal essay and transcript are required.
Exclusive: Visit www.UltimateScholarshipBook.com and enter code NA176712 for updates on this award.

(1768) • NC Student Loan Program for Health, Science and Mathematics

College Foundation of North Carolina
P.O. Box 41966
Raleigh, NC 27629
Phone: 888-234-6400
Fax: 919-821-3139
Email: programinformation@cfnc.org
http://www.cfnc.org
Purpose: To provide financial assistance to students in health, science and mathematics in North Carolina.
Eligibility: Applicants must be North Carolina residents who have been accepted into associate, bachelor's, master's or doctoral degree programs that lead to degrees in qualifying health, science or mathematics majors. Recipients must enroll full-time for fall and spring semesters. Recipients must repay the loans either through service or in cash.
Target applicants: High school students. College students. Graduate school students. Adult students.
Amount: Up to $10,000.
Number of awards: Varies.
Scholarship may be renewable.
Deadline: May 1.
How to apply: Applications are available online.
Exclusive: Visit www.UltimateScholarshipBook.com and enter code CO176812 for updates on this award.

(1769) • Nebraska Actuaries Club Scholarship

Nebraska Actuaries Club
c/o Brian Poppe, ASA
Actuarial Associate
Mutual of Omaha, Mutual of Omaha Plaza
Omaha, NE 68175
Email: svagts@unlnotes.unl.edu
http://www.n-a-c.org
Purpose: To aid Nebraska students who plan to major in actuarial science or a related subject.
Eligibility: Applicants must be U.S. high school seniors who are planning to attend an accredited college or university located in the state of Nebraska. They must be planning to major in actuarial science, economics, mathematics or statistics and must intend to pursue an actuarial career. Applicants must have demonstrated mathematical ability. Selection is based on the overall strength of the application.
Target applicants: High school students.
Amount: $1,000.
Number of awards: 1.
Deadline: March 31.
How to apply: Applications are available online. An application form, recommendation letter and standardized test scores are required.
Exclusive: Visit www.UltimateScholarshipBook.com and enter code NE176912 for updates on this award.

(1770) • Nebraska State Grant

Nebraska Coordinating Commission for Postsecondary Education
P.O. Box 95005
Lincoln, NE 68509
Phone: 402-471-2847
Fax: 402-471-2886
http://www.ccpe.state.ne.us
Purpose: To support Nebraska college students.
Eligibility: Students must be eligible for the Federal Pell Grant and attend a Nebraska postsecondary institution.
Target applicants: High school students. College students. Adult students.
Amount: Varies.
Number of awards: Varies.
Deadline: Varies.
How to apply: Applications are available at college financial aid offices, and students apply through their colleges. Students must complete the Free Application for Federal Student Aid (FAFSA).
Exclusive: Visit www.UltimateScholarshipBook.com and enter code NE177012 for updates on this award.

(1771) • Nebraska Veterans' Aid Fund Waiver of Tuition

Nebraska Department of Veterans' Affairs
State Service Office
5631 S. 48 Street
Lincoln, NE 68516
Phone: 402-420-4021
Fax: 402-471-7070
http://www.vets.state.ne.us/index_html?page=content/benefits.html
Purpose: To provide assistance to children and spouses of Nebraska veterans.
Eligibility: Applicants must be the children, stepchildren, spouses or widows of veterans who died of a service-connected injury or illness, became totally and permanently disabled as a result of military service or was classified as MIA or POW during armed conflict after August 4th, 1964. They must be Nebraska residents and attend a state college, university or community college.
Target applicants: High school students. College students. Adult students.
Amount: Tuition.
Number of awards: Varies.
Scholarship may be renewable.
Deadline: Varies.
How to apply: Applications are available from your County Veterans Service Officer.
Exclusive: Visit www.UltimateScholarshipBook.com and enter code NE177112 for updates on this award.

(1772) • Ned McWherter Scholars Program

Tennessee Student Assistance Corporation
404 James Robertson Parkway
Suite 1510, Parkway Towers
Nashville, TN 37243
Phone: 800-342-1663
Fax: 615-741-6101
Email: tsac.aidinfo@tn.gov
http://www.tn.gov/CollegePays/
Purpose: To assist outstanding Tennessee students who are planning to attend a Tennessee college or university.

Eligibility: Applicants must be U.S. citizens or legal residents and Tennessee residents who are graduating high school seniors. They must have plans to attend an eligible Tennessee undergraduate institution full-time and have a GPA of 3.5 or higher. Applicants must have a combined math and reading SAT score of at least 1280 or an ACT composite score of 29 or higher. Selection is based on the overall strength of the application.
Target applicants: High school students.
Minimum GPA: 3.5
Amount: $6,000.
Number of awards: Varies.
Scholarship may be renewable.
Deadline: February 15.
How to apply: Applications are available online. An application form, official transcripts and standardized test scores are required.
Exclusive: Visit www.UltimateScholarshipBook.com and enter code TE177212 for updates on this award.

(1773) • Need Based Tuition Waiver Program

Massachusetts Department of Higher Education
Office of Student Financial Assistance
454 Broadway
Suite 200
Revere, MA 02151
Phone: 617-727-9420
Fax: 617-727-0667
Email: osfa@osfa.mass.edu
http://www.osfa.mass.edu/default.asp
Purpose: To support Massachusetts students who are in need of supplemental financial aid.
Eligibility: Applicants must live in the state of Massachusetts for at least one year prior to the beginning of the school year, and they must be enrolled in a state funded college. They must be in an undergraduate program with at least three credits per semester. Students must not owe any refunds on prior scholarships and cannot have any defaulted government loans. They must also be able to show proof of financial need.
Target applicants: High school students. College students. Adult students.
Amount: Up to full tuition.
Number of awards: Varies.
Deadline: Varies.
How to apply: Applications are available at college financial aid offices.
Exclusive: Visit www.UltimateScholarshipBook.com and enter code MA177312 for updates on this award.

(1774) • Nettie Tucker Yowell Scholarship

Virginia Business and Professional Women's Foundation
P.O. Box 4842
McLean, VA 22103-4842
Phone: 800-525-3729
Email: bpwfoundation@act.org
http://www.vabpwfoundation.org
Purpose: To support Virginia residents who are pursuing bachelor's degrees.
Eligibility: Applicants must be high school seniors with at least a 3.0 GPA. They must pass all SOL tests and score at least 1000 on the SAT. Students must obtain a letter of recommendation from a guidance counselor or principal. Awards are based on financial need, academic achievements, educational goals and commitment to the Virginia BPW mission.
Target applicants: High school students.
Minimum GPA: 3.0
Amount: $500-$1,000.
Number of awards: Varies.
Deadline: April 1.
How to apply: Applications are available online.
Exclusive: Visit www.UltimateScholarshipBook.com and enter code VI177412 for updates on this award.

(1775) • Nevada Millennium Scholarship

Nevada Office of the State Treasurer
555 E. Washington Avenue
Suite 4600
Las Vegas, NV 89101
Phone: 888-477-2667
Fax: 702-486-3246
Email: millenniumscholarshi@nevadatreasurer.gov
https://nevadatreasurer.gov
Purpose: To assist students who have attained high academic achievement in a Nevada high school.
Eligibility: Applicants must graduate from a Nevada public or private high school with a GPA of 3.25 or higher, pass all areas of the Nevada High School Proficiency Exam and have been a resident of Nevada for at least two years in high school.
Target applicants: High school students.
Minimum GPA: 3.25
Amount: Up to $960 per semester.
Number of awards: Varies.
Scholarship may be renewable.
Deadline: Varies.
How to apply: Applications are not required. Your school district will submit your name to the State Treasurer's office if you are eligible.
Exclusive: Visit www.UltimateScholarshipBook.com and enter code NE177512 for updates on this award.

(1776) • Nevada Women's Fund Scholarships

Nevada Women's Fund
770 Smithridge Drive
Suite 300
Reno, NV 89502
Phone: 775-786-2335
Fax: 775-786-8152
Email: info@nevadawomensfund.org
http://www.nevadawomensfund.org
Purpose: To improve the lives of women and children in northern Nevada.
Eligibility: Northern Nevada residents and those attending northern Nevada schools receive preference.
Target applicants: High school students. College students. Graduate school students. Adult students.
Amount: $500 and up.
Number of awards: Varies.
Deadline: March 31.
How to apply: Applications are available online or from several offices listed on the website.
Exclusive: Visit www.UltimateScholarshipBook.com and enter code NE177612 for updates on this award.

(1777) • New Century Scholarship

Utah State Board of Regents
Board of Regents Building, The Gateway
60 South 400 West
Salt Lake City, UT 84101
Phone: 801-321-7107
http://www.utahsbr.edu
Purpose: To assist Utah high school students.
Eligibility: Applicants must be high school students who have completed the equivalent of an associate's degree at a Utah state institution of higher education by September 1 of their high school graduation year. The award provides assistance for the bachelor's degree at a state college.
Target applicants: High school students.
Amount: Up to $2,500.
Number of awards: Varies.
Scholarship may be renewable.
Deadline: February 1.
How to apply: Applications are available online.
Exclusive: Visit www.UltimateScholarshipBook.com and enter code UT177712 for updates on this award.

(1778) • New England Regional Student Program

New England Board of Higher Education
45 Temple Place
Boston, MA 02111
Phone: 617-357-9620
Fax: 617-338-1577
Email: rsp@nebhe.org
http://www.nebhe.org
Purpose: The program lowers tuition rates for New England students who must travel out of state for their desired major.
Eligibility: Students must be residents of Connecticut, Maine, Massachusetts, New Hampshire, Rhode Island or Vermont and attend a school in another of those states that offers an RSP program in their major. The major must not be available at an in-school state.
Target applicants: High school students. College students. Graduate school students. Adult students.
Amount: $7,000.
Number of awards: Varies.
Scholarship may be renewable.
Deadline: Varies.
How to apply: Students should note that they are interested in the RSP program on their regular college application.
Exclusive: Visit www.UltimateScholarshipBook.com and enter code NE177812 for updates on this award.

(1779) • New Hampshire Charitable Foundation Adult Student Aid Program

New Hampshire Charitable Foundation
37 Pleasant Street
Concord, NH 03301-4005
Phone: 603-225-6641
Fax: 603-225-1700
Email: info@nhcf.org
http://www.nhcf.org/Page.aspx?pid=183
Purpose: To provide financial assistance to adults who are pursuing undergraduate degrees or training.
Eligibility: Applicants must be independent students and legal New Hampshire residents. They must have applied for financial aid and still have unmet financial need. Applicants may be enrolled in a degree or non-degree program, but courses do not have to be taken for credit. Preference is given to single parents, students who have previously received funding through the program and successfully completed coursework and students with little education beyond high school.
Target applicants: College students. Adult students.
Amount: $100-$500.
Number of awards: Varies.
Scholarship may be renewable.
Deadline: May 15, August 15 or December 15.
How to apply: Applications are available online.
Exclusive: Visit www.UltimateScholarshipBook.com and enter code NE177912 for updates on this award.

(1780) • New Hampshire Charitable Foundation Statewide Student Aid Program

New Hampshire Charitable Foundation
37 Pleasant Street
Concord, NH 03301-4005
Phone: 603-225-6641
Fax: 603-225-1700
Email: info@nhcf.org
http://www.nhcf.org/Page.aspx?pid=183
Purpose: To allow New Hampshire students to access over 50 scholarship and loan opportunities through a single application.
Eligibility: Applicants must be New Hampshire residents between the ages of 17 and 23 who plan to pursue a bachelor's degree or graduate students of any age. They must enroll at least half-time to qualify.
Target applicants: High school students. College students. Graduate school students.
Amount: $500-$3,500.
Number of awards: Varies.
Deadline: April 15.
How to apply: Applications are available online.
Exclusive: Visit www.UltimateScholarshipBook.com and enter code NE178012 for updates on this award.

(1781) • New Hampshire Incentive Program

New Hampshire Postsecondary Education Commission
3 Barrell Court
Suite 300
Concord, NH 03301
Phone: 603-271-2555 x352
Fax: 603-271-2696
Email: jknapp@pec.state.nh.us
http://www.state.nh.us/postsecondary
Purpose: To assist New Hampshire students attending eligible New England institutions.
Eligibility: Applicants must be New Hampshire residents, demonstrate financial need and be working towards their first bachelor's degree at an eligible New England institution.
Target applicants: College students. Adult students.
Amount: $125-$1,000.
Number of awards: Varies.
Deadline: May 1.
How to apply: Applicants must complete the Free Application for Federal Student Aid (FAFSA).
Exclusive: Visit www.UltimateScholarshipBook.com and enter code NE178112 for updates on this award.

(1782) • New Jersey Community Bankers Education Foundation Scholarships

New Jersey League of Community Bankers
411 North Avenue E.
Cranford, NJ 07016
Phone: 908-272-8500
Fax: 908-272-6626
http://www.njleague.com/scholarship.htm
Purpose: To provide financial assistance to dependents of deceased service members who are pursuing higher education.
Eligibility: Applicants must have a high school diploma or GED and be pursuing a college degree or technical or vocational training. They must be spouses, children, stepchildren, grandchildren or persons for whom the soldier provided half of their support for the calendar year and have financial need. The applicant must be a permanent resident of New Jersey, or the soldier must have been a permanent resident of or have lived on a military base in New Jersey.
Target applicants: High school students. College students. Adult students.
Amount: Varies.
Number of awards: Varies.
Deadline: December 31.
How to apply: Applications are available online or by mail.
Exclusive: Visit www.UltimateScholarshipBook.com and enter code NE178212 for updates on this award.

(1783) • New Jersey Oratorical Contest

American Legion, Department of New Jersey
135 W. Hanover Street
Trenton, NJ 08618
Phone: 609-695-5418
Fax: 609-394-1532
Email: adjudant@njamericanlegion.org
http://www.njamericanlegion.org
Purpose: To enhance high school students' experience with and understanding of the U.S. Constitution. The contest will help develop students' leadership skills and civic appreciation, as well as the ability to deliver thoughtful, insightful orations regarding U.S. citizenship and its inherent responsibilities.
Eligibility: Applicants must be high school students under the age of 20 who are U.S. citizens or legal residents and residents of the state. Students first give an oration within their state and winners compete at the national level. The oration must be related to the Constitution of the United States focusing on the duties and obligations citizens have to the government. It must be in English and be between eight and ten minutes. There is also an assigned topic which is posted on the website, and it should be between three and five minutes.
Target applicants: High school students.
Amount: Up to $5,500.
Number of awards: 5.
Deadline: Varies.
How to apply: Application information is available by email: ray@njamericanlegion.org.
Exclusive: Visit www.UltimateScholarshipBook.com and enter code AM178312 for updates on this award.

(1784) • New Jersey Physician Assistant Foundation/ New Jersey State Society of Physician Assistants Scholarship

New Jersey State Society of Physician Assistants
760 Alexander Road
P.O. Box 1
Princeton, NJ 08543
Phone: 609-275-4123
Fax: 609-734-0065
Email: info@njsspa.org
http://www.njsspa.org
Purpose: To aid New Jersey physician assistant students.
Eligibility: Applicants must be enrolled in a physician assistant degree program at a school located in the state of New Jersey. They must be student members of the New Jersey State Society of Physician Assistants (NJSSPA). Selection is based on the overall strength of the application.
Target applicants: College students. Graduate school students. Adult students.
Amount: $1,000.
Number of awards: 1.
Deadline: Varies.
How to apply: Applications are available online. An application form, two reference letters and supporting materials are required.
Exclusive: Visit www.UltimateScholarshipBook.com and enter code NE178412 for updates on this award.

(1785) • New Jersey School Counselor Association Scholarships

New Jersey School Counselor Association Inc.
5 Split Rock Place
Moorestown, NJ 08057
Phone: 856-234-8884
Email: jimlukach@msn.com
http://www.njsca.org
Purpose: To spread awareness of the importance of the role of school counselors.
Eligibility: Applicants must be New Jersey residents who will be graduating in the year of application. They must have been accepted to and plan to enroll in an institution of higher learning. A 300-500 word essay is required.
Target applicants: High school students.
Amount: $1,000.
Number of awards: 3.
Deadline: May 11.
How to apply: Applications are available online.
Exclusive: Visit www.UltimateScholarshipBook.com and enter code NE178512 for updates on this award.

(1786) • New Jersey State Elks Handicapped Children's Scholarship

New Jersey State Elks
665 Rahway Avenue
P.O. Box 1596
Woodbridge, NJ 07095
Phone: 732-326-1300
http://www.njelks.org
Purpose: To assist students with physical handicaps in obtaining higher education.
Eligibility: Applicants must be New Jersey residents and high school seniors with physical handicaps. They must demonstrate financial need and excellent academic standing.
Target applicants: High school students.
Amount: Up to $2,500.
Number of awards: 2.

Scholarship may be renewable.
Deadline: April 1.
How to apply: Applications are available online or by phone.
Exclusive: Visit www.UltimateScholarshipBook.com and enter code NE178612 for updates on this award.

(1787) • New Jersey World Trade Center Scholarship

New Jersey Higher Education Student Assistance Authority
P.O. Box 540
Trenton, NJ 08625
Phone: 800-792-8670
Email: clientservices@hesaa.org
http://www.hesaa.org
Purpose: To support the children and spouses of those who died as a result of the World Trade Center attack.
Eligibility: Applicants must be a dependent child or spouse of a New Jersey resident who was killed in the September 11, 2001 attack, died from resulting injuries or exposure to the attack site or are missing and presumed dead as a result of the attack. Students must be full-time undergraduates, and they may attend any eligible school in the U.S.
Target applicants: High school students. College students. Adult students.
Amount: $6,500.
Number of awards: Varies.
Scholarship may be renewable.
Deadline: October 1.
How to apply: Applications are available online.
Exclusive: Visit www.UltimateScholarshipBook.com and enter code NE178712 for updates on this award.

(1788) • New Mexico Children of Deceased Veterans Scholarships

New Mexico Department of Veterans' Services
P.O. Box 2324
Santa Fe, NM 87504
Phone: 505-827-6300
http://www.dvs.state.nm.us
Purpose: To provide higher education opportunities for children of deceased veterans.
Eligibility: Applicants must be children between the ages of 16 and 26 whose parent was a veteran who was killed in action or who died of a battle-related injury. The waiver covers tuition at any state funded college or university as well as a $150 per semester stipend to help cover books or fees.
Target applicants: High school students. College students. Adult students.
Amount: Tuition plus stipend.
Number of awards: Varies.
Scholarship may be renewable.
Deadline: Varies.
How to apply: Applications are available online.
Exclusive: Visit www.UltimateScholarshipBook.com and enter code NE178812 for updates on this award.

(1789) • New Mexico Scholars

New Mexico Higher Education Department
2048 Galisteo Street
Santa Fe, NM 87505
Phone: 800-279-9777
Fax: 505-476-8454
Email: heather.romero@state.nm.us
http://hed.state.nm.us
Purpose: To support New Mexico undergraduate students with financial need attend postsecondary institutions in New Mexico.
Eligibility: Applicants must be undergraduate students attending selected New Mexico public institutions or designated private non-profit colleges, meet family income requirements, be under the age of 22 and have graduated in the top 5 percent of their high school class or have a minimum ACT score of 25.
Target applicants: College students.
Amount: Up to full tuition.
Number of awards: Varies.
Deadline: Varies.
How to apply: Contact your financial aid office.
Exclusive: Visit www.UltimateScholarshipBook.com and enter code NE178912 for updates on this award.

(1790) • New York Legion Auxiliary Department Scholarship

American Legion Auxiliary, Department of New York
112 State Street
Suite 1310
Albany, NY 12207
Phone: 518-463-1162
Fax: 518-449-5406
Email: alanyterry@nycap.rr.com
http://www.deptny.org/Scholarships.htm
Purpose: To assist students whose parents, grandparents or great-grandparents served in the Armed Forces during wartime.
Eligibility: Applicants must be children, grandchildren, or great-grandchildren of veterans who served in the Armed Forces during World War I, World War II, the Korean Conflict, the Vietnam War, Grenada/Lebanon, Panama or the Persian Gulf. Students must be high school seniors and be New York State residents and U.S. citizens.
Target applicants: High school students.
Amount: $1,000.
Number of awards: 1.
Deadline: March 1.
How to apply: Applications are available online.
Exclusive: Visit www.UltimateScholarshipBook.com and enter code AM179012 for updates on this award.

(1791) • New York Legion Auxiliary District Scholarships

American Legion Auxiliary, Department of New York
112 State Street
Suite 1310
Albany, NY 12207
Phone: 518-463-1162
Fax: 518-449-5406
Email: alanyterry@nycap.rr.com
http://www.deptny.org/Scholarships.htm
Purpose: To provide financial assistance to children, grandchildren and great-grandchildren of war veterans.
Eligibility: Applicants must be children, grandchildren or great-grandchildren of Armed Forces veterans of World War I, World War II, the Korean Conflict, the Vietnam War, Grenada/Lebanon, Panama or the Persian Gulf. Students must be high school seniors and must be U.S. citizens and New York State residents.
Target applicants: High school students.
Amount: $1,000.

Number of awards: 1.
Deadline: March 1.
How to apply: Applications are available online.
Exclusive: Visit www.UltimateScholarshipBook.com and enter code AM179112 for updates on this award.

(1792) • New York Oratorical Contest

American Legion, Department of New York
112 State Street, Suite 1300
Albany, NY 12207
Email: info@nylegion.org
http://www.ny.legion.org
Purpose: To enhance high school students' experience with and understanding of the U.S. Constitution. The contest will help develop students' leadership skills and civic appreciation, as well as the ability to deliver thoughtful, insightful orations regarding U.S. citizenship and its inherent responsibilities.
Eligibility: Applicants must be high school students under the age of 20 who are U.S. citizens or legal residents and residents of the state. Students first give an oration within their state and winners compete at the national level. The oration must be related to the Constitution of the United States focusing on the duties and obligations citizens have to the government. It must be in English and be between eight and ten minutes. There is also an assigned topic which is posted on the website, and it should be between three and five minutes.
Target applicants: High school students.
Amount: $2,000-$7,500.
Number of awards: Varies.
Deadline: March 5.
How to apply: Application information is available by contacting the local American Legion Post.
Exclusive: Visit www.UltimateScholarshipBook.com and enter code AM179212 for updates on this award.

(1793) • New York State Association of Agricultural Fairs/New York State Showpeople's Association Scholarships

New York State Association of Agricultural Fairs
http://www.nyfairs.org/scholarship.htm
Purpose: To aid New York students who are preparing for careers in agriculture, fair management or the outdoor amusement business.
Eligibility: Applicants must be New York state residents or must attend school in the state of New York and must be high school seniors or current undergraduate students. They must be enrolled in or planning to enroll in a degree program that is related to agriculture, fair management or the outdoor amusement business. They must be attending or planning to attend an accredited postsecondary institution and must be active in local fairs. Selection is based on fair participation, leadership, citizenship and essay.
Target applicants: High school students. College students. Adult students.
Amount: $1,000.
Number of awards: Up to 6.
Deadline: April.
How to apply: Applications are available online. An application form, personal essay, two recommendation letters and a transcript are required.
Exclusive: Visit www.UltimateScholarshipBook.com and enter code NE179312 for updates on this award.

(1794) • New York State Society of Physician Assistants Scholarship

New York Society of Physician Assistants
251 New Karner Road
Suite 10A
Albany, NY 12205
Phone: 877-769-7722
Fax: 215-564-2175
Email: info@nysspa.org
http://www.nysspa.org
Purpose: To aid New York State Society of Physician Assistants (NYSSPA) student members.
Eligibility: Applicants must be NYSSPA members who are currently enrolled in an ARC-PA accredited physician assistant degree program in the state of New York. They must be in the professional phase of their degree program. Previous NYSSPA Scholarship winners, NYSSPA board members and NYSSPA committee chairs are ineligible. Selection is based on academic achievement, financial need and professional activities.
Target applicants: College students. Graduate school students. Adult students.
Amount: $1,000.
Number of awards: 4.
Deadline: August 20.
How to apply: Applications are available online. An application form, one reference letter, a personal essay and a financial aid award letter are required.
Exclusive: Visit www.UltimateScholarshipBook.com and enter code NE179412 for updates on this award.

(1795) • Nightingale Awards of Pennsylvania Scholarship

Nightingale Awards of Pennsylvania
2090 Linglestown Road
Suite 107
Harrisburg, PA 17110
Phone: 717-909-0350
Email: nightingale@pronursingresources.com
http://www.nightingaleawards.org
Purpose: To support Pennsylvania nursing students.
Eligibility: Applicants must be Pennsylvania residents who are enrolled in or have been accepted into a Pennsylvania nursing program in licensed practical nursing, registered nursing or graduate-level nursing practice. They must have completed at least one course in nursing and must have a B average or better. Previous recipients of this scholarship are ineligible. Selection is based on academic achievement, leadership ability, extracurricular activities and professional dedication to nursing.
Target applicants: College students. Graduate school students. Adult students.
Minimum GPA: 3.0
Amount: Varies.
Number of awards: Varies.
Deadline: January 31.
How to apply: Applications are available online. An application form, official transcript, two recommendation letters, a copy of the applicant's nursing program acceptance letter, a personal statement and a research proposal abstract (Ph.D. applicants only) are required.
Exclusive: Visit www.UltimateScholarshipBook.com and enter code NI179512 for updates on this award.

(1796) • Nissan Hawaii High School Hall of Honor

High School Athletic Association
P.O. Box 62029
Honolulu, HI 96839
http://www.sportshigh.com

Purpose: To support Hawaii high school seniors who are athletes.
Eligibility: Applicants must be graduating high school seniors and athletes in any organized sport in Hawaii. Selection is based primarily on sports achievements. Factors considered include contributions to the team, sportsmanship, character, participation in school activities and community involvement.
Target applicants: High school students.
Amount: $2,000.
Number of awards: 12.
Deadline: April 30.
How to apply: Applications are available by written request.
Exclusive: Visit www.UltimateScholarshipBook.com and enter code HI179612 for updates on this award.

(1797) • Nissan Scholarship

Nissan North America
P.O. Box 685003
Franklin, TN 37068
Phone: 800-647-7261
Email: webmaster@nissanusa.com
http://www.nissanusa.com

Purpose: To assist Mississippi high school seniors in attending public two-year or four-year colleges.
Eligibility: Applicants must have a minimum GPA of 2.5 and a minimum ACT score of 20 or SAT score of 820, have demonstrated financial need and be accepted as a full-time student at a Mississippi public college or university.
Target applicants: High school students.
Minimum GPA: 2.5
Amount: Full tuition.
Number of awards: Varies.
Deadline: March 1.
How to apply: No application is necessary. However, students must mail an essay, resume, high school transcript with ACT or SAT score and FAFSA results to Mississippi Office of Student Financial Aid, 3825 Ridgewood Road, Jackson, MS 39211-6453.
Exclusive: Visit www.UltimateScholarshipBook.com and enter code NI179712 for updates on this award.

(1798) • NJ Student Tuition Assistance Reward Scholarship

New Jersey Higher Education Student Assistance Authority
P.O. Box 540
Trenton, NJ 08625
Phone: 800-792-8670
Email: clientservices@hesaa.org
http://www.hesaa.org

Purpose: To support community college students in New Jersey who graduated from high school with excellent academic standing.
Eligibility: Applicants must have graduated from a New Jersey high school in the top 20 percent of their class, and they must have been state residents for at least 12 months prior to graduation. Students must enroll full-time in their home county college by the fifth semester after graduating from high school.
Target applicants: High school students. College students. Adult students.
Amount: Up to full tuition.
Number of awards: Varies.
Scholarship may be renewable.
Deadline: October 1.
How to apply: Applications are available at college financial aid offices.
Exclusive: Visit www.UltimateScholarshipBook.com and enter code NE179812 for updates on this award.

(1799) • NJ Student Tuition Assistance Reward Scholarship II

New Jersey Higher Education Student Assistance Authority
P.O. Box 540
Trenton, NJ 08625
Phone: 800-792-8670
Email: clientservices@hesaa.org
http://www.hesaa.org

Purpose: To support NJ STARS students who are transferring to four-year colleges.
Eligibility: Applicants must be county college graduates with an associate's degree, and they must have a GPA of at least 3.0. They must either be NJ STARS recipients or have other full state or federal aid during the semester in which they graduate. Students must be enrolled full-time at a New Jersey four-year college within two semesters of graduation.
Target applicants: College students. Adult students.
Minimum GPA: 3.0
Amount: Up to $7,000.
Number of awards: Varies.
Scholarship may be renewable.
Deadline: October 1.
How to apply: Applications are available at college financial aid offices.
Exclusive: Visit www.UltimateScholarshipBook.com and enter code NE179912 for updates on this award.

(1800) • NJVVM Scholarship Program

New Jersey Vietnam Veterans' Memorial Foundation
1 Memorial Lane
P.O. Box 648
Holmdel, NJ 07733
Phone: 800-648-8387
Fax: 732-335-1107
Email: sjsmith2@njvvmf.org
http://www.njvvmf.org

Purpose: To support high school seniors in New Jersey who have visited the New Jersey Vietnam Veterans' Memorial.
Eligibility: Applicants must submit an essay on their experience visiting the New Jersey Vietnam Veterans Memorial.
Target applicants: High school students.
Amount: $2,500.
Number of awards: 2.
Deadline: Varies.
How to apply: Applications are available online.
Exclusive: Visit www.UltimateScholarshipBook.com and enter code NE180012 for updates on this award.

(1801) • NMASBO Scholarship

New Mexico Association of School Business Officials
P.O. Box 7535
Albuquerque, NM 87194-7535

Phone: 505-923-3283
Fax: 505-923-3114
Email: info@nmasbo.org
http://www.nmasbo.org
Purpose: To support graduating high school seniors in New Mexico.
Eligibility: Students must have at least a 3.0 GPA. Applicants must submit an essay and two letters of recommendation. Students must plan to attend a New Mexico college or university on a full-time basis.
Target applicants: High school students.
Minimum GPA: 3.0
Amount: $1,500.
Number of awards: 6-10.
Deadline: March 1.
How to apply: Applications are available online.
Exclusive: Visit www.UltimateScholarshipBook.com and enter code NE180112 for updates on this award.

(1802) • NMPRSA Scholarship

New Mexico Chapter of the Public Relations Society of America
5620 Wyoming NE
Suite A
Albuquerque, NM 87109
Phone: 505-856-9933
Fax: 505-856-9935
Email: oliver@squirescompany.com
http://www.nmprsa.org
Purpose: To support New Mexico students who are majoring in communications fields.
Eligibility: Applicants must be pursuing undergraduate degrees in public relations, mass communications, journalism or visual communications. Preference is given to students who are majoring in public relations.
Target applicants: College students. Adult students.
Amount: $500.
Number of awards: Varies.
Deadline: November 9.
How to apply: Applications are available online.
Exclusive: Visit www.UltimateScholarshipBook.com and enter code NE180212 for updates on this award.

(1803) • NNM American Society of Mechanical Engineers Scholarship

Los Alamos National Laboratory Foundation
1302 Calle de la Merced
Suite A
Espanola, NM 87532
Phone: 505-753-8890
Fax: 505-753-8915
Email: info@lanlfoundation.org
http://www.lanlfoundation.org
Purpose: To support undergraduate students from Northern New Mexico who are majoring in mechanical engineering.
Eligibility: Students must have at least a 3.25 GPA, and they must have either an SAT score of at least 1350 or an ACT score of at least 19. Applicants must submit an essay and two letters of recommendation.
Target applicants: High school students. College students. Adult students.
Minimum GPA: 3.25
Amount: $1,000.
Number of awards: Varies.
Deadline: January 18.
How to apply: Applications are available online.
Exclusive: Visit www.UltimateScholarshipBook.com and enter code LO180312 for updates on this award.

(1804) • Norman and Ruth Good Educational Endowment

Lincoln Community Foundation
215 Centennial Mall South, Suite 100
Lincoln, NE 68508
Phone: 402-474-2345
Fax: 402-476-8532
Email: lcf@lcf.org
http://www.lcf.org
Purpose: To assist Nebraska students.
Eligibility: Applicants must be attending a private college in Nebraska and must be in their junior or senior year. Applicants may not apply if the scholarship money is to be used for summer programs or schools that are not valid degree-granting institutions.
Target applicants: College students. Adult students.
Minimum GPA: 3.5
Amount: Varies.
Number of awards: Varies.
Scholarship may be renewable.
Deadline: April 15.
How to apply: Applications are available online.
Exclusive: Visit www.UltimateScholarshipBook.com and enter code LI180412 for updates on this award.

(1805) • Norman E. Strohmeier, W2VRS Memorial Scholarship

American Radio Relay League Foundation
225 Main Street
Newington, CT 06111
Phone: 860-594-0397
Fax: 860-594-0259
Email: foundation@arrl.org
http://www.arrlf.org
Purpose: To support students from western New York who are involved in amateur radio.
Eligibility: Applicants must have an amateur radio license of Technician Class or higher. Students must have at least a 3.2 GPA, and preference will be given to graduating high school seniors.
Target applicants: High school students.
Minimum GPA: 3.2
Amount: $500.
Number of awards: 1.
Deadline: February 1.
How to apply: Applications are available online.
Exclusive: Visit www.UltimateScholarshipBook.com and enter code AM180512 for updates on this award.

(1806) • Norman S. and Betty M. Fitzhugh Fund

Greater Kanawha Valley Foundation
1600 Huntington Square
900 Lee Street, East
Charleston, WV 25301
Phone: 304-346-3620
Fax: 304-346-3640
Email: tgkvf@tgkvf.org

http://www.tgkvf.org
Purpose: To provide financial assistance to West Virginia residents wishing to earn a college education.
Eligibility: Applicants must be full-time students (12 hours) and demonstrate good moral character and academic excellence.
Target applicants: High school students. College students. Adult students.
Minimum GPA: 2.5
Amount: $850.
Number of awards: 1.
Scholarship may be renewable.
Deadline: January 15.
How to apply: Applications are available online at http://www.tgkvf.org/scholar.htm or by email at shoover@tgkvf.org.
Exclusive: Visit www.UltimateScholarshipBook.com and enter code GR180612 for updates on this award.

(1807) • North Carolina 4-H Development Fund Scholarships

North Carolina 4-H Youth Development
Shannon MCCollum, Extension 4-H Associate
NCSU, Box 7606
512 Brickhaven Drive Suite 230
Raleigh, NC 27695
Phone: 919-515-2801
Email: 4hweb@ces.ncsu.edu
http://www.nc4h.org
Purpose: To help North Carolina students who have been involved with the 4-H Club who want to go to college in the state.
Eligibility: Applicants must be enrolling as undergraduates at a four-year North Carolina college or university or a junior or community college in the state, provided the program of study is transferable to a four-year college. Students must also have a strong record of 4-H Club participation, have an excellent high school academic record and show an aptitude for college work through SAT scores. An application form, transcript, photo page and two recommendation letters are required. For some of the awards, financial need is necessary. Some awards have geographic restrictions to regions of the state while others are for a degree program or a specific college or university. Some scholarships are renewable.
Target applicants: High school students.
Amount: Up to $1,000.
Number of awards: Varies.
Deadline: January 15.
How to apply: Applications are available through each county cooperative extension office in North Carolina by phone or online.
Exclusive: Visit www.UltimateScholarshipBook.com and enter code NO180712 for updates on this award.

(1808) • North Carolina Bar Association Scholarship

College Foundation of North Carolina
P.O. Box 41966
Raleigh, NC 27629
Phone: 888-234-6400
Fax: 919-821-3139
Email: programinformation@cfnc.org
http://www.cfnc.org
Purpose: To provide financial assistance to students whose parents are North Carolina law enforcement officers who were killed or permanently disabled in the line of duty.
Eligibility: Applicants must be children of a North Carolina police officer who was killed or permanently disabled while on duty and must be enrolled or accepted to an institution approved by the scholarship committee. They must also apply before their 27th birthday and demonstrate financial need and merit.
Target applicants: High school students. College students. Adult students.
Amount: Varies.
Number of awards: Varies.
Deadline: April 1.
How to apply: Applications are available online.
Exclusive: Visit www.UltimateScholarshipBook.com and enter code CO180812 for updates on this award.

(1809) • North Carolina Community College Grant

College Foundation of North Carolina
P.O. Box 41966
Raleigh, NC 27629
Phone: 888-234-6400
Fax: 919-821-3139
Email: programinformation@cfnc.org
http://www.cfnc.org
Purpose: To assist North Carolina community college students.
Eligibility: Applicants must be North Carolina residents, demonstrate financial need and attend a North Carolina community college for at least six credit hours per semester. Selection is based on financial need.
Target applicants: College students. Adult students.
Amount: Varies.
Number of awards: Varies.
Deadline: Varies.
How to apply: Application is made by completing the FAFSA.
Exclusive: Visit www.UltimateScholarshipBook.com and enter code CO180912 for updates on this award.

(1810) • North Carolina Education Lottery Scholarship

College Foundation of North Carolina
P.O. Box 41966
Raleigh, NC 27629
Phone: 888-234-6400
Fax: 919-821-3139
Email: programinformation@cfnc.org
http://www.cfnc.org
Purpose: To provide financial assistance to North Carolina residents with financial need who are attending North Carolina colleges and universities.
Eligibility: Applicants must be enrolled for at least six credit hours per semester in an undergraduate degree-seeking program at an eligible North Carolina institution and meet satisfactory academic progress requirements. Students who meet the same criteria as the Federal Pell Grant and those with an Estimated Family Contribution of $5,000 or less are eligible for the scholarship.
Target applicants: College students. Adult students.
Amount: Up to $2,500.
Deadline: Varies.
How to apply: Qualified students who submit the Free Application for Federal Student Aid (FAFSA) will be considered.
Exclusive: Visit www.UltimateScholarshipBook.com and enter code CO181012 for updates on this award.

(1811) • North Carolina Oratorical Contest

American Legion, Department of North Carolina
4 N. Blount Street
P.O. Box 26657
Raleigh, NC 27611
Phone: 919-832-7506
Fax: 919-832-6428
Email: nclegion@nc.rr.com
http://nclegion.org/orate.htm

Purpose: To enhance high school students' experience with and understanding of the U.S. Constitution. The contest will help develop students' leadership skills and civic appreciation, as well as the ability to deliver thoughtful, insightful orations regarding U.S. citizenship and its inherent responsibilities.

Eligibility: Applicants must be high school students under the age of 20 who are U.S. citizens or legal residents and residents of the state. Students first give an oration within their state and winners compete at the national level. The oration must be related to the Constitution of the United States focusing on the duties and obligations citizens have to the government. It must be in English and be between eight and ten minutes. There is also an assigned topic which is posted on the website, and it should be between three and five minutes.

Target applicants: High school students.
Amount: $500-$18,000.
Number of awards: Varies.
Deadline: Varies.
How to apply: Application information is available by contacting the local post by email.
Exclusive: Visit www.UltimateScholarshipBook.com and enter code AM181112 for updates on this award.

(1812) • North Dakota Academic Scholarship

North Dakota Department of Career and Technical Education
600 E. Boulevard Avenue
Department 270
Bismarck, ND 58505
Phone: 701-328-3180
Fax: 701-328-1255
Email: cte@nd.gov
http://www.nd.gov/cte/

Purpose: To assist North Dakota high school seniors.

Eligibility: Applicants must plan to enroll full-time at an accredited North Dakota postsecondary institution and maintain a minimum 2.75 college GPA. The scholarship may not exceed $6,000 nor extend beyond six years. For the class of 2010 graduates, students must receive a minimum ACT score of 24. For the class of 2011 and beyond, students must complete one unit of algebra II, one unit of math for which algebra II is a prerequisite, two units of the same foreign or Native American language, one unit of fine arts or career and technical education and one additional unit of foreign or Native American language, fine arts or career and technical education. Applicants must also earn a C minimum or a half unit in each class, have a minimum cumulative B GPA, have a minimum score of 24 on the ACT and complete one unit of an advanced placement course and exam or a dual-credit course.

Target applicants: High school students.
Minimum GPA: 3.0
Amount: $1,500.
Number of awards: Varies.
Scholarship may be renewable.
Deadline: Varies.
How to apply: Applications are available from your counselor.
Exclusive: Visit www.UltimateScholarshipBook.com and enter code NO181212 for updates on this award.

(1813) • North Dakota Career and Technical Scholarship

North Dakota Department of Career and Technical Education
600 E. Boulevard Avenue
Department 270
Bismarck, ND 58505
Phone: 701-328-3180
Fax: 701-328-1255
Email: cte@nd.gov
http://www.nd.gov/cte/

Purpose: To assist North Dakota students who study career and technical education coursework.

Eligibility: Applicants must plan to enroll full-time at an accredited North Dakota postsecondary institution and maintain a minimum 2.75 college GPA. The scholarship may not exceed $6,000 nor extend beyond six years. For the class of 2010 graduates, students must receive a minimum ACT score of 24 or at least five on each of three WorkKeys assessments recommended by the Department of Career and Technical Education. For the class of 2011 and beyond, students must complete one unit of algebra II, two units of an approved plan of study of career and technical education coursework and three additional units (two of which must be in the area of career and technical education). Applicants must also obtain a minimum grade of C or .5 unit per class, have a minimum cumulative GPA of a B and receive a minimum ACT score of 24 or a score of at least five on each of three WorkKeys assessments.

Target applicants: High school students.
Minimum GPA: 2.75
Amount: $1,500.
Number of awards: 2.
Scholarship may be renewable.
Deadline: Varies.
How to apply: Applications are available from your counselor.
Exclusive: Visit www.UltimateScholarshipBook.com and enter code NO181312 for updates on this award.

(1814) • North Dakota Educational Assistance for Dependents of Veterans

Department of Veterans Affairs
Veterans Benefits Administration
810 Vermont Avenue NW
Washington, DC 20420
Phone: 888-442-4551
http://www.gibill.va.gov

Purpose: To assist dependents of deceased or disabled veterans in obtaining higher education.

Eligibility: Applicants must be dependents of a North Dakota veteran who was killed in action, died or became disabled because of a service-connected injury, was a prisoner of war or was declared missing in action. Students must enroll in a North Dakota public institution of higher learning and earn their degree or certificate within 45 months or ten semesters.

Target applicants: High school students. College students. Adult students.
Amount: Tuition.
Number of awards: Varies.
Scholarship may be renewable.
Deadline: Varies.
How to apply: Applications are available from your financial aid office.

Exclusive: Visit www.UltimateScholarshipBook.com and enter code DE181412 for updates on this award.

(1815) • North Dakota Scholars Program

North Dakota University System
10th Floor, State Capitol
600 East Boulevard Avenue, Dept. 215
Bismarck, ND 58505
Phone: 701-328-2960
Fax: 701-328-2961
Email: ndus.office@ndus.nodak.edu
http://www.ndus.edu
Purpose: To assist outstanding North Dakota high school students.
Eligibility: Applicants must be North Dakota high school seniors who have scored in the top 5 percent of all students in North Dakota who have taken the ACT. They must have plans to attend a North Dakota postsecondary institution. Selection is based on academic merit.
Target applicants: High school students.
Amount: Full-tuition.
Number of awards: 45-50.
Scholarship may be renewable.
Deadline: April.
How to apply: Applications are available by written request. An application form and supporting documents are required.
Exclusive: Visit www.UltimateScholarshipBook.com and enter code NO181512 for updates on this award.

(1816) • North Dakota State Student Incentive Grant

North Dakota University System
10th Floor, State Capitol
600 East Boulevard Avenue, Dept. 215
Bismarck, ND 58505
Phone: 701-328-2960
Fax: 701-328-2961
Email: ndus.office@ndus.nodak.edu
http://www.ndus.edu
Purpose: To assist North Dakota students who have financial need.
Eligibility: Applicants must be U.S. citizens or permanent residents. They must be North Dakota residents who are high school graduates or GED recipients and enrolled as full-time students in a North Dakota undergraduate program that lasts for at least one academic year. They must be first-time undergraduate students who have no defaulted student loans and who owe no Title IV grant or loan refunds. Selection is based on financial need.
Target applicants: High school students. College students. Adult students.
Amount: $800-$1,500.
Number of awards: Varies.
Scholarship may be renewable.
Deadline: March 15.
How to apply: Application is made by completing the Free Application for Federal Student Aid (FAFSA).
Exclusive: Visit www.UltimateScholarshipBook.com and enter code NO181612 for updates on this award.

(1817) • NTA Alexander Harris Undergraduate Scholarship

Tourism Cares
275 Turnpike Street
Suite 307
Canton, MA 02021
Phone: 781-821-5990
Fax: 781-821-8949
Email: carolynv@tourismcares.org
http://www.tourismcares.org
Purpose: To aid New York and New Jersey residents who are studying travel, tourism and hospitality at the undergraduate level.
Eligibility: Applicants must be permanent residents of New York or New Jersey who are enrolled at an accredited, four-year postsecondary institution located in the U.S. They must be rising undergraduate juniors or seniors who are studying travel, tourism or hospitality. By May of the application year, they must have completed 60 or more credits of their program. They must have a GPA of 3.0 or higher on a four-point scale. Selection is based on the overall strength of the application.
Target applicants: College students. Adult students.
Minimum GPA: 3.0
Amount: $1,000.
Number of awards: 1.
Deadline: April 15.
How to apply: Applications are available online. An application form, personal essay, proof of residency, two letters of recommendation, an official transcript and a resume are required.
Exclusive: Visit www.UltimateScholarshipBook.com and enter code TO181712 for updates on this award.

(1818) • NTA California Undergraduate Scholarship

Tourism Cares
275 Turnpike Street
Suite 307
Canton, MA 02021
Phone: 781-821-5990
Fax: 781-821-8949
Email: carolynv@tourismcares.org
http://www.tourismcares.org
Purpose: To aid California residents who are studying hospitality, tourism and travel at the undergraduate level.
Eligibility: Applicants must be permanent residents of California and be enrolled full-time at an accredited two- or four-year postsecondary institution located in California. They must be entering the second year of a two-year program or entering the third or fourth year of a four-year program and must be studying hospitality, tourism or travel at the undergraduate level. By May of the application year, two-year students must have completed 30 or more credits, and four-year students must have completed 60 or more credits. They must have a GPA of 3.0 or higher on a four-point scale. Selection is based on the overall strength of the application.
Target applicants: College students. Adult students.
Minimum GPA: 3.0
Amount: $1,750.
Number of awards: 1.
Deadline: April 15.
How to apply: Applications are available online. An application form, a personal essay, an official transcript, two letters of recommendation, a resume and proof of residency are required.
Exclusive: Visit www.UltimateScholarshipBook.com and enter code TO181812 for updates on this award.

(1819) • NTA Connecticut Undergraduate Scholarship

Tourism Cares
275 Turnpike Street
Suite 307
Canton, MA 02021

Phone: 781-821-5990
Fax: 781-821-8949
Email: carolynv@tourismcares.org
http://www.tourismcares.org
Purpose: To aid Connecticut residents who are studying hospitality, tourism and travel at the undergraduate level.
Eligibility: Applicants must be permanent residents of Connecticut and must be enrolled full-time at an accredited four-year postsecondary institution located in Connecticut. They must be rising undergraduate juniors or seniors who are studying hospitality, tourism or travel and must have a GPA of 3.0 or higher on a four-point scale. Selection is based on the overall strength of the application.
Target applicants: College students. Adult students.
Minimum GPA: 3.0
Amount: $1,000.
Number of awards: 1.
Deadline: April 15.
How to apply: Applications are available online. An application form, personal essay, proof of residency, two letters of recommendation, an official transcript and a resume are required.
Exclusive: Visit www.UltimateScholarshipBook.com and enter code TO181912 for updates on this award.

(1820) • NTA Florida Undergraduate Scholarship

Tourism Cares
275 Turnpike Street
Suite 307
Canton, MA 02021
Phone: 781-821-5990
Fax: 781-821-8949
Email: carolynv@tourismcares.org
http://www.tourismcares.org
Purpose: To aid Florida residents who are studying travel, tourism and hospitality at the undergraduate level.
Eligibility: Applicants must be permanent residents of Florida and be enrolled at an accredited two- or four-year postsecondary institution located in Florida. They must be entering the second year of a two-year program or entering the third or fourth year of a four-year program. They must be studying travel, tourism or hospitality at the undergraduate level. By May of the application year, they must have completed 30 or more credits if in a two-year program or 60 or more credits if in a four-year program. They must have a GPA of 3.0 or higher on a four-point scale. Selection is based on the overall strength of the application.
Target applicants: College students. Adult students.
Minimum GPA: 3.0
Amount: $1,500.
Number of awards: 1.
Deadline: April 15.
How to apply: Applications are available online. An application form, personal essay, a resume, proof of residency, two letters of recommendation and an official transcript are required.
Exclusive: Visit www.UltimateScholarshipBook.com and enter code TO182012 for updates on this award.

(1821) • NTA Hawaii-Chuck Yim Gee Undergraduate Scholarship

Tourism Cares
275 Turnpike Street
Suite 307
Canton, MA 02021
Phone: 781-821-5990
Fax: 781-821-8949
Email: carolynv@tourismcares.org
http://www.tourismcares.org
Purpose: To aid Hawaii residents who are studying hospitality, tourism and travel at the undergraduate level.
Eligibility: Applicants must be permanent residents of Hawaii and must be enrolled at an accredited four-year postsecondary institution located in Hawaii. They must be rising undergraduate juniors or seniors. By May of the application year, they must have completed 60 or more credits of their degree program. They must have a GPA of 3.0 or higher on a four-point scale. Selection is based on the overall strength of the application.
Target applicants: College students. Adult students.
Minimum GPA: 3.0
Amount: $1,500.
Number of awards: 1.
Deadline: April 15.
How to apply: Applications are available online. An application form, personal essay, proof of residency, an official transcript, a resume and two letters of recommendation are required.
Exclusive: Visit www.UltimateScholarshipBook.com and enter code TO182112 for updates on this award.

(1822) • NTA Massachusetts Undergraduate Scholarship

Tourism Cares
275 Turnpike Street
Suite 307
Canton, MA 02021
Phone: 781-821-5990
Fax: 781-821-8949
Email: carolynv@tourismcares.org
http://www.tourismcares.org
Purpose: To aid Massachusetts residents who are studying travel, tourism and hospitality at the undergraduate level.
Eligibility: Applicants must be permanent residents of Massachusetts enrolled at an accredited two- or four-year postsecondary institution located in the state. They must be entering the second year of study if in a two-year program or entering the third or fourth year of study if in a four-year program. By May of the application year, two-year program students must have completed 30 or more credits, and four-year program students must have completed 60 or more credits. They must have a GPA of 3.0 or higher on a four-point scale. Selection is based on the overall strength of the application.
Target applicants: College students. Adult students.
Minimum GPA: 3.0
Amount: $1,000.
Number of awards: 1.
Deadline: April 15.
How to apply: Applications are available online. An application form, proof of residency, a resume, an official transcript, a personal essay and two letters of recommendation are required.
Exclusive: Visit www.UltimateScholarshipBook.com and enter code TO182212 for updates on this award.

(1823) • NTA Michigan Undergraduate Scholarship

Tourism Cares
275 Turnpike Street
Suite 307
Canton, MA 02021
Phone: 781-821-5990
Fax: 781-821-8949

Email: carolynv@tourismcares.org
http://www.tourismcares.org
Purpose: To aid Michigan residents who are studying travel, hospitality and tourism at the undergraduate level.
Eligibility: Applicants must be permanent residents of Michigan, enrolled at an accredited two- or four-year postsecondary institution located in the state and entering the second year of a two-year program or entering the third or fourth year of a four-year program. By May of the application year, they must have completed 30 or more credits if in a two-year program or 60 or more credits if in a four-year program. They must have a GPA of 3.0 or higher on a four-point scale. Selection is based on the overall strength of the application.
Target applicants: College students. Adult students.
Minimum GPA: 3.0
Amount: $1,000.
Number of awards: 1.
Deadline: April 15.
How to apply: Applications are available online. An application form, a resume, proof of residency, two letters of recommendation, a personal essay and an official transcript are required.
Exclusive: Visit www.UltimateScholarshipBook.com and enter code TO182312 for updates on this award.

(1824) • NTA New Jersey Undergraduate Scholarship

Tourism Cares
275 Turnpike Street
Suite 307
Canton, MA 02021
Phone: 781-821-5990
Fax: 781-821-8949
Email: carolynv@tourismcares.org
http://www.tourismcares.org
Purpose: To aid New Jersey residents who are studying hospitality, travel and tourism at the undergraduate level.
Eligibility: Applicants must be permanent residents of New Jersey and enrolled at an accredited two- or four-year postsecondary institution located in the state. They must be entering the second year of a two-year program or entering the third or fourth year of a four-year program. By May of the application year, they must have completed 30 or more credits if in a two-year program or 60 or more credits if in a four-year program. They must have a GPA of 3.0 or higher on a four-point scale. Selection is based on the overall strength of the application.
Target applicants: College students. Adult students.
Minimum GPA: 3.0
Amount: $1,000.
Number of awards: 1.
Deadline: April 15.
How to apply: Applications are available online. An application form, a personal essay, two recommendation letters, proof of residency, an official transcript and a resume are required.
Exclusive: Visit www.UltimateScholarshipBook.com and enter code TO182412 for updates on this award.

(1825) • NTA New York Undergraduate Scholarship

Tourism Cares
275 Turnpike Street
Suite 307
Canton, MA 02021
Phone: 781-821-5990
Fax: 781-821-8949
Email: carolynv@tourismcares.org
http://www.tourismcares.org
Purpose: To aid New York residents who are studying tourism, hospitality and travel at the undergraduate level.
Eligibility: Applicants must be permanent residents of New York and be enrolled full-time at an accredited two- or four-year postsecondary institution located in the state. They must be entering the second year of a two-year program or entering the third or fourth year of a four-year program. By May of the application year, they must have completed 30 or more credits if in a two-year program or 60 or more credits if in a four-year program. They must have a GPA of 3.0 or higher on a four-point scale. Selection is based on the overall strength of the application.
Target applicants: College students. Adult students.
Minimum GPA: 3.0
Amount: $1,000.
Number of awards: 1.
Deadline: April 15.
How to apply: Applications are available online. An application form, personal essay, official transcript, proof of residency, a resume and two recommendation letters are required.
Exclusive: Visit www.UltimateScholarshipBook.com and enter code TO182512 for updates on this award.

(1826) • NTA Ohio Undergraduate Scholarship

Tourism Cares
275 Turnpike Street
Suite 307
Canton, MA 02021
Phone: 781-821-5990
Fax: 781-821-8949
Email: carolynv@tourismcares.org
http://www.tourismcares.org
Purpose: To aid Ohio residents who are studying hospitality, tourism and travel at the undergraduate level.
Eligibility: Applicants must be permanent residents of Ohio and be enrolled at an accredited two- or four-year postsecondary institution located in Ohio. They must be entering the second year of a two-year program or entering the third or fourth year of a four-year program. By May of the application year, they must have completed 30 or more credits if in a two-year program or 60 or more credits if in a four-year program. They must have a GPA of 3.0 or higher on a four-point scale. Selection is based on the overall strength of the application.
Target applicants: College students. Adult students.
Minimum GPA: 3.0
Amount: $1,000.
Number of awards: 1.
Deadline: April 15.
How to apply: Applications are available online. An application form, personal essay, two letters of recommendation, proof of residency, a resume and an official transcript are required.
Exclusive: Visit www.UltimateScholarshipBook.com and enter code TO182612 for updates on this award.

(1827) • NTA Pat and Jim Host Undergraduate or Graduate Scholarship

Tourism Cares
275 Turnpike Street
Suite 307
Canton, MA 02021
Phone: 781-821-5990
Fax: 781-821-8949
Email: carolynv@tourismcares.org

http://www.tourismcares.org
Purpose: To aid Kentucky residents who are studying hospitality, travel and tourism.
Eligibility: Applicants must be permanent residents of Kentucky and be accepted or enrolled full-time at an accredited, four-year postsecondary institution located in the state. They must be entering or returning undergraduate or graduate students who are studying travel, tourism or hospitality and have a GPA of 3.0 or higher on a four-point scale. Selection is based on the overall strength of the application.
Target applicants: High school students. College students. Graduate school students. Adult students.
Minimum GPA: 3.0
Amount: $1,000.
Number of awards: 1.
Deadline: April 15.
How to apply: Applications are available online. An application form, two letters of recommendation, a personal essay, a resume, proof of residency, proof of enrollment (for entering undergraduates only) and an official transcript are required.
Exclusive: Visit www.UltimateScholarshipBook.com and enter code TO182712 for updates on this award.

(1828) • Nurse Education Scholarship Loan Program

College Foundation of North Carolina
P.O. Box 41966
Raleigh, NC 27629
Phone: 888-234-6400
Fax: 919-821-3139
Email: programinformation@cfnc.org
http://www.cfnc.org
Purpose: To reduce the shortage of nurses in the state of North Carolina.
Eligibility: Applicants must be enrolled in an LPN or RN licensure program at a North Carolina college or university. They must demonstrate financial need and adequate academic performance, and they must be U.S. citizens and North Carolina residents. The funds must be paid back after graduation, either through service as a full-time licensed nurse in the state or in cash.
Target applicants: High school students. College students. Adult students.
Amount: $3,000-$5,000.
Number of awards: Varies.
Scholarship may be renewable.
Deadline: Varies.
How to apply: Applications are available from your financial aid office.
Exclusive: Visit www.UltimateScholarshipBook.com and enter code CO182812 for updates on this award.

(1829) • Nurse Support Program II - Graduate Nursing Faculty Scholarship

Maryland Higher Education Commission
Office of Student Financial Assistance
839 Bestgate Road, Suite 400
Annapolis, MD 21401
Phone: 800-974-1024
Fax: 410-260-3200
Email: osfamail@mhec.state.md.us
http://www.mhec.state.md.us
Purpose: To support graduate nursing students who are planning to join the faculty at a Maryland college.
Eligibility: Applicants must be Maryland residents, and they must be enrolled full-time or part-time at a Maryland school as graduate nursing students. Full-time students must agree to complete their graduate program within two years. All students must agree to work in the nursing faculty of a Maryland college within six months of graduation.
Target applicants: College students. Graduate school students. Adult students.
Amount: Up to $13,000.
Number of awards: Varies.
Scholarship may be renewable.
Deadline: Prior to the beginning of the funded semester.
How to apply: Applications are available online.
Exclusive: Visit www.UltimateScholarshipBook.com and enter code MA182912 for updates on this award.

(1830) • Nursing Education Scholarship Program

Illinois Department of Public Health
535 W. Jefferson Street
Springfield, IL 62761
Phone: 217-782-4977
Fax: 217-782-3987
Email: dph.mailus@illinois.gov
http://www.idph.state.il.us
Purpose: To increase the number of nurses in Illinois.
Eligibility: Applicants must be Illinois residents, having lived in the state for one year prior to applying and be U.S. citizens or permanent residents. Applicants must be accepted to or enrolled in an approved nursing program and demonstrate financial need. Scholarship recipients must agree to work as a nurse in Illinois after graduation.
Target applicants: High school students. College students. Graduate school students. Adult students.
Amount: Varies.
Number of awards: Varies.
Scholarship may be renewable.
Deadline: May 31.
How to apply: Applications are available online.
Exclusive: Visit www.UltimateScholarshipBook.com and enter code IL183012 for updates on this award.

(1831) • Nursing Scholarship Fund

State Student Assistance Commission of Indiana
150 W. Market Street
Suite 500
Indianapolis, IN 46204
Phone: 888-528-4719
Fax: 317-232-3260
Email: grants@ssaci.state.in.us
http://www.in.gov/ssaci
Purpose: To support Indiana residents who are pursuing nursing careers.
Eligibility: Applicants must be enrolled full-time or part-time in an Indiana college nursing program. They must demonstrate financial need and have at least a 2.0 GPA. Students must agree to work as nurses in the state of Indiana for at least two years after graduation.
Target applicants: High school students. College students. Adult students.
Minimum GPA: 2.0
Amount: Up to $5,000.
Number of awards: Varies.
Scholarship may be renewable.
Deadline: Varies.
How to apply: Applications are available online.

Exclusive: Visit www.UltimateScholarshipBook.com and enter code ST183112 for updates on this award.

(1832) • NYWEA Major Environmental Career Scholarship

New York Water Environment Association Inc.
525 Plum Street
Suite 102
Syracuse, NY 13204
Phone: 877-556-9932
Fax: 315-422-3851
Email: mah@nywea.org
http://www.nywea.org

Purpose: To support New York students who are planning to pursue a bachelor's degree in an environment-related subject.

Eligibility: Applicants must be residents of the state of New York and must be high school seniors who plan to enroll full-time in an environment-related bachelor's degree program no later than the fall following graduation. The programs could include but are not limited to environmental engineering, civil engineering with an environmental minor, chemical engineering with an environmental minor, hydrogeology with an environmental emphasis or biology or microbiology with an environmental emphasis. Selection is based on the overall strength of the application.

Target applicants: High school students.

Amount: $10,000.

Number of awards: 1.

Deadline: January 20.

How to apply: Applications are available online. An application form, official transcript, two recommendation letters and two personal essays are required.

Exclusive: Visit www.UltimateScholarshipBook.com and enter code NE183212 for updates on this award.

(1833) • Ohio Legion Scholarships

American Legion, Department of Ohio
P.O. Box 8007
Delaware, OH 43015
Phone: 740-362-7478
Fax: 740-362-1429
Email: ohlegion@iwaynet.net
http://www.ohiolegion.com/scholarships/info.htm

Purpose: To provide financial assistance to deserving Ohio students.

Eligibility: Applicants must be high school seniors, Legionnaires or their descendants or spouses or surviving spouses or children of members of the U.S. military who died on active duty or from injuries incurred on active duty.

Target applicants: High school students. College students. Adult students.

Amount: At least $2,000.

Deadline: April 15.

How to apply: Applications are available online, by mail or by phone.

Exclusive: Visit www.UltimateScholarshipBook.com and enter code AM183312 for updates on this award.

(1834) • Ohio Safety Officers College Memorial Fund

Ohio Board of Regents
State Grants and Scholarships Department
P.O. Box 182452
Columbus, OH 43218-2452
Phone: 888-833-1133
Fax: 614-752-5903
http://www.regents.ohio.gov

Purpose: To provide financial assistance to students who are family members of safety officers killed in the line of duty.

Eligibility: Applicants must be spouses or children of peace officers, firefighters or certain other safety officers who died in the line of duty anywhere in the United States. The applicant must be an Ohio resident and attend an Ohio college or university. The award covers full tuition and required fees at public institutions and a portion of tuition and fees at private institutions.

Target applicants: High school students. College students. Adult students.

Amount: Full Tuition.

Number of awards: Varies.

Scholarship may be renewable.

Deadline: Varies.

How to apply: Applications are available from the Ohio Board of Regents State Grants and Scholarships Department.

Exclusive: Visit www.UltimateScholarshipBook.com and enter code OH183412 for updates on this award.

(1835) • Ohio Section Scholarships

Institute of Transportation Engineers - Ohio Section
1799 West 5th Avenue
PMB 157
Columbus, OH 43212
Email: bsliemers@ljbinc.com
http://www.ohioite.org

Purpose: To aid students who are enrolled in a degree program that is related to transportation engineering.

Eligibility: Applicants must be full-time students who are attending an ABET-accredited college or university located in the state of Ohio. They must be enrolled in a civil engineering or other transportation-related degree program and have a GPA of 2.5 or higher. Selection is based on academic achievement, stated career goals and extracurricular activities.

Target applicants: College students. Graduate school students. Adult students.

Minimum GPA: 2.5

Amount: $1,000.

Number of awards: Up to 2.

Deadline: October 19.

How to apply: Applications are available online. An application form, personal statement, official transcript and one recommendation letter are required.

Exclusive: Visit www.UltimateScholarshipBook.com and enter code IN183512 for updates on this award.

(1836) • Ohio State Association/AOTF Scholarships

American Occupational Therapy Foundation
4720 Montgomery Lane
P.O. Box 31220
Bethesda, MD 20824
Phone: 301-652-6611
Fax: 301-656-3620
Email: jcooper@aotf.org
http://www.aotf.org

Purpose: To aid Ohio occupational therapy students who are members of the American Occupational Therapy Foundation.

Eligibility: Applicants must be Ohio residents who are enrolled in an accredited occupational therapy associate's or first professional degree

program at a school located in Ohio. Selection is based on the overall strength of the application.
Target applicants: College students. Graduate school students. Adult students.
Amount: $1,000.
Number of awards: 2.
Deadline: November 21.
How to apply: Applications are available online. An application form, two personal references and a letter from the student's academic program director are required.
Exclusive: Visit www.UltimateScholarshipBook.com and enter code AM183612 for updates on this award.

(1837) • Ohio Turfgrass Foundation Scholarships

Ohio Turfgrass Foundation
OTF Scholarship Committee
1100-H Brandywine Boulevard
Zanesville, OH 43701
Phone: 888-683-3445
Fax: 740-452-2552
Email: info@ohioturfgrass.org
http://www.ohioturfgrass.org
Purpose: To aid Ohio students who are pursuing higher education in subjects related to the turfgrass industry.
Eligibility: Applicants must be Ohio undergraduate or graduate students who are enrolled in a degree program that is related to turfgrass science. They must have a cumulative GPA of 2.5 or higher and a major GPA of 2.75 or higher. Selection is based on academic merit, professional commitment to the turfgrass industry and financial need.
Target applicants: College students. Graduate school students. Adult students.
Minimum GPA: 2.5
Amount: Varies.
Number of awards: Varies.
Deadline: October 22.
How to apply: Applications are available online. An application form, transcript and two recommendation letters are required.
Exclusive: Visit www.UltimateScholarshipBook.com and enter code OH183712 for updates on this award.

(1838) • Ohio War Orphans Scholarship

Ohio Board of Regents
State Grants and Scholarships Department
P.O. Box 182452
Columbus, OH 43218-2452
Phone: 888-833-1133
Fax: 614-752-5903
http://www.regents.ohio.gov
Purpose: To provide tuition assistance to war orphans.
Eligibility: Applicants must be children of deceased or severely disabled Ohio war veterans. They must be Ohio residents under the age of 25 and be enrolled full-time in an undergraduate program at an eligible Ohio institution of higher learning. The award covers all instructional charges and general fees at public institutions and a portion of them at private institutions.
Target applicants: High school students. College students.
Amount: $4,400-80% of full tuition.
Number of awards: Varies.
Scholarship may be renewable.
Deadline: July 1.
How to apply: Applications are available from the Ohio Board of Regents, high school guidance offices, college financial aid offices and veterans service offices.
Exclusive: Visit www.UltimateScholarshipBook.com and enter code OH183812 for updates on this award.

(1839) • Oklahoma Foundation for Excellence Academic All-State Scholarships

Oklahoma Foundation for Excellence
120 N. Robinson Avenue #1420-W
Oklahoma City, OK 73102
Phone: 405-236-0006
Fax: 405-236-8690
Email: info@ofe.org
http://www.ofe.org/awards
Purpose: To reward Oklahoma students with high academic achievement.
Eligibility: Applicants must be high school seniors who are nominated by their school principals or superintendents. They must have an ACT score of 30 or higher or an SAT score of 1350 or higher or be a semi-finalist for a National Merit, National Achievement or National Hispanic Scholarship. An essay is required.
Target applicants: High school students.
Amount: $1,000.
Number of awards: 100.
Deadline: Varies.
How to apply: Applications are available from your school.
Exclusive: Visit www.UltimateScholarshipBook.com and enter code OK183912 for updates on this award.

(1840) • Oklahoma Golf Course Superintendent's Association Scholarships

Oklahoma Golf Course Superintendent's Association
c/o Pam Wooten
1911 West Rockport Place
Broken Arrow, OK 74012
Phone: 800-936-7071
Fax: 800-936-7071
Email: ogcsa@cox.net
http://www.okgcsa.com
Purpose: To aid Oklahoma Golf Course Superintendent's Association members, their family members and students who are pursuing degrees in turfgrass management.
Eligibility: Applicants must be pursuing or planning to pursue a degree in turfgrass management; members of the Oklahoma Golf Course Superintendent's Association (OGCSA) or family members of an OGCSA member. They must be enrolled or planning to enroll as full-time students at an accredited postsecondary institution. Selection is based on academic merit, extracurricular activities and financial need.
Target applicants: High school students. College students. Adult students.
Amount: Varies.
Number of awards: 1.
Deadline: October 31.
How to apply: Applications are available online. An application form, personal statement, transcript and two recommendation letters are required.
Exclusive: Visit www.UltimateScholarshipBook.com and enter code OK184012 for updates on this award.

(1841) • Oklahoma Society of Land Surveyors Scholarships

Oklahoma Society of Land Surveyors
13905 Twin Ridge Road
Edmond, OK 73034
Phone: 405-202-5792
Fax: 405-330-3432
Email: osls@osls.org
http://www.osls.org

Purpose: To aid those who are preparing for careers in land surveying.
Eligibility: Applicants must be high school seniors who are planning to study land surveying in college, or they must be working toward licensure under the direct supervision of a professional land surveyor. High school seniors must be Oklahoma residents who have a GPA of 2.5 or higher and an ACT score of 19 or higher. Applicants who are already working in the field must be associate members of the Oklahoma Society of Land Surveyors (OSLS) and must be recommended by a registered professional land surveyor. Selection is based on citizenship, leadership and commitment to professional land surveying.
Target applicants: High school students. College students. Adult students.
Minimum GPA: 2.5
Amount: Varies.
Number of awards: Varies.
Deadline: Varies.
How to apply: Applications are available online. An application form, official transcript, ACT scores and one recommendation letter are required.
Exclusive: Visit www.UltimateScholarshipBook.com and enter code OK184112 for updates on this award.

(1842) • Oklahoma Tuition Aid Grant Program (OTAG)

Oklahoma State Regents for Higher Education
655 Research Parkway
Suite 200
Oklahoma City, OK 73104
Phone: 405-225-9100
Email: bfair@osrhe.edu
http://www.okhighered.org

Purpose: To assist Oklahoma undergraduates who are pursuing higher education in Oklahoma.
Eligibility: Applicants must be Oklahoma residents who are attending eligible undergraduate institutions in Oklahoma. They must be graduates of Oklahoma high schools and must have resided with their parents in Oklahoma while attending high school for at least two years before graduating. They must demonstrate financial need. Qualified undocumented immigrants are eligible for this award. Selection is based on financial need.
Target applicants: High school students. College students. Adult students.
Amount: Up to $1,300.
Number of awards: Varies.
Deadline: As soon after January 1st.
How to apply: Application is made by completing the FAFSA.
Exclusive: Visit www.UltimateScholarshipBook.com and enter code OK184212 for updates on this award.

(1843) • Oklahoma Tuition Equalization Grant Program (OTEG)

Oklahoma State Regents for Higher Education (OTEG)
655 Research Parkway, Suite 200
Oklahoma City, OK 73104
Phone: 877-622-6231
Fax: 405-225-9230
Email: otaginfo@osrhe.edu
http://www.okhighered.org

Purpose: To provide financial assistance for Oklahoma residents who are attending private institutions in the state.
Eligibility: Applicants must be enrolled in an undergraduate program at a private institution of higher learning full-time. They must have a family income of no more than $50,000, make satisfactory academic progress and not have already earned a bachelor's degree.
Target applicants: High school students. College students. Adult students.
Amount: $2,000.
Number of awards: Varies.
Deadline: Varies.
How to apply: Eligible students who file a Free Application for Federal Student Aid (FAFSA) will be considered.
Exclusive: Visit www.UltimateScholarshipBook.com and enter code OK184312 for updates on this award.

(1844) • Oklahoma Young Farmers and Ranchers Speech Contest

Oklahoma Farm Bureau
2501 North Stiles
Oklahoma City, OK 73105
Phone: 405-523-2405
Fax: 405-523-2362
Email: marcia.irvin@okfb.org
http://www.okfarmbureau.org

Purpose: To recognize youth who are interested in agriculture.
Eligibility: Applicants must be between the ages of 9 and 18. They must give a brief prepared speech on agricultural policy, agricultural production, natural resources or the environment. Selection is based on the overall strength of the presentation.
Target applicants: Junior high students or younger. High school students.
Amount: Varies.
Number of awards: Varies.
Deadline: Varies.
How to apply: Applications are available by request from FFA teachers, county Farm Bureau offices and extension offices. An application form and prepared speech are required.
Exclusive: Visit www.UltimateScholarshipBook.com and enter code OK184412 for updates on this award.

(1845) • Oklahoma Youth with Promise Scholarship Fund

Oklahoma City Community Foundation
P.O. Box 1146
Oklahoma City, OK 73101-1146
Phone: 405-235-5603
Fax: 405-235-5612
Email: info@occf.org
http://www.occf.org/scholarshipcenter.html

Purpose: To provide educational assistance to students who graduated while in foster care.
Eligibility: Applicants must be graduates of Oklahoma high schools who were in the custody of the Oklahoma Department of Human Services at the time of graduation. They must have a minimum GPA of 2.0. Financial need is considered.
Target applicants: High school students. College students. Adult students.
Minimum GPA: 2.0
Amount: $800-$1,200.
Number of awards: Varies.
Deadline: May 15 (graduating seniors) and June 15 (reapplying undergraduates).
How to apply: Applications are available online.
Exclusive: Visit www.UltimateScholarshipBook.com and enter code OK184512 for updates on this award.

(1846) · Oklahoma's Promise

Oklahoma State Regents for Higher Education
655 Research Parkway
Suite 200
Oklahoma City, OK 73104
Phone: 405-225-9100
Email: llangston@osrhe.edu
http://www.okhighered.org
Purpose: To assist children of families with income below $50,000 in preparing for and paying for college.
Eligibility: Applicants must be Oklahoma residents who are enrolled in the eighth, ninth or tenth grade at an Oklahoma high school (or are homeschool students between the ages of 13 and 15) and whose parents' income is less than $50,000 per year. They must take certain college preparatory courses in high school, maintain a GPA of 2.5 or higher and "stay out of trouble" such as gangs, drugs or alcohol.
Target applicants: Junior high students or younger. High school students.
Minimum GPA: 2.5
Amount: Tuition.
Number of awards: Varies.
Scholarship may be renewable.
Deadline: Varies.
How to apply: Applications are available online.
Exclusive: Visit www.UltimateScholarshipBook.com and enter code OK184612 for updates on this award.

(1847) · Oliver Joel and Ellen Pell Denny Healthcare Scholarship Fund

Winston-Salem Foundation
860 West Fifth Street
Winston-Salem, NC 27101
Phone: 336-725-2382
Fax: 336-727-0581
Email: info@wsfoundation.org
http://www.wsfoundation.org
Purpose: To aid North Carolina allied health students.
Eligibility: Applicants must be residents of North Carolina. They must be studying a subject in the field of allied health at an accredited postsecondary institution and have a GPA of 2.5 or higher. They must be seeking a first-time certificate, diploma, associate's degree or bachelor's degree. Master's degree holders are ineligible. Applicants must demonstrate financial need. Preference will be given to residents of Davidson, Davie, Forsyth, Stokes, Surry and Yadkin counties. Selection is based on the overall strength of the application.
Target applicants: High school students. College students. Adult students.
Minimum GPA: 2.5
Amount: Up to $3,000.
Number of awards: Varies.
Deadline: August 15.
How to apply: Applications are available online. An application form, official transcript, tax forms and financial aid award letter are required.
Exclusive: Visit www.UltimateScholarshipBook.com and enter code WI184712 for updates on this award.

(1848) · One Family Scholarship

One Family, Inc.
186 South Street
4th Floor
Boston, MA 02111
Phone: 617-442-1880 x262
Email: ypere@prohope.org
http://www.onefamilyinc.org
Purpose: To provide financial support, mentoring, leadership development and other resources for Massachusetts low income mothers who are returning to school.
Eligibility: Applicants must have family earnings which fall 200 percent or more below the poverty level. They should have clear and obtainable career goals as well as the proven desire and ability to complete the chosen academic program. Students must continue to remain residents of the state of Massachusetts throughout the program, and they must remain active in attendance at required meetings, workshops and retreats.
Target applicants: College students. Adult students.
Amount: Up to $11,000.
Number of awards: Varies.
Scholarship may be renewable.
Deadline: March 16.
How to apply: Applications are available by phone.
Exclusive: Visit www.UltimateScholarshipBook.com and enter code ON184812 for updates on this award.

(1849) · Opportunity Award

Louisiana Office of Student Financial Assistance
P.O. Box 91202
Baton Rouge, LA 70821-9202
Phone: 800-259-5626 x1012
Fax: 225-922-0790
Email: custserv@osfa.la.gov
http://www.osfa.state.la.us
Purpose: To aid Louisiana student residents.
Eligibility: Applicants must be Louisiana residents, U.S. citizens, have a minimum 2.5 GPA, have a minimum ACT score of 20 or equivalent SAT I score and apply during their senior year in high school. Applicants must use the award at a Louisiana college or university.
Target applicants: High school students.
Minimum GPA: 2.5
Amount: Varies.
Number of awards: Varies.
Scholarship may be renewable.
Deadline: July 1.
How to apply: The application is the Free Application for Federal Student Aid (FAFSA). ACT or SAT I scores must also be reported.

Exclusive: Visit www.UltimateScholarshipBook.com and enter code LO184912 for updates on this award.

(1850) · Opportunity Grant

Washington Higher Education Coordinating Board
917 Lakeridge Way
P.O. Box 43430
Olympia, WA 98504
Phone: 360-753-7850
Fax: 360-753-6243
Email: info@hecb.wa.gov
http://www.hecb.wa.gov
Purpose: To assist students with financial need to train for higher-wage careers.
Eligibility: Applicants must be Washington adult students. They must have financial need, be approved for a grant-eligible program with a family income at or below 200 percent of the federal poverty level and maintain a 2.0 GPA.
Target applicants: College students. Adult students.
Amount: Up to full tuition plus $1,000.
Number of awards: Varies.
Scholarship may be renewable.
Deadline: Varies.
How to apply: Applications are available online.
Exclusive: Visit www.UltimateScholarshipBook.com and enter code WA185012 for updates on this award.

(1851) · Opportunity Grant

Washington State Board for Community and Technical Colleges
P.O. Box 42495
1300 Quince Street SE
Olympia, WA 98504-2495
Phone: 360-704-4400
Fax: 360-704-4415
Email: webmaster@sbctc.ctc.edu
http://www.sbctc.ctc.edu
Purpose: To assist Washington adult students.
Eligibility: Applicants must be adult students with financial need who are attending a community or technical college. The grant provides funding for up to 45 credits over a maximum of three years and up to $1,000 for books and supplies per year. In addition, there are support services such as tutoring, career advising, emergency transportation and emergency child care.
Target applicants: College students. Adult students.
Amount: Full Tuition.
Number of awards: Varies.
Scholarship may be renewable.
Deadline: Varies.
How to apply: Applicants must complete the Free Application for Federal Student Aid (FAFSA). Contact your college for more information.
Exclusive: Visit www.UltimateScholarshipBook.com and enter code WA185112 for updates on this award.

(1852) · Opportunity Scholarship

Texas 4-H Youth Development Foundation
7607 Eastmark Drive, Suite 101
College Station, TX 77840
Phone: 979-845-1213
Fax: 979-845-6495
Email: texas4hfoundation@ag.tamu.edu
http://texas4-h.tamu.edu/
Purpose: To support Texas 4-H members who are planning to pursue a bachelor's degree.
Eligibility: Students must be high school seniors who have actively participated in a Texas 4-H program during at least part of the year. They must have formally applied to a Texas college or university, and they must meet the school's admission requirements. Applicants must have a score of at least 1350 on the SAT or 19 on the ACT. Students must provide information about their 4-H achievements, financial need, community service participation and leadership skills.
Target applicants: High school students.
Amount: $1,000-$16,000.
Number of awards: 225.
Deadline: February 11.
How to apply: Applications are available online.
Exclusive: Visit www.UltimateScholarshipBook.com and enter code TE185212 for updates on this award.

(1853) · ORCA Bob Hasson Memorial Scholarship Fund

Oregon Collectors Association
ORCA Scholarship Fund
1541 SW 201st
Beaverton, OR 98660
Phone: 503-201-0858
Email: dcj@pandhbilling.com
http://www.orcascholarshipfund.com
Purpose: To provide financial assistance to Oregon students who are attending a college or university in Oregon.
Eligibility: Applicants must be high school seniors in the state of Oregon who are not children or grandchildren of owners or officers of Oregon collection agencies. Students must write an essay on a specific topic, and if selected as finalists must attend the Oregon Collectors Association Spring Convention and read their essays.
Target applicants: High school students.
Amount: $1,500-$3,000.
Number of awards: 3.
Deadline: March 1.
How to apply: Students must send an essay via mail or email to apply.
Exclusive: Visit www.UltimateScholarshipBook.com and enter code OR185312 for updates on this award.

(1854) · Oregon Association of Student Councils Scholarships

Confederation of Oregon School Administrators
707 13th Street SE
Suite 100
Salem, OR 97301
Phone: 503-581-3141
Fax: 503-581-9840
Email: sera@cosa.k12.or.us
http://www.cosa.k12.or.us
Purpose: To provide financial assistance to Oregon students who plan to attend Oregon colleges or universities.
Eligibility: Applicants must be graduating seniors at an Oregon public high school who plan to attend a public or private institution of higher learning in the state. They must have a 3.5 or higher GPA, be active in school and community activities and be endorsed by a COSA member.
Target applicants: High school students.
Minimum GPA: 3.5

Amount: $1,000.
Number of awards: 2.
Deadline: February 25.
How to apply: Applications are available online.
Exclusive: Visit www.UltimateScholarshipBook.com and enter code CO185412 for updates on this award.

(1855) • Oregon Farm Bureau Memorial Scholarships

Oregon Farm Bureau
3415 Commercial Street SE
Salem, OR 97302
Phone: 800-334-6323
Fax: 503-399-8082
Email: andrea@oregonfb.org
http://www.oregonfb.org
Purpose: To aid Oregon high school graduates who are preparing for careers in agriculture or forestry.
Eligibility: Applicants must be enrolled in or planning to enroll in a degree program that is related to agriculture or forestry. Selection is based on the overall strength of the application.
Target applicants: High school students. College students. Adult students.
Amount: Varies.
Number of awards: 10-12.
Deadline: March 1.
How to apply: Applications are available online. An application form, transcript and three letters of recommendation are required.
Exclusive: Visit www.UltimateScholarshipBook.com and enter code OR185512 for updates on this award.

(1856) • Oregon National Guard State Tuition Program

Oregon Student Assistance Commission
1500 Valley River Drive
Suite 100
Eugene, OR 97401
Phone: 541-687-7400
Fax: 541-687-7414
Email: awardinfo@osac.state.or.us
http://www.osac.state.or.us
Purpose: To support students from Oregon who are in the National Guard.
Eligibility: Students must be new recruits or reenlistments in the National Guard. They must have been residents of Oregon for at least 12 months prior to college enrollment.
Target applicants: High school students. College students. Graduate school students. Adult students.
Amount: Varies.
Number of awards: Varies.
Scholarship may be renewable.
Deadline: Varies.
How to apply: Applications are available online.
Exclusive: Visit www.UltimateScholarshipBook.com and enter code OR185612 for updates on this award.

(1857) • Oregon Opportunity Grant

Oregon Student Assistance Commission
1500 Valley River Drive
Suite 100
Eugene, OR 97401
Phone: 541-687-7400
Fax: 541-687-7414
Email: awardinfo@osac.state.or.us
http://www.osac.state.or.us
Purpose: To provide financial assistance to Oregon residents in need.
Eligibility: Applicants must have financial need and be enrolled at least half-time in an undergraduate program at a participating Oregon college or university. They must be Oregon residents and U.S. citizens or eligible noncitizens, and they must be eligible for a Federal Pell Grant.
Target applicants: College students. Graduate school students. Adult students.
Amount: Varies.
Number of awards: Varies.
Deadline: January 21, January 29, February 24.
How to apply: Qualified students who submit a Free Application for Federal Student Aid (FAFSA) will be considered.
Exclusive: Visit www.UltimateScholarshipBook.com and enter code OR185712 for updates on this award.

(1858) • Oregon Scholarship Fund Community College Student Award

Oregon Student Assistance Commission
1500 Valley River Drive
Suite 100
Eugene, OR 97401
Phone: 541-687-7400
Fax: 541-687-7414
Email: awardinfo@osac.state.or.us
http://www.osac.state.or.us
Purpose: To assist Oregon community college students.
Eligibility: Applicants must be U.S. citizens or legal residents, enrolled at or planning to enroll at a community college in Oregon and enrolled at least part-time. They must owe no educational grant refunds and must have no defaulted student loans. Selection is based on financial need.
Target applicants: High school students. College students. Adult students.
Amount: Varies.
Number of awards: Varies.
Scholarship may be renewable.
Deadline: March 1.
How to apply: Applications are available online. An application form and completed FAFSA are required.
Exclusive: Visit www.UltimateScholarshipBook.com and enter code OR185812 for updates on this award.

(1859) • Osher Scholarship

Maine Community College System
323 State Street
Augusta, ME 04330-7131
Phone: 207-629-4000
Fax: 207-629-4048
Email: info@mccs.me.edu
http://www.mccs.me.edu
Purpose: To aid liberal arts students at Maine community colleges.
Eligibility: Students must be Maine residents who are not currently enrolled in any college or university program and who have completed no more than 24 college credits. They must also qualify for and be accepted into the associate of arts degree program in liberal/general studies at a Maine community college.
Target applicants: High school students. College students. Adult students.
Amount: $504.

Number of awards: Varies.
Deadline: Varies.
How to apply: Applications are available from community colleges.
Exclusive: Visit www.UltimateScholarshipBook.com and enter code MA185912 for updates on this award.

(1860) • Outrigger Duke Kahanamoku Scholarship

Outrigger Duke Kahanamoku Foundation
Scholarship Committee
PMB 202
350 Ward Avenue, Suite106
Honolulu, HI 96814
Phone: 808-545-4880
Fax: 888-624-0181
Email: info@dukefoundation.org
http://www.dukefoundation.org
Purpose: To support Hawaii students who are involved in water sports.
Eligibility: Applicants must be Hawaii residents and demonstrate financial need and athletic involvement. Preference is given to the water sports.
Target applicants: High school students. College students. Adult students.
Amount: Varies.
Number of awards: Varies.
Deadline: April 1.
How to apply: Applications are available online.
Exclusive: Visit www.UltimateScholarshipBook.com and enter code OU186012 for updates on this award.

(1861) • Pacers TeamUp Scholarship

Pacers Foundation
125 S. Pennsylvania Street
Indianapolis, IN 46204
Phone: 317-917-2864
Fax: 317-917-2599
Email: foundation@pacers.com
http://www.nba.com/pacers/news/Foundation_Index.html
Purpose: The Pacers TeamUp Scholarship rewards students for community service.
Eligibility: Applicants must be Indiana residents in their senior year of high school planning to attend an accredited four-year college or two-year community or junior college.
Target applicants: High school students.
Amount: $2,000.
Number of awards: 5.
Deadline: March 1.
How to apply: Application information is available by email at foundation@pacers.com, by phone at 317-917-2864 or online.
Exclusive: Visit www.UltimateScholarshipBook.com and enter code PA186112 for updates on this award.

(1862) • Pacific National Bank Scholarship

Pacific National Bank
345 California Street, 7th Floor
San Francisco, CA 94104
Phone: 415-774-2203
Email: calmojuela@pacificnational.com
http://www.pacificnational.com
Purpose: To assist students from low to moderate income families in the Bay Area.
Eligibility: Applicants must attend a college or university on a full-time basis, have a minimum 3.0 GPA and reside in San Francisco, Marin, San Mateo, Alameda, Contra Costa, San Benito, Santa Clara or Napa county.
Target applicants: High school students. College students. Adult students.
Minimum GPA: 3.0
Amount: $500-$1,500.
Number of awards: Varies.
Deadline: April 30.
How to apply: Applications are available online.
Exclusive: Visit www.UltimateScholarshipBook.com and enter code PA186212 for updates on this award.

(1863) • Palmetto Fellows Scholarship Program

South Carolina Commission on Higher Education
1333 Main Street
Suite 200
Columbia, SC 29201
Phone: 803-737-2260
Fax: 803-737-2297
Email: shubbard@che.sc.gov
http://www.che400.state.sc.us
Purpose: Monetary assistance is awarded to academically talented South Carolina high school seniors in an effort to encourage them to go to South Carolina colleges.
Eligibility: Applicants must have a minimum SAT score of 1200 or ACT score of 27, have a minimum 3.5 GPA, rank in the top 5 percent of their class, be residents of South Carolina, be enrolled in a public or private high school, be U.S. citizens or permanent residents and plan to attend a college in South Carolina.
Target applicants: High school students.
Minimum GPA: 3.5
Amount: $6,700-$7,500.
Number of awards: Varies.
Scholarship may be renewable.
Deadline: Varies.
How to apply: Applications are available through your high school guidance office.
Exclusive: Visit www.UltimateScholarshipBook.com and enter code SO186312 for updates on this award.

(1864) • Paraprofessional Teacher Preparation Grant

Massachusetts Department of Higher Education
Office of Student Financial Assistance
454 Broadway
Suite 200
Revere, MA 02151
Phone: 617-727-9420
Fax: 617-727-0667
Email: osfa@osfa.mass.edu
http://www.osfa.mass.edu/default.asp
Purpose: To assist Massachusetts public school paraprofessionals who wish to become certified as full-time teachers.
Eligibility: Applicants must be employed for at least two years as a paraprofessional in a Massachusetts public school and enroll in an undergraduate program leading to teacher certification, or be employed as a paraprofessional for less than two years and enroll in an undergraduate course of study leading to teacher certification in a high need discipline. Applicants must not have previously earned a bachelor's degree.
Target applicants: College students. Adult students.

Amount: Up to $7,500.
Number of awards: Varies.
Scholarship may be renewable.
Deadline: Varies.
How to apply: Applications are available online.
Exclusive: Visit www.UltimateScholarshipBook.com and enter code MA186412 for updates on this award.

(1865) • Part-Time Grant

Maryland Higher Education Commission
Office of Student Financial Assistance
839 Bestgate Road, Suite 400
Annapolis, MD 21401
Phone: 800-974-1024
Fax: 410-260-3200
Email: osfamail@mhec.state.md.us
http://www.mhec.state.md.us
Purpose: To assist part-time, degree-seeking undergraduates.
Eligibility: All applicants and their parents (if applicants are dependents of their parents) must be Maryland residents. Part-time applicants must complete the Free Application for Federal Student Aid (FAFSA) and contact the financial aid office of the college attending and request to be considered for the Part-Time Grant. Selection is based on financial need.
Target applicants: College students. Adult students.
Amount: $200-$2,000.
Number of awards: Varies.
Scholarship may be renewable.
Deadline: Varies.
How to apply: Applications are available by request from the applicant's financial aid office. An application form and a completed FAFSA are required.
Exclusive: Visit www.UltimateScholarshipBook.com and enter code MA186512 for updates on this award.

(1866) • Part-Time Grant Program

State Student Assistance Commission of Indiana
150 W. Market Street
Suite 500
Indianapolis, IN 46204
Phone: 888-528-4719
Fax: 317-232-3260
Email: grants@ssaci.state.in.us
http://www.in.gov/ssaci
Purpose: To help part-time Indiana students pursue higher education.
Eligibility: Applicants must be undergraduates taking at least 6 but not more than 12 credit hours per term at eligible institutions. This is a need-based award.
Target applicants: College students. Adult students.
Amount: Varies.
Number of awards: Varies.
Scholarship may be renewable.
Deadline: Varies.
How to apply: Complete the Free Application for Federal Student Aid (FAFSA).
Exclusive: Visit www.UltimateScholarshipBook.com and enter code ST186612 for updates on this award.

(1867) • Part-Time Grants

Vermont Student Assistance Corporation
10 East Allen Street
P.O. Box 2000
Winooski, VT 05404
Phone: 800-882-4166
Fax: 802-654-3765
Email: info@vsac.org
http://www.vsac.org
Purpose: To assist Vermont part-time undergraduate students.
Eligibility: Applicants must be Vermont residents enrolled in or planning to enroll in an undergraduate degree or certificate program part-time (for less than 12 credits per semester). Those who have earned a bachelor's degree previously are ineligible. Selection is based on financial need.
Target applicants: High school students. College students. Adult students.
Amount: Varies.
Number of awards: Varies.
Deadline: Varies.
How to apply: Applications are available online. An application form, a completed FAFSA and supporting documents are required.
Exclusive: Visit www.UltimateScholarshipBook.com and enter code VE186712 for updates on this award.

(1868) • Part-Time Student Instructional Grant

Ohio Board of Regents
State Grants and Scholarships Department
P.O. Box 182452
Columbus, OH 43218-2452
Phone: 888-833-1133
Fax: 614-752-5903
http://www.regents.ohio.gov
Purpose: To assist part-time Ohio undergraduate students.
Eligibility: Applicants must be Ohio residents who attend an eligible Ohio public or private university part-time and who have financial need.
Target applicants: College students. Adult students.
Amount: Varies.
Number of awards: Varies.
Deadline: Varies.
How to apply: Contact your financial aid office.
Exclusive: Visit www.UltimateScholarshipBook.com and enter code OH186812 for updates on this award.

(1869) • Part-Time TAP Program

New York State Higher Education Services Corporation (HESC)
99 Washington Avenue
Albany, NY 12255
Phone: 888-697-4372
Email: hescwebmail@hesc.org
http://www.hesc.com/content.nsf/
Purpose: To support undergraduate students in the state of New York.
Eligibility: Applicants may attend the State University of New York, the City University of New York or any other public New York school. Students must be enrolled in 6-12 credits per semester, and they must have at least a 2.0 GPA. Applicants must have earned 12 credits per semester in at least two consecutive prior semesters. Students must demonstrate financial need through the FAFSA.
Target applicants: College students. Adult students.
Minimum GPA: 2.0

Amount: Varies.
Number of awards: Varies.
Scholarship may be renewable.
Deadline: Varies.
How to apply: Applications are available online.
Exclusive: Visit www.UltimateScholarshipBook.com and enter code NE186912 for updates on this award.

(1870) • Part-Time Tuition Aid Grant

New Jersey Higher Education Student Assistance Authority
P.O. Box 540
Trenton, NJ 08625
Phone: 800-792-8670
Email: clientservices@hesaa.org
http://www.hesaa.org
Purpose: To support part-time students who are attending county colleges in New Jersey.
Eligibility: Applicants must be residents of New Jersey for at least 12 months prior to college enrollment. They cannot have any previous degrees or defaulted student loans. Students must be enrolled in 6-11 credits per semester at an approved New Jersey county college, and they cannot be majoring in theology or divinity.
Target applicants: High school students. College students. Adult students.
Amount: Up to full tuition.
Number of awards: Varies.
Scholarship may be renewable.
Deadline: Varies.
How to apply: Applications are available through completion of the FAFSA.
Exclusive: Visit www.UltimateScholarshipBook.com and enter code NE187012 for updates on this award.

(1871) • Passport for Foster Youth Promise Program

Washington Higher Education Coordinating Board
917 Lakeridge Way
P.O. Box 43430
Olympia, WA 98504
Phone: 360-753-7850
Fax: 360-753-6243
Email: info@hecb.wa.gov
http://www.hecb.wa.gov
Purpose: To encourage students who have been in foster care to get ready for college.
Eligibility: Applicants must have spent one year or more in foster care since their 16th birthdays, be Washington residents who will enroll at least half-time in an eligible college by their 22nd birthdays, not have earned a bachelor's degree and not be seeking a degree in theology.
Target applicants: High school students. College students.
Amount: Varies.
Number of awards: Varies.
Scholarship may be renewable.
Deadline: Varies.
How to apply: Applications are available online.
Exclusive: Visit www.UltimateScholarshipBook.com and enter code WA187112 for updates on this award.

(1872) • Past Department Presidents' Junior Scholarship Award

American Legion Auxiliary, Department of California
401 Van Ness Avenue
Room 113
San Francisco, CA 94102
Phone: 415-861-5092
Fax: 415-861-8365
Email: calegionaux@calegionaux.org
http://www.calegionaux.org
Purpose: To reward American Legion Auxiliary Juniors.
Eligibility: Applicants must be California resident high school students planning to attend a California college or university, be American Legion Auxiliary members with three years as a Junior and be the children, grandchildren or great grandchildren of a veteran.
Target applicants: High school students.
Amount: Varies.
Number of awards: 1.
Deadline: Varies.
How to apply: Applications are available online.
Exclusive: Visit www.UltimateScholarshipBook.com and enter code AM187212 for updates on this award.

(1873) • Past Presidents' Parley Nursing Scholarships

American Legion Auxiliary, Department of California
401 Van Ness Avenue
Room 113
San Francisco, CA 94102
Phone: 415-861-5092
Fax: 415-861-8365
Email: calegionaux@calegionaux.org
http://www.calegionaux.org
Purpose: To provide support to the U.S. Armed Forces members and their spouses and children.
Eligibility: Applicants must be residents of California, enrolled or planning to enroll in a nursing program and be the wife, husband, widow, widower or child of a veteran or be veterans themselves.
Target applicants: High school students. College students. Graduate school students. Adult students.
Amount: $500-$1,000.
Number of awards: Varies.
Deadline: April 5.
How to apply: Applications are available online.
Exclusive: Visit www.UltimateScholarshipBook.com and enter code AM187312 for updates on this award.

(1874) • Patty and Melvin Alperin First Generation Scholarship

Rhode Island Foundation
One Union Station
Providence, RI 02903
Phone: 401-274-4564
Fax: 401-331-8085
Email: libbym@rifoundation.org
http://www.rifoundation.org
Purpose: To provide opportunities for students whose parents did not graduate from college.
Eligibility: Applicants must be Rhode Island high school seniors and first-generation college students. They must be enrolled in an accredited

institution of higher learning that offers either two-year or four-year degrees.
Target applicants: High school students.
Amount: $1,000.
Number of awards: 2-3.
Scholarship may be renewable.
Deadline: May 8.
How to apply: Applications are available online.
Exclusive: Visit www.UltimateScholarshipBook.com and enter code RH187412 for updates on this award.

(1875) • Paul and Betty Honzik Scholarship

Hawaii Community Foundation - Scholarships
1164 Bishop Street, Suite 800
Honolulu, HI 96813
Phone: 888-731-3863
Fax: 808-521-6286
Email: scholarships@hcf-hawaii.org
http://www.hawaiicommunityfoundation.org
Purpose: To support Presbyterian students in Hawaii.
Eligibility: Students must attend a four-year college or university. Applicants must have at least a 3.0 GPA. A letter of reference from a church or pastor is required.
Target applicants: High school students. College students. Adult students.
Minimum GPA: 3.0
Amount: Varies.
Number of awards: Varies.
Deadline: March 1.
How to apply: To apply, register online, complete the online application and select the scholarships to which you wish to apply. In addition, mail the supporting materials: printed confirmation page from the online application, personal statement, letter of reference from church or pastor, copy of Student Aid Report (SAR) available at www.fafsa.ed.gov and official transcript.
Exclusive: Visit www.UltimateScholarshipBook.com and enter code HA187512 for updates on this award.

(1876) • Paul Flaherty Athletic Scholarship

American Legion, Department of Kansas
1314 SW Topeka Boulevard
Topeka, KS 66612
Phone: 785-232-9315
Fax: 785-232-1399
http://www.ksamlegion.org
Purpose: To support student athletes.
Eligibility: Applicants must be high school seniors or college freshmen or sophomores and have participated in high school athletics. Students must be average or better students and submit three letters of recommendation, one of which must be from a coach, a high school transcript, a 1040 income statement and an essay on the topic, "Why I Want to Go to College."
Target applicants: High school students. College students. Adult students.
Amount: $250.
Number of awards: 1.
Deadline: July 15.
How to apply: Applications are available online.
Exclusive: Visit www.UltimateScholarshipBook.com and enter code AM187612 for updates on this award.

(1877) • Paulina L. Sorg Scholarship

Hawaii Community Foundation - Scholarships
1164 Bishop Street, Suite 800
Honolulu, HI 96813
Phone: 888-731-3863
Fax: 808-521-6286
Email: scholarships@hcf-hawaii.org
http://www.hawaiicommunityfoundation.org
Purpose: To support nursing or physical therapy students in Hawaii.
Eligibility: Applicants must be college juniors, college seniors or graduate students.
Target applicants: College students. Graduate school students. Adult students.
Amount: Varies.
Number of awards: Varies.
Deadline: March 1.
How to apply: To apply, register online, complete the online application and select the scholarships to which you wish to apply. In addition, mail the supporting materials: printed confirmation page from the online application, personal statement, copy of Student Aid Report (SAR) available at www.fafsa.ed.gov and official transcript.
Exclusive: Visit www.UltimateScholarshipBook.com and enter code HA187712 for updates on this award.

(1878) • Pauline Thompson Nursing Education Scholarship

Nursing Foundation of Pennsylvania
2578 Interstate Drive
Suite 101
Harrisburg, PA 17110
Phone: 717-827-4369
Fax: 717-657-3796
Email: nfp@panurses.org
http://www.panurses.org
Purpose: To support Pennsylvania nursing students.
Eligibility: Applicants must be members of the Student Nurses Association of Pennsylvania (SNAP) or the National Student Nurses Association (NSNA). They must be enrolled in an associate's or bachelor's degree program in nursing at a postsecondary institution located in Pennsylvania. They must have completed at least one year of undergraduate study at the time of application. Students must have a GPA of 3.0 or higher on a four-point scale, must have leadership experience and must be involved in community service. Selection is based on academic merit, leadership and service to the community.
Target applicants: College students. Adult students.
Minimum GPA: 3.0
Amount: $1,000.
Number of awards: 1.
Deadline: May 28.
How to apply: Applications are available online. An application form, personal statement, official transcript, three reference letters and proof of SNAP or NSNA membership are required.
Exclusive: Visit www.UltimateScholarshipBook.com and enter code NU187812 for updates on this award.

(1879) • Pennsylvania Educational Gratuity for Veterans' Dependents

Bureau for Veterans Affairs
Building S-0-47
Fort Indiantown Gap
Annville, PA 17003

Phone: 717-861-8719
Fax: 717-861-9457
Email: bfoster@state.pa.us
http://www.milvet.state.pa.us/DMVA/201.htm
Purpose: To provide financial assistance to children of veterans.
Eligibility: Applicants must be dependents of honorably discharged veterans who served during wartime or armed conflict and have service-connected disabilities or who died in service during war or armed conflict. They must be 16 to 23 years of age and have lived in and attended school in Pennsylvania for five years prior to application, and they must demonstrate financial need.
Target applicants: High school students. College students.
Amount: Up to $1,000.
Number of awards: Varies.
Scholarship may be renewable.
Deadline: Varies.
How to apply: Applications are available from your local Department of Military and Veterans Affairs.
Exclusive: Visit www.UltimateScholarshipBook.com and enter code BU187912 for updates on this award.

(1880) · Pennsylvania Engineering Foundation Grant

Pennsylvania Society of Professional Engineers
908 North Second Street
Harrisburg, PA 17102
Phone: 717-441-6051
Fax: 717-236-2046
Email: jennifer@wannerassoc.com
http://www.pspe.org/scholarships.shtml
Purpose: To aid Pennsylvania students who are planning to major in engineering.
Eligibility: Applicants must be Pennsylvania residents and must be rising undergraduate freshmen who plan to attend a Pennsylvania college or university that has an ABET-accredited engineering degree program. They must have a GPA of 3.6 or higher, an SAT Verbal score (or ACT equivalent) of 600 or higher and an SAT Math score (or ACT equivalent) of 700 or higher. Selection is based on the overall strength of the application.
Target applicants: High school students.
Minimum GPA: 3.6
Amount: $2,000.
Number of awards: 2.
Deadline: April 15.
How to apply: Applications are available online. An application form, official transcript, personal essay and standardized test scores are required.
Exclusive: Visit www.UltimateScholarshipBook.com and enter code PE188012 for updates on this award.

(1881) · Pennsylvania Engineering Foundation Upperclassman Grant

Pennsylvania Society of Professional Engineers
908 North Second Street
Harrisburg, PA 17102
Phone: 717-441-6051
Fax: 717-236-2046
Email: jennifer@wannerassoc.com
http://www.pspe.org/scholarships.shtml
Purpose: To aid Pennsylvania engineering students.
Eligibility: Applicants must be sophomores, juniors or seniors enrolled in an ABET-accredited engineering degree program at a college or university located in Pennsylvania. Selection is based on the overall strength of the application.
Target applicants: College students. Adult students.
Amount: $2,000.
Number of awards: Varies.
Scholarship may be renewable.
Deadline: April 15.
How to apply: Applications are available online. An application form, personal essay and one letter of recommendation are required.
Exclusive: Visit www.UltimateScholarshipBook.com and enter code PE188112 for updates on this award.

(1882) · Pennsylvania Knights Templar Educational Foundation Scholarships

Pennsylvania Masonic Youth Foundation
1244 Bainbridge Road
Elizabethtown, PA 17022-9423
Phone: 717-367-1536
Fax: 717-367-0616
Email: pmyf@pagrandlodge.com
http://www.pagrandlodge.org
Purpose: To assist students in pursuing higher education.
Eligibility: Applicants must be working toward a two- or four-year college degree, graduate degree or trade school education. This award is open to students regardless of financial circumstances, Masonic ties, age, race or religion.
Target applicants: High school students. College students. Graduate school students. Adult students.
Amount: Varies.
Number of awards: Varies.
Deadline: Varies.
How to apply: Applications are available by mail.
Exclusive: Visit www.UltimateScholarshipBook.com and enter code PE188212 for updates on this award.

(1883) · Pennsylvania Land Surveyors' Foundation Scholarships

Pennsylvania Society of Land Surveyors
2040 Linglestown Road
Suite 200
Harrisburg, PA 17110
Phone: 717-540-6811
Fax: 717-540-6815
Email: ksherman@psls.org
http://www.psls.org
Purpose: To aid Pennsylvania students who are planning for careers as land surveyors.
Eligibility: Applicants must be U.S. citizens and residents of Pennsylvania. They must be accepted into or enrolled in a two- or four-year degree program in land surveying. Selection is based on academic merit, statement of purpose, extracurricular activities and recommendations.
Target applicants: High school students. College students. Adult students.
Amount: Varies.
Number of awards: Varies.
Deadline: March 1.
How to apply: Applications are available online. An application form, transcript, standardized test scores (high school applicants only) and a guidance counselor evaluation form are required.

Exclusive: Visit www.UltimateScholarshipBook.com and enter code PE188312 for updates on this award.

(1884) • Pennsylvania Oratorical Contest

American Legion, Department of Pennsylvania
P.O. Box 2324
Harrisburg, PA 17105
Phone: 717-730-9100
Fax: 717-975-2836
Email: hq@pa-legion.com
http://www.pa-legion.com

Purpose: To enhance high school students' experience with and understanding of the U.S. Constitution. The contest will help develop students' leadership skills and civic appreciation, as well as the ability to deliver thoughtful, insightful orations regarding U.S. citizenship and its inherent responsibilities.
Eligibility: Applicants must be high school students under the age of 20 who are U.S. citizens or legal residents and residents of the state. Students first give an oration within their state and winners compete at the national level. The oration must be related to the Constitution of the United States focusing on the duties and obligations citizens have to the government. It must be in English and be between eight and ten minutes. There is also an assigned topic which is posted on the website, and it should be between three and five minutes.
Target applicants: High school students.
Amount: $4,000-$7,500.
Number of awards: 3.
Deadline: January 15.
How to apply: Applications are available from school coordinators and online.
Exclusive: Visit www.UltimateScholarshipBook.com and enter code AM188412 for updates on this award.

(1885) • Pennsylvania State Grant Program

Pennsylvania Higher Education Assistance Agency (PHEAA)
Pennsylvania State Grant Program
P.O. Box 8157
Harrisburg, PA 17105
Phone: 800-692-7392
http://www.pheaa.org

Purpose: To assist Pennsylvania undergraduates who demonstrate financial need.
Eligibility: Applicants must be current Pennsylvania residents who have lived in the state for at least 12 consecutive months. They must be graduates of an approved high school or GED recipients and be enrolled in or plan to enroll in a two-year or longer degree program at an approved college or university. They must be enrolled for at least six credit hours per academic term and must meet financial need criteria. Applicants who have earned a bachelor's degree previously or who have a defaulted student loan are ineligible. Selection is based on financial need.
Target applicants: High school students. College students. Adult students.
Amount: Varies.
Number of awards: Varies.
Deadline: Varies.
How to apply: Applications are available online. An application form, a completed FAFSA and supporting documents are required.
Exclusive: Visit www.UltimateScholarshipBook.com and enter code PE188512 for updates on this award.

(1886) • Philip P. Barker Memorial Scholarship

Los Alamos National Laboratory Foundation
1302 Calle de la Merced
Suite A
Espanola, NM 87532
Phone: 505-753-8890
Fax: 505-753-8915
Email: info@lanlfoundation.org
http://www.lanlfoundation.org

Purpose: To support undergraduate students from Northern New Mexico.
Eligibility: Students must have at least a 3.25 GPA, and they must have either an SAT score of at least 1350 or an ACT score of at least 19. Applicants must submit an essay and two letters of recommendation.
Target applicants: High school students. College students. Adult students.
Minimum GPA: 3.25
Amount: $1,000.
Number of awards: Varies.
Deadline: January 18.
How to apply: Applications are available online.
Exclusive: Visit www.UltimateScholarshipBook.com and enter code LO188612 for updates on this award.

(1887) • Phillips/Laird Scholarship

Minnesota Nurses Association
345 Randolph Avenue
Suite 200
Saint Paul, MN 55102
Phone: 651-414-2800
Fax: 651-695-7000
Email: linda.owens@mnnurses.org
http://www.mnnurses.org

Purpose: To support Minnesota Nurses Association members who are nursing students.
Eligibility: Applicants must be members of the Minnesota Nurses Association (MNA) who are enrolled in a bachelor's or graduate degree program in nursing. Preference will be given to applicants who live or work in MNA District 13. Selection is based on academic merit, extracurricular activities, stated career goals and leadership.
Target applicants: College students. Graduate school students. Adult students.
Amount: $2,000.
Number of awards: Varies.
Scholarship may be renewable.
Deadline: June 1.
How to apply: Applications are available by request from the MNA. An application form and supporting materials are required.
Exclusive: Visit www.UltimateScholarshipBook.com and enter code MI188712 for updates on this award.

(1888) • Physician Assistant Academy of Vermont Student Scholarship Award

Physician Assistant Academy of Vermont
45 Lyme Road
Suite 304
Hanover, NH 03755
Phone: 603-643-2325
Fax: 603-643-1444
Email: paav@conmx.net

http://www.paav.org
Purpose: To aid current and recent Vermont physician assistant students.
Eligibility: Applicants must be Vermont residents and must be currently enrolled in a physician assistant program in Vermont or must be recent graduates of such a program who have outstanding student loans and are working or intending to work in Vermont. Previous winners of this scholarship are ineligible. Selection is based on the overall strength of the application.
Target applicants: College students. Graduate school students. Adult students.
Amount: $1,000.
Number of awards: 1.
Deadline: June 30.
How to apply: Applications are available online. An application form, personal statement, school enrollment verification (if applicable) and employment verification (if applicable) are required.
Exclusive: Visit www.UltimateScholarshipBook.com and enter code PH188812 for updates on this award.

(1889) • Pinnacol Foundation Scholarship Program

Pinnacol Foundation
7501 E. Lowry Boulevard
Denver, CO 80230
Phone: 303-361-4775
Email: starkey@pinnacol.com
http://www.pinnacol.com/foundation
Purpose: To provide assistance for students whose parent was killed or injured in a work-related accident.
Eligibility: Applicants must be dependents of workers killed or permanently injured in compensable work-related accidents during employment with Colorado-based employers. They must be between the ages of 16 and 25 and have a diploma or GED or be high school seniors in good standing. Letter of recommendation, essay, transcripts and documentation of the parent's injury or death are required.
Target applicants: High school students. College students.
Amount: Varies.
Number of awards: Varies.
Deadline: March 31.
How to apply: Applications are available online.
Exclusive: Visit www.UltimateScholarshipBook.com and enter code PI188912 for updates on this award.

(1890) • Pizza Hut Scholarship Fund

Hawaii Community Foundation - Scholarships
1164 Bishop Street, Suite 800
Honolulu, HI 96813
Phone: 888-731-3863
Fax: 808-521-6286
Email: scholarships@hcf-hawaii.org
http://www.hawaiicommunityfoundation.org
Purpose: To support students in Hawaii with financial need.
Eligibility: Applicants must attend a two- or four-year college or university and have a GPA between 2.5 and 3.5.
Target applicants: High school students. College students. Adult students.
Minimum GPA: 2.5
Amount: Varies.
Number of awards: Varies.
Deadline: March 1.
How to apply: To apply, register online, complete the online application and select the scholarships to which you wish to apply. In addition, mail the supporting materials: printed confirmation page from the online application, personal statement, copy of Student Aid Report (SAR) available at www.fafsa.ed.gov and official transcript.
Exclusive: Visit www.UltimateScholarshipBook.com and enter code HA189012 for updates on this award.

(1891) • Portuguese Foundation Scholarships

Portuguese Foundation of Connecticut
P.O. Box 331441
West Hartford, CT 06133-1441
Phone: 860-236-5514
http://www.pfict.org/scholar.html
Purpose: To provide financial assistance to Portuguese students.
Eligibility: Applicants must be of Portuguese ancestry and demonstrate financial need. They must be U.S. citizens or permanent residents and residents of Connecticut. They must be applying to or already attending college as a full-time undergraduate student or part-time graduate student. Applicants may not have previously received more than four scholarships from the Portuguese Foundation. Applicants must have taken the SAT.
Target applicants: High school students. College students. Graduate school students. Adult students.
Amount: $1,000.
Number of awards: 4.
Deadline: March 15.
How to apply: Applications are available online.
Exclusive: Visit www.UltimateScholarshipBook.com and enter code PO189112 for updates on this award.

(1892) • Professional Engineers in Private Practice Grant

Pennsylvania Society of Professional Engineers
908 North Second Street
Harrisburg, PA 17102
Phone: 717-441-6051
Fax: 717-236-2046
Email: jennifer@wannerassoc.com
http://www.pspe.org/scholarships.shtml
Purpose: To aid Pennsylvania students who are planning to major in engineering.
Eligibility: Applicants must be Pennsylvania residents who are incoming undergraduate freshmen at a Pennsylvania college or university that has an ABET-accredited engineering program. They must have plans to study engineering, have a GPA of 3.6 or higher and have an SAT Math score of 700 or higher and an SAT Verbal score of 600 or higher. Selection is based on the overall strength of the application.
Target applicants: High school students.
Minimum GPA: 3.6
Amount: $1,000.
Number of awards: 2.
Deadline: April 15.
How to apply: Applications are available online. An application form, official transcript and standardized test scores are required.
Exclusive: Visit www.UltimateScholarshipBook.com and enter code PE189212 for updates on this award.

(1893) • Professional Scholarships

California Mathematics Council - Southern Section
Dr. Sik Kolpas, CMC-S Scholarships
Glendale Community College Math Department

1500 N. Verdugo Road
Glendale, CA 91208-2894
Phone: 888-CMC-MATH
Email: skolpas@glendale.edu
http://www.cmc-math.org

Purpose: To support math teachers pursuing coursework and degree accreditation programs.

Eligibility: Applicants must be current teachers of mathematics and active CMC-S members. They must submit a course of study that includes educational goals and specifies the college, classes and estimated cost. Applicants must also submit verification from an administrator that at least 60 percent of their teaching schedules are in mathematics.

Target applicants: Graduate school students. Adult students.

Amount: Varies.

Number of awards: Varies.

Deadline: January 31.

How to apply: Applications are available online. An application form, proposal, confirmation of teaching program and two letters of recommendation are required.

Exclusive: Visit www.UltimateScholarshipBook.com and enter code CA189312 for updates on this award.

(1894) • Progress Energy Power Careers Program

North Carolina Community College System
200 West Jones Street
Raleigh, NC 27603
Phone: 919-807-7100
Fax: 919-807-7164
Email: kuryp@nccommunitycolleges.edu
http://www.ncccs.cc.nc.us

Purpose: To aid community college students who are preparing for careers in the power utility industry.

Eligibility: Applicants must be at least 18 years old, be high school graduates and hold a valid driver's license. They must be attending or planning to attend a North Carolina community or technical college and must be enrolled in or planning to enroll in an associate's degree program in electric power production technology, electrical-electronics technology or industrial systems technology. They must have a proven interest in pursuing a career in power plant operations. Preference will be given to applicants having a GPA of 3.2 or higher. Selection is based on the overall strength of the application.

Target applicants: College students. Adult students.

Amount: Varies.

Number of awards: Varies.

Scholarship may be renewable.

Deadline: Varies.

How to apply: Applications are available by request from Progress Energy. An application form and supporting materials are required.

Exclusive: Visit www.UltimateScholarshipBook.com and enter code NO189412 for updates on this award.

(1895) • PRSA-Hawaii/Roy Leffingwell Public Relations Scholarship

Hawaii Community Foundation - Scholarships
1164 Bishop Street, Suite 800
Honolulu, HI 96813
Phone: 888-731-3863
Fax: 808-521-6286
Email: scholarships@hcf-hawaii.org
http://www.hawaiicommunityfoundation.org

Purpose: To support Hawaii students who are pursuing careers in public relations.

Eligibility: Applicants must be college juniors, college seniors or graduate students. They must be majoring in public relations, journalism or communications.

Target applicants: College students. Graduate school students. Adult students.

Amount: Varies.

Number of awards: Varies.

Deadline: March 1.

How to apply: To apply, register online, complete the online application and select the scholarships to which you wish to apply. In addition, mail the supporting materials: printed confirmation page from the online application, personal statement, copy of Student Aid Report (SAR) available at www.fafsa.ed.gov and official transcript.

Exclusive: Visit www.UltimateScholarshipBook.com and enter code HA189512 for updates on this award.

(1896) • R. Flake Shaw Scholarship

North Carolina Farm Bureau
P.O. Box 27766
Raleigh, NC 27611
Phone: 919-782-1705
Fax: 919-783-3593
http://www.ncfb.org

Purpose: To aid North Carolina students who are preparing for careers in agriculture.

Eligibility: Applicants must be North Carolina students who are pursuing an associate's or bachelor's degree in an agriculture-related subject. They must be planning to pursue a career in agriculture and demonstrate leadership ability and financial need. Preference will be given to applicants who are the family members of Farm Bureau members. Selection is based on academic merit, character, stated career goals and financial need.

Target applicants: College students. Adult students.

Amount: Up to $12,000.

Number of awards: 8.

Scholarship may be renewable.

Deadline: March 15.

How to apply: Applications are available online. An application form, transcript, personal statement and financial information are required.

Exclusive: Visit www.UltimateScholarshipBook.com and enter code NO189612 for updates on this award.

(1897) • R. Preston Woodruff, Jr. Scholarships

Arkansas Student Loan Authority
3801 Woodland Heights, Suite 200
Little Rock, AR 72212
Phone: 800-443-6030
Email: info@asla.info
http://www.asla.info

Purpose: To support students who live in Arkansas or are planning to attend school there.

Eligibility: Students must be enrolled or planning to enroll in an undergraduate program with at least a half-time schedule. Applicants must be a high school senior or current college student.

Target applicants: High school students. College students. Adult students.

Amount: $1,000.

Number of awards: Varies.

Scholarship may be renewable.

Deadline: April 1.
How to apply: Applications are available online.
Exclusive: Visit www.UltimateScholarshipBook.com and enter code AR189712 for updates on this award.

(1898) • R. Ray Singleton Fund

Greater Kanawha Valley Foundation
1600 Huntington Square
900 Lee Street, East
Charleston, WV 25301
Phone: 304-346-3620
Fax: 304-346-3640
Email: tgkvf@tgkvf.org
http://www.tgkvf.org
Purpose: To provide financial assistance to residents of Kanawha, Boone, Clay, Putnam, Lincoln and Fayette counties in West Virginia who are interested in pursuing a college education.
Eligibility: Applicants must be full-time students and possess good moral character as well as proven academic achievement.
Target applicants: High school students. College students. Graduate school students. Adult students.
Minimum GPA: 2.5
Amount: $1,000.
Number of awards: 4.
Scholarship may be renewable.
Deadline: January 15.
How to apply: Applications are available online at http://www.tgkvf.org/scholar.htm or via email at shoover@tgkvf.org.
Exclusive: Visit www.UltimateScholarshipBook.com and enter code GR189812 for updates on this award.

(1899) • Rachel E. Lemieux Youth Scholarship

Business and Professional Women/Maine Futurama Foundation
103 County Road
Oakland, ME 04963
Email: webmaster@bpwmaine.org
http://www.bpwmaine.org/files/index.php?id=10
Purpose: To honor the memory of Rachel E. Lemieux and to provide financial assistance to Maine high school seniors and recent graduates.
Eligibility: Applicants must be female Maine residents who are high school seniors or who have recently graduated.
Target applicants: High school students.
Amount: $1,200.
Number of awards: Varies.
Deadline: April 20.
How to apply: Applications are available from your local BPW chapter.
Exclusive: Visit www.UltimateScholarshipBook.com and enter code BU189912 for updates on this award.

(1900) • Rae Lee Siporin Award

Los Alamos National Laboratory Foundation
1302 Calle de la Merced
Suite A
Espanola, NM 87532
Phone: 505-753-8890
Fax: 505-753-8915
Email: info@lanlfoundation.org
http://www.lanlfoundation.org
Purpose: To support undergraduate students from Northern New Mexico.
Eligibility: Students must have at least a 3.25 GPA, and they must have either an SAT score of at least 1350 or an ACT score of at least 19. Applicants must submit an essay and two letters of recommendation.
Target applicants: High school students. College students. Adult students.
Minimum GPA: 3.25
Amount: $1,000.
Number of awards: Varies.
Deadline: January 18.
How to apply: Applications are available online.
Exclusive: Visit www.UltimateScholarshipBook.com and enter code LO190012 for updates on this award.

(1901) • Random House Inc. Creative Writing Competition

Random House Inc. Creative Writing Competition
c/o Scholarship America
One Scholarship Way
St. Peter, MN 56082
Phone: 888-369-3434
Fax: 212-940-7590
Email: worldofexpression@randomhouse.com
http://www.worldofexpression.org
Purpose: To recognize students of New York City Public High Schools for creativity in literature.
Eligibility: Applicants must be seniors in a New York City Public High School who are 21 years old or younger and must not have family members employed by Bertelsmann or its subsidiaries. Students must submit a literary composition. Possible formats include poetry/spoken word, fiction/drama or personal essay/memoir. College essays, book reports, myths and legends will not be accepted. Foreign language submissions are not allowed, and all work must not have been previously published or awarded.
Target applicants: High school students.
Amount: $500-$10,000.
Number of awards: 47.
Deadline: February 11 and April 1.
How to apply: Applications are available online.
Exclusive: Visit www.UltimateScholarshipBook.com and enter code RA190112 for updates on this award.

(1902) • Ranelius Scholarship Program

Minnesota Turkey Growers Association
108 Marty Drive
Buffalo, MN 55313
Phone: 763-682-2171
Fax: 763-682-5546
Email: lara@minnesotaturkey.com
http://www.minnesotaturkey.com
Purpose: To aid Minnesota students who are preparing for careers in the poultry industry.
Eligibility: Applicants must be Minnesota residents. They must be enrolled in or planning to enroll in a postsecondary educational program that provides adequate preparation for a career in the turkey or poultry industry. Preference will be given to applicants who have not won the award previously, members of the Minnesota Turkey Growers Association (MTGA), family members of MTGA members and employees of MTGA members. Selection is based on academic merit, extracurricular activities and demonstrated interest in the poultry industry.
Target applicants: High school students. College students. Adult students.

Amount: Varies.
Number of awards: Varies.
Scholarship may be renewable.
Deadline: February 15.
How to apply: Applications are available online. An application form, personal essay and one recommendation letter are required.
Exclusive: Visit www.UltimateScholarshipBook.com and enter code MI190212 for updates on this award.

(1903) • Raymond F. Cain Scholarship Fund

Hawaii Community Foundation - Scholarships
1164 Bishop Street, Suite 800
Honolulu, HI 96813
Phone: 888-731-3863
Fax: 808-521-6286
Email: scholarships@hcf-hawaii.org
http://www.hawaiicommunityfoundation.org
Purpose: To support students in Hawaii who are majoring in fields related to landscape architecture.
Eligibility: Applicants must have at least a 2.7 GPA, and they must have financial need.
Target applicants: High school students. College students. Adult students.
Minimum GPA: 2.7
Amount: Varies.
Number of awards: Varies.
Deadline: March 1.
How to apply: To apply, register online, complete the online application and select the scholarships to which you wish to apply. In addition, mail the supporting materials: printed confirmation page from the online application, personal statement, copy of Student Aid Report (SAR) available at www.fafsa.ed.gov and official transcript.
Exclusive: Visit www.UltimateScholarshipBook.com and enter code HA190312 for updates on this award.

(1904) • Raymond J. Faust Scholarship

American Water Works Association - Michigan Section
Attn.: Faust Scholarship Committee
P.O. Box 16337
Lansing, MI 48901
Phone: 616-355-1698
Fax: 616-355-1559
Email: jvandewege@hollandbpw.com
http://www.mi-water.org/miawwa/index.html
Purpose: To aid Michigan Section American Water Works Association members who are preparing for careers in the water utility industry.
Eligibility: Applicants must be members of the Michigan Section of the American Water Works Association (AWWA). They must be current water utility employees, the dependents of current water utility employees or prospective water utility professionals. They must be pursuing or planning to pursue a college degree in a subject that relates to the drinking water field. Selection is based on commitment to the water supply industry.
Target applicants: High school students. College students. Adult students.
Amount: Varies.
Number of awards: Varies.
Deadline: June 1.
How to apply: Applications are available online. An application form is required.
Exclusive: Visit www.UltimateScholarshipBook.com and enter code AM190412 for updates on this award.

(1905) • Raymond T. Wellington, Jr. Memorial Scholarship

American Legion Auxiliary, Department of New York
112 State Street
Suite 1310
Albany, NY 12207
Phone: 518-463-1162
Fax: 518-449-5406
Email: alanyterry@nycap.rr.com
http://www.deptny.org/Scholarships.htm
Purpose: To provide financial assistance to students who are children, grandchildren and great-grandchildren of war veterans.
Eligibility: Applicants must be children, grandchildren or great grandchildren of Armed Forces veterans who served in World War I, World War II, the Korean Conflict, the Vietnam War, Grenada/Lebanon, Panama or the Persian Gulf. Students must be high school seniors and must be U.S. citizens and New York State residents.
Target applicants: High school students.
Amount: $1,000.
Number of awards: 1.
Deadline: March 1.
How to apply: Applications are available online.
Exclusive: Visit www.UltimateScholarshipBook.com and enter code AM190512 for updates on this award.

(1906) • RBC Dain Rauscher Colorado Scholarships

Denver Foundation
55 Madison
8th Floor
Denver, CO 80206
Phone: 303-300-1790
Fax: 303-300-6547
Email: information@denverfoundation.org
http://www.denverfoundation.org/grants/page/scholarships
Purpose: To provide assistance to outstanding Colorado high school seniors who plan to pursue degrees in science or engineering.
Eligibility: Applicants must be graduating seniors at a Colorado high school who have a 3.75 or higher GPA and have completed college preparatory coursework.
Target applicants: High school students.
Minimum GPA: 3.75
Amount: $3,000.
Number of awards: 5.
Deadline: March 5.
How to apply: Applications are available online.
Exclusive: Visit www.UltimateScholarshipBook.com and enter code DE190612 for updates on this award.

(1907) • Regents Award for Children of Veterans

New York State Higher Education Services Corporation (HESC)
99 Washington Avenue
Albany, NY 12255
Phone: 888-697-4372
Email: hescwebmail@hesc.org
http://www.hesc.com/content.nsf/
Purpose: To assist students whose parents served in the Armed Forces during times of war or national emergency.

Eligibility: Applicants must have a parent who served in the United States Armed Forces during the Persian Gulf, Vietnam or Korean Conflicts, World War I or II or as a Merchant Seaman during World War II. The parent must be or have been a resident of New York State and have died or suffered a disability of 40 percent or more as a result of service, been classified as missing in action or been a prisoner of war. Students with a parent who has received the expeditionary medal for participation in operations in Lebanon, Grenada or Panama and students born with spina bifida whose parent is a Vietnam Veteran are also eligible.
Target applicants: Junior high students or younger. High school students. College students. Graduate school students. Adult students.
Amount: $450.
Number of awards: Varies.
Scholarship may be renewable.
Deadline: April 30.
How to apply: Applications are available by phone.
Exclusive: Visit www.UltimateScholarshipBook.com and enter code NE190712 for updates on this award.

(1908) • Regional University Baccalaureate Scholarship

Oklahoma State Regents for Higher Education
655 Research Parkway
Suite 200
Oklahoma City, OK 73104
Phone: 405-225-9100
Email: llangston@osrhe.edu
http://www.okhighered.org
Purpose: To provide financial assistance to students of regional universities.
Eligibility: Applicants must be Oklahoma residents who are enrolled in a bachelor's degree program at one of the following schools: Cameron University, East Central University, Langston University, Northeastern State University, Northwestern Oklahoma State University, Oklahoma Panhandle State University, Rogers State University, Southeastern Oklahoma State University, Southwestern Oklahoma State University, University of Central Oklahoma or the University of Science and Arts of Oklahoma. They must also either have an ACT score of 30 or higher or be a National Merit Semifinalist or Commended Student.
Target applicants: High school students.
Amount: Tuition plus $3,000.
Number of awards: Up to 165.
Scholarship may be renewable.
Deadline: Varies.
How to apply: Applications are available from your university.
Exclusive: Visit www.UltimateScholarshipBook.com and enter code OK190812 for updates on this award.

(1909) • Rehabilitation Assistance for the Blind and Visually Impaired

College Foundation of North Carolina
P.O. Box 41966
Raleigh, NC 27629
Phone: 888-234-6400
Fax: 919-821-3139
Email: programinformation@cfnc.org
http://www.cfnc.org
Purpose: To assist North Carolina undergraduate and graduate students who are blind or visually impaired.
Eligibility: Applicants must be North Carolina residents who are enrolled full-time at a North Carolina college or university. They must be legally blind or have a condition that could result in blindness, and they must be in need of vocational rehabilitation services.
Target applicants: College students. Graduate school students. Adult students.
Amount: Up to full tuition.
Number of awards: Varies.
Deadline: Varies.
How to apply: Applications are available from the State Division of Services for the Blind at http://www.dhhs.state.nc.us/dsb/.
Exclusive: Visit www.UltimateScholarshipBook.com and enter code CO190912 for updates on this award.

(1910) • Retail Chapter Awards

Oregon Association of Nurseries
29751 SW Town Center Loop West
Wilsonville, OR 97070
Phone: 800-342-6401
Fax: 503-682-5099
Email: info@oan.org
http://www.oan.org
Purpose: To aid students who are majoring in ornamental horticulture or a related subject.
Eligibility: Applicants must be majoring in ornamental horticulture or a related subject. Selection is based on the overall strength of the application.
Target applicants: College students. Adult students.
Amount: $1,000.
Number of awards: 3.
Deadline: April 1.
How to apply: Applications are available online. An application form, official transcript and three references letters are required.
Exclusive: Visit www.UltimateScholarshipBook.com and enter code OR191012 for updates on this award.

(1911) • Rhode Island Foundation Association of Former Legislators Scholarship

Rhode Island Foundation
One Union Station
Providence, RI 02903
Phone: 401-274-4564
Fax: 401-331-8085
Email: lmonahan@rifoundation.org
http://www.rifoundation.org
Purpose: To assist Rhode Island high school seniors with an excellent track record of community service.
Eligibility: Applicants must be Rhode Island high school seniors who have been accepted into college, have demonstrated need and have a substantial amount of community service.
Target applicants: High school students.
Amount: $1,500.
Number of awards: 5.
Deadline: May 3.
How to apply: Applications are available online.
Exclusive: Visit www.UltimateScholarshipBook.com and enter code RH191112 for updates on this award.

(1912) • Richard Goolsby Scholarship Fund

Foundation for the Carolinas
217 South Tryon Street
Charlotte, NC 28202

Phone: 704-973-4500
Email: mmccrorey@fftc.org
http://www.fftc.org
Purpose: To support students who are interested in the plastics industry.
Eligibility: Applicants must be full-time graduate students or rising undergraduate sophomores, juniors or seniors. They must have completed science, business or engineering coursework that is related to plastics and must be interested in the plastics industry. Selection is based on the overall strength of the application.
Target applicants: College students. Graduate school students. Adult students.
Amount: Varies.
Number of awards: Varies.
Deadline: Varies.
How to apply: Applications are available online. An application form and supporting materials are required.
Exclusive: Visit www.UltimateScholarshipBook.com and enter code FO191212 for updates on this award.

(1913) • Richard W. Tyler Principals Scholarship Program

MELMAC Education Foundation
188 Whitten Road
Augusta, ME 04330
Phone: 866-622-3066
Fax: 207-622-3053
Email: info@melmacfoundation.org
http://www.melmacfoundation.org/Default.aspx
Purpose: To assist Maine students and encourage them to continue their college education beyond the first year.
Eligibility: Applicants must be Maine high school students nominated by their school's principal. They must be accepted to a college or university and demonstrate exceptional financial need. They must face challenges or obstacles in their pursuit of an education and be committed to public service.
Target applicants: High school students.
Amount: $1,000.
Number of awards: Varies.
Deadline: Varies.
How to apply: Applications are made on the student's behalf by his or her high school principal.
Exclusive: Visit www.UltimateScholarshipBook.com and enter code ME191312 for updates on this award.

(1914) • Richie Gregory Fund

Hawaii Community Foundation - Scholarships
1164 Bishop Street, Suite 800
Honolulu, HI 96813
Phone: 888-731-3863
Fax: 808-521-6286
Email: scholarships@hcf-hawaii.org
http://www.hawaiicommunityfoundation.org
Purpose: To support students who are majoring in art.
Eligibility: Applicants must be residents of Hawaii.
Target applicants: High school students. College students. Adult students.
Amount: Varies.
Number of awards: Varies.
Deadline: March 1.
How to apply: To apply, register online, complete the online application and select the scholarships to which you wish to apply. In addition, mail the supporting materials: printed confirmation page from the online application, personal statement, copy of Student Aid Report (SAR) available at www.fafsa.ed.gov and official transcript.
Exclusive: Visit www.UltimateScholarshipBook.com and enter code HA191412 for updates on this award.

(1915) • Rick Pankow Foundation Scholarships

Rick Pankow Foundation
18654 NW Bernina Court
Issaquah, WA 98027
Email: chris@rickpankowfoundation.org
http://www.rickpankowfoundation.org
Purpose: To aid students of horticulture and landscaping.
Eligibility: Applicants must be high school seniors in the state of Washington. They must be planning to pursue a two- or four-year college degree in horticulture or landscaping. Selection is based on academic merit, extracurricular activities, recommendations, leadership and financial need.
Target applicants: High school students.
Amount: $1,000.
Number of awards: Varies.
Deadline: March 30.
How to apply: Applications are available online. An application form, transcript and one recommendation letter are required.
Exclusive: Visit www.UltimateScholarshipBook.com and enter code RI191512 for updates on this award.

(1916) • Rob Branham Scholarship

Advertising Club of Connecticut
P.O. Box 298
Marlborough, CT 06447
Phone: 860-723-2190
Fax: 860-721-7406
Email: jirobinson@tribune.com
http://www.adclubct.org
Purpose: To help students planning careers in advertising, marketing and supporting industries.
Eligibility: Applicants must attend or be accepted to an accredited university or technical or trade school. They must major in advertising, marketing, broadcast media or print production. They must be sponsored by a member of the Advertising Club of Connecticut. Selection is based on GPA (20 percent), essay (30 percent), work experience and activities (30 percent) and SAT/ACT scores (20 percent).
Target applicants: High school students. College students. Adult students.
Amount: Varies.
Number of awards: Varies.
Deadline: April 23.
How to apply: Applications are available online. An application form, referral letter, two letters of recommendation, essay, transcript and SAT/ACT scores are required.
Exclusive: Visit www.UltimateScholarshipBook.com and enter code AD191612 for updates on this award.

(1917) • Robanna Fund

Hawaii Community Foundation - Scholarships
1164 Bishop Street, Suite 800
Honolulu, HI 96813
Phone: 888-731-3863
Fax: 808-521-6286

Email: scholarships@hcf-hawaii.org
http://www.hawaiicommunityfoundation.org
Purpose: To support Hawaii students who plan to work in health care.
Eligibility: Applicants must be in an undergraduate health-related program.
Target applicants: High school students. College students. Adult students.
Amount: Varies.
Number of awards: Varies.
Deadline: March 1.
How to apply: To apply, register online, complete the online application and select the scholarships to which you wish to apply. In addition, mail the supporting materials: printed confirmation page from the online application, personal statement, copy of Student Aid Report (SAR) available at www.fafsa.ed.gov and official transcript.
Exclusive: Visit www.UltimateScholarshipBook.com and enter code HA191712 for updates on this award.

(1918) • Robert C. Byrd Honors Scholarship Program - Alaska

Alaska Department of Education and Early Development
801 W. 10th Street, Suite 200
P.O. Box 110500
Juneau, AK 99811
Phone: 907-465-3826
Fax: 907-465-2989
Email: kay.holmes@alaska.gov
http://www.eed.state.ak.us
Purpose: To support Alaskan high school students in their pursuit of higher education.
Eligibility: Applicants must be high school seniors with the promise of future excellence and achievement. They must be residents of Alaska and U.S. citizens accepted into a college, university or technical school as a full-time student. Applicants must not be in default on any federal student loans. They must include an essay on a social issue of importance to them and three letters of recommendation with their application.
Target applicants: High school students.
Amount: $1,500.
Number of awards: 18.
Scholarship may be renewable.
Deadline: April 2.
How to apply: Applications are available online.
Exclusive: Visit www.UltimateScholarshipBook.com and enter code AL191812 for updates on this award.

(1919) • Robert C. Byrd Honors Scholarship Program - Arizona

Arizona Department of Education
1535 W. Jefferson Street
Phoenix, AZ 85007
Phone: 800-352-4558
Fax: 602-364-1532
Email: byrd@azed.gov
http://www.ade.state.az.us
Purpose: To reward Arizona high school students who demonstrate academic excellence.
Eligibility: Applicants must be graduating high school seniors or students who have received a GED who have applied to or been accepted at a post-secondary institution as a full-time student. They must be Arizona residents and U.S. citizens or permanent residents.
Target applicants: High school students.
Amount: $1,500.
Number of awards: Varies.
Scholarship may be renewable.
Deadline: March 26.
How to apply: Applicants must be nominated by their high schools.
Exclusive: Visit www.UltimateScholarshipBook.com and enter code AR191912 for updates on this award.

(1920) • Robert C. Byrd Honors Scholarship Program - Arkansas

Arkansas Department of Education
4 Capitol Mall
Little Rock, AR 72201
Phone: 501-682-4475
Email: ade.communications@arkansas.gov
http://www.arkansased.org
Purpose: To support high-achieving Arkansas high school graduates.
Eligibility: Applicants must be graduating seniors or recipients of the equivalent of a high school diploma. They must be residents of Arkansas admitted to a post-secondary school. Applicants must show current academic achievement with a promise of future achievement. Students with full scholarship awards or who will be attending military academies are not eligible for the scholarship.
Target applicants: High school students.
Amount: $1,500.
Number of awards: Varies.
Scholarship may be renewable.
Deadline: Varies.
How to apply: Applications are available online.
Exclusive: Visit www.UltimateScholarshipBook.com and enter code AR192012 for updates on this award.

(1921) • Robert C. Byrd Honors Scholarship Program - California

California Student Aid Commission (CSAC)
Attn.: Robert C. Byrd Honors Scholarship Program
P.O. Box 419029
Rancho Cordova, CA 95741-9029
Phone: 888-224-7268
Email: studentsupport@csac.ca.gov
http://www.csac.ca.gov
Purpose: To aid outstanding California resident students.
Eligibility: Applicants must be legal residents of California who are U.S. citizens or eligible noncitizens. Applicants must enroll in and attend a U.S. postsecondary institution on a full-time basis as freshmen, have registered with the Selective Service System and submit a certification form attesting that they are not delinquent or in default on a federal scholarship or educational loan. The Commission reviews applicants by grade point average.
Target applicants: High school students.
Amount: $1,500.
Number of awards: Varies.
Scholarship may be renewable.
Deadline: April 2.
How to apply: Students must apply through their high school program coordinator. Students not currently enrolled in a California high school may obtain an application directly from the California Student Aid Commission.
Exclusive: Visit www.UltimateScholarshipBook.com and enter code CA192112 for updates on this award.

(1922) • Robert C. Byrd Honors Scholarship Program - Colorado

Colorado Department of Education
High School Reform/Counselor Corps
201 East Colfax Avenue, Room 400C
Denver, CO 80203
Phone: 303-866-6142
Email: dukes_c@cde.state.co.us
http://www.cde.state.co.us/cdeawards/byrd.htm

Purpose: To promote academic excellence in Colorado high school seniors.

Eligibility: Applicants must be Colorado residents graduating from high school or receiving a GED. They must also be U.S. citizens or national or permanent residents of the U.S. Applicants must have an unweighted GPA of at least 3.8 or a weighted GPA of at least 4.0 and have received a score of 31 or above on the ACT or a score of 2040 or above on the SAT. Students receiving a GED must score in the top 5 percent of Colorado GED scores. Applicants must be accepted into an accredited post-secondary institution and provide proof of acceptance with the application.

Target applicants: High school students.
Minimum GPA: 3.8
Amount: $1,500.
Number of awards: Varies.
Scholarship may be renewable.
Deadline: Early April.
How to apply: Applications are available online.
Exclusive: Visit www.UltimateScholarshipBook.com and enter code CO192212 for updates on this award.

(1923) • Robert C. Byrd Honors Scholarship Program - Connecticut

Connecticut Department of Higher Education
61 Woodland Street
Hartford, CT 06105-2326
Phone: 860-947-1855
Fax: 860-947-1838
Email: byrd@ctdhe.org
http://www.ctdhe.org

Purpose: To assist Connecticut student residents.

Eligibility: Applicants must be Connecticut residents who are high school seniors ranking in the top 2 percent of their class or with SAT scores of at least 2100. Selection is based on SAT scores and class rank.

Target applicants: High school students.
Amount: $1,500.
Number of awards: Varies.
Deadline: April 1.
How to apply: Applications are available online.
Exclusive: Visit www.UltimateScholarshipBook.com and enter code CO192312 for updates on this award.

(1924) • Robert C. Byrd Honors Scholarship Program - Delaware

Delaware Higher Education Commission
Carvel State Office Building
5th Floor
820 North French Street
Wilmington, DE 19801-3509
Phone: 800-292-7935
Fax: 302-577-6765
Email: dhec@doe.k12.de.us
http://www.doe.k12.de.us/infosuites/students_family/dhec/

Purpose: To support high-achieving Delaware resident students.

Eligibility: Applicants must be residents of Delaware, U.S. citizens or eligible noncitizens, high school seniors who rank in the upper quarter of their class or GED recipients who score at least 300 on the GED examination, score a minimum of 1200 on the SAT and enroll at least half-time at a regionally-accredited institution of higher education. The program is dependent on U.S. Congressional funding.

Target applicants: High school students. College students. Graduate school students. Adult students.
Amount: $1,500.
Number of awards: 20.
Scholarship may be renewable.
Deadline: March 28.
How to apply: Applications are available online.
Exclusive: Visit www.UltimateScholarshipBook.com and enter code DE192412 for updates on this award.

(1925) • Robert C. Byrd Honors Scholarship Program - Florida

Florida Department of Education
Office of Student Financial Assistance
1940 N. Monroe Street
Suite 70
Tallahassee, FL 32303-4759
Phone: 888-827-2004
Fax: 850-245-9667
Email: osfa@fldoe.org
http://www.floridastudentfinancialaid.org

Purpose: To support Florida high school graduates who show academic promise.

Eligibility: Applicants must meet Florida's residency requirements for receiving state financial aid as determined by the student's postsecondary school and must not be in default on federal or state student loan programs.

Target applicants: High school students. College students. Adult students.
Amount: Up to $1,500.
Number of awards: Varies.
Scholarship may be renewable.
Deadline: Varies.
How to apply: Applicants must be nominated by their high school principal, adult education director or principal or headmaster and complete the Florida Financial Aid Application.
Exclusive: Visit www.UltimateScholarshipBook.com and enter code FL192512 for updates on this award.

(1926) • Robert C. Byrd Honors Scholarship Program - Georgia

Georgia Student Finance Commission
2082 East Exchange Place
Tucker, GA 30084
Phone: 800-505-4732
Fax: 770-724-9089
Email: support@gacollege411.org
http://www.gacollege411.org

Purpose: To aid outstanding Georgia high school students.

Eligibility: Applicants must be U.S. citizens, have recently graduated from a Georgia secondary school and be enrolled at a postsecondary institution. Applicants must also demonstrate academic achievement.

Target applicants: High school students.
Amount: $1,500.
Number of awards: 200.
Scholarship may be renewable.
Deadline: February 1.
How to apply: Applications are available by telephone request.
Exclusive: Visit www.UltimateScholarshipBook.com and enter code GE192612 for updates on this award.

(1927) • Robert C. Byrd Honors Scholarship Program - Hawaii

Hawaii Department of Education
Office of Curriculum, Instruction and Student Support
Student Support Section
641 18th Avenue V-201
Honolulu, HI 96816
Phone: 808-586-3230
Fax: 808-586-3234
http://doe.k12.hi.us
Purpose: To promote academic excellence among Hawaii students.
Eligibility: Applicants must be graduating high school seniors or planning to earn a GED. They must have a GPA of 3.3 or higher and have scored above 1270 on the SAT and/or above 29 on the ACT. GED applicants must score at least 60 points. Applicants must be legal Hawaiian residents, but they may attend high schools outside of Hawaii.
Target applicants: High school students.
Minimum GPA: 3.3
Amount: $1,500.
Number of awards: Varies.
Scholarship may be renewable.
Deadline: March 15.
How to apply: Applications are available online.
Exclusive: Visit www.UltimateScholarshipBook.com and enter code HA192712 for updates on this award.

(1928) • Robert C. Byrd Honors Scholarship Program - Idaho

Idaho State Board of Education
P.O. Box 83720
Boise, ID 83720
Phone: 208-334-2270
Fax: 208-334-2632
Email: dkelly@osbe.state.id.us
http://www.boardofed.idaho.gov
Purpose: To recognize outstanding Idaho high school seniors.
Eligibility: Applicants must be U.S. citizens who are graduating seniors of Idaho high schools and who demonstrate outstanding academic achievement. Selection is based on merit.
Target applicants: High school students.
Amount: Up to $1,500.
Number of awards: Varies.
Scholarship may be renewable.
Deadline: January 15.
How to apply: Applications are available online.
Exclusive: Visit www.UltimateScholarshipBook.com and enter code ID192812 for updates on this award.

(1929) • Robert C. Byrd Honors Scholarship Program - Illinois

Illinois Department of Public Health
535 W. Jefferson Street
Springfield, IL 62761
Phone: 217-782-4977
Fax: 217-782-3987
Email: dph.mailus@illinois.gov
http://www.idph.state.il.us
Purpose: To aid outstanding Illinois high school students.
Eligibility: Applicants must be U.S. citizens, be graduating Illinois high school seniors, demonstrate outstanding academic achievement and be enrolled or accepted for enrollment full-time as undergraduate students.
Target applicants: High school students.
Amount: $1,500.
Number of awards: Varies.
Scholarship may be renewable.
Deadline: July 15.
How to apply: Applicants are nominated by their high schools.
Exclusive: Visit www.UltimateScholarshipBook.com and enter code IL192912 for updates on this award.

(1930) • Robert C. Byrd Honors Scholarship Program - Indiana

State Student Assistance Commission of Indiana
150 W. Market Street
Suite 500
Indianapolis, IN 46204
Phone: 888-528-4719
Fax: 317-232-3260
Email: grants@ssaci.state.in.us
http://www.in.gov/ssaci
Purpose: Monetary assistance is provided to help academically worthy Indiana resident high school seniors with their college expenses.
Eligibility: Applicants must be U.S. citizens who are graduating Indiana high school seniors and have a minimum SAT score of 1300 or a minimum ACT score of 29. Applicants must apply to and enroll in a higher education institution full-time.
Target applicants: High school students.
Amount: $1,500.
Number of awards: Varies.
Scholarship may be renewable.
Deadline: April 26.
How to apply: Applications are available online.
Exclusive: Visit www.UltimateScholarshipBook.com and enter code ST193012 for updates on this award.

(1931) • Robert C. Byrd Honors Scholarship Program - Iowa

Iowa College Student Aid Commission
200 10th Street, 4th Floor
Des Moines, IA 50309
Phone: 515-242-3344
Fax: 515-242-3388
Email: info@iowacollegeaid.org
http://www.iowacollegeaid.org
Purpose: To recognize top Iowa high school seniors.
Eligibility: Applicants must be ranked in the top 10 percent of their graduating Iowa high school class, have taken required academic courses,

have a minimum ACT score of 28 or minimum SAT score of 1240 and have a minimum 3.5 GPA.
Target applicants: High school students.
Minimum GPA: 3.5
Amount: $1,500.
Number of awards: Varies.
Scholarship may be renewable.
Deadline: April 1.
How to apply: Applications are available from your high school guidance counselor and online.
Exclusive: Visit www.UltimateScholarshipBook.com and enter code IO193112 for updates on this award.

(1932) • Robert C. Byrd Honors Scholarship Program - Kansas

Kansas State Department of Education
120 SE 10th Avenue
Topeka, KS 66612
Phone: 785-296-3201
Fax: 785-296-7933
Email: contact@ksde.org
http://www.ksde.org
Purpose: To provide scholarship funds to high-achieving seniors in Kansas.
Eligibility: Applicants must be graduating high school seniors or have obtained the equivalent of a high school diploma. They must demonstrate academic achievement and show promise of continued academic achievement and be planning to attend a post-secondary school. Applicants must have an unweighted GPA of at least 3.85 and score of 32 or above on the ACT. Applicants must be U.S. citizens or legal residents.
Target applicants: High school students.
Minimum GPA: 3.85
Amount: $1,500.
Number of awards: Varies.
Scholarship may be renewable.
Deadline: February 7.
How to apply: Applications are available online. Two letters of reference and an essay are required.
Exclusive: Visit www.UltimateScholarshipBook.com and enter code KA193212 for updates on this award.

(1933) • Robert C. Byrd Honors Scholarship Program - Kentucky

Kentucky Higher Education Assistance Authority
P.O. Box 798
Frankfort, KY 40602
Phone: 800-928-8926
Email: blane@kheaa.com
http://www.kheaa.com
Purpose: To assist high-achieving high school seniors and GED recipients.
Eligibility: Applicants must be residents of Kentucky and U.S. citizens or nationals. Students must have a GPA of 3.5 or higher and a score of 23 or higher on the ACT or a score of 1060 or higher on the SAT. GED recipients must receive a score of 2700 or higher. Applicants must be nominated by a high school official or GED coordinator, cannot be in default on a federal loan and males must be in compliance with Selective Service requirements.
Target applicants: High school students.
Minimum GPA: 3.5
Amount: Up to $1,500.
Number of awards: Varies.
Scholarship may be renewable.
Deadline: February 1 for high school and June 30 for GED.
How to apply: Applications are available online.
Exclusive: Visit www.UltimateScholarshipBook.com and enter code KE193312 for updates on this award.

(1934) • Robert C. Byrd Honors Scholarship Program - Louisiana

Louisiana Department of Education
P.O. Box 94064
Baton Rouge, LA 70804
Phone: 877-453-2721
Fax: 225-342-0193
http://www.doe.state.la.us
Purpose: To provide financial support to students who have demonstrated academic achievement.
Eligibility: Applicants must be high school students or GED recipients who are Louisiana residents and U.S. citizens. They must have a GPA of at least 3.5 and score above 23 on the ACT or above 970 on the SAT. GED recipients should have a score above 620. Applicants must be planning to attend an accredited post-secondary institution.
Target applicants: High school students.
Minimum GPA: 3.5
Amount: $1,500.
Number of awards: Varies.
Scholarship may be renewable.
Deadline: Varies.
How to apply: Applications are available from high school guidance counselors and GED coordinators.
Exclusive: Visit www.UltimateScholarshipBook.com and enter code LO193412 for updates on this award.

(1935) • Robert C. Byrd Honors Scholarship Program - Maine

Maine Education Assistance Division
Finance Authority of Maine (FAME)
5 Community Drive
P.O. Box 949
Augusta, ME 04332
Phone: 800-228-3734
Fax: 207-623-0095
Email: education@famemaine.com
http://www.famemaine.com
Purpose: To provide support to high-achieving high school seniors.
Eligibility: Applicants must be graduating high school seniors. Home-schooled seniors are eligible if they submit GED scores and high school transcripts, if available. Applicants must be Maine residents who have demonstrated academic achievement and participation in community service activities. They must submit an essay and ACT or SAT scores.
Target applicants: High school students.
Amount: $1,500.
Number of awards: Varies.
Scholarship may be renewable.
Deadline: May 1.
How to apply: Applications are available online.
Exclusive: Visit www.UltimateScholarshipBook.com and enter code MA193512 for updates on this award.

(1936) • Robert C. Byrd Honors Scholarship Program - Maryland

Maryland State Department of Education
William Cappe
200 W. Baltimore Street
Baltimore, MD 21201
Email: wcappe@msde.state.md.us
http://www.msde.state.md.us

Purpose: To recognize student achievement and scholastic excellence.
Eligibility: Applicants must be high school seniors who are Maryland residents and in the top 1 percent of their class. They must be admitted full-time to a post-secondary school, excluding military academies.
Target applicants: High school students.
Amount: $1,000-$1,500.
Number of awards: 118.
Deadline: Varies.
How to apply: Applicants must be nominated by school officials.
Exclusive: Visit www.UltimateScholarshipBook.com and enter code MA193612 for updates on this award.

(1937) • Robert C. Byrd Honors Scholarship Program - Massachusetts

Massachusetts Department of Education
350 Main Street
Malden, MA 02148
Phone: 781-338-6304
Email: steixeira@doe.mass.edu
http://www.doe.mass.edu

Purpose: To reward academic achievement in high school seniors.
Eligibility: Applicants must be high school seniors or be earning the equivalent of a high school diploma. They must be Massachusetts residents, having lived in the state at least one year prior to beginning college. Applicants must apply to or be accepted at an accredited post-secondary institution. They must have a GPA of at least 3.5, and the scholarship committee will consider school activities, leadership, community service, employment, awards and honors.
Target applicants: High school students.
Minimum GPA: 3.5
Amount: $1,500.
Number of awards: Varies.
Deadline: Varies.
How to apply: Applications are sent to schools, and schools must nominate students.
Exclusive: Visit www.UltimateScholarshipBook.com and enter code MA193712 for updates on this award.

(1938) • Robert C. Byrd Honors Scholarship Program - Michigan

Michigan Tuition Grant Program
Office of Scholarships and Grants
P.O. Box 30462
Lansing, MI 48909
Phone: 888-447-2687
Email: osg@michigan.gov
http://www.michigan.gov/osg

Purpose: To assist outstanding Michigan high school seniors.
Eligibility: Applicants must be U.S. citizens or eligible noncitizens, Michigan residents, high school seniors and demonstrate academic excellence.
Target applicants: High school students.
Amount: Up to $1,500.
Number of awards: Varies.
Scholarship may be renewable.
Deadline: March 19.
How to apply: Each Michigan high school principal may nominate one outstanding senior.
Exclusive: Visit www.UltimateScholarshipBook.com and enter code MI193812 for updates on this award.

(1939) • Robert C. Byrd Honors Scholarship Program - Minnesota

Minnesota Office of Higher Education Services
1450 Energy Park Drive
Suite 350
Saint Paul, MN 55108
Phone: 651-642-0567
Fax: 651-642-0675
Email: ginny.dodds@state.mn.us
http://www.mheso.state.mn.us

Purpose: To assist outstanding Minnesota high school seniors.
Eligibility: Applicants must be U.S. citizens or eligible noncitizens, Minnesota residents, high school seniors and demonstrate academic excellence.
Target applicants: High school students.
Amount: Varies.
Number of awards: 125.
Scholarship may be renewable.
Deadline: March.
How to apply: The Minnesota Department of Children, Families and Learning sends out the nomination information in January. Applicants apply through their high school and should contact their principal or counselor for application forms.
Exclusive: Visit www.UltimateScholarshipBook.com and enter code MI193912 for updates on this award.

(1940) • Robert C. Byrd Honors Scholarship Program - Mississippi

Mississippi Department of Education
P.O. Box 771
Jackson, MS 39205
Phone: 601-359-3513
Email: askmde@mde.k12.ms.us
http://www.mde.k12.ms.us

Purpose: To recognize and promote academic excellence and achievement.
Eligibility: Applicants must be residents of Mississippi and U.S. citizens or permanent residents. They must be graduating high school seniors or have earned their GED during the application year and have applied or been accepted to a post-secondary school. Applications must include ACT or SAT scores, high school transcript or GED test results, extracurricular activities, leadership activities, honors and awards and a one-page essay.
Target applicants: High school students.
Amount: $1,100-$1,500.
Number of awards: Varies.
Scholarship may be renewable.
Deadline: March 31.
How to apply: Applications are available online.
Exclusive: Visit www.UltimateScholarshipBook.com and enter code MI194012 for updates on this award.

(1941) • Robert C. Byrd Honors Scholarship Program - Missouri

Missouri Department of Elementary and Secondary Education
P.O. Box 480
Jefferson City, MO 65102
Phone: 573-751-1668
Fax: 573-751-8613
Email: webreplyqualtrr@dese.mo.gov
http://www.dese.mo.gov
Purpose: To recognize and promote academic excellence and achievement.
Eligibility: Applicants must be Missouri high school graduates or GED recipients. They must be U.S. citizens or permanent residents. Applicants must be in the top 10 percent of their class and score above the 90th percentile on the ACT.
Target applicants: High school students.
Amount: Varies.
Number of awards: Varies.
Scholarship may be renewable.
Deadline: April 15.
How to apply: Applications are available online.
Exclusive: Visit www.UltimateScholarshipBook.com and enter code MI194112 for updates on this award.

(1942) • Robert C. Byrd Honors Scholarship Program - Montana

Montana Department of Education
The Montana Office of Public Instruction
P.O. Box 202501
Helena, MT 59620
http://opi.mt.gov/Programs/SchoolPrograms/#gpm1_10
Purpose: To assist outstanding Montana high school seniors.
Eligibility: Applicants must be U.S. citizens or eligible noncitizens, Montana residents, high school seniors and have a GPA of at least 3.6 in a college preparatory curriculum, and a cumulative score of 1380 on the SAT or 30 on the ACT.
Target applicants: High school students.
Minimum GPA: 3.6
Amount: Varies.
Number of awards: Varies.
Scholarship may be renewable.
Deadline: Varies.
How to apply: Applications are available at your high school counseling office or online.
Exclusive: Visit www.UltimateScholarshipBook.com and enter code MO194212 for updates on this award.

(1943) • Robert C. Byrd Honors Scholarship Program - Nebraska

Nebraska Department of Education
301 Centennial Mall South
P.O. Box 94987
Lincoln, NE 68509
Phone: 402-471-2295
Email: mardi.north@nde.ne.gov
http://www.education.ne.gov/
Purpose: To honor academic excellence and potential.
Eligibility: Applicants must be Nebraska residents who are graduating from high school or receiving a GED with a minimum ACT score of 30. They must be U.S. citizens, nationals or permanent residents. Applicants must have applied or been accepted to a post-secondary school, planning to attend full-time. They must fulfill all Selective Service requirements and not be in default on any student loans.
Target applicants: High school students.
Amount: Up to $1,500.
Number of awards: 40.
Scholarship may be renewable.
Deadline: Varies.
How to apply: Applications are available online.
Exclusive: Visit www.UltimateScholarshipBook.com and enter code NE194312 for updates on this award.

(1944) • Robert C. Byrd Honors Scholarship Program - Nevada

Nevada Department of Education
700 E. Fifth Street
Carson City, NV 89701
Phone: 775-687-9200
Fax: 775-687-9101
http://www.doe.nv.gov
Purpose: To recognize and promote excellence and achievement among Nevada students.
Eligibility: Applicants must be legal residents of the State of Nevada, be Nevada High School Scholars Program recipients and be accepted into an institution of higher education.
Target applicants: High school students.
Amount: $1,500.
Number of awards: 60.
Scholarship may be renewable.
Deadline: Varies.
How to apply: Contact your high school guidance counselor.
Exclusive: Visit www.UltimateScholarshipBook.com and enter code NE194412 for updates on this award.

(1945) • Robert C. Byrd Honors Scholarship Program - New Hampshire

New Hampshire Postsecondary Education Commission
3 Barrell Court
Suite 300
Concord, NH 03301
Phone: 603-271-2555 x352
Fax: 603-271-2696
Email: jknapp@pec.state.nh.us
http://www.state.nh.us/postsecondary
Purpose: To assist exceptional New Hampshire students in postsecondary study.
Eligibility: Applicants must be New Hampshire residents, U.S. citizens or eligible noncitizens and high school seniors who plan to be full-time college students.
Target applicants: High school students.
Amount: $1,500.
Number of awards: Varies.
Deadline: First Friday in April.
How to apply: Contact the New Hampshire Department of Education for more information and an application.
Exclusive: Visit www.UltimateScholarshipBook.com and enter code NE194512 for updates on this award.

(1946) • Robert C. Byrd Honors Scholarship Program - New Jersey

State of New Jersey Department of Education
P.O. Box 500
Trenton, NJ 08625
Phone: 609-292-4469
http://www.state.nj.us/education

Purpose: To reward academic achievement in graduating seniors and GED recipients.

Eligibility: Applicants must be New Jersey residents who are U.S. citizens or permanent residents. Scholarships are awarded based on merit and are renewable for four years of undergraduate study.

Target applicants: High school students.
Amount: Up to $1,500.
Number of awards: Varies.
Scholarship may be renewable.
Deadline: Varies.

How to apply: Applications are available from the department of education and school officials. Students must be nominated to apply.

Exclusive: Visit www.UltimateScholarshipBook.com and enter code ST194612 for updates on this award.

(1947) • Robert C. Byrd Honors Scholarship Program - New Mexico

New Mexico Public Education Department
300 Don Gaspar
Santa Fe, NM 87501
Phone: 505-827-5800
http://www.ped.state.nm.us

Purpose: To recognize the educational accomplishments of outstanding students.

Eligibility: Applicants must be New Mexico residents who are graduating high school seniors or who have received a GED. They must have a GPA of at least 3.5 and score higher than 1220 on the SAT or higher than 27 on the ACT.

Target applicants: High school students.
Minimum GPA: 3.5
Amount: $1,500.
Number of awards: Varies.
Scholarship may be renewable.
Deadline: March 31.

How to apply: Applications are available from school officials and the public education department.

Exclusive: Visit www.UltimateScholarshipBook.com and enter code NE194712 for updates on this award.

(1948) • Robert C. Byrd Honors Scholarship Program - New York

New York State Higher Education Services Corporation (HESC)
99 Washington Avenue
Albany, NY 12255
Phone: 888-697-4372
Email: hescwebmail@hesc.org
http://www.hesc.com/content.nsf/

Purpose: To assist outstanding New York State high school graduates.

Eligibility: Applicants must be high school seniors, New York residents, plan to attend an institution of higher education and have a minimum high school average of 95 or GED of 310 and minimum SAT score of 1250.

Target applicants: High school students.
Minimum GPA: 3.7
Amount: Up to $1,500.
Number of awards: Varies.
Scholarship may be renewable.
Deadline: Varies.

How to apply: Contact your high school guidance counselor.

Exclusive: Visit www.UltimateScholarshipBook.com and enter code NE194812 for updates on this award.

(1949) • Robert C. Byrd Honors Scholarship Program - North Carolina

North Carolina Department of Public Instruction
Center for Recruitment and Retention
Division of Human Resource Management, Department of Public Instruction
301 N. Wilmington Street
Wilmington, NC 27601
Phone: 919-807-3300
Fax: 919-807-3362
Email: scholars@dpi.state.nc.us
http://www.ncpublicschools.org

Purpose: To assist academically outstanding North Carolina high school students.

Eligibility: Applicants must be legal North Carolina residents, graduate from a North Carolina high school, have a minimum SAT score of 900 and a minimum 3.0 GPA and be accepted to an approved postsecondary institution in the U.S.

Target applicants: High school students.
Minimum GPA: 3.0
Amount: $1,500.
Number of awards: 200.
Scholarship may be renewable.
Deadline: February 25.

How to apply: Students must be nominated by their schools. Contact your high school guidance counselor.

Exclusive: Visit www.UltimateScholarshipBook.com and enter code NO194912 for updates on this award.

(1950) • Robert C. Byrd Honors Scholarship Program - North Dakota

North Dakota Department of Public Instruction
600 E. Boulevard Avenue, Dept. 201
Floors 9, 10, and 11
Bismarck, ND 58505
Phone: 701-328-2260
Fax: 701-328-2461
http://www.dpi.state.nd.us

Purpose: To recognize outstanding academic achievement.

Eligibility: Applicants must be North Dakota residents who are graduating seniors or have earned a GED. Academic achievement, potential for future academic achievement, leadership, extracurricular involvement and community service will all be considered in awarding the scholarship.

Target applicants: High school students.
Amount: $1,500.
Number of awards: At least 8.
Scholarship may be renewable.
Deadline: Late April.

How to apply: Applications are available from school officials and the department of public instruction.

Exclusive: Visit www.UltimateScholarshipBook.com and enter code NO195012 for updates on this award.

(1951) • Robert C. Byrd Honors Scholarship Program - Ohio

Ohio Department of Education
25 S. Front Street
Columbus, OH 43128
Phone: 614-466-4590
Email: contact.center@ode.state.oh.us
http://www.ode.state.oh.us
Purpose: To assist outstanding Ohio high school students.
Eligibility: Applicants must be Ohio high school seniors who plan to attend an accredited U.S. undergraduate college or university. This award is given to at least one student in each of Ohio's congressional districts. Selection is based on academic achievement and participation in leadership activities.
Target applicants: High school students.
Amount: $1,500.
Number of awards: Varies.
Scholarship may be renewable.
Deadline: Varies.
How to apply: Contact your high school guidance counselor.
Exclusive: Visit www.UltimateScholarshipBook.com and enter code OH195112 for updates on this award.

(1952) • Robert C. Byrd Honors Scholarship Program - Oklahoma

Oklahoma State Department of Education
Professional Services Division
Oliver Hodge Building
2500 North Lincoln Boulevard
Oklahoma City, OK 73105
Phone: 405-521-2808
Email: studentinfo@osrhe.edu
http://www.okhighered.org
Purpose: To assist outstanding Oklahoma high school students.
Eligibility: Applicants must be high school seniors who are outstanding academically, U.S. citizens or eligible noncitizens, legal residents of Oklahoma, plan to attend full-time an institution of higher education and meet academic requirements.
Target applicants: High school students.
Amount: $1,500.
Number of awards: Varies.
Scholarship may be renewable.
Deadline: Varies.
How to apply: Contact your high school guidance counselor.
Exclusive: Visit www.UltimateScholarshipBook.com and enter code OK195212 for updates on this award.

(1953) • Robert C. Byrd Honors Scholarship Program - Oregon

Oregon Student Assistance Commission
1500 Valley River Drive
Suite 100
Eugene, OR 97401
Phone: 541-687-7400
Fax: 541-687-7414
Email: awardinfo@osac.state.or.us
http://www.osac.state.or.us
Purpose: To assist Oregon high school students.
Eligibility: Applicants must be Oregon high school seniors, have a minimum 3.85 GPA or minimum GED score of 325 and have a minimum SAT score of 1300 or ACT score of 29.
Target applicants: High school students.
Minimum GPA: 3.85
Amount: $1,500.
Number of awards: 75.
Scholarship may be renewable.
Deadline: March 2.
How to apply: Applications are available online.
Exclusive: Visit www.UltimateScholarshipBook.com and enter code OR195312 for updates on this award.

(1954) • Robert C. Byrd Honors Scholarship Program - Pennsylvania

Pennsylvania Higher Education Assistance Agency
P.O. Box 8114
Harrisburg, PA 17105
Phone: 800-692-7392
http://www.pheaa.org
Purpose: To assist outstanding Pennsylvania high school students.
Eligibility: Applicants must be high school seniors, Pennsylvania residents, accepted for enrollment at an eligible institution of higher education and U.S. citizens or permanent residents. Applicants must also rank in the top 5 percent of their class, have a minimum 3.5 GPA and have a minimum SAT score of 1150, ACT score of 25 or GED score of 355.
Target applicants: High school students.
Minimum GPA: 3.5
Amount: Varies.
Number of awards: Varies.
Deadline: April 1.
How to apply: Applications are available through your high school counselor or by written request.
Exclusive: Visit www.UltimateScholarshipBook.com and enter code PE195412 for updates on this award.

(1955) • Robert C. Byrd Honors Scholarship Program - Rhode Island

Rhode Island Department of Elementary and Secondary Education
255 Westminster Street
Providence, RI 02903
Phone: 401-222-4600
http://www.ride.ri.gov/
Purpose: To reward high scholastic achievement.
Eligibility: Applicants must be graduating high school seniors or GED recipients who are residents of Rhode Island and U.S. citizens. The scholarship is awarded based on academic achievements and the student's potential for continued achievement in post-secondary education.
Target applicants: High school students.
Amount: $1,500.
Number of awards: Varies.
Scholarship may be renewable.
Deadline: Varies.
How to apply: Applications are available from the Department of Elementary and Secondary Education and from school officials.
Exclusive: Visit www.UltimateScholarshipBook.com and enter code RH195512 for updates on this award.

(1956) • Robert C. Byrd Honors Scholarship Program - South Carolina

South Carolina Department of Education
Beth Cope, Education Associate
Suite 701
1429 Senate Street
Columbia, SC 29201
Phone: 803-734-8116
Fax: 803-734-8701
Email: info@ed.sc.gov
http://www.ed.sc.gov

Purpose: To help outstanding high school seniors pursue higher education.
Eligibility: Applicants must be graduating seniors in a South Carolina high school. Public, private and home-schooled students are eligible. Applicants must have a score of at least 1300 on the SAT or a score of at least 29 on the ACT and a GPA of 3.5 or higher.
Target applicants: High school students.
Minimum GPA: 3.5
Amount: $1,500.
Number of awards: 96.
Scholarship may be renewable.
Deadline: February 1.
How to apply: Schools and home-school associations select applicants.
Exclusive: Visit www.UltimateScholarshipBook.com and enter code SO195612 for updates on this award.

(1957) • Robert C. Byrd Honors Scholarship Program - South Dakota

South Dakota Department of Education and Cultural Affairs
700 Governors Drive
Pierre, SD 57501
Phone: 605-773-3426
http://doe.sd.gov

Purpose: To assist outstanding South Dakota high school students.
Eligibility: Applicants must be South Dakota high school seniors who plan to attend full-time an eligible institution of higher education, meet course requirements, have a minimum 3.5 GPA and have a minimum ACT score of 24.
Target applicants: High school students.
Minimum GPA: 3.5
Amount: $1,500.
Number of awards: Varies.
Scholarship may be renewable.
Deadline: May 1.
How to apply: Applications are available online.
Exclusive: Visit www.UltimateScholarshipBook.com and enter code SO195712 for updates on this award.

(1958) • Robert C. Byrd Honors Scholarship Program - Tennessee

Tennessee Student Assistance Corporation
404 James Robertson Parkway
Suite 1510, Parkway Towers
Nashville, TN 37243
Phone: 800-342-1663
Fax: 615-741-6101
Email: tsac.aidinfo@tn.gov
http://www.tn.gov/CollegePays/

Purpose: To assist outstanding Tennessee high school students.
Eligibility: Applicants must be U.S. citizens or permanent residents, be Tennessee residents, be graduating high school seniors or GED recipients and have a minimum 3.5 GPA and minimum ACT score of 24.
Target applicants: High school students.
Minimum GPA: 3.5
Amount: $1,500.
Number of awards: Varies.
Deadline: March 1.
How to apply: Contact your high school guidance counselor.
Exclusive: Visit www.UltimateScholarshipBook.com and enter code TE195812 for updates on this award.

(1959) • Robert C. Byrd Honors Scholarship Program - Texas

Texas Higher Education Coordinating Board
1200 East Anderson Lane
Austin, TX 78752
Phone: 512-427-6101
Fax: 512-427-6127
Email: marylou.guerra@thecb.state.tx.us
http://www.collegefortexans.com

Purpose: To assist outstanding Texas high school students.
Eligibility: Applicants must be U.S. citizens or permanent residents who are Texas residents, graduating high school seniors or GED recipients and be nominated by their school.
Target applicants: High school students.
Amount: $1,500.
Number of awards: Varies.
Scholarship may be renewable.
Deadline: Varies.
How to apply: Contact your high school guidance counselor.
Exclusive: Visit www.UltimateScholarshipBook.com and enter code TE195912 for updates on this award.

(1960) • Robert C. Byrd Honors Scholarship Program - Utah

Utah State Office of Education
250 East 500 South
P.O. Box 144200
Salt Lake City, UT 84114
http://www.usoe.k12.ut.us

Purpose: To recognize graduating seniors who have demonstrated academic excellence.
Eligibility: Applicants must be graduating high school seniors in Utah or have an equivalent certificate of graduation. They must be accepted at a post-secondary institution and be planning to attend full-time. Applicants must show evidence of outstanding academic achievement, including a GPA of at least 3.7 and an ACT score of 25 or higher. Applicants must be U.S. citizens or permanent residents.
Target applicants: High school students.
Minimum GPA: 3.7
Amount: $1,500.
Number of awards: Varies.
Scholarship may be renewable.
Deadline: March 26.
How to apply: Applications are available online.
Exclusive: Visit www.UltimateScholarshipBook.com and enter code UT196012 for updates on this award.

(1961) • Robert C. Byrd Honors Scholarship Program - Vermont

Vermont Student Assistance Corporation
10 East Allen Street
P.O. Box 2000
Winooski, VT 05404
Phone: 800-882-4166
Fax: 802-654-3765
Email: info@vsac.org
http://www.vsac.org

Purpose: To recognize students who achieve academic excellence.
Eligibility: Applicants must be graduating high school seniors who have demonstrated academic excellence and show promise for future academic achievements. They must attend an accredited post-secondary institution full-time. Applicants must be residents of Vermont and U.S. citizens or permanent residents.
Target applicants: High school students.
Amount: $1,500.
Number of awards: 12.
Scholarship may be renewable.
Deadline: March 5.
How to apply: Applications are available online.
Exclusive: Visit www.UltimateScholarshipBook.com and enter code VE196112 for updates on this award.

(1962) • Robert C. Byrd Honors Scholarship Program - Virginia

Virginia Department of Education
P.O. Box 2120
Richmond, VA 23218
Phone: 804-225-3349
Fax: 804-371-2456
Email: joseph.wharff@doe.virginia.gov
http://www.pen.k12.va.us

Purpose: To assist Virginia high school students.
Eligibility: Applicants must be U.S. citizens or eligible noncitizens, Virginia residents, high school seniors and demonstrate academic excellence.
Target applicants: High school students.
Amount: Varies.
Number of awards: Varies.
Deadline: April 9.
How to apply: Contact your high school guidance counselor.
Exclusive: Visit www.UltimateScholarshipBook.com and enter code VI196212 for updates on this award.

(1963) • Robert C. Byrd Honors Scholarship Program - Washington

Office of Superintendent of Public Instruction
Old Capitol Building
P.O. Box 47200
Olympia, WA 98504
Phone: 360-725-6000
http://www.k12.wa.us

Purpose: To assist outstanding Washington high school students.
Eligibility: Applicants must be U.S. citizens or eligible noncitizens, Washington residents, high school seniors and demonstrate academic excellence.
Target applicants: High school students.
Amount: $1,500.
Number of awards: Varies.
Deadline: Varies.
How to apply: Contact your high school guidance counselor.
Exclusive: Visit www.UltimateScholarshipBook.com and enter code OF196312 for updates on this award.

(1964) • Robert C. Byrd Honors Scholarship Program - West Virginia

West Virginia Higher Education Policy Commission
1018 Kanawha Boulevard, East
Suite 700
Charleston, WV 25301
Phone: 304-558-2101
Fax: 304-558-5719
Email: financialaiddirector@hepc.wvnet.edu
http://www.hepc.wvnet.edu

Purpose: To assist outstanding West Virginia high school students.
Eligibility: Applicants must be U.S. citizens or eligible noncitizens, be West Virginia residents, be high school seniors and demonstrate academic excellence.
Target applicants: High school students.
Amount: $1,500.
Number of awards: Varies.
Deadline: March 1.
How to apply: Contact your high school guidance counselor.
Exclusive: Visit www.UltimateScholarshipBook.com and enter code WE196412 for updates on this award.

(1965) • Robert C. Byrd Honors Scholarship Program - Wisconsin

Wisconsin Department of Public Instruction
125 S. Webster Street
P.O. Box 7841
Madison, WI 53707
Phone: 800-441-4563
http://www.dpi.state.wi.us

Purpose: To assist outstanding Wisconsin students.
Eligibility: Applicants must be U.S. citizens or eligible noncitizens, be Wisconsin residents, be high school seniors and demonstrate academic excellence.
Target applicants: High school students.
Amount: Varies.
Number of awards: Varies.
Deadline: Third week in February.
How to apply: Applicants are nominated by their high schools.
Exclusive: Visit www.UltimateScholarshipBook.com and enter code WI196512 for updates on this award.

(1966) • Robert C. Byrd Honors Scholarship Program - Wyoming

Wyoming Department of Education
2300 Capitol Avenue
Hathaway Building, 2nd Floor
Cheyenne, WY 82002
Phone: 307-777-7673
Fax: 307-777-6234
Email: webmaster@educ.state.ky.us
http://www.k12.wy.us

Purpose: To assist outstanding Wyoming students.

Eligibility: Applicants must be U.S. citizens or eligible noncitizens, be Wyoming residents, be high school seniors and demonstrate academic excellence.
Target applicants: High school students.
Amount: $1,500.
Number of awards: 9.
Scholarship may be renewable.
Deadline: March 19.
How to apply: Individual applications are NOT available from the Wyoming Department of Education. Contact your high school guidance counselor for an application.
Exclusive: Visit www.UltimateScholarshipBook.com and enter code WY196612 for updates on this award.

(1967) · Robert D. Blue Scholarship

Treasurer of State
Capitol Building
Des Moines, IA 50319
Phone: 515-281-3067
Fax: 515-281-6962
Email: treasurer@tos.state.ia.us
http://www.rdblue.org
Purpose: To provide financial assistance to deserving Iowa students.
Eligibility: Applicants must be Iowa residents who plan to attend an Iowa institution of higher learning the following school year. They may be high school seniors or current college students. An essay and two references are required.
Target applicants: High school students. College students. Adult students.
Amount: $1,000.
Number of awards: 20.
Deadline: May 10.
How to apply: Applications are available online.
Exclusive: Visit www.UltimateScholarshipBook.com and enter code TR196712 for updates on this award.

(1968) · Robert M. Voorhees/Standard Golf Company Scholarship

Iowa Golf Course Superintendents Association
Iowa Turfgrass Office
17017 US Highway 69
Ames, IA 50010
Phone: 515-232-8222
Fax: 515-232-8228
Email: patti@iowaturfgrass.org
http://www.iowagcsa.org
Purpose: To aid Iowa turfgrass management students.
Eligibility: Applicants must be members of the Iowa Golf Course Superintendents Association (GCSA). They must be Iowa residents who are studying at a school located outside of Iowa or must be non-residents of Iowa who are enrolled at a postsecondary institution located in Iowa. They must be studying turfgrass management or a related subject. Selection is based on the overall strength of the application.
Target applicants: College students. Adult students.
Amount: Varies.
Number of awards: Varies.
Deadline: October 31.
How to apply: Applications are available online. An application form and supporting materials are required.
Exclusive: Visit www.UltimateScholarshipBook.com and enter code IO196812 for updates on this award.

(1969) · Rockefeller State Wildlife Scholarship

Louisiana Office of Student Financial Assistance
P.O. Box 91202
Baton Rouge, LA 70821-9202
Phone: 800-259-5626 x1012
Fax: 225-922-0790
Email: custserv@osfa.la.gov
http://www.osfa.state.la.us
Purpose: To assist Louisiana students in wildlife, forestry or marine science.
Eligibility: Applicants must be Louisiana residents for at least one year, be enrolled as full-time undergraduate or graduate students in a Louisiana public college or university, earn a degree in wildlife, forestry or marine science and have a minimum 2.5 GPA. Applicants must also submit the Free Application for Federal Student Aid (FAFSA) and be U.S. citizens.
Target applicants: High school students. College students. Graduate school students. Adult students.
Minimum GPA: 2.5
Amount: $2,000-$12,000.
Number of awards: Varies.
Scholarship may be renewable.
Deadline: July 1.
How to apply: Applications are available online or by written request.
Exclusive: Visit www.UltimateScholarshipBook.com and enter code LO196912 for updates on this award.

(1970) · Rocky Mountain Chapter ASHRAE Scholarships

American Society of Heating, Refrigerating and Air-Conditioning Engineers, Inc. - Rocky Mountain Chapter
c/o Craig Wanklyn
M-E Engineers Inc.
10055 W. 43rd Avenue
Wheat Ridge, CO 80033
Phone: 303-421-6655
Email: craig.wanklyn@me-engineers.com
http://www.rockymtnashrae.com
Purpose: To aid students in the Rocky Mountain chapter area who are interested in heating, ventilation and air-conditioning (HVAC).
Eligibility: Applicants must be postsecondary students at a school located in the American Society of Heating, Refrigerating and Air-Conditioning Engineers' (ASHRAE) Rocky Mountain chapter area. They must be interested in the field of HVAC. Selection is based on demonstrated interest in HVAC, communication skills and financial need.
Target applicants: College students. Adult students.
Amount: $1,000.
Number of awards: 4.
Deadline: October 27.
How to apply: Applications are available online. An application form and supporting materials are required.
Exclusive: Visit www.UltimateScholarshipBook.com and enter code AM197012 for updates on this award.

(1971) · Rosa L. Parks Scholarships

Rosa L. Parks Scholarship Foundation
P.O. Box 950
Detroit, MI 48231
Phone: 313-222-2538
Email: rpscholarship@dnps.com

http://www.rosaparksscholarshipfoundation.org
Purpose: To provide education funds for students who hold ideals close to those of Rosa Parks.
Eligibility: Applicants must be Michigan high school seniors who will graduate by August of the application year. They must have a GPA of 2.5 or higher and have taken the SAT or ACT. An essay is required.
Target applicants: High school students.
Minimum GPA: 2.5
Amount: Varies.
Number of awards: Varies.
Deadline: Varies.
How to apply: Applications are available online.
Exclusive: Visit www.UltimateScholarshipBook.com and enter code RO197112 for updates on this award.

(1972) • Rosedale Post 346 Scholarship

American Legion, Department of Kansas
1314 SW Topeka Boulevard
Topeka, KS 66612
Phone: 785-232-9315
Fax: 785-232-1399
http://www.ksamlegion.org
Purpose: To assist the children of members of the Kansas American Legion or American Legion Auxiliary.
Eligibility: Applicants must be high school seniors or college freshmen or sophomores who are enrolling or enrolled in an approved post-secondary school. They also must be average or better students who are the children of veterans. The children of deceased parents are also eligible if the parent was a paid member at the time of death. Applicants must submit three letters of recommendation, with at least one from a teacher, an essay on "Why I Want to Go to College," a 1040 income statement, documentation of parent's veteran status and a certified high school transcript.
Target applicants: High school students. College students. Adult students.
Amount: $1,500.
Number of awards: 2.
Deadline: February 15.
How to apply: Applications are available online.
Exclusive: Visit www.UltimateScholarshipBook.com and enter code AM197212 for updates on this award.

(1973) • Rosemary and Nellie Ebrie Foundation

Hawaii Department of Education (DOE)
900 Fort Street Mall
Suite 1300
Honolulu, HI 96813
Phone: 808-566-5570
Email: hern@hawaii.edu
http://doe.k12.hi.us
Purpose: To assist college and graduate students who have Hawaiian ancestry or were born or have been a long-time residents of the Island.
Eligibility: Applicants must be residents of the Island of Hawaii and be of Hawaiian or part-Hawaiian ancestry. Applicants must also submit a four-sheet application and financial form, personal statement, recommendations and transcript.
Target applicants: High school students. College students. Graduate school students. Adult students.
Amount: Varies.
Number of awards: Varies.
Deadline: Varies.
How to apply: Applications are available by written request.
Exclusive: Visit www.UltimateScholarshipBook.com and enter code HA197312 for updates on this award.

(1974) • Rosewood Family Scholarship Program

Florida Department of Education
Office of Student Financial Assistance
1940 N. Monroe Street
Suite 70
Tallahassee, FL 32303-4759
Phone: 888-827-2004
Fax: 850-245-9667
Email: osfa@fldoe.org
http://www.floridastudentfinancialaid.org
Purpose: To help Florida minority students especially direct descendants of Rosewood families.
Eligibility: Applicants must be full-time, undergraduate minority students (Black, Hispanic, Asian, Pacific Islander, American Indian or Alaskan native) who attend state universities, public community colleges or public postsecondary vocational-technical schools. Direct descendants of Rosewood families affected by the incidents of January, 1923 receive preference. The descendants must provide family information on the Florida Financial Aid Application.
Target applicants: High school students. College students. Adult students.
Amount: Varies.
Number of awards: 25.
Scholarship may be renewable.
Deadline: April 1.
How to apply: Applicants must submit the Initial Student Florida Financial Aid Applications online by April 1. Florida residents must submit the Free Application for Federal Student Aid (FAFSA) online by May 15. Non-residents must submit the FAFSA in time to receive the Student Aid Report (SAR) from the processor and send a copy of the SAR to the Office of Student Financial Assistance by May 15.
Exclusive: Visit www.UltimateScholarshipBook.com and enter code FL197412 for updates on this award.

(1975) • Roy W. Likins Scholarship

American Water Works Association - Florida Section
1300 Ninth Street
Suite B-124
St. Cloud, FL 34769
Phone: 407-957-8448
Fax: 407-957-8415
Email: byoung@co.st-johns.fl.us
http://www.fsawwa.org
Purpose: To aid Florida students who are preparing for careers in the drinking water industry.
Eligibility: Applicants must be undergraduate upperclassmen or graduate students who are enrolled at an accredited postsecondary institution located in Florida. They must be majoring in a subject that is related to the drinking water industry and have a GPA of 3.0 or higher on a four-point scale. Previous recipients of this award are ineligible. Selection is based on academic achievement, extracurricular activities, character and stated career goals.
Target applicants: College students. Graduate school students. Adult students.
Minimum GPA: 3.0
Amount: $1,000-$2,000.
Number of awards: Varies.

Scholarship may be renewable.
Deadline: May 15.
How to apply: Applications are available online. An application form, personal statement, official transcript and two recommendation letters are required.
Exclusive: Visit www.UltimateScholarshipBook.com and enter code AM197512 for updates on this award.

(1976) • RSF Memorial Scholarship

Missouri Society of Professional Engineers
200 East McCarty Street
Suite 200
Jefferson, MO 65101
Phone: 573-636-4861
Fax: 573-636-5475
http://www.mspe.org
Purpose: To aid Missouri engineering students.
Eligibility: Applicants must be U.S. citizens who are active or retired members of the U.S. Armed Forces or a member of ROTC or the National Guard. They must be undergraduate sophomores or juniors who are majoring in engineering at one of Missouri's state universities. They must be enrolled in a program that is accredited by ABET-EAC. Selection is based on academic merit, military service, extracurricular activities and financial need.
Target applicants: College students. Adult students.
Amount: $1,500.
Number of awards: 1.
Deadline: Varies.
How to apply: Applications are available online. An application form, personal essay, proof of military service and two recommendation letters are required.
Exclusive: Visit www.UltimateScholarshipBook.com and enter code MI197612 for updates on this award.

(1977) • Ruppert Educational Grant Program

Silicon Valley Community Foundation
2440 W. El Camino Real
Suite 300
Mountain View, CA 94040
Phone: 650-450-5400
Fax: 650-450-5401
Email: scholarships@siliconvalleycf.org
http://www.siliconvalleycf.org
Purpose: To assist California students who are "late bloomers."
Eligibility: Applicants must be U.S. citizens, be high school seniors in San Mateo County or northern Santa Clara County (Daly City through Mountain View) and have a maximum GPA of 3.3. Students must demonstrate financial need; evidence of partial self-support such as savings from summer jobs, part-time work, etc.; community service and academic promise and GPA improvement during high school years.
Target applicants: High school students.
Amount: Up to $5,000.
Number of awards: Up to 30.
Deadline: Varies.
How to apply: Applications are available online.
Exclusive: Visit www.UltimateScholarshipBook.com and enter code SI197712 for updates on this award.

(1978) • Russ Brannen/KENT FEEDS Memorial Beef Scholarship

Iowa Foundation for Agricultural Advancement
Winner's Circle Scholarships
c/o SGI
30805 595th Avenue
Cambridge, IA 50046
Phone: 515-685-3719
Email: linda@slweldon.net
http://www.iowastatefair.org
Purpose: To aid incoming freshmen at Iowa four-year colleges and universities.
Eligibility: Applicants must be incoming freshmen at an Iowa four-year college or university. They must have been actively involved in FFA beef cattle projects. Preference will be given to applicants who have experience in cattle showmanship contest and expositions. Selection is based on livestock project participation, academic merit and leadership.
Target applicants: High school students.
Amount: $1,000.
Number of awards: 1.
Deadline: June 1.
How to apply: Applications are available online. An application form, extracurricular activities list and personal essay are required.
Exclusive: Visit www.UltimateScholarshipBook.com and enter code IO197812 for updates on this award.

(1979) • Ruth Lutes Bachmann Scholarship

Grand Lodge of Missouri: Ancient, Free and Accepted Masons
6033 Masonic Drive
Suite B
Columbia, MO 65202
Phone: 573-474-8561
Email: grlodge@momason.org
http://www.momason.org/programs.asp
Purpose: To aid Missouri high school seniors who are planning to become nurses or school teachers.
Eligibility: Applicants must have plans to pursue higher education in nursing or school teaching. Selection is based on academic merit and promise.
Target applicants: High school students.
Amount: Varies.
Number of awards: Varies.
Deadline: March 31.
How to apply: Applications are available online. An application form, personal statement, transcript and standardized test scores are required.
Exclusive: Visit www.UltimateScholarshipBook.com and enter code GR197912 for updates on this award.

(1980) • Safety Essay Contest

American Legion, Department of New Jersey
135 W. Hanover Street
Trenton, NJ 08618
Phone: 609-695-5418
Fax: 609-394-1532
Email: adjudant@njamericanlegion.org
http://www.njamericanlegion.org
Purpose: To award students for exceptional essays regarding safety.
Eligibility: Applicants must be in the 6th, 7th or 8th grade and enrolled in a New Jersey school.
Target applicants: Junior high students or younger.

Amount: Varies.
Number of awards: Varies.
Deadline: Varies.
How to apply: Application information is available from the local Department.
Exclusive: Visit www.UltimateScholarshipBook.com and enter code AM198012 for updates on this award.

(1981) • Sallie Mae Bank Scholarships

Sallie Mae Bank
P.O. Box 9500
Wilkes-Barre, PA 18773-9500
Phone: 703-984-5628
http://www.salliemae.com/content/salliemaebank
Purpose: To provide financial assistance to engineering, nursing and teaching students.
Eligibility: Applicants must be undergraduate students who are majoring in engineering, nursing or teaching. They must provide proof of application and acceptance from an approved, accredited institution of higher learning in Salt Lake County or Utah County, Utah. Students enrolling in an online school must provide proof of residence in one of these counties.
Target applicants: High school students. College students. Adult students.
Amount: $5,000.
Number of awards: 15.
Deadline: March 31.
How to apply: Applications are available from financial aid departments of qualifying schools.
Exclusive: Visit www.UltimateScholarshipBook.com and enter code SA198112 for updates on this award.

(1982) • San Antonio Chapter NAWIC Scholarship

National Association of Women in Construction - San Antonio Chapter
c/o Becky Wynne
4315 Sandy Crest
San Antonio, TX 78217
http://www.nawicsatx.org
Purpose: To aid female Texas students who are pursuing higher education in a construction-related subject.
Eligibility: Applicants must be Texas residents or non-residents who are attending school in Texas and must be full-time students. They must be studying a construction-related subject and must have a GPA of 3.0 or higher on a four-point scale. Selection is based on the overall strength of the application.
Target applicants: College students. Adult students.
Minimum GPA: 3.0
Amount: Varies.
Number of awards: Varies.
Scholarship may be renewable.
Deadline: December 1.
How to apply: Applications are available online. An application form, transcript and one or more letters of recommendation are required.
Exclusive: Visit www.UltimateScholarshipBook.com and enter code NA198212 for updates on this award.

(1983) • San Francisco Section Daniel Cubicciotti Student Award

Electrochemical Society
65 South Main Street, Building D
Pennington, NJ 08534-2839
Phone: 609-737-1902
Fax: 609-737-2743
Email: awards@electrochem.org
http://www.electrochem.org
Purpose: To help a deserving student in Northern California to pursue a career in the physical sciences or engineering.
Eligibility: Applicants must be full- or part-time graduate or advanced undergraduate students in good standing at a university or college in Northern California. Students must major in metallurgy, materials science, chemical engineering or chemistry and be involved in thesis research or other academic activities that relate to electrochemistry. Applicants may be nominated by anyone familiar with their qualifications. The applicant does not have to be a member of The Electrochemical Society. The award is based on academic excellence, quality of research activities, a demonstrated interest in the study of electrochemistry and personal characteristics that reflect Dan Cubicciotti's integrity. Community service and participation in other activities will also be considered.
Target applicants: College students. Graduate school students. Adult students.
Amount: $500-$2,000.
Number of awards: 1.
Deadline: February 15.
How to apply: Applicants should submit transcripts, a short description of their history and interests and a letter of recommendation from a university or college faculty member from the appropriate department.
Exclusive: Visit www.UltimateScholarshipBook.com and enter code EL198312 for updates on this award.

(1984) • Sara E. Jenne Scholarship

Montana State Elks Association
P.O. Box 1274
Polson, MT 59860
Phone: 406-849-5276
Email: robert058@centurytel.net
http://www.elksmt.com
Purpose: To support undergraduate students in Montana.
Eligibility: Students must have completed one year of college or technical school with at least 30 semester hours, and they must have at least a 2.0 GPA. Applicants must show financial need and good character.
Target applicants: College students. Adult students.
Minimum GPA: 2.0
Amount: Varies.
Number of awards: Varies.
Deadline: Varies.
How to apply: Applications are available online.
Exclusive: Visit www.UltimateScholarshipBook.com and enter code MO198412 for updates on this award.

(1985) • Scan | Design Foundation by Inger and Jens Bruun Scholarship for Study in Denmark

Northwest Danish Foundation
Meridian Office Building
1833 North 105th Street, Suite 203
Seattle, WA 98133

Phone: 800-564-7736
Fax: 206-729-6997
Email: seattle@nwdanish.org
http://www.northwestdanishfoundation.org
Purpose: To provide funds for students who wish to study in Denmark.
Eligibility: Applicants must be 18 years of age or older and be Washington or Oregon residents or students who wish to study in Denmark. They may pursue academic, vocational, cultural or artistic studies.
Target applicants: High school students. College students. Adult students.
Amount: $5,000.
Number of awards: 1.
Deadline: March 31.
How to apply: Applications are available online.
Exclusive: Visit www.UltimateScholarshipBook.com and enter code NO198512 for updates on this award.

(1986) • Schlutz Family Beef Breeding Scholarship

Iowa Foundation for Agricultural Advancement
Winner's Circle Scholarships
c/o SGI
30805 595th Avenue
Cambridge, IA 50046
Phone: 515-685-3719
Email: linda@slweldon.net
http://www.iowastatefair.org
Purpose: To aid Iowa entering undergraduate freshmen who have experience in beef projects.
Eligibility: Applicants must be rising undergraduate freshmen at an Iowa postsecondary institution. They must have experience in beef projects and activities. Preference will be given to applicants who demonstrate an interest in continuing an involvement in the beef cattle industry after graduation from college. Selection is based on the overall strength of the application.
Target applicants: High school students.
Amount: $1,000.
Number of awards: 1.
Deadline: June 1.
How to apply: Applications are available online. An application form and supporting materials are required.
Exclusive: Visit www.UltimateScholarshipBook.com and enter code IO198612 for updates on this award.

(1987) • Schneider-Emanuel American Legion Scholarship

American Legion, Department of Wisconsin
2930 American Legion Drive
P.O. Box 388
Portage, WI 53901
Phone: 608-745-1090
Fax: 608-745-0179
Email: info@wilegion.org
http://www.wilegion.org
Purpose: To award scholarships to American Legion members and their children or grandchildren and members of the Sons of the American Legion or Auxiliary.
Eligibility: Applicants must have graduated from an accredited Wisconsin high school and plan to earn an undergraduate degree at a U.S. college or university. Applicants must also have participated in one or more American Legion-sponsored activities listed in the eligibility requirements.
Target applicants: High school students. College students. Adult students.
Minimum GPA: 3.0
Amount: $1,000.
Number of awards: 3.
Deadline: March 1.
How to apply: Applications are available online.
Exclusive: Visit www.UltimateScholarshipBook.com and enter code AM198712 for updates on this award.

(1988) • Scholarships for Academic Excellence

New York State Higher Education Services Corporation (HESC)
99 Washington Avenue
Albany, NY 12255
Phone: 888-697-4372
Email: hescwebmail@hesc.org
http://www.hesc.com/content.nsf/
Purpose: To assist outstanding New York State high school graduates.
Eligibility: Applicants must be New York residents who are high school seniors, plan to study at an eligible undergraduate program in New York State and are U.S. citizens or eligible noncitizens. Selection is based on grades in Regents exams.
Target applicants: High school students.
Amount: $500-$1,500.
Number of awards: 8,000.
Scholarship may be renewable.
Deadline: Varies.
How to apply: Students are nominated by their high schools.
Exclusive: Visit www.UltimateScholarshipBook.com and enter code NE198812 for updates on this award.

(1989) • Scholarships for Orphans of Veterans

New Hampshire Postsecondary Education Commission
3 Barrell Court
Suite 300
Concord, NH 03301
Phone: 603-271-2555 x352
Fax: 603-271-2696
Email: jknapp@pec.state.nh.us
http://www.state.nh.us/postsecondary
Purpose: To provide financial assistance to children of veterans of armed conflict who died while on active duty or from a service-related disability.
Eligibility: Applicants must be New Hampshire residents between the ages of 16 and 25, enrolled in college at least half-time at a New Hampshire public institution of higher learning and have a parent or parents who died while on active duty or from service-related disability.
Target applicants: High school students. College students.
Amount: Up to $2,500.
Number of awards: Varies.
Scholarship may be renewable.
How to apply: Applications are available by phone.
Exclusive: Visit www.UltimateScholarshipBook.com and enter code NE198912 for updates on this award.

(1990) • Scholarships in Mathematics Education

Illinois Council of Teachers of Mathematics
ICTM Scholarship
c/o Sue and Randy Pippen

24807 Winterberry Lane
Plainfield, IL 60585
http://www.ictm.org/scholarship.html
Purpose: To aid Illinois mathematics education students.
Eligibility: Applicants must be enrolled at an accredited Illinois postsecondary institution in an undergraduate mathematics education curriculum that provides preparation for becoming a teacher. They must be rising juniors or seniors who have a GPA of 3.0 or higher on a four-point scale. Applicants must be pursuing a first bachelor's degree. Selection is based on the overall strength of the application.
Target applicants: College students. Adult students.
Minimum GPA: 3.0
Amount: $1,500.
Number of awards: 2-5.
Deadline: March 6.
How to apply: Applications are available online. An application form, lesson planning form, personal essay, two recommendation letters and a transcript are required.
Exclusive: Visit www.UltimateScholarshipBook.com and enter code IL199012 for updates on this award.

(1991) • Science or Other Studies Scholarship

Los Alamos National Laboratory Foundation
1302 Calle de la Merced
Suite A
Espanola, NM 87532
Phone: 505-753-8890
Fax: 505-753-8915
Email: info@lanlfoundation.org
http://www.lanlfoundation.org
Purpose: To support undergraduate students in Northern New Mexico.
Eligibility: Students must have at least a 3.25 GPA, and they must have either an SAT score of at least 1350 or an ACT score of at least 19. Applicants must submit an essay and two letters of recommendation.
Target applicants: High school students. College students. Adult students.
Minimum GPA: 3.25
Amount: $1,000-$2,500.
Number of awards: Varies.
Scholarship may be renewable.
Deadline: January 18.
How to apply: Applications are available online.
Exclusive: Visit www.UltimateScholarshipBook.com and enter code LO199112 for updates on this award.

(1992) • Secondary Education Scholarships

California Mathematics Council - Southern Section
Dr. Sik Kolpas, CMC-S Scholarships
Glendale Community College Math Department
1500 N. Verdugo Road
Glendale, CA 91208-2894
Phone: 888-CMC-MATH
Email: skolpas@glendale.edu
http://www.cmc-math.org
Purpose: To encourage students to pursue careers in math education.
Eligibility: Applicants must reside, teach or attend school in one of the following California counties: Imperial, Los Angeles, Orange, Riverside, San Bernardino, San Diego, Santa Barbara or Ventura. They must be accepted into a secondary credential program at an accredited college or university in Southern California and have an undergraduate degree in work toward a single subject credential in mathematics.
Target applicants: Graduate school students. Adult students.
Amount: $100-$2,000.
Number of awards: Varies.
Deadline: January 31.
How to apply: Applications are available online. An application form, transcript and three letters of recommendation are required.
Exclusive: Visit www.UltimateScholarshipBook.com and enter code CA199212 for updates on this award.

(1993) • Senator George J. Mitchell Scholarship Research Institute Scholarships

Mitchell Institute
22 Monument Square, Suite 200
Portland, ME 04101
Phone: 888-220-7209
Email: info@mitchellinstitute.org
http://www.mitchellinstitute.org
Purpose: To provide educational opportunities to students in Maine.
Eligibility: Applicants must be legal residents of Maine graduating from a public high school in Maine and attending a two- or four-year program at an accredited college. Scholarships are based on academic performance, community service and financial need. One scholarship is given out at every Maine public high school, with one extra scholarship per county intended for first-generation college students. While the deadline for the application is April 1, supporting materials have a deadline of May 1.
Target applicants: High school students.
Amount: $1,250-$1,500.
Number of awards: 1.
Scholarship may be renewable.
Deadline: April 1.
How to apply: Applications are available online.
Exclusive: Visit www.UltimateScholarshipBook.com and enter code MI199312 for updates on this award.

(1994) • Senator Patricia K. McGee Nursing Faculty Scholarship

New York State Higher Education Services Corporation (HESC)
99 Washington Avenue
Albany, NY 12255
Phone: 888-697-4372
Email: hescwebmail@hesc.org
http://www.hesc.com/content.nsf/
Purpose: To increase the number of nursing educators and clinical faculty members in the State of New York.
Eligibility: Applicants must be U.S. citizens or eligible non-citizens and residents of New York for one year or more. They must be registered nurses who are licensed in New York, and they must be accepted into a graduate nursing program at an approved college or university in New York. Students must also agree to four years of service as nursing faculty in the state.
Target applicants: Graduate school students. Adult students.
Amount: Up to $20,000.
Number of awards: Varies.
Scholarship may be renewable.
Deadline: June 15.
How to apply: Applications are available online after June of each year.
Exclusive: Visit www.UltimateScholarshipBook.com and enter code NE199412 for updates on this award.

(1995) • Senatorial Scholarship

Maryland Higher Education Commission
Office of Student Financial Assistance
839 Bestgate Road, Suite 400
Annapolis, MD 21401
Phone: 800-974-1024
Fax: 410-260-3200
Email: osfamail@mhec.state.md.us
http://www.mhec.state.md.us

Purpose: To assist Maryland undergraduate and graduate students who can demonstrate financial need.

Eligibility: Applicants must be U.S. citizens or eligible noncitizens, legal residents of the state of Maryland and complete the Free Application for Federal Student Aid (FAFSA). Some senators have supplementary forms. Contact your area's senator's office for complete details. All applicants must enroll at a two- or four-year Maryland college or university as degree-seeking undergraduate or graduate student, or attend certain private career schools. Applicants must show financial need. High school applicants must also take the SAT I or the ACT.

Target applicants: High school students. College students. Graduate school students. Adult students.

Amount: $400-$9,000.

Number of awards: Varies.

Scholarship may be renewable.

Deadline: Varies.

How to apply: Complete and file the Free Application for Federal Student Aid (FAFSA). Contact senator for specific application forms. The Office of Student Financial Assistance (OSFA) can provide a list of all State legislators.

Exclusive: Visit www.UltimateScholarshipBook.com and enter code MA199512 for updates on this award.

(1996) • Service League Nursing Scholarship

Akron General Medical Center
400 Wabash Avenue
Akron, OH 44307
Phone: 330-344-6000
http://www.agmc.org

Purpose: To aid Ohio nursing school students.

Eligibility: Applicants must be enrolled in or accepted into an accredited school of nursing located in Ohio. They must be pursuing a bachelor's degree in nursing and must have a GPA of 3.0 or higher. Selection is based on academic achievement and financial need.

Target applicants: High school students. College students. Adult students.

Minimum GPA: 3.0

Amount: Varies.

Number of awards: Varies.

Deadline: March 1.

How to apply: Applications are available online. An application form, personal statement, official transcript, income tax information and three reference letters are required.

Exclusive: Visit www.UltimateScholarshipBook.com and enter code AK199612 for updates on this award.

(1997) • SGT Felix Delgreco Jr. Scholarship

Connecticut National Guard Foundation Inc.
State Armory
360 Broad Street
Hartford, CT 06105
Phone: 860-241-1550
Fax: 860-293-2929
Email: scholarship.committee@ctngfoundation.org
http://www.ctngfoundation.org/Scholarship.asp

Purpose: To provide financial assistance to children of Connecticut National Guard members.

Eligibility: Applicants must be sons or daughters of a member of the Connecticut Army National Guard. They must be enrolled in or plan to attend an accredited degree or technical program.

Target applicants: High school students. College students. Adult students.

Amount: $3,000.

Number of awards: 1.

Deadline: March 15.

How to apply: Applications are available online.

Exclusive: Visit www.UltimateScholarshipBook.com and enter code CO199712 for updates on this award.

(1998) • Sharon D. Banks Memorial Undergraduate Scholarship

Women's Transportation Seminar - Puget Sound Chapter
P.O. Box 3461
Bellevue, WA 98009
Phone: 206-802-1730
Email: koverleese@shorelinewa.gov
http://www.wtsinternational.org

Purpose: To support female undergraduates who are preparing for careers in the field of transportation.

Eligibility: Applicants must be female undergraduates who are enrolled in a transportation-related degree program (such as transportation finance, engineering, logistics or planning). They must have a GPA of 3.0 or higher and must have plans to pursue a transportation-related career. Selection is based on academic merit, stated career goals and extracurricular activities.

Target applicants: College students. Adult students.

Minimum GPA: 3.0

Amount: $4,000.

Number of awards: 1.

Deadline: November 23.

How to apply: Applications are available online. An application form, official transcript, one recommendation letter, personal statement and proof of college enrollment are required.

Exclusive: Visit www.UltimateScholarshipBook.com and enter code WO199812 for updates on this award.

(1999) • Shirely McKown Scholarship Fund

Hawaii Community Foundation - Scholarships
1164 Bishop Street, Suite 800
Honolulu, HI 96813
Phone: 888-731-3863
Fax: 808-521-6286
Email: scholarships@hcf-hawaii.org
http://www.hawaiicommunityfoundation.org

Purpose: To support Hawaii students who are majoring in journalism, advertising or public relations.

Eligibility: Applicants must be attending a four-year college or university with at least a 3.0 GPA. They must be college juniors, college seniors or graduate students.

Target applicants: College students. Graduate school students. Adult students.

Minimum GPA: 3.0

Amount: Varies.

Number of awards: Varies.
Deadline: March 1.
How to apply: To apply, register online, complete the online application and select the scholarships to which you wish to apply. In addition, mail the supporting materials: printed confirmation page from the online application, personal statement, copy of Student Aid Report (SAR) available at www.fafsa.ed.gov and official transcript.
Exclusive: Visit www.UltimateScholarshipBook.com and enter code HA199912 for updates on this award.

(2000) • Shoe City-WB54/WB50 Scholarship

Central Scholarship Bureau
1700 Reisterstown Road
Suite 220
Baltimore, MD 21208-2903
Phone: 410-415-5558
Fax: 410-415-5501
Email: info@centralsb.org
http://www.centralsb.org
Purpose: To help high school seniors who live in Maryland or Washington, DC.
Eligibility: Applicants must be permanent residents of Maryland or Washington, DC, plan to attend an accredited college or university full-time and demonstrate financial need. An application, budget form, school bill, transcript, school financial aid award letter and essay are required. Selection is based on financial need, teamwork/community service and academic excellence.
Target applicants: High school students.
Amount: $1,500.
Number of awards: 4.
Deadline: May 10.
How to apply: Applications are available online.
Exclusive: Visit www.UltimateScholarshipBook.com and enter code CE200012 for updates on this award.

(2001) • Shook Construction Harry F. Gaeke Memorial Scholarship

Associated General Contractors of Ohio
1755 Northwest Boulevard
Columbus, OH 43212
Phone: 614-486-6446
Fax: 614-486-6498
Email: web@agcohio.com
http://www.agcohio.com
Purpose: To aid students preparing for careers in the construction industry.
Eligibility: Applicants must be U.S. citizens either living in or attending school in Ohio, Kentucky or Indiana. They must be in at least the second year of an undergraduate degree program that is related to construction and have a GPA of 2.5 or higher. Selection is based on the overall strength of the application.
Target applicants: College students. Adult students.
Minimum GPA: 2.5
Amount: Varies.
Number of awards: 1.
Deadline: March 31.
How to apply: Applications are available online. An application form, transcript and personal essay are required.
Exclusive: Visit www.UltimateScholarshipBook.com and enter code AS200112 for updates on this award.

(2002) • Shuichi, Katsu and Itsuyo Suga Scholarship

Hawaii Community Foundation - Scholarships
1164 Bishop Street, Suite 800
Honolulu, HI 96813
Phone: 888-731-3863
Fax: 808-521-6286
Email: scholarships@hcf-hawaii.org
http://www.hawaiicommunityfoundation.org
Purpose: To support Hawaii students who are majoring in math, physics or science and technology.
Eligibility: Applicants must have at least a 3.0 GPA.
Target applicants: High school students. College students. Adult students.
Minimum GPA: 3.0
Amount: Varies.
Number of awards: Varies.
Deadline: March 1.
How to apply: To apply, register online, complete the online application and select the scholarships to which you wish to apply. In addition, mail the supporting materials: printed confirmation page from the online application, personal statement, copy of Student Aid Report (SAR) available at www.fafsa.ed.gov and official transcript.
Exclusive: Visit www.UltimateScholarshipBook.com and enter code HA200212 for updates on this award.

(2003) • Silver Knight Award

Miami Herald and El Herald Newspapers
One Herald Plaza
Miami, FL 33132
Phone: 305-376-2905
Email: silverknight@miamiherald.com
http://www.miamiherald.com/silverknights/
Purpose: To recognize students for their academic achievement and contributions to their school and community.
Eligibility: Applicants must be high school seniors in Miami-Dade and Broward counties in Florida and be nominated by their schools.
Target applicants: High school students.
Amount: $500-$2,000.
Number of awards: Varies.
Deadline: January 24.
How to apply: Contact your high school guidance counselor.
Exclusive: Visit www.UltimateScholarshipBook.com and enter code MI200312 for updates on this award.

(2004) • Sister Helen Marie Pellicer Scholarship

Florida Dietetic Association
Scholarship Chair
P.O. Box 12608
Tallahassee, FL 32317
Phone: 850-386-8850
Fax: 850-386-7918
Email: cstapell@eatrightflorida.org
http://www.eatrightflorida.org
Purpose: To aid Florida dietetics students.
Eligibility: Applicants must be U.S. citizens or permanent residents, Florida residents and undergraduate upperclassmen who are majoring in dietetics. They must have a GPA of 2.5 or higher on a four-point scale. Selection is based on the overall strength of the application.
Target applicants: College students. Adult students.
Minimum GPA: 2.5

Amount: $1,000.
Number of awards: 1.
Deadline: November 1.
How to apply: Applications are available online. An application form, official transcript and two recommendation letters are required.
Exclusive: Visit www.UltimateScholarshipBook.com and enter code FL200412 for updates on this award.

(2005) • Sister Mary Petronia Van Straten Scholarship

Wisconsin Mathematics Council Inc.
W175 N11117 Stonewood Drive
Suite 204
Germantown, WI 53022
Phone: 262-437-0174
Fax: 262-532-2430
Email: wmc@wismath.org
http://www.wismath.org
Purpose: To aid Wisconsin teacher education students.
Eligibility: Applicants must be Wisconsin legal residents, be enrolled in a teacher education program and have completed or be in the process of completing a course in mathematics teaching methods. They must have a GPA of 3.0 or higher. Selection is based on the overall strength of the application.
Target applicants: College students. Adult students.
Minimum GPA: 3.0
Amount: $2,000.
Number of awards: 1.
Deadline: March 1.
How to apply: Applications are available online. An application form, official transcript, two letters of recommendation, a plan of study and a personal essay are required.
Exclusive: Visit www.UltimateScholarshipBook.com and enter code WI200512 for updates on this award.

(2006) • Six Meter Club of Chicago Scholarship

American Radio Relay League Foundation
225 Main Street
Newington, CT 06111
Phone: 860-594-0397
Fax: 860-594-0259
Email: foundation@arrl.org
http://www.arrlf.org
Purpose: To support Illinois residents who are involved in amateur radio.
Eligibility: Applicants must have an active amateur radio license in any class. Students must be enrolled in an Illinois university or technical school for undergraduate study.
Target applicants: High school students. College students. Adult students.
Amount: $500.
Number of awards: 1.
Deadline: February 1.
How to apply: Applications are available online.
Exclusive: Visit www.UltimateScholarshipBook.com and enter code AM200612 for updates on this award.

(2007) • Skandalaris Family Foundation Scholarships

Skandalaris Family Foundation
840 West Long Lake Road
Suite 601
Troy, MI 48098
Phone: 248-220-2004
Fax: 248-220-2038
Email: info@skandalaris.com
http://www.skandalaris.com
Purpose: To recognize students for their special talents, leadership skills, values and commitment to excellence.
Eligibility: Applicants must be U.S. citizens and high school seniors who have a GPA of 3.5 or higher and an ACT score of 27 or higher, or an SAT score of 1200 or higher. Involvement in school, sports and community service is also considered. Most scholarships are granted to Michigan residents.
Target applicants: High school students.
Minimum GPA: 3.5
Amount: Varies.
Number of awards: Varies.
Scholarship may be renewable.
Deadline: May 1.
How to apply: Applications are available online.
Exclusive: Visit www.UltimateScholarshipBook.com and enter code SK200712 for updates on this award.

(2008) • Society of American Military Engineers Arkansas Post Scholarships

Society of American Military Engineers-Arkansas Post
P.O. Box 867
Little Rock, AR 72203-0867
Phone: 501-324-5842 x1064
Email: craig.pierce@usace.army.mil
http://www.same.org/arkansas
Purpose: To aid architecture and engineering students.
Eligibility: Applicants must be Arkansas high school seniors, be U.S. citizens or permanent residents and have applied to a college offering a four- to five-year architectural or engineering program or a college with a cooperative program to transfer credits to such a school. Scholarship winners must be accepted to an architecture or construction-related engineering program to receive funds.
Target applicants: High school students.
Amount: $1,000.
Number of awards: 2.
Deadline: March 31.
How to apply: Applications are available online. An application form, transcript, essay and letter of recommendation from a math or science teacher are required.
Exclusive: Visit www.UltimateScholarshipBook.com and enter code SO200812 for updates on this award.

(2009) • Society of American Military Engineers, Albuquerque Post Scholarship

New Mexico Engineering Foundation
P.O. Box 3828
Albuquerque, NM 87190
Email: info@nmef.net
http://www.nmef.net
Purpose: To support New Mexico students who plan to pursue college degrees in science, engineering or mathematics.
Eligibility: Applicants must be high school seniors and residents of New Mexico. They must plan to enroll in a math, science or engineering undergraduate degree program. Selection is based on academic achievement, leadership experiences at school, involvement in the community and financial need.

Target applicants: High school students.
Amount: $1,000.
Number of awards: 1.
Deadline: March 1.
How to apply: Applications are available online. An application form, a transcript and one letter of recommendation are required.
Exclusive: Visit www.UltimateScholarshipBook.com and enter code NE200912 for updates on this award.

(2010) • Sol J. Barer Scholarship in Life Sciences

Independent College Fund of New Jersey
797 Springfield Avenue
Summit, NJ 07901
Phone: 908-277-3424
Fax: 908-277-0851
Email: scholarships@njcolleges.org
http://www.njcolleges.org
Purpose: To aid life sciences students who are attending a New Jersey independent college or university.
Eligibility: Applicants must be rising undergraduate juniors or seniors at a New Jersey independent college or university. They must be majoring in one of the life sciences and have a GPA of 3.25 or higher on a four-point scale. Selection is based on academic merit and career potential.
Target applicants: College students. Adult students.
Minimum GPA: 3.25
Amount: $2,500.
Number of awards: 3.
Deadline: March 31.
How to apply: Applications are available online. An application form, transcript, resume, one recommendation letter and personal statement are required.
Exclusive: Visit www.UltimateScholarshipBook.com and enter code IN201012 for updates on this award.

(2011) • South Carolina Farm Bureau Foundation Scholarships

South Carolina Farm Bureau Foundation
P.O. Box 754
Columbia, SC 29202
Email: sanderson@scfb.org
http://www.scfb.org
Purpose: To aid agriculture students from South Carolina Farm Bureau member families.
Eligibility: Applicants must be from a South Carolina Farm Bureau member family. They must be rising undergraduate sophomores, juniors or seniors. They must be majoring in agriculture or a related subject. Selection is based on commitment to the field of agriculture, character and demonstrated leadership ability.
Target applicants: College students. Adult students.
Amount: $1,000.
Number of awards: 4.
Deadline: April 30.
How to apply: Applications are available by request from the South Carolina Farm Bureau. An application form and supporting materials are required.
Exclusive: Visit www.UltimateScholarshipBook.com and enter code SO201112 for updates on this award.

(2012) • South Carolina Hope Scholarship

South Carolina Commission on Higher Education
1333 Main Street
Suite 200
Columbia, SC 29201
Phone: 803-737-2260
Fax: 803-737-2297
Email: shubbard@che.sc.gov
http://www.che400.state.sc.us
Purpose: Monetary assistance is provided to those freshmen who do not qualify for LIFE or Palmetto Fellows Scholarships.
Eligibility: Applicants must attend an eligible South Carolina public or private college full-time, be South Carolina residents and have a minimum 3.0 GPA. The award is only applicable to the first year of college.
Target applicants: High school students.
Minimum GPA: 3.0
Amount: Up to $2,800.
Number of awards: Varies.
Deadline: Varies.
How to apply: Your college will determine your eligibility based on your high school transcript. There is no application form.
Exclusive: Visit www.UltimateScholarshipBook.com and enter code SO201212 for updates on this award.

(2013) • South Carolina Nurses Foundation Nurses Care Scholarship

South Carolina Nurses Foundation Inc.
Chairperson, SCNF Awards Committee
1821 Gadsden Street
Columbia, SC 29201
http://www.scnursesfoundation.org
Purpose: To aid South Carolina nursing students.
Eligibility: Applicants must be South Carolina residents and be enrolled in an undergraduate registered nurse (RN) degree program or a graduate degree program in nursing. They must be in good academic standing, have plans to practice nursing in South Carolina after graduation and must demonstrate financial need. Selection is based on the overall strength of the application.
Target applicants: College students. Graduate school students. Adult students.
Amount: $1,500.
Number of awards: 15.
Deadline: May 30.
How to apply: Applications are available online. An application form, personal statement, transcript and two recommendation letters are required.
Exclusive: Visit www.UltimateScholarshipBook.com and enter code SO201312 for updates on this award.

(2014) • South Carolina Tuition Grants Program

South Carolina Tuition Grants Commission
101 Business Park Boulevard
Suite 2100
Columbia, SC 29203
Phone: 803-896-1120
Fax: 803-896-1126
Email: info@sctuitiongrants.org
http://www.sctuitiongrants.com

Purpose: To assist students who wish to attend independent South Carolina colleges.
Eligibility: Students must be legal residents of South Carolina with financial need. High school seniors must graduate in the top 75 percent of their class or score a minimum of 900 on the SAT or 19 on the ACT. College applicants must complete and pass a minimum of 24 semester hours each year.
Target applicants: High school students. College students. Adult students.
Amount: Varies.
Number of awards: Varies.
Scholarship may be renewable.
Deadline: June 30.
How to apply: Fill out the FAFSA, which is available online.
Exclusive: Visit www.UltimateScholarshipBook.com and enter code SO201412 for updates on this award.

(2015) • South Carolina Tuition Program for Children of Certain War Veterans

South Carolina Office of Veterans Affairs
VA Regional Office Building, Room 141
1801 Assembly Street
Columbia, SC 29201
Phone: 803-255-4255
Fax: 803-255-4257
Email: va@oepp.sc.gov
http://www.govoepp.state.sc.us/vetaff.htm
Purpose: To support the children of war veterans.
Eligibility: Veterans must have been killed, injured, taken prisoner, pronounced missing in action or awarded the Purple Heart or Congressional Medal of Honor. Students must attend a state-supported college, university or technical school in South Carolina. Applicants must be 25 years old or younger.
Target applicants: High school students. College students.
Amount: Full Tuition Waiver.
Number of awards: Varies.
Scholarship may be renewable.
Deadline: Varies.
How to apply: Applications are available online.
Exclusive: Visit www.UltimateScholarshipBook.com and enter code SO201512 for updates on this award.

(2016) • South Dakota Free Tuition for Children of Residents Who Died During Service in the Armed Forces

South Dakota Board of Regents
306 East Capitol Ave, Suite 200
Pierre, SD 57501-2545
Phone: 605-773-3455
Fax: 605-773-5320
Email: info@sdbor.edu
http://www.sdbor.edu
Purpose: To provide education assistance to children whose parents died during service in the United States military.
Eligibility: Applicants must be South Dakota residents who are under the age of 25. The deceased parent must have been a resident of South Dakota for at least six months before entering the service and must have died while enlisted from any cause.
Target applicants: High school students. College students.
Amount: Full Tuition.
Number of awards: Varies.
Scholarship may be renewable.
Deadline: Varies.
How to apply: Applications are available from your financial aid office.
Exclusive: Visit www.UltimateScholarshipBook.com and enter code SO201612 for updates on this award.

(2017) • South Dakota Free Tuition for Dependents of Prisoners or Missing in Action

South Dakota Board of Regents
306 East Capitol Ave, Suite 200
Pierre, SD 57501-2545
Phone: 605-773-3455
Fax: 605-773-5320
Email: info@sdbor.edu
http://www.sdbor.edu
Purpose: To provide assistance for children of prisoners of war and those missing in action.
Eligibility: Applicants must be children of veterans who were declared POW or MIA. They may receive benefits for up to eight semesters or twelve quarters.
Target applicants: High school students. College students. Adult students.
Amount: Full Tuition.
Number of awards: Varies.
Scholarship may be renewable.
Deadline: Varies.
How to apply: Applications are available online.
Exclusive: Visit www.UltimateScholarshipBook.com and enter code SO201712 for updates on this award.

(2018) • South Dakota Free Tuition for Survivors of Deceased Fire Fighters, Certified Law Enforcement Officers and Emergency Medical Technicians

South Dakota Board of Regents
306 East Capitol Ave, Suite 200
Pierre, SD 57501-2545
Phone: 605-773-3455
Fax: 605-773-5320
Email: info@sdbor.edu
http://www.sdbor.edu
Purpose: To provide financial assistance to students who are survivors of public servants who died while on duty.
Eligibility: Applicants must be survivors of firefighters, law enforcement officers or emergency medical technicians who died as a result of injuries received while on official duty. They must be seeking a bachelor's or vocational degree, and funding is only available to those who earn such degrees within a 36-month or eight semester period.
Target applicants: High school students. College students. Adult students.
Amount: Full Tuition.
Number of awards: Varies.
Scholarship may be renewable.
Deadline: Varies.
How to apply: Applications are available from your financial aid office.
Exclusive: Visit www.UltimateScholarshipBook.com and enter code SO201812 for updates on this award.

(2019) · South Dakota Free Tuition for Veterans and Others Who Performed War Service

South Dakota Board of Regents
306 East Capitol Ave, Suite 200
Pierre, SD 57501-2545
Phone: 605-773-3455
Fax: 605-773-5320
Email: info@sdbor.edu
http://www.sdbor.edu

Purpose: To allow veterans and others who served in war the opportunity to receive higher education.
Eligibility: Applicants must be veterans or others who performed active war service. They must South Dakota residents who qualify for resident tuition and not be entitled to have their tuition or expenses paid by the United States.
Target applicants: High school students. College students. Graduate school students. Adult students.
Amount: Full Tuition.
Number of awards: Varies.
Scholarship may be renewable.
Deadline: Varies.
How to apply: Applications are available from your financial aid office.
Exclusive: Visit www.UltimateScholarshipBook.com and enter code SO201912 for updates on this award.

(2020) · Southern Scholarship Foundation Scholarship

Southern Scholarship Foundation
322 Stadium Drive
Tallahassee, FL 32304
Phone: 850-222-3833
Fax: 850-222-6750
Email: ssmith@southernscholarship.org
http://www.southernscholarship.org

Purpose: To provide rent-free housing scholarships to students attending Florida State, University of Florida, Florida A&M, Bethune-Cookman or Florida Gulf Coast University.
Eligibility: Applicants must have financial need, have a minimum 3.0 high school GPA or 2.85 college GPA, demonstrate high character and attend or plan to attend Florida State, the University of Florida, Florida Gulf Coast University, Florida A&M or Bethune-Cookman.
Target applicants: High school students. College students. Adult students.
Minimum GPA: 2.85
Amount: Varies.
Number of awards: Varies.
Scholarship may be renewable.
Deadline: March 1.
How to apply: Applications are available online.
Exclusive: Visit www.UltimateScholarshipBook.com and enter code SO202012 for updates on this award.

(2021) · Southside Tobacco Forgiveness Loan

Southwest Virginia Higher Education Center
P.O. Box 1987
Arlington, VA 24212
Phone: 276-619-4300
Fax: 276-619-4309
Email: educationinfo@swcenter.edu
http://www.swcenter.edu

Purpose: To support students from the Southside region of Virginia.
Eligibility: Applicants must be attending a public or private four-year college. They must be permanent residents of one of the 24 Southside areas, and they must have been residents of Virginia for at least 12 months. Students must agree to work in the Southside region after graduation. Preference will be given to applicants with the highest GPA's.
Target applicants: High school students. College students. Adult students.
Amount: Up to $3,750.
Number of awards: Varies.
Scholarship may be renewable.
Deadline: June 1.
How to apply: Applications are available online.
Exclusive: Visit www.UltimateScholarshipBook.com and enter code SO202112 for updates on this award.

(2022) · Space Coast Chapter of the Florida Surveying and Mapping Society Scholarships

Florida Surveying and Mapping Society
Space Coast Chapter
4450 West Eau Gallie Boulevard
Suite 232
Melbourne, FL 32934
Phone: 321-255-5434
Fax: 321-255-7751
Email: dirwin@creechinc.com
http://www.spacecoast-fsms.com

Purpose: To help Florida residents who are enrolled in a geomatics or land surveying degree program.
Eligibility: Applicants must be residents of Brevard County or the state of Florida. They must be pursuing a degree in land surveying or geomatics and must maintain an overall GPA of 2.5 or better and a GPA of 3.0 or better in surveying courses. Selection is based on the overall strength of the application. Preference is given to full-time students and students who are active members of the Florida Surveying and Mapping Society.
Target applicants: College students. Adult students.
Minimum GPA: 2.5
Amount: Varies.
Number of awards: Varies.
Deadline: Varies.
How to apply: Applications are available online. An application form, transcript, proof of FSMS membership (if applicable), class schedule, proof of registration and personal statement are required.
Exclusive: Visit www.UltimateScholarshipBook.com and enter code FL202212 for updates on this award.

(2023) · St. Mary-Corwin Medical Center Nightingale Scholarship

Colorado Nurses Foundation
7400 East Arapahoe Road
Suite 211
Centennial, CO 80112
Phone: 303-694-4728
Fax: 303-694-4869
Email: mail@cnfound.org
http://www.cnfound.org/

Purpose: To aid Colorado nursing students who are planning to work in Canon City, Florence, Pueblo or the surrounding area.
Eligibility: Applicants must be Colorado residents who are enrolled in an associate's, bachelor's, master's or doctoral degree program in nursing at an approved Colorado postsecondary institution. Undergraduates

must have a GPA of 3.25 or higher, and graduate students must have a GPA of 3.5 or higher. Applicants must intend to work in the Canon City, Florence or Pueblo area after graduation. Selection is based on commitment to professional practice in Colorado, community involvement, academic merit and financial need.
Target applicants: College students. Graduate school students. Adult students.
Minimum GPA: 3.25
Amount: $1,000.
Number of awards: 1.
Deadline: October 29.
How to apply: Applications are available online. An application form, resume, personal essay, transcript and two recommendation letters are required.
Exclusive: Visit www.UltimateScholarshipBook.com and enter code CO202312 for updates on this award.

(2024) • Stanley O. McNaughton Community Service Award

Independent Colleges of Washington
600 Stewart Street, Suite 600
Seattle, WA 98101
Phone: 206-623-4494
Fax: 206-625-9621
Email: info@icwashington.org
http://www.icwashington.org
Purpose: To reward students who are committed to community service and who attend an independent college of Washington.
Eligibility: Applicants must be juniors or seniors who have participated in community service in high school and college. Students attending Gonzaga University, Heritage University, Pacific Lutheran University, Saint Martin's University, Seattle Pacific University, Seattle University, University of Puget Sound, Walla Walla University, Whitman College or Whitworth University are eligible.
Target applicants: College students. Adult students.
Amount: $2,500.
Number of awards: 2.
Deadline: Varies.
How to apply: Applications are available online or from your school's financial aid office.
Exclusive: Visit www.UltimateScholarshipBook.com and enter code IN202412 for updates on this award.

(2025) • Stanley Z. Koplik Certificate of Mastery Tuition Waiver Program

Massachusetts Department of Higher Education
Office of Student Financial Assistance
454 Broadway
Suite 200
Revere, MA 02151
Phone: 617-727-9420
Fax: 617-727-0667
Email: osfa@osfa.mass.edu
http://www.osfa.mass.edu/default.asp
Purpose: To support Massachusetts students who have demonstrated academic merit.
Eligibility: Applicants must be currently enrolled in a public high school in the state of Massachusetts. Students must receive an "Advanced" score on at least one part of the 10th grade MCAS test, and they must score "Proficient" on all of the other sections. They must also have good scores on at least two AP exams, two SAT II exams or combinations of one of those tests and other achievements determined by the Koplik program. Students must maintain a 3.3 GPA while participating in the scholarship.
Target applicants: High school students.
Minimum GPA: 3.3
Amount: Up to full tuition.
Number of awards: Varies.
Deadline: Varies.
How to apply: Applications are available from high schools.
Exclusive: Visit www.UltimateScholarshipBook.com and enter code MA202512 for updates on this award.

(2026) • State Contractual Scholarship Fund Program

College Foundation of North Carolina
P.O. Box 41966
Raleigh, NC 27629
Phone: 888-234-6400
Fax: 919-821-3139
Email: programinformation@cfnc.org
http://www.cfnc.org
Purpose: To provide financial assistance to needy students attending private colleges and universities in North Carolina.
Eligibility: Applicants must be North Carolina residents who are enrolled in an undergraduate program at an approved North Carolina private postsecondary institution and have unmet financial need. They must not be enrolled in a program that is designed primarily to prepare students for religious vocations. Licensure students may also apply if they have a bachelor's degree and are enrolled in undergraduate classes in a licensure program for teachers or nurses.
Target applicants: College students. Adult students.
Amount: Varies.
Number of awards: Varies.
Deadline: Varies.
How to apply: See your financial aid office for application details.
Exclusive: Visit www.UltimateScholarshipBook.com and enter code CO202612 for updates on this award.

(2027) • State Employees Association of North Carolina (SEANC) Scholarships

State Employees Association of North Carolina
P.O. Drawer 27727
Raleigh, NC 27611
Phone: 919-833-6436
Email: rvaughan@seanc.org
http://www.seanc.org
Purpose: To provide financial assistance to SEANC members, their spouses and their children who plan to attend college.
Eligibility: Applicants must be the spouses or children of members and demonstrate either financial need or merit, or applicants must be members working full-time and enrolled in six or more semester hours of undergraduate work or three or more hours of graduate work. Students who are spouses or children must be enrolled full-time.
Target applicants: High school students. College students. Graduate school students. Adult students.
Amount: Varies.
Number of awards: Varies.
Deadline: April 15.
How to apply: Applications are available online or from your guidance counselor or financial aid office.
Exclusive: Visit www.UltimateScholarshipBook.com and enter code ST202712 for updates on this award.

(2028) • State Grant Program

Rhode Island Higher Education Assistance Authority
560 Jefferson Boulevard
Warwick, RI 02886
Phone: 401-736-1100
Fax: 401-732-3541
Email: scholarships@riheaa.org
http://www.riheaa.org

Purpose: To assist Rhode Island students with financial need.

Eligibility: Applicants must be U.S. citizens or eligible noncitizens, Rhode Island residents, enrolled or accepted for enrollment in a degree or certificate program and attend the program at least half-time.

Target applicants: High school students. College students. Adult students.

Amount: $250-$900.

Number of awards: Varies.

Deadline: March 1.

How to apply: Complete the Free Application for Federal Student Aid (FAFSA).

Exclusive: Visit www.UltimateScholarshipBook.com and enter code RH202812 for updates on this award.

(2029) • State Need Grant

Washington Higher Education Coordinating Board
917 Lakeridge Way
P.O. Box 43430
Olympia, WA 98504
Phone: 360-753-7850
Fax: 360-753-6243
Email: info@hecb.wa.gov
http://www.hecb.wa.gov

Purpose: To assist low-income students to pursue undergraduate degrees or train for new careers.

Eligibility: Applicants must be Washington residents who have a family income of 70 percent or less of the state median, enroll at least half-time as an undergraduate student in an eligible program and be pursuing a certificate, associate's degree or bachelor's degree.

Target applicants: High school students. College students. Adult students.

Amount: Up to $6,876.

Number of awards: Varies.

Deadline: Varies.

How to apply: Eligible students who have filed a Free Application for Federal Student Aid (FAFSA) are considered.

Exclusive: Visit www.UltimateScholarshipBook.com and enter code WA202912 for updates on this award.

(2030) • State Need-based Grants

South Carolina Commission on Higher Education
1333 Main Street
Suite 200
Columbia, SC 29201
Phone: 803-737-2260
Fax: 803-737-2297
Email: shubbard@che.sc.gov
http://www.che400.state.sc.us

Purpose: Monetary assistance for higher education is provided to South Carolina resident students.

Eligibility: Applicants must be obtaining their first baccalaureate or professional degree, complete the Free Application for Federal Student Aid (FAFSA) and be residents of South Carolina.

Target applicants: High school students. College students. Adult students.

Amount: $2,500.

Number of awards: Varies.

Scholarship may be renewable.

Deadline: Varies.

How to apply: Complete the FAFSA and contact your college's financial aid office if you plan to attend a public college or the South Carolina Commission on Higher Education if you plan to attend a private college.

Exclusive: Visit www.UltimateScholarshipBook.com and enter code SO203012 for updates on this award.

(2031) • State Scholarship

Kansas Board of Regents
Curtis State Office Building
Suite 520
1000 SW Jackson Street
Topeka, KS 66612
Phone: 785-296-3421
Fax: 785-296-0983
Email: dlindeman@ksbor.org
http://www.kansasregents.org

Purpose: To aid needy Kansas students designated as state scholars.

Eligibility: Applicants must have taken the ACT, completed the Regents Scholars Curriculum and be graduating seniors. Applicants are ranked by an index combining ACT score and GPA. The top students are chosen.

Target applicants: High school students.

Amount: $1,000.

Number of awards: Varies.

Scholarship may be renewable.

Deadline: May 1.

How to apply: Complete the Free Application for Federal Student Aid (FAFSA).

Exclusive: Visit www.UltimateScholarshipBook.com and enter code KA203112 for updates on this award.

(2032) • State Work Study

Washington Higher Education Coordinating Board
917 Lakeridge Way
P.O. Box 43430
Olympia, WA 98504
Phone: 360-753-7850
Fax: 360-753-6243
Email: info@hecb.wa.gov
http://www.hecb.wa.gov

Purpose: To help low and middle income students earn money for college while gaining work experience.

Eligibility: Applicants must have demonstrated financial need according to the FAFSA, enroll at least half-time in an eligible undergraduate or graduate program and not be seeking a degree in theology.

Target applicants: High school students. College students. Graduate school students. Adult students.

Amount: $2,000-$5,000.

Number of awards: Varies.

Deadline: Varies.

How to apply: Eligible students who have filed a Free Application for Federal Student Aid (FAFSA) will be considered.

Exclusive: Visit www.UltimateScholarshipBook.com and enter code WA203212 for updates on this award.

(2033) • Stephen Phillips Memorial Scholarship Fund

Stephen Phillips Memorial Scholarship Fund
P.O. Box 870
Salem, MA 01970
Phone: 978-744-2111
Fax: 978-744-0456
Email: info@spscholars.org
http://www.phillips-scholarship.org
Purpose: To aid New England residents pursuing higher education.
Eligibility: Applicants must be U.S. residents or resident aliens who are permanent residents of Connecticut, Massachusetts, Maine, New Hampshire, Rhode Island or Vermont. They must be enrolled in a demanding undergraduate course of study pursuing their first degrees. A GPA of 3.0 or higher is required. Applicants must demonstrate citizenship, character, serious-mindedness and financial need.
Target applicants: High school students. College students. Adult students.
Minimum GPA: 3.0
Amount: $3,000-$10,000.
Number of awards: 145.
Deadline: April 30.
How to apply: Applications are available online. An application form, essay, transcript, counselor or professor recommendation, additional letter of recommendation, FAFSA Student Aid Report, financial aid award letter, documentation of college costs and student's and parents' tax forms are required.
Exclusive: Visit www.UltimateScholarshipBook.com and enter code ST203312 for updates on this award.

(2034) • Sterling Scholar Award Program

Hawaii Department of Education
Office of Curriculum, Instruction and Student Support
Student Support Section
641 18th Avenue V-201
Honolulu, HI 96816
Phone: 808-586-3230
Fax: 808-586-3234
http://doe.k12.hi.us
Purpose: To support outstanding Hawaii high school seniors.
Eligibility: Applicants must be graduating high school seniors and demonstrate leadership and citizenship in English, industrial arts, speech/drama, business education, foreign language, visual arts, mathematics, science, music, social science, Hawaiian studies or computer science and technology.
Target applicants: High school students.
Amount: $2,000-$4,000.
Number of awards: 65.
Deadline: December.
How to apply: Applications are available from the department heads of each high school.
Exclusive: Visit www.UltimateScholarshipBook.com and enter code HA203412 for updates on this award.

(2035) • Sterling Scholar Awards of Utah

Deseret News
P.O. Box 1257
Salt Lake City, UT 84110
Phone: 801-237-2135
http://www.deseretnews.com/home/
Purpose: To aid outstanding Utah students.
Eligibility: Applicants must be Utah public high school seniors. They must be nominated by their schools in one of 13 categories. Selection is based on scholarship (50 percent), leadership (25 percent) and community service/citizenship (25 percent).
Target applicants: High school students.
Amount: Up to full tuition.
Number of awards: Varies.
Deadline: January 31.
How to apply: Applications are available from your school's Sterling Awards organizer. An ID page, application form, transcript, proof of ACT scores, principal's report, standardized test data sheet and letter of recommendation are required.
Exclusive: Visit www.UltimateScholarshipBook.com and enter code DE203512 for updates on this award.

(2036) • Steve Dearduff Scholarship Fund

Community Foundation for Greater Atlanta Inc.
50 Hurt Plaza
Suite 449
Atlanta, GA 30303
Phone: 404-688-5525
Fax: 404-688-3060
Email: info@cfgreateratlanta.org
http://www.cfgreateratlanta.org
Purpose: To aid students who are preparing for careers in the fields of medicine and social work.
Eligibility: Applicants must be legal residents of Georgia and be enrolled at or accepted into an accredited postsecondary institution. They must be majoring in medicine or social work, have a GPA of 2.0 or higher and have a demonstrated commitment to community service. They must demonstrate financial need. Selection is based on academic merit, career potential, community service involvement and financial need.
Target applicants: College students. Graduate school students. Adult students.
Minimum GPA: 2.0
Amount: $2,500.
Number of awards: 3.
Scholarship may be renewable.
Deadline: March 15.
How to apply: Applications are available online. An application form and supporting materials are required.
Exclusive: Visit www.UltimateScholarshipBook.com and enter code CO203612 for updates on this award.

(2037) • Steve Fasteau Past Presidents' Scholarship

California Association for Postsecondary Education and Disability
71423 Biskra Road
Rancho Mirage, CA 92270
Phone: 760-346-8206
Fax: 760-340-5275
Email: bjaworski@csub.edu
http://www.caped.net
Purpose: To support disabled students.
Eligibility: Applicants must be college students with high academic achievement. They must demonstrate leadership and dedication to the advancement of students with disabilities in higher education. Undergraduate students must have a minimum GPA of 2.5 and at least six semester units, and graduate students must have a minimum GPA of

3.0 and at least three semester units from a public or private California college or university.
Target applicants: College students. Graduate school students. Adult students.
Minimum GPA: 2.5 for undergraduate students and 3.0 for graduate students
Amount: $1,000.
Number of awards: 1.
Deadline: September 19.
How to apply: Applications are available online. An application form, letter of application, letter of recommendation, verification of disability, transcript and proof of enrollment are required.
Exclusive: Visit www.UltimateScholarshipBook.com and enter code CA203712 for updates on this award.

(2038) • Student Incentive Grant

College Foundation of North Carolina
P.O. Box 41966
Raleigh, NC 27629
Phone: 888-234-6400
Fax: 919-821-3139
Email: programinformation@cfnc.org
http://www.cfnc.org
Purpose: To assist outstanding North Carolina high school graduates.
Eligibility: Successful applicants must be North Carolina residents enrolled full-time at a state college or university. Study programs cannot be in preparation for a religious career. Students must demonstrate financial need and maintain adequate academic progress.
Target applicants: High school students. College students. Adult students.
Amount: $700.
Number of awards: Varies.
Scholarship may be renewable.
Deadline: Varies.
How to apply: Contact your financial aid office.
Exclusive: Visit www.UltimateScholarshipBook.com and enter code CO203812 for updates on this award.

(2039) • Student Incentive Grants

New Mexico Higher Education Department
2048 Galisteo Street
Santa Fe, NM 87505
Phone: 800-279-9777
Fax: 505-476-8454
Email: heather.romero@state.nm.us
http://hed.state.nm.us
Purpose: To support New Mexico undergraduate students with financial need to attend postsecondary institutions in New Mexico.
Eligibility: Applicants must be New Mexico resident undergraduate students and attend public and selected private nonprofit postsecondary institutions in New Mexico at least half-time. Students must also be U.S. citizens.
Target applicants: College students. Adult students.
Amount: $200-$2,500.
Number of awards: Varies.
Deadline: Varies.
How to apply: Submit the FAFSA and contact your financial aid office. Deadlines are set by individual institutions.
Exclusive: Visit www.UltimateScholarshipBook.com and enter code NE203912 for updates on this award.

(2040) • Sun Student College Scholarship Program

Phoenix Suns Charities
P.O. Box 1369
Phoenix, AZ 85001
http://www.suns.com
Purpose: As part of the series of grants offered by the Phoenix Suns to help children in Arizona, the Student College Scholarship Program assists Arizona high school seniors with their college expenses.
Eligibility: Eligible candidates must be seniors in an Arizona high school.
Target applicants: High school students.
Minimum GPA: 2.5
Amount: $2,000-$5,000.
Number of awards: Varies.
Deadline: Varies.
How to apply: Contact the Phoenix Suns Charities via their website.
Exclusive: Visit www.UltimateScholarshipBook.com and enter code PH204012 for updates on this award.

(2041) • Susan Thompson Buffett Foundation Scholarship Program

Susan Thompson Buffett Foundation
222 Kiewit Plaza
Omaha, NE 68131
Phone: 402-943-1300
Email: scholarships@stbfoundation.org
http://www.buffettscholarships.org
Purpose: To support Nebraska students.
Eligibility: Applicants must be Nebraska residents pursuing undergraduate studies at a Nebraska public institution of higher learning who have not yet earned a bachelor's degree. They must be in need of financial assistance in order to obtain education. Students must have applied for federal aid and have a 2.5 or higher GPA.
Target applicants: High school students. College students. Adult students.
Minimum GPA: 2.5
Amount: $7,200.
Number of awards: Varies.
Scholarship may be renewable.
Deadline: March 1.
How to apply: Applications are available online. An application form, transcript, two letters of reference and essay are required.
Exclusive: Visit www.UltimateScholarshipBook.com and enter code SU204112 for updates on this award.

(2042) • Susan Vincent Memorial Scholarship

DownEast Association of Physician Assistants
30 Association Drive
Manchester, ME 04351
Phone: 207-620-7577
Fax: 207-622-3332
Email: info@deapa.com
http://www.deapa.com
Purpose: To aid Maine physician assistant students.
Eligibility: Applicants must be residents of Maine. They must have been accepted into a physician assistant degree program. Selection is based on the overall strength of the application.
Target applicants: College students. Graduate school students. Adult students.
Amount: $1,000.
Number of awards: 1.

Deadline: June 1.
How to apply: Application instructions are available online. A personal essay and a copy of the student's degree program acceptance letter are required.
Exclusive: Visit www.UltimateScholarshipBook.com and enter code DO204212 for updates on this award.

(2043) • Sussman-Miller Educational Assistance Award

Albuquerque Community Foundation (ACF)
P.O. Box 36960
Albuquerque, NM 87176
Phone: 505-883-6240
Email: foundation@albuquerquefoundation.org
http://www.albuquerquefoundation.org
Purpose: To assist New Mexico high school graduates and college undergraduates.
Eligibility: Students must be New Mexico residents for a minimum of one year, have been awarded a financial package that does not satisfy demonstrated need and be accepted by and have chosen to attend a U.S. post-secondary, accredited, nonprofit educational institution full-time. High school applicants need to graduate from an accredited public or private high school and have a 3.0 minimum GPA. Undergraduate applicants must have completed a minimum of one semester of undergraduate study with a 2.5 minimum GPA and cannot be applying for residency in another state.
Target applicants: High school students. College students. Adult students.
Minimum GPA: 3.0 for high school applicants and 2.5 for undergraduate applicants
Amount: $500-$3,000.
Number of awards: Varies.
Deadline: April 25.
How to apply: Applications are available online.
Exclusive: Visit www.UltimateScholarshipBook.com and enter code AL204312 for updates on this award.

(2044) • Swine Industry Scholarship

Iowa Foundation for Agricultural Advancement
Winner's Circle Scholarships
c/o SGI
30805 595th Avenue
Cambridge, IA 50046
Phone: 515-685-3719
Email: linda@slweldon.net
http://www.iowastatefair.org
Purpose: To aid Iowa 4-H and FFA students who are planning to go to college.
Eligibility: Applicants must be Iowa entering undergraduate freshmen. They must have a history of involvement in 4-H or FFA, with experience in swine projects. Selection is based on the overall strength of the application.
Target applicants: High school students.
Amount: $1,500.
Number of awards: 1.
Deadline: June 1.
How to apply: Applications are available online. An application form and supporting materials are required.
Exclusive: Visit www.UltimateScholarshipBook.com and enter code IO204412 for updates on this award.

(2045) • Tadeusz Sendzimir Fund

Connecticut Community Foundation Center for Philanthropy
43 Field Street
Waterbury, CT 06702
Phone: 203-753-1315
Fax: 203-756-3054
Email: info@conncf.org
http://www.conncf.org
Purpose: To provide financial assistance to students who are studying Polish language, history or culture.
Eligibility: Applicants must be Connecticut residents who are either in the U.S. during the academic year or in Poland during the summer. Academic year applicants must be taking undergraduate courses in Polish history, culture and language or be graduate students majoring in Slavic studies with an emphasis on Polish culture. Preference is given to students of Polish descent.
Target applicants: College students. Graduate school students. Adult students.
Amount: $3,000-$5,000.
Number of awards: 2.
Deadline: March 15.
How to apply: Applications are available online.
Exclusive: Visit www.UltimateScholarshipBook.com and enter code CO204512 for updates on this award.

(2046) • Talent Incentive Program Grant

State of Wisconsin Higher Educational Aids Board
P.O. Box 7885
Madison, WI 53707
Phone: 608-267-2206
Fax: 608-267-2808
Email: heabmail@wisconsin.gov
http://heab.state.wi.us
Purpose: To assist Wisconsin students who have financial need.
Eligibility: Applicants must be Wisconsin residents who are first-time college freshmen at a Wisconsin postsecondary institution. They must be enrolled at least part-time and must demonstrate financial need. Selection is based on financial need.
Target applicants: College students. Adult students.
Amount: Up to $1,800.
Number of awards: Varies.
Scholarship may be renewable.
Deadline: Varies.
How to apply: Applicants must complete the FAFSA and must be nominated for this award by their financial aid office or by a Wisconsin Educational Opportunities Program (WEOP) counselor.
Exclusive: Visit www.UltimateScholarshipBook.com and enter code ST204612 for updates on this award.

(2047) • Tech High School Alumni Association/W.O. Cheney Merit Scholarship

Community Foundation for Greater Atlanta Inc.
50 Hurt Plaza
Suite 449
Atlanta, GA 30303
Phone: 404-688-5525
Fax: 404-688-3060
Email: info@cfgreateratlanta.org
http://www.cfgreateratlanta.org

Purpose: To aid future college students who are planning to major in engineering, mathematics or one of the physical sciences.
Eligibility: Applicants must be U.S. citizens, Georgia residents and high school seniors who have been accepted at an accredited four-year postsecondary institution. They must be planning to major in mathematics, one of the physical sciences or engineering and must be full-time students who have a proven interest in community service. They must have an SAT composite (math and critical reading) score of 1300 or higher and must either be in the top 10 percent of their class or have a GPA of 3.7 or higher. Selection is based on the overall strength of the application.
Target applicants: High school students.
Minimum GPA: 3.7
Amount: $5,000.
Number of awards: 4.
Scholarship may be renewable.
Deadline: March 15.
How to apply: Applications are available online. An application form and supporting materials are required.
Exclusive: Visit www.UltimateScholarshipBook.com and enter code CO204712 for updates on this award.

(2048) • Technical Award

Louisiana Office of Student Financial Assistance
P.O. Box 91202
Baton Rouge, LA 70821-9202
Phone: 800-259-5626 x1012
Fax: 225-922-0790
Email: custserv@osfa.la.gov
http://www.osfa.state.la.us
Purpose: To assist Louisiana resident students.
Eligibility: Applicants must be Louisiana residents, apply during their junior or senior year in a public high school and pursue an industry-based occupational or vocational credential in a public college or university that meets certain standards. They must also have a minimum 2.0 GPA, score at least 15 on the English and Mathematics subsections of the ACT PLAN Assessment, have at least minimum passing scores in English and Mathematics on the GEE and have prepared a 5-year education and career plan.
Target applicants: High school students.
Minimum GPA: 2.0
Amount: $600.
Number of awards: Varies.
Scholarship may be renewable.
Deadline: July 2.
How to apply: Applications are available online or from guidance counselors.
Exclusive: Visit www.UltimateScholarshipBook.com and enter code LO204812 for updates on this award.

(2049) • Ted and Nora Anderson Scholarships

American Legion, Department of Kansas
1314 SW Topeka Boulevard
Topeka, KS 66612
Phone: 785-232-9315
Fax: 785-232-1399
http://www.ksamlegion.org
Purpose: To support worthy and needy children of American Legion and American Legion Auxiliary members as they pursue their educations.
Eligibility: Applicants must be high school seniors or college freshmen or sophomores who are average or better students. They must be enrolling or enrolled in a post-secondary school in Kansas and the son or daughter of a veteran. At least one parent must have been a member of the Kansas American Legion or American Legion Auxiliary for the past three years. The children of deceased parents are also eligible as long as the parent was a paid member at the time of death. Applicants must submit three letters of recommendation, with only one from a teacher, a 1040 income statement, documentation of parent's veteran status, an essay on "Why I Want to Go to College" and a high school transcript.
Target applicants: High school students. College students. Adult students.
Amount: $500.
Number of awards: 4.
Deadline: February 15.
How to apply: Applications are available online.
Exclusive: Visit www.UltimateScholarshipBook.com and enter code AM204912 for updates on this award.

(2050) • Ted Brickley/Bernice Shickora Scholarship

New Jersey Chapter of the American Society of Safety Engineers
Liberty Mutual Insurance Company
Attn.: Frank Gesualdo
3 Becker Farm Road, 2nd Floor
Roseland, NJ 07068
Email: info@njasse.org
http://www.njasse.org
Purpose: To aid New Jersey students who are majoring in industrial hygiene, occupational safety, environmental science or a related subject.
Eligibility: Applicants must be New Jersey residents who are enrolled at an accredited New Jersey college or university and must be graduate students or rising undergraduate juniors or seniors. They must be majoring in industrial hygiene, occupational safety, environmental science or a related subject and must be involved in extracurricular activities pertaining to occupational safety. They must have a major GPA of 3.0 or higher on a four-point scale. Selection is based on the overall strength of the application.
Target applicants: College students. Graduate school students. Adult students.
Minimum GPA: 3.0
Amount: Varies.
Number of awards: Varies.
Deadline: April 14.
How to apply: Applications are available online. An application form, transcript and one reference letter are required.
Exclusive: Visit www.UltimateScholarshipBook.com and enter code NE205012 for updates on this award.

(2051) • Tennessee HOPE Access Grant

Tennessee Student Assistance Corporation
404 James Robertson Parkway
Suite 1510, Parkway Towers
Nashville, TN 37243
Phone: 800-342-1663
Fax: 615-741-6101
Email: tsac.aidinfo@tn.gov
http://www.tn.gov/CollegePays/
Purpose: To support students who do not qualify for the Tennessee HOPE Grant.
Eligibility: Applicants must be entering freshmen who have a GPA between 2.75 and 2.99. They must also have either an ACT score between 18 and 20 or an SAT score between 860 and 970. Independent

students or the parents of dependent students must have an adjusted gross income under $36,000.
Target applicants: High school students.
Minimum GPA: 2.75
Amount: $1,750-$2,750.
Number of awards: Varies.
Deadline: September 1 and Feburary 1.
How to apply: Applications are available through completion of the FAFSA.
Exclusive: Visit www.UltimateScholarshipBook.com and enter code TE205112 for updates on this award.

(2052) • Tennessee HOPE Lottery Scholarship

Tennessee Student Assistance Corporation
404 James Robertson Parkway
Suite 1510, Parkway Towers
Nashville, TN 37243
Phone: 800-342-1663
Fax: 615-741-6101
Email: tsac.aidinfo@tn.gov
http://www.tn.gov/CollegePays/
Purpose: To support undergraduate students in Tennessee.
Eligibility: Applicants must be entering freshmen and either have at least a 3.0 GPA, a score of 21 on the ACT or a score of 980 on the SAT. GED students must also score at least a 525 on the GED test. Home-schooled students and some private school students must meet additional requirements. Applicants must be Tennessee residents for at least one year prior to the application deadline.
Target applicants: High school students.
Minimum GPA: 3.0
Amount: $2,000-$4,000.
Number of awards: Varies.
Scholarship may be renewable.
Deadline: September 1 and February 1.
How to apply: Applications are available through completion of the FAFSA.
Exclusive: Visit www.UltimateScholarshipBook.com and enter code TE205212 for updates on this award.

(2053) • Tennessee Hope Scholarships

Tennessee Student Assistance Corporation
404 James Robertson Parkway
Suite 1510, Parkway Towers
Nashville, TN 37243
Phone: 800-342-1663
Fax: 615-741-6101
Email: tsac.aidinfo@tn.gov
http://www.tn.gov/CollegePays/
Purpose: To aid Tennessee students with financial need.
Eligibility: Applicants must be high school seniors with a GPA of 3.0 or higher and an ACT score of 21 or higher or an ACT score of 980 or higher. GED applicants must score a 525 or better.
Target applicants: High school students.
Minimum GPA: 3.0
Amount: $2,000-$4,000.
Number of awards: Varies.
Scholarship may be renewable.
Deadline: Varies.
How to apply: Applications are available online. A Free Application for Federal Student Aid (FAFSA) is required.
Exclusive: Visit www.UltimateScholarshipBook.com and enter code TE205312 for updates on this award.

(2054) • Tennessee Need-Based Supplemental Aspire Awards

Tennessee Student Assistance Corporation
404 James Robertson Parkway
Suite 1510, Parkway Towers
Nashville, TN 37243
Phone: 800-342-1663
Fax: 615-741-6101
Email: tsac.aidinfo@tn.gov
http://www.tn.gov/CollegePays/
Purpose: To supplement the Tennessee HOPE Scholarship.
Eligibility: Applicants must have a minimum ACT score of 21 or SAT score of 980. Entering freshmen may substitute a GPA of 3.0 or higher. GED students must also have a GED test score of 525 or higher. Family adjusted gross income may not be more than $36,000.
Target applicants: High school students. College students. Adult students.
Minimum GPA: 3.0
Amount: $1,500.
Number of awards: Varies.
Scholarship may be renewable.
Deadline: Varies.
How to apply: Applications are available online. A Free Application for Federal Student Aid (FAFSA) is required.
Exclusive: Visit www.UltimateScholarshipBook.com and enter code TE205412 for updates on this award.

(2055) • Tennessee Student Assistance Awards

Tennessee Student Assistance Corporation
404 James Robertson Parkway
Suite 1510, Parkway Towers
Nashville, TN 37243
Phone: 800-342-1663
Fax: 615-741-6101
Email: tsac.aidinfo@tn.gov
http://www.tn.gov/CollegePays/
Purpose: To aid Tennessee students.
Eligibility: Applicants must be Tennessee residents who have applied for federal aid and have an Expected Family Contribution of $2,100 or less. They must be enrolled at least half time at an eligible Tennessee institution of higher learning and maintain satisfactory academic progress. They may not be in default on a loan or owe a refund on any grant previously received for education.
Target applicants: High school students. College students. Adult students.
Amount: Varies.
Number of awards: Varies.
Scholarship may be renewable.
Deadline: February 15.
How to apply: Applications are available online. A Free Application for Federal Student Aid (FAFSA) is required.
Exclusive: Visit www.UltimateScholarshipBook.com and enter code TE205512 for updates on this award.

(2056) • Terry L. McKanna Scholarship

American Water Works Association - Kansas Section
c/o David Cox, Scholarship Committee Chair

City of Olathe
P.O. Box 768
Olathe, KS 66051
Phone: 913-971-9056
Fax: 913-971-9099
Email: dcox@olatheks.org
http://www.ksawwa.org
Purpose: To aid students who are preparing for careers in the water industry.
Eligibility: Applicants must be undergraduate or graduate students who are preparing for careers in the water industry. Selection is based on the overall strength of the application.
Target applicants: College students. Graduate school students. Adult students.
Amount: Varies.
Number of awards: Varies.
Deadline: Varies.
How to apply: Applications are available by request from the Kansas chapter of the American Water Works Association. An application form and supporting materials are required.
Exclusive: Visit www.UltimateScholarshipBook.com and enter code AM205612 for updates on this award.

(2057) · Tese Caldarelli Memorial Scholarship

National Association for Campus Activities
13 Harbison Way
Columbia, SC 29212
Phone: 803-732-6222
Fax: 803-749-1047
Email: info@naca.org
http://www.naca.org
Purpose: To provide financial assistance to student leaders.
Eligibility: Students must hold a significant campus leadership position and demonstrate significant leadership skills and abilities. Students must also be making significant contributions through on- or off-campus volunteering. Applicants must also be current undergraduate or graduate students in Kentucky, Michigan, Ohio, Western Pennsylvania or West Virginia.
Target applicants: College students. Graduate school students. Adult students.
Minimum GPA: 3.0
Amount: Varies.
Number of awards: Varies.
Deadline: November 1.
How to apply: Applications are available online.
Exclusive: Visit www.UltimateScholarshipBook.com and enter code NA205712 for updates on this award.

(2058) · Texas Broadcast Education Foundation Scholarships

Texas Association of Broadcasters
502 E. 11th Street
Suite 200
Austin, TX 78701
Phone: 512-322-9944
Fax: 512-322-0522
http://www.tab.org
Purpose: To support promising Texas students.
Eligibility: Applicants must be TAB student members or attend a TAB member college or university. They must have a GPA of 3.0 or higher.
Target applicants: College students. Adult students.
Minimum GPA: 3.0
Amount: $2,000.
Number of awards: 8.
Deadline: May 2.
How to apply: Applications are available online. An application form is required.
Exclusive: Visit www.UltimateScholarshipBook.com and enter code TE205812 for updates on this award.

(2059) · Texas Elks State Association Scholarship Program

Texas Elks State Association
1963 FM 1586
Gonzales, TX 78629
Phone: 830-875-2425
http://www.texaselks.org
Purpose: To support Texas students.
Eligibility: Applicants must be seniors in Texas high schools who are not in the top 5 percent of their class. They must be U.S. citizens and Texas residents.
Target applicants: High school students.
Amount: $1,250.
Number of awards: 6.
Scholarship may be renewable.
Deadline: March 5.
How to apply: Applications are available online. An application form, transcript, SAT or ACT scores, applicant statement and parent statement are required.
Exclusive: Visit www.UltimateScholarshipBook.com and enter code TE205912 for updates on this award.

(2060) · Texas Elks State Association Teenager of the Year Contest

Texas Elks State Association
1963 FM 1586
Gonzales, TX 78629
Phone: 830-875-2425
http://www.texaselks.org
Purpose: To support outstanding high school students.
Eligibility: Applicants must be graduating high school seniors from Texas. Selection criteria include SAT/ACT scores, honors and awards, participation and leadership in extracurricular activities and neatness and organization of application.
Target applicants: High school students.
Amount: $500-$1,500.
Number of awards: 6.
Deadline: March 1.
How to apply: Applications are available online. An application form and documentation of awards and activities are required.
Exclusive: Visit www.UltimateScholarshipBook.com and enter code TE206012 for updates on this award.

(2061) · Texas Elks State Association Vocational Grant Program

Texas Elks State Association
1963 FM 1586
Gonzales, TX 78629
Phone: 830-875-2425

http://www.texaselks.org
Purpose: To support students pursuing vocational education.
Eligibility: Applicants must be U.S. citizens and Texas residents 18 years of age or older. They must plan to enroll full-time in a two-year or less vocational or technical program that results in a certificate, diploma or bachelor's degree.
Target applicants: High school students. College students. Adult students.
Amount: Varies.
Number of awards: Varies.
Deadline: Varies.
How to apply: Applications are available online. An application form, personal statement, letter from parent or other person with knowledge of family background, letter of recommendation and grade or work records for previous two years are required.
Exclusive: Visit www.UltimateScholarshipBook.com and enter code TE206112 for updates on this award.

(2062) • Texas Emergency Nurses Association Continuing Development Scholarships

Texas Emergency Nurses Association
c/o Malissa Aing, Scholarship Chair
16543 Chalk Maple Lane
Houston, TX 77095
http://www.txena.org
Purpose: To aid Texas registered nurses who are pursuing additional education in nursing or a complementary subject.
Eligibility: Applicants must be Texas residents or attending school in Texas and be members of the Emergency Nurses Association (ENA). They must be registered nurses who are pursuing an additional degree in nursing or a degree in a complementary subject (such as business or law). They must have a GPA of 2.5 or higher. Selection is based on the overall strength of the application.
Target applicants: College students. Graduate school students. Adult students.
Minimum GPA: 2.5
Amount: Up to $4,000.
Number of awards: 6.
Deadline: September 15.
How to apply: Applications are available online. An application form, official transcript, three references, a resume and proof of ENA membership are required.
Exclusive: Visit www.UltimateScholarshipBook.com and enter code TE206212 for updates on this award.

(2063) • Texas Emergency Nurses Association Initial Nursing Degree Scholarships

Texas Emergency Nurses Association
c/o Malissa Aing, Scholarship Chair
16543 Chalk Maple Lane
Houston, TX 77095
http://www.txena.org
Purpose: To aid Texas students who are pursuing an entry-level degree in nursing.
Eligibility: Applicants must be members of the Texas Nursing Students' Association (TNSA) or the Emergency Nurses Association (ENA). They must be Texas residents or attending school in Texas and be pursuing a diploma, associate's degree or bachelor's degree in nursing as their first nursing degree. They must have senior status in their degree program and must have a GPA of 2.5 or higher. Selection is based on the overall strength of the application.
Target applicants: College students. Adult students.
Minimum GPA: 2.5
Amount: $500-$1,000.
Number of awards: 2.
Deadline: September 15.
How to apply: Applications are available online. An application form, official transcript, three recommendation letters, a resume and proof of TNSA or ENA membership are required.
Exclusive: Visit www.UltimateScholarshipBook.com and enter code TE206312 for updates on this award.

(2064) • Texas History Essay Scholarship

Sons of the Republic of Texas
1717 8th Street
Bay City, TX 77414
Phone: 979-245-6644
http://www.srttexas.org
Purpose: To aid high school students and promote awareness of Texas history.
Eligibility: Applicants must be graduating seniors. They must submit an essay exploring the relevance of Texas history in the building of the state. Selection is based on research, originality and organization.
Target applicants: High school students.
Amount: $1,000-$3,000.
Number of awards: 3.
Deadline: January 31.
How to apply: Applications are available online. An application form and essay are required.
Exclusive: Visit www.UltimateScholarshipBook.com and enter code SO206412 for updates on this award.

(2065) • Texas Mutual Insurance Company Scholarship Program

Texas Mutual Insurance Company
Office of the President
6210 E. Highway 290
Austin, TX 78723-1098
Phone: 800-859-5995
http://www.texasmutual.com
Purpose: To assist the families of work-related accident victims.
Eligibility: Applicants must be spouses or children of persons who died or became disabled as a result of a compensable work-related accident or illness. Children must be unmarried and age 25 or younger. Spouses must not have remarried if the worker is deceased and must still be eligible for workers' compensation benefits.
Target applicants: High school students. College students. Adult students.
Amount: Up to full tuition plus $500.
Number of awards: Varies.
Scholarship may be renewable.
Deadline: Rolling.
How to apply: Applications are available online. An application form, transcript, financial aid report, letter of admission, SAT/ACT scores, tuition and fees information and death certificate (if applicable) are required.
Exclusive: Visit www.UltimateScholarshipBook.com and enter code TE206512 for updates on this award.

(2066) • Texas Occupational Therapy Association Scholarships

American Occupational Therapy Foundation
4720 Montgomery Lane
P.O. Box 31220
Bethesda, MD 20824
Phone: 301-652-6611
Fax: 301-656-3620
Email: jcooper@aotf.org
http://www.aotf.org
Purpose: To aid Texas occupational therapy students.
Eligibility: Applicants must be members of the Texas Occupational Therapy Association (TOTA). They must be Texas residents who are enrolled in an occupational therapy certificate, associate's or professional degree program at an accredited Texas school. Selection is based on the overall strength of the application.
Target applicants: College students. Graduate school students. Adult students.
Amount: $2,000.
Number of awards: 2.
Deadline: Varies.
How to apply: Applications are available by request from Jeanne Cooper, who is the scholarship coordinator at the American Occupational Therapy Association. An application form and supporting materials are required.
Exclusive: Visit www.UltimateScholarshipBook.com and enter code AM206612 for updates on this award.

(2067) • Texas Oratorical Contest

American Legion, Department of Texas
3401 Ed Bluestein Boulevard
Austin, TX 78721
Phone: 512-472-4138
Fax: 512-472-0603
Email: programs@txlegion.org
http://www.txlegion.org
Purpose: To enhance high school students' experience with and understanding of the U.S. Constitution. The contest will help develop students' leadership skills and civic appreciation, as well as the ability to deliver thoughtful, insightful orations regarding U.S. citizenship and its inherent responsibilities.
Eligibility: Applicants must be high school students under the age of 20 who are U.S. citizens or legal residents and residents of the state. Students first give an oration within their state and winners compete at the national level. The oration must be related to the Constitution of the United States focusing on the duties and obligations citizens have to the government. It must be in English and be between eight and ten minutes. There is also an assigned topic which is posted on the website, and it should be between three and five minutes.
Target applicants: High school students.
Amount: $500-$18,000.
Number of awards: Varies.
Deadline: November.
How to apply: Application information is available online or by contacting the local post.
Exclusive: Visit www.UltimateScholarshipBook.com and enter code AM206712 for updates on this award.

(2068) • Texas Physician Assistant Foundation Educational Scholarship

Texas Academy of Physician Assistants
401 West 15th Street
Austin, TX 78701
Phone: 512-370-1537
Fax: 512-370-1626
Email: kristina.haley@texmed.org
http://www.tapa.org
Purpose: To aid Texas physician assistant students.
Eligibility: Applicants must be student members of the Texas Academy of Physician Assistants (TAPA). They must be enrolled in an accredited physician assistant (PA) program in Texas. Selection is based on academic merit, stated career goals, extracurricular activities and recommendation letter.
Target applicants: College students. Graduate school students. Adult students.
Amount: Varies.
Number of awards: Varies.
Deadline: January 15.
How to apply: Applications are available online. An application form, transcript and recommendation letter are required.
Exclusive: Visit www.UltimateScholarshipBook.com and enter code TE206812 for updates on this award.

(2069) • Texas Professional Nursing Scholarships

Texas Higher Education Coordinating Board
1200 East Anderson Lane
Austin, TX 78752
Phone: 512-427-6101
Fax: 512-427-6127
Email: marylou.guerra@thecb.state.tx.us
http://www.collegefortexans.com
Purpose: To aid Texas nursing students.
Eligibility: Applicants must be Texas residents who are attending a Texas college or university. They must be enrolled in coursework that leads to licensure as a professional nurse. They must be attending school at least part-time and must demonstrate financial need. Selection is based on the overall strength of the application.
Target applicants: High school students. College students. Graduate school students. Adult students.
Amount: Up to $2,500.
Number of awards: Varies.
Deadline: Varies.
How to apply: Applications are available from the student's financial aid office. An application form and supporting materials are required.
Exclusive: Visit www.UltimateScholarshipBook.com and enter code TE206912 for updates on this award.

(2070) • Texas Public Educational Grant

Texas Higher Education Coordinating Board
1200 East Anderson Lane
Austin, TX 78752
Phone: 512-427-6101
Fax: 512-427-6127
Email: marylou.guerra@thecb.state.tx.us
http://www.collegefortexans.com
Purpose: To assist Texas students who have financial need.

Eligibility: Applicants must attend a public college or university in Texas and demonstrate financial need. Individual institutions determine additional eligibility criteria. Selection is based on financial need.
Target applicants: High school students. College students. Graduate school students. Adult students.
Amount: Varies.
Number of awards: Varies.
Deadline: April 1.
How to apply: Application is made by completing the FAFSA and contacting your school's financial aid office.
Exclusive: Visit www.UltimateScholarshipBook.com and enter code TE207012 for updates on this award.

(2071) • Texas Vocational Nursing Scholarships

Texas Higher Education Coordinating Board
1200 East Anderson Lane
Austin, TX 78752
Phone: 512-427-6101
Fax: 512-427-6127
Email: marylou.guerra@thecb.state.tx.us
http://www.collegefortexans.com
Purpose: To aid Texas students who are preparing for careers as vocational nurses.
Eligibility: Applicants must be Texas residents, be attending a Texas college or university on at least a part-time basis and be enrolled in coursework that provides preparation for licensure as a vocational nurse. They must demonstrate financial need. Selection is based on the overall strength of the application.
Target applicants: College students. Adult students.
Amount: Up to $1,500.
Number of awards: Varies.
Deadline: Varies.
How to apply: Applications are available by request from the student's financial aid office. An application form and supporting materials are required.
Exclusive: Visit www.UltimateScholarshipBook.com and enter code TE207112 for updates on this award.

(2072) • Thaddeus Colson and Isabelle Saalwaechter Fitzpatrick Memorial Scholarship

Community Foundation of Louisville
Waterfront Plaza
325 West Main Street
Suite 1110
Louisville, KY 40202
Phone: 502-585-4649
Fax: 502-587-7484
Email: gails@cflouisville.org
http://www.cflouisville.org
Purpose: To aid female undergraduates in Kentucky who are majoring in environment-related subjects.
Eligibility: Applicants must be Kentucky residents who are attending a public college or university in Kentucky. They must be full-time undergraduate students who are rising sophomores, juniors or seniors and be majoring in a subject that is related to the environment (such as agriculture, horticulture, environmental engineering, biology or environmental studies). They must have a GPA of 3.0 or higher. Selection is based on the overall strength of the application.
Target applicants: College students. Adult students.
Minimum GPA: 3.0
Amount: Up to $5,000.
Number of awards: Varies.
Deadline: March 15.
How to apply: Applications are available online. An application form and supporting materials are required.
Exclusive: Visit www.UltimateScholarshipBook.com and enter code CO207212 for updates on this award.

(2073) • The Arc of Washington State Trust Fund Stipend Award

Arc of Washington State
2638 State Avenue NE
Olympia, WA 98506
Phone: 360-357-5596
Fax: 360-357-3279
Email: diana@arcwa.org
http://www.arcwa.org
Purpose: To help students attending school in Alaska, Idaho, Oregon and Washington state who wish to pursue careers working with the developmentally disabled.
Eligibility: Applicants must be undergraduate juniors or above (including graduate-level students) and must be enrolled in a college or university located in Idaho, Washington state, Alaska or Oregon. They must be interested in working with the developmentally disabled. Selection is based on the overall strength of the application.
Target applicants: College students. Graduate school students. Adult students.
Amount: Up to $5,000.
Number of awards: Varies.
Deadline: February 28.
How to apply: Applications are available online. An application form, official transcripts, personal statement and two letters of recommendation are required.
Exclusive: Visit www.UltimateScholarshipBook.com and enter code AR207312 for updates on this award.

(2074) • The Francis Ouimet Scholarship Fund

Francis Ouimet Scholarship Fund
300 Arnold Palmer Boulevard
Norton, MA 02766
Phone: 774-430-9090
Fax: 774-430-9091
Email: marionm@ouimet.org
http://www.ouimet.org
Purpose: To provide merit- and need-based scholarships to students who have worked at Massachusetts golf clubs.
Eligibility: Applicants must have served at least two years as golf caddies, as golf pro shop workers or in course superintendent operations. The award is to be used for undergraduate study.
Target applicants: High school students. College students. Adult students.
Amount: Up to $20,000.
Number of awards: Varies.
Scholarship may be renewable.
Deadline: December 1.
How to apply: Applications are available by mail or by online request.
Exclusive: Visit www.UltimateScholarshipBook.com and enter code FR207412 for updates on this award.

(2075) • The Heart of a Marine Foundation Scholarship

Heart of a Marine Foundation
P.O. Box 1732
Elk Grove Village, IL 60007
Phone: 847-621-7324
Email: theheartofamarine@comcast.net
http://www.heartofamarine.org

Purpose: To support students from New Jersey and Illinois who have outstanding character.

Eligibility: Applicants must be graduating high school seniors or discharged military personnel. Students must demonstrate loyalty, patriotism, honor, respect and compassion for others.

Target applicants: High school students.

Amount: $1,000.

Number of awards: 2.

Deadline: March 15.

How to apply: Applications are available online.

Exclusive: Visit www.UltimateScholarshipBook.com and enter code HE207512 for updates on this award.

(2076) • Theodore Gordon Flyfishers Inc. Founders Fund Scholarship

Environmental Consortium of Hudson Valley Colleges and Universities Gordon Flyfishers
c/o Pace Academy for the Environment
861 Bedford Road
Choate 221N
Pleasantville, NY 10570
Phone: 914-773-3738
Fax: 914-773-3265
Email: envtlconsortium@pace.edu
http://www.environmentalconsortium.org

Purpose: To support a student who excels in the environmental field at one of the member institutions of the consortium.

Eligibility: Applicants must be U.S. citizens enrolled full-time and at least in the second year of college or in graduate school. Students must major in an area of environmental studies such as, but not limited to, ecology, hydrology, conservation biology, natural resource management, zoology or environmental law and policy. A list of member institutions is online.

Target applicants: College students. Graduate school students. Adult students.

Minimum GPA: 3.0

Amount: $3,500.

Number of awards: 1.

Deadline: April 1.

How to apply: Applications are available online.

Exclusive: Visit www.UltimateScholarshipBook.com and enter code EN207612 for updates on this award.

(2077) • Theodore R. and Vivian M. Johnson Scholarship Program

Scholarship America Johnson Scholarship
One Scholarship Way
P.O. Box 297
Saint Peter, MN 56082
Phone: 507-931-1682
http://www.johnsonscholarships.org

Purpose: To support the children of UPS employees.

Eligibility: Applicants must be high school seniors or graduates who are enrolled or plan to enroll in a full-time undergraduate course of study at an accredited institution. One parent must be a regular full-time or permanent part-time UPS employee who has resided in Florida for at least twelve months. They must have been employed at UPS at least one year and must be employed there when the awards are announced. Children of UPS retirees and deceased UPS workers are also eligible. Applicants must demonstrate financial need.

Target applicants: High school students. College students. Adult students.

Amount: $1,000-$10,000.

Number of awards: Varies.

Deadline: April 15.

How to apply: Applications are available online. An application form is required.

Exclusive: Visit www.UltimateScholarshipBook.com and enter code SC207712 for updates on this award.

(2078) • Thomara Latimer Cancer Foundation Scholarship

Thomara Latimer Cancer Foundation
Franklin Plaza Center
29193 Northwestern Highway #528
Southfield, MI 48034
Phone: 248-557-2346
Email: info@thomlatimercares.org
http://www.thomlatimercares.org

Purpose: To aid African-American students in Michigan who are preparing for careers in medicine or a related field.

Eligibility: Applicants must be African-American students between the ages of 17 and 30, have a minimum 3.0 GPA and be Michigan residents who are enrolled at or have been accepted at an accredited postsecondary institution. They must be studying or planning to study allied health, medicine, nursing, occupational therapy, physical therapy, physician assisting or a related subject. Selection is based on the overall strength of the application.

Target applicants: High school students. College students. Graduate school students. Adult students.

Minimum GPA: 3.0

Amount: Varies.

Number of awards: Varies.

Deadline: December 17.

How to apply: Applications are available online. An application form, official transcript, personal essay, two recommendation letters and proof of college acceptance or enrollment are required.

Exclusive: Visit www.UltimateScholarshipBook.com and enter code TH207812 for updates on this award.

(2079) • Thomas E. Desjardins Memorial Scholarship

Institute of Transportation Engineers - New England Section
Email: rod.emery@jacobs.com
http://www.neite.org

Purpose: To aid New England civil engineering students who are interested in transportation engineering.

Eligibility: Applicants must be civil engineering undergraduates or graduate students who are enrolled at an accredited postsecondary institution in Connecticut, Maine, Massachusetts, New Hampshire, Rhode Island or Vermont. They must demonstrate an interest in transportation engineering through their coursework or extracurricular activities. Selection is based on academic merit, character and extracurricular activities.

Target applicants: College students. Graduate school students. Adult students.
Amount: Varies.
Number of awards: Varies.
Deadline: Varies.
How to apply: Applications are available by request from the New England section of the Institute of Transportation Engineers. An application form and supporting materials are required.
Exclusive: Visit www.UltimateScholarshipBook.com and enter code IN207912 for updates on this award.

(2080) • Timmins, Kroll & Jacobsen Scholarship

Iowa Foundation for Agricultural Advancement
Winner's Circle Scholarships
c/o SGI
30805 595th Avenue
Cambridge, IA 50046
Phone: 515-685-3719
Email: linda@slweldon.net
http://www.iowastatefair.org
Purpose: To aid Iowa students who have been active in 4-H or FFA.
Eligibility: Applicants must be Iowa residents, be incoming freshmen at an Iowa college or university and have experience in 4-H and/or FFA livestock projects. They must have plans to major in animal science, agriculture or a related subject. Preference will be given to applicants from Polk County. Selection is based on the overall strength of the application.
Target applicants: High school students.
Amount: $2,000.
Number of awards: 1.
Deadline: June 1.
How to apply: Applications are available online. An application form and supporting materials are required.
Exclusive: Visit www.UltimateScholarshipBook.com and enter code IO208012 for updates on this award.

(2081) • Toby Wright Scholarship

Workers' Compensation Association of New Mexico
P.O. Box 35757
Station D
Albuquerque, NM 87176
Phone: 800-640-0724
Email: scibrock@qwest.net
http://www.wcaofnm.com
Purpose: To support the children of injured New Mexico workers.
Eligibility: Applicants must have a parent who was badly injured or killed in a work-related accident which resulted in economic hardship and New Mexico worker's compensation. Students must be between the ages of 16 and 25, and they must attend college or technical school in New Mexico.
Target applicants: High school students. College students.
Amount: Up to full tuition.
Number of awards: Varies.
Scholarship may be renewable.
Deadline: Varies.
How to apply: Applications are available online.
Exclusive: Visit www.UltimateScholarshipBook.com and enter code WO208112 for updates on this award.

(2082) • Tongan Cultural Society Scholarship

Hawaii Community Foundation - Scholarships
1164 Bishop Street, Suite 800
Honolulu, HI 96813
Phone: 888-731-3863
Fax: 808-521-6286
Email: scholarships@hcf-hawaii.org
http://www.hawaiicommunityfoundation.org
Purpose: To support students of Tongan ancestry.
Eligibility: Applicants must attend school in Hawaii.
Target applicants: High school students. College students. Adult students.
Amount: Varies.
Number of awards: Varies.
Deadline: March 1.
How to apply: To apply, register online, complete the online application and select the scholarships to which you wish to apply. In addition, mail the supporting materials: printed confirmation page from the online application, personal statement, copy of Student Aid Report (SAR) available at www.fafsa.ed.gov and official transcript.
Exclusive: Visit www.UltimateScholarshipBook.com and enter code HA208212 for updates on this award.

(2083) • TOPS Performance Award

Louisiana Office of Student Financial Assistance
P.O. Box 91202
Baton Rouge, LA 70821-9202
Phone: 800-259-5626 x1012
Fax: 225-922-0790
Email: custserv@osfa.la.gov
http://www.osfa.state.la.us
Purpose: To aid Louisiana student residents.
Eligibility: Applicants must be Louisiana residents, U.S. citizens, apply during their senior year in high school, use the award at a Louisiana college or university, have a minimum 3.0 GPA and have a minimum ACT score of 23 or an equivalent SAT I score.
Target applicants: High school students.
Minimum GPA: 3.0
Amount: Tuition plus $400.
Number of awards: Varies.
Scholarship may be renewable.
Deadline: July 1.
How to apply: The application is the Free Application for Federal Student Aid (FAFSA). ACT or SAT I scores must also be reported.
Exclusive: Visit www.UltimateScholarshipBook.com and enter code LO208312 for updates on this award.

(2084) • Toward Excellence, Access and Success (TEXAS) Grant II Program (TGII)

Texas Higher Education Coordinating Board
1200 East Anderson Lane
Austin, TX 78752
Phone: 512-427-6101
Fax: 512-427-6127
Email: marylou.guerra@thecb.state.tx.us
http://www.collegefortexans.com
Purpose: To assist Texas two-year college students with financial need.
Eligibility: Applicants must be Texas residents, enrolled at least half-time in a public Texas two-year community college, technical college or public state college and demonstrate financial need.

Target applicants: College students. Adult students.
Amount: $1,500.
Number of awards: Varies.
Deadline: May 25.
How to apply: Complete the Free Application for Federal Student Aid (FAFSA).
Exclusive: Visit www.UltimateScholarshipBook.com and enter code TE208412 for updates on this award.

(2085) • Towards EXcellence, Access and Success (TEXAS) Grant Program

Texas Higher Education Coordinating Board
1200 East Anderson Lane
Austin, TX 78752
Phone: 512-427-6101
Fax: 512-427-6127
Email: marylou.guerra@thecb.state.tx.us
http://www.collegefortexans.com
Purpose: To assist Texas students who have financial need.
Eligibility: Applicants must be Texas residents and high school graduates. They must demonstrate financial need by having an Expected Family Contribution (EFC) of $4,000 or less. They must be enrolled at a public, non-profit Texas college or university and cannot have earned more than 30 semester credits at the time of application submission. Those who have earned an associate's degree at a Texas two-year institution and who intend to enroll in a Texas bachelor's degree program within 12 months of graduation are also eligible. Selection is based on financial need.
Target applicants: High school students. College students. Adult students.
Amount: $3,150-$6,780.
Number of awards: Varies.
Scholarship may be renewable.
Deadline: Varies.
How to apply: Application is made by completing the FAFSA.
Exclusive: Visit www.UltimateScholarshipBook.com and enter code TE208512 for updates on this award.

(2086) • Township Officials of Illinois Scholarship

Township Officials of Illinois
408 S. 5th Street
Springfield, IL 62701
Phone: 217-744-2212
Fax: 217-744-7419
Email: bryantoi@toi.org
http://www.toi.org
Purpose: To promote the ideas of quality local government and civic duty and to recruit young people into the TOI.
Eligibility: Applicants must be high school seniors attending an Illinois college or university in the fall.
Target applicants: High school students.
Amount: $2,000.
Number of awards: Varies.
Deadline: Varies.
How to apply: Applications are available online in January.
Exclusive: Visit www.UltimateScholarshipBook.com and enter code TO208612 for updates on this award.

(2087) • Tsung Tsin Association Scholarship

Tsung Tsin Association
Chairperson, Scholarship Committee
47-701 Hui Alala Street
Kaneohe, HI 96744
Phone: 808-533-3998
http://165.248.6.166/data/bulletin15/index.asp
Purpose: To help outstanding Hawaii students pay for college.
Eligibility: Applicants must be high school seniors, college undergraduates or graduate students and must be attending or planning to attend a post-secondary institution. Applicants must provide a transcript, SAT scores, recommendations and autobiographical sketch. Community service and career goals are taken into consideration.
Target applicants: High school students. College students. Graduate school students. Adult students.
Amount: $750.
Number of awards: 1.
Deadline: April 20.
How to apply: Applications are available by written request.
Exclusive: Visit www.UltimateScholarshipBook.com and enter code TS208712 for updates on this award.

(2088) • Tuition Aid Grant

New Jersey Higher Education Student Assistance Authority
P.O. Box 540
Trenton, NJ 08625
Phone: 800-792-8670
Email: clientservices@hesaa.org
http://www.hesaa.org
Purpose: To support New Jersey students who are unable to pay the full cost of tuition.
Eligibility: Students must be residents of New Jersey for at least 12 months prior to college enrollment, enroll in an approved New Jersey school and remain in school full-time in an undergraduate program. Applicants cannot have any previous degrees, and they cannot be enrolled in theology or divinity programs.
Target applicants: High school students. College students. Adult students.
Amount: Up to full tuition.
Number of awards: Varies.
Scholarship may be renewable.
Deadline: Varies.
How to apply: Applications are available through completion of the FAFSA.
Exclusive: Visit www.UltimateScholarshipBook.com and enter code NE208812 for updates on this award.

(2089) • Tuition Assistance Program (TAP)

New York State Higher Education Services Corporation (HESC)
99 Washington Avenue
Albany, NY 12255
Phone: 888-697-4372
Email: hescwebmail@hesc.org
http://www.hesc.com/content.nsf/
Purpose: To assist New York resident students in attending in-state postsecondary institutions.
Eligibility: Applicants must be U.S. citizens or eligible noncitizens, be legal residents of New York State, study full-time at an eligible New York State postsecondary institution as undergraduate or graduate students, meet income eligibility requirements and maintain a "C" average in college.
Target applicants: High school students. College students. Graduate school students. Adult students.
Amount: Up to $5,000.

Number of awards: Varies.
Scholarship may be renewable.
Deadline: May 1.
How to apply: Complete the Free Application for Federal Student Aid (FAFSA), including a New York school on the application and then complete the Express TAP Application.
Exclusive: Visit www.UltimateScholarshipBook.com and enter code NE208912 for updates on this award.

(2090) · Tuition Equalization Grant Program

Texas Higher Education Coordinating Board
1200 East Anderson Lane
Austin, TX 78752
Phone: 512-427-6101
Fax: 512-427-6127
Email: marylou.guerra@thecb.state.tx.us
http://www.collegefortexans.com
Purpose: To assist students with financial need who are attending private, non-profit colleges or universities in Texas.
Eligibility: Applicants must be Texas residents or nonresident National Merit Finalists. They must be enrolled at a private, non-profit Texas institution in a first associate's, bachelor's, master's or doctoral degree program. Applicants cannot be athletic scholarship recipients and must demonstrate financial need. Selection is based on financial need.
Target applicants: High school students. College students. Graduate school students. Adult students.
Amount: Up to $3,808.
Number of awards: Varies.
Deadline: Varies.
How to apply: Application is made by completing the FAFSA.
Exclusive: Visit www.UltimateScholarshipBook.com and enter code TE209012 for updates on this award.

(2091) · Tuition Reduction for Non-Resident Nursing Students

Maryland Higher Education Commission
Office of Student Financial Assistance
839 Bestgate Road, Suite 400
Annapolis, MD 21401
Phone: 800-974-1024
Fax: 410-260-3200
Email: osfamail@mhec.state.md.us
http://www.mhec.state.md.us
Purpose: To support non-resident nursing students who are attending college in Maryland.
Eligibility: Applicants cannot be residents of the state of Maryland, but they must be enrolled in a two-year or four-year undergraduate nursing program in Maryland. Students must agree to work full-time at a Maryland hospital after graduation, for a period of four years for full-time students and two years for part-time students.
Target applicants: High school students. College students. Adult students.
Amount: Varies.
Number of awards: Varies.
Scholarship may be renewable.
Deadline: Varies.
How to apply: Applications are available online.
Exclusive: Visit www.UltimateScholarshipBook.com and enter code MA209112 for updates on this award.

(2092) · Tuition Waiver for Foster Care Recipients

Maryland Higher Education Commission
Office of Student Financial Assistance
839 Bestgate Road, Suite 400
Annapolis, MD 21401
Phone: 800-974-1024
Fax: 410-260-3200
Email: osfamail@mhec.state.md.us
http://www.mhec.state.md.us
Purpose: To assist students who have resided in foster care in attending a public college.
Eligibility: Applicants must be under the age of 21 and have lived in foster care in the state of Maryland when they graduated high school or have lived in foster care on their 14th birthday and subsequently been adopted.
Target applicants: High school students. College students.
Amount: Up to full tuition.
Number of awards: Varies.
Scholarship may be renewable.
Deadline: March 1.
How to apply: Students may apply by filing the FAFSA and contacting the financial aid office at the institution they plan to attend.
Exclusive: Visit www.UltimateScholarshipBook.com and enter code MA209212 for updates on this award.

(2093) · Tweet Coleman Aviation Scholarship

American Association of University Women - Honolulu Branch
1802 Keeaumoku Street
Honolulu, HI 96822
Phone: 808-537-4702
http://www.aauwhonolulu.org
Purpose: To aid female undergraduates who are pursuing a private pilot's license.
Eligibility: Applicants must be currently attending a college or university in Hawaii. Selection is based on the overall strength of the application.
Target applicants: College students. Adult students.
Amount: Varies.
Number of awards: Varies.
Deadline: Varies.
How to apply: Applications are available by online request. An application form and supporting materials are required.
Exclusive: Visit www.UltimateScholarshipBook.com and enter code AM209312 for updates on this award.

(2094) · Twenty-first Century Scholars Program

State Student Assistance Commission of Indiana
150 W. Market Street
Suite 500
Indianapolis, IN 46204
Phone: 888-528-4719
Fax: 317-232-3260
Email: grants@ssaci.state.in.us
http://www.in.gov/ssaci
Purpose: To support Indiana middle school students from families with low to moderate incomes.
Eligibility: Applicants must be in 7th or 8th grade at a school recognized by the Indiana Department of Education. Students must meet the maximum income requirements, be wards of the state or county or be in foster care. Scholarship funds may only be used at eligible Indiana colleges or technical schools.

Target applicants: Junior high students or younger.
Amount: Varies.
Number of awards: Varies.
Scholarship may be renewable.
Deadline: June 30.
How to apply: Applications are available at Indiana middle schools.
Exclusive: Visit www.UltimateScholarshipBook.com and enter code ST209412 for updates on this award.

(2095) • Two-Year College Academic Scholarship Program

State of Alabama
Commission on Higher Education
100 N. Union Street
P.O. Box 302000
Montgomery, AL 36130-2000
Phone: 334-242-1998
Fax: 334-242-0268
http://www.ache.state.al.us
Purpose: To assist students attending two-year colleges in Alabama.
Eligibility: Applicants must be accepted for enrollment at a public two-year postsecondary educational institution in Alabama. Selection is based on academic merit and is not based on financial need. Priority is given to in-state residents.
Target applicants: High school students.
Amount: Up to full tuition.
Number of awards: Varies.
Scholarship may be renewable.
Deadline: Varies.
How to apply: Contact the college financial aid office.
Exclusive: Visit www.UltimateScholarshipBook.com and enter code ST209512 for updates on this award.

(2096) • UDC Virginia Division Gift Scholarships

Virginia Division, United Daughters of the Confederacy
c/o Mrs. Jean Frawner
6501 Norman Bridge Road
Hanover, VA 23069
Email: 2vp@vaudc.org
http://www.vaudc.org
Purpose: To aid descendants of worthy Confederates.
Eligibility: Applicants must be direct descendants of Confederates or indirect descendants who are UDC members. They must receive an endorsement from a Virginia UDC chapter and demonstrate financial need. Applicants must maintain a GPA of 3.0 or higher.
Target applicants: High school students. College students. Adult students.
Minimum GPA: 3.0
Amount: Varies.
Number of awards: Varies.
Scholarship may be renewable.
Deadline: Varies.
How to apply: Applications are available online. An application form, proof of ancestor's Confederate military record, transcript, two letters of recommendation and a personal statement are required.
Exclusive: Visit www.UltimateScholarshipBook.com and enter code VI209612 for updates on this award.

(2097) • University of North Carolina Need Based Grant

College Foundation of North Carolina
P.O. Box 41966
Raleigh, NC 27629
Phone: 888-234-6400
Fax: 919-821-3139
Email: programinformation@cfnc.org
http://www.cfnc.org
Purpose: To provide financial assistance to students attending a campus of the University of North Carolina.
Eligibility: Applicants must be enrolled in six or more credit hours at one of the 16 campuses of the University of North Carolina. They must also demonstrate financial need.
Target applicants: High school students. College students. Adult students.
Amount: Varies.
Number of awards: Varies.
Deadline: Varies.
How to apply: Applicants must complete the Free Application for Federal Student Aid and list at least one campus of the University of North Carolina on it.
Exclusive: Visit www.UltimateScholarshipBook.com and enter code CO209712 for updates on this award.

(2098) • University Scholarship and Research Grant

Michigan Council of Women in Technology Foundation
Attn.: Scholarship Committee
19011 Norwich Road
Livonia, MI 48152
Fax: 248-281-5391
Email: info@mcwt.org
http://www.mcwtf.org
Purpose: To support female information technology students.
Eligibility: Applicants must be high school seniors or undergraduate or graduate students who are Michigan residents and U.S. citizens with a GPA of 2.8 or higher. Students must enroll in a degree program in information systems, business applications, computer science, computer engineering, software engineering or information security.
Target applicants: High school students. College students. Graduate school students. Adult students.
Minimum GPA: 2.8
Amount: $3,000-$5,000.
Number of awards: Varies.
Scholarship may be renewable.
Deadline: January 31.
How to apply: Applications are available online. An application form, transcript, two letters of recommendation and research project description (for research grant applicants only) are required.
Exclusive: Visit www.UltimateScholarshipBook.com and enter code MI209812 for updates on this award.

(2099) • Upper Midwest Chapter Scholarships

National Academy of Television Arts and Sciences-Upper Midwest Chapter
4967 Kensington Gate
Shorewood, MN 55331
Phone: 952-474-7126
Email: twv@mktgbydesign.com
http://www.midwestemmys.org

Purpose: To aid students interested in television, broadcasting and electronic media careers.
Eligibility: Applicants must be high school seniors. They must have applied or been accepted to a college or university that offers a broadcasting, television or other electronic media curriculum and intend to pursue one of these fields. A GPA of 3.0 or higher is preferred, but not required.
Target applicants: High school students.
Amount: $2,500.
Number of awards: Varies.
Deadline: March 13.
How to apply: Applications are available online. An application form is required.
Exclusive: Visit www.UltimateScholarshipBook.com and enter code NA209912 for updates on this award.

(2100) • Urban Scholars Award

New Jersey Higher Education Student Assistance Authority
P.O. Box 540
Trenton, NJ 08625
Phone: 800-792-8670
Email: clientservices@hesaa.org
http://www.hesaa.org
Purpose: To support New Jersey high school seniors from urban or economically depressed areas.
Eligibility: Applicants must be New Jersey residents for at least 12 months prior to college enrollment, and they must enroll full-time in an approved state college. Students must show outstanding academic achievement in high school through SAT scores and transcripts.
Target applicants: High school students.
Amount: Up to $1,000.
Number of awards: Varies.
Scholarship may be renewable.
Deadline: Varies.
How to apply: Applications are available from high school guidance counselors.
Exclusive: Visit www.UltimateScholarshipBook.com and enter code NE210012 for updates on this award.

(2101) • Utah Centennial Opportunity Program for Education (UCOPE) Grants

Utah Higher Education Assistance Authority
P.O. Box 145112
Salt Lake City, UT 84114
Phone: 877-336-7378
Fax: 801-366-8430
Email: uheaa@utahsbr.edu
http://www.uheaa.org
Purpose: To assist Utah students who are attending Utah colleges.
Eligibility: Applicants must be residents of Utah who are attending college in Utah. It is recommended that students apply early because there are limited funds. Selection is based on financial need.
Target applicants: High school students. College students. Adult students.
Amount: Varies.
Number of awards: Varies.
Deadline: Varies.
How to apply: Applicants must complete the FAFSA and contact their financial aid office.
Exclusive: Visit www.UltimateScholarshipBook.com and enter code UT210112 for updates on this award.

(2102) • Valedictorial Tuition Waiver Program

Massachusetts Department of Higher Education
Office of Student Financial Assistance
454 Broadway
Suite 200
Revere, MA 02151
Phone: 617-727-9420
Fax: 617-727-0667
Email: osfa@osfa.mass.edu
http://www.osfa.mass.edu/default.asp
Purpose: To provide comprehensive financial aid to Massachusetts valedictorians.
Eligibility: Applicants must be designated as a valedictorian by a public or private high school in the state of Massachusetts, and they must be residents of the state for at least one year prior to the beginning of the school year. Students must enroll in a Massachusetts public college and meet individual requirements for the program imposed by the school. They cannot owe refunds on previous financial aid or have any defaulted government loans.
Target applicants: High school students.
Amount: Full Tuition.
Number of awards: Varies.
Scholarship may be renewable.
Deadline: Varies.
How to apply: Applications are available at college financial aid offices.
Exclusive: Visit www.UltimateScholarshipBook.com and enter code MA210212 for updates on this award.

(2103) • VCTA Virginia's Future Leaders Scholarship

Virginia's Cable Telecommunications Association
1001 E. Broad Street
Suite 210
Richmond, VA 23219
Phone: 877-861-5464
Fax: 804-225-8036
http://www.vcta.com
Purpose: To support Virginia students seeking higher education.
Eligibility: Applicants must be Virginia residents. They must be attending or plan to attend a Virginia two- or four-year college or university, graduate or technical school. Financial need is required.
Target applicants: High school students. College students. Graduate school students. Adult students.
Amount: Varies.
Number of awards: Varies.
Deadline: Varies.
How to apply: Applications are available online.
Exclusive: Visit www.UltimateScholarshipBook.com and enter code VI210312 for updates on this award.

(2104) • Vermont Incentive Grants

Vermont Student Assistance Corporation
10 East Allen Street
P.O. Box 2000
Winooski, VT 05404
Phone: 800-882-4166
Fax: 802-654-3765
Email: info@vsac.org
http://www.vsac.org
Purpose: To assist Vermont students who are attending college full-time.
Eligibility: Applicants must be Vermont residents who are accepted into or enrolled in an undergraduate degree program, a certificate program,

a Doctor of Veterinary Medicine degree program or a University of Vermont College of Medicine degree program. They must attend or plan to attend school full-time. Applicants who have earned a bachelor's degree previously are ineligible. Selection is based on financial need.
Target applicants: High school students. College students. Graduate school students. Adult students.
Amount: Varies.
Number of awards: Varies.
Deadline: Varies.
How to apply: Applications are available online. An application form and a completed FAFSA are required.
Exclusive: Visit www.UltimateScholarshipBook.com and enter code VE210412 for updates on this award.

(2105) • Vermont Oratorical Contest

American Legion, Department of Vermont
P.O. Box 396
126 State Street
Montpelier, VT 05601
Phone: 802-223-7131
Fax: 802-223-0318
Email: alvthq@verizon.net
http://www.legionvthq.com
Purpose: To enhance high school students' experience with and understanding of the U.S. Constitution. The contest will help develop students' leadership skills and civic appreciation, as well as the ability to deliver thoughtful, insightful orations regarding U.S. citizenship and its inherent responsibilities.
Eligibility: Applicants must be high school students under the age of 20 who are U.S. citizens or legal residents and residents of the state. Students first give an oration within their state and winners compete at the national level. The oration must be related to the Constitution of the United States focusing on the duties and obligations citizens have to the government. It must be in English and be between eight and ten minutes. There is also an assigned topic which is posted on the website, and it should be between three and five minutes.
Target applicants: High school students.
Amount: $100-$18,000.
Number of awards: Varies.
Deadline: Varies.
How to apply: Applications are available from district representatives.
Exclusive: Visit www.UltimateScholarshipBook.com and enter code AM210512 for updates on this award.

(2106) • Vernon T. Swain, P.E./Robert E. Chute, P.E. Scholarship

Maine Society of Professional Engineers
Colin C. Hewett, P.E.
Chairman, Scholarship Committee
P.O. Box 318
Winthrop, ME 04364
Email: chewett@ahgeng.com
http://www.mespe.org
Purpose: To aid Maine students who are preparing for careers in engineering.
Eligibility: Applicants must be Maine residents who are graduating high school seniors. They must have plans to enroll in an ABETEAC-accredited degree program in engineering and to pursue a career in engineering. Applicants have to have applied to at least one school that offers engineering degrees. These are the minimum acceptable standardized test scores: SAT Math 600, SAT Writing 500, SAT Critical Reading 500, ACT Math 29, ACT English 25, PAA Quantitative 750 and PAA Verbal 640. Selection is based on standardized test scores, GPA, personal essay, recommendations, extracurricular activities and work experience.
Target applicants: High school students.
Amount: Varies.
Number of awards: Varies.
Deadline: March 4.
How to apply: Applications are available online. An application form, official transcript, personal statement, two recommendation letters and official SAT or ACT scores are required.
Exclusive: Visit www.UltimateScholarshipBook.com and enter code MA210612 for updates on this award.

(2107) • Veterans Tuition Awards

New York State Higher Education Services Corporation (HESC)
99 Washington Avenue
Albany, NY 12255
Phone: 888-697-4372
Email: hescwebmail@hesc.org
http://www.hesc.com/content.nsf/
Purpose: To assist veterans in obtaining higher education.
Eligibility: Applicants must be veterans from New York State who have been honorably discharged and served in Indochina between December 22, 1961 and May 7, 1975, the Persian Gulf on or after August 2, 1990 or Afghanistan on or after September 11, 2001. Applicants must also have applied for the Tuition Assistant Program if studying full-time, and the Federal Pell Grant whether studying full-time or part-time, unless enrolled in a vocational training program.
Target applicants: College students. Graduate school students. Adult students.
Amount: Up to $4,895.
Number of awards: Varies.
Scholarship may be renewable.
Deadline: May 1.
How to apply: Applications are available from your institution's financial aid office or by phone from HESC.
Exclusive: Visit www.UltimateScholarshipBook.com and enter code NE210712 for updates on this award.

(2108) • Veterinary Education Program

New Hampshire Postsecondary Education Commission
3 Barrell Court
Suite 300
Concord, NH 03301
Phone: 603-271-2555 x352
Fax: 603-271-2696
Email: jknapp@pec.state.nh.us
http://www.state.nh.us/postsecondary
Purpose: To support veterinary medicine students in New Hampshire.
Eligibility: Applicants must have been New Hampshire residents for at least 12 months prior to the beginning of the school year and must have graduated from a New Hampshire high school within the last six years. Funding is available to attend Tufts and Cornell Universities.
Target applicants: College students. Graduate school students. Adult students.
Amount: $12,000.
Number of awards: Varies.
Scholarship may be renewable.
Deadline: Varies.

How to apply: Applications are available at the University of New Hampshire College of Life Sciences and Agriculture.
Exclusive: Visit www.UltimateScholarshipBook.com and enter code NE210812 for updates on this award.

(2109) • Victoria S. and Bradley L. Geist Foundation

Hawaii Community Foundation - Scholarships
1164 Bishop Street, Suite 800
Honolulu, HI 96813
Phone: 888-731-3863
Fax: 808-521-6286
Email: scholarships@hcf-hawaii.org
http://www.hawaiicommunityfoundation.org
Purpose: To support students who have been in the Hawaii foster care system.
Eligibility: Applicants must be residents of Hawaii. Students must not have been legally adopted before the age of 18.
Target applicants: High school students. College students. Adult students.
Amount: Varies.
Number of awards: Varies.
Scholarship may be renewable.
Deadline: June 1.
How to apply: Applications are available online. In addition, mail the supporting materials: confirmation letter from a case worker, personal statement and official transcript.
Exclusive: Visit www.UltimateScholarshipBook.com and enter code HA210912 for updates on this award.

(2110) • Vietnam Veterans' Scholarship

New Mexico Higher Education Department
2048 Galisteo Street
Santa Fe, NM 87505
Phone: 800-279-9777
Fax: 505-476-8454
Email: heather.romero@state.nm.us
http://hed.state.nm.us
Purpose: To support Vietnam veterans who are attending college in New Mexico.
Eligibility: Applicants must have been honorably discharged from the armed forces, and they must have received a Vietnam campaign medal for serving in Vietnam anytime between August 5, 1964 and the official end of the war. Students must be attending either a public school or one of the following private schools in New Mexico: the College of Santa Fe, St. John's College or the College of the Southwest. They must have been New Mexico residents when entering the armed forces or have lived in the state for at least 10 years.
Target applicants: College students. Graduate school students. Adult students.
Amount: Full tuition.
Number of awards: Varies.
Scholarship may be renewable.
Deadline: Varies.
How to apply: Applications are available at college financial aid offices.
Exclusive: Visit www.UltimateScholarshipBook.com and enter code NE211012 for updates on this award.

(2111) • Vincent L. Hawkinson Scholarship for Peace and Justice

Vincent L. Hawkinson Foundation for Peace and Justice
324 Harvard Street S.E.
Minneapolis, MN 55414
Phone: 612-331-8125
Email: info@graceattheu.org
http://www.graceattheu.org
Purpose: To provide financial assistance to undergraduate and graduate students who share the ideals of the Rev. Vincent L. Hawkinson, a leader of Grace University Lutheran Church for more than 30 years.
Eligibility: Applicants must advocate peace, reside in or attend school in Iowa, Minnesota, North Dakota, South Dakota or Wisconsin and attend an interview in Minneapolis and the fall awards ceremony.
Target applicants: High school students. College students. Graduate school students. Adult students.
Amount: Up to $3,000.
Number of awards: 5-10.
Deadline: March 15.
How to apply: Applications are available by sending a self-addressed stamped envelope, by email or online.
Exclusive: Visit www.UltimateScholarshipBook.com and enter code VI211112 for updates on this award.

(2112) • Virginia Commonwealth Award

State Council of Higher Education for Virginia
101 N. 14th Street
James Monroe Building
Richmond, VA 23219
Phone: 804-225-2600
Fax: 804-225-2604
Email: communications@schev.edu
http://www.schev.edu
Purpose: To assist Virginia students.
Eligibility: Undergraduate applicants must be admitted to a Virginia public two- or four-year college or university, be enrolled at least half-time, be residents of Virginia, be U.S. citizens or eligible noncitizens and demonstrate financial need. Graduate applicants must be enrolled full-time in an eligible Virginia graduate degree program. The selection process varies by school.
Target applicants: High school students. College students. Graduate school students. Adult students.
Amount: Varies.
Number of awards: Varies.
Scholarship may be renewable.
Deadline: Varies.
How to apply: Application instructions are available by request from the student's financial aid office.
Exclusive: Visit www.UltimateScholarshipBook.com and enter code ST211212 for updates on this award.

(2113) • Virginia Daughters of the American Revolution Scholarships

Virginia Daughters of the American Revolution
DAR Scholarship Committee
5268 Albright Drive
Virginia Beach, VA 23464-8120
Phone: 757-479-4167
Email: nancy72miller@alumni.umw.edu
http://www.vadar.org

Purpose: To support Virginia high school students in pursuing higher education.
Eligibility: Applicants must be high school seniors and U.S. citizens who are sponsored by a Virginia DAR chapter. They may pursue an undergraduate degree in any field except nursing at any Virginia college or university.
Target applicants: High school students.
Amount: $500-$1,000.
Number of awards: 3.
Deadline: February 1.
How to apply: Applications are available online. An application form, letter of sponsorship, written statement, transcript, financial need form and letter of recommendation are required.
Exclusive: Visit www.UltimateScholarshipBook.com and enter code VI211312 for updates on this award.

(2114) • Virginia Guaranteed Assistance Program

State Council of Higher Education for Virginia
101 N. 14th Street
James Monroe Building
Richmond, VA 23219
Phone: 804-225-2600
Fax: 804-225-2604
Email: communications@schev.edu
http://www.schev.edu
Purpose: To provide a financial incentive for economically disadvantaged students to consider attending college.
Eligibility: Applicants must have graduated from a Virginia high school with at least a 2.5 GPA, and they must be enrolled full-time in a two-year or four-year college in the state. Students must be classified as dependents. Preference will be given to students with the greatest financial need.
Target applicants: High school students. College students. Adult students.
Minimum GPA: 2.5
Amount: Up to full tuition.
Number of awards: Varies.
Scholarship may be renewable.
Deadline: Varies.
How to apply: Applications are available at college financial aid offices.
Exclusive: Visit www.UltimateScholarshipBook.com and enter code ST211412 for updates on this award.

(2115) • Virginia High School League Achievement Award

Virginia High School League Foundation
1642 State Farm Boulevard
Charlottesville, VA 22911
Phone: 434-977-8475
Fax: 434-977-5943
Email: ktilley@vhsl.org
http://www.vhsl.org
Purpose: To support students who have made outstanding achievements in sports, academics or courageousness.
Eligibility: Students must be from a Virginia high school in Group A, AA or AAA. Applicants must show participation in VHSL activities and other school or community activities. They must have at least a 3.0 GPA.
Target applicants: High school students.
Minimum GPA: 3.0
Amount: $1,000.
Number of awards: 10.
Deadline: March 15.
How to apply: Applications are available online.
Exclusive: Visit www.UltimateScholarshipBook.com and enter code VI211512 for updates on this award.

(2116) • Virginia High School League Charles E. Savedge Journalism Scholarship

Virginia High School League Foundation
1642 State Farm Boulevard
Charlottesville, VA 22911
Phone: 434-977-8475
Fax: 434-977-5943
Email: ktilley@vhsl.org
http://www.vhsl.org
Purpose: To support student journalists in Virginia.
Eligibility: Applicants must be active members of a high school newspaper, yearbook or other publication. Students must be in their senior year and have plans to study journalism in college.
Target applicants: High school students.
Amount: Up to $500.
Number of awards: Varies.
Deadline: March 1.
How to apply: Applications are available online.
Exclusive: Visit www.UltimateScholarshipBook.com and enter code VI211612 for updates on this award.

(2117) • Virginia Part-Time Assistance Program

State Council of Higher Education for Virginia
101 N. 14th Street
James Monroe Building
Richmond, VA 23219
Phone: 804-225-2600
Fax: 804-225-2604
Email: communications@schev.edu
http://www.schev.edu
Purpose: To assist part-time Virginia students who have financial need.
Eligibility: Applicants must be Virginia residents. They must attend a school in Virginia's community college system part-time (three to five credit hours per term) and must demonstrate financial need. Selection is based on financial need.
Target applicants: High school students. College students. Adult students.
Amount: Varies.
Number of awards: Varies.
Deadline: Varies.
How to apply: Applications are available from the student's financial aid office. An application form and supporting materials are required.
Exclusive: Visit www.UltimateScholarshipBook.com and enter code ST211712 for updates on this award.

(2118) • Virginia Tuition Assistance Grant Program

State Council of Higher Education for Virginia
101 N. 14th Street
James Monroe Building
Richmond, VA 23219
Phone: 804-225-2600
Fax: 804-225-2604
Email: communications@schev.edu
http://www.schev.edu

Purpose: To assist Virginia students who are attending eligible private postsecondary institutions in Virginia.
Eligibility: Applicants must be Virginia residents and enrolled full-time as undergraduate, graduate or professional school students at an eligible private, non-profit Virginia postsecondary institution. Applicants who are enrolled in a religious or theological degree program are ineligible as are graduate students who are enrolled in a degree program that is not related to health care. Selection is based on the overall strength of the application.
Target applicants: High school students. College students. Graduate school students. Adult students.
Amount: Up to $3,000.
Number of awards: Varies.
Scholarship may be renewable.
Deadline: July 31.
How to apply: Applications are available by request from the student's college financial aid office. An application form and supporting materials are required.
Exclusive: Visit www.UltimateScholarshipBook.com and enter code ST211812 for updates on this award.

(2119) • Vocational Nurse Scholarship

Health Professions Education Foundation
400 R Street
Suite 460
Sacramento, CA 95811
Phone: 916-326-3640
Fax: 916-324-6585
Email: stran@oshpd.ca.gov
http://www.oshpd.ca.gov
Purpose: To aid California vocational nursing students.
Eligibility: Applicants must be accepted or enrolled in an accredited California vocational nurse (VN) degree program and must be enrolled at least part-time (six credits per term). They must maintain a GPA of 2.0 or higher while enrolled in the degree program and must commit to two years of practice in an underserved area of California after graduation. Selection is based on academic merit, stated career goals, community involvement, work experience and financial need.
Target applicants: College students. Adult students.
Minimum GPA: 2.0
Amount: Up to $4,000.
Number of awards: Varies.
Deadline: September 11.
How to apply: Applications are available online. An application form, personal statement, official transcript, two recommendation letters and financial information are required.
Exclusive: Visit www.UltimateScholarshipBook.com and enter code HE211912 for updates on this award.

(2120) • Vocational Rehabilitation Program

College Foundation of North Carolina
P.O. Box 41966
Raleigh, NC 27629
Phone: 888-234-6400
Fax: 919-821-3139
Email: programinformation@cfnc.org
http://www.cfnc.org
Purpose: To provide financial assistance to students with mental and physical disabilities that hinder their ability to obtain employment.
Eligibility: The program provides assistance with counseling, job placement and some support services that is not based on financial need. Need is considered for assistance with tuition and fees, transportation and books.
Target applicants: High school students. College students. Graduate school students. Adult students.
Amount: Up to $2,428.
Number of awards: Varies.
Deadline: Varies.
How to apply: Applications are available from your local Vocational Rehabilitation Office or by mail or phone. The website for the office is www.dhhs.state.nc.us/docs/divinfo/dvr.htm.
Exclusive: Visit www.UltimateScholarshipBook.com and enter code CO212012 for updates on this award.

(2121) • Vocational Scholarship

Kansas Board of Regents
Curtis State Office Building
Suite 520
1000 SW Jackson Street
Topeka, KS 66612
Phone: 785-296-3421
Fax: 785-296-0983
Email: dlindeman@ksbor.org
http://www.kansasregents.org
Purpose: To assist Kansas students to attend vocational colleges.
Eligibility: Applicants must be enrolled in approved vocational programs and take the vocational exam. Selection is based on exam scores.
Target applicants: High school students. College students. Adult students.
Amount: $500.
Number of awards: 240.
Scholarship may be renewable.
Deadline: February 18.
How to apply: Applications are available online.
Exclusive: Visit www.UltimateScholarshipBook.com and enter code KA212112 for updates on this award.

(2122) • VSAC Board of Directors Bette Matkowski Scholarship

Vermont Student Assistance Corporation
10 East Allen Street
P.O. Box 2000
Winooski, VT 05404
Phone: 800-882-4166
Fax: 802-654-3765
Email: info@vsac.org
http://www.vsac.org
Purpose: To honor the contributions of board member Bette Matkowski to the VSAC.
Eligibility: Applicants must be adult students who attend a Title IV eligible college or university and demonstrate financial need. An essay is required.
Target applicants: College students. Adult students.
Amount: $1,000.
Number of awards: 2.
Deadline: March 4.
How to apply: Applications are available online.
Exclusive: Visit www.UltimateScholarshipBook.com and enter code VE212212 for updates on this award.

(2123) • W.P. Black Scholarship Fund

Greater Kanawha Valley Foundation
1600 Huntington Square
900 Lee Street, East
Charleston, WV 25301
Phone: 304-346-3620
Fax: 304-346-3640
Email: tgkvf@tgkvf.org
http://www.tgkvf.org
Purpose: To aid West Virginia students.
Eligibility: Applicants must be residents of West Virginia who are full-time students, have a minimum 2.5 GPA, have a minimum ACT score of 20, be of good moral character and demonstrate significant financial need.
Target applicants: High school students. College students. Adult students.
Minimum GPA: 2.5
Amount: $1,000.
Number of awards: 68.
Scholarship may be renewable.
Deadline: January 15.
How to apply: Applications are available online.
Exclusive: Visit www.UltimateScholarshipBook.com and enter code GR212312 for updates on this award.

(2124) • Wachovia Citizenship Scholarship

Virginia Department of Education
P.O. Box 2120
Richmond, VA 23218
Phone: 804-225-3349
Fax: 804-371-2456
Email: joseph.wharff@doe.virginia.gov
http://www.pen.k12.va.us
Purpose: To assist high school seniors in paying for higher education.
Eligibility: Applicants must be graduating high school seniors at Virginia High School League A, AA or AAA schools. Students must demonstrate outstanding citizenship.
Target applicants: High school students.
Amount: $1,000.
Number of awards: 6.
Deadline: March 15.
How to apply: Applications are available by phone at 434-977-8475.
Exclusive: Visit www.UltimateScholarshipBook.com and enter code VI212412 for updates on this award.

(2125) • Wachovia Technical Scholarship

College Foundation of North Carolina
P.O. Box 41966
Raleigh, NC 27629
Phone: 888-234-6400
Fax: 919-821-3139
Email: programinformation@cfnc.org
http://www.cfnc.org
Purpose: To assist students with financial need who are enrolled in two-year technical programs in North Carolina community colleges.
Eligibility: Applicants must be enrolled full-time in their second year of a technical program. Financial need and academic merit are required. The award may be used for books, tuition or transportation.
Target applicants: College students. Adult students.
Amount: $500.
Number of awards: 58.
Deadline: Varies.
How to apply: Recipients are selected by a committee at each individual community college. Contact your college for more information.
Exclusive: Visit www.UltimateScholarshipBook.com and enter code CO212512 for updates on this award.

(2126) • Wachovia Wells Fargo Scholars

Virginia Foundation for Independent Colleges
8010 Ridge Road
Suite B
Richmond, VA 23229-7288
Phone: 800-230-6757
Fax: 804-282-4635
Email: info@vfic.org
http://www.vfic.org/scholarships/scholarships_vfic.html
Purpose: To support students interested in careers in the financial services industry.
Eligibility: Applicants must be full-time students at VFIC member colleges and be first semester juniors studying on campus and U.S. citizens with a GPA of 3.0 or higher. They must major in business, finance, accounting, economics or mathematics.
Target applicants: College students. Adult students.
Minimum GPA: 3.0
Amount: $5,000.
Number of awards: 2.
Scholarship may be renewable.
Deadline: October 15.
How to apply: Applications are available online. An online application, resume and two letters of recommendation are required.
Exclusive: Visit www.UltimateScholarshipBook.com and enter code VI212612 for updates on this award.

(2127) • Walter and Ruby Behlen Memorial Scholarship

National FFA Organization
P.O. Box 68960
6060 FFA Drive
Indianapolis, IN 46268-0960
Phone: 317-802-6060
Fax: 317-802-6051
Email: scholarships@ffa.org
http://www.ffa.org/
Purpose: To support Nebraska students who are majoring in agriculture.
Eligibility: Applicants must be current FFA members and high school seniors or college students planning to enroll or currently enrolled full-time. They may be pursuing two-year or four-year degrees in any field of agriculture. Students only need to complete the online application one time to be considered for all FFA-administered scholarships. The application requires information about the students' activities and a 1,000-word essay. Awards may be used for books, supplies, tuition, fees and room and board.
Target applicants: High school students. College students. Adult students.
Amount: $1,000.
Number of awards: 1.
Deadline: February 15.
How to apply: Applications are available online.
Exclusive: Visit www.UltimateScholarshipBook.com and enter code NA212712 for updates on this award.

(2128) • Washington Award for Vocational Excellence

Washington Higher Education Coordinating Board
917 Lakeridge Way
P.O. Box 43430
Olympia, WA 98504
Phone: 360-753-7850
Fax: 360-753-6243
Email: info@hecb.wa.gov
http://www.hecb.wa.gov

Purpose: To reward students for outstanding achievement in vocational or technical education.

Eligibility: Applicants must be enrolled in a Washington high school, skills center or public community or technical college, graduate high school with at least 360 hours in an approved vocational program or have completed at least one year in an eligible vocational program by June 30th of the award year and not have previously received a WAVE scholarship.

Target applicants: High school students. College students. Adult students.

Amount: Up to $7,600.

Number of awards: 147.

Scholarship may be renewable.

Deadline: Varies.

How to apply: Students must be nominated by a counselor or administrator.

Exclusive: Visit www.UltimateScholarshipBook.com and enter code WA212812 for updates on this award.

(2129) • Washington BPW Foundation Mature Woman Educational Scholarship

Washington Business and Professional Women's Foundation
1181 Sudden Valley
Bellingham, WA 98229
Phone: 360-714-8901
Fax: 360-714-8901
Email: cdleeper@hotmail.com
http://www.bpwwa.com

Purpose: To assist non-traditional female students.

Eligibility: Applicants must be female students age 35 or older who are pursuing retraining or continuing education. Students must be U.S. citizens and Washington state residents for at least two years and must be accepted into a program at an accredited Washington state institution of higher learning or enrolled in an accredited online program from a Washington state school. They must demonstrate scholastic ability and financial need.

Target applicants: College students. Adult students.

Amount: $1,000.

Number of awards: Varies.

Deadline: April 1.

How to apply: Applications are available online. An application form, essay, proof of income, financial aid and expense estimates, three letters of recommendation, transcript and proof of acceptance or enrollment are required.

Exclusive: Visit www.UltimateScholarshipBook.com and enter code WA212912 for updates on this award.

(2130) • Washington College Bound Scholarship

Washington Higher Education Coordinating Board
917 Lakeridge Way
P.O. Box 43430
Olympia, WA 98504
Phone: 360-753-7850
Fax: 360-753-6243
Email: info@hecb.wa.gov
http://www.hecb.wa.gov

Purpose: To provide an incentive for students and their families who might not consider college due to financial concerns.

Eligibility: Applicants must be Washington students in the seventh or eighth grades who are eligible for free or reduced-price lunch, and they must sign a pledge to participate in the program. The student's family income must be 65 percent or less of the state's median income when he or she graduates high school, and his or her GPA must be 2.0 or higher in order to receive the scholarship.

Target applicants: Junior high students or younger.

Minimum GPA: 2.0

Amount: Full tuition plus $500 for books.

Number of awards: Varies.

Scholarship may be renewable.

Deadline: Varies.

How to apply: Applications are available online.

Exclusive: Visit www.UltimateScholarshipBook.com and enter code WA213012 for updates on this award.

(2131) • Washington Oratorical Contest

American Legion, Department of Washington
P.O. Box 3917
Lacey, WA 98509
Phone: 360-491-4373
Fax: 360-491-7442
Email: americanismchairman@americanism-alwa.org
http://www.walegion.org/

Purpose: To enhance high school students' experience with and understanding of the U.S. Constitution. The contest will help develop students' leadership skills and civic appreciation, as well as the ability to deliver thoughtful, insightful orations regarding U.S. citizenship and its inherent responsibilities.

Eligibility: Applicants must be high school students under the age of 20 who are U.S. citizens or legal residents and residents of the state. Students first give an oration within their state and winners compete at the national level. The oration must be related to the Constitution of the United States focusing on the duties and obligations citizens have to the government. It must be in English and be between eight and ten minutes. There is also an assigned topic which is posted on the website, and it should be between three and five minutes.

Target applicants: High school students.

Amount: Up to $2,000.

Number of awards: Varies.

Deadline: December 15.

How to apply: Application information is available online.

Exclusive: Visit www.UltimateScholarshipBook.com and enter code AM213112 for updates on this award.

(2132) • Washington Scholars Grant Program

Washington Higher Education Coordinating Board
917 Lakeridge Way
P.O. Box 43430
Olympia, WA 98504
Phone: 360-753-7850
Fax: 360-753-6243
Email: info@hecb.wa.gov
http://www.hecb.wa.gov

Purpose: To assist Washington high school students.

Eligibility: Applicants must be Washington high school seniors planning to enroll in an eligible Washington college or university. Selection is based on academic achievements, leadership and community activities.
Target applicants: High school students.
Amount: 90% of full tuition.
Number of awards: Varies.
Scholarship may be renewable.
Deadline: Varies.
How to apply: Students are nominated by their high schools.
Exclusive: Visit www.UltimateScholarshipBook.com and enter code WA213212 for updates on this award.

(2133) • Washington State Achievers Program

College Success Foundation
1605 NW Sammamish Road
Suite 100
Issaquah, WA 98027
Phone: 425-416-2000
Fax: 425-416-2001
Email: info@collegesuccessfoundation.org
http://www.collegesuccessfoundation.org
Purpose: To provide financial assistance to students in high schools serving large low-income populations in Washington state, encouraging these high schools to raise efforts to improve academic achievement.
Eligibility: Applicants must be a junior or senior in high school at a foundation-designated Achievers high school in Washington state, have a family income that is in the lowest 35 percent of Washington state's family income level and plan to enroll in a Washington public or independent college for at least two years of their college education.
Target applicants: High school students.
Amount: $5,000.
Number of awards: Varies.
Scholarship may be renewable.
Deadline: October 23.
How to apply: Applications are available at the selected high schools and on the Washington Education Foundation's website at http://www.waedfoundation.org.
Exclusive: Visit www.UltimateScholarshipBook.com and enter code CO213312 for updates on this award.

(2134) • Washington State Auto Dealers Association Awards

Washington State Auto Dealers Association
P.O. Box 58170
Seattle, WA 98138
Phone: 206-433-6300
Fax: 206-433-6301
Email: info@wsada.org
http://www.wsada.org
Purpose: To provide financial assistance for business majors.
Eligibility: Recipients must be Washington state residents who are majoring in business or a related field or graduate students who have received the award as undergraduates. Preference is given to minority students. Students attending Gonzaga University, Heritage University, Pacific Lutheran University, Saint Martin's University, Seattle Pacific University, Seattle University, University of Puget Sound, Walla Walla University, Whitman College or Whitworth University are eligible.
Target applicants: College students. Graduate school students. Adult students.
Amount: $500.
Number of awards: 10.
Deadline: Varies.
How to apply: No application is necessary. ICW colleges and universities select recipients from their schools.
Exclusive: Visit www.UltimateScholarshipBook.com and enter code WA213412 for updates on this award.

(2135) • Washington State PTA Scholarship

Washington State PTA
2003 65th Avenue West
Tacoma, WA 98466-6215
Phone: 253-565-2153
Email: wapta@wastatepta.org
http://www.wastatepta.org
Purpose: To provide financial assistance to graduates of Washington public high schools.
Eligibility: Applicants must meet maximum household income requirements and be entering their freshman year of college. Academic performance and community service are also considered.
Target applicants: High school students.
Amount: $1,000-$2,000.
Number of awards: Varies.
Deadline: March 1.
How to apply: Applications are available online.
Exclusive: Visit www.UltimateScholarshipBook.com and enter code WA213512 for updates on this award.

(2136) • West Virginia Higher Education Grant

West Virginia Higher Education Policy Commission
1018 Kanawha Boulevard, East
Suite 700
Charleston, WV 25301
Phone: 304-558-2101
Fax: 304-558-5719
Email: financialaiddirector@hepc.wvnet.edu
http://www.hepc.wvnet.edu
Purpose: To assist West Virginia students who have financial need.
Eligibility: Applicants must be U.S. citizens or permanent residents and West Virginia residents who have lived in the state for at least 12 months before the application submission date. They must be high school graduates or GED recipients who are enrolled full-time in an undergraduate degree program at a participating postsecondary institution located in West Virginia or Pennsylvania. They must demonstrate financial need. Applicants who have earned a bachelor's degree previously are ineligible. Selection is based on financial need.
Target applicants: College students. Adult students.
Amount: Up to $3,300.
Number of awards: Varies.
Scholarship may be renewable.
Deadline: April 15.
How to apply: Application is made by completing the FAFSA.
Exclusive: Visit www.UltimateScholarshipBook.com and enter code WE213612 for updates on this award.

(2137) • West Virginia PROMISE Scholarship

West Virginia Higher Education Policy Commission PROMISE Scholarship
1018 Kanawha Boulevard, East
Suite 700
Charleston, WV 25301
Phone: 304-558-2101
Fax: 304-558-5719

Email: canderson@hepc.wvnet.edu
http://wvhepcnew.wvnet.edu
Purpose: To assist outstanding West Virginia high school students who are planning to attend college in the state.
Eligibility: Applicants must be West Virginia residents and high school seniors or GED recipients who are planning to attend a West Virginia postsecondary institution. They must have a GPA of 3.0 or higher or a GED score of 2500 or higher. Applicants must also have a combined reading and math SAT score of 1020 or higher or a composite ACT score of 22 or higher. Selection is based on academic merit and financial need.
Target applicants: High school students.
Minimum GPA: 3.0
Amount: Up to $4,750.
Number of awards: Varies.
Scholarship may be renewable.
Deadline: March 1.
How to apply: Applications are available online. An application form, supporting materials and a completed FAFSA are required.
Exclusive: Visit www.UltimateScholarshipBook.com and enter code WE213712 for updates on this award.

(2138) · Wilder-Naifeh Technical Skills Grant

Tennessee Student Assistance Corporation
404 James Robertson Parkway
Suite 1510, Parkway Towers
Nashville, TN 37243
Phone: 800-342-1663
Fax: 615-741-6101
Email: tsac.aidinfo@tn.gov
http://www.tn.gov/CollegePays/
Purpose: To support students enrolled in Tennessee Technology Centers.
Eligibility: Applicants cannot be prior recipients of the Wilder-Naifeh Grant or the Tennessee HOPE Scholarship. Students must be Tennessee residents for at least one year prior to the beginning of the school term. A list of Tennessee Technology Centers is available online.
Target applicants: High school students. College students. Adult students.
Amount: Up to $2,000.
Number of awards: Varies.
Deadline: September 1 and February 1.
How to apply: Applications are available through completion of the FAFSA.
Exclusive: Visit www.UltimateScholarshipBook.com and enter code TE213812 for updates on this award.

(2139) · William A. and Vinnie E. Dexter Scholarship

Community Foundation of Western Massachusetts
1500 Main Street
P.O. Box 15769
Springfield, MA 01115
Phone: 413-732-2858
Fax: 413-733-8565
Email: scholar@communityfoundation.org
http://www.communityfoundation.org
Purpose: To help graduating high school seniors in western Massachusetts.
Eligibility: Applicants must plan to attend college part-time or full-time. Application forms, transcripts and Student Aid Reports (from completing the FAFSA) are required.
Target applicants: High school students.
Amount: Varies.
Number of awards: Varies.
Deadline: March 31.
How to apply: Applications are available online and by phone.
Exclusive: Visit www.UltimateScholarshipBook.com and enter code CO213912 for updates on this award.

(2140) · William D. and Jewell Brewer Scholarship

American Legion, Department of Michigan
212 N. Verlinden Avenue, Ste. A
Lansing, MI 48915
Phone: 517-371-4720 x11
Fax: 517-371-2401
Email: programs@michiganlegion.org
http://www.michiganlegion.org
Purpose: To support Michigan students who are the sons, daughters or grandchildren of veterans.
Eligibility: Applicants must be sons, daughters or grandchildren of wartime veterans, residents of Michigan, have a minimum 2.5 GPA and plan to attend a college or university. Scholarships are based on financial need, academic standing and applicant's goals. Applicants must also provide proof of a parent's military service record. They should send scholarship information to the county district committee person.
Target applicants: High school students. College students. Graduate school students. Adult students.
Minimum GPA: 2.5
Amount: $500.
Number of awards: Varies.
Deadline: January 17.
How to apply: Applications are available online.
Exclusive: Visit www.UltimateScholarshipBook.com and enter code AM214012 for updates on this award.

(2141) · William D. Squires Scholarship

William D. Squires Educational Foundation
P.O. Box 2940
Jupiter, FL 33468-2940
Phone: 561-741-7751
Email: wmdsquires@comcast.net
http://www.wmdsquiresfoundation.org
Purpose: To provide financial assistance to needy Ohio students with specific career goals.
Eligibility: Applicants must be Ohio high school seniors with demonstrated financial need who have specific career goals and are highly motivated. They must plan to enroll in a degree, diploma or certificate program at an accredited college or university, and they must have a minimum GPA of 3.2.
Target applicants: High school students.
Minimum GPA: 3.2
Amount: $3,000.
Number of awards: 12.
Scholarship may be renewable.
Deadline: April 5.
How to apply: Applications are available online.
Exclusive: Visit www.UltimateScholarshipBook.com and enter code WI214112 for updates on this award.

(2142) · William G. Saletic Scholarship

Independent Colleges of Washington
600 Stewart Street, Suite 600
Seattle, WA 98101

Phone: 206-623-4494
Fax: 206-625-9621
Email: info@icwashington.org
http://www.icwashington.org
Purpose: To provide financial assistance to students who are studying politics or history at an independent college of Washington.
Eligibility: Applicants must be juniors or seniors who are studying or majoring in politics or history. Students attending Gonzaga University, Heritage University, Pacific Lutheran University, Saint Martin's University, Seattle Pacific University, Seattle University, University of Puget Sound, Walla Walla University, Whitman College or Whitworth University are eligible.
Target applicants: College students. Adult students.
Amount: Up to $1,000.
Number of awards: Varies.
Deadline: Varies.
How to apply: Applications are available online or from your school's financial aid office.
Exclusive: Visit www.UltimateScholarshipBook.com and enter code IN214212 for updates on this award.

(2143) • William James and Dorothy Bading Lanquist Fund

Hawaii Community Foundation - Scholarships
1164 Bishop Street, Suite 800
Honolulu, HI 96813
Phone: 888-731-3863
Fax: 808-521-6286
Email: scholarships@hcf-hawaii.org
http://www.hawaiicommunityfoundation.org
Purpose: To support students who are majoring in physical sciences and related fields.
Eligibility: Applicants must be residents of Hawaii.
Target applicants: High school students. College students. Adult students.
Amount: Varies.
Number of awards: Varies.
Deadline: March 1.
How to apply: To apply, register online, complete the online application and select the scholarships to which you wish to apply. In addition, mail the supporting materials: printed confirmation page from the online application, personal statement, copy of Student Aid Report (SAR) available at www.fafsa.ed.gov and official transcript.
Exclusive: Visit www.UltimateScholarshipBook.com and enter code HA214312 for updates on this award.

(2144) • William L. Boyd, IV, Florida Resident Access Grant

Florida Department of Education
Office of Student Financial Assistance
1940 N. Monroe Street
Suite 70
Tallahassee, FL 32303-4759
Phone: 888-827-2004
Fax: 850-245-9667
Email: osfa@fldoe.org
http://www.floridastudentfinancialaid.org
Purpose: Provides monetary assistance to Florida undergraduate college students enrolled at eligible, private, non-profit Florida schools.
Eligibility: Applicants must attend an eligible private, nonprofit Florida college or university, be Florida residents and not be in default on any state or federal grant, loan or scholarship. Requirements vary by institution.
Target applicants: High school students. College students. Adult students.
Amount: $2,529.
Number of awards: Varies.
Scholarship may be renewable.
Deadline: Varies.
How to apply: Contact your financial aid office.
Exclusive: Visit www.UltimateScholarshipBook.com and enter code FL214412 for updates on this award.

(2145) • William M. Evans Scholarship

Coles Marketing Communications
3950 Priority Way
Suite 106
Indianapolis, IN 46240
Phone: 317-571-0051
http://www.boselaw.com
Purpose: To aid special education students.
Eligibility: Applicants must be students in Indiana public high schools who are classified as special education students under 511 IAC 7 and Indiana residents. They must be graduating seniors in the year of application and must be accepted to a college, university, junior college or vocational school for the upcoming academic year.
Target applicants: High school students.
Amount: $2,000.
Number of awards: 1.
Deadline: March 20.
How to apply: Applications are available online. An application form, transcript with GPA and three letters of recommendation are required.
Exclusive: Visit www.UltimateScholarshipBook.com and enter code CO214512 for updates on this award.

(2146) • William P. Willis Scholarship Program

Oklahoma State Regents for Higher Education
655 Research Parkway
Suite 200
Oklahoma City, OK 73104
Phone: 405-225-9100
Email: llangston@osrhe.edu
http://www.okhighered.org
Purpose: To provide financial assistance to low-income students attending institutions in the Oklahoma State system.
Eligibility: Applicants must be Oklahoma residents who are enrolled full-time in an undergraduate program at an Oklahoma State System institution. They must also meet low-income criteria.
Target applicants: College students. Adult students.
Amount: Up to full tuition.
Number of awards: Varies.
Scholarship may be renewable.
Deadline: Varies.
How to apply: Students must be nominated by their college's president.
Exclusive: Visit www.UltimateScholarshipBook.com and enter code OK214612 for updates on this award.

(2147) • William Winter Teacher Scholarship

Mississippi Office of Student Financial Aid
3825 Ridgewood Road
Jackson, MS 39211

Phone: 800-327-2980
Fax: 601-432-6527
Email: sfa@ihl.state.ms.us
http://www.ihl.state.ms.us
Purpose: To increase the supply of teachers for public schools in Mississippi.
Eligibility: Applicants must be enrolled as full-time students in programs leading to a Class 'A' teaching license and must have a high school GPA of 3.0 or higher and an ACT score of 21 or higher. Sophomores, juniors, seniors and persons seeking a second baccalaureate degree leading to a Class "A" teaching license must have a cumulative college GPA of 2.5 or higher. Applicants must also agree to serve for one year in any Mississippi public school for each year they receive the scholarship. Awards are made on a first come, first served basis.
Target applicants: High school students. College students. Adult students.
Minimum GPA: 2.5
Amount: $1,000-$3,000.
Number of awards: Varies.
Scholarship may be renewable.
Deadline: March.
How to apply: Contact the Mississippi Office of Student Financial Aid for an application.
Exclusive: Visit www.UltimateScholarshipBook.com and enter code MI214712 for updates on this award.

(2148) • Wisconsin Amusement and Music Operators Scholarships

Wisconsin Amusement and Music Operators
P.O. Box 620830
Middleton, WI 53562
Phone: 800-827-8011
http://www.westerntc.edu/scholarships/wamo.asp
Purpose: To assist students of Wisconsin technical schools.
Eligibility: Applicants must be enrolled in for a minimum of six credits or plan to attend one of the 16 Wisconsin Technical College campuses. They must be family members, employees or players of a WAMO member business. They must have a recommendation from a WAMO member.
Target applicants: High school students. College students. Adult students.
Amount: Varies.
Number of awards: Varies.
Deadline: Open until awarded.
How to apply: Applications are available online. Two copies of application form, a transcript and two letters of recommendation are required.
Exclusive: Visit www.UltimateScholarshipBook.com and enter code WI214812 for updates on this award.

(2149) • Wisconsin Broadcasters Association Foundation College/University Student Scholarship Program

Wisconsin Broadcasters Association
44 E. Mifflin Street
Suite 900
Madison, WI 53703
Phone: 608-255-2600
Fax: 608-256-3986
http://www.wi-broadcasters.org
Purpose: To assist broadcasting students.
Eligibility: Applicants must attend a four-year college or university. They must major in broadcasting, communications or a related field and have completed 60 credits by the application deadline. Students must have graduated from a Wisconsin high school or be attending a Wisconsin institution of higher learning. They must plan a career in radio or television broadcasting and must not have previously won a WBA scholarship.
Target applicants: College students. Adult students.
Amount: $1,000-$2,000.
Number of awards: 4.
Deadline: October 16.
How to apply: Applications are available online. An application form, transcript, essay and two letters of recommendation are required.
Exclusive: Visit www.UltimateScholarshipBook.com and enter code WI214912 for updates on this award.

(2150) • Wisconsin Foundation for Independent Colleges Scholarship

Wisconsin Foundation for Independent Colleges
4425 North Port Washington Road
Suite 402
Glendale, WI 53212
Phone: 414-273-5980
Email: wfic@wficweb.org
http://www.wficweb.org
Purpose: To support students who are attending private colleges in Wisconsin.
Eligibility: Students must meet various college-specific requirements for each scholarship including residency, GPA and area of study.
Target applicants: High school students. College students. Adult students.
Amount: Varies.
Number of awards: Varies.
Deadline: Varies.
How to apply: Applications are available at college financial aid offices.
Exclusive: Visit www.UltimateScholarshipBook.com and enter code WI215012 for updates on this award.

(2151) • Wisconsin Higher Education Grant

State of Wisconsin Higher Educational Aids Board
P.O. Box 7885
Madison, WI 53707
Phone: 608-267-2206
Fax: 608-267-2808
Email: heabmail@wisconsin.gov
http://heab.state.wi.us
Purpose: To assist Wisconsin students who have financial need.
Eligibility: Applicants must be Wisconsin residents and certificate- or degree-seeking undergraduate students with financial need who are enrolled at least part-time. They must be attending a Wisconsin technical college, tribal college or University of Wisconsin system institution. Selection is based on financial need.
Target applicants: College students. Adult students.
Amount: $250-$3,000.
Number of awards: Varies.
Scholarship may be renewable.
Deadline: Varies.
How to apply: Application is made by completing the FAFSA.
Exclusive: Visit www.UltimateScholarshipBook.com and enter code ST215112 for updates on this award.

(2152) • Wisconsin National Guard Scholarships

Department of Military Affairs
WING-SBF
P.O. Box 14587
Madison, WI 53708-14587
Phone: 800-292-9464
Fax: 608-242-3154
Email: education@wi.ngb.army.mil
http://dma.wi.gov

Purpose: To help Wisconsin National Guard members with their education.

Eligibility: Applicants must be Wisconsin National Guard enlisted members and warrant officers in good standing who do not have a bachelor's degree. Recipients may use the grant at any campus of the University of Wisconsin System, a public institution of higher education under the Minnesota-Wisconsin student reciprocity agreement, or an accredited institution of higher education in Wisconsin.

Target applicants: High school students. College students. Adult students.

Minimum GPA: 2.0

Amount: Up to full tuition.

Number of awards: Varies.

Scholarship may be renewable.

Deadline: Varies.

How to apply: Applications are available online.

Exclusive: Visit www.UltimateScholarshipBook.com and enter code DE215212 for updates on this award.

(2153) • Wisconsin Oratorical Contest

American Legion, Department of Wisconsin
2930 American Legion Drive
P.O. Box 388
Portage, WI 53901
Phone: 608-745-1090
Fax: 608-745-0179
Email: info@wilegion.org
http://www.wilegion.org

Purpose: To enhance high school students' experience with and understanding of the U.S. Constitution. The contest will help develop students' leadership skills and civic appreciation, as well as the ability to deliver thoughtful, insightful orations regarding U.S. citizenship and its inherent responsibilities.

Eligibility: Applicants must be high school students under the age of 20 who are U.S. citizens or legal residents and residents of the state. Students first give an oration within their state and winners compete at the national level. The oration must be related to the Constitution of the United States focusing on the duties and obligations citizens have to the government. It must be in English and be between eight and ten minutes. There is also an assigned topic which is posted on the website, and it should be between three and five minutes.

Target applicants: High school students.

Amount: Varies.

Number of awards: Varies.

Deadline: Varies.

How to apply: Application information is available by contacting the local American Legion Post.

Exclusive: Visit www.UltimateScholarshipBook.com and enter code AM215312 for updates on this award.

(2154) • Wisconsin Region Student Leadership Scholarship

National Association for Campus Activities
13 Harbison Way
Columbia, SC 29212
Phone: 803-732-6222
Fax: 803-749-1047
Email: info@naca.org
http://www.naca.org

Purpose: To help students who are working toward undergraduate or graduate degrees that lead to careers in student activities or services.

Eligibility: Applicants must be undergraduate or graduate students taking at least six credits per semester and be enrolled in or have previously earned a degree from a college or university in Wisconsin or the Upper Peninsula of Michigan. Applicants must also have demonstrated leadership and service to their campus community.

Target applicants: College students. Graduate school students. Adult students.

Amount: Varies.

Number of awards: Varies.

Deadline: January 15.

How to apply: Applications are available online.

Exclusive: Visit www.UltimateScholarshipBook.com and enter code NA215412 for updates on this award.

(2155) • Wisconsin Tuition Grant

State of Wisconsin Higher Educational Aids Board
P.O. Box 7885
Madison, WI 53707
Phone: 608-267-2206
Fax: 608-267-2808
Email: heabmail@wisconsin.gov
http://heab.state.wi.us

Purpose: To assist Wisconsin undergraduate students who have financial need.

Eligibility: Applicants must be Wisconsin residents. They must be degree- or certificate-seeking undergraduate students who are attending a Wisconsin school at least part-time, and they must demonstrate financial need. Selection is based on financial need.

Target applicants: College students. Adult students.

Amount: At least $250.

Number of awards: Varies.

Scholarship may be renewable.

Deadline: Varies.

How to apply: Application is made by completing the FAFSA.

Exclusive: Visit www.UltimateScholarshipBook.com and enter code ST215512 for updates on this award.

(2156) • Wisconsin Veterans Education Reimbursement Grants

Wisconsin Department of Veterans Affairs
30 W. Mifflin Street
P.O. Box 7843
Madison, WI 53707-7843
Phone: 800-947-8387
Email: wdvaweb@dva.state.wi.us
http://www.dva.state.wi.us/default.asp

Purpose: To support Wisconsin veterans.

Eligibility: Applicants must be Wisconsin residents and must have served in the U.S. armed forces in active duty for two consecutive

years, completed their initial active service obligations, accumulated at least 90 days of active duty during wartime or have received or become qualified to receive an expeditionary or service medal. Students must have received an honorable discharge and be working toward a degree or certificate. A minimum 2.0 GPA is required. Funds are awarded upon course completion.
Target applicants: College students. Adult students.
Minimum GPA: 2.0
Amount: Up to full tuition.
Number of awards: Varies.
Deadline: No later than 60 days after the start of classes.
How to apply: Applications are available online. An application form is required.
Exclusive: Visit www.UltimateScholarshipBook.com and enter code WI215612 for updates on this award.

(2157) · Women in Science and Technology Scholarship

Virginia Business and Professional Women's Foundation
P.O. Box 4842
McLean, VA 22103-4842
Phone: 800-525-3729
Email: bpwfoundation@act.org
http://www.vabpwfoundation.org
Purpose: To support women who are pursuing careers in science and technology.
Eligibility: Applicants must be at least 18 years of age, and they must be officially accepted into a bachelor's, master's or doctoral program in the state of Virginia. Students must be majoring in biology, bio-engineering, chemistry, computer science, dentistry, engineering, mathematics, medicine, physics or similar scientific and technical fields. Applicants must show financial need and have concrete plans to use their education in a science or technical career. Recipients must complete their course of study within two years.
Target applicants: High school students. College students. Graduate school students. Adult students.
Amount: $500-$1,000.
Number of awards: Varies.
Deadline: April 1.
How to apply: Applications are available online.
Exclusive: Visit www.UltimateScholarshipBook.com and enter code VI215712 for updates on this award.

(2158) · Workforce Incentive Program

New Hampshire Postsecondary Education Commission
3 Barrell Court
Suite 300
Concord, NH 03301
Phone: 603-271-2555 x352
Fax: 603-271-2696
Email: jknapp@pec.state.nh.us
http://www.state.nh.us/postsecondary
Purpose: To encourage New Hampshire students to enter career shortage areas in special education, foreign language, mathematics, chemistry, science, physics and nursing. The scholarship repays education loans.
Eligibility: Applicants must have completed at least one year of service in an approved shortage area for each year of repayment.
Target applicants: College students. Graduate school students. Adult students.
Minimum GPA: 3.0
Amount: Up to $1,500-$3,000.
Number of awards: Varies.
Scholarship may be renewable.
Deadline: July 1 through September 30.
How to apply: Applications are available online.
Exclusive: Visit www.UltimateScholarshipBook.com and enter code NE215812 for updates on this award.

(2159) · Workforce Shortage Student Assistance Grant Program

Maryland Higher Education Commission
Office of Student Financial Assistance
839 Bestgate Road, Suite 400
Annapolis, MD 21401
Phone: 800-974-1024
Fax: 410-260-3200
Email: osfamail@mhec.state.md.us
http://www.mhec.state.md.us
Purpose: To support students in Maryland who plan to work in jobs which are needed on a statewide or regional basis.
Eligibility: Applicants must be currently enrolled or planning to enroll in a Maryland postsecondary school. Dependent students must have parents who also live in Maryland. Eligible majors are chosen to address current state or regional needs and usually include the following: child care, human services, teaching, nursing, physical and occupational therapy and public service. Students must agree to begin working within that employment field within one year of graduation at a rate of one year for every year that the scholarship was granted.
Target applicants: High school students. College students. Graduate school students. Adult students.
Amount: $1,000-$19,000.
Number of awards: Varies.
Scholarship may be renewable.
Deadline: July 1.
How to apply: Applications are available online in January.
Exclusive: Visit www.UltimateScholarshipBook.com and enter code MA215912 for updates on this award.

(2160) · World Trade Center Memorial Scholarship

New York State Higher Education Services Corporation (HESC)
99 Washington Avenue
Albany, NY 12255
Phone: 888-697-4372
Email: hescwebmail@hesc.org
http://www.hesc.com/content.nsf/
Purpose: To support the families and dependents of those who were injured or died as a result of the attacks on September 11, 2001.
Eligibility: Applicants must be full-time undergraduate students. Students must attend school in the state of New York, but they may be residents of any state or country.
Target applicants: College students. Adult students.
Amount: Up to full tuition plus room and board.
Number of awards: Varies.
Scholarship may be renewable.
Deadline: Varies.
How to apply: Applications are available online.
Exclusive: Visit www.UltimateScholarshipBook.com and enter code NE216012 for updates on this award.

(2161) • WSTLA President's Scholarship

Washington State Trial Lawyers Association
1809 7th Avenue #1500
Seattle, WA 98101-1328
Phone: 206-464-1011
Fax: 206-464-0703
Email: wstla@wstla.org
http://www.wstla.org
Purpose: To provide assistance to needy Washington students who have overcome challenges.
Eligibility: Applicants must be residents of Washington state who are attending high school at the time of application and have achieved advanced placement toward a degree. They must have financial need, and they must have overcome a disability, handicap or similar challenge. They must plan to use their education to help people.
Target applicants: High school students.
Amount: $2,000.
Number of awards: Varies.
Deadline: March 18.
How to apply: Applications are available online.
Exclusive: Visit www.UltimateScholarshipBook.com and enter code WA216112 for updates on this award.

(2162) • You've Got a Friend in Pennsylvania Scholarship

American Radio Relay League Foundation
225 Main Street
Newington, CT 06111
Phone: 860-594-0397
Fax: 860-594-0259
Email: foundation@arrl.org
http://www.arrlf.org
Purpose: To support Pennsylvania students who are involved in amateur radio.
Eligibility: Applicants must have an amateur radio license in General Class or higher and an active American Radio Relay League membership.
Target applicants: High school students. College students. Adult students.
Amount: $2,000.
Number of awards: 1.
Deadline: February 1.
How to apply: Applications are available online.
Exclusive: Visit www.UltimateScholarshipBook.com and enter code AM216212 for updates on this award.

(2163) • Zagunis Student Leader Scholarship

National Association for Campus Activities
13 Harbison Way
Columbia, SC 29212
Phone: 803-732-6222
Fax: 803-749-1047
Email: info@naca.org
http://www.naca.org
Purpose: To provide financial assistance to student leaders.
Eligibility: Applicants must hold a significant campus leadership position, demonstrate significant leadership skills and abilities and make significant contributions through on- or off-campus volunteering. Students must attend school in Kentucky, Michigan, Ohio, West Virginia or Western Pennsylvania.
Target applicants: College students. Adult students.
Minimum GPA: 3.0
Amount: Varies.
Number of awards: Varies.
Deadline: November 1.
How to apply: Applications are available online.
Exclusive: Visit www.UltimateScholarshipBook.com and enter code NA216312 for updates on this award.

MEMBERSHIP

(2164) · AFL-CIO Skilled Trades Exploring Scholarship

Explorers Learning for Life
P.O. Box 152079
Irving, TX 75015
Phone: 972-580-2433
Fax: 972-580-2137
Email: pchestnu@lflmail.org
http://www.learningforlife.org/exploring

Purpose: To assist explorers in obtaining an education that will help them start a career in skilled trades.
Eligibility: Applicants must be graduating seniors who plan to attend an accredited public or proprietary institution or a union apprentice program. They must provide three recommendations and a 500-word essay.
Target applicants: High school students.
Amount: $1,000.
Number of awards: 2.
Deadline: April 30.
How to apply: Applications are available online.
Exclusive: Visit www.UltimateScholarshipBook.com and enter code EX216412 for updates on this award.

(2165) · AFSA Financial Aid Scholarships

American Foreign Service Association (AFSA)
2101 East Street NW
Washington, DC 20037
Phone: 202-944-5504
Fax: 202-338-6820
Email: dec@afsa.org
http://www.afsa.org/

Purpose: To provide financial aid to university students who are the children or dependents of Foreign Service employees.
Eligibility: Applicants must be dependents of U.S. government Foreign Service employees with a minimum 2.0 GPA. Students must attend or plan to attend full-time an undergraduate U.S. college, university, community college, art school, conservatory or other post-secondary institution. Applicants must submit applications, transcripts and financial need reports. Recipients must complete their undergraduate degree within four years and must demonstrate financial need.
Target applicants: High school students. College students. Adult students.
Minimum GPA: 2.0
Amount: Varies.
Number of awards: Varies.
Scholarship may be renewable.
Deadline: February 6.
How to apply: Applications are available after November 1.
Exclusive: Visit www.UltimateScholarshipBook.com and enter code AM216512 for updates on this award.

(2166) · AFSA/AAFSW Merit Award

American Foreign Service Association (AFSA)
2101 East Street NW
Washington, DC 20037
Phone: 202-944-5504
Fax: 202-338-6820
Email: dec@afsa.org
http://www.afsa.org/

Purpose: To recognize the academic and artistic achievements of high school seniors who are the children or dependents of Foreign Service employees.
Eligibility: Applicants must be dependents of U.S. government Foreign Service employees who are members of AFSA or AAFSW. Students must be high school seniors with a minimum 2.0 GPA. Applicants can also submit an art entry under the categories of visual arts, musical arts, drama, dance or creative writing. Awards are based on GPA, SAT scores, a two-page essay, letters of recommendation and extra-curricular activities.
Target applicants: High school students.
Minimum GPA: 2.0
Amount: $800-$1,800.
Number of awards: Varies.
Deadline: February 6.
How to apply: Applications are available online after November 1.
Exclusive: Visit www.UltimateScholarshipBook.com and enter code AM216612 for updates on this award.

(2167) · AFSCME Family Scholarship Program

American Federation of State, County and Municipal Employees (AFSCME), AFL-CIO
Attn: Education Department
1625 L Street NW
Washington, DC 20036-5687
Phone: 202-429-1000
Fax: 202-429-1293
Email: education@afscme.org
http://www.afscme.org

Purpose: To offer financial assistance to the dependents of AFSCME members.
Eligibility: Applicants must be graduating high school seniors who are the daughters, sons or financially dependent grandchildren of AFSCME members who intend to enroll in a full-time, four-year degree program in any accredited college or university. Applicants should submit applications, essays, transcripts, test scores and recommendation letters. Selection is based on information provided on the application form, high school transcript, SAT/ACT scores and a required essay.
Target applicants: High school students.
Amount: $2,000.
Number of awards: At least 10.
Scholarship may be renewable.
Deadline: December 31.
How to apply: Applications are available online and by written request.
Exclusive: Visit www.UltimateScholarshipBook.com and enter code AM216712 for updates on this award.

(2168) · AFTRA/Heller Memorial Foundation Scholarships

American Federation of Television and Radio Artists
260 Madison Avenue
7th Floor
New York, NY 10016
Phone: 212-532-0800
Fax: 212-532-2242
Email: info@aftra.com
http://www.aftra.com

Purpose: To support AFTRA members and their children.
Eligibility: Applicants must be AFTRA members in good standing with five years of membership or the children of members. Scholarships are awarded based on academic achievement and financial need and can

be used to study any academic field or for professional training in the performing arts at an accredited higher education institution.
Target applicants: High school students. College students. Graduate school students. Adult students.
Amount: Up to $2,500.
Number of awards: 12-15.
Deadline: May 1.
How to apply: Applications are available online.
Exclusive: Visit www.UltimateScholarshipBook.com and enter code AM216812 for updates on this award.

(2169) • AGCO Corporation FFA Scholarship

National FFA Organization
P.O. Box 68960
6060 FFA Drive
Indianapolis, IN 46268-0960
Phone: 317-802-6060
Fax: 317-802-6051
Email: scholarships@ffa.org
http://www.ffa.org/
Purpose: To support students in select majors who are in the FFA.
Eligibility: Applicants must be current FFA members and high school seniors or college students planning to enroll or currently enrolled full-time. They must have one of the following undergraduate majors: agronomy, crop science, general agriculture, agricultural communications, education, journalism, extension, public relations, business management, economics, sales and marketing, engineering, mechanization, agriculture power and equipment or welding. Students only need to complete the online application one time to be considered for all FFA-administered scholarships. The application requires information about the student's activities and a 1,000-word essay. Awards may be used for books, supplies, tuition, fees and room and board. Students must show financial need and evidence of community service participation.
Target applicants: High school students. College students. Adult students.
Amount: $2,000.
Number of awards: 12.
Deadline: February 15.
How to apply: Applications are available online.
Exclusive: Visit www.UltimateScholarshipBook.com and enter code NA216912 for updates on this award.

(2170) • Agrium U.S. Inc. FFA Scholarship

National FFA Organization
P.O. Box 68960
6060 FFA Drive
Indianapolis, IN 46268-0960
Phone: 317-802-6060
Fax: 317-802-6051
Email: scholarships@ffa.org
http://www.ffa.org/
Purpose: To support students who are members of the FFA.
Eligibility: Applicants must be current FFA members and high school seniors or college students planning to enroll or currently enrolled full-time. They must have at least a 3.0 GPA and be pursuing a bachelor's degree in one of the following subjects: agricultural sales, marketing, engineering, agronomy or crop science. Students only need to complete the online application one time to be considered for all FFA-administered scholarships. The application requires information about the students' activities and a 1,000-word essay. Awards may be used for books, supplies, tuition, fees and room and board. Applicants must show proof of community service participation.
Target applicants: High school students. College students. Adult students.
Minimum GPA: 3.0
Amount: $1,000.
Number of awards: 5.
Deadline: February 15.
How to apply: Applications are available online.
Exclusive: Visit www.UltimateScholarshipBook.com and enter code NA217012 for updates on this award.

(2171) • Airbus Leadership Grant

Women in Aviation, International
Morningstar Airport
3647 State Route 503 South
West Alexandria, OH 45381
Phone: 937-839-4647
Fax: 937-839-4645
Email: dwallace@wai.org
http://www.wai.org
Purpose: To help Women in Aviation, International members who are college sophomores or above.
Eligibility: Applicants must be WAI members, have a GPA of 3.0 or higher, have demonstrated leadership skills and be enrolled in an aviation-related degree program. Selection is based on academic and aviation-related achievements, leadership skills, commitment to professional goals, the motivation to succeed and financial need.
Target applicants: College students. Adult students.
Minimum GPA: 3.0
Amount: $5,000.
Number of awards: 1.
Deadline: November 15.
How to apply: Applications are available online or can be sent by mail by request. An application form, three recommendation letters, a resume and an essay are required.
Exclusive: Visit www.UltimateScholarshipBook.com and enter code WO217112 for updates on this award.

(2172) • All-Teke Academic Team

Tau Kappa Epsilon Educational Foundation
8645 Founders Road
Indianapolis, IN 46268
Phone: 317-872-6533
Fax: 317-875-8353
Email: tef@tke.org
http://www.tkefoundation.org
Purpose: To recognize the scholastic achievement of the top ten members academically.
Eligibility: Applicants must be initiated Tau Kappa Epsilon members in good standing and full-time students. Applicants must also have a GPA of at least 3.0 and demonstrate outstanding positive contributions to their chapter, campus and community. A statement describing how they have benefited from TKE membership is required.
Target applicants: College students. Adult students.
Minimum GPA: 3.0
Amount: $150.
Number of awards: 10.
Deadline: March 1.
How to apply: Applications are available online.

Exclusive: Visit www.UltimateScholarshipBook.com and enter code TA217212 for updates on this award.

(2173) • Allan Jerome Burry Scholarship

United Methodist Church
Office of Loans and Scholarships
P.O. BOX 340007
Nashville, TN 37203-0007
Phone: 615-340-7344
Fax: 615-340-7367
Email: umscholar@gbhem.org
http://www.gbhem.org

Purpose: To support students in ministry or chaplaincy programs who are members of the United Methodist Church.

Eligibility: Applicants must be college undergraduates who show evidence of financial need, leadership qualities, academic excellence and church participation. They must have a GPA of 3.0 or higher. Students must have been active members of the United Methodist Church for at least three years and be nominated by the campus chaplain or minister.

Target applicants: College students. Adult students.

Minimum GPA: 3.0

Amount: Varies.

Number of awards: Varies.

Deadline: January 15.

How to apply: Applications are available from campus ministers or chaplains.

Exclusive: Visit www.UltimateScholarshipBook.com and enter code UN217312 for updates on this award.

(2174) • ALPA Scholarship Program

Air Line Pilots Association
1625 Massachusetts Avenue NW
Washington, DC 20036
Phone: 703-689-2270
http://www.alpa.org

Purpose: To support the children of medically retired, long-term disabled or deceased pilot members of the Air Line Pilots Association.

Eligibility: Applicants must be pursuing a baccalaureate degree. Selection is based on academic achievements and financial need. The award is renewable for four years with a minimum 3.0 GPA.

Target applicants: High school students. College students. Adult students.

Minimum GPA: 3.0

Amount: Varies.

Number of awards: Varies.

Scholarship may be renewable.

Deadline: Varies.

How to apply: Applications are available by mail.

Exclusive: Visit www.UltimateScholarshipBook.com and enter code AI217412 for updates on this award.

(2175) • Alpha Gamma Rho Educational Foundation

National FFA Organization
P.O. Box 68960
6060 FFA Drive
Indianapolis, IN 46268-0960
Phone: 317-802-6060
Fax: 317-802-6051
Email: scholarships@ffa.org
http://www.ffa.org/

Purpose: To support male students who are majoring in agriculture.

Eligibility: Applicants must be current FFA members and high school seniors or college students planning to enroll or currently enrolled full-time. Students must enroll in a college which has an Alpha Gamma Rho chapter, and they should be pursuing a four-year degree in any field related to agriculture. Students only need to complete the online application one time to be considered for all FFA-administered scholarships. The application requires information about the student's activities and a 1,000-word essay. Awards may be used for books, supplies, tuition, fees and room and board.

Target applicants: High school students. College students. Adult students.

Amount: $1,000.

Number of awards: 1.

Deadline: February 15.

How to apply: Applications are available online.

Exclusive: Visit www.UltimateScholarshipBook.com and enter code NA217512 for updates on this award.

(2176) • Alvin E. Heaps Memorial Scholarship

Retail, Wholesale and Department Store Union District Council (RWDSU)
30 E. 29th Street
New York, NY 10016
Phone: 212-684-5300
Fax: 212-779-2809
http://www.rwdsu.info

Purpose: To provide scholarships for RWDSU members and their children.

Eligibility: Applicants must be RWDSU members or their children. Recipients are determined through consideration of academic performance, involvement in extracurricular activities and completion of a 500-word essay.

Target applicants: High school students. College students. Adult students.

Amount: Varies.

Number of awards: Varies.

Deadline: June 1.

How to apply: Applications are available online or by written request.

Exclusive: Visit www.UltimateScholarshipBook.com and enter code RE217612 for updates on this award.

(2177) • American Family Insurance FFA Scholarship

National FFA Organization
P.O. Box 68960
6060 FFA Drive
Indianapolis, IN 46268-0960
Phone: 317-802-6060
Fax: 317-802-6051
Email: scholarships@ffa.org
http://www.ffa.org/

Purpose: To support students who are members of the FFA.

Eligibility: Applicants must be current FFA members and high school seniors or college students planning to enroll or currently enrolled full-time. They may be pursuing a four-year degree in any major in the state of Wisconsin, Minnesota or Missouri. Students only need to complete the online application one time to be considered for all FFA-administered scholarships. The application requires information about the students' activities and a 1,000-word essay. Awards may be used for books, supplies, tuition, fees and room and board.

Target applicants: High school students. College students. Adult students.
Amount: $1,000.
Number of awards: 3.
Deadline: February 15.
How to apply: Applications are available online.
Exclusive: Visit www.UltimateScholarshipBook.com and enter code NA217712 for updates on this award.

(2178) • American Legion Eagle Scout of the Year

American Legion
Attn.: Americanism and Children and Youth Division
P.O. Box 1055
Indianapolis, IN 46206
Phone: 317-630-1249
Fax: 317-630-1369
Email: acy@legion.org
http://www.legion.org
Purpose: To provide scholarships for Eagle Scouts.
Eligibility: Applicants must be registered, active members of a Boy Scout Troop, Varsity Scout Team or Venturing crew chartered to an American Legion Post or Auxiliary or Scouts who are the sons or grandsons of Legionnaires or Auxiliary Members. Applicants must receive the Eagle Scout Award, be active members of their religious institutions, receiving the appropriate Boy Scouts religious emblem, demonstrate citizenship, be at least 15 years old and be high school students.
Target applicants: High school students.
Amount: $2,500-$10,000.
Number of awards: 4.
Deadline: March 1.
How to apply: Applications are available online.
Exclusive: Visit www.UltimateScholarshipBook.com and enter code AM217812 for updates on this award.

(2179) • American Veterinary Medical Association FFA Scholarship

National FFA Organization
P.O. Box 68960
6060 FFA Drive
Indianapolis, IN 46268-0960
Phone: 317-802-6060
Fax: 317-802-6051
Email: scholarships@ffa.org
http://www.ffa.org/
Purpose: To support students who are pursuing degrees related to animal science.
Eligibility: Applicants must be current FFA members and high school seniors or college students planning to enroll or currently enrolled full-time. They must be pursuing a four-year degree in one of the following subject areas: animal nutrition; animal, dairy, equine or poultry science; animal breeding and genetics; animal pathology or veterinary sciences. Preference will be given to students who are planning to work in the fields of veterinary medicine and veterinary food supply. Students only need to complete the online application one time to be considered for all FFA-administered scholarships. The application requires information about the student's activities and a 1,000-word essay. Awards may be used for books, supplies, tuition, fees and room and board.
Target applicants: High school students. College students. Adult students.
Amount: $1,000.
Number of awards: 3.
Deadline: February 15.
How to apply: Applications are available online.
Exclusive: Visit www.UltimateScholarshipBook.com and enter code NA217912 for updates on this award.

(2180) • AMVETS National Ladies Auxiliary Scholarship

AMVETS Auxiliary
4647 Forbes Boulevard
Lanham, MD 20706
Phone: 301-459-6255
http://www.amvetsaux.org
Purpose: To promote educational opportunities for students interested in or involved with a national service organization.
Eligibility: Applicants must be the child or grandchild of a current member of the AMVETS Ladies Auxiliary.
Target applicants: High school students. College students. Adult students.
Amount: $750-$1,000.
Number of awards: 5-7.
Deadline: July 1.
How to apply: Applications are available by mail.
Exclusive: Visit www.UltimateScholarshipBook.com and enter code AM218012 for updates on this award.

(2181) • Anderson Foundation FFA Scholarship

National FFA Organization
P.O. Box 68960
6060 FFA Drive
Indianapolis, IN 46268-0960
Phone: 317-802-6060
Fax: 317-802-6051
Email: scholarships@ffa.org
http://www.ffa.org/
Purpose: To support students who are majoring in agriculture.
Eligibility: Applicants must be current FFA members and high school seniors or college students planning to enroll or currently enrolled full-time. They must be pursuing a four-year degree in agriculture in the state of Illinois, Indiana, Michigan or Ohio. Applicants must show proof of community service participation. Students only need to complete the online application one time to be considered for all FFA-administered scholarships. The application requires information about the student's activities and a 1,000-word essay. Awards may be used for books, supplies, tuition, fees and room and board.
Target applicants: High school students. College students. Adult students.
Amount: $1,250.
Number of awards: 2.
Deadline: February 15.
How to apply: Applications are available online.
Exclusive: Visit www.UltimateScholarshipBook.com and enter code NA218112 for updates on this award.

(2182) • ARA Scholarship

ARA Scholarship Foundation Inc.
ARA Scholarship Advisor
109 Defiant Way
Grass Valley, CA 95945
Phone: 703-385-1001
Email: arascholar@sbcglobal.net

http://www.a-r-a.org
Purpose: To support the children of Automotive Recyclers Association (ARA) members.
Eligibility: Applicants must be high school seniors and/or planning to attend college full-time and have earned a minimum 3.0 GPA in their last educational program. Applicants must also be the children of employees of a Direct Member of ARA who were hired at least one year prior to March 15 of the application year. Scholarships are based on academic merit, not financial need.
Target applicants: High school students. College students. Graduate school students. Adult students.
Minimum GPA: 3.0
Amount: Varies.
Number of awards: Varies.
Scholarship may be renewable.
Deadline: March 15.
How to apply: Applications are available online and by email request.
Exclusive: Visit www.UltimateScholarshipBook.com and enter code AR218212 for updates on this award.

(2183) • Archer Daniels Midland Company FFA Scholarship

National FFA Organization
P.O. Box 68960
6060 FFA Drive
Indianapolis, IN 46268-0960
Phone: 317-802-6060
Fax: 317-802-6051
Email: scholarships@ffa.org
http://www.ffa.org/
Purpose: To support students who are majoring in agriculture.
Eligibility: Applicants must be current FFA members and high school seniors or college students planning to enroll or currently enrolled full-time in an agriculture program. They must have at least a 2.8 GPA and a history of leadership and community service. Students only need to complete the online application one time to be considered for all FFA-administered scholarships. The application requires information about the student's activities and a 1,000-word essay. Awards may be used for books, supplies, tuition, fees and room and board.
Target applicants: High school students. College students. Adult students.
Minimum GPA: 2.8
Amount: $1,000.
Number of awards: 80.
Deadline: February 15.
How to apply: Applications are available online.
Exclusive: Visit www.UltimateScholarshipBook.com and enter code NA218312 for updates on this award.

(2184) • Armstrong Achievement Scholarships

Armstrong Foundation
2500 Columbia Avenue
Lancaster, PA 17603
Phone: 717-396-5536
Fax: 717-396-6124
Email: foundation@armstrongfoundation.com
http://www.armstrongfoundation.com
Purpose: The Armstrong Foundation awards four-year awards for college to children of employees and retirees of Armstrong and its subsidiaries.
Eligibility: Applicants must be sons or daughters of full-time or retired employees of Armstrong or its subsidiaries. Eligible students must also meet all requirements for participation in the Merit Program as sponsored by the National Merit Scholarship Corporation.
Target applicants: High school students.
Amount: $2,500.
Number of awards: Varies.
Scholarship may be renewable.
Deadline: January 31.
How to apply: Applications are available online.
Exclusive: Visit www.UltimateScholarshipBook.com and enter code AR218412 for updates on this award.

(2185) • Arysta LifeScience North America FFA Scholarship

National FFA Organization
P.O. Box 68960
6060 FFA Drive
Indianapolis, IN 46268-0960
Phone: 317-802-6060
Fax: 317-802-6051
Email: scholarships@ffa.org
http://www.ffa.org/
Purpose: To support students in the FFA who are studying agriculture or business.
Eligibility: Applicants must be current FFA members and high school seniors or college students planning to enroll or currently enrolled full-time. They must be majoring in one of the following subject areas: agronomy, crop science, horticulture, nursery and landscape management, plant science, turf management, agricultural communications, public relations or sales and marketing, entomology or plant pathology. Applicants must have at least a 3.0 GPA. Students only need to complete the online application one time to be considered for all FFA-administered scholarships. The application requires information about the student's activities and a 1,000-word essay. Awards may be used for books, supplies, tuition, fees and room and board.
Target applicants: High school students. College students. Adult students.
Minimum GPA: 3.0
Amount: $1,275.
Number of awards: 5.
Deadline: February 15.
How to apply: Applications are available online.
Exclusive: Visit www.UltimateScholarshipBook.com and enter code NA218512 for updates on this award.

(2186) • Ashby B. Carter Memorial Scholarship

National Alliance of Postal and Federal Employees (NAPFE)
1628 11th Street NW
Washington, DC 20001
Phone: 202-939-6325
Email: headquarters@napfe.org
http://www.napfe.com
Purpose: To aid the dependents of National Alliance members in furthering their education.
Eligibility: Applicants must be dependents of members of the National Alliance of Postal and Federal Employees who have been in good standing for at least three years. Applicants must take the Aptitude Test of the College Board Entrance Examination at their local high school before March 1 and be high school seniors.
Target applicants: High school students.
Amount: $2,000-$5,000.
Number of awards: 3.

Deadline: April 1.
How to apply: Applications are available online.
Exclusive: Visit www.UltimateScholarshipBook.com and enter code NA218612 for updates on this award.

(2187) • Association of Flight Attendants Annual Scholarship

Association of Flight Attendants
501 Third Street NW
Washington, DC 20001
Phone: 202-434-1300
Email: afatalk@afanet.org
http://www.afanet.org
Purpose: To provide financial assistance to the children of members of the AFA.
Eligibility: Applicants must be the dependents of AFA members in good standing. Applicants must also be in the top 15 percent of their class, have or expect to have excellent SAT/ACT scores, demonstrate financial need and provide a 300-word essay along with the completed application.
Target applicants: High school students.
Amount: Up to $5,000.
Number of awards: 1.
Scholarship may be renewable.
Deadline: April 10.
How to apply: Applications are available online.
Exclusive: Visit www.UltimateScholarshipBook.com and enter code AS218712 for updates on this award.

(2188) • Astrid G. Cates Scholarship Fund and the Myrtle Beinhauer Scholarship

Sons of Norway Foundation
1455 West Lake Street
Minneapolis, MN 55408
Phone: 800-945-8851
Fax: 612-827-0658
Email: foundation@sofn.com
http://www.sofn.com
Purpose: To support the members and children and grandchildren of members of the Sons of Norway.
Eligibility: Applicants must have a certificate of completion from high school and be enrolled in post-secondary training or education (college, vocational school or trade school) and be current members of Sons of Norway or the children or grandchildren of current Sons of Norway members in Sons of Norway districts 1-6. Membership must be in effect for one calendar year prior to application. Students must also have strong financial need. Selection is based on financial need, a statement of education and career goals, applicants' grade-point averages, a letter of recommendation and applicants' extracurricular involvements.
Target applicants: College students. Adult students.
Amount: $1,000-$3,000.
Number of awards: 8.
Deadline: March 1.
How to apply: Applications are available online and by mail.
Exclusive: Visit www.UltimateScholarshipBook.com and enter code SO218812 for updates on this award.

(2189) • Awards of Excellence Scholarship Program

International Order of the Golden Rule
Education Department
P.O. Box 28689
St. Louis, MO 631461189
Phone: 800-637-8030
Fax: 314-209-7213
Email: jgabbert@ogr.org
http://www.ogr.org
Purpose: To provide aid for students in mortuary science and who intend to pursue a career in the funeral service profession.
Eligibility: Applicants must be currently enrolled in a mortuary science school and have a minimum 3.0 GPA. The award is based on community service, honors, grades and potential contributions to the funeral service profession.
Target applicants: College students. Adult students.
Minimum GPA: 3.0
Amount: Up to $3,500.
Number of awards: Varies.
Deadline: January 31.
How to apply: Applications are available online or by email.
Exclusive: Visit www.UltimateScholarshipBook.com and enter code IN218912 for updates on this award.

(2190) • Beatrice S. Jacobson Memorial Fund

American Guild of Musical Artists
1430 Broadway, 14th Floor
New York, NY 10018
Phone: 212-265-3687
Fax: 212-262-9088
Email: agma@musicalartists.org
http://www.musicalartists.org
Purpose: To provide scholarships to AGMA members.
Eligibility: Applicants must be AGMA members in good standing for at least two years who are full- or part-time, traditional or adult students working toward either undergraduate or graduate degrees. The award is based on financial need and GPA. Applicants don't have to be music majors.
Target applicants: College students. Graduate school students. Adult students.
Amount: Varies.
Number of awards: Varies.
Deadline: April 1.
How to apply: Applications are available by written request.
Exclusive: Visit www.UltimateScholarshipBook.com and enter code AM219012 for updates on this award.

(2191) • Bernard Rotberg Memorial Scholarship Fund

Jewish War Veterans of the USA
1811 R Street NW
Washington, DC 20009
Phone: 202-265-6280
Fax: 202-234-5662
Email: jwv@jwv.org
http://www.jwv.org
Purpose: To provide scholarships for descendents of members of the Jewish War Veterans of the USA.
Eligibility: Applicants must be a direct descendent of a JWV member in good standing. Candidates must also have been accepted to an accredited college, university or nursing school, be in the upper 25 percent of their class and be active in activities at school and within the Jewish community.
Target applicants: High school students.
Amount: $1,000.

Number of awards: 1.
Deadline: May 4.
How to apply: Applications are available online and should be submitted by the applicant's school to the department commander in the local post.
Exclusive: Visit www.UltimateScholarshipBook.com and enter code JE219112 for updates on this award.

(2192) • Berrien Fragos Thorn Arts Scholarships for Migrant Farmworkers

BOCES Geneseo Migrant Center
27 Lackawanna Avenue
Mt. Morris, NY 14510
Phone: 800-245-5681
Fax: 585-658-7969
Email: info@migrant.net
http://www.migrant.net
Purpose: To foster and encourage the creative talents of students with migrant histories.
Eligibility: Applicants must be at least 16 years old and must have a history of movement to obtain agricultural work. Applicants need not be enrolled in school at the time of application.
Target applicants: High school students. College students. Adult students.
Amount: $500-$2,500.
Number of awards: Varies.
Deadline: No deadline for grants under $500, applications reviewed case-by-case.
How to apply: Applications are available online.
Exclusive: Visit www.UltimateScholarshipBook.com and enter code BO219212 for updates on this award.

(2193) • Bill Moon Scholarship

NATSO Foundation
Heather Mooney
c/o Bill Moon Scholarship Committee
60 Main Street
Farmington, CT 06032
Phone: 703-549-2100
Fax: 703-684-9667
http://www.natsofoundation.org
Purpose: To assist Truck Stop Operators industry employees and their families.
Eligibility: Applicants must be Truck Stop Operators industry employees or their family members and must submit applications, essays, recommendation letters, transcripts and financial information. The award is based on academic merit, financial need, community activities and essays.
Target applicants: High school students. College students. Graduate school students. Adult students.
Amount: Varies.
Number of awards: Varies.
Deadline: April 16.
How to apply: Applications are available online.
Exclusive: Visit www.UltimateScholarshipBook.com and enter code NA219312 for updates on this award.

(2194) • BLET Auxiliary Scholarships

Brotherhood of Locomotive Engineers and Trainmen
3341 S. 112th Street
Omaha, NE 68144-4709
Phone: 402-330-6348
Email: bunziegia@cox.net
http://www.ble.org
Purpose: To provide scholarships to the children of members of the BLE.
Eligibility: Applicants must be the children of both a Grand International Auxiliary (GIA) and BLE member (living or deceased) and enrolled or accepted by an accredited university, college or institute of higher learning. If the applicant is a graduate student or returning to school as a sophomore, junior or senior, he or she must have a minimum 3.0 GPA. Selection is based on academic record, leadership, character and personal achievement. Applicants must have a parent participating in the IWC.
Target applicants: High school students. College students. Graduate school students. Adult students.
Minimum GPA: 3.0
Amount: $1,000.
Number of awards: Varies.
Scholarship may be renewable.
Deadline: April 1.
How to apply: Applications are available online and by written request through your local GIA auxiliary or BLE division.
Exclusive: Visit www.UltimateScholarshipBook.com and enter code BR219412 for updates on this award.

(2195) • BNSF Railway Company FFA Scholarship

National FFA Organization
P.O. Box 68960
6060 FFA Drive
Indianapolis, IN 46268-0960
Phone: 317-802-6060
Fax: 317-802-6051
Email: scholarships@ffa.org
http://www.ffa.org/
Purpose: To support FFA members who are majoring in agriculture.
Eligibility: Applicants must be current FFA members and high school seniors or college students planning to enroll or currently enrolled full-time. Students must be pursuing a four-year degree in one of the following agricultural fields: business management, economics, sales and marketing or finance. They must be residents of California, Illinois, Iowa, Kansas, Minnesota, Montana, Nebraska, North Dakota, South Dakota or Texas. Applicants must have at least a 3.0 GPA. Students only need to complete the online application one time to be considered for all FFA-administered scholarships. The application requires information about the student's activities and a 1,000-word essay. Awards may be used for books, supplies, tuition, fees and room and board.
Target applicants: High school students. College students. Adult students.
Minimum GPA: 3.0
Amount: $5,000.
Number of awards: 10.
Scholarship may be renewable.
Deadline: February 15.
How to apply: Applications are available online.
Exclusive: Visit www.UltimateScholarshipBook.com and enter code NA219512 for updates on this award.

(2196) • Boilermakers, Iron Ship Builders, Blacksmiths, Forgers and Helpers, International Brotherhood of (IBB) Scholarship Awards

Boilermakers, Iron Ship Builders, Blacksmiths, Forgers and Helpers, (IBB)

753 State Avenue
Suite 570
Kansas City, KS 66101
Phone: 913-371-2640
http://www.boilermakers.org
Purpose: To provide scholarships to the children of members of the International Brotherhood.
Eligibility: Applicants must be the children or dependents of members of the IBB and high school seniors who will be entering their first year of college as full-time students within one year of graduation from high school. U.S. applicants are required to take the SAT or ACT. Recipients are selected on the basis of academic achievement, career goals, extracurricular activities, outside school activities and essay.
Target applicants: High school students.
Amount: Up to $5,000.
Number of awards: Varies.
Deadline: March 1.
How to apply: Applications are available by written request.
Exclusive: Visit www.UltimateScholarshipBook.com and enter code BO219612 for updates on this award.

(2197) • Boys and Girls Clubs of America National Youth of the Year Award

Boys and Girls Clubs of America
1275 Peachtree Street NE
Atlanta, GA 30309
Phone: 404-487-5700
Email: info@bgca.org
http://www.bgca.org
Purpose: To reward club members who demonstrate good academic performance, perform services for both their club and community and who are active in both family and spiritual life.
Eligibility: Applicants must be a member of a BGCA and be selected by their local club to compete for the regional and national scholarships.
Target applicants: High school students.
Amount: $1,000-$26,000.
Number of awards: Varies.
Deadline: Varies.
How to apply: Contact your local club for more information.
Exclusive: Visit www.UltimateScholarshipBook.com and enter code BO219712 for updates on this award.

(2198) • BRIDGE Endowment Fund FFA Scholarship

National FFA Organization
P.O. Box 68960
6060 FFA Drive
Indianapolis, IN 46268-0960
Phone: 317-802-6060
Fax: 317-802-6051
Email: scholarships@ffa.org
http://www.ffa.org/
Purpose: To support disabled students who are studying agriculture.
Eligibility: Applicants must be current FFA members and high school seniors or college students planning to enroll or currently enrolled full-time. They must be physically disabled or handicapped. Students only need to complete the online application one time to be considered for all FFA-administered scholarships. The application requires information about the student's activities and a 1,000-word essay. Awards may be used for books, supplies, tuition, fees and room and board.
Target applicants: High school students. College students. Adult students.
Amount: $5,000.
Number of awards: 1.
Deadline: February 15.
How to apply: Applications are available online.
Exclusive: Visit www.UltimateScholarshipBook.com and enter code NA219812 for updates on this award.

(2199) • Bridgestone/Firestone Trust Fund FFA Scholarship

National FFA Organization
P.O. Box 68960
6060 FFA Drive
Indianapolis, IN 46268-0960
Phone: 317-802-6060
Fax: 317-802-6051
Email: scholarships@ffa.org
http://www.ffa.org/
Purpose: To support students from families that are involved in farming.
Eligibility: Applicants must be current FFA members and high school seniors or college students planning to enroll or currently enrolled full-time. They must live on the family farm and show financial need, leadership skills and community service participation. Students only need to complete the online application one time to be considered for all FFA-administered scholarships. The application requires information about the student's activities and a 1,000-word essay. Awards may be used for books, supplies, tuition, fees and room and board.
Target applicants: High school students. College students. Adult students.
Amount: $2,500.
Number of awards: 5.
Deadline: February 15.
How to apply: Applications are available online.
Exclusive: Visit www.UltimateScholarshipBook.com and enter code NA219912 for updates on this award.

(2200) • Bruce B. Melchert Scholarship

Tau Kappa Epsilon Educational Foundation
8645 Founders Road
Indianapolis, IN 46268
Phone: 317-872-6533
Fax: 317-875-8353
Email: tef@tke.org
http://www.tkefoundation.org
Purpose: To award a member of Tau Kappa Epsilon for outstanding academic achievement and leadership within the chapter as a recruitment chair, prytanis, major officer or leader in IFC or other organizations.
Eligibility: Applicants must have a GPA of at least 3.0, be sophomores or above and be seeking an undergraduate degree in political science or government. Applicants must also plan to pursue a career in political or government service. Preference is first given to members of the Beta-Theta Chapter.
Target applicants: College students. Adult students.
Minimum GPA: 3.0
Amount: $150.
Number of awards: 1.
Deadline: March 1.
How to apply: Applications are available online.
Exclusive: Visit www.UltimateScholarshipBook.com and enter code TA220012 for updates on this award.

(2201) • Buckingham Memorial Scholarship

Air Traffic Control Association
1101 King Street
Suite 300
Alexandria, VA 22134
Phone: 703-299-2430
Fax: 703-299-2437
Email: info@atca.org
http://www.atca.org

Purpose: To provide education assistance for children of ATCA Specialists.

Eligibility: Applicants must be U.S. citizens who are half- or full-time students enrolled in an accredited institution of higher learning. They may pursue an undergraduate degree in any major.

Target applicants: High school students. College students. Adult students.

Amount: Varies.

Number of awards: Varies.

Deadline: May 1.

How to apply: Applications are available from the ATCA.

Exclusive: Visit www.UltimateScholarshipBook.com and enter code AI220112 for updates on this award.

(2202) • Business Achievement Awards

Golden Key National Honour Society
Scholarship Program Administrators
Golden Key Scholarships/Awards
P.O. Box 23737
Nashville, TN 37202-3737
Phone: 800-377-2401
Email: scholarships@goldenkey.org
http://www.goldenkey.org

Purpose: To support Golden Key members who are studying business.

Eligibility: Applicants must be undergraduate, graduate or post-graduate members who are currently attending classes in a degree-granting program. The award is based on academic achievement and a business-related paper or report.

Target applicants: College students. Graduate school students. Adult students.

Amount: $1,000-$2,000.

Number of awards: 3.

Deadline: March 1.

How to apply: Applications are available online.

Exclusive: Visit www.UltimateScholarshipBook.com and enter code GO220212 for updates on this award.

(2203) • Carrol C. Hall Memorial Scholarship

Tau Kappa Epsilon Educational Foundation
8645 Founders Road
Indianapolis, IN 46268
Phone: 317-872-6533
Fax: 317-875-8353
Email: tef@tke.org
http://www.tkefoundation.org

Purpose: To award a member of Tau Kappa Epsilon for outstanding academic achievement and for leadership within the organization, campus or community.

Eligibility: Applicants must have a minimum 3.0 GPA and be undergraduates seeking a degree in education or science with the intention of pursuing a career in teaching or the sciences.

Target applicants: College students. Adult students.

Minimum GPA: 3.0

Amount: $250.

Number of awards: 1.

Deadline: March 1.

How to apply: Applications are available online.

Exclusive: Visit www.UltimateScholarshipBook.com and enter code TA220312 for updates on this award.

(2204) • Casey's General Stores Inc. FFA Scholarship

National FFA Organization
P.O. Box 68960
6060 FFA Drive
Indianapolis, IN 46268-0960
Phone: 317-802-6060
Fax: 317-802-6051
Email: scholarships@ffa.org
http://www.ffa.org/

Purpose: To support agriculture students.

Eligibility: Applicants must be current FFA members and high school seniors or college students planning to enroll or currently enrolled full-time. They must be pursuing a two-year or four-year degree in agriculture and have plans to work in agriculture or agribusiness. Applicants must be residents of one of the following states: Illinois, Indiana, Iowa, Kansas, Minnesota, Missouri, Nebraska, South Dakota or Wisconsin. Students only need to complete the online application one time to be considered for all FFA-administered scholarships. The application requires information about the student's activities and a 1,000-word essay. Awards may be used for books, supplies, tuition, fees and room and board.

Target applicants: High school students. College students. Adult students.

Amount: $1,000.

Number of awards: 3.

Deadline: February 15.

How to apply: Applications are available online.

Exclusive: Visit www.UltimateScholarshipBook.com and enter code NA220412 for updates on this award.

(2205) • Catholic Aid Association College Tuition Scholarship

Catholic Aid Association
Scholarship Program
3499 Lexington Avenue North
St. Paul, MN 55126
Phone: 800-568-6670
Email: caa@catholicaid.com
http://www.catholicaid.com

Purpose: To award scholarships to members of the Catholic Aid Association.

Eligibility: Applicants must be members of the Catholic Aid Association for at least two years prior to the date of application, have completed high school and be entering their first or second year in any accredited college, university, state college or technical college other than a private, non-Catholic college/university.

Target applicants: High school students. College students. Adult students.

Amount: $300-$500.

Number of awards: Varies.

Deadline: February 15.

How to apply: Applications are available online.

Exclusive: Visit www.UltimateScholarshipBook.com and enter code CA220512 for updates on this award.

(2206) • Catholic Workman Scholarship

First Catholic Slovak Ladies Association
Attn.: Scholarships
24950 Chagrin Blvd
Beachwood, OH 44122
Phone: 800-464-4642
Fax: 216-464-9260
Email: info@fcsla.org
http://www.fcsla.org
Purpose: To assist insured members of Catholic Workman.
Eligibility: Applicants must be a member of First Catholic Slovak Ladies Association for three years prior to date of application. An application and supporting documents are required. Selection is based on academic standing (50 percent), financial need (20 percent), family membership (15 percent), leadership (10 percent) and extenuating circumstances (5 percent). There are scholarships for elementary school, junior high, high school and college students.
Target applicants: Junior high students or younger. High school students. College students. Adult students.
Minimum GPA: 2.5
Amount: $750-$1,750.
Number of awards: 221.
Scholarship may be renewable.
Deadline: March 1.
How to apply: Applications are available online or by phone.
Exclusive: Visit www.UltimateScholarshipBook.com and enter code FI220612 for updates on this award.

(2207) • Central Atlantic Region National Garden Clubs Scholarship Award

National Garden Clubs Inc.
4401 Magnolia Avenue
St. Louis, MO 63110
Phone: 314-776-7574
Fax: 314-776-5108
Email: headquarters@gardenclub.org
http://www.gardenclub.org
Purpose: To support students in the National Garden Club's Central Atlantic Region.
Eligibility: Applicants must be residents of Delaware, Maryland, New Jersey, New York, Ohio, Pennsylvania or Washington, DC. They must be members of a National Garden Clubs member organization. Students who have won a National Garden Club scholarship are not eligible for a Central Atlantic Region scholarship.
Target applicants: High school students. College students. Adult students.
Amount: $1,000.
Number of awards: 1.
Deadline: July 1.
How to apply: Applications are available from Central Atlantic Region garden clubs. An application form, transcript, personal statement, financial aid form, list of extracurricular activities, honors and recognitions and three letters of recommendation are required.
Exclusive: Visit www.UltimateScholarshipBook.com and enter code NA220712 for updates on this award.

(2208) • Chairman's Award

National Association of Blacks in Criminal Justice
North Carolina Central University
P.O. Box 19788
Durham, NC 27707
Phone: 919-683-1801
Fax: 919-683-1903
Email: office@nabcj.org
http://www.nabcj.org
Purpose: To support an individual who has shown leadership, dedication and made contributions to NABCJ at the chapter or regional level.
Eligibility: Applicants must be nominated by a member of NABCJ.
Target applicants: College students. Adult students.
Amount: Varies.
Number of awards: 1.
Deadline: May 1.
How to apply: Nomination applications are available online.
Exclusive: Visit www.UltimateScholarshipBook.com and enter code NA220812 for updates on this award.

(2209) • Charles Bradley Memorial Scholarship

Harness Horse Youth Foundation
16575 Carey Road
Westfield, IN 46074
Phone: 317-867-5877
Fax: 317-867-5896
Email: ellen@hhyf.org
http://www.hhyf.org
Purpose: To support the children and relatives of horse racing officials.
Eligibility: Applicants must be related to a member of the North American Judges and Stewards Association or a licensed USTA pari-mutuel official in one of the following areas: presiding judges, associate judges, paddock judges and starters. Students must be at least in their senior year of high school. Applicants must submit an essay and two letters of recommendation.
Target applicants: High school students. College students. Adult students.
Amount: Varies.
Number of awards: Varies.
Deadline: April 30.
How to apply: Applications are available online.
Exclusive: Visit www.UltimateScholarshipBook.com and enter code HA220912 for updates on this award.

(2210) • Charles J. Trabold Scholarship

Tau Kappa Epsilon Educational Foundation
8645 Founders Road
Indianapolis, IN 46268
Phone: 317-872-6533
Fax: 317-875-8353
Email: tef@tke.org
http://www.tkefoundation.org
Purpose: To recognize academic achievement and leadership in members.
Eligibility: Applicants must be initiated Tau Kappa Epsilon members in good standing and full-time students with a GPA of at least 3.0. They must also demonstrate outstanding leadership and include a statement describing how they have benefited from TKE membership. First preference will be given to members of Kappa-Kappa Chapter.
Target applicants: College students. Adult students.
Minimum GPA: 3.0

Amount: $600.
Number of awards: 1.
Deadline: March 1.
How to apply: Applications are available online.
Exclusive: Visit www.UltimateScholarshipBook.com and enter code TA221012 for updates on this award.

(2211) • Charles R. Walgreen Jr. Leadership Award

Tau Kappa Epsilon Educational Foundation
8645 Founders Road
Indianapolis, IN 46268
Phone: 317-872-6533
Fax: 317-875-8353
Email: tef@tke.org
http://www.tkefoundation.org
Purpose: To honor Charles R. Walgreen's support of Tau Kappa Epsilon by recognizing academic achievement in members.
Eligibility: Applicants must be initiated Tau Kappa Epsilon members in good standing and full-time students. They must have a GPA of at least 3.0 and demonstrate leadership in their chapter, campus and community. Applicants must also include a statement describing how they have benefited from TKE membership.
Target applicants: College students. Adult students.
Amount: $875.
Number of awards: 1.
Deadline: March 1.
How to apply: Applications are available online.
Exclusive: Visit www.UltimateScholarshipBook.com and enter code TA221112 for updates on this award.

(2212) • Charlie Logan Scholarship Program for Dependents

Seafarers International Union of North America
Mr. Lou Delma, Administrator
Seafarers Welfare Plan Scholarship Program
5201 Auth Way
Camp Springs, MD 20746
Phone: 301-899-0675
Fax: 301-899-7355
http://www.seafarers.org
Purpose: To offer scholarships to the dependents of members of the SIU.
Eligibility: Applicants must be the dependent children or spouses of members of the Seafarers International Union. The union member must be eligible for the Seafarer's Plan and must have credit for three years with an employer who is obligated to make a contribution to the Seafarer's Plan on behalf of the employee. Recipients may attend any U.S. accredited institution. Selection is based upon review of secondary school records, SAT or ACT test scores, college transcripts, if any, character references, extracurricular activities and autobiography.
Target applicants: High school students. College students. Adult students.
Amount: $5,000.
Number of awards: 4.
Scholarship may be renewable.
Deadline: April 15.
How to apply: Applications are available by written request.
Exclusive: Visit www.UltimateScholarshipBook.com and enter code SE221212 for updates on this award.

(2213) • Chester M. Vernon Memorial Eagle Scout Scholarship

Boy Scouts of America Vernon Scholarship
1325 W. Walnut Hill Lane
P.O. Box 152079
Irving, TX 75015-2079
Phone: 972-580-2000
Fax: 972-580-7886
Email: scholarships@jewishscouting.org
http://www.jewishscouting.org
Purpose: To aid Jewish Eagle Scouts.
Eligibility: Applicants must registered and active members of a Boy Scout troop, Varsity Scout team or Venturing crew who have received the Eagle Scout award. They must be active members of a synagogue and have received their Ner Tamid or Etz Chaim religious emblems. Students must be high school seniors and demonstrate good citizenship and financial need.
Target applicants: High school students.
Amount: $1,000.
Number of awards: 1.
Scholarship may be renewable.
Deadline: February 28.
How to apply: Applications are available online. An application form, two letters of recommendation, essays and a self-addressed stamped postcard are required.
Exclusive: Visit www.UltimateScholarshipBook.com and enter code BO221312 for updates on this award.

(2214) • Chief Industries FFA Scholarship

National FFA Organization
P.O. Box 68960
6060 FFA Drive
Indianapolis, IN 46268-0960
Phone: 317-802-6060
Fax: 317-802-6051
Email: scholarships@ffa.org
http://www.ffa.org/
Purpose: To support FFA members who are majoring in agriculture.
Eligibility: Applicants must be current FFA members and high school seniors or college students planning to enroll or currently enrolled full-time. They must be residents of Indiana, Iowa or Nebraska. Students only need to complete the online application one time to be considered for all FFA-administered scholarships. The application requires information about the student's activities and a 1,000-word essay. Awards may be used for books, supplies, tuition, fees and room and board.
Target applicants: High school students. College students. Adult students.
Amount: $1,000.
Number of awards: 1.
Deadline: February 15.
How to apply: Applications are available online.
Exclusive: Visit www.UltimateScholarshipBook.com and enter code NA221412 for updates on this award.

(2215) • Christian Connector Undergraduate Scholarship

Christian Connector Inc.
627 24 1/2 Road
Suite D
Grand Junction, CO 81505

Phone: 800-667-0600
http://www.christianconnector.com
Purpose: To provide financial assistance for students attending Christian or Bible colleges.
Eligibility: Applicants must be enrolling as a first-time student at a Christ-centered Christian or Bible college, including but not limited to CCCU, NACCAP or AABC member institutions, within 16 months of winning the scholarship. To enter the drawing, the student must fill out an information request form.
Target applicants: High school students.
Amount: $2,500.
Number of awards: 1.
Deadline: Varies.
How to apply: Applications are available online.
Exclusive: Visit www.UltimateScholarshipBook.com and enter code CH221512 for updates on this award.

(2216) • Christopher Grasso Scholarship

Tau Kappa Epsilon Educational Foundation
8645 Founders Road
Indianapolis, IN 46268
Phone: 317-872-6533
Fax: 317-875-8353
Email: tef@tke.org
http://www.tkefoundation.org
Purpose: To recognize a member of Tau Kappa Epsilon for outstanding leadership in the local chapter or community.
Eligibility: Applicants must have a GPA of at least 2.5. Preference is first given to members of the Alpha-Tau Chapter.
Target applicants: College students. Adult students.
Minimum GPA: 2.5
Amount: $125.
Number of awards: 1.
Deadline: March 1.
How to apply: Applications are available online.
Exclusive: Visit www.UltimateScholarshipBook.com and enter code TA221612 for updates on this award.

(2217) • Church and Dwight Company Inc. FFA Scholarship

National FFA Organization
P.O. Box 68960
6060 FFA Drive
Indianapolis, IN 46268-0960
Phone: 317-802-6060
Fax: 317-802-6051
Email: scholarships@ffa.org
http://www.ffa.org/
Purpose: To support FFA members who are pursuing degrees related to agricultural science or business.
Eligibility: Applicants must be current FFA members and high school seniors or college students planning to enroll or currently enrolled full-time. They must be majoring in one of the following areas: animal nutrition, animal or dairy science, agricultural business management, finance, sales and marketing or agricultural engineering. Students must have at least a 3.0 GPA. Preference will be given to applicants who show strong leadership skills and an interest in pursuing a dairy-related career. Students only need to complete the online application one time to be considered for all FFA-administered scholarships. The application requires information about the student's activities and a 1,000-word essay. Awards may be used for books, supplies, tuition, fees and room and board.
Target applicants: High school students. College students. Adult students.
Minimum GPA: 3.0
Amount: $1,000.
Number of awards: 3.
Deadline: February 15.
How to apply: Applications are available online.
Exclusive: Visit www.UltimateScholarshipBook.com and enter code NA221712 for updates on this award.

(2218) • Cindy Shemansky Travel Scholarship

National Gerontological Nursing Association (NGNA)
7794 Grow Drive
Pensacola, FL 32514
Phone: 800-723-0560
Fax: 850-484-8762
Email: ngna@puetzamc.com
http://www.ngna.org
Purpose: To provide assistance to NGNA members who wish to attend the annual convention but who need financial assistance with travel expenses.
Eligibility: Applicants must have been members of NGNA for at least one year.
Target applicants: College students. Adult students.
Amount: $1,000.
Number of awards: Varies.
Deadline: July 1.
How to apply: Applications are available online.
Exclusive: Visit www.UltimateScholarshipBook.com and enter code NA221812 for updates on this award.

(2219) • Clara Abbott Foundation Educational Grant Program

Clara Abbott Foundation
1505 South White Oak Drive
Waukegan, IL 60085
Phone: 800-972-3859
Fax: 847-938-6511
http://clara.abbott.com/
Purpose: To help children of eligible Abbott employees and retirees worldwide receive a college-level education by providing scholarships on the basis of financial need.
Eligibility: Applicants must be full- or part-time students at an accredited college, university, community college, vocational school or trade school. Applicants must also be 24 years of age or younger, be the children or dependents of retirees or full-time/part-time employees with at least a year's service to Abbott Laboratories and be residents of the United States or Puerto Rico. Scholarships are awarded according to financial need. Applicants may first apply as high school seniors.
Target applicants: High school students. College students.
Amount: Varies.
Number of awards: Varies.
Scholarship may be renewable.
Deadline: March 15.
How to apply: Applications are available online.
Exclusive: Visit www.UltimateScholarshipBook.com and enter code CL221912 for updates on this award.

(2220) • Collegian of the Year

Delta Sigma Pi
330 S. Campus Avenue
Oxford, OH 45056
Phone: 513-523-1907
Fax: 513-523-7292
Email: centraloffice@dspnet.org
http://www.dspnet.org

Purpose: To honor the most outstanding collegian member of Delta Sigma Pi who exemplifies the ideals of the organization.

Eligibility: Nominees must be members in good standing and be nominated by their chapter by October 15. Demonstrated fraternity involvement, demonstrated college/university and/or community involvement, demonstrated pursuit of professional development and scholastic average will all be considered along with other desirable characteristics like moral character and professional attitude.

Target applicants: College students. Adult students.

Amount: $3,000.

Number of awards: 1.

Deadline: November 15.

How to apply: Applications are available online.

Exclusive: Visit www.UltimateScholarshipBook.com and enter code DE222012 for updates on this award.

(2221) • Community Service Award

Golden Key National Honour Society
Scholarship Program Administrators
Golden Key Scholarships/Awards
P.O. Box 23737
Nashville, TN 37202-3737
Phone: 800-377-2401
Email: scholarships@goldenkey.org
http://www.goldenkey.org

Purpose: To support a Golden Key member who has served the community.

Eligibility: Applicants must be undergraduate or graduate Golden Key members who were enrolled during the previous academic year. Selection is based on the impact of the community service. Applicants must provide an essay of up to 500 words describing the community service project, recommendation letters and list of extracurricular activities.

Target applicants: College students. Graduate school students. Adult students.

Amount: $2,000.

Number of awards: 1.

Deadline: March 1.

How to apply: Applications are available online.

Exclusive: Visit www.UltimateScholarshipBook.com and enter code GO222112 for updates on this award.

(2222) • Continuing Education Grant/Loan Program

Presbyterian Church (USA)
100 Witherspoon Street
Louisville, KY 40202
Phone: 888-728-7228 x5776
Email: finaid@pcusa.org
http://www.pcusa.org/financialaid

Purpose: To aid Presbyterian Church (U.S.A.) pastors serving small (150 member or less) congregations.

Eligibility: Applicant must be enrolled in a D.Min. program at an ATS accredited institution. Funding is limited to the first three years of the program and will be used for tuition, fees, books and travel and lodging expenses for the in-residence portion of the program.

Target applicants: Graduate school students. Adult students.

Amount: Up to $1,500.

Number of awards: 15.

Deadline: November 15.

How to apply: Applications are available online.

Exclusive: Visit www.UltimateScholarshipBook.com and enter code PR222212 for updates on this award.

(2223) • Continuing Education Scholarships

Federation of American Consumers and Travelers (FACT)
P.O. Box 104
318 Hillsboro Avenue
Edwardsville, IL 62025
Phone: 800-872-3228
Email: cservice@fact-org.org
http://www.fact-org.org

Purpose: To help FACT members and their families.

Eligibility: Applicants must be FACT members or their immediate families in the following categories: current high school seniors, students already in college, students who graduated from high school four or more years ago or students planning to attend a trade or technical school.

Target applicants: High school students. College students. Graduate school students. Adult students.

Amount: $2,500-$10,000.

Number of awards: Varies.

Deadline: Varies.

How to apply: Contact the organization for more information.

Exclusive: Visit www.UltimateScholarshipBook.com and enter code FE222312 for updates on this award.

(2224) • CSE Insurance Youth Automobile Safety Scholarship Program

Civil Service Employees Insurance Company (CSE)
P.O. Box 8041
Walnut Creek, CA 94596-8041
Phone: 800-282-6848
http://www.cseinsurance.com/scholarship.htm

Purpose: To support children of government employees.

Eligibility: Applicants must be California, Arizona or Nevada residents and high school seniors, have a GPA of 3.0 or higher and be accepted to and plan to enroll full-time in a four-year institution of higher learning in the U.S. in the fall following application. The applicant's parent or legal guardian must be employed full-time by a government entity or be retired or deceased and have been employed full-time by a government entity. Students must write an essay about how the teenage automobile accident rate can be reduced.

Target applicants: High school students.

Minimum GPA: 3.0

Amount: $500-$1,500.

Number of awards: 15.

Deadline: April 5.

How to apply: Applications are available online. An application form, essay, letter of recommendation, letter of acceptance and transcript are required.

Exclusive: Visit www.UltimateScholarshipBook.com and enter code CI222412 for updates on this award.

(2225) • CTA Scholarship for Dependent Children

California Teachers Association (CTA)
CTA Human Rights Department
P.O. Box 921
Burlingame, CA 94011-0921
Phone: 650-697-1400
Fax: 650-552-5001
http://www.cta.org

Purpose: To support the children of CTA members.
Eligibility: Students must be the dependents of active, retired or deceased California Teachers Association members. Applicants must have a 3.5 high school GPA or high academic achievement in college, although there is the opportunity to explain any extenuating circumstances affecting grades. Scholarships are based on a personal statement, school and community activities and letters of recommendation.
Target applicants: High school students. College students. Graduate school students. Adult students.
Minimum GPA: 3.5
Amount: $5,000.
Number of awards: Up to 35.
Deadline: February 4.
How to apply: Applications are available online.
Exclusive: Visit www.UltimateScholarshipBook.com and enter code CA222512 for updates on this award.

(2226) • CTA Scholarship for Members

California Teachers Association (CTA)
CTA Human Rights Department
P.O. Box 921
Burlingame, CA 94011-0921
Phone: 650-697-1400
Fax: 650-552-5001
http://www.cta.org

Purpose: To support CTA members as they further their education.
Eligibility: Applicants must be current active members of the California Teachers Association who are attending college. Their coursework must show high academic achievement, although they may explain any extenuating circumstances affecting their grades. Scholarships are awarded based on a personal statement, school and community activities and letters of recommendation.
Target applicants: College students. Graduate school students. Adult students.
Amount: $3,000.
Number of awards: Up to 5.
Deadline: February 4.
How to apply: Applications are available online.
Exclusive: Visit www.UltimateScholarshipBook.com and enter code CA222612 for updates on this award.

(2227) • Cunat Visionary Scholarship

Circle K International
3636 Woodview Trace
Indianapolis, IN 46268
http://www.circlek.org

Purpose: This scholarship, provided by Kiwanis International Past President Brian Cunat and Miki Cunat, was established to recognize Kiwanis members who aspire to make a difference in people's lives and create a better world for all.
Eligibility: Applicants must be either college-attending Circle K International members or graduating Key Club members.
Target applicants: High school students. College students. Adult students.
Amount: Varies.
Number of awards: Varies.
Deadline: Varies.
How to apply: Applications are available online.
Exclusive: Visit www.UltimateScholarshipBook.com and enter code CI222712 for updates on this award.

(2228) • CWA Joe Beirne Foundation Scholarship

Communications Workers of America
Attn.: George Kohl
501 Third Street NW
Washington, DC 20001
Phone: 202-434-1158
Fax: 202-434-1139
Email: kadams@cwa-union.org
http://www.cwa-union.org

Purpose: To provide scholarships for CWA members and their families.
Eligibility: Applicants may be Communications Workers of America (CWA) members, their spouses, their children or their grandchildren. Applicants must be high school graduates or at least high school students who will graduate during the year in which they apply. Winners are selected by a lottery drawing. This is a two-year scholarship.
Target applicants: High school students. College students. Graduate school students. Adult students.
Amount: $3,000.
Number of awards: 15.
Scholarship may be renewable.
Deadline: March 31.
How to apply: Contact a CWA Local or write (referencing CWA local number, member name and Social Security number) for an application. Applications are available online.
Exclusive: Visit www.UltimateScholarshipBook.com and enter code CO222812 for updates on this award.

(2229) • Delta Gamma Foundation Scholarship

Delta Gamma Foundation
3250 Riverside Drive
P.O. Box 21397
Columbus, OH 43221
Phone: 614-481-8169
Fax: 614-481-0133
Email: dgscholarships08@aol.com
http://www.deltagamma.org

Purpose: To support student members.
Eligibility: Applicants must be initiated members of Delta Gamma, have maintained a 3.0 GPA and have completed three semesters or five quarters of college coursework. Applicants should also be active participants in chapter, campus and community leadership activities. Awards are based on academic achievement and participation in activities.
Target applicants: College students. Adult students.
Minimum GPA: 3.0
Amount: Varies.
Number of awards: Varies.
Deadline: January 15.
How to apply: Applications are available online.
Exclusive: Visit www.UltimateScholarshipBook.com and enter code DE222912 for updates on this award.

(2230) • Delta Phi Epsilon Educational Foundation Scholarship

Delta Phi Epsilon Educational Foundation
16A Worthington Drive
Maryland Heights, MO 63043
Phone: 314-275-2626
Fax: 314-275-2655
Email: fausbury@dphie.org
http://www.dphie.org

Purpose: To award members of Delta Phi Epsilon.

Eligibility: Applicants must be members or the sons or daughters of members of Delta Phi Epsilon who are applying for undergraduate or graduate study. The award is based on service and involvement, academics and financial need. Applicants should submit transcripts, letters of introduction and financial need, autobiographical sketches, two recent photos, at least two letters of recommendation and the contact information of the financial aid director for the school.

Target applicants: High school students. College students. Graduate school students. Adult students.

Amount: $1,000.

Number of awards: Varies.

Deadline: March 17.

How to apply: Applications are available online.

Exclusive: Visit www.UltimateScholarshipBook.com and enter code DE223012 for updates on this award.

(2231) • Descendants of the Signers of the Declaration of Independence Scholarships

Descendants of the Signers of the Declaration of Independence
7157 S.E. Reed College Place
Portland, OR 97202-8354
Email: registrar@dsdi1776.com
http://www.dsdi1776.com/Scholarship/scholarship.html

Purpose: To support Descendants of the Signers of the Declaration of Independence members.

Eligibility: Applicants must be DSDI members and actual descendants of Declaration of Independence signers. Senior members' dues must be current, and junior annual members must convert to senior status on their 18th birthdays.

Target applicants: High school students. College students. Adult students.

Amount: Varies.

Number of awards: Varies.

Deadline: April 3.

How to apply: Applications are available online. An application form, three letters of recommendation and transcript are required.

Exclusive: Visit www.UltimateScholarshipBook.com and enter code DE223112 for updates on this award.

(2232) • Diocese of the Armenian Church of America (Eastern) Scholarships

Diocese of the Armenian Church of America (Eastern)
630 Second Avenue
New York, NY 10016
Phone: 212-686-0710
Fax: 212-686-0245
Email: info@armenianchurch.net
http://www.armenianchurch.net

Purpose: To support young Armenian Church members who are seeking higher education.

Eligibility: Applicants must be Armenian Americans who are currently attending or plan to attend a four-year college or university. Preference is given to applicants who are U.S. citizens and are active in the Armenian Church.

Target applicants: High school students. College students. Adult students.

Amount: Varies.

Number of awards: Varies.

Deadline: June 15.

How to apply: Applications are available from the Diocese of the Armenian Church of America (Eastern).

Exclusive: Visit www.UltimateScholarshipBook.com and enter code DI223212 for updates on this award.

(2233) • Distinct Advantage Scholarship

Alpha Tau Omega Fraternity
One North Pennsylvania Street
12th Floor
Phone: 800-508-5131
Fax: 317-684-1862
Email: cheri@atofoundation.org
http://www.joinato.org

Purpose: To aid male students who are planning to attend a school that has an active chapter of the Alpha Tau Omega fraternity.

Eligibility: Applicants must be male high school seniors. They must be planning to attend a college or university that has an active chapter of the Alpha Tau Omega fraternity. Selection is based on the overall strength of the application.

Target applicants: High school students.

Amount: Varies.

Number of awards: Varies.

Deadline: September 4.

How to apply: Applications are available online. An application form is required.

Exclusive: Visit www.UltimateScholarshipBook.com and enter code AL223312 for updates on this award.

(2234) • Don Forsyth "Circle K" Scholarship Fund

Community Foundation for the Greater Capital Region
6 Tower Place
Albany, NY 12203
Phone: 518-446-9638
Fax: 518-446-9708
Email: info@cfgcr.org
http://www.cfcr.org/grants_scholarships/scholarships.htm

Purpose: To provide recognition and financial assistance for outstanding Circle K members.

Eligibility: Applicants must be members of Circle K clubs at New York colleges who are in good standing with the club and their schools. They must have an exceptional community service record and be enrolled in college full-time.

Target applicants: College students. Adult students.

Amount: $4,500.

Number of awards: 1.

Deadline: March 5.

How to apply: Applications are available online.

Exclusive: Visit www.UltimateScholarshipBook.com and enter code CO223412 for updates on this award.

(2235) • Donald A. and John R. Fisher Memorial Scholarship

Tau Kappa Epsilon Educational Foundation
8645 Founders Road
Indianapolis, IN 46268
Phone: 317-872-6533
Fax: 317-875-8353
Email: tef@tke.org
http://www.tkefoundation.org

Purpose: To recognize academic achievement and leadership in honor of father and son members Donald A. and John R. Fisher.
Eligibility: Applicants must be initiated Tau Kappa Epsilon members in good standing and full-time students with a GPA of at least 3.0. They must demonstrate outstanding leadership in their chapter, campus and community. Applicants must also include a statement describing how they have benefited from TKE membership.
Target applicants: College students. Adult students.
Minimum GPA: 3.0
Amount: $500.
Number of awards: 1.
Deadline: March 1.
How to apply: Applications are available online.
Exclusive: Visit www.UltimateScholarshipBook.com and enter code TA223512 for updates on this award.

(2236) • Doris and Elmer H. Schmitz, Sr. Memorial Scholarship

Tau Kappa Epsilon Educational Foundation
8645 Founders Road
Indianapolis, IN 46268
Phone: 317-872-6533
Fax: 317-875-8353
Email: tef@tke.org
http://www.tkefoundation.org

Purpose: To award a member of Tau Kappa Epsilon for academic achievement and outstanding leadership within the organization as a chapter officer.
Eligibility: Applicants must have a GPA of at least 2.5. First preference is given to applicants from Wisconsin.
Target applicants: College students. Adult students.
Minimum GPA: 2.5
Amount: $175.
Number of awards: 1.
Deadline: March 1.
How to apply: Applications are available online.
Exclusive: Visit www.UltimateScholarshipBook.com and enter code TA223612 for updates on this award.

(2237) • Dorothy Patricia Brewster Scholarships

La Leche League
c/o Lynn Nicholson
4643 Elspeth Way
Covina, CA 91722
Phone: 626-332-0304
Email: nchlynn@aol.com
http://breastfeedingsituations.blogspot.com

Purpose: To support children of La Leche League Leaders.
Eligibility: Applicants must be high school seniors who plan to attend a two- or four-year institution of higher learning. The Leader must have served in LLL actively for at least three years, part of which must have been in the Southern California/Nevada area.
Target applicants: High school students.
Amount: $500-$1,500.
Number of awards: 2.
Deadline: April 15.
How to apply: Applications are available online. An application form, essay and transcript are required.
Exclusive: Visit www.UltimateScholarshipBook.com and enter code LA223712 for updates on this award.

(2238) • Duke Energy Scholars

Duke Energy Corporation
526 S. Church Street
Charlotte, NC 28202-1904
Phone: 704-594-6200
Email: contactus@duke-energy.com
http://www.duke-energy.com

Purpose: To support the children of Duke Energy employees and retirees.
Eligibility: Applicants should be children of Duke Energy employees and retirees who are undergraduates at accredited, two-year technical schools or community colleges or four-year colleges or universities in the U.S. and Canada. The awards are based on academics, references, community service and financial need.
Target applicants: College students. Adult students.
Amount: Up to $20,000.
Number of awards: 15.
Scholarship may be renewable.
Deadline: Varies.
How to apply: Contact the company for more information.
Exclusive: Visit www.UltimateScholarshipBook.com and enter code DU223812 for updates on this award.

(2239) • Dwayne R. Woerpel Memorial Scholarship

Tau Kappa Epsilon Educational Foundation
8645 Founders Road
Indianapolis, IN 46268
Phone: 317-872-6533
Fax: 317-875-8353
Email: tef@tke.org
http://www.tkefoundation.org

Purpose: To award a member of Tau Kappa Epsilon for outstanding academic achievement and leadership within the fraternity, civic and religious communities.
Eligibility: Applicants must have a GPA of at least 3.0. Preference is first given to graduates of the TKE Leadership Academy.
Target applicants: College students. Adult students.
Minimum GPA: 3.0
Amount: $500.
Number of awards: 1.
Deadline: March 16.
How to apply: Applications are available online.
Exclusive: Visit www.UltimateScholarshipBook.com and enter code TA223912 for updates on this award.

(2240) • E. Craig Brandenburg Scholarship

United Methodist Church
Office of Loans and Scholarships
P.O. BOX 340007
Nashville, TN 37203-0007

Phone: 615-340-7344
Fax: 615-340-7367
Email: umscholar@gbhem.org
http://www.gbhem.org
Purpose: To support adult students who are members of the United Methodist Church.
Eligibility: Applicants must be at least 35 years old, and they must have been members of the United Methodist Church for at least one year. Students may be pursuing undergraduate or graduate degrees.
Target applicants: College students. Graduate school students. Adult students.
Amount: Varies.
Number of awards: Varies.
Deadline: February 15.
How to apply: Applications are available online.
Exclusive: Visit www.UltimateScholarshipBook.com and enter code UN224012 for updates on this award.

(2241) · Eagle Scout Scholarship

National Society of the Sons of the American Revolution
1000 S. Fourth Street
Louisville, KY 40203
Phone: 502-589-1776
Email: contests@sar.org
http://www.sar.org
Purpose: To reward exceptional students who have reached the status of Eagle Scout.
Eligibility: Applicants must have reached Eagle Scout status, must currently be registered in an active unit and can't have reached their 19th birthday during the year of application. Applicants can apply multiple years as long as they are under the age limit, but the maximum award amount is $8,000. Applicants usually apply at the chapter level. Applicants will be required to submit an essay and four-generation ancestor chart with their application.
Target applicants: Junior high students or younger. High school students.
Amount: $2,000-$8,000.
Number of awards: Varies.
Deadline: December 31.
How to apply: Applications are available online.
Exclusive: Visit www.UltimateScholarshipBook.com and enter code NA224112 for updates on this award.

(2242) · Edith M. Allen Scholarship

United Methodist Church
Office of Loans and Scholarships
P.O. BOX 340007
Nashville, TN 37203-0007
Phone: 615-340-7344
Fax: 615-340-7367
Email: umscholar@gbhem.org
http://www.gbhem.org
Purpose: To support African American students who are attending United Methodist colleges.
Eligibility: Applicants must have been active members of the United Methodist Church for at least three years. They must be majoring in education, social work, medicine or other health fields. Students may be pursuing undergraduate or graduate degrees. They must have at least a B+ average.
Target applicants: High school students. College students. Graduate school students. Adult students.
Minimum GPA: 3.3
Amount: Varies.
Number of awards: Varies.
Deadline: April 15-May 1.
How to apply: Applications are available online.
Exclusive: Visit www.UltimateScholarshipBook.com and enter code UN224212 for updates on this award.

(2243) · Education Achievement Awards

Golden Key National Honour Society
Scholarship Program Administrators
Golden Key Scholarships/Awards
P.O. Box 23737
Nashville, TN 37202-3737
Phone: 800-377-2401
Email: scholarships@goldenkey.org
http://www.goldenkey.org
Purpose: To support members studying education.
Eligibility: Applicants must be undergraduate, graduate or post-graduate Golden Key members who are taking classes in a degree-granting program. Selection is based on academic achievement and education-related paper or report.
Target applicants: College students. Graduate school students. Adult students.
Amount: $1,000-$2,000.
Number of awards: 3.
Deadline: March 1.
How to apply: Applications are available online.
Exclusive: Visit www.UltimateScholarshipBook.com and enter code GO224312 for updates on this award.

(2244) · Elizabeth Ahlemeyer Quick/Gamma Phi Beta Scholarship

National Panhellenic Conference
8777 Purdue Road
Suite 117
Indianapolis, IN 46268
Phone: 317-872-3185
Fax: 317-872-3192
Email: npccentral@npcwomen.org
http://www.npcwomen.org
Purpose: To support collegiate members of the National Panhellenic Conference.
Eligibility: Applicants must be members of an NPC member group in good standing, be nominated by their College Panhellenics and have displayed outstanding service. Students must be rising full-time juniors or seniors in college with a 3.0 or higher GPA.
Target applicants: College students. Adult students.
Minimum GPA: 3.0
Amount: $2,000.
Number of awards: 1.
Deadline: January 10.
How to apply: Applications are available online. An application form, transcript and two letters of recommendation are required.
Exclusive: Visit www.UltimateScholarshipBook.com and enter code NA224412 for updates on this award.

(2245) • Elks' Eagle Scout Scholarship

Boy Scouts of America, Eagle Scout Service
1325 West Walnut Hill Lane
P.O. Box 152079
Irving, TX 75015-2079
Phone: 972-580-2401
Fax: 972-580-2413
http://www.nesa.org/religious.html

Purpose: To support Boy Scouts who have achieved Eagle Scout rank.
Eligibility: Applicants must be registered Boy Scouts with an Eagle rank, have a minimum SAT score of 1090 and/or an ACT score of 26, be high school seniors and demonstrate financial need.
Target applicants: High school students.
Amount: $1,000-2,000.
Number of awards: 8.
Scholarship may be renewable.
Deadline: February 28.
How to apply: Applications are available from the local Scout Council Service Center and online.
Exclusive: Visit www.UltimateScholarshipBook.com and enter code BO224512 for updates on this award.

(2246) • Emergency Educational Fund Grants

Elks National Foundation Headquarters
2750 North Lakeview Avenue
Chicago, IL 60614
Phone: 773-755-4732
Fax: 773-755-4733
Email: scholarship@elks.org
http://www.elks.org

Purpose: To assist children of deceased and incapacitated Elks.
Eligibility: Applicants must be the children of deceased or incapacitated Elks who were/are members in good standing for at least one year, unmarried, under 23 years old and full-time undergraduate students at a U.S. school. Applicants must also demonstrate financial need.
Target applicants: High school students. College students.
Amount: Up to $4,000.
Number of awards: Varies.
Scholarship may be renewable.
Deadline: December 31.
How to apply: Applications are available from the local Elks Lodge or by phone or e-mail request.
Exclusive: Visit www.UltimateScholarshipBook.com and enter code EL224612 for updates on this award.

(2247) • Ethnic Minority Scholarship

United Methodist Church
Office of Loans and Scholarships
P.O. BOX 340007
Nashville, TN 37203-0007
Phone: 615-340-7344
Fax: 615-340-7367
Email: umscholar@gbhem.org
http://www.gbhem.org

Purpose: To support minority students who belong to the United Methodist Church.
Eligibility: Applicants must belong to one of the following minority groups: Native American, Asian, African American, Hispanic or Pacific Islander. They must have been members of the United Methodist Church for at least one year. Students must be currently pursuing their first undergraduate degree at an accredited school in the United States, and they must be attending school full-time with a GPA of at least 2.5.
Target applicants: High school students. College students. Adult students.
Minimum GPA: 2.5
Amount: Varies.
Number of awards: Varies.
Deadline: April 15-May 1.
How to apply: Applications are available online.
Exclusive: Visit www.UltimateScholarshipBook.com and enter code UN224712 for updates on this award.

(2248) • Eugene C. Beach Memorial Scholarship

Tau Kappa Epsilon Educational Foundation
8645 Founders Road
Indianapolis, IN 46268
Phone: 317-872-6533
Fax: 317-875-8353
Email: tef@tke.org
http://www.tkefoundation.org

Purpose: To award a member of Tau Kappa Epsilon for outstanding academic achievement and leadership within the chapter, campus and community.
Eligibility: Applicants must have a minimum GPA of 3.0.
Target applicants: College students. Adult students.
Minimum GPA: 3.0
Amount: $150.
Number of awards: 1.
Deadline: March 1.
How to apply: Applications are available online.
Exclusive: Visit www.UltimateScholarshipBook.com and enter code TA224812 for updates on this award.

(2249) • Fadel Educational Foundation Annual Award Program

Fadel Educational Foundation
P.O. Box 212135
Augusta, GA 30917-2135
Phone: 484-694-1783
http://www.fadelfoundation.org

Purpose: To support Muslim U.S. citizens and permanent residents.
Eligibility: Applicants must be non-incarcerated students pursuing higher education. Selection is based on need and merit. Applicants should provide application forms, two teacher recommendation forms, one masjid official recommendation letter and financial need reports.
Target applicants: High school students. College students. Graduate school students. Adult students.
Amount: Up to $3,000.
Number of awards: Varies.
Deadline: April 20.
How to apply: Applications are available online.
Exclusive: Visit www.UltimateScholarshipBook.com and enter code FA224912 for updates on this award.

(2250) • Faith and Education Scholarship Fund

Faith and Education Scholarship Fund
P.O. Box 25555
San Mateo, CA 94402
Phone: 650-341-8702

Email: chris@faithandeducation.org
http://www.faithandeducation.org
Purpose: To support students who are active members of churches of Christ.
Eligibility: Applicants must be active members of churches of Christ and be enrolled full-time at four-year liberal arts colleges or universities. Students must submit the application form, transcripts, copy of SAT or ACT scores from high school applicants and a recommendation letter from a leader of their congregation.
Target applicants: High school students. College students. Adult students.
Amount: $5,000.
Number of awards: 1.
Deadline: March 31.
How to apply: Applications are available online.
Exclusive: Visit www.UltimateScholarshipBook.com and enter code FA225012 for updates on this award.

(2251) • FEEA Scholarship

Federal Employee Education and Assistance Fund
8441 W. Bowles Avenue
Suite 200
Littleton, CO 80123
Phone: 303-933-7580
Fax: 303-933-7587
http://www.feea.org
Purpose: The FEEA scholarship program aids postal employees and their family members.
Eligibility: Applicants must be current civilian federal and postal employees with three years of service or their children or spouses. Applicants must also be enrolled or plan to enroll in an accredited post secondary school, have a minimum 3.0 GPA and may be high school seniors, college students or graduate students.
Target applicants: High school students. College students. Graduate school students. Adult students.
Minimum GPA: 3.0
Amount: $250-$5,000.
Number of awards: Varies.
Deadline: March.
How to apply: Applications are available online or by sending a self-addressed and stamped envelope.
Exclusive: Visit www.UltimateScholarshipBook.com and enter code FE225112 for updates on this award.

(2252) • Fellowship of United Methodists in Music and Worship Arts Scholarship

Fellowship of United Methodists in Music and Worship Arts
Robert A. Schilling
4702 Graceland Avenue
Indianapolis, IN 46208-3504
Phone: 800-952-8977
Fax: 615-749-6874
Email: info@fummwa.org
http://www.fummwa.org
Purpose: To support students who want to pursue church music and/or worship arts as a career.
Eligibility: Applicants must be full-time music students pursuing a career in sacred music who are either entering freshmen or already enrolled in an accredited college, university or school of theology or pursuing an academic education in worship; be members of the United Methodist Church or be employed in the United Methodist Church for at least a year before applying and show Christian character and participation in Christian activities. Students must also demonstrate musical or other artistic talent and leadership potential. Applicants must submit applications, transcripts, personal statements and three reference letters.
Target applicants: High school students. College students. Graduate school students. Adult students.
Amount: $1,000.
Number of awards: Varies.
Deadline: March 1.
How to apply: Applications are available online.
Exclusive: Visit www.UltimateScholarshipBook.com and enter code FE225212 for updates on this award.

(2253) • Fleet Reserve Association Scholarship

Fleet Reserve Association
FRA Scholarship Administrator
125 N. West Street
Alexandria, VA 22314
Phone: 800-372-1924
http://www.fra.org
Purpose: To provide financial support for post-secondary education to FRA members and their dependents and grandchildren.
Eligibility: Applicants must be either FRA members or the dependents or grandchildren of an FRA member who is in good standing or was in good standing at time of death. Applicants are judged on the basis of leadership skills, financial need, academic record and character.
Target applicants: High school students. College students. Graduate school students. Adult students.
Amount: Varies.
Number of awards: Varies.
Deadline: April 15.
How to apply: Applications are available online.
Exclusive: Visit www.UltimateScholarshipBook.com and enter code FL225312 for updates on this award.

(2254) • Ford Motor Company Business and Leadership Scholarship

Golden Key National Honour Society
Scholarship Program Administrators
Golden Key Scholarships/Awards
P.O. Box 23737
Nashville, TN 37202-3737
Phone: 800-377-2401
Email: scholarships@goldenkey.org
http://www.goldenkey.org
Purpose: To provide opportunities for undergraduate and graduate students majoring in business.
Eligibility: Applicants must be Golden Key members and must be majoring in business. The award is based on academic achievement, leadership, Golden Key involvement and extracurricular activities.
Target applicants: College students. Graduate school students. Adult students.
Amount: $10,000.
Number of awards: 4.
Deadline: October 15.
How to apply: Applications are available online.
Exclusive: Visit www.UltimateScholarshipBook.com and enter code GO225412 for updates on this award.

(2255) • Ford Motor Company Engineering and Leadership Scholarship

Golden Key National Honour Society
Scholarship Program Administrators
Golden Key Scholarships/Awards
P.O. Box 23737
Nashville, TN 37202-3737
Phone: 800-377-2401
Email: scholarships@goldenkey.org
http://www.goldenkey.org

Purpose: To provide opportunities for undergraduate and graduate students majoring in engineering.

Eligibility: Applicants must be Golden Key members and must be majoring in engineering. Award is based on academic achievement, leadership, Golden Key involvement and extracurricular activities.

Target applicants: College students. Graduate school students. Adult students.

Amount: $10,000.

Number of awards: 4.

Deadline: October 15.

How to apply: Applications are available online.

Exclusive: Visit www.UltimateScholarshipBook.com and enter code GO225512 for updates on this award.

(2256) • Ford Truck Scholarship Program

National FFA Organization
P.O. Box 68960
6060 FFA Drive
Indianapolis, IN 46268-0960
Phone: 317-802-6060
Fax: 317-802-6051
Email: scholarships@ffa.org
http://www.ffa.org/

Purpose: To provide educational assistance to FFA members.

Eligibility: Applicants must be high school seniors who plan to pursue a two- or four-year degree in any major. They must apply online and obtain a signature and dealer code from a local participating Ford Truck dealer. If there is no participating Ford dealer in the applicant's area, he or she may obtain a signature from any local Ford dealer and be eligible for one of five national scholarships.

Target applicants: High school students.

Amount: $1,000.

Number of awards: Varies.

Deadline: February 15.

How to apply: Applications are available online.

Exclusive: Visit www.UltimateScholarshipBook.com and enter code NA225612 for updates on this award.

(2257) • Ford Trucks/Built Ford Tough FFA Scholarship Program

National FFA Organization
P.O. Box 68960
6060 FFA Drive
Indianapolis, IN 46268-0960
Phone: 317-802-6060
Fax: 317-802-6051
Email: scholarships@ffa.org
http://www.ffa.org/

Purpose: To support students who are members of the FFA.

Eligibility: Applicants must be current FFA members and high school seniors or college students planning to enroll or currently enrolled full-time. Students only need to complete the online application one time to be considered for all FFA-administered scholarships. The application requires information about the student's activities and a 1,000-word essay. Awards may be used for books, supplies, tuition, fees and room and board. Applicants must obtain a signature from a local Ford dealer.

Target applicants: High school students. College students. Adult students.

Amount: $1,000.

Number of awards: Up to 500.

Deadline: February 15.

How to apply: Applications are available online.

Exclusive: Visit www.UltimateScholarshipBook.com and enter code NA225712 for updates on this award.

(2258) • Foundation Scholarship Program

Kappa Alpha Theta Foundation
Attn.: Undergraduate Scholarship Application
8740 Founders Road
Indianapolis, IN 46268
Phone: 888-526-1870 x119
Fax: 317-876-1925
Email: cthoennes@kappaalphatheta.org
http://www.kappaalphatheta.org

Purpose: To provide merit-based scholarships for undergraduate, graduate and alumna Kappa Alpha Theta members.

Eligibility: The award is based on academics, fraternity activities, campus and community activities and references.

Target applicants: College students. Graduate school students. Adult students.

Amount: Varies.

Number of awards: Varies.

Deadline: February 1.

How to apply: Applications are available online.

Exclusive: Visit www.UltimateScholarshipBook.com and enter code KA225812 for updates on this award.

(2259) • Fourth Degree Pro Deo and Pro Patria Scholarships

Knights of Columbus
Department of Scholarships
P.O. Box 1670
New Haven, CT 06507
Phone: 203-752-4000
Email: info@kofc.org
http://www.kofc.org

Purpose: To provide aid to members or the children of members of the Knights of Columbus.

Eligibility: Applicants must be members or the children of current or deceased members of the Knights of Columbus or, in some cases, be members of the Columbian Squires. Applicants must be entering their freshmen year at a U.S. Catholic college.

Target applicants: High school students. College students. Adult students.

Amount: $1,500.

Number of awards: 62.

Scholarship may be renewable.

Deadline: March 1.

How to apply: Applications are available by mail.

Exclusive: Visit www.UltimateScholarshipBook.com and enter code KN225912 for updates on this award.

(2260) • Francis J. Flynn Memorial Scholarship

Tau Kappa Epsilon Educational Foundation
8645 Founders Road
Indianapolis, IN 46268
Phone: 317-872-6533
Fax: 317-875-8353
Email: tef@tke.org
http://www.tkefoundation.org

Purpose: To recognize academic achievement and chapter leadership in members pursuing degrees in mathematics and education.
Eligibility: Applicants must be initiated Tau Kappa Epsilon members in good standing and full-time undergraduate students pursuing a degree in mathematics or education. They must have a GPA of at least 2.75 and demonstrate outstanding chapter leadership. Applicants must also include a statement describing how they have benefited from TKE membership. First preference will be given to members of Theta-Sigma Chapter.
Target applicants: College students. Adult students.
Minimum GPA: 2.75
Amount: $475.
Number of awards: 1.
Deadline: March 1.
How to apply: Applications are available online.
Exclusive: Visit www.UltimateScholarshipBook.com and enter code TA226012 for updates on this award.

(2261) • Frank Kamierczak Memorial Migrant Scholarship

BOCES Geneseo Migrant Center
27 Lackawanna Avenue
Mt. Morris, NY 14510
Phone: 800-245-5681
Fax: 585-658-7969
Email: info@migrant.net
http://www.migrant.net

Purpose: To provide financial aid to migrant youth.
Eligibility: Applicants must be the children of migrant workers or migrant workers themselves and must have teaching as a career goal. Selection is based upon scholastic achievement, financial need and recent history of movement for agricultural employment, with priority given to applicants who have moved within the last three years before applying.
Target applicants: High school students. College students. Adult students.
Amount: $1,000.
Number of awards: 1.
Deadline: February 1.
How to apply: Applications are available online.
Exclusive: Visit www.UltimateScholarshipBook.com and enter code BO226112 for updates on this award.

(2262) • Frank S. Land Scholarships

DeMolay Foundation
10200 NW Ambassador Drive
Kansas City, MO 64153
Phone: 800-336-6529
Fax: 816-891-9062
Email: demolay@demolay.org
http://www.demolay.org

Purpose: To award DeMolay members.
Eligibility: Applicants must be active male members of DeMolay and be under the age of 21. DeMolay is an organization with more than 1,000 chapters in the world that helps prepare young men ages 12 to 21 to "lead successful, happy and productive lives." The group aims to help members develop civic awareness, personal responsibility and leadership skills.
Target applicants: Junior high students or younger. High school students. College students.
Amount: $800.
Number of awards: Varies.
Deadline: April 1.
How to apply: Applications are available online.
Exclusive: Visit www.UltimateScholarshipBook.com and enter code DE226212 for updates on this award.

(2263) • Gaston/Nolle Scholarships

Alpha Chi
Harding University Box 12249
915 E. Market Avenue
Searcy, AR 72149-2249
Phone: 800-477-4225
Fax: 501-279-4589
Email: dorgan@harding.edu
http://www.alphachihonor.org

Purpose: To assist Alpha Chi members who are entering their senior year of undergraduate study.
Eligibility: Applicants must be members of Alpha Chi who are enrolled full-time in a bachelor's degree program.
Target applicants: College students. Adult students.
Amount: $1,500-$2,500.
Number of awards: 12.
Deadline: February 22.
How to apply: Application requirements are available online, and applicants must be nominated by the faculty sponsor.
Exclusive: Visit www.UltimateScholarshipBook.com and enter code AL226312 for updates on this award.

(2264) • GCSAA Legacy Awards

Golf Course Superintendents Association of America
GCSAA Career Development Department
1421 Research Park Drive
Lawrence, KS 66049
Phone: 800-472-7878
Fax: 785-832-3643
Email: mbrhelp@gcsaa.org
http://www.gcsaa.org

Purpose: To support the children and grandchildren of GCSAA members.
Eligibility: The applicant's parents or grandparents must have been GCSAA members for five or more consecutive years. Applicants must also be full-time college students or high school seniors already accepted into a postsecondary school.
Target applicants: High school students. College students. Adult students.
Amount: $1,500.
Number of awards: Varies.
Deadline: April 15.
How to apply: Applications are available by contacting Pam Smith, 800-472-7878, x3678.

Exclusive: Visit www.UltimateScholarshipBook.com and enter code GO226412 for updates on this award.

(2265) • GEICO Life Scholarship

Golden Key National Honour Society
Scholarship Program Administrators
Golden Key Scholarships/Awards
P.O. Box 23737
Nashville, TN 37202-3737
Phone: 800-377-2401
Email: scholarships@goldenkey.org
http://www.goldenkey.org

Purpose: To support undergraduate students who balance family, career or other life commitments with pursuing a degree.
Eligibility: Applicants must be members of Golden Key, be enrolled in a baccalaureate program and have completed at least 12 hours at the time of application. The award is based on academic achievement, extracurricular activities and family and/or career commitments.
Target applicants: College students. Adult students.
Amount: $1,000.
Number of awards: 10.
Deadline: April 1.
How to apply: Applications are available online.
Exclusive: Visit www.UltimateScholarshipBook.com and enter code GO226512 for updates on this award.

(2266) • General Conference Women's Ministries Scholarship Program

General Conference of Seventh-Day Adventists Women's Ministries
12501 Old Columbia Pike
Silver Spring, MD 20904
Phone: 301-680-6672
Fax: 301-680-6600
Email: womensministries@gc.adventist.org
http://wm.gc.adventist.org

Purpose: To support female Seventh-day Adventists who are pursuing Christian education.
Eligibility: Applicants must be women who are planning to study at a Seventh-day Adventist college in their division. Students in their final two years of study will be given preference. Applicants must show financial need, academic achievement and willingness to serve the Lord.
Target applicants: High school students. College students. Graduate school students. Adult students.
Amount: Varies.
Number of awards: Varies.
Deadline: Varies.
How to apply: Applications are available online and from Women's Ministries Directors in each division.
Exclusive: Visit www.UltimateScholarshipBook.com and enter code GE226612 for updates on this award.

(2267) • George W. Woolery Memorial Scholarship

Tau Kappa Epsilon Educational Foundation
8645 Founders Road
Indianapolis, IN 46268
Phone: 317-872-6533
Fax: 317-875-8353
Email: tef@tke.org
http://www.tkefoundation.org

Purpose: To award a member of Tau Kappa Epsilon for academic achievement and outstanding leadership within the chapter and campus.
Eligibility: Applicants must have a GPA of at least 2.5 and must be seeking an undergraduate degree in marketing or communications. Preference is first given to members of the Beta-Sigma Chapter.
Target applicants: College students. Adult students.
Minimum GPA: 2.5
Amount: $200.
Number of awards: 1.
Deadline: March 1.
How to apply: Applications are available online.
Exclusive: Visit www.UltimateScholarshipBook.com and enter code TA226712 for updates on this award.

(2268) • Gift of Hope: 21st Century Scholars Program

United Methodist Higher Education Foundation
P.O. Box 340005
Nashville, TN 37203-0005
Phone: 615-340-7385
Fax: 615-340-7330
Email: umscholar@gbhem.org
http://www.umhef.org

Purpose: To support United Methodist students who are leaders in the church.
Eligibility: Applicants must have been full, active members and leaders in the United Methodist Church for at least three years. They must be U.S. citizens, permanent residents or members of the Central Conferences. Students must be enrolled in a full-time undergraduate degree program at an accredited U.S. institution with a GPA of 3.0 or higher.
Target applicants: High school students. College students. Adult students.
Minimum GPA: 3.0
Amount: $1,000.
Number of awards: Varies.
Deadline: April 15 and May 1.
How to apply: Applications are available online. An application form, transcript, essay and three letters of recommendation are required.
Exclusive: Visit www.UltimateScholarshipBook.com and enter code UN226812 for updates on this award.

(2269) • Girl Scout Achievement Award

American Legion Auxiliary
8945 N. Meridian Street
Indianapolis, IN 46260
Phone: 317-569-4500
Fax: 317-569-4502
Email: alahq@legion-aux.org
http://www.legion-aux.org

Purpose: To reward Girl Scout Gold Award winners.
Eligibility: Applicants must be Cadet or Senior Girl Scouts who have received the Girls Scout Gold Award, be active members of their religious institution and have received the appropriate religious emblem and demonstrate citizenship. Applicants must submit four letters of recommendation from a religious institution, a school, the community and scouting.
Target applicants: High school students.
Amount: Varies.
Number of awards: Varies.
Deadline: March 15.
How to apply: Applications are available online.

Exclusive: Visit www.UltimateScholarshipBook.com and enter code AM226912 for updates on this award.

(2270) • Glass, Molders, Pottery, Plastics and Allied Workers Memorial Scholarship Fund

Glass, Molders, Pottery, Plastics and Allied Workers International Union
608 E. Baltimore Pike
P.O. Box 607
Media, PA 19063
Phone: 610-565-5051
Fax: 610-565-0983
Email: gmpiu@ix.netcom.com
http://www.gmpiu.org
Purpose: To provide financial assistance to the children of members.
Eligibility: Applicants must be children, step-children or legally-adopted children of Glass, Molders, Pottery, Plastics and Allied Workers members.
Target applicants: High school students.
Amount: $2,000-$4,000.
Number of awards: 10.
Scholarship may be renewable.
Deadline: November 1.
How to apply: Applications are available by written request or by contacting your local union office.
Exclusive: Visit www.UltimateScholarshipBook.com and enter code GL227012 for updates on this award.

(2271) • Gloria and Joseph Mattera National Scholarship for Migrant Children

BOCES Geneseo Migrant Center
27 Lackawanna Avenue
Mt. Morris, NY 14510
Phone: 800-245-5681
Fax: 585-658-7969
Email: info@migrant.net
http://www.migrant.net
Purpose: To assist migrant youth in attending college.
Eligibility: Applicants must be enrolling in college or another institute of post-secondary education or be high school dropouts or potential dropouts who show promise in intending to pursue higher education. Recipients are chosen based upon scholastic ability, financial need and recent history of movement for agricultural employment, with priority given to current interstate migrant youth.
Target applicants: High school students.
Amount: $150-$500.
Number of awards: 100.
Deadline: None, applications are reviewed on a case-by-case basis.
How to apply: Applications are available online.
Exclusive: Visit www.UltimateScholarshipBook.com and enter code BO227112 for updates on this award.

(2272) • Golden Key Engineering/Technology Achievement Awards

Golden Key International Honour Society
621 North Avenue NE
Suite C-100
Atlanta, GA 30308
Phone: 800-377-2401
Fax: 678-420-6757
Email: memberservices@goldenkey.org
http://www.goldenkey.org
Purpose: To aid Golden Key members who are engineering or technology students.
Eligibility: Applicants must be Golden Key members who are studying engineering or technology at the postsecondary level. They must be enrolled in a degree-granting program at the time of application submission. Selection is based on academic merit and the quality of the academic paper submitted along with the application.
Target applicants: College students. Adult students.
Amount: Up to $2,000.
Number of awards: 3.
Deadline: March 1.
How to apply: Applications are available online. An application form, academic paper, official transcript and one letter of recommendation are required.
Exclusive: Visit www.UltimateScholarshipBook.com and enter code GO227212 for updates on this award.

(2273) • Golden Key Graduate Scholar Award

Golden Key National Honour Society
Scholarship Program Administrators
Golden Key Scholarships/Awards
P.O. Box 23737
Nashville, TN 37202-3737
Phone: 800-377-2401
Email: scholarships@goldenkey.org
http://www.goldenkey.org
Purpose: To support Golden Key members' graduate studies at accredited universities in the U.S. or abroad.
Eligibility: Applicant must be a Golden Key member. Selection is based on academic achievement, involvement in Golden Key and extracurricular activities.
Target applicants: College students. Graduate school students. Adult students.
Amount: $10,000.
Number of awards: At least 10.
Deadline: January 15.
How to apply: Applications are available online.
Exclusive: Visit www.UltimateScholarshipBook.com and enter code GO227312 for updates on this award.

(2274) • Golden Key Math Scholarship

Golden Key International Honour Society
621 North Avenue NE
Suite C-100
Atlanta, GA 30308
Phone: 800-377-2401
Fax: 678-420-6757
Email: memberservices@goldenkey.org
http://www.goldenkey.org
Purpose: To support Golden Key members who are studying math.
Eligibility: Applicants must be Golden Key members who are math students enrolled in a degree-granting program at the postsecondary level. Selection is based on academic merit and the strength of the academic paper that is submitted along with the application.
Target applicants: College students. Adult students.
Amount: $1,000.
Number of awards: 2.
Deadline: April 1.

How to apply: Applications are available online. An application form, official transcript, academic paper and one recommendation letter are required.
Exclusive: Visit www.UltimateScholarshipBook.com and enter code GO227412 for updates on this award.

(2275) • Grange Insurance Group Scholarship

Grange Insurance Association
Scholarship Committee
P.O. Box 21089
Seattle, WA 98111-3089
Phone: 800-247-2643
http://www.grange.com
Purpose: To help those associated with Grange Insurance Group.
Eligibility: Applicants must be current Grange Insurance Group (GIG) policyholders (or children or grandchildren of GIG policyholders) in California, Colorado, Idaho, Oregon, Washington or Wyoming; Grange members (or children or grandchildren of Grange members) or children or grandchildren of current GIG employees and residents in California, Colorado, Idaho, Oregon, Washington and Wyoming. Applicants can apply for scholarships in either academic or vocational studies. Three of the awards will be for students wishing to pursue vocational studies and 22 will be for academic studies. The top scoring student in each category receives $1,500 and each additional winner receives $1,000. Scholarships may be used toward a certificate or degree in a recognized profession or vocation, including community colleges, business colleges and technical institutes, as well as institutions offering an academic degree program. Vocational scholarships are intended for use at community colleges, technical or business schools or other institutions that offer vocational training which does not lead to a two- or four-year academic degree. Selection is based on academic achievement and essays.
Target applicants: High school students. College students. Adult students.
Amount: $1,000-$1,500.
Number of awards: 25.
Deadline: April 15.
How to apply: Applications are available online.
Exclusive: Visit www.UltimateScholarshipBook.com and enter code GR227512 for updates on this award.

(2276) • Guistwhite Scholarships

Phi Theta Kappa Honor Society
1625 Eastover Drive
Jackson, MS 39211
Phone: 601-984-3504
Fax: 601-984-3548
Email: scholarship.programs@ptk.org
http://www.ptk.org
Purpose: To aid Phi Theta Kappa members who plan to pursue bachelor's degrees.
Eligibility: Applicants must be active members of Phi Theta Kappa who will remain enrolled at a community college through December of the application year. They must have completed at least 30 semester credits (or 45 quarter credits) over the past five years and must have maintained a GPA of 3.5 or higher on a four-point scale over the past five years. Students must have plans to transfer to a four-year postsecondary institution during the calendar year following the submission of the scholarship application and must have junior status at the time of transfer. Applicants must have a community college record that is free of any disciplinary action and must not have a criminal record. Selection is based on academic merit and Phi Theta Kappa participation.
Target applicants: College students. Adult students.
Minimum GPA: 3.5
Amount: $5,000.
Number of awards: Up to 20.
Deadline: December 1.
How to apply: Applications are available online. An application form, official transcript, two recommendation letters and personal essay are required.
Exclusive: Visit www.UltimateScholarshipBook.com and enter code PH227612 for updates on this award.

(2277) • Guy and Gloria Muto Memorial Scholarship

Guy and Gloria Muto Memorial Scholarship Foundation Inc.
P.O. Box 60159
Sacramento, CA 95860
Email: ggmuto@aol.com
http://www.ggmuto.org
Purpose: To provide scholarships for pool and spa industry employees and their immediate families.
Eligibility: Applicants or their immediate family must have been employed full-time in the pool and spa industry for at least one year. Students must have the endorsement of an officer of a chapter of a recognized pool and spa association. Scholarships may be used for college, graduate school, trade school or vocational education.
Target applicants: High school students. College students. Graduate school students. Adult students.
Amount: Varies.
Number of awards: Varies.
Deadline: May 31.
How to apply: Applications are available online.
Exclusive: Visit www.UltimateScholarshipBook.com and enter code GU227712 for updates on this award.

(2278) • HANA Scholarship

United Methodist Church
Office of Loans and Scholarships
P.O. BOX 340007
Nashville, TN 37203-0007
Phone: 615-340-7344
Fax: 615-340-7367
Email: umscholar@gbhem.org
http://www.gbhem.org
Purpose: To support students in the United Methodist Church who are of Hispanic, Asian, Native American or Pacific Island parentage.
Eligibility: Applicants must be in at least their junior year of college or in graduate school, and they must have at least a 2.85 GPA. They must have been members of the United Methodist Church for at least three years. Students must plan to take on leadership roles in their church and ethnic communities.
Target applicants: College students. Graduate school students. Adult students.
Minimum GPA: 2.85
Amount: Varies.
Number of awards: Varies.
Deadline: April 15.
How to apply: Applications are available online.
Exclusive: Visit www.UltimateScholarshipBook.com and enter code UN227812 for updates on this award.

(2279) • Harold Davis Memorial Scholarship

National FFA Organization
P.O. Box 68960
6060 FFA Drive
Indianapolis, IN 46268-0960
Phone: 317-802-6060
Fax: 317-802-6051
Email: scholarships@ffa.org
http://www.ffa.org/

Purpose: To provide financial assistance to students who have livestock backgrounds and are seeking degrees in animal science, agricultural education and agribusiness.
Eligibility: Applicants must be current FFA members and high school seniors or college students planning to enroll or currently enrolled full-time. Students only need to complete the online application one time to be considered for all FFA-administered scholarships. The application requires information about the student's activities and a 1,000-word essay. Awards may be used for books, supplies, tuition, fees and room and board.
Target applicants: High school students. College students. Adult students.
Amount: $400.
Number of awards: 1.
Deadline: February 15.
How to apply: Applications are available online.
Exclusive: Visit www.UltimateScholarshipBook.com and enter code NA227912 for updates on this award.

(2280) • Harry C. Bates Merit Scholarships

International Union of Bricklayers and Allied Craftworkers (BAC)
Education Department
1776 Eye Street NW
Washington, DC 2006
Phone: 888-880-8222 x3111
Email: askbac@bacweb.org
http://www.bacweb.org

Purpose: To award scholarships to the children of BAC members.
Eligibility: U.S. applicants must be the children of a member, living or deceased, of BAC and among the semifinalists in the PSAT/NMSQT.
Target applicants: High school students.
Amount: $2,500.
Number of awards: 3.
Scholarship may be renewable.
Deadline: February 28.
How to apply: For U.S. students: There is no application. NMSQT semi-finalists should notify their local BAC office. The application for Canadian students is available online.
Exclusive: Visit www.UltimateScholarshipBook.com and enter code IN228012 for updates on this award.

(2281) • Harry J. Donnelly Memorial Scholarship

Tau Kappa Epsilon Educational Foundation
8645 Founders Road
Indianapolis, IN 46268
Phone: 317-872-6533
Fax: 317-875-8353
Email: tef@tke.org
http://www.tkefoundation.org

Purpose: To honor the "father" of the TKE Educational Foundation by recognizing outstanding current members.
Eligibility: Applicants must be initiated Tau Kappa Epsilon members in good standing and full-time students. They must be undergraduate students in accounting or graduate students in law and plan to be full-time students in the following academic year. Applicants must have a GPA of at least 3.0, demonstrate outstanding leadership in their chapter, campus and community and include a statement describing how they have benefited from TKE membership.
Target applicants: College students. Graduate school students. Adult students.
Minimum GPA: 3.0
Amount: $300.
Number of awards: 1.
Deadline: March 1.
How to apply: Applications are available online.
Exclusive: Visit www.UltimateScholarshipBook.com and enter code TA228112 for updates on this award.

(2282) • Highway Worker Memorial Scholarship Program

American Road and Transportation Builders Association
1219 28th Street NW
Washington, DC 20007
Phone: 202-289-4434
Email: rbritton@artba.org
http://www.artba.org

Purpose: To support the children of injured or deceased highway workers.
Eligibility: Students must have a parent who was killed or seriously injured in a highway construction zone accident, and the parent must have been employed by a transportation construction firm or a transportation public agency at the time of the accident. Applicants must demonstrate financial need, and they must have at least a 2.5 GPA.
Target applicants: High school students. College students. Adult students.
Minimum GPA: 2.5
Amount: Up to $5,000.
Number of awards: Varies.
Deadline: March 19.
How to apply: Applications are available online.
Exclusive: Visit www.UltimateScholarshipBook.com and enter code AM228212 for updates on this award.

(2283) • Hites Transfer Scholarship

Phi Theta Kappa Honor Society
1625 Eastover Drive
Jackson, MS 39211
Phone: 601-984-3504
Fax: 601-984-3548
Email: scholarship.programs@ptk.org
http://www.ptk.org

Purpose: To aid Phi Theta Kappa members who intend to transfer to a four-year postsecondary institution.
Eligibility: Applicants must be Phi Theta Kappa members who are in good standing, have a GPA of 3.5 or higher and have completed 50 or more semester credits over the past five years. They must be enrolled at an accredited community college through March of the application year, have plans to transfer to a four-year postsecondary institution in the fall and have plans to pursue a bachelor's degree on a full-time basis. Applicants cannot have a criminal record. Selection is based on the overall strength of the application.
Target applicants: College students. Adult students.

Minimum GPA: 3.5
Amount: $7,500.
Number of awards: Up to 5.
Deadline: March 1.
How to apply: Applications are available online. An application form and supporting documents are required.
Exclusive: Visit www.UltimateScholarshipBook.com and enter code PH228312 for updates on this award.

(2284) · Howard Coughlin Memorial Scholarship Fund

Office and Professional Employees International Union
1660 L Street NW
Suite 801
Washington, DC 20036
Phone: 202-393-4464
Fax: 202-347-0649
http://www.opeiu.org
Purpose: To offer scholarships to OPEIU members and their children.
Eligibility: Applicants must either be members of OPEIU in good standing, or the children, stepchildren or legally adopted children of an OPEIU member in good standing or associate members. Applicants must also be high school seniors, high school graduates entering a college, university or a recognized technical or vocational post-secondary school as full-time students, or presently in a college, university or a recognized technical or vocational post-secondary school as a full-time or part-time student. Part-time scholarships are defined as a minimum of three credits and no more than two courses. Selection is based on transcripts, high school class rank and SAT/ACT scores or evidence of an equivalent exam by a recognized technical or vocational post-secondary school.
Target applicants: High school students. College students. Adult students.
Amount: $1,200-$3,000.
Number of awards: 18.
Scholarship may be renewable.
Deadline: March 31.
How to apply: Applications are available at the local union office, at the secretary-treasurer's office of the International Union or online.
Exclusive: Visit www.UltimateScholarshipBook.com and enter code OF228412 for updates on this award.

(2285) · International Association of Machinists and Aerospace Workers Scholarship for Members

International Association of Machinists and Aerospace Workers
9000 Machinists Place
Room 117
Upper Marlboro, MD 20772
Phone: 301-967-4500
http://www.iamaw.org
Purpose: To offer scholarships to members of the International Association of Machinists and Aerospace Workers (IAM).
Eligibility: Applicants must have two years of continuous good standing membership and must be working for a company under contract with the IAM. Applicants may be entering college or vocational/technical school as a freshman or at a higher level with some college credits already completed. Grades, attitude, references, test scores, activities and participation in local lodge are considered in selecting scholarship recipients.
Target applicants: High school students. College students. Adult students.
Amount: $2,000.
Number of awards: Varies.
Deadline: February 25.
How to apply: Applications are available by written request.
Exclusive: Visit www.UltimateScholarshipBook.com and enter code IN228512 for updates on this award.

(2286) · International Association of Machinists and Aerospace Workers Scholarship for Members' Children

International Association of Machinists and Aerospace Workers
9000 Machinists Place
Room 117
Upper Marlboro, MD 20772
Phone: 301-967-4500
http://www.iamaw.org
Purpose: To offer scholarships to children of the members of the IAM.
Eligibility: The applicant's parent member must have two years of continuous good standing membership, and applicants must be in their senior year of high school. Selection is based on grades, attitude, references, test scores and activities outside of school.
Target applicants: High school students.
Amount: $1,000-$2,000.
Number of awards: Varies.
Deadline: February 25.
How to apply: Applications are available by written request.
Exclusive: Visit www.UltimateScholarshipBook.com and enter code IN228612 for updates on this award.

(2287) · Isabella M. Gillen Memorial Scholarship Fund

Aviation Boatswain Mates Association (ABMA)
Scholarship Chairman
Lanny Vines
144 CR 1515
Alba, TX 75410
Email: secretary@abma-usn.org
http://www.abma-usn.org
Purpose: To support family members of ABMA.
Eligibility: Applicants must be the spouses or dependent children of ABMA members who have paid dues for at least two years. In addition to the application, applicants must write a letter stating their professional goals and how they plan to reach them.
Target applicants: High school students. College students. Graduate school students. Adult students.
Amount: $2,500.
Number of awards: Varies.
Deadline: June 1.
How to apply: Applications are available online.
Exclusive: Visit www.UltimateScholarshipBook.com and enter code AV228712 for updates on this award.

(2288) · Islamic Scholarship Fund

Islamic Scholarship Fund
P.O. Box 802
Alamo, CA 94507
Phone: 650-995-6782
Email: contact@islamicscholarshipfund.org
http://www.islamicscholarshipfund.org
Purpose: To aid Muslim students in pursuing degrees in humanities, social sciences, liberal arts and law.

Eligibility: Applicants must be accepted by or attend a top-ranked four-year college or university for undergraduate or graduate studies. They must be practicing Muslims and U.S. citizens or permanent residents. They must have college junior standing or higher and maintain a minimum GPA of 3.4. Applicants should be active members of their communities. Selection is based on academic record, school and extracurricular activities, extenuating circumstances and a personal interview.
Target applicants: College students. Graduate school students. Adult students.
Minimum GPA: 3.4
Amount: $1,000-$10,000.
Number of awards: Varies.
Deadline: March 21.
How to apply: Applications are available online. An application form is required.
Exclusive: Visit www.UltimateScholarshipBook.com and enter code IS228812 for updates on this award.

(2289) · IUE-CWA International Paul Jennings Scholarship

IUE-CWA
1275 K Street NW
Suite 600
Washington, DC 20005
Phone: 202-513-6300
Fax: 202-513-6357
http://www.iue-cwa.org
Purpose: To provide scholarships for the children and grandchildren of local IUE-CWA union elected officials.
Eligibility: Applicants must be the children or grandchildren of IUE-CWA members who are now or have been local union elected officials. Applicants must also be accepted for admission or already enrolled as full-time students at an accredited college, university, nursing school or technical school offering college credit courses. All study must be completed at the undergraduate level. Applicants should demonstrate an interest in equality, improving the quality of life of others and community service. Applicants will also be evaluated on character, leadership and a desire to improve.
Target applicants: High school students. College students. Adult students.
Amount: $3,000.
Number of awards: 1.
Deadline: Varies.
How to apply: Applications are available online.
Exclusive: Visit www.UltimateScholarshipBook.com and enter code IU228912 for updates on this award.

(2290) · J. Robert Ashcroft National Youth Scholarship

Assemblies of God
1445 N. Boonville Avenue
Springfield, MO 65802
Phone: 417-862-2781
Email: colleges@ag.org
http://www.ag.org
Purpose: To provide financial assistance to college-bound seniors who attend Assemblies of God churches.
Eligibility: Applicants must be high school seniors who attend an Assemblies of God church, either in the United States or abroad as dependents of Assemblies of God missionaries or chaplains. Applicants must also attend an institution of higher learning that is endorsed by the Assemblies of God the fall immediately following their high school graduation.
Target applicants: High school students.
Amount: $2,000-$8,000.
Number of awards: 3.
Deadline: February 1.
How to apply: Applications are available online. Applications must be sent to their AG District Council first, and the top candidates are then sent to us for review.
Exclusive: Visit www.UltimateScholarshipBook.com and enter code AS229012 for updates on this award.

(2291) · James C. Borel FFA Leaders Scholarship Fund

National FFA Organization
P.O. Box 68960
6060 FFA Drive
Indianapolis, IN 46268-0960
Phone: 317-802-6060
Fax: 317-802-6051
Email: scholarships@ffa.org
http://www.ffa.org/
Purpose: To support FFA officers who are studying agriculture.
Eligibility: Applicants must be current FFA members and high school seniors or college students planning to enroll or currently enrolled full-time. They must have served as a chapter, state or national FFA officer, and preference will be given to students who have demonstrated leadership skills. Applicants must have at least a 3.5 GPA, and they must show proof of community service participation. Students only need to complete the online application one time to be considered for all FFA-administered scholarships. The application requires information about the student's activities and a 1,000-word essay. Awards may be used for books, supplies, tuition, fees and room and board.
Target applicants: High school students. College students. Adult students.
Minimum GPA: 3.5
Amount: $1,000.
Number of awards: 1.
Deadline: February 15.
How to apply: Applications are available online.
Exclusive: Visit www.UltimateScholarshipBook.com and enter code NA229112 for updates on this award.

(2292) · John A. Courson Top Scholar Award

Tau Kappa Epsilon Educational Foundation
8645 Founders Road
Indianapolis, IN 46268
Phone: 317-872-6533
Fax: 317-875-8353
Email: tef@tke.org
http://www.tkefoundation.org
Purpose: To recognize academic achievement in members.
Eligibility: Applicants must be initiated Tau Kappa Epsilon members in good standing and full-time students with a GPA of 3.0 or higher. They must include a statement describing how they have benefited from TKE membership and demonstrate leadership on their campus, in their community and in their chapter.
Target applicants: College students. Adult students.
Minimum GPA: 3.0
Amount: $1,200.
Number of awards: 1.
Deadline: February 15.

How to apply: Applications are available online.
Exclusive: Visit www.UltimateScholarshipBook.com and enter code TA229212 for updates on this award.

(2293) • John H. Lyons, Sr., Scholarship Program

Iron Workers, International Association of Bridge, Structural, Ornamental and Reinforcing
1750 New York Avenue NW
Suite 400
Washington, DC 20006
Phone: 203-383-4000
Fax: 202-638-4856
http://www.ironworkers.org
Purpose: To offer scholarships to the children of members of the Iron Workers Union.
Eligibility: Applicants must be the children, stepchildren or adopted children of an active member of the Iron Workers who has had five or more years of continuous membership. Children of deceased members who were in members in good standing at the time of their death are also eligible. Applicants must also be in their senior year of high school and rank in the upper half of their graduating classes. Selection is based on academic record, SAT/ACT scores, extracurricular activities, references, leadership and citizenship.
Target applicants: High school students.
Amount: $1,500-$5,000.
Number of awards: 18.
Scholarship may be renewable.
Deadline: January 31.
How to apply: Applications are available by written request.
Exclusive: Visit www.UltimateScholarshipBook.com and enter code IR229312 for updates on this award.

(2294) • John Kelly Labor Studies Scholarship Fund

Office and Professional Employees International Union
1660 L Street NW
Suite 801
Washington, DC 20036
Phone: 202-393-4464
Fax: 202-347-0649
http://www.opeiu.org
Purpose: To offer scholarships to OPEIU members and associate members.
Eligibility: Applicants must be members of OPEIU in good standing or associate members for at least two years, and applicants must be either undergraduate or graduate students in one of the following areas of study: labor studies, industrial relations, union leadership and administration or non-degree programs sponsored by the National Labor College at the George Meany Center or similar institution. The selections shall be based on recommendations of an academic scholarship committee.
Target applicants: College students. Graduate school students. Adult students.
Amount: $3,000.
Number of awards: 10.
Deadline: March 31.
How to apply: Applications are available by phone or written request from the local union office, at the secretary-treasurer's office of the International Union or online.
Exclusive: Visit www.UltimateScholarshipBook.com and enter code OF229412 for updates on this award.

(2295) • John L. Dales Scholarship Fund

Screen Actors Guild Foundation
5757 Wilshire Boulevard
Suite 124
Los Angeles, CA 90036
Phone: 323-549-6649
Fax: 323-549-6710
Email: dlloyd@sag.org
http://www.sagfoundation.org
Purpose: To award scholarships to the families of the SAG.
Eligibility: Applicants must be a member of the Screen Actors Guild or a child of a member of the Screen Actors Guild. Members under the age of 22 must have been a member of the Screen Actors Guild for five years and have a lifetime earnings of $30,000. The parent of an applicant must have ten vested years of pension credits OR a lifetime earnings of $150,000 earned in the Guild's jurisdiction. Applicants must submit an essay of 350 to 750 words on a topic of their choice. The award may be used during college or graduate school.
Target applicants: High school students. College students. Graduate school students. Adult students.
Amount: Varies.
Number of awards: Varies.
Deadline: March 15.
How to apply: Applications are available online.
Exclusive: Visit www.UltimateScholarshipBook.com and enter code SC229512 for updates on this award.

(2296) • John Sarrin Scholarship

Society of Friends (Quakers)
Attn.: Dinah Geiger
2757 South 1050 East
Indianapolis, IN 46231
Phone: 765-962-7573
Fax: 765-966-1293
Email: info@usfwi.org
http://www.usfwi.org
Purpose: To support the education of ministers, missionaries, the children of ministers and other Friends who aspire to full-time Christian service.
Eligibility: Applicants must belong to the Society of Friends. They must be committed to staying drug and alcohol free, and they must agree to never join the armed forces of any country. Students must possess good moral character in order to receive and keep the scholarship.
Target applicants: Junior high students or younger. High school students. College students. Graduate school students. Adult students.
Amount: Varies.
Number of awards: Varies.
Deadline: January 1.
How to apply: Applications are available by written request.
Exclusive: Visit www.UltimateScholarshipBook.com and enter code SO229612 for updates on this award.

(2297) • John W McDevitt (Fourth Degree) Scholarship Fund

Knights of Columbus
Department of Scholarships
P.O. Box 1670
New Haven, CT 06507
Phone: 203-752-4000

Email: info@kofc.org
http://www.kofc.org
Purpose: To provide financial assistance to college students who are Knights of Columbus members or family members of a member.
Eligibility: Applicants must be a Knights of Columbus member, or the wife, widow or child of a member in good standing. New applicants must also be entering their freshman year at a Catholic college or university.
Target applicants: High school students. College students. Adult students.
Amount: $1,500.
Number of awards: 36.
Scholarship may be renewable.
Deadline: March 1.
How to apply: Applications are available by mail.
Exclusive: Visit www.UltimateScholarshipBook.com and enter code KN229712 for updates on this award.

(2298) • Jones-Laurence Award for Scholastic Achievement

Sigma Alpha Epsilon (SAE)
Dave Sandell
Sigma Alpha Epsilon Foundation Scholarships
1856 Sheridan Road
Evanston, IL 60201-3837
Phone: 800-233-1856 x234
Fax: 847-475-2250
Email: dsandell@sae.net
http://www.sae.net
Purpose: To improve scholarship among active Sigma Alpha Epsilon members.
Eligibility: Applicants must be brothers of Sigma Alpha Epsilon in good standing and either must have junior standing or higher or must be pursuing full-time graduate study. This award is merit-based, with an emphasis on combining academic excellence, leadership, service and campus involvement. Applicants are nominated by their chapters and have a minimum 3.9 GPA.
Target applicants: College students. Graduate school students. Adult students.
Minimum GPA: 3.9
Amount: $1,000-$2,000.
Number of awards: 2.
Deadline: March 1.
How to apply: Applications are available online.
Exclusive: Visit www.UltimateScholarshipBook.com and enter code SI229812 for updates on this award.

(2299) • JWV Grant

Jewish War Veterans of the USA
1811 R Street NW
Washington, DC 20009
Phone: 202-265-6280
Fax: 202-234-5662
Email: jwv@jwv.org
http://www.jwv.org
Purpose: To provide scholarships for descendents of members of the Jewish War Veterans of the USA.
Eligibility: Applicants must be direct descendents of a JWV member in good standing. Candidates must also have been accepted to an accredited college, university or nursing school, be in the upper 25 percent of their class and be active in activities at school and within the Jewish community.
Target applicants: High school students.
Amount: $500.
Number of awards: 1.
Deadline: May 4.
How to apply: Applications are available online and should be submitted by the applicant's school to the department commander in the local post.
Exclusive: Visit www.UltimateScholarshipBook.com and enter code JE229912 for updates on this award.

(2300) • Kenneth L. Duke, Sr., Memorial Scholarship

Tau Kappa Epsilon Educational Foundation
8645 Founders Road
Indianapolis, IN 46268
Phone: 317-872-6533
Fax: 317-875-8353
Email: tef@tke.org
http://www.tkefoundation.org
Purpose: To award a member of Tau Kappa Epsilon for academic achievement and outstanding leadership within the chapter, campus or community.
Eligibility: Applicants must have a GPA of at least 2.5.
Target applicants: College students. Adult students.
Minimum GPA: 2.5
Amount: $150.
Number of awards: 1.
Deadline: March 1.
How to apply: Applications are available online.
Exclusive: Visit www.UltimateScholarshipBook.com and enter code TA230012 for updates on this award.

(2301) • Koven L. Brown Scholarship Program

International Order of the Golden Rule
Education Department
P.O. Box 28689
St. Louis, MO 631461189
Phone: 800-637-8030
Fax: 314-209-7213
Email: jgabbert@ogr.org
http://www.ogr.org
Purpose: To assist mortuary science students with financial need.
Eligibility: Applicants must be studying mortuary science and have a minimum 3.0 GPA. The award is based on community service, honors, grades and potential contributions to the funeral service profession.
Target applicants: College students. Adult students.
Minimum GPA: 3.0
Amount: Varies.
Number of awards: Varies.
Deadline: October 1.
How to apply: Applications are available online.
Exclusive: Visit www.UltimateScholarshipBook.com and enter code IN230112 for updates on this award.

(2302) • Kyutaro and Yasuo Abiko Memorial Scholarship

Japanese American Citizens League (JACL)
1765 Sutter Street
San Francisco, CA 94115
Phone: 415-921-5225
Fax: 415-931-4671

Email: jacl@jacl.org
http://www.jacl.org
Purpose: To aid National Japanese American Citizens League (JACL) members who are pursuing higher education.
Eligibility: Applicants must be National JACL members who are enrolled as full-time undergraduates at a U.S. institution of higher learning. Preference will be given to applicants who are studying agriculture or journalism. Selection is based on the overall strength of the application.
Target applicants: College students. Adult students.
Amount: Varies.
Number of awards: Varies.
Deadline: April 1.
How to apply: Applications are available online. An application form, official transcript, personal statement, one recommendation letter and proof of JACL membership are required.
Exclusive: Visit www.UltimateScholarshipBook.com and enter code JA230212 for updates on this award.

(2303) • L. Gordon Bittle Memorial Scholarship for Student CTA (SCTA)

California Teachers Association (CTA)
CTA Human Rights Department
P.O. Box 921
Burlingame, CA 94011-0921
Phone: 650-697-1400
Fax: 650-552-5001
http://www.cta.org
Purpose: To support members of the Student California Teachers Association.
Eligibility: Applicants must be planning to work in public education and have a minimum 3.5 high school GPA or show high academic achievement in college coursework, explaining any special circumstances affecting their grades. Scholarships are based on a personal statement, school and community activities and letters of recommendation.
Target applicants: High school students. College students. Graduate school students. Adult students.
Minimum GPA: 3.5
Amount: $3,000.
Number of awards: Up to 3.
Deadline: February 4.
How to apply: Applications are available online.
Exclusive: Visit www.UltimateScholarshipBook.com and enter code CA230312 for updates on this award.

(2304) • Leaders of Promise/GEICO Business Student Scholarship

Phi Theta Kappa Honor Society
1625 Eastover Drive
Jackson, MS 39211
Phone: 601-984-3504
Fax: 601-984-3548
Email: scholarship.programs@ptk.org
http://www.ptk.org
Purpose: To aid Phi Theta Kappa members.
Eligibility: Applicants must be Phi Theta Kappa members who are in good standing. They must be enrolled in an associate's degree program at a community college, have a GPA of 3.5 or higher and have completed no more than 36 semester hours (54 quarter hours) of study by January of the application year. They must have plans to enroll for at least six credits during the fall semester of the application year. Applicants must have a community college record that is free of disciplinary action and cannot have a criminal record. Students who already have earned an associate's or bachelor's degree are ineligible. All applicants meeting the above criteria are eligible for the Leaders of Promise award, but only declared business majors are eligible for the GEICO Business Student Scholarship. Selection is based on the overall strength of the application.
Target applicants: College students. Adult students.
Minimum GPA: 3.5
Amount: $1,000.
Number of awards: Up to 30.
Deadline: May 1.
How to apply: Applications are available online. An application form and supporting materials are required.
Exclusive: Visit www.UltimateScholarshipBook.com and enter code PH230412 for updates on this award.

(2305) • Legacy Award

Elks National Foundation Headquarters
2750 North Lakeview Avenue
Chicago, IL 60614
Phone: 773-755-4732
Fax: 773-755-4733
Email: scholarship@elks.org
http://www.elks.org
Purpose: To assist the descendants of Elk members.
Eligibility: Applicants must be children or grandchildren (including step-children/grandchildren and legal wards) of Elk members in good standing and be high school seniors planning to attend accredited U.S. postsecondary institutions (with the exception of some non-U.S. Elks Lodges). Applicants must also take or have taken the SAT or ACT. The selection committee will evaluate applicants on the core values of knowledge, charity, community and integrity. Financial need is not a consideration.
Target applicants: High school students.
Amount: $1,000.
Number of awards: Up to 250.
Deadline: February 1.
How to apply: Applications are available from local Elks Lodges, online or by written request.
Exclusive: Visit www.UltimateScholarshipBook.com and enter code EL230512 for updates on this award.

(2306) • Lenwood S. Cochran Scholarship

Tau Kappa Epsilon Educational Foundation
8645 Founders Road
Indianapolis, IN 46268
Phone: 317-872-6533
Fax: 317-875-8353
Email: tef@tke.org
http://www.tkefoundation.org
Purpose: To award a member of Tau Kappa Epsilon for outstanding academic achievement and leadership within the chapter, including serving as an officer.
Eligibility: Applicants must have a GPA of at least 3.0. Preference is first given to members of the Gamma-Mu Chapter.
Target applicants: College students. Adult students.
Minimum GPA: 3.0
Amount: $175.
Number of awards: 1.
Deadline: March 1.

How to apply: Applications are available online.
Exclusive: Visit www.UltimateScholarshipBook.com and enter code TA230612 for updates on this award.

(2307) • Life Members' Scholarship

American Atheists
P.O. Box 5733
Parsippany, NJ 07054
Phone: 908-276-7300
Fax: 908-276-7402
Email: info@athiests.org
http://www.atheists.org
Purpose: To support Atheist students who are activists.
Eligibility: Applicants must be high school seniors or college students who are Atheists, have a minimum 2.5 GPA and be student activists. The award is based on the level of activism and requires a 500- to 1,000-word essay. In addition to the scholarship, the winner will receive a free trip to the American Atheists National Convention.
Target applicants: High school students. College students. Adult students.
Minimum GPA: 2.5
Amount: $1,000-$2,000.
Number of awards: 1-3.
Deadline: January 31.
How to apply: Applications are available online.
Exclusive: Visit www.UltimateScholarshipBook.com and enter code AM230712 for updates on this award.

(2308) • Lillian and Arthur Dunn Scholarship

National Society Daughters of the American Revolution
Committee Services Office
Attn.: Scholarships
1776 D Street NW
Washington, DC 20006-5303
Phone: 202-628-1776
http://www.dar.org
Purpose: To assist the children of members with their education.
Eligibility: Applicants must be sons or daughters of current women members of NSDAR, must be U.S. citizens and plan to attend an accredited U.S. college or university. All applicants must obtain a letter of sponsorship from their local DAR chapter.
Target applicants: High school students. College students. Adult students.
Amount: $2,000.
Number of awards: Varies.
Scholarship may be renewable.
Deadline: February 15.
How to apply: Applications are available by written request with a self-addressed, stamped envelope.
Exclusive: Visit www.UltimateScholarshipBook.com and enter code NA230812 for updates on this award.

(2309) • Literacy Grants

Honor Society of Phi Kappa Phi
7576 Goodwood Boulevard
Baton Rouge, LA 70806
Phone: 800-804-9880
Fax: 225-388-4900
Email: awards@phikappaphi.org
http://www.phikappaphi.org
Purpose: To award grants to Phi Kappa Phi members and chapters to offer literacy programs.
Eligibility: The project leader must be a member of Phi Kappa Phi. Previous winners have provided books and book bags to literacy programs, organized literacy fairs and conducted research on literacy.
Target applicants: College students. Graduate school students. Adult students.
Amount: Up to $2,500.
Number of awards: Varies.
Deadline: April 1.
How to apply: Applications are available online.
Exclusive: Visit www.UltimateScholarshipBook.com and enter code HO230912 for updates on this award.

(2310) • Literary Achievement Awards

Golden Key National Honour Society
Scholarship Program Administrators
Golden Key Scholarships/Awards
P.O. Box 23737
Nashville, TN 37202-3737
Phone: 800-377-2401
Email: scholarships@goldenkey.org
http://www.goldenkey.org
Purpose: To support members who demonstrate literary talents.
Eligibility: Applicants must be undergraduate, graduate or post-graduate members who are taking classes in a degree-granting program. Selection is based on an original composition. One winner is selected in each of four categories: fiction, non-fiction, poetry and news writing.
Target applicants: College students. Graduate school students. Adult students.
Amount: $1,000.
Number of awards: 4.
Deadline: March 1.
How to apply: Applications are available online.
Exclusive: Visit www.UltimateScholarshipBook.com and enter code GO231012 for updates on this award.

(2311) • Lorin E. Kerr Scholarship Fund

United Mine Workers of America/BCOA T.E.F.
8315 Lee Highway
Fairfax, VA 22031-2215
Phone: 703-208-7200
http://www.umwa.org
Purpose: To offer scholarships to UMWA members and their families.
Eligibility: Applicants must be UMWA members or dependents who pursue undergraduate degrees. Selection is based on academic potential and financial need.
Target applicants: High school students. College students. Adult students.
Amount: $2,500.
Number of awards: 2.
Deadline: February 18.
How to apply: Applications are available online.
Exclusive: Visit www.UltimateScholarshipBook.com and enter code UN231112 for updates on this award.

(2312) • Louis S. Silvey Grant

Jewish War Veterans of the USA
1811 R Street NW
Washington, DC 20009

Phone: 202-265-6280
Fax: 202-234-5662
Email: jwv@jwv.org
http://www.jwv.org
Purpose: To provide scholarships for descendents of members of the Jewish War Veterans of the USA.
Eligibility: Applicants must be direct descendents of a JWV member in good standing. Candidates must also have been accepted to an accredited college, university or nursing school, be in the upper 25 percent of their class and be active in activities at school and within the Jewish community.
Target applicants: High school students.
Amount: $750.
Number of awards: 1.
Deadline: May 4.
How to apply: Applications are available online and should be submitted by the applicant's school to the department commander in the local post.
Exclusive: Visit www.UltimateScholarshipBook.com and enter code JE231212 for updates on this award.

(2313) · Maids of Athena Scholarships

American Hellenic Education Progressive Association
1909 Q Street NW
Suite 500
Washington, DC 20009
Phone: 202-232-6300
Fax: 202-232-2140
Email: ahepa@ahepa.org
http://www.ahepa.org
Purpose: To support members of the Maids of Athena.
Eligibility: Students must demonstrate financial need and academic achievement. Applicants must be high school seniors, college undergraduates or graduate students. Selection is based on academic achievement, financial need and participation in the organization.
Target applicants: High school students. College students. Graduate school students. Adult students.
Amount: $1,000.
Number of awards: 3.
Deadline: Varies.
How to apply: Applications are available online.
Exclusive: Visit www.UltimateScholarshipBook.com and enter code AM231312 for updates on this award.

(2314) · Margaret Jerome Sampson Scholarship

Phi Upsilon Omicron Inc.
National Office
P.O. Box 329
Fairmont, WV 26555
Phone: 304-368-0612
Email: info@phiu.org
http://www.phiu.org
Purpose: To aid Phi Upsilon Omicron members who are working toward bachelor's degrees in family and consumer sciences.
Eligibility: Applicants must be Phi Upsilon Omicron (Phi U) members. They must be full-time students who are enrolled in a family and consumer sciences degree program at the baccalaureate level. Preference will be given to applicants who are majoring in food and nutrition or dietetics. Selection is based on academic merit, participation in Phi U and stated career goals.
Target applicants: College students. Adult students.
Amount: $4,000.
Number of awards: 5.
Deadline: February 1.
How to apply: Applications are available online. An application form, three recommendation letters, an official transcript and a financial statement are required.
Exclusive: Visit www.UltimateScholarshipBook.com and enter code PH231412 for updates on this award.

(2315) · Martin Luther King, Jr. Memorial Scholarship

California Teachers Association (CTA)
CTA Human Rights Department
P.O. Box 921
Burlingame, CA 94011-0921
Phone: 650-697-1400
Fax: 650-552-5001
http://www.cta.org
Purpose: To encourage ethnic minority students to become teachers and support the continuing education of ethnic minority teachers.
Eligibility: Applicants must be African American, American Indian/ Alaska Native, Asian/Pacific Islander or Hispanic students pursuing a teaching-related career in public education. Candidates must also be active members of the California Teachers Association or Student California Teachers Association or the dependents of an active, retired-life or deceased California Teachers Association member.
Target applicants: High school students. College students. Graduate school students. Adult students.
Amount: Varies.
Number of awards: Varies.
Deadline: Varies.
How to apply: Applications are available online.
Exclusive: Visit www.UltimateScholarshipBook.com and enter code CA231512 for updates on this award.

(2316) · Mattie J.C. Russell Scholarship

Woman's Missionary Union Foundation
P. O. Box 11346
Birmingham, AL 35202-1346
Phone: 1-877-482-4483
Fax: 205-408-5508
Email: llucas@wmu.org
http://www.wmufoundation.com
Purpose: To reward the sons or daughters of international and North American missionaries who have achieved academic excellence.
Eligibility: The foundation offers several scholarships for the children of missionaries. The Elizabeth Lowndes Award is for college seniors. The Julia C. Pugh Scholarship is open to the children of international or North American missionaries. The Mattie J.C. Russell Scholarship supports the children of North American missionaries. The Mary B. Rhodes Medical Scholarship is for medical students and students majoring in nursing, dentistry or pharmacy. Transcripts and recommendation letters are required.
Target applicants: High school students. College students. Adult students.
Amount: $400.
Number of awards: 4.
Deadline: March 1.
How to apply: Applications are available online.
Exclusive: Visit www.UltimateScholarshipBook.com and enter code WO231612 for updates on this award.

(2317) • Michael Hakeem Memorial College Essay Contest

Freedom from Religion Foundation
P.O. Box 750
Madison, WI 53701
Phone: 608-256-5800
Email: info@ffrf.org
http://www.ffrf.org

Purpose: To assist current college students who write an essay about freedom from religion.

Eligibility: Applicants must write a four- to five-page essay on the provided topic. Recent topic choices have been, "Why I am an atheist/agnostic/unbeliever," "Growing up a freethinker" or "Rejecting religion." More details about the topic are available online.

Target applicants: College students. Adult students.

Amount: $200-$2,000.

Number of awards: 4.

Deadline: July 1.

How to apply: There is no application form. In addition to the essay, applicants must submit a one-paragraph biography and should not include a resume.

Exclusive: Visit www.UltimateScholarshipBook.com and enter code FR231712 for updates on this award.

(2318) • Michael J. Morin Memorial Scholarship

Tau Kappa Epsilon Educational Foundation
8645 Founders Road
Indianapolis, IN 46268
Phone: 317-872-6533
Fax: 317-875-8353
Email: tef@tke.org
http://www.tkefoundation.org

Purpose: To award a member of Tau Kappa Epsilon for outstanding academic achievement and leadership within the chapter, community and campus.

Eligibility: Applicants must have a GPA of at least 3.0.

Target applicants: College students. Adult students.

Minimum GPA: 3.0

Amount: $150.

Number of awards: 1.

Deadline: March 1.

How to apply: Applications are available online.

Exclusive: Visit www.UltimateScholarshipBook.com and enter code TA231812 for updates on this award.

(2319) • Michael J. Quill Scholarship Fund

Transport Workers Union of America
1700 Broadway, Second Floor
New York, NY 10019-5905
http://www.twu.org

Purpose: To provide financial assistance to the dependents of TWU members.

Eligibility: Applicants must be high school seniors and may be the children of present, retired or deceased TWU members in good standing or meet other eligibility requirements. Recipients are selected by a public drawing.

Target applicants: High school students.

Amount: $4,800.

Number of awards: 15.

Scholarship may be renewable.

Deadline: May 1.

How to apply: Applications are available from local unions and the union publication. They're also available online.

Exclusive: Visit www.UltimateScholarshipBook.com and enter code TR231912 for updates on this award.

(2320) • Michelin/TIA Scholarship Program

Tire Association of North America
Michelin/TIA Scholarship Program
P.O. Box 1465
Taylors, SC 29687-0031
Phone: 864-268-3363
Email: susanjlee@bellsouth.net
http://www.tireindustry.org

Purpose: To offer financial assistance to children of full-time TIA employees and part-time TIA employees.

Eligibility: Applicants must be part-time employees or dependent children of full-time employees of the Tire Industry Association. Applicants must also be seniors in high school with a minimum 3.0 GPA and be pursuing further education at an accredited two-year or four-year school. Academic achievement, scholarship performance, scholastic aptitude, essays and leadership skills will all be considered.

Target applicants: High school students.

Minimum GPA: 3.0

Amount: $1,250-$2,500.

Number of awards: 3.

Scholarship may be renewable.

Deadline: March 22.

How to apply: Applications are available online.

Exclusive: Visit www.UltimateScholarshipBook.com and enter code TI232012 for updates on this award.

(2321) • Migrant Farmworker Baccalaureate Scholarship

BOCES Geneseo Migrant Center
27 Lackawanna Avenue
Mt. Morris, NY 14510
Phone: 800-245-5681
Fax: 585-658-7969
Email: info@migrant.net
http://www.migrant.net

Purpose: To assist students with migrant histories.

Eligibility: Applicants must have a recent history of movement for agricultural employment, a good academic record and financial need. Applicants must also have successfully completed one year of schooling at an accredited post-secondary institution and may also use the award in graduate school.

Target applicants: College students. Adult students.

Amount: $2,000.

Number of awards: 1.

Scholarship may be renewable.

Deadline: July 1.

How to apply: Applications are available online.

Exclusive: Visit www.UltimateScholarshipBook.com and enter code BO232112 for updates on this award.

(2322) • Miles Gray Memorial Scholarship

Tau Kappa Epsilon Educational Foundation
8645 Founders Road
Indianapolis, IN 46268

Phone: 317-872-6533
Fax: 317-875-8353
Email: tef@tke.org
http://www.tkefoundation.org
Purpose: To award a member of Tau Kappa Epsilon for outstanding academic achievement and leadership within the chapter, campus and community.
Eligibility: Applicants must have a GPA of at least 3.0.
Target applicants: College students. Adult students.
Minimum GPA: 3.0
Amount: $150.
Number of awards: 1.
Deadline: March 1.
How to apply: Applications are available online.
Exclusive: Visit www.UltimateScholarshipBook.com and enter code TA232212 for updates on this award.

(2323) · Mitchell-Beall Scholarship

NASA Federal Credit Union
Mitchell-Beall Memorial Scholarship
P.O. Box 1588
Bowie, MD 20717-1588
Phone: 888-627-2328
Fax: 301-249-0799
Email: support@nasafcu.com
http://www.nasafcu.com
Purpose: To assist younger members of the NASA FCU to further their educations.
Eligibility: Applicants must be the primary owners of NASA Federal Credit Union accounts, high school seniors under the age of 21 and have a minimum 2.0 GPA.
Target applicants: High school students.
Minimum GPA: 2.0
Amount: Up to $7,000.
Number of awards: Varies.
Deadline: February 12.
How to apply: Applications are available online.
Exclusive: Visit www.UltimateScholarshipBook.com and enter code NA232312 for updates on this award.

(2324) · Modern Woodmen of America Scholarship

Modern Woodmen of America
1701 1st Avenue
P.O. Box 2005
Rock Island, IL 61204
Phone: 309-786-6481
Email: memberservice@modern-woodmen.org
http://www.modern-woodmen.org
Purpose: To support beneficial members of Modern Woodmen.
Eligibility: Applicants must be high school seniors and be beneficial members of Modern Woodmen for at least two years. Applicants should be in the upper half of their graduating class.
Target applicants: High school students.
Amount: Up to $4,000.
Number of awards: 139.
Deadline: January 1.
How to apply: Applications are available online.
Exclusive: Visit www.UltimateScholarshipBook.com and enter code MO232412 for updates on this award.

(2325) · Moris J. and Betty Kaplun Scholarship

Kaplun Foundation
Essay Contest Committee
P.O. Box 234428
Great Neck, NY 11023
http://www.kaplunfoundation.org
Purpose: To award essays about Jewish-related topics.
Eligibility: Applicants must be in grades 7 through 12. Grades 7 through 9 are level one, and grades 10 through 12 are level two. Applicants must submit essays on Jewish-related topics listed on the website, and essays must be typed, double-spaced and a minimum of 250 words. Level one essays may not be more than 1,000 words. Level two essays may not be more than 1,500 words. A recent level one topic has been, "What person of importance to the Jewish people, past or present, would you like to meet and why?" A recent level two topic has been, "Antisemitism plagues all Jews regardless of religious adherence. How do you see yourself reacting to it?"
Target applicants: Junior high students or younger. High school students.
Amount: Up to $1,800.
Number of awards: Varies.
Deadline: March 19.
How to apply: Essays must be submitted by mail.
Exclusive: Visit www.UltimateScholarshipBook.com and enter code KA232512 for updates on this award.

(2326) · Mortin Scholarship

Triangle Education Foundation
Chairman, Scholarship and Loan Committee
120 S. Center Street
Plainfield, IN 46168-1214
Phone: 317-837-9640
Fax: 317-837-9642
Email: scholarships@triangle.org
http://www.triangle.org
Purpose: To help deserving active members of Triangle Fraternity in completing their education.
Eligibility: Applicants must be active members of the Triangle Fraternity, enrolled in a course of study leading to a degree. Applicants must have at least a 3.0 GPA, have completed at least two full academic years of school and be undergraduates in the year following their application. Selection is based on financial need, grades and participation in campus and Triangle activities.
Target applicants: College students. Adult students.
Minimum GPA: 3.0
Amount: $2,500.
Number of awards: 1.
Deadline: February 15.
How to apply: Applications are available online.
Exclusive: Visit www.UltimateScholarshipBook.com and enter code TR232612 for updates on this award.

(2327) · Nancy Lorraine Jensen Memorial Scholarship

Sons of Norway Foundation
1455 West Lake Street
Minneapolis, MN 55408
Phone: 800-945-8851
Fax: 612-827-0658
Email: foundation@sofn.com
http://www.sofn.com

Purpose: To support female students who are pursuing higher education in chemistry, physics or engineering.
Eligibility: Applicants must be females who are between the ages of 17 and 35 at the time of application submission. They must be members, the daughters of members or the granddaughters of members of Sons of Norway. They must be full-time undergraduates who have completed at least one semester of coursework within their declared major and must be majoring in chemistry, physics, chemical engineering, electrical engineering or mechanical engineering. They must have an ACT score of 26 or higher or an SAT score of 1800 or higher (including a math score of 600 or higher). Selection is based on academic potential, stated career goals and recommendations.
Target applicants: College students. Adult students.
Amount: Varies.
Number of awards: Varies.
Scholarship may be renewable.
Deadline: April 1.
How to apply: Applications are available online. An application form, personal essay, official transcript, standardized test scores and three recommendation letters are required.
Exclusive: Visit www.UltimateScholarshipBook.com and enter code SO232712 for updates on this award.

(2328) • National Eagle Scout Association Academic Scholarships

Boy Scouts of America
1325 W. Walnut Hill Lane
P.O. Box 152079
Irving, TX 75015-2079
Phone: 972-580-2000
Fax: 972-580-7886
http://www.nesa.org/scholarships.html
Purpose: To support Eagle Scouts.
Eligibility: Applicants must be Eagle Scouts who have received credentials from the national office. They must be graduating high school and entering college in the year of application and have an SAT score of 1200 or higher or an ACT score of 28 or higher. Demonstrated leadership ability in scouting and record of participation in activities outside of scouting are required.
Target applicants: High school students.
Amount: $1,000-$12,000.
Number of awards: Up to 100.
Scholarship may be renewable.
Deadline: January 31.
How to apply: Applications are available online. An application form, transcript and letter of recommendation from a scout leader are required.
Exclusive: Visit www.UltimateScholarshipBook.com and enter code BO232812 for updates on this award.

(2329) • National Eagle Scout Scholarship

Boy Scouts of America, Eagle Scout Service
1325 West Walnut Hill Lane
P.O. Box 152079
Irving, TX 75015-2079
Phone: 972-580-2401
Fax: 972-580-2413
http://www.nesa.org/religious.html
Purpose: To support Jewish Boy Scouts who have received their Eagle Scout award based on their commitment to scouting ideals and community and religious service.
Eligibility: Applicants must be seniors in high school and active members of the Boy Scouts or Varsity Scouts who have received the Eagle Scout award. In addition, applicants must be an active member of a synagogue or have received the Ner Tamid or Etz Chaim religious emblem.
Target applicants: High school students.
Amount: $500-$1,000.
Number of awards: Varies.
Scholarship may be renewable.
Deadline: February 28.
How to apply: Applications are available online.
Exclusive: Visit www.UltimateScholarshipBook.com and enter code BO232912 for updates on this award.

(2330) • National Honor Society Scholarship

National Honor Society
c/o National Association of Secondary School Principals
1904 Association Drive
Reston, VA 20191
Phone: 703-860-0200
Fax: 703-476-5432
Email: nhs@nhs.us
http://www.nhs.us
Purpose: To recognize NHS members.
Eligibility: Each high school chapter may nominate two senior members. Nominees must demonstrate character, scholarship, service and leadership.
Target applicants: High school students.
Amount: $1,000-$13,000.
Number of awards: Varies.
Deadline: January 14.
How to apply: Nomination forms are available from your local NHS chapter adviser.
Exclusive: Visit www.UltimateScholarshipBook.com and enter code NA233012 for updates on this award.

(2331) • National Presbyterian College Scholarship

Presbyterian Church (USA)
100 Witherspoon Street
Louisville, KY 40202
Phone: 888-728-7228 x5776
Email: finaid@pcusa.org
http://www.pcusa.org/financialaid
Purpose: To recognize young students preparing to enter as full-time incoming freshmen in one of the participating colleges related to the Presbyterian Church.
Eligibility: Applicants must be members of the Presbyterian Church, U.S. citizens or permanent residents and high school seniors planning to attend a participating college related to PCUSA. Applicants must also demonstrate financial need and take the SAT or ACT exam no later than December 15 of their senior year in high school. Applicants must have recommendations from both their church pastors and high school guidance counselors.
Target applicants: High school students.
Minimum GPA: 3.0
Amount: Up to $1,500.
Number of awards: 25-30.
Scholarship may be renewable.
Deadline: March 1.
How to apply: Applications are available online.

Exclusive: Visit www.UltimateScholarshipBook.com and enter code PR233112 for updates on this award.

(2332) • National Scholars and Awards Program

Girls Inc.
120 Wall Street
New York, NY 10005
Phone: 800-374-4475
http://www.girlsinc.org

Purpose: To support young members of Girls Incorporated.
Eligibility: Applicants must be young women who are in their junior or senior year of high school and members of a Girls Incorporated affiliate.
Target applicants: High school students.
Amount: $2,500-$15,000.
Number of awards: 25.
Deadline: Varies.
How to apply: Applications are available by written request.
Exclusive: Visit www.UltimateScholarshipBook.com and enter code GI233212 for updates on this award.

(2333) • National Temperance Scholarship

United Methodist Higher Education Foundation
P.O. Box 340005
Nashville, TN 37203-0005
Phone: 615-340-7385
Fax: 615-340-7330
Email: umscholar@gbhem.org
http://www.umhef.org

Purpose: To provide financial assistance for Methodist students.
Eligibility: Applicants must have been members of the United Methodist Church for at least one year and be enrolled or plan to enroll in a United Methodist-affiliated institution of higher learning. They must have a GPA of 3.0 or higher and be U.S. citizens or permanent residents.
Target applicants: High school students. College students. Adult students.
Minimum GPA: 3.0
Amount: Varies.
Number of awards: Varies.
Deadline: April 1.
How to apply: Applications are available online.
Exclusive: Visit www.UltimateScholarshipBook.com and enter code UN233312 for updates on this award.

(2334) • NESA Hall/McElwain Merit Scholarships

Boy Scouts of America
1325 W. Walnut Hill Lane
P.O. Box 152079
Irving, TX 75015-2079
Phone: 972-580-2000
Fax: 972-580-7886
http://www.nesa.org/scholarships.html

Purpose: To assist Eagle Scouts.
Eligibility: Applicants must have received credentials from the national office. They must be graduating high school and entering college in the year of application. A minimum SAT score of 1200 or ACT score of 28 is required. Applicants must have demonstrated leadership ability in scouting and a record of participation in activities outside of scouting.
Target applicants: High school students.
Amount: $1,000.
Number of awards: Varies.
Deadline: January 31.
How to apply: Applications are available online. An application form, transcript and letter of recommendation from a scout leader are required.
Exclusive: Visit www.UltimateScholarshipBook.com and enter code BO233412 for updates on this award.

(2335) • NIADA Scholarship

National Independent Automobile Dealers Association
2521 Brown Boulevard
Arlington, TX 76006-5203
Phone: 817-640-3838
Fax: 817-649-5866
Email: rachel@niada.com
http://www.niada.com

Purpose: To support high school seniors with academic achievement and ties to NIADA members.
Eligibility: Applicants must be the son, daughter or grandchild of a NIADA member, have an excellent high school academic record and have high SAT or ACT scores. Applications, transcripts, test scores and a maximum of five recommendation letters are required.
Target applicants: High school students.
Amount: $3,500.
Number of awards: 4.
Deadline: Varies.
How to apply: Applications are available online and should be submitted to the state association.
Exclusive: Visit www.UltimateScholarshipBook.com and enter code NA233512 for updates on this award.

(2336) • Non-Traditional Student Scholarship

American Legion Auxiliary
8945 N. Meridian Street
Indianapolis, IN 46260
Phone: 317-569-4500
Fax: 317-569-4502
Email: alahq@legion-aux.org
http://www.legion-aux.org

Purpose: To support students resuming formal schooling after an interruption.
Eligibility: Applicants must be members of The American Legion, the American Legion Auxiliary or Sons of The American Legion and be undergraduate students who are enrolled in at least six hours per semester or four hours per quarter. Applicants must also be students resuming formal schooling after an interruption or who have had at least one year of college schooling and need financial assistance to continue their degree. Selection is based on financial need, scholastic achievement, character and goals.
Target applicants: College students. Adult students.
Amount: $1,000.
Number of awards: 5.
Deadline: March 1.
How to apply: Applications are available online.
Exclusive: Visit www.UltimateScholarshipBook.com and enter code AM233612 for updates on this award.

(2337) • NPC Foundation Regional Scholarships

National Panhellenic Conference
8777 Purdue Road
Suite 117
Indianapolis, IN 46268

Phone: 317-872-3185
Fax: 317-872-3192
Email: npccentral@npcwomen.org
http://www.npcwomen.org
Purpose: To provide financial assistance to NPC members.
Eligibility: Requirements vary by region. Some regions require applicants to have graduated from certain high schools while others require attendance at specific colleges or residence in certain counties.
Target applicants: High school students. College students. Adult students.
Amount: $1,000-$2,000.
Number of awards: 2.
Deadline: January 10.
How to apply: Applications are available online.
Exclusive: Visit www.UltimateScholarshipBook.com and enter code NA233712 for updates on this award.

(2338) • Oliver and Esther R. Howard Scholarship

Fleet Reserve Association
FRA Scholarship Administrator
125 N. West Street
Alexandria, VA 22314
Phone: 800-372-1924
http://www.fra.org
Purpose: To provide financial aid to the dependent children of FRA members or LA FRA members.
Eligibility: Applicants must be the dependent children of members of either the Fleet Reserve Association or the Ladies' Auxiliary of the Fleet Reserve Association who are in good standing. This scholarship is alternated between male and female recipients each year (males - odd years) (females - even years). Recipients must be high school seniors or college undergraduates pursuing undergraduate degrees and are selected on the basis of academic record, financial need, leadership skills and character.
Target applicants: High school students. College students. Adult students.
Amount: Varies.
Number of awards: Varies.
Deadline: April 15.
How to apply: Applications are available online.
Exclusive: Visit www.UltimateScholarshipBook.com and enter code FL233812 for updates on this award.

(2339) • Opportunity Scholarships for Lutheran Laywomen

Women of the Evangelical Lutheran Church in America
8765 W. Higgins Road
Chicago, IL 60631
Phone: 800-638-3522 x2730
Fax: 773-380-2419
Email: women.elca@elca.org
http://www.womenoftheelca.org
Purpose: To assist Lutheran women in studying for careers other than ordained ministry.
Eligibility: Applicants must be U.S. citizens, members of the Evangelical Lutheran Church and at least 21 years of age. They must also have had an interruption in education of two years or more since graduating from high school.
Target applicants: College students. Graduate school students. Adult students.
Amount: Varies.
Number of awards: Varies.
Deadline: Varies.
How to apply: Applications are available online.
Exclusive: Visit www.UltimateScholarshipBook.com and enter code WO233912 for updates on this award.

(2340) • Outstanding Scouts Awards

Veterans of Foreign Wars
406 W. 34th Street
Kansas City, MO 64111
Phone: 816-968-1117
Fax: 816-968-1149
Email: kharmer@vfw.org
http://www.vfw.org
Purpose: To recognize outstanding Boy Scouts and support the common bonds between the Boy Scouts of America and the VFW: belief in God, respect for others, honesty and patriotism.
Eligibility: Applicants must be nominated as the top Scout by a VFW organization.
Target applicants: Junior high students or younger. High school students.
Amount: $1,000-$5,000.
Number of awards: 3.
Deadline: March 1.
How to apply: Applications are available online.
Exclusive: Visit www.UltimateScholarshipBook.com and enter code VE234012 for updates on this award.

(2341) • Owens-Bell Award

National Association of Blacks in Criminal Justice
North Carolina Central University
P.O. Box 19788
Durham, NC 27707
Phone: 919-683-1801
Fax: 919-683-1903
Email: office@nabcj.org
http://www.nabcj.org
Purpose: To award an individual NABCJ member for outstanding chapter development and leadership.
Eligibility: Applicants must be nominated by a member of NABCJ.
Target applicants: College students. Adult students.
Amount: Varies.
Number of awards: 1.
Deadline: May 1.
How to apply: Nomination applications are available online.
Exclusive: Visit www.UltimateScholarshipBook.com and enter code NA234112 for updates on this award.

(2342) • Phi Kappa Phi Fellowship

Honor Society of Phi Kappa Phi
7576 Goodwood Boulevard
Baton Rouge, LA 70806
Phone: 800-804-9880
Fax: 225-388-4900
Email: awards@phikappaphi.org
http://www.phikappaphi.org
Purpose: To provide fellowships for Phi Kappa Phi members entering their first year of graduate or professional studies.
Eligibility: Applicants may enter any professional or graduate field and must not have completed one full term of graduate study. Selection

is based on academic achievement, service, leadership, letters of recommendation, personal statement and career goals.
Target applicants: College students. Graduate school students. Adult students.
Amount: $5,000-$15,000.
Number of awards: 60.
Deadline: April 1.
How to apply: Applications are available online.
Exclusive: Visit www.UltimateScholarshipBook.com and enter code HO234212 for updates on this award.

(2343) • Phyllis J. Jones Memorial Scholarships for Head Start Graduates

National Head Start Association
1651 Prince Street
Alexandria, VA 22314
Phone: 703-739-0875 x7507
Fax: 703-739-0878
Email: chutchinson@nhsa.org
http://www.nhsa.org
Purpose: To honor the memory of Phyllis J. Jones, former NHSA president.
Eligibility: Applicants must be Head Start graduates of an NHSA program or individual members of NHSA. They must prove acceptance or enrollment at a college or university. Three letters of reference are required.
Target applicants: High school students. College students. Adult students.
Amount: $1,500.
Number of awards: Varies.
Deadline: February 1.
How to apply: Applications are available online.
Exclusive: Visit www.UltimateScholarshipBook.com and enter code NA234312 for updates on this award.

(2344) • Power Systems Professional Scholarship

National Strength and Conditioning Association (NSCA) Foundation
1885 Bob Johnson Drive
Colorado Springs, CO 80906
Phone: 800-815-6826
Fax: 719-632-6367
Email: nsca@nsca-lift.org
http://www.nsca-lift.org
Purpose: To support students interested in becoming strength and conditioning coaches.
Eligibility: Applicants must be undergraduate or graduate students and be working under a coach in the school's athletic department. Applicants must be members of the National Strength and Conditioning Association for one year prior to applying for a scholarship. Applications must include a resume, transcript, personal essay and letter from the head strength coach. The application must also be submitted by the head strength coach.
Target applicants: College students. Adult students.
Amount: $1,500.
Number of awards: 1.
Deadline: March 15.
How to apply: Applications are available online.
Exclusive: Visit www.UltimateScholarshipBook.com and enter code NA234412 for updates on this award.

(2345) • Presbyterian Church USA Student Opportunity Scholarships

Presbyterian Church (USA)
100 Witherspoon Street
Louisville, KY 40202
Phone: 888-728-7228 x5776
Email: finaid@pcusa.org
http://www.pcusa.org/financialaid
Purpose: To aid students pursuing disciplines that further the mission of the Presbyterian Church.
Eligibility: Applicants must be members of the Presbyterian Church (USA) who have completed their second year of college. They must be enrolled full-time and have a GPA of 2.5 or greater. Students must be pursuing a bachelor's degree in education, health service/science, religious studies, sacred music or social service/sciences. Financial need is required. Preference is given to members of racial and ethnic minorities.
Target applicants: College students. Adult students.
Minimum GPA: 2.5
Amount: Up to $3,000.
Number of awards: Varies.
Scholarship may be renewable.
Deadline: June 15.
How to apply: Applications are available by mail or email.
Exclusive: Visit www.UltimateScholarshipBook.com and enter code PR234512 for updates on this award.

(2346) • Priscilla R. Morton Scholarship

United Methodist Higher Education Foundation
P.O. Box 340005
Nashville, TN 37203-0005
Phone: 615-340-7385
Fax: 615-340-7330
Email: umscholar@gbhem.org
http://www.umhef.org
Purpose: To help students who are members of the United Methodist Church.
Eligibility: Applicants must be active, full members of the United Methodist Church for at least a year before applying and enrolled or planning to enroll in an accredited institution working towards a degree full-time. The scholarship may be used for undergraduate, graduate or professional study. Applicants should provide application forms, transcripts, references, membership proof and essays. A minimum 3.5 GPA and financial need are required. Preference is given to students who enroll at a United Methodist-related college, university, seminary or theological school.
Target applicants: High school students. College students. Graduate school students. Adult students.
Minimum GPA: 3.5
Amount: Varies.
Number of awards: Varies.
Deadline: April 1.
How to apply: Applications are available online.
Exclusive: Visit www.UltimateScholarshipBook.com and enter code UN234612 for updates on this award.

(2347) • Professional and Technical Engineers, International Federation Scholarship

International Federation of Professional and Technical Engineers
8630 Fenton Street
Suite 400
Silver Spring, MD 20910

Phone: 301-565-9016
Fax: 301-565-0018
Email: gjunemann@ifpte.org
http://www.ifpte.org
Purpose: To offer scholarships to the children and grandchildren of IFPTE members.
Eligibility: Applicants must be high school seniors who are the children or grandchildren of IFPTE members.
Target applicants: High school students.
Amount: $2,500.
Number of awards: 3.
Deadline: March 15.
How to apply: Applications are available online.
Exclusive: Visit www.UltimateScholarshipBook.com and enter code IN234712 for updates on this award.

(2348) • Pryor Fellowships

Alpha Chi
Harding University Box 12249
915 E. Market Avenue
Searcy, AR 72149-2249
Phone: 800-477-4225
Fax: 501-279-4589
Email: dorgan@harding.edu
http://www.alphachihonor.org
Purpose: To assist alumni and graduate Alpha Chi members who are seeking doctoral, master's or first professional degrees.
Eligibility: Applicants must be Alpha Chi members who are enrolled or planning to enroll full-time in a doctoral, terminal master's or first professional degree program.
Target applicants: College students. Graduate school students. Adult students.
Amount: $3,000-$5,000.
Number of awards: 2.
Deadline: February 1.
How to apply: Applications are available online.
Exclusive: Visit www.UltimateScholarshipBook.com and enter code AL234812 for updates on this award.

(2349) • Racial/Ethnic History Research Grant

General Commission on Archives and History, The United Methodist Church
P.O. Box 127
36 Madison Avenue
Madison, NJ 07940
Phone: 973-408-3189
Fax: 973-408-3909
Email: research@gcah.org
http://www.gcah.org
Purpose: To promote excellence in research and writing in the history of Asians, Blacks, Hispanics and Native Americans in The United Methodist Church.
Eligibility: Applicants must submit an application in English which includes biographical information, a detailed description of the project, the expected date of completion, a budget and letters of recommendation.
Target applicants: Junior high students or younger. High school students. College students. Graduate school students. Adult students.
Amount: At least $1,000.
Number of awards: Varies.
Deadline: December 31.
How to apply: Submit materials to the General Secretary at the address listed.
Exclusive: Visit www.UltimateScholarshipBook.com and enter code GE234912 for updates on this award.

(2350) • Rev. Dr. Karen Layman Gift of Hope 21st Century Scholars Program

United Methodist Church
Office of Loans and Scholarships
P.O. BOX 340007
Nashville, TN 37203-0007
Phone: 615-340-7344
Fax: 615-340-7367
Email: umscholar@gbhem.org
http://www.gbhem.org
Purpose: To support students who have demonstrated leadership within the United Methodist Church.
Eligibility: Applicants must have been members of the United Methodist Church for at least three years. They must be full-time undergraduates with at least a 3.0 GPA.
Target applicants: High school students. College students. Adult students.
Minimum GPA: 3.0
Amount: $1,000.
Number of awards: Varies.
Deadline: April 15-May 1.
How to apply: Applications are available online.
Exclusive: Visit www.UltimateScholarshipBook.com and enter code UN235012 for updates on this award.

(2351) • Richard F. Walsh, Alfred W. DiTolla, Harold P. Spivak Foundation Award

International Alliance of Theatrical Stage Employees, Artists and Allied Crafts of the U.S.
1430 Broadway
20th Floor
New York, NY 10018
http://www.iatse-intl.org
Purpose: To provide scholarships for the children of IATSE members.
Eligibility: Applicants must be the sons or daughters of IATSE members in good standing, be high school seniors and apply for admission to an accredited college or university full-time leading towards a bachelor's degree.
Target applicants: High school students.
Amount: $1,750.
Number of awards: 2.
Scholarship may be renewable.
Deadline: December 31.
How to apply: Applications are available by written request (through an online form).
Exclusive: Visit www.UltimateScholarshipBook.com and enter code IN235112 for updates on this award.

(2352) • Robert G. Porter Scholars Program for Members

American Federation of Teachers
555 New Jersey Avenue NW
Washington, DC 20001
Phone: 202-879-4400

http://www.aft.org
Purpose: To provide grants to AFT members.
Eligibility: Applicants must be AFT members who have been in good standing for at least one year and intend to pursue courses in their field of work. Applicants must submit an essay on a labor-related topic.
Target applicants: Graduate school students. Adult students.
Amount: $1,000.
Number of awards: 10.
Deadline: March 31.
How to apply: Applications are available by written request.
Exclusive: Visit www.UltimateScholarshipBook.com and enter code AM235212 for updates on this award.

(2353) • Robert G. Porter Scholars Program for Members' Dependents

American Federation of Teachers
555 New Jersey Avenue NW
Washington, DC 20001
Phone: 202-879-4400
http://www.aft.org
Purpose: To provide scholarships to AFT members' dependents.
Eligibility: Applicants must be graduating high school seniors. The award is merit-based and will consider academics, community service and performance on the required labor-related essay. Applicant's parents or guardians must be AFT members for at least one year.
Target applicants: High school students.
Amount: $8,000.
Number of awards: 4.
Scholarship may be renewable.
Deadline: March 31.
How to apply: Applications are available by written request.
Exclusive: Visit www.UltimateScholarshipBook.com and enter code AM235312 for updates on this award.

(2354) • Ronald Reagan Leadership Award

Tau Kappa Epsilon Educational Foundation
8645 Founders Road
Indianapolis, IN 46268
Phone: 317-872-6533
Fax: 317-875-8353
Email: tef@tke.org
http://www.tkefoundation.org
Purpose: To honor Ronald Reagan's dedication and loyalty as a Tau Kappa Epsilon member.
Eligibility: Applicants must be initiated Tau Kappa Epsilon members in good standing and full-time students. Applicants must also have a GPA of at least 3.0 and demonstrate leadership in their chapter, campus and community. A statement describing how they have benefited from TKE membership is required.
Target applicants: College students. Adult students.
Minimum GPA: 3.0
Amount: $700.
Number of awards: 1.
Deadline: February 15.
How to apply: Applications are available online.
Exclusive: Visit www.UltimateScholarshipBook.com and enter code TA235412 for updates on this award.

(2355) • Rosalie Bentzinger Scholarship

United Methodist Church
Office of Loans and Scholarships
P.O. BOX 340007
Nashville, TN 37203-0007
Phone: 615-340-7344
Fax: 615-340-7367
Email: umscholar@gbhem.org
http://www.gbhem.org
Purpose: To support United Methodist students who are pursuing doctoral degrees in Christian education.
Eligibility: Applicants must be attending a graduate school of theology which is approved by the University Senate. They must be full-time students with at least a B+ grade average. Students must have been members of the United Methodist Church for at least three years, and they must have attained one of the following positions: deacon in full connection, diaconal minister or deaconess.
Target applicants: Graduate school students. Adult students.
Minimum GPA: 3.3
Amount: $5,000.
Number of awards: 1.
Deadline: January 15.
How to apply: Applications are available online.
Exclusive: Visit www.UltimateScholarshipBook.com and enter code UN235512 for updates on this award.

(2356) • Rust Scholarship

Triangle Education Foundation
Chairman, Scholarship and Loan Committee
120 S. Center Street
Plainfield, IN 46168-1214
Phone: 317-837-9640
Fax: 317-837-9642
Email: scholarships@triangle.org
http://www.triangle.org
Purpose: To help deserving active members of Triangle Fraternity in completing their education.
Eligibility: Applicants must be active members of the Triangle Fraternity who have completed at least two full academic years of school and will be undergraduates in the school year following their application. Selection is based on financial need, grades and participation in campus and Triangle activities. Preference is given to applicants in engineering and the hard sciences. Applicants must have at least a 3.0 GPA.
Target applicants: College students. Adult students.
Minimum GPA: 3.0
Amount: $6,000.
Number of awards: 1.
Deadline: February 15.
How to apply: Applications are available online.
Exclusive: Visit www.UltimateScholarshipBook.com and enter code TR235612 for updates on this award.

(2357) • S. Frank Bud Raftery Scholarship

International Union of Painters and Allied Trades of the United States and Canada
1750 New York Avenue NW
Washington, DC 20006
http://www.iupat.org
Purpose: To provide scholarships for the children of IUPAT members.

Eligibility: Applicants must be the children or legally-adopted dependents of an IUPAT member in good standing. Selection is based on a 1,000- to 2,000-word essay on a subject chosen by the IUPAT.
Target applicants: High school students. College students. Graduate school students. Adult students.
Amount: $2,000.
Number of awards: 10.
Deadline: December.
How to apply: Applications are available by written request.
Exclusive: Visit www.UltimateScholarshipBook.com and enter code IN235712 for updates on this award.

(2358) • Sam Rose Memorial Scholarship

Ladies Auxiliary of the Fleet Reserve Association
125 N. West Street
Alexandria, VA 22314
Phone: 800-372-1924 x123
Email: mserfra@fra.org
http://www.la-fra.org
Purpose: To support the descendants of Fleet Reserve Association members.
Eligibility: Applicants must have a deceased father or grandfather who was a member of the Fleet Reserve Association or was eligible for membership at the time of death.
Target applicants: High school students. College students. Adult students.
Amount: Varies.
Number of awards: Varies.
Deadline: April 15.
How to apply: Applications are available online.
Exclusive: Visit www.UltimateScholarshipBook.com and enter code LA235812 for updates on this award.

(2359) • Schuyler S. Pyle Award

Fleet Reserve Association
FRA Scholarship Administrator
125 N. West Street
Alexandria, VA 22314
Phone: 800-372-1924
http://www.fra.org
Purpose: To support members of the FRA, their spouses and their dependent children or grandchildren.
Eligibility: Applicants must be members of the FRA in good standing, or the spouse or dependent children/grandchildren of a member who is in good standing or was in good standing at time of death. Recipients are determined on the basis of academic record, leadership skills, character and financial need.
Target applicants: High school students. College students. Graduate school students. Adult students.
Amount: Varies.
Number of awards: Varies.
Deadline: April 15.
How to apply: Applications are available online.
Exclusive: Visit www.UltimateScholarshipBook.com and enter code FL235912 for updates on this award.

(2360) • SEIU-Jesse Jackson Scholarship Program

Service Employees International Union
c/o Scholarship Program Administrators Inc.
P.O. Box 23737
Nashville, TN 37202-3737
Phone: 800-424-8592
http://www.seiu.org
Purpose: To honor the Rev. Jesse Jackson by giving a scholarship to those SEIU members and their children who exemplify his values in the pursuit of social justice.
Eligibility: Applicants must be members or the children of members of the SEIU and must be enrolled in an accredited two- or four-year college or university. The scholarship is for undergraduate work only.
Target applicants: High school students. College students. Adult students.
Amount: $5,000.
Number of awards: 1.
Scholarship may be renewable.
Deadline: March 1.
How to apply: Applications are available online.
Exclusive: Visit www.UltimateScholarshipBook.com and enter code SE236012 for updates on this award.

(2361) • Service Employees International Union Scholarships

Service Employees International Union
c/o Scholarship Program Administrators Inc.
P.O. Box 23737
Nashville, TN 37202-3737
Phone: 800-424-8592
http://www.seiu.org
Purpose: To give financial assistance to members of the SEIU and their children.
Eligibility: For the $1,000 scholarship, applicants must be members or the children of members of SEIU who have been in good standing for at least three years. Applicants must also be enrolled in an accredited college or university and should not have completed more than one year of college. For the $1,500 scholarship, applicants must be members or the children of members of SEIU returning full time to an accredited college or university as a sophomore, junior or senior or attending an accredited community college, trade or technical school. This scholarship is not renewable. All applicants must read a report online and answer questions.
Target applicants: High school students. College students. Adult students.
Amount: $1,000-$1,500.
Number of awards: 48.
Deadline: March 1.
How to apply: Applications are available online.
Exclusive: Visit www.UltimateScholarshipBook.com and enter code SE236112 for updates on this award.

(2362) • SEVEN-CIFA Essay Competition

Social Equity Venture Fund (SEVEN Fund)
1770 Massachusetts Avenue, 247
Cambridge, MA 02140
Email: info@sevenfund.org
http://www.sevenfund.org
Purpose: To aid those who have written the best essays on the subject of poverty reduction through faith-based efforts.
Eligibility: Applicants must submit a first-person essay on faith-based initiatives that have helped to decrease poverty. Selection is based on the strength of the essay.
Target applicants: High school students. College students. Graduate school students. Adult students.

Amount: $5,000.
Number of awards: 2.
Deadline: October 15.
How to apply: Application instructions are available online. An essay, essay abstract and author biographical statement are required.
Exclusive: Visit www.UltimateScholarshipBook.com and enter code SO236212 for updates on this award.

(2363) • Sheet Metal Workers' International Scholarship Fund

Sheet Metal Workers' International Association
1750 New York Avenue NW
6th Floor
Washington , DC 20006-5389
Phone: 202-783-5880
Email: scholarship@smwia.org
http://www.smwia.org
Purpose: To provide scholarships for members of the SMWIA and their families.
Eligibility: Applicants must be SMWIA members, covered employees, or dependent spouses or children under the age of 25 of SMWIA members or covered employees. Applicants must also be full-time students or accepted to be full-time students at an accredited college or university. Only qualified applicants from local unions that participate in the one-cent check off are eligible for these four-year scholarships. Selection is based on information on SMWIA membership, including information on the local union's jurisdiction and family member's SMWIA membership, high school transcript, SAT/ACT scores or college transcript if already enrolled in college, an essay on the importance of SMWIA to the applicant's family and a letter of recommendation.
Target applicants: High school students. College students. Adult students.
Amount: $4,000.
Number of awards: 32.
Scholarship may be renewable.
Deadline: March 1.
How to apply: Applications are available by email and written request.
Exclusive: Visit www.UltimateScholarshipBook.com and enter code SH236312 for updates on this award.

(2364) • Shopko Scholarships

ShopKo Stores, Inc.
http://www.shopko.com
Purpose: To provide educational opportunities for Shopko employees and their families.
Eligibility: Applicants must be Shopko employees who have been with the company for at least one year or their dependents under the age of 24. Factors considered include academic record, leadership and community activities, honors, work experience and future goals.
Target applicants: High school students. College students. Adult students.
Amount: Up to $2,500.
Number of awards: Varies.
Deadline: March 1.
How to apply: Applications are available online or from Shopko stores.
Exclusive: Visit www.UltimateScholarshipBook.com and enter code SH236412 for updates on this award.

(2365) • Shropshire Scholarship

Civitan
Civitan International Foundation
P.O. Box 130744
Birmingham, AL 35213-0744
Phone: 205-591-8910
Fax: 205-592-6307
Email: civitan@civitan.org
http://www.civitan.org
Purpose: The Shropshire Scholarship assists deserving Civitan members who will pursue careers that further the ideals of Civitan International, such as working toward world peace and unity, fighting for justice and building better citizenship.
Eligibility: Applicants must be Civitans or a Civitan's immediate family member, have been Civitan or Junior Civitan members for at least two years, be enrolled in a college or university and pursue careers which help further the ideals of Civitan International.
Target applicants: College students. Graduate school students. Adult students.
Amount: $1,000.
Number of awards: Varies.
Deadline: January 31.
How to apply: Applications are available online.
Exclusive: Visit www.UltimateScholarshipBook.com and enter code CI236512 for updates on this award.

(2366) • Sledge/Benedict Fellowships

Alpha Chi
Harding University Box 12249
915 E. Market Avenue
Searcy, AR 72149-2249
Phone: 800-477-4225
Fax: 501-279-4589
Email: dorgan@harding.edu
http://www.alphachihonor.org
Purpose: To assist Alpha Chi members who are entering their first year of graduate study.
Eligibility: Applicants must be Alpha Chi members in their final year of undergraduate study and must be enrolled full-time as a graduate student the following fall semester.
Target applicants: College students. Adult students.
Amount: $2,500-$3,500.
Number of awards: 12.
Deadline: February 22.
How to apply: Application requirements are available online, and applicants must be nominated by the faculty advisor.
Exclusive: Visit www.UltimateScholarshipBook.com and enter code AL236612 for updates on this award.

(2367) • Spirit of Youth Scholarship for Junior Members

American Legion Auxiliary
8945 N. Meridian Street
Indianapolis, IN 46260
Phone: 317-569-4500
Fax: 317-569-4502
Email: alahq@legion-aux.org
http://www.legion-aux.org
Purpose: To assist Junior members of the American Legion Auxiliary.
Eligibility: Applicants must be or have been Junior members of the American Legion Auxiliary for three years, be high school seniors, have

a minimum 3.0 GPA and demonstrate character. Selection is based on character/leadership (30 percent), essay/application (30 percent) and scholarship (40 percent).
Target applicants: High school students.
Minimum GPA: 3.0
Amount: $1,000.
Number of awards: 5.
Scholarship may be renewable.
Deadline: March 1.
How to apply: Applications are available online.
Exclusive: Visit www.UltimateScholarshipBook.com and enter code AM236712 for updates on this award.

(2368) • Stanfield and D'Orlando Art Scholarship

Unitarian Universalist Association
25 Beacon Street
Boston, MA 02108
Phone: 617-742-2100
Email: info@uua.org
http://www.uua.org
Purpose: To help graduate and undergraduate Unitarian Universalist artists.
Eligibility: Applicants must be preparing for a career in fine arts which includes painting, drawing, photography and sculpture. Applicants must submit applications, transcripts, recommendations, slide portfolios and a list of works.
Target applicants: College students. Graduate school students. Adult students.
Amount: Varies.
Number of awards: Varies.
Deadline: February 15.
How to apply: Applications are available online.
Exclusive: Visit www.UltimateScholarshipBook.com and enter code UN236812 for updates on this award.

(2369) • Stanley A. Doran Memorial Scholarship

Fleet Reserve Association
FRA Scholarship Administrator
125 N. West Street
Alexandria, VA 22314
Phone: 800-372-1924
http://www.fra.org
Purpose: To provide financial aid to the dependents of FRA members.
Eligibility: Applicants must be the dependent children of a member in good standing of the FRA or a member who was in good standing at time of death. Recipients are selected on the basis of academic achievement, leadership skills, financial need and character.
Target applicants: High school students. College students. Graduate school students. Adult students.
Amount: Varies.
Number of awards: Varies.
Deadline: April 15.
How to apply: Applications are available online.
Exclusive: Visit www.UltimateScholarshipBook.com and enter code FL236912 for updates on this award.

(2370) • Steven J. Muir Scholarship

Tau Kappa Epsilon Educational Foundation
8645 Founders Road
Indianapolis, IN 46268
Phone: 317-872-6533
Fax: 317-875-8353
Email: tef@tke.org
http://www.tkefoundation.org
Purpose: To recognize a member of Tau Kappa Epsilon for academic achievement and outstanding leadership within the organization.
Eligibility: Applicants must be sophomores or above and have at least a 3.0 GPA. Members must be seeking an undergraduate degree in engineering or another of the pure sciences. Applicants must have served as a chapter officer or committee chair; preference will be given to members of the Beta-Eta Chapter.
Target applicants: College students. Adult students.
Minimum GPA: 3.0
Amount: $2,300.
Number of awards: 1.
Deadline: March 1.
How to apply: Applications are available online.
Exclusive: Visit www.UltimateScholarshipBook.com and enter code TA237012 for updates on this award.

(2371) • Student CEC Graduation Awards

Council for Exceptional Children
1110 North Glebe Road
Suite 300
Arlington, VA 22201
Phone: 888-232-7733
Fax: 703-264-9494
Email: mbrship@cec.sped.org
http://www.cec.sped.org
Purpose: To provide financial aid to student members transitioning to professional membership status in the Council for Exceptional Children.
Eligibility: Applicants must be undergraduate or graduate students enrolled at an accredited college or university graduating in the academic year the award is given. Applicants must be members of the Student CEC with a minimum 3.0 GPA. Selection is based on an essay, GPA, letters of recommendation and extracurricular activities.
Target applicants: College students. Graduate school students. Adult students.
Minimum GPA: 3.0
Amount: Varies.
Number of awards: 2.
Deadline: October 30.
How to apply: Applications are available online.
Exclusive: Visit www.UltimateScholarshipBook.com and enter code CO237112 for updates on this award.

(2372) • Student Leader Award

Golden Key National Honour Society
Scholarship Program Administrators
Golden Key Scholarships/Awards
P.O. Box 23737
Nashville, TN 37202-3737
Phone: 800-377-2401
Email: scholarships@goldenkey.org
http://www.goldenkey.org
Purpose: To support student members who have demonstrated leadership.
Eligibility: Applicants must be currently or previously involved in Golden Key and be currently enrolled in an undergraduate or graduate program at an accredited college or university. There are awards for both U.S. and international students. U.S. applicants must submit

an application form, personal statement, description of Golden Key involvement, list of activities, recommendation letter and transcript.
Target applicants: College students. Graduate school students. Adult students.
Amount: $1,000.
Number of awards: 13.
Deadline: April 1.
How to apply: Applications are available online.
Exclusive: Visit www.UltimateScholarshipBook.com and enter code GO237212 for updates on this award.

(2373) • Study Abroad Scholarships

Golden Key National Honour Society
Scholarship Program Administrators
Golden Key Scholarships/Awards
P.O. Box 23737
Nashville, TN 37202-3737
Phone: 800-377-2401
Email: scholarships@goldenkey.org
http://www.goldenkey.org
Purpose: To assist members who study abroad.
Eligibility: Applicants must be undergraduate members who plan to be or are currently enrolled in a study abroad program. Selection is based on academic achievement and relevance of the study abroad program to the applicant's major.
Target applicants: College students. Adult students.
Amount: $1,000.
Number of awards: 10.
Deadline: April 15 and October 20.
How to apply: Applications are available online.
Exclusive: Visit www.UltimateScholarshipBook.com and enter code GO237312 for updates on this award.

(2374) • Subway Scholarship Fund

Subway Restaurants
Susan Lee
Center for Scholarship Administration, Subway Scholarship Fund
P.O. Box 1465
Taylors, SC 29687-0031
Phone: 864-268-3363
Fax: 864-268-7160
Email: susanjlee@bellsouth.net
http://www.subway.com
Purpose: To provide scholarships for Subway employees.
Eligibility: Applicants must be either high school seniors or full-time college students and must be Subway employees who work a minimum of 15 hours a week and have worked at least six months prior to December 31. Academic achievement, scholarship performance, scholastic aptitude, essays and letters of recommendation will be considered.
Target applicants: High school students. College students. Adult students.
Minimum GPA: 2.75
Amount: $1,000.
Number of awards: Varies.
Deadline: November 30.
How to apply: Applications are available online.
Exclusive: Visit www.UltimateScholarshipBook.com and enter code SU237412 for updates on this award.

(2375) • T.J. Schmitz Scholarship

Tau Kappa Epsilon Educational Foundation
8645 Founders Road
Indianapolis, IN 46268
Phone: 317-872-6533
Fax: 317-875-8353
Email: tef@tke.org
http://www.tkefoundation.org
Purpose: To award a member of Tau Kappa Epsilon for oustanding academic achievement and leadership within the organization, campus and community.
Eligibility: Applicants must have a GPA of at least 3.0.
Target applicants: College students. Adult students.
Minimum GPA: 3.0
Amount: $250.
Number of awards: 1.
Deadline: March 1.
How to apply: Applications are available online.
Exclusive: Visit www.UltimateScholarshipBook.com and enter code TA237512 for updates on this award.

(2376) • Tall Club International Scholarship

Tall Clubs International
6770 River Terrace Drive
Franklin, WI 53132
Phone: 888-468-2552
Email: info@tcifoundation.org
http://www.tall.org
Purpose: To support students of tall stature.
Eligibility: Applicants must be high school seniors or college students under the age of 21 attending or planning to attend a two- or four-year institution of higher learning for their first year of college. Female applicants must meet the height requirement of 5'10" and male applicants must meet the requirement of 6'2". Applicants must live within the geographic area of a participating club.
Target applicants: High school students. College students.
Amount: Up to $1,000.
Number of awards: Varies.
Deadline: Varies.
How to apply: Applications are available by emailing the closest TCI club.
Exclusive: Visit www.UltimateScholarshipBook.com and enter code TA237612 for updates on this award.

(2377) • Tau Beta Pi Scholarships

Tau Beta Pi Association
Attn.: D. Stephen Pierre Jr., P.E.
Alabama Power Company
150 Joseph Street, P.O. Box 2247
Mobile, AL 36652-2247
Phone: 865-546-4578
Fax: 865-546-4579
Email: fellowships@tbp.org
http://www.tbp.org
Purpose: To assist members who are studying engineering.
Eligibility: Applicants must be undergraduate members of Tau Beta Pi and be juniors at the time of application who are planning to remain in or return to school for a senior year of full-time study in engineering.
Target applicants: College students. Adult students.
Amount: $2,000.
Number of awards: 150.

Deadline: March 1.
How to apply: Applications are available online.
Exclusive: Visit www.UltimateScholarshipBook.com and enter code TA237712 for updates on this award.

(2378) • Terrill Graduate Fellowship

Phi Sigma Kappa International Headquarters
2925 E. 96th Street
Indianapolis, IN 46240
Phone: 317-573-5420
Fax: 317-573-5430
Email: vershun@phisigmakappa.org
http://www.phisigmakappa.org
Purpose: To award money to graduating senior and alumni members entering graduate school or members already enrolled in graduate school.
Eligibility: Applicants must graduate from college by August of the year during which they apply, plan to begin graduate or professional study during the next academic year or already be in graduate school and have a minimum B GPA for all undergraduate work. Scholarships are awarded based on scholastic performance.
Target applicants: College students. Graduate school students. Adult students.
Minimum GPA: 3.0
Amount: $3,000.
Number of awards: 1.
Deadline: January 31.
How to apply: Applications are available online.
Exclusive: Visit www.UltimateScholarshipBook.com and enter code PH237812 for updates on this award.

(2379) • Thomas H. Dunning, Sr., Memorial Scholarship

Tau Kappa Epsilon Educational Foundation
8645 Founders Road
Indianapolis, IN 46268
Phone: 317-872-6533
Fax: 317-875-8353
Email: tef@tke.org
http://www.tkefoundation.org
Purpose: To award a member of Tau Kappa Epsilon for academic achievement and service within the chapter as an officer or committee chair.
Eligibility: Applicants must have a GPA of at least 2.75 and be at least sophomores. Applicants must also be undergraduates seeking a degree in engineering, computer science or any of the pure sciences. Preference is first given to members of the Beta-Eta Chapter and then to other Tekes at colleges/universities in Indiana or Missouri.
Target applicants: College students. Adult students.
Minimum GPA: 2.75
Amount: $275.
Number of awards: 1.
Deadline: March 1.
How to apply: Applications are available online.
Exclusive: Visit www.UltimateScholarshipBook.com and enter code TA237912 for updates on this award.

(2380) • Timothy L. Taschwer Scholarship

Tau Kappa Epsilon Educational Foundation
8645 Founders Road
Indianapolis, IN 46268
Phone: 317-872-6533
Fax: 317-875-8353
Email: tef@tke.org
http://www.tkefoundation.org
Purpose: To award a member of Tau Kappa Epsilon for academic achievement and outstanding leadership within the organization as a chapter officer.
Eligibility: Applicants must have a GPA of at least 2.75 and be seeking an undergraduate degree in natural resources, earth sciences or similar fields. Preference is first given to graduates of the TKE Leadership Academy.
Target applicants: College students. Adult students.
Minimum GPA: 2.75
Amount: $500.
Number of awards: 1.
Deadline: March 1.
How to apply: Applications are available online.
Exclusive: Visit www.UltimateScholarshipBook.com and enter code TA238012 for updates on this award.

(2381) • Tri Delta Graduate Scholarship

Tri Delta
Delta Delta Delta Foundation
P.O. Box 5987
Arlington, TX 76005
Phone: 817-633-8001
Fax: 817-652-0212
Email: info@trideltaeo.org
http://www.tridelta.org
Purpose: To offer scholarships to graduate student members.
Eligibility: The Mary Margaret Hafter Fellowship, Luella Akins Key Scholarship, Second Century Graduate Scholarship, Margaret Stafford Memorial Scholarship and Sarah Shinn Marshall Scholarship may be awarded to Tri Delta members who are admitted or current graduate students. Applicants to the Durning Sisters Scholarship must be unmarried Tri Delta members who have completed at least 12 graduate credits and who will be continuing graduate study during the year in which the award is given. There is usually one winner for each award.
Target applicants: College students. Graduate school students. Adult students.
Amount: Varies.
Number of awards: Varies.
Deadline: March 1.
How to apply: Applications are available online.
Exclusive: Visit www.UltimateScholarshipBook.com and enter code TR238112 for updates on this award.

(2382) • Tri Delta Undergraduate Scholarship

Tri Delta
Delta Delta Delta Foundation
P.O. Box 5987
Arlington, TX 76005
Phone: 817-633-8001
Fax: 817-652-0212
Email: info@trideltaeo.org
http://www.tridelta.org
Purpose: To offer scholarships to undergraduate members.
Eligibility: Applicants must be sophomores or juniors in good standing with the organization.
Target applicants: College students. Adult students.
Amount: Varies.
Number of awards: Varies.

Deadline: March 1.
How to apply: Applications are available online.
Exclusive: Visit www.UltimateScholarshipBook.com and enter code TR238212 for updates on this award.

(2383) • Truckload Carriers Association Scholarship Fund

Truckload Carriers Association
Attn: Scholarship Applications
2200 Mill Road
Alexandria, VA 22314
Phone: 703-838-1950
Fax: 703-836-6610
Email: TCA@truckload.org
http://www.truckload.org
Purpose: To support college students affiliated with the trucking industry.
Eligibility: Applicants must attend or plan to attend college, be in good standing and be the children, grandchildren or spouses of an employee of a trucking company; applicants may also be the children, grandchildren or spouses of an independent contractor or independent contractors affiliated with a trucking company and attending a four-year college.
Target applicants: High school students. College students. Adult students.
Minimum GPA: 3.3
Amount: $1,500-$2,500.
Number of awards: Varies.
Deadline: June 12.
How to apply: Applications are available online.
Exclusive: Visit www.UltimateScholarshipBook.com and enter code TR238312 for updates on this award.

(2384) • Tuition Exchange Scholarships

Tuition Exchange
1743 Connecticut Avenue NW
Washington, DC 20009
Phone: 202-518-0135
Email: info@tuitionexchange.org
http://www.tuitionexchange.org
Purpose: To assist the children or other family members of the faculty and staff at participating colleges and universities to encourage employment of parents and guardians in higher education.
Eligibility: Eligibility varies by institution. Applicants must be family members of the home institution where they are applying. However specific details about employment status, years of service or other requirements are determined solely by the home institution.
Target applicants: High school students. College students. Adult students.
Amount: Full tuition or up to $29,000.
Number of awards: 5,400.
Scholarship may be renewable.
Deadline: Varies.
How to apply: Applications are available from the liaison officer at the home institution.
Exclusive: Visit www.UltimateScholarshipBook.com and enter code TU238412 for updates on this award.

(2385) • UCC Seminarian Scholarship

United Church of Christ
700 Prospect Avenue
Cleveland, OH 44115
Phone: 216-736-3839
Email: jeffersv@ucc.org
http://www.ucc.org
Purpose: To support members of the United Church of Christ who are preparing for ministry.
Eligibility: Applicants must be members of a United Church of Christ congregation for at least one year prior to receipt of the scholarship. They must be currently enrolled in an ATS accredited seminary in a course of study to become an ordained minister, and they must maintain at least a B average to receive and keep the scholarship. Applicants should be able to show that they have demonstrated leadership abilities in a church or academic environment. Students must also agree to serve the United Church of Christ or one of its partners after the completion of their studies.
Target applicants: High school students. College students. Graduate school students. Adult students.
Minimum GPA: 3.0
Amount: Varies.
Number of awards: Varies.
Scholarship may be renewable.
Deadline: Varies.
How to apply: Applications are available by mail.
Exclusive: Visit www.UltimateScholarshipBook.com and enter code UN238512 for updates on this award.

(2386) • UFCW Suffridge Scholarship

United Food and Commercial Workers Union
Scholarship Program - Education Office
1775 K Street NW
Washington, DC 20006
Email: scholarship@ufcw.org
http://www.ufcw.org/scholarship
Purpose: To provide financial assistance for members of the UFCW and their children.
Eligibility: Applicants must be members of good standing of the UFCW with a membership of one continuous year or more or the unmarried children of a member. Applicants must also be graduating high school in the year of the competition and be less than 20 years old. Academic achievement, community involvement and essays are part of the selection process.
Target applicants: High school students.
Amount: $2,000.
Number of awards: 14.
Scholarship may be renewable.
Deadline: April 15.
How to apply: Applications are available online.
Exclusive: Visit www.UltimateScholarshipBook.com and enter code UN238612 for updates on this award.

(2387) • UMWA/BCOA Training and Education Fund

United Mine Workers of America/BCOA T.E.F.
8315 Lee Highway
Fairfax, VA 22031-2215
Phone: 703-208-7200
http://www.umwa.org
Purpose: To offer scholarships to UMWA members and their families.

Eligibility: Applicants must be miners unemployed from the coal industry with at least five years in classified employment. The spouses or children (below age 25) of eligible unemployed or working miners are also eligible for benefits. Grants are awarded based on the recommendation of one or more panels chosen by UMWA and the Bituminous Coal Association.
Target applicants: High school students. College students. Graduate school students. Adult students.
Amount: Varies.
Number of awards: Varies.
Deadline: Varies.
How to apply: Applications are available by phone or written request.
Exclusive: Visit www.UltimateScholarshipBook.com and enter code UN238712 for updates on this award.

(2388) • Undergraduate Fellows Program

Fund for Theological Education Inc.
825 Houston Mill Road, Suite 250
Atlanta, GA 30329
Phone: 404-727-1450
Fax: 404-727-1490
Email: fte@thefund.org
http://www.thefund.org
Purpose: To support students who are considering ministry as a possible career.
Eligibility: Applicants must be juniors or seniors in an accredited undergraduate program at a North American college or university who are considering ministry as a career, have a minimum 3.0 GPA and be citizens of the U.S. or Canada. Applicants are evaluated on the basis of ability and character.
Target applicants: College students. Adult students.
Minimum GPA: 3.0
Amount: $2,000.
Number of awards: Up to 40.
Deadline: March 15.
How to apply: Applicants must be nominated by a college faculty member, administrator, campus minister or chaplain or current pastor. Nomination forms and application forms are available online.
Exclusive: Visit www.UltimateScholarshipBook.com and enter code FU238812 for updates on this award.

(2389) • Undergraduate Research Grants

Golden Key National Honour Society
Scholarship Program Administrators
Golden Key Scholarships/Awards
P.O. Box 23737
Nashville, TN 37202-3737
Phone: 800-377-2401
Email: scholarships@goldenkey.org
http://www.goldenkey.org
Purpose: To assist members in their thesis research or in presenting their research at a professional conference.
Eligibility: Applicants must be undergraduate student members. Selection is based on academic achievement and the quality of the research.
Target applicants: College students. Adult students.
Amount: $1,000.
Number of awards: Varies.
Deadline: April 1 October 15.
How to apply: Applications are available online.
Exclusive: Visit www.UltimateScholarshipBook.com and enter code GO238912 for updates on this award.

(2390) • Undergraduate Scholarship

Delta Sigma Pi
330 S. Campus Avenue
Oxford, OH 45056
Phone: 513-523-1907
Fax: 513-523-7292
Email: centraloffice@dspnet.org
http://www.dspnet.org
Purpose: To assist student members.
Eligibility: Applicants must be members in good standing of Delta Sigma Pi with at least one semester or quarter of undergraduate studies remaining. Applicants are judged on scholastic achievement, financial need, fraternal service, service activities, letters of recommendation and overall presentation of required materials.
Target applicants: College students. Adult students.
Amount: $250-$3,000.
Number of awards: 10.
Deadline: June 30.
How to apply: Applications are available online.
Exclusive: Visit www.UltimateScholarshipBook.com and enter code DE239012 for updates on this award.

(2391) • Undergraduate Scholarships

American Baptist Churches USA
P.O. Box 851
Valley Forge, PA 19482
Phone: 800-222-3872
Fax: 610-768-2453
Email: karen.drummond@abc-usa.org
http://www.nationalministries.org
Purpose: To support American Baptist students pursuing educational opportunities.
Eligibility: Applicants must be members of an American Baptist church for at least one year before applying for aid, be enrolled at an accredited educational institution in the U.S. or Puerto Rico, be U.S. citizens and retain a 2.75 GPA to remain eligible for the scholarships.
Target applicants: High school students. College students. Adult students.
Minimum GPA: 2.75
Amount: Varies.
Number of awards: Varies.
Scholarship may be renewable.
Deadline: May 29.
How to apply: Applications are available by request.
Exclusive: Visit www.UltimateScholarshipBook.com and enter code AM239112 for updates on this award.

(2392) • Union Plus Scholarship

Union Plus
1125 15th Street, NW
Suite 300
Washington, DC 20005
Fax: 202-293-5311
http://www.unionplus.org
Purpose: To help the families of union members.
Eligibility: Applicants must be members of unions participating in a Union Plus program or the spouses or children of such union members.

Applicants must be accepted to or attending an undergraduate course of study at an accredited college or university, community college or recognized technical or trade school. Selection is based on academic ability, social awareness, financial need and appreciation of labor.
Target applicants: High school students. College students. Adult students.
Amount: $500-$4,000.
Number of awards: Varies.
Deadline: January 31.
How to apply: Applications are available online.
Exclusive: Visit www.UltimateScholarshipBook.com and enter code UN239212 for updates on this award.

(2393) • United Agribusiness League and United Agricultural Benefit Trust Scholarships

United Agribusiness League
54 Corporate Park
Irvine, CA 92606
Phone: 949-975-1424
Fax: 949-975-1671
Email: info@ual.org
http://www.ual.org
Purpose: To aid undergraduate students who are affiliated with the United Agribusiness League (UAL) or the United Agricultural Benefit Trust (UABT).
Eligibility: Applicants must be current undergraduate students at an accredited college or university and must be affiliated with the United Agribusiness League (UAL) or the United Agricultural Benefit Trust (UABT) through a member or an employee of a member. They must have a GPA of 2.5 or higher. Selection is based on the overall strength of the application.
Target applicants: College students. Adult students.
Minimum GPA: 2.5
Amount: Varies.
Number of awards: Varies.
Deadline: March 31.
How to apply: Applications are available online. An application form, three reference letters, a personal essay and a resume are required.
Exclusive: Visit www.UltimateScholarshipBook.com and enter code UN239312 for updates on this award.

(2394) • United Methodist General Scholarship

United Methodist Church
Office of Loans and Scholarships
P.O. BOX 340007
Nashville, TN 37203-0007
Phone: 615-340-7344
Fax: 615-340-7367
Email: umscholar@gbhem.org
http://www.gbhem.org
Purpose: To support students who are members of a United Methodist Church.
Eligibility: Applicants must be active, full members of a United Methodist Church for at least one year prior to applying, be admitted to a full-time degree program in an accredited college or university and have a minimum 2.5 GPA. Students must also be U.S. citizens or permanent residents and be undergraduate, graduate or doctoral students. Online applications are due by April 15, and supporting documents are due by May 1.
Target applicants: College students. Graduate school students. Adult students.
Minimum GPA: 2.5
Amount: Varies.
Number of awards: Varies.
Deadline: April 15.
How to apply: Applications are available online.
Exclusive: Visit www.UltimateScholarshipBook.com and enter code UN239412 for updates on this award.

(2395) • United Transportation Union Scholarships

United Transportation Union Insurance Association
UTUIA Scholarship Program
14600 Detroit Avenue
Cleveland, OH 44107-4250
http://www.utuia.org
Purpose: To provide financial aid to the children and grandchildren of UTU/UTUIA members.
Eligibility: Applicants must be at least high school seniors or the equivalent and be age 25 or less. Applicants must also be UTU or UTUIA-insured members, the children or grandchildren of a UTU or UTUIA-insured member or the children of a deceased UTU or UTUIA-insured member. UTU or UTUIA-insured members must be U.S. residents. Applicants must be accepted for admittance or already enrolled for at least 12 credit hours per quarter or semester at a recognized institution of higher learning (university, college or junior college, nursing or technical school offering college credit). Scholarships are awarded on the basis of chance, not grades. A UTUIA scholar, however, is expected to maintain a satisfactory academic record to keep the scholarship for the full four years.
Target applicants: High school students. College students.
Amount: $500.
Number of awards: 50.
Scholarship may be renewable.
Deadline: Last business day in March.
How to apply: Applications are available from the UTU news or by written request.
Exclusive: Visit www.UltimateScholarshipBook.com and enter code UN239512 for updates on this award.

(2396) • Utility Workers Union of America Scholarships

Utility Workers Union of America
815 16th Street NW
Washington, DC 20006
Phone: 202-974-8200
Fax: 202-974-8201
Email: webmaster@uwua.net
http://www.uwua.net
Purpose: To offer scholarships to the children of UWUA members.
Eligibility: Applicants must be the sons or daughters of active Utility Workers Union members. Recipients are selected from those who participate in the National Merit Scholarship Competition by taking the PSAT/NMSQT as high school juniors, complete high school and are enrolled in a regionally accredited college in the United States.
Target applicants: High school students.
Amount: Varies.
Number of awards: Varies.
Scholarship may be renewable.
Deadline: Varies.
How to apply: Applications are available online.
Exclusive: Visit www.UltimateScholarshipBook.com and enter code UT239612 for updates on this award.

(2397) • VFW Scout of the Year Scholarship

Veterans of Foreign Wars
406 W. 34th Street
Kansas City, MO 64111
Phone: 816-968-1117
Fax: 816-968-1149
Email: kharmer@vfw.org
http://www.vfw.org

Purpose: To reward an outstanding Boy Scout, Venture Scout or Sea Scout.

Eligibility: Applicants must have received the Eagle Scout Award, the Venture Silver Award or the Sea Scout Quartermaster Award and demonstrated practical citizenship. Applicants must also have reached their 15th birthday and be enrolled in high school.

Target applicants: High school students.

Amount: $1,000-$5,000.

Number of awards: 3.

Deadline: March 1.

How to apply: Applications are available online.

Exclusive: Visit www.UltimateScholarshipBook.com and enter code VE239712 for updates on this award.

(2398) • Visual and Performing Arts Achievement Awards

Golden Key National Honour Society
Scholarship Program Administrators
Golden Key Scholarships/Awards
P.O. Box 23737
Nashville, TN 37202-3737
Phone: 800-377-2401
Email: scholarships@goldenkey.org
http://www.goldenkey.org

Purpose: To assist members who are talented in the visual and performing arts.

Eligibility: Applicants must be undergraduate, graduate or post-graduate members who are currently taking classes at a degree-granting program. Selection is based on the work submitted. For the visual arts, students must submit a slide or slides of their artwork. For the performing arts, students must submit a videotape or DVD of a performance up to 10 minutes. The competition categories are: painting, drawing, photography, sculpture, computer-generated art/graphic design/ illustration, mixed media, instrumental performance, vocal performance and dance.

Target applicants: College students. Graduate school students. Adult students.

Amount: $1,000.

Number of awards: 9.

Deadline: March 1.

How to apply: Applications are available online.

Exclusive: Visit www.UltimateScholarshipBook.com and enter code GO239812 for updates on this award.

(2399) • Vocations Scholarship Funds

Knights of Columbus
Department of Scholarships
P.O. Box 1670
New Haven, CT 06507
Phone: 203-752-4000
Email: info@kofc.org
http://www.kofc.org

Purpose: To support theology students on their path to the priesthood.

Eligibility: Applicants must be males studying with ecclesiastical approval at a major seminary for a diocese or religious institute in the United States, its territories and Canada. The Father Michael J. McGivney Vocations Scholarship Fund awards scholarships based on financial need, and applicants must provide proof of need. The Bishop Thomas V. Daily Scholarships Fund awards recipients on the basis of merit, and applicants must submit their most recent transcript and two letters of recommendation. Both funds give preference to Knights of Columbus members and their sons, but membership is not required.

Target applicants: High school students. College students. Graduate school students. Adult students.

Amount: $2,500.

Number of awards: Varies.

Scholarship may be renewable.

Deadline: June 1.

How to apply: Applications are available from seminary rectors and diocesan vocations directors starting in February.

Exclusive: Visit www.UltimateScholarshipBook.com and enter code KN239912 for updates on this award.

(2400) • W. Allan Herzog Scholarship

Tau Kappa Epsilon Educational Foundation
8645 Founders Road
Indianapolis, IN 46268
Phone: 317-872-6533
Fax: 317-875-8353
Email: tef@tke.org
http://www.tkefoundation.org

Purpose: To assist Tau Kappa Epsilon members entering the fields of accounting and finance.

Eligibility: Applicants must be initiated Tau Kappa Epsilon members in good standing and full-time undergraduate students majoring in accounting or finance. They must have a GPA of at least 2.75 and demonstrate a record of leadership in their chapter and other campus organizations. Applicants must also include a statement describing how they have benefited from TKE membership.

Target applicants: College students. Adult students.

Minimum GPA: 2.75

Amount: $3,000.

Number of awards: 1.

Deadline: March 1.

How to apply: Applications are available online.

Exclusive: Visit www.UltimateScholarshipBook.com and enter code TA240012 for updates on this award.

(2401) • Wallace G. McCauley Memorial Scholarship

Tau Kappa Epsilon Educational Foundation
8645 Founders Road
Indianapolis, IN 46268
Phone: 317-872-6533
Fax: 317-875-8353
Email: tef@tke.org
http://www.tkefoundation.org

Purpose: To award a member of Tau Kappa Epsilon for outstanding academic achievement who has participated in developing and improving alumni relations and participation.

Eligibility: Applicants must have a GPA of 3.0 and be in the junior or senior year. If no "alumni relations" applicants are recognized, the GPA requirement will be 2.5 and the award will be given in honor of academic achievement and chapter or community leadership.

Target applicants: College students. Adult students.
Minimum GPA: 3.0
Amount: $200.
Number of awards: 1.
Deadline: March 1.
How to apply: Applications are available online.
Exclusive: Visit www.UltimateScholarshipBook.com and enter code TA240112 for updates on this award.

(2402) • Walter L. Mitchell Memorial Scholarship Awards

Chemical Workers Union Council, International, of the UFCW
Research and Education Department
1799 Akron Peninsula Road
Akron, OH 44313
Phone: 330-926-1444
Fax: 330-926-0816
http://www.icwuc.org
Purpose: To offer scholarships to the children or step-children of members of the UFCW.
Eligibility: Applicants must be children or step-children of members of at least a year who intend to enter college the fall following application. Recipients are selected on the basis of biographical information, ACT/SAT scores and high school records.
Target applicants: High school students.
Amount: $1,500.
Number of awards: 12.
Deadline: March 5.
How to apply: Applications are available online.
Exclusive: Visit www.UltimateScholarshipBook.com and enter code CH240212 for updates on this award.

(2403) • Warren Poslusny Award for Outstanding Achievement

Sigma Alpha Epsilon (SAE)
Dave Sandell
Sigma Alpha Epsilon Foundation Scholarships
1856 Sheridan Road
Evanston, IL 60201-3837
Phone: 800-233-1856 x234
Fax: 847-475-2250
Email: dsandell@sae.net
http://www.sae.net
Purpose: To recognize collegians who have demonstrated outstanding leadership and service and have exemplified a dedication to the values established by the founders of Sigma Alpha Epsilon.
Eligibility: Applicants must be brothers of Sigma Alpha Epsilon in good standing, have a minimum 3.0 GPA and either must have junior standing or higher or must be pursuing full-time graduate study. This award is merit-based, with an emphasis on combining academic excellence, leadership, service and campus involvement.
Target applicants: College students. Graduate school students. Adult students.
Minimum GPA: 3.0
Amount: $1,000.
Number of awards: 5.
Deadline: March 1.
How to apply: Contact the coordinator of educational programs and services.
Exclusive: Visit www.UltimateScholarshipBook.com and enter code SI240312 for updates on this award.

(2404) • Wenderoth Undergraduate Scholarship

Phi Sigma Kappa International Headquarters
2925 E. 96th Street
Indianapolis, IN 46240
Phone: 317-573-5420
Fax: 317-573-5430
Email: vershun@phisigmakappa.org
http://www.phisigmakappa.org
Purpose: To give financial aid to college sophomore and junior members.
Eligibility: Applicants must be sophomores or juniors in college for the year that the scholarship will apply to, have completed two semesters or three quarters of study and have a minimum B GPA. Scholarships are awarded on the basis of academic accomplishments and essays.
Target applicants: College students. Adult students.
Minimum GPA: 3.0
Amount: $1,750-$5,000.
Number of awards: 4.
Deadline: January 31.
How to apply: Applications are available online.
Exclusive: Visit www.UltimateScholarshipBook.com and enter code PH240412 for updates on this award.

(2405) • William C. Doherty Scholarship Fund

National Association of Letter Carriers
100 Indiana Avenue NW
Washington, DC 20001-2144
Phone: 202-393-4695
Email: nalcinf@nalc.org
http://www.nalc.org
Purpose: To offer scholarships to the children of members of the Letter Carriers Union.
Eligibility: Applicants must be the children or legally adopted children of an active, retired or deceased letter carrier and high school seniors. The applicant's parents must be members in good standing at least one year prior to applying. Selection is based on SAT/ACT scores, high school transcript and questionnaire.
Target applicants: High school students.
Amount: $4,000.
Number of awards: 5.
Scholarship may be renewable.
Deadline: December 31.
How to apply: Preliminary applications are available online.
Exclusive: Visit www.UltimateScholarshipBook.com and enter code NA240512 for updates on this award.

(2406) • William V. Muse Scholarship

Tau Kappa Epsilon Educational Foundation
8645 Founders Road
Indianapolis, IN 46268
Phone: 317-872-6533
Fax: 317-875-8353
Email: tef@tke.org
http://www.tkefoundation.org
Purpose: To award a member of Tau Kappa Epsilon for outstanding academic achievement and leadership within the organization as a chapter officer.

Eligibility: Applicants must have a GPA of at least 3.0 and must have earned at least 30 semester-credit hours. Preference is first given to members of the Epsilon-Upsilon Chapter.
Target applicants: College students. Adult students.
Minimum GPA: 3.0
Amount: $225.
Number of awards: 1.
Deadline: March 1.
How to apply: Applications are available online.
Exclusive: Visit www.UltimateScholarshipBook.com and enter code TA240612 for updates on this award.

(2407) • William Wilson Memorial Scholarship

Tau Kappa Epsilon Educational Foundation
8645 Founders Road
Indianapolis, IN 46268
Phone: 317-872-6533
Fax: 317-875-8353
Email: tef@tke.org
http://www.tkefoundation.org
Purpose: To award a member of Tau Kappa Epsilon for outstanding academic achievement who has participated in developing and improving alumni relations and participation.
Eligibility: Applicants must have a GPA of 3.0 and be in the junior or senior year. If no "alumni relations" applicants are recognized, the GPA requirement will be 2.5 and the award will be given in honor of academic achievement and chapter or community leadership.
Target applicants: College students. Adult students.
Minimum GPA: 3.0
Amount: $175.
Number of awards: 1.
Deadline: March 1.
How to apply: Applications are available online.
Exclusive: Visit www.UltimateScholarshipBook.com and enter code TA240712 for updates on this award.

(2408) • Wilson W. Carnes Scholarship

National FFA Organization
P.O. Box 68960
6060 FFA Drive
Indianapolis, IN 46268-0960
Phone: 317-802-6060
Fax: 317-802-6051
Email: scholarships@ffa.org
http://www.ffa.org/
Purpose: To support students who are majoring in agricultural communications.
Eligibility: Applicants must be current FFA members and high school seniors or college students planning to enroll or currently enrolled full-time. Students only need to complete the online application one time to be considered for all FFA-administered scholarships. The application requires information about the student's activities and a 1,000-word essay. Awards may be used for books, supplies, tuition, fees and room and board.
Target applicants: High school students. College students. Adult students.
Amount: $300.
Number of awards: 1.
Deadline: February 15.
How to apply: Applications are available online.
Exclusive: Visit www.UltimateScholarshipBook.com and enter code NA240812 for updates on this award.

(2409) • Women in Sports Media Scholarship/Internship Program

Association for Women in Sports Media
P.O. Box 601557
Dallas, TX 75360
Email: awsmintern@hotmail.com
http://www.awsmonline.org
Purpose: To encourage females interested in sports media careers.
Eligibility: Applicants must be female students working full-time toward a graduate or undergraduate degree with the goal of becoming a sports writer, editor, broadcaster or public relations representative. Applicants must submit a resume, an essay on a memorable experience in sports or sports media, three references, two letters of recommendation and up to five samples of their work. Application fee is waived for AWSM members.
Target applicants: College students. Graduate school students. Adult students.
Amount: $1,000-$2,000+internship pay and expenses for convention attendance.
Number of awards: Varies.
Deadline: October 31.
How to apply: Applications are available online.
Exclusive: Visit www.UltimateScholarshipBook.com and enter code AS240912 for updates on this award.

(2410) • Women in United Methodist History Research Grant

General Commission on Archives and History, The United Methodist Church
P.O. Box 127
36 Madison Avenue
Madison, NJ 07940
Phone: 973-408-3189
Fax: 973-408-3909
Email: research@gcah.org
http://www.gcah.org
Purpose: To provide seed money for research projects relating specifically to the history of women in the United Methodist Church.
Eligibility: Applicants must submit an application that includes a resume, a description of the project, a timetable for the project, a budget and letters of recommendation.
Target applicants: Junior high students or younger. High school students. College students. Graduate school students. Adult students.
Amount: At least $1,000.
Number of awards: Varies.
Deadline: December 31.
How to apply: Submit materials to the General Secretary at the address listed.
Exclusive: Visit www.UltimateScholarshipBook.com and enter code GE241012 for updates on this award.

(2411) • Women in United Methodist History Writing Award

General Commission on Archives and History, The United Methodist Church
P.O. Box 127
36 Madison Avenue
Madison, NJ 07940

Phone: 973-408-3189
Fax: 973-408-3909
Email: research@gcah.org
http://www.gcah.org
Purpose: To reward research and writing on the history of women in The United Methodist Church.
Eligibility: Applicants must submit completed, original manuscripts no longer than 20 double-spaced, typewritten pages with footnotes and bibliography about the history of women in the United Methodist Church or its antecedents.
Target applicants: Junior high students or younger. High school students. College students. Graduate school students. Adult students.
Amount: $500.
Number of awards: 1.
Deadline: December 31.
How to apply: Send manuscript to the General Secretary at the address listed.
Exclusive: Visit www.UltimateScholarshipBook.com and enter code GE241112 for updates on this award.

(2412) • Youth of the Year Award

National Exchange Club
3050 Central Avenue
Toledo, OH 43606
Phone: 800-924-2643
Fax: 419-535-1989
Email: info@nationalexchangeclub.org
http://www.nationalexchangeclub.org
Purpose: To recognize students who excel in academics, leadership and community service.
Eligibility: Applicants are chosen by their local Exchange Clubs. The process begins with Youth of the Month Awards. At the end of the year, a Youth of the Year nominee is selected from Youth of the Month winners. Applicants are judged based on participation in activities, community service, special achievements/awards, grades and a required essay. To be eligible to win, applicants must be able to attend national convention to accept the award.
Target applicants: High school students.
Amount: $10,000.
Number of awards: 1.
Deadline: June 1.
How to apply: Applications are available online.
Exclusive: Visit www.UltimateScholarshipBook.com and enter code NA241212 for updates on this award.

(2413) • Youth Partners Accessing Capital

Alpha Kappa Alpha Educational Advancement Foundation Inc.
5656 S. Stony Island Avenue
Chicago, IL 60637
Phone: 800-653-6528
Fax: 773-947-0277
Email: akaeaf@akaeaf.net
http://www.akaeaf.org
Purpose: To provide financial assistance to Alpha Kappa Alpha members with exceptional academic achievement or extreme financial need.
Eligibility: Applicants must be Alpha Kappa Alpha members who are in their sophomore year of college or higher with a GPA of 3.0 or higher. They must have either high academic achievement or extreme financial need, and they must participate in leadership, volunteer, civic or campus activities.
Target applicants: College students. Adult students.
Minimum GPA: 3.0
Amount: $750-$1,500.
Number of awards: Varies.
Deadline: April 15.
How to apply: Applications are available online.
Exclusive: Visit www.UltimateScholarshipBook.com and enter code AL241312 for updates on this award.

ETHNICITY / RACE / GENDER / FAMILY

(2414) • A.T. Anderson Memorial Scholarship

American Indian Science and Engineering Society
P.O. Box 9828
Albuquerque, NM 87119-9828
Phone: 505-765-1052
Fax: 505-765-5608
http://www.aises.org
Purpose: To provide scholarships for Native American and Alaskan Native students majoring in science, engineering, medicine, natural resources, math and technology.
Eligibility: Applicants must be full-time undergraduate or graduate students at an accredited college or university. Applicants must also be members of a Native American tribe or Alaskan Native and members of AISES.
Target applicants: College students. Graduate school students. Adult students.
Minimum GPA: 2.7
Amount: $1,000-$2,000.
Number of awards: Varies.
Deadline: June 15.
How to apply: Applications are available online.
Exclusive: Visit www.UltimateScholarshipBook.com and enter code AM241412 for updates on this award.

(2415) • AAJA Newhouse National Scholarship And Internship Awards

Asian American Journalists Association
1182 Market Street
Suite 230
San Francisco, CA 94102
Phone: 415-346-2051
Fax: 415-346-6343
Email: lilac@aaja.org
http://www.aaja.org
Purpose: Offers monetary assistance to print journalism college students from historically underrepresented Asian Pacific American groups.
Eligibility: The AAJA encourages students from historically underrepresented Asian Pacific American groups, including Vietnamese, Cambodians, Hmong and other Southeast Asians, South Asians and Pacific Islanders to apply. Applicants must demonstrate a commitment to the field of journalism, sensitivity to Asian American issues as demonstrated by community involvement, journalistic ability, scholastic ability and financial need. Applicants may be high school seniors, college students or graduate students.
Target applicants: High school students. College students. Graduate school students. Adult students.
Amount: Up to $5,000.
Number of awards: Varies.
Deadline: Varies.
How to apply: Applications are available online.
Exclusive: Visit www.UltimateScholarshipBook.com and enter code AS241512 for updates on this award.

(2416) • AAUW Educational Foundation Career Development Grants

American Association of University Women (AAUW) Educational Foundation
Dept. 60
301 ACT Drive
Iowa City, IA 52243-4030
Phone: 319-337-1716 x60
Fax: 202-872-1425
Email: aauw@act.org
http://www.aauw.org
Purpose: To support college-educated women who need additional training to advance their careers, re-enter the workforce or change careers.
Eligibility: Applicants must be U.S. citizens, hold a bachelor's degree and enroll in courses at a regionally-accredited program related to their professional development, including two- and four-year colleges, technical schools and distance learning programs. Special preference is given to women of color, AAUW members and women pursuing their first advanced degree or credentials in a nontraditional field.
Target applicants: Graduate school students. Adult students.
Amount: $2,000-$12,000.
Number of awards: Varies.
Deadline: December 15.
How to apply: Applications are available online from August 1-December 15.
Exclusive: Visit www.UltimateScholarshipBook.com and enter code AM241612 for updates on this award.

(2417) • Actuarial Diversity Scholarship

Actuarial Foundation
475 N. Martingale Road, Suite 600
Schaumburg, IL 60173-2226
Phone: 847-706-3581
Fax: 847-706-3599
Email: scholarships@actfnd.org
http://www.beanactuary.org
Purpose: To promote diversity through an annual scholarship program for African American, Hispanic and Native American Indian students and encourage academic achievements by awarding scholarships to full-time undergraduate and graduate students pursuing a degree in the actuarial profession.
Eligibility: Applicants must have at least one birth parent who is a member of one of the minority groups listed and a minimum GPA of 3.0. High school seniors must have a minimum ACT math score of 28 or SAT math score of 600. An award will be provided in the recipient's name to any accredited U.S. educational institution to cover educational expenses. An application, a personal statement, two letters of recommendation and official school transcripts (sealed) are required.
Target applicants: High school students. College students. Graduate school students. Adult students.
Minimum GPA: 3.0
Amount: Varies.
Number of awards: Varies.
Scholarship may be renewable.
Deadline: May 4.
How to apply: Applications are available online.
Exclusive: Visit www.UltimateScholarshipBook.com and enter code AC241712 for updates on this award.

(2418) • Ada I. Pressman Memorial Scholarship

Society of Women Engineers
120 South LaSalle Street
Suite 1515
Chicago, IL 60603
Phone: 877-793-4636
Email: scholarshipapplication@swe.org

http://www.swe.org
Purpose: To support female engineering students.
Eligibility: Applicants may major in any type of engineering. They must be U.S. citizens and must be college sophomores, juniors, seniors or graduate students. A GPA of 3.0 or higher is required.
Target applicants: College students. Graduate school students. Adult students.
Minimum GPA: 3.0
Amount: $5,000.
Number of awards: 6.
Deadline: February 15.
How to apply: Applications are available online. An application form is required.
Exclusive: Visit www.UltimateScholarshipBook.com and enter code SO241812 for updates on this award.

(2419) • Admiral Grace Murray Hopper Memorial Scholarships

Society of Women Engineers
120 South LaSalle Street
Suite 1515
Chicago, IL 60603
Phone: 877-793-4636
Email: scholarshipapplication@swe.org
http://www.swe.org
Purpose: To support women in engineering.
Eligibility: Applicants must be females who are enrolled in their freshman year at an accredited engineering or computer science program. They must have a GPA of 3.5 or higher.
Target applicants: College students. Adult students.
Minimum GPA: 3.5
Amount: $1,000.
Number of awards: 5.
Deadline: May 15.
How to apply: Applications are available online. An application form is required.
Exclusive: Visit www.UltimateScholarshipBook.com and enter code SO241912 for updates on this award.

(2420) • Adolph Van Pelt Scholarship

Association on American Indian Affairs
Lisa Wyzlic, Director of Scholarship Programs
966 Hungerford Drive, Suite 12-B
Rockville, MD 20850
Phone: 240-314-7155
Fax: 240-314-7159
Email: general.aaia@verizon.net
http://www.indian-affairs.org
Purpose: To assist Native American/Alaska Native undergraduate students based on merit and financial need.
Eligibility: Applicants must be full-time students and provide proof of tribal enrollment, a Certificate of Indian Blood (showing 1/4 Indian blood) and an essay on educational goals.
Target applicants: College students. Adult students.
Amount: $1,500.
Number of awards: Varies.
Scholarship may be renewable.
Deadline: June 18.
How to apply: Applications are available online.
Exclusive: Visit www.UltimateScholarshipBook.com and enter code AS242012 for updates on this award.

(2421) • Afro-Academic, Cultural, Technological and Scientific Olympics (ACT-SO)

National Association for the Advancement of Colored People
The United Negro College Fund
Scholarships and Grants Administration
8260 Willow Oaks Corporate Drive
Fairfax, VA 22031
Phone: 800-331-2244
Email: youth@naacpnet.org
http://www.naacp.org
Purpose: To recognize and reward the academic and cultural achievements of African American high school students.
Eligibility: Students must be in grades 9 through 12, 19 years of age or younger and of African-American descent. They must compete in one of 25 categories including business, sciences, humanities and performing and visual arts. Winners receive scholarships, internships and apprenticeships.
Target applicants: High school students.
Amount: Varies.
Number of awards: Varies.
Deadline: Varies.
How to apply: Applications are available from the NAACP.
Exclusive: Visit www.UltimateScholarshipBook.com and enter code NA242112 for updates on this award.

(2422) • AGBU Scholarship Program

Armenian General Benevolent Union (AGBU)
55 E. 59th Street, 7th Floor
New York, NY 10022-1112
Phone: 212-319-6383
Fax: 212-319-6507
Email: scholarship@agbu.org
http://www.agbu.org
Purpose: To help students of Armenian descent.
Eligibility: Applicants should be international full-time students or high school seniors of Armenian descent who attend academic institutions and graduate programs. Applications, two recommendation letters, transcripts, college acceptance letters, financial award letters, resumes and photographs are required.
Target applicants: High school students. College students. Graduate school students. Adult students.
Amount: Varies.
Number of awards: Varies.
Scholarship may be renewable.
Deadline: April 15 to May 31.
How to apply: Applications are available online.
Exclusive: Visit www.UltimateScholarshipBook.com and enter code AR242212 for updates on this award.

(2423) • AGI Minority Participation Program

American Geological Institute
4220 King Street
Alexandria, VA 22302
Phone: 703-379-2480
Fax: 703-379-7563
Email: mpp@agiweb.org
http://www.agiweb.org

Purpose: To aid minority students who are pursuing higher education in the geosciences.
Eligibility: Applicants must be U.S. citizens. They must be of African-American, Latino or Native American (American Indian, Eskimo, Hawaiian or Samoan) heritage. They must be full-time undergraduate or graduate students who are majoring in geoscience or an eligible subdiscipline (hydrology, planetary geology, geology, earth-science education, geochemistry, physical oceanography or geophysics). Selection is based on the overall strength of the application.
Target applicants: College students. Graduate school students. Adult students.
Amount: Varies.
Number of awards: Varies.
Scholarship may be renewable.
Deadline: March 15.
How to apply: Applications are available online. An application form, official transcript, personal essay and two recommendation letters are required.
Exclusive: Visit www.UltimateScholarshipBook.com and enter code AM242312 for updates on this award.

(2424) • Agnes Jones Jackson Scholarship

National Association for the Advancement of Colored People
The United Negro College Fund
Scholarships and Grants Administration
8260 Willow Oaks Corporate Drive
Fairfax, VA 22031
Phone: 800-331-2244
Email: youth@naacpnet.org
http://www.naacp.org
Purpose: To reward NAACP members with financial need.
Eligibility: Students must be members of the NAACP, U.S. citizens and attending an accredited U.S. college. Undergraduates must attend college full-time, while graduates may be full- or part-time students. High school seniors and undergraduates must have a minimum 2.5 GPA while graduate students must have a minimum 3.0 GPA. Applicants must demonstrate financial need according to the formula in the application form.
Target applicants: High school students. College students. Graduate school students.
Minimum GPA: 2.5 for high school and undergraduate applicants and 3.0 for graduate student applicants
Amount: $1,500-$2,500.
Number of awards: Varies.
Scholarship may be renewable.
Deadline: Last Friday in March.
How to apply: Applications are available online.
Exclusive: Visit www.UltimateScholarshipBook.com and enter code NA242412 for updates on this award.

(2425) • Agnes Missirian Scholarship

Armenian International Women's Association
65 Main Street
#3A
Watertown, MA 02472
Phone: 617-926-0171
Email: aiwainc@aol.com
http://www.aiwa-net.org/scholarshipinfo.html
Purpose: To honor the memory of Professor Agnes Missirian and assist Armenian women in obtaining higher education.
Eligibility: Applicants must be full-time students at accredited colleges or universities who are females of Armenian descent. They must be juniors, seniors or graduate students.
Target applicants: College students. Graduate school students. Adult students.
Amount: $2,000.
Number of awards: Varies.
Deadline: April.
How to apply: Applications are available online.
Exclusive: Visit www.UltimateScholarshipBook.com and enter code AR242512 for updates on this award.

(2426) • Alliance Data Scholarship

United Negro College Fund (UNCF)
8260 Willow Oaks Corporate Drive
P.O. Box 10444
Fairfax, VA 22031-8044
Phone: 800-331-2244
http://www.uncf.org/
Purpose: To assist African American students who are enrolled at a UNCF institution.
Eligibility: Applicants must have a minimum 3.0 GPA, complete the Free Application for Federal Student Aid (FAFSA) and have unmet financial need that is verified by the college or university financial aid office. UNCF students are encouraged to complete the UNCF General Scholarship application to be matched with scholarships for which they meet the criteria.
Target applicants: High school students. College students. Adult students.
Minimum GPA: 3.0
Amount: $5,000.
Number of awards: Varies.
Deadline: Varies.
How to apply: Applications are available online.
Exclusive: Visit www.UltimateScholarshipBook.com and enter code UN242612 for updates on this award.

(2427) • Allison E. Fisher Scholarship

National Association of Black Journalists
1100 Knight Hall
Suite 3100
College Park, MD 20742
Phone: 301-405-7520
Fax: 301-314-1714
Email: iwashington@nabj.org
http://www.nabj.org
Purpose: To aid print and broadcast journalism students.
Eligibility: Applicants must be student members of the National Association of Black Journalists (NABJ). They must be undergraduate or graduate students enrolled at a four-year institution majoring in broadcast or print journalism. They must have a GPA of 3.0 or higher and must demonstrate a commitment to community service. Selection is based on the overall strength of the application.
Target applicants: College students. Graduate school students. Adult students.
Minimum GPA: 3.0
Amount: $2,500.
Number of awards: 1.
Deadline: Varies.
How to apply: Applications are available online. An application form and supporting materials are required.

Exclusive: Visit www.UltimateScholarshipBook.com and enter code NA242712 for updates on this award.

(2428) • Allogan Slagle Memorial Scholarship

Association on American Indian Affairs
Lisa Wyzlic, Director of Scholarship Programs
966 Hungerford Drive, Suite 12-B
Rockville, MD 20850
Phone: 240-314-7155
Fax: 240-314-7159
Email: general.aaia@verizon.net
http://www.indian-affairs.org

Purpose: To assist Native American/Alaska Native undergraduate and graduate students from tribes that are not recognized by the federal government.
Eligibility: Applicants must submit a financial need analysis form, Certificate of Indian Blood or documents proving their lineal descent, proof of tribal enrollment, essay, two letters of recommendation, current financial aid award letter, transcripts and class schedule.
Target applicants: College students. Graduate school students. Adult students.
Amount: $1,500.
Number of awards: Varies.
Deadline: June 18.
How to apply: Applications are available online.
Exclusive: Visit www.UltimateScholarshipBook.com and enter code AS242812 for updates on this award.

(2429) • Alton and Dorothy Higgins MD Scholarship

United Negro College Fund (UNCF)
8260 Willow Oaks Corporate Drive
P.O. Box 10444
Fairfax, VA 22031-8044
Phone: 800-331-2244
http://www.uncf.org/

Purpose: To assist UNCF students or UNCF graduates in attending medical school.
Eligibility: The award may be used for tuition, room and board, books or to repay a federal student loan.
Target applicants: College students. Graduate school students. Adult students.
Amount: $5,000-$10,000.
Number of awards: Varies.
Deadline: Varies.
How to apply: Applications are available online.
Exclusive: Visit www.UltimateScholarshipBook.com and enter code UN242912 for updates on this award.

(2430) • America's Junior Miss Scholarship Program

America's Junior Miss
P.O. Box 2786
Mobile, AL 36652
Phone: 251-438-3621
Fax: 251-431-0063
Email: lynne@ajm.org
http://www.ajm.org

Purpose: To provide scholarship opportunities and encourage personal development for high school girls through a competitive pageant stressing academics and talent as well as poise and fitness.
Eligibility: Teen girls are selected from state competitions to participate in a national pageant. Contestants are judged on a combination of scholastics, personal interview, talent, fitness and poise. Applicants should be high school students at least in their sophomore year.
Target applicants: High school students.
Amount: Varies.
Number of awards: Varies.
Deadline: Varies.
How to apply: Applications are available from the local Junior Miss Program offices. A list of local contacts is available online.
Exclusive: Visit www.UltimateScholarshipBook.com and enter code AM243012 for updates on this award.

(2431) • American Chemical Society Scholars Program

American Chemical Society
1155 Sixteenth Street, NW
Washington, DC 20036
Phone: 800-227-5558
Fax: 614-447-3713
Email: crobinson@rubber.org
http://www.acs.org

Purpose: To encourage minority students to pursue careers in the sciences and to help them acquire the skills necessary for success in these fields.
Eligibility: Applicants must be African American, Hispanic/Latino or American Indian and graduating high school seniors or college freshmen, sophomores or juniors enrolled full-time at an accredited institution. Students must major in chemistry, biochemistry, chemical engineering or a chemically-related science and plan to work in a chemistry-related field. Those entering pre-med programs or pursuing pharmacy degrees are not eligible. A minimum GPA of 3.0 or "B" or better with high academic achievement in chemistry or science is required. Students must also demonstrate financial need through the Free Application for Federal Student Aid (FAFSA).
Target applicants: High school students. College students. Adult students.
Minimum GPA: 3.0
Amount: Up to $5,000.
Number of awards: Varies.
Scholarship may be renewable.
Deadline: March 1.
How to apply: Applications are available online.
Exclusive: Visit www.UltimateScholarshipBook.com and enter code AM243112 for updates on this award.

(2432) • American Hotel Foundation Scholarship

United Negro College Fund (UNCF)
8260 Willow Oaks Corporate Drive
P.O. Box 10444
Fairfax, VA 22031-8044
Phone: 800-331-2244
http://www.uncf.org/

Purpose: To promote the study of hotel management.
Eligibility: Applicants must be major in hotel management at United Negro College Fund (UNCF) member colleges and universities. Students must also have a minimum 2.5 GPA, complete the Free Application for Federal Student Aid (FAFSA) and have unmet financial need that is verified by the college or university financial aid office. UNCF students are encouraged to complete the UNCF General Scholarship application to be matched with scholarships for which they meet the criteria.

Target applicants: High school students. College students. Adult students.
Minimum GPA: 2.5
Amount: $1,500.
Number of awards: Varies.
Deadline: Varies.
How to apply: Applications are available online.
Exclusive: Visit www.UltimateScholarshipBook.com and enter code UN243212 for updates on this award.

(2433) • American Indian Scholarship

National Society Daughters of the American Revolution
Committee Services Office
Attn.: Scholarships
1776 D Street NW
Washington, DC 20006-5303
Phone: 202-628-1776
http://www.dar.org
Purpose: To assist Native American students.
Eligibility: Applicants must be Native Americans with papers proving Native American blood, have a minimum 2.75 GPA and demonstrate financial need and academic achievement. Graduate students are eligible, but preference is given to undergraduate students. Undergraduate students may attend a college, university or technical school. No affiliation with DAR is required.
Target applicants: College students. Graduate school students. Adult students.
Minimum GPA: 2.75
Amount: $1,000.
Number of awards: Varies.
Deadline: April 1.
How to apply: Applications are available by written request with a self-addressed, stamped envelope. Please specify that you are requesting information on the American Indian Scholarship.
Exclusive: Visit www.UltimateScholarshipBook.com and enter code NA243312 for updates on this award.

(2434) • American Society of Criminology Fellowships for Ethnic Minorities

American Society of Criminology
Department of Sociology and Criminal Justice C.O. Ronet Bachman
University of Delaware
Newark, DE 19717-5242
Email: ronet@udel.edu
http://www.asc41.com
Purpose: To encourage minorities to study criminology or criminal justice.
Eligibility: Applicants must be African American, Asian American, Latino or Native American. Recipients must have been accepted into a doctoral studies program. Selection is based on curriculum vitae, college transcripts, financial need, references and letter describing career plans, experiences and interest in criminology.
Target applicants: College students. Graduate school students. Adult students.
Amount: $6,000.
Number of awards: 3.
Deadline: March 1.
How to apply: Applications are available by written request.
Exclusive: Visit www.UltimateScholarshipBook.com and enter code AM243412 for updates on this award.

(2435) • Anne Maureen Whitney Barrow Memorial Scholarship

Society of Women Engineers
120 South LaSalle Street
Suite 1515
Chicago, IL 60603
Phone: 877-793-4636
Email: scholarshipapplication@swe.org
http://www.swe.org
Purpose: To support female engineering students.
Eligibility: Applicants must be enrolled in an accredited engineering or computer science program. A minimum GPA of 3.5 is required.
Target applicants: College students. Adult students.
Minimum GPA: 3.5
Amount: $5,000.
Number of awards: 1.
Scholarship may be renewable.
Deadline: May 15.
How to apply: Applications are available online.
Exclusive: Visit www.UltimateScholarshipBook.com and enter code SO243512 for updates on this award.

(2436) • Armenian Educational Foundation Scholarships

Armenian Educational Foundation Inc.
600 W. Broadway
Suite 130
Glendale, CA 91204
Phone: 818-242-4154
Email: aef@aefweb.org
http://www.aefweb.org
Purpose: To support Armenian students throughout the world.
Eligibility: Students must be of Armenian descent either on their mother's side, father's side or both. Selection is based on academic performance and financial need. Applicants must be at least college sophomores or graduate students who attend the colleges or universities listed on the website.
Target applicants: College students. Graduate school students. Adult students.
Amount: Varies.
Number of awards: Varies.
Deadline: May 27.
How to apply: Applications are available online.
Exclusive: Visit www.UltimateScholarshipBook.com and enter code AR243612 for updates on this award.

(2437) • Armenian Relief Society Undergraduate Scholarship

Armenian Relief Society Of North America Inc.
80 Bigelow Avenue
Watertown, MA 02472
Phone: 617-926-5892
Fax: 617-926-4855
Email: ars1910@aol.com
http://www.ars1910.org
Purpose: To provide merit and need-based scholarships for students of Armenian ancestry.
Eligibility: Applicants must be of Armenian ancestry and not related to the ARS Central Executive or Eremian Scholarship Committee members. Specific requirements may vary by region.

Target applicants: Junior high students or younger. High school students. College students. Adult students.
Amount: Varies.
Number of awards: Varies.
Deadline: May 31.
How to apply: Applications are available by mail.
Exclusive: Visit www.UltimateScholarshipBook.com and enter code AR243712 for updates on this award.

(2438) • ASA Scholarships

Armenian Students' Association of America
333 Atlantic Avenue
Warwick, RI 02888
Phone: 401-461-6114
Email: asa@asainc.org
http://www.asainc.org
Purpose: To provide scholarships for students of Armenian descent.
Eligibility: Applicants must be college sophomores or beyond in the year of application and be of Armenian descent.
Target applicants: College students. Graduate school students. Adult students.
Amount: Varies.
Number of awards: Varies.
Deadline: March 15.
How to apply: Request forms for applications are available online.
Exclusive: Visit www.UltimateScholarshipBook.com and enter code AR243812 for updates on this award.

(2439) • Asian and Pacific Islander American Scholarships

Asian and Pacific Islander American Scholarship Fund
1900 L Street NW
Suite 210
Washington, DC 20036-5002
Phone: 202-986-6892
Fax: 202-530-0643
Email: info@apiasf.org
http://www.apiasf.org
Purpose: To provide financial assistance to Asian and Pacific Island Americans.
Eligibility: Applicants must be of Asian or Pacific Islander ethnicity as defined by the U.S. Census, and they must be legal citizens, nationals or permanent residents of the United States. Citizens of the Marshall Islands, Micronesia and Palau are also eligible. Applicants must be enrolling full-time as a first-year degree-seeking student in an accredited college or university in the U.S. They must have a GPA of 2.7 or higher or have earned a GED, and they must apply for federal financial aid.
Target applicants: High school students.
Minimum GPA: 2.7
Amount: $2,500-$8,000.
Number of awards: Varies.
Deadline: January 14.
How to apply: Applications are available online.
Exclusive: Visit www.UltimateScholarshipBook.com and enter code AS243912 for updates on this award.

(2440) • Association of Cuban Engineers Scholarship Foundation Scholarships

Association of Cuban Engineers
P.O. Box 557575
Miami, FL 33255
Phone: 305-597-9858
Email: president@a-i-c.org
http://www.a-i-c.org
Purpose: To help undergraduate and graduate students of Hispanic heritage who are pursuing degrees in engineering.
Eligibility: Applicants must be U.S. citizens or legal residents of Hispanic heritage who have completed at least 30 units of coursework towards a bachelor's degree or higher in engineering at an ABET-accredited institution located in the United States or Puerto Rico. They must have a GPA of 3.0 or higher and must be current, full-time students (carrying 12 or more semester hours if an undergraduate and 6 or more semester hours as a graduate student). Selection is based on the overall strength of the application.
Target applicants: College students. Graduate school students. Adult students.
Minimum GPA: 3.0
Amount: $500-$2,000.
Number of awards: Varies.
Deadline: December 31.
How to apply: Applications are available online. An application form, official transcript and financial aid award letter are required.
Exclusive: Visit www.UltimateScholarshipBook.com and enter code AS244012 for updates on this award.

(2441) • B.J. Harrod Scholarships

Society of Women Engineers
120 South LaSalle Street
Suite 1515
Chicago, IL 60603
Phone: 877-793-4636
Email: scholarshipapplication@swe.org
http://www.swe.org
Purpose: To aid female engineering students.
Eligibility: Applicants may major in any type of engineering at an accredited institution of higher learning. They must be freshmen and have a GPA of 3.5 or higher.
Target applicants: College students. Adult students.
Minimum GPA: 3.5
Amount: $2,000.
Number of awards: 2.
Deadline: May 15.
How to apply: Applications are available online. An application form is required.
Exclusive: Visit www.UltimateScholarshipBook.com and enter code SO244112 for updates on this award.

(2442) • B.K. Krenzer Reentry Scholarship

Society of Women Engineers
120 South LaSalle Street
Suite 1515
Chicago, IL 60603
Phone: 877-793-4636
Email: scholarshipapplication@swe.org
http://www.swe.org
Purpose: To support reentering female engineering students.
Eligibility: Applicants must have been out of school and out of the job market for at least two years. They must enroll in an accredited engineering or computer science program. A GPA of 3.0 or higher is required. Preference is given to degreed engineers.

Target applicants: High school students. College students. Adult students.
Minimum GPA: 3.0
Amount: $300-$500.
Number of awards: 2.
Scholarship may be renewable.
Deadline: April 1.
How to apply: Applications are available from high school counselors, from departments of education at participating colleges, from the Brown Foundation and online.
Exclusive: Visit www.UltimateScholarshipBook.com and enter code BR244712 for updates on this award.

(2448) • Bruce Lee Scholarship

U.S. Pan Asian American Chamber of Commerce
1329 18th Street NW
Washington, DC 20036
Phone: 800-696-7818
Fax: 202-296-5225
Email: info@uspaacc.com
http://uspaacc.com/scholarships/overview/
Purpose: To support the higher education goals of Asian American students.
Eligibility: Applicants must be U.S. citizens or permanent residents and be high school seniors of Asian or Pacific Heritage who will pursue post-secondary educations at an accredited institution in the U.S. Selection is based on character, the ability to persevere over adversity, academic excellence with at least a 3.0 GPA, community service involvement and financial need. Applicants must be able to attend the Excellence Awards and Scholarships Dinner during the CelebrAsian Annual Conference (in May).
Target applicants: High school students.
Minimum GPA: 3.0
Amount: $5,000.
Number of awards: 1.
Deadline: March 31.
How to apply: Applications are available online.
Exclusive: Visit www.UltimateScholarshipBook.com and enter code U.244812 for updates on this award.

(2449) • Burlington Northern Santa Fe (BNSF) Foundation Scholarship

American Indian Science and Engineering Society
P.O. Box 9828
Albuquerque, NM 87119-9828
Phone: 505-765-1052
Fax: 505-765-5608
http://www.aises.org
Purpose: To provide a four-year scholarship for an American Indian student attending an accredited four-year college or university in a state where Burlington Northern Santa Fe operates.
Eligibility: Applicants must reside in one of the following states: Arizona, California, Colorado, Kansas, Minnesota, Montana, New Mexico, North Dakota, Oklahoma, Oregon, South Dakota or Washington. Applicants must also major in one of the following areas: business, engineering, math, medicine/health administration, natural/physical sciences, technology or education and belong to AISES.
Target applicants: High school students. College students. Adult students.
Minimum GPA: 2.0
Amount: $2,500.
Number of awards: 5.
Scholarship may be renewable.
Deadline: Varies.
How to apply: Applications are available online.
Exclusive: Visit www.UltimateScholarshipBook.com and enter code AM244912 for updates on this award.

(2450) • California Chafee Grant Program

California Student Aid Commission
P.O. Box 419026
Rancho Cordova, CA 95741-9026
Phone: 888-224-7268
Fax: 916-464-8002
Email: studentsupport@csac.ca.gov
http://www.csac.ca.gov
Purpose: To provide educational assistance for students who have been in foster care in California.
Eligibility: Applicants must be current or former foster youth who are under 22 years of age as of July 1 of the award year. Dependency must have been established by the court between the ages of 16 and 18. Financial need is required. Applicants must enroll at least half-time in a program that is at least one academic year long, and they must attend class regularly and maintain good grades.
Target applicants: High school students. College students.
Amount: Up to $5,000.
Number of awards: Varies.
Scholarship may be renewable.
Deadline: Varies.
How to apply: Applications are available online.
Exclusive: Visit www.UltimateScholarshipBook.com and enter code CA245012 for updates on this award.

(2451) • Carmen E. Turner Scholarship

Conference of Minority Transportation Officials
818 18th Street NW, Suite 850
Washington, DC 20006
Phone: 202-530-0551
Fax: 202-530-0617
Email: comto@comto.org
http://www.comto.org
Purpose: To support students who are members of COMTO.
Eligibility: Applicants must have been COMTO members in good standing for at least the past year. Students must be enrolled in an undergraduate or graduate program for at least six credits per semester with at least a 2.5 GPA.
Target applicants: College students. Graduate school students. Adult students.
Minimum GPA: 2.5
Amount: $3,500.
Number of awards: Varies.
Deadline: April 16.
How to apply: Applications are available online.
Exclusive: Visit www.UltimateScholarshipBook.com and enter code CO245112 for updates on this award.

(2452) • Carolyn Bailey Thomas Scholarship

United Negro College Fund (UNCF)
8260 Willow Oaks Corporate Drive
P.O. Box 10444
Fairfax, VA 22031-8044

Target applicants: College students. Graduate school students. Adult students.
Minimum GPA: 3.0
Amount: $2,000.
Number of awards: 1.
Deadline: May 15.
How to apply: Applications are available online. An application form is required.
Exclusive: Visit www.UltimateScholarshipBook.com and enter code SO244212 for updates on this award.

(2443) • Bechtel Foundation Scholarship

Society of Women Engineers
120 South LaSalle Street
Suite 1515
Chicago, IL 60603
Phone: 877-793-4636
Email: scholarshipapplication@swe.org
http://www.swe.org
Purpose: To support female engineering students.
Eligibility: Applicants must be enrolled in an accredited engineering program in their sophomore, junior or senior year. They must be SWE members. A minimum GPA of 3.0 is required.
Target applicants: College students. Adult students.
Minimum GPA: 3.0
Amount: $1,400.
Number of awards: 2.
Deadline: May 15.
How to apply: Applications are available online. An application form is required.
Exclusive: Visit www.UltimateScholarshipBook.com and enter code SO244312 for updates on this award.

(2444) • Berbeco Senior Research Fellowship

United Negro College Fund (UNCF)
8260 Willow Oaks Corporate Drive
P.O. Box 10444
Fairfax, VA 22031-8044
Phone: 800-331-2244
http://www.uncf.org/
Purpose: To encourage African Americans to conduct independent research internationally.
Eligibility: Applicants must be college juniors who attend United Negro College Fund (UNCF) member colleges or universities. The need-based award is for students to work on their senior thesis or research projects outside the U.S. during the summer between their junior and senior years.
Target applicants: College students. Adult students.
Minimum GPA: 2.5
Amount: Up to $6,000.
Number of awards: Varies.
Deadline: Varies.
How to apply: Applications are available online.
Exclusive: Visit www.UltimateScholarshipBook.com and enter code UN244412 for updates on this award.

(2445) • Bertha Lamme Memorial Scholarship

Society of Women Engineers
120 South LaSalle Street
Suite 1515
Chicago, IL 60603
Phone: 877-793-4636
Email: scholarshipapplication@swe.org
http://www.swe.org
Purpose: To aid female engineering students.
Eligibility: Applicants must be college freshmen majoring in electrical engineering at an accredited institution. They must be U.S. citizens. A minimum GPA of 3.5 is required.
Target applicants: College students. Adult students.
Minimum GPA: 3.5
Amount: $1,200.
Number of awards: 1.
Deadline: May 15.
How to apply: Applications are available online. An application form is required.
Exclusive: Visit www.UltimateScholarshipBook.com and enter code SO244512 for updates on this award.

(2446) • Bessie Irene Smith Trust Scholarship

United Negro College Fund (UNCF)
8260 Willow Oaks Corporate Drive
P.O. Box 10444
Fairfax, VA 22031-8044
Phone: 800-331-2244
http://www.uncf.org/
Purpose: To help African American students attending United Negro College Fund (UNCF) member colleges and universities.
Eligibility: Applicants must have a minimum 2.5 GPA, complete the Free Application for Federal Student Aid (FAFSA) and have unmet financial need that is verified by the college or university financial aid office. Students are encouraged to complete the UNCF General Scholarship application to be matched with scholarships for which they meet the criteria.
Target applicants: High school students. College students. Adult students.
Minimum GPA: 2.5
Amount: Varies.
Number of awards: Varies.
Deadline: Varies.
How to apply: Applications are available online.
Exclusive: Visit www.UltimateScholarshipBook.com and enter code UN244612 for updates on this award.

(2447) • Brown Foundation Scholarships

Brown Foundation Scholarship Program
P.O. Box 4862
Topeka, KS 66604
Phone: 785-235-3939
Fax: 785-235-1001
Email: brownfound@juno.com
http://www.brownvboard.org/foundatn/sclrbroc.htm
Purpose: To help minority students who are either high school seniors or college juniors who want to teach.
Eligibility: High school seniors should have a demonstrated desire to enter a teacher education program through volunteer experience, work experience and/or references and should plan to enroll in college at least half-time. The high school senior scholarship is $300 for the freshman year. College juniors must be accepted to a teacher education program and attend at least half-time. The college award is $500 per year for two academic years. Selection for both awards is based on GPA, school, community and extracurricular activities, career plans and goals in education, essays and two recommendations.

Phone: 800-331-2244
http://www.uncf.org/
Purpose: To help African Americans attending United Negro College Fund (UNCF) member colleges and universities.
Eligibility: Applicants must have a minimum 3.0 GPA, complete the Free Application for Federal Student Aid (FAFSA) and have unmet financial need that is verified by the college or university financial aid office. Students are encouraged to complete the UNCF General Scholarship application to be matched with scholarships for which they meet the criteria.
Target applicants: High school students. College students. Adult students.
Minimum GPA: 3.0
Amount: Varies.
Number of awards: Varies.
Deadline: Varies.
How to apply: Applications are available online.
Exclusive: Visit www.UltimateScholarshipBook.com and enter code UN245212 for updates on this award.

(2453) • Catherine W. Pierce Scholarship

United Negro College Fund (UNCF)
8260 Willow Oaks Corporate Drive
P.O. Box 10444
Fairfax, VA 22031-8044
Phone: 800-331-2244
http://www.uncf.org/
Purpose: To help African American students majoring in art or history.
Eligibility: Applicants must have a minimum 3.0 GPA, complete the Free Application for Federal Student Aid (FAFSA) and have unmet financial need that is verified by the college or university financial aid office. UNCF students are encouraged to complete the UNCF General Scholarship application to be matched with scholarships for which they meet the criteria.
Target applicants: High school students. College students. Adult students.
Minimum GPA: 3.0
Amount: Up to $5,000.
Number of awards: Varies.
Deadline: Varies.
How to apply: Applications are available online.
Exclusive: Visit www.UltimateScholarshipBook.com and enter code UN245312 for updates on this award.

(2454) • CDM Scholarship/Internship

United Negro College Fund (UNCF)
8260 Willow Oaks Corporate Drive
P.O. Box 10444
Fairfax, VA 22031-8044
Phone: 800-331-2244
http://www.uncf.org/
Purpose: To support African Americans studying engineering, science or construction disciplines.
Eligibility: Applicants must be undergraduates majoring in engineering, science or construction fields, such as chemical, civil, electrical, environmental, geotechnical, geology/hydrogeology, geography, GIS, mechanical, mining and structural or must be planning to pursue a master's degree in one of these disciplines at United Negro College Fund (UNCF) member colleges and universities. A minimum 3.0 GPA is required. There is also an internship as a part of the program.
Target applicants: High school students. College students. Graduate school students. Adult students.
Minimum GPA: 3.0
Amount: $6,000 plus $2,500 living stipend.
Number of awards: 6.
Deadline: January 14.
How to apply: Applications are available online.
Exclusive: Visit www.UltimateScholarshipBook.com and enter code UN245412 for updates on this award.

(2455) • CHCI Scholarship Award

Congressional Hispanic Caucus Institute Inc.
911 2nd Street NE
Washington, DC 20002
Phone: 202-543-1771
Email: shernandez@chci.org
http://www.chci.org
Purpose: To award Latino students for public service activities in their communities.
Eligibility: Applicants must be Latinos who have actively participated in public service; be accepted as full-time students into an accredited community college, four-year university or a graduate/professional program; demonstrate financial need and have good writing skills. Students should submit applications, resumes, essays, Student Aid Reports, two recommendation letters, transcripts and a self-addressed stamped postcard to be notified when application is received.
Target applicants: College students. Graduate school students. Adult students.
Amount: $1,000-$5,000.
Number of awards: Varies.
Deadline: Varies.
How to apply: Applications are available online.
Exclusive: Visit www.UltimateScholarshipBook.com and enter code CO245512 for updates on this award.

(2456) • Cherokee Nation PELL Scholarship

Cherokee Nation
Cherokee Nation Undergraduate Scholarship Programs
Attn.: Higher Education
P.O. Box 948
Tahlequah, OK 74465
Phone: 918-456-0671
Email: highereducation@cherokee.org
http://www.cherokee.org
Purpose: To support students who are Cherokee Nation Tribal Members.
Eligibility: Applicants must be high school senior Cherokee Nation tribal members planning to attend an institution of higher education.
Target applicants: High school students.
Amount: Varies.
Number of awards: Varies.
Deadline: Varies.
How to apply: Applications are available online.
Exclusive: Visit www.UltimateScholarshipBook.com and enter code CH245612 for updates on this award.

(2457) • Chickasaw Nation Education Foundation Program

Chickasaw Nation Education Foundation
P.O. Box 1726
Ad, OK 74821

Phone: 580-421-9031
http://www.chickasaw.net
Purpose: To assist Chickasaw students who demonstrate academic excellence, community service, dedication to learning and a commitment to Native Americans.
Eligibility: Applicants must be full-time Chickasaw students. Other eligibility requirements vary by scholarship.
Target applicants: High school students. College students. Graduate school students. Adult students.
Amount: Varies.
Number of awards: Varies.
Deadline: Varies.
How to apply: Applications are available online.
Exclusive: Visit www.UltimateScholarshipBook.com and enter code CH245712 for updates on this award.

(2458) · Chief Manuelito Scholarship Program

Office of Navajo Nation Scholarship and Financial Assistance
http://www.onnsfa.org
Purpose: The scholarship was created to help high-achieving Navajo students.
Eligibility: Students must be enrolled members of the Navajo nation, submit a Certificate of Indian Blood, attend a regionally-accredited school and complete a FAFSA form. Students must also complete a Navajo Government course (available online).
Target applicants: High school students. College students. Graduate school students. Adult students.
Amount: $7,000.
Number of awards: Varies.
Scholarship may be renewable.
Deadline: Varies.
How to apply: Applications are available online and must be submitted to your agency, which is listed online.
Exclusive: Visit www.UltimateScholarshipBook.com and enter code OF245812 for updates on this award.

(2459) · Chrysler Corporation Scholarship

United Negro College Fund (UNCF)
8260 Willow Oaks Corporate Drive
P.O. Box 10444
Fairfax, VA 22031-8044
Phone: 800-331-2244
http://www.uncf.org/
Purpose: To help African Americans attending United Negro College Fund (UNCF) member colleges and universities.
Eligibility: Applicants must have a minimum 2.5 GPA, complete the Free Application for Federal Student Aid (FAFSA) and have unmet financial need that is verified by the college or university financial aid office. UNCF students are encouraged to complete the UNCF General Scholarship application to be matched with scholarships for which they meet the criteria.
Target applicants: High school students. College students. Adult students.
Minimum GPA: 2.5
Amount: $3,900.
Number of awards: 10.
Deadline: Varies.
How to apply: Applications are available online.
Exclusive: Visit www.UltimateScholarshipBook.com and enter code UN245912 for updates on this award.

(2460) · Citizen Potawatomi Nation Tribal Rolls Scholarship

Citizen Potawatomi Nation
1601 S. Gordon Cooper Drive
Shawnee, OK 74801
Phone: 405-275-3121
Fax: 405-878-4653
Email: lcapps@potawatomi.org
http://www.potawatomi.org
Purpose: To assist Citizen Potawatomi Nation tribal members who are pursuing higher education.
Eligibility: Applicants must be Citizen Potawatomi Nation tribal members who are getting vocational training or earning an academic degree at an accredited postsecondary institution. Selection is based on the overall strength of the application.
Target applicants: High school students. College students. Graduate school students. Adult students.
Amount: Up to $1,500.
Number of awards: Varies.
Scholarship may be renewable.
Deadline: December 1, June 1, August 1.
How to apply: Applications are available online. An application form, proof of enrollment, federal tax return information and transcript are required.
Exclusive: Visit www.UltimateScholarshipBook.com and enter code CI246012 for updates on this award.

(2461) · Coleman Entrepreneurial Scholarship

Coleman Entrepreneurial Scholarship Program
Scholarship Management Services
One Scholarship Way
P.O. Box 297
Saint Peter, MN 56082
Phone: 800-537-4180
http://www.thecolemanscholarship.org
Purpose: To support students majoring or concentrating in entrepreneurship.
Eligibility: Applicants must be current sophomores or juniors in qualifying Historically Black Colleges and Universities. They must be U.S. citizens of African-American or Hispanic descent. Applicants must also have a GPA of 3.0 or higher and enroll full-time for the upcoming academic year.
Target applicants: College students. Adult students.
Minimum GPA: 3.0
Amount: $5,000.
Number of awards: Up to 10.
Deadline: February 28.
How to apply: Applications are available online. An application form, appraisal and transcript are required.
Exclusive: Visit www.UltimateScholarshipBook.com and enter code CO246112 for updates on this award.

(2462) · Colgate-Palmolive Company/UNCF Scholarship

United Negro College Fund (UNCF)
8260 Willow Oaks Corporate Drive
P.O. Box 10444
Fairfax, VA 22031-8044
Phone: 800-331-2244
http://www.uncf.org/

Purpose: To help African American sophomores, juniors and seniors majoring in business with a concentration in marketing.
Eligibility: Applicants must have a minimum 3.0 GPA and attend United Negro College Fund (UNCF) member colleges and universities. Students must complete the Free Application for Federal Student Aid (FAFSA) and have unmet financial need that is verified by the college or university financial aid office. UNCF students are encouraged to complete the UNCF General Scholarship application to be matched with scholarships for which they meet the criteria.
Target applicants: College students. Adult students.
Minimum GPA: 3.0
Amount: Varies.
Number of awards: Varies.
Deadline: Varies.
How to apply: Applications are available online.
Exclusive: Visit www.UltimateScholarshipBook.com and enter code UN246212 for updates on this award.

(2463) • Community College Transfer Scholarship Program

Hispanic Scholarship Fund (HSF)
55 Second Street
Suite 1500
San Francisco, CA 94105
Phone: 877-473-4636
Fax: 415-808-2302
Email: scholar1@hsf.net
http://www.hsf.net
Purpose: To support students of Hispanic heritage who plan to transfer from a community college program to a four-year college or university.
Eligibility: Applicants must be of Hispanic heritage (one parent fully Hispanic or each parent half-Hispanic) and be a part-time or full-time community college student with a minimum 3.0 GPA. Applicants must plan to transfer to a four-year college or university the following academic year.
Target applicants: College students. Adult students.
Minimum GPA: 3.0
Amount: $1,000-$2,500.
Number of awards: Varies.
Deadline: December 15.
How to apply: Applications are available online.
Exclusive: Visit www.UltimateScholarshipBook.com and enter code HI246312 for updates on this award.

(2464) • Consortium Fellowship

Consortium for Graduate Study in Management
5585 Pershing
Suite 240
St. Louis, MO 63112-4621
Phone: 314-877-5500
Email: frontdesk@cgsm.org
http://www.cgsm.org
Purpose: To support graduate business students at member schools.
Eligibility: Applicants must be African Americans, Hispanic Americans or Native Americans and U.S. citizens and U.S. permanent residents of other races and ethnicities who fulfill the Consortium's mission. Applicants must have a bachelor's degree, and the degree may be in any academic discipline from an accredited institution recognized by Consortium member schools. The fellowship supports full-time graduate business studies at member schools only. Applicants must submit two references, transcripts, copies of GMAT scores and application fees. All applicants must also interview with a Consortium representative. Note: We do not recommend applying to scholarships that charge application fees. However, some scholarships of this type charge fees and are included for completeness.
Target applicants: Graduate school students. Adult students.
Amount: Full tuition and fees.
Number of awards: Varies.
Deadline: January 5 and November 15.
How to apply: Applications are available online.
Exclusive: Visit www.UltimateScholarshipBook.com and enter code CO246412 for updates on this award.

(2465) • Continuing Education Award

Slovenian Women's Union of America
Mary Turvey, SWUA Scholarship Director
4 Lawrence Drive
Marquette, MI 49855
Email: mturvey@aol.com
http://www.swua.org
Purpose: To promote Slovenian culture.
Eligibility: Applicants must be returning to an accredited college in the fall as full- or part-time students and must have been a member of the SWUA for at least three years or an active participant. Students must include a photograph, resume, FAFSA, income tax return and a letter of recommendation from their SWU branch president or secretary. The awards committee considers life goals and involvement in school, church and community.
Target applicants: College students. Graduate school students. Adult students.
Amount: $500.
Number of awards: Varies.
Deadline: March 1.
How to apply: Applications are available online and from SWUA branch secretaries.
Exclusive: Visit www.UltimateScholarshipBook.com and enter code SL246512 for updates on this award.

(2466) • Coy G. Eklund Scholarship

United Negro College Fund (UNCF)
8260 Willow Oaks Corporate Drive
P.O. Box 10444
Fairfax, VA 22031-8044
Phone: 800-331-2244
http://www.uncf.org/
Purpose: To help African Americans majoring in business at United Negro College Fund (UNCF) Member Colleges and Universities.
Eligibility: Applicants must have a minimum 2.5 GPA, complete the Free Application for Federal Student Aid (FAFSA) and have unmet financial need that is verified by the college or university financial aid office. UNCF students are encouraged to complete the UNCF General Scholarship application to be matched with scholarships for which they meet the criteria.
Target applicants: High school students. College students. Adult students.
Minimum GPA: 2.5
Amount: Varies.
Number of awards: Varies.
Deadline: Varies.
How to apply: Applications are available online.
Exclusive: Visit www.UltimateScholarshipBook.com and enter code UN246612 for updates on this award.

(2467) • David Risling Emergency Aid Scholarship

Association on American Indian Affairs
Lisa Wyzlic, Director of Scholarship Programs
966 Hungerford Drive, Suite 12-B
Rockville, MD 20850
Phone: 240-314-7155
Fax: 240-314-7159
Email: general.aaia@verizon.net
http://www.indian-affairs.org

Purpose: To provide emergency financial assistance to Native Americans who face temporary circumstances which would prevent them from going to school.
Eligibility: Applicants must be full-time students in the continental U.S. or Alaska, and they must not be in a technical, trade or seminary program.
Target applicants: College students. Adult students.
Amount: $100-$400.
Number of awards: Varies.
Deadline: Varies.
How to apply: Applications are available online.
Exclusive: Visit www.UltimateScholarshipBook.com and enter code AS246712 for updates on this award.

(2468) • Displaced Homemaker Scholarship

Association on American Indian Affairs
Lisa Wyzlic, Director of Scholarship Programs
966 Hungerford Drive, Suite 12-B
Rockville, MD 20850
Phone: 240-314-7155
Fax: 240-314-7159
Email: general.aaia@verizon.net
http://www.indian-affairs.org

Purpose: To provide assistance to Native American/Alaska Native undergraduate men and women in any curriculum who would be unable to complete college due to family responsibilities.
Eligibility: Applicants must be full-time students able to prove financial need, proof of tribal enrollment and Certificate of Indian Blood (showing 1/4 Indian blood).
Target applicants: College students. Adult students.
Amount: $1,500.
Number of awards: Varies.
Deadline: June 18.
How to apply: Applications are available online.
Exclusive: Visit www.UltimateScholarshipBook.com and enter code AS246812 for updates on this award.

(2469) • Donald Malcolm MacArthur Scholarship

St. Andrew's Society of Washington, DC
Charity and Education Committee
P.O. Box 372
Glen Echo, MD 20812
Email: secretary@saintandrewsociety.com
http://www.saintandrewsociety.com

Purpose: To encourage foster study between the U.S. and Scotland, monies are awarded to third and fourth year college students and full-time graduate students who are either Scots wishing to study in the U.S., or U.S. students intending to study in Scotland.
Eligibility: Eligible U.S. candidates must live or attend school within a 200 mile radius of Washington, DC and be of Scottish descent.
Target applicants: College students. Graduate school students. Adult students.
Amount: $2,500.
Number of awards: Varies.
Deadline: April 30.
How to apply: Applications are available online.
Exclusive: Visit www.UltimateScholarshipBook.com and enter code ST246912 for updates on this award.

(2470) • Doris and John Carpenter Scholarship

United Negro College Fund (UNCF)
8260 Willow Oaks Corporate Drive
P.O. Box 10444
Fairfax, VA 22031-8044
Phone: 800-331-2244
http://www.uncf.org/

Purpose: To help African Americans with the most financial need.
Eligibility: Applicants must be freshmen at United Negro College Fund (UNCF) member colleges or universities and must have a minimum 2.5 GPA.
Target applicants: High school students.
Minimum GPA: 2.5
Amount: $2,000-$5,000.
Number of awards: Varies.
Deadline: Varies.
How to apply: Applications are available online.
Exclusive: Visit www.UltimateScholarshipBook.com and enter code UN247012 for updates on this award.

(2471) • Dorothy N. McNeal Scholarship

United Negro College Fund (UNCF)
8260 Willow Oaks Corporate Drive
P.O. Box 10444
Fairfax, VA 22031-8044
Phone: 800-331-2244
http://www.uncf.org/

Purpose: To support students interested in pursuing community service careers.
Eligibility: Applicants must be African American students attending a UNCF member college or university with a GPA of at least 2.5. Students must complete the Free Application for Federal Student Aid (FAFSA) and have unmet financial need that is verified by the college or university financial aid office. Applicants are encouraged to complete the UNCF General Scholarship application to be matched with scholarships for which they meet the criteria.
Target applicants: High school students. College students. Adult students.
Minimum GPA: 2.5
Amount: Varies.
Number of awards: Varies.
Deadline: Varies.
How to apply: Applications are available online.
Exclusive: Visit www.UltimateScholarshipBook.com and enter code UN247112 for updates on this award.

(2472) • Dr. James M. Rosin Scholarship

United Negro College Fund (UNCF)
8260 Willow Oaks Corporate Drive
P.O. Box 10444
Fairfax, VA 22031-8044

Phone: 800-331-2244
http://www.uncf.org/
Purpose: To help African American students pursuing bachelor's degrees in the health sciences and who plan for careers in the health sciences field.
Eligibility: Applicants must have a minimum 3.0 GPA, complete the Free Application for Federal Student Aid (FAFSA) and have unmet financial need that is verified by the college or university financial aid office. UNCF students are encouraged to complete the UNCF General Scholarship application to be matched with scholarships for which they meet the criteria. Applicants must show dedication to personal growth, helping others and education.
Target applicants: High school students. College students. Adult students.
Minimum GPA: 3.0
Amount: $5,000.
Number of awards: 1.
Deadline: Varies.
How to apply: Applications are available online.
Exclusive: Visit www.UltimateScholarshipBook.com and enter code UN247212 for updates on this award.

(2473) • Dr. Joe Ratliff Challenge

United Negro College Fund (UNCF)
8260 Willow Oaks Corporate Drive
P.O. Box 10444
Fairfax, VA 22031-8044
Phone: 800-331-2244
http://www.uncf.org/
Purpose: To help African American students attending United Negro College Fund (UNCF) Member Colleges and Universities and majoring in religion.
Eligibility: Applicants must have a minimum 2.5 GPA, complete the Free Application for Federal Student Aid (FAFSA) and have unmet financial need that is verified by the college or university financial aid office. Students are encouraged to complete the UNCF General Scholarship application to be matched with scholarships for which they meet the criteria.
Target applicants: High school students. College students. Adult students.
Minimum GPA: 2.5
Amount: Up to $3,000.
Number of awards: Varies.
Deadline: Varies.
How to apply: Applications are available online.
Exclusive: Visit www.UltimateScholarshipBook.com and enter code UN247312 for updates on this award.

(2474) • Dr. Scholl Foundation Scholarship

United Negro College Fund (UNCF)
8260 Willow Oaks Corporate Drive
P.O. Box 10444
Fairfax, VA 22031-8044
Phone: 800-331-2244
http://www.uncf.org/
Purpose: To help African American students attending United Negro College Fund (UNCF) member colleges and universities.
Eligibility: Applicants must have a minimum 2.5 GPA, complete the Free Application for Federal Student Aid (FAFSA) and have unmet financial need that is verified by the college or university financial aid office. Students are encouraged to complete the UNCF General Scholarship application to be matched with scholarships for which they meet the criteria.
Target applicants: High school students. College students. Adult students.
Minimum GPA: 2.5
Amount: Varies.
Number of awards: Varies.
Deadline: Varies.
How to apply: Applications are available online.
Exclusive: Visit www.UltimateScholarshipBook.com and enter code UN247412 for updates on this award.

(2475) • Drs. Poh Shien and Judy Young Scholarship

U.S. Pan Asian American Chamber of Commerce
1329 18th Street NW
Washington, DC 20036
Phone: 800-696-7818
Fax: 202-296-5225
Email: info@uspaacc.com
http://uspaacc.com/scholarships/overview/
Purpose: To support the higher education goals of Asian American students.
Eligibility: Applicants must be U.S. citizens or permanent residents and be high school seniors of Asian or Pacific Heritage who will pursue post-secondary educations at an accredited institution in the U.S. Selection is based on academic excellence, leadership in extracurricular activities, community service involvement and financial need. Minimum 3.5 GPA required. Applicants must be able to attend the Excellence Awards and Scholarships Dinner during the CelebrAsian Annual Conference (in May).
Target applicants: High school students.
Minimum GPA: 3.5
Amount: Up to $5,000.
Number of awards: 1.
Deadline: March 31.
How to apply: Applications are available online.
Exclusive: Visit www.UltimateScholarshipBook.com and enter code U.247512 for updates on this award.

(2476) • Earl and Patricia Armstrong Scholarship

United Negro College Fund (UNCF)
8260 Willow Oaks Corporate Drive
P.O. Box 10444
Fairfax, VA 22031-8044
Phone: 800-331-2244
http://www.uncf.org/
Purpose: To promote the health sciences among African American students.
Eligibility: Applicants must major in pre-medicine, biology or health, have a minimum 3.0 GPA, complete the Free Application for Federal Student Aid (FAFSA) and have unmet financial need that is verified by the college or university financial aid office. UNCF students are encouraged to complete the UNCF General Scholarship application to be matched with scholarships for which they meet the criteria.
Target applicants: High school students. College students. Adult students.
Minimum GPA: 3.0
Amount: Up to $3,000.
Number of awards: 1.
Deadline: Varies.
How to apply: Applications are available online.

Exclusive: Visit www.UltimateScholarshipBook.com and enter code UN247612 for updates on this award.

(2477) • Earl Graves Scholarship

National Association for the Advancement of Colored People
The United Negro College Fund
Scholarships and Grants Administration
8260 Willow Oaks Corporate Drive
Fairfax, VA 22031
Phone: 800-331-2244
Email: youth@naacpnet.org
http://www.naacp.org

Purpose: The NAACP created its scholarships to promote equal opportunity in education.
Eligibility: Applicants must be junior or senior business majors or accepted into a business master's or doctoral program at an accredited U.S. college or university, in the top 20 percent of their class and attend school full-time.
Target applicants: College students. Graduate school students. Adult students.
Amount: $5,000.
Number of awards: Varies.
Deadline: The last Friday in the month of March.
How to apply: Applications are available online and by written request.
Exclusive: Visit www.UltimateScholarshipBook.com and enter code NA247712 for updates on this award.

(2478) • Edward and Hazel Stephenson Scholarship

United Negro College Fund (UNCF)
8260 Willow Oaks Corporate Drive
P.O. Box 10444
Fairfax, VA 22031-8044
Phone: 800-331-2244
http://www.uncf.org/

Purpose: To help African American seniors at United Negro College Fund (UNCF) member colleges or universities.
Eligibility: Applicants must have a minimum 2.5 GPA, complete the Free Application for Federal Student Aid (FAFSA) and have unmet financial need that is verified by the college or university financial aid office. Students are encouraged to complete the UNCF General Scholarship application to be matched with scholarships for which they meet the criteria.
Target applicants: College students. Adult students.
Minimum GPA: 2.5
Amount: $1,000-$3,000.
Number of awards: Varies.
Deadline: Varies.
How to apply: Applications are available online.
Exclusive: Visit www.UltimateScholarshipBook.com and enter code UN247812 for updates on this award.

(2479) • Edward D. Grigg Scholarship

United Negro College Fund (UNCF)
8260 Willow Oaks Corporate Drive
P.O. Box 10444
Fairfax, VA 22031-8044
Phone: 800-331-2244
http://www.uncf.org/

Purpose: To support needy African American students.
Eligibility: Applicants must have a minimum 2.5 GPA, complete the Free Application for Federal Student Aid (FAFSA) and have unmet financial need that is verified by the college or university financial aid office. Applicants must be UNCF students and are encouraged to complete the UNCF General Scholarship application to be matched with scholarships for which they meet the criteria.
Target applicants: High school students. College students. Adult students.
Minimum GPA: 2.5
Amount: Varies.
Number of awards: Varies.
Deadline: Varies.
How to apply: Applications are available online.
Exclusive: Visit www.UltimateScholarshipBook.com and enter code UN247912 for updates on this award.

(2480) • Edward N. Ney Scholarship

United Negro College Fund (UNCF)
8260 Willow Oaks Corporate Drive
P.O. Box 10444
Fairfax, VA 22031-8044
Phone: 800-331-2244
http://www.uncf.org/

Purpose: To support African American students at UNCF member schools.
Eligibility: Applicants must have a minimum 3.5 GPA, complete the Free Application for Federal Student Aid (FAFSA) and have unmet financial need that is verified by the college or university financial aid office. Students are encouraged to complete the UNCF General Scholarship application to be matched with scholarships for which they meet the criteria.
Target applicants: High school students. College students. Adult students.
Minimum GPA: 3.5
Amount: Varies.
Number of awards: Varies.
Deadline: Varies.
How to apply: Applications are available online.
Exclusive: Visit www.UltimateScholarshipBook.com and enter code UN248012 for updates on this award.

(2481) • Elizabeth and Sherman Asche Memorial Scholarship

Association on American Indian Affairs
Lisa Wyzlic, Director of Scholarship Programs
966 Hungerford Drive, Suite 12-B
Rockville, MD 20850
Phone: 240-314-7155
Fax: 240-314-7159
Email: general.aaia@verizon.net
http://www.indian-affairs.org

Purpose: To provide financial assistance to American Indians who are seeking undergraduate or graduate degrees in public health or science.
Eligibility: Applicants must be American Indians who are studying full-time in public health or science programs. They must be full-time students and must not be enrolled in a technical or trade program or seminary. The scholarship is open to undergraduate and graduate students.
Target applicants: High school students. College students. Graduate school students. Adult students.
Amount: $1,500.

Number of awards: Varies.
Deadline: Varies.
How to apply: Applications are available online.
Exclusive: Visit www.UltimateScholarshipBook.com and enter code AS248112 for updates on this award.

(2482) • Ella Fitzgerald Charitable Foundation Scholarship

United Negro College Fund (UNCF)
8260 Willow Oaks Corporate Drive
P.O. Box 10444
Fairfax, VA 22031-8044
Phone: 800-331-2244
http://www.uncf.org/
Purpose: To support music students as a testament to Ella Fitzgerald's love of music.
Eligibility: Applicants must be African American students majoring in music with a minimum 2.5 GPA. Students must attend a UNCF member college or university and demonstrate financial need.
Target applicants: High school students. College students. Adult students.
Minimum GPA: 2.5
Amount: Varies.
Number of awards: Varies.
Deadline: Varies.
How to apply: Applications are available online.
Exclusive: Visit www.UltimateScholarshipBook.com and enter code UN248212 for updates on this award.

(2483) • Emilie Hesemeyer Memorial Scholarship

Association on American Indian Affairs
Lisa Wyzlic, Director of Scholarship Programs
966 Hungerford Drive, Suite 12-B
Rockville, MD 20850
Phone: 240-314-7155
Fax: 240-314-7159
Email: general.aaia@verizon.net
http://www.indian-affairs.org
Purpose: To provide financial assistance to Native Americans, especially those who are studying education.
Eligibility: Applicants must be Native Americans who are full-time students from the continental U.S. or Alaska. Preference is given to those who are studying education.
Target applicants: High school students. College students. Adult students.
Amount: $1,500.
Number of awards: Varies.
Scholarship may be renewable.
Deadline: Varies.
How to apply: Applications are available online.
Exclusive: Visit www.UltimateScholarshipBook.com and enter code AS248312 for updates on this award.

(2484) • Eugene and Elinor Kotur Scholarship Trust Fund

Ukrainian Fraternal Association
371 N. 9th Avenue
Scranton, PA 18504-2005
Phone: 570-342-0937
Fax: 570-347-5649
http://www.members.tripod.com/~ufa_home
Purpose: To support Ukrainian students.
Eligibility: Applicants must be in their sophomore year of college or higher at one of 30 participating schools. They must be of Ukrainian descent and have been members of the Ukrainian Fraternal Association for two years.
Target applicants: College students. Adult students.
Amount: At least $1,000.
Number of awards: Varies.
Deadline: Varies.
How to apply: Applications are available by mail or phone.
Exclusive: Visit www.UltimateScholarshipBook.com and enter code UK248412 for updates on this award.

(2485) • Fannie Mae Foundation Scholarship

United Negro College Fund (UNCF)
8260 Willow Oaks Corporate Drive
P.O. Box 10444
Fairfax, VA 22031-8044
Phone: 800-331-2244
http://www.uncf.org/
Purpose: To help African American rising juniors planning careers in the fields of housing and community development.
Eligibility: Applicants must be full-time students attending Benedict College, Bethune-Cookman College, Johnson C. Smith University, LeMoyne-Owen College or United Negro College Fund (UNCF) Member Colleges and Universities. Students should have community development/community service experience, financial need and a minimum 3.0 GPA. Applicants must also submit transcripts, essays, two recommendation letters and small photos.
Target applicants: College students. Adult students.
Minimum GPA: 3.0
Amount: Varies.
Number of awards: 12.
Deadline: Varies.
How to apply: Applications are available online.
Exclusive: Visit www.UltimateScholarshipBook.com and enter code UN248512 for updates on this award.

(2486) • Financial Services Institution

United Negro College Fund (UNCF)
8260 Willow Oaks Corporate Drive
P.O. Box 10444
Fairfax, VA 22031-8044
Phone: 800-331-2244
http://www.uncf.org/
Purpose: To help African Americans majoring in Finance at United Negro College Fund (UNCF) Member Colleges and Universities.
Eligibility: Applicants must have a minimum 2.5 GPA, complete the Free Application for Federal Student Aid (FAFSA) and have unmet financial need that is verified by the college or university financial aid office. UNCF students are encouraged to complete the UNCF General Scholarship application to be matched with scholarships for which they meet the criteria.
Target applicants: High school students. College students. Adult students.
Minimum GPA: 2.5
Amount: Varies.
Number of awards: Varies.
Deadline: Varies.

How to apply: Applications are available online.
Exclusive: Visit www.UltimateScholarshipBook.com and enter code UN248612 for updates on this award.

(2487) • Florence Young Memorial Scholarship

Association on American Indian Affairs
Lisa Wyzlic, Director of Scholarship Programs
966 Hungerford Drive, Suite 12-B
Rockville, MD 20850
Phone: 240-314-7155
Fax: 240-314-7159
Email: general.aaia@verizon.net
http://www.indian-affairs.org
Purpose: To provide financial assistance to Native Americans who are working toward a master's degree in art, public health or law.
Eligibility: Applicants must be full-time students from the continental U.S. or Alaska.
Target applicants: Graduate school students. Adult students.
Amount: $1,500.
Number of awards: Varies.
Deadline: Varies.
How to apply: Applications are available online.
Exclusive: Visit www.UltimateScholarshipBook.com and enter code AS248712 for updates on this award.

(2488) • Forum for Concerns of Minorities Scholarship

American Society for Clinical Laboratory Science
6701 Democracy Boulevard, Suite 300
Bethesda, MD 20817
Phone: 301-657-2768
Fax: 301-657-2909
Email: ascls@ascls.org
http://www.ascls.org
Purpose: To assist minority students in becoming clinical laboratory scientists and clinical laboratory technicians.
Eligibility: Applicants must be minority students accepted to an NAACLS-accredited Clinical Laboratory Science/Medical Technology program or a Clinical Laboratory Technician/Medical Laboratory Technician program. They must also demonstrate financial need.
Target applicants: High school students. College students. Graduate school students. Adult students.
Amount: Varies.
Number of awards: 2.
Deadline: April 1.
How to apply: Applications are available online.
Exclusive: Visit www.UltimateScholarshipBook.com and enter code AM248812 for updates on this award.

(2489) • Foundation Scholarships

CIRI Foundation
3600 San Jeronimo Drive
Suite 256
Anchorage, AK 99508-2870
Phone: 800-764-3382
Fax: 907-793-3585
Email: tcf@thecirifoundation.org
http://www.thecirifoundation.org
Purpose: To provide financial aid for Alaska Natives.
Eligibility: Applicants must be qualified Alaska Native beneficiaries who plan to attend or are currently attending undergraduate or graduate institutions. There are a number of awards based on field of study or career goal. Applicants must submit applications, proof of eligibility, reference letter, transcripts, purpose statements and proof of enrollment.
Target applicants: High school students. College students. Graduate school students. Adult students.
Amount: $500-$20,000.
Number of awards: Varies.
Scholarship may be renewable.
Deadline: June 1.
How to apply: Applications are available online.
Exclusive: Visit www.UltimateScholarshipBook.com and enter code CI248912 for updates on this award.

(2490) • Frances Crawford Marvin American Indian Scholarship

National Society Daughters of the American Revolution
Committee Services Office
Attn.: Scholarships
1776 D Street NW
Washington, DC 20006-5303
Phone: 202-628-1776
http://www.dar.org
Purpose: To assist Native American students.
Eligibility: Applicants must be Native Americans able to prove Native American blood, demonstrate financial need and academic achievement, be enrolled full-time at a college or university and have a minimum 3.0 GPA. Students must obtain a letter of sponsorship from their local DAR chapter. However, affiliation with DAR is not required.
Target applicants: College students. Adult students.
Minimum GPA: 3.0
Amount: Varies.
Number of awards: 1.
Deadline: February 1.
How to apply: Applications are available by written request with a self-addressed, stamped envelope.
Exclusive: Visit www.UltimateScholarshipBook.com and enter code NA249012 for updates on this award.

(2491) • Frederick D. Patterson Scholarship

United Negro College Fund (UNCF)
8260 Willow Oaks Corporate Drive
P.O. Box 10444
Fairfax, VA 22031-8044
Phone: 800-331-2244
http://www.uncf.org/
Purpose: To help African Americans attending United Negro College Fund (UNCF) Member Colleges and Universities.
Eligibility: Applicants must have a minimum 2.5 GPA, complete the Free Application for Federal Student Aid (FAFSA) and have unmet financial need that is verified by the college or university financial aid office. Students are encouraged to complete the UNCF General Scholarship application to be matched with scholarships for which they meet the criteria.
Target applicants: High school students. College students. Adult students.
Minimum GPA: 2.5
Amount: Varies.
Number of awards: Varies.
Deadline: Varies.
How to apply: Applications are available online.

Exclusive: Visit www.UltimateScholarshipBook.com and enter code UN249112 for updates on this award.

(2492) • GAPA's George Choy Memorial Scholarship

Horizons Foundation
870 Market Street
Suite 728
San Francisco, CA 94102
Phone: 415-398-2333
Fax: 415-398-4733
Email: info@horizonsfoundation.org
http://www.horizonsfoundation.org

Purpose: To assist Bay Area gay, lesbian, bisexual and transgender Asian and Pacific Islander graduating high school students.

Eligibility: Applicants should have at least 25 percent Asian/Pacific Islander ancestry, plan to attend or currently attend a post-secondary institution as a freshman or sophomore and reside in one of the nine Bay Area counties (Alameda, Contra Costa, Marin, San Francisco, San Mateo, Santa Clara, Napa, Sonoma or Solano). Preference is given to those who are lesbian, gay, bisexual or transgender or who are involved in the LGBT community.

Target applicants: High school students. College students. Adult students.

Minimum GPA: 2.75

Amount: $1,000.

Number of awards: Varies.

Deadline: Varies.

How to apply: Applications are available by phone.

Exclusive: Visit www.UltimateScholarshipBook.com and enter code HO249212 for updates on this award.

(2493) • Gates Millennium Scholars Program

Gates Foundation
P.O. Box 10500
Fairfax, VA 22031
Phone: 877-690-4677
http://www.gmsp.org

Purpose: To provide outstanding minority students with opportunities to complete their undergraduate college educations.

Eligibility: Applicants must be African American, American Indian/ Alaska Native, Asian Pacific Islander American or Hispanic American students with a minimum 3.3 GPA, enter an accredited college or university and have significant financial need. Applicants must also be eligible for federal Pell Grants.

Target applicants: High school students.

Minimum GPA: 3.3

Amount: Varies.

Number of awards: 1000.

Deadline: January 10.

How to apply: Students are nominated by teachers, principals or other education professionals. Nomination materials are available online.

Exclusive: Visit www.UltimateScholarshipBook.com and enter code GA249312 for updates on this award.

(2494) • GEM Fellowship Program

National Consortium for Graduate Degrees for Minorities in Engineering and Science Inc. (GEM)
GEM Consortium
P.O. Box 537
Notre Dame, IN 46556
Phone: 574-631-7771
Fax: 574-287-1486
http://www.gemfellowship.org

Purpose: To provide fellowships for minority students pursuing graduate degrees in engineering, physical science or natural science.

Eligibility: Applicants must be college sophomore, junior or senior or graduate student majors in engineering, physical science or natural science and be members of one of the following minority groups: African American, Native American or Puerto Rican, Latino or other Hispanic American.

Target applicants: College students. Graduate school students. Adult students.

Amount: Varies.

Number of awards: Varies.

Deadline: November 15.

How to apply: Applications are available online.

Exclusive: Visit www.UltimateScholarshipBook.com and enter code NA249412 for updates on this award.

(2495) • Gena Wright Memorial Scholarship

United Negro College Fund (UNCF)
8260 Willow Oaks Corporate Drive
P.O. Box 10444
Fairfax, VA 22031-8044
Phone: 800-331-2244
http://www.uncf.org/

Purpose: To support students interested in working with children.

Eligibility: Applicants must be African American students interested in working with children. They must attend a UNCF member college or university, have a GPA of at least 3.0 and demonstrate financial need.

Target applicants: High school students. College students. Adult students.

Minimum GPA: 3.0

Amount: Varies.

Number of awards: 2.

Deadline: Varies.

How to apply: Applications are available online.

Exclusive: Visit www.UltimateScholarshipBook.com and enter code UN249512 for updates on this award.

(2496) • General Electric Foundation Scholarship

Society of Women Engineers
120 South LaSalle Street
Suite 1515
Chicago, IL 60603
Phone: 877-793-4636
Email: scholarshipapplication@swe.org
http://www.swe.org

Purpose: To support female freshman undergraduates who plan to study engineering.

Eligibility: Applicants must be U.S. citizens who are rising undergraduate freshmen planning to major in engineering. Selection is based on the overall strength of the application.

Target applicants: High school students.

Amount: $1,500.

Number of awards: 3.

Scholarship may be renewable.

Deadline: Mid-May.

How to apply: Applications are available online. An application form and supporting documents are required.

Exclusive: Visit www.UltimateScholarshipBook.com and enter code SO249612 for updates on this award.

(2497) • General Mills Technology Scholars Award

United Negro College Fund (UNCF)
8260 Willow Oaks Corporate Drive
P.O. Box 10444
Fairfax, VA 22031-8044
Phone: 800-331-2244
http://www.uncf.org/
Purpose: To recognize outstanding students in technology-related fields.
Eligibility: Applicants must be African American undergraduate students majoring in engineering, information systems, computer science/MIS, computer science, food service, information technology or management information systems. They must have a GPA of at least 3.0 and demonstrate financial need. Academics, career aspirations, leadership and achievement will be considered in awarding the scholarship.
Target applicants: College students. Adult students.
Minimum GPA: 3.0
Amount: $5,000.
Number of awards: 1.
Deadline: March 15.
How to apply: Applications are available online.
Exclusive: Visit www.UltimateScholarshipBook.com and enter code UN249712 for updates on this award.

(2498) • Gerald W. and Jean Purmal Endowed Scholarship

United Negro College Fund (UNCF)
8260 Willow Oaks Corporate Drive
P.O. Box 10444
Fairfax, VA 22031-8044
Phone: 800-331-2244
http://www.uncf.org/
Purpose: To help African Americans attending United Negro College Fund (UNCF) Member Colleges and Universities.
Eligibility: Applicants must have a minimum 2.5 GPA, complete the Free Application for Federal Student Aid (FAFSA) and have unmet financial need that is verified by the college or university financial aid office. Students are encouraged to complete the UNCF General Scholarship application to be matched with scholarships for which they meet the criteria.
Target applicants: High school students. College students. Adult students.
Minimum GPA: 2.5
Amount: $1,000-$4,000.
Number of awards: Varies.
Deadline: Varies.
How to apply: Applications are available online.
Exclusive: Visit www.UltimateScholarshipBook.com and enter code UN249812 for updates on this award.

(2499) • Girls Going Places Entrepreneurship Awards

Guardian Life Insurance Company of America
Attn: Girls Going Places
7 Hanover Square, Mailstop 26-3
New York, NY 10004
Phone: 212-598-8000
http://www.guardianlife.com
Purpose: To support budding female entrepreneurs.
Eligibility: Applicants must be females between the ages of 12 and 18 who are nominated by an adult. They must be legal U.S. residents who are enrolled in a middle or high school or equivalent homeschooling and must not be enrolled in a post-secondary institution. Judging criteria include demonstration of budding entrepreneurship, taking the first steps toward financial independence, making a difference in the school or community, initiation of a new business or service, relevance of achievements to theme of contest, demonstrated potential for success, significance of achievements and contributions, originality and clarity of essay, supplemental data and presentation of application.
Target applicants: Junior high students or younger. High school students.
Amount: $1,000-$10,000.
Number of awards: 15.
Deadline: February 26.
How to apply: Applications are available online. An application form, personal statement and letter of recommendation are required.
Exclusive: Visit www.UltimateScholarshipBook.com and enter code GU249912 for updates on this award.

(2500) • Glamour's Top Ten College Women Competition

Glamour
The Conde Nast Publications Inc.
4 Times Square
New York, NY 10036
Phone: 800-244-4526
Fax: 212-286-6922
Email: ttcw@glamour.com
http://www.glamour.com/about/top-10-college-women
Purpose: To recognize outstanding female college students.
Eligibility: Applicants must be college juniors at an accredited U.S. or Canadian college or university. They must be enrolled full-time and may not be scheduled to graduate before May of the year following application.
Target applicants: College students. Adult students.
Amount: $3,000.
Number of awards: 10.
Deadline: December 1.
How to apply: Applications are available online. An application form, transcript, list of activities on- and off-campus, essay, photograph and letter of recommendation are required.
Exclusive: Visit www.UltimateScholarshipBook.com and enter code GL250012 for updates on this award.

(2501) • Goldman Sachs Scholarships

Society of Women Engineers
120 South LaSalle Street
Suite 1515
Chicago, IL 60603
Phone: 877-793-4636
Email: scholarshipapplication@swe.org
http://www.swe.org
Purpose: To aid Society of Women Engineers members who are majoring in computer engineering, computer science or electrical engineering.
Eligibility: Applicants must be female and rising undergraduate juniors or seniors enrolled in an ABET-accredited program in electrical engineering, computer engineering or computer science. They must be full-time students and must have a GPA of 3.2 or higher on a four-point scale. They cannot be current recipients of a renewable scholarship awarded by the SWE. Those receiving full funding from another

organization (such as the U.S. military) are ineligible. Selection is based on the overall strength of the application.
Target applicants: College students. Adult students.
Minimum GPA: 3.2
Amount: $2,000.
Number of awards: 4.
Deadline: February 15.
How to apply: Applications are available online. An application form, official transcript and two recommendation letters are required.
Exclusive: Visit www.UltimateScholarshipBook.com and enter code SO250112 for updates on this award.

(2502) · Google Scholarship

United Negro College Fund (UNCF)
8260 Willow Oaks Corporate Drive
P.O. Box 10444
Fairfax, VA 22031-8044
Phone: 800-331-2244
http://www.uncf.org/
Purpose: To encourage diversity in the computer field.
Eligibility: Applicants must be African American students who are juniors at a UNCF member school or HBCU. They must be computer science or computer engineering majors with a GPA of at least 3.5 and demonstrate financial need.
Target applicants: College students. Adult students.
Minimum GPA: 3.5
Amount: $5,000.
Number of awards: Varies.
Deadline: October 6.
How to apply: Applications are available online.
Exclusive: Visit www.UltimateScholarshipBook.com and enter code UN250212 for updates on this award.

(2503) · Hagiwara Student Aid Award

Japanese American Citizens League (JACL)
1765 Sutter Street
San Francisco, CA 94115
Phone: 415-921-5225
Fax: 415-931-4671
Email: jacl@jacl.org
http://www.jacl.org
Purpose: To aid students who otherwise would have to delay or terminate their education due to lack of financing.
Eligibility: Applicants must be National JACL members and must be attending a college, university, trade school, business school or any other institution of higher learning. A personal statement, letter of recommendation, academic performance, work experience and community involvement are considered. Applicants should have extreme financial need.
Target applicants: College students. Graduate school students. Adult students.
Amount: Varies.
Number of awards: Varies.
Deadline: April 1.
How to apply: Applications are available online.
Exclusive: Visit www.UltimateScholarshipBook.com and enter code JA250312 for updates on this award.

(2504) · Harry C. Jaecker Scholarship

United Negro College Fund (UNCF)
8260 Willow Oaks Corporate Drive
P.O. Box 10444
Fairfax, VA 22031-8044
Phone: 800-331-2244
http://www.uncf.org/
Purpose: To assist pre-medical students attending a UNCF member school.
Eligibility: Applicants must be African American, have a minimum 2.5 GPA, complete the Free Application for Federal Student Aid (FAFSA) and have unmet financial need that is verified by the college or university financial aid office. Students are encouraged to complete the UNCF General Scholarship application to be matched with scholarships for which they meet the criteria.
Target applicants: High school students. College students. Adult students.
Minimum GPA: 2.5
Amount: $2,000-$5,000.
Number of awards: Varies.
Deadline: Varies.
How to apply: Applications are available online.
Exclusive: Visit www.UltimateScholarshipBook.com and enter code UN250412 for updates on this award.

(2505) · Harry L. Morrison Scholarship

National Society of Black Physicists
1100 North Glebe Road
Suite 1010
Arlington, VA 22201
Phone: 703-536-4207
Fax: 703-536-4203
Email: scholarship@nsbp.org
http://www.nsbp.org
Purpose: To aid undergraduate students majoring in physics.
Eligibility: Applicants must be physics majors who are undergraduate sophomores or juniors. Selection is based on the overall strength of the application.
Target applicants: College students. Adult students.
Amount: $1,000.
Number of awards: 3.
Deadline: January 8.
How to apply: Applications are available online. An application form, official transcript and three letters of recommendation are required.
Exclusive: Visit www.UltimateScholarshipBook.com and enter code NA250512 for updates on this award.

(2506) · Harvey H. and Catherine A. Moses Scholarship

United Negro College Fund (UNCF)
8260 Willow Oaks Corporate Drive
P.O. Box 10444
Fairfax, VA 22031-8044
Phone: 800-331-2244
http://www.uncf.org/
Purpose: To support African American students at UNCF member schools.
Eligibility: Applicants must have a minimum 2.5 GPA, complete the Free Application for Federal Student Aid (FAFSA) and have unmet financial need that is verified by the college or university financial aid

office. UNCF students are encouraged to complete the UNCF General Scholarship application to be matched with scholarships for which they meet the criteria.
Target applicants: High school students. College students. Adult students.
Minimum GPA: 2.5
Amount: Varies.
Number of awards: Varies.
Deadline: Varies.
How to apply: Applications are available online.
Exclusive: Visit www.UltimateScholarshipBook.com and enter code UN250612 for updates on this award.

(2507) • Hawaiian Homes Commission Scholarship

Hawaii Community Foundation - Scholarships
1164 Bishop Street, Suite 800
Honolulu, HI 96813
Phone: 888-731-3863
Fax: 808-521-6286
Email: scholarships@hcf-hawaii.org
http://www.hawaiicommunityfoundation.org
Purpose: To provide financial assistance to students of Hawaiian ancestry.
Eligibility: Applicants must be native Hawaiians or homestead lessees but do not have to live in Hawaii. They must be enrolled full-time at an accredited college or university as classified students and have a minimum GPA of 2.0 (3.0 if graduate students). Additional awards are available for students with high academic achievement and a proven commitment to the native Hawaiian community.
Target applicants: High school students. College students. Graduate school students. Adult students.
Minimum GPA: 2.0 for undergraduate students and 3.0 for graduate students
Amount: Varies.
Number of awards: Varies.
Deadline: March 1.
How to apply: To apply, register online, complete the online application and select the scholarships to which you wish to apply. In addition, mail the supporting materials: printed confirmation page from the online application, personal statement, copy of Student Aid Report (SAR) available at www.fafsa.ed.gov and official transcript.
Exclusive: Visit www.UltimateScholarshipBook.com and enter code HA250712 for updates on this award.

(2508) • Health Professions Pre-Graduate Scholarship Program

Indian Health Service
Scholarship Program Office
801 Thompson Avenue
Suite 120
Rockville, MD 20852
Phone: 301-443-6197
Fax: 301-443-6048
Email: dawn.kelly@ihs.gov
http://www.ihs.gov
Purpose: To aid Native Americans and Alaska Natives who are enrolled in selected health-related pre-professional degree programs.
Eligibility: Applicants must be U.S. citizens who are enrolled in or accepted into a pre-medicine, pre-dentistry, pre-optometry, pre-podiatry or other health-related pre-professional degree program. Applicants must have plans to work in the Native American or Alaska Native community as a health care provider in the chosen field of study. Selection is based on academic achievement, recommendation letters and the applicant's stated career goals.
Target applicants: High school students. College students. Adult students.
Amount: Varies.
Number of awards: Varies.
Scholarship may be renewable.
Deadline: April 28.
How to apply: Applications are available online. An application form, course curriculum outline, two recommendation forms, proof of Native American/Alaska Native status, an official transcript, proof of acceptance into an academic program and other supporting documents are required.
Exclusive: Visit www.UltimateScholarshipBook.com and enter code IN250812 for updates on this award.

(2509) • Health Professions Preparatory Scholarship Program

Indian Health Service
Scholarship Program Office
801 Thompson Avenue
Suite 120
Rockville, MD 20852
Phone: 301-443-6197
Fax: 301-443-6048
Email: dawn.kelly@ihs.gov
http://www.ihs.gov
Purpose: To aid Native Americans and Alaska Natives who are preparing for careers in one of the health professions.
Eligibility: Applicants must be U.S. citizens accepted into or enrolled in a compensatory or pre-professional general education course of study at an accredited college or university. The applicant must be studying or have plans to study a subject that has been designated as a priority career category by the Indian Health Service. Applicants must plan to serve Native American or Alaska Native communities as a professional healthcare provider after completing the necessary training. Selection is based on academic achievement, recommendation letters and stated career goals.
Target applicants: High school students. College students. Adult students.
Amount: Varies.
Number of awards: Varies.
Scholarship may be renewable.
Deadline: April 28.
How to apply: Applications are available online. An application form, two letters of recommendation, proof of Native American or Alaska Native status, an official transcript, proof of acceptance into a postsecondary educational program and other supporting documents are required.
Exclusive: Visit www.UltimateScholarshipBook.com and enter code IN250912 for updates on this award.

(2510) • Hellenic Times Scholarship

Hellenic Times Scholarship Fund
823 Eleventh Avenue
Attn.: Nick Katsoris
New York, NY 10019
Fax: 212-977-3662
Email: htsfund@aol.com
http://www.htsfund.org
Purpose: To financially help Greek American students.

Eligibility: Applicants must be undergraduate or graduate students of Greek descent between the ages of 17 and 25 and may not win any other full scholarships. Applicants must submit transcripts and may be required to submit tax returns.
Target applicants: College students. Graduate school students. Adult students.
Amount: Varies.
Number of awards: Varies.
Deadline: February 25.
How to apply: Applications are available online.
Exclusive: Visit www.UltimateScholarshipBook.com and enter code HE251012 for updates on this award.

(2511) • Herbert Lehman Scholarships

NAACP Legal Defense and Educational Fund
99 Hudson Street, Suite 1600
New York, NY 10013
Phone: 212-965-2200
Email: mbagley@naacpldf.org
http://www.naacpldf.org
Purpose: To support African American students who are attending college for the first time.
Eligibility: Applicants must have a strong academic record and clear educational goals, and they must show leadership potential through involvement in school and extracurricular activities. Students must show good character through positive recommendations from teachers, employers or community representatives.
Target applicants: High school students. College students. Adult students.
Amount: Varies.
Number of awards: Varies.
Scholarship may be renewable.
Deadline: March 31.
How to apply: Applications are available by sending a written request.
Exclusive: Visit www.UltimateScholarshipBook.com and enter code NA251112 for updates on this award.

(2512) • HIAS Scholarship

Hebrew Immigrant Aid Society
333 Seventh Avenue, 16th Floor
New York, NY 10001-5004
Phone: 212-613-1358
Fax: 212-967-4483
Email: scholarship@hias.org
http://www.hias.org
Purpose: To award scholarships to Jewish immigrant students.
Eligibility: Applicants must have completed one year of high school or college in the United States and have arrived in the United States after January 1, 1992. Selection is based on academic achievement, financial need and service within the Jewish community.
Target applicants: High school students. College students. Graduate school students. Adult students.
Amount: $1,000-$2,000.
Number of awards: Varies.
Deadline: March 1.
How to apply: Applications are available online.
Exclusive: Visit www.UltimateScholarshipBook.com and enter code HE251212 for updates on this award.

(2513) • Higher Education Grant

Bureau of Indian Affairs
1849 C Street NW/MS-3512 MIB
Washington, DC 20240-0001
Phone: 202-208-6123
Fax: 202-208-3312
Email: gking@bia.edu
http://www.bia.gov/
Purpose: To assist American Indian and Alaska Native students obtaining their undergraduate degrees.
Eligibility: Applicants must be members of a tribe or at least one-quarter degree Indian blood descendents of members of an American Indian tribe, be accepted into a college or another similar institution that provides an associate's or bachelor's degrees and show financial need.
Target applicants: High school students. College students. Adult students.
Amount: Varies.
Number of awards: Varies.
Deadline: Varies.
How to apply: Applications are available through tribes.
Exclusive: Visit www.UltimateScholarshipBook.com and enter code BU251312 for updates on this award.

(2514) • Hispanic College Fund Scholarships

Hispanic College Fund
1301 K Street NW
Suite 450-A
Washington, DC 20005
Phone: 800-644-4223
Fax: 202-296-3774
Email: hcf-info@hispanicfund.org
http://www.hispanicfund.org
Purpose: To develop future Hispanic business leaders by aiding students who have demonstrated excellence and potential.
Eligibility: Applicants must be Hispanic students applying to or enrolled at a college or university in the U.S. or Puerto Rico. Applicants must be U.S. citizens or permanent residents, plan to attend school full-time during the next academic year and have a minimum 3.0 GPA. Selection is based on academics and financial need. Some specific awards have additional eligibility requirements.
Target applicants: High school students. College students. Adult students.
Minimum GPA: 3.0
Amount: $500-$10,000.
Number of awards: Varies.
Scholarship may be renewable.
Deadline: March 1.
How to apply: Applications are available online.
Exclusive: Visit www.UltimateScholarshipBook.com and enter code HI251412 for updates on this award.

(2515) • Hispanic Health Professional Student Scholarship

National Hispanic Medical Association at New York University
Robert F. Wagner Graduate School of Public Service
The Puck Building
295 Lafayette Street
New York, NY 10012
Phone: 212-992-8706
Fax: 212-992-8715

Email: nhhf@nyu.edu
http://www.nhmafoundation.org
Purpose: To support Hispanic students who are planning to pursue careers in health care.
Eligibility: Applicants must be Hispanic students who are enrolled in a postsecondary degree program in allied health, dentistry, medicine, nursing, health research, public health or health management and policy analysis. Selection is based on academic achievement, leadership skills and commitment to improving health care in the Hispanic community.
Target applicants: College students. Graduate school students. Adult students.
Amount: Varies.
Number of awards: Varies.
Deadline: Varies.
How to apply: Applications are available online. An application form and supporting materials are required.
Exclusive: Visit www.UltimateScholarshipBook.com and enter code NA251512 for updates on this award.

(2516) • Hispanic Heritage Youth Awards

Hispanic Heritage Awards Foundation
2600 Virginia Avenue NW
Suite 406
Washington, DC 20037
Phone: 202-861-9797
Fax: 202-861-9799
Email: contact@hispanicheritageawards.org
http://www.hispanicheritage.org
Purpose: To promote Hispanic excellence and recognize the contributions of Hispanic American youth.
Eligibility: Applicants must be high school seniors who are U.S. citizens or permanent residents, reside in Chicago, Denver, Dallas, Los Angeles, Miami, New York City, Philadelphia, Phoenix, San Antonio, San Diego, San Jose or Washington DC and have Hispanic parentage (Hispanic parentage can be one parent of Mexican, Central American, Cuban, Puerto Rican, South American, Spanish or Caribbean Hispanic descent). Selection criteria include achievement in the applicant's discipline, involvement in community, ability to overcome adversity and character. The disciplines are: Academic Excellence, Sports, the Arts, Literature/ Journalism, Mathematics, Leadership/Community Service and Science and Technology.
Target applicants: High school students.
Amount: Up to $3,000.
Number of awards: Varies.
Deadline: July 1.
How to apply: Applications are available by request.
Exclusive: Visit www.UltimateScholarshipBook.com and enter code HI251612 for updates on this award.

(2517) • Honeywell International Inc. Scholarships

Society of Women Engineers
120 South LaSalle Street
Suite 1515
Chicago, IL 60603
Phone: 877-793-4636
Email: scholarshipapplication@swe.org
http://www.swe.org
Purpose: To aid female students planning to pursue undergraduate degrees in computer science and engineering.
Eligibility: Applicants must be female U.S. citizens. They must be rising undergraduate freshmen and must plan to major in computer science, computer engineering, electrical engineering, chemical engineering, manufacturing engineering, mechanical engineering, architectural engineering, aerospace engineering, industrial engineering or materials science and engineering. Applicants must demonstrate financial need. Selection is based on the overall strength of the application.
Target applicants: High school students.
Amount: $5,000.
Number of awards: 3.
Deadline: February 15.
How to apply: Applications are available online. An application form and supporting documents are required.
Exclusive: Visit www.UltimateScholarshipBook.com and enter code SO251712 for updates on this award.

(2518) • Hopi Scholarship

Hopi Tribe Grants and Scholarship Program
P.O. Box 123
Kykotsmovi, AZ 86039
Phone: 800-762-9630
Fax: 928-734-9575
Email: info@hopi.nsn.us
http://www.hopieducationfund.org
Purpose: To help Hopi students with academic achievement.
Eligibility: Applicants must be enrolled members of the Hopi tribe, be high school graduates or have earned a GED, have been accepted to a regionally accredited college and plan to attend full-time and have completed the Free Application for Federal Student Aid. Students must be in top 10 percent of their high school class or score 930 on the SAT or 21 on the ACT as entering freshmen; have a minimum 3.0 GPA as undergraduates or have a minimum 3.2 GPA as graduate, post graduate or professional degree students. Applications, statements of goals, financial needs analysis, proof of Hopi enrollment and transcripts are required.
Target applicants: High school students. College students. Graduate school students. Adult students.
Minimum GPA: 3.0
Amount: Varies.
Number of awards: Varies.
Deadline: July 1, November 1, December 1, May 1.
How to apply: Applications are available by mail.
Exclusive: Visit www.UltimateScholarshipBook.com and enter code HO251812 for updates on this award.

(2519) • Houghton Mifflin Company Fellows Program/ Internship

United Negro College Fund (UNCF)
8260 Willow Oaks Corporate Drive
P.O. Box 10444
Fairfax, VA 22031-8044
Phone: 800-331-2244
http://www.uncf.org/
Purpose: To introduce college students to careers in the publishing industry.
Eligibility: Applicants must be African American juniors with a GPA of at least 3.0 interested in the publishing industry. They must attend a UNCF member college or university and demonstrate financial need. The scholarship will be awarded upon successful completion of a summer internship.
Target applicants: College students. Adult students.
Minimum GPA: 3.0
Amount: $3,700+internship pay.

Number of awards: Varies.
Deadline: Varies.
How to apply: Applications are available online.
Exclusive: Visit www.UltimateScholarshipBook.com and enter code UN251912 for updates on this award.

(2520) • Howard County PFLAG Academic Scholarship

Parents, Family and Friends of Lesbians and Gays (PFLAG) Howard County/Maryland
Attention: Colette Roberts
7303 Swan Point Way
Columbia, MD 21045
Phone: 410-290-8292
Email: robertscp@aol.com
http://www.pflagmd.org
Purpose: To support outstanding gay, lesbian, bisexual and transgendered students and their straight allies.
Eligibility: Applicants must be Maryland residents who are attending or plan to attend an institution of higher learning during the upcoming academic year. They must not be receiving a scholarship or other assistance that pays their tuition in full. Prior Howard County PFLAG scholarship recipients may not apply.
Target applicants: High school students. College students. Adult students.
Amount: $1,000.
Number of awards: 1.
Deadline: May 1.
How to apply: Applications are available online. An application form, questionnaire, transcript and two letters of recommendation are required.
Exclusive: Visit www.UltimateScholarshipBook.com and enter code PA252012 for updates on this award.

(2521) • HSF/Association of Latino Professionals in Finance and Accounting (ALPFA) Scholarship Program

Hispanic Scholarship Fund (HSF)
55 Second Street
Suite 1500
San Francisco, CA 94105
Phone: 877-473-4636
Fax: 415-808-2302
Email: scholar1@hsf.net
http://www.hsf.net
Purpose: To aid outstanding Latino students who are majoring in finance, accounting, economics, business administration or management.
Eligibility: Applicants must be of Latino descent and be U.S. citizens or legal permanent residents. They must be enrolled full-time at an accredited postsecondary institution located in the U.S. or Puerto Rico. They must be entering a master's degree program or be rising undergraduate sophomores, juniors or seniors. They must be studying economics, management, business administration, finance or accounting and have a GPA of 3.0 or higher on a four-point scale. Selection is based on the overall strength of the application.
Target applicants: College students. Graduate school students. Adult students.
Minimum GPA: 3.0
Amount: $1,000-$10,000.
Number of awards: Varies.
Deadline: January 31.
How to apply: Applications are available online. An application form, supporting materials and submission of the Free Application for Federal Student Aid (FAFSA) are required.
Exclusive: Visit www.UltimateScholarshipBook.com and enter code HI252112 for updates on this award.

(2522) • HSF/BB&T Charitable Scholarship

Hispanic Scholarship Fund (HSF)
55 Second Street
Suite 1500
San Francisco, CA 94105
Phone: 877-473-4636
Fax: 415-808-2302
Email: scholar1@hsf.net
http://www.hsf.net
Purpose: To aid outstanding Latino and African-American undergraduates who are studying law, business or liberal arts.
Eligibility: Applicants must be U.S. citizens or legal permanent residents and full-time undergraduate students. They must be attending an accredited, four-year postsecondary institution located in the U.S. or Puerto Rico. They must reside in or attend school in Alabama, Florida, Georgia, Indiana, Kentucky, Maryland, North Carolina, Puerto Rico, South Carolina, Tennessee, Virginia, Washington, DC or West Virginia. They must be sophomores who are enrolled in a degree program in liberal arts, law or business and have a GPA of 3.0 or higher on a four-point scale. Selection is based on the overall strength of the application.
Target applicants: College students. Adult students.
Minimum GPA: 3.0
Amount: Varies.
Number of awards: Varies.
Deadline: December 15.
How to apply: Applications are available online. An application form, supporting materials and submission of the Free Application for Federal Student Aid (FAFSA) are required.
Exclusive: Visit www.UltimateScholarshipBook.com and enter code HI252212 for updates on this award.

(2523) • HSF/Cummins Scholarship

Hispanic Scholarship Fund (HSF)
55 Second Street
Suite 1500
San Francisco, CA 94105
Phone: 877-473-4636
Fax: 415-808-2302
Email: scholar1@hsf.net
http://www.hsf.net
Purpose: To aid Hispanic undergraduates who are studying business, human resources, engineering and computer science subjects.
Eligibility: Applicants must be U.S. citizens or legal permanent residents, be of Hispanic descent and be full-time undergraduate students who are majoring in business administration, finance, marketing, computer science, human resources management, electrical engineering, mechanical engineering or industrial engineering. They must be attending an accredited four-year institution, be freshmen or sophomores and have a GPA of 3.0 or higher on a four-point scale. Selection is based on the overall strength of the application.
Target applicants: College students. Adult students.
Minimum GPA: 3.0
Amount: $2,500.
Number of awards: Varies.
Deadline: December 1.

How to apply: Applications are available online. An application form, resume and other supporting materials are required.
Exclusive: Visit www.UltimateScholarshipBook.com and enter code HI252312 for updates on this award.

(2524) • HSF/General College Scholarship Program

Hispanic Scholarship Fund (HSF)
55 Second Street
Suite 1500
San Francisco, CA 94105
Phone: 877-473-4636
Fax: 415-808-2302
Email: scholar1@hsf.net
http://www.hsf.net

Purpose: To support students of Hispanic heritage.
Eligibility: Applicants must be high school seniors, entering college students or current college undergraduate or graduate students who are of Hispanic heritage and U.S. citizens or permanent residents. Students must have a GPA of 3.0 or higher and plan to enroll full-time in a degree program at a two- or four- year accredited institution in the U.S., Puerto Rico, the Virgin Islands or Guam in the upcoming academic year. Applicants must also apply for federal financial aid and be pursuing their first undergraduate or graduate degree.
Target applicants: High school students. College students. Graduate school students. Adult students.
Minimum GPA: 3.0
Amount: $1,000-$5,000.
Number of awards: Varies.
Deadline: December 15.
How to apply: Applications are available online. An application form, letter of recommendation, transcript, enrollment verification form and copy of FAFSA Student Aid Report are required.
Exclusive: Visit www.UltimateScholarshipBook.com and enter code HI252412 for updates on this award.

(2525) • HSF/General Motors Scholarship

Hispanic Scholarship Fund (HSF)
55 Second Street
Suite 1500
San Francisco, CA 94105
Phone: 877-473-4636
Fax: 415-808-2302
Email: scholar1@hsf.net
http://www.hsf.net

Purpose: To help Latinos pursuing degrees in engineering and business.
Eligibility: Applicants must be of Hispanic heritage, enrolled full-time at a four-year U.S. accredited college or university in the U.S., Puerto Rico or U.S. Virgin Islands and major in engineering (electrical, industrial, manufacturing or mechanical) or business (accounting, business administration, economics or finance). Applicants or their families must have ethnic backgrounds from Spain, Mexico, Guatemala, Honduras, El Salvador, Costa Rica, Nicaragua, Panama, Colombia, Venezuela, Ecuador, Peru, Argentina, Chile, Bolivia, Uruguay, Paraguay, Brazil, Cuba, Puerto Rico or the Dominican Republic. Students from Belize, Guyana, Suriname and French Guiana are ineligible. Semifinalists must complete the GM online assessment.
Target applicants: High school students. College students. Adult students.
Minimum GPA: 3.0
Amount: $2,500.
Number of awards: Varies.
Deadline: June 30.
How to apply: Applications are available online.
Exclusive: Visit www.UltimateScholarshipBook.com and enter code HI252512 for updates on this award.

(2526) • HSF/Haz La U Scholarship

Hispanic Scholarship Fund (HSF)
55 Second Street
Suite 1500
San Francisco, CA 94105
Phone: 877-473-4636
Fax: 415-808-2302
Email: scholar1@hsf.net
http://www.hsf.net

Purpose: To aid college-bound Hispanic students.
Eligibility: Applicants must be of Hispanic heritage, be U.S. citizens or legal permanent residents and be high school seniors who are planning to attend an accredited two- or four-year postsecondary institution in the U.S., Puerto Rico, the U.S. Virgin Islands or Guam. They must have plans to enroll full-time and have a GPA of 3.0 or higher on a four-point scale. Selection is based on the overall strength of the application.
Target applicants: High school students.
Minimum GPA: 3.0
Amount: Up to $15,000.
Number of awards: 11.
Deadline: December 31.
How to apply: Applications are available online. An application form, submission of the FAFSA and supporting materials are required.
Exclusive: Visit www.UltimateScholarshipBook.com and enter code HI252612 for updates on this award.

(2527) • HSF/Honda Award Scholarship

Hispanic Scholarship Fund (HSF)
55 Second Street
Suite 1500
San Francisco, CA 94105
Phone: 877-473-4636
Fax: 415-808-2302
Email: scholar1@hsf.net
http://www.hsf.net

Purpose: To aid Hispanic undergraduates who are planning for careers in the automotive industry.
Eligibility: Applicants must be U.S. citizens or legal permanent residents, be of Latino heritage and be full-time undergraduate juniors or seniors who are enrolled at a four-year, accredited U.S. institution located in the U.S., Puerto Rico, the U.S. Virgin Islands or Guam. They must be majoring in business, industrial engineering or technology, electrical engineering, mechanical engineering or chemical engineering. They must also be attending school in or residents of Ohio, Michigan, Indiana, Pennsylvania or Illinois. They must be degree-seeking students who have a GPA of 3.0 or higher on a four-point scale and have plans to pursue a career in the automotive industry. Selection is based on the overall strength of the application.
Target applicants: College students. Adult students.
Minimum GPA: 3.0
Amount: $5,000.
Number of awards: Varies.
Deadline: December 15.
How to apply: Applications are available online. An application form, submission of the Free Application for Federal Student Aid (FAFSA) and other supporting materials are required.

Exclusive: Visit www.UltimateScholarshipBook.com and enter code HI252712 for updates on this award.

(2528) • HSF/Hormel Scholarship

Hispanic Scholarship Fund (HSF)
55 Second Street
Suite 1500
San Francisco, CA 94105
Phone: 877-473-4636
Fax: 415-808-2302
Email: scholar1@hsf.net
http://www.hsf.net

Purpose: To aid Hispanic undergraduate students.
Eligibility: Applicants must be U.S. citizens or legal permanent residents, be of Hispanic heritage and be undergraduate juniors who are majoring in business, finance, accounting, marketing, engineering, agriculture, computer science, information technology, zoology or hospitality administration. They must have a GPA of 3.0 or higher on a four-point scale. Selection is based on the overall strength of the application.
Target applicants: College students. Adult students.
Minimum GPA: 3.0
Amount: $2,500.
Number of awards: Varies.
Deadline: December 15.
How to apply: Applications are available online. An application form, resume, submission of the Free Application for Federal Student Aid (FAFSA) and other supporting materials are required.
Exclusive: Visit www.UltimateScholarshipBook.com and enter code HI252812 for updates on this award.

(2529) • HSF/Marathon Oil Corporation College Scholarship Program

Hispanic Scholarship Fund (HSF)
55 Second Street
Suite 1500
San Francisco, CA 94105
Phone: 877-473-4636
Fax: 415-808-2302
Email: scholar1@hsf.net
http://www.hsf.net

Purpose: To aid minority undergraduates who are studying selected subjects.
Eligibility: Applicants must be U.S. citizens or legal permanent residents who are Hispanic, African-American, Native American, Asian, Pacific Islanders or Alaska Natives and who are undergraduate sophomores or seniors. Sophomores must be majoring in accounting, engineering, computer science, energy management, environmental health, finance, physical sciences, information technology, marketing, transportation and logistics or supply chain management. Seniors must have plans to pursue a master's degree in geology or geophysics. Applicants must have a GPA of 3.0 or higher on a four-point scale. Selection is based on the overall strength of the application.
Target applicants: College students. Adult students.
Minimum GPA: 3.0
Amount: Up to $15,000.
Number of awards: Varies.
Scholarship may be renewable.
Deadline: November 1.
How to apply: Applications are available online. An application form, submission of the Free Application for Federal Student Aid (FAFSA) and other supporting materials are required.
Exclusive: Visit www.UltimateScholarshipBook.com and enter code HI252912 for updates on this award.

(2530) • HSF/McNamara Family Creative Arts Grant Project

Hispanic Scholarship Fund (HSF)
55 Second Street
Suite 1500
San Francisco, CA 94105
Phone: 877-473-4636
Fax: 415-808-2302
Email: scholar1@hsf.net
http://www.hsf.net

Purpose: To aid outstanding Latino creative arts students.
Eligibility: Applicants must be U.S. citizens or legal permanent residents, be of Hispanic descent and be full-time undergraduate or graduate degree-seeking students who are enrolled at a U.S.-accredited institution located in the U.S., Puerto Rico, the U.S. Virgin Islands or Guam. They must be studying the creative arts (communications, media, performing arts, film, writing, etc.) and have a GPA of 3.0 or higher on a four-point scale. Selection is based on the overall strength of the application.
Target applicants: College students. Graduate school students. Adult students.
Minimum GPA: 3.0
Amount: Up to $15,000.
Number of awards: Varies.
Deadline: December 15.
How to apply: Applications are available online. An application form, submission of the Free Application for Federal Student Aid (FAFSA) and other supporting materials are required.
Exclusive: Visit www.UltimateScholarshipBook.com and enter code HI253012 for updates on this award.

(2531) • HSF/Monsanto Fund Scholarship Program

Hispanic Scholarship Fund (HSF)
55 Second Street
Suite 1500
San Francisco, CA 94105
Phone: 877-473-4636
Fax: 415-808-2302
Email: scholar1@hsf.net
http://www.hsf.net

Purpose: To aid Hispanic undergraduate students.
Eligibility: Applicants must be U.S. citizens or legal permanent residents, be of Hispanic heritage and be undergraduate sophomores who are majoring in agriculture, biological sciences, chemistry, horticulture, engineering, business, finance, accounting, computer science or information technology. They must have a GPA of 3.0 or higher on a four-point scale. Selection is based on the overall strength of the application.
Target applicants: College students. Adult students.
Minimum GPA: 3.0
Amount: $10,000.
Number of awards: Varies.
Scholarship may be renewable.
Deadline: November 1.

How to apply: Applications are available online. An application form, submission of the Free Application for Federal Student Aid (FAFSA) and other supporting materials are required.
Exclusive: Visit www.UltimateScholarshipBook.com and enter code HI253112 for updates on this award.

(2532) • HSF/Qualcomm Q Awards Scholarship

Hispanic Scholarship Fund (HSF)
55 Second Street
Suite 1500
San Francisco, CA 94105
Phone: 877-473-4636
Fax: 415-808-2302
Email: scholar1@hsf.net
http://www.hsf.net
Purpose: To aid Hispanic students who are majoring in computer science, computer engineering or electrical engineering.
Eligibility: Applicants must be U.S. citizens or legal permanent residents, be of Latino heritage and be graduate students or rising undergraduate sophomores, juniors or seniors at a U.S.-accredited four-year postsecondary institution. They must be full-time students who are majoring in electrical engineering, computer engineering or computer science. They must have a GPA of 3.0 or higher on a four-point scale. Preference will be given to students who are enrolled at the University of California-Berkeley or the University of California-San Diego. Selection is based on the overall strength of the application.
Target applicants: College students. Graduate school students. Adult students.
Minimum GPA: 3.0
Amount: $5,000.
Number of awards: Varies.
Deadline: December 15.
How to apply: Applications are available online. An application form, resume, submission of the Free Application for Federal Student Aid (FAFSA) and other supporting materials are required.
Exclusive: Visit www.UltimateScholarshipBook.com and enter code HI253212 for updates on this award.

(2533) • HSF/Shell Scholarship

Hispanic Scholarship Fund (HSF)
55 Second Street
Suite 1500
San Francisco, CA 94105
Phone: 877-473-4636
Fax: 415-808-2302
Email: scholar1@hsf.net
http://www.hsf.net
Purpose: To aid Hispanic undergraduate students.
Eligibility: Applicants must be U.S. citizens or legal permanent residents, be of Latino heritage and be full-time undergraduate freshmen, sophomores or juniors at an accredited two- or four-year institution. They must be residents of Texas, Oklahoma or Louisiana or must be attending school in one of these states. They must be majoring in accounting, chemical engineering, civil engineering, distribution, electrical engineering, finance, logistics, mechanical engineering, petroleum engineering or supply chain management. They must have a GPA of 3.2 or higher on a four-point scale. Selection is based on the overall strength of the application.
Target applicants: College students. Adult students.
Minimum GPA: 3.2
Amount: Varies.
Number of awards: Varies.
Deadline: November 9.
How to apply: Applications are available online. An application form, submission of the Free Application for Federal Student Aid (FAFSA) and supporting materials are required.
Exclusive: Visit www.UltimateScholarshipBook.com and enter code HI253312 for updates on this award.

(2534) • HSF/Verizon Foundation Scholarship

Hispanic Scholarship Fund (HSF)
55 Second Street
Suite 1500
San Francisco, CA 94105
Phone: 877-473-4636
Fax: 415-808-2302
Email: scholar1@hsf.net
http://www.hsf.net
Purpose: To aid outstanding Latino undergraduates.
Eligibility: Applicants must be of Hispanic heritage, be U.S. citizens or legal permanent residents and be undergraduate sophomores, juniors or seniors enrolled full-time at an accredited four-year institution located in the U.S., Puerto Rico, the U.S. Virgin Islands or Guam. They must be majoring in accounting, business administration, finance, hospitality administration, human resources management, management, marketing, computer science, computer engineering, information technology, electrical engineering, industrial engineering or mechanical engineering. They must have a GPA of 3.0 or higher on a four-point scale. Selection is based on the overall strength of the application.
Target applicants: College students. Adult students.
Minimum GPA: 3.0
Amount: $5,000.
Number of awards: Varies.
Deadline: August 14.
How to apply: Applications are available online. An application form, submission of the Free Application for Federal Student Aid (FAFSA) and supporting materials are required.
Exclusive: Visit www.UltimateScholarshipBook.com and enter code HI253412 for updates on this award.

(2535) • HSF/Wells Fargo Scholarship

Hispanic Scholarship Fund (HSF)
55 Second Street
Suite 1500
San Francisco, CA 94105
Phone: 877-473-4636
Fax: 415-808-2302
Email: scholar1@hsf.net
http://www.hsf.net
Purpose: To aid Hispanic undergraduates who are preparing for careers in banking and finance.
Eligibility: Applicants must be of Hispanic descent, be U.S. citizens or legal permanent residents and be undergraduate sophomores who are enrolled full-time at an accredited four-year postsecondary institution. They must be majoring in business, economics, finance, accounting or information technology. They must have a GPA of 3.0 or higher on a four-point scale. Selection is based on the overall strength of the application.
Target applicants: College students. Adult students.
Minimum GPA: 3.0
Amount: $2,000.
Number of awards: Varies.

Deadline: December 15.
How to apply: Applications are available online. An application form, submission of the Free Application for Federal Student Aid (FAFSA) and supporting materials are required.
Exclusive: Visit www.UltimateScholarshipBook.com and enter code HI253512 for updates on this award.

(2536) • Hubertus W.V. Wellems Scholarship for Male Students

National Association for the Advancement of Colored People
The United Negro College Fund
Scholarships and Grants Administration
8260 Willow Oaks Corporate Drive
Fairfax, VA 22031
Phone: 800-331-2244
Email: youth@naacpnet.org
http://www.naacp.org
Purpose: To aid male students who are studying certain math and science subjects at the undergraduate and graduate levels.
Eligibility: Applicants must be U.S. citizens who are high school seniors, undergraduates or graduate students. They must be enrolled in or plan to enroll in a mathematics, chemistry, physics or engineering degree program at an accredited four-year institution of higher learning located in the U.S. Undergraduate applicants must be full-time students. High school seniors and undergraduate students must have a GPA of 2.5 or higher, and graduate students must have a GPA of 3.0 or higher. All applicants must demonstrate financial need. Selection is based on the overall strength of the application.
Target applicants: High school students. College students. Graduate school students. Adult students.
Minimum GPA: 2.5
Amount: Varies.
Number of awards: Varies.
Deadline: The last Friday in the month of March.
How to apply: Applications are available online. An application form, personal essay, official transcript and two letters of recommendation are required.
Exclusive: Visit www.UltimateScholarshipBook.com and enter code NA253612 for updates on this award.

(2537) • IBM Corporation Scholarship

Society of Women Engineers
120 South LaSalle Street
Suite 1515
Chicago, IL 60603
Phone: 877-793-4636
Email: scholarshipapplication@swe.org
http://www.swe.org
Purpose: To aid female undergraduates who are majoring in computer science, computer engineering and electrical engineering.
Eligibility: Applicants must be female undergraduate sophomores or juniors enrolled full-time in a CSAB-accredited computer science degree program or in an ABET-accredited computer engineering or electrical engineering degree program. They must have a GPA of 3.4 or higher. Preference will be given to members of underrepresented groups. Selection is based on the overall strength of the application.
Target applicants: College students. Adult students.
Minimum GPA: 3.4
Amount: $1,000.
Number of awards: 4.
Deadline: February 15.
How to apply: Applications are available online. An application form, official transcript and two recommendation letters are required.
Exclusive: Visit www.UltimateScholarshipBook.com and enter code SO253712 for updates on this award.

(2538) • Ida M. Pope Memorial Scholarship

Hawaii Community Foundation - Scholarships
1164 Bishop Street, Suite 800
Honolulu, HI 96813
Phone: 888-731-3863
Fax: 808-521-6286
Email: scholarships@hcf-hawaii.org
http://www.hawaiicommunityfoundation.org
Purpose: To assist female students of Hawaiian ancestry in obtaining higher education.
Eligibility: Applicants must attend an accredited college or university and have a GPA of 3.0 or higher.
Target applicants: High school students. College students. Adult students.
Minimum GPA: 3.0
Amount: Varies.
Number of awards: Varies.
Deadline: March 1.
How to apply: To apply, register online, complete the online application and select the scholarships to which you wish to apply. In addition, mail the supporting materials: printed confirmation page from the online application, personal statement, copy of Student Aid Report (SAR) available at www.fafsa.ed.gov and official transcript.
Exclusive: Visit www.UltimateScholarshipBook.com and enter code HA253812 for updates on this award.

(2539) • Isabella Carvalho Health Scholarship

North Carolina Society of Hispanic Professionals
8450 Chapel Hill Road
Suite 209
Cary, NC 27513
Phone: 919-467-8424
Email: mailbox@thencshp.org
http://www.thencshp.org
Purpose: To aid Hispanic students who are preparing for careers in the healthcare field.
Eligibility: Applicants must be Hispanic students who have graduated from high school within the past two years. They must have had a cumulative four-year GPA of 2.5 or higher on a four-point scale and must desire to pursue undergraduate education in a healthcare-related field. They must be committed to serving their communities. Preference will be given to female applicants. Selection is based on academic merit, community involvement, leadership ability and financial need.
Target applicants: High school students.
Minimum GPA: 2.5
Amount: Up to $2,500.
Number of awards: Varies.
Scholarship may be renewable.
Deadline: January 15.
How to apply: Applications are available online. An application form, official transcript, personal statement and two letters of recommendation are required.
Exclusive: Visit www.UltimateScholarshipBook.com and enter code NO253912 for updates on this award.

(2540) • Ivy M. Parker Memorial Scholarship

Society of Women Engineers
120 South LaSalle Street
Suite 1515
Chicago, IL 60603
Phone: 877-793-4636
Email: scholarshipapplication@swe.org
http://www.swe.org

Purpose: To aid female undergraduates who are majoring in engineering.
Eligibility: Applicants must be be full-time students who are enrolled in an ABET-accredited engineering program. They must be rising juniors or seniors who have a GPA of 3.0 or higher on a four-point scale. Applicants cannot be currently receiving another scholarship awarded by the Society of Women Engineers (SWE), and they cannot be receiving full funding from another source (such as an employee reimbursement program or the U.S. military). Selection is based on academic merit and financial need.
Target applicants: College students. Adult students.
Minimum GPA: 3.0
Amount: $1,500.
Number of awards: 1.
Deadline: February 15.
How to apply: Applications are available online. An application form, official transcript and two letters of recommendation are required.
Exclusive: Visit www.UltimateScholarshipBook.com and enter code SO254012 for updates on this award.

(2541) • Jack and Jill of America Foundation Scholarship

United Negro College Fund (UNCF)
8260 Willow Oaks Corporate Drive
P.O. Box 10444
Fairfax, VA 22031-8044
Phone: 800-331-2244
http://www.uncf.org/

Purpose: To help African American high school seniors attend college.
Eligibility: Applicants must plan to attend college full-time, have a minimum 3.0 GPA, complete the Free Application for Federal Student Aid (FAFSA) and have unmet financial need that is verified by the college or university financial aid office. UNCF students are encouraged to complete the UNCF General Scholarship application to be matched with scholarships for which they meet the criteria.
Target applicants: High school students.
Minimum GPA: 3.0
Amount: $1,500-$2,500.
Number of awards: Varies.
Deadline: March 14.
How to apply: Applications are available online.
Exclusive: Visit www.UltimateScholarshipBook.com and enter code UN254112 for updates on this award.

(2542) • Jackie Robinson Scholarship

Jackie Robinson Foundation
3 W. 35th Street
11th Floor
New York, NY 10001
Phone: 212-290-8600
Fax: 212-290-8081
Email: general@jackierobinson.org
http://www.jackierobinson.org

Purpose: To help minority students who have shown leadership skills in their communities.
Eligibility: Applicants must be minority high school seniors with demonstrated financial need and academic achievement and who have already been accepted to a four-year college or university.
Target applicants: High school students.
Amount: Up to $7,500.
Number of awards: 30-60.
Deadline: March 15.
How to apply: Applications are available online, by email to requests@jackierobinson.org or by mail.
Exclusive: Visit www.UltimateScholarshipBook.com and enter code JA254212 for updates on this award.

(2543) • Japanese American Citizens League Creative and Performing Arts Awards

Japanese American Citizens League (JACL)
1765 Sutter Street
San Francisco, CA 94115
Phone: 415-921-5225
Fax: 415-931-4671
Email: jacl@jacl.org
http://www.jacl.org

Purpose: To recognize and encourage performing arts and creative projects among JACL members.
Eligibility: Applicants must be National JACL members and must be attending a college, university, trade school, business school or any other institution of higher learning. A personal statement, letter of recommendation, academic performance, work experience and community involvement are considered. Professional artists are ineligible.
Target applicants: College students. Graduate school students. Adult students.
Amount: Varies.
Number of awards: Varies.
Deadline: April 1.
How to apply: Applications are available online or by sending a self-addressed, stamped envelope.
Exclusive: Visit www.UltimateScholarshipBook.com and enter code JA254312 for updates on this award.

(2544) • Japanese American Citizens League Entering Freshman Awards

Japanese American Citizens League (JACL)
1765 Sutter Street
San Francisco, CA 94115
Phone: 415-921-5225
Fax: 415-931-4671
Email: jacl@jacl.org
http://www.jacl.org

Purpose: To recognize and encourage education as a key to greater opportunities among JACL members.
Eligibility: Applicants must be National JACL members and must be planning to attend a college, university, trade school, business school, or any other institution of higher learning at the undergraduate level. A personal statement, letter of recommendation, academic performance, work experience and community involvement will all be considered.
Target applicants: High school students.
Amount: Varies.
Number of awards: Varies.
Deadline: March 1.

How to apply: Applications are available through local JACL chapters, regional offices, National JACL Headquarters and website.
Exclusive: Visit www.UltimateScholarshipBook.com and enter code JA254412 for updates on this award.

(2545) • Japanese American Citizens League Graduate Awards

Japanese American Citizens League (JACL)
1765 Sutter Street
San Francisco, CA 94115
Phone: 415-921-5225
Fax: 415-931-4671
Email: jacl@jacl.org
http://www.jacl.org
Purpose: To provide monetary assistance for graduate studies to JACL members.
Eligibility: Applicants must be National JACL members and must attend a college or university at the graduate level. A personal statement, letter of recommendation, academic performance, work experience and community involvement are considered.
Target applicants: Graduate school students. Adult students.
Amount: Varies.
Number of awards: 7.
Deadline: April 1.
How to apply: Applications are available online and by sending a self-addressed, stamped envelope.
Exclusive: Visit www.UltimateScholarshipBook.com and enter code JA254512 for updates on this award.

(2546) • Japanese American Citizens League Law Scholarships

Japanese American Citizens League (JACL)
1765 Sutter Street
San Francisco, CA 94115
Phone: 415-921-5225
Fax: 415-931-4671
Email: jacl@jacl.org
http://www.jacl.org
Purpose: To help JACL members who are studying law.
Eligibility: Applicants must be National JACL members and must be studying law at a college or university. A personal statement, letter of recommendation, academic performance, work experience and community involvement will all be considered.
Target applicants: Graduate school students. Adult students.
Amount: Varies.
Number of awards: 4.
Deadline: April 1.
How to apply: Applications are available online and by sending a self-addressed, stamped envelope.
Exclusive: Visit www.UltimateScholarshipBook.com and enter code JA254612 for updates on this award.

(2547) • Japanese American Citizens League Undergraduate Awards

Japanese American Citizens League (JACL)
1765 Sutter Street
San Francisco, CA 94115
Phone: 415-921-5225
Fax: 415-931-4671
Email: jacl@jacl.org
http://www.jacl.org
Purpose: To recognize and encourage education as a key to greater opportunities among JACL members.
Eligibility: Applicants must be National JACL members and must be attending a college, university, trade school, business school, or any other institution of higher learning at the undergraduate level. A personal statement, letter of recommendation, academic performance, work experience and community involvement will all be considered.
Target applicants: College students. Adult students.
Amount: Varies.
Number of awards: 8.
Deadline: April 1.
How to apply: Applications are available through local JACL chapters, regional offices, National JACL Headquarters and website.
Exclusive: Visit www.UltimateScholarshipBook.com and enter code JA254712 for updates on this award.

(2548) • Jeannette Rankin Foundation Award

Jeannette Rankin Foundation
1 Huntington Road, Suite 701
Athens, GA 30606
Phone: 706-208-1211
Email: info@rankinfoundation.org
http://www.rankinfoundation.org
Purpose: To support the education of low-income women 35 years or older.
Eligibility: Applicants must be women 35 years of age or older, plan to obtain an undergraduate or vocational education and meet maximum household income guidelines.
Target applicants: College students. Adult students.
Amount: $2,000.
Number of awards: Varies.
Scholarship may be renewable.
Deadline: March 1.
How to apply: Applications are available online or by sending a self-addressed and stamped envelope to the foundation.
Exclusive: Visit www.UltimateScholarshipBook.com and enter code JE254812 for updates on this award.

(2549) • Jesse Jones, Jr. Scholarship

United Negro College Fund (UNCF)
8260 Willow Oaks Corporate Drive
P.O. Box 10444
Fairfax, VA 22031-8044
Phone: 800-331-2244
http://www.uncf.org/
Purpose: To assist business students at UNCF member schools.
Eligibility: Applicants must be African American, have a minimum 2.5 GPA, complete the Free Application for Federal Student Aid (FAFSA) and have unmet financial need that is verified by the college or university financial aid office. UNCF students are encouraged to complete the UNCF General Scholarship application to be matched with scholarships for which they meet the criteria.
Target applicants: High school students. College students. Adult students.
Minimum GPA: 2.5
Amount: $2,000-$5,000.
Number of awards: Varies.
Deadline: Varies.
How to apply: Applications are available online.

Exclusive: Visit www.UltimateScholarshipBook.com and enter code UN254912 for updates on this award.

(2550) • Jimi Hendrix Endowment Fund Scholarship

United Negro College Fund (UNCF)
8260 Willow Oaks Corporate Drive
P.O. Box 10444
Fairfax, VA 22031-8044
Phone: 800-331-2244
http://www.uncf.org/

Purpose: To assist students studying music at UNCF member schools.
Eligibility: Applicants must have a minimum 2.5 GPA, complete the Free Application for Federal Student Aid (FAFSA) and have unmet financial need that is verified by the college or university financial aid office. Students are encouraged to complete the UNCF General Scholarship application to be matched with scholarships for which they meet the criteria.
Target applicants: High school students. College students. Adult students.
Minimum GPA: 2.5
Amount: $2,000-$5,000.
Number of awards: Varies.
Deadline: Varies.
How to apply: Applications are available online.
Exclusive: Visit www.UltimateScholarshipBook.com and enter code UN255012 for updates on this award.

(2551) • Juanita Robles-Lopez Scholarship

National Association of Hispanic Nurses
Attn: Maria Castro, NAHN Awards and Scholarship Committee Chair
1501 Sixteenth Street NW
Washington, DC 20036
Phone: 202-387-2477
Fax: 202-483-7183
Email: info@thehispanicnurses.org
http://www.thehispanicnurses.org

Purpose: To support graduate students enrolled in a maternal-child nursing program.
Eligibility: Students must be members of NAHN, although they may apply for membership at the time of application. Selection is based on an essay describing the maternal-child needs in Hispanic communities and the applicant's potential leadership in this field, recommendations, academic achievement and application form.
Target applicants: Graduate school students. Adult students.
Minimum GPA: 3.0
Amount: $2,000.
Number of awards: 1.
Deadline: March 14.
How to apply: Applications are available online or by mail.
Exclusive: Visit www.UltimateScholarshipBook.com and enter code NA255112 for updates on this award.

(2552) • Judith Resnik Memorial Scholarship

Society of Women Engineers
120 South LaSalle Street
Suite 1515
Chicago, IL 60603
Phone: 877-793-4636
Email: scholarshipapplication@swe.org
http://www.swe.org

Purpose: To help female undergraduates who are majoring in astronautical, aeronautical or aerospace engineering.
Eligibility: Applicants must be rising undergraduate sophomores, juniors or seniors and have a GPA of 3.0 or higher on a four-point scale. They must be enrolled in an ABET-accredited degree program in aeronautical engineering, aerospace engineering or astronautical engineering. They cannot be receiving a renewable scholarship from the Society of Women Engineers. Applicants who are receiving full funding from another source (such as the U.S. military or an employee reimbursement plan) are ineligible. Selection is based on the overall strength of the application.
Target applicants: College students. Adult students.
Minimum GPA: 3.0
Amount: $3,000.
Number of awards: 1.
Deadline: February 15.
How to apply: Applications are available online. An application form, official transcript and two recommendation letters are required.
Exclusive: Visit www.UltimateScholarshipBook.com and enter code SO255212 for updates on this award.

(2553) • Julianne Malveaux Scholarship

National Association of Negro Business and Professional Women's Clubs Inc.
1806 New Hampshire Avenue NW
Washington, DC 20009-3298
Phone: 202-483-4206
Email: info@nanbpwc.org
http://www.nanbpwc.org

Purpose: To award scholarships to college students majoring in journalism, economics or a related field.
Eligibility: Applicants must be enrolled as sophomores or juniors at an accredited college or university and have a minimum 3.0 GPA. Students may major in related fields such as public policy or creative writing.
Target applicants: College students. Adult students.
Minimum GPA: 3.0
Amount: Varies.
Number of awards: Varies.
Deadline: March 1.
How to apply: Applications are available online.
Exclusive: Visit www.UltimateScholarshipBook.com and enter code NA255312 for updates on this award.

(2554) • Kellogg Scholarship

Society of Women Engineers
120 South LaSalle Street
Suite 1515
Chicago, IL 60603
Phone: 877-793-4636
Email: scholarshipapplication@swe.org
http://www.swe.org

Purpose: To aid female undergraduates who are majoring in chemical or mechanical engineering.
Eligibility: Applicants must be female rising undergraduate sophomores or juniors who are enrolled in an ABET-accredited degree program in chemical engineering or mechanical engineering. They must have a GPA of 3.2 or higher on a four-point scale, must not be receiving a renewable SWE scholarship and must not be receiving full academic funding from another source. Selection is based on the overall strength of the application.

Target applicants: College students. Adult students.
Minimum GPA: 3.2
Amount: $1,000-$3,000.
Number of awards: 3.
Deadline: February 15.
How to apply: Applications are available online. An application form, official transcript and two recommendation letters are required.
Exclusive: Visit www.UltimateScholarshipBook.com and enter code SO255412 for updates on this award.

(2555) • Kirsten Lorentzen Award

Association for Women in Science
1442 Duke Street
Alexandria, VA 22314
Phone: 202-326-8940
Fax: 202-326-8960
Email: awisedfd@awis.org
http://www.awis.org
Purpose: To aid female undergraduates who are studying physics or geosciences.
Eligibility: Applicants must be undergraduate sophomores or juniors and U.S. citizens or foreign nationals who are attending a U.S. institution of higher learning. They must be studying physics or geosciences and must have plans to pursue a career in teaching at the postsecondary level or in research. Previous applicants are ineligible. Selection is based on the overall strength of the application.
Target applicants: College students. Adult students.
Amount: $1,000.
Number of awards: Varies.
Deadline: January 29.
How to apply: Applications are available online. An application form, transcripts and three recommendation letters are required.
Exclusive: Visit www.UltimateScholarshipBook.com and enter code AS255512 for updates on this award.

(2556) • Knights of Lithuania Scholarship Program

Knights of Lithuania
93 Princess Pine Circle
Taunton, MA 02780
Email: veronicacote@comcast.net
http://www.knightsoflithuania.com/ScholarshipCommittee.html
Purpose: To assist Lithuanian-Americans in obtaining higher education.
Eligibility: Applicants must be members of the Knights of Lithuania for at least two years. They must receive recommendations from their council president or vice president, a pastor or spiritual adviser and a former teacher in addition to a separate character reference.
Target applicants: High school students. College students. Adult students.
Amount: Varies.
Number of awards: Varies.
Deadline: June 15.
How to apply: Applications are available online.
Exclusive: Visit www.UltimateScholarshipBook.com and enter code KN255612 for updates on this award.

(2557) • Kuntz Foundation Scholarship

United Negro College Fund (UNCF)
8260 Willow Oaks Corporate Drive
P.O. Box 10444
Fairfax, VA 22031-8044
Phone: 800-331-2244
http://www.uncf.org/
Purpose: To support African American college students at UNCF member colleges and universities.
Eligibility: Applicants must have a minimum 2.5 GPA, complete the Free Application for Federal Student Aid (FAFSA) and have unmet financial need that is verified by the college or university financial aid office. Students are encouraged to complete the UNCF General Scholarship application to be matched with scholarships for which they meet the criteria.
Target applicants: High school students. College students. Adult students.
Minimum GPA: 2.5
Amount: Varies.
Number of awards: Varies.
Deadline: Varies.
How to apply: Applications are available online.
Exclusive: Visit www.UltimateScholarshipBook.com and enter code UN255712 for updates on this award.

(2558) • Larry Whiteside Scholarship

National Association of Black Journalists
1100 Knight Hall
Suite 3100
College Park, MD 20742
Phone: 301-405-7520
Fax: 301-314-1714
Email: iwashington@nabj.org
http://www.nabj.org
Purpose: To assist students who are planning for careers in sports journalism.
Eligibility: Applicants must be student members of the National Association of Black Journalists (NABJ). They must be graduate students or rising undergraduate juniors or seniors at an accredited four-year institution who are planning to pursue careers in sports journalism. They must be majoring in journalism or communications or must have demonstrated an interest in journalism by working for a media outlet. They must have a major GPA of 2.5 or higher. Selection is based on the overall strength of the application.
Target applicants: College students. Graduate school students. Adult students.
Minimum GPA: 2.5
Amount: $2,500.
Number of awards: 1.
Deadline: Varies.
How to apply: Applications are available online. An application form, resume, official transcript, personal essay, three writing samples and three references are required.
Exclusive: Visit www.UltimateScholarshipBook.com and enter code NA255812 for updates on this award.

(2559) • Lee Dubin Scholarship

Children of Lesbians and Gays Everywhere (COLAGE)
COLAGE Scholarship Committee
3543 18th Street, #1
San Francisco, CA 94110
Email: colage@colage.org
http://www.colage.org
Purpose: To acknowledge the achievements of gay and lesbian families.

Eligibility: Applicants must have one or more lesbian, gay, bisexual or transgender parent. Applicants must be an undergraduate with a minimum 2.0 GPA.
Target applicants: College students. Adult students.
Minimum GPA: 2.0
Amount: $500-$1,000.
Number of awards: 5 or more.
Deadline: April 15.
How to apply: Applications are available online.
Exclusive: Visit www.UltimateScholarshipBook.com and enter code CH255912 for updates on this award.

(2560) • Letty Garofalo Scholarship

United Negro College Fund (UNCF)
8260 Willow Oaks Corporate Drive
P.O. Box 10444
Fairfax, VA 22031-8044
Phone: 800-331-2244
http://www.uncf.org/
Purpose: To support students in need of financial assistance.
Eligibility: Applicants must have a minimum 2.5 GPA, complete the Free Application for Federal Student Aid (FAFSA) and have unmet financial need that is verified by the college or university financial aid office. UNCF students are encouraged to complete the UNCF General Scholarship application to be matched with scholarships for which they meet the criteria.
Target applicants: High school students. College students. Adult students.
Minimum GPA: 2.5
Amount: Varies.
Number of awards: Varies.
Deadline: Varies.
How to apply: Applications are available online.
Exclusive: Visit www.UltimateScholarshipBook.com and enter code UN256012 for updates on this award.

(2561) • Lillian Moller Gilbreth Memorial Scholarship

Society of Women Engineers
120 South LaSalle Street
Suite 1515
Chicago, IL 60603
Phone: 877-793-4636
Email: scholarshipapplication@swe.org
http://www.swe.org
Purpose: To aid female students who are majoring in engineering.
Eligibility: Applicants must be rising undergraduate juniors or seniors who are enrolled in an ABET-accredited engineering degree program. They must have a GPA of 3.0 or higher on a four-point scale. Applicants cannot be receiving full academic funding from another source, and they cannot be receiving another renewable SWE scholarship at the time of award disbursement. Selection is based on the overall strength of the application.
Target applicants: College students. Adult students.
Minimum GPA: 3.0
Amount: $10,000.
Number of awards: 1.
Scholarship may be renewable.
Deadline: February 15.
How to apply: Applications are available online. An application form, official transcript and two letters of recommendation are required.
Exclusive: Visit www.UltimateScholarshipBook.com and enter code SO256112 for updates on this award.

(2562) • Limited Inc. and Intimate Brands Inc. Scholarship

United Negro College Fund (UNCF)
8260 Willow Oaks Corporate Drive
P.O. Box 10444
Fairfax, VA 22031-8044
Phone: 800-331-2244
http://www.uncf.org/
Purpose: To support students at UNCF member schools in Ohio.
Eligibility: Applicants must be African American students, have a minimum 2.5 GPA, complete the Free Application for Federal Student Aid (FAFSA) and have unmet financial need that is verified by the college or university financial aid office. UNCF students are encouraged to complete the UNCF General Scholarship application to be matched with scholarships for which they meet the criteria.
Target applicants: High school students. College students. Adult students.
Minimum GPA: 2.5
Amount: Varies.
Number of awards: Varies.
Deadline: Varies.
How to apply: Applications are available online.
Exclusive: Visit www.UltimateScholarshipBook.com and enter code UN256212 for updates on this award.

(2563) • Lockheed Martin Freshman Scholarship

Society of Women Engineers
120 South LaSalle Street
Suite 1515
Chicago, IL 60603
Phone: 877-793-4636
Email: scholarshipapplication@swe.org
http://www.swe.org
Purpose: To aid female students who are planning to pursue higher education in engineering.
Eligibility: Applicants must be rising undergraduate freshmen who are planning to major in engineering. Selection is based on the overall strength of the application.
Target applicants: High school students.
Amount: $3,000.
Number of awards: 2.
Deadline: Mid-May.
How to apply: Applications are available online. An application form and supporting materials are required.
Exclusive: Visit www.UltimateScholarshipBook.com and enter code SO256312 for updates on this award.

(2564) • Louis Dreyfus Natural Gas Company Scholarship

United Negro College Fund (UNCF)
8260 Willow Oaks Corporate Drive
P.O. Box 10444
Fairfax, VA 22031-8044
Phone: 800-331-2244
http://www.uncf.org/
Purpose: To support African American college students at UNCF member colleges and universities.

Eligibility: Applicants must have a minimum 2.5 GPA, complete the Free Application for Federal Student Aid (FAFSA) and have unmet financial need that is verified by the college or university financial aid office. Students are encouraged to complete the UNCF General Scholarship application to be matched with scholarships for which they meet the criteria.
Target applicants: High school students. College students. Adult students.
Minimum GPA: 2.5
Amount: Varies.
Number of awards: Varies.
Deadline: Varies.
How to apply: Applications are available online.
Exclusive: Visit www.UltimateScholarshipBook.com and enter code UN256412 for updates on this award.

(2565) • Louise Moritz Molitoris Leadership Scholarship for Undergraduates

WTS Advancing Women in Transportation
1701 K Street, NW
Suite 800
Washington, DC 20006
Phone: 202-955-5085
Fax: 202-955-5088
Email: membership@wtsinternational.org
http://www.wtsinternational.org
Purpose: To aid female undergraduates who are pursuing transportation-related degrees.
Eligibility: Applicants must be currently enrolled in a transportation-related degree program, have a GPA of 3.0 or higher and have plans to pursue a career in the field of transportation. Selection is based on academic merit, proven leadership in transportation-related activities and stated career goals.
Target applicants: College students. Adult students.
Minimum GPA: 3.0
Amount: $3,000.
Number of awards: 1.
Deadline: Varies.
How to apply: Applications are available from local WTS chapters by request. An application form and supporting materials are required.
Exclusive: Visit www.UltimateScholarshipBook.com and enter code WT256512 for updates on this award.

(2566) • Lucile B. Kaufman Women's Scholarship

Society of Manufacturing Engineers Education Foundation
One SME Drive
P.O. Box 930
Dearborn, MI 48121
Phone: 313-425-3300
Fax: 313-425-3411
Email: foundation@sme.org
http://www.smeef.org
Purpose: To aid female undergraduates who are majoring in manufacturing engineering or manufacturing engineering technology.
Eligibility: Applicants must be full-time undergraduates who have completed at least 30 credit hours of study at an accredited postsecondary institution located in the U.S. or Canada. They must have a GPA of 3.0 or higher on a four-point scale. Applicants must have plans to pursue a career in manufacturing engineering technology or manufacturing engineering. Selection is based on the overall strength of the application.
Target applicants: College students. Adult students.
Minimum GPA: 3.0
Amount: At least $1,000.
Number of awards: Varies.
Deadline: February 1.
How to apply: Applications are available online. An application form, resume, personal statement, two recommendation letters and a transcript are required.
Exclusive: Visit www.UltimateScholarshipBook.com and enter code SO256612 for updates on this award.

(2567) • Lucy Kasparian Aharonian Scholarship

Armenian International Women's Association
65 Main Street
#3A
Watertown, MA 02472
Phone: 617-926-0171
Email: aiwainc@aol.com
http://www.aiwa-net.org/scholarshipinfo.html
Purpose: To aid female students of Armenian descent who are studying selected subjects.
Eligibility: Applicants must be full-time undergraduate juniors, undergraduate seniors or graduate students who are enrolled at an accredited postsecondary institution. They must be pursuing a degree in architecture, computer science, engineering, mathematics or technology. Selection is based on academic merit and financial need.
Target applicants: College students. Graduate school students. Adult students.
Amount: $2,000-$10,000.
Number of awards: 2.
Deadline: April 5.
How to apply: Applications are available online. An application form and supporting materials are required.
Exclusive: Visit www.UltimateScholarshipBook.com and enter code AR256712 for updates on this award.

(2568) • LULAC GE Scholarship

League of United Latin American Citizens
2000 L Street NW
Suite 610
Washington, DC 20036
Phone: 202-835-9646
Fax: 202-835-9685
Email: scholarships@lnesc.org
http://www.lnesc.org
Purpose: To assist minority students who are majoring in business or engineering.
Eligibility: Applicants must be entering their sophomore year of college at an accredited institution and majoring in business or engineering.
Target applicants: College students. Adult students.
Amount: $5,000.
Number of awards: Varies.
Deadline: March 31.
How to apply: Applications are available from LULAC.
Exclusive: Visit www.UltimateScholarshipBook.com and enter code LE256812 for updates on this award.

(2569) • LULAC General Awards

League of United Latin American Citizens
2000 L Street NW
Suite 610

Washington, DC 20036
Phone: 202-835-9646
Fax: 202-835-9685
Email: scholarships@lnesc.org
http://www.lnesc.org
Purpose: To provide assistance to Hispanic students who are seeking or plan to seek degrees.
Eligibility: Students must have applied to or be enrolled in a two- or four-year college or graduate school and be U.S. citizens or legal residents. Grades and academic achievement may be considered, but emphasis is placed on motivation, sincerity and integrity as demonstrated by the interview and essay.
Target applicants: High school students. College students. Graduate school students. Adult students.
Amount: $250-$1,000.
Number of awards: Varies.
Deadline: March 31.
How to apply: Applications are available from LULAC.
Exclusive: Visit www.UltimateScholarshipBook.com and enter code LE256912 for updates on this award.

(2570) • LULAC Honors Awards

League of United Latin American Citizens
2000 L Street NW
Suite 610
Washington, DC 20036
Phone: 202-835-9646
Fax: 202-835-9685
Email: scholarships@lnesc.org
http://www.lnesc.org
Purpose: To provide assistance to all levels of degree seeking Latino students.
Eligibility: Applicants must be U.S. citizens or legal residents, have applied to or attend a college or graduate school and have a GPA of 3.25 or better. Applicants who are entering freshmen must also have an ACT score of 23 or higher or an SAT score of 1000 or higher.
Target applicants: High school students. College students. Graduate school students. Adult students.
Minimum GPA: 3.25
Amount: $500-$2,000.
Number of awards: Varies.
Deadline: March 31.
How to apply: Applications are available from LULAC.
Exclusive: Visit www.UltimateScholarshipBook.com and enter code LE257012 for updates on this award.

(2571) • LULAC National Scholastic Achievement Awards

League of United Latin American Citizens
2000 L Street NW
Suite 610
Washington, DC 20036
Phone: 202-835-9646
Fax: 202-835-9685
Email: scholarships@lnesc.org
http://www.lnesc.org
Purpose: To aid Hispanic students attending colleges, universities and graduate schools.
Eligibility: Applicants must have applied to or be enrolled in a college, university or graduate school and be U.S. citizens or legal residents. Students must also have a minimum 3.5 GPA and if entering freshmen a minimum ACT score of 29 or minimum SAT score of 1350. Eligible candidates cannot be related to scholarship committee members, the Council President or contributors to the Council funds. Since applications must be sent from local LULAC Councils, students without LULAC Councils in their states are ineligible.
Target applicants: College students. Graduate school students. Adult students.
Minimum GPA: 3.5
Amount: $2,000+.
Number of awards: Varies.
Deadline: March 31.
How to apply: Applications are available online.
Exclusive: Visit www.UltimateScholarshipBook.com and enter code LE257112 for updates on this award.

(2572) • Mae Maxey Memorial Scholarship

United Negro College Fund (UNCF)
8260 Willow Oaks Corporate Drive
P.O. Box 10444
Fairfax, VA 22031-8044
Phone: 800-331-2244
http://www.uncf.org/
Purpose: To provide assistance to African American students at UNCF member colleges and universities who are interested in poetry.
Eligibility: Applicants must have a minimum 2.5 GPA, complete the Free Application for Federal Student Aid (FAFSA) and have unmet financial need that is verified by the college or university financial aid office. Students are encouraged to complete the UNCF General Scholarship application to be matched with scholarships for which they meet the criteria.
Target applicants: High school students. College students. Adult students.
Minimum GPA: 2.5
Amount: $1,000-$5,000.
Number of awards: Varies.
Deadline: Varies.
How to apply: Applications are available online.
Exclusive: Visit www.UltimateScholarshipBook.com and enter code UN257212 for updates on this award.

(2573) • MAES Scholarship Program

Society of Mexican American Engineers and Scientists Inc. (MAES)
711 W. Bay Area Boulevard
Suite #206
Webster, TX 77598-4051
Phone: 281-557-3677
Fax: 281-557-3757
Email: execdir@maes-natl.org
http://www.maes-natl.org
Purpose: To assist Hispanic students in the fields of science and engineering.
Eligibility: Applicants must be current Hispanic MAES student members who are full-time undergraduate and graduate students in an accredited U.S. college or university majoring in science or engineering. Community college applicants must be enrolled in majors that are transferable to a four-year institution offering bachelor's degrees. There are various scholarships in the program. Some sponsors require students to be U.S. citizens or permanent residents. Awards are based on financial need, academic achievement, personal qualities, strengths and leadership abilities. Applicants should submit applications, financial information, recommendations and transcripts.

Target applicants: College students. Graduate school students. Adult students.
Amount: $1,000-$4,000.
Number of awards: Varies.
Deadline: September 11.
How to apply: Applications are available online.
Exclusive: Visit www.UltimateScholarshipBook.com and enter code SO257312 for updates on this award.

(2574) · Malcolm X Scholarship for Exceptional Courage

United Negro College Fund (UNCF)
8260 Willow Oaks Corporate Drive
P.O. Box 10444
Fairfax, VA 22031-8044
Phone: 800-331-2244
http://www.uncf.org/
Purpose: To assist students who attend UNCF member colleges and universities and have overcome extreme circumstances and hardships.
Eligibility: Applicants must be African American students, have a minimum 2.5 GPA, complete the Free Application for Federal Student Aid (FAFSA) and have unmet financial need that is verified by the college or university financial aid office. Students are encouraged to complete the UNCF General Scholarship application to be matched with scholarships for which they meet the criteria. Academic excellence and leadership on campus and in the community are also required.
Target applicants: College students. Adult students.
Minimum GPA: 2.5
Amount: $4,000.
Number of awards: Varies.
Deadline: Varies.
How to apply: Applications are available online.
Exclusive: Visit www.UltimateScholarshipBook.com and enter code UN257412 for updates on this award.

(2575) · Margaret Mcnamara Memorial Fund Fellowships

Margaret Mcnamara Memorial Fund
1818 H Street NW, MSN H2-204
Washington, DC 20433
Phone: 202-473-8751
Fax: 202 522-3142
Email: familynetwork@worldbank.org
http://go.worldbank.org/4EZTOTYEF0
Purpose: To provide financial assistance to women from developing countries who are currently studying to earn a college degree in the U.S.
Eligibility: Applicants must be from an eligible nation, have a record of community service in their country and be U.S. or Canadian residents at the time of application, while intending to return to their country of origin with two years. Individuals under the age of 25 and relatives of World Bank employees are not eligible.
Target applicants: College students. Graduate school students. Adult students.
Amount: $4,000-$12,000.
Number of awards: Varies.
Deadline: February 18 (U.S. or Canada) and August 25 (Africa).
How to apply: Applications are available online.
Exclusive: Visit www.UltimateScholarshipBook.com and enter code MA257512 for updates on this award.

(2576) · Maria Elena Salinas Scholarship Program

National Association of Hispanic Journalists
Scholarship Committee
1000 National Press Building
Washington, DC 20045
Phone: 202-662-7145
Fax: 202-662-7144
Email: ntita@nahj.org
http://www.nahj.org
Purpose: To support Spanish speaking students who plan to become broadcast journalists.
Eligibility: Applicants must be high school seniors, undergraduates or first-year graduate students who plan to pursue careers in journalism in Spanish-language television or radio. The award includes an opportunity to intern with the news division of Univision or an affiliate. Applicants must write an essay in Spanish outlining their career goals and provide Spanish-language samples of their work.
Target applicants: High school students. College students. Graduate school students. Adult students.
Amount: $5,000.
Number of awards: 3.
Scholarship may be renewable.
Deadline: March 31.
How to apply: Applications are available online.
Exclusive: Visit www.UltimateScholarshipBook.com and enter code NA257612 for updates on this award.

(2577) · Marriott Scholars Program

United Negro College Fund (UNCF)
8260 Willow Oaks Corporate Drive
P.O. Box 10444
Fairfax, VA 22031-8044
Phone: 800-331-2244
http://www.uncf.org/
Purpose: To assist future hospitality industry professionals.
Eligibility: Applicants must be incoming African American students majoring in hotel management, restaurant management or a similar hospitality field. They must have a GPA of at least 3.0 and demonstrate financial need.
Target applicants: High school students.
Minimum GPA: 3.0
Amount: Up to $9,000.
Number of awards: Varies.
Scholarship may be renewable.
Deadline: March 1.
How to apply: Applications are available online.
Exclusive: Visit www.UltimateScholarshipBook.com and enter code UN257712 for updates on this award.

(2578) · Mary E. Scott Memorial Scholarship

United Negro College Fund (UNCF)
8260 Willow Oaks Corporate Drive
P.O. Box 10444
Fairfax, VA 22031-8044
Phone: 800-331-2244
http://www.uncf.org/
Purpose: To help African American students attending United Negro College Fund (UNCF) member colleges and universities.
Eligibility: Applicants must have a minimum 2.5 GPA, complete the Free Application for Federal Student Aid (FAFSA) and have unmet

financial need that is verified by the college or university financial aid office. Students are encouraged to complete the UNCF General Scholarship application to be matched with scholarships for which they meet the criteria.
Target applicants: High school students. College students. Adult students.
Minimum GPA: 2.5
Amount: $1,500-$5,000.
Number of awards: Varies.
Deadline: Varies.
How to apply: Applications are available online.
Exclusive: Visit www.UltimateScholarshipBook.com and enter code UN257812 for updates on this award.

(2579) • Mary Moy Quan Ing Memorial Scholarship

Asian American Journalists Association
1182 Market Street
Suite 230
San Francisco, CA 94102
Phone: 415-346-2051
Fax: 415-346-6343
Email: lilac@aaja.org
http://www.aaja.org
Purpose: Monetary assistance is awarded to a high school senior pursuing college studies that lead to a journalism career.
Eligibility: Applicants must be high school seniors intending to major in journalism. Applicants must also demonstrate a commitment to the field of journalism, sensitivity to Asian American issues as demonstrated by community involvement, journalistic ability, scholastic ability and financial need.
Target applicants: High school students.
Amount: $1,000.
Number of awards: 3.
Deadline: Varies.
How to apply: Applications are available online.
Exclusive: Visit www.UltimateScholarshipBook.com and enter code AS257912 for updates on this award.

(2580) • Mary R. Norton Memorial Scholarship Award for Women

ASTM International
100 Barr Harbor Drive
P.O. Box C700
West Conshohocken, PA 19428
Phone: 610-832-9500
Email: awards@astm.org
http://www.astm.org
Purpose: To aid female students who are pursuing graduate studies in materials science or physical metallurgy.
Eligibility: Applicants must be full-time undergraduate seniors or first-year graduate students. They must be enrolled in or planning to enroll in a graduate program in physical metallurgy or materials science, with an emphasis on the relationship between properties and microstructures. Selection is based on faculty recommendation and personal statement.
Target applicants: College students. Graduate school students. Adult students.
Amount: $1,000.
Number of awards: Varies.
Deadline: December 15.
How to apply: Applications are available online. An application form, one faculty recommendation, personal statement and transcripts are required.
Exclusive: Visit www.UltimateScholarshipBook.com and enter code AS258012 for updates on this award.

(2581) • Mas Family Scholarships

Jorge Mas Canosa Freedom Foundation
P.O. Box 14-1898
Miami, FL 33114
Phone: 305-529-0075
Fax: 305-529-0085
Email: gparlapiano@gablesfinancial.com
http://www.jorgemascanosa.org
Purpose: To aid undergraduate and graduate students of Cuban descent who are studying selected subjects.
Eligibility: Applicants must be majoring in or have plans to major in business, communications, economics, engineering, international relations or journalism. They must demonstrate leadership potential and a commitment to success in a democratic, free enterprise society. Selection is based on academic merit, personal essay, leadership ability, professional potential and character.
Target applicants: High school students. College students. Graduate school students. Adult students.
Amount: Varies.
Number of awards: Varies.
Scholarship may be renewable.
Deadline: February 12.
How to apply: Applications are available online. An application form, official transcript, SAT scores, personal essay, three recommendation forms, proof of Cuban descent, proof of college acceptance (for incoming freshmen only), cost of tuition statement and statement of financial need are required.
Exclusive: Visit www.UltimateScholarshipBook.com and enter code JO258112 for updates on this award.

(2582) • MCCA Lloyd M. Johnson, Jr. Scholarship Program

United Negro College Fund (UNCF)
8260 Willow Oaks Corporate Drive
P.O. Box 10444
Fairfax, VA 22031-8044
Phone: 800-331-2244
http://www.uncf.org/
Purpose: To support first-year entering law students.
Eligibility: Applicants must be African American students entering their first year of law school at an accredited institution. They must have a GPA of at least 3.0 and demonstrate financial need.
Target applicants: College students. Graduate school students. Adult students.
Minimum GPA: 3.0
Amount: $10,000-$20,000.
Number of awards: Varies.
Scholarship may be renewable.
Deadline: May 31.
How to apply: Applications are available online.
Exclusive: Visit www.UltimateScholarshipBook.com and enter code UN258212 for updates on this award.

(2583) • McClare Family Trust Scholarship

United Negro College Fund (UNCF)
8260 Willow Oaks Corporate Drive
P.O. Box 10444
Fairfax, VA 22031-8044
Phone: 800-331-2244
http://www.uncf.org/

Purpose: To provide funding to humanities students.

Eligibility: Applicants must be African American college freshmen at a UNCF member college or university majoring in the humanities, with an interest in English literature. Students must have a GPA of at least 3.0 and demonstrate financial need.

Target applicants: College students. Adult students.

Minimum GPA: 3.0

Amount: Varies.

Number of awards: Varies.

Deadline: October 29.

How to apply: Applications are available online.

Exclusive: Visit www.UltimateScholarshipBook.com and enter code UN258312 for updates on this award.

(2584) • Medicus Student Exchange

Swiss Benevolent Society of New York
Scholarship Committee
500 Fifth Avenue, Room 1800
New York, NY 10110
http://www.swissbenevolentny.com

Purpose: To provide need and merit-based scholarships for students from Swiss-American backgrounds.

Eligibility: Applicants or one of their parents must be a Swiss national. The Medicus grant for study in Switzerland is only open to U.S. residents and is a need-based award. Applicants must be college juniors or seniors or graduate-level students accepted to a Swiss university or the Federal Institute of Technology.

Target applicants: College students. Graduate school students. Adult students.

Amount: Varies.

Number of awards: Varies.

Deadline: March 31.

How to apply: Applications are available online.

Exclusive: Visit www.UltimateScholarshipBook.com and enter code SW258412 for updates on this award.

(2585) • Medtronic Foundation Scholarship

United Negro College Fund (UNCF)
8260 Willow Oaks Corporate Drive
P.O. Box 10444
Fairfax, VA 22031-8044
Phone: 800-331-2244
http://www.uncf.org/

Purpose: To support African American sophomores and juniors at UNCF member colleges and universities majoring in a science, engineering or medical field.

Eligibility: Eligible majors include: engineering, pre-medicine, science, chemistry, biochemistry, biology, microbiology, biomedical research, medicine, physical sciences, electrical engineering, civil engineering, chemical engineering and mechanical engineering. Applicants must have a GPA of at least 3.3 and demonstrate financial need.

Target applicants: College students. Adult students.

Minimum GPA: 3.3

Amount: Up to $5,000.

Number of awards: Varies.

Deadline: November 12.

How to apply: Applications are available online.

Exclusive: Visit www.UltimateScholarshipBook.com and enter code UN258512 for updates on this award.

(2586) • MESBEC Program

Catching the Dream
Attn.: Scholarship Affairs Office
8200 Mountain Road NE
Suite 203
Albuquerque, NM 87110
Phone: 505-262-2351
Email: nscholarsh@aol.com
http://www.catchingthedream.org

Purpose: To provide scholarships to high-achieving American Indians in the fields of math, engineering, science, business, education and computers.

Eligibility: Applicants must be 1/4 or more degree American Indian, enrolled in a tribe and attend or plan to attend college full-time. Students must apply to all other sources of funding at the same time they apply for this scholarship. Selection is based on grades, SAT or ACT scores, work experience, leadership, clear goals, commitment to the American Indian community and the potential to improve the lives of American Indian people.

Target applicants: High school students. College students. Graduate school students. Adult students.

Amount: $500-$5,000.

Number of awards: Varies.

Deadline: March 15, April 15 and September 15.

How to apply: Applications are available online.

Exclusive: Visit www.UltimateScholarshipBook.com and enter code CA258612 for updates on this award.

(2587) • Michael and Donna Griffith Scholarship

United Negro College Fund (UNCF)
8260 Willow Oaks Corporate Drive
P.O. Box 10444
Fairfax, VA 22031-8044
Phone: 800-331-2244
http://www.uncf.org/

Purpose: To support African American college students.

Eligibility: Applicants must have a minimum 2.5 GPA, complete the Free Application for Federal Student Aid (FAFSA) and have unmet financial need that is verified by the college or university financial aid office. Applicants must be UNCF students and are encouraged to complete the UNCF General Scholarship application to be matched with scholarships for which they meet the criteria.

Target applicants: High school students. College students. Adult students.

Minimum GPA: 2.5

Amount: $1,000-$2,500.

Number of awards: Varies.

Deadline: Varies.

How to apply: Applications are available online.

Exclusive: Visit www.UltimateScholarshipBook.com and enter code UN258712 for updates on this award.

(2588) • Michael Jackson Scholarship

United Negro College Fund (UNCF)
8260 Willow Oaks Corporate Drive
P.O. Box 10444
Fairfax, VA 22031-8044
Phone: 800-331-2244
http://www.uncf.org/

Purpose: To assist students majoring in communications, English or performing arts.

Eligibility: Applicants must be African American students at a UNCF member college or university majoring in communications, English or performing arts. Applicants must have a GPA of at least 3.0 and demonstrate financial need.

Target applicants: High school students. College students. Adult students.

Minimum GPA: 3.0

Amount: Up to $4,000.

Number of awards: Varies.

Deadline: Varies.

How to apply: Applications are available online.

Exclusive: Visit www.UltimateScholarshipBook.com and enter code UN258812 for updates on this award.

(2589) • Mike and Stephanie Bozic Scholarship

United Negro College Fund (UNCF)
8260 Willow Oaks Corporate Drive
P.O. Box 10444
Fairfax, VA 22031-8044
Phone: 800-331-2244
http://www.uncf.org/

Purpose: To assist African American students with financial need.

Eligibility: Applicants must attend United Negro College Fund (UNCF) member colleges and universities, have a minimum 2.5 GPA, complete the Free Application for Federal Student Aid (FAFSA) and have unmet financial need that is verified by the college or university financial aid office. UNCF students are encouraged to complete the UNCF General Scholarship application to be matched with scholarships for which they meet the criteria.

Target applicants: High school students. College students. Adult students.

Minimum GPA: 2.5

Amount: Varies.

Number of awards: Varies.

Deadline: Varies.

How to apply: Applications are available online.

Exclusive: Visit www.UltimateScholarshipBook.com and enter code UN258912 for updates on this award.

(2590) • Minority Affairs Committee Award for Outstanding Scholastic Achievement

American Institute of Chemical Engineers - (AIChE)
3 Park Avenue
New York, NY 10016
Phone: 212-591-7634
Fax: 212-591-8890
Email: awards@aiche.org
http://www.aiche.org

Purpose: Recognizes outstanding achievements by a chemical engineering student who serves as a role model for minority students.

Eligibility: Applicants must be ethnic minorities, major in chemical engineering and be undergraduate or graduate students.

Target applicants: College students. Graduate school students. Adult students.

Amount: $1,000-$1,500.

Number of awards: 10.

Deadline: July 1.

How to apply: Applications are available online or by telephone or written request.

Exclusive: Visit www.UltimateScholarshipBook.com and enter code AM259012 for updates on this award.

(2591) • Minority Scholarship

National Strength and Conditioning Association (NSCA) Foundation
1885 Bob Johnson Drive
Colorado Springs, CO 80906
Phone: 800-815-6826
Fax: 719-632-6367
Email: nsca@nsca-lift.org
http://www.nsca-lift.org

Purpose: To encourage minorities to enter the field of strength and conditioning.

Eligibility: Applicants must be African American, Hispanic, Asian American or Native American students working toward a graduate degree related to strength and conditioning. Students must be NSCA members for one year before applying and be pursuing careers in strength and conditioning. Applications are evaluated based on grades, courses, experience, honors, recommendations and involvement in the community and with NSCA.

Target applicants: College students. Graduate school students. Adult students.

Amount: $1,500.

Number of awards: Varies.

Deadline: March 15.

How to apply: Applications are available with membership.

Exclusive: Visit www.UltimateScholarshipBook.com and enter code NA259112 for updates on this award.

(2592) • Minority Scholarship and Training Program

LinTV
8 Elm Street
New Haven, CT 06510
Phone: 203-784-8958
Email: gail.brekke@lintv.com
http://www.lintv.com

Purpose: To help educate outstanding minority students who plan to enter the television broadcast field.

Eligibility: Applicants must have a minimum 3.0 GPA, major in journalism or a related broadcast field at an accredited university or college, be college sophomores, be U.S. citizens and of non-white origin.

Target applicants: College students. Adult students.

Minimum GPA: 3.0

Amount: Varies.

Number of awards: Varies.

Deadline: Varies.

How to apply: Applications are available online.

Exclusive: Visit www.UltimateScholarshipBook.com and enter code LI259212 for updates on this award.

(2593) • Minority Scholarship Awards for College Students

American Institute of Chemical Engineers - (AIChE)
3 Park Avenue
New York, NY 10016
Phone: 212-591-7634
Fax: 212-591-8890
Email: awards@aiche.org
http://www.aiche.org

Purpose: To offer financial aid to minority students in chemical engineering.
Eligibility: Applicants must be AIChE national student members, undergraduates in chemical engineering and members of a minority group (i.e., African American, Hispanic, Native American or Alaskan Native) that is underrepresented in chemical engineering. Selection is based on academic record, participation in AIChE student and professional activities, career objectives and financial need.
Target applicants: College students. Adult students.
Amount: $1,000.
Number of awards: 10.
Deadline: July 1.
How to apply: Applications are available online or by telephone or written request.
Exclusive: Visit www.UltimateScholarshipBook.com and enter code AM259312 for updates on this award.

(2594) • Minority Scholarship Awards for Incoming College Freshmen

American Institute of Chemical Engineers - (AIChE)
3 Park Avenue
New York, NY 10016
Phone: 212-591-7634
Fax: 212-591-8890
Email: awards@aiche.org
http://www.aiche.org

Purpose: To offer financial aid to minority students in chemical engineering.
Eligibility: Applicants must be members of a minority group (i.e. African American, Hispanic, Native American or Alaskan Native) that is underrepresented in chemical engineering. Applicants must also be high school graduates during the academic year of application and plan to enroll in a four-year college or university. Applicants are encouraged to major in science or engineering. Selection is also based on academic record, reason for choosing science or engineering, work or activities and financial need.
Target applicants: High school students.
Amount: $1,000.
Number of awards: 10.
Deadline: Varies.
How to apply: Applications are available online or by telephone or written request.
Exclusive: Visit www.UltimateScholarshipBook.com and enter code AM259412 for updates on this award.

(2595) • Mitsubishi Motors U.S.A. Foundation Leadership Awards

United Negro College Fund (UNCF)
8260 Willow Oaks Corporate Drive
P.O. Box 10444
Fairfax, VA 22031-8044
Phone: 800-331-2244
http://www.uncf.org/

Purpose: To support African American students at UNCF member schools who have leadership roles in their communities.
Eligibility: Applicants must have a minimum 2.5 GPA, complete the Free Application for Federal Student Aid (FAFSA) and have unmet financial need that is verified by the college or university financial aid office. Students are encouraged to complete the UNCF General Scholarship application to be matched with scholarships for which they meet the criteria.
Target applicants: College students. Adult students.
Minimum GPA: 2.5
Amount: $2,000.
Number of awards: 39.
Deadline: October 29.
How to apply: Applications are available online.
Exclusive: Visit www.UltimateScholarshipBook.com and enter code UN259512 for updates on this award.

(2596) • Morgan Stanley Scholarship/Internship

United Negro College Fund (UNCF)
8260 Willow Oaks Corporate Drive
P.O. Box 10444
Fairfax, VA 22031-8044
Phone: 800-331-2244
http://www.uncf.org/

Purpose: To help African American students attending United Negro College Fund (UNCF) member colleges and universities who are majoring in finance or banking.
Eligibility: Applicants must have a minimum 2.5 GPA, complete the Free Application for Federal Student Aid (FAFSA) and have unmet financial need that is verified by the college or university financial aid office. Students are encouraged to complete the UNCF General Scholarship application to be matched with scholarships for which they meet the criteria. This program includes a summer internship. Funds may be used for tuition, room and board, books or to repay a federal student loan.
Target applicants: High school students. College students. Adult students.
Minimum GPA: 2.5
Amount: Up to $10,000.
Number of awards: Varies.
Deadline: Varies.
How to apply: Applications are available online.
Exclusive: Visit www.UltimateScholarshipBook.com and enter code UN259612 for updates on this award.

(2597) • Morris K. Udall Scholarship

Morris K. Udall Foundation
130 S. Scott Avenue
Tucson, AZ 85701-1922
Phone: 520-901-8500
Fax: 520-670-5530
Email: info@udall.gov
http://www.udall.gov

Purpose: To aid students committed to careers related to the environment, tribal public policy or Native American health care.
Eligibility: Students must be juniors or sophomores studying full-time for an associate's or bachelor's degree at an accredited two- or four-year institution. They must be U.S. citizens, nationals or permanent residents and be committed to a career related to the environment, tribal public

policy or Native American health care. Students must be nominated by a college or university faculty representative and must have a grade point average equivalent to a "B" or higher. Selection is based on demonstrated commitment to the environment, tribal public policy or Native Americal healthcare. Selection is also based on potential of applicant to make significant contributions, leadership, character, desire to make a difference and demonstration of diverse interests and activities.
Target applicants: College students. Adult students.
Minimum GPA: 3.0
Amount: Up to $5,000.
Number of awards: 80.
Scholarship may be renewable.
Deadline: March 2.
How to apply: Applications are available online. An application form, essay, college transcript(s) and three recommendation letters are required.
Exclusive: Visit www.UltimateScholarshipBook.com and enter code MO259712 for updates on this award.

(2598) • Mutual of Omaha Actuarial Scholarship for Minority Students

Mutual of Omaha
Mutual of Omaha Plaza
Strategic Staffing - Actuarial Recruitment
Omaha, NE 68175
Phone: 402-351-3300
http://www.mutualofomaha.com
Purpose: To support undergraduate students who are preparing for actuarial careers.
Eligibility: Applicants must be African-American, Native American, Hispanic, Asian American or from another underrepresented minority group. They must be U.S. citizens, permanent residents, temporary residents, asylees or refugees and must be full-time undergraduate students who have completed 24 or more credit hours (including 18 or more graded hours). They must be pursuing a degree in mathematics or an actuarial-related subject and must have a GPA of 3.0 or more. Applicants must have plans to pursue a career in an actuarial field and must have passed at least one actuarial exam. Scholarship recipients must be willing to complete a summer internship at the Mutual of Omaha offices in Omaha. Selection is based on the overall strength of the application.
Target applicants: College students. Adult students.
Minimum GPA: 3.0
Amount: $5,000.
Number of awards: Varies.
Scholarship may be renewable.
Deadline: November 15.
How to apply: Applications are available online. An application form, personal statement, one recommendation letter and a resume are required.
Exclusive: Visit www.UltimateScholarshipBook.com and enter code MU259812 for updates on this award.

(2599) • NAACP/HBCU Scholarship Fund

United Negro College Fund (UNCF)
8260 Willow Oaks Corporate Drive
P.O. Box 10444
Fairfax, VA 22031-8044
Phone: 800-331-2244
http://www.uncf.org/
Purpose: To support incoming freshmen at HBCUs.
Eligibility: Applicants must be incoming African American freshmen at a Historically Black College or University (HBCU). Students must have a GPA of at least 2.5 and demonstrate financial need.
Target applicants: High school students.
Minimum GPA: 2.5
Amount: $2,000.
Number of awards: 1.
Deadline: Last Friday in March.
How to apply: Applications are available online.
Exclusive: Visit www.UltimateScholarshipBook.com and enter code UN259912 for updates on this award.

(2600) • NABJ/Carole Simpson Scholarship

National Association of Black Journalists
1100 Knight Hall
Suite 3100
College Park, MD 20742
Phone: 301-405-7520
Fax: 301-314-1714
Email: iwashington@nabj.org
http://www.nabj.org
Purpose: To aid broadcast journalism students.
Eligibility: Applicants must be student members of the National Association of Black Journalists (NABJ). They must be undergraduate or graduate students who are enrolled in a degree program in broadcast journalism and have a GPA of 2.5 or higher. Selection is based on the overall strength of the application.
Target applicants: College students. Graduate school students. Adult students.
Minimum GPA: 2.5
Amount: $2,500.
Number of awards: 1.
Deadline: April 4.
How to apply: Applications are available online. An application form and supporting materials are required.
Exclusive: Visit www.UltimateScholarshipBook.com and enter code NA260012 for updates on this award.

(2601) • NACME Pre-Engineering Student Scholarships

National Action Council for Minorities in Engineering Inc. (NACME)
Pre-Engineering Scholarship Program
440 Hamilton Avenue, Suite 302
White Plains, NY 10601-1813
Phone: 914-539-4010
Fax: 914-539-4032
Email: scholarships@nacme.org
http://www.nacmebacksme.org
Purpose: To aid minority high school seniors who are planning to pursue higher education in engineering.
Eligibility: Applicants must be high school seniors. They must be African-American, Latino or Native American. They must be in the top 10 percent of their graduating class and must have been accepted into an ABET-accredited engineering school. They must have demonstrated leadership skills. Applicants must be formally nominated by their high school guidance counselor. Selection is based on the overall strength of the application.
Target applicants: High school students.
Amount: $1,500.
Number of awards: Varies.

Deadline: May 10.
How to apply: Applicants must be formally nominated by their high school guidance counselors. Nomination instructions are available online.
Exclusive: Visit www.UltimateScholarshipBook.com and enter code NA260112 for updates on this award.

(2602) • NAHJ General Scholarships - Rubén Salazar Fund

National Association of Hispanic Journalists
Scholarship Committee
1000 National Press Building
Washington, DC 20045
Phone: 202-662-7145
Fax: 202-662-7144
Email: ntita@nahj.org
http://www.nahj.org
Purpose: To support Hispanic students who plan to enter the broadcast journalism field.
Eligibility: Applicants must be high school seniors, college undergraduate or graduate students who plan to pursue careers in English or Spanish-language broadcast journalism.
Target applicants: High school students. College students. Graduate school students. Adult students.
Amount: $1,000-$2,000.
Number of awards: Varies.
Deadline: March 31.
How to apply: Applications are available online.
Exclusive: Visit www.UltimateScholarshipBook.com and enter code NA260212 for updates on this award.

(2603) • NAHJ Newhouse Scholarship Program

National Association of Hispanic Journalists
Scholarship Committee
1000 National Press Building
Washington, DC 20045
Phone: 202-662-7145
Fax: 202-662-7144
Email: ntita@nahj.org
http://www.nahj.org
Purpose: To support Hispanic students who plan to enter the journalism field.
Eligibility: Applicants must be current college sophomores. Recipients are required to intern at a Newhouse newspaper the summer following their junior year. The program provides a stipend to attend NAHJ's annual convention.
Target applicants: College students. Adult students.
Amount: Up to $5,000.
Number of awards: Varies.
Scholarship may be renewable.
Deadline: March 31.
How to apply: Applications are available online.
Exclusive: Visit www.UltimateScholarshipBook.com and enter code NA260312 for updates on this award.

(2604) • NAHN Scholarship

National Association of Hispanic Nurses
Attn: Maria Castro, NAHN Awards and Scholarship Committee Chair
1501 Sixteenth Street NW
Washington, DC 20036
Phone: 202-387-2477
Fax: 202-483-7183
Email: info@thehispanicnurses.org
http://www.thehispanicnurses.org
Purpose: To aid Hispanic nursing students who demonstrate the potential to make contributions to the nursing profession and who will act as positive role models for other nursing students.
Eligibility: Applicants must be members of the NAHN and be enrolled in a diploma, associate, baccalaureate, graduate or practical/vocational nursing program.
Target applicants: College students. Graduate school students. Adult students.
Minimum GPA: 3.0
Amount: $1,000.
Number of awards: Varies.
Deadline: March 14.
How to apply: Applications are available online or by mail.
Exclusive: Visit www.UltimateScholarshipBook.com and enter code NA260412 for updates on this award.

(2605) • NAJA Scholarship Fund

Native American Journalists Association
555 Dakota Street
Al Neuharth Media Center
Vermillion, SD 57069
Phone: 605-677-5282
Fax: 866-694-4262
Email: info@naja.com
http://www.naja.com
Purpose: To assist Native American students pursuing journalism degrees.
Eligibility: Applicants must be current members of NAJA.
Target applicants: College students. Adult students.
Amount: $500-$5,000.
Number of awards: Varies.
Deadline: April 2.
How to apply: Applications are available online.
Exclusive: Visit www.UltimateScholarshipBook.com and enter code NA260512 for updates on this award.

(2606) • NAMEPA Beginning Freshmen Engineering Student Award

National Association of Multicultural Engineering Program Advocates Inc.
341 North Maitland Avenue
Suite 130
Maitland, FL 32751
Phone: 407-647-8839
Fax: 407-629-2502
Email: namepa@namepa.org
http://www.namepa.org
Purpose: To aid minority students who are planning to pursue higher education in engineering.
Eligibility: Applicants must be graduating high school seniors who are African-American, Latino or Native American. They must have been accepted into a National Association of Multicultural Engineering Program Advocates (NAMEPA) member institution and designated as an engineering major. They must have a GPA of 2.7 or higher on a four-point scale and must have a cumulative ACT score of 25 or higher or a cumulative SAT score of 1000 or higher. Selection is based on coursework, extracurricular activities and recommendations.

Target applicants: High school students.
Minimum GPA: 2.7
Amount: $1,000.
Number of awards: Varies.
Deadline: May 26.
How to apply: Applications are available online. An application form, official transcript, standardized test scores, personal essay, resume and one letter of recommendation are required.
Exclusive: Visit www.UltimateScholarshipBook.com and enter code NA260612 for updates on this award.

(2607) • NANBPWC National Scholarships

National Association of Negro Business and Professional Women's Clubs Inc.
1806 New Hampshire Avenue NW
Washington, DC 20009-3298
Phone: 202-483-4206
Email: info@nanbpwc.org
http://www.nanbpwc.org
Purpose: To provide assistance to African American students who wish to pursue higher education.
Eligibility: Applicants must be graduating African American high school seniors with a GPA of 3.0 or higher. A 300-word essay is required.
Target applicants: High school students.
Minimum GPA: 3.0
Amount: Varies.
Number of awards: Varies.
Deadline: March 1.
How to apply: Applications are available online.
Exclusive: Visit www.UltimateScholarshipBook.com and enter code NA260712 for updates on this award.

(2608) • National AAJA General Scholarship Awards

Asian American Journalists Association
1182 Market Street
Suite 230
San Francisco, CA 94102
Phone: 415-346-2051
Fax: 415-346-6343
Email: lilac@aaja.org
http://www.aaja.org
Purpose: Monetary assistance is awarded to students pursuing studies that lead to careers in print, broadcast or photo journalism.
Eligibility: Applicants must demonstrate a commitment to the field of journalism, sensitivity to Asian American issues demonstrated by community involvement, journalistic ability, scholastic ability and financial need. Applicants may be high school seniors, college students or graduate students.
Target applicants: High school students. College students. Graduate school students. Adult students.
Amount: Varies.
Number of awards: Varies.
Deadline: Varies.
How to apply: Applications are available online.
Exclusive: Visit www.UltimateScholarshipBook.com and enter code AS260812 for updates on this award.

(2609) • National and District Scholarships

American Hellenic Education Progressive Association
1909 Q Street NW
Suite 500
Washington, DC 20009
Phone: 202-232-6300
Fax: 202-232-2140
Email: ahepa@ahepa.org
http://www.ahepa.org
Purpose: To support projects furthering the goals of AHEPA: studies concerning Hellenism, Hellenic culture or Greek-American life.
Eligibility: Applicants must be high school seniors, college students, post-graduate students or adult students of Greek descent.
Target applicants: High school students. College students. Graduate school students. Adult students.
Amount: Varies.
Number of awards: Varies.
Scholarship may be renewable.
Deadline: March 31.
How to apply: Applications are available online.
Exclusive: Visit www.UltimateScholarshipBook.com and enter code AM260912 for updates on this award.

(2610) • National Association of Black Accountants National Scholarship Program

National Association of Black Accountants
7249-A Hanover Parkway
Greenbelt, MD 20770
Phone: 301-474-NABA
Fax: 301-474-3114
http://www.nabainc.org
Purpose: To support African Americans and other minorities in the accounting and finance professions.
Eligibility: Applicants must be ethnic minorities currently enrolled as full-time undergraduates in accounting, finance or business or as graduate students in a Master's of Accountancy program. Applicants must also be NABA members and have a minimum 3.5 major GPA and 3.3 cumulative GPA.
Target applicants: College students. Graduate school students. Adult students.
Minimum GPA: 3.3
Amount: $3,000-$6,000.
Number of awards: Varies.
Deadline: January 1-January 31.
How to apply: Applications are available online.
Exclusive: Visit www.UltimateScholarshipBook.com and enter code NA261012 for updates on this award.

(2611) • National Association of Black Journalists Scholarship Program

National Association of Black Journalists
1100 Knight Hall
Suite 3100
College Park, MD 20742
Phone: 301-405-7520
Fax: 301-314-1714
Email: iwashington@nabj.org
http://www.nabj.org
Purpose: To support African American students who are planning to pursue careers in journalism.
Eligibility: Applicants must be African American high school seniors, college students or graduate students who plan to pursue careers in journalism and who are journalism majors or in staff positions on the school newspaper or campus television, radio or website.

Target applicants: High school students. College students. Graduate school students. Adult students.
Amount: $1,250-$5,000.
Number of awards: Varies.
Deadline: Varies.
How to apply: Applications are available online.
Exclusive: Visit www.UltimateScholarshipBook.com and enter code NA261112 for updates on this award.

(2612) • National Foster Parent Association (NFPA) College Scholarship

National Foster Parent Association (NFPA)
2313 Tacoma Avenue South
Tacoma, WA 98418
Phone: 253-683-4246
Fax: 253-853-4001
Email: info@nfpainc.org
http://www.nfpainc.org
Purpose: To support foster youth.
Eligibility: Applicants must be foster children who are high school seniors planning to attend a college or university.
Target applicants: High school students.
Amount: Varies.
Number of awards: Varies.
Deadline: March 31.
How to apply: Applications are available online.
Exclusive: Visit www.UltimateScholarshipBook.com and enter code NA261212 for updates on this award.

(2613) • National Foster Parent Association Vocational/Job Training Scholarship

National Foster Parent Association (NFPA)
2313 Tacoma Avenue South
Tacoma, WA 98418
Phone: 253-683-4246
Fax: 253-853-4001
Email: info@nfpainc.org
http://www.nfpainc.org
Purpose: To support foster youth in furthering their education through technical or vocational programs.
Eligibility: Applicants must be foster children at least 17 years old planning to enroll in vocational, job training or correspondence courses, including the GED.
Target applicants: High school students. College students. Adult students.
Amount: $1,000.
Number of awards: 5.
Deadline: March 31.
How to apply: Applications are available online.
Exclusive: Visit www.UltimateScholarshipBook.com and enter code NA261312 for updates on this award.

(2614) • National Leadership Grant

Order Sons of Italy in America (OSIA)
219 E Street NE
Washington, DC 20002
Phone: 202-547-5106
Fax: 202-546-8168
Email: scholarships@osia.org
http://www.osia.org
Purpose: To provide awards to college students of Italian descent.
Eligibility: Applicants must be enrolled in an undergraduate or graduate program at a four-year university and of Italian descent. Students must submit official transcripts, test scores, letters of recommendation and an essay. Awards are given based on academic merit. There is a non-refundable $30 processing fee. Note: We do not recommend applying to scholarships that charge application fees. However, some scholarships of this type charge fees and are included for completeness.
Target applicants: College students. Graduate school students. Adult students.
Amount: $5,000-$25,000.
Number of awards: 10-12.
Deadline: February 28.
How to apply: Applications are available online.
Exclusive: Visit www.UltimateScholarshipBook.com and enter code OR261412 for updates on this award.

(2615) • National Scholarship

National Association of Negro Business and Professional Women's Clubs Inc.
1806 New Hampshire Avenue NW
Washington, DC 20009-3298
Phone: 202-483-4206
Email: info@nanbpwc.org
http://www.nanbpwc.org
Purpose: To award scholarships to aspiring business and professional college or university students.
Eligibility: Applicants must be graduating high school seniors and have a minimum 3.0 GPA. Students must submit a transcript, an application form, two letters of recommendation and an essay that is at least 300 words on "Why is education important to me?"
Target applicants: High school students.
Minimum GPA: 3.0
Amount: Varies.
Number of awards: Varies.
Deadline: March 1.
How to apply: Applications are available online.
Exclusive: Visit www.UltimateScholarshipBook.com and enter code NA261512 for updates on this award.

(2616) • Native American Education Grant

Presbyterian Church (USA)
100 Witherspoon Street
Louisville, KY 40202
Phone: 888-728-7228 x5776
Email: finaid@pcusa.org
http://www.pcusa.org/financialaid
Purpose: To aid Alaska Natives and Native Americans pursuing full-time post-secondary education.
Eligibility: Applicants must be U.S. citizens who are high school graduates or GED recipients and demonstrate financial need. Applicants must present proof of tribal membership, and preference will be given to active members of the Presbyterian Church. Students are awarded based on the availability of funds and best match to donor restrictions.
Target applicants: College students. Adult students.
Minimum GPA: 2.5
Amount: Up to $1,500.
Number of awards: 35.
Deadline: June 15.
How to apply: Subscribe to the list serve to get an application.

Exclusive: Visit www.UltimateScholarshipBook.com and enter code PR261612 for updates on this award.

(2617) • Native American Leadership Education Program

Catching the Dream
Attn.: Scholarship Affairs Office
8200 Mountain Road NE
Suite 203
Albuquerque, NM 87110
Phone: 505-262-2351
Email: nscholarsh@aol.com
http://www.catchingthedream.org

Purpose: To increase the number of American Indian teachers in American Indian schools.

Eligibility: Applicants must be at least 1/4 degree American Indian, enrolled in a tribe and current paraprofessionals in an American Indian school who are attending or plan to attend college full-time studying education, counseling or school administration. Students are required to apply for all other sources of funding at the same time as applying for this scholarship. Scholarships are based on grades, ACT or SAT scores, work experience, leadership, commitment to the American Indian community, goals and potential to improve the lives of American Indian people.

Target applicants: College students. Graduate school students. Adult students.

Amount: $500-$5,000.

Number of awards: Varies.

Deadline: March 15, April 15 and September 15.

How to apply: Applications are available online.

Exclusive: Visit www.UltimateScholarshipBook.com and enter code CA261712 for updates on this award.

(2618) • Nelnet Scholarship

United Negro College Fund (UNCF)
8260 Willow Oaks Corporate Drive
P.O. Box 10444
Fairfax, VA 22031-8044
Phone: 800-331-2244
http://www.uncf.org/

Purpose: To support African American students attending UNCF member schools.

Eligibility: Applicants must have a minimum 2.5 GPA, complete the Free Application for Federal Student Aid (FAFSA) and have unmet financial need that is verified by the college or university financial aid office. Students are encouraged to complete the UNCF General Scholarship application to be matched with scholarships for which they meet the criteria.

Target applicants: High school students. College students. Adult students.

Minimum GPA: 2.5

Amount: $1,000.

Number of awards: Varies.

Deadline: Varies.

How to apply: Applications are available online.

Exclusive: Visit www.UltimateScholarshipBook.com and enter code UN261812 for updates on this award.

(2619) • Newhouse Foundation Scholarship

National Association of Black Journalists
1100 Knight Hall
Suite 3100
College Park, MD 20742
Phone: 301-405-7520
Fax: 301-314-1714
Email: iwashington@nabj.org
http://www.nabj.org

Purpose: To aid students who are preparing for careers in print journalism.

Eligibility: Applicants must be student members of the National Association of Black Journalists (NABJ). They must be enrolled in or planning to enroll in a four-year print journalism degree program at an accredited school and have a GPA of 3.0 or higher. They must work for or have plans to work for the campus newspaper and must demonstrate financial need. Selection is based on the overall strength of the application.

Target applicants: High school students. College students. Adult students.

Minimum GPA: 3.0

Amount: Up to $5,000.

Number of awards: Varies.

Scholarship may be renewable.

Deadline: Varies.

How to apply: Applications are available online. An application form and supporting materials are required.

Exclusive: Visit www.UltimateScholarshipBook.com and enter code NA261912 for updates on this award.

(2620) • NOAA Educational Partnership Program Undergraduate Scholarships

NOAA Educational Partnership Program
1315 East-West Highway
Room 10703
Silver Spring, MD 20910
Phone: 301-713-9437
Fax: 301-713-9465
Email: studentscholarshipprograms@noaa.gov
http://www.epp.noaa.gov

Purpose: To aid undergraduates who are attending a minority serving institution and are pursuing undergraduate degrees in subjects related to the atmospheric, oceanic or environmental sciences.

Eligibility: Applicants must be U.S. citizens and full-time undergraduates who are in the second year of a four-year degree program or in the third year of a five-year degree program. They must be attending an accredited minority serving institution (MSI), and they must have a GPA of 3.0 or higher on a four-point scale. Applicants must be majoring in a discipline that is related to environmental, atmospheric or oceanic sciences. Selection is based on relevant coursework completed, stated career goals, recommendations and extracurricular activities.

Target applicants: College students. Adult students.

Minimum GPA: 3.0

Amount: Varies.

Number of awards: Up to 15.

Scholarship may be renewable.

Deadline: January 31.

How to apply: Applications are available online. An application form, two personal essays, two recommendation letters and an official transcript are required.

Exclusive: Visit www.UltimateScholarshipBook.com and enter code NO262012 for updates on this award.

(2621) · Northrop Grumman Foundation Scholarship

Society of Women Engineers
120 South LaSalle Street
Suite 1515
Chicago, IL 60603
Phone: 877-793-4636
Email: scholarshipapplication@swe.org
http://www.swe.org

Purpose: To aid female undergraduate computer science and engineering students.

Eligibility: Applicants must be rising undergraduate sophomores, juniors or seniors. They must be enrolled in an accredited degree program in computer science, chemical engineering, manufacturing engineering, aerospace engineering, electrical engineering, computer engineering, mechanical engineering or industrial engineering. They must have a GPA of 3.0 or higher on a four-point scale. Selection is based on the overall strength of the application.

Target applicants: College students. Adult students.

Minimum GPA: 3.0

Amount: $5,000.

Number of awards: 1.

Deadline: Varies.

How to apply: Applications are available online. An application form and supporting materials are required.

Exclusive: Visit www.UltimateScholarshipBook.com and enter code SO262112 for updates on this award.

(2622) · Northrop Grumman Freshman Scholarship

Society of Women Engineers
120 South LaSalle Street
Suite 1515
Chicago, IL 60603
Phone: 877-793-4636
Email: scholarshipapplication@swe.org
http://www.swe.org

Purpose: To aid female freshmen undergraduates who are planning to major in computer science or engineering.

Eligibility: Applicants must be rising undergraduate freshmen who are planning to major in computer science, computer engineering, aerospace engineering, industrial engineering, mechanical engineering, systems engineering or electrical engineering. Selection is based on the overall strength of the application.

Target applicants: High school students.

Amount: $5,000.

Number of awards: 1.

Deadline: Varies.

How to apply: Applications are available online. An application form and supporting materials are required.

Exclusive: Visit www.UltimateScholarshipBook.com and enter code SO262212 for updates on this award.

(2623) · Northrop Grumman/HENAAC Scholars Program

Great Minds in STEM (HENAAC)
3900 Whiteside Street
Los Angeles, CA 90063
Phone: 323-262-0997
Fax: 323-262-0946
Email: jcano@greatmindsinstem.org
http://www.greatmindsinstem.org

Purpose: To aid Hispanic undergraduates who are studying naval architecture, computer science, computer engineering, electrical engineering or systems engineering.

Eligibility: Applicants must be undergraduates who have completed at least one academic year of college. They must demonstrate leadership experience. Selection is based on the overall strength of the application.

Target applicants: College students. Adult students.

Amount: Up to $5,000.

Number of awards: Varies.

Deadline: April 30.

How to apply: Applications are available online. An application form, personal essay, transcript, letters of recommendation and resume are required.

Exclusive: Visit www.UltimateScholarshipBook.com and enter code GR262312 for updates on this award.

(2624) · OCA-AXA Achievement Scholarship

OCA (formerly Organization of Chinese Americans)
1322 18th Street NW
Washington, DC 20036
Phone: 202-223-5500
Fax: 202-296-0540
Email: oca@ocanational.org
http://www.ocanational.org

Purpose: To help Asian Pacific American students.

Eligibility: Applicants must be entering their first year of college and be U.S. citizens or permanent residents. They must have a GPA of 3.0 or higher and demonstrate academic achievement, leadership ability and community service.

Target applicants: High school students.

Minimum GPA: 3.0

Amount: $2,000.

Number of awards: 10.

Deadline: Varies.

How to apply: Applications are available online. An application form, resume, essay, transcript, copy of acceptance letter, summary of college costs and Student Aid Report are required.

Exclusive: Visit www.UltimateScholarshipBook.com and enter code OC262412 for updates on this award.

(2625) · OCA-Verizon Scholarship

OCA (formerly Organization of Chinese Americans)
1322 18th Street NW
Washington, DC 20036
Phone: 202-223-5500
Fax: 202-296-0540
Email: oca@ocanational.org
http://www.ocanational.org

Purpose: To support Asian Pacific American students.

Eligibility: Applicants must be Asian Pacific Americans who are entering their second, third or fourth year of college. They must be U.S. citizens or permanent residents. They must demonstrate financial need and have an unweighted GPA of 3.0 or higher.

Target applicants: College students. Adult students.

Minimum GPA: 3.0

Amount: $2,000.

Number of awards: 12.

Deadline: Varies.

How to apply: Applications are available by mail. An application form, essay, transcript and Student Aid Report are required.
Exclusive: Visit www.UltimateScholarshipBook.com and enter code OC262512 for updates on this award.

(2626) • OCA/UPS Gold Mountain Scholarship

OCA (formerly Organization of Chinese Americans)
1322 18th Street NW
Washington, DC 20036
Phone: 202-223-5500
Fax: 202-296-0540
Email: oca@ocanational.org
http://www.ocanational.org
Purpose: To support first generation Asian American students.
Eligibility: Applicants must be Asian Pacific Americans who intend to begin college in the fall of the year of application and must demonstrate significant financial need. Applicants must also be the first in their family to attend college and have a minimum 3.0 GPA.
Target applicants: High school students.
Minimum GPA: 3.0
Amount: $2,000.
Number of awards: 12.
Deadline: April 1.
How to apply: Applications are available online or by written request.
Exclusive: Visit www.UltimateScholarshipBook.com and enter code OC262612 for updates on this award.

(2627) • Office Depot Scholarship

United Negro College Fund (UNCF)
8260 Willow Oaks Corporate Drive
P.O. Box 10444
Fairfax, VA 22031-8044
Phone: 800-331-2244
http://www.uncf.org/
Purpose: To help African American students attending United Negro College Fund (UNCF) member colleges and universities who have performed service to the community.
Eligibility: Applicants must have a minimum 2.5 GPA, complete the Free Application for Federal Student Aid (FAFSA) and have unmet financial need that is verified by the college or university financial aid office. Students are encouraged to complete the UNCF General Scholarship application to be matched with scholarships for which they meet the criteria. Applicants should submit two recommendation letters, a personal statement, a transcript, a resume and a small photo.
Target applicants: High school students. College students. Adult students.
Minimum GPA: 2.5
Amount: $2,000-$3,000.
Number of awards: Varies.
Deadline: March 31.
How to apply: Applications are available online.
Exclusive: Visit www.UltimateScholarshipBook.com and enter code UN262712 for updates on this award.

(2628) • Office of Hawaiian Affairs Scholarship Fund

Hawaii Community Foundation - Scholarships
1164 Bishop Street, Suite 800
Honolulu, HI 96813
Phone: 888-731-3863
Fax: 808-521-6286
Email: scholarships@hcf-hawaii.org
http://www.hawaiicommunityfoundation.org
Purpose: To support students of Hawaiian ancestry.
Eligibility: Students may attend any two- or four-year college in the United States. Ancestry must be verified through the office's Hawaiian Registry Program, which is available online.
Target applicants: High school students. College students. Adult students.
Amount: Varies.
Number of awards: Varies.
Deadline: March 1.
How to apply: To apply, register online, complete the online application and select the scholarships to which you wish to apply. In addition, mail the supporting materials: printed confirmation page from the online application, personal statement, copy of Student Aid Report (SAR) available at www.fafsa.ed.gov and official transcript.
Exclusive: Visit www.UltimateScholarshipBook.com and enter code HA262812 for updates on this award.

(2629) • Olive Lynn Salembier Memorial Reentry Scholarship

Society of Women Engineers
120 South LaSalle Street
Suite 1515
Chicago, IL 60603
Phone: 877-793-4636
Email: scholarshipapplication@swe.org
http://www.swe.org
Purpose: To aid female engineering students.
Eligibility: Applicants must be female high school seniors, undergraduates or graduate students who are studying or planning to study engineering. Undergraduate and graduate applicants must have a GPA of 3.0 or higher on a four-point scale. Selection is based on the overall strength of the application.
Target applicants: High school students. College students. Graduate school students. Adult students.
Minimum GPA: 3.0
Amount: $2,000.
Number of awards: 3.
Deadline: Varies.
How to apply: Applications are available online. An application form and supporting materials are required.
Exclusive: Visit www.UltimateScholarshipBook.com and enter code SO262912 for updates on this award.

(2630) • Outstanding Student Member of the Year Award

Council for Exceptional Children
1110 North Glebe Road
Suite 300
Arlington, VA 22201
Phone: 888-232-7733
Fax: 703-264-9494
Email: mbrship@cec.sped.org
http://www.cec.sped.org
Purpose: To recognize a student CEC member.
Eligibility: Applicants must be undergraduate or graduate students enrolled in an accredited college or university and be U.S. or Canadian citizens. Students must also be student CEC members who have contributed to the organization and exceptional children. Applicants must submit a list of their Student CEC activities and/or other

involvement with programs for those with disabilities and a short autobiography focusing on their interest in special education.
Target applicants: College students. Graduate school students. Adult students.
Minimum GPA: 2.5
Amount: $500.
Number of awards: 2.
Deadline: October 31.
How to apply: Applications are available online.
Exclusive: Visit www.UltimateScholarshipBook.com and enter code CO263012 for updates on this award.

(2631) • P.A. Margaronis Scholarships

American Hellenic Education Progressive Association
1909 Q Street NW
Suite 500
Washington, DC 20009
Phone: 202-232-6300
Fax: 202-232-2140
Email: ahepa@ahepa.org
http://www.ahepa.org
Purpose: To support undergraduate and graduate students who are of Greek descent.
Eligibility: Applicants must submit an essay and two letters of recommendation.
Target applicants: High school students. College students. Graduate school students. Adult students.
Amount: Varies.
Number of awards: Varies.
Deadline: March 31.
How to apply: Applications are available online.
Exclusive: Visit www.UltimateScholarshipBook.com and enter code AM263112 for updates on this award.

(2632) • P.E.O. Program for Continuing Education

P.E.O. Sisterhood
3700 Grand Avenue
Des Moines, IA 50312
Phone: 515-255-3153
Fax: 515-255-3820
http://www.peointernational.org
Purpose: To assist women whose education has been interrupted.
Eligibility: Applicants must be women who are resuming studies to improve their marketable skills due to changing demands in their lives. They must have financial need and cannot use the funds to pay living expenses or repay educational loans. They must be sponsored by a P.E.O. chapter and be citizens and students of the United States or Canada. They must have had at least two consecutive years as a non-student in their adult lives and be able to complete their educational goals in two consecutive years or less. Doctoral degree students are not eligible.
Target applicants: College students. Graduate school students. Adult students.
Amount: Up to $3,000.
Number of awards: Varies.
Deadline: 10 weeks before the start of classes.
How to apply: Applications are available from your local P.E.O. Chapter. An application form, income and expense statement and chapter recommendation are required. See website to locate nearest P.E.O. Chapter.
Exclusive: Visit www.UltimateScholarshipBook.com and enter code P.263212 for updates on this award.

(2633) • PBS&J Achievement Scholarship

Conference of Minority Transportation Officials
818 18th Street NW, Suite 850
Washington, DC 20006
Phone: 202-530-0551
Fax: 202-530-0617
Email: comto@comto.org
http://www.comto.org
Purpose: To support high school, undergraduate and graduate students who are pursuing careers in transportation.
Eligibility: High school and undergraduate students must have at least a 2.0 GPA. Undergraduate students must be enrolled in at least 12 credits per semester. Undergraduate and graduate students must have majors related to transportation.
Target applicants: High school students. College students. Graduate school students. Adult students.
Minimum GPA: 2.0
Amount: $4,000.
Number of awards: Varies.
Deadline: April 4.
How to apply: Applications are available online.
Exclusive: Visit www.UltimateScholarshipBook.com and enter code CO263312 for updates on this award.

(2634) • PEO International Peace Scholarship

PEO International Peace Scholarship Fund
3700 Grand Avenue
Des Moines, IA 50312
Phone: 515-255-3153
Fax: 515-255-3820
http://www.peointernational.org
Purpose: Women from countries other than the U.S. or Canada are assisted in their graduate studies within North America.
Eligibility: Applicants must be female, attend a North American graduate school or Cottey College and be from a country other than the U.S. or Canada. Eligibility must be established by submitting an eligibility form between August 15 and December 15.
Target applicants: Graduate school students. Adult students.
Amount: Up to $10,000.
Number of awards: Varies.
Scholarship may be renewable.
Deadline: January 31.
How to apply: Applicants must first submit an eligibility form, available online. If found eligible, students will be mailed application materials.
Exclusive: Visit www.UltimateScholarshipBook.com and enter code PE263412 for updates on this award.

(2635) • Physician Assistants for Latino Health Scholarships

Physician Assistants for Latino Health
950 North Washington Street
Alexandria, VA 22314
Phone: 800-596-7494
Fax: 703-684-1924
Email: palh@aapa.org
http://www.pasforlatinohealth.com
Purpose: To aid physician assistant students who are interested in Latino health.
Eligibility: Applicants must be members of Physician Assistants for Latino Health (PALH) and the American Academy of Physician

Assistants (AAPA). They must be currently enrolled in a physician assistant program and have leadership experience in the Latino community or be interested in Latino health concerns. They must have a GPA of 3.0 or higher. Selection is based on the overall strength of the application.
Target applicants: College students. Graduate school students. Adult students.
Minimum GPA: 3.0
Amount: $500.
Number of awards: 2.
Deadline: April 1.
How to apply: Applications are available online. An application form, statement of purpose, one letter of recommendation and a transcript are required.
Exclusive: Visit www.UltimateScholarshipBook.com and enter code PH263512 for updates on this award.

(2636) · Polish National Alliance Scholarship

Polish National Alliance
Educational Department
6100 Cicero Avenue
Chicago, IL 60646
Phone: 800-621-3723
Email: pna@pna-znp.org
http://www.pna-znp.org
Purpose: To assist members of the Polish National Alliance with their undergraduate studies.
Eligibility: Applicants must be college sophomores, juniors or seniors and have been paying members in good standing with the Polish National Association for at least three years. If the applicant has been in good standing with the PNA for at least two years, his or her parents must have been paying PNA members for at least five years.
Target applicants: College students. Adult students.
Amount: Varies.
Number of awards: Varies.
Scholarship may be renewable.
Deadline: April 15.
How to apply: Applications are available by email at mary.srodon@pna-znp.org.
Exclusive: Visit www.UltimateScholarshipBook.com and enter code PO263612 for updates on this award.

(2637) · Possible Woman Foundation International Scholarship

Possible Woman Enterprises
1054 Redwood Drive
Norcross, GA 30093
Email: info@possiblewomanfoundation.org
http://www.possiblewomanfoundation.org
Purpose: To provide financial assistance to women who are returning to school to change or further their careers and to stay-at-home moms who need additional training.
Eligibility: Applicants must be women at least 25 years of age who plan to study in the United States. Students from other countries are eligible but must be referred by an educational institution or organization. Applicants should not be eligible for significant funding from other sources. Selection is based on financial need, other funding received, goals, essay, leadership and participation in community activities, honors and awards.
Target applicants: College students. Adult students.
Amount: $2,000-$5,000.
Number of awards: Varies.
Deadline: January 7.
How to apply: Applications are available online. An application form and essay are required.
Exclusive: Visit www.UltimateScholarshipBook.com and enter code PO263712 for updates on this award.

(2638) · Premedical Summer Institute Program/ Internship

United Negro College Fund (UNCF)
8260 Willow Oaks Corporate Drive
P.O. Box 10444
Fairfax, VA 22031-8044
Phone: 800-331-2244
http://www.uncf.org/
Purpose: To help African American students attending United Negro College Fund (UNCF) Member Colleges and Universities who are pre-med and who are interested in medical careers.
Eligibility: Applicants must have a minimum 3.0 GPA, complete the Free Application for Federal Student Aid (FAFSA) and have unmet financial need that is verified by the college or university financial aid office. Students are encouraged to complete the UNCF General Scholarship application to be matched with scholarships for which they meet the criteria. The program allows access to pre-med education through an eight-week internship during the summer.
Target applicants: High school students. College students. Adult students.
Minimum GPA: 3.0
Amount: $1,000.
Number of awards: Varies.
Deadline: March 1.
How to apply: Applications are available online.
Exclusive: Visit www.UltimateScholarshipBook.com and enter code UN263812 for updates on this award.

(2639) · Prince Kuhio Hawaiian Civic Club Scholarship

Prince Kuhio Hawaiian Civic Club
P.O. Box 4728
Honolulu, HI 96812
Email: cypakele@ksbe.edu
http://www.pkhcc.com
Purpose: To provide funds for higher education to Hawaiians.
Eligibility: Applicants must be high school seniors or current college students from Hawaii. Preference is given to students who have some Hawaiian ancestry and have participated in community service or volunteer work. Studies of Hawaiian language, studies and culture, journalism and education are encouraged. Applicants must enroll full-time at a two- or four-year institution.
Target applicants: High school students. College students. Adult students.
Amount: $500-$1,000.
Number of awards: Varies.
Scholarship may be renewable.
Deadline: April 1.
How to apply: Applications are available online or by mail.
Exclusive: Visit www.UltimateScholarshipBook.com and enter code PR263912 for updates on this award.

(2640) • Que Llueva Cafe Scholarship

Chicano Organizing and Research in Education
P.O. Box 160144
Sacramento, CA 95816
Email: jdelrazo@ca-core.org
http://www.ca-core.org

Purpose: To aid undocumented Latino students who wish to attend college.

Eligibility: Applicants must be graduating high school seniors, high school graduates or GED recipients who are legally undocumented residents of the U.S. They must have plans to enroll at an accredited postsecondary institution located in the U.S. or Puerto Rico. They must show academic promise and demonstrate financial need. Selection is based on the overall strength of the application.

Target applicants: High school students.

Amount: $500-$1,000.

Number of awards: Varies.

Deadline: February 26.

How to apply: Applications are available online. An application form, transcript, one letter of recommendation, a personal essay and a financial need statement are required.

Exclusive: Visit www.UltimateScholarshipBook.com and enter code CH264012 for updates on this award.

(2641) • Queen of the Highlands Scholarship

St. Andrew's Society of Detroit
30161 Southfield Road
Cranbrook Center - Suite 112
Southfield, MI 48076
Phone: 248-593-5064
Email: queenofthehighlands@hotmail.com
http://www.queenofthehighlands.com

Purpose: To support young ladies of Scottish descent.

Eligibility: Applicants must be 18 to 22 years of age. They must not be present Queens or members of the court from other organizations. Children or grandchildren of members of St. Andrew's Society Executive Board, its trustees and directors may not apply. Finalists must be available for an interview session and the crowning ceremony.

Target applicants: High school students. College students.

Amount: Up to $1,500.

Number of awards: Up to 3.

Deadline: March 6.

How to apply: Applications are available online. An application form, resume, essay, transcript, photograph and two letters of recommendation are required.

Exclusive: Visit www.UltimateScholarshipBook.com and enter code ST264112 for updates on this award.

(2642) • RA Consulting Service Maria Riley Scholarship

National Forum for Black Public Administrators
777 North Capitol Street NE
Suite 807
Washington, DC 20002
Phone: 202-408-9300
Fax: 202-408-8558
Email: vreed@nfbpa.org
http://www.nfbpa.org

Purpose: To support African-American engineering technology and information technology students.

Eligibility: Applicants must be full-time undergraduate or graduate students who are majoring in information technology or engineering technology. They must have a GPA of 3.0 or higher. Selection is based on the overall strength of the application.

Target applicants: College students. Graduate school students. Adult students.

Minimum GPA: 3.0

Amount: $2,500.

Number of awards: 1.

Deadline: February 28.

How to apply: Applications are available online. An application form, cover letter, official transcript, three recommendation letters, a personal essay, a resume and a copy of the applicant's student ID card are required.

Exclusive: Visit www.UltimateScholarshipBook.com and enter code NA264212 for updates on this award.

(2643) • Raymond W. Cannon Memorial Scholarship

United Negro College Fund (UNCF)
8260 Willow Oaks Corporate Drive
P.O. Box 10444
Fairfax, VA 22031-8044
Phone: 800-331-2244
http://www.uncf.org/

Purpose: To help African American student leaders.

Eligibility: Applicants must be juniors majoring in pharmacy or pre-law at United Negro College Fund (UNCF) member colleges or universities or Historically Black Colleges or Universities (HBCU Schools) and who have shown leadership in high school and college.

Target applicants: College students. Adult students.

Minimum GPA: 2.5

Amount: $2,000-$5,000.

Number of awards: Varies.

Deadline: Varies.

How to apply: Applications are available online.

Exclusive: Visit www.UltimateScholarshipBook.com and enter code UN264312 for updates on this award.

(2644) • Reader's Digest Scholarship

United Negro College Fund (UNCF)
8260 Willow Oaks Corporate Drive
P.O. Box 10444
Fairfax, VA 22031-8044
Phone: 800-331-2244
http://www.uncf.org/

Purpose: To help African American students attending United Negro College Fund (UNCF) Member Colleges and Universities and majoring in communications, journalism or English who have shown an interest in print journalism.

Eligibility: Applicants must have a minimum 3.0 GPA, complete the Free Application for Federal Student Aid (FAFSA) and have unmet financial need that is verified by the college or university financial aid office. Students are encouraged to complete the UNCF General Scholarship application to be matched with scholarships for which they meet the criteria. Funds may be used for tuition, room and board, books or to repay a federal student loan.

Target applicants: High school students. College students. Adult students.

Minimum GPA: 3.0

Amount: $5,000.

Number of awards: Varies.

Deadline: Varies.

How to apply: Applications are available online.
Exclusive: Visit www.UltimateScholarshipBook.com and enter code UN264412 for updates on this award.

(2645) · Richard R. Tufenkian Memorial Scholarship

Armenian Educational Foundation Inc.
600 W. Broadway
Suite 130
Glendale, CA 91204
Phone: 818-242-4154
Email: aef@aefweb.org
http://www.aefweb.org
Purpose: To support Armenian undergraduate students.
Eligibility: Applicants must be full-time undergraduate students of Armenian descent at U.S. universities, have a minimum 3.0 GPA, demonstrate financial need and be involved in the Armenian community. Tax returns, transcripts, two reference letters, essays and applications are required.
Target applicants: College students. Adult students.
Minimum GPA: 3.0
Amount: $2,000.
Number of awards: 5.
Deadline: July 29.
How to apply: Applications are available online.
Exclusive: Visit www.UltimateScholarshipBook.com and enter code AR264512 for updates on this award.

(2646) · Robert Dole Scholarship for Disabled Students

United Negro College Fund (UNCF)
8260 Willow Oaks Corporate Drive
P.O. Box 10444
Fairfax, VA 22031-8044
Phone: 800-331-2244
http://www.uncf.org/
Purpose: To help physically and/or mentally challenged African Americans at United Negro College Fund (UNCF) member colleges or universities.
Eligibility: Applicants must have a minimum 2.5 GPA, complete the Free Application for Federal Student Aid (FAFSA) and have unmet financial need that is verified by the college or university financial aid office. UNCF students are encouraged to complete the UNCF General Scholarship application to be matched with scholarships for which they meet the criteria.
Target applicants: High school students. College students. Adult students.
Minimum GPA: 2.5
Amount: Up to $3,500.
Number of awards: Varies.
Deadline: March 1.
How to apply: Applications are available online.
Exclusive: Visit www.UltimateScholarshipBook.com and enter code UN264612 for updates on this award.

(2647) · Robert Half International

United Negro College Fund (UNCF)
8260 Willow Oaks Corporate Drive
P.O. Box 10444
Fairfax, VA 22031-8044
Phone: 800-331-2244
http://www.uncf.org/
Purpose: To support African American business and accounting students.
Eligibility: Applicants must be majoring in business or accounting at a UNCF member college or university. They must have a GPA of at least 2.5 and demonstrate financial need.
Target applicants: High school students. College students. Adult students.
Minimum GPA: 2.5
Amount: $1,000-$1,750.
Number of awards: Varies.
Deadline: Varies.
How to apply: Applications are available online.
Exclusive: Visit www.UltimateScholarshipBook.com and enter code UN264712 for updates on this award.

(2648) · Rockwell Automation Scholarship

Society of Women Engineers
120 South LaSalle Street
Suite 1515
Chicago, IL 60603
Phone: 877-793-4636
Email: scholarshipapplication@swe.org
http://www.swe.org
Purpose: To aid female undergraduates who are studying engineering, computer science or engineering technology.
Eligibility: Applicants must be juniors or seniors who are majoring in computer engineering, computer science, electrical engineering, engineering technology, industrial engineering, mechanical engineering, manufacturing engineering or software engineering. They must have a GPA of 3.0 or higher on a four-point scale and must demonstrate leadership ability. Selection is based on the overall strength of the application.
Target applicants: College students. Adult students.
Minimum GPA: 3.0
Amount: $2,500.
Number of awards: 2.
Deadline: Varies.
How to apply: Applications are available online. An application form and supporting materials are required.
Exclusive: Visit www.UltimateScholarshipBook.com and enter code SO264812 for updates on this award.

(2649) · Rockwell Collins Scholarship

Society of Women Engineers
120 South LaSalle Street
Suite 1515
Chicago, IL 60603
Phone: 877-793-4636
Email: scholarshipapplication@swe.org
http://www.swe.org
Purpose: To aid female undergraduates who are majoring in engineering, engineering technology or computer science.
Eligibility: Applicants must be sophomores or juniors who are majoring in mechanical engineering, industrial engineering, manufacturing engineering, software engineering, computer engineering, electrical engineering, engineering technology or computer science. They must have a GPA of 3.0 or higher on a four-point scale. Selection is based on the overall strength of the application.
Target applicants: College students. Adult students.
Minimum GPA: 3.0

Amount: $2,500.
Number of awards: 3.
Deadline: Varies.
How to apply: Applications are available online. An application form and supporting materials are required.
Exclusive: Visit www.UltimateScholarshipBook.com and enter code SO264912 for updates on this award.

(2650) • Ron Brown Scholar Program

CAP Charitable Foundation
Ron Brown Scholar Program
1160 Pepsi Place
Suite 206
Charlottesville, VA 22901
Phone: 434-964-1588
Fax: 434-964-1589
Email: franh@ronbrown.org
http://www.ronbrown.org
Purpose: To award scholarships to academically talented, highly motivated African American high school seniors.
Eligibility: Applicants must be African American collegebound high school seniors. Selection is based on academic promise, leadership, communication skills, school and community involvement and financial need.
Target applicants: High school students.
Amount: $10,000.
Number of awards: 10-20.
Scholarship may be renewable.
Deadline: January 9.
How to apply: Applications are available online.
Exclusive: Visit www.UltimateScholarshipBook.com and enter code CA265012 for updates on this award.

(2651) • Rosa L. Parks Scholarship

Conference of Minority Transportation Officials
818 18th Street NW, Suite 850
Washington, DC 20006
Phone: 202-530-0551
Fax: 202-530-0617
Email: comto@comto.org
http://www.comto.org
Purpose: To support graduating high school students whose parents are COMTO members and college or graduate students who are studying fields related to transportation.
Eligibility: Applicants must have at least a 3.0 GPA. High school students must be accepted into a college or technical school, and their parents must have been COMTO members in good standing for at least the past year. College students must have at least 60 credits, and graduate students must have at least 15 credits.
Target applicants: High school students. College students. Graduate school students. Adult students.
Minimum GPA: 3.0
Amount: $4,500.
Number of awards: Varies.
Deadline: April 16.
How to apply: Applications are available online.
Exclusive: Visit www.UltimateScholarshipBook.com and enter code CO265112 for updates on this award.

(2652) • Roy Wilkins Scholarship

National Association for the Advancement of Colored People
The United Negro College Fund
Scholarships and Grants Administration
8260 Willow Oaks Corporate Drive
Fairfax, VA 22031
Phone: 800-331-2244
Email: youth@naacpnet.org
http://www.naacp.org
Purpose: The NAACP created its scholarships to promote equal opportunity in education.
Eligibility: Students must be entering college freshmen at an accredited U.S. college and be full-time students. Membership in the NAACP is not required, but highly recommended.
Target applicants: High school students. College students. Adult students.
Minimum GPA: 2.5
Amount: $1,000.
Number of awards: Varies.
Deadline: The last Friday in the month of March.
How to apply: Applications are available online or by mail.
Exclusive: Visit www.UltimateScholarshipBook.com and enter code NA265212 for updates on this award.

(2653) • Scholarships for Social Justice

Higher Education Consortium for Urban Affairs
2233 University Avenue W, Suite 210
St. Paul, MN 55114
Phone: 651-646-8832
Email: info@hecua.org
http://www.hecua.org/scholarships.php
Purpose: To support students from low-income families, students from ethnic minorities and students who are the first in their families to attend college.
Eligibility: Students must have submitted an application to one of HECUA's semester programs, and they must be enrolled at an HECUA member institution. A list of member institutions is available online.
Target applicants: College students. Adult students.
Amount: $1,500.
Number of awards: 2.
Deadline: April 15.
How to apply: Applications are available online. An essay, letter of recommendation and Student Aid Report from completing the Free Application for Federal Student Aid are required.
Exclusive: Visit www.UltimateScholarshipBook.com and enter code HI265312 for updates on this award.

(2654) • Sequoyah Graduate Fellowships for American Indian and Alaskan Natives

Association on American Indian Affairs
Lisa Wyzlic, Director of Scholarship Programs
966 Hungerford Drive, Suite 12-B
Rockville, MD 20850
Phone: 240-314-7155
Fax: 240-314-7159
Email: general.aaia@verizon.net
http://www.indian-affairs.org
Purpose: To provide graduate fellowships for students of American Indian and Alaskan Native heritage.

Eligibility: Applicants must be full-time students who can provide proof of tribal enrollment, a Certificate of Indian Blood (showing 1/4 Indian blood) and an essay on educational goals.
Target applicants: Graduate school students. Adult students.
Amount: $1,500.
Number of awards: Varies.
Deadline: June 18.
How to apply: Applications are available online.
Exclusive: Visit www.UltimateScholarshipBook.com and enter code AS265412 for updates on this award.

(2655) • SHPE/CDM Scholars Program

Advancing Hispanic Excellence in Technology, Engineering, Math and Science, Inc.
The University of Texas at Arlington
College of Engineering, Box 19019
Nedderman Hall, Room 634
Arlington, TX 76019
Phone: 817-272-1116
Fax: 817-272-2548
Email: ahetems@shpe.org
http://www.ahetems.org
Purpose: To aid Hispanic students who are majoring in science, engineering or construction-related subjects.
Eligibility: Applicants must be members of the Society of Hispanic Professional Engineers (SHPE). They must be current undergraduates or entering graduate students who are pursuing degrees in engineering, science or a construction-related discipline. They must have a GPA of 3.0 or higher. Selection is based on the overall strength of the application.
Target applicants: College students. Graduate school students. Adult students.
Minimum GPA: 3.0
Amount: Up to $8,000.
Number of awards: Varies.
Deadline: February 1.
How to apply: Applications are available online. An application form, official transcript, resume, personal statement and two recommendation letters are required.
Exclusive: Visit www.UltimateScholarshipBook.com and enter code AD265512 for updates on this award.

(2656) • Siemens Corporation Scholarship

Society of Women Engineers
120 South LaSalle Street
Suite 1515
Chicago, IL 60603
Phone: 877-793-4636
Email: scholarshipapplication@swe.org
http://www.swe.org
Purpose: To aid entering undergraduate female students who are planning to major in electrical engineering, industrial engineering or manufacturing engineering.
Eligibility: Applicants must be U.S. citizens and be members of the Society of Women Engineers (SWE). They must be entering undergraduate freshmen who are planning to major in manufacturing engineering, electrical engineering or industrial engineering. Selection is based on the overall strength of the application.
Target applicants: High school students.
Amount: $2,500.
Number of awards: 2.
Deadline: Varies.
How to apply: Applications are available online. An application form and supporting materials are required.
Exclusive: Visit www.UltimateScholarshipBook.com and enter code SO265612 for updates on this award.

(2657) • Siemens Teacher Education Scholarship Program

United Negro College Fund (UNCF)
8260 Willow Oaks Corporate Drive
P.O. Box 10444
Fairfax, VA 22031-8044
Phone: 800-331-2244
http://www.uncf.org/
Purpose: To help African American students who are rising juniors or seniors who plan to teach in science, technology or math.
Eligibility: Applicants must plan to teach and may major in mathematics, science, information systems, education, chemistry, biology, science technology, computer engineering or chemical engineering. Applicants must have a minimum 2.75 GPA, complete the Free Application for Federal Student Aid (FAFSA) and have unmet financial need that is verified by the college or university financial aid office. UNCF students are encouraged to complete the UNCF General Scholarship application to be matched with scholarships for which they meet the criteria.
Target applicants: College students. Adult students.
Minimum GPA: 2.75
Amount: $4,400 average.
Number of awards: Varies.
Scholarship may be renewable.
Deadline: August 30.
How to apply: Applications are available online.
Exclusive: Visit www.UltimateScholarshipBook.com and enter code UN265712 for updates on this award.

(2658) • Sikh Education Aid Fund

Association of Sikh Professionals
2917 Oak Brook Hills Road
Oak Brook, IL 60523
Email: contact@sikhprofessionals.org
http://www.sikhprofessionals.org
Purpose: To recognize Sikh students for academic achievement.
Eligibility: Applicants must be accepted by or attend an accredited U.S. institution. Recipients are usually high school seniors or college students. Financial documents, a photo, copies of recent transcripts, essays and names and addresses of five Sikhs in the community are required. Financial need is the most important criteria, but academic ability and involvement in Sikh activities is also considered. Candidates may be interviewed.
Target applicants: High school students. College students. Graduate school students. Adult students.
Amount: $400-$4,000.
Number of awards: Varies.
Scholarship may be renewable.
Deadline: June 1.
How to apply: Applications are available online.
Exclusive: Visit www.UltimateScholarshipBook.com and enter code AS265812 for updates on this award.

(2659) • Siragusa Foundation Scholarship

United Negro College Fund (UNCF)
8260 Willow Oaks Corporate Drive
P.O. Box 10444
Fairfax, VA 22031-8044
Phone: 800-331-2244
http://www.uncf.org/

Purpose: To help African American students attending United Negro College Fund (UNCF) member colleges and universities.

Eligibility: Applicants must have a minimum 2.5 GPA, complete the Free Application for Federal Student Aid (FAFSA) and have unmet financial need that is verified by the college or university financial aid office. Students are encouraged to complete the UNCF General Scholarship application to be matched with scholarships for which they meet the criteria.

Target applicants: High school students. College students. Adult students.

Minimum GPA: 2.5

Amount: $2,000.

Number of awards: Varies.

Deadline: Varies.

How to apply: Applications are available online.

Exclusive: Visit www.UltimateScholarshipBook.com and enter code UN265912 for updates on this award.

(2660) • Slovenian Women's Union of America Scholarship Program

Slovenian Women's Union of America
Mary Turvey, SWUA Scholarship Director
4 Lawrence Drive
Marquette, MI 49855
Email: mturvey@aol.com
http://www.swua.org

Purpose: To promote Slovenian culture.

Eligibility: Students must be high school seniors or current college students at an accredited school. Applicants must have been members of the SWUA for at least three years. High school senior applications must include a photo, FAFSA, a letter of recommendation from high school principal or teacher, brief autobiography, including personal and educational goals, a high school transcript including SAT and ACT scores, a letter of recommendation from an SWUA branch officer and a financial statement from their parents. College student applications must include a photo, FAFSA, a brief autobiography including personal and educational goals, letters of recommendation from a college professor/ instructor and an SWUA branch officer and grade transcripts from the last two semesters. The committee considers life goals, scholastic achievement, financial need and involvement in school, church and community.

Target applicants: High school students. College students. Graduate school students. Adult students.

Amount: $500-$2,000.

Number of awards: Varies.

Deadline: March 1.

How to apply: Applications are available online and from SWUA branch secretaries.

Exclusive: Visit www.UltimateScholarshipBook.com and enter code SL266012 for updates on this award.

(2661) • Sodexho Scholarship

United Negro College Fund (UNCF)
8260 Willow Oaks Corporate Drive
P.O. Box 10444
Fairfax, VA 22031-8044
Phone: 800-331-2244
http://www.uncf.org/

Purpose: To help African American freshmen, especially those who have helped with community service programs dealing with hunger, attending Historically Black Colleges and Universities (HBCU) or United Negro College Fund (UNCF) member colleges and universities.

Eligibility: Applicants must have a minimum 3.0 GPA, complete the Free Application for Federal Student Aid (FAFSA) and have unmet financial need that is verified by the college or university financial aid office. UNCF students are encouraged to complete the UNCF General Scholarship application to be matched with scholarships for which they meet the criteria. Priority will be given to students who have participated in community service programs dealing with hunger. Applicants must submit a transcript, two recommendation letters, an essay and college or university acceptance letters.

Target applicants: High school students. College students. Adult students.

Minimum GPA: 3.0

Amount: Up to $5,000.

Number of awards: Varies.

Deadline: April 30.

How to apply: Applications are available online.

Exclusive: Visit www.UltimateScholarshipBook.com and enter code UN266112 for updates on this award.

(2662) • Sports Illustrated Scholarship

National Association of Black Journalists
1100 Knight Hall
Suite 3100
College Park, MD 20742
Phone: 301-405-7520
Fax: 301-314-1714
Email: iwashington@nabj.org
http://www.nabj.org

Purpose: To aid female students who are planning for careers in sports journalism.

Eligibility: Applicants must be student members of the National Association of Black Journalists (NABJ). They must be rising undergraduate seniors at an accredited college or university who are majoring in journalism or planning to pursue a career in sports journalism. Selection is based on the overall strength of the application.

Target applicants: College students. Adult students.

Amount: $5,000.

Number of awards: 1.

Deadline: Varies.

How to apply: Application instructions are available online. A resume, personal essay, five writing samples, an official transcript and three references are required.

Exclusive: Visit www.UltimateScholarshipBook.com and enter code NA266212 for updates on this award.

(2663) • Sterling Bank Scholarship

United Negro College Fund (UNCF)
8260 Willow Oaks Corporate Drive
P.O. Box 10444
Fairfax, VA 22031-8044
Phone: 800-331-2244
http://www.uncf.org/

Purpose: To help African American students attending United Negro College Fund (UNCF) member colleges and universities.
Eligibility: Applicants must have a minimum 2.5 GPA, complete the Free Application for Federal Student Aid (FAFSA) and have unmet financial need that is verified by the college or university financial aid office. Students are encouraged to complete the UNCF General Scholarship application to be matched with scholarships for which they meet the criteria.
Target applicants: High school students. College students. Adult students.
Minimum GPA: 2.5
Amount: Varies.
Number of awards: Varies.
Deadline: Varies.
How to apply: Applications are available online.
Exclusive: Visit www.UltimateScholarshipBook.com and enter code UN266312 for updates on this award.

(2664) • Student CEC Ethnic Diversity Scholarship

Council for Exceptional Children
1110 North Glebe Road
Suite 300
Arlington, VA 22201
Phone: 888-232-7733
Fax: 703-264-9494
Email: mbrship@cec.sped.org
http://www.cec.sped.org
Purpose: To recognize a student CEC member from an ethnically diverse background who is currently pursuing a degree in special education.
Eligibility: Applicants must be U.S. or Canadian citizens, junior, senior or graduate students enrolled in an accredited college or university, members of an ethnically diverse group and pursuing a degree in special education. Students must be student CEC members in good standing with a minimum 2.5 GPA. Applicants must also submit a list of their Student CEC activities and/or other involvement with those with disabilities and a short autobiography focusing on their interest in special education.
Target applicants: College students. Graduate school students. Adult students.
Minimum GPA: 2.5
Amount: Varies.
Number of awards: 1.
Deadline: October 30.
How to apply: Applications are available online.
Exclusive: Visit www.UltimateScholarshipBook.com and enter code CO266412 for updates on this award.

(2665) • Sutton Scholarship

National Association for the Advancement of Colored People
The United Negro College Fund
Scholarships and Grants Administration
8260 Willow Oaks Corporate Drive
Fairfax, VA 22031
Phone: 800-331-2244
Email: youth@naacpnet.org
http://www.naacp.org
Purpose: To support African Americans entering the field of education.
Eligibility: Applicants must be education majors at an accredited college and U.S. citizens. Undergraduates must be full-time students with a GPA of 2.5, while graduates may be full- or part-time students and must maintain a GPA of 3.0. NAACP membership is not required but is highly desirable.
Target applicants: High school students. College students. Graduate school students. Adult students.
Minimum GPA: 2.5 for undergraduate students and 3.0 for graduate students
Amount: $1,000-$2,000.
Number of awards: Varies.
Scholarship may be renewable.
Deadline: Last Friday in March.
How to apply: Applications are available online.
Exclusive: Visit www.UltimateScholarshipBook.com and enter code NA266512 for updates on this award.

(2666) • SWE Past Presidents Scholarship

Society of Women Engineers
120 South LaSalle Street
Suite 1515
Chicago, IL 60603
Phone: 877-793-4636
Email: scholarshipapplication@swe.org
http://www.swe.org
Purpose: To aid female engineering students.
Eligibility: Applicants must be U.S. citizens and be graduate students or undergraduate sophomores, juniors or seniors. They must be enrolled in an ABET-accredited engineering degree program and have a GPA of 3.0 or higher on a four-point scale. Selection is based on the overall strength of the application.
Target applicants: College students. Graduate school students. Adult students.
Minimum GPA: 3.0
Amount: $2,000.
Number of awards: 2.
Deadline: Varies.
How to apply: Applications are available online. An application form and supporting materials are required.
Exclusive: Visit www.UltimateScholarshipBook.com and enter code SO266612 for updates on this award.

(2667) • Sylvia Shapiro Scholarship

United Negro College Fund (UNCF)
8260 Willow Oaks Corporate Drive
P.O. Box 10444
Fairfax, VA 22031-8044
Phone: 800-331-2244
http://www.uncf.org/
Purpose: To help African American students attending United Negro College Fund (UNCF) member colleges and universities.
Eligibility: Applicants must have a minimum 2.5 GPA, complete the Free Application for Federal Student Aid (FAFSA) and have unmet financial need that is verified by the college or university financial aid office. Students are encouraged to complete the UNCF General Scholarship application to be matched with scholarships for which they meet the criteria.
Target applicants: High school students. College students. Adult students.
Minimum GPA: 2.5
Amount: Varies.
Number of awards: Varies.
Deadline: Varies.
How to apply: Applications are available online.

Exclusive: Visit www.UltimateScholarshipBook.com and enter code UN266712 for updates on this award.

(2668) • The Maureen L. and Howard N. Blitman, P.E., Scholarship

National Society of Professional Engineers
1420 King Street
Alexandria, VA 22314-2794
Phone: 703-684-2885
Fax: 703-836-4875
Email: memserv@nspe.org
http://www.nspe.org

Purpose: To encourage minority students to pursue careers in engineering.

Eligibility: Applicants must be African-American, Hispanic or Native American high school seniors who have been accepted into an accredited engineering program at a four-year institution. Students are evaluated based on academic achievement, community involvement and recommendations and must have a minimum 3.5 GPA.

Target applicants: High school students.

Minimum GPA: 3.5

Amount: $5,000.

Number of awards: 1.

Deadline: March 1.

How to apply: Applications are available online.

Exclusive: Visit www.UltimateScholarshipBook.com and enter code NA266812 for updates on this award.

(2669) • The MillerCoors National Scholarship

Adelante U.S. Educational Leadership Fund
8415 Datapoint Drive
Suite 400
San Antonio, TX 78229
Phone: 877-692-1971
Fax: 210-692-1951
Email: info@adelantefund.org
http://www.adelantefund.org

Purpose: To assist Latino students attending participating institutions who are pursuing degrees in business, economics, marketing or communications.

Eligibility: Applicants must be college juniors or seniors pursuing a business, marketing, economics, or communications degree. Students must have a 3.0 GPA or above and be full-time students attending one of the partnering universities.

Target applicants: College students. Adult students.

Minimum GPA: 3.0

Amount: Up to $3,000.

Number of awards: Varies.

Deadline: May 31.

How to apply: Applications are available online starting March 1.

Exclusive: Visit www.UltimateScholarshipBook.com and enter code AD266912 for updates on this award.

(2670) • Thomas G. Neusom Scholarship

Conference of Minority Transportation Officials
818 18th Street NW, Suite 850
Washington, DC 20006
Phone: 202-530-0551
Fax: 202-530-0617
Email: comto@comto.org
http://www.comto.org

Purpose: To support college students who are members of COMTO.

Eligibility: Applicants must have been COMTO members in good standing for at least the past year. Students must be enrolled in at least six credits per semester at a college, vocational school or graduate school. They must have at least a 2.5 GPA. Applicants must submit a short essay and two letters of recommendation.

Target applicants: College students. Graduate school students. Adult students.

Minimum GPA: 2.5

Amount: $5,500.

Number of awards: Varies.

Deadline: April 16.

How to apply: Applications are available online.

Exclusive: Visit www.UltimateScholarshipBook.com and enter code CO267012 for updates on this award.

(2671) • Thurgood Marshall College Scholarship Fund Scholarship

Thurgood Marshall Scholarship Fund
80 Maiden Lane
Suite 2204
New York, NY 10038
Phone: 212-573-8888
Fax: 212-573-8497
Email: studentinfo@tmsf.org
http://www.thurgoodmarshallfund.org

Purpose: To provide support to the nation's 45 historically black public colleges and universities by offering merit-based scholarships.

Eligibility: Applicants must be currently enrolled or planning to enroll as full-time students at one of the 45 TMSF member schools, have a minimum 3.0 high school GPA and have a minimum SAT score of 1100 or ACT score of 25. Applicants must demonstrate a commitment to academic excellence and community service and show financial need. Winners need to maintain a 3.0 GPA for the duration of the scholarship. Applicants must submit a head shot photograph, letters of recommendation, essay and resume.

Target applicants: High school students. College students. Adult students.

Minimum GPA: 3.0

Amount: Average awrard of $4,400.

Number of awards: Varies.

Scholarship may be renewable.

Deadline: August 30.

How to apply: Applications are available through the member schools.

Exclusive: Visit www.UltimateScholarshipBook.com and enter code TH267112 for updates on this award.

(2672) • Time Warner Scholars Program

United Negro College Fund (UNCF)
8260 Willow Oaks Corporate Drive
P.O. Box 10444
Fairfax, VA 22031-8044
Phone: 800-331-2244
http://www.uncf.org/

Purpose: To help African American sophomores attending historically black colleges and universities.

Eligibility: Applicants must attend historically black colleges and universities (HBCU): Benedict College, Bennett College for Women, Bethune-Cookman College, Claflin University, Clark Atlanta University, Dillard University, Edward Waters College, Fisk University, Florida

Memorial College, Huston-Tillotson University, Johnson C. Smith University, Lane College, LeMoyne-Owen College, Livingstone College, Miles College, Morehouse College, Morris College, Oakwood College, Paine College, Paul Quinn College, Philander Smith College, Rust College, Saint Augustine's College, Saint Paul's College, Shaw University, Spelman College, Stillman College, Talladega College, Tougaloo College, Tuskegee University, Virginia Union University, Voorhees College, Wilberforce University, Wiley College, Xavier University, Florida A & M University or Norfolk State University. Applicants must also have a minimum 3.0 GPA, complete the Free Application for Federal Student Aid (FAFSA) and have unmet financial need that is verified by the college or university financial aid office.
Target applicants: College students. Adult students.
Minimum GPA: 3.0
Amount: $2,500.
Number of awards: Over 100.
Deadline: Varies.
How to apply: Applications are available online.
Exclusive: Visit www.UltimateScholarshipBook.com and enter code UN267212 for updates on this award.

(2673) • Trailblazer Scholarship

Conference of Minority Transportation Officials
818 18th Street NW, Suite 850
Washington, DC 20006
Phone: 202-530-0551
Fax: 202-530-0617
Email: comto@comto.org
http://www.comto.org
Purpose: To support undergraduate and graduate students in the field of transportation.
Eligibility: Students must be in an undergraduate or graduate program enrolled in at least six credits per semester, and they must have at least a 2.5 GPA.
Target applicants: College students. Graduate school students. Adult students.
Minimum GPA: 2.5
Amount: $2,500.
Number of awards: Varies.
Deadline: April 16.
How to apply: Applications are available online.
Exclusive: Visit www.UltimateScholarshipBook.com and enter code CO267312 for updates on this award.

(2674) • Transfer Engineering Student Award

National Association of Multicultural Engineering Program Advocates Inc.
341 North Maitland Avenue
Suite 130
Maitland, FL 32751
Phone: 407-647-8839
Fax: 407-629-2502
Email: namepa@namepa.org
http://www.namepa.org
Purpose: To aid African-American, Native American and Latino transfer students who are studying engineering.
Eligibility: Applicants must be transferring from a junior college, community college or three/two dual degree program to a National Association of Multicultural Engineering Program Advocates (NAMEPA) member institution. They must be planning to major in engineering and have a GPA of 2.7 or higher on a four-point scale. Selection is based on the overall strength of the application.
Target applicants: College students. Adult students.
Minimum GPA: 2.7
Amount: $1,000.
Number of awards: Varies.
Deadline: May 26.
How to apply: Applications are available online. An application form, personal essay, one recommendation, a resume and an official transcript are required.
Exclusive: Visit www.UltimateScholarshipBook.com and enter code NA267412 for updates on this award.

(2675) • Tribal Business Management Program

Catching the Dream
Attn.: Scholarship Affairs Office
8200 Mountain Road NE
Suite 203
Albuquerque, NM 87110
Phone: 505-262-2351
Email: nscholarsh@aol.com
http://www.catchingthedream.org
Purpose: To support American Indian students majoring in business, finance, management, economics, banking, hotel management and related fields who plan to work in economic development for tribes.
Eligibility: Applicants must be 1/4 or more degree American Indian, enrolled in a U.S. tribe and attending or planning to attend college full-time. Candidates are required to apply for all other forms of funding in addition to applying for this scholarship. Scholarships are based on grades, SAT or ACT scores, work experience, leadership, commitment to the tribe, personal goals and potential to improve the lives of American Indian people.
Target applicants: High school students. College students. Graduate school students. Adult students.
Amount: $500-$5,000.
Number of awards: Varies.
Deadline: March 15, April 15 and September 15.
How to apply: Applications are available online.
Exclusive: Visit www.UltimateScholarshipBook.com and enter code CA267512 for updates on this award.

(2676) • Trull Foundation Scholarship

United Negro College Fund (UNCF)
8260 Willow Oaks Corporate Drive
P.O. Box 10444
Fairfax, VA 22031-8044
Phone: 800-331-2244
http://www.uncf.org/
Purpose: To help African American students attending United Negro College Fund (UNCF) member colleges and universities.
Eligibility: Applicants must have a minimum 2.5 GPA, complete the Free Application for Federal Student Aid (FAFSA) and have unmet financial need that is verified by the college or university financial aid office. Students are encouraged to complete the UNCF General Scholarship application to be matched with scholarships for which they meet the criteria.
Target applicants: High school students. College students. Adult students.
Minimum GPA: 2.5
Amount: Varies.
Number of awards: Varies.

Deadline: Varies.
How to apply: Applications are available online.
Exclusive: Visit www.UltimateScholarshipBook.com and enter code UN267612 for updates on this award.

(2677) • Truman D. Picard Scholarship

Intertribal Timber Council
Attn.: Education Committee
1112 NE 21st Avenue, Suite 4
Portland, OR 97232
Phone: 503-282-4296
Fax: 503-282-1274
Email: itc1@teleport.com
http://www.itcnet.org
Purpose: To promote the field of natural resources.
Eligibility: Applicants must be high school seniors or college students and must pursue the natural resources field. Applicants must submit a resume, letters of reference, validated enrollment in Tribe/Native Alaska Corporation, letter about interest in natural resources, education, academics and financial need.
Target applicants: High school students. College students. Graduate school students. Adult students.
Amount: $1,500-$2,000.
Number of awards: Varies.
Deadline: March 18.
How to apply: There is no official application form.
Exclusive: Visit www.UltimateScholarshipBook.com and enter code IN267712 for updates on this award.

(2678) • UBS/PaineWebber Scholarship

United Negro College Fund (UNCF)
8260 Willow Oaks Corporate Drive
P.O. Box 10444
Fairfax, VA 22031-8044
Phone: 800-331-2244
http://www.uncf.org/
Purpose: To help African American sophomores and juniors attending United Negro College Fund (UNCF) institutions and majoring in the field of business.
Eligibility: Applicants should demonstrate leadership skills and may major in accounting, business administration, economics, finance or any business-related major. Students should submit two recommendation letters, an essay, a resume, two small photos and a transcript. Applicants must have a minimum 3.0 GPA, complete the Free Application for Federal Student Aid (FAFSA) and have unmet financial need that is verified by the college or university financial aid office. Students are encouraged to complete the UNCF General Scholarship application to be matched with scholarships for which they meet the criteria.
Target applicants: College students. Adult students.
Minimum GPA: 3.0
Amount: $8,000.
Number of awards: Varies.
Scholarship may be renewable.
Deadline: Varies.
How to apply: Applications are available online.
Exclusive: Visit www.UltimateScholarshipBook.com and enter code UN267812 for updates on this award.

(2679) • UNCF-Foot Locker Foundation Inc. Scholarship

United Negro College Fund (UNCF)
8260 Willow Oaks Corporate Drive
P.O. Box 10444
Fairfax, VA 22031-8044
Phone: 800-331-2244
http://www.uncf.org/
Purpose: To support African American students attending UNCF member schools.
Eligibility: Applicants must be high school seniors or current college students planning to attend or attending a UNCF member college or university. Students must also have a minimum 2.5 GPA, complete the Free Application for Federal Student Aid (FAFSA) and have unmet financial need that is verified by the college or university financial aid office. Students are encouraged to complete the UNCF General Scholarship application to be matched with scholarships for which they meet the criteria.
Target applicants: High school students. College students. Adult students.
Minimum GPA: 2.5
Amount: Up to $5,000.
Number of awards: Varies.
Deadline: April 9.
How to apply: Applications are available online.
Exclusive: Visit www.UltimateScholarshipBook.com and enter code UN267912 for updates on this award.

(2680) • UNCF/Merck Graduate Science Research Dissertation Fellowships

United Negro College Fund (UNCF)
8260 Willow Oaks Corporate Drive
P.O. Box 10444
Fairfax, VA 22031-8044
Phone: 800-331-2244
http://www.uncf.org/
Purpose: To assist African American graduate students completing dissertations in biomedically-related life or physical sciences.
Eligibility: Applicants must be full-time Ph.D. students in a life or physical science or M.D./Ph.D. candidates who are within one to three years of completing their dissertation research. Students must also be U.S. citizens or permanent residents. Selection is based on academic record, accomplishments and proposed doctoral research plan. Recipients are mentored by a Merck scientist.
Target applicants: Graduate school students. Adult students.
Amount: Up to $52,000 plus stipend.
Number of awards: 12.
Deadline: December 1.
How to apply: Applications are available online.
Exclusive: Visit www.UltimateScholarshipBook.com and enter code UN268012 for updates on this award.

(2681) • United Parcel Service Foundation

United Negro College Fund (UNCF)
8260 Willow Oaks Corporate Drive
P.O. Box 10444
Fairfax, VA 22031-8044
Phone: 800-331-2244
http://www.uncf.org/

Purpose: To provide financial assistance to African American students at UNCF member schools.
Eligibility: Applicants must have a minimum 2.5 GPA, complete the Free Application for Federal Student Aid (FAFSA) and have unmet financial need that is verified by the college or university financial aid office. Students are encouraged to complete the UNCF General Scholarship application to be matched with scholarships for which they meet the criteria.
Target applicants: High school students. College students. Adult students.
Minimum GPA: 2.5
Amount: Varies.
Number of awards: Varies.
Deadline: Varies.
How to apply: Applications are available online.
Exclusive: Visit www.UltimateScholarshipBook.com and enter code UN268112 for updates on this award.

(2682) • United Parcel Service Scholarship for Minority Students

Institute of Industrial Engineers
3577 Parkway Lane
Suite 200
Norcross, GA 30092
Phone: 800-494-0460
Fax: 770-441-3295
Email: bcameron@iienet.org
http://www.iienet2.org
Purpose: To help minority undergraduate students in industrial engineering.
Eligibility: Applicants must be full-time undergraduate minority students enrolled in a college in the United States, Canada or Mexico with an accredited industrial engineering program, major in industrial engineering and be active members. Students may not apply directly for this scholarship and must be nominated. The award is based on academic ability, character, leadership, potential service to the industrial engineering profession and financial need.
Target applicants: College students. Adult students.
Minimum GPA: 3.4
Amount: $4,000.
Number of awards: 1.
Deadline: February 1.
How to apply: Nomination forms are available online.
Exclusive: Visit www.UltimateScholarshipBook.com and enter code IN268212 for updates on this award.

(2683) • UPS Hallmark Scholarship

U.S. Pan Asian American Chamber of Commerce
1329 18th Street NW
Washington, DC 20036
Phone: 800-696-7818
Fax: 202-296-5225
Email: info@uspaacc.com
http://uspaacc.com/scholarships/overview/
Purpose: To provide financial assistance to Asian American students.
Eligibility: Applicants must be high school seniors at least 16 years of age who are of Asian or Pacific heritage. They must be U.S. citizens or permanent residents and plan to enroll full-time at an accredited college or university in the United States in the fall following graduation. A minimum GPA of 3.3 is required, and applicants should demonstrate academic excellence, leadership, community service involvement and financial need.
Target applicants: High school students.
Minimum GPA: 3.3
Amount: Up to $5,500.
Number of awards: 1.
Deadline: March 31.
How to apply: Applications are available online.
Exclusive: Visit www.UltimateScholarshipBook.com and enter code U.268312 for updates on this award.

(2684) • USA Funds Scholarship

United Negro College Fund (UNCF)
8260 Willow Oaks Corporate Drive
P.O. Box 10444
Fairfax, VA 22031-8044
Phone: 800-331-2244
http://www.uncf.org/
Purpose: To help African American students attain a post-secondary education at a UNCF member college or university.
Eligibility: Applicants must have a minimum 2.5 GPA, complete the Free Application for Federal Student Aid (FAFSA) and have unmet financial need that is verified by the college or university financial aid office. Students are encouraged to complete the UNCF General Scholarship application to be matched with scholarships for which they meet the criteria.
Target applicants: High school students. College students. Adult students.
Minimum GPA: 2.5
Amount: Varies.
Number of awards: Varies.
Deadline: Varies.
How to apply: Applications are available online.
Exclusive: Visit www.UltimateScholarshipBook.com and enter code UN268412 for updates on this award.

(2685) • USENIX Association Scholarship

United Negro College Fund (UNCF)
8260 Willow Oaks Corporate Drive
P.O. Box 10444
Fairfax, VA 22031-8044
Phone: 800-331-2244
http://www.uncf.org/
Purpose: To encourage African American computer science and information systems students.
Eligibility: Applicants must major in computer science, computer science/MIS or information systems at a UNCF member college or university. Applicants must have a minimum 3.5 GPA, complete the Free Application for Federal Student Aid (FAFSA) and have unmet financial need that is verified by the college or university financial aid office. Students are encouraged to complete the UNCF General Scholarship application to be matched with scholarships for which they meet the criteria.
Target applicants: High school students. College students. Adult students.
Minimum GPA: 3.5
Amount: Up to $10,000.
Number of awards: Varies.
Deadline: Varies.
How to apply: Applications are available online.

Exclusive: Visit www.UltimateScholarshipBook.com and enter code UN268512 for updates on this award.

(2686) • Verizon Scholarship

Society of Women Engineers
120 South LaSalle Street
Suite 1515
Chicago, IL 60603
Phone: 877-793-4636
Email: scholarshipapplication@swe.org
http://www.swe.org
Purpose: To aid female undergraduate engineering students.
Eligibility: Applicants must be rising undergraduate sophomores, juniors or seniors who are majoring in civil, computer, electrical, industrial or mechanical engineering. They must have a GPA of 3.0 or higher on a four-point scale. Selection is based on the overall strength of the application.
Target applicants: College students. Adult students.
Minimum GPA: 3.0
Amount: $2,500.
Number of awards: 2.
Deadline: Varies.
How to apply: Applications are available online. An application form and supporting materials are required.
Exclusive: Visit www.UltimateScholarshipBook.com and enter code SO268612 for updates on this award.

(2687) • Visual Task Force Scholarship

National Association of Black Journalists
1100 Knight Hall
Suite 3100
College Park, MD 20742
Phone: 301-405-7520
Fax: 301-314-1714
Email: iwashington@nabj.org
http://www.nabj.org
Purpose: To aid visual journalism students.
Eligibility: Applicants must be student members of the National Association of Black Journalists (NABJ). They must be enrolled in a four-year undergraduate degree program or a graduate program and must be concentrating in visual journalism. They must have a GPA of 2.75 or higher, have experience working in an on-campus media outlet, and have completed an internship. Selection is based on the overall strength of the application.
Target applicants: College students. Graduate school students. Adult students.
Minimum GPA: 2.7
Amount: Up to $1,250.
Number of awards: 2.
Deadline: Varies.
How to apply: Applications are available online. An application form and supporting materials are required.
Exclusive: Visit www.UltimateScholarshipBook.com and enter code NA268712 for updates on this award.

(2688) • Wells Fargo Scholarship

United Negro College Fund (UNCF)
8260 Willow Oaks Corporate Drive
P.O. Box 10444
Fairfax, VA 22031-8044
Phone: 800-331-2244
http://www.uncf.org/
Purpose: To support African American students at HBCUs.
Eligibility: Applicants must be college sophomores or juniors or first-year MBA students, have a minimum 2.5 GPA, complete the Free Application for Federal Student Aid (FAFSA) and have unmet financial need that is verified by the college or university financial aid office. Students may major in business, finance, accounting, architecture, electrical engineering, computer engineering or systems engineering. UNCF Students are encouraged to complete the UNCF General Scholarship application to be matched with scholarships for which they meet the criteria.
Target applicants: College students. Adult students.
Minimum GPA: 2.5
Amount: $2,000.
Number of awards: Varies.
Deadline: October 31.
How to apply: Applications are available online.
Exclusive: Visit www.UltimateScholarshipBook.com and enter code UN268812 for updates on this award.

(2689) • Wendell Scott, Sr./NASCAR Scholarship

United Negro College Fund (UNCF)
8260 Willow Oaks Corporate Drive
P.O. Box 10444
Fairfax, VA 22031-8044
Phone: 800-331-2244
http://www.uncf.org/
Purpose: To provide financial support for upper-level African American students at UNCF member colleges or universities.
Eligibility: Applicants must be juniors, seniors or graduate students. Graduate students may be part-time students. Applicants must have a GPA of at least 3.0 for undergraduates and at least 3.2 for graduate students and demonstrate financial need.
Target applicants: College students. Graduate school students. Adult students.
Minimum GPA: 3.0
Amount: $10,230.
Number of awards: Varies.
Deadline: Varies.
How to apply: Applications are available online.
Exclusive: Visit www.UltimateScholarshipBook.com and enter code UN268912 for updates on this award.

(2690) • Willems Scholarship

National Association for the Advancement of Colored People
The United Negro College Fund
Scholarships and Grants Administration
8260 Willow Oaks Corporate Drive
Fairfax, VA 22031
Phone: 800-331-2244
Email: youth@naacpnet.org
http://www.naacp.org
Purpose: To encourage African-American males in scientific and technical fields.
Eligibility: Students must be males majoring in engineering, chemistry, physics or mathematical sciences. Applicants must be U.S. citizens attending an accredited U.S. school. Undergraduates must be full-time students with a 2.5 GPA. Graduate students may be full- or part-time students and must maintain a 3.0 GPA. Students must display financial

need according to the chart included in the application materials. Membership in the NAACP is not required but preferred.
Target applicants: High school students. College students. Graduate school students. Adult students.
Minimum GPA: 2.5
Amount: $2,000-$3,000.
Number of awards: Varies.
Deadline: Last Friday in March.
How to apply: Applications are available online.
Exclusive: Visit www.UltimateScholarshipBook.com and enter code NA269012 for updates on this award.

(2691) • William Randolph Hearst Endowed Scholarship for Minority Students

Aspen Institute
Nonprofit Sector Research Fund
Attn.: John Russell, Program Coordinator
One Dupont Circle, Suite 700
Washington, DC 20036
Phone: 202-736-5800
Fax: 202-293-0525
Email: hearstinfo@aspeninstitute.org
http://www.nonprofitresearch.org
Purpose: To provide fellowships for minority students interested in philanthropy, volunteerism and the nonprofit sector.
Eligibility: Applicants must be undergraduate or graduate students belonging to a minority group. Hearst fellows work as interns at the Fund, providing assistance with research and outreach programs. Awards are based on academic excellence and financial need.
Target applicants: College students. Graduate school students. Adult students.
Amount: $2,000-$4,000.
Number of awards: Varies.
Deadline: March 15 and July 15.
How to apply: Application information is available online.
Exclusive: Visit www.UltimateScholarshipBook.com and enter code AS269112 for updates on this award.

(2692) • William Wrigley Jr. Scholarship/Internship

United Negro College Fund (UNCF)
8260 Willow Oaks Corporate Drive
P.O. Box 10444
Fairfax, VA 22031-8044
Phone: 800-331-2244
http://www.uncf.org/
Purpose: To support African American engineering, business and chemistry students with scholarships and paid internships.
Eligibility: Applicants must be sophomores or juniors at a UNCF member college or university. They must demonstrate financial need and have a GPA of at least 3.0.
Target applicants: College students. Adult students.
Minimum GPA: 3.0
Amount: Up to $3,000.
Number of awards: Varies.
Deadline: Varies.
How to apply: Applications are available online.
Exclusive: Visit www.UltimateScholarshipBook.com and enter code UN269212 for updates on this award.

(2693) • Women's Opportunity Awards Program

Soroptimist International of the Americas
1709 Spruce Street
Philadelphia, PA 19103
Phone: 215-893-9000
Fax: 215-893-5200
Email: siahq@soroptimist.org
http://www.soroptimist.org
Purpose: To assist women entering or re-entering the workforce with educational and skills training support.
Eligibility: Applicants must be attending or been accepted by a vocational/skills training program or an undergraduate degree program. Applicants must be the women heads of household who provide the primary source of financial support for their families and demonstrate financial need. Applicants must submit their application to the appropriate regional office.
Target applicants: College students. Adult students.
Amount: Varies.
Number of awards: Varies.
Deadline: December 1.
How to apply: Applications are available online.
Exclusive: Visit www.UltimateScholarshipBook.com and enter code SO269312 for updates on this award.

(2694) • Young Women in Public Affairs Fund

Zonta International
1211 West 22nd Street
Oak Brook, IL 60523
Phone: 630-928-1400
Fax: 630-928-1559
Email: zontaintl@zonta.org
http://www.zonta.org
Purpose: To encourage young women to participate in politics and public service.
Eligibility: Applicants must be pre-college women between the ages of 16 and 20. District award winners receive at least $500, and international award winners receive $1,000. Selection is based on volunteerism, volunteer leadership and dedication to "advancing the status of women worldwide."
Target applicants: High school students.
Amount: $500-$1,000.
Number of awards: 30.
Deadline: April 1.
How to apply: Applications are available online or from your local Zonta Club.
Exclusive: Visit www.UltimateScholarshipBook.com and enter code ZO269412 for updates on this award.

DISABILITY / ILLNESS

(2695) • AG Bell College Scholarship Program

Alexander Graham Bell Association for the Deaf and Hard of Hearing
Youth and Family Programs Manager
3417 Volta Place NW
Washington, DC 20007
Phone: 202-337-5220
Fax: 202-337-8314
Email: financialaid@agbell.org
http://www.agbell.org

Purpose: To recognize students with moderate to profound hearing loss who have academically excelled.
Eligibility: Applicants must have moderate to profound hearing loss since birth or before learning to speak with a hearing loss of 60 dB or greater. Students must use spoken communication as their primary means of communicating and be enrolled in an accredited mainstream university. The TTY phone number is 202-337-5221.
Target applicants: High school students. College students. Graduate school students. Adult students.
Amount: $1,000-$10,000.
Number of awards: Varies.
Deadline: Varies.
How to apply: Applications are available online.
Exclusive: Visit www.UltimateScholarshipBook.com and enter code AL269512 for updates on this award.

(2696) • American Council of the Blind Scholarships

American Council of the Blind
Scholarship Program
1155 15th Street NW
Suite 1004
Washington, DC 20005
Phone: 202-467-5081
Fax: 202-467-5085
Email: info@acb.org
http://www.acb.org

Purpose: To reward outstanding blind students.
Eligibility: Students must be legally blind in both eyes and admitted full-time to a post-secondary academic or vocational program. A minimum GPA of 3.3 is required, except in extenuating circumstances. Students who work full-time and attend school part-time may apply for the John Hebner Memorial Scholarship. Scholarship recipients are expected to attend a national convention if they are over 18.
Target applicants: High school students. College students. Graduate school students. Adult students.
Minimum GPA: 3.3
Amount: Varies.
Number of awards: Over two dozen.
Deadline: March 1.
How to apply: Applications are available online and by phone.
Exclusive: Visit www.UltimateScholarshipBook.com and enter code AM269612 for updates on this award.

(2697) • Andre Sobel Award

Andre Sobel River of Life Foundation
8899 Beverly Boulevard
Suite 11
Los Angeles, CA 90048
Phone: 310-276-7111
Fax: 310-276-0244
Email: info@andreriveroflife.org
http://www.andreriveroflife.org

Purpose: To provide financial assistance for young survivors of catastrophic illness.
Eligibility: Applicants must be between the ages of 12 and 21 as of June 30 of the year of application. They must be survivors of cancer or some other critical or life-threatening illness. Friends, family members and caregivers of those who meet these qualifications may also participate. All applicants must be United States residents. An essay is required.
Target applicants: Junior high students or younger. High school students. College students.
Amount: Up to $5,000.
Number of awards: Varies.
Deadline: April 1.
How to apply: Applications are available online.
Exclusive: Visit www.UltimateScholarshipBook.com and enter code AN269712 for updates on this award.

(2698) • Ann and Matt Harbison Scholarship

P. Buckley Moss Society
20 Stoneridge Drive, Suite 102
Waynesboro, VA 22980
Phone: 540-943-5678
Fax: 540-949-8408
Email: society@mosssociety.org
http://www.mosssociety.org

Purpose: This scholarship recognizes the persistence and dedication to academic or extracurricular pursuits of students with a learning disability.
Eligibility: Applicants must be nominated by a P. Buckley Moss Society member, have a language-related learning difference and pursue a post-secondary education.
Target applicants: High school students.
Amount: $1,500.
Number of awards: 1.
Scholarship may be renewable.
Deadline: March 31.
How to apply: Applications are available online.
Exclusive: Visit www.UltimateScholarshipBook.com and enter code P.269812 for updates on this award.

(2699) • Anne and Allegra Ford Scholarship Program

National Center for Learning Disabilities
381 Park Avenue South, Suite 1401
New York, NY 10016-8806
Phone: 888-575-7373
Fax: 212-545-9665
Email: afscholarship@ncld.org
http://www.ncld.org

Purpose: To provide financial assistance to students with learning disabilities who plan to pursue undergraduate degrees.
Eligibility: Applicants must be U.S. citizens who are academically successful in public or private secondary schools and with an identified learning disability. Financial need is considered.
Target applicants: High school students.
Minimum GPA: 3.0
Amount: $10,000.
Number of awards: 2.
Deadline: December 31.
How to apply: Applications are available online.

Exclusive: Visit www.UltimateScholarshipBook.com and enter code NA269912 for updates on this award.

(2700) • Association of Blind Citizens Scholarships

Association of Blind Citizens
P.O. Box 246
Holbrook, MA 02343
Email: scholarship@blindcitizens.org
http://www.blindcitizens.org/abc_scholarship.htm
Purpose: To assist blind individuals who wish to pursue higher education.
Eligibility: Applicants must be legally blind U.S. residents who have been accepted to an accredited institution of higher learning or vocational program. A 300- to 500- word autobiographical sketch, a certificate of legal blindness, a letter from an ophthalmologist and two letters of reference are required.
Target applicants: High school students. College students. Adult students.
Amount: $1,000-$2,000.
Number of awards: 9.
Deadline: April 15.
How to apply: Applications are available online.
Exclusive: Visit www.UltimateScholarshipBook.com and enter code AS270012 for updates on this award.

(2701) • Boomer Esiason Foundation Scholarship Program

Boomer Esiason Foundation
c/o Jerry Cahill
52 Vanderbilt Avenue, 15th Floor
New York, NY 10017
Phone: 646-292-7930
Fax: 646-292-7945
Email: jcahillbef@aol.com
http://www.esiason.org
Purpose: To provide assistance to students with cystic fibrosis.
Eligibility: Applicants may be pursuing undergraduate or graduate degrees. They must demonstrate financial need. Selection is based on scholastic achievement, character, leadership, community service and financial need. Scholarships are awarded in March, June, September and December of each year.
Target applicants: High school students. College students. Graduate school students. Adult students.
Amount: $500-$2,000.
Number of awards: 10-15.
Deadline: March 15, June 15, September 15, December 15.
How to apply: Applications are available online. An application form, recent photo, letter from doctor, essay, transcript, tuition breakdown and W2 from both parents are required.
Exclusive: Visit www.UltimateScholarshipBook.com and enter code BO270112 for updates on this award.

(2702) • Cancer for College Scholarships

Cancer for College
1345 Specialty Drive
Suite E
Vista, CA 92081
Phone: 760-599-5096
Fax: 760-599-9208
Email: melissa@cancerforcollege.org
http://www.cancerforcollege.org
Purpose: To support current and former cancer patients and amputees.
Eligibility: Applicants must be U.S. residents. They must be enrolled in a university, community college or trade school. Recipients must agree to attend regional events and be available for interviews and media coverage. All eligible applicants receive a one-time $250 scholarship. There are also $1,500 one-time scholarships and $4,000 four-year scholarships.
Target applicants: College students. Adult students.
Amount: $250-$16,000.
Number of awards: 48.
Scholarship may be renewable.
Deadline: May 1.
How to apply: Applications are available online. An application form, summary of cancer treatment, personal statement, details of college financing and two letters of recommendation are required.
Exclusive: Visit www.UltimateScholarshipBook.com and enter code CA270212 for updates on this award.

(2703) • Chair Scholars Scholarship

Chair Scholars Foundation Inc.
16101 Carencia Lane
Odessa, FL 33556-3278
Phone: 813-920-0544
Fax: 813-920-7661
Email: chairscholars@tampabay.rr.com
http://www.chairscholars.org
Purpose: To allow financially disadvantaged, physically challenged students a chance to obtain a college education.
Eligibility: Applicants must be significantly physically challenged (although not necessarily in a wheelchair), demonstrate severe financial need (such that they could not attend college without financial aid), and have at least a B+ average in previous scholastic work. Applicants must also be under age 21 and be high school seniors or college freshmen with previous community contributions. Applicants must submit applications, parents'/guardians' tax returns, test scores, photos, three recommendations and transcripts.
Target applicants: High school students. College students.
Minimum GPA: 3.33
Amount: $1,000-$5,000.
Number of awards: 15 to 20.
Scholarship may be renewable.
Deadline: February 15.
How to apply: Applications are available online.
Exclusive: Visit www.UltimateScholarshipBook.com and enter code CH270312 for updates on this award.

(2704) • Chairscholars Foundation National Scholarships

Chair Scholars Foundation Inc.
16101 Carencia Lane
Odessa, FL 33556-3278
Phone: 813-920-0544
Fax: 813-920-7661
Email: chairscholars@tampabay.rr.com
http://www.chairscholars.org
Purpose: To provide educational opportunities for physically challenged students.
Eligibility: Applicants must have major disabilities and serious financial difficulties that would prevent them from going to college without financial aid. They must have a B+ or higher average. They must be high school seniors or college freshmen age 21 or younger, and they

must have participated in some form of major community service or other social contribution.
Target applicants: High school students. College students.
Minimum GPA: 3.3
Amount: $1,000-$5,000.
Number of awards: 15-20.
Scholarship may be renewable.
Deadline: February 15.
How to apply: Applications are available online.
Exclusive: Visit www.UltimateScholarshipBook.com and enter code CH270412 for updates on this award.

(2705) • Challenge Met Scholarship

American Radio Relay League Foundation
225 Main Street
Newington, CT 06111
Phone: 860-594-0397
Fax: 860-594-0259
Email: foundation@arrl.org
http://www.arrlf.org
Purpose: To provide assistance to amateur radio operators with learning disabilities.
Eligibility: Applicants must be licensed amateur radio operators who are accepted to or enrolled in a two- or four-year college, technical school or university. Preference is given to students with documented learning disabilities who are putting forth effort.
Target applicants: High school students. College students. Adult students.
Amount: $500.
Number of awards: Varies.
Deadline: February 1.
How to apply: Applications are available online.
Exclusive: Visit www.UltimateScholarshipBook.com and enter code AM270512 for updates on this award.

(2706) • CRS Scholarship

Christian Record Services
Melisa Welch
4444 S. 52nd Street
Lincoln, NE 68516-1302
Phone: 402-488-0981
Fax: 402-488-7582
Email: info@christianrecord.org
http://www.christianrecord.org
Purpose: To assist legally blind youths in obtaining a college education.
Eligibility: Applicants must be legally blind and intend to attend undergraduate institutions to gain independence and self sufficiency. Applicants should submit application forms and character reference forms.
Target applicants: High school students. College students. Adult students.
Amount: Varies.
Number of awards: Varies.
Deadline: April 1.
How to apply: Applications are available online.
Exclusive: Visit www.UltimateScholarshipBook.com and enter code CH270612 for updates on this award.

(2707) • Curtis Pride Scholarship for the Hearing Impaired

National Head Start Association
1651 Prince Street
Alexandria, VA 22314
Phone: 703-739-0875 x7507
Fax: 703-739-0878
Email: chutchinson@nhsa.org
http://www.nhsa.org
Purpose: To aid hearing impaired students.
Eligibility: Applicants must be individual National Head Start Association members. They must provide proof of acceptance to or enrollment in a college or university. Judging criteria include statement of financial need (30 points), statement of goals (40 points) and letters of reference (30 points).
Target applicants: High school students. College students. Adult students.
Amount: $1,000.
Number of awards: 1.
Deadline: December 28.
How to apply: Applications are available online. An application form, statement of financial need, statement of goals, proof of acceptance or enrollment and three letters of recommendation are required.
Exclusive: Visit www.UltimateScholarshipBook.com and enter code NA270712 for updates on this award.

(2708) • Cystic Fibrosis Foundation Scholarship

Cystic Fibrosis Scholarship Foundation
1555 Sherman Avenue #116
Evanston, IL 60201
Phone: 847-328-0127
Fax: 847-328-0127
Email: mkbcfsf@aol.com
http://www.cfscholarship.org
Purpose: To aid to students with cystic fibrosis.
Eligibility: Applicants must be high school seniors or college undergraduates who have cystic fibrosis. Recipients are chosen on the basis of academic achievement, leadership skills and financial need.
Target applicants: High school students. College students. Adult students.
Amount: $1,000.
Number of awards: Varies.
Deadline: March 21.
How to apply: Applications are available online.
Exclusive: Visit www.UltimateScholarshipBook.com and enter code CY270812 for updates on this award.

(2709) • Cystic Fibrosis Scholarships

Cystic Fibrosis Scholarship Foundation
1555 Sherman Avenue #116
Evanston, IL 60201
Phone: 847-328-0127
Fax: 847-328-0127
Email: mkbcfsf@aol.com
http://www.cfscholarship.org
Purpose: To provide educational opportunities for young adults with cystic fibrosis.
Eligibility: Applicants may be high school seniors or current college students. A doctor's note indicating a diagnosis of cystic fibrosis

is required. Criteria for selection include financial need, academic achievement and leadership.
Target applicants: High school students. College students. Adult students.
Amount: $1,000.
Number of awards: Varies.
Scholarship may be renewable.
Deadline: March 21.
How to apply: Applications are available online.
Exclusive: Visit www.UltimateScholarshipBook.com and enter code CY270912 for updates on this award.

(2710) • Dr. Mae Davidow Memorial Scholarship

American Council of the Blind
Scholarship Program
1155 15th Street NW
Suite 1004
Washington, DC 20005
Phone: 202-467-5081
Fax: 202-467-5085
Email: info@acb.org
http://www.acb.org
Purpose: To provide financial assistance for visually impaired students.
Eligibility: Applicants must be blind or visually impaired. They must submit letters of recommendation, autobiographical sketches and copies of their academic transcripts.
Target applicants: High school students. College students. Adult students.
Amount: $1,500.
Number of awards: 1.
Deadline: March.
How to apply: Applications are available online.
Exclusive: Visit www.UltimateScholarshipBook.com and enter code AM271012 for updates on this award.

(2711) • Duane Buckley Memorial Scholarship

American Council of the Blind
Scholarship Program
1155 15th Street NW
Suite 1004
Washington, DC 20005
Phone: 202-467-5081
Fax: 202-467-5085
Email: info@acb.org
http://www.acb.org
Purpose: To assist students who work to overcome challenges.
Eligibility: Applicants must be legally blind college freshmen. A letter of recommendation, autobiographical sketch and copies of transcripts are required.
Target applicants: College students. Adult students.
Amount: $1,000.
Number of awards: 1.
Deadline: March.
How to apply: Applications are available online.
Exclusive: Visit www.UltimateScholarshipBook.com and enter code AM271112 for updates on this award.

(2712) • Educator of Tomorrow Award

National Federation of the Blind
200 East Wells Street
Baltimore, MD 21230
Phone: 410-659-9314
Fax: 410-685-5653
Email: scholarships@nfb.org
http://www.nfb.org
Purpose: To assist legally blind education students.
Eligibility: Applicants must be legally blind, full-time post-secondary students pursuing a career in education at any level. They must live in and attend college in the U.S. or Puerto Rico. Academic excellence, financial need and community service involvement are considered.
Target applicants: High school students. College students. Graduate school students. Adult students.
Amount: $3,000.
Number of awards: 1.
Deadline: March 31.
How to apply: Applications are available online. Applicants must submit the official application form (online or print), a personal essay, two letters of recommendation, transcripts and a letter from a federation state president or designee. High school seniors only must submit ACT, SAT or similar test score reports.
Exclusive: Visit www.UltimateScholarshipBook.com and enter code NA271212 for updates on this award.

(2713) • Elizabeth Nash Foundation Scholarship Program

Elizabeth Nash Foundation
P.O. Box 1260
Los Gatos, CA 95031-1260
Email: info@elizabethnashfoundation.org
http://www.elizabethnashfoundation.org
Purpose: To support students with cystic fibrosis.
Eligibility: Applicants must be current or entering graduate or undergraduate students at an accredited U.S. institution of higher learning. They must be U.S. citizens, and they must be pursuing a bachelor's degree or higher. Selection criteria include scholastic achievement, character, leadership, community service, service to cystic fibrosis-related causes and financial need.
Target applicants: High school students. College students. Graduate school students. Adult students.
Amount: $1,000-$2,500.
Number of awards: Varies.
Deadline: April 5.
How to apply: Applications are available online. An application form, essay, letter of recommendation, documentation of cystic fibrosis diagnosis, transcript, copy of FAFSA and details of tuition costs are required.
Exclusive: Visit www.UltimateScholarshipBook.com and enter code EL271312 for updates on this award.

(2714) • Eric Dostie Memorial College Scholarship

NuFACTOR
41093 County Center Drive
Temecula, CA 92591
Phone: 800-323-6832
Fax: 951-296-2565
http://www.kelleycom.com

Purpose: To assist students who suffer from hemophilia or related bleeding disorders as well as their immediate families.
Eligibility: Applicants must be individuals with hemophilia or related to said individuals, enrolled full-time in an accredited college or university and demonstrate academic achievement, financial need and a history of community service.
Target applicants: College students. Adult students.
Amount: $1,000.
Number of awards: 10.
Deadline: March 1.
How to apply: Applications are available after November 1 by telephone or mail.
Exclusive: Visit www.UltimateScholarshipBook.com and enter code NU271412 for updates on this award.

(2715) • Ethel Louise Armstrong Foundation Scholarship

Ethel Louise Armstrong Foundation
2460 N. Lake Avenue, PMB #128
Altadena, CA 91001
Phone: 626-398-8840
Email: executivedirector@ela.org
http://www.ela.org
Purpose: To promote the inclusion of people with disabilities and to expand the opportunities of female graduate students with disabilities.
Eligibility: Applicants must be female with a physical disability, active in a disability organization, currently enrolled in or applying to a graduate school in the U.S. and willing to work with the foundation on future research work.
Target applicants: Graduate school students. Adult students.
Amount: $500-$2,000.
Number of awards: Varies.
Deadline: June 1.
How to apply: Applications are available online.
Exclusive: Visit www.UltimateScholarshipBook.com and enter code ET271512 for updates on this award.

(2716) • Ferdinand Torres Scholarship

American Foundation for the Blind Scholarship Committee
11 Penn Plaza
Suite 1102
New York, NY 10021
Phone: 800-232-5463
Fax: 888-545-8331
Email: afbinfo@afb.net
http://www.afb.org
Purpose: The foundation addresses the issues of literacy, independent living, employment and access for visually impaired Americans.
Eligibility: Applicants must be full-time, post-secondary students with proof of legal blindness. Students must reside in the U.S. and provide evidence of economic need. Preference is given to applicants living in the New York metropolitan area and new immigrants to the U.S. Applicants must submit applications, essays, transcripts, enrollment letters and two recommendation letters.
Target applicants: College students. Graduate school students. Adult students.
Amount: $2,500.
Number of awards: 1.
Deadline: April 30.
How to apply: Applications are available online.
Exclusive: Visit www.UltimateScholarshipBook.com and enter code AM271612 for updates on this award.

(2717) • Flicker of Hope Foundation Scholarships

Flicker of Hope Foundation
8624 Janet Lane
Vienna, VA 22180
Phone: 703-698-1626
Fax: 703-698-6225
Email: info@flickerofhope.org
http://www.flickerofhope.org
Purpose: To support burn survivors.
Eligibility: Applicants must be current high school seniors or graduates or current college students. Winners must be accepted to an accredited college or university prior to disbursement of funds. Selection is based on severity of burn injury, academic performance, community service and economic need.
Target applicants: High school students. College students. Adult students.
Amount: Varies.
Number of awards: Varies.
Deadline: June 1.
How to apply: Applications are available online. An application form, list of other sources and amounts of financial aid, transcript, college acceptance letter, listing of college costs, two letters of recommendation, letter from a medical professional and a copy of most recent tax return on which student is claimed as a dependent are required.
Exclusive: Visit www.UltimateScholarshipBook.com and enter code FL271712 for updates on this award.

(2718) • Fred Scheigert Scholarships

Council of Citizens with Low Vision International
1155 15th Street NW
Suite 1004
Washington, DC 20005
Phone: 800-733-2258
Email: ncclv@yahoo.com
http://www.cclvi.org
Purpose: To provide educational assistance for students with low vision.
Eligibility: Applicants must be registered in a full-time undergraduate or graduate course of study at a college, trade or vocational school. They must have a GPA of 3.2 or higher. Those with extenuating circumstances may be exempt from these requirements. Applicants must have 20/70 or worse vision in the better eye with the best possible correction, or a field of vision of 30 degrees or less.
Target applicants: High school students. College students. Graduate school students. Adult students.
Minimum GPA: 3.2
Amount: $3,000.
Number of awards: 3.
Deadline: March 1.
How to apply: Applications are available online.
Exclusive: Visit www.UltimateScholarshipBook.com and enter code CO271812 for updates on this award.

(2719) • Graeme Clark Scholarship

Cochlear Americas
13059 E. Peakview Avenue
Centennial, CO 80111
Phone: 800-523-5798

Fax: 303-790-9010
http://www.cochlearamericas.com
Purpose: To support cochlear implant recipients.
Eligibility: Applicants must have received a Nucleus cochlear implant. They may be high school seniors, current college students or students who have been accepted into an institution of higher learning. Students must pursue a minimum of a three-year undergraduate degree at an accredited university. Criteria for selection include academic achievement and commitment to leadership and humanity.
Target applicants: High school students. College students. Adult students.
Amount: Varies.
Number of awards: Varies.
Deadline: August 31.
How to apply: Applications are available online. An application form, transcript, proof of university admission, list of activities and awards, personal statement, proof of age and citizenship and three letters of reference are required.
Exclusive: Visit www.UltimateScholarshipBook.com and enter code CO271912 for updates on this award.

(2720) • Immune Deficiency Foundation Scholarship

Immune Deficiency Foundation
40 W. Chesapeake Avenue
Suite 308
Towson, MD 21204
Phone: 800-296-4433
Email: idf@primaryimmune.org
http://www.primaryimmune.org
Purpose: To provide financial assistance to undergraduate students afflicted with a primary immune deficiency disease.
Eligibility: Applicant must have been admitted or must currently be enrolled in an accredited college or university as an undergraduate student. Applicants must also have demonstrated financial need and a record of community involvement.
Target applicants: High school students. College students. Adult students.
Amount: Varies.
Number of awards: Varies.
Scholarship may be renewable.
Deadline: Varies.
How to apply: Applications are available online, by email or by telephone.
Exclusive: Visit www.UltimateScholarshipBook.com and enter code IM272012 for updates on this award.

(2721) • Ina Brudnick Scholarship Award

Great Comebacks Award Program
100 Headquarters Park Drive
Skillman, NJ 08558
Phone: 858-259-2092
Email: professional.services@bms.com
http://www.greatcomebacks.com
Purpose: To support students who have undergone ostomy surgery or are suffering from inflammatory bowel disease.
Eligibility: Students must be 24 years old or younger, and they must be planning to attend an institution of higher education.
Target applicants: High school students. College students.
Amount: $1,000.
Number of awards: 4.
Deadline: July 15.
How to apply: Applications are available online.
Exclusive: Visit www.UltimateScholarshipBook.com and enter code GR272112 for updates on this award.

(2722) • Incight Go-Getter Scholarship

Incight Company
310 S.W. 4th Avenue
Suite 530
Portland, OR 97204
Phone: 971-244-0305
Fax: 971-244-0304
Email: questions@incight.org
http://www.incight.com
Purpose: To support students with physical or learning disabilities.
Eligibility: Applicants must have a documented disability that may include physical, learning or cognitive. Students must also attend a trade school, college or university on a full-time basis and have at least a 2.5 GPA. Recipients are placed with internships related to their field of study.
Target applicants: High school students. College students. Adult students.
Minimum GPA: 2.5
Amount: $750.
Number of awards: Varies.
Scholarship may be renewable.
Deadline: April 1.
How to apply: Applications are available online.
Exclusive: Visit www.UltimateScholarshipBook.com and enter code IN272212 for updates on this award.

(2723) • Karen D. Carsel Memorial Scholarship

American Foundation for the Blind Scholarship Committee
11 Penn Plaza
Suite 1102
New York, NY 10021
Phone: 800-232-5463
Fax: 888-545-8331
Email: afbinfo@afb.net
http://www.afb.org
Purpose: The foundation addresses the issues of literacy, independent living, employment and access for visually impaired Americans.
Eligibility: Applicants must be full-time graduate students who are legally blind and can present evidence of financial need. Students must submit applications, transcripts, enrollment letters, proof of U.S. citizenship, proof of legal blindness, two letters of recommendation and a typed statement describing educational and personal goals, work experience, extracurricular activities and how the scholarship funds will be used.
Target applicants: Graduate school students. Adult students.
Amount: $500.
Number of awards: 1.
Deadline: April 30.
How to apply: Applications are available online.
Exclusive: Visit www.UltimateScholarshipBook.com and enter code AM272312 for updates on this award.

(2724) • Keppra Family Epilepsy Scholarship Program

Hudson Medical Communications
200 White Plains Road
Tarrytown, NY 10591
Phone: 866-825-1920

Email: questions@hudsonmc.com
http://www.ucb.com
Purpose: To provide financial assistance to people with epilepsy who wish to obtain higher education.
Eligibility: Applicants must be U.S. citizens or legal and permanent residents who have epilepsy, or family members or caregivers of persons with epilepsy. They must be graduating high school in the year of application or have already graduated and be enrolled in or awaiting acceptance from a U.S. institution of higher learning. They must have demonstrated academic achievement, participate in extracurricular activities and be positive role models.
Target applicants: High school students. College students. Adult students.
Amount: $5,000.
Number of awards: 30.
Deadline: April 10.
How to apply: Applications are available online.
Exclusive: Visit www.UltimateScholarshipBook.com and enter code HU272412 for updates on this award.

(2725) • Kermit B. Nash Academic Scholarship

Sickle Cell Disease Association of America
231 E. Baltimore Street
Suite 800
Baltimore, MD 21202
Phone: 800-421-8453
Fax: 410-528-1495
Email: scdaa@sicklecelldisease.org
http://www.sicklecelldisease.org
Purpose: To encourage individuals with sickle cell disease to pursue their educational goals.
Eligibility: Applicants must be U.S. citizens or permanent residents who have sickle cell disease. They must be graduating high school seniors with a GPA of 3.0 or higher (unless they can demonstrate special hardship), a record of leadership and community service and SAT scores. An essay is required.
Target applicants: High school students.
Minimum GPA: 3.0
Amount: $5,000.
Number of awards: 4.
Scholarship may be renewable.
Deadline: April 30.
How to apply: Applications are available online.
Exclusive: Visit www.UltimateScholarshipBook.com and enter code SI272512 for updates on this award.

(2726) • Kevin Child Scholarship

National Hemophilia Foundation
116 W. 32nd Street
11th Floor
New York, NY 10001
Phone: 212-328-3700
Fax: 212-328-3777
Email: webmaster@hemophilia.org
http://www.hemophilia.org
Purpose: To support students who have been diagnosed with hemophilia or von Willebrand disease.
Eligibility: Applicants must be high school seniors or enrolled undergraduate students.
Target applicants: High school students. College students. Adult students.
Amount: Varies.
Number of awards: 1.
Deadline: June 1.
How to apply: Applications are available online.
Exclusive: Visit www.UltimateScholarshipBook.com and enter code NA272612 for updates on this award.

(2727) • Kyle Lee Foundation Scholarship

Kyle Lee Foundation Inc.
c/o Arnold Uy
85 Sansovino
Ladera Ranch, CA 92694
Phone: 714-433-3204
Email: foundation@kylelee28.com
http://www.kylelee28.com
Purpose: To provide financial assistance to college-bound cancer survivors, especially survivors of Ewing's sarcoma.
Eligibility: Applicants must be cancer survivors who have taken the SAT, ACT or GRE and plan to attend an institution of higher learning.
Target applicants: High school students. College students. Graduate school students. Adult students.
Amount: Varies.
Number of awards: 5.
Deadline: May 31.
How to apply: Applications are available online.
Exclusive: Visit www.UltimateScholarshipBook.com and enter code KY272712 for updates on this award.

(2728) • Lawrence Madeiros Scholarship

Adirondack Spintacular
P.O. Box 11
Mayfield, NY 12117
Phone: 518-661-6005
Email: carol@adirondackspintacular.com
http://www.adirondackspintacular.com
Purpose: To support students who are living with a bleeding disorder or other chronic disorder.
Eligibility: Applicants must be graduating high school seniors.
Target applicants: High school students.
Amount: Varies.
Number of awards: Varies.
Deadline: May 1.
How to apply: Applications are available online.
Exclusive: Visit www.UltimateScholarshipBook.com and enter code AD272812 for updates on this award.

(2729) • Lilly Moving Lives Forward Reintegration Scholarships

Center for Reintegration Inc.
609 72nd Street
Floor 1
North Bergen, NJ 07047
Phone: 201-869-2333
Fax: 201-869-2123
Email: reintegration@reintegration.com
http://www.reintegration.com/resources/scholarships/scholarship.asp
Purpose: To encourage people with schizophrenia and similar disorders to obtain higher education.
Eligibility: Applicants must be diagnosed with schizophrenia, schizophreniform, schizoaffective disorder or bipolar disorder and

be receiving treatment for the disease. They must be involved in reintegrative efforts such as work, school or volunteer programs. Three recommendations and an essay are required.
Target applicants: High school students. College students. Adult students.
Amount: Varies.
Number of awards: Varies.
Deadline: January 24.
How to apply: Applications are available online.
Exclusive: Visit www.UltimateScholarshipBook.com and enter code CE272912 for updates on this award.

(2730) • Lilly Reintegration Scholarship

Lilly Reintegration Programs
PMB 327
310 Busse Highway
Park Ridge, IL 60068
Phone: 800-809-8202
Email: lillyscholarships@reintegration.com
http://www.reintegration.com
Purpose: To provide aid to students with schizophrenia or similar disorders who are seeking to advance themselves academically and vocationally.
Eligibility: Applicants must have been diagnosed with schizophrenia, schizophreniform, schizoaffective disorder or bipolar disorder, be undergoing medical treatment for their disease(s) and be involved in other rehabilitative efforts, such as working part-time or volunteering with a civic organization.
Target applicants: High school students. College students. Graduate school students. Adult students.
Amount: Varies.
Number of awards: Varies.
Deadline: January 24.
How to apply: Applications are available online or by phone, mail or email.
Exclusive: Visit www.UltimateScholarshipBook.com and enter code LI273012 for updates on this award.

(2731) • Linda Cowden Memorial Scholarship

Hearing Bridges (formerly League for the Deaf and Hard of Hearing and EAR Foundation)
415 4th Avenue South, Suite A
Nashville, TN 37201
Phone: 615-248-8828
Fax: 615-248-4797
Email: nr@hearingbridges.org
http://www.hearingbridges.org
Purpose: To support students who are deaf or hard of hearing and hearing persons who serve them.
Eligibility: Applicants must live in one of the following Tennessee counties: Cheatham, Davidson, Dekalb, Dickson, Houston, Macon, Maruy, Montgomery, Robertson, Rutherford, Smith, Stewart, Sumner, Trousdale, Williamson or Wilson. They must be a deaf or hard of hearing person who has been accepted into a post-secondary education program or a hearing person accepted into a program leading to a profession that serves the deaf or hard of hearing.
Target applicants: High school students. College students. Adult students.
Amount: $1,000.
Number of awards: 1.
Deadline: Varies.
How to apply: Applications are available from the League for the Deaf. An application form is required.
Exclusive: Visit www.UltimateScholarshipBook.com and enter code HE273112 for updates on this award.

(2732) • Little People of America Scholarships

Little People of America
250 El Camino Real
Suite 201
Tustin, CA 92780
Phone: 888-572-2001
Fax: 714-368-3367
Email: info@lpaonline.org
http://www.lpaonline.org
Purpose: To aid those affected by dwarfism.
Eligibility: Applicants may be junior high, high school or college students who have been involved with Little People of America. Preference is given in the following order: LPA members with medically diagnosed dwarfism, immediate family members of LPA members diagnosed with dwarfism, non-LPA members with dwarfism, students with disabilities and non-disabled students with demonstrated financial need.
Target applicants: Junior high students or younger. High school students. College students. Adult students.
Amount: Up to $1,000.
Number of awards: Varies.
Deadline: April 22.
How to apply: Applications are available online. An application form, personal statement and three letters of recommendation are required.
Exclusive: Visit www.UltimateScholarshipBook.com and enter code LI273212 for updates on this award.

(2733) • Manne Family Foundation Scholarships

SuperSibs!
4300 Lincoln Avenue
Suite 1
Rolling Meadows, IL 60008
Phone: 866-444-7427
Fax: 847-776-7084
http://www.supersibs.org
Purpose: To provide education opportunities for siblings of cancer patients.
Eligibility: Applicants must be siblings of children who have or have had cancer. They must be U.S. residents who are graduating high school in the year of application. A minimum GPA of 3.5 is required. Applicants must have financial need and plan to attend a four-year college or university immediately following high school.
Target applicants: High school students.
Minimum GPA: 3.5
Amount: $5,000.
Number of awards: 4.
Deadline: February 1.
How to apply: Applications are available online.
Exclusive: Visit www.UltimateScholarshipBook.com and enter code SU273312 for updates on this award.

(2734) • Marion Huber Learning Through Listening Awards

Recording for the Blind and Dyslexic
20 Roszel Road
Princeton, NJ 08540
Phone: 866-RFBD-585
Fax: 609-520-7990
Email: custserv@rfbd.org
http://www.rfbd.org

Purpose: To assist learning-disabled high school seniors.
Eligibility: Applicants must demonstrate leadership skills, scholarship and a desire to help others and attend a two- or four-year college or vocational school. Students must have a specific learning disability and be registered with RFB&D for at least one year prior to the application deadline.
Target applicants: High school students.
Minimum GPA: 3.0
Amount: $2,000-$6,000.
Number of awards: 6.
Deadline: Varies.
How to apply: Applications are available online.
Exclusive: Visit www.UltimateScholarshipBook.com and enter code RE273412 for updates on this award.

(2735) • Mary Ellen Locher Foundation Scholarship

Mary Ellen Locher Foundation
P.O. Box 4032
Chattanooga, TN 37405
http://www.maryellenlocherfoundation.org

Purpose: To provide scholarship assistance to children whose mothers have died of breast cancer and children whose mothers are breast cancer survivors.
Eligibility: Applicants must have lost a parent to breast cancer or complications of the disease or have a parent who has survived breast cancer. They must be high school seniors who have been accepted as a full-time student at an accredited college or university.
Target applicants: High school students.
Amount: Varies.
Number of awards: Varies.
Deadline: January 15.
How to apply: Applications are available online.
Exclusive: Visit www.UltimateScholarshipBook.com and enter code MA273512 for updates on this award.

(2736) • Mary P. Oenslanger Scholastic Achievement Awards

Recording for the Blind and Dyslexic
20 Roszel Road
Princeton, NJ 08540
Phone: 866-RFBD-585
Fax: 609-520-7990
Email: custserv@rfbd.org
http://www.rfbd.org

Purpose: Assistance for graduate study is awarded to blind college senior students who have shown leadership skills, scholarship and a desire to help others.
Eligibility: Applicants must be legally blind, have been registered with RFB&D for at least one year prior to the application deadline and hold a bachelor's degree from an accredited U.S. college or university.
Target applicants: Graduate school students. Adult students.
Minimum GPA: 3.0
Amount: $1,000-$6,000.
Number of awards: 9.
Deadline: Varies.
How to apply: Applications are available online.
Exclusive: Visit www.UltimateScholarshipBook.com and enter code RE273612 for updates on this award.

(2737) • MedPro Rx Inc. Education Is Power Scholarships

MedProRx Inc.
140 Northway Court
Raleigh, NC 27615-4916
Phone: 866-528-4963
Email: educationispower@medprorx.com
http://www.medprorx.com

Purpose: To aid students with bleeding disorders.
Eligibility: Applicants must have hemophilia or von Willebrand disease and be United States residents who are entering or attending a college, university or vocational school in the fall following application. Students must have participated in community service or volunteer work.
Target applicants: High school students. College students. Adult students.
Amount: $500-$2,500.
Number of awards: 78.
Deadline: May 1.
How to apply: Applications are available online. An application form, documentation of bleeding disorder, copy of diploma, GED or most recent transcript, proof of admission and college tuition, essay and letter of recommendation are required.
Exclusive: Visit www.UltimateScholarshipBook.com and enter code ME273712 for updates on this award.

(2738) • Michael A. Hunter Memorial Scholarship Fund

Orange County Community Foundation
30 Corporate Park, Suite 410
Irvine, CA 92606
Phone: 949-553-4202
Fax: 949-553-4211
Email: cmontesano@oc-cf.org
http://www.oc-cf.org

Purpose: To support those who have been affected by leukemia as they pursue an education.
Eligibility: Applicants must be high school seniors or current college students who are leukemia patients and/or are the children of non-surviving leukemia patients. Applicants must be full-time students with a GPA of at least 3.0 and demonstrate financial need. They must submit an essay describing how leukemia has impacted their life, a doctor's note verifying the leukemia diagnosis and two letters of recommendation.
Target applicants: High school students. College students. Adult students.
Minimum GPA: 3.0
Amount: Varies.
Number of awards: Varies.
Deadline: March 23.
How to apply: Applications are available online.
Exclusive: Visit www.UltimateScholarshipBook.com and enter code OR273812 for updates on this award.

(2739) • Mike Hylton and Ron Niederman Scholarships

Factor Support Network Pharmacy
900 Avenida Acaso, Suite A
Camarillo, CA 93012
Phone: 877-376-4968
Fax: 805-482-6324
Email: scholarships@factorsupport.com
http://www.factorsupport.com/scholarships.htm

Purpose: To support men with hemophilia or von Willebrand disease and their families.
Eligibility: Students must provide proof of diagnosis by a physician. Applicants must submit an essay and two letters of recommendation.
Target applicants: High school students. College students. Adult students.
Amount: $1,000.
Number of awards: 10.
Deadline: April 30.
How to apply: Applications are available online.
Exclusive: Visit www.UltimateScholarshipBook.com and enter code FA273912 for updates on this award.

(2740) • Millie Brother Scholarship

Children of Deaf Adults, International
Dr. Jennie E. Pyers
Assistant Professor of Psychology, Wellesley College
106 Central Street, SCI480
Wellesley, MA 02842
Phone: 781-283-3736
Email: coda.scholarship@gmail.com
http://www.coda-international.org

Purpose: To assist hearing children of deaf parents to pursue post-secondary educational opportunities.
Eligibility: Applicants must be graduating high school seniors and the hearing children of deaf parents. Applicants must submit a transcript, letters of recommendation and essay. Essays should describe applicants' Coda experience and future career goals.
Target applicants: High school students.
Amount: $1,500.
Number of awards: 2.
Deadline: April 2.
How to apply: Applications are available by written request.
Exclusive: Visit www.UltimateScholarshipBook.com and enter code CH274012 for updates on this award.

(2741) • Millie Gonzales Memorial Scholarships

Factor Support Network Pharmacy
900 Avenida Acaso, Suite A
Camarillo, CA 93012
Phone: 877-376-4968
Fax: 805-482-6324
Email: scholarships@factorsupport.com
http://www.factorsupport.com/scholarships.htm

Purpose: To support women with hemophilia or von Willebrand Disease.
Eligibility: Students must provide proof of diagnosis by a physician. Applicants must submit an essay and two letters of recommendation.
Target applicants: High school students. College students. Adult students.
Amount: $1,000.
Number of awards: 5.
Deadline: April 30.
How to apply: Applications are available online.
Exclusive: Visit www.UltimateScholarshipBook.com and enter code FA274112 for updates on this award.

(2742) • Minnie Pearl Scholarship

Hearing Bridges (formerly League for the Deaf and Hard of Hearing and EAR Foundation)
415 4th Avenue South, Suite A
Nashville, TN 37201
Phone: 615-248-8828
Fax: 615-248-4797
Email: nr@hearingbridges.org
http://www.hearingbridges.org

Purpose: To support students with hearing loss as they strive to achieve their full potential.
Eligibility: Applicants must be high school seniors with a minimum 3.0 GPA and be accepted to a college, university or technical school and be planning to attend full-time. Applicants must also be U.S. citizens, be mainstreamed students and have significant (severe to profound) bilateral hearing loss.
Target applicants: High school students.
Minimum GPA: 3.0
Amount: Up to $10,000.
Number of awards: 1.
Deadline: March 12.
How to apply: Applications are available online.
Exclusive: Visit www.UltimateScholarshipBook.com and enter code HE274212 for updates on this award.

(2743) • National Collegiate Cancer Foundation Scholarship

National Collegiate Cancer Foundation
P.O. Box 14190
Silver Spring, MD 20911
Phone: 717-215-0943
Email: info@collegiatecancer.org
http://www.collegiatecancer.org

Purpose: To provide financial assistance to college students who have been diagnosed with cancer.
Eligibility: Applicants must demonstrate financial need. Selection is based on financial need, quality of essay and recommendations, demonstrating a "will win" attitude and overall story of cancer survivorship.
Target applicants: College students. Adult students.
Amount: $1,000.
Number of awards: Varies.
Deadline: Varies.
How to apply: Applications are available online.
Exclusive: Visit www.UltimateScholarshipBook.com and enter code NA274312 for updates on this award.

(2744) • National Federation of the Blind Computer Science Scholarship

National Federation of the Blind
200 East Wells Street
Baltimore, MD 21230
Phone: 410-659-9314
Fax: 410-685-5653

Email: scholarships@nfb.org
http://www.nfb.org
Purpose: To aid legally blind computer science students.
Eligibility: Applicants must be residents of the U.S. or Puerto Rico who are legally blind in both eyes. They must be enrolled in or planning to enroll in a full-time postsecondary degree program in computer science. Selection is based on the overall strength of the application.
Target applicants: High school students. College students. Adult students.
Amount: $3,000.
Number of awards: 1.
Deadline: March 31.
How to apply: Applications are available online. An application form, proof of legal blindness, a transcript, two recommendation letters and standardized test scores (high school seniors only) are required.
Exclusive: Visit www.UltimateScholarshipBook.com and enter code NA274412 for updates on this award.

(2745) · National Federation of the Blind Scholarship

National Federation of the Blind
200 East Wells Street
Baltimore, MD 21230
Phone: 410-659-9314
Fax: 410-685-5653
Email: scholarships@nfb.org
http://www.nfb.org
Purpose: The National Federation of the Blind offers thirty scholarships to exceptional blind scholars.
Eligibility: Applicants must be legally blind and pursue a full-time postsecondary study in the following semester in the U.S. One scholarship may be given to a part-time student. There are no additional restrictions for most of the scholarships. However, a few require study in certain fields or other special traits. Awards are based on academic excellence, community service and financial need. Applicants must reside in the United States or Puerto Rico and attend college in the United States or Puerto Rico. Students make one application for any of the 30 awards; the members of the NFB Scholarship Committee choose the 30 winners and decide which person will receive which award. Legally blind means one is blind in both eyes according to the legal definition, which is available on the organization's website.
Target applicants: High school students. College students. Graduate school students. Adult students.
Amount: $3,000-$12,000.
Number of awards: 30.
Deadline: March 31.
How to apply: Applications are available online.
Exclusive: Visit www.UltimateScholarshipBook.com and enter code NA274512 for updates on this award.

(2746) · National MS Society Scholarship Program

National Multiple Sclerosis Society
733 Third Avenue
New York, NY 10017
Phone: 800-344-4867
http://www.nationalmssociety.org
Purpose: To provide educational opportunities for students affected by multiple sclerosis.
Eligibility: Applicants must be high school seniors or graduates who have MS, or who have a parent with MS and will be attending college for the first time. They must be U.S. citizens or legal residents who plan to enroll in an undergraduate program at an accredited institution of higher learning. Applicants must take at least six credit hours per semester, and the courses taken must lead to a degree, license or certificate.
Target applicants: High school students.
Amount: $1,000-$3,000.
Number of awards: Varies.
Deadline: January 14.
How to apply: Applications are available online.
Exclusive: Visit www.UltimateScholarshipBook.com and enter code NA274612 for updates on this award.

(2747) · NFMC Hinda Honigman Award for the Blind

National Federation of Music Clubs (NC)
Regina Einig
864 Schoolhouse Road
Carbondale, IL 62902-7928
Phone: 618-549-5082
Fax: 317-638-0503
Email: reinig@siu.edu
http://www.nfmc-music.org
Purpose: To support blind instrumentalists or vocalists.
Eligibility: Applicants must be between the ages of 16 and 25, be an instrumentalist or vocalist and submit an affidavit from an ophthalmologist stating that they are blind. Applicants must also be affiliated with the National Federation of Music Clubs.
Target applicants: High school students. College students. Graduate school students.
Amount: $350-$650.
Number of awards: Varies.
Deadline: February 1.
How to apply: Applications are available online.
Exclusive: Visit www.UltimateScholarshipBook.com and enter code NA274712 for updates on this award.

(2748) · Optimist International Communications Contest

Optimist International
4494 Lindell Boulevard
St. Louis, MO 63108
Phone: 314-371-6000
Fax: 314-371-6006
Email: programs@optimist.org
http://www.optimist.org
Purpose: To reward students based on their communications performance.
Eligibility: Applicants must be students up to grade 12 in the U.S. and Canada, to CEGEP in Quebec and to grade 13 in the Caribbean who are recognized by their schools as deaf or hard of hearing.
Target applicants: High school students.
Amount: $2,500.
Number of awards: Varies.
Deadline: June 15.
How to apply: Contact your local Optimist Club.
Exclusive: Visit www.UltimateScholarshipBook.com and enter code OP274812 for updates on this award.

(2749) · Paul and Ellen Ruckes Scholarship

American Foundation for the Blind Scholarship Committee
11 Penn Plaza
Suite 1102
New York, NY 10021

Phone: 800-232-5463
Fax: 888-545-8331
Email: afbinfo@afb.net
http://www.afb.org
Purpose: To support visually impaired engineering, computer science, life sciences or physical sciences students.
Eligibility: Applicants must be U.S. citizens who are blind or visually impaired. They must be undergraduate or graduate students who are majoring in computer science, life sciences, physical sciences or engineering. Selection is based on the overall strength of the application.
Target applicants: High school students. College students. Graduate school students. Adult students.
Amount: $1,000.
Number of awards: 1.
Deadline: April 30.
How to apply: Applications are available online. An application form, official transcript, personal statement, two reference letters, proof of college acceptance, proof of U.S. citizenship and proof of legal blindness are required.
Exclusive: Visit www.UltimateScholarshipBook.com and enter code AM274912 for updates on this award.

(2750) • Pfizer Epilepsy Scholarship

Pfizer Epilepsy Scholarship Award
c/o The Eden Communications Group
515 Valley Street
Suite 200
Maplewood, NJ 07040
Phone: 800-292-7373
Email: czoppi@edencomgroup.com
http://www.epilepsy-scholarship.com
Purpose: To recognize outstanding students who demonstrate how they have overcome the challenge of epilepsy in their lives.
Eligibility: Applicants must be high school seniors or college undergraduates currently under a physician's care for epilepsy, demonstrate achievement in academic and extracurricular activities and submit verification of academic status and two letters of recommendation. Selection is made by a panel of judges composed of opinion leaders in the fields of medicine and education.
Target applicants: High school students. College students. Adult students.
Amount: $2,000.
Number of awards: 40.
Deadline: June 15.
How to apply: Applications are available online.
Exclusive: Visit www.UltimateScholarshipBook.com and enter code PF275012 for updates on this award.

(2751) • Project Red Flag Academic Scholarship for Women with Bleeding Disorders

National Hemophilia Foundation
116 W. 32nd Street
11th Floor
New York, NY 10001
Phone: 212-328-3700
Fax: 212-328-3777
Email: webmaster@hemophilia.org
http://www.hemophilia.org
Purpose: To assist women with bleeding disorders in pursuing higher education.
Eligibility: Applicants must be female U.S. residents who have a bleeding disorder that has been diagnosed by a hematologist. Preference is given to those who have participated in community service or volunteer work pertaining to bleeding disorders. The funds may be used to pay for undergraduate or graduate studies.
Target applicants: High school students. College students. Graduate school students. Adult students.
Amount: $2,500.
Number of awards: 2.
Deadline: May 14.
How to apply: Applications are available online.
Exclusive: Visit www.UltimateScholarshipBook.com and enter code NA275112 for updates on this award.

(2752) • Robert Guthrie PKU Scholarship and Awards

National PKU News
6869 Woodlawn Avenue NE #116
Seattle, WA 98115-5469
Email: schuett@pkunews.org
http://www.pkunews.org
Purpose: In honor of the doctor who created the newborn screening test for PKU, the scholarship gives support to bright students living with PKU.
Eligibility: Students must have PKU, follow the diet and attend an accredited school. Financial need is considered along with academic excellence.
Target applicants: High school students. College students. Graduate school students.
Amount: Varies.
Number of awards: Varies.
Deadline: November 1.
How to apply: Applications are available by mail.
Exclusive: Visit www.UltimateScholarshipBook.com and enter code NA275212 for updates on this award.

(2753) • Rudolph Dillman Memorial Scholarship

American Foundation for the Blind Scholarship Committee
11 Penn Plaza
Suite 1102
New York, NY 10021
Phone: 800-232-5463
Fax: 888-545-8331
Email: afbinfo@afb.net
http://www.afb.org
Purpose: To aid blind or visually impaired students who are preparing for careers in the rehabilitation or education of the blind or visually impaired.
Eligibility: Applicants must be U.S. citizens who are blind or visually impaired. They must be undergraduate or graduate students who are preparing for careers in the education or rehabilitation of visually impaired or blind people. Previous recipients of this award are ineligible. Selection is based on the overall strength of the application.
Target applicants: College students. Graduate school students. Adult students.
Amount: $2,500.
Number of awards: 4.
Deadline: April 30.
How to apply: Applications are available online. An application form, official transcript, personal essay, two recommendation letters, proof of legal blindness and proof of U.S. citizenship are required.
Exclusive: Visit www.UltimateScholarshipBook.com and enter code AM275312 for updates on this award.

(2754) • Sara Conlon Memorial Scholarship

Foundation for Exceptional Children
1110 N. Glebe Road
Suite 300
Arlington, VA 22201
Phone: 800-224-6830
Email: yesican@cec.sped.org
http://www.cec.sped.org

Purpose: To help disabled students who major in special education.
Eligibility: Applicants must be enrolled in two- or four-year undergraduate college programs or vocational, technical or fine arts training programs. Students should submit the application form, transcript, three letters of recommendation, goals statement, statement verifying disability and statement verifying financial need.
Target applicants: High school students. College students. Adult students.
Amount: $500.
Number of awards: 1.
Deadline: February 1.
How to apply: Applications are available online.
Exclusive: Visit www.UltimateScholarshipBook.com and enter code FO275412 for updates on this award.

(2755) • SBAA One-Year Scholarship

Spina Bifida Association of America
4590 MacArthur Boulevard NW
Suite 250
Washington, DC 20007-4226
Phone: 800-621-3141
Fax: 202-944-3295
Email: tcoogan@sbaa.org
http://www.sbaa.org

Purpose: To create opportunities for high school students with spina bifida to attend a college that is otherwise outside of the applicants' financial reach.
Eligibility: Applicants must have spina bifida with a statement of disability from a physician and be high school seniors or have a GED at the time of application. Awards are based on academic record, financial need, work history, community service, leadership and commitment to personal goals.
Target applicants: High school students.
Amount: Up to $2,000.
Number of awards: Up to 6.
Scholarship may be renewable.
Deadline: March 3.
How to apply: Applications are available online.
Exclusive: Visit www.UltimateScholarshipBook.com and enter code SP275512 for updates on this award.

(2756) • Scholarship and Careeer Awards

Lighthouse International
111 E. 59th Street
New York, NY 10022
Phone: 212-821-9200
Fax: 212-821-9707
Email: info@lighthouse.org
http://www.lighthouse.org

Purpose: To assist blind or partially-sighted collegiate or college-bound students.
Eligibility: Applicants must be blind or have low vision capabilities and be in one of three categories: college-bound high school student, undergraduate college student or graduate student. They must also be U.S. citizens and residents and attend an accredited college or university in the U.S. or its territories. Selection is based on academic and personal achievements.
Target applicants: High school students. College students. Graduate school students. Adult students.
Amount: $5,000.
Number of awards: 5.
Deadline: March 14.
How to apply: Applications are available online.
Exclusive: Visit www.UltimateScholarshipBook.com and enter code LI275612 for updates on this award.

(2757) • Scholarships for Survivors

Patient Advocate Foundation
Ruth Anne Reed, Vice President of Special Programs
700 Thimble Shoals Boulevard
Suite 200
Newport News, VA 23606
Phone: 800-532-5274
Fax: 757-873-8999
Email: help@patientadvocate.org
http://www.patientadvocate.org

Purpose: This group of scholarships seeks to assist students who have been diagnosed with cancer or another life-threatening illness.
Eligibility: Students must be under the age of 25 and have a current or former diagnosis of cancer or another life-threatening illness. If awarded a scholarship, the student must maintain a 3.0 GPA, be enrolled full time and perform 20 hours of community service each year.
Target applicants: High school students. College students. Graduate school students. Adult students.
Amount: $3,000.
Number of awards: 11.
Scholarship may be renewable.
Deadline: April 12.
How to apply: Applications are available online.
Exclusive: Visit www.UltimateScholarshipBook.com and enter code PA275712 for updates on this award.

(2758) • School-Age Financial Aid Program

Alexander Graham Bell Association for the Deaf and Hard of Hearing
Youth and Family Programs Manager
3417 Volta Place NW
Washington, DC 20007
Phone: 202-337-5220
Fax: 202-337-8314
Email: financialaid@agbell.org
http://www.agbell.org

Purpose: To assist students who are deaf or hard of hearing.
Eligibility: Applicants must be students with pre-lingual hearing loss between the ages of 6 and 21 who are enrolled in parochial, independent or private schools.
Target applicants: Junior high students or younger. High school students.
Amount: Varies.
Number of awards: Varies.
Deadline: May 26.
How to apply: Applications are available online.

Exclusive: Visit www.UltimateScholarshipBook.com and enter code AL275812 for updates on this award.

(2759) • Sertoma Hearing Impaired Scholarship

Sertoma International
1912 E. Meyer Boulevard
Kansas City, MO 64132
Phone: 816-333-8300
Fax: 816-333-4320
Email: infosertoma@sertomahq.org
http://www.sertoma.org

Purpose: The organization's focus is to concentrate on communicative disorders.
Eligibility: Applicants must be entering or continuing as full-time undergraduates in the U.S., show proof that they have a clinically significant (40dB) bilateral hearing loss and have a minimum 3.2 GPA for all high school and college courses.
Target applicants: High school students. College students. Adult students.
Minimum GPA: 3.2
Amount: $1,000.
Number of awards: Varies.
Deadline: May 1.
How to apply: Applications are available online.
Exclusive: Visit www.UltimateScholarshipBook.com and enter code SE275912 for updates on this award.

(2760) • Soozie Courter Sharing a Brighter Tomorrow Hemophilia Scholarship

Wyeth Pharmaceuticals
Hemophilia Scholarship Program (Bioanalytical Solutions)
P.O. Box 26825
Collegeville, PA 19426-0825
Phone: 888-999-2349
http://www.hemophiliavillage.com

Purpose: To provide financial assistance to students with hemophilia.
Eligibility: Applicants must be high school seniors or graduates, GED recipients or college or vocational school students who have been diagnosed with hemophilia A or B.
Target applicants: High school students. College students. Adult students.
Amount: $2,500-$4,000.
Number of awards: 17.
Deadline: Varies.
How to apply: Applications are available online.
Exclusive: Visit www.UltimateScholarshipBook.com and enter code WY276012 for updates on this award.

(2761) • The Barbara Palo Foster Memorial Scholarship

Ulman Cancer Fund for Young Adults
4725 Dorsey Hall Drive, Suite A
Ellicott City, MD 21042
Phone: 410-964-0202
Email: scholarship@ulmanfund.org
http://www.ulmanfund.org

Purpose: To support students who have a parent with cancer and those who have lost a parent to cancer.
Eligibility: Students must show financial need, community service participation, commitment to education and career goals and how they have used their experience to help others.
Target applicants: High school students. College students. Adult students.
Amount: Varies.
Number of awards: Varies.
Deadline: May 3.
How to apply: Applications are available online.
Exclusive: Visit www.UltimateScholarshipBook.com and enter code UL276112 for updates on this award.

(2762) • The Marilyn Yetso Memorial Scholarship

Ulman Cancer Fund for Young Adults
4725 Dorsey Hall Drive, Suite A
Ellicott City, MD 21042
Phone: 410-964-0202
Email: scholarship@ulmanfund.org
http://www.ulmanfund.org

Purpose: To support students who have a parent with cancer and those who have lost a parent to cancer.
Eligibility: Students must show financial need, community service participation, commitment to education and career goals and how they have used their experience to help others.
Target applicants: High school students. College students. Adult students.
Amount: Varies.
Number of awards: Varies.
Deadline: May 3.
How to apply: Applications are available online.
Exclusive: Visit www.UltimateScholarshipBook.com and enter code UL276212 for updates on this award.

(2763) • The Vera Yip Memorial Scholarship

Ulman Cancer Fund for Young Adults
4725 Dorsey Hall Drive, Suite A
Ellicott City, MD 21042
Phone: 410-964-0202
Email: scholarship@ulmanfund.org
http://www.ulmanfund.org

Purpose: To support students who are cancer survivors and students whose parents have been afflicted with cancer.
Eligibility: Students must show financial need, community service participation, personal or family medical hardship, commitment to education and career goals and how they have used their experience to help others.
Target applicants: High school students. College students. Adult students.
Amount: $2,500.
Number of awards: Varies.
Deadline: May 10.
How to apply: Applications are available online.
Exclusive: Visit www.UltimateScholarshipBook.com and enter code UL276312 for updates on this award.

(2764) • TPA Scholarship Trust for the Deaf and Near Deaf

TPA Scholarship Trust for the Deaf and Near Deaf
3755 Lindell Boulevard
St. Louis, MO 63108-3476
Phone: 314-371-0533
Fax: 314-371-0537
Email: support@tpahq.org
http://www.tpahq.org
Purpose: To provide financial aid to children and adults who are deaf or hearing impaired and who need assistance in obtaining mechanical devices, treatment or specialized education.
Eligibility: Applicants must suffer from deafness or hearing impairment.
Target applicants: Junior high students or younger. High school students. College students. Graduate school students. Adult students.
Amount: Varies.
Number of awards: Varies.
Deadline: March 1.
How to apply: Applications are available by written request or online.
Exclusive: Visit www.UltimateScholarshipBook.com and enter code TP276412 for updates on this award.

(2765) • Will to Win Scholarship

Merck
P.O. Box 6503
Carlstadt, NJ 07072
Phone: 908-229-2862
Email: replytomerck@willtowinscholarship.com
http://www.willtowinscholarship.com
Purpose: To demonstrate that asthma need not affect one's ability to excel in life.
Eligibility: Applicants must be high school seniors with asthma who demonstrate outstanding performance and achievements in performing arts, community service, athletics, visual arts or science. They must plan to attend college in the fall following application. A GPA of 3.5 or higher and at least one award related to entry category are required.
Target applicants: High school students.
Minimum GPA: 3.5
Amount: $5,000.
Number of awards: 10.
Deadline: April 30.
How to apply: Applications are available online.
Exclusive: Visit www.UltimateScholarshipBook.com and enter code SC276512 for updates on this award.

(2766) • William and Dorothy Ferrell Scholarship

Association for Education and Rehabilitation of the Blind and Visually Impaired
1703 N. Beauregard Street
Suite 440
Alexandria, VA 22311
Phone: 877-493-2708
Fax: 703-671-6391
http://www.aerbvi.org
Purpose: To assist visually-impaired students who plan to assist others who are visually impaired.
Eligibility: Applicants must be legally blind, with a vision of 20/200 or less in the best eye or 20 degrees or less in the visual field. Applicants must also study in college or a similar institution and must be in the field of services for the blind or visually impaired. Scholarships are only awarded in the even numbered years.
Target applicants: College students. Graduate school students. Adult students.
Amount: Varies.
Number of awards: 2.
Deadline: March 15.
How to apply: Applications are available online or by phone request.
Exclusive: Visit www.UltimateScholarshipBook.com and enter code AS276612 for updates on this award.

(2767) • Young Soloists Awards

VSA Arts
818 Connecticut Avenue NW
Suite 600
Washington, DC 20006
Phone: 800-933-8721
Fax: 202-429-0868
Email: info@vsarts.org
http://www.vsarts.org
Purpose: To award promising young musicians with disabilities with scholarship funds and a chance to perform in Washington, DC, at the John F. Kennedy Center for the Performing Arts.
Eligibility: Applicants must be instrumentalists or vocalists no older than 25 years of age and have physical or mental disabilities that limit one or more of their major life activities. Applicants need to include audio or videocassette recordings of three musical selections along with a one-page biography explaining why they feel they should be selected for the award. Awards are based on technique, tone, intonation, rhythm and interpretation from the taped performances.
Target applicants: Junior high students or younger. High school students. College students. Graduate school students.
Amount: $5,000.
Number of awards: Varies.
Deadline: November 15 (inside USA) and December 1 (outside USA).
How to apply: Applications are available online.
Exclusive: Visit www.UltimateScholarshipBook.com and enter code VS276712 for updates on this award.

Scholarship Indexes

What would you rather do: read the description of every single scholarship in this book or use an index to quickly zero in on scholarships that fit you? That's what we thought, which is why we put together a set of indexes that make it easy for you to find the perfect scholarships. We strongly recommend that you use all of the indexes. This is because every scholarship can be categorized in numerous ways and often the decision is unavoidably subjective. So to make sure that you don't miss out on a great scholarship, spend the time to consult each of the following indexes:

GENERAL CATEGORY INDEX

This is one of the most useful indexes since it organizes the scholarships by common fields of study or career areas. It does not list any state specific scholarships since there is another index just for state of residence. Here are the general categories:

Academics/General

Chemistry (Physical Sciences)

Communications

EDUCATION/TEACHING

Also See Scholarships Listed Under:
Academics/General
English/Writing
Public Administration/Social Work
Public Service/Community Service

ENGINEERING

Also See Scholarships Listed Under:
Aerospace/Aviation
Computer and Information Science
Sciences/Physical Sciences

English/Writing

Ethnic and Area Studies

Mathematics

Medicine/Nursing/Health Professions

Military/Police/Fire (Includes Protective Services which is Main CIP)

Also See Scholarships Listed Under:
Leadership

Organizations/Clubs/Employers

Also See Scholarships Listed Under: Unions

Race/Ethnicity/Gender/Family Status

Also See Scholarships Listed Under: Academics/General

Real Estate (Business/Mgt.)

Also See Scholarships Listed Under:
Business/Management

Religion and Churches

Also See Scholarships Listed Under:
Academics/General

Sciences/Physical Sciences

Also See Scholarships Listed Under:
Engineering
Chemistry
Computer and Information Science
Mathematics

Social Science/History

Also See Scholarships Listed Under:
Education/Teaching
English/Writing
Foreign Language
Ethnic and Area Studies
State of Residence

FIELD OF STUDY INDEX

This index organizes the scholarships by fields of study. It lists both general areas of study (in bold) as well as specific areas of study. If you cannot find a specific area of study that matches your major simply look at the scholarships under the closest matching general area.

In addition to this index be sure to use the Career Index since many scholarships are targeted to specific careers but do not have specific field of study requirements.

ENGINEERING -- AEROSPACE, AERONAUTICAL AND ASTRONAUTICAL ENGINEERING

ENGINEERING -- AGRICULTURAL/ BIOLOGICAL ENGINEERING AND BIOENGINEERING

ENGINEERING -- BIOMEDICAL/MEDICAL ENGINEERING

ENGINEERING -- CHEMICAL ENGINEERING

ENGINEERING -- CIVIL ENGINEERING

HEALTH PROFESSIONS AND RELATED CLINICAL SCIENCES -- NURSING ADMINISTRATION (MSN, MS, PHD)

HEALTH PROFESSIONS AND RELATED CLINICAL SCIENCES -- NURSING SCIENCE (MS, PHD)

HEALTH PROFESSIONS AND RELATED CLINICAL SCIENCES -- NURSING/ REGISTERED NURSE (RN, ASN, BSN, MSN)

HEALTH PROFESSIONS AND RELATED CLINICAL SCIENCES -- OCCUPATIONAL HEALTH AND INDUSTRIAL HYGIENE

HEALTH PROFESSIONS AND RELATED CLINICAL SCIENCES -- OCCUPATIONAL THERAPY/THERAPIST

HEALTH PROFESSIONS AND RELATED CLINICAL SCIENCES -- OPTOMETRY (OD)

HEALTH PROFESSIONS AND RELATED CLINICAL SCIENCES -- PHARMACY (PHARMD (USA), PHARMD OR BS/ BPHARM (CANADA))

CAREER INDEX

This index organizes the scholarships by common career fields. If you cannot find your specific career listed simply look at the scholarships under the closest matching career area.

In addition to this index be sure to use the Major Index since many scholarships are targeted to fields of study but do not have specific career requirements.

INTERESTS / HOBBIES INDEX

This index lists awards that are geared toward students who are active in specific pasttimes and hobbies.

SPECIAL CIRCUMSTANCES

This index lists a variety of special circumstances that are used as eligibility limits for these scholarships.

STATE OF RESIDENCE INDEX

This index lists awards that are restricted to students who are residents of the state or who are planning to study in the state.

Georgia

Guam

Hawaii

New Mexico

New York

North Carolina

MILITARY RELATED INDEX

Most of the awards in this index require that you have a parent. grandparent or spouse who has served in the military. There are also awards if you want to enter the armed services.

ETHNICITY AND RACE INDEX

This index lists awards for members of minority and non-minority ethnic groups.

African-American

Italian

Japanese

Korean

Lithuanian

Mexican

RELIGION INDEX

This index lists awards from various churches and religious organizations.

DISABILITY INDEX

This index lists awards for students with physical, hearing, vision, mental and learning disabilities. It also includes awards for students who have been afflicted with certain illnesses.

MEMBERSHIP INDEX

If you or your parents are members of any of the groups in this index, you may qualify for a scholarship.

INDEX BY SPONSOR

SCHOLARSHIP NAME INDEX

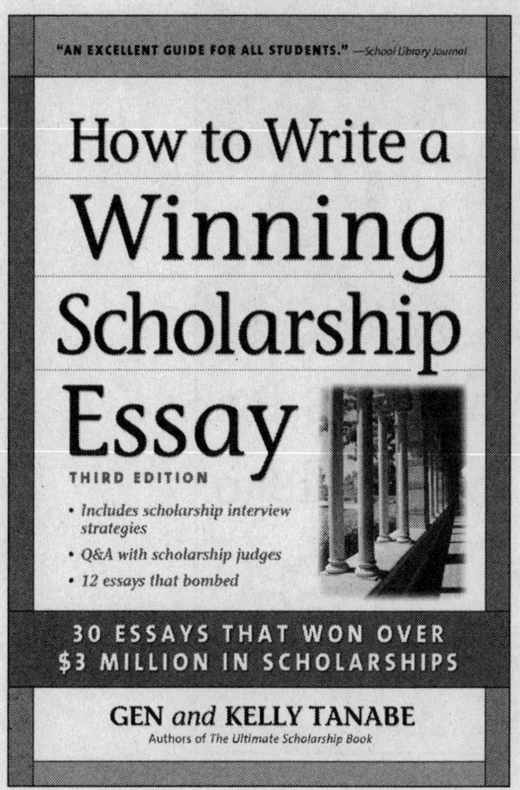

YOU WIN OR LOSE A SCHOLARSHIP WITH YOUR ESSAY AND INTERVIEW. LEARN TO ACE BOTH!

- Complete instructions on crafting a powerful scholarship essay
- 30 money-winning essays that won $3 million in scholarships
- Scholarship judges reveal what separates winners from runner-ups
- 12 essays that bombed and how to avoid these mistakes
- Master the interview with sample questions and answers

Get your copy at bookstores nationwide or visit www.supercollege.com

ISBN: 978-1-932662-37-5

$17.95

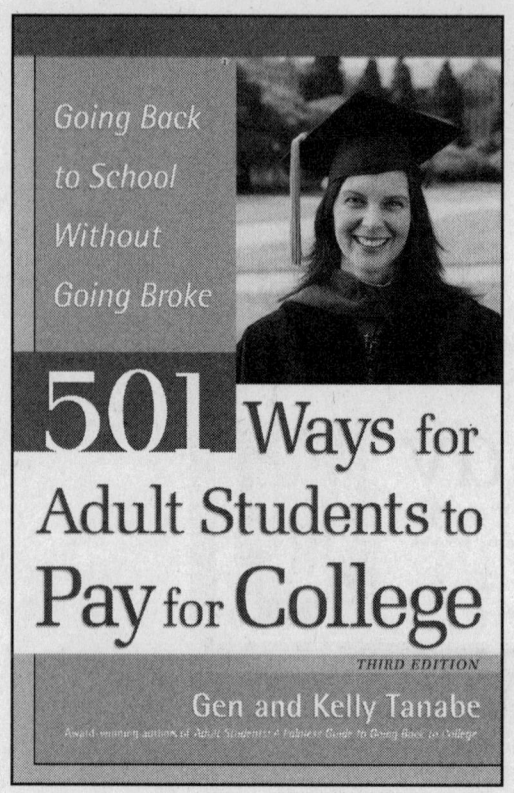

GET MORE TOOLS AND RESOURCES AT SUPERCOLLEGE.COM

Visit **www.supercollege.com** for more free resources on college admission, scholarships, and financial aid. And, apply for the SuperCollege Scholarship.

ABOUT THE AUTHORS

Harvard graduates and husband and wife team Gen and Kelly Tanabe are the founders of SuperCollege and award-winning authors of twelve books including: *Get Free Cash for College, 1001 Ways to Pay for College, How to Write a Winning Scholarship Essay, Get into Any College, Accepted! 50 Successful College Admission Essays, 501 Ways for Adult Students to Pay for College* and *Accepted! 50 Successful Business School Admission Essays.*

Together, Gen and Kelly were accepted to every school to which they applied, including all the Ivy League colleges and won over $100,000 in merit-based scholarships. They were able to graduate from Harvard debt-free.

Gen and Kelly give workshops across the country and write the nationally syndicated "Ask the SuperCollege Experts" column. They have made hundreds of appearances on television and radio and have served as expert sources for *USA Today*, the *New York Times*, *U.S. News & World Report*, *New York Daily News*, *San Jose Mercury News*, *Chronicle of Higher Education*, *CNN* and *Seventeen.*

Gen grew up in Waialua, Hawaii. A graduate of Waialua High School, he was the first student from his school to be accepted at Harvard, where he graduated magna cum laude with a degree in both History and East Asian Studies.

Kelly attended Whitney High School, a nationally ranked public high school in her hometown of Cerritos, California. She graduated magna cum laude from Harvard with a degree in Sociology.

The Tanabes approach financial aid from a practical, hands-on point of view. Drawing on the collective knowledge and experiences of students, they provide real strategies students can use to pay for their education.

Gen and Kelly live in Belmont, California with their sons Zane and Kane and dog Sushi.